PIMLICO

357

THE PIMLICO DICTIONARY OF 20TH-CENTURY COMPOSERS

Mark Morris is a Welsh librettist and writer, now living in Canada. He was Wales correspondent of *Classical Music Fortnightly* from 1979 to 1986, and in 1995 completed the first English Creative Writing PhD in Canada. His many collaborations with composers include the operas *The Skin Drum* with composer Julian Grant, winner of the 1988 Opera Association of North America Chamber Opera Competition, and *Kafka's Chimp* with composer John Metcalf, for the 1996 Banff Festival of the Arts. In addition to his writing activities, he teaches opera singing and acting techniques, and has regularly directed both theatre and opera.

THE PIMLICO
DICTIONARY OF
20TH-CENTURY
COMPOSERS

―――――

MARK MORRIS

PIMLICO

Published by Pimlico 1999

2 4 6 8 10 9 7 5 3 1

Copyright © Mark Morris 1996

Mark Morris has asserted his right
under the Copyright, Designs and Patents Act 1988
to be identified as the author of this work

First published in Great Britain as
A Guide to 20th-Century Composers by
Methuen London 1996
Pimlico edition 1999

Pimlico
Random House, 20 Vauxhall Bridge Road,
London SW1V 2SA

Random House Australia (Pty) Limited
20 Alfred Street, Milsons Point, Sydney,
New South Wales 2061, Australia

Random House New Zealand Limited
18 Poland Road, Glenfield,
Auckland 10, New Zealand

Random House South Africa (Pty) Limited
Endulini, 5A Jubilee Road, Parktown 2193, South Africa

Random House UK Limited Reg. No. 954009

A CIP catalogue record for this book
is available from the British Library

ISBN 0-7126-6568-4

Papers used by Random House UK Limited are natural,
recyclable products made from wood grown in sustainable forests.
The manufacturing processes conform to the environmental
regulations of the country of origin

Printed and bound in Great Britain by
Mackays of Chatham PLC

To Ken and Anne Loveland
and
Christopher and Gillian Butler
for all their support and encouragement

Acknowledgements

This book could not have been written without the very many people who answered my queries or pointed me in the right direction to find information, and without those among my friends who encouraged me to keep on with it. It took a number of years to research, compile and write; if, in these acknowledgements, there are those whom, through time and distance, I have forgotten to include, I hope they will forgive me, and rest content that their contribution is, nevertheless, to be found in the book itself.

I would like especially to thank the staff of the Banff Centre Library, and of the Performing Arts (formerly the Music) Library of The University of Calgary, for their patience and cheerful assistance, and for the foresightedness that has made the holdings of both libraries so interesting and comprehensive. Many of the International Music Centres provided useful help, notably the Australian, British, Czech, Donemus (Holland) and Icelandic. In the early stages of the book, a number of recording companies also provided answers to queries or material I could not otherwise obtain, notably BIS, Bulgariton, Chandos, Claves, Crystal Records and Marco Polo. I would also like to thank the Alberta Foundation for the Arts for their assistance in the early stages of writing.

I have been extremely fortunate in my editors, Penelope Hoare, Kate Goodhart and Charlotte Mendelson, who have made the relationship between author and publisher not only professionally fulfilling by their guidance through the various stages of the book's creation, but personally rewarding by their good humour and encouragement. Three other people have made major contributions. Anthony Mulgan, on behalf of the publishers, used his considerable knowledge and expertise to ferret out every date and reference in the manuscript, and to query and suggest when my writing was unclear or when I went off at a tangent; an invaluable and unenviable task. My two copy-editors, Chris Wood and Steve Dobell, then performed a similar task on the final manuscript; all three succeeded in that rare achievement, making the author enjoy their corrections, emendations, and comments. Last, but not least, my agent, Deborah Rogers, has steered me over these years through all the difficulties of getting a book like this launched, and I, and this *Guide*, are gratefully indebted to her.

Equally important has been the personal encouragement of friends, four of whom are to be found in the dedication of this *Guide*. At the inception of the book, John and Jenny Morris, Eric Jenkins and his family, and especially Carolyn Landrum, got me going. Once the book was underway, it would not have continued without the input and kindness, in another field, of Sandra Hayes-Gardiner. Keith Turnbull and Graham Cozzubbo, of the Banff Centre, and Dr Zoltan Roman at the University of Calgary, have all kept me writing during its later stages, and, I suspect, have impatiently waited for me to finish it. Finally Janice Tole has followed the creation of the manuscript with me, suffered hours and hours of often strange music issuing from the stereo, worked her pencil where I had been dyslexic, shared the excitement, and ensured I continued when the task seemed overwhelming. Every writer who takes on such a crazy undertaking as this *Guide* needs friends and companions like these. I hope they will all find pleasure in the result.

Mark Morris, June 1996

Contents

Introduction

There are few cultural experiences more exciting and more difficult than discovering the art of our own times. Exciting, because contemporary or near-contemporary art addresses our own experience, our own concerns, our own possibilities. It speaks to the tenor of our age, and it opens new horizons. Difficult, because sometimes it involves new languages and expressions with which we have to become familiar, because sometimes it evokes feelings and emotions we may prefer not to acknowledge, and because it does not carry the evaluation and familiarity of a century or more of acknowledgment.

Of all the art-forms, serious classical music has perhaps suffered most from misunderstanding, ignorance and neglect in the general culturally-aware populace, for a variety of reasons (some of which are touched upon in 'A Brief history of 20th-century music' later in this guide). How many times has one heard 'Oh, I can't stand any of that modern stuff' or 'I won't go if there's any 20th-century music in it', even though that 'modern stuff' may have been written in 1917? Yet, guilty though we may all have been of such sentiments at one time or another, they are the product of dogma, not common sense. Take anyone who enjoys Mozart and Beethoven, with a smattering of the later 19th-century composers (a little Brahms and Tchaikovsky, and perhaps some Verdi and Wagner), a couple of hours of their time, and some appropriate recordings, and I guarantee they will soon become hooked on one classic 20th-century score or another. Those works may not be very extreme (though they will be in a language almost unimaginable to the 19th century), but from them it is but a short series of steps to understanding, appreciating, and loving 20th-century music with more complex idioms.

The problem with encountering 20th-century music has been one of access, of knowing where to start without being put off, of developing one's knowledge. This *Guide to 20th-Century Composers* is, in part, an attempt to provide something of that access, by giving an idea of what listeners might encounter in the music of a particular composer, and by suggesting what composers and what works an interested person might explore (see 'How to use this guide', below).

But it has also been written in response to all those, from composers, conductors and musicians to ordinary music lovers who already have a knowledge of 20th-century music, who wish to explore further, be it the other works of a composer they have enjoyed, or the music of a particular period or country in which they are interested. I also hope it will be of value to those who already have a considerable knowledge of 20th-century music, by introducing yet more composers.

It is, however, a *guide*, and not a dictionary or an encyclopedia. A guide should have practical application, and this one has been designed so that when confronted with a variety of situations – whether to go to the concert with the unfamiliar modern composer's work, whether to buy that 20th-century recording in the second-hand store, what to listen to by that unfamiliar composer whose work on the radio you so liked – it will at least provide some idea of the music and what to explore. Consequently, there is little biography in the guide; there are many other publications (some of them discussed at the end of this introduction) which give biographical information. This one concentrates solely on the music. I have tried to avoid getting bogged down in technical description, which properly belongs to the realm of musicology: to hear a work with the sole intent of recognizing the retrograde inversion of the second tone-row may be a cerebral experience, but it is hardly a musical one. To try and describe music in descriptive phrases (rather than by technical exposition) is always a thankless task, and one that has become unfashionable; but words are still the major vehicle for transmitting ideas, experiences and enthusiasms to others, and if they will never match the music, that is no reason not to try.

The other feature of guides is that they are personal. This is not an objective book, and it would be boring if it were. I have attempted to be as objective as I can, but if the majority of opinions and assessments will meet with general concurrence, some will not. I am fortunate in finding excitement in all the myriad styles of 20th-century classical music, but I am not immune to bias, including the belief that if a piece of contemporary music is so conservative that it belongs to a bygone era then it is almost certain not to speak to us or our age except on the most superficial level. Guides should come from personal experience, and to write the guide I have listened to virtually all the works discussed in the main entries; I trust it will be clear where I have been unable to do so, and was unable to consult a score. However, such subjectivity can also be a virtue: if the guide starts an argument at a musical dinner-table over the exclusion of that composer and the inclusion of another, and the CD player is turned on, it will have achieved at least one of its objectives.

I have undertaken all the research and typing myself. I could not have done so without many writers on various aspects of the subject whose works I consulted. Sometimes in that research I came across a paragraph that had migrated from one book to another, and yet another; I hope I have avoided following such a dubious example. But any errors that escaped the eagle eyes of my copy-editors – and errors there will inevitably be in any work of this size – should be lain at my door, and mine alone.

Who has been included in the guide and why

The exact term '20th-century composer' is a debatable one. For this guide I set the following criteria for the inclusion or exclusion of a particular composer.

First, the composer had to live in the 20th century, with a date of death at least 1917 or later. The only exceptions to this are those composers who died before 1917 but whose works, written in the 20th century, had a conspicuous influence on the development of 20th-century music. Mahler is a prime example. Similarly, composers who lived well into the 20th century, but wrote nothing of significance in this century, are excluded. Saint-Säens is an obvious example.

Second, there would have to be a reasonable expectation of access to that composer's work, in concert or recording form, not just in the country of origin, but outside. In some cases, such access will require considerable perseverance, and lesser composers have been relegated to a brief survey in the introductions to each country, rather than in a lengthier main entry.

These criteria still left so many composers that the guide would have been unusable and untransportable. Consequently, the exclusion of other lesser-known composers has been made on a personal basis. In particular, composers in their forties or younger have generally been excluded; in many cases it is still too early to get a comprehensive overview of their work, and a moment's reflection will confirm that the majority will be 21st-century, not 20th-century composers, with the height of their powers and fame expected in the 2010s and life-expectancy to the 2030s. The guide is not therefore comprehensive; but if a reader started at the beginning and listened once to every work mentioned in the main entries, listening for a couple of hours each and every day, it would still take virtually a decade to reach the end.

One of the regrets of this guide is the relative paucity of women composers, which reflects an historical fact. But one of the delights of the contemporary classical music scene is that this barrier seems at last to be broken, with the emergence of many women composers still too young or too little known to meet the criteria of this guide – something that will, I am sure, no longer hold in twenty years' time.

It should be noted that in music, more than all the other arts, the work of a particular composer is invariably and identifiably fertilised by the work of other composers, especially in the earlier years of a composer's career. This is in part because music is a complex abstract art that requires the starting point of patterns and models, and in part because the human mind has an extraordinary ability to store and recall sounds, consciously or subconsciously. Consequently, when this guide suggests that a composer's work is influenced by another composer, or has echoes of another composer, there is no derogatory critical intention. Such comparisons can also be useful to readers unfamiliar with a particular composer's work, by placing the music within the general sphere of a more familiar composer. Of course, sometimes a composer is so influenced by the style of another that their own individuality is almost completely suppressed; such situations should be clear in this guide.

It proved too lengthy to include in the guide lists of the works of a given composer, in addition to those works recommended. However, readers with access to the Internet will find such lists of works of all composers with a main entry in the book in the guide's World Wide Web site.

The address is: http://www.reedbooks.com/methuen/morris/index.html

Mark Morris

Conventions used in this guide

CLASSICAL MUSIC
For the purposes of this guide 'classical music' means music with a serious intent and expectation, written within the western tradition that emerged from European antecedents. There are, of course, other classical traditions (such as those of the rāga of India). 'Classical music' (with a capital C), following convention, refers specifically to the music of the end of the 18th and very beginning of the 19th centuries, the time of Haydn and Mozart.

DATES
The dates given with a particular work are, wherever possible, the dates of composition.

SONATA
Following general usage, the expression 'sonata', as in *Violin Sonata*, refers to a work for violin and piano. If the work is for solo instrument, it is stated, as in *Sonata for Solo Clarinet*.

SERIALISM AND 12-TONE MUSIC
The language used for Schoenberg's harmonic innovations and their subsequent development has become confusing, with expressions overlapping in meaning. This guide follows what seems to be developing as the convention. '12-tone' refers to the harmonic system of organizing melodic motivational material into rows of 12 notes ('tone-rows'), using all the notes of the chromatic scale, as invented by Schoenberg (and also known as 'dodecaphonic' music, or '12-note' rows). 'Serial music' or 'serialism' refers to the system, developed by composers following Webern, of organizing not just the melodic motivational material according to such rules, but also other parameters of the music, such as rhythm, dynamics, or timbre.

'AVANT-GARDE'
The expression 'avant-garde' has historically described contemporary advanced new art. However, in terms of 20th-century music, it has become exclusively used for the period of extreme experimentation in the 1950s and 1960s, and is used in this context in this guide.

TITLES
The titles of works are generally given in their original language. However, this can be confusing when referring to better-known works that are invariably titled in English in the English-speaking world (Prokofiev's *Peter and the Wolf*, for example). In these cases English titles have been used.

How to use this guide

Countries

The guide is divided into COUNTRIES, in alphabetical order of country.

At the beginning of each country there is a short INTRODUCTION to the history of 20th-century music in that country, indicating the main trends and composers. These introductions also include briefer information on those 20th-century composers of that country who do not seem to warrant, for one reason or another, a major entry.

Where applicable, at the end of the introduction to the country there is the address of that country's International Music Centre, an organisation dedicated to the modern music of that country, and the best place to address a detailed query about one of that country's composers. The International Association of Music Information Centres (IAMIC) maintains its own page on the Internet at http://www.lab.sce.nyu.edu/stacie/iamic/iamic.html ; readers should note that Internet addresses are subject to change, and if they have difficulty, should search for the address using the keyword IAMIC.

Following the historical summary, individual COMPOSERS of that country have their own entry in alphabetical order of composer.

Composers

The entry for each individual composer is arranged as follows:

NAME of composer with DATE and PLACE of BIRTH and DEATH:

Stravinsky Igor Fedorovich***
born 17th June 1882 at Oranienbaum
died 6th April 1971 in New York

MAIN ENTRY describing the works and development of the composer:

Igor Stravinsky was for many years the most influential and highly acclaimed of 20th-century composers, the touchstone by which others were judged. The residue of this eminence remains, in that the older generation of current musicians, composers, and critics formed their musical outlook when Stravinsky was to all intents and purposes infallible. Yet that. . . . .

References to other composers who have their own entries in the guide are in bold type:

. . . the orchestra while emphasizing the rhythmic element. Those who respond to the music of **Orff** will enjoy this work, the direct predecessor of **Orff**'s idiom.

LIST OF RECOMMENDED WORKS in alphabetical order with dates:

RECOMMENDED WORKS:
'monodrama' *Erwartung* (1909)
Five Pieces (1949) for orchestra
oratoria *Gurre-lieder* (1900–1911)
opera *Moses und Aron* (1930–1932)
Ode to Napoleon (1942) for reciter and orchestra
Pelleas und Mellisande (1902–1903) for orchestra
Piano Concerto (1942)
staged song-cycle *Pierrot lunaire* (1912)

BIBLIOGRAPHY (where applicable). The books chosen are generally the standard works on the composer concerned, so that the reader who discovers a special affinity for a particular composer can have a more comprehensive overview of the life and works of the composer than this guide can provide. For the more academically minded, such books will usually include a full bibliography of articles in journals, books, etc.

FINDING A PARTICULAR COMPOSER

If you know the composer's country turn to that country and then to that composer.

If you don't know the composer's country go to the index at the back of the guide. Composers with main entries are in capitals (upper case). The main entry for that composer is in **bold** type and listed first. Other references to the composer follow in normal type, and then references to individual works:

STRAVINSKY, Igor **416–425**, 12, 94, 119, 343, 579, 603, 911
    Agon, 419, 895, *Apollo*, 418, 421 etc.

If you want a list of a composer's works: it has not been possible to include a list of a given composer's works in this guide. However, such information can be found on the guide's WWW site at http://www.reedbooks.com/methuen/morris/index.html

If you know the name of a work, but not the composer: there is an index of 20th-century works by name, with that of the composer concerned, on the guide's WWW site at http://www.reedbooks.com/methuen/morris/index.html

EXPLORING THE WORKS OF A COMPOSER

The recommended works of each composer are given at the end of each composer entry. Most, if not all, of these will be discussed in the main portion of the entry, and it is suggested that readers who want to explore a composer's work, perhaps because they have heard a work that has attracted them, or because they are already familiar with some of the composer's output, follow this recommended list first. Similarly, works that are *not* included in these recommendations might be better avoided until the reader is familiar with the composer's important works.

Many 20th-century composers have drastically changed their styles during the course of their output, and works from one period might attract the reader, while those from another may not. A combination of the recommended works list and the main entry should point the reader to those periods and changes of style.

EXPLORING THE WORKS OF UNFAMILIAR COMPOSERS

The main entry should give a clear indication of the style(s) of the composer concerned, and a general evaluation of their work. If this seems attractive, the reader should explore the works in the list of recommended works first.

EXPLORING THE MUSIC OF THE 20TH CENTURY

For those who wish to explore the music of our century, and encounter composers and works unfamiliar to them, there are various levels of personal recommendation to make this fascinating experience easier. Alongside each composer entry is a bullet-point 'rating', as follows:

••• indicates a composer who is among the best known and most influential composers of our century. It is suggested that those relatively unfamiliar with 20th-century music might start with these major figures; their music will provide a secure foundation of knowledge of modern music.

•• indicates a composer who is less well known, but still of considerable stature, often of importance in their own country but less heard abroad. Many readers will already be familiar with the music of the major composers; they may care to explore the works of these composers.

• indicates a composer who will be of significance mainly to those with a considerable involvement in 20th-century music and with an already broad knowledge of the repertoire, who may find these composers of particular interest.

(No bullet-point) indicates a composer who may be encountered, but whose music is not recommended except to specialists.

To facilitate such an exploration, there are lists of composers marked with ••• and •• on p. 21.

Finding Recordings

For many, recordings will be the major resource for listening to 20th-century music.

RECORDINGS CURRENTLY AVAILABLE

To find a current recording, there are two invaluable publications, regularly updated. The *Gramophone Classical Music Catalogue* is published in Britain, and will be found in most good record stores on both sides of the Atlantic. *Opus* is its American equivalent. Less easy to find outside Germany, but extremely comprehensive, is the German *Bielefelder* catalogue. All three catalogues list the works of composers currently available, with the name of the recording company and its recording number. If your record store does not stock the item, most good stores will order it in; alternatively, there are many mail-order companies on both sides of the Atlantic.

In the case of major composers, there may sometimes be dozens of different recordings of the same work; in this situation the recording guides published by

Penguin are invaluable, offering sensible evaluations and with regular supplements, though weaker on less well-known 20th-century composers. Most good record stores have their own copies; alternatively, they can be found in most good book stores from the Orkneys to the Yukon.

To keep up-to-date on new recordings, there are a number of magazines reviewing new classical releases. Two are especially recommended, though both can sometimes fall into the annoying trap of assuming that readers are familiar with the styles of 20th-century composers known only to specialists:

Gramophone, published monthly in the UK but available world-wide, has comprehensive, sober, and informed reviews and articles. On 20th-century music it is inclined to be conservative but informative.

Fanfare, published bi-monthly in paperback in the USA is even more comprehensive, including issues from the most obscure companies, and with a vast knowledge of past recordings. Always entertaining and informative, its bias is the opposite of that of *Gramophone*, sometimes allowing personal enthusiasm or specialist interest to overcome objective evaluation, but it will be of especial interest to the musician, the specialist, or the collector. The *American Record Guide* also regularly covers 20th-century music in a less imposing format than *Fanfare*, as do such magazines as *CD Review*. The *BBC Music Magazine* has well-balanced articles and reviews in an attractive format.

RECORDINGS OUT OF PRINT

A remarkable amount of 20th-century music has already been issued (or re-issued) on CD. Unfortunately, recordings of 20th-century music often do not stay in the catalogue, even in CD format, and are quickly deleted (out of print). However, virtually all the recommended works in this guide have been recorded at one time or another (there are some exceptions). Fortunately, many of these will be found in the libraries of major cities, and especially university libraries. The catalogue systems of such libraries can be difficult to browse through, and it is recommended that you take with you the name of the composer and the work(s) in which you are interested.

In addition, there are a number of major mail-order stores in the USA and Europe specializing in older second-hand recordings, usually with a huge inventory. These stores issue lists for a modest fee which can be browsed through at home. Such recordings can be relatively inexpensive, though some rare items can fetch very high prices, and since many of them are in LP format, a good turntable is mandatory. The major mail-order stores advertise in both *Gramophone* and *Fanfare*.

Finally, second-hand record stores carrying records almost invariably have some interesting 20th-century music hidden away somewhere, but since this is often a case of turning up an interesting record rather than finding something specific, it is recommended that readers take the guide with them. These are often in LP format; with the advent of the CD, many people are selling their LP collections, and this is a particularly fruitful period for those prepared to buy LPs, as well as an inexpensive way of exploring modern music. Those developing a collection of 20th-century recordings should consider investing in a really good turntable and cartridge while they are still available.

A brief history of 20th-century music

The music of the 20th century has seen more developments, more divergent styles, more ferment and contrasts of idea, than any prior century except perhaps the 16th. The disparity between, say, a work of 1905 and a **Kagel** piece of the 1960s is so vast that it has no parallel in earlier times, not even between the music of Bach and Beethoven, divided by a similar time-period. With such a span to cover, any attempt to outline the history of 20th-century music in a brief introduction will be inadequate. But it may still be useful, provided the danger of over-simplification is noted, if it can give some order and perspective to what can seem, especially to someone unfamiliar with the music of the century, a very confusing picture.

Musically, the latter half of the 19th century was dominated by the Romanticism of German-speaking Europe, and by two composers, Wagner and Brahms, both of whom had in their own particular fashions developed the German tradition stemming from Beethoven. Other countries had their own veins of Romanticism, notably the Russian, and the Czech (Smetana and Dvořák), but in lesser musical countries such as Britain, the USA or Sweden, composers attempted to emulate German models. The other major force of the 19th century, Italian opera, remained a law unto itself, barely affecting the course of musical history outside Italy. French composers thrived, many with conspicuous success in their time, but (with the exception of Berlioz) without lasting influence outside their own sphere: there is no French composer in his maturity in the second half of the 19th century of the stature of the major German composers.

The continuity of the German tradition through the 19th century, from the birth of Romanticism to the brink of its collapse, is striking, and has its parallels in the relative but considerable peace, stability and continuous economic growth and development of Europe from the Treaty of Vienna (1815) until the outbreak of World War I. It is not difficult to trace the progression of musical idiom and idea through the 19th century, as each new development in the areas of both harmony and form unfurls in a logical and linear flow. Indeed the basic forms of music and the different genres remained essentially unchanged through the century, even if their content evolved: the main exception was the continuous flow of the music-dramas of Wagner.

The Romantic aesthetic, in both form and content, continues to echo to this day. But, at the beginning of the 20th century, these 19th-century traditions underwent such a huge upheaval, setting the course for all the progressive elements of 20th-century composition throughout the century, that it amounted to a second Renaissance of classical music.

By the turn of the century, the traditional harmonic system had been stretched to its limits in the search for more extensive modes of expression. In that traditional system, known as the tonal system, the melodic and harmonic progression follows a predetermined pattern (exemplified by the music of Mozart). It is a fundamental basis of the tonal system that a recognizable key is set up, then modified or departed from, and finally returned to, both on a long-term scale (for example, movements) and in short-term passages. The exception of that return is always present, exemplified by the final cadences in any Classical work. This principle of calculated tension and release has its obvious satisfactions, which is why it has remained so popular, and it informs popular music to this day.

Any notes outside the seven notes of the key concerned are perceived as dissonance, and such dissonance can create colour and effect. Through the 19th century the dissonances gradually became more complex, and were increasingly used to reflect more complex ideas. The piling up of tension upon tension, with limited or long-delayed release, entirely suited the late Romantic aesthetic, moving far from the collective 'natural' order of the Enlightenment to an appreciation of the power and force of nature and of the individual psyche. This increased use of the extra five notes available in a scale is known as 'chromatic', after the Greek work for colour. In a famous turning-point, the opening chord of the Prelude to Wagner's *Tristan und Isolde* (premièred in 1865), the sense of key is almost completely dissolved. But however complex the tensions, the traditional key structure still remained the foundation of composition at the end of the 19th century, with any departures eventually returning to provide a sense of resolution. Parallel with these developments, and in the search for deeper and more varied forms of expression, works became longer and the forces larger, especially in orchestral and operatic works.

At the beginning of the 20th century, the complexities of the late-Romantic tensions became untenable and collapsed, and the centre of that collapse was located in two cities, Paris and Vienna. The French musical reaction to Romanticism was much more subtle and less dramatic than the Viennese, and has received less attention, but in terms of changing the way musicians and composers think, its effects on 20th-century music have been just as far-reaching. Its central figure was **Debussy**: to encapsulate his contribution, he reasserted the ability and the right of music to state effects without recourse to the patterns of tension and release, and without the Romantic emphasis of constantly developing internal psychological states. He redefined the possibilities of motion (and thus of beginnings and endings) in classical music, but in doing so he maintained the basis of key (the triadic structure), which is why his contribution is not so obviously dramatic as those who abandoned it. Rather, he simply broke almost every rule governing how such triadic structures were to be organized, reordering progression using juxtapositions that were not supposed to work, but patently did; in this he is rightly compared to the contemporary movement of Impressionism in painting. In addition, in a process of profound importance to later composers, he drew on the experience of musics outside the prevailing German classical tradition: earlier French musics, folk scales (pentatonic sales), the music of Bali. In other words, he opened up to composers a new palette of freedoms, immediately utilised in a less revolutionary way by his younger contemporary **Ravel**.

The focus of new European ideas in all fields at the turn of the century was to be found in Vienna. It has been stated, without too much exaggeration, that all the principal developments of 20th-century thought can be traced back to there, from atomic physics to architecture to psychology. What was happening in Vienna was revolutionary: a rethinking of the nature and place of the individual, drawn from the experience of Romanticism, but in reaction to the failures and inadequacies of the Romantic approach. Psychology and the concept of the subconscious were being developed by Freud; Otto Wagner led the movement for functionalism in architecture; the Vienna *Sezession* revolutionized painting: and the *Jugendstil* movement in literature turned into Expressionism. Building on Nietzsche and Darwin, humankind's relationship with God was being completely reappraised. The new science of sociology was emerging, and the older one of mathematics was rewriting the knowledge of the physical universe. Major thinkers and artists from outside Austria, such as Einstein (who taught at Prague, one of the three great cities of the Austro-Hungarian Empire), Ibsen, Oscar Wilde, Charles Rennie Mackintosh, Max Weber, or Bertrand Russell, were as well known (in some cases better known) in Vienna as in their home countries. The exodus of so many artists and thinkers following the rise of the Nazis helped disseminate the influence of this Viennese intellectual tradition, notably in the USA. In the political sphere, Vienna's turmoil at the beginning of the century continues to resonate, not least in the Balkans. In those terms our current European political history is still a continuation of events set in motion in and around 1914, and this is equally true of musical history.

Artistic technical developments rarely occur outside a social and cultural context. The tonal discipline of the Classical age of Mozart reflected the preoccupation with Rational social order and grace; the darker and more complex harmonies of Beethoven, the changes wrought by Napoleon and French thought; the tone-poems of the later part of the century, the increasing Romantic awareness of the darker internal recesses of the soul that were to emerge in concrete fashion in the work of Freud. The crisis that engulfed composition in the first two decades of the 20th century can be seen in part as a response to the technical impasse: the tonal system could be stretched no further without destroying the very basis of the system, and forces were already so large as to be unextendable. But it can also be seen as a reflection of the age: an awareness that the orders of European empires, the social and intellectual structures of élite aristocracies, and the patterns of thought that had developed through 19th-century Europe, were no longer viable. It is no coincidence that such a musical crisis occurred in the period of the slaughter and massive social change of World War I and the Russian Revolution. But the locus of that change at the turn of the century was undoubtedly Vienna, the centre of a decadent Empire in a state of collapse.

Musically, the hinge of that crisis was **Mahler**, who died in 1911. In one sense, he represents the culmination of the Romantic development, in his huge, psychologically turbulent, religiously and philosophically striving symphonies and song-cycles. In another, he heralded what was to come, in his use of musical sound-sources that had been considered outside the area of serious music, in his extension of chromaticism to the edge of atonality, and in his reversion to chamber forces within the large-scale orchestration. It was **Schoenberg**, together with his pupils **Berg** and **Webern**, who wrought the revolution. At the end of the first decade of the century they broke down the whole concept of key (and thus of traditional tension and release) in the so-called 'atonal' works. Crucial to this change was an appreciation that dissonances were not an adjunct to the consonance of tonality, a departure from the norm, but perfectly worthy musical elements in their own right. In other words, the tonal system was in itself a construct, sanctified by much usage and the passage of time but not necessarily given by nature. This is a concept still argued about, and still very difficult for many to understand, so steeped are we in that tonal tradition. But the concept of tonality as a natural order is a very Western ethnocentric view: other systems exist perfectly viably elsewhere, such as in some Eastern European folk musics, in the classical rāga of India, or in most Eastern musics. Consequently, once this concept had been established, 20th-century Western composers have found it possible and profitable to learn from those other musics.

The problem for Schoenberg and his followers was that the traditional structures of music had been inextricably linked to the harmonic system, and the collapse of the latter led to problems with the former. Their return to a primacy of small-scale, often chamber, works was in part a reaction to Romantic inflation, in part a response to the economic stresses of the period, but also a necessity. Traditionally, larger-scale structures had been based on harmonic progression; it was not clear how one could build new, larger-scale works using the new harmonies. In the 1920s Schoenberg responded to this by inventing the 12-tone system, which organized the ordering, or patterning of the 12 notes of the complete chromatic scale, each carrying equal weight (i.e. without any note acting as a traditional dissonant), and being arranged according to mathematical and strict rules. This system was developed by all three composers in their different fashions during the next two decades. Schoenberg largely followed his system until late in his life. Berg developed the more expressive possibilities and the interweaving of 12-tone principles with echoes of a tonal base. Webern created complex and compressed miniatures. There are still composers (albeit not many) following Schoenberg's system. Webern, however, opened up new possibilities, for he realized the potential of the system to be extended to parameters of music other than harmony (dynamics, duration, rhythm).

The possibilities of Webern's developments were exploited by a whole new generation of younger composers after World War I, notably by **Boulez** in France and **Stockhausen** in Germany; **Messiaen** had already, to a large extent, combined the legacy of Debussy and that of Webern in his own very individual fashion. This strand of modern music has become known as 'total serialism', or more commonly simply 'serialism'. When these developments were married to ideas from other developments in 20th-century music, they produced the avant-garde period of the 1960s. Thus the first of the continuities of 20th-century music can be drawn, from Mahler through to the avant-garde composers of the 1960s. The influence of Berg has perhaps been even greater, for he showed later composers not prepared to be as experimental as the main figures of the avant-garde that some of the controls and organization of the 12-tone system could be fruitfully merged with elements of more traditional harmonic organizations.

Although Schoenberg's followers continued their developments in the city, the importance of Vienna as a cultural centre waned after 1918, its empire defeated and dismembered. Its place was taken by the capital of one of the major victors.

Paris attracted artists, writers, and composers from all over the world in a remarkable ferment of new artistic ideas in the 1920s and early 1930s, from Cubism to Surrealism, from Joyce to Hemingway. Paris became the focus of alternatives to Austrian developments in the musical reaction to Romanticism; here was the place where serious music was recast to reflect new views of the world and humanity's place in it. An immediate influence was that of jazz, whose new rhythmic and instrumental sounds briefly flared in the works of a number of composers (for example, **Milhaud**). The major figure working in Paris in this period was undoubtedly **Stravinsky**, whose continuous exploration of new ideas was of enormous influence internationally for four decades between the 1920s and the 1960s. His earlier works (especially the ballet *The Rite of Spring*, 1911–13) had caused sensation and scandal, though in retrospect they can be seen as a continuation (or culmination) of the late-Romantic Russian tradition. What was new, and of immense influence, was Stravinsky's development of rhythm, from an element largely circumscribed and ordered, into something much more potent and malleable. He put it on an equal footing with the other elements of a musical composition; at the same time the percussion section of the orchestra, and the use of percussion in instrumental works, was developed and extended. Stravinsky also employed the new ideas of polytonality, in which two or more keys are heard simultaneously, and polyrhythms, in which two or more rhythms are heard simultaneously.

Equally influential was Stravinsky's adoption and development, from the 1920s, of what has become known as neo-classicism. The basic intent was decidedly anti-Romantic: to return music to an abstract art, divorced from the expression of internal emotional states that had so dominated later Romantic works; in this, Stravinsky was influenced by the example of Debussy. He, like others of his generation, looked back to earlier musics for examples of such abstract music-making, and then emulated the smaller forces and some of the grace and style of the Classical and pre-Classical masters. He also adopted their forms, combined with more modern harmonic effects and instrumental colours, while staying within the tonal harmonic tradition if not all the traditional procedures. One of Stravinsky's major contributions within this style was his use of two or more simultaneous planes of musical event, which fold over each other and replace each other (in Stravinsky's case, partly as a substitute for the traditional classical harmonic progression). This concept has been utilised in widely varying musical contexts ever since. Stravinsky was not the first to develop a neo-classical idiom (**Prokofiev**, among others, had already demonstrated his brilliance in such an arena), but he was the most conspicuous and influential, and many other composers turned to a similar idiom in the 1920s and 1930s, though their usage encompassed a wide range; **Honegger** is a representative example. Neo-classical works continue to be written.

After World War II, in an ironic and unexpected development, Stravinsky eventually turned to 12-tone structures and procedures. His influence then waned, and the place of his actual music, rather than his influence on other composers, is much less secure than was once thought, aside from the early ballets. In part this is because neo-classicism is now seen as something of a musical dead-end, more a reflection of the particular cultural and artistic circumstances of the time than of universal profundity. In part it is due to mid-century critics and musicologists, who found his music easier to understand (and promote) than that of more experimental contemporaries such as Schoenberg, and consequently over-estimated his value, if not his influence.

The 1920s also saw the emergence of new musical ideas in areas other than Vienna or Paris. It seemed to be the new age of machinery and technology, and a vogue emerged for music that reflected the mechanics of machinery. This motoric music, with notable examples in the fervent young Soviet Union (where it was part of the artistic movement of Constructivism) but also from such composers as **Honegger,** is now often ridiculed. However, it had considerable influence on the rhythmic palette open to later composers, and motoric rhythmic effects have permeated later 20th-century music. In the same period, there emerged an interest in micro-tones, divisions of the scale into intervals smaller than a semi-tone, usually quarter-tones. This was seen as a potential way out of the chromatic impasse, and its main proponents were led by the Czech **Hába**, who had instruments such as pianos specially constructed to include quarter-tones. The drawback to such experiments was the familiarity among audiences and musicians of scales based on the semi-tone. They thus heard quarter-tones as mistuning (rather than dissonance), especially on string intruments. Although a tradition of micro-tone music did not emerge, these experiments did lead the way to a general acceptance of intervals of less than a semi-tone in the avant-garde period of the 1950s and 1960s (especially in electronic music) in a less systematized fashion, often for colour or decorative effect. The gradual assimilation of folk musics and Eastern musics, which often divide the scale into intervals different to those traditional in Western classical music, had a similar effect.

In Berlin, which itself became a decadent artistic centre in the late 1920s until the Nazis emasculated cultural life, styles arose influenced by Berlin cabaret jazz. These were associated with more working-class, less élitist music-making. The most notable exponent was **Weill**, especially in the operas written in collaboration with Bertolt Brecht; although others had developed stage works on a similar scale (Stravinsky, for one), they showed that a new art-form – small-scale music theatre – was viable, and the genre has since continued to develop and expand. Another composer who briefly adopted the idiom of Berlin cabaret jazz was **Hindemith**, but he also turned to his own style of neo-classicism, looking back to Baroque models and often combining them with the new motoric rhythms. In doing so, he developed a German neo-classicism parallel to the Parisian-based neo-classicism of Stravinsky. With his mastery of traditional harmony, his developments of that tradition, and his teaching and writing powers, Hindemith had widespread influence. He also had an additional agenda: to produce music that was modern, but which could be played or sung by amateurs, thus attempting to give contemporary music a broader base than specialist audiences. This agenda has been widely emulated. In the field of children's music, two composers in particular developed systems of teaching music using modern means, **Kodály** in Hungary and **Orff** in Germany.

Meanwhile, other composers were following their own paths, redirecting the Romantic legacy rather than revolutionizing it. One phenomenon initiated in the 19th century that has continued through the 20th has been the development of consciously national styles. As the emerging musical cultures of various countries have arrived at a sense of self-identity, distinct national styles have arisen. Generally such nationalistic idioms have drawn on the mainstream advanced styles of the period, and added some particular, original, nationalistic element to create a new style (which may in turn then influence composers in other countries). Thus, just after the turn of the century British composers (such as **Vaughan Williams** and **Holst**) and Italian composers (**Respighi** and **Malipiero**) turned to earlier glorious periods of their musical histories in a renaissance of their own musics, drawing on old church music and indigenous folk music. Similarly in the same period, and reflecting the widespread interest in folk music at the start of the century, **Bartók** in Hungary, **Szymanowski** in Poland and **Enescu** in Romania revitalized their countries' serious music-making by absorbing their own folk musics, in each case with unusual harmonic patterns. The Spanish-speaking countries also discovered nationalistically idiomatic styles drawing on the rich, Moorish-influenced heritage of Spanish folk music, **Falla** leading the way in Spain. In an even more potent development (because it included the influence of non-western musics of indigenous South and Central American cultures), **Villa-Lobos** in Brazil and **Chávez** in Mexico developed idioms originating in the Iberian heritage.

But the major country to transform its classical music from clones of the mainstream European trends to idioms unmistakably its own was the United States, in the 1920s and 1930s. Led by **Copland**, a number of composers went to France to study with the extraordinary teacher Nadia Boulanger, thus adding a progressive French element to the prevailing German cast of American composition. The new, purely American, elements of the works of these composers were first of all jazz, a revolutionary and especially American idiom, and, second, a style we now associate with the expanses of the American West, again exemplified by Copland, that had much of its origins in the post-Spanish developments of Mexican music and of Chávez, however reluctant Americans have been to acknowledge the fact. At the same time **Ives**, besides experimenting to an extreme extent, had shown the potency of such indigenous American traditions as hymn musics, though his works were little known until later in the century. These three indigenous strands formed the basis for the emergence of the United States as a major force in contemporary composition immediately after World War II, with its own developments to offer 20th-century music. Some of the composers of Japan have also, since 1945, embraced the idioms of Western music and allied them with elements of their own, very different, musical traditions. The process of developing national styles continues: recently Australia has seen such an emergence, with influences drawn from its unique landscape and its aboriginal heritage.

A completely different form of nationalism has dominated about half the Western world for much of the century. As already noted, Russia had been a seedbed of experimental ideas in all the arts immediately after the Revolution, but with the complete control by Stalin of the USSR from the beginning of the 1930s, and the communist control, with varying degrees of Stalinism, of Eastern Europe in the four decades following the end of World War Two, any participation of those countries in the progressive development of classical music was effectively stamped out. There was a similar situation in those areas dominated by the Nazis before or during World War II, when any taint of experimentation beyond the point reached by the late 19th century was ruthlessly expunged. The Communist creed was one of Socialist Realism, art forms that would ostensibly speak to and for the people, without bourgeois élitism. In effect this meant freezing harmony, rhythms and forms in 19th-century idioms, with an emphasis on memorable tunes and patriotic and communist themes. This was, of course, the idiom that Stalin and his cultural arbitrators had grown up with; it was also thought to be accessible to the general populace. The results were predictable and fairly disastrous: a huge corpus of vacuous music, in which only a very few composers managed to subvert the process and develop in their own constrained fashions, often with compelling expressive effect. The most significant of these is undoubtedly **Shostakovich,** who in part developed the legacy of Mahler to express, in an extraordinarily powerful fashion, those very angers, tensions, frustrations and despairs that the system engendered. The relaxation of such controls was gradual and occurred at different times in different countries: in Czechoslovakia (with its own strong musical tradition) in the 1960s, in the USSR in the 1980s. One result was that the composers of these countries were suddenly exposed to the Western developments of the previous decades that had been denied to them. In almost all cases, they went through a period of discovering **Webern**, in turn reinvigorating the influence of such ideas in Western composition: the Hungarian **Kurtág**, who discovered Webern in the late 1950s and whose music came into prominence in the West in the late 1970s, is an example.

These, then, were the main trends in the development of 20th-century music until the end of World War II, besides the continuation of essentially 19th-century Romantic idioms, exemplified in the music of **Rachmaninov**. While they have all continued in some fashion or another (with the exception of Socialist Realism, now thankfully consigned to history), a new movement developed in the 1950s and came into full prominence in the 1960s: what has become known as the 'avant-garde', an expression now applied in musical circles exclusively to this period of experimentation. This was essentially an international movement, observing few stylistic boundaries apart from the unscalable barrier of the Iron Curtain, though its main centres were in Paris, Germany (especially Cologne) and to a lesser extent in New York. As has already been suggested, it originated in the development of strict organizational and procedural controls, parallel to those of 12-tone techniques, in the areas of music other than harmony – rhythm, dynamics, duration, timbre – with Webern as the original inspiration. In one sense this was just the logical development of the potential unleashed when Schoenberg and his followers took the step beyond the brink of tonality, but it coincided with a number of other developments.

The most important was the invention of the first electronic instruments, which had already seen such pioneers as **Varèse**, and then of the electronic manipulation of conventional instruments. Initially, electronic music embraced two genres: pure electronically generated sounds, and sounds (whether musical or otherwise) recorded on tape and then manipulated electronically to create a new tape (called *musique-concrète*). Either way, this was a complete and absolute divorce from the music of all preceding ages, the earlier part of the 20th century included, as the types of sounds produced had literally never been heard or realized before, and the traditional procedures for organizing music turned out to be inadequate or inappropriate to the new medium; the problems of structure this posed have still not been fully solved. At the same time, instrumentalists and singers were learning to perform excessively complex scores, and developing the range and colours of their instruments far beyond what had been imagined possible before World War II – in the case of instruments, often in ways their original designers had never intended. This also opened up a whole new range of effect, colour, and timbre; the combination of electronics and these new 'extended techniques' effectively revolutionized the types of sounds available to composers, which had remained relatively stable ever since the invention of the piano. A natural extension of this was the awareness that other things besides traditional instruments, such as household items, could equally well make musical sounds if one was not so hidebound by the notion of a musical 'instrument' as to ignore them.

In addition, a number of composers, often influenced by non-Western thought and led by **Cage** (the second great American contribution to Western music after jazz), realized that they were not necessarily constrained by the accepted structures of music, but could draw on other, non-musical, structures and patterns for the basis of their music. Most extreme among these was the concept of chance (for example, the fall of a pack of cards determining the order of sections of a composition), which reintroduced improvisatory elements into serious music-making. This chance element (which can also be a question of choice on the part of the performer rather than chance) has become known as 'aleatory', after the Latin word for dice. More important, this very concept challenged the whole basis of all Western classical music: that compositions were pre-determined by the composer, and thus considered, fixed, and predictable before performance. This indeterminacy was the exact obverse of the strict control of all parameters developed from Webern, and because of this, the two could happily coexist (the strict control and determinacy of all aspects of a section of a work that itself appeared or did not appear according to chance principles, for example). The logical extension of these ideas was to question the traditional forms and venues of music-making, so that works were written for completely new forces and for non-auditorium venues. Most important, they started to include major non-musical elements, such as visual effects, film and drama (with the instrumentalists performing), in what has become known as 'multi-media' works, a process flirted with in Paris in the 1920s, but not fully developed until the 1960s. One of the results of all these developments was that scores abandoned traditional notation, which could no longer encompass or express the music.

The conglomeration of these developments made the avant-garde period of the late 1950s and the 1960s the most experimental, the most fertile and the most exciting since the 1920s. From the assured electronic soundscapes of **Stockhausen**, through the complex constructs of **Xenakis**, to the ethereal vocal scores of **Ligeti**, to name but three of the experimentalists, there was a ferment of new ideas. Often each work had to be taken on its own reference points, as the connections with traditional procedures were so tenuous. Yet this explosion of revolutionary ideas reached a crisis as great as that of the first decade of the century. First, it had not achieved anything like widespread acceptance with more traditionally minded musicians, let alone audiences; the developments were so fast that it was almost impossible for many people to adjust to the new musical demands made on them. Second, the new sounds and ideas had not yet found new, generally accepted and widely understood systems of containment and organization (a situation parallel to the atonal period of the Viennese experimentalists). The experimentation and new directions largely collapsed, almost overnight, at the beginning of the 1970s.

All of this, of course, reflected the contemporary questioning of established patterns of thought and political and social structures so prevalent in the 1960s, as well as the change in human thinking engendered by the electronic revolution (especially computers) and by the trip to the moon. The reaction to avant-garde music exactly paralleled the conservative political and social reaction to the sixties; many composers quite literally returned to the music of prior times, in a movement known as neo-Romanticism, saying very little new, and rarely saying it well. Some composers, of course, had continued to develop their idiom within a more mainstream style, often drawing on the kind of synthesis **Berg** had initiated, but now informed by the appropriate techniques explored by the experimenters: the Pole **Lutosławski**, for example, or the American **Carter**, who developed a new and influential technique of forward motion that uses overlapping changes of pulse and metre (known as 'metric modulation').

One geographical area where this mainstream has been in continuous development to interesting effect, allied to some avant-garde experimentation, has been the Scandinavian countries. At the beginning of the century they produced two major figures who advanced the development of the symphony, the Dane **Nielsen** and the Finn **Sibelius**. They created a different way of looking at the world, with nationalistic elements, often drawn from northern mythology, and a particular evocation of the northern landscape and light. The Scandinavian mainstream tradition of their successors is beginning to get the attention it deserves.

In a very different idiom, electronic music has been undergoing development, with new computer techniques changing the interaction between instruments and electronics, but as yet it is unclear where this is leading, and this development remains on the fringe of audience experience. The main new movement that has emerged from the 1970s and 1980s is essentially a reactionary one: Minimalism, where long, often very long, swathes of ostinati unfurl and transmute, in a markedly tonal harmonic structure. It has proved instantly attractive, produced one populist composer (Philip **Glass**), but has seemed incapable of enriching ideas, whether musical, social or philosophical, with more than just a surface gloss, though Steve **Reich** may prove an exception. Minimalism has been a fitting movement for what has emerged as the most regressive and disappointing 20th-century period in Western culture and intellect. Recently, Minimalism has influenced a new development that also seemed to hold promise: an ethereal, spartan and often polyphonic musical style exemplified by **Pärt** and more recently by **Tavener**, both from societies undergoing profound change (Estonia and Britain). However, in both cases the impetus for their meditative contemplations is as much religious as musical, and their styles seem to have reached a musical impasse. The experience and development of the avant-garde period remains a sleeping giant, perhaps waiting for the right genius of a composer to reawaken it.

Two other important phenomena of the history of 20th-century music remain to be mentioned. The first is the internationalization of styles: cultural boundaries are increasingly being broken down, and idioms are cross-fertilizing each other in widely differing regions. This process is much more marked, and much more rapid, than in earlier ages. In part it is due to the improvements in transport and the ease of movement around the world, but much more it is caused by the ease of hearing far-away developments almost immediately. Radio started this process, but the emergence of the LP record, and especially of magnetic tape recording, was far more significant, allowing the very swift dissemination and availability of new works: the first significantly international (i.e. non-national) movement – the avant-garde – combined with these developments and greatly benefited from them.

The second has been the decline of interest in contemporary music among general audiences, rather than specialists, a decline that seems to have accelerated with the passing of the century. Many reasons have been put forward for this; undoubtedly the difficulty of assimilating new sounds, musical patterns and ideas is one of them, though previous eras almost exclusively listened to new music (Schubert was surprised that anybody still listened to Mozart). This does not mean that modern and contemporary music has been ignored: quite the contrary, the availability of modern music is unparalleled, and to the surprise of many who had predicted otherwise, the emergence of the CD as the main carrier of recordings has seen an unprecedented surge of releases of modern music, with the exception of the avant-garde period. In Europe especially the availability of modern music on the radio is considerable. Rather, the problem is that the progressive music of the century has not entered the regular repertoire, or become familiar to a general listening public. Those works that have entered the general consciousness and regular programming have essentially been those with strong after-echoes of the 19th-century tradition: **Shostakovich** is an obvious example.

The availability of modern music is not in question: rather it is the dissemination of the newer idioms to a wider public. Some may argue that it is the nature of modern music to be too arcane for a general listener, but that has been the argument ever since Monteverdi's time, and it is simply untrue: children who have not been steeped in traditional music often respond to modern music in a manner inexplicable to their elders, who have to make the transition from traditional ideas to new musical languages. Rather, alongside the echoes of the Classical and Romantic idioms, the thought-patterns, the substance, the foundations of modern music have undergone a profound change. It is that recasting of thought and idea which has not been disseminated to a wider public, for, I would suggest, two main reasons.

The first is one of education. Most music training is still based on the concept of traditional harmony, often with the deeply ingrained delusion that the traditional Western tonal system is the 'natural' basis of all music. A general appreciation of modern music requires a change of paradigm in which traditional tonality is seen – and taught – as but one facet (albeit one that dominated historically for three centuries) of the Western tradition that has since been superseded. Such fundamental changes of thought do not come swiftly; we are perhaps in an analogous situation to that of the Renaissance, where the scholastic modes of thought continued to be taught as the fundamental basis of human existence long after they had been made redundant by new developments. The obsession with increasingly arcane mathematical analysis by those musicologists who have specialized in new music (an unfortunate by-product of the developments of Schoenberg and Webern) has also hindered the creation of such a new aesthetic. The emotional power, as well as the cerebral construction, of new music needs to be demonstrated (hence this guide); unfortunately it is easier to explore the minutiae of construction than explain the emotional power and cultural experience of modern music. A corollary of this has been the role of the critic, the intermediary between modern music and the potential audience. Many critics – especially outside the major musical centres – have understandably found it difficult to make the switch from a mode of thought trained in traditional harmony to new musical languages, and even more difficult to express the experience of a new work in words. The influence of academe has, for some time, made it more fashionable to describe music in factual rather than descriptive terms; modern music needs the kind of advocacy that such word-masters as George Bernard Shaw and the American critic Paul Rosenfeld brought to earlier generations.

The second reason is more contentious, and more insidious. Western European cultures have traditionally valued the arts beyond their immediate financial rewards as essential to the health of those cultures; North American culture since World War II has not. Increasingly, North American thinking has been dominated by financial considerations, and controlled by accountants. Consequently, in the search for large audiences, the culture has aimed at a lower and lower common denominator. In terms of classical music, this has meant an increasing reliance on the standard 'classics' that will bring in audiences. New works are increasingly aimed at entertainment as much as challenge; this is one of the reasons the United States has produced so comparatively few composers of stature. A culture that should take the lead in disseminating new ideas – including new music – is almost totally incapable of doing so with such cultural attitudes. For much of the century Europe was largely immune from this blight, and has celebrated her new composers (one only has to think of Stravinsky or **Britten**; potential German celebration of Schoenberg and Webern was extinguished by the Nazis). Since the 1960s – exactly that period when general audiences might have begun to assimilate the developments of music in the 1930s and 1950s – American culture has started to dominate internationally, bringing with it a cast of mind that downgrades the culturally experimental in favour of the financially acute – gratification rather than challenge. This has been a slow process, but as American thinking, based on the primacy of economic values, has begun to permeate Europe, so its cultural attitudes have followed in the wake (as the French fully understand). The process is not yet complete, but such frames of mind are a major, if lateral, factor in the demise of introducing new music to a wider audience, not only in actual performance, but more especially in the attitudes that might make such performances possible. The social woes and problems that such cultural imperial-ism (for that is what is emerging) brings with it are beyond the scope of this book, but suffice it to say that a culture that does not constantly renew itself with new forms of expression is a culture in crisis.

For the serious art of any time should address its time, to propel and inform it, and needs a climate in which it is able to do just that. Every culture that wishes to understand changes in human thought needs to listen to that art if it is to remain viable. There is a very real danger that classical music will be relegated in its contemporary manifestations to the ivory tower, and in the wider world to musics of the past. These cannot speak to those needs, or foster new ideas, except in the most general way, and classical music is in danger of becoming a medium to entertain, rather than to expand our horizons.

This should be reason enough to explore the music of our times, but quite apart from such lofty considerations, contemporary music – indeed the 'modern' music of our century – has the power to uplift, frustrate, challenge, anger, extend, instruct, enthral and even entertain us. To embrace those effects may take a little courage, and a little perseverance, but it is not too difficult, and to deny those experiences is to deny something of ourselves, and the cogency of the art and times that are our own.

Further Reading

The standard reference work in English on classical music in general is the *New Grove Dictionary of Music and Musicians* (ed. S. Sadie, London, 1980, new edition in preparation). This gigantic publication is beyond the budget of the ordinary music-lover, but is to be found in most major libraries. Its coverage of 20th-century music is comprehensive and on the whole reliable, though some of the composers included here are not to be found in its pages. It is inevitably technical, and in a few cases conveys absolutely no idea of what the music is actually like, but it remains the paramount reference work, recently joined by the exemplary *New Grove Dictionary of Opera* (London, 1994).

The major reference work on living composers is *Contemporary Composers* (eds Brian Morton and Pamela Collins, 1992), with extensive lists of works; however, some notable composers are missing, and the accompanying surveys of the composers' music are often written by specialists or enthusiasts too close to their subjects for an objective view.

The Dictionary of Twentieth-Century Music (ed. J. Vinton, London, 1974) was a comprehensive one-volume reference work that unfortunately did not remain long in print. It is to be found in libraries, but is difficult otherwise to acquire.

The best short paperback reference work on 20th-century music is Paul Griffiths's *Encyclopedia of 20th-Century Music* (London, 1986), which is especially good at explaining terms and technicalities. Griffiths has also written a number of other useful works on modern music and on individual composers.

Of the very many introductions to 20th-century music, the standard university textbook is Eric Salzman's *Twentieth-Century Music: An Introduction* (New Jersey, 1967, revised 1974), better at outlining the means than evoking or conveying the aural results. *The Companion to 20th-Century Music* by Norman Lebrecht (1992) provides highly idiosyncratic quick references to 20th-century composers, and *Greene's Biographical Encyclopedia of Composers* by Daniel Mason Greene (1985), equally quirky in its writing style, includes biographies of a large number of 20th-century composers.

Argentina

Introduction

Argentina had a vigorous musical life in the 19th century, and the opera at Buenos Aires became (and remains) world famous. The 1880s saw the rise of a nationalist music style drawing on indigenous folk music, especially that of the gauchos and their ranching life. The father figure of this movement was Alberto Williams (1862–1952), of Basque and British descent, whose mantle was taken over by Alberto **Ginastera** (1916–83), the Argentinian composer with greatest international stature. In reaction to this movement, the composer Juan Carlos Paz (1901–72), who considered nationalist material a dead form, introduced the latest ideas current in Europe, especially 12-tone techniques. After co-founding the Grupo Renovación in 1929, and as director of the Concerts of New Music from the 1930s and of the acclaimed Teatro Colón (founded in Buenos Aires in 1908), he presided over the performance of foreign contemporary works; through his own compositions he influenced a subsequent generation of Argentinian composers. It was he who introduced Mauricio **Kagel** (born 1931), the other major Argentinian composer beside Ginastera, to contemporary music.

The most fertile period of new music in Argentina was probably the period 1950 to 1970, especially with the foundation in 1962 of the Latin American Center for Advanced Musical Studies, which included an electronic music studio and maintained contacts with visiting foreign composers until its closure in 1970. In spite of this, such composers as Kagel preferred the freer musical atmosphere of Europe to their politically troubled homeland. Like Kagel, Carlos Alsina (born 1941) left Argentina for Germany in 1964. He has also followed Kagel in embracing the extremes of the avant-garde movement of the 1960s, though without the same notoriety, and in composing works for music theatre. In 1969 he formed with Drouet, Globokar, and Portal an improvisation group, New Phonic Art, for performances of both improvised music and their own works. His music has embraced most of the new techniques developed in the 1960s, including aleatoric devices and free improvisation, thereby exploring the possibility of dramatised performance of music works in addition to more overt stage works. His music often employs extreme instrumental ranges and unconventional instruments, and the merging of apparently antipathetical instrumental timbres.

As with so many South American countries, the paucity of composers in this section does not reflect the quality of Argentinian composition, but rather the near impossibility of encountering works by such composers as Williams and Juan Carlos Paz, who would otherwise be in the guide, either on the concert platform or on recordings outside South America.

Bautista Julián
see under Spain

Ginastera Alberto**
born 11th April 1916 at Buenos Aires
died 25th June 1983 at Geneva

Although Ginastera has long been recognised as the major exponent of Argentinian naturalism in music, the label is misleading and his international reputation rests as much on the international style of his later works as on the expression of local colour.

In his early nationalist works, the style of Argentinian folk music is blended into his music, rather than the genuine or quasi-folk music so prevalent elsewhere in South America in the 1930s and 1940s. These folk-influenced effects included polytonality, the melodic feel of the *música criolla*, rhythmic effects, and the chord of the open strings of the guitar. Ginastera himself called this style 'objective nationalist', expressed both in music suggesting primitive ritual and in music with a more contemplative, lyrical character. Two such works, the *Danzas Argentinas* for piano (1937), and the ballet *Panambí* (1934–36), established his reputation. *Panambí* is a heady and vivid piece that pits sections of sensuous, thick-textured Impressionistic colour, with marvellous descriptive touches and effects (bird calls, rain-forest sounds), against the primitive violence of a heavy percussive bass or a rather spare, languid lyricism. The works between 1937 and 1947 confirmed this nationalist reputation, notably the ballet *Estancia* (1941, suite 1943), which included spoken and sung evocations of the pampas and the use of the popular gaucho dance, the *malambo*, and *Las horas de una estancia* (1943) for voice and piano.

In 1945, with the rise to power of Perón,

Ginastera left Argentina for the USA. He travelled extensively before returning to Argentina after the overthrow of Perón in 1955. These wanderings coincided with a second period in his music. With the first of three *Pampeana* (*No. 1* for violin and piano, 1947) and the *String Quartet No. 1* (1948) the indigenous influences became assimilated into his personal style in a process he called 'subjective nationalism'. The overall feel may have an Argentinian character, but the folk elements are no longer individually recognisable, apart from general ideas such as the continued use of the 'guitar chord'. The most often heard work of this period is the tense *Piano Sonata No. 1* (1952), whose dense and percussive writing is characterised by a nervous rhythmic flow. A sparse slow movement recalls **Prokofiev** and the work ends with a *malambo* and characteristic ostinati.

Pampeana No. 3 (1954) for orchestra introduced elements of 12-tone techniques into Ginastera's music, although the total effect remained tonal. This change of direction seems temporarily to have halted Ginastera's output, for the only work in the next four years was the *Harp Concerto* (1956), a brilliantly orchestrated work with an atmospheric slow movement, and writing for harp that sometimes recalls guitar effects. It heralded a third stage in Ginastera's development, in which 12-tone and serial techniques were employed for dramatic, ritualistic (sometimes surrealistic), and above all expressive effect, while the traits of his earlier music, particularly the nervous rhythmic energy and the use of ostinati, were maintained.

With the *String Quartet No. 2* (1958) 12-tone technique was openly embraced, the nervous rhythmic drive continued. The individuality of his new 'neo-expressionist' style was announced in the *Cantata para América mágica* (1960) for soloists and a total of 52 percussion instruments, including two pianos and a celesta. Based on pre-Columbian poems, the cantata is overtly serial (pitch, rhythm and dynamics are treated serially, as well as the melodic material), but has an extraordinary undercurrent of expressive primitivism, especially in the pervasive rhythmic effects (polyrhythms and irregular metres) and in the difficult and dramatic vocal writing, with wide leaps and subtle inflections. This cantata is a genuine marriage of ancient emotions and modern techniques, in which the power of expression may attract many listeners who are otherwise hostile to serial techniques. The

dramatic elements of this cantata were developed in four operas, highly successful on their débuts if now largely ignored. They present strong formal structures, surrealistic situations arising from characters on the edge of sanity, and a pervasive theme of sex and violence, mixing the Expressionist with the dreamlike and the fantastical; all use elements of 12-tone techniques. *Don Rodrigo*, (1963–64) has a precise palindromic formal structure, its scenes separated by instrumental interludes, while *Bomarzo* (1966–67) caused the greatest stir (one critic called it 'Porno in Belcanto', though it has also been compared to the architecture of Antonio Gaudi). Inspired by the grotesque garden statues in a palace belonging to the Orsini family, the libretto, by Manuel Mujica Láinez and based on his novel of the same title, traces the life of the 16th-century Duke, combining his actual life with his sexual fantasies, imaginations, hallucinations, and the machinations of the court around him. The chorus is placed in the orchestra and employs extended techniques, and the orchestra includes a very large battery of percussion. It was followed by *Beatrix Cenci* (1971) and the incomplete *Barabbas* (1977).

The other element of Ginastera's later music is its virtuoso writing, a natural ally to strong expressive intent. The brilliant and expressive solo part of the *Piano Concerto No. 1* (1961) is initially heard against the orchestra in a dialogue of variations, then in an 'hallucinatory' slow movement before a rhythmic finale. The long *Piano Concerto No. 2* (1972) is more florid, shot through with nervous energy and dense, sometimes dissonant textures. The virtuoso solo writing employs clusters against an orchestra providing single tone colours or emphatic points. Its second movement consists of 32 variations on a chord from the fourth movement of Beethoven's *Symphony No. 9*. While more difficult than its predecessor, the concerto is both a more introvert (in spite of its massive effects) and more rewarding work. Similarly personal is the spiky *Piano Quintet* (1963), in which the strings explore tense intimate effects in the central slow section, while the piano is dense and complex in the outer movements, with a suggestion of the maniacal. The tense energy of these works, notes piled on notes, corresponds to the primitive aspects of his earlier work. Much clearer in texture and structure is the powerful *Concerto for Strings* (1965), more obviously lyrical within its dramatic and rugged mould (with swooping effects, and the glistening of high harmonics). The *Violin Concerto* (1963) requires brilliant technique, while the *Estudios sinfónicos* (*Symphonic Studies*, 1967) for orchestra include clusters and microtones. The technical difficulties of these works have limited their wider dissemination.

His final works, the last two piano sonatas (1981 and 1982) and *Iubilum* for orchestra (1980), showed a mixture of this uncompromising language with a return to the accessibility of his early works; *Iubilum* contrasts dissonant fanfares with quiet meditations, and includes tonal climaxes and Impressionist writing.

Ginastera was professor of composition at the National Conservatory (1941, dismissed 1945), and in 1958 was appointed dean of the Faculty of Arts and Science at the Argentine Catholic University. In 1968 he again left Argentina and in 1970 settled in Geneva, where he lived until his death. Ginastera's music appears to be currently neglected, but it seems only a matter of time before it resurfaces, for the primitivism of the earlier works and more especially the individuality in the later. If its language shares many of the styles and techniques of contemporary Western music, its statement – nervous, dramatic, surrealist – is unique.

RECOMMENDED WORKS
> *Cantata para América mágica*, op. 27 (1960)
> *Concerto per corde*, op. 33 (1965)
> Harp Concerto, op. 35 (1956, revised 1968)
> *Panambi* (1934–36) (suite from ballet)
> Piano Concerto No. 1, op. 28 (1961)
> Piano Concerto No. 2, op. 39 (1972)
> Piano Quintet, op. 29 (1963)
> Piano Sonata No. 1 op. 22 (1952)
> Piano Sonato No. 2 (1981)

BIBLIOGRAPHY
> P Suárez, *Alberto Ginastera*, Buenos Aires, 1967
> P Suárez, *Alberto Ginastera en circeo movimientos*, Buenos Aires, 1972

Kagel Mauricio**
born 24th December 1931 at Buenos Aires

Mauricio Kagel properly belongs to the European avant-garde as much as to Argentinian musical life, for in 1957 he moved to Cologne, quickly became an integral part of the German musical scene, and has continued to live in Germany. He has been one of the most colourful and extreme musical experimenters, whose works have often shocked and horrified, but elements of which have had wide influence on other composers. In 1969 he was appointed director of the Institute for New Music at the Cologne Musikschule. His work has shown a consistent thread of restructuring what might be described as the dialectic of music. Initially, and in common with many other composers, this involved the extension of instruments into new ranges and sounds, including the human voice (unusual texts and vocal techniques), and, abstractly, the exploration of free forms and chance happenings of musical events. He extended this to the restructuring of the ambience of the performance, creating dramatic events out of concert works, and redefining music theatre. As this process involved irony and surrealist humour, it has infuriated those who have seen it as insincere or a negation of the weight of received tradition. He has broadened these concerns to include film and the crossover of various media. Finally, he has filtered earlier music through these techiques to redefine it too, causing further furore.

His experimentation started while he was still in Argentina, while choral director of the Teatro Colón (1949–56). *Palimsestos* (1950) mixed speech patterns, while *Música para la torre* (*Tower Music*, 1953) was an early electronic work using concrete sounds and distortions, broadcast from a tower with a light show – an early indication of a preoccupation with unconventional sounds and dramatic effects. The *String Sextet* (1952, revised 1957) contrasted structured sounds (including microtones and polymetric patterns) against free expression.

The first work to attract wider attention after his move to Germany was the influential *Anagrama* (1955–58) for four voices, chorus, and orchestra, in which unconventional texts – the sounds, not the sense, of anagrams – were performed by unconventional vocal techniques, including whispering and declamatory, shouted passages. The purely electronic *Transición I* (1958–60) explored the evolution of timbre changing into timbre, in a revolving roll-over of sound, since used by many composers but at the time quite new. *Improvisation ajoutée* (1961–62) not only used the extremes of organ sounds, and a large element of random interplay as two assistants improvise registration changes while a third plays (all to prearranged instructions), but also included their voices and hand-clapping, creating a haunting effect like some Inquisition nightmare. The element of action in sound was even more overt in another organ piece, *Phantasie*, which caused a considerable stir when it appeared in 1967. The purely organ part, signifying the organist's official duties, is contrasted with a tape prerecorded by the organist, that might typically include the sounds of breakfast, commuting, the church bells, the noises of the services – the background to official duties. The effect is surprisingly evocative. The major and most extended work concerned with new vocal sounds was *Hallelujah* (1967), an arcane hymn of praise for sixteen soloists and also a film. The major score exploring new instrumental sound was *Acustica* (1968–70), which used experimental sound-makers (from bull-roarers to blowtorches), loudspeakers and tape, the musical events precisely delineated on 200 file cards, but then distributed randomly and played in a random order against the fixed sequence of the tape.

His first stage work – and one of his major successes – was *Sur scène* (1959–60), which employed music-hall elements to ridicule the pretensions of critics, a process culminating in the anti-opera *Staatstheater* (1967–70), whose nine scenes include a satirical swipe at earlier opera, and whose musical instruments – all household objects – include a chamber pot. In other stage works, the music itself has become the drama. In *Match* (1964) two cellist/table-tennis players and a drummer/referee play out the tensions found in chamber groups, while in *Pas de cinq* (1965) the players walk around in pentagrams, the rhythm of their footfalls and the tapping of their walking-sticks – precisely notated – creating the music.

Kagel's re-evaluation of older music through avant-garde eyes was first apparent in *Heterophonie* (1959–61), in which the forty-two traditional instruments play as soloists in a work concerned with spatial changes of timbre. *Music for Renaissance Instruments* (1965–66) employed an orchestra of disparate historical instruments, while *Der Schall* (*Sound*, 1968) for five players with fifty-four instruments of the most varied kind imaginable, whose combinations only appear once, suggests the breakup of some old symphonic work, like a once shiny piece of metal dug up unrecognisable and rusted. This led to

Ludwig van, Homage to Beethoven (1969), which processed Beethoven's music for a film as well as a score. Similarly, *Variations ohne Fugue* (1971–72) for orchestra arose out of Brahms's *Hungarian Variations*. Catalogue effects appear in *1898* written in strict two parts for a number of instruments for the 75th anniversary of Deutsche Grammophon.

In common with many avant-garde composers, Kagel dropped from the limelight during the middle 1970s. If the swirling voices of the short *Intermezzo* (1983) for chorus, orchestra and narrator continue the choral techniques developed earlier, and *Ex-position* (1978) the unusual performing groups, such works as '*Rrrrrrr . . .*' (title abbreviated – forty-one movements for various forces) suggest a mellowing of the extremes of sound. The opera *Aus Deutschland* (1981) filters Schubert and the *lied* through his perspective. But his most remarkable work of recent years continues the preoccupation of re-evaluation. *Nach einer Sankt-Bach-Passion* (1985) is a huge oratorio consisting of the unmistakable ambience of a Bach Passion filtered through modern techniques, without being overtly dissonant or extreme. As a passion of the life of Bach, it is both reverent and moving, if one can accept the modern, sometimes kitsch, elements.

None of the unfamiliar sounds of Kagel's avant-garde music is easy to listen to. The large element of the dramatic, in concert as well as stage works, makes them more effective live than on radio or recording. As a result, it is likely that Kagel's work will occupy a diminishing place in the repertoire, although the products of this inquiring and irreverent imagination will remain important for their influence on other, less extreme composers.

RECOMMENDED WORKS

   Acustica for experimental sound producers and loudspeakers (1968–70)

   Hallelujah for 16 solo singers a capella (1967–68)

   Ludwig van, Homage to Beethoven (1969)

   Phantasie for organ (1967)

   oratorio *Nach einer Sankt-Bach-Passion* (1985)

   electronic *Transición I* (1958–60)

BIBLIOGRAPHY
D Schnebel, *Mauricio Kagel: Musik, Theatre, Film*, Cologne, 1970

Armenia

Introduction

Armenia has a strong tradition of folk music and folk song. The most prominent 20th-century Armenian composer is Aram **Khatchaturian** (1903–78), whose colourful music, infused with the harmonies and melodies of that folk music, achieved international prominence. Michael Ippolitov-Ivanov (1859–1935, see under Russian Republic), though not Armenian, incorporated a number of Armenian folk songs and influences in his music, notably in the *Caucasian Sketches* and the *Armenian Rhapsody*. Alexander Arturyunian (born 1920) also absorbed Armenian folk music into his idiom; his best-known work is probably the innocuous *Trumpet Concerto* (1949).

Khatchaturian Aram Ilich*
(also spelt Khachaturian)
born 6th June 1903 at Tiflis
died 1st May 1978 at Moscow

The talents of Aram Khatchaturian suggest that if he had been born in America rather than the USSR, he would, with his penchant for bright colours, traditional harmonies and bold tunes, have made a consummate composer in the heyday of that capitalist counterpart to Soviet Socialist Realism, the Hollywood epic. Indeed, a large proportion of his output was for Soviet films. As it was, one aspect of his art in particular marks him out from the run of Soviet composers, and has brought a handful of his works international popularity.

His harmonies are coloured by the inflections of Armenian music, and in particular the interval of the minor second and the minor seventh, reflecting Armenian rather than traditional Western scales. This, with his sense of vivid colour and melodious flow, gives his music a touch of exotic piquancy, but it must be said that once one has heard one of Khatchaturian's works one has, to all intents and purposes, heard them all, as a quick comparison with the better-known passages of the ballet *Spartacus* and the opening of his graduation work, the *Symphony No. 1* (1933–34) of two decades earlier, will show.

That symphony, though marred by academic passages that betray Khatchaturian's inexperience, is an attractive and characteristic work, with folk inflections,

syncopated rhythms and colourful orchestration. Cheerfully bombastic at times, it
also has moments of delicate Romantic
lyricism, the impulse of the dance, and an
exotic third movement. It was followed by
a colourful and technically more assured
Piano Concerto (1936), in the grand
Romantic virtuoso tradition, saturated
with Armenian folk influence and with a
memorable use of the flexitone (musical
saw) in the lovely slow movement, full of a
hushed delight and wonder. The *Violin
Concerto* (1940) sounds too much like the
Piano Concerto for comfort, but is equally
as attractive and felicitous, and is the finer
work of the two: the musical argument is
tauter, and the lyrical tone of the violin
better suits Khatchaturian's idiom. It also
exists in a version for flute, the *Flute
Concerto*, transcribed by the flautist
Jean-Pierre Rampal at the composer's
suggestion. The *Cello Concerto* (1946) follows similar lines, but is less inspired in its
colours and its material.

Khatchaturian later produced three
Concerto-Rhapsodies, for violin (1961–62),
cello (1963) and piano (1965). The *Symphony No. 2* (1943, revised 1944) is a huge,
epic wartime symphony, known in Russia
as the *Bell Symphony* after the bell motive
that runs through the work. All colour,
sonority and effect, it has a stirring immediacy, a noble bombast, and is full of
sincere fervour. That bombastic element
was given full-blown and hideous sway in
the *Symphony No. 3* (1947, originally titled
Symphony-Poem) for orchestra, organ
and sixteen extra trumpets, a piece best
forgotten.

The summit of Khatchaturian's output is
in the ballets *Gayaneh* and *Spartacus*.
Both have reached a wider audience
through other media, the former from the
spare, haunted, monochromatic landscape
music in the film *2001: A Space Odyssey*,
the latter from use in the British television
series *The Onedin Line*. Both also have
complex histories. Some of the music for
Gayaneh (1940–41) originated in an earlier
ballet, *Happiness* (1936). The new ballet
was set on an Armenian collective farm,
telling the story of Gayaneh, her malicious
traitor of a husband, and her love for a
Russian officer. In 1957 a new version
appeared, to a completely different story
telling of a man racked with guilt for a
crime, and containing considerable additional music. Both contained the justly
famous *Sabre Dance*, a *tour de force* of
orchestral rhythmic energy and colour.

The first version is more often encountered, and Khatchaturian drew three
suites from the ballet.

Spartacus, based on the uprising of the
slaves against the Romans led by Spartacus, exists in an original version of 1956, a
version of 1957 with the story heavily
altered, and another version of 1958. It is
best known as an orchestral suite. The
beautiful 'Adagio of Spartacus and Phry-
gia', with its upward surge of excitement
and epic orchestration, is unforgettable; its
association with the sea in *The Onedin
Line* seemed so appropriate that it will be
difficult for many to imagine it in its
original stage context.

Of his other works, the early *Piano Trio*
(1932) is effective, while the waltz from the
suite *Masquerade*, based on incidental
music to Lermontov's play, is occasionally
heard. One of Khatchaturian's songs from
the film score of *Pepo* (1936) became so
popular that when the composer heard
some vineyard workers singing it, and
enquired what it was, he was told it was a
very old folk song.

Khatchaturian never quite fulfilled the
early promise of the *Symphony No. 1* and
the *Piano Concerto*, but his handful of
major works are vivid, undemanding, and
entertaining, and seem destined to remain
in the popular repertoire. He taught in
Moscow from 1950, and was an accomplished conductor of his own music. His
wife, Nina Makarova (1907–76), was also a
composer, as is his nephew, Karen Khatchaturian (born 1920).

RECOMMENDED WORKS
> ballet *Gayaneh* (1939–42, rev. 1952
>   and 1957)
> Piano Concerto (1936)
> ballet suite *Spartacus* (1954)
> Violin Concerto (1940)

Australia

Introduction

The pattern of Australian classical music has much in common with other countries that entered the 20th century without a classical music tradition of their own, such as Canada and Mexico. The earlier part of the century was characterised by music that essentially belonged to European traditions, with the best-known figures working outside Australia. A nationalist period, discovering indigenous traditions (in the case of Australia, Aboriginal legends and music), has been followed by a generation of younger composers either following the mainstream European avant-garde, or combining elements of that very international language with a continued exploration of Australia's own cultural and native heritage. However, followers of 12-tone developments have been rare in Australia; by the time younger composers studied in Europe, the influences were **Boulez, Stockhausen, Lutosławski** and similar models, who in many cases had themselves moved beyond serialism. Thanks to Australia's geographical position, many recent composers have also been influenced by traditional and contemporary music from the Pacific Rim countries, notably that of Balinese and Japanese cultures.

Of the earliest generation recognised as Australian composers, the two best known, Percy **Grainger** (1882–1961) and Arthur **Benjamin** (1893–1960), spent most of their lives working in Britain or the USA, and both came to prominence initially as pianists as much as composers. Peggy Glanville-Hicks (1912–90), a tireless critic and supporter of new music, spent most of her life in the USA and Greece, and is best known for her chamber music (including settings of some of fellow-critic Virgil Thomson's reviews) and later operas, notably *Nausicaa* (after Robert Graves, 1960). The main composer to stay in Australia was Alfred **Hill** (1879–1960) who retained throughout his life the musical language he had learnt in Germany at the end of the 19th century. Virtually unknown outside Australia is Margaret Sutherland (1897–1984), whose main legacy is her chamber music, and whose opera *The Young Kabbarli* (1964) was the first Australian opera to be recorded in Australia. Her pioneering example in a country not noted historically for its emancipation of women is reflected in the large number of contemporary Australian women composers. Other composers of this generation include William Lovelock (1899–1986).

The rediscovery of Aboriginal ideas and legends was spearheaded by the landmark ballet *Corroboree* (1935–46) by John Antill (1904–86), still one of the most successful and evocative of all Australian scores. Its basis is the opposition of percussion and high woodwind to the rest of a big orchestra; its colours are bright and bold, offset by the rattles and hisses of percussion. The atmosphere is one of sensuous headiness, of a primitivism driven by motoric rhythms, and if it has sometimes been called the Australian *Rite of Spring*, it is much more accurate to compare it with similar ballet works by **Ginastera** and **Villa-Lobos**, both of whom were responding to similar discoveries of a rich and earthy natural heritage. Of the next generation of composers, Malcolm **Williamson** (born 1931) is the senior figure, who attracted sufficient attention with his large-scale orchestral works to be appointed Master of the Queen's Music in Britain in 1975. Since the 1960s, his music has become increasingly conservative and lightweight, and has included operas for children and works with audience participation. Besides Williamson, the best known are Don **Banks** (1923–80), whose influences included jazz; Richard **Meale** (born 1932), whose language is international rather than identifiably Australian; and, perhaps the most familiar, Peter **Sculthorpe** (born 1929), who has been heavily influenced by music of the Pacific Rim. All three composers have regularly been heard in Europe and the USA.

During the 1970s and 1980s, Australia saw an explosion of artistic activity and cultural self-confidence, with Australian film and television attracting international attention. The building of the extraordinary Sydney Opera House, begun in 1957 and completed in 1973 with four concert halls and two recording halls, designed by the Danish architect Joern Utzon and one of the most imaginative buildings of its kind anywhere in the world, marked the maturity of Australia as a musical country. The explosion in cultural activity has had ramifications in composition, notably the opening of a national 24-hour serious music radio station by the Australian Broadcasting Corporation in 1976. However, familiarity with composers currently working in

Australia is greatly hampered by the failure to disseminate Australia's new music outside Australia. The Australian Broadcasting Corporation has made many excellent recordings, but they have appeared outside Australia only in private issues, and are found only in the largest university libraries.

Among the current generation of composers who deserve more interest are Nigel Butterley (born 1935), whose recent works have included settings of Walt Whitman, Barry Conyngham (born 1944); who has explored the Australian heritage in music theatre and opera (notably the opera *Ned*, 1974–78); and Douglas Knehans (born 1957), who is also turning to opera and music theatre. Helen Gifford (born 1935) is influenced by Balinese traditions, while John Crocker (1944–84) was an experimenter in sound as an art form using electronics and multimedia. Larry Sitsky (born 1934) is known for his keyboard music and his studies of Busoni. Martin Wesley-Smith (born 1945) concentrates on computer music and audio-visual works, and runs the group WATT and environmental group TREE. Michael Whiticker is influenced by the music of the Pacific Rim and the Korean composer Isang **Yun**. Betty Beath has written environmental works and a number of stage works for children to librettos by the writer David Cox, notably with indigenous, Balinese and Javanese themes. Ross Edwards (born 1943) has written in both a sparse, introspective style with Far Eastern influences, and a much more extrovert and traditional idiom.

Australian Music Centre Ltd
1st Floor, 18 Argyle St
The Rocks
New South Wales, 2000
Australia
tel: +61 2 247 4677
fax: +61 2 241 2873

Banks Don*

born 25th October, 1923 at Melbourne
died 5th September, 1980 at Sydney

Don Banks spent many years in Britain (1949–72), where he first came to attention with the *Duo for Violin and Cello* (1951–52), which uses a 14-note row. On his return to Australia, he became established as a leading figure in new music. His earliest acknowledged works were chamber pieces, but included transcriptions of Elizabethan works in *Elizabethan Miniatures* (1961), for flute, lute, viola da gamba and strings. With *Equation I* (1963–64) for jazz group and chamber ensemble he initiated a number of works that use jazz musicians (his father was a jazz player). These include *Settings from Roget* (1966), combining serialism with jazz, *Three Short Songs* (1971) for female jazz singer and jazz quartet, *Meeting Place* (1970) for chamber orchestra, jazz groups and sound synthesizer, and *Take Eight* (1973) for string quartet and jazz quartet. A flirtation with aleatoric elements was reflected in *Form X* (1964), a 'graphic score' for two to ten players. *Assemblies* (1966) for orchestra was designed to introduce student players to contemporary techniques, including semi-improvisatory elements, but is entertaining in its own right. The *Violin Concerto* (1966) is unusually constructed (the equivalent of a slow movement comes in the middle of the last of three movements), with melodic solo writing designed to avoid extended instrumental techniques, while at the same time building a complex of interrelated series expanding from a single cell. *Tirade* (1968) for voice, piano, harp, and percussionists (using some fifty instruments) is a kind of polemic against Australia, with texts by Peter Porter. It presents, amid a welter of percussion, a picture of Australia as an 'ever-present' museum, attacks the exploitation and rape of the Australian landscape, and savages the traditional treatment of Australia's culture and heritage. Its mood ranges from stark simplicity with characteristic slow progressions, to frenzy, including a siren. An element of that violence had earlier appeared in the short, atonal *Pezzo dramatico* (1956) for piano.

With *Intersections* (1969) for electronic sound and orchestra, Banks added electronic media to his palette, eventually leading to *Shadows of Space* (1972) for tape. *Limbo* (1972) for soloists, chamber ensemble and pre-recorded tape – pretentious existentialist text notwithstanding – shows an eclectic diversity, including half-spoken chattering, pop elements, tape interjections and lyrical vocal writing, which echoes, perhaps intentionally, Benjamin **Britten**, complete with distant snarling brass.

A more straightforward development of 12-tone principles appears in the *String Quartet* (1975), a flowing work in one continuous movement divided into two sections. It uses two tone-rows designed to overlap and conflict, enhanced by contrasting timbres and sonorities, at times melodically reminiscent of **Schoenberg**. A satisfying if unstartling work, it shows Banks's skill at combining clarity of thought and structure with easy lyricism.

Banks initiated an electronic music studio in Canberra, and taught at the Australian National University and Canberra School of Music from 1973. He was chairman of the Music Board of the Australian Council for the Arts from 1972 to 1974.

RECOMMENDED WORKS
   Violin Concerto (1966)
   Tirade (1968) for voice, harp, piano
      and percussion

Benjamin Arthur
   born September 18th 1893 at Sydney
   died April 19th 1960 at London

Arthur Benjamin was a virtuoso pianist and conductor as well as composer, and together with **Grainger** was one of the first Australian composers to be noticed internationally, partly through his residence in Britain from 1921 (teaching at the Royal Academy from 1926), and a period in North America (1941–46). Today he is primarily remembered for his operas and his lighter music. Of the former, the comic *The Devil Take Her* (1931) and *Prima Donna* (1933), enjoyed some success, while *Mañana* (1956) was the first opera televised by the BBC. The most highly regarded is *A Tale of Two Cities* (1948–49), but none has survived in the repertoire. His lighter music includes *Cotillon* (1938), a suite of dances for orchestra based on 17th-century tunes, an uninspiring diversion that has retained some popularity in Australia, and the humorous *Overture to an Italian Comedy* (1937). The jazzy and entertaining little *Concertino* (1927) for piano and orchestra is heavily influenced by **Gershwin** and **Ravel**'s piano concertos. His *Harmonica Concerto* (1953), with a beautiful slow movement, has retained its place as one of the very few serious concertante works for that instrument.

The works most likely to be encountered today are the series of Caribbean dances and rags, mostly for piano, though a number, notably *Two Jamaican Pieces* (1938), are scored for orchestra. Benjamin had encountered this music while touring in the area as a Music Board Examiner, but he himself wrote the pastiche tune for the most celebrated, *Jamaican Rumba* (the second of the *Jamaican Pieces*). The calypso style is enormously infectious, and there is a delight in the pianistic adaptation. Of his more serious works, which include a *Violin Concerto* (1932) and a *Symphony* (1944–45), the *Concerto quasi una fantasia* (1949) for piano and orchestra was written as a showpiece for his own pianistic powers. Tautly constructed with predominantly lyrical virtuoso piano writing that is indebted to **Rachmaninov**, it is not individual or interesting enough to warrant more than the rarest revival. His *Oboe Concerto* (1940) for oboe and strings is actually a reworking of keyboard sonatas by Domenico Cimarosa (1749–1801), and, though far more Cimarosa than Benjamin, is a lithe and gently delightful diversion.

Benjamin flew as a pilot in World War One, and was shot down and captured by the Germans.

RECOMMENDED WORKS
   calypso piano works
   Harmonica Concerto (1953)

Grainger Percy Aldridge*
   born 8th July 1882 at Melbourne
   died 20th February 1961 at White
      Plains, New York

Percy Grainger is a complete anomaly. His name is familiar to many, his music to few, apart from his orchestral arrangements of traditional folk songs or original pieces in similar styles that are known everywhere, especially *Country Gardens* (1925), *Handel in the Strand* (1913), *Molly on the Shore* (1913) and the suite *Lincolnshire Posy* (1937–38). In these his art is that of the miniature. His ability at arranging such material is considerable, retaining the rhythmic, vocal, and sometimes dialect irregularities that made the original folk songs so distinctive. The result was to give his arrangements an infectious life and vitality. He was an important early collector of folk songs in England (1905–09), recording songs on portable wax cylinder gramophone equipment, and later in Denmark (1922, 1925, 1927).

However, there was a completely different side to Grainger's work, which has been obscured by his habit of constant revision, the subsequent chaos of material, and the failure to pursue ideas to a completed form. This was entirely experimental, including microtones and electronic (using an early electronic instrument, the theremin, in *Free Music II*, 1935–36), with the aim of creating a 'free music' with a flow of sonorities beyond conventional techniques. Many of these early experiments used folk song or similar material as their base (a contemporary parallel to **Ives**'s experiments in the USA, using hymns or popular tunes as a base), or explored instrumental ideas advanced for their time (such as the arrangement of Debussy's *Pagodes* for mallet instruments and harmonium, 1918).

The orchestral score *The Warriors* (begun 1901, reworked 1906, otherwise 1912–16) shows many of these eclectic ideas, and will come as something of a surprise to those who know only his popular miniatures. Some of the orchestral ideas it contains, while familiar today, were revolutionary at the time: the extra scoring of what Grainger called 'tuneful percussion' (a battery of tuned instruments), a minimum of three pianos, sometimes played with marimba sticks, and two assistant conductors to control offstage forces. These offstage forces sometimes move at a different speed and in a different key to the main body in polyrhythmic and polytonal echoes. It is Grainger's longest continuous score, and has a typical energy and love of bright effect, its use of orchestral forces and polytonal effects sometimes anticipating general practice by two or more decades. But it also shows the weakness of Grainger's experiments: the basic material, sometimes using the type of melody and material preferred in the miniatures, is conventional underneath all the exploration of colour and sonority. *The Warriors* is a product of the late Edwardian era and, in terms of large-scale architecture, somewhat out of control. It is perhaps Grainger's failure to find a new musical language to match his aural ideas that has doomed this aspect of his output to relative obscurity. Nonetheless, *The Warriors* will fascinate the curious, and will be of particular interest to those exploring early experiments in ideas that have become familiar later in the century.

Similar in concept is *The Power of Rome and the Christian Heart* (1918–43) for orchestra, shorter in length but using even larger orchestral forces (including wind band, organ, piano ad lib and tuned percussion) that includes free sections for the percussion. The basic material is again straightforward but less interesting than that of *The Warriors*; any value lies in the colour effects. Although much has been made of this experimental aspect of Grainger in some quarters, it had no influence in his lifetime, and little (apart from

historical curiosity) since. It may be that the effectiveness of these experiments will become clearer with time; in the meantime, he will continue to be remembered for those catchy miniatures.

Grainger left Australia at the age of 13, and after a period settled in the USA in 1914, becoming a US citizen in 1918. He was celebrated as an international concert pianist of flair, including among his concerts one in the Hollywood Bowl to an audience of 20,000, at which he was married. He taught at the Chicago Musical College (1919–31) and at New York University.

RECOMMENDED WORKS
orchestral miniatures based on folk songs or similar materials
The Warriors (1912–16) for orchestra

BIBLIOGRAPHY
J Bird, *Percy Grainger, the Man and the Music*, London, 1976

Hill Alfred*
born 16th November 1870 at Melbourne
died 30th October 1960 at Sydney

Alfred Hill is the grandfather of Australian classical music, occupying a similar position to Sir Ernest **MacMillan** in Canada. He had the distinction of being born almost exactly a century after Beethoven, and his staunchly Romantic compositional style was formed by studies in Germany and by playing in the Leipzig Gewandhaus Orchestra (1887–91). This was followed by his discovery of Maori music during periods spent in New Zealand (1892–96, 1902–07).

His chief legacy is symphonies (of which ten are numbered); eleven are actually reworkings of music written mostly in the 1930s for string quartet or chamber groupings, though their origins are well disguised. Partly reflecting this reworking process, there was a long gap between the *Symphony No. 1 'The Maori'* (1896–1900) and *Symphony No. 2 'The Joy of Life'* (1941, based on *Life, 1912* for string quartet, piano, and eight voices) for soloists, chorus and orchestra. *Symphony No. 3 'Australia'* appeared in 1951, and the rest of the symphonies in the last fifteen years of Hill's long life. The *Symphony No. 4 'The Pursuit of Happiness'* (1955) was an original composition rather than a reworking. It is cast in the unmistakable lyrical style of the late 19th century, with touches of Dvořák, is exceptionally well crafted, with a logical flow and a lucidity of conventional orchestration that make it an appealing work. *Symphony No. 6 'Celtic'* recasts a string quartet of 1938 and makes extensive use of Irish folk material, especially jig rhythms, with a direct quotation in the slow movement. Those who enjoy the symphonies of **Parry** or **Harty** will respond. *Symphony in E flat* (unofficially No. 12, from *String Quartet No. 13*, 1936) has a more intimate, almost neo-classical feel in spite of a short-lived chromatic opening. The *Symphony in A minor*, unofficially No. 13, is for strings alone, and is based on the *String Quartet No. 9* (1935). It also has neo-classical overtones, and a rather beautiful and mournful *Andantino*, its mood immediately contradicted by the jaunty *Scherzo*.

Hill occupies an important position in the musical heritage of Australia and New Zealand, even if his work is virtually unknown elsewhere. If his idiom is anachronistic, it is wrought with skill and a sense of buoyancy. Historically he is a good example of a composer maintaining the ideas of his youthful training when attempting to forge a place for his compositions in a very young classical music culture, with no traditions of its own but close ties to a European heritage. Hill was a scholar of Maori music, was director of the New Zealand Orchestra and from 1915 taught at the newly founded New South Wales Conservatory. Among his pupils was Antill. From its foundation in 1931 he was active in the Australian Broadcasting Commission.

RECOMMENDED WORK
Symphony No. 4 (*The Pursuit of Happiness*, 1955)

Meale Richard
born 24th August 1932 at Sydney

A pianist as well as composer, Richard Meale is of all Australian composers the one most clearly influenced by the mainstream advances in European orchestral writing. A programmatic element, sometimes based on historical associations, plays a strong role in his works, which prefer rugged and atmospheric ideas to the picturesque.

Following the composition of his *Flute Sonata* (1960), the first work to suggest a European influence, he withdrew all his earlier music. Spanish influence appears in *Los Alboradas* (1963) for flute, violin, horn and piano and *Homage to García Lorca* (1964), which exists in versions for two string orchestras and two string groups. *Nocturnes* (1967) for orchestra, solo harp, vibraphone and celesta is highly regarded in Australia, its six sections describing the movements of the sun and moon, and their symbolic associations. The rather startling *Very High Kings* (1968) for orchestra was the first of an intended cycle, *The Mystical Voyage of Christopher Columbus*. It opens with a massive organ chord against a orchestra holding a hushed chord that emphasises the minor 7th, reminiscent of **Messiaen**, before launching into an atmospheric sequence of short disjointed phrases struggling against subdued sonorities. There is a wide range of orchestral effect, notably bells and two amplified pianos. *Clouds Now and Then* (1969) and *Soon It Will Die* (1969), both for orchestra, are inspired by Japanese haiku poetry.

A two-year compositional silence preceded *Evocations* (1972) for oboe and chamber orchestra with violin obligato, commissioned by Paul Sacher with the virtuoso oboist Heinz Holliger in mind as soloist. The evocations of the title refer to the interaction of soloists and orchestra (the latter evoking the former), and musical ideas (notes, chords, fragments) evoking other similar musical materials. *Veridian* (1978–79 – the title is a play on various connotations of 'green') is similarly atmospheric, with Messiaen again an influence. In comparison to *Evocations*, it has a stronger sense of linear progression, with less reliance on fragmentation. With the *String Quartet No. 2* (1980), Meale, like many other mainstream contemporary composers, switched to a neo-Romantic, lyrical style. Among his more recent projects has been an opera based on Patrick White's novel *Voss*; a major undertaking, as Meale's only other acknowledged vocal work (*This I*, three songs for soprano and piano on verses by Spender) was written in 1955.

Meale is a noted interpreter of the piano works of Messiaen, and the influence of the French composer is again evident in *Coruscations* for piano (1971 – its title refers to rapid flashes of light, as in the aurora borealis), Messiaen's technique of fragmentation of material here extended into very short phrases and ideas.

Meale has taught at the University of Adelaide since 1969.

RECOMMENDED WORK
Very High Kings (1968) for orchestra

Sculthorpe Peter Joshua**
born 19th April 1929 at Launceston,
Tasmania

Peter Sculthorpe is one of the best known of his generation of Australian composers. His music has been widely performed outside Australia, and he has taught at Yale (1965–67) and at Sussex University (1971–72). He is also one of the major Australian composers who, in applying an antipodean orientation to European models, has merged the concepts and traditions of the Pacific Rim countries with a personal and evocative response to the Australian landscape and its indigenous traditions. He remains the most impressive of all Australian composers, who has forged an idiom that is individual and recognisable, draws on European roots, and yet belongs entirely to its own emerging cultural and geographic origins.

His oriental interest was announced in the *Sonata for Viola and Percussion* (1960), but he came to wider prominence with a series of works titled *Sun Music* for orchestra. Part of the inspiration was the stark Australian landscape, and the Aboriginal concept of 'Dreamtime'; much of the musical means stems from the Far East. The impressive *Sun Music I* (1965) is rich in the sonorities of Far Eastern ceremonial court music, translated into dense orchestral textures with a strong sense of ritual developed by alteration of sonorities and textures rather than melodic or rhythmic momentum. *Sun Music II* (1966–69) has echoes of Eastern processional street music, the percussion dominating in sounds used to ward off evil spirits. *Sun Music III 'Anniversary Music'* (1966) sets delicate gamelan sounds, woodwind reminiscent of Chinese or Japanese models, and high strings against gentle static textures, with a favourite device of high scraping strings suggesting bird calls. The melodic content is more direct, and magically and gradually evolves from that Eastern influence to a highly atmospheric evocation of the Australian outback – bird calls prominent, the rattle of indigenous percussion instruments adding their own unmistakable timbre – before the Far Eastern ritual re-emerges. The more intense *Sun Music IV* (1967) collects together many of the elements of the earlier works. The four works, with their inherent contrasts, work well as a series to be played in succession,

the overwhelming sense of ritual combining with the evocation of landscape to create a forty-minute score of impressive power that manages to be international in its implications while specific in its origins. *Sun Music for Voices and Percussion* (1966) is a supplement to the series.

The influence of indigenous and Aboriginal sounds is overt in *The Song of Tailitnama* (1974, the title refers to an Aboriginal totemic centre) for high voice, six cellos and percussion (version for voice and piano, 1984). Originally written for a television documentary, its vivid opening sets a lyrical wordless voice against the clicking sounds of percussion and high scoops using harmonic overtones on the cellos, before a solo cello takes over the melody. The subsequent verses are a wallaby song in Aranda. With the tangible integration of a very different aural culture, this would make a fascinating companion piece to **Villa Lobos**'s *Bachianas brasileiras No. 5*, which influenced Sculthorpe's work. *How the Stars Were Made* (1971), written for the virtuoso percussion ensemble Percussions de Strasbourg, is also based on Aboriginal legend, while *Port Essington* (1977) for string trio and string orchestra is a musical reflection of historical events. The town of the title, an early settlement, was gradually given up to the encroaching bush; the string trio, recalling salon music, is gradually overcome by the more primitive cast of the string orchestra. *Mangrove* (1979) for orchestra without wind is a reflection of the many associations with that tree, from Sidney Nolan paintings to a New Guinea concept that people are descended from mangroves. Cast in one movement, the piece contrasts short phrases for brass and percussion with longer, darker passages, including a melody that uses a gradual phase shift to create echo effects. The multitudinous bird sounds of a mangrove swamp are marvellously evoked by the use of high strings. The sense of tropical primitivism is expressed by a section for drums against increasingly wild calls, joined by long string phrases and finally brass, to round off a graphic score.

More obviously neo-Romantic in mood is the *Piano Concerto* (1983), partly reflecting the deaths of three friends during its composition. Within its traditional European five-movement form, some of the ideas stem from traditional Japanese court music, and the repetitions and slow transformations of the piano writing from Balinese gamelan music. The result is an unusual and disconcerting mixture, the bright, detailed figurations of the piano regularly setting up textures against lengthier and more conventional material in the orchestra. The shifts between echoes of the Romantic tradition and a soundscape of more dense and unaccustomed origins produce impressive colours and sonorities. *Kakadu* (1988) for orchestra is an evocation of the sounds of Australia's north, especially birds.

Of his string quartets, the *String Quartet No. 8* (1969, subtitled *String Quartet Music*) has been widely heard through the advocacy of the popular Canadian Kronos Quartet. It too evokes bird calls, with high string trills and harmonics against more conventional melodic material, later combined with gamelan influences and Balinese 'rice-pounding' music. However, the predominant mood in this strongly evocative quartet is lyrical, with its sectional structure lending a haunting atmosphere. His major stage works have been *Rites of Passage* (1972–73) for soloists, chorus, orchestra and dancers, using Latin texts from Boethius and Southern Aranda poetry, and a television opera, *Quiros* (1982).

Sculthorpe's voice is distinctive and individual, and his combination of the sounds of the Pacific Rim cultures and his native land has created an idiom of its own. His powers of recreating sound images suggest the tactile and visual qualities of sculpture. For those unfamiliar with contemporary Australian serious music it is a rewarding place to start.

RECOMMENDED WORKS
   The Song of Tailitnama (1974) for
      high voice, six cellos and
      percussion
   String Quartet No. 8 *String Quartet
      Music* (1969)
   Sun Music I–IV (1965–67)

BIBLIOGRAPHY
   P Sculthorpe, *Sun Music*
   M Hannan, *Peter Sculthorpe, His
      Music and Ideas 1929–1979*, 1982

Williamson (Sir) Malcolm Benjamin Graham Christopher*
born 21st November 1931 at Sydney

Malcolm Williamson in 1975, was the first Australian composer to be appointed Master of the Queen's Music in Britain, succeeding Sir Arthur Bliss. Settling in London in his early twenties, his earliest works were influenced by **Messiaen** (Williamson, like Messiaen, became a virtuoso organist), but his large output quickly became divided into lighter pieces designed to entertain, or to be performed by amateur players, and more weighty works, notably symphonies and concertos. Gradually, from the 1960s on, the former dominated and, in spite of his flirtations with modernism, his idiom has emerged as essentially conservative. His music increasingly reflects that quasi-amateur light-heartedness or jolliness that has bedevilled English music for two centuries.

The *Symphony No. 1* (1957), titled *Elevamini*, is one of Williamson's finest works. It is based, as are some subsequent works, on a tone-row, in this case of eight notes, although the row is designed to give a modal cast. The three movements are programmatic, describing a soul's journey after death. In the contrast between the more searching weight of the outer movements and the lightness of the central movement, a lively *Allegretto* that delights in dance cross-rhythms are the seeds of the later split in his style, and the moments of less taut, focused writing presage those of his later, less inspired output. The one-movement *Symphony No. 2* (1969) is quite different, thoughtful and thick-textured. Two other symphonies are not numbered. The *Organ Symphony* (1960) for solo organ is in six movements, while the *Symphony for Voices* (1960) is a setting for unaccompanied choir of poems by the Australian James McAuley. The *Organ Concerto* (1961), written for Williamson himself to play, was a tribute to the conductor Sir Adrian Boult. It has an imposing timpani opening, offset by the unlikely colours of a solo harp. Entertaining enough on first hearing, the work cannot sustain interest and at times sounds dangerously similar to **Poulenc's** incomparably better concerto. It is a frustrating experience, as so many of the individual moments are full of promise and interest. It is only fair to say that others may react differently to this curious work, imbued with both Williamson's strengths and weaknesses, and it is therefore recommended to those interested.

Among Williamson's finest works is the *Violin Concerto* (1965), written as a tribute to Edith Sitwell, which inserts a playful scherzo amongst its otherwise melodious and thoughtful movements. Rich and lyrical solo lines are set against tough and tragic orchestral writing in the opening movement. Of his other concertos, the *Sinfonia Concertante* (1958–61) for piano and orchestra is a vigorous, terse work, recalling **Stravinsky**. The *Concerto for Piano and String Orchestra (Piano Concerto No. 2*, 1960) was written for Australian amateurs and students. The *Piano Concerto No. 3* (1962), for all its Romantic overtones combined with gently dissonant features, emerges as a piece of light music. With its pseudo jazz and aimless strings, it is a completely valueless piece apart from the infuriatingly delightful, simple, limpid opening idea of the slow movement, reminiscent of Shostakovich's *Piano Concerto No. 2* (the rest of the movement is as bombastic as its surroundings). The rather disappointing *Concerto for Two Pianos and Strings* (1973) has a middle movement based on a slow waltz, and shades of **Bartók** in the finale.

His early operas, *Our Man in Havana* (1963, based on Graham Greene's famous novel) and *English Eccentrics* (1964, after Sitwell) were widely admired when they appeared, but failed to maintain a place in the repertoire. His subsequent stage works concentrated on operas for children. His works for smaller instrumental forces include the *Piano Sonata No. 2* (1957, revised 1971). Later works, including three more symphonies (No. 3, 1972, *The Icy Mirror*, for soloists, chorus and orchestra; No. 4, 1977; No. 5 *Aquero*, 1977), and a considerable body of choral music and masses, as well as music for ceremonial duties as Master of the Queen's Music, have failed to have any impact.

RECOMMENDED WORKS
Organ Concerto (1961)
Symphony No. 1 *Elevamini* (1957)
Violin Concerto (1965)

Austria

Introduction

Vienna was the city of Mozart, Beethoven and Schubert, and Austria had already been the cradle of European music-making for over a century when, at the beginning of the 20th century, it became the centre of intellectual progress in Europe in all artistic fields, including new music.

The late Romantic musical idiom, large in scale, employing huge forces, turbulent, eclectic, and soul-searching, found its spiritual centre in Vienna, coinciding with a burgeoning in contemporary poetry and painting. **Mahler** (1860–1911) and **Schoenberg** (1874–1951) – the latter in his early works – took the parameters of this idiom, especially the harmonic foundations of traditional tonality, to their limits, and in so doing in part reconciled the division that had split the musical world in the latter part of the 19th century, between the hedonistic spirit of Wagner and the furtherance of the classical tradition, founded on counterpoint and represented by Brahms. A number of lesser but still potent composers such as **Zemlinsky** (1871–1942), **Schreker** (1878–1934), the young **Korngold** (1897–1957), and Karl Weigl (1881–1949), whose output includes six symphonies and eight string quartets, continued this luxuriant and psychologically turbulent idiom. The major German exponent of late Romanticism, Richard **Strauss** (1864–1949), himself became increasingly influential in, and influenced by, Viennese musical life, directing the Vienna State Opera from 1919–24, and becoming an Austrian citizen in 1947. The more classical tradition of Austro-German composition was continued and developed by Franz **Schmidt** (1874–1939), and the Viennese staple of operetta by a number of composers, notably Franz Lehár (1870–1948), whose major work, *Die lustige Witwe (The Merry Widow*, 1905) has sufficient depth and insight to be classed an opera rather than an operetta.

The major contribution of Austria to 20th-century classical music (still resonating through composition today) was the response to the crisis of reaching the limits of traditional tonal harmony effected by Schoenberg and his two main pupils, **Berg** (1885–1935) and **Webern** (1883–1945), who have become collectively (and rather misleadingly) known as 'The Second Viennese School'. Their initial move was towards atonality, abandoning any sense of key and thus using the entire chromatic scale of twelve notes in the harmonic palette; at the same time they reverted to smaller forces, especially chamber forces, a medium hardly touched by Mahler or Strauss, and to much shorter durations. The next step, developed by Schoenberg, was to formalise rules for the use and manipulation of rows, or melodies, based on all twelve notes of the chromatic scale (12-note rows – for fuller details, see **Schoenberg**). A similar system had been simultaneously and independently developed by a little-known Austrian composer, J. M. Hauer (1883–1959), who produced over seventy 12-tone works, notably the cantata *Wandlungen* (1927). Webern concentrated on concise miniatures using this system, moving towards the serialisation and the systematisation of other parameters besides harmony (dynamics, rhythm, etc.), fully developed by his followers in the avant-garde movement of the 1950s and 1960s. Berg eventually evolved the system to allow suggestions of a tonal base within the row, in a style that has proved perhaps the most durable.

A number of other Schoenberg pupils should correctly be included in the Second Viennese School, notably Egon Wellesz (1885–1974), whose large output includes nine symphonies and more quartets and some works that returned to tonality; he is better known as a musicologist and teacher than as a composer. Ernst **Krenek** (1900–92) was also a Schoenberg pupil, but achieved fame with the successful opera *Jonny spielt auf* which incorporated jazz. The surrealist movement was represented by Max Brand (1896–1980), whose opera *Maschinist Hopkins* (first performed 1929) was equally successful, with its machines among the singing character and its working-class subject matter, is a powerful work worth encountering.

The experimentation that so much of this musical activity represented was cut short by the rise of the Nazis and their control of Austria (1938–45). Most of the major intellectual and artistic figures fled, including Schoenberg, Krenek, Korngold, Weigl and Zemlinsky to the United States, and Wellesz to the UK. Since the Second World War Austrian composers have not been nearly so prominent: von **Einem** (1918–96), a major opera composer, is probably the most widely heard, though more recently H. K. Gruber (born 1943) has attracted attention, notably with his compelling surrealist *Frankenstein!!* (1976–77), for narrator and orchestra, and

as one of the first avant-garde composers to return to tonality.

Austrian Music Information Centre:
Österreichische Gesellschaft für Musik
Stiftgasse 29
A-1070 Wien
tel: +43 1 521 04 52
fax: +43 1 512 04 59

Berg Alban Maria Johannes***
born 9th February 1885 at Vienna
died 24th December 1935 at Vienna

The name and the music of Alban Berg are inextricably linked with those of his teacher **Schoenberg** and fellow pupil **Webern**. Of the three, Berg most completely fused the emotional inheritance of the late Romantic composers – in particular the emotional if not always the musical legacy of **Mahler** – with the new ideas and explorations of Schoenberg. Collectively the three composers have become known as the Second Viennese School, a tag that has hindered appreciation of the individuality of each composer, and of Berg in particular.

Berg produced a very small number of works of astonishing power and emotional and technical range, less strictly tied to the minutiae of systems than those of Schoenberg and Webern. Unfortunately, his name is so inextricably linked with 12-tone ideas in the popular imagination that many have shied away from the discovery of his music for fear of a dissonance and complexity comparable to that of Webern. This has been reinforced by the tendency of academics to treat Berg's music in terms of quasi-mathematical formulae, to the detriment of the emotional content and the expressive word setting that inform his most powerful works. A couple of works apart (discussed below), the actuality is quite different. Indeed, much of Berg's sound has passed into the common currency of subsequent mainstream composers and his music provides an excellent introduction to that mainstream, as well as a comfortable initiation into atonal and 12-tone ideas.

Berg's earliest music consists of a large number of songs, long unpublished but recently unearthed, that follow the tradition of Schumann and Brahms. However, in 1904 he started studying with Schoenberg, developing his idiom through the late Romantic German tradition, and then following his teacher's lead to increasingly atonal works. The *Seven Early Songs*

(1905–08, orchestrated in 1928) have the feel of a grand outpouring of emotion, the intensity heightened by a tense restraint, and are rich in colour, especially in the version for voice and orchestra. The influential one-movement *Piano Sonata* op. 1 (1907–08), a model for later composers making a similar break with tonality, is built on the transformation of a few seminal ideas. This concise and fascinating work has a sense of transition, from the echoes of late Romanticism in the melodic cast and broken chords, to a more astringent, angular idiom in which the emotional content has become compressed. Any tonal associations are almost lost, apart from clear moments of restful resolution, like a snake in the process of sloughing off its skin. The last of the *Four Songs* op. 2 (1909–10), is totally atonal, without any key signature, and was followed by the original and inventive *String Quartet* op. 3 (1910). Developing concepts initiated in the *Piano Sonata*, Berg used themes and ideas without any tonal implications, but constructed in such a way that they act as points of reference analogous to traditional tonal development, thus providing the listener with a clear aural map.

Berg's next work is a masterpiece that remained virtually unknown until its first complete performance by the Swiss conductor Ernest Ansermet in 1952. The *Fünf Orchesterlieder nach Ansichtkartentexten von Peter Altenberg* (1912) for soprano and orchestra, usually known as the *Five Altenberg Songs*, are based on Expressionist texts by Altenberg. Berg takes the huge apparatus of Mahlerian orchestral song-cycle and compresses it into five short songs (whose brevity led to the tag 'aphoristic'), extending the harmonic ideas into spare and alienated regions. Quite apart from the multiplicity of fascinating technical devices that meld into an extraordinary cohesion, these emotionally intense and varied songs are knife-edged and tortured, expressing the intense introversion, psychological turmoil, and alienation of the age. Overlaid is a sense of the vastness of the nature in which this vision is placed, aided by the simple bright colours of the huge orchestra, the magical and mysterious ostinato opening (prefiguring more recent musical developments, with no two patterns the same), by the climactic Mahlerian outburst in the last song, and by the latent lyricism. In this song-cycle Berg expressed a universal aspect of the troubled human experience, verging on the neurotic and the despairing but pulling back from the brink. He does so in a fashion

that has rarely been equalled by any other composer, and the *Five Altenberg Songs* are one of the masterpieces of the 20th century.

Schoenberg was scathing of the *Altenberg Songs*, and Berg's response was to attempt in the *Four Pieces for Clarinet and Piano*, op. 5 (1913) the kind of genuine aphorisms that his teacher and Webern had explored. The pieces are exceedingly short (12, 9, 18 and 20 bars). The technical brilliance is undoubted (the pieces correspond to a four-movement classical sonata) but the results are completely sterile, especially when set alongside Webern's similar works. They are primarily interesting as a musical example of psychological dependence. Berg followed with a controlled explosion of emotional intensity: the *Three Orchestral Pieces* (1914–15, revised 1929). This wonderful work bridges the sultry turbulence of late Romanticism and the asceticism of Webern and Schoenberg. The *Three Orchestral Pieces* are unmistakably a development of the idiom of late Mahler, most obviously in the use of a Ländler and a march, more covertly in the conjunction of fragmentary emotional ideas swirling around a central core of progression, and in the orchestral colours. The genesis of the thematic material is contained in the opening 'Präludium', to be unravelled in threads in the subsequent movements. Above all, the impact is emotional, not intellectual – the passion of the *Altenberg Songs* revisited – from the opening, like a hollow groan, to the strands of resolution that precede the dissonant close.

The *Altenberg Songs* are a prelude to the works for which Berg is perhaps best known, the operas *Wozzeck* (1917–22) and *Lulu* (1929–35). At the heart of these operas is a similar emotional intensity, a study of the human psyche on the edge of neurosis, viewed against the dysfunctional world around. *Wozzeck* is a seminal work, as central to 20th-century opera as Wagner's *Tristan und Isolde* had been to the late 19th century. Its place as the first atonal operatic masterpiece has often been attested, being seen either as a break with the Romantic tradition of grand opera or as the culmination of opera itself. Less often remarked is the revolution created by its plot (though Schoenberg was quick to recognise it), based on Georg Büchner's incomplete 1837 play, which had received its first stage performance only in 1913. *Wozzeck* is the first truly proletarian opera, its main characters coming from the seamy underside of social life, presented without a trace of sentimentality or patronisation. The characters of a higher social order – the Doctor, the Captain – are equally starkly drawn, their social position doubtful. In this, *Wozzeck* destroyed the conventions of large-scale opera, attacked the complacency of opera audiences, demanded their compassion, and questioned the normality of social order. Wozzeck, an ordinary private soldier, is naïve, trusting, but entirely human. His gullibility is preyed upon by the neurotic Captain and by the obsessive Doctor, who performs experiments on him. His essentially passive nature is incapable of satisfying the more wanton dreams of his young wife, Marie, who is wooed by a visiting Drum Major. Goaded on by those around him, tormented by his bewilderment at the evil world in which he finds himself and by the inexorable progression of events, Wozzeck is overwhelmed by paranoia and murders Marie. The opera ends with the voices of children, playing with Wozzeck's daughter and running off to see her dead mother.

Berg was aided in his setting by the fragmentary nature of the incomplete play, in which only individual scenes, and thus the plot, were complete. This entirely suited his musical conception, which again made a break with operatic tradition. The work is divided into three acts, further divided to follow the scenes of the play. The five scenes of Act II are the psychological centrepiece; Act I sets the background, and Act III expounds the inevitable consequences of those five scenes. For the musical realisation of this structure, Berg used forms that were associated with abstract music, and not with opera. The opening five scenes are self-contained musical units ('character sketches'), including a suite and a passacaglia. The second act constitutes a five-movement symphony, and is constructed as such. In Act III each of the five scenes is an 'invention': on a theme, on a sound, on a rhythm, a tone, and a perpetuum mobile, the interlude being an invention on a key. Musical motifs and their manipulations and variations bind this structure together, and each act ends with a cadence on the same chord. The danger of such a scheme is that adherence to the formal musical requirements will override the suitability for the dramatic action. This Berg brilliantly avoids in an astonishing synthesis of form and content, the structural elements providing a musical symbolism for the characterisation. His formal innovations have since been widely emulated. Such technical considerations should not disguise the expressive intent of the opera, as Berg himself was at pains to point out. Indeed, it is not necessary to be even aware of them for the work to have extraordinary impact. The atonal language with its varied vocal lines, from wide leaps to *Sprechgesang* (half-speech, half-song), is completely suited to the psychological torment of the work, and many who have found such a musical language otherwise difficult have found it perfectly acceptable in such a dramatic context. Berg, who generally uses the orchestra on a chamber scale, avoids musical judgement, presenting the characters, their good or their evil sides, for what they are, with compassion and understanding. Recordings provide a marvellous opportunity to follow and understand the formal constructs of *Wozzeck*; but they can only hint at the emotional impact a good production of this most important of 20th-century operas can have.

Berg's next work, the *Chamber Concerto* (1923–25) for piano, violin and 13 wind instruments, is, after the *Four Pieces for Clarinet and Piano*, the second odd work in his canon. Given its dedicatory purpose for the occasion of Schoenberg's 50th birthday, it is tempting to see it as another attempt to please the master rather than follow his own compositional instincts. With its abstract formal designs and lean instrumental textures, it has more than a hint of neo-classicism. The result sounds curiously stilted for such an emotionally fluid composer.

Berg used the full 12-tone system first in a song, *Schliesse mir die Augen beide* (1925; he had set the same song tonally in 1905), and then, using for the first movement the same 12-note series as the song, in the *Lyric Suite* (1925–26) for string quartet. Berg does not adopt the strict constraints of the 12-tone technique that were self-imposed by Schoenberg and Webern. Instead, he evolved a less rigid (but intellectually equally well-ordered) use of the main elements of 12-tone technique, better suited to his expressive idiom, with its late Romantic roots. He used smaller-scale integrated structures, usually echoing Classical models, building up a series of these units to create an overall form (often using symmetry or palindromes): this is a primary technical break with the Mahlerian late Romantic tradition, which had preferred a sonata-form symphonic structure. Onto this formal scaffolding he built 12-tone techniques to extend the harmonic language. Berg had used such a construction in *Wozzeck*; in the six-movement *Lyric Suite* the 12-tone elements are used to build the material that is placed within that structure, and to unify the individual units (*Lulu* has similar structural priorities). Thus only the first, third (less its trio) and the sixth movements are built entirely on 12-tone principles, and the first movement has three 12-note series, rather than the single one preferred by Schoenberg. There are 12-tone ideas in the second and fifth movements that prefigure those of the following movements, and themes and longer sections are shared by more than one otherwise autonomous movement to give an overall cohesion to the work. The aesthetic is very different from that of Webern, where the structural base and the 12-tone usage are inextricably interwoven. From this crucial difference stem two of the main trends of post-1945 composition, the serialists following the lead of Webern, and, as it has turned out, a larger and more influential number of composers following Berg in integrating 12-tone elements into languages and structures derived from, or inspired by, other sources.

The *Lyric Suite* has a secret programme: the basic cell (B–F–A–B flat, in German H–F–A–B) is based on Berg's own initials and those of the object of his passion, Hanna Fuchs-Robettin, the wife of an industrialist. It is an intense and dramatic work, as if the quartet were together telling some dramatic tale, and this drama is reflected in the titles of the movements (*giovale, amoroso, misterioso, appassionato, delirando, desolato*) which describe the emotional progression. Berg himself suggested that the changes to the initial 12-tone series that occur through the work represented a 'submission to fate'. It is also a technically dramatic work, stretching the expressive range of the string instruments by a plethora of techniques and sonic effects, most obvious in the fragmentary, hallucinatory effects of the 'Allegro misterioso', with its use of harmonics. In 1928 Berg orchestrated three of the movements (the 'Andante amoroso', the 'Allegro misterioso' and the 'Adagio appassionato') to form an orchestral suite. This is probably more often encountered than the full suite for string quartet; unfortunately it is usually billed as the *Lyric Suite* rather than its full title of *Three Pieces from the 'Lyric Suite'*, which can cause some confusion.

Berg's next vocal work, *Der Wein* (1929) for soprano and orchestra, is an extended dramatic aria to three poems by Baudelaire (in German), equating wine with its power over world-weariness. It anticipates some of the concepts used in *Lulu*, notably the use of a saxophone and piano in the orchestration. Berg uses a 12-note row freely, as a source of thematic material. A connection with a tonal language is maintained, anticipating the *Violin Concerto*, in that the row chosen has the possibility of tonal chordal implications. The work thus still has its origins in an extension of a late Romantic idiom, particularly in the orchestral flow and the flowing vocal line, with echoes of Mahler in the climaxes and the falling orchestral swoops. Against these, the angular nature of the intervals in the vocal line and the juxtaposition of thematic ideas create a nervous energy and a disassociated, unsettled atmosphere that takes the work far beyond a purely Romantic aesthetic.

The opera *Lulu* (1929–35) extends the musical and dramatic world of *Wozzeck*. For many years it was given in a truncated two-act form, as Berg did not finish the orchestration or short sections of the final act. This was completed by Friedrich Cerha, and first given in 1979 (Cerha had secretly completed it some years earlier, but had to wait until the death of Berg's widow before publishing it). Such is the formal and emotional importance of that third act that any two-act version is best avoided. The central theme of the opera, distilled from two controversial plays by Frank Wedekind, is of the sexual obsession of men, with the associated themes of power and death. Through the often lurid scenes weaves the object of that obsession, Lulu, at one and the same time a victim and an instigator of her liaisons. Berg makes no moral judgement on her or on her surroundings, and in modern terms *Lulu* might be described as a study of a series of co-dependent relationships. The first act describes Lulu's rise, the death of her husband when he discovers her making love to a painter, her marriage to the painter, his suicide when he discovers that she has a patron, and her manipulation of that patron to cast aside his fiancée. The second act is her triumph, with marriage to her patron, and a bevy of admirers and lovers of both sexes. She murders her husband and is jailed, but her lesbian lover, the Countess, takes her place, allowing her to escape. The third act is her fall. Living with the son of her murdered patron, she is blackmailed in an attempt to sell her into white slavery, but again she escapes. In the final scene she has been reduced to living as a prostitute in London. She is visited by the Countess, but, offstage, she is murdered by one of her clients, Jack the Ripper, who then kills the Countess.

Such a plot could easily emerge as melodramatic. That it does not is due to a host of structural devices, including an introduction by a circus-master, the duplication of Lulu's three admirers in the opening of the opera by her three clients at the end (with the same singers, and musical associations), and a kind of substitute father figure from Lulu's past who stalks through the work unscathed. The depth of characterisation is also considerable; Berg creates an extraordinary expressive atmosphere, a world in which such crazy behaviour seems the norm. Relatively short, self-contained scenes allow a series of snap-shots of the long time-span of the story. The arch symmetry of the plot is emphasised, with a three-minute film designated for the central point of the opera, showing Lulu's trial and imprisonment, and its retrograde, her escape from prison.

A major change from the earlier opera is that Berg now employs the 12-tone system developed since *Wozzeck* by Schoenberg. The use of material derived from 12-note series and other core cells binds the work together. Analysis of that usage has prompted endless argument and discussion, which although fascinating, is of scant relevance to *Lulu* as a work of operatic art. More important is the overall scheme. Each act has a central musical structure (a sonata-allegro in Act I, a rondo in Act II, a theme and variations in Act III), used less rigidly than in *Wozzeck*, as they are surrounded and interrupted by other self-contained musical events. These shorter units hark back to earlier, Classical conceptions: ariettas, canzonettas, duets, interludes. The vocal writing is wide-ranging; jazz is employed in the theatre scene, though for purely dramatic purposes, as a distant backdrop to the foreground action. All these devices serve one single purpose: the expressive realisation of the drama and characters, of a slice of the human dilemma, presented in a close marriage of music and word.

Of all operas *Lulu* perhaps comes closest to the fast interplay of human speech, dialogue, interruption and argument. This is due partly to the libretto, partly to the flexibility of the vocal lines, again wide-ranging in technique, but most of all to the extraordinary elasticity of Berg's musical setting. The instrumental language, kept for the most part to chamber proportions, wraps itself around the vocal lines like an outer skin, acting as a kind of musical body-language to our encounter with the characters and their emotions. The genius of Berg's setting is that these constant fluctuations flow so naturally into each other. The ending of the opera, with the Countess crying out for Lulu, has the musical ambience of, and quotes directly from, the final *Altenberg Song*, which itself describes the emptiness of oblivion. This magnificent opera, more wide ranging, clearer, musically more lucid and ultimately more harrowing than *Wozzeck*, clearly had autobiographical associations for Berg. Wedekind's character Alwa is altered by Berg to a composer and there are connections with the lives of his own family, as there are echoes of Berg's passion for Hanna Fuchs-Robettin. The suite of five symphonic pieces from *Lulu* (*Symphonische Stücke aus der Oper 'Lulu'*, 1934, for soprano and orchestra) utilises music from the orchestral interludes, Lulu's *Lied* from Act II, and the Countess's final words from the end of the opera.

Berg's final completed work, the *Violin Concerto* (1935), is subtitled *To The Memory of an Angel*, and was written following the death from polio of Manon Gropius, the daughter of Mahler's widow and her second husband, the architect Walter Gropius. Berg incorporates a quote from the opening of the Bach chorale *Es ist genug!* (*'It is enough'*) and a Carpathian folksong. There is also a second, secret autobiographical programme, contained in the numerology of the bar numbers, in some of the markings, and in the (unprinted) actual words to the Carpathian folk song. This programme reflects Berg's first major love affair, with a servant-woman, that led to the birth of his illegitimate child, and his last, with Hanna Fuchs-Robettin. Musically, the concerto is founded on a 12-tone row with strong tonal associations; its penultimate three notes form the motif of the Bach chorale. The subsequent material interlaces tonal and 12-tone elements within a strict framework that provided Berg with the base for expressive and harmonic freedom. The four movements are divided into two pairs, with the only break between the second and third. The first pair of movements portray Manon Gropius; the second pair suggest death and transfiguration, returning us to the principal philosophical theme of late Romanticism. The rocking opening of the concerto, leading to the first recognition of the Bach chorale, is steeped in warm affection, and the work progresses through the development of that mood, a lyrical sense of reminiscence, echoes of the Viennese

Ländler, and the chorale-variations final movement, with its feeling of acceptance and reconciliation. The solo line provides a continuous thread among these changes of emotional expression, and is not merely fluid, but has something of the freedom of flight, like a swallow or a swift spontaneously darting and soaring over a pond, buoyed up by the eddies and gullies and thunderstorms of the orchestral air in which it moves, eventually gliding in the calm of sunset.

Now that over sixty years have passed since Berg's death, it is clear that Berg's ties to Schoenberg and Webern existed primarily on two levels. The first was psychological: a strange triangle of dominance and submission, with Schoenberg as the tyrannical father-figure, who seems to have answered some psychological need in both his pupils. The second, stemming from this, is the common exploration of certain new techniques, generated by Schoenberg and developed to their own ends by Berg and Webern. But, as the experience of the development of music since then has made clearer, as far as the actual music goes there is little other than technical means to link the mature works of the three composers. It is high time Berg was divorced from such close associations; then a wider audience might begin to appreciate the composer of some of the most emotionally intense and psychologically compelling music written in this century.

There is an International Alban Berg Society, which has published since 1968 a newsletter devoted to Berg studies.

RECOMMENDED WORKS

All Berg's mature output is recommended. For those new to Berg, it is suggested that they start with the *Altenberg Songs*, the *Three Pieces for Orchestra*, and the *Violin Concerto*, and continue with *Wozzeck* and *Lulu*. Specialists may care to note that there is a recording of Webern conducting the *Violin Concerto* and the *Lyric Suite*.

BIBLIOGRAPHY

T. Adorno, *Alban Berg*, Vienna, 1978 (revised edition)
D. Jarman, *The Music of Alban Berg*, London, 1979
W. Reich, *Alban Berg: the Man and his Music* (Eng. trans.), Vienna, 1957
A short but detailed survey of Berg's life and works by G. Perle will be found in *The New Grove Second Viennese School* (London 1980) which includes an extensive bibliography.

Einem Gottfried von[*]
born 24th January 1918 at Bern (Switzerland)
died 12th July 1996

Von Einem is best known as a composer of operas that have enjoyed success in Austria and Germany, and some limited exposure elsewhere. The most celebrated of these is probably *Dantons Tod* (*Danton's Death*, 1944–46), his first opera, to a libretto by his teacher Boris **Blacher**. Based on the 1835 play by Georg Büchner, the music of this rather earnest work does not match the dramatic libretto, set in Revolutionary France. Its colours are dark and monochromatic, only occasionally relieved by a contrasting brightness. Its generally diatonic harmonic language is leavened with dramatically appropriate dissonances. Musical action is heavily reliant on rhythmic action, creating rather obvious, two-dimensional musical events. However, the large choral spectacular of the second half is theatrically exciting, and the work has had many passionate advocates since its original success at the 1947 Salzburg Festival.

Einem's next opera, *Der Prozess* (*The Trial*, 1950–52), based on Kafka, included Expressionist and jazz elements that hark back to the interwar German cabaret operas. *Der Zerrissene* (*The Man Torn by Conflicts*, 1961–64) was a comedy based on Nestroy, and in contrast to the earlier Expressionist dramas follows the Viennese tradition of tuneful delight, and has more in common with Einem's neoclassical orchestral works. His fourth opera, *Der Besuch der alten Dame* (*The Old Lady's Visit*, 1970) is less extreme in its dark language, though retaining the sense of heightened emotions. It is based on a play by the Swiss writer Friedrich Dürrenmatt, who adapted the play for the libretto. Its subject is a blistering, black comment on the universality of materialistic greed. The old woman of the title, brilliantly characterised (her name, Zachanassian, is a compound of Zaharoff, Onassis and Gulbenkian) returns as a billionairess to her home town, now in deep economic depression. She had left it penniless and pregnant, and it turns out that she has been responsible for its current circumstance. She will give the town a billion if they kill the grocer, Ill, who was responsible for her original state. The town (Güllen, Swiss for 'liquid manure') at first refuses, but eventually works out a judicial sacrificial murder of the grocer, and the woman leaves. Musically, the opera is not innovatory, but the drama is effectively drawn together by short linking orchestral interludes (the first is scored for percussion alone, and then gradually instruments are added and percussion withdrawn during the subsequent interludes) and by harmonic motifs, including one from Bach's *St Matthew Passion*. The strength of the opera lies in its close marriage of musical characterisation and plot; as such, it is probably more effective on stage than on recording but it is a fine example of a mid-century opera with a strong social message. Of his later operas, *Kabale und Liebe* (*Intrigue and Love*, 1975) is based on a 'domestic tragedy' by Schiller, while *Jesu Hochzeit* (*Jesus's Wedding*, 1979), is a 'mystery opera'.

Of von Einem's non-operatic works, the *Piano Concerto No. 1* (1955) turns to the neo-Romanticism of **Rachmaninov** in the piano writing, with a grand solo opening pitted against spartan orchestration. The contrast of soloist and orchestra sets up a strange tension, in an alluring work whose material constantly seems to parody or echo snatches of famous piano concertos, without being either directly identifiable or upsetting the generally lyrical flow. The *Philadelphia Symphony* (1960) is a short work and unimpressively nondescript. The lyrical *Violin Concerto* (1961–67) also has a generally Romantic character, with two slower movements framing two faster ones. The importance of the solo line is underlined by the long solo cadenza that opens the work, and the spirit of the dance hovers over much of the concerto (with bongos set against the solo violin in the third movement), but it is more interesting in individual moments and in its clear orchestration than in overall effect, like a novel with some interesting characterisation but a weak plot.

From 1946 to 1951 von Einem was on the board of the Salzburg Festival (becoming chairperson of the Kunstrat, 1954), and from 1960 to 1964 he was director of the Vienna Festival. He taught at the Vienna Musikhochschule (1965–73).

RECOMMENDED WORKS
  opera *Der Besuch der alten Dame*
    (1970)
  opera *Dantons Tod* (1947)

Korngold Erich Wolfgang*
born 29th May 1897 at Brno
died 29th November 1957 in Hollywood

Korngold was one of the most admired of film composers during the heyday of Hollywood, winning two Academy Awards, and it is for his film music that he is still best remembered. Before moving to the USA in 1934, he had a startling compositional career, first as a child prodigy and then as a young composer of late Romantic, Expressionist operas that attracted world-wide attention. Korngold was to a certain extent the victim of fashion: whereas his early works were considered the height of modernity, their large-scale, voluptuous idiom was quickly eclipsed in the 1920s and 1930s by the very different trends towards jazz-inspired works and neo-classicism. In 1947, after completing twenty-one major film scores, he gave up the silver screen and attempted to regain some of his previous prestige as a composer for the concert platform. Unfortunately, the Romantic idiom he then cultivated, heavily influenced by the style of the Hollywood epic and romantic film music he had himself helped create, was completely out of touch with developments in concert music, and old-fashioned even by the standards of his own early works. He made one return to the studios in 1955, to work on a film biography of Wagner.

Korngold's earliest published work, the *Piano Trio* (1909–10) is an astonishingly assured work for a child of twelve, and never suggests the age of its composer. It is harmonically a more daring extension of Brahms, chiefly of historical interest in that its lyrical, angular themes, with wide leaps, are recognisably from the same milieu as those of **Webern**'s early chamber music. The luscious *String Sextet* (1917) is again influenced by Brahms, pleasant and passionate but less remarkable than the earlier work. However, it was *Violanta* (1916) that signalled an opera composer of considerable talents. Korngold had already written a ballet-pantomime *Der Schneeman* (1910), and the lengthy one-act *Violanta* was originally given in a double billing with *Der Ring des Polykrates* (1916). The melodramatic story, set in Venice in Carnival time during the Renaissance, equates love and death: the heroine cannot give herself fully to her husband until the roué who seduced her is murdered. The score is an amalgam of Wagner and **Strauss**, with a lyricism derived from **Puccini**, although the opening has an Impressionist feel that is more

French than German. Sensuous, heady and passionate, its sometimes clumsy transitions betray Korngold's inexperience, but it has the turbulent passion of a teenager and is an opera worth hearing.

None of that inexperience lingered in Korngold's masterpiece, written when he was twenty-three. *Die tote Stadt* (*The Dead City*, 1920) is built around a powerful and succinct libretto by Korngold and his father, music critic Julius Korngold, based on George Rodenbach's dark Symbolist novel 'Bruges la Morte'. The story, set in Bruges, the 'city of the dead' of the title, is very much of its time and influenced by Edgar Allan Poe. However, its major theme – the excessive love of a widower for his dead wife, to the detriment of his subsequent life – goes beyond the constraints of the period. The widower Paul woos a lively young dancer because she looks just like his dead wife. Paul murders the replacement (so she, too, will be dead), only to find her walking in: the entire story has been a mirage, Paul is cured of his necrofatuation, and the ending is one of personal reconciliation. This vivid psychological exploration, seen entirely through the eyes of the hero, is clothed in a heady score of sumptuous richness, handled with a sure touch for the dramatic, and for atmospheric tone-painting (notably the marvellous orchestral portrait of the dead city that opens Act II). The major influence is **Strauss**, but Korngold often uses his very large orchestra on a more restrained scale. Unlike Strauss, he also had an instinct for the big tune in the Italian style (there are two here, persuasively integrated into the flow so that they remain a component of the dramatic action). The vivacity of orchestral imagination is compelling, sometimes twisting into the grotesque, as in the waltz that ends Act I. With its concise drama and hedonistic atmosphere, this remains a major 20th-century opera, in spite of its many detractors. What prevents frequent performance is the huge forces required (including a battery of percussion and keyboard instruments) and the very high writing for the soloists which places great demands on the cast.

By the completion of his next opera, *Das Wunder der Heliane* (1927), Korngold's late Romantic idiom was already considered out of date. Meanwhile Korngold had scored considerable success with reworkings of arrangements of operettas, and unfortunately the spark of genius that had produced *Die tote Stadt* was not again rekindled. His major orchestral work of the period, the *Concerto for Piano Left Hand and Orchestra* (1923), is in the tradition of the big Romantic virtuouso concerto and, lacking the rich, heady sonorities of his operatic writing, is of lesser interest.

The best known of Korngold's works written after he had ceased writing for films is the sickly-sweet *Violin Concerto* (1946), an unashamedly Romantic work based on the music of four of his film scores. The *Cello Concerto* (1946) is taken from the film *Deception*, where it formed part of the plot. The four-movement *Symphonic Serenade* (1947) is interesting for its very beautiful Brucknerian slow movement. This pleasant, completely anachronistic, and beautifully wrought large-scale work is perhaps the best of Korngold's later music, with a pizzicato scherzo and an energetic, purposeful finale, all without a trace of Hollywood sentimentality. The *Symphony in F sharp* (1950) also has Brucknerian overtones, especially in the slow movement, allied to Hollywood gestures. Of his three string quartets, the *String Quartet No. 3* (1945) rather unsuccessfully incorporates two film tunes. More interesting is the *String Quartet No. 1* (1924), with a patchwork of influences, notably **Mahler**, and the rich lushness of the period.

Korngold's importance to the Hollywood film industry lay in his contribution to the establishment of the grand Romantic style, with 'big' tunes, rich orchestration, and vivid colours, which has remained the Hollywood norm. The first of his twenty-two scores consisted of arrangements of Mendelssohn; the rest were original, apart from the late *Magic Fire* (1956), which arranges music by Wagner. The best of the music is probably to be found in the scores for *The Sea Hawk* (1940) and *Kings Row* (1942), both of which will satisfy urges for a Romantic wallow.

RECOMMENDED WORKS
    film score *Kings Row* (1942)
    Symphonic Serenade (1947)
    opera *Die tote Stadt* (1920)

BIBLIOGRAPHY
    L. Korngold, *Erich Wolfgang Korngold*, Vienna, 1967

Krenek Ernst**

born 23rd August 1900 at Vienna
died 23rd December 1991 at Palm
    Springs (California)

Ernst Krenek's compositional career spanned most of the 20th century, and so varied was his style, and so large his output, that many aware of his activities in Vienna of the 1920s and 1930s are unaware that the same composer continued his compositional career for five decades after World War II in the USA, where he lived from 1937. His most conspicuous success remains the opera *Jonny spielt auf* (1926).

Krenek's early music represents an attempt to move beyond the late Romanticism of contemporary Vienna, without making a major break with that style (as his contemporaries grouped around **Schoenberg** were doing). This led to extending chromaticism into atonality (notably in the opera *Orpheus und Eurydike*, 1923, to a libretto by the painter Oskar Kokoschka). He then became influenced by jazz, and it is the works of this period that are probably of the most immediate interest. Following a period in Paris, he was influenced by Stravinsky's neo-classicism, and then in 1933 turned to 12-note methods (one of the first composers outside Schoenberg's immediate circle to do so), and continued to develop a serial style after his move to the USA. Throughout, he showed a predilection for polyphonic writing, and sometimes for two-part structures, which occur in some of his operas and in other works, such as the *Trio for Clarinet, Violin and Piano* (1946).

The first phase of his career is represented by three symphonies, written in the space of two years. They were an attempt to develop the form beyond the point at which **Mahler** had arrived, extending the chromaticism into atonal areas. The *Symphony No. 1* (1921) is a rather uneasy combination of late Romanticism, concise orchestration, and motoric rhythms and ideas. A rather fragmentary feel is heightened by the structure, one movement divided into nine sections with diverse material, though the aim is partly achieved in the large scale and imposing fugue towards the end. The *Symphony No. 2* (1922) is in a more conventional three-movement structure, while the *Symphony No. 3* includes a dance-like section that has some of the irony of Mahler with more steely colours. All these three symphonies have moments of interest, often of a technical nature, but none of them suggest a particularly convincing overall idiom or a strong individual character.

The first three string quartets (*No. 1*, 1921; *No. 2*, 1921; *No. 3*, 1923) inhabit much the same dour world. They are, however, more interesting than these early symphonies, the mild atonalism having a genuine bite within the tighter constraints of the form; the overall impulse is stronger, influenced by **Bartók**, especially in the propulsive, droning, dissonant opening of the third quartet. The rather diffuse seven-movement *String Quartet No. 4*, (1923) is in a lyrical, formal idiom, with shades of neo-classicism. The fifth movement has intentional echoes of Spanish music; its final eighth movement has remained missing.

The influence of jazz transformed Krenek's idiom. This was immediately evident in the fine *Symphony for Wind Instruments and Percussion* (1924–25), his fourth symphony but not numbered as such. Its jazzy feel, more an integrated influence than an overt style, leans towards the kind of insistent vertical rigidity of rhythm that **Stravinsky** had developed. Distinct colours, short, apparently inconsequential phrases, and little overlap of those phrases, give that contemporary Berlin sense of mechanical marionettes. The following year Krenek completed the opera *Jonny spielt auf* (*Johnny Strikes Up*), to his own libretto, which catapulted him to international fame, being performed right across Europe, in the USSR, and in the USA. The story is an ironic satire in which jazz conquers the world, led by its hero, the high-living black jazz player Jonny. Its central theme is the freedom of the artist, with the symbolic contrasts of the jazz player, a virtuoso violinist, a composer, and a beautiful soprano opera singer among the main characters. The music combines lyrical opera and a Berlin cabaret jazz (rather than the more fiery American jazz), which appears when the scene changes to a bar in a Paris hotel, and then accompanies the protagonists through the work. The mixture of realism, fantasy and farce presented a new view of opera, in contrast to the historical or mythological plots usually associated with the genre. One brilliant touch is when the composer, high on a mountainside (in an anti-nature message), hears one of his own arias coming from a radio far down in the valley. Prophetically, the opera ends with the main characters taking a train to the USA. Besides being an important historical document, *Jonny spielt auf*, though certainly flawed – the combination of idioms is unconvincing – is also entertaining, with its swift-moving and skilful story-line, its bursts of light-hearted jazz, and its moments that look forward to the idiom of music-theatre. The opera *Leben des Orest* (*The Life of Orestes*, 1929) has a similar jazzy feel.

Just before turning to 12-tone techniques, Krenek moved away from jazz-inspired works to a kind of neo-Romanticism, rooted in Schubert, which included the song-cycle *Reisebuch aus den österreichischen Alpen* (*Travel Book from the Austrian Alps*, 1935), modelled on Schubert's *Winterreise*, and the lovely Schubertian *String Quartet No. 5* (1930), whose first movement has a song-like intensity and lyricism, while the second movement is a theme and variations, and the third (which quotes from Monteverdi) a 'Phantasie' adagio, with at times a strong feel of the blues.

Krenek's use of 12-tone technique was initiated in the opera *Karl V* (*Charles V*, 1930–33) which incurred the wrath of the authorities when first performed in 1938. The *String Quartet No. 6* (1936–37) is the most severe of the 12-tone works; following this period, Krenek's use of 12-tone techniques is free, often breaking down the rows into smaller groups, which are themselves used as the basis for thematic material and regularly introduce ideas not connected with the original 12-tone idea. These techniques give an elasticity to his idiom, making it less severe than some of his contemporaries working within a serial framework.

A major work composed during the war years is the long and austere *Lamentatio Jeremiae Prophetae* (*Lamentations of the Prophet Jeremiah*, 1941) for unaccompanied choir. With the influence of Gregorian chant, a unifying 12-note row, slow-moving textures, and unrelieved atmosphere of gloom, it is of interest for its anticipations of later serial and avant-garde choral writing. The *String Quartet No. 7* (1943–44) is in five linked movements, the thematic material of the opening being developed in later movements, and using a 12-tone row that is usually divided into smaller series of notes for development and manipulation. The work is not as daunting as such a description might suggest: the drive is created by the counterpoint, and the harmonies have a suggestion of a tonal base. The second movement is an expressive and dark adagio, and the central movement a fugue.

Krenek's works after World War II covered a wide range of genre, and are mostly in his developed, free serial style. Works such as *Aus drei mach sieben* (*From Three Make Seven*, 1961) for orchestra show the fragmentary orchestral serial style, building up patterns from a succession of instrumental blocks that is typical of the serial scores of the time. The avant-garde concepts of chance were used in *Sestina* (1957) for voice and ten players, while in some scores elements are left to the performers' choice, as in the orchestral work that gave Krenek the title for his autobiography, *Horizon Circled* (1967). A slightly impish humour also appeared, for example in *Kithauraulos* (1971), which exists in two versions, one for oboe, harp and orchestra, and one for oboe, harp and tape. The humour appears in the tape section, with whistles and bleeps that comment on the instrumental lines.

Later operas ranged widely – *Pallas Athene weint* (1955) comments on the eclipse of Greek democracy, *Der goldene Bock* (1963) is an absurdist treatment of the story of the Argonauts, while *Der Zauberspiegel* (1966), written for television, has sci-fi elements, and ranges from 13th-century China to modern times. There are also a number of concertante works, of which the *Capriccio for Cello and Orchestra* (1955) shows the integration of the various elements of Krenek's idiom, with a lyrical, conversational line for the cello, a 12-note structure, suggestions of a jazz rhythm and concise and clear orchestration. In 1980 he returned to the string quartet medium, after an absence of thirty-six years, with the *String Quartet No. 8*. In one movement divided into ten loose sections, it uses a 12-tone row sporadically, in a deliberately episodic work with a variety of mood.

Throughout his career, Krenek wrote songs and song-cycles, following the different styles of his output, and his sensitivity to the medium is often rewarding. For those wishing to explore this multi-faceted composer, the *Symphony for Wind Instruments and Percussion* and the opera *Jonny spielt auf* provide an immediate and attractive introduction to the jazz-influenced works. But it is the string quartets, covering the whole range of Krenek's stylistic changes, which provide an overview of his achievement. They are often fascinating in their technical means (especially in their sense of unity), and consistently compelling in their musical impact. Even so, they only hint at the extraordinarily wide compass of this composer's multiple musical personality, which never quite seems to achieve striking individuality, but whose music is consistently interesting.

Krenek was also active as a writer, critic, poet and playwright. Among his many books are those on Mahler (with the conductor Bruno Walter), Ockeghem, and modal counterpoint in the 16th century. Among his pupils were Henry Mancini, the arranger and film composer, and the American composer and musicologist George Perle.

RECOMMENDED WORKS
opera *Jonny spielt auf* (1926)
String Quartet No. 1 (1921)
String Quartet No. 2 (1921)
String Quartet No. 3 (1923)
String Quartet No. 5 (1930)
String Quartet No. 6 (1936–37)
String Quartet No. 7 (1943–44)
String Quartet No. 8 (1980)
Symphony for Wind Instruments and
Percussion (1924–25)

BIBLIOGRAPHY
E Krenek, *Horizons Circled: Reflections on my Music*, Berkeley, California, 1974

Mahler Gustav···
born 7th July 1860 at Kalischt (Bohemia)
died 18th May 1911 at Vienna

Debussy and Mahler are the two major figures that span the end of the 19th century and the start of the 20th, and each had a profound influence on the subsequent development of 20th-century music. Debussy's music has been widely heard throughout the century, but the works of Mahler were known only to a few champions, composers and music specialists until the 1960s. Since then, aided by recordings, Mahler has taken his rightful place as one of the major composers of any century.

Mahler appears a colossus, the composer of huge symphonies on a vast scale, taking the musical inflation of the 19th century to its limits. But he was also the composer of myriad details of an intimate and far from epic nature. It was Mahler's genius to recognise that a grand scale and chamber-like intimacy were but two aspects of the same whole, and to reconcile them in his music. Behind this lay an artistic aim: the expression in music of the most profound philosophical questions, humankind's place in nature and the cosmos, and the contradictory human experiences that place entails: tragedy, joy, turbulence, redemption. From these spring the necessity for the grand scale and the involvement of intimacy. There is also an inherent contradiction between the gaiety of the world and its suffering which Mahler expressed through irony, a recurring component in his work, alongside the beatific vision and the tormented tragedy. There is also a strong spiritual element in Mahler's music (most directly in the *Symphony No. 8*), that reflects the symbolic and spiritual attractions of Catholicism, to which Mahler converted from Judaism. He himself stated that he was merely the vessel through which the music emerged.

A philosophical quest propels all his music; consequently, his output embraces only two genres, apart from a handful of chamber works. The first is the song and the song-cycle, especially the orchestral song-cycle. The words Mahler chose to set almost always allow entry into a wider, more abstract, spiritual experience. Although himself an opera conductor, he never completed an original stage work. The second genre is that of the symphony, which had been since the time of Haydn the chief musical vehicle for philosophical comment or abstraction. Four of Mahler's ten symphonies use words, one has a vocal format throughout, and material from Mahler's earlier or contemporaneous song-cycles continually informs the symphonies. In addition, Mahler's symphonies all started with programmatic, philosophical conceptions. Mahler's later suppression of such programmes, which mainly exist in early drafts or in letters, was in part a response to an age which was beginning to frown on such programmatic music, in part a need to avoid confusion for audiences when the actual music had developed beyond the original impulse, and contained only a programmatic essence rather than substance.

Combined with this impulse is a singular consistency of voice. Although his idiom developed and expanded in emotional range, every single Mahler work is instantly recognisable as coming from his pen and no other. His main melodic lines are founded on song, whether in vocal works or in symphonies, and are characterised by the interval of the falling fourth, and by the technique of starting a melody with a series of short rising notes (again, often encompassing a fourth) before slowing the melody down with longer note-values (a technique derived from Bruckner), creating a sensation of expectation and then expansion. The progression of the melody often includes large interval leaps, heightening the expressive power. His idiom is founded on counterpoint, and often more than one melody will intertwine and unravel simultaneously. A second major characteristic is eclecticism, drawing material from sources that hitherto had not been included in serious works. Chief among these are bird-calls and bird-song, created by woodwind; march themes, often instrumented more like a band than the customary symphonic orchestral treatment; and the lilting Viennese Ländler. To these are added such devices as the chorale and the funeral march, all fully integrated into his own voice to create a music where the extramusical associations emphasise and reinforce the philosophical content.

It is Mahler's use of orchestral colour that probably most contributes to the instant recognition of his music. Far from using his huge forces *en masse*, as Wagner and Bruckner had been inclined to do, Mahler divided them into a number of chamber-sized forces, reserving the full orchestra for moments of special impact. This division allows for varied combinations of simple colours (emphasised by his use of the extreme registers of instruments, often contrasting with each other), and sudden changes in the texture. It also creates the sense of intimacy and lucidity for which Mahler was so often striving, furthered by the addition of instruments not traditionally found in a symphony orchestra: cowbells, piano, guitar or mandolin, even the harmonium.

Mahler's harmony remained rooted in the traditional tonal system, but is regularly on the edge of subversion by extreme chromaticism: he took tonality to the brink of its elastic limits. A favourite device is to end a movement in a different key from that in which it began; although this broke the traditional rules of symphonic harmonic progression, it was a perfectly logical extension of the tonal system, creating a goal at which the harmony aims with an expressive as well as a technical purpose.

The earliest Mahler work likely to be encountered is the youthful ballad-cantata *Das klagende Lied* (1880) for soloists, chorus and orchestra. It tells of a minstrel whose new flute describes a fratricide and describes the consequences of that knowledge, as the murderer is about to marry. Mahler's atmospheric setting of this Gothic tale is permeated by stylistic traits from the late Romantic heritage (notably that of Bruckner) while containing many foretastes of Mahler's own later idiom (notably the use of off-stage brass).

In the period after *Das klagende Lied*, the literary impulse behind much of Mahler's work came from a famous collection of German folk poetry, *Des Knaben Wunderhorn (The Youth's Magic Horn)*, which recount and praise the lives of ordinary folk, usually in simple situational tales, looking back with a certain amount of nostalgia to former, golden days when lives were simpler. The dates of Mahler's earliest settings of this material are uncertain. The gentle and ingenuous *Lieder eines fahrenden Gesellen (Songs of the Wayfarer*, 1884–85) for voice and orchestra or piano, have texts whose origins are in the *Wunderhorn* collection, while direct settings appear in Volumes II and III of *Lieder und Gesänge* (before 1890) for voice and piano. Mahler reached a maturity in the handling of such material in the thirteen songs that form *Des Knaben Wunderhorn* (1892–1901) for soloists and orchestra. Mahler resisted any Romantic temptation to pander to the nostalgic or folksy elements inherent in the texts. Instead, he cut to the kernel of the tales, recognising the elemental truths they contained and eliciting the dramatic potential of the situations in settings that are realistic, vivid and direct. The orchestration is lucid, preferring small groups of instruments or solos to the mass use of the orchestra, giving a chamber-like clarity and swift changes in the predominant colours. The songs fall into three stylistic groups: those containing elements of a march (often with percussion prominent), humorous songs, and purely lyrical songs. These stylistic types were to recur throughout Mahler's works. The orchestration of the cycle provided the origins of Mahler's later orchestral idiom, and the vocal lines the foundation of his later lyrical melodies. Two of the thirteen songs and three other settings of *Wunderhorn* texts occur in Mahler's first four symphonies. One result is that *Des Knaben Wunderhorn* is usually heard as a cycle of twelve songs, leaving *Urlicht* in its place as the fourth movement of the second symphony.

Mahler's next song-cycle is perhaps his most poignant. *Kindertotenlieder (Songs on the Death of Children*, 1901–04) for voice and orchestra or piano, sets five poems by Rückert describing the anguished feelings of a parent who has lost a child. Sadly, Mahler's own daughter was to die shortly after he composed the cycle. The cycle is more sophisticated than previous ones: its harmonic language is more chromatic, the counterpoint and the rhythmic effects more interwoven, the vivid orchestral poster-paint colours now mixed with more subtle pastels, the passions more intimate and introvert. Four other Rückert songs provide the texts for the *Rückert-Lieder* (1901–02), similar in both musical and literary tone.

Kindertotenlieder was Mahler's last song-cycle, apart from the quasi-symphony *Das Lied von der Erde*. However, it is worth noting that his song-cycles, with their themes of love and departure, of grief and resignation, anticipated the moods and themes of a number of later 20th-century song-cycles. The influence is direct in the works of **Shostakovich** and **Britten**, and still palpable in many English settings of AE Housman, which express moods and emotions similar to those of the *Wunderhorn* collection – an ethos perhaps more properly understood after the experience of the First World War.

There has long been discussion as to whether Mahler's symphonies are primarily abstract (apart from No. 8) or programmatic. The simple reality (as so often in such cases) is that they are both. The symphonies can be listened to, enjoyed, and admired purely as abstract music, for their formal construction as symphonies, and equally they can be enjoyed without any knowledge of those formal processes, as evocative music with programmatic or descriptive content, where some knowledge of Mahler's original extra-musical conception is useful.

The symphonies fall into three major groups: the first four (with 2, 3, and 4 known as the 'Wunderhorn' symphonies, and the fourth standing as a bridge to the second group); the fifth, sixth and seventh, which omit vocal forces; and the quasi-symphony *Das Lied von der Erde*, the ninth and the incomplete tenth forming the final group. The eighth symphony stands on its own, though it has connections with the preceding three symphonies. Moreover, each group, besides having musical connections or stylistic resemblances, also has a philosophical unity. The pattern in each group is (crudely) the struggles of life; the mystery and horror of death; and the puzzle of the afterlife. Each group presents these seminal questions in a different fashion, reflecting Mahler's increasing understanding.

The *Symphony No. 1* (1886–88, revised 1893–96), which has close thematic links with the *Lieder eines fahrenden Gesellen*, is a largely happy work that reflects Mahler's joy in nature. Sometimes titled 'Titan',

it was conceived by Mahler as having a Hero. The impulse of the first movement is a reflection of the landscape Mahler loved, with a hushed opening of bird-calls, horn cries and offstage brass, followed by a typically lyrical, flowing dance. The scherzo has a strong rustic feel, while the slow movement, haunted by a late 19th-century sense of the macabre, introduces irony with a distortion into an eerie funeral march of the famous round 'Frère Jacques'. The more turbulent finale is the least successful movement. The symphony originally had five movements, but after the first performance Mahler withdrew the second movement, and this beautiful but rather sentimental adagio (known as *Blumine*) is now sometimes heard on its own, and very occasionally restored into the symphony.

The *Symphony No. 2* (1888–94, revised 1903) for soprano, contralto, chorus and orchestra, expands the scale of musical and philosophical content. Often subtitled 'Resurrection' on account of the final movement's setting of Klopstock's *Resurrection Hymn*, it opens with an extended funeral march that covers a wide range of mood (Mahler himself described it as the funeral of the hero of his first symphony). It is remarkable for the power of its opening, with an emphatic, broken, rising line from the cellos that bursts onto the silence, for its multiplicity of themes and sub-themes derived from the major ideas, and for the compression of the development section in such a long movement. The progression of the symphony is towards the goal of the final two (linked) movements: the gentle beauty of the *Wunderhorn* song *Urlicht* in the fourth, and the monumental cry of the Day of Judgement and the subsequent Resurrection in the fifth. The intervening movements act as a kind of reflection on the life that led to his journey, with a lilting Beethovenian andante, and a swirling scherzo based (without the words) on one of the *Wunderhorn* songs, touched with a satirical humour and infected with the macabre, like some witches' dance.

The *Symphony No. 3* (1893–96, revised 1906) for contralto, women's chorus, boys' chorus, and orchestra, extends the number of movements to six (Mahler dropped a seventh, later using it as the finale of the fourth symphony). This is more obviously a nature symphony, combining pictorial representation with the emotions aroused by the natural world – he once called it 'A Summer Morning Dream'. In the sonata-form first movement the driving force of its opening is largely founded on military marches but encompasses counter-passages of descriptive beauty. The build-up of turbulence is given more potency towards the end of the development by the superimposition of themes, creating a series of almost independent lines. This first movement, and the last of the second symphony, are the longest that Mahler wrote, each lasting half an hour. This monumental construct is immediately contrasted by a touching little minuet, classical in feel and orchestration, that forms the basis of the second movement. The scherzo also has the general feel of an interlude, until a final progression to a climactic outburst, where Mahler explores the atmospheric possibilities of off-stage brass. The following two movements are paired: a slow-moving song for contralto (to words by Nietzsche expressing the eternity of night), and a *Wunderhorn* song for the soloists and chorus expressing heavenly joy, which has the overtones of a sophisticated choral folk song. The finale was the first of Mahler's large-scale adagios, dominated by strings and using the whole of its considerable span to expand emotionally to an eventual climax of sublime achievement, rather than triumph. Although the individual movements contain finer music and a more developed idiom than those of the second symphony, this is the one Mahler symphony where the accusation of inflation has some validity, not through the sheer size but due to the overall disparity of its parts.

The *Symphony No. 4* (1899–1900, revised 1901–10) for soprano and orchestra remains the most popular of Mahler's symphonies. Although fifty minutes long, it is more concise than all but the first symphony: the movements are cut to four, the forces are smaller, and the sense of huge climax is absent. It is also the most radiantly happy of his symphonies, a more direct, less philosophical evocation after the terrors and triumphs of the second and the drive and sublimity of the third. The other-worldly still hovers at its edge – the Devil's dance in the second movement, to a violin tuned a whole tone higher, the suggestions of heavenly joys in the *Wunderhorn* words of the finale – but these are subservient to direct expression of nature.

Mahler then embarked on a trilogy of purely instrumental symphonies. The *Symphony No. 5* (1901–02, revised 1904–10) again opens with a funeral march, but it is one of new confidence, breadth and poise, broken into by the tumultuous and the macabre. There is a clear grouping into three in the five-movement layout: the opening two movements, the hinge of the scherzo, and the adagio introducing the finale. The harmonic progression of the key of each movement describes a large-scale modal cadence, from C sharp minor at the opening to D major at the ending. The long scherzo, more robust and less tortured than those of the earlier symphonies, is imbued with the swirl of the dance. The fourth movement is the famous adagietto, scored only for strings and harp. It is extraordinarily beautiful, and the poignancy of the main theme, nostalgic and hauntingly regretful, is all the more marked when heard after the emphatic ending of the scherzo. The cheerful finale (which has thematic connections with the adagietto) reaffirms the overall tone of the symphony: the joy present in the kernel of life, even when, as in the adagietto, that depth of intense feeling is recalled rather than presently lived. The *Symphony No. 5* is the most fluent and the most contrapuntal of all Mahler's symphonies, and, perhaps because audiences have come to expect more tortured expression from Mahler, is paid less attention than it deserves.

The *Symphony No. 6* (1903–04, revised 1906) is sometimes subtitled 'Tragic' (following Mahler's own lead), which describes its overall mood, the obverse of the more luminous emotions laid out in the fifth. The opening movement is tense and turbulent, founded on march rhythms. Mahler specifies a repeat of the exposition, which takes on a different hue after the intervening martial rhythms on the timpani – a prime example of Mahler's understanding of the emotional impact of his technical procedures. The movement is countered by the wide-ranging, fragmentary moods of the scherzo, from the menace of the march to the chamber-like grace of the trio, with a suggestion of Wagner's *Ring* cycle along the way. The sometimes hollow laughter of the scherzo gives way to another beautiful slow movement, less regretful than its predecessor, the flow of strings alloyed by woodwind. The inherent threat of tragedy, lying in wait in the first three movements, is unleashed in the huge finale. It opens with an Impressionistic swirl, countered by a theme from the first movement, and moves swiftly through ominous calls, a funereal miasma in dark orchestral colours, a dance, and arrives at a sudden explosion, where, to the stroke of the drum, a small figure from the first movement suddenly takes on ominous import. From these beginnings the movement, one of Mahler's finest creations, passes through strange haunted interludes of distant bells and horn calls, building in passionate intensity to what seems a song of joyful triumph. But that triumph disintegrates, and the apparently quiet brass close is shattered by the return of that ominous stroke, carrying the whole weight of the previous movements on its shoulders. So pictorially vivid is this movement, with its cowbells, its timpani strokes of mortality, its snatches of angry percussion, a moment of Turkish exoticism, its harp swirls, its fanning into passionate flames, that it is difficult to conceive that this music did not have a programmatic base. If it did, Mahler did not admit to it. Mahler made a late revision to the symphony, cutting the final great stroke and reversing the order of the middle movements. Both versions may be encountered.

The *Symphony No. 7* (1904–05, revised 1909) turns the tragedy of its predecessor into a kind of cynical counter-display. The structure pairs the outer movements, and then the second and fourth movements (both nocturnes), with a central scherzo. After the enigmatic opening movement, the symphony slithers into the first of the nocturnes, a sinuous movement scored with extraordinary lucidity and economy. It is announced by a series of disillusioned fanfares, and the subsequent march-like themes seem to evoke soldiers returning to the wars, carrying with them the faded recall of dances behind the lines. The scherzo declares itself with broken, disjointed rhythms and raucous instrumentation. There is a suggestion of more than mere satire in this movement, with its distortions of the Ländler and the waltz: evil seems to stalk somewhere in the background. The second nocturne is still somewhat unsettled, without much of the stillness of the night that its title might imply, until the peaceful close. The large finale combines elements of sonata and variation form, and includes parodies of a theme from Wagner's *Die Meistersinger* and the waltz from Lehár's *The Merry Widow*. Just as in Elgar there can be an underlying sense of uncertainty that undermines any triumphal conviction, so in the finale to this work. Of all Mahler's symphonies, this is the one that most benefits from some knowledge of the symphonies that preceded and succeeded it, when its strange atmosphere can then be placed in context.

From this Mahler moved to an expression of faith and praise in the mighty

Symphony No. 8 (1906–07). The huge forces – two sopranos, two contraltos, tenor, baritone, bass, two large choirs and boys' choir, orchestra and organ – have led to its name of the 'Symphony of a Thousand'. The work is in two parts. The first is a setting of the 9th-century Whitsuntide Vesper hymn *Veni, Creator Spiritus* (*Come, Holy Ghost*), attributed to Hrabanus Maurus, and acts as a sonata-form first movement. It is an affirmation of the traditional Catholic faith in God's love. The second, much longer section combines a slow movement, a scherzo, and finale in a setting of the final scene from Goethe's *Faust*, which in Romantic and humanist fashion contemplates that love, finally concluding in affirmation. The first part is a triumphant, optimistic web of vocal strands, often repeating lines and words out of the linear flow of the hymn. A section for the soloists near the beginning seems to invoke the spirit of Beethoven's ninth symphony, dissolved by a typical rising Mahler string line. The second part starts orchestrally, eventually joined by a half-whispering chorus. A series of solo and choral ecstasies of various kinds follows, all pointing to the climax of the ending, the sublime and triumphant 'mystical choir', echoing, in Goethe's words, the expression of the hymn that opened the work. Throughout, Mahler binds the symphony with a weave of thematic reference and idea, and not the least achievement of the symphony is the clarity of vocal and choral textures achieved with such massive forces, something that eluded almost every other late Romantic composer of choral works. Magnificent though the work is, there is the uncomfortable feeling of something absent: the constant texture of voices, especially in the bulk of the second part, as opposed to their appearance in a single movement, limits Mahler's mastery of symphonic colour, and denies the kind of imagic detail and inspiration that the poetry of the song-cycles supplied. **Brian's** *Gothic Symphony*, also inspired by Goethe and setting a Latin spiritual text, provides an interesting comparison.

No such doubts can be attached to Mahler's next work, *Das Lied von der Erde* (*The Song of the Earth*, 1908–09) for tenor, contralto or baritone, and orchestra. Its six movements are symphonic in construction, and the only reason that Mahler did not call it his ninth symphony was his superstition over writing nine symphonies (the number that Beethoven completed). It forms, with the ninth and the incomplete tenth, the final trilogy of symphonies, and was coloured by Mahler's discovery just after the completion of the eighth symphony that he suffered from a fatal heart disease. A setting of German versions by Hans Bethge of Chinese poems whose main theme is the quick passing of youth and happiness, it is a passionate combination of regretful resignation and celebration of the beauties of nature and life. A major theme in the violins near the opening provides unification throughout the work: its exotic, pentatonic character suggests the oriental, and it is later found in various guises, including its inversion (upside-down) and retrograde (backwards) forms.

A mixture of the sorrowful and the affirmative opens the *Symphony No. 9* (1908–09), in the most breathtakingly inspired of all Mahler's symphonic movements. Throughout there is an underlying pulse, mostly given to the lower strings, that suggests not only the pulse of Mahler's heart but the pulse of time itself, but even when impending death seems to break in with ominous timpani strokes, Mahler insists on leading it out into a more glorious light. This movement has rightly been compared in its depth of illumination to Beethoven's late works. The second movement is a dance, an earthy Ländler that gradually whirls, through a waltz, into darker and more obscure harmonic regions, distorting tonality and swinging the mood from rustic pleasure into something far more disturbing. The rondo-burlesque third movement is one of the angriest Mahler wrote, with moments of gallows humour, sometimes bitingly satirical, sometimes tongue-in-cheek. In the middle of this comes a beautifully sublime passage, countering the anger, until the raucous has the last word. All this is assuaged by the last movement, a luminous redemption through which a vein of uncertainty runs half-submerged until the visionary final pages.

Throughout this symphony, the polyphonic textures become more complex and convoluted, the harmonies at times more dissonant, heralding later 20th-century developments. In the *Symphony No. 10* (1910) the exploration goes still further, into regions of extreme chromaticism that stand on the very threshold of the collapse of traditional harmony. For it would be quite wrong to see the ninth symphony as Mahler's swan song. Although the *Symphony No. 10* remained unfinished apart from the adagio (often played on its own), enough was completed to give a comprehensive idea of the whole work. There

have been a number of attempts to complete the symphony, but one in particular stands out, the 'realisation' by Deryck Cooke (1960–64, revised 1976) that now stands alongside the other symphonies to complete the canon. Those who have objected to the very idea seem more concerned with propriety than music, for the experience of the tenth symphony immediately places the ninth in its proper context as the central work in a trilogy, whose overall trend only becomes apparent through the last work of the triptych. The symphony returns to a five-movement structure, with an opening adagio whose first bars, for strings alone, probe and wander until reaching the adagio proper, which in a less sublime fashion picks up the mood of the end of the ninth symphony. Its inexorable build-up is shattered by the unexpected arrival of a climax in a different key, allowing the movement finally to embrace the sublimity that had marked the end of its predecessor. The second movement is remarkable chiefly for its abruptly altering tempi, the third ('Purgatorio') for its clashes of key and its tortured dance-like feel. The fourth movement makes allusions to the previous movements, *Das Lied von der Erde*, the ninth symphony, and Dvořák's ninth symphony. This movement is also turbulent, ending with a great drum stroke. That sound of the drum dominates the last movement, starting it and returning in the middle. This finale is the most remarkable section of the symphony, ending with a sense of joy and a kind of bliss absent in the earlier works: it is this conclusion, full of more than just acceptance, that offers a different perspective on the ninth symphony.

Mahler's impact on succeeding composers has been in three disparate directions. First, he stood behind the transition of **Schoenberg, Webern,** and **Berg** from the late Romantic idiom into completely new harmonic directions, his own solutions to the breaking-point of tonality acting as the springboard for their developments. Second, a number of composers, notably **Zemlinsky,** continued the large-scale late Romantic aural landscapes Mahler had epitomised. Third, he had a direct influence on a number of subsequent composers who attempted to continue the symphonic idiom and the humanist ethic without recourse to either 12-tone harmonies or late Romantic Expressionism, most notably **Shostakovich** and **Pettersson.**

Mahler was a distinguished conductor, considered by many the greatest of his times; his period as director of the Vienna

Court Opera (1897–1907) revolutionised opera in the city and is still considered a golden age. He had earlier worked at opera houses in Prague (1885–86), Leipzig (1886–88), Budapest (1888–91) and Hamburg (1891–97), and subsequently became conductor of the New York Metropolitan Opera (1908–10) and the New York Philharmonic (1909–11).

RECOMMENDED WORKS
Those new to Mahler might care to start with the first and fourth symphonies and the song cycle *Das Lied von der Erde.*
song cycle *Kindertotenlieder* (1901–04)
song cycle *Das klangende Lied* (1880)
song cycle *Lieder eines fahrenden Geselle* (c. 1884–85)
song cycle *Das Lied von der Erde* (1908–09)
song collection *Das Knaben Wunderhorn* (1892–1901)
song cycle *Five Rückert Lieder* (1901–02)
symphonies 1–10 (1886–1910)

BIBLIOGRAPHY
M. Kennedy, *Mahler*, London, 1974
D. Mitchell, *Gustav Mahler*, 3 vols, 1958, rep. 1975, 1980

Schmidt Franz**
born 22nd December 1874 at Bratislava
died 11th February 1939 at Vienna

Franz Schmidt studied under Bruckner, and was cellist under **Mahler** with the Vienna Philharmonic Orchestra (1896–1911). He belongs to that group of composers who maintained the large-scale 19th-century ethos during the first half of the 20th century, and which includes **Pfitzner** and **Zemlinsky**. While not as interesting as either of these composers, he may yet appeal to those who enjoy late Romanticism. There is a Franz Schmidt Society, based in the Archives of the Society of Viennese Music-Lovers.

His music is an amalgam of a number of late 19th-century Germanic traditions: **Strauss** and Wagner in some of the thematic ideas and in the orchestration, Bruckner in the long breadth of melodic construction, Brahms and Reger in the use of variation forms and fugues. Magyar folk music sometimes influenced his work, as in the *Variations on a Hussar Song* (1930–31) for orchestra. Unusually for an Austrian composer of the period, *lieder* are absent from his output.

His *Symphony No. 1* (1896–99) is a bold and vivacious work, showing the influence of **Strauss** and Beethoven. Although an assured score for a young composer, it is overlong (especially in the finale), something that also mars the two succeeding symphonies, relegating them to the status of curiosities. The *Symphony No. 2* (1911–13) is richer and smoother in its textures, again indebted to Strauss and Wagner. Its chief interest lies in the second of the three movements, cast in the form of variations with a neo-classical opening which revert to a lush Romantic idiom, and include a Dvořák-like Czech waltz. The highly chromatic opening to the finale is also of interest, but again the movement outstays its welcome. The rather dull *Symphony No. 3* (1928) was written for a Schubert competition in the USA (won by **Atterberg**). In keeping with the Schubertian inspiration, the orchestra is smaller, the textures dense and sinuous, the melodic lines long. All these three symphonies are essentially joyous; it is the injection of tragedy that makes his *Symphony No. 4 in C major* (1933–34), written as the requiem for his daughter, stand out. The orchestral sound is still Romantic, extremely conservative for its date, but heartfelt tragedy lifts the work beyond anachronism. The form, too, is unusual. The symphony is cast in one movement, divided into three sections built around a central funereal adagio, and integrating variations and sonata form (as other composers of the period were attempting to do). The tone is set by the mournful elegiac opening, and throughout there is a breadth of line, a slow unfolding of material reminiscent of Bruckner, and a predominance of the string colours of the orchestra.

The other work for which Schmidt is still known is a vast oratorio based on the Book of Revelation, *Das Buch mit sieben Siegeln* (*The Book with Seven Seals*, 1938). It carries the great weight of the German–Austrian oratorio tradition on its shoulders while anticipating the apocalypse that was about to engulf Europe. After a long-winded Romantic opening, at times it harks back to Haydn, and includes highly chromatic Bach-like fugues. The orchestra accompanies the vocal writing in a highly dramatic style, with generally rich and heavy colours that gradually evolve into an individual sound world with unusual touches, such as an extraordinary clinking percussion and pizzicato strings against dark low brass. Organ interludes act as independent elements. Anachronistic though much of the work may be, it is utterly intense and genuine, a profound work whose dramatic subject is matched by its music.

The intermezzo from his opera *Notre Dame* (*Our Lady of Paris*, 1904–06, based on Hugo's *The Hunchback of Notre Dame*) is still sometimes heard (it was written before the rest of the opera). The opera itself suffers from an absurd libretto, but does have a lyrically attractive idiom, usually slow-moving, and a restraint in the orchestration which allows clarity to the long-flowing vocal lines. For those exploring the bywaters of post-Wagnerian opera, it is worth the acquaintance. Its successor, *Fredigundis* (1916–21), set beside the Seine of the 6th century with 19th-century sensibilities, is less interesting. Schmidt used its fanfare leitmotif as the basis of a set of organ variations. Of his other works, much of Schmidt's writing for piano was composed for the one-armed pianist Paul Wittgenstein, including a piano concerto (1934), three piano quintets (1926, 1932, 1938), and a *Toccata* (1938) for solo piano. His output also includes a number of organ compositions.

Schmidt taught at the Vienna Academy (1914–37), where he was successively professor of piano, composition, and the director (1925–27), and rector of the Musikhochschule (1927–31).

RECOMMENDED WORKS
    oratorio *Das Buch mit sieben Siegen* (1935–37)
    Symphony No. 4 (1932–33)

Schoenberg Arnold Franz Walter (also spelt Schönberg)***

born September 13th 1874 at Vienna
died July 14th 1951 in Los Angeles

Schoenberg is one of those unfortunate composers whose name is better known than his music. Indubitably and irrevocably he changed the course of classical music, for no subsequent composer could be unaffected by the existence, if not the practice, of first the purely atonal works and then the 12-tone system of harmonic usage that he developed. Yet the music of composers who built on those developments is still more likely to be encountered than that of the instigator. In addition, the very name of Schoenberg still sends a chill down the musical backbone of many a potential listener, a prejudice (for that is what it is) all the more remarkable when one considers that his earlier music is in

the rich, sumptuous *fin de siècle* idiom now so widely appreciated; that his late works, even if intellectually complex, are filled with markers the average musically literate will recognise; and that even the most difficult of his 12-tone works (a mere handful) now sound tame compared with **Webern**, let alone more recent developments. It is perhaps ironic, and a comment on the gulf between musicology and musical practice, that there can scarcely be a composer more written about, and whose music has been more minutely analysed, in the last fifty years.

Aside from his very earliest works, Schoenberg's output falls into four general periods throughout which his overall development was consistent; changes represent a rapid evolution rather than the abrupt departures of some of his contemporaries. In his earliest mature works, sometimes employing huge forces for effects of colour and drama, he took traditional harmony to its limits (often with a favourite key of D minor as the basis). The emotional tensions, and the corresponding harmonic relationship between expectation and resolution, became virtually unsustainable. The next logical stage (in emotional terms) would have been the depiction of emotional breakdown, and (in harmonic terms) such a total chromaticism that musical anarchy would occur. In fact, the end of this period was a retrenchment into smaller forces and tauter forms, and a relaxation of the emotional tension in the first steps towards an alternative solution to this problem. The second period can be dated from 1908. In it he took the logical and deliberate step of divorcing dissonance from resolution, abandoning any key structure, and then sought ways of integrating what had traditionally been thought of as dissonance as an active principal participant. This is the period of the atonal works. At the same time, and equally logically, he also explored in Expressionist stage works the possibilities of using the resultant dissonant language to reflect states of mind that had entered a world of dreams or neurosis.

Shortly after the end of World War I Schoenberg abandoned the attempts on which he was then engaged to utilise atonal language in large-scale late Romantic works. The problem of freeing a musical language from traditional harmony was to find an order, both structural and harmonic, to contain the freed sounds within the boundaries that music requires. Two concepts had provided containment during the atonal period: that of continual variation, in which ideas evolve into other ideas continuously; and the written text, which imposes its own structural demands. The problem with the first (though Schoenberg did not totally abandon it) was that it restricted the *development* of a particular idea through the course of a piece. The problem with the second was that it did not provide solutions to the structures of abstract music. As he moved away from Expressionism to more strict control of material, Schoenberg's solution was to return to Classical and Baroque forms, and to create a self-imposed discipline of construction using all 12 notes of the chromatic scale: the 12-tone system. In this the basic material is a melody (a 'row' or a 'set') composed of all 12 notes, in a predetermined order, in which no note may be repeated. This row can also be used in its inversion (upside-down), retrograde (back-to-front) and retrograde-inversion, thus giving four basic rows. Each of these can be transposed. The basic material can apply to a whole work, a movement, or indeed part of a movement. Such a manipulation of melodic material was endemic to Classical and pre-Classical composers; the enormous difference was that they were working within a tonal harmonic system, while Schoenberg was using a system in which all 12 notes, and their combinations, create the harmonic interplay, without recourse to a traditional, externally imposed, harmonic scheme. There is clearly a parallel with the contemporary neo-classical movement; however, the neoclassical composers also returned to the Classical harmonic system, and to a sense of the aesthetic of Classical music, absent in Schoenberg's works. In addition, Schoenberg became increasingly concerned to integrate the vertical possibilities arising from the material contained in the rows with the horizontal flow of those rows, and it is this interaction, an alternative system to the tonal harmonic structure, that marks his music and that of his followers.

The works that explore and consolidate the new technique occupied the period 1923–36 and include all genres from the string quartet to opera, with the exception of the symphony. By 1936 he was resident in the United States, having, as a Jew, fled Nazi domination, and the final phase of Schoenberg's output suggests at least a partial reconciliation with tonality, as if the composer, having grappled with, formulated, and developed an alternative, could then afford to relax and explore the possibilities of interactive elements. Thus Schoenberg no longer paid strict observance to his own rules, and rows were sometimes chosen to suggest the possibility of tonal resonances. The very fact that Schoenberg had so consistently adapted Classical and Baroque forms to contain the new 12-tone system perhaps, with the benefit of hindsight, made it inevitable that he would then explore the interactive possibilities those forms might suggest. This fascinating period of Schoenberg's music is perhaps the least known.

Schoenberg's output is relatively large, and some of the works are more interesting for the light they shed on his development than for general listening (particularly the choral works). Therefore, in the discussion of his output that follows, only the major works are emphasised.

Schoenberg's earliest works, only some of which survive, culminated in the fluent, Brahmsian *String Quartet in D major* (1897). He then embarked on a series of programmatic works influenced by Wagner and by the example of **Strauss**, which if he had written nothing else would have placed him firmly as a major *fin de siècle*, late Romantic composer. They depict heightened human emotions in a language that matches the emotional extremity by stretching tonal harmonies to their brink, and, for three of the works, employing huge orchestral forces that allow dense textures and vivid colours. The first, the string sextet *Verklärte Nacht* (*Transfigured Night*, 1899), is based on poetry by Dehmal, recounting a man's conversation with his lover, who is pregnant by another man; its five movements correspond to the five sections of the poem. Headily sensual, dripping with nostalgia, regret, passion, and a transfiguring reconciliation, as if the emotional humidity had reached saturation point, it is with *Pierrot lunaire*, the Schoenberg work most often encountered, either in its original form or arranged for string orchestra (1917, revised 1943), in which the intimacy of the original scoring is lessened, but the emotional drama developed in the massed string sonorities.

The oratorio *Gurrelieder* (1900–01, orchestration completed 1911) is for enormous forces, five soloists, a speaker, large chorus, and huge orchestra, and is a setting of a long ballad poem by the Danish poet Jens Peter Jacobsen. Its subject, conveyed through a mythical Danish story in which the detail of the nature imagery is more potent than the actual tale, is the equation of love and death, and the rebellion against God represented by the passions, though it ends with summer light. Schoenberg's response is a work of expansive power and range, one of the finest pieces of its type and period. The long tone poem *Pelleas und Melisande* (based on Maeterlinck, 1902–03) is less successful, its length unable to sustain the material without the structure of a text.

In these last two works Schoenberg had been developing his contrapuntal mastery, and his structural ideas were taken a stage further in the *String Quartet No. 1 in D minor* (1904–05), which is in a single movement in a sonata form into which are inserted a scherzo, a rondo, and a slow section (which, to illustrate the integration, acts as a second subject). The *Chamber Symphony No. 1* (1906) uses a similar structure, and its opening includes a falling theme, reminiscent of *Verklärte Nacht*, that would seem to herald a continuation of the late Romantic expression. Instead, there is a new-found concentration, a drastic reduction of orchestral forces, and a further, but not complete, dissolution of the traditional harmonic structure in which dissonances begin not to resolve, but themselves become part of the harmonic idiom. The vertical structure is being freed from the melodic line, and at the same time becomes more interrelated with it. The result is a bouncing, confident work, with a lovely, delicately textured slow movement.

The *String Quartet No. 2* (1907–08) is both a personal work and transitionally experimental: it includes a popular melody that had reference to his personal life, as well as settings of two Stefan George poems for soprano and string quartet that again describe transfiguration from worldly toils. The four-movement quartet begins tonally (in F sharp minor); but its final movement, notable for the dark abandon of its opening, the delicacy of the vocal setting, and the luminosity of the ending, abandons tonality for much of its span, and there is no key signature. This movement towards the abandonment of the traditional harmonic structure was completed in the *Three Piano Pieces* op. 11 (1909), and the song-cycle *Das Buch der hängenden Gärten* (*The Book of the Hanging Gardens*, 1908–09), again to poems by Stefan George. The first piano piece explores the possibilities of generating material from motivic cells; the song-cycle, for the most part pale and ghostly in atmosphere and slow and fragmentary in rhythmic impulse, regularly avoids any sense of tonal resolution. The expressive settings of the texts, shifting and distilling the

emotions of the poetry, allows this lack of resolution to appear natural. The effect is to distance, to alienate the listener in a manner entirely suited to the subject matter.

In the *Five Pieces for Orchestra* op. 16 (1909, revised 1922, version for reduced orchestra, 1949) the emotive passion of the early works is toned down and honed into a new emerging language in one of Schoenberg's most satisfying works that can be heard purely for its evocative qualities, without any knowledge of its technical fascination. Each piece has a descriptive title, and in each the material is derived from the opening in the principle of continuous variation. In spite of the atonal idiom there are ghosts of a lost key (D minor) throughout. Especially effective is the central slow *Farben* ('colours'), a kind of German Impressionism using a technique known as *Klangfarben*, referring to an underpinning chord which is sustained, or imperceptibly changed. Schoenberg's 1949 title for this piece, 'Morning by a Lake', exactly describes it, complete with a jumping fish motive.

The monodrama *Erwartung* (1909), based on a libretto by Marie Pappenheim, also uses perpetual variation technique. But much more striking in this extraordinary work is the use of the extremes of Expressionist tension, reinforced by the atonality, to express the nightmare story of murder and necrophilia expressed by a woman entering a forest to find her lover: this is one of the first operas influenced by Freud, a masterpiece of the expression of extreme neurosis. The text is an intense study of breakdown caused by extreme emotion; the music matches and amplifies it, apparently spontaneous in its rapid illustrations of the woman's anguish.

It was followed by an even more extraordinary work, *Pierrot lunaire* (1912), for speaker/singer and five instrumentalists (playing eight instruments), and intended for stage performance. Based on twenty-one expressionist poems by Albert Giraud that look back to *comedia dell'arte*, its protagonist is the Pierrot of the title, whose abstract foil is the moon. The short poems encompass a gamut of human emotions, in a style sometimes bordering on the surrealistic. The overall atmosphere is of extremes, the no man's land between what is normally considered sane and what is touched by madness. Divided into three parts, the first presents the Pierrot as lover and poet; the second is suffused with images of guilt and punishment; while in the third the Pierrot reaches back to the lost world of the *commedia*, the moon threading in and out of the Pierrot's fantasies. The soloist employs *Sprechgesang* ('speech-song'), fully notated but delivered with speech-like freedom of declamation, while the instrumental writing often opposes the vocal line. An extraordinary variety of colour and idea is achieved in the various songs, partly by a continuous change of instrumental combinations, the entire group coming together only in the final song. Parody and humour are also important components in establishing the fantastical atmosphere. Schoenberg's musical world is between sleeping and waking, close to substantiality yet insubstantial, fantastical but half-real, a region where semi-submerged emotions and fantasies are allowed a brief reign. The effect of the *Sprechgesang*, half-spoken, half-sung, heightens the sense of limbo. *Pierrot lunaire* is a seminal work of the 20th century, first for opening up this nether region of the psyche, second for showing the musical means for doing so, and third for creating a form of small-scale yet highly potent music-theatre, five years before **Stravinsky's** *The Soldier's Tale*.

The dramatic elements of *Pierrot lunaire* were considerably extended in *Die glückliche Hand* (*The Knack*, 1910–13), a symbolic drama for singer, mime-artists, and orchestra. Techniques similar to film are employed (swift cutting, rapid changes of scene, careful consideration of visual angles), while the sphere of action largely belongs to the mime-artists, emotional expression to the singer and orchestra. The overall Expressionist effect is heavily dependent on the detailed stage and visual requirements, especially symbolic lighting. At the time of composition, these must have seemed both extreme and impossible, but recent multimedia theatrical developments have made this a much more viable piece, perhaps best suited to television.

Schoenberg then planned and started a gigantic symphony, which in design would have followed the Mahlerian pattern. Some of the material for this abandoned project was incorporated into the equally huge oratorio *Die Jakobsleiter* (*Jacob's Ladder*, 1917–22), which originally envisaged forces of 720 (including 20 flutes), Schoenberg abandoned this, too; he was interrupted by the war, and when he returned to it he was already moving onwards to the concept of the 12-tone system. But the first half of the fragmentary score has been rendered into a usable form by Winfried Zilling, and is interesting in showing the continuity from a late Mahlerian idiom to the 12-tone system.

With the abandonment of *Jakobsleiter*, Schoenberg turned to smaller-scale structures. The *Five Piano Pieces* op. 23 (1920 and 1923), the *Serenade* op. 24 (1920–23) for seven instruments and bass voice, and the *Piano Suite* op. 25 (1921) signal this change and the development of the 12-tone system. Four of the *Five Piano Pieces*, for example, use the principles of 12-tone procedures, while the fifth, a waltz, uses a strict row in a fairly simple manner. The *Piano Suite* is composed of dances whose forms echo the late Baroque, complete with repeats, and every one of the dances is composed from the same 12-note series, which includes the retrograde of the notes (in German notation) B–A–C–H (B flat –A–C–B), deliberately asserting the continuity of German music in the new system. The tone of both sets of piano pieces is of an introverted exploration of the new constraints. The seven-movement *Serenade*, also utilising dance forms, has as its central movement a 12-note vocal setting of a Petrarch sonnet. Its instrumentation, reflecting the desire for distinctive new sonorities, includes the mandolin. There is a jauntiness to the *Serenade* that perhaps makes it an easier introduction to this important period in Schoenberg's development than the more austere piano pieces.

In the works that followed, Schoenberg consolidated and developed his understanding of the system that he had evolved. The first movement of the *Wind Quintet* op. 26 (1923–24) is in sonata form, the last a rondo, and with its short-phrased, light textures, its purely abstract exploration, it is far removed from the emotional Expressionism of earlier works. In tone, if not in harmonic structure, it has strong affinities to the works of contemporary neo-classical composers. The *Suite* op. 29 (1924–26) for piccolo, clarinet, bass clarinet, violin, viola, cello and piano, also uses Baroque forms, but is more flowing, more obviously lyrical, the emphasis on colour, with a sense of spontaneous flow that belies the technical complexities. The rather dour but fluently integrated *String Quartet No. 3* (1927) is modelled on Schubert's A minor quartet, D 804, its four movements being a sonata, a set of variations, a scherzo, and a rondo. In the powerful *Variations for Orchestra* op. 31 (1926–28), Schoenberg combined the techniques of the immediately preceding works with something of the grandeur and emotional expression of his earlier music. Scored for a large orchestra, including celesta and mandolin, it is in the form of an introduction, nine variations, and finale, with a solo cello presenting the 12-note row theme, subsequently manipulated in all the mirror versions as well as in transposition. With its wide range of mood, from a suggestion of abstract playfulness to moments of high drama, it is capable of a wide range of interpretation.

The relative paucity of works in the early Thirties is partly a reflection of the political and social atmosphere of the time, but also of a return to the stage, first with the small, and largely forgotten, one-act domestic comedy of manners, *Von heute auf morgen* (1928–29), and then with Schoenberg's only full-scale opera, *Moses und Aron* (1930–32). This major work is rarely performed, partly because Schoenberg never wrote the third act (eventually authorising a purely dramatic performance of the end of the libretto), although the previous two acts feel complete in themselves. More daunting is the nature of the libretto itself: based on the biblical story of Moses and Aaron, it is in part Schoenberg's profession of faith. Central to the opera is the conflict between the two brothers, Moses exhorting the people to understand an abstract God, Aaron requiring concrete images (faith versus materialism). The libretto is earnest, the moral severe, and as a drama it seems to have been thought rather than felt. On the one hand it fails to involve the audience in the psychological struggles it portrays, and on the other it removes the story completely from the resonances of myth. Dramatic elements are created by powerful visual effects (sacrifices, burnt offerings, orgies of destruction), but this fails to disguise the uncomfortable feeling that the opera stage is the wrong arena for this particular statement. This is unfortunate, for Schoenberg invested the score with some of his finest music, drawing on all his experience of the previous decade. Moses and Aaron are contrasted in voice, the former, a bass, almost always employing *Sprechgesang*, the latter a lyrical tenor. Technically the opera is based on a single 12-note row, with a complex evolution of the possible permutations of that row; expressively, the music is wide-ranging and powerful, with an extraordinary range of emotion, and especially effective choral writing that ranges from the ethereal to the savage and destructive. It is difficult not to see a parallel between Moses and Schoenberg's own artistic position, or between the stern

father figure of Moses and the psychological hold that Schoenberg had over Berg and Webern.

In 1934 Schoenberg left for the United States, and his first work in his new country, the *Violin Concerto* (1934–36), continued the consolidation of the 12-tone technique in the new format of the concerto, laid out in a traditional three-movement scheme. The opening, with the row first divided between violin and orchestra, and then played by the soloist, announces the nature of the solo writing, technically virtuoso, but imbued with the traditional rich and soaring character of the instrument. Dense, gritty, uncompromising, but with a sense of freedom and flight in the extremely difficult solo writing, this concerto is not for the casual listener, but is nonetheless an engrossing work. It was followed by Schoenberg's last string quartet, the four-movement *String Quartet No. 4* (1936). As with the violin concerto, the classical layout is not followed strictly, and in this closely constructed, austere, but lyrical work Schoenberg achieved a fluid linear melodic flow using the parameters of the 12-tone system, the culmination of this period of his output.

In 1938 he wrote the rather bitty, overemphatic, and undistinguished *Kol nidre* for speaker, chorus and orchestra, which is unmistakably tonal, even if the main chant theme is open to the kinds of manipulation Schoenberg had used in his 12-tone rows. In 1939 he reworked the unfinished *Chamber Symphony No. 2* (1906–16 and 1939), thus returning to his own pre-atonal period. In the strange *Ode to Napoleon* (1942), for reciter, piano and string quartet or string orchestra (a setting of Byron's poem), Schoenberg returned to elements of *Sprechgesang*, but without the associated sumptuous Expressionism. The instrumental accompaniment is often emotive, but in a more dry, incisive and ironic manner, occasionally recalling *Pierrot lunaire*, using a 12-tone series in a very free fashion, and eventually ending in E flat. This process of a partial backward glance while progressing forward is continued in the *Piano Concerto* (1942), where Schoenberg continued his preoccupation with compressing material into a one-movement form while implying four distinct sections. There is again the feel of a tonal base, largely created by a sense of cadence and resolution. The character of this demanding but rewarding concerto is again incisive: each incident emerges with a calculated precision, and at times the concerto debate seems to be as much between the desire for linear flow and accurate determinacy of detail as between solo and orchestra.

In 1946 Schoenberg recovered from a serious heart attack, and the experience was reflected in one of his most completely satisfying works, the *String Trio* (1946). In many ways it is a summary of his work. The overall shape is a distant derivation of Schoenberg's compression of classical forms, with one long movement shaped into three sections, of which the last reflects the first, redistributed among the instruments and using an inversion of the opening idea. More important, he achieved a synthesis of the vivid Expressionist episodes of the much earlier works with the terser, angular style of the 12-tone period, and in a manner that sounds spontaneous and fresh; the experience of the immediately preceding works allows (through the triad implications of the tone-row) a tonal atmosphere without any tonal procedures. This dense and concentrated work is by no means easy to grasp overall, although many of its moments have immediate impact or attraction; but it has something of the visionary quality given to some composers at the end of their lives, and deserves in its own fashion to stand alongside **Strauss's** *Four Last Songs*.

Dramatic narration returned in the six-minute *Survivor from Warsaw* (1946–47) for narrator, chorus and orchestra, Schoenberg's protest against the Nazi experience, to his own text. The dense, expressive, harrowing score, full of instrumental effects, entirely matches the intensity of the text, and ends with 'Shema Yisroel' sung in Hebrew by the chorus to an original melody, the orchestra being used in full for the first time.

It may turn out that Schoenberg's current position, his music more written about than heard, will prove lasting. For, aesthetically, there really does seem to be some essential element missing in his music. He does not have the single-minded fascination and focus of **Webern**, the vision of **Berg**, the passion of **Bartók**, or even the humanism of **Shostakovich**. For much of his music, one senses a wall between his own psyche and its expression in music, seeking solutions through the pure application of intellect. It is perhaps this, rather than his 'difficultness', that is responsible for the relative paucity of performances, for his idiom has long been easily encompassed by musicians. Schoenberg comes closest to letting down his guard in the passionate early works, when he can let it slip past through Expressionism or, in

Pierrot lunaire, through an ironic slant (in both cases exploring the edge of madness, the flip side to the coin of iron control), and in works such as the *Five Pieces for Orchestra* or the *String Trio* where the means merge with the ends. It is perhaps no coincidence that in one of his own paintings (for he was an accomplished painter) he depicts himself with his back to the viewer. The mighty flaws and the strengths of *Moses und Aron* stand as an allegory for the composer himself, quite apart from the overt autobiographical symbolism.

Schoenberg was active in promoting new music, founding the Society for the Private Performance of Music in Vienna in 1917. He was also an important teacher, first as a private tutor, then as professor at the Prussian Academy of Fine Arts (1924–33), and finally teaching at the University of California (1936–44). He published five books on composition. Many subsequently distinguished composers were among his pupils, of whom the best known are **Webern** and **Berg**. He himself was the brother-in-law of the composer **Zemlinsky** by his first marriage, and father-in-law to **Nono** through his second. There is an Arnold Schoenberg Institute that since 1976 has regularly published a *Journal of the Arnold Schoenberg Institute* with scholarly articles on the composer and his works.

RECOMMENDED WORKS
  Erwartung op. 17 (1909)
  Five Pieces op. 16 (1909) for orchestra
  oratorio *Gurrelieder* (1900–11)
  opera *Moses und Aron* (1930–32)
  Ode to Napoleon op. 41 (1942) for
     reciter and orchestra
  Pelleas und Melisande op. 5 (1902–03)
     for orchestra
  Piano Concerto op. 42 (1942)
  Pierrot lunaire op. 21 (1912)
  Serenade op. 24 (1920–23) for septet
  String Quartet No. 1 op. 7 (1904–05)
  String Quartet No. 2 op. 10 (1907–08)
  String Quartet No. 3 op. 30 (1927)
  String Quartet No. 4 op. 37 (1936)
  String Trio op. 45 (1946)
  A Survivor from Warsaw op. 46 (1947)
     for reciter, chorus and orchestra
  Variations op. 31 (1926–28) for
     orchestra
  Violin Concerto op. 36 (1935–36)
  Verklärte Nacht op. 4 for string sextet
     (1899) or string orchestra (1917,
     rev. 1943)
  Wind Quintet op. 26 (1925–26)

SELECTED BIBLIOGRAPHY

A. Schoenberg, *Letters* (ed. E. Stein),
English trans., 1964

Style and Idea (ed. L. Stein), 1975

W. Reich, *Arnold Schoenberg: A.
Critical Biography*, trans. L.
Black, 1971

C. Rosen, *Schoenberg*, 1976

H. H. Stuckenschmidt, *Arnold
Schoenberg*, trans. H. Searle and E.
Temple-Roberts, 1959

A short but detailed survey of
Schoenberg's life and works by O.
Neighbour will be found in *The
New Grove Second Viennese
School* (1980), which includes an
extensive bibliography.

Schreker Franz*

born 23rd March 1878 at Monaco
died 21st March 1934 at Berlin

An important and successful opera composer in the first two decades of the
century, Schreker is now better remembered for his *Chamber Symphony* of 1916
than for his stage works, although in
recent years there has been a revival of
interest in the latter. His musical idiom is
late Romantic, following the inheritance of
Wagnerian Germanic opera; his stage
works are music dramas, with a continuous
flow of idea and action rather than obvious
divisions into arias. His plots extend the
Wagnerian inheritance. Mostly folk-tale
subjects, they focus on extremes of human
motivation and human sexuality, with an
emphasis on individual characterisation
rather than archetypes. Schreker's
orchestral style is luxuriant, influenced by
Strauss and **Mahler**, and in turn influencing
Berg. Using very large forces, the orchestration is rich in detail, sometimes dividing
instruments into chamber groups in an
almost pointillistic style. He also extended
the use of percussion, with large batteries
of instruments, especially the tuned percussion.

His first success was with his second
opera, *Der ferne Klang* (*The Distant
Sound*, 1901–10), which makes striking use
of extra orchestras both onstage and off-
stage and is full of subtleties of orchestral
detail. The hero of the opera is himself an
opera composer. *Das Spielwerk und die
Prinzessin* (*The Carillon and the Princess*, 1909–12) is a 'mystery play' in one act
set in the Middle Ages. It has a marvellous
seamless flow, touches of **Mahler** in the
orchestration, and typical moments when
Schreker produces passages of magical

orchestral timbre, around a story that
ends with the soul of a dead violinist being
laid to rest, and the Princess and the
Apprentice starting a new life. But its very
luxuriance becomes wearing, unrelieved
by contrast of incident or idiom. *Die
Gezeichneten* (*The Marked Men*, 1913–15)
is marred by its complicated plot (concerning the orgies of a Genoese nobleman), but
the best of its music is found in the
orchestral suite *Vorspiel zu einem Drama*
(*Prelude to a Drama*). Its successor, *Der
Schatzgräber* (*The Treasure Digger*,
1915–18), is his major work, and received
385 performances in fifty locations during
the Weimar Republic. The story (again
with a fairy-tale medieval setting) is a
combination of elements of the tales of
Lady Macbeth and of Orpheus, its central
characters being an over-sensual murder-
ess and a minstrel with semi-magical
powers. Again there is a wealth of fascinating orchestral detail, but also a considerable variety of mood and dramatic situation and location, and a strong Straussian
influence (reminiscent of the contemporary *Die Frau ohne Schatten*, which has
some parallels in its basic plot). Ultimately, the vocal writing and the plot do
not match the interest of the orchestral
sound, but those who enjoy a late-Romantic idiom in the manner of **Pfitzner** or
Zemlinsky will find the work of interest.

By the 1920s the heyday of the large-
scale late Romantic opera was over, and in
his later operas Schreker turned to a more
neo-classical idiom. None of these was a
success, partly because their sexual liber-
ality (and Schreker's Jewishness) came
under increasing criticism from the emerging Nazi movement. Apart from some
songs, occasionally heard, and a handful of
chamber music, notably the pleasant *Der
Wind* (1908–09) for violin, cello, clarinet,
horn, and piano, it is the *Chamber Symphony* (1916) for twenty-three instruments that has prevented Schreker's
music from falling into obscurity. Again,
the delight in the changing textures and
instrumental combinations (including
piano, harp and harmonium) are greater
than the overall effect, but it is full of
charm and subtle pleasure. Of his songs,
the song-cycle *Fünf Gesänge für tiefe
Stimme* (*Five Cantos for Low Voice*, 1909),
setting one tale from the Arabian Nights
and three poems by Edith Ronsperger, is
quietly passionate and intense, and luminous in Schreker's 1920 orchestration,
where washes of orchestral colour, sometimes languid, sometimes dark, support a

sensuous vocal line devoid of Expressionist extremes of emotion.

Schreker was active as a conductor, founding the Vienna Philharmonic Choir in 1902, and conducting it until 1920, including the first performance of Schoenberg's *Gurrelieder*. He had a considerable influence as a teacher at the Vienna Academy of Music (from 1917) and at the Berlin Hochschule für Musik, although his teaching was cut short by the rise to power of the Nazis. Among his pupils was **Hába**, while **Berg**, who prepared the piano reduction of *Der ferne Klang*, was influenced by his orchestration and the sensual nature of his operatic subject-matter. As a composer, Schreker's position is an ambiguous one: although close to the circle of Schoenberg, he did not succeed in breaking out of the mould of late Romanticism, with its rich chromatic palette, into new harmonic conceptions. His operatic plots now seem dated, and the luxuriance too continuously rich for the musical stomach. But the prowess of his orchestral skills will interest students of orchestration and of that fertile, decadent period of Vienna's musical history.

RECOMMENDED WORKS
   Chamber Symphony (1916)
   song-cycle *Fünf Gesänge für tiefe
      Stimme* (1909, orchestrated 1920)
   opera *Der Schatzgräber* (1915–18)
   opera *Das Spielwerk und die
      Prinzessin* (1909–12)

Webern Anton (Friedrich Wilhelm von)•••
born 3rd December 1883 at Vienna
died 15th September 1945 at Mittersill

The art of Anton Webern is the most elusive of any 20th-century composer. It profoundly influenced the generation of composers who emerged in the 1950s and 1960s, and through them it resounds today. It has baffled the majority of audiences, totally unequipped for its means and techniques, for its concept, and for its purpose of expression; yet it weaves a fascination over those who have learned to enter its strange world.

Webern was the supreme composer of the miniature. Yet he is not a miniaturist in the sense of taking some small aspect of the world and offering an exquisite glimpse of that facet. Rather he is an imploder, attempting to take the enormity and wonder of the world and convert that

wonder into the smallest possible distillation. Faced with one of the expansive mountain landscapes that he loved, he describes musically not the profundity of the vast scene, but rather a single mountain flower, showing how that flower is a perfect microcosm of the landscape, the distillation of the glory of God. Such an analogy is pertinent to Webern's aesthetic: in 1926 he found a poet, Hildegarde Jone, who expressed just such a vision, and many of his later works are settings of her poetry.

This art emerges as much less a break from the late Romantic tradition than is popularly supposed: rather it is the inversion of that tradition, the Mahlerian world turned inside out, an aesthetic and emotional involvement that Webern's followers have almost universally ignored. New thinking in art often parallels new thinking in other human fields, and Webern's musical discoveries are analogous to contemporary developments in physics, particularly subatomic physics, where in place of the huge conception of the universe, the basis of the entire physical world has been shown to be encapsulated in a minuscule structure. The implosion in Webern's music accounts for the brevity of his works, and the desire for perfection their relative paucity: Webern's entire output can be heard in a little over four hours.

The elements of Webern's music are not easy to assimilate, but much easier to understand when their overall purpose is grasped. The major problem of such a distillation into the miniature is that every aspect of that miniature must be perfect, without a single element that could be substituted by another. Webern's entire mature output can be seen, on this level, as an attempt to find forms that would most completely fulfil this vision in its different aspects; unfortunately, most of the attention has been given to those formal elements, to the detriment of expressive content, since in the final analysis it is easier to discuss the building blocks than the building. Webern found the way to those forms through the ideas of his teacher **Schoenberg**, and throughout Webern's career Schoenberg developed new formal ideas that Webern was able to embrace and evolve for his own purposes. A second, sometimes latent, influence on Webern's formal structures was his knowledge of the Renaissance polyphonists, who in their own sphere had similar problems to overcome.

Webern's output can be divided into

four periods: the earliest works that represent the final breakdown of late Romantic tonality; the move to atonality and increasing brevity; the earliest 12-tone works; and the maturation of Webern's use of the 12-tone system. Within this development, his main output is of chamber music and song, both solo and choral, and five orchestral works.

His first mature work was the *Passacaglia for Orchestra* op. 1 (1908). Its techniques are derived from those of Brahms, its sensuous atmosphere, held in check until bursting out in climax, from late Romantic tone poems, and in particular Schoenberg's *Verklärte Nacht.* The tonal basis is bursting at the seams, and its use of the passacaglia, as well as **Schoenberg's** technique of continuous variations, give it a formal ruggedness that marks the work out from its late Romantic antecedents. The *Six Pieces* op. 6 (1909) for orchestra are also for Mahlerian-sized forces, but they are put to quite different uses. The elements that might have formed a late Romantic work are presented in fleeting wisps, with constant change of colours. Nothing is repeated; ideas slip and clash; the emotional expression changes from moment to moment, from the sweetest lyricism to raucous expression, with the extreme of instrumental range and rapid deployment of instrumental groups. Although there is a tonal undercurrent, the harmonic language is atonal, and there is a powerful sense in these pieces of the collapse of the late Romantic idiom, as if we are hearing the pieces of the musical landscape actually imploding as a prelude to the later miniaturism. By the *Five Pieces* op. 10 (1911–13) for orchestra, this connection with Romanticism has been almost entirely broken. What are left are fragments reduced to their utmost brevity, introducing the device of 'pointillism' in which each note is assigned to a different instrument. No. 4 lasts only seven bars, and uses all 12 notes in the opening. Newcomers to Webern might listen to these three orchestral works in succession: the power and beauty of the language of the *Five Pieces* is then naturally evident, whereas a plunge into them can be bewildering.

By the *Symphony* op. 21 (1928), for clarinet, bass clarinet, two horns, harps, and strings, Webern had adopted 12-tone principles, especially the use of mirror reflections of 12-note rows, and symmetrical relationships between rows. The symphony is in two short movements (Webern planned a third, but abandoned it), the second loosely a mirror of the first. Notes are often very widely spaced (with, for example, an octave shift of any given note of the row), pointillism is much in evidence, and silences between individual notes are an integral device. The second movement is especially tightly constructed. Cast as a theme with seven short variations and a coda, it uses complex interrelationships of the theme, so that, for example, the fourth variation uses mirror images, and the rest of the piece is a mirror image of the preceding theme and variations, while the initial presentation of the theme is accompanied by its retrograde. The complexity of this formal scheme is impossible to follow without a score (and indeed, a prior analysis of that score), but what the interrelationships seem to achieve is cohesion in what might otherwise, on the aural surface, be totally isolated points of music. The effect is of a meditative eeriness, with a faded echo of a waltz in the second movement.

The *Orchestral Variations* op. 30 (1940) represent Webern's final paring down of material in orchestral form. The theme and six variations are played without a break, and last around six minutes. The theme, a four-note phrase, is handed around the different components of the orchestra (thus becoming a variation through timbre and colour), and in the variations the rhythmic pattern of the theme is subject to careful modification, thus making the work approach the total serialism that was adopted in a more systematic and controlled fashion by Webern's followers. The orchestration is especially lucid in this most rarefied of Webern's orchestral works, and the chordal effects give it a strong lineal impetus.

It was with the crepuscular *Five Movements* op. 5 (1909) for string quartet (also arranged for strings, 1928) that Webern started to apply his own aesthetic to the chamber medium. In the earlier *String Quartet* (1905) he had attempted to bind differing tonalities and speeds within a single movement, but the sound world is indebted to Schoenberg's *Verklärte Nacht*; the equally attractive *Piano Quintet* (1907) is Brahmsian. In the *Five Movements*, with the use of unusual string sounds, the range of timbre is extended in an expressive work in which every detail carries weight. The slow movements create a haunting mood, heightened by the string technique (especially the use of harmonics); there are echoes of Mahler in the scherzo. The *Six Bagatelles* op. 9 (1913) for string quartet use similar extended timbres, and are built on two- or three-note motifs using all 12 notes. The six pieces use ostinati, and the sense of reduction in both musical technique and expression is overt, notably in the extraordinary nothingness of the fifth bagatelle, just impressions of sound in an otherwise empty vision. The atonal experimentation is even more marked in the *Four Pieces* op. 7 (1910) for violin and piano. These very short and bare Expressionist pieces, like dying shards of sound, are characterised by wide leaps and extreme changes of dynamics. The limits of such compression are reached in the two and a quarter minute *Three Little Pieces* op. 11 (1914) for cello and piano, where every note carries a different weight of dynamic and attack, silences become of integral importance, and the last piece consists of just twenty notes.

By the *String Trio* op. 20 (1926–27), Webern had adopted 12-tone techniques, and the characteristic 7ths and minor 9ths are prominent. It is perhaps the most difficult of Webern's work to grasp (the cellist of the first London performance gave up in disgust). The two movements are based on a classical rondo and sonata form (including a straight repeat), although these may appear quite inaudible. The most jagged of all Webern's works, it is technically full of mirror reflections. The music will almost certainly seem incomprehensible on first acquaintance, but if followed with a score Webern's patterns can be recognised and the abstract intensity, once experienced, is difficult to forget.

The *Quartet* op. 22 (1930) for clarinet, tenor, saxophone, piano and violin, is as rarefied as the *String Trio*, though both the two movements have a gentle, swaying nature that is appealing. The *Concerto* op. 24 (1931–34) is a nonet for flute, oboe, clarinet, horn, trumpet, trombone, piano, violin and viola. The reduction to single points of instrumental colour is almost complete: they are dispersed widely on the vertical scale, silence moving in as the linear progression shifts to another vertical mark, emphasised by the different combinations of instruments involved. It rather unexpectedly arrives at an almost humorous, rumbustious, swinging feel in the last of its three movements, as if Webern was both showing that his idiom was capable of such a mood, and delighting in turning his own technique emotionally on its head.

In the *String Quartet* op. 28 (1936–38) the technique is again formidable, the series based on the four notes (in German notation) of B–A–C–H (B flat–A–C–B), and brilliantly using sections within its row to reflect that motif in multiple forms (it has become a model for later serial composers). It is more flowing and opaque than the *String Trio*, but at the same time it does feel more sterile, the whole subordinated to the demands of the 12-tone writing without the internal wonder of the earlier work.

Apart from some early music, Webern wrote only one work for piano, the late *Piano Variations* op. 27 (1935–36). 'Variations' is a little misleading, unless it refers to the mirror imaging of the first of three movements, and the development of ideas in the last: Webern himself referred to it as a kind of suite. The second movement is particularly notable for its strong pointillistic contrasts, constant tension, and resolution created by alternating dynamics.

The largest body of music by Webern is for the voice, yet these are the works least likely to be encountered. One of the reasons is their sheer difficulty, although Webern always uses the voice melodically, without *Sprechgesang* or other extended techniques. Nonetheless, the solo lines are extremely taxing, in spite of modern developments in vocal technique. A more important failing is the texts he chose after 1926; all are by Hildegard Jone, wordy in their combination of Christian and pantheistic mysticism, and of dubious quality.

The first published songs are (like those of **Schoenberg**) settings of Stefan George. The wispy, short *Entflieht auf Leichten Kähnen* op. 2 (1908) for chorus introduces Webern's love of four-part canon, still with elements of tonality (and bitonality) and with prominent 3rds and 6ths. With the *Five Lieder* op. 3 (1908) and *Five Lieder* op. 4 (1908–09) he moved to pure atonality. There is a gossamer feel to these works, the rhythmic sense broken down, with wide intervals and the use of 7ths and minor 9ths that became so characteristic of Webern's writing. The op. 3 songs are strictly linear; the op. 4 songs more dramatic, with a chordal feel at points. Expressionism is the dominant aesthetic, the anti-Romantic music stripping the poetry of its more Romantic elements.

As soon as Webern replaces the piano with instrumentation, his settings take on a different dimension. In the *Two Songs* op. 8 (1910) for voice and eight instruments, to verses by Rilke, the solo line is again full of wide leaps, but now woven through a fragmented instrumentation, whose points of timbre and individual colour effectively counter the soloist. The *Four Songs* op. 12 (1915–17) are rather more full and flowing. One of the summits of Webern's output is the *Four Songs* op. 13 (1914–18) for soprano and small orchestra, in which the instruments create the atmosphere behind the vocal line rather than amplifying it or commenting on it. The use of the celesta and harp add unexpected delicacies of colour in settings whose extreme economy of means is paradoxically so rich in weight of detail that there is a strong impression of the vocal line being one of those actual instruments. The *Six Songs* op. 14 (1917–21) for soprano, two clarinets, and two strings (to verses by Trakl) feature a more extreme vocal line, darker colours and more marked dynamics for each individual note. The solo part is extremely taxing; the overall effect is of allusions rather than emotions.

The next two groups of songs are on sacred texts, and in them Webern returned to the use of canon as a major structural device. A double canon ends the *Fünf Geistliche Lieder* op. 15 (*Five Sacred Songs*, 1917–22) for voice and five instruments, which demand high purity from the soloist, whose line is more obviously continuous than in preceding works, while retaining the wide leaps. The *Five Canons on Latin Texts* op. 16 (1923–24) for soprano, clarinet and bass clarinet are another highpoint in Webern's vocal output. These chips hewn off a block of runic stone employ strict canonic structures, stark in their instrumental simplicity, that bind the group. There is a wonderful simplicity and flow to the immensely difficult and high vocal line, which darts up and back in a very wide leaps at fairly fast speeds.

The *Three Traditional Rhymes* op. 17 (1924–25) for soprano, clarinet, bass clarinet and violin doubling viola, were Webern's first 12-tone pieces, and continue the use of canonic techniques. The continuity from op. 16 is obvious, but the effect is more jagged and angular. In the *Three Songs* op. 18 (1925) for soprano, E flat clarinet, and guitar, the connection between the music and the folk texts has almost totally disappeared, and they are chiefly interesting for the use of the guitar in such an unexpected context. Webern ended this series of vocal works with a work for chorus, violin, two clarinets, celesta and guitar, the *Two Songs* op. 19 (1926), which set two short Goethe texts. Both songs use the same 12-note row, the orchestral accompaniment is detailed and pointillistic, the canonic choral writing densely stranded, and there is a closer

connection between words and music (for example in the rhythms of the instrumental opening to the second song, evoking the sheep leaving the meadow in the verse).

Webern's return to vocal writing in 1933 reflected his discovery of Hildegard Jone's writing: all his remaining vocal works are settings of her words. In keeping with the soulfulness of the texts, the *Three Songs from 'Viae inviae'* op. 23 (1933–34) for voice and piano are less extreme and compressed in both form and content than the preceding vocal works, with a more obviously tuneful flow to the vocal writing. More successful are the *Three Songs* op. 25 (1934) for voice and piano, partly because the words are more succinct. Whether the musical process is here more important than the word-setting is debatable; certainly the correlation between words and music veers by now between the extremely tenuous (the opening of the first song) and the clearly apposite (the butterfly movement of the piano of the second song). The 12-note row is used with considerable freedom, shared by voice and piano, each supplying the missing notes of the other.

Webern's final three vocal works are all for chorus. The intense four and a half minutes of *Das Augenlicht* op. 26 (1935) for chorus and orchestra combine drama, especially in the brass, with delicate events created by the orchestration. The chordal density of the chorus contrasts markedly with the particularism of the instruments. The impressive three-movement *Cantata No. 1* op. 29 (1938–39) for soprano, chorus and orchestra, is more extended, with an explosive choral opening to its first movement, after a quiet instrumental introduction. There is a pulse to this opening movement, created by the alternation of quiet meditation and emphatic outburst, while the solo lines of the second canonic movement return to the lifting and falling flow of the *Five Canons*. The form is a fusion of fugue, scherzo and variations, and again is dramatic, building in a step-like manner to a central climax and gradually falling to an ending of tranquillity. The larger *Cantata No. 2* op. 31 (1941–43) for soprano, bass, chorus and orchestra is in six short movements, in which the vocal line of the bass is pitted against instrumental writing that constantly shifts in its time-values. The atmosphere is more mystical, summarised by two lines from the text: 'The hives of bees are like constellations / so full of drops of light that creation brings.'

Webern's importance to the succeeding generation of composers is considerable.

The carefully constructed rhythmic irregularities and the detailed changes of dynamics in the later works led the way for serialism (or, as it is sometimes called, 'total serialism') in which these aspects of the construction of a piece were subject to a systematisation similar to that of the harmonic structure. But few of those successors have had such a deep aesthetic instinct as Webern (**Kurtág** is a notable exception), or created such a particular and individual sound world.

Webern was active as a conductor, working at Prague's Deutsches Theater (1917–18) and with Austrian radio (1927–38). He directed a number of groups, notably the Vienna Workers' Symphony Concerts (1922–34) and the Vienna Workers' Chorus (1923–34), where he brought new (and old) music-making to social strata not usually associated with the contemporary musical life of Vienna. He taught musical theory at the Jewish Cultural Institute for the Blind from 1926, and his private pupils included **Hartmann**. He died in tragic circumstances, shot in error by an American soldier.

RECOMMENDED WORKS

All Webern's mature output is recommended, and has been quite widely recorded. Those new to Webern might consider listening to the sequence of orchestral works outlined above.

BIBLIOGRAPHY

H. Moldenhauer, *Anton von Webern: Chronicle of his Life and Works*, 1978

A short but detailed survey of Webern's life and works by Paul Griffiths will be found in *The New Grove Second Viennese School*, which includes an extensive bibliography.

Zemlinsky Alexander von**

born 14th October 1871 at Vienna
died 15th March 1942 at Larchmont (New York)

For many years Zemlinsky was best known as **Schoenberg**'s teacher (for a brief period) and brother-in-law, and as the composer of a single work, the *Lyrische Symphonie* (*Lyric Symphony*, 1922). He emerged into musical maturity just as the late Romantic style was about to be eclipsed by the new developments of Schoenberg and **Stravinsky**, and his

neglect is partly due to his continuation of that idiom. Recently, as the conservatism of his idiom has been mellowed by time, he has emerged as one of the few composers continuing in the late Romantic vein with an individual and sometimes striking voice, especially in the allegory and symbolism of his operas: his distinctiveness comes from a sumptuous sense of orchestration, backed by marvellous orchestral craftsmanship, and the ability to create unfolding kaleidoscopes of sound perhaps akin to the constant shifting of dreams. His opera subjects reflect this aspect, and in almost all his operas there are marvellous moments when the dream world suddenly opens out into a broader and more ordered musical landscape. This is a subtle art, belied by the very luxuriance of his orchestral usage, and not always an immediate one, and he perhaps reflects better than anyone the hothouse intellectual atmosphere and internal self-questioning of the Vienna of his day.

The early *Clarinet Trio* (1895) is assured but derivative of Brahms and Dvořák, and while melodious and attractive, is not of especial interest. The big and expressive *Symphony in B flat* (*Symphony No. 2*, 1897) also shows youthful influences, with Wagnerian, Brucknerian and many Brahmsian touches, and the springing rhythmic vitality and melodic organisation of Dvořák. Like most Zemlinsky works, it has a markedly atmospheric opening. With its big slow movement and energetic finale, it is more than just a curiosity.

The first signs of his mature style emerged in the sumptuous tone poem *Die Seejungfrau* (*The Mermaid*, 1903), whose programme is based on the Andersen fairy-tale. Requiring an enormous orchestra, this rich and often beautiful work is well worth the discovery, but it is in his vocal works that Zemlinsky's idiom found its ideal genre. His third opera, *Der Traumgörge* (1903–06) coincides with the maturing of his musical style. To a libretto by Leo Feld, its subject is a mill-owner who writes fairy tales, and seeks to apply them to real life: reality and dream become intertwined. With its passionate, swirling, long, high vocal lines, and a more obvious division into aria-like passages than the later operas, it has echoes of Czech pastoral, an almost Scandinavian sense of light and colour, and passages of considerable beauty. His next opera, *Kleider machen Leute* (*Clothes Make the Man*, 1907–10), also to a libretto by Feld, is based on the comic story by Gottfried Keller.

The next two operas (and two of Zemlinsky's most effective works) are based on the writings of Oscar Wilde, which, with their willingness to unleash psychological motivations, echoed the self-tormenting tone of Freudian Vienna. *Eine florentinische Tragödie* (*A Florentine Tragedy*, 1914–15), is a powerful and compact one-act work based on Wilde's decadent play of a love triangle in Renaissance Florence, uniting sex and power and with a disturbing parody of the 'happy ending': through the murder of the lover by the husband, the husband recognises his wife's beauty, and his wife her husband's strength and her own sexual reaction to the violence. The music is swift-moving and sumptuous, closely matching the psychological undercurrents and developments of the plot. Its build-up of passions, power, and anger is subtle, gradual, and inexorable, and when the climax arrives, it is to music of impact and conviction, the thematic network becoming recognisable and cogent. In the same vein, and finer still, is Zemlinsky's sixth opera, *The Birthday of the Infanta* (1920–21), also known as *Der Zwerg* (*The Dwarf*). Short and succinct, it is based on Wilde's story in which a misshapen dwarf is carried off as a birthday present for an Infanta. In the palace, he sees a mirror for the first time and, realising his ugliness, dies. The Infanta continues her birthday, unmoved by what the dwarf has in the meantime shown her: the power of imagination and creativity. It was his most successful opera during his own lifetime.

Zemlinsky's last completed opera, *Der Kreidekreis* (*The Chalk Circle*, 1931–32) was based on a successful play by 'Klabund' (Alfred Henschke), itself based on an old Chinese drama (later made famous by Brecht). It tells the story of a woman sold to a merchant as a second wife, who is accused of the murder of the merchant and is saved by a Prince who had fallen in love with her at the time of her sale. The powerful drama is a combination of symbolist tale and social and political comment; with the exception of the heroine, the characters are largely archetypes. Zemlinsky responded with a setting that moves with considerable fluidity between a tough, direct style (including shades of Weill) and passages of rich expressiveness, combined with touches of humour and stylistic devices, such as the characters introducing themselves to the audience. The marriage between music and words is close, considerable use being made of spoken sections. *Der König Kandaules*

(1935–42) was based on Gide, but its orchestration remained incomplete.

The *Lyrische Symphonie* (*Lyric Symphony*, 1922) for soprano, baritone and orchestra is Zemlinsky's masterpiece, and if by the time of its composition its style was already outdated, it nonetheless inspired **Berg**, whose *Lyric Suite* was dedicated to Zemlinsky, and quotes from the symphony. Zemlinsky himself suggested the work was in the tradition of Mahler's *Das Lied von der Erde*, but if the general tone is similar, the layout and the emotion are its own. The structure combines a one-movement symphony with a song-cycle, with seven songs separated by orchestral interludes. The songs to poems by the Bengali writer Rabindranath Tagore concern love and dreams, and especially the distance between dreams and reality. They have little of the self-searching angst that informed earlier Viennese song-cycles: rather their tone is ecstatic, whether the ecstasy of sadness or joy. An emphatic orchestral opening gives way to loneliness and longing in the song that follows, with its uneasy harmonies and restless orchestral movement. Throughout the orchestration is rich and complex, turning from huge swellings to delicate underpinnings to illustrate and amplify the ecstatic vocal lines. This exceptionally beautiful work will be too rich for many, but those who respond to Strauss or to Mahler's song-cycles will find it a discovery to be treasured.

The most important of Zemlinsky's songs are in the cycle *Six Songs to Poems of Maurice Maeterlinck* (1910–13) for mezzo or baritone and orchestra, Straussian in feel and beautifully crafted, their subject women and death; the later *Sinfonietta* uses a melody from the last song.

Zemlinsky wrote four string quartets which reflect the different periods of his musical development. The *String Quartet No. 1* (1895) reflects various formative influences, while the Expressionistic *String Quartet No. 2* (1914) derives inspiration from Schoenberg's *String Quartet No. 1*. The *String Quartet No. 3* (1923), with its beautiful slow movement and a sense of emotional withdrawal, is perhaps the most immediate of the four. The *String Quartet No. 4* (1936) is in the shape of a Classical suite in six movements, with echoes of early Webern in the rapidly changing string effects of the driving second movement.

The only mature piano work is the *Fantasien über Gedichte von Richard*

Dehmel (1900) for piano, in which chromaticism is extended to a point where any sense of tonality is almost dissolved in the dark exploration. Of the handful of later works, the effective *Sinfonietta* (1934) is a neo-classical tone-painting, with moments of Mahlerian lilt. The slow movement has phrases reminiscent of Webern's *Passacaglia*. The fine *Psalm 13* (1935) for chorus and orchestra remained unperformed until 1971, and has thematic correspondences with Zemlinsky's two earlier psalm settings (*Psalm 83*, 1900; *Psalm 23*, 1910). As in the *Sinfonietta*, the idiom is less Romantically luxuriant, the harmonies more tart.

Zemlinsky was a conductor of opera in Vienna (1899–1911), Prague (1911–27), and Berlin (1927–30), and taught in Prague (1920–27) and at the Berlin Musikhochschule (1927–33). His reputation as a conductor, especially of new works stylistically far more advanced than his own, was considerable, and with **Schoenberg** he founded the Vereinigung Schaffender Tonkünstler in Vienna in 1904 to promote new music. To escape the Nazi regime, he left Berlin and fled to the USA in 1938.

RECOMMENDED WORKS
    opera *The Birthday of the Infanta*
      (*Der Zwerg*, 1920–21)
    opera *Eine florentinische Tragödie*
      (1914–15)
    opera *Der Kreidekreis* (1931–32)
    Lyrische Symphonie (1922)
    tone poem *Die Seejungfrau* (1903)
    Sinfonietta (1934)
    Six Songs to Poems of Maurice
      Maeterlinck (1910–13)
    opera *Der Traumgörge* (1904–06)

Azerbaijan

Azerbaijan has a tradition of colourful and flamboyant folk music, studied and used in the Soviet period by a number of composers. The major nationalist Azerbaijan composer was Uzeir Gadzhibekov (1885–1948), who became director of the Baku Conservatory and wrote seven operas on nationalistic subjects. Fikret Dzhamil Amirov (born 1922) has written colourful music heavily influenced by Azerbaijani folk music, including *Kyurdi Ovshari* and *Shur* for orchestra, both based on national modes ('*mugama*'), and the ballet *Thousand and One Nights* (1979). One of the most important Azerbaijani works was written by a Ukrainian: **Glière's** opera *Shah-Senem* (1925, revised 1934), which utilised Azerbaijani folk songs following Glière's study of the music and *mugama* of the area.

Belgium

Introduction

As a musical country, Belgian has been dominated by its neighbours Germany and France, particularly the latter: for two centuries Belgium composers have studied and worked in Paris. One aspect of that connection has been the tradition of organ music and composition, and Belgium's best known composer, César Franck (1822–90), exemplified that tradition, spending almost his entire adult life in France and becoming a famous organist and professor of the organ at the Paris Conservatoire. Another Belgian tradition has been of virtuoso performers, notably on the violin: the most famous of these in the 19th century was Henri Vieuxtemps (1820–81), composer of well-known display concertos as well as a soloist. An indigenous and quite prolific late 19th-century opera tradition arose, represented by such composers as François Gevaert (1828–1908), now best remembered for his interest in old music, and Fernand Le Borne (1862–1929).

The tradition of performer-composer was taken into the 20th century by one of the outstanding violinists of any age, Eugène **Ysaÿe** (1858–1931), and his brother, the pianist, conductor and composer Théo Ysaÿe (1865–1918). Eugène Ysaÿe's only opera was in the Walloon dialect, reflecting the nationalistic interests of the period; the chief exponents of Flemish nationalism, building on the lead of Peter Benoit (1834–1901), were Jan Blockx (1851–1912) who concentrated on operas and vocal music in the Flemish language, and Flor Alpaerts (1876–1954).

The major Belgian composer of the first part of the 20th century was Joseph **Jongen** (1873–1953), who worked initially in the idiom of his teacher Franck, and absorbed developing trends throughout his life, including French Impressionism and atonality; his brother Léon Jongen (1884–1969) was also a composer and pianist. Paul Gilson (1865–1942) was influenced by the Russian nationalists, and invoked some of their rich orchestral colour, notably in his best-known orchestral work, *La mer* (1892); he became a prominent teacher who numbered many of the next generation of Belgian composers among his pupils. Jean Absil (1893–1974) developed an atonal and polytonal style in three symphonies, before turning to folk music, especially Bulgarian and Rumanian;

included in his large output is a huge radio opera, *Peter Breughel the Elder* (1950). Also prominent were a group of composers who formed the group 'Synthétiste' in the 1920s, modelled on the French 'Les Six', and including Marcel Poot (1901–88). The tradition of organ and church music was continued by Flor Peeters (1903–86).

The major figure of the second half of the century has been Henri **Pousseur** (born 1929), who was an important figure in the avant-garde movement, as was Karel Goeyvaerts (1923–93), one of the earliest composers to see the possibilities, following **Webern**, of serialism ('total serialism'), notably in his *Sonata for Two Pianos* (1951). Their lead has been followed by Philippe **Boesmans** (born 1936), who with Pousseur established the Musical Research Centre of Wallonie in 1971, and Pierre Bartholomée (born 1937), director of the ensemble 'Musiques Nouvelles', who has been interested in microtones and whose unusual *Tombeau de Marin Marais*, for an ensemble of baroque instruments, divides the octave in twenty-one equal parts.

Belgian Music Information Centre:
Centre Belge de Documentation Musicale
Rue d'Arlon 75–77
B–1040 Bruxelles
Belgium
tel: +32 2 2309430
fax: +32 2 2309437

Boesmans Philippe*
born 17th May 1936 at Tongeren

Boesmans is an interesting and largely self-taught composer who deserves to be better known outside Belgium. The foundation of his idiom is post-Webern serialism, evident in his piano music (*Étude I* for piano, 1963; *Sonance I* for two pianos, 1964; and *Sonance II* for three pianos, 1967), which he developed into a loose serialism in which the often lyrical linear flow is contrasted with, and sometimes interrupted by, vertical blocks of ideas. The atmospheric, dreamy quality of this style is exemplified in *Conversations* (1980) for orchestra, that uses repetitive rhythmic and melodic patterns, with small intervals, set against tone clusters in a variation form. The effect is of two related series of events happening at a different pace in a kind of serial Impressionism.

The *Violin Concerto* (1979) is an exceptionally fine work, in part because of the technique of its construction. The feel of different simultaneous layers is present, the orchestra often providing a back projection against the isolated solo part, continuity being maintained by the transformation of material in the orchestra that had been initiated by the soloist. This technique is used in other Boesmans concertante works, such as *Eléments-Extensions* (1976) for piano and chamber orchestra. The transformation from the focus on almost chamber-like interaction to the sudden opening out of the soundscape can be rapid, as in an unusual passage in the *Violin Concerto* where the soloist has agitated repeated patterns intertwining with similar patterns of solo strings in the orchestra. As the entire work seems to grow in scale the solo part, almost unnoticed, has converted the solo material into a lyrical line. Boesmans also uses a technique of what he calls 'harmonic travels', in which a basic 12-tone row is played several times, becoming enlarged until it takes on chromatic and then diatonic hues. The solo virtuosity was inspired by the Liège violin tradition of Vieuxtemps and **Ysaÿe**, from rapid passage work to rich lyricism. There are also humorous touches, such as an on-stage trumpet muddling up with an off-stage trumpet.

The opera *La passion de Gilles* (1983) is a dark story of perversion, malice, and child abuse, set in the 15th century and providing a commentary on the present day. Its colours are dark, intense, and sparse, in keeping with the subject, the orchestra often used in distinct colour groups or single instruments highlighted. The orchestra (at points joined by a distant children's choir) acts as a continual commentator, almost another protagonist, and the vocal lines emerge as foreground against this backdrop, following a French tradition of lyrical flow of speech that looks back to **Ravel** and beyond. The orchestral writing is often tortured and interjectory, the overall effect powerful and harrowing, as if the dreaming of earlier works had become nightmare.

Boesmans' more recent works include the fine *Trakl-Lieder* (1986–87, revised 1989) for soprano and orchestra. The song-cycle is in the tradition of **Mahler** and **Berg**, using a large orchestra, with off-stage effects that continue Boesman's mastery of layered instrumental sounds. The passionate vocal lines are set against a wide range of orchestral colours and tones. The suite from the ballet-mime *Attitudes* (1979) for soprano and ensemble is a throwback to the experimentation of the avant-garde 1960s in its exploration of the various ways words can be sounded and in its aleatoric procedures. Very different in feel are the two-movement *String Quartet* (1989, revised 1990) and *Surfing* (1990) for viola and instrumental ensemble, both of which use extra-musical sources as inspiration for their structure and which have a nervous, edgy energy.

Boesmans has been a producer for Belgian Radio, and collaborated with Henri **Pousseur** in founding the Musical Research Centre of Wallonie in 1971.

RECOMMENDED WORKS
  Conversations (1980) for orchestra
  opera *La passion de Gilles* (1983)
  Violin Concerto (1979)

Jongen Joseph Marie Alphonse Nicholas •
born 14th December 1873 at Liège
died 12th July 1953 at Sart-lez-Spa

The best-known Belgian composer of his time, Joseph Jongen became known in England when he lived there during World War I, founding his own piano quartet. A self-critical composer, he withdraw 104 of his 241 works towards the end of his life. Initially influenced by César Franck and then the German post-Romantics, his music reflects an awareness of contemporary trends, eventually absorbing the French Impressionists and adding touches of atonality while continuing a happy lyricism.

Although perhaps best represented by chamber works, notably the hazy beauty of the *String Quartet No. 2* (1916) and the polyphony of the *Rhapsody* for piano and wind quintet (1922), influenced by Impressionism, his music is now probably more likely to be encountered in organ recitals. A child prodigy, he showed an early aptitude for the organ, especially the French art of improvisation. His own organ music is gratifying both to play and hear, the best-known probably being the menuet-scherzo *Chant de Mai* (1917). Two of his orchestral pieces may occasionally be heard, the popular *Fantaisie sur deux noëls populaires wallons* (1902) for orchestra, based on two Walloon Christmas carols, and the intense *Symphonie concertante* (1926) for organ and orchestra, his best-known work. In four movements, it includes virtuoso writing for the soloist, an atmospheric slow movement using a solemn hymn-like theme, and an exciting final toccata.

Jongen conducted the Concert Spirituels, specialising in religious music and including contemporary works, from 1920–25. He was professor at the Conservatoire Royal of Liège (1903–14), and professor at (appointed 1920) and then director of the Conservatoire Royal of Brussels (1925–39).

RECOMMENDED WORKS
    Symphonie concertante for organ and orchestra (1926)

Pousseur Henri Léon Marie •
born 23rd June 1929 at Malmédy

Henri Pousseur has been the leading exponent of avant-garde ideas in Belgium, and has achieved a wide prominence abroad after studying with **Boulez, Stockhausen** and **Berio**. Throughout his career, he has seen a correspondence between complex musical structures and complex social structures, and believes that solutions to the latter may be mirrored in solutions to the former.

The early works of a large and eclectic output show echoes of **Webern** (the canonic effects of the pre-serial, ruminating *Sept versets des psaumes de la pénitence*, 1950, for four-part mixed chorus, or the *Quintet in Memory of Anton Webern*, 1955), and the influence of his meeting with Boulez in 1951 (the serial and pointillist *Trois chants sacrés*, 1951). He saw in the precision of total serialism an abstraction of sounds akin to aleatory effects, and so developed chance elements in his own work, such as *Scambi* (1957), in which the sixteen prerecorded tape sections can be put together in any order, and *Répons* for seven instrumentalists, who each take various roles (such as conductor) according to set rules in different sections, with an actor coordinating the events in a second version (1965).

Increasingly Pousseur used extramusical materials as sources, such as the children's poems using old Liège street names in the electronic *Trois visages de Liège* (it was commissioned for a *son et lumière*; the Liège authorities found the music too modern, and instead tried passages of **Debussy** and Bach before settling on **Gershwin's** *Rhapsody in Blue*). His major work of the Sixties, using the concept of mobile forms (alterations in such parameters as the order of self-contained

structures within the overall cast) and chance elements, was the opera *Votre Faust*, for five actors, singers, and twelve instrumentalists, written in collaboration with the writer Michel Butor between 1960 and 1967. The story is of a composer commissioned to write a new opera with all the money and resources he needs on the condition that it has a Faust theme. The audience has an important role to play: they must at one point decide whether the composer obeys his girlfriend, who wants him to give up the commission, or the theatre director. The opera aims for the unification and continuity of the Western musical tradition on the one hand, and on the other for potential spin-offs in various directions (including earlier musics) from the application of serial principles. In one section, a puppet play on the Faust legend ('La chevauchée fantastique'), there are four possible taped backgrounds: Gounod's *Faust*; Mozart's *Don Giovanni*; snatches showing the progression of 19th-century harmony; and early church music. Anticipating **Stockhausen**, a number of sections of the opera can be taken in their own right as concert works. *Miroir de Votre Faust* (1964–65) uses in modified form three of the opera's sections, 'Le tarot d'Henri' for piano, 'La chevauchée fantastique' for soprano ad lib and piano, and 'Souvenirs d'une marionette' (which combines elements of the previous two) for piano. There is also a tape version that includes other voices, instrumentalists, and electronics, *Jeu de miroirs de Votre Faust* (1967). Other self-contained concert works include *Echoes de Votre Faust* in two variants (1967 and 1969), the first for cello, the second for mezzo-soprano, piano and cello, *Ombres de Votre Faust* for tape, and *Fresques de Votre Faust* for organ, violin, and two amplified instruments. An illustration of Pousseur's parallel between complex musical structures and complex social structures is provided by *Jeu de miroirs de Votre Faust*, where in 'Le tarot d'Henri' (a series of separate sheets of score which, in the concert version, can be played in any order) the musical *objets trouvées* range from the tonal to the Webernesque, in order to show the central character's 'quest for a homogeneous, harmonic field of action'. In *Jeu de miroirs de Votre Faust*, the form in which the work is now most likely to be encountered, the effects of these techniques are often startling, with a mosaic of musical elements set in a serial cast.

The possibilities of complex harmonic diversity within structural unity were further explored in a number of divergent works. *Couleurs croisées* (1967) for orchestra takes the song 'We shall overcome' and manipulates it in six sections. *Les éphémérides d'Icare II* (1970) for piano and eighteen instruments predetermines intervals and rhythms and then allows collective improvisation within those parameters. *Invitation à l'utopie* (1970) for speaker, soloists, chorus, piano and eighteen instruments, is actually the addition of voices (texts again by Michel Butor) to *Les éphémérides d'Icare II* and echoes contemporary anthropological and linguistic ideas in a sequence of spoken language–sung language–sung phonemes–purely instrumental sound.

Like many avant-garde composers, Pousseur has been less prominent in recent years, and the more startling aspects of his music would seem to have mellowed. The eighty-one units, gaining in length from ten seconds to five minutes and divided by the tinkle of small cymbals, of *Agonie* (1981) for voices, percussionist and synthesizers, have a consistency and a gentle flow not found in the work of the sixties. Its subject is death from two viewpoints: those around the dying person and the actual dying person. The texts are from a variety of sources, from modern writers to the Tibetan Book of the Dead, and the structure is determined by a 'timetable' divided into sections into which the singers cast dice. Behind the whole work, sometimes emerging overtly, is an air by the 16th-century composer John Dowland. In keeping with its title, it includes unkind music in the electronic distortion of voices in an effective and unostentatiously dramatic work.

In 1958 Pousseur founded the Studio de Musique Electronique (SME) at Brussels. He taught at the Basle Conservatory (1963–64) and at the State University of New York at Buffalo (1966–68), and became professor of composition at the Liège Conservatory in 1971. He has written widely on avant-garde music.

RECOMMENDED WORKS
> *Agonie* (1981) for voices, percussion and synthesizers
> *Miroirs de Votre Faust* (1964–65)/*Jeu de miroirs de Votre Faust* (1967) for various forces
> *Sept versets des psaumes de la pénitence* (1950) for chorus

opera *Votre Faust* (1960–67)

BIBLIOGRAPHY
> H. Pousseur, *Musique, sémantique, société*, 1972

Ysaÿe Eugène Auguste *
born 16th July 1858 at Liège
died 12th May 1931 at Brussels

Considered by many the greatest violinist of his time, and a champion of the music of his contemporaries (notably **Elgar's** *Violin Concerto*), Ysaÿe the composer has largely been forgotten except for one set of works, the six *Sonatas* for solo violin, op. 27, written in 1923. Like the Bach sonatas for solo violin that are their ancestors (No. 2 quotes from the Prelude of Bach's *Partita in E major*, its dedicatee, Jacques Thibaud, used the Bach piece for his preconcert warm-up), these works are among the most effective violin works of their time, and among the most important works of the chamber violin repertoire. Each sonata is dedicated to a famous violinist of his age (each from a different country), and highlights elements of their individual styles; as a group, the sonatas cover a wide range of expression and technique, while maintaining a sense of consistency.

The inspiration of Bach is evident in the form and phrasing of the ruminative and introspective *Sonata No. 1 in G minor*, giving it a neo-classical feel. Dedicated to the Hungarian Joseph Szigeti, it has moments of harmonic shading that hint at Hungarian folk music. The late Romantic *Sonata No. 2 in A minor*, dedicated to Thibaud, opens with the alternation of the Bach quote and an elaboration of the plainchant *Dies Irae*. The four movements have descriptive as opposed to abstract musical titles ('obsession', 'melancholy', 'dance of the shades', 'the furies'). The overall cast is emotionally expressive, nocturnal in the shades of the middle movement, with a slow quasi-folk dance in the third, and an equally slow but nightmarish treatment of the plainchant in the finale. The ballade-form *Sonata No. 3 in D minor*, dedicated to the Romanian Georges **Enescu**, is short and in one movement, a flight of fancy with the soaring main line supported by double or triple stopping.

The *Sonata No. 4 in E minor*, for the Austrian Fritz Kreisler, is neo-Baroque in form, and the grandest in the cycle. Its decorative but emphatic writing hints at

Kreisler's own bravura compositional style in the consistent arpeggio motion. The two-movement *Sonata No. 5 in G major*, dedicated to the Belgian Mathieu Crickboom, reverts to descriptive titles ('The Dawn', 'Rustic Dance'), and is the most daring of the series, closest perhaps to **Bartók** in its intensity of expression and variety of means. 'The Dawn' opens with double stopping and pizzicato support before gradually building in intensity and thickness of texture – it would be a perceptive listener who, coming blind to it, recognised that this was being played by only one instrument. The 'Rustic Dance' has little in common with the neo-Baroque dance forms used elsewhere in the suite; rather it has the improvisatory feel and inner descriptive logic of a folk instrumentalist (especially in the changes of rhythmic flow). The extrovert *Sonata No. 6 in E major* was the only one never played by its dedicatee, the Spaniard Manuel Quiroga, due to injury. In one movement, it uses a *habanera* rhythm in the exceptionally high range used by gypsy fiddlers. All these sonatas are technically extremely difficult, and the combination of virtuoso demands and absorbing content, each sonata with its own particular character, makes them well worth the encounter.

Of Ysaÿe's other works, sometimes highly chromatic and turbulent in style, a number are violin showpieces, following the tradition of Kreisler, of which the most celebrated is the *Caprice d'après l'étude en forme de valse de Saint-Saëns*, while the *Poème élégiaque* (before 1896) inspired the famous *Poème* for violin and orchestra by Ernest Chausson (1855–99), written for Ysaÿe to play. He also wrote eight violin concertos, some of which he himself performed early in his career, but these have remained unpublished, as has his opera (in the Walloon dialect), *Piére li houïeu (Peter the Miner*, 1930). It was produced, and Ysaÿe managed to attend the second performance just before his death.

Apart from his many concert tours, Ysaÿe was a founder member of the Berlin Philharmonic Orchestra, and directed the Cincinnati Symphony Orchestra from 1918 to 1922. He taught at the Brussels Conservatoire (1886–98) and founded the Concerts Ysaÿe in the same city. His Stradivarius violin (the 'Hercules' Stradivarius) was stolen while he was on a concert tour in Russia in 1908; it turned up in Berlin in 1947. A Fondation E. Ysaÿe was formed in 1961.

RECOMMENDED WORKS
Six Sonatas op. 27 (1923) for solo violin

BIBLIOGRAPHY
L. Ginsberg, *Ysaÿe*, trans. X. M. Danko, 1980
A. Ysaÿe and B. Ratcliffe, *Ysaÿe: His Life, Work and Influence*, 1947

Brazil

Introduction

Like many other South American countries, Brazil had a flourishing musical life in the 19th century, centred on opera and producing one opera composer of international repute, Antonio Carlos Gomes (1836–96). The next generation still looked to European and Romantic models for their music, and it was not until the ascendance of the most famous of all South American composers, Heitor **Villa-Lobos** (1887–1959), that a Brazilian nationalism was heard, reflecting parallel movements in other South American countries.

The Brazilian folk tradition was rich, ranging from the samba, which entered popular cultures internationally during the 20th century, to the itinerant streetbands of varying instrumentation, the *chôros*, mixed with echoes of Portuguese popular dances and African influences (though virtually no indigenous South American Indian music). One popular Brazilian instrument, the marimba, also became internationally familiar through its use in jazz and popular music. The adoption of nationalistic themes, and the reflection of the Brazilian landscape and culture in serious music, was most notably proclaimed in the Week of Modern Art at São Paulo in 1922, with Villa-Lobos as one of the main organisers. Villa-Lobos also introduced his version of Brazilian primitivism to Parisian audiences in the 1920s, generating considerable excitement and interest. But with the revolution of October 1930 the climate for a consciously Brazilian aesthetic became more favourable. The movement was again led by Villa-Lobos, who organised huge public rallies to sing popular Brazilian choruses (*concentraes civicas*), and instigated both a system of music teaching in schools and concerts in which classics of the repertoire (from Palestrina onwards) that had not been heard in Brazil were introduced, alongside contemporary Brazilian compositions. A number of other composers followed Villa-Lobos's example, notably Francisco Mignone (1897–1986), the composer of two successful operas and a number of orchestral works with Brazilian themes, including the *Suite brasiliera* (1933); Oscar Lorenzo Fernandez (also spelt Fernandos, 1897–1948) who founded the Conservatorio Brasileiro in Rio in 1936 to rival the National Institute of Music;

and Camargo Guarnieri (1907–93), who was at one time heard quite widely in the United States; his output concentrates on large-scale orchestral forms (symphonies and concertos) but he is noted for his songs.

The subsequent reaction to nationalism centred around the group of composers called Musica Viva, led by Hans Joachim Koellreutter, who was born in Germany. Composers such as Cláudio Santoro (1919–89) introduced the 12-tone system into Brazil. Marlos Nombre (born 1939) is the leading composer of the following generation.

Nonetheless it remains surprising that such a large country as Brazil should have produced only one 20th-century composer whose music is regularly heard outside its boundaries. One does not find, either in quality or in quantity, the depth of compositional talent that Mexico (with a similar musical history) has shown, or the kind of figures that, leaving their native Argentina, have made a mark on European music. Perhaps some of the cause lies in relatively poor standards of music-making (with some obvious individual exceptions who have made their careers on the international circuit) – there is, for example, no parallel to **Chávez's** work with the National Orchestra of Mexico.

Villa-Lobos Heitor[**]
born 5th March 1887 at Rio de Janeiro
died 17th November 1959 at Rio de Janeiro

Villa-Lobos was one of the most prodigious composers of the 20th century, producing around 2,000 compositions and arrangements. Inevitably his music is uneven; but not only did he establish a nationalist musical style in Brazil, but like his contemporary the Mexican **Chávez**, he introduced to a wider audience a new kind of sound, composed of an amalgam of popular South American influences (such as native Indian music and instruments, popular songs) and modernistic European techniques.

He eschewed formal studies and instead travelled in Brazil from 1906–13, absorbing the indigenous music. Among his earlier works were the tone poem *Amazonas* (1917), and the marvellous ballet *Uirapurú* (1917) that tells the tale of the legendary bird of the title, the 'king of love' who draws people into the forest and who has incarnations as an old man and as a beautiful youth. The legacy of the 19th century occasionally strays into the score, but the driving rhythms of the opening recall **Stravinsky**, the heady sensuousness **Szymanowski**, the Impressionistic textures **Respighi**. (Szymanowisky's *First Violin Concerto* and Respighi's *The Pines of Rome* were written in the same year.) What makes *Uirapurú* so individual and appealing is the vivid evocation of the Amazonian forest, with exotic bird-calls, Brazilian folk percussion instruments, the effective use of the piano in the orchestra, and a willingness to suspend conventional rhythmic progression. It makes an interesting comparison with a much later suite with a similar setting, the evocative *Song of the Amazons* for soprano and orchestra, drawn from the music to the film *Green Mansions*, where the textures are much leaner, almost neo-classical, and the rhythms more straightforward.

The *Nonetto* (1922) included chorus and percussion with Brazilian instruments and shows indigenous influences in the rhythms and woodwind colours. The two piano sets *A Prole do Bebê* (*The Baby's Family*, 1918 and 1921) were inspired by the pianist Rubinstein, whom Villa-Lobos had met in Rio. The first is based on children's popular tunes, while the second is about toy animals, with Brazilian rhythms and ostinati, and a characteristic alternation of white and black keys. A sophisticated nationalist primitivism is strikingly exemplified in the *Suite for Voice and Violin* (1923).

While the primitivism of some of these works showed an affinity with Stravinsky, Villa-Lobos absorbed something of Impressionism from his friendship with **Milhaud** (in Rio during World War I). He then spent 1923 to 1930 mainly in Paris, where his music was enthusiastically greeted, also encountering African music in Dakar. In this period his style matured, combining an unstable harmonic language (including bitonality and polytonality), Impressionism, and Brazilian folk melodies with colourful and complex rhythms, syncopations, ostinati, polyrhythms, and percussive dissonances. His orchestration remained generally dense, and he delighted in unusual effects (percussive strings, the extremes of woodwind registers, elements of the harmonic structures in different instrumental blocks).

The centre of his huge output are two series of works. The sixteen *Chôros* (1920–29), fourteen numbered plus an *Introduction* and the supplementary *Chôros Bis*) are a striking and original series and broad in scope. They are based on folk

music and on the *chôro* popular form, an improvisatory serenade with a solo instrument often taking the lead. The sources for the *chôro* range from folk music, spirituals and hymns to African rhythms. The series gradually expands in forces from a solo guitar (No. 1, 1920) through wind chamber forces (No. 2, 1921; No. 3 with male chorus, 1925; No. 4, 1926; No. 7, 1924) to a full orchestra (No. 6, 1926; No. 8, 1925, with two pianos; No. 9, 1929) with chorus (No. 10 *Rasga o Coracão*, 1926) and further to a piano concerto (No. 11), and a work for orchestra, band, and chorus with off-stage fanfares (No. 14, 1928, now lost along with No. 13). There is a similar expansion in duration, from the two minutes in No. 1 to over an hour in No. 11. They are all beguiling, from the intimacy of the writing of No. 5 (for piano, 1926) to the very French Impressionist flutes of the orchestral No. 12 (1929); but the finest is No. 10. It opens with an Impressionistic evocation of the Brazilian landscape, with sonorous orchestral effects (including bird-calls), which is turned into a savage, primitive and powerful crescendo, the chorus singing onomatopoeic lines, before a broad melody contrasts with this aboriginal vision.

The nine highly attractive suites that form the *Bachianas brasileiras* (1930–45) are Villa-Lobos's most popular works, intrinsically less interesting than the *Chôros*, but, with their simpler harmonic language, more immediate in their appeal. They are at the same time both a tribute to Bach (in their suite forms, and sometimes in orchestration and feel, especially in the slow movements), and a celebration of Brazilian folklore (in their melodies and colours). For Villa-Lobos, the music of Bach was a universal folklore for later composers, and he perceived similarities between it and Brazilian popular music. To reinforce the connection, each movement has both a traditional European and a Brazilian title. The Baroque influence is most overt in the polyphony of No. 1 (1930) for eight cellos, and in the prelude and fugue of No.9 for string orchestra (1945). No.2 (1934) includes the famous *Little Train of the Caipira*, which exemplifies the clarity of his graphic use of complex native rhythms. No. 5 (1938–45) for soprano and eight cellos shows his use of broad and lovely melodies in its cantilena, with a feeling of improvisation and irregular metres. No. 3 (1934, a virtuoso piano concerto, Romantic in scale and tone) is the largest and stylistically the most remote of the series.

Of his other works of this period, his symphonies (including a war triptych) are rarely encountered, but the fantasy for piano and orchestra *Mômoprecóce* (1930) is particularly vivacious and rewarding. His music after 1945 became increasingly abstract in inspiration and tonal in feel, and includes a number of virtuoso concertos, notably the *Guitar Concerto* (1951), whose easy-going style does not merit the frequency with which it is performed. The *Cello Concerto No. 2* (1954) is equally pleasant, its opening invoking the rain forest, its solo writing often harking back to Bach, but is equally unremarkable. If these large number of later works do not seem to have the interest or the colour of his earlier, more nationalistic music, there is still much that is fine among them, notably the ballet *Emperor Jones* (1955), the sonorous, whimsical and perky *Fantasie concertante* (1953) for clarinet, bassoon and piano, some of the choral music, and the last quartets.

Of his seventeen string quartets (1915–57), No. 5 (1931) and No. 6 (1938) use popular Brazilian elements, while No. 17 (1957) uses an uncharacteristically spartan language. Among his other chamber music, the stylistically related *Trio* (1921), *Quartet* (1928) and *Quintet en forme de chôros* (1928), all for wind instruments, are quirkily delightful. His piano music includes the sixteen *Cirandas* (1926), nationalistic, based on children's tunes, rhythmically unusual, and varied in colour, and *Rudepoema* (1921–26), complex and large in scale, dense in texture, varied in mood. His guitar music is often to be heard, especially the gentle *Suite populaire brésiliene* (1908–12), the *Twelve Études* (1929), combining attractive music in the Spanish classical tradition with technical studies, and the *Five Preludes* (1939–40 – a sixth is lost).

His many musical activities included the promotion of both Brazilian music and his own works on foreign tours, the organisation of music teaching in schools in Rio – and by training and example, in the rest of Brazil – and the foundation in 1945 and directorship until his death of the Brazilian Academy of Music.

It is still extremely difficult to assess Villa-Lobos' overall achievement, for so much has still to be heard. Faced with this multiplicity, together with the unfamiliarity of idiom and style, many coming to his works for the first time have experienced difficulty – but perseverance is rewarded. Those who look for insight into the human soul will be disappointed. Rather he attempts a fusion of the European contemporary experience with the indigenous tradition to create a modern Brazilian reflection in serious music of the multiplicity of his native culture. Arriving at his music is like arriving in a new country: totally new colours and a bewildering array of new experiences. But, just as when one becomes familiar with a new country, the relationships of the new elements becomes clear, so with the music of Villa-Lobos, and in it are then found many delights.

RECOMMENDED WORKS
Bachianas brasileiras No. 1 (1930) for eight cellos
Bachianas brasileiras No. 2 (1934) for orchestra
Bachianas brasileiras No. 3 (1934) for piano and orchestra
Bachianas brasileiras No. 5 (1938–45) for soprano and eight cellos
Bachianas brasileiras No. 6 (1938) for flute and bassoon
Bachianas brasileiras No. 9 (1944) for string orchestra
Chôros 3 (1925) for male chorus and seven wind instruments
Chôros 7 (1924) for chamber ensemble
Chôros 10 (Rasga o Coracão) (1926) for chorus and orchestra
Chôros 12 (1929) for orchestra
Mômoprecóce (1930) for piano and orchestra
A Prole do Bebê (Book 1) for piano (1918)
Quintette en forme de Chôros (1928 revised 1953)
Suite for Voice and Violin (1923)

BIBLIOGRAPHY
V. Mariz, *Heitor Villa-Lobos: Life and Work of the Brazilian Composer*, 3rd ed. (in Eng. trans.) 1970, 5th ed., 1977
A. Muricy, *Villa-Lobos*, 1961
S. Wright, *Villa-Lobos*, 1988

Bulgaria

Introduction

As a country, the modern history of Bulgaria, for centuries dominated by the Turks, only dates from the end of the 19th century, and her classical musical history is even more recent: the country's first generation of emerging composers, some of whom studied in Paris in the 1920s and 1930s, reached their maturity under first a pro-Nazi regime and then communist control, in both cases isolating them from the developments in Western music. Most drew on the heritage of Bulgarian folk music to forge an indigenous idiom.

The principal composers of this generation were Pancho **Vladigerov** (1899–1978), the father figure of modern Bulgarian music, Vesselin Stoyanov (1902–69), whose output includes early examples of Bulgarian chamber music as well as some colourful and zestful orchestral suites, Lyubomir Pipkov (1904–74), Marin **Goleminov** (born 1908), and Parashkev Hadjiev (born 1912), whose work ranges from an early *String Quartet No. 1* that has strong affinities with the English pastoral composers to *Paradoxes* (1982), a trilogy of gently humorous short operas in any easygoing style based on the short stories of the American, O. Henry. Pipkov has been held in high esteem in Bulgaria (his *String Quartet No. 1*, 1928, is said to be the first by a Bulgarian composer), and is perhaps best known elsewhere for his second opera *Momchil*. It is an epic historical opera in the tradition of Russian 19th-century models in both form and content, with grand, heroic arias touched with darker hues, stirring choruses, many with liturgical influence, passages integrating Bulgarian folk idioms, and an orchestration of primary colours. While none of it is particularly remarkable, it has a ruggedness and a vitality that makes its popularity in Bulgaria, where the historical material would have a stronger resonance, understandable. The same cannot be said for such socialist realist banalities as the *Oratorio on Our Time* (1959).

Stalinist socialist realist principles (populist, simplistic music dominated by historical and patriotic subjects) maintained its hold until the break-up of the communist system, and its deadening effects are evident in the music of the composers born in the 1920s and 1930s, such as Ivan Marinov

(born 1928), Jules Levy (born 1930) or the prolific Alexander **Yossifov** (born 1940). Alexander Tanev (born 1928) includes large-scale patriotic historical oratorios (such as *The Bequest*) among his works, as well as works with a showpiece dazzle and humour, such as the *Concerto for Winds and Percussion* (1972) or the *Divertimento-Concertante* (1976) for piano and orchestra, influenced by **Stravinsky**. Simeon Pironkov (born 1927) may prove to be one exception when more of his work is disseminated, for his *Concerto Rustica* for cello and orchestra is an arresting, powerful, orchestrally assured, and decidedly unpastoral work in six short linked movements, firmly in the European progressive mainstream and well worth the discovery. Similarly Dmitri Hristov (born 1933) has written an interesting, rather frenetic *Cello Concerto*, an *Overture with Fanfares*, powerful and strident in its massed sonorities, and an alluring set of *Concert Miniatures* for orchestra, all of which suggest familiarity with more recent Western trends. It is still difficult to hear the works of these composers, and the major changes in the social and political climate have been too recent to judge the potential compositional future of the country.

Bulgaria has a rich choral tradition, nurtured by the Bulgarian Orthodox musical heritage. Its folk music is full of colour and variety, its exotic touches reflecting the long domination by Turkish and oriental influences. Bulgarian opera singers have a considerable reputation in Eastern Europe, but their generic style (a harder, more nasal sound) has not always been accepted in the West.

Modern Bulgarian music is extremely difficult to encounter at the best of times. There are suggestions that some composers are aware of modern trends, and the mixture of these into the populist idiom is fascinating in itself. For example, Dimiter Sagayev (born 1915) is a composer of large-scale patriotic works in a populist style that nevertheless reflect contemporary developments. His works include vocal symphonies (No. 3 *Khan Asparouh*; No. 6 *September*) that are essentially neo-Romantic socialist realist cantatas, with rudimentary symphonic development. The rare modernist moments, exemplified by the *Symphony No. 6* (*September*, 1982) with its strong orchestral dissonances, cluster effects, atonal sections, and percussive effects influenced by late

Shostakovich, are used primarily for colour, and sit uneasily with his exotic folk and oriental influences, simple and fetching tunes, and general unchallenging neo-Romantic feel and harmonic language.

Goleminov Marin
born September 28th 1908 at Kjunstendil

Although Goleminov's works have increased in complexity, his idiom is conservative and rooted in Romanticism. The ballet *Nestinarka (The Fire Dance,* 1940) was a major landmark in Bulgarian ballet, with the stong influence of folk idioms, but its unadventurous cast is only of interest on those occasions when the broad swathes of orchestration take on the piquancy of the colours of Bulgarian folk music. The chief interest of such works as the *String Quartet No. 3 (Old Bulgarian,* 1944) is also in the influence of folk music on the rhythms and melodic material.

More effective is the opera *Zografat Zahariy* (1972), an important work in the modern history of Bulgarian music. Its story is loosely based on the life of the 19th-century Bulgarian icon painter of the title and his love for his brother's wife, and dwells on the place of the artist and the clash of new artistic ideas and received tradition. The idiom is less obviously conservative, with the occasional passage of acerbic harmonies, used for colour or psychological effect. With its free-flowing vocal lines contrasted with sparingly used church chant, the psychological drama is musically effective. What prevents it from being a better opera is the orchestration, so often the bane of cultures under former Soviet cultural sway: the reliance on bare string textures, so predictably giving way to woodwind or brass, adds little to the overall effect.

The gradual interweaving of contemporary influences – acerbic harmonies, angular melodic lines, and adventurous non-folk rhythmic effects – as well as the integration of older musics, are evident in such works as the appealing if unremarkable *Concerto for String Orchestra* (1980), whose opening and close use a Gregorian chant, or the *Symphony No. 1* (1963), based on Bulgarian children's songs.

Goleminov studied with d'Indy in Paris, and taught at the Sofia Conservatory. His music will be chiefly of interest to students of Eastern Europe and the history of communist aesthetics.

RECOMMENDED WORKS
opera *Zografat Zahariy* (1972)

Vladigerov Pancho*
born 13th March 1899 at Zurich
died 8th September 1978 at Sofia

It is a measure of the esteem in which Pancho Vladigerov is held in Bulgaria that his complete works have been recorded in a special Bulgarian issue, yet his name is completely unknown outside Bulgaria. He is considered the father of modern Bulgarian music, helping to forge an indigenous compositional tradition, and integrating specifically Bulgarian folk idioms to create a national classical music identity.

The youthful and energetic *Piano Concerto No. 1* (1918) is an assured work for a 19-year-old, in the style of **Rachmaninov**, with touches of Liszt, the occasional clumsy transition passage not detracting from an appealing if derivative work that was the first Bulgarian instrumental concerto. Of much more interest is the *Violin Concerto No. 1* (1921). If the shadow of **Strauss** lingers behind the work, much more prominent is that of **Szymanowski**, with a similar palette of sensuous, heady orchestration and long, lyrical, ecstatically singing solo lines. Those interested in the period when Impressionistic techniques merged with the heritage of late Romanticism might well investigate this often beautiful and beguiling work.

Vardar (1922) for violin and piano (versions for orchestra, 1928, and violin and orchestra, 1951) is a Bulgarian rhapsody that established itself as a quintessential Bulgarian nationalist piece, equivalent to (if not as brilliant as) **Enescu's** *Romanian Rhapsodies*. There is a zest, a raw enthusiasm, to these works, equally discernible in the early Impressionistic works, the orchestral triptych *Three Impressions* (1920) and *Six Exotic Preludes* for piano (1924, orchestrated 1955).

The works that followed failed to fulfil the promise of these youthful works, lapsing into a Romanticism in which gesture has more sway than content. The *Piano Concerto No. 2* (1930) is better constructed than its predecessor, but lacks its zest; the *Piano Concerto No. 3*, a brilliant virtuoso work, is heavily influenced by **Rachmaniov's** third concerto, and suffers in the comparison. The *Symphony No. 1* is large, tuneful, and bombastic. There are, however, a number of works of specifically Bulgarian content, drawing on folk music, such as the colourful *Seven Bulgarian*

Symphonic Dances as well as two entertaining and exotic sets of Romanian dances, inspired in part by his friend **Enescu**.

The chief work of this period is the opera
Tsar Kaloyan (1936), whose story concerns the repulse of the forces of the
Emperor Baldwin and his capture by the
Bulgarian Tsar Kaloyan. Its Romantic
inflatedness, touches of **Strauss**, and concentration on surface colour rather than
psychology make it of little interest to
anyone for whom the historical context has
no relevance. More interesting, with their
Impressionism and folk dances, are the
two suites drawn from the ballet *The
Legend of the Lake* (ballet 1946, unperformed until 1962, suites 1947 and 1953),
which tells the story of the deliberate
flooding by the soldier Vlad of the town
containing his lover and the enemy who
had just captured it, and the subsequent
appearance of his lover from the resulting
lake as a water nymph. The works following communist control continue a similar
idiom, with more rhythmic spice in the
Piano Concerto No. 4 (1953), and a *Violin
Concerto No. 2* (1968) that is jauntier but
less effective than its predecessor, in spite
of the seamless song-like flow of the solo
writing.

From 1920–32 Vladigerov worked as the
orchestra director of Max Reinhardt's
famous Deutsches Theater in Berlin, and
produced incidental music for ten productions, ranging from Ibsen to Shaw. They
are of historical interest, showing that the
Deutsches Theater used music that was a
precursor of Hollywood Romantic film
music.

Vladigerov taught at the Bulgarian
State Conservatory, and many of the succeeding generation of Bulgarian composers were among his pupils.

RECOMMENDED WORKS
Violin Concerto No. 1 (1921)
Four Romanian Symphonic Dances
(1942) for orchestra

Yossifov Alexander
born 12 August 1940 at Sofia

Yossifov is highly regarded in Bulgaria,
and has written in most genres in a conservative Romantic style that incorporates a
watered-down folk idiom. His cantatas,
however well-crafted, exemplify a grandiose socialist realism of banal tunes, bright
orchestral colours, and a harmonic language rooted in Romanticism, as does the
appalling *To the Heroes of Stanlingrad* for
orchestra. Bulgarian folk styles emerge in
the overblown and rigid *Symphony No. 5
(Proto-Bulgarians)*, especially in the
rhythms and colour, which are strongly
reminiscent in melodic line and general
feel of **Khachaturian** at his worst. In spite
of the imaginative percussion opening, and
the occasional interest of the Bulgarian
folk music (especially in the last movement), the paucity of musical imagination
hardly earns it the name of a symphony – it
is more akin to a film score with local
colour.

His works for children have included
piano teaching pieces, the trite *Youth
Overture*, and the attractive children's
suite *The Bells Are Singing* (1979) for
bells, triangle, gong, small drum, cymbals,
and glockenspiel, in which the balance
between unusual sounds and simplicity of
playing is nicely judged. The banality of
the opera *Khan Kroum Youvigi (Khan
Kroum the Supreme*, 1980), an historical
drama set in AD 811, but whose musical
language is a cross between that of 1880
and a 1940s film score for a romantic B-
movie, is beyond description. He has written many songs in a popular style. From
1969 Yossifov was director of the state
recording company Balkanton and is
therefore one of the Bulgarian composers
that readers may come across; they are
advised not to.

Canada

Introduction

Canada provides an example of a country attempting to create an autonomous modern classical music of its own, analogous to the process that such countries as Czechoslovakia underwent in the 19th century, Mexico in the 1920s, or Australia in the 1960s and 1970s.

Canadian music was initially influenced by European, particularly German, developments rather than by the United States. Although the history of opera performance dates back to 1798, the groundwork for indigenous composition was laid by Calixa Lavallée (1842–91), who wrote the Canadian national anthem, and Guillaume Couture (1851–1915). But the father figures of Canadian composition were from the following generation, Healey **Willan** (1880–1968), who emigrated from Britain to Canada, Sir Ernest **MacMillan** (1893–1973), both of whom wrote under the influence of the emerging English tradition, and Claude Champagne (1891–1965), who in contrast followed the French tradition of **Debussy** and **Ravel**, and was an important influence on the next generation of French-Canadian composers.

The following generation of composers, who were often taught by Canadians rather than exclusively studying abroad, in the main clustered around two centres, Toronto and Montreal, reflecting two of Canada's cultures, the English and the French-Canadian. The variety of styles in this generation has been considerable. Among the English-Canadians, John Weinzweig (born 1913) was one of first in Canada to use atonal and 12-tone methods (1939), notably in a series of *Divertimentos*, though from the late 1960s he increasingly incorporated new contemporary ideas, descriptive rather than generic titles, and theatrical elements, as in *Around the stage in twenty-five minutes during which a variety of instruments are struck* (1970). He has become important as a teacher, passing on his concepts of clarity and economy to many of his younger contemporaries.

Jean Coulthard (born 1908) has retained neo-Romantic leanings, and her best-known work, *Prayer for Elizabeth* (1952) for strings, shows the influence of her teacher **Vaughan Williams**. Barbara Pentland (born 1912) has preferred traditional forms (the symphony, the string quartet) as a framework for first 12-tone, and then serial and aleatory techniques in an increasingly refined language. Violet Archer (born 1913) has been influenced by the concept of *Gebrauchsmusik* (music designed to be useful in social applications, including music for amateurs: the term was coined by **Hindemith**, with whom she studied), and has included serial techniques and, from the 1970s, electronics in her palette. Harry **Somers** (1925–99), one of Weinzweig's pupils, has drawn on various sources, frequently mixing atonal or 12-tone methods with tonal elements. Harry Freedman (born in Poland, 1922) started under the influence of jazz, but became attracted to 12-tone composition, until in the early 1950s he found the strict application inappropriate to his concerns. He then turned to landscape painting for musical inspiration, before returning to a freer usage of 12-tone composition in 1964. He is also well-known as a composer for film and television. John Beckwith (born 1927) has sometimes used extra-musical sources of inspiration, and has been interested in the dualities of the public and private and the expression of Canadian life and society in music. His output includes many collaborations with writers, notably the poet James Reaney, and his formal designs often have collage structures, sometimes likened to quilting designs. The pianist and composer Bruce Mather (born 1939) came under the influence of **Boulez**. The bulk of his output is for small ensembles, including much vocal music initially based on English poetry (especially Robert Graves in the cantata *The White Goddess*, 1960–61) and then on French poetry, notably (from 1967) a series of *Madrigals* for one or two voices and instrumental ensembles.

Among the French-Canadians, François Morel (born 1926) moved from quasi-Impressionism to serial techniques, while Serge Garant (1929–86) was one of the first to come under the influence of **Boulez** and has become one of Canada's major conductors of new music. André Prévost (born 1934) has written large-scale avant-garde works that concentrate on colour and sonority, and whose forms have been predicated by the content and context of each piece. Perhaps the finest of this generation of composers working in a mainstream idiom is Jacques Hétu (born 1938), who has synthesized 12-tone and modal elements into a largely lyrical idiom, often for large orchestral forces handled with considerable powers of colour and effect. The large orchestral song-cycle *Les abîmes du rêve* (*The Abyss of Dream*, 1981–82) is strongly recommended. Before his murder in Paris, Claude Vivier (1948–83) produced works in an idiom recognisably influenced by **Messiaen**, and, after the mid-1970s, by Eastern and gamelan musics, with affinities to the American minimalists; *Lonely Child* (1980) for soprano and small orchestra is recommended. The most interesting of this group is Gilles **Tremblay** (born 1932), who has pursued a single-minded preoccupation with space, duration and sonority.

The most recent generation of composers is equally eclectic, and ranges from Michael Longtin (born 1946), who started as an electronic composer and whose experience in that field has spilled over into his conventional scores, such as the distinct colours, percussion effects and dramatic incident of the fine *Pohjatuuli* (1983) for instrumental ensemble, to Michael Conway Baker (born 1941 in the USA), whose idiom is often so conservative that he can be mistaken for a composer writing at the beginning, not the end, of the 20th century. Alexina Louie (born 1949) has attracted attention for an idiom that combines modern effects with popular appeal.

In addition, a lively electro-acoustic composition school has emerged, centred on the Canadian Electroacoustic Community (CEC) in Montreal, and tracing their ancestry back to an early pioneer of electronic music, Hugh LeCaine (1914–77), who helped establish the first genuine electronic-music studio in North America in Toronto in 1959.

Within this pattern there have been attempts to forge music that would reflect the individuality of the country. Some works have reflected Canadian history, notably Harry **Somers**'s grand opera *Louis Riel*, which dressed 19th-century epic opera in modern garb. Many have been arrangements of folk songs, particularly Newfoundland folk songs, but most of these reflect a British or Irish rather than an indigenous tradition. Others, especially during the 1950s, attempted to evoke the Canadian landscape. A few have attempted to draw on the heritage of Canada's indigenous peoples, sometimes using melody and text, sometimes influenced by native Indian rhythms. **MacMillan**'s *Three Indian Songs from the West Coast* remains one of the best examples, while the *Songs of the Central Eskimos* (1971) and the *Indian Legends* (1971), both for solo voice

and piano are an interesting response by Alexander Brott (born 1915). By and large these attempts at the assimilation of a traditional heritage have not been successful, and, with the exception of Murray **Schafer** (born 1933), Canada has failed as yet to produce a modern idiom that has a strong Canadian character.

Canada is experiencing the teething pains of a musical culture struggling to gain self-identity: the large number of composers working in Canada, as well as the success already achieved in other artistic fields, may augur well for the future. Meanwhile, a large number of recordings of Canadian music have been produced, especially by the Canadian Broadcasting Company and the Canadian Music Centre, but there has been a relative failure to distribute them with any success inside the country, let alone outside.

Canadian Music Centre:
Chalmers House
20 St Joseph Street
Toronto
Ontario M4Y 1J9
tel: +1 416 961–6601
fax: +1 416 961–7198

Hambraeus Bengt
see under Sweden

MacMillan (Sir) Ernest*
born 18th August 1893 at Mimico (Toronto)
died 6th May 1973 at Toronto

Sir Ernest MacMillan's activities as composer, teacher, educator and administrator qualify him as the father figure of modern Canadian music: he was one of the first Canadian composers of note actually to be born in Canada. His compositional output was small and reflected his English training, essentially late Romantic with an English fluidity and sensibility of colour. A number of his works utilised or arranged Canadian folk songs, especially after his meeting with the folk musicologist Marius Barbeau in 1927.

The best known of MacMillan's folk-influenced works is the *Two Sketches on Canadian Folksongs* (1927), written for string quartet but later arranged for string orchestra. The first sketch is based on a song of the legend of Christ disguising himself as a beggar, the second on a folk song popular in Quebec describing the Breton port of St-Malo, from where many Canadian immigrants sailed. But the pieces are essentially abstract: the string orchestra version has something of the English pastoral, reminiscent of **Vaughan Williams**, while the string quartet version is more rugged and individual. They were followed by a sequel, with actual word settings, the *Six Bergerettes du Bas Canada* (1928) for three soloists and four instruments. Among other works likely to be encountered is the *String Quartet* (1915–19), conventional in its construction (with sonata form outer movements, and a ternary slow movement), broadly lyrical, light-textured and attractive with moments that suggest MacMillan knew the **Ravel** string quartet. It deserves to be better known in Canada as one of the foundations of the Canadian string quartet.

Much of MacMillan's vocal and choral output remains unheard, but among the most interesting of his works, and one of the most successful of all Canadian song-cycles, is the short *Three Indian Songs of the West Coast* (1928) for high voice and piano. The native melodies and the words, translated by Duncan Campbell Scott, were collected on a trip with Marius Barbeau to British Columbia; the three powerful texts are intimate but dramatic, and MacMillan's arrangements succeed in retaining their vitality, nobility, and, in the second song, tenderness, while merging the rhythmic energy with the form of the art-song and elevating both traditions.

MacMillan's life was extraordinarily energetic. He was captured at the outbreak of World War I – he had been attending the Bayreuth Festival – and managed as a prisoner to produce enough work to gain a further degree from Oxford on his release in 1918. He was principal of the Toronto Conservatory (1926–42), dean of the Faculty of Music at the University of Toronto (1927–52), conductor of the Toronto Symphony Orchestra (1931–56), toured widely and edited the first book of essays on Canadian music. He was knighted in 1935.

RECOMMENDED WORKS
String Quartet (1915–19)
Three Indian Songs of the West Coast (1928) for high voice and piano
Two Sketches on Canadian Folksongs (1927) for string quartet

Schafer (Raymond) Murray**
born 18th July 1933 at Sarnia (Ontario)

Murray Schafer is probably the best-known Canadian composer, respected for his many writings and publications on Canadian and other music, on the environment, and on music education, as well as for his compositions. A number of his works have become, or have been designed as, individual items in a huge ongoing cycle of works, *Patria*, which represents the core of his aesthetics and concerns.

His early works were conventional – the powerful *In Memoriam: Alberto Guerro* (1959) for strings, for example, is tonal, while concentrating on varying sonority. They announced a distinctive musical personality, albeit at the time influenced by **Sibelius** and **Mahler**, the latter conspicuously and overtly in the 12 *Minnelieder* (1956) for mezzo-soprano and woodwind quintet, settings of medieval German love songs, where the use of the woodwind quintet creates an individual sense of timbre within the Mahlerian cast. During the 1960s, Schafer started exploring the techniques and the sounds of the contemporary avant-garde, and at the same time turned to extra-musical subjects, often with political and social content, and to the uses of language. *Protest and Incarceration* (1960) for mezzo-soprano and orchestra is a setting of Romanian poets; the sombre and pointillistic *Canzoni for Prisoners* (1962) for orchestra, in five linked sections, concerns prisoners of conscience.

Communication is the main theme of what started as the trilogy *Patria*, eventually developed into an extended cycle. In *Patria I* ('The Characteristics of Man', 1974) for mezzo-soprano, mime, actors, chorus and chamber ensemble, an immigrant can communicate with the audience, but not with the other characters. In *Requiems for the Party Girl* (1966) for mezzo-soprano and chamber ensemble (subsequently incorporated into *Patria II* as *Requiems for a Party Girl*, 1972, with actors and tape) the schizophrenic central character is unable to communicate with her medical helpers; she collapses and commits suicide, representing the alienation of contemporary society. The score, closely allying vocal line and instrumental response, as if the vocal line is trapped in the instrumental writing, graphically reflects her fears and neurosis.

Schafer's music also revealed an interest in Eastern philosophy, as in *From the Tibetan Book of the Dead* (1968) for soprano, chorus, alto flute, clarinet and tape (later included in altered form in *Patria II*). *Music for the Morning of the World* (1969) for soprano and tape, is the second of a trilogy inspired by the 13th-century Sufi mystic Jalâl al-Dîn Rûmi; the texts chosen relate the inner self to the outer heavens, with an ecstatic, Oriental decorative solo line against the wide sonorities and expressive commentary of the electronic tape. The complete trilogy (part one is titled *Divan i Shams i Tabriz*, 1969, revised 1970, for six soloists, orchestra and tape, and part three *Beyond the Great Gate of Light*, 1972, for six soloists, orchestra and tape) is entitled *Lustro. Arcana* (1972) for soprano and instrumental ensemble or chamber orchestra is a set of fourteen songs (from which the singer may chose) using a secret ancient Egyptian text, where each phoneme of the text has two associated notes. Again, vocal and instrumental lines are structurally integrated: when the singer sings one note, often the paired note is heard in the instrumentation. *East* (1972) for chamber orchestra is a meditation on texts from the Ishna-Upanishad, in which each letter is given a specific pitch; a gong is sounded every ten seconds, and the instrumentalists hum and sing the letters in a powerful, sonorous score of shifting colours.

A growing interest in the theatrical power of text, and in unconventional dramatic treatment, emerged in his first stage work, the 'audio-visual poem' *Loving* (1963–65) for actor, actress, singers and chamber orchestra, with a bilingual text by the composer, which might be described as post-serial. Its subject, the stages of a relationship, is non-linear (there is no plot as such) and is designed to reflect states and projections of the psyche rather than actual characters, an early indication of a preoccupation with the Jungian aspects of interaction and myth. The musical means are mainly short scraps of instrumental colour and texture used to support the free-flowing vocal lines. That the intrinsic interest of the work is not realised is in part due to the text – Schafer is a fine composer and writer, but not a good poet – but it pointed to his special and original contribution: a series of works employing multimedia and specifically removed from traditional venues.

The sense of space that these works employ, and sometimes the inspiration of Canadian landscape and myth, give them a hue that makes them unique to their country of origin, the genesis of a Canadian music that unfortunately has been little encouraged in Canada by performances.

The primary motivation is myth, the primary structure ritual. The form of these pieces is determined by the spatial context, using a combination of influences from traditional ethnic musics and avant-garde techniques.

An early example of Schafer's environmental concerns was *North/White* (1973) for harp, piano, snowmobile and strings, that introduced a snowmobile to illustrate the destruction of the myth of the Canadian north. *Music for a Wilderness Lake* (1979) placed the members of a trombone ensemble around an Ontario lake, making use of the large distances separating them, the sonic effects of water and echo, and the interaction with natural sounds, such as bird-song. This was developed in the most celebrated of these outdoor performances, *The Princess of the Stars* (1981), which now also acts as the prologue to the *Patria* cycle. Its basis is the story of the Princess of the Stars, who is taken into the lake by a Three-Horned Enemy, leaving dew in her wake in her struggles. A Wolf looks for her, and the rising sun joins in the action. Although invented by Schafer, this story is inspired by native Indian myths. The action is set around a large lake before dawn, and the performers are ranged around the lake and in canoes on the lake, with masks and effigies representing the main protagonists: a Presenter, or storyteller, links the action for the audience placed on one shore. Again, there is intentional interaction with the natural state and sounds of the setting, the Princess's voice at the opening coming from a great distance across the water, the rising sun coinciding with its actual rising. For obvious reasons, it is a work that needs to be experienced rather than heard in recording, but it would cause a sensation if anyone had the courage to do it in Britain's Lake District, or in the Alps.

Ra (1983) for singers, dancers, actors and instrumentalists, is based on the Egyptian myth of the journey of the sun god through the netherworld between dusk and dawn. The audience is limited to seventy-five (corresponding to the seventy-five names of the sun god) who are expected to take part in the ritual. The inspiration of the 'Procession' section clearly comes from Canadian native Indian music, and successfully transfers to its present setting; elsewhere the musical sources are eclectic, with spare textures emphasising the ritual of the vocal lines.

At the same time as exploring the concept of an indigenous myth (which Schafer sees as exemplified by the figure of the

Wolf) he has written a number of works inspired by the Greek myth of Theseus, Ariadne, and the Labyrinth. These include *La testa d'Ariane* (1980) for soprano, narrator and accordion; *Theseus* (1988) for harp and string quartet; and the effective *The Crown of Ariadne* (1979) for harp. In the latter the harpist plays percussion instruments in addition to the harp, thus reverting to two elemental and ancient musical elements. Individual sounds and ideas are separated to give a delicate sense of space, high percussion adding a ritualistic feeling with occasional exotic colouring or modal shades.

Similar preoccupations with ritual and the environment occur in Schafer's concert music. *Epitaph for Moonlight* (1969) for chorus and high tuned percussion is an exploration of the kind of block chordal writing developed by **Ligeti**, an epitaph for a moon no longer untouched, following the lunar landings. The beautiful *Sun* (1982) for unaccompanied choir sets the names of the sun in different languages, with sustained textures heard against verbally-driven rhythmic figures. Water has been a consistent inspiration: the electronic *Okeanos* (1971) utilises the sounds of the sea and various sea poets. *Miniwanka or the Moments of Water* (1971) for chorus is a successful emulation of various states of water, from rain to ocean swells, using the words for water of several North American Indian languages. The gentle *String Quartet No. 2* (1976), with its wave and trough-like motion, was in part inspired by Schafer's 'soundscape' studies of the timings that ocean waves exhibit between trough and crest. The *String Quartet No. 3* (1981) contains elements of ritual in its arch form, with the drone-like opening played by the cello, joined by off-stage viola and then two violins, all eventually arriving on-stage by the end of the first movement, while in the turbulent and sometimes motoric central movement the players add new layers and effects by constant vocalisations. *Le cri de Merlin* (1987) for guitar uses a tape of bird-songs with the solo instrument.

If such concerns have been central to Schafer's aesthetic, he has also written works with a more conventional concert context. *Son of Heldenleben* (1968) is a forceful transformation of elements of Strauss's tone poem into a modern orchestral idiom, using a series drawn from the main theme of the tone poem, in a tribute to the German composer. The *String Quartet No. 4* (1988–89) for string quartet,

violin (which may be pre-taped) and soprano seems to be a reworking of **Bartók** and especially **Shostakovich**. It also uses themes from the *Patria* cycle, and ends with an off-stage soprano and a third violin. The compelling *String Quartet No. 5 'Rosalind'* (1989) is stylistically similar. His more recent music also includes the attractive *Flute Concerto* (1985) and a *Harp Concerto* (1988), as well as a music-theatre work in two parts, *Apocalypsis*, the first part being *John's Vision* (1981) for sound-poets, singers, mime, dancers, multiple choruses, instruments and pre-recorded tape, the second *Credo* (1986) for twelve mixed choirs with optional tape, synthesizers and/or string instruments.

Schafer has also written a number of works for children or younger players, such as *The star princess & the waterlilies* (1984) for narrator, adult singer, children's chorus and percussion, designed to introduce new sounds, aleatory techniques and graphic as well as traditional notation.

Murray Schafer was artist-in-residence at Newfoundland's Memorial University (1963–65), and professor of Communication Studies at Simon Frazer University (1966–75), where he started the World Soundscape Project to investigate the relationship between humans and their sonic landscape.

RECOMMENDED WORKS

> *The Crown of Ariadne* (1979) for harp
> *East* (1972) for chamber orchestra
> *In Memoriam: Alberto Guerro* (1959) for strings
> *Music for the Morning of the World* (1969) for soprano and tape
> *The Princess of the Stars* (1981)
> ritual *Ra* (1983)
> String Quartet No. 3 (1981)
> String Quartet No. 4 (1988–89)
> String Quartet No. 5 *Rosalind* (1989)
> *Sun* (1982) for unaccompanied choir

BIBLIOGRAPHY

> R. Murray Schafer, *The New Soundscape*, 1969
> — *The Book of Noise*, 1970
> — *The Tuning of the World*, 1977
> — *On Canadian Music*, 1984

Somers Harry Stuart*

born 11th September 1925 at Toronto
died 9th March 1999 at Toronto

A prolific composer who worked in most genres, Harry Somers is, with Murray **Schafer**, the only Canadian composer who has received more than passing attention outside Canada.

In his earlier work he mixed elements of a free atonality with those of a tonal base: the beautiful and carefully paced *North Country* (1948) for string orchestra, one of the most effective of Canadian landscape evocations, contrasts neo-classical contrapuntal passages with sparse suggestions of the northern wilderness that inspired it. Passages of the exploratory and eclectic *Suite for Harp and Chamber Orchestra* (1949), which draws on a variety of styles, point to a recurring feature of Somers' music: a slow melodic line either unsupported or very sparsely supported. A feature of his operas, this reached its most extended form in the twenty-one-minute *Music for Solo Violin* (1973), in which the Muezzin call which inspired the opening gradually evolves in a quasi-improvisatory fashion.

Following those early works, Somers's output has been marked by eclecticism, different pieces often being in highly contrasted styles and driven more by context of commission and performance than by compositional pattern. There has been a gradual integration of techniques originally inspired by the avant-garde, spatial and theatrical effects increasingly used in the 1960s. Some features, though, have remained consistent, especially generating and maintaining tension in the listener by rhythmic interjections, declamatory effects, contrasting styles, and abrupt changes in dynamics, which Somers has called 'dynamic unrest'. His harmonic vocabulary is also wide-ranging, and has drawn on 12-tone and atonal techniques.

The best known of his orchestral works is perhaps the rather bombastic *Fantasia for Orchestra* (1958); more interesting is the grittier and less compromising *Symphony for Woodwinds, Brass and Percussion* (1961), whose first two movements use juxtaposition and superimposition of rhythms and declamatory and spatial effects within the orchestra, although the last two movements are closer to Somers's avowed intent to write a piece 'suitable for a wide audience'. The *Picasso Suite* (1964) for small orchestra is particularly attractive: based on music written for a television documentary, the suite is in nine short sections, seven of which depict different periods in the painter's style. The suite includes gentle pastiche, from rag-time to neo-classical **Stravinsky**. Of his chamber music, the rather dark *String Quartet No.*

2 (1950) in five movements played continuously, is lean and introverted, regularly threatening to break out into more emphatic writing, but pulling away from it. The *String Quartet No. 3* (1959) contains interesting ideas and construction, but is rather colourless; based on themes from his earlier opera *The Fool*, it uses 12-tone techniques in a single movement, ending with a fugue.

Listeners to the two early violin sonatas (No. 1, 1953; No. 2 1955) should beware Somers's disarming statement that they belong more to the 19th century than the 20th; with the *String Quartet No. 2* they are akin to the later **Shostakovich** chamber works in harmonic language, formal construction, and general feel, though they lack the Russian's ability to suddenly change gear or produce a passage of searing memorability.

Somers's vocal music illustrates his practice of changing idioms. The short, beautiful cycle *Three Songs on Words by Walt Whitman* (1946) for baritone and piano has the clarity, lean textures, and something of the luminous quality of **Britten's** Donne or Hardy settings. The *Five Songs for Dark Voice* (1956) for contralto and orchestra, to specially written texts by Michael Fram, are avowedly Mahlerian in their style and cast, the five songs acting as the movements of a symphonic structure; the liquid textures of the fifth song in particular are atmospherically beguiling. *Twelve Miniatures* (1963) for soprano, flute, spinet and cello are settings of Japanese haikus, grouped into four sets of three to follow the seasons and the months respectively. Those seasonal contrasts are not overt in the music, which is deliberately rarefied in texture and rhythm to match the haiku style. *Evocations* (1966) for mezzo-soprano and piano is based on words by the composer which evoke the Canadian landscape and are often fragmented into constituent syllables. Special effects figure in the piano writing – the singer sings into the piano (in a haunting echo of the bird-call of the Canadian loon), and rubber hammers are used. *Voiceplay* (1971) for solo vocalist takes the reduction to the constituents of words considerably further, using thirteen different pitches for thirteen vowel sounds, the vocalist taking the roles of lecturer, actor, and demonstrator; the experimentation echoes earlier avant-garde vocal explorations without being particularly effective. In complete contrast, the *Five Songs of the*

Newfoundland Outports (1968) for chorus and piano, Somers's best-known work, are based on songs from a collection of traditional songs published four years earlier. The arrangements are very free, with the choir using Newfoundland techniques of emulating instruments vocally.

Somers's first opera was *The Fool* (1953), a chamber opera for four characters which represent various levels: the personal, the psychologically symbolic, and the political. Both libretto (by Michael Fram) and music are highly stylised, with a chamber ensemble (ten players) whose colours recall the neo-classical **Stravinsky**. The mood veers between the grotesque and the lyrical, in a work which successfully integrates music of earlier times, from the 17th century through quasi folk song to a suggestion of **Milhaud's** *The Creation of the World*.

One of the landmarks of Canadian music was Somers's second opera, *Louis Riel* (1966–67), commissioned for the centenary of Canadian Confederation. The libretto, by Mavor Moore, concerns a pivotal and still contentious event in Canadian history, the second uprising (1884–85) of the *métis* ('half-breeds') under their charismatic leader Louis Riel, and his subsequent capture and hanging. Though symbolically important, the opera has not become a staple in the Canadian repertoire, receiving only one production (1967, revived in 1975 and shown at a Canadian festival in Washington). *Louis Riel* complicatedly switches between different settings in seventeen scenes; the libretto, while theatrically colourful and imposing, fails to home in on a convincing musico-dramatic thread. Musically, the idiom is modernistic, with cluster effects and small bursts of orchestral comment; but all too often it has little or no memorable character. A major failing is that at many of the heightened moments for which opera is so suited, the possibilities are not realised or are passed over. It is recommended below for historical reasons.

The sense of theatre superseding music is perpetuated in Somers's fourth opera, the three-act *Mario the Magician* (1988–92), also to a libretto by Mavor Moore based on the Thomas Mann novel of the same title, (and just predated by an opera on the same subject by the English composer Stephen Oliver, 1950–92). It received almost as much attention and promotion as *Louis Riel*, and a million dollar budget. Again, the plot – of a family caught in Fascist Italy in 1929 – is theatrically imposing, its theme the outsider in a xenophobic society and the manipulation of individuals by an individual (the magician of the title). The style is not as eclectic as *Louis Riel*, the action more continuous; theatrical effects include the use of the cast in the audience. For much of the opera the tension that is a component of Somers's style extends into an almost continuous hysteria, which creates constant theatrical tension, but not musical interest or characterisation. The third act gives a powerful ending to the work without an especially individual musical style. Hopes that Somers might prove a powerhouse for indigenous Canadian opera have not yet been realised.

RECOMMENDED WORKS
 song-cycle *Five Songs for Dark Voice* (1956)
 opera *Louis Riel* (1966–67)
 North Country (1948) for orchestra
 Picasso Suite (1964) for small orchestra
 song-cycle *Three Songs on Words by Walt Whitman* (1946)

BIBLIOGRAPHY
 B. Cherney, *Harry Somers*, Toronto, 1975

Tremblay Gilles Léonce*
born 6th September 1932 at Arvida, Quebec

If **Schafer** is the major Canadian composer who has allied avant-garde techniques with specifically Canadian imagery and concerns, Gilles Tremblay is the one who has most consistently embraced the international, abstract explorations generated by the European avant-garde. His relatively small output has showed a consistency of idiom and purpose, and a concern with spatial and temporal concepts that has affinities with Eastern thought and music; as do his favourite colours and timbral effects, recalling the clashing cymbals of China, the temple horns of Tibet, the delicate tracery of gamelan, the flutes of Japan.

He was one of the very few Canadian composers who launched straight into a contemporary idiom without an early period of a more traditional style, and his immediate influences were **Varèse** and **Messiaen**. The short piano pieces *Phases* (1956) and *Réseaux* (*Networks*, 1956) echo Messiaen in their construction, with sharp cluster-bursts contrasted with slow progressions of isolated notes. Their concentration on the spaces between the notes, particularly the resonances of the piano, heralds Tremblay's preoccupation with sonority and timbre, and especially the relationship between event and its echo and pre-echo. This duality, between sound and its shadow, resonates throughout Tremblay's work. On first encounter it may seem (incorrectly) somewhat bitty, as events are inclined to flare up and die away, like astronomical incidents, but since the space between those events is of such importance, it requires (like many other avant-garde explorations of sonorities) a change of perception on the part of the listener.

Cantique de durées (1960) for orchestra applied spatial concepts in the orchestra within a serial framework, with seven groups of players, five on stage, three (wind and ondes martenot) ranged around the audience. *Kékoba* ('Evening Star' in Hebrew, 1965, revised 1967) for three soloists, ondes martenot and percussion contrasts precise events (especially percussive) with more fluid sonorities (especially created by the ondes martenot). A flow of action and reaction is created by the use of limited choice: one player choosing a particular percussion instrument for a passage determines the instrument of the next percussionist. The final section is a setting of '*Ave maris stella*' in which the word 'star' is treated in several languages.

A cycle of works entitled *Champs* (in the sense of electromagnetic or similar 'fields') explored the fields of pitch, duration and timbre and their interactions. The rather restrained *Champs I* (1965, revised 1969), for piano and two percussionists, with its pitter-patter of events like the rhythmic effects of a collection of wind chimes, uses 'reflexes' in which one player reacts to another, extending in *Champ III, Vers* (*Towards*, 1969) for instrumental ensemble, to a chain of reactions, growing out from earthy sonorities and bright chimes in a kind of avant-garde spring rite. *Champs II, Souffles* (*Breaths*, 1968) includes blowing effects in wind instruments without creating concrete notes.

The interaction of these elements reached a further stage in *Solstices* (1971, subtitled *Les jours et les saisons tournent*) for flute, clarinet, horn, bass and two percussionists. Each instrument represents a season. The starting point of the work is determined by the date and time of performance, and a relay system is used, passing activity from one season to

another and creating interplays between the 'seasons'. This may be extended to other instrumental groups, either in the same location or distant locations, connected electronically. The effect is of a spontaneity of event within a generality of framework. *Jeux de solstices* (1974) is for full orchestra; here the four seasons are represented by four different techniques, the form and development of the performance controlled by the conductor. *Oralleluiants* (1974–75) for soprano, tenor and ensemble with microphones, juxtaposes slow-moving textures (emulating breathing) with rapturous or excited interjections, combined with suggestions of ritual with gongs and the flute prominent.

While continuing the general patterns of his idiom – dualities, contrasts, resonances, and mobile forms – the correspondences between Trembly's techniques and the interactions of the natural world were explored further in *Compostelle I* (1978) for clarinet and ensemble, written for **Messiaen's** seventieth birthday, and in perhaps the most effective score from this period, *Fleuves (Great Rivers*, 1976) for orchestra, which ranges from grand statement to the delicacy of wind chimes at its close. Equally effective, but on a much smaller scale, is '. . . *le sifflement des vents porteurs de l'amour . . .*' ('. . . *the whistling of the winds, bearers of love . . .*', 1971) for flute and percussion with microphones, which takes its title from St John of the Cross. Here frost (delicate sounds) is contrasted with warmth (more linear melodic lines), using extended flute techniques (such as breath harmonics) and a wide range of lighter percussive colours. These two works perhaps provide the best introduction to Tremblay's methods. The imposing *Vêpres de la Vierge* (1986) for soprano, chorus, flute, organ and orchestra was written for the 850th anniversary of the foundation of the Abbey of Our Lady at Sylvanès, France. Contemporary effects intertwine with the influence of Gregorian chant in sonorities which reflect the acoustics of the Abbey. It opens with a long and inspired flute solo, using extended techniques and influenced by Eastern musics, which itself is worthy of attention by flautists; the whole work is a powerful addition to the modern choral repertoire.

Among his other works was the electronic 'sound-environment' (*Centre-élan*, 1967) for the Quebec Pavilion at Expo 67, which was in five sequences drawn from a widespread variety of Quebec sounds, from the sea to industry, and ending with an evocation of the northern lights.

RECOMMENDED WORKS

Fleuves (1976) for orchestra
Jeux de solstices (1974) for orchestra
Phases (1966) for piano
'. . . *le sifflement des vents porteurs de l'amour . . .*' (1971) for flute, percussion and microphones
Vêpres de la Vierge (1986) for soprano, chorus, flute, organ and orchestra

Willan Healey

born 12th October 1880 at Balham (London, UK)
died 16th February 1968 at Toronto

Willan's huge output (over 900 works) divides into two groups; the secular works, which follow the English late Victorian traditions of **Stanford** and Parry, and the considerable body of religious works, either choral or for organ, that are more eclectic in idiom.

Among the most often heard of Willan's secular works is the *Piano Concerto* (1944, revised 1949), heavily influenced by **Rachmaninov** and a pale clone of the Russian composer. Of his two symphonies, the *Symphony No. 2* (1941, revised 1948) is more likely to be heard; in ethos and idiom, it belongs to a pre-World War I aesthetic, with a Brucknerian opening movement, a jauntiness in the scherzo combined with Elgarian turns of phrase, and, after a slow mysterious opening to the finale (the most interesting section of the symphony), a huge, blazingly triumphant finale. The two violin sonatas may occasionally be encountered, the rather dull *Violin Sonata No. 1* (1916) being late Romantic idiom, while Baroque elements pervade the *Violin Sonata No. 2* (1923).

There was also a Celtic streak in Willan's interests, which, combined with the influence of Wagner, emerges in the rather beautiful *Poem* for string quartet (1904, revised 1930), and more overtly in his major work, the opera *Deirdre*. Based on the Irish legends of Deirdre of the Sorrows, it started as incidental music to a radio drama by John Coulter (1941), was then recast as a radio opera (1945), and finally revised as a three-act stage opera (1962–65). It uses leitmotifs, though sparingly, lush orchestration, and has been criticised for its dramatic weakness. He also wrote six ballad-operas (two have been lost), using folk music as the source of the songs.

More highly regarded than these is Willan's organ music, especially the virtuoso *Introduction, Passacaglia and Fugue* (1916), and the two *Prelude and Fugues* (1908 and 1909), which reflect a European late Romantic chromaticism. The fine *Introduction, Passacaglia and Fugue* is an imposing work, taking full advantage of the resources of the late Victorian organ in a taut musical construction. The opening is dramatic, the hushed mystery of the initial chords suddenly blazing out. The eighteen variations on the passacaglia ground bass contrast the delicate and the imposing, the climax placed in the penultimate variation to allow a gentle link to the fugue, which eventually sheds its chromatic garb in a final blaze of triumph. Among his later organ works, the *Choral Preludes* of the 1950s are the most successful.

Willan's sacred vocal music is in the English tradition, but with the additional influence of Renaissance polyphony, sometimes overt in such unaccompanied choral works as the five-part motet *Gloria Deo per immensa sæcula* (1950). But the range of style is considerable, from the spartan textures of the Lutheran *Missa Brevis in G* (1954) to the more personal style he adopted in compositions for his own church, St Mary Magdalene, Toronto, where the influence of early polyphony and plainsong is evident. They include fourteen settings of the *Missa brevis* (1928–63) and a set of eleven *Liturgical Motets* (1928–37). His most celebrated choral work is perhaps *An Apostrophe to the Heavenly Hosts* (1921) for unaccompanied double choir, using texts and musical influences drawn from Eastern Orthodox rites. Its four parts are linked by ethereal amens, the final section being based on the hymn 'Ye Watchers and Ye Holy Ones'. Those who enjoy **Holst's** choral music might consider investigating this work.

Willan was an organist and conductor, notably at St Mary Magdalene (1921–68), and taught at Toronto, where his pupils included many of the later generations of English-speaking Canadian composers, including John Beckwith, Godfrey Ridout and John Weinzweig.

RECOMMENDED WORKS

An Apostrophe to the Heavenly Hosts (1921) for unaccompanied double choir
Introduction, Passacaglia and Fugue for organ (1916)

Poem (1904, revised 1930) for string
quartet or string orchestra (1959)

Chile

The development of composition in Chile
has followed lines similar to that of Mexico
or Argentina, although Chilean composers
have not had the exposure of some of their
colleagues from other South or Central
American countries. The father of modern
Chilean music was Humberto Allende
(1885–1959), who made folk song collections and composed in a nationalistic style,
notably in the tone poems *Escenas campe-
sinas chilenas* (1913) and *La voz de las
calles* (1920), which uses the songs of
Chilean street vendors. He also taught at
the Santiago Conservatory (1925–46).
Domingo Santa Cruz Wilson (1899–1987),
who wrote in a neo-classical style with only
occasional use of Chilean melodies, studied
in Madrid, and on his return to Chile did
much to further the cause of indigenous
music, especially in the area of music
education. Of the younger generation, the
best known is Juan Allende-Blin (nephew
of Humberto Allende), who studied mathematics, architecture and music in Chile,
and then music in West Germany,
returned to Chile to teach at the Santiago
Conservatory (1954), but then settled in
West Germany (1957). He was one of the
avant-garde composers who rethought the
potential and possibilities of the organ, and
among his works written for the foremost
organist of new techniques, Gerd Zacher,
are the study of sonorities and vibrations
Sonorités (1962), and *Sons brisés – in
memoriam Lothar Schreyer* (1967),
another study in sonorities utilising overtone and breathing effects by varying the
wind pressure in the organ box. Some of
his works have been written for the
outdoor water organ of which he was
co-inventor.

Croatia

Introduction

Croatia has had a lively compositional history in the 20th century, even if few of its composers are known elsewhere. Classical Croatian music dates back to Vatroslav Lisinski (1819–54), but the major figure of the 19th and early 20th centuries was the prolific Ivan Zajc (1832–1914, also known as Giovanni von Zaytz), best known for his operas in a grand Romantic style, often with Croatian subjects: the most famous is *Nikola Šubiç Zrinjski* (1876), describing the defence of Siget against the Turks by the hero in 1566, a tuneful and colourful work in the style of Verdi. Opera predominated at the turn of the century, mainly because of the success and standards of the Zagreb Opera, founded in 1870. Modern Croatian opera began with *Ogani* (*Fire*, 1911) by Blagoje Bersa (1873–1934), using a continuous style with leitmotifs influenced by Wagner, married to the influence of **Puccini**, which has claims to be the first 20th-century opera dealing with factory workers and the proletariat. Of the many subsequent Croatian operas, the best known is probably the comic *Ero s onoga svijeta* (*Ero the Joker*, 1935) by Jakov Gotovac (1895–1982), who conducted the Zagreb Opera from 1923 to 1958.

Croatian composition in other genres, such as chamber music and symphonies, dates from the end of World War I, and that generation of composers can be divided between those using Croatian and other local folk music and those more influenced by new styles elsewhere in Europe. Among the former were Antun Dobroni (1879–1955), Gotovac, Krešimir Baranović (1894–1975), best known for his folk ballet *Licitarsko srce* (*Gingerbread Heart*, 1924) and who pioneered Croatian symphonic music, and Ivan Brkanović (born 1906), whose output includes five symphonies. The more cosmopolitan composers include Stjepan Šulek (born 1914), whose neo-classical works include six symphonies, three *Classical Concertos* and the opera *Coriolanus* (1957), based on Shakespeare's play. Boris Papandopulo (1906–91) also adopted a neo-classical style with abstract forms, notably in the *Sinfonietta* (1939), but also wrote operas, including *Rona* (1955), whose main characters are beggars.

That broad division continued after the establishment of communist Yugoslavia, one of the few communist states allowing a freedom of musical style. The Zagreb Biennial, founded in 1971, has become an important forum for modern European works. Communist themes have been most overt in the choral music (including, for example, the later choral works of Papandopulo) and in opera. The two most important composers of modern Croatian music have been Ivo **Malec** (born 1925), who settled in Paris in 1959 but has maintained close contact with his home country, and Milko Kelemen (born 1924), one of the founders of the Biennial, who moved to Germany in 1970. Kelemen started in a neo-classical style, but after studying in Paris he introduced serial and avant-garde techniques to Croatia; the *Tri plesa* (*Three Dances*, 1956) for viola and strings attempts to merge folk music and 12-tone technique. His *Concerto Improvisations* (1955) for strings, which uses continuous variations, was once widely heard, while *Equilibrium* (1961) for two orchestras explored unusual colours and stereophonic effects, with stone and metal objects in addition to conventional instruments. *Sub Rosa* (1965), in which Kelemen went beyond the serial techniques he had been using, was originally for a small instrumental group, but was extended by the appearance (in mid-performance) of an enlarged orchestra, with amplification effects. Among his vocal works, the cantata *Les mots* (*Words*, 1956) is based on Sartre, and uses television effects, while the opera *Novi stanar* (*The New Tenant*, 1964) is to a theatre-of-the-absurd libretto by Ionesco. His music needs to be more widely disseminated. The Yugoslav Music Centre (SOKOJ) at one time carried information on Croatian composers (see under Yugoslavia); the current position is unclear.

Malec Ivo
born March 30th 1925 at Zagreb

Malec is, with Milko Kelemen, the Croatian composer best known outside the country, and the one who has most comprehensively embraced the avant-garde. He studied in Paris, settling there permanently in 1959 while maintaining close contacts with the then Yugoslavia.

Starting with *Mavena* (1957), many of his early works were electronic, and often in the *musique concrète* style. Among these is *Dahovi II* (*Breaths II*, 1961), an effective score combining electronics with *musique concrète* reworkings of actual instruments, set against the breathing effects of the title, and with spatial qualities creating a varied sense of distance. He then combined electronics with conventional forces in a number of works, notably the short *Tutti* (1962) for orchestra and tape.

Colour has played an important role in Malec's non-electronic works. Each of the five movements of the ballet *Makete* (*Models*, 1956) for seventeen solo instruments is associated with a different colour. *Mouvements en couleur* (1959) for the unusual combination of woodwind, brass, percussion, and nine cellos, explores gradually changing instrumental colours, interrupted by harsher ideas. *Miniatures for Lewis Carroll* (1964) for chamber orchestra is a tribute to the author of *Alice in Wonderland*, with material transformations analogous to those in Alice's world. *Cantata pour elle* (1966) for soprano, harp and magnetic tape combines three layers: tape transformation of pre-recorded harp sounds, the live harp, and the solo voice, using extended techniques in all three and with the vocal line concentrating on emotional sounds rather than words. The generally ecstatic tone is enlivened by the discreet use of sound 'objects' in the electronic transformation.

Oral (1966–67) uses the combination of reciter and orchestra, popular in the 19th century, but unusual in contemporary music. It is based on sections and fragments drawn by the composer from André Breton's *Nadja*, creating a Kafkaesque verbal montage of idea and surrealist incident. A reciter provides the rhythmic and declamatory effects of sound-poetry which combine with an orchestration whose sounds are drawn from Malec's earlier electronic experience. In the pulsating *Arco 11* (1975) for eleven solo strings, Malec applied his experience of electronic sonorities and effects to a string group, drawing from them an impressive range of sounds that nonetheless remain firmly within the string tradition. It opens with the energy and drive of a Minimalist piece, and shifts into an ethereal slow section of overlapping sonorities (layering harmonic effects) and gentle slides that emerge and die away, often with considerable beauty; the following frenetic section of fragmented string layers is gradually but not conclusively resolved as the instruments are reduced to thinner and thinner textures. This powerful, ultimately enigmatic piece is highly recommended. A similar extension of sonorities occurs in *Ottava Bassa* (1983–84) for double-bass and large orchestra extending the expressive range of the solo instrument with a number of extended techniques, set against largely dark-hued massed effects from the orchestra.

Malec has been a professor at the Paris Conservatoire since 1972.

RECOMMENDED WORKS
  Acro 11 (1975) for eleven solo strings
  Cantata pour elle (1966) for soprano,
    harp and magnetic tape
  electronic *Dahovi II* (1961)
  Oral (1966–67) for reciter and
    orchestra

Cuba

Modern indigenous Cuban composition dates from the 1920s and 1930s, led by the conductor, teacher and composer Amadeo Roldán (1900–39), who was born in Spain. His music used Afro-Cuban musical idioms and vigorous rhythms, and his *Ritmicas V–VI* (1930) for percussion were among the first Western works for percussion alone. He founded the Havana String Quartet (1927), and the Havana Conservatory was renamed after him. José Ardévol (1911–81) was a founding member of the Grupo de Renovaćión, set up to play the music of the group; after the 1959 revolution, his music followed revolutionary themes, including settings for words by Fidel Castro. The neo-classical composer Julián Orbón (de Soto) (born 1925) was another founding member, but left Cuba following the revolution. The best known of the following generation of composers is the guitarist Leo Brouwer (born 1939), who has acted as a musical spokesperson for the revolution; his own music is influenced by European avant-garde composers and by left-wing politics. He was in charge of the music wing of the Cuban film industry, and has taught in Havana University.

Czech Republic

Introduction

The geographical area of the former Czechoslovakia has had a remarkable and long music history; the Berlin–Prague–Vienna –Budapest axis has been the major location of new musical ideas from the 18th century onwards, only recently eroded by World War II and its consequences. The Czech musical tradition has been continued in the 20th century, and, like that of Hungary, is notable not just for the internationally known composers, but for the quality in depth of its lesser figures, who, while never likely to achieve widespread attention, provide consistently satisfying and invigorating musical experiences little matched by countries of a similar size.

The recent division of the former Czechoslovakia has left many, though not all, of these composers to be claimed by the Czech Republic rather than Slovakia (q.v.), in part due to the prominence of the musical centres of Prague and Brno. The folk music of Bohemia and Moravia has been especially fruitful for 20th-century composers, and it should be noted that the sources of such folk music are now divided by the Czech–Slovak border. The other main legacy of popular music has been the tradition (dating back to the 15th century) of the chorales of the Hussites, who believed in the power of popular song and vernacular languages in religious worship.

Modern Czech music can trace its sources to the extraordinary resurgence of Czech music in the second half of the 19th century, connected with the rise of Czech nationalism within the Austro-Hungarian Empire. The leading figure of this resurgence was Bedřich Smetana (1824–84), whose tone poem cycle *Má Vlast* is the quintessential Czech nationalist orchestral work, while his *The Bartered Bride* is the classical Czech national folk opera. As important to Czech musical life, Antonin Dvořák (1841–1904) placed that nationalism into an international context, in such works as his *Slavonic Dances*, but even more prominently in his nine symphonies, a staple of the international repertoire, of which the *Symphony No. 9 'The New World'* (1893) is one of the best known of all symphonies. The significance of these two composers for Czech music was that, while following German models, they established an overall tone that is specifically and recognisably Czech, and which remains potent to this day: deeply rooted in the Czech and Slovakian landscapes, it is characterised by clarity and a joyful brightness, by a rhythmic surge and excitement of happiness, even in tragic works seeking the positive.

Their legacy was immediately taken up by three composers working in a late Romantic chromatic idiom: Vítězslav **Novák** (1870–1949), best remembered for his orchestral works; Josef **Suk** (1874–1935), Dvořák's son-in-law and a celebrated violinist who, in addition to orchestral works inspired by nature, produced important chamber and violin works; and Josef **Foerster** (1859–1951) whose choral works are of significance in the Czech Republic. But by far the most significant Czech composer in the first three decades of the 20th century was Leoš **Janáček** (1854–1928), one of the four most important opera composers of the 20th century. His musical language, rooted in Moravian folk music and patterns of speech, is completely idiomatic and individual, and all the more remarkable in that almost all his important works were written after the age of 60. With their social and psychological concerns, his operas belong firmly to the 20th century.

The reaction to late Romanticism centred on Alois **Hába** (1893–1973) and his followers; Hába started with atonal techniques and athematic works (paralleling the path already taken by **Schoenberg**), but in the search for a new harmonic language quickly adopted microtones (intervals smaller than a semitone), while intentionally using forms (the string quartet, for example) that emphasised continuity. An alternative reaction to Romanticism was exemplified by Bohuslav **Martinů** (1890–1959), who with **Janáček** is the major Czech 20th-century composer. Working in Paris, he absorbed jazz and neo-classicism, and then, from the middle 1930s, developed a powerful personal idiom.

The overtly experimental was represented by Emil Burian (1904–59) a theatre and film director, magazine editor, and jazz-band leader as well as composer. After studying with **Foerster**, he founded the Prague theatre group 'D'. In 1927 he developed the 'voice-band' for choral recitation (speech set to music), composing works for the group, notably *May* (1936). His earliest music used Richard **Strauss** as a model, but he soon became more experimental, incorporating jazz, negro spiritual, and Dadaesque influences. In turn, this gave way to a more obviously Czech style, absorbing folk music (folk play with music

The War, 1935). In the post-war period his language became more conventional, influenced by **Martinů** and **Janáček**, notably in the fine *String Quartet No. 4* (1947).

Miloslav Kabeláč (1908–79) explored the influences of Oriental and primitive folk music, combined with Gregorian chant and elements of 12-tone composition. The hallmarks of his symphonies and a mass of choral and vocal music are conciseness and economy. His instrumental skill is exemplified in the odd combinations that his symphonies use: *No. 1* for string orchestra and percussion (1941–42), *No. 3* for organ, brass and timpani (1948–57), *No. 5 'Dramatica'* for soprano and orchestra (1960), *No. 6 'Concertante'* for clarinet and orchestra (1961–62), *No. 7* for speaker and orchestra (Old Testament texts) (1967–68), *No. 8 'Antiphonies'* for soprano, chorus, percussion and organ (1969–70). He was influential in introducing younger Czech composers to electronic music and *musique concrète*.

Czech music was seriously disrupted by the German occupation (1939–45), with some composers (notably **Martinů**) leaving, and others being imprisoned or killed, notably Pavel Haas (1899–1944), who had combined Hebraic and Moravian influences. But Czech music-making continued, often with overtones of a nationalist resistance. The establishment of communist rule in Czechoslovakia in 1949 further cut Czech composers off from European developments: composers had to adapt to the demands of socialist realism, and a younger generation (exemplified by Petr **Eben**, born 1929) emerged unaware of serial developments, and thus continued a mainstream Czech tradition. However, Czechoslovakia slackened its cultural restraint earlier than many Eastern Bloc countries, and knowledge of **Webern** and the European avant-garde filtered through in the 1960s, allowing the teaching of the principles of electronic music.

The first electronic studios opened in 1964, following French rather than German lines. New music compositional groups sprang up, such as 'Group A' in Brno, 1963, that included Citrad Kohoutek (born 1929); the Prague New Music Group, 1965, that included Marek **Kopelent** (born 1932) and Zbyněk Vostřák (1920–85); and the multi-art group Syntéza ('synthesis'). Kohoutek published a survey of modern western European musical techniques in 1962 as well as his ideas on the application of modern techniques to children's music in 1966. He developed what he calls 'project music composition', which includes the pre-planning by graph of the formal structure, dynamics, and tone-colours, before any purely musical ideas or realisations. *Memento* (1967) for wind and percussion utilised this method, which he has since increasingly applied to large-scale orchestral pieces, culminating in the three-part *Slavnosti světla* (*Festivals of Light*, 1974–75). The moments of banality in this rather quirky piece are rescued by interesting orchestral textures and bold effective colours. Vostřák is one of the few Czech composers to be directly influenced by the German avant-garde, notably **Stockhausen**, and by the ideas of **Boulez** and **Cage**. In the 1950s he concentrated on stage works in a lyrical neo-classical style, but then started using serial and 12-note techniques in the early sixties, *Zrozeni měsice* (*Moon Birth*, 1967) for chamber orchestra receiving wide attention. His interest in electronic music led to work in the Electronic Music Studio of Prague Radio from 1977.

Václav Kučera (born 1929) is a leading figure among Czech composers involved in electronic music and *musique concrète*. Whereas most electronic composers have followed German examples, the Czechs have been influenced by the French, and in particular the ballet works of Pierre **Henry** and his major collaborator, the choreographer Maurice Béjart. This is exemplified in Kučera's *Kinetic Ballet* (1968) – a major change from his earlier music, which had reflected the requirements of social realism. His *Obraz (Picture)* for piano and large orchestra won a prize in Geneva in 1970, and *Invariant* (1969) for bass clarinet, piano and tape was heard at the London ISCM in 1971. *Lidice*, a 'radio musical–dramatic fresco' for forces that include reporters and electronic sounds, won the Prix d'Italia in 1973 and is recommended. His recent works (for example, *Maluje Malíř* for a cappella children's choir, 1985, or the song cycle *Hořké a Jiné Pisně* [*Bitter and Other Songs*], 1987) have seemed dull in comparison.

Of the more conservative composers of this generation, Jindřich Feld (born 1925), initially influenced by **Bartók**, came to prominence with a radio opera, *Pohádka o Budulinkovi* (*A Fairytale about Budulinkovi*, 1955), followed by a children's opera *Poštáchká Pohádka* (*The Postman's Tale* 1956). The *Concerto for Chamber Orchestra* (1957) incorporated serial and 12-tone techniques, though these have subsequently been assimilated into a fairly traditional style. From the *Concerto for Orchestra* (1950) he has specialised in the

concerto form, and among his more recent works the *Harp Concerto* (1985) is particularly interesting for its integration of solo instrument and orchestra in a modern idiom, and is recommended.

The earliest compositions of Jaromir Podešva (born 1927) follow the line of **Novák** and **Janáček**, and his interest in poetry culminated in *Symphony No. 3* (1966, subtitled *Parallels to ideas by M. Kundera and B. Hrabal*). In the sixties he developed a more individual and dynamically vigorous style, with an element of introspection, progressing from a free tonality to combining tonality with 12-tone techniques. This was expressed in the *String Quartet No. 5* (1965) and in a series of symphonies starting with No. 2 (1960–61) of which the recommended *Sinfonia da Camera No. 4, Hudba Solán* (*Solan's Flute*) is an individually atmospheric and largely lyrical reflection of the composer's native Moravia, laced with gritty harmonies.

During the 1950s the music of Klement Slavický (born 1910) was influenced by Moravian folk-music, and its rhythmic subtlety and its sense of drama attracted considerable debate in Czechoslovakia. His fine *Sinfonietta No. 3* (1972) shows his expressive qualities and his use of motoric rhythms and moments of hushed lyricism. It was followed in 1984 by a fourth sinfonietta for unusual forces – soprano solo, reciter, strings, keyboard and percussion instruments. Three of the meticulously crafted works of Vladimir Sommer (1921–97) have entered the regular Czech repertoire. The first was the melodic *Violin Concerto* (1950), followed by the dramatic tragic prelude *Antigona* (1956–57) for orchestra. His best known work is *Vokální symfonie* (*Vocal Symphony*, 1957–58), setting Kafka, Dostoyevsky and Pavese. It is a dramatic, harrowing, and innovative work, effective on first acquaintance although on repetition its material is too limited for its stridency. His more recent work, such as the rather solemn and affecting *Cello Concerto* (1977) or *String Quartet No. 3* (1981), is less dramatic and more introverted. One of the most exciting piano concertos of the second half of the 20th-century is the *Piano Concerto 'Na pamět Gideona Kleina'* (*'In Memory of Gideon Klein'*, 1987) by Vojtěch Saudek, influenced by **Messiaen**, but of stunning impact in its use of virtuoso avant-garde piano techniques and in its depth of emotional expression.

Since the 1960s Czech music has fully caught up with European developments, and synthesized them with their own Czech traditions, reflected in the gramophone industry, nationalised as Supraphon (1946), which has been exemplary in issuing new music.

Czech Music Information Centre:
Ceského hudebniho fondu
Besedni 3, CS–11800
Praha 1
The Czech Republic
tel: + 420 2 573 200 08
fax: + 420 2 53 97 20

Eben Petř
born 22nd January 1929 at Žamberk
(Bohemia)

Petř Eben is one of the better-known Czech composers of his generation, and is a practising pianist (especially in chamber music) and organist as well as a composer. He initially attracted attention in 1954 with *Six Love Songs*. His first major large-scale work, *Sinfonia gregoriana* for organ and orchestra (1954), later revised as an organ concerto, initiated a life-long interest in Gregorian chant. He then concentrated on vocal music (including children's songs and folk songs, influenced by Silesian folk music), but turned to a *Piano Concerto* in 1961, which, within a conventional framework, has some powerful moments. It was followed by another large-scale work, the oratorio *Apologia Sokratus* (1961–67), based on Socrates' trial. His style is modern without being extreme, with echoes of music of earlier periods; recent works have included *Landscapes of Patmos* (1984) for organ and percussion instruments. Recordings of his work have been regularly available outside Czechoslovakia, and are worth hunting out as representative of the music of his generation of Czech composers. He was imprisoned by the Nazis, and many of his works reflect his strong religious faith; he has taught at Charles University, Prague, since 1955.

RECOMMENDED WORKS
oratorio *Apologia Sokratus* (1961–67)
String Quartet (1981)

Fišer Luboš*
born 30th September 1935 at Prague

Fišer is an interesting composer with a strong dramatic bent, even in such works as the fine, if conventional, *Sonata for solo cello*, 1985. His music shows an awareness

of the modern techniques of such composers as **Ligeti** and **Penderecki**, but is also influenced by **Janáček**'s technique of building up by short, pithy phrases. His violin sonata *Ruce* (*Hands*, 1961) quickly entered the Czech repertoire, and his *Fifteen Prints after Dürer's 'Apocalypse'* (1965) brought international recognition; built on a six-note theme, it is constructed in fifteen related episodes, and has a rugged strength paired with a feeling of isolation or loneliness. It formed the first of a triptych, of which the second part, *Caprichos*, is inspired by Goya. The final section, *Requiem* (1968) is a powerful work contrasting massed sound and clusters against simple, ritual textures. His choral interests continued in a large cantata, *Ná ek nad zkazow mesta Ur*, (*Lament for the destruction of the City of Ur*, 1969). Fišer is also noted in Czechoslovakia for his piano sonatas and the *Sonata* for piano, mixed chorus, and orchestra (1984).

RECOMMENDED WORKS
Fifteen Prints after Dürer's 'Apocalypse' (1965) for orchestra
Requiem (1968)

Foerster Josef Bohuslav**
born 30th December 1859 at Detenice
died 29th May 1951 at Novy Vestec

Foerster has been overshadowed by his major contemporaries, but his music is very much in the Czech Romantic tradition and is worth discovering, especially his masterpiece, the opera *Eva*. His early work (pre–1897) is unexceptional, but the large corpus of music that followed (influenced by periods spent in Hamburg and Vienna, and the friendship of such composers as **Mahler**) combine a lyrical nationalism with late Romantic ideas. His handling of material and orchestration is always thoroughly professional and sometimes inspired, displaying an assured command of large or massed forces and often delighting in polyphony. His style remained essentially consistent during a long working life, though it takes on a new dimension in *Eva*, partly through the influence of Moravian folk music. The theme of the power of love as a spiritual motivator appears throughout his work, often expressed with an elegiac lyricism.

In the Czech Republic his large number of choral works and songs for both professional and amateur singers have been widely influential. His lyricism is exemplified in the slow and lovely introduction, viola and harp prominent, to the cantata *Máj* (*May*, 1936) for baritone, reciter, male chorus and orchestra. A setting of a section of the best-known poem by the most famous of Czech Romantic poets, Karel Mácha (1810–36), it is the farewell of the condemned outlaw 'the King of the Forest', who had become an outlaw after killing his lover's seducer only to discover that he had committed patricide. The cantata is dramatic, warmly passionate, and combines a nationalist ecstasy with haunting sadness, especially in the farewell baritone solo. The *Mass* (1923) pre-dates Janáček's better-known use of the ancient Moravian language, Glagolitic.

Outside the former Czechoslovakia Foerster is more often encountered in orchestral works. Of these, the finest is the *Symphony No. 4 'Easter'* (1904–05). Its big, brazen opening movement, filled with Romantic tragedy, Czech lyricism, and a tumultuous joy, describes the feelings elicited in an adult by Easter and has a Mahlerian grandeur. The second movement (Easter through the eyes of a child) has a lithe and very Czech sense of joyous dance, a natural continuation of the kind of orchestral painting at which Smetana excelled. The slow movement ('in praise of solitude and magic') is expansive, with a sense of joyous triumph; the large and sometimes Mahlerian final movement, which swiftly and powerfully changes moods, is suddenly and unexpectedly illuminated by a solo organ playing a Czech chorale ('On the third day was the Lord arisen') before the final orchestral paean of praise. This work should be on the list of anyone exploring major 20th-century symphonies.

The other orchestral work most often encountered is the symphonic suite *Cyrano de Bergerac* (1903). Divided into five movements describing various events in the play, it is sometimes grand, often contemplative, and full of Czech colour and clarity. The *Violin Concerto No. 2* (1918–26) is also attractive, and unusual for a Romantic concerto in having more in common with the form of the tone poem than with a virtuoso work.

Of Foerster's six operas, the third, *Jessica*, is based on Shakespeare's *Merchant of Venice*, but the most important, and the only one to have remained in the repertoire, is *Eva* (1895–97). In contrast to earlier 'folk' operas (such as those of Smetana) its deeply drawn characters are treated entirely from within. It predates Janáček's *Jenůfa*, usually considered the earliest opera to employ such natural portrayal. It provides a musical link between Smetana and Janáček, and the similarities with the latter are considerable. The libretto is based on a play by Gabriela Preissová (as is *Jenůfa*), but whereas Janáček retained the prose and the flow of speech, Foerster rewrote the prose of the stage drama into poetry, toning down the dialect. The story is of a poor young woman, Eva, in love with a young man, Mánek, whose mother (who holds the inheritance of the family farm) does not think Eva is good enough for her son. Eva accepts the love of another admirer, the furrier Samko, and in Act II has had a baby by him that has died. She is however still in love with the now married Mánek, and he with her; they decide to leave together. In Act II they have moved away from the village and are living together beside the Danube, unmarried but happy except for Eva's doubts and premonitions, when Mánek's mother arrives to tell them that his petition for divorce has been refused by the village council. Mánek must return, and Eva throws herself into the river Danube in despair.

The core of the opera is the internal tension of the three main characters: Eva's constant turmoil, her shame over her unmarried state, and despair over her dead baby; Samko's infatuated love and eventual frustration at his sharing a life with a woman who does not love him; and Mánek's inability to take decisive action against his mother. These are strongly drawn in both text and music, with a free flow of action and interaction only occasionally broken for a more extended aria. Eva's final song of despair before she commits suicide is one of the finest passages in Czech opera. The magnificent ending must surely have influenced the ending of *Jenůfa*, and although *Eva* is not of the same quality as *Jenůfa*, it is a most convincing opera that deserves to be better known.

Foerster was an accomplished visual artist and music critic, and worked as a teacher and critic in Hamburg (1893–1902) and in Vienna (1902–18) before becoming professor and then director (1922) at the Prague Conservatory.

RECOMMENDED WORKS
 opera *Eva* (1895–97)
 cantata *May* (1935)
 Symphony No. 4 *Easter* (1904–05)

Hába Alois**

born 21st June 1893 at Vizovice
died 18th November 1973 at Prague

Alois Hába is one of those figures whose place in the history of music is assured, but whose own innovations have never captured the public imagination. After an early interest in folk music (his father was a Moravian folk musician), he studied with **Novák**, and then in Vienna and Berlin with **Schreker**, whose ideas greatly influenced him, and through whom he learnt of **Schoenberg**'s harmonic developments.

His early works, such as the *Symphonic Fantasy for Piano and Orchestra*, explored atonality, but also athematicism (the lack of developed or repeated themes) which became characteristic of his work. For Hába the new musical ideas were associated with the philosophy of the theosophist Rudolf Steiner (1861–1925), whose concept of 'anthroposophy' sought (through cognitive development) to return people to the spiritual realities from which they had become divorced. This influence culminated in the symphonic fantasy *Cesta Života* (*The Path of Life*, 1933) and in the still-unperformed anthroposophist opera *New Earth*. Hába saw thematic development and repetition as a legacy of primitivistic instincts that needed to be overthrown for full personal development.

At the same time, Hába continued to explore Moravian and Slovak folk music, not for their melodies and harmonic progressions, but for their use of microtones. Whereas for **Schoenberg** the natural development from atonality was the 12-tone system, Hába decided to integrate the use of such microtones in his own music as intervals of equal importance to more usual intervals, and not (as so often in Moravian folk music) as inflections or decorations to the main melodic line. This was developed in the quarter-tone *String Quartet No. 2* (1921) and *String Quartet No. 3* (1922), and then in the orchestral *Symphonic Music for Orchestra* (1922) and the *Choral Suite on Onomatopoeic Folk Texts* (1923). The culmination of this period was the quarter-tone opera *Matka* (*The Mother*, 1929–30) and the sixth-tone opera *Thy Kingdom Come* (1938–42). *Matka* is perhaps Hába's major work, and would be interesting even without the athematic progression and the use of quarter-tones. These create strange colours in the orchestral opening, but the ear becomes quickly accustomed to their use through a rising quarter-tone phrase or row in the strings, which returns from time to time and is eventually given in a full scale. The story, in ten scenes, is of the realities of farming life, influenced by Hába's own childhood experiences. It concerns the rebuilding of a family after the death of the farmer's wife through overwork, and his remarriage to the mother of the title. The opera has an almost Expressionist intensity, enhanced by the use of quarter-tones, as are the colours to match the darker sides of a farming life. It is the most effective of his quarter-tone works.

In the 1930s Hába, while continuing to utilise microtones, also started to use elements of 12-tone techniques in such works as the *Toccata quasi una fantasia* (1931) for piano, and *Cesta života* (*The Path of Life*, 1933) for orchestra. This symphonic fantasy is in one movement, divided into seven sections; the 12-tone influence is here mainly in the melodic progression, spinning a flow of lines of non-repeated notes, where rhythmic vitality and repetition, reminiscent of the neo-classical **Stravinsky**, propels the piece. The effect is angular and unsettled, as if traditional elements had been distorted. The athematic *Nonet No. 1* (1931) also uses 12-tone melodies and again is in one movement, divided into four sections corresponding to a classical four-movement structure, the pattern of the first corresponding (by use of a new theme at each traditional point) to the progression of sonata form. It is a lithe and engaging work alternating moments of dissonant harmonic tension with harmonic repose. The one-movement *Nonet No. 2*, written in the same year, uses 7-tone rows in a similar cast, which gives it an attractive Oriental hue (Hába was aware of the affinities of his musical interests and philosophies with those of the East). In the 1950s Hába continued alternating 12-tone works (such as *Violin Concerto*, 1954, and *Viola Concerto*, 1956) with microtonal works, but also introduced more orthodox folk music elements in such works as the *Wallachian Suite* (1952) for orchestra. The jaunty, jazzy and improvisatory *Suite for Solo Bass Clarinet* shows a similar return to simpler idioms, while remaining athematic.

The bulk of Hába's microtonal ideas are to be found in the piano music and the string quartets. The microtonal piano music is virtually impossible to encounter, as special pianos are required to play it: Hába had three quarter-tone pianos especially constructed, as well as other instruments (brass, guitar, harmonium) to play microintervals. Of his sixteen string quartets, some use 12-note rows (*Nos, 7, 8, 9,*

13), some are in quarter-tones (*2*, *3*, *13*), another in sixth-tone (*11*), while *No. 16* is in fifth-tones. The works in conventional intervals present few problems, and are interesting for their athematic construction as well as their rugged, expressive qualities. The middle sections of the programmatic *String Quartet No. 13* '*Astronautic*' (1961), for example, draw continuously changing melodic material from a 12-tone row, and the quartet draws on both tonal and atonal harmonic ideas. With the microtonal works problems do occur for listeners, as well as players. The danger is that the microtones can be perceived as poor intonation, especially as the general layout and rhythmic processes are relatively conventional. The opening movement of the *String Quartet No. 11* (1958) in sixth-tones illustrates these dangers. But in the fine *String Quartet No. 12* (1960) in quarter-tones, written in part as a reaction to the international tension that led to the Cuban missile crisis, such criticisms are less valid, as the microtones take on cluster-like effects in the opening, and moments of repose are created by moving away from the quarter-tones.

Hába taught his microtonal and athematic principles at the Prague Conservatory (1924–45) and the Prague Academy of Music (1945–51), and headed the '5th of May' Opera company (1945–48). He wrote widely on his musical ideas.

RECOMMENDED WORKS
> opera *Matka* (*The Mother*, 1929–30)
> *Nonet No. 2* (1931)
> String Quartet No. 12 (1960)
> String Quartet No. 13 (1961)

Hanuš Jan
born 2nd May 1915 at Prague

Jan Hanuš has been active in Czech music as an organiser (notably in the Prague Spring Festival) and as a musicologist (including work on the critical edition of Dvořák's music), as well as a composer, and after the collapse of communism he became head of the Czech League of Composers. His music has a direct appeal in an undemanding Czech idiom, full of light, colour and Czech melodic progressions in the tradition of Smetana and Dvořák. His harmonies are only occasionally touched by dissonance, though he has more recently used modern devices in such works as *Poseltvi* (*The Message*, 1969), for baritone, chorus, two prepared pianos, electric guitar, percussion and tape, and

the *Concertino*, 1972, for two percussionists and tape.

He is noted as a symphonist: the *Symphony No. 6* (1979) introduces unusual instruments (including the flexitone and electric bass guitar) and sonorities within a traditional framework. He recently reconstructed the lost choral finale of the *Symphony No. 1* (1943) from memory. The *Symphony No. 2* (1950–51), written during a period when Hanuš was inspired by St Francis of Assisi, has an infectious springtime bounce and a Czech lyricism within a conventional format. The lively and attractive scherzo employs a Bohemian folk dance and has the vigour of similar works by **Martinů**. Among his larger-scale works is a major oratorio, *Ecce Homo* (1977–80) for soloists, reciter, choruses, orchestra, organ and electronics, and an admired *Glagolitic Mass* (1986). He has a special interest in music for children, exemplified in the cantata *The Czech Year*, 1949–52.

RECOMMENDED WORK
> Symphony No. 2 (1950–51)

Janáček Leoš•••
born 3rd July 1854 at Hukvaldy
died 12th August 1928 at Moravská Ostrava

Leoš Janáček was a composer of genius, whose operas, alongside those of **Strauss**, **Britten** and **Berg**, form the basis of the 20th-century operatic repertoire. His achievement is all the more remarkable because the music he composed before reaching the age of forty is relatively conventional, if well constructed, and most of his finest and most individual works were written after he was sixty. Those earlier works were initially in a Romantic style, and then from 1888 came under the influence of Moravian folk music, which he had begun to collect. Heralded by the cantata *Amarus* (1897), the opera *Jenůfa* (1894–1903, later revised) introduced his personal voice, and after 1918 it became internationally recognised as a masterpiece, boosting Janáček's own compositional confidence.

The key elements of Janáček's mature style are tension, a sense of yearning, and a constant feeling of a momentum that is on the edge of unbalance. Melodic lines are built up from short units, often shifted out of step with their accompaniment to create a tension in the flow. The harmonies increasingly omit key signatures, but while including whole-tone passages (an influence from the French Impressionists) and sometimes scales drawn from folk music, are founded on a tonal base. The tension and edge that his harmonic colours so often invoke are created first by the characteristic melodic progression of 4ths, 5ths and 2nds, and second by pitting blocks of contrasting harmonies against each other, sometimes with dissonant elements.

Janáček's structures and rhythms follow a similar pattern. He rarely used traditional forms or motifs, and there is little use of counterpoint. Instead, structural tension is created by the contrast of disparate ideas placed against the main blocks, and by the use of ostinati rhythms: structural progression is achieved by changes in these contrasts. Repeats of melodic ideas are often accompanied by changes of rhythm, which themselves are often mirrored (repeated back to front – a technique found in Moravian folk music). The result is a constant shifting of the flow of similar material to give an urgent sense of progression.

His orchestration supports this approach. Blocks of the orchestra regularly overlay each other without merging. Further expressiveness is created by the use of instruments in their extreme registers. His operas reject the traditional aria, preferring dramatic progression through a flowing vocal line (foreshadowed in Czechoslovakia by **Foerster's** *Eva*, first performed in 1899). This developed into an avoidance of overlapping voices, and the substitution of a realistic concentration on a single voice at any given moment, sometimes contrasting with an off-stage chorus. Most revolutionary is the use of what Janáček called 'speech melody': the irregular patterns and musical structures of everyday speech. This led to the setting of prose, as opposed to the poetry that was then standard for libretti. Another characteristic that creates tension is his habit of ending vocal phrases on a weak rather than an emphatic beat. All his operas are relatively short, a reflection of the tautness and tension of much of the material. An anomaly in some of his operas is the presence of minor inconsistencies and contradictions in the plots, reflecting the concentration on the psychological and social comment rather than story-line. A personal stylistic device is the quick repetition of a crucial phrase (something Janáček employed in his own speech).

Janáček's exploration of Moravian folk music was reflected in a series of collections of arrangements of folk songs in the late 1880s and early 1890s, and emerged in an orchestral suite, the lively *Lachian*

Dances (1889) for orchestra with organ. It is heavily influenced by Dvořák's *Slavonic Dances*, and not as accomplished. Some of the dances were then incorporated into the ballet *Rákocz Rákoczy* (1891).

Janáček's first opera, *Šárka* (1887–88), was based on a play by Julius Zeyer. The story is a Czech myth with Wagnerian overtones, and the failings of the libretto, as well as Janáček's inexperience, have relegated it to being completely overshadowed by the opera of the same title and subject by Zdeněk Fibich (1850–1900). His second, *The Beginning of a Romance* (1891), is also marred by its libretto, based on a short story by Gabriela Preissová. The folkish tale tells of the love of a shepherd's daughter and a Count's son, and is very much a 19th-century treatment, peasants viewed from the city, complete with the moral that people should marry their equals. Fortunately the best of the themes found their way into the *Suite for Orchestra* (1891), a four-movement work that is a good introduction to Janáček's earlier style. The third movement uses an extended version of one of the *Lachian Dances*. The major transitional work is the cantata *Amarus* (1897, revised 1901, 1906) for soprano, tenor, baritone, chorus and orchestra, which tells of Amarus, forced as a young man to become a monk, who longs for a life beyond his vows. It lacks the rhythmic pungency and rapid juxtaposition of orchestral blocks that makes his mature style so idiomatic, but the melodic lines anticipate his later work.

Nonetheless, the development of an original idiom in his next opera, *Jenůfa* (1894–1903), is remarkable. It was inspired by a folk play by Gabriela Preissová which presented its characters as real people, whose concerns and psychology involve us regardless of their origins, as opposed to the then-usual treatment of villagers as 'objects' pursuing a colourful, distant lifestyle. Central to *Jenůfa* is the tension between social norms and the individual desire for self-fulfilment; here, and in other Janáček operas, the focus is on the constraints placed on women. Jenufa is in love with a young mill-owner, Števa, whose step-brother Laca is in love with her. Jenůfa's step-mother, the Kostelnička (a nickname reflecting her position as churchwarden) forbids her to marry Števa without a year's engagement, unaware that Jenůfa is already pregnant by him. In Act II Jenufa has had her baby, and is being kept hidden away for shame by Kostelnička. Števa is told, in the hopes he will marry her, but is now not interested and anyway already engaged. Kostelnička tries to pursuade Laca to take Jenůfa, but he is put off by the fact of the baby. In a fit of madness, Kostelnička drowns the baby, telling Jenůfa it had died while she was bedridden with fever. Jenůfa accepts Laca, and Act III opens with the impending wedding. But at that moment the body of the baby is dragged from the river, and Laca has to save Jenůfa, who admits the baby is hers, from the fury of the villagers. Kostelnička announces her guilt, and at this moment Janáček builds the orchestra into an urgent, emphatic climax, and it seems clear that the curtain is about to fall. Instead, to delicate orchestral strains, completely changing the focus in one of the most moving moments in opera, Laca turns to Jenůfa and offers her his hand in spite of all that has happened. Jenůfa has learnt the true meaning of love, and the opera closes to music of magnificent warmth and fulfilment.

Janáček's next opera *Osud* (*Fate*, 1903–06) is an oddity, being the rather bizarre story of an opera writer and his unfinishable opera, and was closely connected with actual events and people in Prague. Its verse libretto destroys its credibility as a stage work, in spite of later attempts to improve it, though the music shows many of Janáček's hallmarks. Janáček then turned to works that showed a growing political and social awareness. The rather unpianistic piano sonata *Sonata 1.X.1905 'On the Streets'* (1905) reflects the violent suppression of a Czech nationalist demonstration (the cycle *On an Overgrown Path*, 1901–11, is a much more effective piano work). Janáček then wrote three short choral works of importance inside Czechoslovakia, but little known outside, all based on nationalist poems by Petr Bezruč attacking a thinly disguised Archduke Ferdinand. They are for unaccompanied male voice choir, an idiom at which Janáček excelled, with his sense of rhythm and sonorous chordal polyphony. *Kantor Halfar* (*Schoolmaster Halfar*, 1906, revised 1917) tells the (apparently true) story of an assistant schoolmaster whose use of Czech (as opposed to the required Polish) prevents him finding a full teaching position, and leads to his losing his fiancée and committing suicide. *Maryčka Magdónova* (1906, second version 1907) is about an orphaned woman who steals wood from the Baron's estates to keep warm, but is caught, and to avoid the shame of having to face the aristocracy, she throws herself into the river and is

drowned. *Sedmdesát tisíc* (*Seventy Thousand*, 1909, rewritten 1913) is a revolutionary work, and perhaps the most effective of the three: the 70,000 are those left who have not abandoned their native language, but will have to if they are to survive. The text is direct and heavily spiced with irony, with music of hope and protest overlaid with a resignation as tenors at the top of their range add the anguished words 'seventy thousand'.

Janáček's next opera might have been expected to adopt a similar socially potent subject, but instead he turned to a satirical work in which the target is a certain type of his fellow countryman. *The Excursions of Mr Brouček to the Moon and the Fifteenth Century* (1908–17, usually known simply as *The Excursions of Mr Brouček*) has the element of fantasy and unusual mental and physical environments that were to be a feature of the last three operas. The story is based on a novel by Svatoplukčech, and its complicated libretto history ended up with a work in two parts, with parallel subsidiary characters played by the same singers in each half, who are also contemporary characters in the tavern of the opening and close. The central character is a type unusual in opera, but no less cogent for that: an ordinary, self-satisfied, comfortably middle-class philistine. In the first part, Brouček, who has fallen into an inebriated sleep, is transported to the moon, where his materialistic outlook and stodgy mental views are the derision of the highly refined moon people. In the second half, dramatically more effective, Brouček is dropped into the middle of the Hussite rebellion, and finds himself expected to fight. The opera has been overshadowed by Janáček's other major works, in part because of the oddity of the story, but its neglect is not justified. The delightful music is wide ranging, from hard-hitting satire to the glory of the Hussite chorale, and the combination of fantasy and satire is dramatically effective. In particular, Mr Brouček emerges as a character whom we can condemn, but for whom at the same time we can have a sneaking sympathy and affection.

Janáček turned to another patriotic subject in the tone poem *Taras Bulba* (1915–18) for orchestra with organ. In part inspired by Czech nationalism, the grim story (based on Gogol) is of a Ukrainian Slav hero who loses his two sons, one by his own hand, in a siege of a Polish-held town, and is himself captured, nailed to a tree, and burnt. Divided into three movements (the death of each son and the death of the father), the score is Janáček in his most pungent Czech idiom, graphically vivid, with tender love themes, raucously martial brass, dissonant blocks, interjectory or ostinati percussion, and gloriously uplifting.

The end of World War I, when the composer was already 68, marks the beginning of Janáček's final intense and luminous compositional phase, in part inspired by his love for a much younger married woman, Kamila Stösslova, which lasted from 1917 until his death. His love was not requited (though a close friendship developed), but this does not seem to have been crucial: it was the intensity of loving that generated much of the following music. The first musical outcome was one of the finest of 20th-century song-cycles, *The Diary of One Who Disappeared* (1917–19) for tenor, contralto, three off-stage women's voices and piano. The twenty-two poems that form the diary were ostensibly by an industrious farmer, and were discovered after his disappearance; the actual authorship has never been conclusively determined. They tell of the infatuation of a farmer for a gypsy, his torment in his desire, her seduction of him, and (in a poem consisting just of punctuation) their consummation. He is torn further away from his farmer's life by his continuing desire, and when she bears his child, he leaves, giving himself up to his fate. Janáček's treatment, especially with the extra voices, makes it a kind of compressed opera for the concert platform, and he provided instructions for darkened lighting and the entry of the alto onto the stage only in the seventh song. The tone is immediately set by the tense opening, describing the meeting, encapsulating the suppressed energy and physical excitement. The vocal lines are free, following the natural lines of the verse, impassioned, often full of pent-up agitation; the piano writing is mostly light and delicate in texture, sometimes word-painting (fireflies, the wind in the cornfield, the cock's crow), but usually following or anticipating the vocal line. The wordless thirteenth poem is set for piano alone, starting lightly, but becoming more earthy, disjointed, and urgent in describing the consummation.

The opera *Katya Kabanova* (1920–21) is based on the powerful play *The Storm* by the Russian A.N. Ovstrovsky, set on the banks of the Volga, and tells of a woman (Katya) married to a weak man dominated by his mother. Suffocated by this situation, Katya falls in love with the cultured Boris,

himself plagued by his drunkard uncle. However, she refuses to be unfaithful, in spite of the encouragement of a friend who is herself having an affair. When her husband goes on a business journey, and resists her pleas to take her along with him, she succumbs to her passion for Boris. But she is stricken by her conscience, confesses, and commits suicide in the Volga. Janáček's preoccupation is with the tension between personal and social requirements and the ambivalent tug between a hollow duty and desire. Again, the plot is relatively simple, and the focus is on the psychology of the characters. Janáček's score is the most warm and lyrical of his operas, with a flow of glowing colours, especially in the purely orchestral writing. This is combined with an intensity of vocal writing and characterisation: Katya is vividly portrayed, making this one of the great singing–acting roles. The intoxication of love and the counter-pull of a kind of spiritual duty suffuse the work, and time and time again the orchestral writing caresses and inflames the passionate vocal lines, and when they become so overwrought as to be on the verge of breakdown, the orchestra lets them sink back into the warmer flow. Knife-edged domestic tensions have rarely been so well caught as in Act I and the meeting of the lovers in Act III has something of the quality of the end of *Jenůfa* with a sensuous edge.

Janáček then turned to a combination of pure fantasy and down-to-earth symbolic reality in one of the most magical of all operas, a work whose apparent simplicity appeals to children, and whose psychological complexity captivates adults. The *Liška Bystrouška* (*Cunning Little Vixen*, 1922–24) is Janáček's tribute to Nature as the generator of all things, including human emotions. The libretto originated in a series of drawings by Stanislav Lolek in a newspaper, to which Rudolf Těsnohlídek wrote prose stories in the dialect of the local lumberjacks. The central character is the vixen of the title, living in a world filled by butterflies, crows, a dragonfly, a mosquito, a frog, a badger, a forester, a gamekeeper and his dog, and other creatures of the woods, all portrayed on stage. In Act I this magic scenario is set, and the vixen as a cub is caught by the gamekeeper as a pet for his children. The lonely vixen tries to escape but is tied up and then teased by the farmyard animals, especially the cock and hens. She kills the cock, and manages to escape into the forest. In Act II the vixen tries to find a home in the badger's set. The gamekeeper shoots at the vixen, missing, and the vixen meets a fox, who tries to seduce her. He soon succeeds, and the woodpecker announces their forthcoming marriage. In Act III the vixen and her new cubs evade a trap set for her, but she is shot by the gamekeeper and killed. The humans in the inn discuss these events, and in the last scene the gamekeeper, seeing a little fox cub, muses on the miracle of rebirth. Again, the theme of a female caught in an inappropriate social situation (the farmyard) is treated, but here with the celebration of her freedom, even if it will lead to her eventual death, and of the continuing cycle of that freedom (the fox-cubs). The animals are closely intertwined with the humans (the badger and the schoolmaster are sung by the same singer), and act as psychological archetypes as well as having their own sharply drawn characters. Musically, it is the opera in which Janáček most suffused into his idiom the Czech qualities of light and clarity, and the happiness of sunlight and nature pervade the score, the rhythms often gently lilting, the occasional moments of folk song more direct than was his custom. It is also full of gentle humour and satire, from the gaggle of crows raucously commenting on events to the bantering and tipsy humans. *The Cunning Little Vixen* is a magical experience not to be missed.

Janáček's next opera had another, but much more rigorous, sense of the fantastic. *Věc Makropulos* (*The Makropulos Case*, 1923–25) is based on the play by Karel Čapek. It revolves around an inheritance litigation, Prus v. Gregor, which, if it turns out against the Gregor family, will leave Albert Gregor with no choice but to commit suicide over his debts, as his father had done. The verdict depends on a will lost a century ago, and a young and beautiful woman, Emila Marty, says she knows where it is; she wants some old Greek papers that were with it. The will is found, but mentions an illegitimate son, and Emila says she will prove that this is Albert's father. In Act II, the Prus claimant, who, like Albert, has fallen under Emila's spell, finds out the surname of the illegitimate son was Makropulos, and his mother Emila Makropulos. He also has the Greek papers, which he will give to Emila in return for her giving herself to him. In the beginning of Act II she has done so, icecoldly, and the document identifying Ferdinand is discovered to be a fraud. Emila's luggage is ransacked and found to be full of letters addressed to various women with

the initials E.M. Emila then declares the truth – she was born in Crete in 1575, and has been kept alive and young by a potion developed by her father. She was Emila Makropulos, the mother of Ferdinand. She declares that such a long life has no meaning, and that she does not want the Greek papers with the formula; neither does anyone else, and they are burnt, as Emila rapidly ages and dies, at peace at last.

This complex story provided the framework for Janáček's most acid opera, exposing the petty meanness and avarice of the lesser characters, and the spiritual bankruptcy and cynicism of Emila. The central theme is the sufficiency and wonder of life as it is; it also allowed Janáček to produce a portrait of a different kind of woman, more sophisticated, eventually world-weary, but in the end suffering a similar tension between natural fulfilment and the constraints of circumstance to his earlier portrayals. The ending, as Emila reveals her secret, stunning and subduing her listeners, and then, changing from a young and beautiful woman into an ancient and withered old lady, is of compelling force, a kind of cathartic redemption, and the whole of the rest of the opera necessarily leads to this point.

Janáček's final opera, *From the House of the Dead* (1927–28), has as its material one of the most unlikely of operatic sources, Dostoyevsky's novel of a prison camp. Yet Janáček's treatment turns it into one of the most harrowing and yet most uplifting of all operas. There are no concessions to the audience – this is not an opera to see for its story or melodies. Instead, it is a kind of extended musical portrait of the camp, in which prisoners recount their life experiences and undertake camp tasks. Throughout is the spectre of the containment of freedom and man's inhumanity to man. The music is not often lyrical and never sentimental, yet portrays the power and wonder of life even in the most adverse circumstances. *From the House of the Dead*, with great prescience, stands as the opera which condemns so much of the worst of the 20th century, while still celebrating hope and the power of the spirit.

The extraordinary vitality of Janáček's last two decades also produced four non-operatic masterpieces. The *Sinfonietta* (1925–26) is Janáček's finest orchestral work, that developed from a set of fanfares into a full-length work ecstatically celebrating the force of life. The first movement is a series of fanfares that fold over each other, theme engendering theme, using nine trumpets, two tenor tubas, two bass trumpets and two pairs of timpani. The lighter second movement involves the whole orchestra, while the third is nocturnal, spinning short woodwind figures in a description of night around the old monastery at Brno. The fourth acts as a scherzo, while the final movement returns to the fanfares of the opening. Throughout, Janáček's technique of short phrases, switching around the orchestra, is used to pump power, momentum and excitement into the flow in a culmination of his orchestral technique.

Equally remarkable are Janáček's string quartets. As might be expected from a composer with such a dramatic instinct, both are programmatic in inspiration and passionate and expressive. The *String Quartet No. 1* (1923) – an earlier quartet of 1880 had been lost – was inspired by Tolstoy's story, *The Kreutzer Sonata*, itself inspired by Beethoven's violin sonata (echoed in the slow movement of the quartet). The quartet had an intended message, a protest against men's despotic attitude to women. It contrasts dark colours and tense writing with the dance, moments of aggression with passages of tenderness. The *String Quartet No. 2 'Intimate Letters'* (1928) is Janáček's most personal expression of the experience of love, with passion and unerring musical logic encapsulating the emotions from anguish and nostalgia to great beauty. It is one of the finest quartets ever written, combining purely abstract music with the most intense expression.

The *Glagolitic Mass* (*Glagolská mše*, 1926) for four soloists, chorus, orchestra and organ, is a setting of the Mass in Old Slavonic, the five parts divided by orchestral interludes with a fanfare introduction and, to end, an Intrada preceded by an organ postludum. This highly charged work is the choral equivalent of the *Sinfonietta*, in its general stylistic features, its celebration of the Slav spirit, and especially in its atmosphere of fervent uplift; Janáček seems to be exalting not so much a specific religion as the joy of created nature itself. The ending is preceded by a thundering organ solo with furious pedal work, before orchestra and organ join forces in the final Intrada, whose tremendous excitement seems to renew the promise of the cycle of birth.

Mention should also be made of the light-hearted and attractive wind sextet *Mládí* (*Youth*, 1924) and the equally happy *Concertino* (1925) for piano and six instruments, inspired by little incidents in the lives of the animals in Janáček's garden.

Janáček's final work, *Danube* (1928) for orchestra, left incomplete and usually heard in the version by Osvald Chlubna, will be of interest to those who already know his work.

Some of the editions of Janáček's operas are problematic, the personal idiom of *Jenůfa* for example, being smoothed out in some versions, and changes being made to the ending of *From the House of the Dead*. The original versions promoted by the conductor Sir Charles Mackerras are to be preferred.

Janáček conducted the Brno Philharmonic Orchestra, and was connected with the Brno Organ school (1881–1920), which he helped found. He was not an influential teacher; of all the composers in this *Guide*, his very personal idiom is perhaps the least imitable.

RECOMMENDED WORKS
Seventy Thousand (1909) for male voice chorus
Concertino (1925) for piano and six instruments
song-cycle *The Diary of One Who Disappeared* (1917–19)
opera *The Excursions of Mr Brouček* (1908–17)
opera *From the House of the Dead* (1927–28)
Glagolitic Mass (1926) for soloists, chorus, orchestra and organ
opera *Jenůfa* (1894–1903)
opera *Katya Kabanova* (1919–21)
String Quartet No. 1 *Kreutzer Sonata* (1923)
String Quartet No. 2 *Intimate Letters* (1928)
Suite for Orchestra (1891)
Taras Bulba (1915–18) for orchestra
wind sextet *Youth* (1924)

BIBLIOGRAPHY
M. Brod, *Leoš Janáček, His Life and Works*, Prague, 1924 (Vienna, 1956)
E. Chisholm, *The Operas of Leoš Janáček*, London, 1971
H. Hollander, *Janáček, His Life and Works*, London, 1963
J. Vogel, *Leoš Janáček*, London, 1962

Jirášek Ivo*
born 16th July, 1920 at Prague

Jirášek is known in Czechoslovakia for his operas (he conducted opera at Opava, 1946–55) and for his vocal works. In the 1960s he concentrated on works for chamber-sized forces (*Four Studies* for string quartet, 1963–66; *Music for Soprano, Flute and Harp*, 1967). His *Stabat Mater* (1968) is a powerful combination of modern and ancient styles and aleatoric devices. It was followed by another major large-scale work, the *Symphony 'Mother Hope'*, 1973–74, since revised to exclude the vocal part), a striking and urgent work in a mainstream European idiom. The opening adagio is brutal, uneasy and motoric, contrasted by a thoughtful lento that breaks out into a turbulent, aggressive climax in the middle of the movement before closing in a lyrical, mysterious atmosphere. The powerful third movement opens with a march handed around the orchestra, moves through a contrasting trio, reestablishes the mood of brutal aggression, before ending with a very beautiful and mysterious atmosphere of slow rising woodwind phrases against held strings. The finale only partially resolves this turbulence, and the symphony, if uneven, is well worth investigating.

The *Concertino for Harpsichord and Eleven Strings* (1987) has a similar ruggedness and rhythmic energy, together with nostalgic string writing, a satirical, slightly grotesque middle movement, and a rather quirky last movement. Jirásek has also produced a number of humorous and ironic works, such as *Hudba k odpoledni kávě* (*Music for Afternoon Coffee*, 1972) for four clarinets. More recently he has concentrated on stage works.

RECOMMENDED WORKS
   *Concertino for Harpsichord and
      Eleven Strings* (1987)
   Stabat Mater (1968)
   Symphony *Mother Hope* (1973–74)

Kalabis Viktor*
born 27th February 1923 at Cerveny Kostelec

Viktor Kalabis's style has evolved from the mainstream evolutionary line influenced by **Bartók** and **Stravinsky** towards the use of some serial features, in pieces to which he has brought a tough and rigorous intellect. This is exemplified in the impressive *Violin Concerto No. 1* (1958), whose explosive orchestral opening is immediately countered by a flowing lyrical solo violin line, as if the two were in debate, the orchestra angry, the solo line a more considered and beautiful appraisal, mollifying the orchestra. The very beautiful, sometimes anguished, slow movement reconciles some of that orchestral anger, and

if the finale is not as inspired, it makes an interesting work for those exploring the violin concerto beyond the usual repertoire. It was followed by a second violin concerto in 1978.

Kalabis's relatively small output has concentrated on symphonic and chamber music, the former including nine concertos (among the most recent being for piano and chamber ensemble, 1987). The *Concerto for Orchestra* (1966), with its explosive opening, a slow movement that starts in a lyrical vein but turns into an angry march, a sometimes perky, sometimes aggressive third movement, and emphatic finale that leads to a quiet close and a final moment of orchestral outburst, is one of his better-known works, strong in technique and orchestral effect, but short on memorable invention. The *Symphony No. 2 'Sinfonia Pacis'* of 1960 was widely heard outside Czechoslovakia, while the fine *Symphony No. 4* (1972–73) has the unusual shape of two movements. The first, in a loose rondo form, opens and closes with the strings in the mood and atmosphere of the slow movement of **Shostakovich**'s *Symphony No. 5*, but builds up inexorably to a great climax, its technique of surging forward following those of **Martinů**'s symphonies, with ostinati bass pedal figures. The balancing but more frenetic second movement has a similar sense of progression.

The chamber music has reflected an interest in the neo-Baroque, and includes a number of works that use a harpsichord (his wife is the well-known harpsichordist Zuzana Růžičková), such as the *Concerto for Harpsichord and String Instruments* (1975), and the *Sonata for Violin and Harpsichord* (1967). Harpsichord players might consider investigating the *Six Two-Part Canonic Inventions for Harpsichord* (1962).

From 1953 to 1972 Kalabis was manager of the music department of Radio Prague.

RECOMMENDED WORKS
   Violin Concerto No. 1 (1958)
   *Six Two-Part Canonic Inventions for
      Harpsichord* (1962)
   Symphony No. 4 (1972–73)

Kapr Jan*
born 12th March 1914 at Prague
died 29th April 1988

Kapr startled the Czech musical world in the 1960s by changing his style from the nationalist school to a new personal system

of composing that included serial procedures. His earliest works, *String Quartet
No. 1* (1937), *Piano Concerto No. 1* (1938),
had shown the influence of French music
and **Martinů**, but during World War II he
concentrated on folk music. His works
immediately after the war reflected the
current climate in *Song of my Native Land*
(1950) and *In the Soviet Land* (1950). His
eight symphonies, the first written in 1943,
showed a steady progression to simpler
textures and harmonic styles, so that by
the *Symphony No. 7 Krajina dětství
(Country of Childhood)* spare textures
and serial techniques combine into a moving and very accessible idiom, with a taut
and economical structure. *Symphony No.
8* (1970) includes a chorus and taped bells.
Works such as *Chiffres* (1965) and *Oscilla-
tions* (1966) attracted considerable attention among other Czech composers.

Kapr was a music critic (1946–49), a
music producer with Czech Radio
(1939–46), an editor with the publishing
house Orbis (1950–54), and a teacher. His
works have been heard quite widely outside Czechoslovakia (he won a UNESCO
prize in 1968). As a leading figure of his
generation, his music, especially that written after the middle 1960s, deserves more
widespread attention.

RECOMMENDED WORK
   Symphony No. 7 *Country of
      Childhood* (1968)

Kopelent Marek*
born 28th April 1932 at Prague

Since his discovery of the techniques of
Webern in the early 1960s, Kopelent has
been at the forefront of the Czech avant-
garde. His *String Quartet No. 3* of 1963
used serial techniques, non-periodic
rhythms, and an element of performer
choice – a far cry from Czech music of only
a few years earlier – and subsequently
gained wider attention at Stockholm in
1966. The atmospheric and effective (if not
highly individual) choral piece *Matka
(Mother)* of the following year, pitting
modern vocal textures against a solo flute
and employing 12-tone rows and performer rhythmic choice, was also heard
outside Czechoslovakia. The *String Quartet No. 4* of 1967 uses theatrical gestures,
an interest reflected in music for experimental films, radio plays, poetry recitals,
and other multi-media events.

In 1969 he received a grant from the
German Academy of Arts in West Berlin
to concentrate on his compositional activities. From 1956–71 he was editor of contemporary music for the publishing house
Supraphon, and in 1965 became director of
the ensemble Musica Viva Pragensis. He is
interesting as a Czech composer who has
decided not to encase his modern ideas in
more traditional forms. Perhaps because of
this, his music is woefully neglected in
recordings, in spite of the fact that many
pieces have been heard in Western
Europe. His recent works have been for
more conventional forces, while retaining
their modernity. They include the *Toccata*
(1978) for viola and piano, the unusual and
appealing *Concertino* (1984) for cor anglais
and chamber ensemble and the *String
Quartet No. 5*. His individual approach has
been recently exemplified in the *Agnus
Dei* for soprano and chamber ensemble,
which moves from astringent atonalism to
a moving tonal close.

RECOMMENDED WORKS
   Concertino for cor anglais and
      chamber ensemble (1984)
   Matka (Mother) for flute and chorus
      (1964)

Krejčí Isa*
born 10th July 1904 at Prague
died 6th March 1968 at Prague

Krejčí was a leading Czech neo-classicist
and a member of a group of composers
associated with **Martinů** before World War
II. Neo-classical ideas are woven together
with a lively sense of joy in the *Cessation*
for orchestra (1925), the *Symphony No. 1*
(1954–55), the opera *Pozdviženi v Efesu
(Revolt at Ephesus*, 1939–43) and in the
five string quartets. The *Symphony No. 2*
(1956–57) is an undemanding and vivacious
work that should appeal to many with its
classical elements, strong echoes of **Prokofiev** and **Shostakovich**, and deft scoring
tinged with unmistakable Czech elements.
He also absorbed influences from Czech
folk music, especially the chorales of the
Bohemian Brethren, and from ancient
classical culture (opera *Antigone* 1934;
song-cycle *Antické motivy) Ancient
Motifs*, (1936).

His influence was widely felt through his
other musical activities. He was conductor
of the Bratislava Opera (1928–32), music
director and conductor of Prague Radio
(1934–45), artistic director of Olomouc
Opera (1945–57), and conductor and dram-
aturge at the Prague National Theatre
(1957–68).

Symphony No 2 (1956–57)

Martinů Bohuslav***
born 8th December 1890 at Polička
died 28th August 1959 at Liestal,
Switzerland

If there is a 20th-century composer whose mastery has still to be discovered by a wider public, that composer is Martinů. It took forty years for the music of **Janáček** to become well known; perhaps the same fate awaits Martinů, whose compositions after the mid-1930s, if developing no startling innovations, show a uniformity of a totally individual, instantly recognisable voice.

The situation has been exacerbated by his huge output (over 400 works), by his reputation as a leading composer in Paris in the 1920s and 1930s, and by claims of his unevenness. His mature style, for all its elements of deep tragedy, is founded on the basis of expressing joy, and at times ecstatic pleasure in life and nature. His predominant tone extends the Czech tradition in a fundamentally new direction. His formal structures, founded on a mastery of counterpoint, look back to the free forms of the Baroque. All these elements have been unfashionable in the musical world of the last three decades.

Martinů was expelled from the Prague Conservatory for 'incorrigible negligence' – he was stifled by the prevailing German Romanticism – and after playing second violin in the Czech Philharmonic (1918–23) he found his milieu in Paris in 1923, studying with **Roussel**. His *String Quintet* (1927) won a Coolidge Prize in 1932, and his *String Quartet No. 2* was heard at an International Society for Contemporary Music concert in 1928. The most striking pieces of this period are influenced by jazz, such as the marvellous *Revue de Cuisine* (1927, written as a short ballet), and the instantly attractive *Concertino* for cello, wind instruments and piano (1924), important as the first of thirty-three works using the solo cello, and including musical fingerprints that are to be found throughout his output, such as the side drum and the use of a four-note rhythmic device.

Martinů continued to experiment in a number of stage works, using his particular gift for musical comedy, employing advanced dramatic techniques and surrealist subjects. At the same time, he started to incorporate Czech elements into his music in a wide variety of genres. In parallel with this appeared a number of

orchestral and concertante neo-classical works which reflected the influence of his teacher **Roussel** and looked back to Baroque forms (e.g. the *Concerto for String Quartet and Orchestra*, 1931, and the *Sinfonia Concertante* for two orchestras, 1932), with development by *ritornello* or by treatment that is episodic rather than thematic.

At the end of the Thirties, Martinů fused the neo-classical elements (notably the influence of the concerto grosso), the Czech melodic tinges, and technical devices learnt from his earlier music (especially germinal development from cells of ideas gradually extending to become the motivating impulse of the music, first tried out in the *Piano Trio No. 1 'Cinq Pièces Brèves'*, 1930) into a totally individual style, and his music took on a new authority. The *Double Concerto* for two string orchestras, piano and timpani (1938) has all the characteristics of the works that were to follow; a simplified melodic vocabulary, an intense rhythmic momentum, with 'sprung' rhythms, heightened by the germinal development of melodic ideas, and strong Moravian folk intervals. Combined with his natural lyricism is a powerful musical awareness of the tension of the times both immediately before and during World War II, most consciously in the *Polni mše* (*Field Mass*, 1939) and in *Památník Lidicem* (*Memorial to Lidice*, 1943).

Between 1940, when he fled Paris for the States via Lisbon, and 1953, he concentrated on a series of six symphonies, in which the principle of developing cells reached a culmination in the *Symphony No. 3* (1944), and in what many regard as his masterpiece, the *Symphony No. 6* (*Fantaisies symphoniques*, 1951–53), when his voice is to be heard at its most natural and spontaneous. His luminous orchestration also reached its culmination in this period, with blocks of solo instruments (especially wind) pitted against the general orchestra, octave doubling, and the use of the piano as a colour instrument. In 1945 Martinů suffered a serious accident, cracking his skull, and this affected the quality of his output in the immediately subsequent years.

After 1953, his final works show a more conscious return to the atmosphere of his Czech homeland, which after the arrival of the communist regime, he never revisited. This culminated, together with Greek colours, in the opera *The Greek Passion* (*Recké pasije*, 1956–59). From this period also come two major works with voices, looking to new sources of inspiration, *Gil-games* (*The Epic of Gilgamesh*, 1954) and *Proroctvi Izaiásovo* (*The Prophecy of Isaiah*, 1959).

These, then, are the general outlines of Martinů's development, and within these lines his works are best discussed by genre. Chief among these are the group of five symphonies, all composed between 1942 and 1946, and joined by a sixth in 1953. Although still relatively unknown, they are among the finest symphonies of the century, consistent and completely individual. In technical terms they represent, even more than those of **Shostako-vich**, a regeneration of the form, building on **Sibelius's** concept of growth from germ cells, and on the idea of progressive tonality (ending in a key different from the opening). Their sound world (the piano and often the harp prominent in the orchestration) has no parallel in the symphonic repertoire, one of the advantages of coming to the genre at the age of 52.

The *Symphony No. 1* (1942) is the most classical in construction, the principle of development by germ cell used only in the first two movements. It is largely lyrical in conception, its atmospheric opening using the Bohemian St Wenceslas chorale that recurs throughout Martinů's work and which is of Czech nationalist significance; the symphony also uses a Moravian cadence, first heard in the opera *Julietta*, that also recurs in Martinů's later work. The scherzo has an arresting syncopated lilt, and a trio without strings; there is a sense of Mediterranean colour in the slow movement, and of folk song in the finale. The *Symphony No. 2* (1943) is more chamber-like in character, aptly described as his 'pastoral' symphony, and is cast in three movements, with a boisterous march and a brief quote from the Marseillaise in the third.

With the emotionally more searching *Symphony No. 3* (1944) Martinů found his individual voice. Apart from his own two earlier symphonies, there is nothing in the symphonic repertoire to herald it, and its only antecedents are in the symphonies of **Sibelius**, and then only distantly. The entire orchestra is used as a huge organic complex, generating germ cells and growing them with passionate logic and marvellous clarity of orchestral texture, flowering when the growth is momentarily complete and major chords arrive. The orchestra is used in step-like blocks, the generating impulse passed from block to block, and then opened out in more flowing, lyrical culminations. Whenever such moments of relative stasis are reached, a new ostinato phrase with its own particular colours inevitably starts up again. Suddenly in the final movement, in the midst of this wonderful and sometimes troubled organic progression, the entire canvas is taken onto a different plane, with shimmering orchestral textures as if the world had suddenly been hushed and held still. This is one of the finest symphonies of the century, quite unlike those of any other composer in construction and tone, deeply rooted in the Czech tradition of brightness and hope.

The *Symphony No. 4* (1945) returns to a lyrical, happier tone announced by the light textures and boisterous opening. In the scherzo and again in the finale, Martinů's use of swirling ostinato figures reaches its most sophisticated development, whirring around like little dust-devils across a field. The slow movement opens with complex slow-moving chromaticism, like a fog in which the chromatic drops are held in suspension. Gradually this clears, and turns into the spirit of Dvořák redefined in 20th century terms. The finale has thematic connections with Martinů's opera *Julietta* and the third symphony.

The *Symphony No. 5* (1946) is the most difficult and complex, continuing the general idiom and including moments of grandeur not often found in his output. The culmination of this symphonic experience is the *Symphony No. 6*, subtitled *Fantaisies symphoniques* (1951–53), the best known of these works. This extraordinary score defies conventional analysis. The element of fantasy of the title is given free rein, the construction and choice of musical event based entirely on instinctive response, which at this stage in Martinů's career was of unerring sureness. Martinů's symphonies bear a similar relationship to the Czech symphony as Janáček's operas do to Czech opera; their idiom, while retaining a tonal base, is still sufficiently unusual to require adjustments by listeners unused to it.

Of Martinů's other orchestral works, the brilliant, sometimes harsh *Sinfonia concertante* (1932) pits two orchestras antiphonally, while the *Concerto grosso* (1937) for wind, brass, strings, and two pianos exemplifies his modernisation of Baroque principles, alternating solo and tutti passages, and using a short germ motif. The *Tre ricercari* (1938), the piano prominent in the orchestra, is the culmination of his neo-

Baroque period, combining Baroque elements with his later style in a generally bright and uplifting tone. In *Les Fresques de Piero dalla Francesca* (1955), a three-movement work inspired by three of the 15th-century artist's paintings, there is a marvellous melding of Impressionistic Mediterranean colour and Czech yearning and drama, Martinů's tribute to the joys of the creative spirit. All these works show Martinů at his best.

Concertos formed a considerable part of Martinů's output, often harking back to the concerto grosso rather than to the Romantic conflict between soloist and orchestra. Of his concerto works for piano, the *Sinfonietta giocosa* (1940) was written while Martinů was waiting in Nice to escape Vichy France; his happy anticipation of leaving is reflected in the perky score. A more stunning work in an equally extrovert mood is the *Concerto for Two Pianos and Orchestra* (1943). From its emphatic opening, full of urgency and rhythmic drive, it presents vivid solo writing, a sense of pent-up excitment, and in the central adagio glittering colours evolving from the Impressionistic opening. Throughout it explores the sonic possibilities of the two solo instruments. The rather grand *Piano Concerto No. 3* (1943–46) is less convincing than either of these two works. The *Piano Concerto No. 4 'Incantation'* (1955–56), on the other hand, is his finest work for piano and orchestra. In two movements, it expresses the composer's search 'for truth and the meaning of life', and is complex but flowing in its coalescence of a multiplicity of ideas, colours, and timbres, with a wide range of effects for the largely percussive piano writing, including the depression of silent chord clusters to add sympathetic colours. Its moods are equally wide-ranging, with an element of imaginative and meditative fantasy that preoccupied Martinů in this period. This is not the easiest Martinů work on first encounter, but it is one of the most satisfying. The *Piano Concerto No. 5* (1957, titled *Fantasia concertante*) also has fine passages in a more conventional structure, the fantasy elements being suggested in the brittle piano writing of the opening. Uncharacteristically virtuoso passages combine with ideas of tenderness and simplicity, with a slow movement whose haunting textures suggest a nocturne.

The two violin concertos are contrasted in idiom and tone. The *Violin Concerto No. 1* (1932–33, but not performed until rediscovered in 1973) comes from the composer's neo-Baroque period. It is dominated by the jerky, nervous, constantly agitated but nonetheless lyrical solo line, permeated by technical challenges and syncopated rhythms. The *Violin Concerto No. 2* (1943) is a yearningly lyrical work reflecting Martinů's own considerable gift on the instrument, with a much more Romantic interplay between soloist and orchestra, pitting solo line against transforming but heavily textured orchestral sonorities. The predominant mood is one of rhapsodic nostalgia, in which echoes of the folk music of his native country are never far away. A lithe, dancing finale returns to the understated grandeur of the opening of the concerto in one of Martinů's finest works.

Of Martinů's four concerto works for cello, the influence of jazz predominates in the little *Concertino* (1924) for cello, wind instruments, piano and percussion, mixed with a cantabile lyricism for the soloist. The *Cello Concerto No. 2* (1944–45) is in a similar idiom to the second violin concerto and shares its qualities, although it is perhaps a little long for its material. His other concertos include two related concertinos for the unusual combination of piano trio and string orchestra. The lithe and vital *Concertino for Piano Trio and String Orchestra No. 2* (1933) is in four movements, with a neo-classical rhythmic urgency initially reminiscent of **Stravinsky** and with skilful use of the available forces, the piano being used mainly in short notes, reminiscent of harpsichord writing, and a joyous, folk-like lilt to the finale. The *Concerto for Harpsichord and Small Orchestra* (1935) belongs to the period when Martinů was exploring the concerto grosso, and is a piece full of charm and interest. More effective and biting, until the more playful final movement, is the *Concerto for String Quartet and Orchestra* (1931). The short *Oboe Concerto* (1955), for a small orchestra that includes piano, suffers from over-thick orchestration (Martinů had intended to revise it), but has a rustic simplicity to the solo writing in the first movement and a slow movement of magical textures and a very beautiful main theme.

Unlike the symphonies, the seven string quartets span Martinů's compositional career, and therefore provide an overview of his changing styles and concerns within one medium. They are much finer than their reputation would suggest, full of the vigour of life while never being light-weight, and are marked by their use of counterpoint to thrust the music forward. The long *String Quartet No. 1* (1918, revised 1927) is Romantic in style and inspiration, imbued with a gentle Czech 19th-century lyricism, influenced by both Dvořák and **Debussy**. The *String Quartet No. 2* (1925) is idiomatically more ambitious, built around a weighty and dark central andante, flanked by two movements that oscillate between lightheartedness and rhythmic aggression. The *String Quartet No. 3* (1929) continued the exploration of sonority initiated in the slow movement of its predecessor, and is of interest in his development, having features in common with his later concerto grosso style. The *String Quartet No. 4* (1937), subtitled *Concerto da camera*, anticipates the early symphonies, especially in the short phrases of the opening, darting between instruments. This fine quartet has drive and bright vigour in the first two movements and the last, with a more contemplative slow movement of an almost religious cast, solo cello lines like a cantor being answered by the remainder of the quartet. The more anguished *String Quartet No. 5* (1938) was the response to a passionate love affair and is tragic in tone, the style of the previous quartet taken to new depths by the addition of much more dissonant and fragmentary writing and a wider range of string effects. The fast-paced and often restless *String Quartet No. 6* (1946) is also introverted, but in a very different fashion, and is the quartet in which Martinů seems to be expressing his longing for his homeland, using his technique of long, developing repeated rhythmic phrases that thrust towards luminosity. After two such personal quartets, the last, the graceful *String Quartet No. 7* (1947), also subtitled *Concerto da camera*, is more abstract. It combines Martinů's technique of short abutting phrases in the outer movements with the strong influence of Haydn, especially in the lovely andante, a kind of tribute to the 18th-century composer and quite unlike any of his earlier quartet slow movements.

Of his other chamber music, the madrigal form features in his later works, notably in the attractive *Madrigal-Sonata* (1942) for flute, violin and piano, which has become popular with performers, as have the *Three Madrigals* (1947) for violin and viola, combining virtuosity with depths of expression. The circumstances of the composition of the *Bergerettes* (1939–40) for

piano trio, written as Martinů was leaving for the USA, completely belie their bubbling, sunlit atmosphere; the turbulent *Piano Quartet* (1942) reflects the actual upheaval of the period.

Martinů's extensive piano music is of less interest, and mostly consists of miniatures, usually with a distant basis in folk-music rhythms. It displays a full range of pianistic techniques, exemplified in the three books of cheerful *Etudes and Polkas* (1945), in which the longest piece is under three minutes.

Martinů wrote fourteen operas (a further two are incomplete). It is still difficult to assess their worth, particularly the earlier experimental works which often use techniques easier to achieve with modern technology than at the time of their writing. *Voják a tanečnice* (*The Soldier and the Dancer*, 1926–27) to a libretto by J.L. Budín based on Plautus, is a riot of crazy incidents parodying the artistic idioms of the 1920s, involving audience, critics, moon, stars, knives, forks, spoons and a Dixieland jazzband. *Les Larmes du couteau* (*The Tears of the Knife*, 1928), to a libretto by Ribemont-Dessaignes, is a 20–minute Dadaesque tale of horror, necrophilia and erotic violence. *Les Trois souhaits* (*The Three Wishes*, 1929), also to a libretto by Ribemont-Dessaignes, applied film techniques to operatic structure, with an actual film-crew as part of the action. In complete contrast, *The Miracle of Our Lady*, more correctly titled *Plays of Mary* (*Hry o Marii*, 1933–34) is an attractive and deliberately simplistic trilogy of miracle plays based on three legends about Mary, using dance, narration, mime, and a commenting chorus; Martinů was consciously trying to create a popular, folk-based music theatre (as **Britten** was later to do), and succeeds.

Hlas lesa (*The Voice of the Forest*, 1935), to a libretto by Vítězslav Nezval was one of the first operas written especially for radio, using a folk story as its basis. More effective was his next one-act radio play, *Veselohra na mostě* (*Comedy on the Bridge*, 1935), in six linked scenes based on a classic Czech play by Václav Klicpera, again with a slightly fantastic situation, but one resonant to this day. Neighbours try to visit each other across a bridge, but the two river banks are in different and now mutually hostile territories. The various characters have exit visas from their respective sides, but no entry visas, and so find themselves stranded in the middle of the bridge, and there, in fear of their lives, make various personal confessions, until with the victory of one side they are pushed off the bridge to make way for troops. The bright, lively music, with martial overtones and often passionate vocal lines, uses a chamber ensemble. It is one of Martinů's better-known works in the USA, having won the New York Critics' Prize for the best new opera in 1951.

It was followed by Martinů's operatic masterpiece, the surrealistic *Julietta* (1936–37), where his interest in fantasy and its relationship to the actuality of existence found a perfect text in the French play *Juliette ou le clé des songes* by Georges Neveux. A book salesman revisits a town where he once been captivated by the sight of a young woman, Julietta. However, everyone has lost their memory. They are aware only of the moment, with many disconcerting consequences such as a fortune-teller foretelling the past, an engineer who gazes at the blank pages of a photo album, a memory seller who invents journeys. The book salesman gradually gets sucked into this real, yet unreal world, with the affair with Julietta a linking thread (she is apparently shot at one point, but this too hovers between reality and fantasy). The ending (invented by Martinů) is inconclusive, as all that has happened turns into a dream which itself restarts the action. This profoundly disturbing drama explores the edges of reality. Martinů treats it very directly, letting the music build character and the fantasy speak for itself, often with warm, yearning music (especially in the interaction with Julietta), and with strong musical characterisation of the many protagonists. This profound, questioning, and yet affirming work has few parallels in the operatic repertoire.

What Men Live By (1952), based on a version of the legend of St Martin by Tolstoy, is an opera for television (one of the first), but neither it nor its successor, the television opera *The Marriage* (1952), after Gogol, really make use of the new medium. The comedy *Mirandolina* (1954) is based on Goldoni. The title role of *Ariadne* (1958), to a libretto in French by the composer based on a version of the Greek myth by Neveux, was inspired by the singing of Callas. The compressed, swift-moving story is deceptively simple, hinging on verbal and psychological ambiguities which gradually unfold into a complex and disturbing metaphor. Ariadne has a fantasy love for the Minotaur (she has heard his voice, but never seen him); Theseus also has an appointment with him. The two recognise their common cause, and are engaged following an unexpected decree from the King of Crete. Theseus sets aside his quest in favour of love, but when one of his companions is killed, Theseus is stirred into action. The Minotaur appears as his own double, the Theseus who loves Ariadne (who says she knew the two would be alike). He has to kill the Minotaur, and in doing so kills his relationship with Adriadne, who is left abandoned, watching the departing Greek ships. Martinů's score to this swift one-act opera starts in disarming fashion, bouncy and lyrical, but gradually gets more complex and dark, culminating in a beautiful extended aria for Ariadne, whose changes of mood and intuitive knowledge have been subtly portrayed throughout the work.

The best known of the later operas is the grand opera *The Greek Passion* (1956–59), based on Nikos Kazantzakis's novel *Christ Recrucified*. It uses a play within a play: the Greek villagers are staging their Passion play, with competition in the village to play the parts, and an overall plot of interaction between the characters that parallels the crucifixion story. Added to this is a third layer, the story of a refugee group of Greeks fleeing the Turks who, with their priest, seek shelter in the village. It is a flawed work but contains some of Martinů's finest music and most affective character portraits.

Of Martinu's many other works, mention should be made of three very attractive scores based on the colours and relative simplicity of folk music. The undemanding but enchanting ballet *Špalíček* (*Little Block*, 1931–32, revised 1940 as two suites) uses fairy tales and nursery rhymes, and the cantata *Kytice* (*Bouquet of Flowers*, 1937) for four soloists, children's chorus, chorus, and orchestra with two pianos and harmonium, uses echoes of a wordless cry or greeting called across the Bohemian–Moravian mountains within the folk texts. The *Songs of the Highlands* (1955–59), four chamber cantatas using soloists, chorus, and chamber forces, to words by the poet Miloslav Bureš are better known by their individual titles (*The Opening of the Wells, The Legend of the Smoke from the Potato-tops, Dandelion Romance*, for soprano and chorus a cappella, and *Mikeš from the Mountains*).

They are the culmination of Martinů's nostalgia for his homeland. In all these unaffected works the colours are vivid and the zest of life shines through.

Martinů's idiom is not a difficult one, though the very individual cast of the later works may require familiarity for their strengths to emerge. Generally, readers are advised to avoid works not recommended below, at least until they have experienced those works which reveal the full range and scope of the life-affirming idiom of this most underrated of all major 20th-century composers.

RECOMMENDED WORKS
    opera *Ariadne* (1958)
    cantata *Bouquet of Flowers* (1937)
    Cello Concerto No. 2 (1944–45)
    opera *The Comedy on the Bridge* (1935)
    Concertino for cello, wind instruments and piano (1924)
    Double Concerto for two string orchestras, piano and timpani (1938)
    cantata *Epic of Gilgamesh* (1954–55)
    Field Mass (1939)
    Les Fresques de Piero della Francesca for orchestra (1955)
    opera *Julietta* (1936–37)
    opera *The Greek Passion* (1956–59)
    Memorial to Lidice (1943) for orchestra
    opera trilogy *The Miracle of Our Lady* (1934)
    Piano Concerto No. 4 (1956)
    Rhapsody Concerto for viola and orchestra (1952)
    ballet *La Revue de Cuisine* for chamber orchestra (1927)
    Sinfonia concertante for two string orchestras (1932)
    ballet *Špaliček* (1931–32, revised. 1940 as two suites)
    String Quartet No. 4 (*Concerto da camera*, 1937)
    String Quartet No. 5 (1938)
    String Quartet No. 6 (1946)
    Symphony No. 3 (1944)
    Symphony No. 4 (1945)
    Symphony No. 5 (1946)
    Symphony No. 6 (*Fantaisies symphoniques*, 1951–53)
    Tre ricercari for orchestra (1938)

BIBLIOGRAPHY
    B. Large, *Martinů*, 1975
    J. Milhule, *Martinů*, 1972
    M. Safránck, *Bohuslav Martinů: his Life and Works*, 1962

Novák Vitězslav**
born 5th December 1870 at Kamenice
died 18th July 1949 at Skuteč

Vitězslav Novák is, with **Suk**, the most important Czech composer of the generation that followed Dvořák (with whom he studied) and **Janáček**. Coming from a poor background (and hating his forced music lessons as a small child), he studied jurisprudence and philosophy as well as music to fulfil the terms of a scholarship. His early works are in the style of German Romanticism (Brahms recognised his talent, and introduced him to his publisher). Following a study of Moravian and Slovak folk music discovered when on holiday (and with the encouragement of Janáček), he found a nationalistic voice based on the colours and rhythms of Slovak folk music. The results of this change of style were the large *Sonata Eroica* (1900) for piano and three orchestral works. The vividly atmospheric symphonic poem *V Tatrách* (*In the Tatras*, 1903–05 – Novák himself made the first ascent of the difficult Ostry peak in the Tatra mountains) showed Novák's powers of musical landscape painting, and *Slovácká svitá* (*Slovak Suite*, 1903), where the small orchestra is used with restraint but a strong sense of colour, his growing awareness of nationalist themes. The third work in this group, the symphonic poem *O vecné touze* (*About the Eternal Longing*, 1908) applied the same descriptive techniques to a Hans Christian Andersen tale. This vivid tone poem combines Impressionism with the power of the late Romantic orchestra, using a wide palette of often mystical orchestral colours and effects.

At the same time Novák produced a number of song arrangements and chamber works with characteristic Slovak folk elements, notably bare fourths and fifths. While sometimes using actual folk melodies or themes, Novák preferred to invent his own in a similar style. To the natural sensuality of his music was added an erotic element in the tone poem *Toman a lesni panna* (*Toman and the Wood Nymph*, 1906–07), the overture *Lady Godiva* (1907) and, combined with his feel for the emotive aspects of nature, in a piano cycle (later orchestrated) with strong dramatic elements, *Pan* (1910). The culmination of this period is perhaps Novák's finest work, the powerful and beautiful cantata *Bowře* (*The Storm*, 1908–10), for soloist, chorus and orchestra, which has been aptly described as a sea symphony with obbligato chorus. The scoring is especially vivid and controlled, much of the material built on thematic fragments heard at the opening.

At the age of 45, Novák turned to opera. *Zvíkovský rarášek* (*The Imp of Zvíkov*, 1913–14) was a comic-ironic opera, as was *Karlštejn* (1914–15); but his most striking opera is the nationalist fairy tale *Lucerna* (*The Lantern*, 1919–22), reflecting the sufferings of the Czechs. *Dědův odkaz* (*Grandfather's Legacy*, 1922–25) is about a man who inherits a violin and becomes a virtuoso, and satirises the hypocrisies of a virtuoso's life and audience.

From the same period comes a major orchestral work, highly regarded in Czechoslovakia, *Podzimní Sinfonie* (*Autumn Symphony*, 1931–34) for chorus and orchestra. The final flowering of his symphonic talent is the effective *De Profundis* (1941) for orchestra and organ, a patriotic assertion of eventual victory over the Nazis, that starts with a long, dark and foreboding search for harmonic resolution, turbulently building to a climax during which bright ideas slide in among the darkness. This opens out to an unmistakably Czech landscape which in turn builds to a huge climax, the organ prominent, of hope and joy. During this last period folk influences were largely replaced by Hussite chorales, reflecting Novák's recognition of the threat current political events posed to his country.

Throughout his life Novák was fascinated by nature, and depictions of mountains, forests and water abound in his music. His work, full of polyphonic skill and the interlacing of textures and melodic ideas, is primarily an expression of the emotions engendered by that fascination. Such an approach has long been out of fashion, but his high standards will be appreciated and enjoyed by those who are not expecting music of great intellectual depth.

Novák taught at the Prague Conservatory (1909–20) and was professor of composition at the Czech State Conservatory (1918–39). The legacy of his teaching was almost as great as that of his music, with many of the next generation of composers his pupils, including **Hába**, **Kapr** and **Suchon**. With Suk, he helped found the Society of Modern Music.

RECOMMENDED WORKS
  symphonic poem *About the Eternal Longing* (1903–05)
  tone poem *De Profundis* (1941)
  symphonic poem *In the Tatras* (1902)

Slovak Suite (1903)
cantata *The Storm* for soloists, male chorus and orchestra (1908–10)

BIBLIOGRAPHY
  Vladimir Lébl, *Vitězslav Novák*, 1968 (in English)

Slavický Milan[*]
born 7th May 1947 at Prague

Milan Slavický, son of Klement Slavický (see introduction), is one of the most interesting of the younger Czech composers. He has concentrated on orchestral and chamber music, and won acclaim outside Czechoslovakia, including a UNESCO prize and the Prix d'Italia. He studied with **Kapr** and **Kohoutek**, and gained attention with an orchestral work, *Poctat Saint-Expérymu* (*Homage to Saint-Exupéry*). It was followed by an arresting one-movement violin concerto, subtitled *Ceste srdce* (*The Way of the Heart*, 1978). It is a taut and dramatic work, with the linear and harmonically unsettled solo line passing through a number of fragmentary episodes. Percussion and insistent, sometimes violent, rhythms are much in evidence, as is a deft, pointed use of the limited colours available (wind, percussion, celesta and harp).

The symphonic triptych *Terre des Hommes* (1979–83), grander in conception, descriptive in its scoring, followed a similar pattern without being so immediately alluring. It has been followed by another triptych, *Sinfonia mortis et vitae* (*The Well of Life*, 1986). The darker moments of these works are also observable in the chamber music, exploring expressive effects from the brooding piano trio *Brightening I* (1986) to the dark colours of *Dialogues with Silence* (1978) for string quartet. In these works his approachable, non-tonal harmonic palette is founded on a sense of tonal centres. The interest in colours and rhythms has been explored in *Tre Toccate* (1964) for percussion instruments. He has also been active as a recording producer in Czechoslovakia.

RECOMMENDED WORKS
  Violin Concerto *The Way of the Heart* (1979)
  Dialogues with Silence for string quartet (1978)

Suk Joseph[**]
born 4th January 1874 at Křečovice u Neveklova

died 29th May 1935 at Benešov
(Prague)

Jospeh Suk was both Dvořák's favourite
pupil and his son-in-law. With **Novák**, he is
the most important Czech composer in the
generation following Dvořák and **Janáček**.
Whereas Novák found his voice through
Moravian folk song, Suk largely avoided
folk influences (although he used Bohemian rhythms), extending the tradition of
Dvořák mainly through chamber music,
including freer forms such as ballads and
rhapsodies, and a number of orchestral
works – there are very few songs or choral
works, and he wrote no operas. Much of his
music is programmatic, but its programmes are of inner emotions and personal events, rather than external inspiration. The sonorities of his string writing
reflect his own exceptional abilities as a
violinist (he was also a fine pianist). He was
the second violinist of the famous Czech
Quartet, giving over 4,000 performances
before his retirement in 1933. The violin
virtuoso tradition has been carried on by
his grandson, Josef Suk (born 1929).

The earliest works of his small output
(39 opus numbers) show the influence of
Dvořák, and his *Serenade for Strings*
(1892) has remained one of his most popular works. The discovery of Julius Zeyer's
stage fairy tale *Radúz and Mahulena*,
with its theme of faithful love and the
triumph of good over evil, started a period
of Romantic and lyrically happy works. It
remained an influence throughout his life,
and themes from his music to the play
(*Radúz and Mahulena*, 1897–98, suite
titled *A Fairy Tale*, 1900) regularly recur
in his later music. From the same period
come a number of works with limpid and
singing solo violin writing, notably the
Four Pieces (1890) for violin and piano.
The twin culminations of this period are
the *Fantasy* (1902–03) for violin and
orchestra, a most attractive work in which
he avoided concerto form in favour of a free
fantasy, with common motifs in each of the
three movements, and the symphonic
poem *Prague* (1904).

The death of Dvořák in 1905 affected
Suk deeply, and it was followed in 1906 by
the death of his wife. From that point his
music has a sterner, more tragic element,
and he moves from Romanticism to a more
complex polytonal idiom with dense harmonies. The immediate result was the
tragic and powerful symphony *Asrael*
(*The Angel of Death*, 1907), with linking
thematic motifs, including one of Fate and
the Death motif from *Radúz and Mahulena*. It is a score of great emotional impact

and structural mastery with an ending of
reconciliation and represents the culmination of the late Romantic tradition in the
Czech symphony. It was followed by an
Impressionistic and beautiful meditation
on nature, the symphonic poem *Pohádka
léta* (*A Summer's Tale*, 1907–09), and the
best of his piano music, the introspective
cycle *Things Lived and Dreamed*, 1909,
with irregular rhythms and rich and
ambiguous harmonies.

Pod jabloní (*Under the Apple Tree*,
1911) for contralto, chorus and orchestra is
drawn from the music for a play by Zeyer
(1902) consisting of three ecstatic poems
concerning nature and heaven. It opens
with a long and gorgeous Romantic
orchestral introduction, full of light and
happiness, solo violin prominent in delicate
textures that gradually thicken; the vocal
writing ranges from a similar delicacy to
the uplifting nobility of the close in a work
that would be ideal for larger choral societies. The *War Triptych* consists of three
separate works drawn together under the
same opus number (35). The first part,
*Meditation on the Old Czech Chorale St
Wenceslas* (usually known as *Meditation*,
1914) is a beautiful and intense version of
the chorale for strings (originally string
quartet), and has become one of Suk's best-
known works. *Legend of the Dead Victors*
(1919) is rather bombastic (it was commissioned as an official commemoration), but
has moments of quiet luminosity, especially at the close. The third part, the
infectious festival march *Towards a New
Life* (1919), has become one of the best
known of all Czech marches.

Suk's masterpiece is the symphonic
poem *Zráni* (*The Ripening*, 1913–18) for
orchestra with wordless chorus, with a
personal programme indicated in the titles
of its five sections ('youth', 'love', 'pain',
'determination', and 'victory'). The thematic structure matches the title, with seeds
of ideas growing and coming to fruition in a
rich web of complex harmonies and with an
intense message describing both the
brightness and the tragic shades of life. It
opens and closes with trumpet fanfares,
and the last movement – victory – includes
a fugue followed by near silence and then a
final hymn. Throughout, the sense of ger-
mination and fulfilment is palpable. His
last major work, *Epilogue* (1920–32), for
soloists, chorus and orchestra, expresses
Suk's vision of love, and is almost as fine.

Suk's later works represent one of the
final flowerings of the Romantic tradition,
but in a more pastoral idiom than the late
Romantic German works more usually

encountered. They are imbued with an intensely personal expression both of the tragedy of life and the power of reconciliation, rebirth and love, in an increasingly complex, individual and effective language. With the immediate attractions of the earlier and less profound works, it seems surprising that his music, revered in Czechoslovakia, is so neglected outside.

Suk became professor at the Prague Conservatory in 1922, and was its director from 1924–26. Among his many pupils was **Martinů**, and his teaching, especially of his concepts of freer forms and thematic growth, had an abiding influence on the next generation of Czech composers.

RECOMMENDED WORKS
Epilogue for soloists, chorus and
  orchestra (1920–32)
suite *A Fairy Tale* (1900 from *Radúz*
  and Mahulena, 1897–98)
Fantasy for violin and orchestra
  (1902–03)
Four Pieces for violin and piano (1890)
Meditation on the Old Czech Chorale
  St Wenceslas (1914) for orchestra
symphonic poem *The Ripening*
  (1913–18)
symphonic poem *A Summer's Tale*
  (1905–06)
Symphony No. 2 (*Asrael*) (1905–06)
piano cycle *Things Lived and*
  Dreamed (1909)
cantata *Under the Apple Tree* (1911)
  for contralto, chorus and orchestra

BIBLIOGRAPHY
Jiři Berkovec, *Joseph Suk*, 1969

Válek Jiři*
born 28th May 1923 at Prague

The composer and musicologist Jiři Válek is one of Czechoslovakia's major symphonists, although his pieces should be approached with caution. For in common with many other East European composers, the primary stimulus for his symphonies has been extra-musical, and those expecting abstract symphonic developments and structures will be disappointed. His major inspiration has been from history, and at best he has the capacity to conjure up a vivid musical picture using a smattering of modern techniques and effects. The *Symphony No. 6* (1969), for flute and chamber orchestra, is an atmospheric meditation on Herakleitos, and exemplifies his approachable atonality and his spare use of harder sounds (percussion, percussive piano) and short woodwind phrases against a wide orchestral background. The less effective and more rambling *Symphony No. 7* on Pompeii introduced an element of violence, and in subsequent symphonies the uninteresting structures and elements of banality (heard at their worst in the ballet music from his opera *Hamlet Our Contemporary*, 1984) outweigh the elements of expressive interest. At the same time, he has produced chamber works in parallel with the symphonies (*Villa dei misteri* for violin and piano matching the *Symphony No. 7*, fragments of ancient Chinese chants in *Symphony No. 8* being echoed in the song-cycle *La Partenza della Primavera* 1970–71). With the reservations outlined, his music is interesting as an example of modernism officially acceptable during the Communist period.

RECOMMENDED WORK
Symphony No. 6 *Ekpyrosis* (1969)

Denmark

Introduction

Historically, Denmark has been a Scandinavian country looking over its shoulder at the more dominant mainland European cultures, usually Germany, but sometimes France. A leading Danish Romantic composer was Johan Peter Emilius Hartmann (1805–1900), who came from a family with a Danish tradition of composition stretching back to the 18th century. Hartmann is best remembered for his songs (often drawing on Old Norse literature) and his operas, two of which had librettos by Hans Christian Andersen. One of his most nationalist works was the folk ballet *Et Folkesagn*, written in collaboration with his son-in-law, the best-known of the 19th-century Danish composers, Niels Wilhelm Gade (1817–90). The foundation of Gade's output is eight symphonies, now largely forgotten but quite widely admired in their time. Gade was also an important teacher and influence on the following generation of Danish composers. The dominant figure of this generation was Carl **Nielsen** (1865–1931), who with **Sibelius** is the most important Scandinavian composer of any age, and who provided a crucial link between the symphonies of Brahms and Dvořák and the late 20th century. His contemporary August Enna (1859–1939) was once widely known for his sentimental opera, based on Andersen, *The Little Match Girl* (1897).

The French influence appeared in the next generation, notably in the vivacious music of Knudage Riisåger (1897–1974) who studied with **Roussel** and admired the Gallic wit of Les Six. He is best known for his sparkling *Concerto for Trumpet and String Orchestra* (1933) and his ballet music, including *Qarrtsiluni* (1938), originally a purely orchestral score but turned into a celebrated ballet in 1942; the work was inspired by the writings of the Arctic explorer Knud Rassmussen, and the title is an Inuit word referring to the silence of expectation before the summer sun returns after the long night of the Arctic winter. Jørgen Bentzon (1897–1951) looked more to Germany and **Hindemith**, and was the first Danish modernist composer, experimenting, largely in chamber music, with what he called 'character polyphony', exploiting the character of a particular instrument by assigning material suited to that character, and different (simultaneous) material suited to the character of each other instrument. The concept is developed in a chamber series, *Racconto* (No. 1, 1935). He later toned down the experimentation, partly motivated by his democratic political ideas, leading to such works as the *Dickens Symphony* (1939). The most unusual composer of this generation. who has recently received more attention, is the mystical maverick Rued **Langgaard** (1893–1952).

The only one of this generation of composers to receive more than a passing attention outside Denmark has been Vagn Holmboe (1909–96), whose idiom recognisably follows on from **Nielsen**, but who has forged an individual voice in his symphonies and string quartets. Two of the better-known Danish composers have embraced a more European outlook, influenced by the avant-garde. Niels Viggo **Bentzon** (born 1919) has produced a vast, eclectic and uneven output, while Per Nørgård (born 1932) has developed a personal, static idiom. Danish 12-tone composers have included Jan Maegaard (born 1926), while the first Danish serial work was *Elegy* (1953) for organ by Poul Rovsing Olsen (1922–82), who was influenced by non-European musics, especially the classical rāgs of northern India; the nonet *Patet* (1966), for example, is based on Indonesian music and Watusi rhythms.

Among the younger composers, Poul Ruders (born 1949) is beginning to attract attention. His two-movement *String Quartet No. 2* suggested a composer of promise whose textures echoed the distant influence of the minimalists, also apparent in his *Violin Concerto No. 1* (1981), a tribute to Vivaldi's *Four Seasons*. In his *Concerto for clarinet and twin orchestras* (1985) the soloist represents the voice of humanity squeezed in an orchestral grip, and among his other works is a trilogy of concertos, *Drama-Trilogy*, the last the *Cello Concerto 'Polydrama'* (1988).

In contrast to the other Scandinavian countries, Denmark has been singularly reticent about disseminating its music, and **Nielsen** is still far too little known, especially in North America. Vagn **Holmboe**, while admittedly likely to appeal to a narrower audience, has not received the kind of international attention and performance that he deserves, and the lesser composers can be difficult to encounter.

Danish Music Information Centre:
Dansk Musik Information Centre
Graabroedre Torv 16

DK–1154 Copenhagen K.
Denmark
tel: +45 33 112066
fax: +45 33 322016

Bentzon Niels Viggo*
born 24th August 1919 at Copenhagen

Niels Viggo Bentzon (not to be confused with his cousin, the composer Jørgen Bentzon, 1897–1951), has been a colourful figure in Danish composition, and his huge, uneven, sometimes provocative output has drawn on a very wide variety of influences and sources. His earliest music was influenced by **Hindemith**, but his discovery of **Schoenberg**, partly through his activities as a pianist, led to the use of 12-tone principles, and he wrote a treatise on the technique in 1950; it eventually became only one element in his eclectic palette. From the late 1940s he also adopted the technique of 'metamorphosis', the continuous development and evolution of material (a technique already employed by **Holmboe**). From the 1960s his music took two directions: a continuation of the more mainstream style, often tonally based, and a more avant-garde approach that has included the use of pop and jazz, 'happenings', and unconventional performance venues. This latter aspect has been very difficult to encounter outside Denmark. The consistent features of this eclectic output have been an improvisatory feeling, contrasting moods, and an often Classical or Baroque basis of structure, especially variation form. The neo-classical strain was exemplified in the concerto grosso impetus to the *Chamber Concerto* (1948) for eleven instruments, coloured by the use of three pianos, or in such works as the *Pezzi sinfonici* (*Symphonic Pieces*, 1956), a work whose architectural clarity and vigour is more impressive than its rather colourless overall effect.

The works currently most admired date from before 1960, especially his symphonies and piano sonatas, which now number at least fifteen and twenty-two respectively. The *Symphony No. 3* (1947) is impressively built from a pastoral opening, transformed into a number of effective themes. The *Symphony No. 4 'Metamorfosen'* (1948) builds on three themes heard at the outset, and was the work which brought him more international attention. By the time of *Kronik om René Descartes* (*Feature Article on René Descartes*, 1975), his orchestral style had absorbed some of the mainstream European elements originating in the avant-garde. The four movements of the work reflect different aspects of Descartes' philosophy and philosophical life, and the moods of the work are as diverse as the stylistic sources, including tongue-in-cheek humour through instrumental effects and a fairly dreadful jazz passage. While one can admire the inventiveness, there is a lack of strong character in the music, especially for such a potent subject; but it has some fine moments, and it shows the composer's fluency as well as his flaws. The piano sonatas have something of the mercurial quality and pianistic brilliance of **Prokofiev**, an influence that Bentzon has acknowledged. Of his other piano music, *The Tempered Piano* (1964) is a gigantic (eighty-minute) series of twenty-four preludes and fugues using metamorphosis techniques, and is one of a number of works that reflect Bentzon's appreciation of Bach, including the *Fifteen Two-Part Inventions* (1964),and the *Fifteen Three-Part Inventions* (1964), both for piano. His later piano writing includes works for prepared piano.

Bentzon taught at the Århus Conservatory from 1945–1949, and then at the Copenhagen Conservatory. He has been active as a painter, writer, poet and critic as well as a composer.

RECOMMENDED WORKS
> *Feature Article on René Descartes*
> (1975) for orchestra
> Symphony No. 4 *Metamorfosen* (1948)

Holmboe Vagn**
born 20th December 1909 at Horsens
died 1st September 1996 at Ramløse

Vagn Holmboe is the leading Danish symphonist after **Nielsen**, and his considerable achievement has received less general recognition than its deserves. Largely unaffected by changing trends around him, his music shows a continuous development and refinement of a personal idiom, seeking tauter and more concentrated means of expression within parameters established fairly early in his career. This unflinching attitude left him somewhat isolated in the rapidly developing experimentation of the 1960s, and partly accounts for his neglect. A second reason is a studied dryness in his style. Emotions arise, so to speak, from the subconscious, as if it is the play of forms that allows their expression. This is the antithesis of a composer such as **Shostakovich**, where form often has to contain a welter of expression, and the interplay of the cerebral and the expressive in Holmboe's music is not so immediately appealing. Symphonies and string quartets are at the core of Holmboe's output, and they share similar qualities and techniques.

Holmboe's earlier music was influenced by **Nielsen,** whose clarity of orchestration he has continued to develop, and by **Bartók,** furthered by studies of folk music that Holmboe made in Romania in the 1930s (his wife was Romanian). The more obvious residue of these influences died out by the early 1950s. The chief feature of his idiom is a very Scandinavian clarity, best compared to the quality of light in northern lands, with sharp outlines, a lack of hazy shadows, a starkness, at times a draining of colour in a clear whitening brilliance that will be familiar to anyone who has lived in northern latitudes.

The guiding principle behind Holmboe's structures, fully developed by the time of the sixth string quartet and the sixth symphony, has been described by him as 'metamorphosis': the continuous evolution and development of material, often subtle and complex, from a theme or idea expressed at the beginning of a work; the obvious antecedent is to be found in **Sibelius's** *Symphony No. 7.* Taken with the emotional reticence, this can produce in Holmboe's music a feeling of satisfaction often much greater than the individual events would seem to warrant, even allowing for the haunting passages Holmboe often produces. The other features of his style are a rhythmic vitality, sometimes almost nervous; melodies shaped by modal scales, at times allowing a line to follow the key in the minor, while the main body pursues the major (or vice versa – all these techniques are traceable back to **Nielsen**); precise, clear orchestration of lean textures, often sharply differentiating between sections of the orchestra; moods of controlled tension; luminosity; and a Danish sense of humour, occasionally slightly sardonic or melancholy. The overall effect is to invite us in to survey the prospect he is offering, not the presentation of emotions we are expected to share.

The *Symphony No. 1* (1935) uses chamber forces, while the *Symphony No. 4 'Sinfonia sacra'* is a choral work, but the first of his symphonies to receive wider attention was the three-movement *Symphony No. 5* (1944). It exemplifies his clear, incisive lines, the forceful opening movement sculpted with bold precision, especially in the compelling climax. The slow

movement, reminiscent of **Nielsen,** is suffused with a noble quality, and includes a funeral march with reiterated timpani strokes. The dark, polyphonic *Symphony No. 6* (1947) developed Holmboe's technique of metamorphosis in two taut movements, with a quote in the first movement paying tribute to **Nielsen's** two movement fifth symphony. The *Symphony No. 7* (1950), again developing from the initial germ material, is one of his finest. In one overall movement divided into three sections, themselves linked by what Holmboe called 'intermedia', it opens with a section of penetrating clarity and rhythmic vitality, including a suggestion of the mawkish and moments of arresting delicacy, celesta and high violins setting the atmosphere, woodwind carrying the progression. The central slow section is limpid and mysterious, building to luminous textures; the final section is forceful, arriving at what seems to be the climax of an ending. The strings are held on from the climactic chord for a moment of warmth, and then a marvellous equivalent to an epilogue emerges, haunting, fragmented, and unforgettable.

The much larger *Symphony No. 8 'Sinfonia boreale'* (1952) reverts to a more conventional usage of thematic material, each of its four movements introducing new themes, but within each movement using the principle of thematic metamorphosis. An element of the mawkish or sardonic emerges in the second movement, the elegiac in the slow movement. The three-movement *Symphony No. 10* (1970–71) is prefaced by a quote from Walt Whitman referring to the mutability of the universe, and the movements are separated by a general pause rather than by breaks (a device **Nielsen** had also used). There is here an added texture, a layer of fluttering wind or strings that replaces the silences between the orchestral sections. The symphony has the quality of the stars suggested by its preface, with trumpet calls over long dark lines and a weave of subdued patterns in the slow movement. The typical nervous percussive tension is joined by a sense of uplift and the expansive vista of the heavens in the last movement. There is a new tone, too, in the warm textures of the fine *Symphony No. 11* (1980), its opening (reminiscent of **Britten**) setting a positive, unaggressive rhythmic figure against the type of whirling textures found in the tenth symphony. This rhythmic figure recurs in the symphony and is devoid of the nervous tension found in earlier works. Slower sections have a pastoral, almost bucolic, air, and the symphony fades away with a mellow light not often found in Holmboe's output.

Besides the symphonies, Holmboe has written a number of other orchestral works, including a series of concertos recalling the spirit of Bach's *Brandenberg Concertos*. The restrained and thoughtful *Cello Concerto* (1974) is worth encountering. Its dramatic opening, orchestral crashes against slow-spinning figures led by the cello, belies the general mood, the lyrical cello line weaving in short phrases, and often visiting ruminative or light-hearted regions.

Holmboe's most important contribution after the symphonies has been his string quartets, now numbering twenty. They share the stylistic and procedural features of the symphonies within the more intimate setting of the form, and are characterised by the thoroughness with which they explore their material. The *String Quartet No. 1* (1949) was influenced by **Bartók**, and the *String Quartet No. 2* (1949) is lyrical. Holmboe's individual voice emerged in the concentrated *String Quartet No. 3* (1949), pitting major triads against minor and with a chaconne at its centre, and especially in the dark *String Quartet No. 4* (1953–54, revised 1956) and in the drive of the *String Quartet No. 5* (1954–55). By the *String Quartet No. 6* (1961) Holmboe had refined his technique of metamorphosis, and all the material in its four movements is developed from the opening theme. The next two string quartets are related. The *String Quartet No. 7* (1964) shows a relaxation from its astringent predecessor in its broader feel, with darker emotions in the adagio, while the *String Quartet No. 8* (1965) returns to a five-movement plan, with luminous clear textures, especially in the second movement. Of the later quartets, the *String Quartet No. 14* (1979), with its very stark opening, occupies a refined, introspective and subdued world analogous to that of the late quartets of **Shostakovich**.

Holmboe also wrote a considerable body of vocal music, including a series of works on biblical texts written in the early 1950s under the collective title *Liber canticorum*, of which the best known is the eight-part motet *Vanitas vanitatum* (1953). While some are dry and austere, others are warm and very beautiful, such as the luminous, undulating *Domine non superbit*, or the folk-like opening of *Omnia flumina* for six voices, a long line over a drone conjuring the rivers of the title. Of his other choral music, the spirited *Three*

Inuit Songs (1956) for the energetic combination of baritone, male chorus and timpani is worth discovering.

Holmboe was music critic of *Politiken* (1947–55), and from 1950 taught at the Copenhagen Conservatory.

RECOMMENDED WORKS
   Cello Concerto (1974)
   the string quartets
   Symphony No. 5 (1944)
   Symphony No. 7 (1950)
   Symphony No. 10 (1970–71)
   Symphony No. 11 (1980)
   Three Inuit Songs (1956) for baritone,
      male chorus and timpani

Langgaard Rued Immanuel
born 28th July 1893 at Copenhagen
died 10th July 1952 at Ribe

An eccentric, something of a visionary or a little crazed (depending on your point of view), composer and organist Rued Langgaard has started to receive more attention in his native Denmark, and now occupies a place analogous to Havergal **Brian** in Britain. His early music was Romantic, including the *Symphony No. 4, Løvfald* (*The Fall of the Leaf*, 1916), but by the end of World War I he had started experimenting with such devices as dissonant polyphony, tone clusters and static bodies of sonority, mostly prompted by the cosmic scope of his themes (especially the clash between good and evil). This period included *Sfaerernes Musik* (*Music for the Spheres*, 1918) for soprano, chorus and orchestra, which opens with a tone cluster but shows his limitations in the handling of large-scale forms; the busy *Symphony No. 6 'Det Himmelrivende'* (*Heaven-Storming*, 1919); and the first stages of his major work, the one-act Expressionist opera–oratorio *Antikrist* (*Antichrist*, 1921–39), based on the Book of Revelation. By the mid-1920s, apparently disenchanted with neo-classicism, he reverted to the late Romantic style of his earlier works, while retaining the apocalyptic and religious themes. His five string quartets (numbered 2 to 6; the material of *No. 1*, 1914, was reworked in *Nos 4 and 5*) originally dated from 1914 to 1925, and show a considerable stylistic diversity, from the emulation of a passing train in *No. 2* to the late Romantic style of the last three. His piano music includes the *Insectarium*, a collection of unusual miniatures describing various insects. His major organ work is the *Messis* (*Mass*, 1934–37), an 'organ drama' showing French organ and Romantic Nordic influences, intended to be played over three evenings.

Much of the dating of Langgaard's work is obscure due to his habit of multiple revisions. His music is a mixture of ideas of interest and a vision quite beyond his technical means; like many such visionaries, he has passionate adherents.

RECOMMENDED WORKS
opera *Antikrist* (1921–39)
Symphony No. 6 *Det Himmelrivende* (*Heaven–Storming*) (1919)

Nielsen Carl August•••
born 9th June 1865 at Norre-Lyndelse
died 3rd October 1931 at Copenhagen

Nielsen is the one Danish composer of unquestionable international reputation. While **Mahler** took the symphony to its late Romantic culmination, it was Nielsen and his exact contemporary **Sibelius** who took the form of the symphony and sought new procedures to mould it into a rejuvenated genre. Nielsen's output is relatively small but of consistently high quality, and at its core lie the six symphonies, which, spread over his compositional life, exemplify his artistic development.

Nielsen stands on the cusp of Romanticism, and he represents not so much a reaction against the full lushness of the late Romantic idiom, but an evolution out of it, influenced in part by his admiration for the crisp precision of the Classical period. That precision is the hallmark of Nielsen's writing; he increasingly stripped away the accumulations of the late Romantic idiom, so that ideas are less encumbered by a wealth of colour effects and thick-textured detail, and every facet of the orchestra has a precision of purpose. Yet at the same time, and using these means, he could produce an atmosphere that was the legacy of the Scandinavian Romantic heritage. What propels this aesthetic evolution is Nielsen's underlying philosophy, a return to a more direct and simple (but never simplistic) view of the human condition, cutting away the angst that was the heritage of the German late Romantics. Implicit in this is a sense of hope, even when menace, distress, and sometimes titanic conflict enter his music during and after World War I, which affected him deeply.

However, stripping the late Romantic idiom left a void in terms of emotional expression, especially as Nielsen was continuing a tradition, rather than forging a new one. His response was to develop those aspects he had at hand, in particular the harmonic. In his symphonies he applied the principle of progressive tonality, where the whole work (or a movement) ends in a different key to that in which it began (a technique also explored by **Mahler**). This has two main effects: a sense of momentum established by the progression of keys to a new goal while the work is in progress; and a different atmosphere from the traditional symphonic harmonic layout after the work is finished. Instead of arriving back where we started harmonically, having experienced various musical events and emotions on the way, we now use those experiences to arrive at a new destination. In addition, he used polytonality (the simultaneous use of two or more keys) as an element of the progression and also for conflict and for expressive effect. A third harmonic idiom is his use of church modes and the pentatonic scale; which maintains the tonal system while often leaving the key hovering between major and minor.

At the same time Nielsen developed his use of light, spacious and precise textures as in the use of glockenspiel in the *Symphony No. 6* (1924–5). He had an awareness of the potential and power of silences and developed the use of the percussion section, in particular the snare-drum (side-drum). On the one hand this instrument could inject the underlying menace already mentioned; on the other, it is a harmonically neutral instrument, and can thus act independently of the progressions of tonality, most obviously in the *Symphony No. 5* (1921–2) or in the *Clarinet Concerto* (1928). It also allows strongly emphasized rhythmic elements, another area of development for Nielsen, culminating in the *Symphony No. 5* (where a section of the important snare-drum part is left to the performer, and not notated), but also clear in the structural momentum generated by changing rhythmic ideas in passages of the *Symphony No. 6*. By the end of his life Nielsen had arrived at a fluidity and ease of flow, with an almost instinctive sense of the progress of events, that has been disconcerting to those used to more conventional structuring of material, but which can in hindsight be seen as prophetic of later developments in music.

Nielsen's earliest music was heavily influenced by Niels Gade and Edvard Grieg, the main Scandinavian proponents of Romanticism, and shows the same sunny disposition, in the *Little Suite* op. 1 (1888) for strings, still a popular work, and the first two string quartets (1888, revised 1890). The forceful *String Quartet No. 3* (1897–98) shows his command of conterpoint, and the warm *String Quartet No. 4* (1906, revised 1923), subtitled *Piacevolezza*, the increasing influence of Classical precision. But it is in the short tone poems that the Scandinavian Romantic legacy never completely abandoned by Nielsen is best displayed. The *Helios Overture* (1903) is a short and beautiful descriptive work inspired by a Greek holiday, best described in Nielsen's own words: 'Silence and darkness – then the sun rises with a joyous song of praise – it wanders its golden way – and sinks quietly into the sea'. *Saga Drøm* (1908) was inspired by a passage from the famous Icelandic *Njal's Saga*, in which Gunner rides home, sleeps, and recounts a prophetic dream in which he was pursued by wolves and had to fight them off. After the slow opening that sets the landscape, the story is closely followed, concentrating on nature tone painting and a dreamy atmosphere admirers of **Sibelius**'s tone poems will enjoy. *Andante Lamentoso, Ved en ung Kunstners Baare* (*At the bier of a young artist*, 1910) for strings (originally string quartet) is a powerful funeral tribute to the young painter Oluf Hartmann. The finest of these orchestral works is *Pan and Syrinx* (1918) for orchestra, which Nielsen described as a 'nature scene for orchestra', though it is a fiercely dramatic work; it deserves to stand alongside the best of his symphonies. It tells the story (from Ovid's *Metamorphoses*) of how Pan got his pipes, chasing the unwilling nymph Syrinx until the gods, taking pity on her, turned her into a reed. By this stage Nielsen's command of contrast in orchestral ideas and their more fragmentary placement was highly developed, and percussion plays an important colour and structural role.

If *Pan and Syrinx* is the finest of these works, easily the most immediately evocative is *En Fantasirejse til Faerøerne* (*An Imaginary Trip to the Faroes*, 1927). It opens with the dark swelling of the grey North Sea, woodwind joining in to scatter light on the crest of the waves, building up to a climax joined by a marching bass. Horns announce a noble Faroese folk song ('Easter bells chimed softly') over shimmering upper strings, taken up by the whole orchestra and sighing away to the tinkle of the triangle. Suddenly the piece bursts into a Faroese dance (surely land has been sighted), the earlier quieter

material weaving in and out and creating the quiet close. This little nature picture deserves to stand alongside **Sibelius**'s better-known shorter tone poems, and would make a show-stopper of an orchestral encore. These orchestral works are essentially Nielsen in a more relaxed, Romantic mood; it is in the six symphonies that his genius is to be found.

The *Symphony No. 1* (1890–92) is the most derivative, showing the influence of Brahms and Dvořák, unmistakable at the end of the first movement. It is constructed with great sureness, displaying a spacious freshness, clean textures, and joy and vivacity in the finale. In the pastoral third movement there is entirely individual writing in the suggestion of a sudden storm in the falling flutes. It also introduced progressive tonality (the first symphony to use the principle). The *Symphony No. 2* (1901–02), titled *The Four Temperaments*, was inspired by paintings depicting the four humours – choleric, phlegmatic, melancholic and sanguine. Its tonality moves from B minor to A major, from the big, expansive opening full of vitality and energy, through the nobility of the opening of the third movement, turning into a more pastoral vein, to the boldness of the finale. There is an analogy with the kind of sound that **Elgar** was producing in the same period.

The *Symphony No. 3 'Sinfonia espansiva'* (1910–11) for orchestra with soprano and tenor has a philosophical content, the title referring to the expansion of the mind and thus of the appreciation of life; the progressive tonality of the whole symphony is announced in the harmonic evolution of the first movement (from D minor to A major). This movement has tremendous force and energy, including a majestic waltz and passages that suggest that Nielsen had absorbed the idiom of **Mahler**. The slow movement is a beautiful and atmospheric evocation that includes a wordless soprano and tenor to add colour and texture. The third movement is a wonderful dancing praise of the joys of life, propelling its assured self-confidence with exuberant brass, while the finale, again with hints of the dance, arrives at a moment when all this heady vitality almost overwhelms itself, the woodwind dying away exhausted. Slowly the dancing, delighted atmosphere picks itself up again and eventually arrives at a climactic assertion of the overall mood. No one in a 20th-century symphony has managed to express such a powerful and untroubled assertion of the explosive joy of life and nature with such a complete absence of banality or cliché.

In the *Symphony No. 4 'Inextinguishable'* (1914–16) the spirit of vitality triumphant comes under threat from darker and more menacing material (a reflection of the events in Europe) and has to strive to emerge; but it does, and hence the title of the work. Nielsen makes a further expressive evolution of the form, linking the four movements so that they are played continuously. The menace is underlined by the use of timpani in the third and fourth movements; in the last, the pair in the body of the orchestra are joined by another at the side of the orchestra, creating a stereophonic effect. Technically, the strife is characterised by the attempt to establish the key of E major; expressively, the symphony moves from the statement of a gentle pastoral theme in A major, heard near the beginning of the first movement, to its triumphant full brilliance in E major at the end of the work. In the journey is a reflective slow movement, and two passages of great turbulence in the first and last movements, both using fragments of themes already heard, that display Nielsen's powers of precise control at their best.

The struggle inherent in the fourth symphony is continued in the *Symphony No. 5* (1921–22); its entire cast is a conflict between two ideas expressed musically in two tonal centres, and indirectly by the construction in two massive movements. Nielsen intended the opening, with violas repeating the interval C–A joined by elements of the orchestra drifting in and out, to express inertia or lack of purpose. What he actually produces is a state of aimless anxiety, filled with insecurity and fears, of which lassitude and inertia can be a psychological consequence; this aspect of the symphony is centred around the key of F. Its opposite, the energy of fulfilment, is centred on the key of B (conflicting with F). That insecure opening is joined by martial percussion, leading to a controlled menacing chaos, an emotionally deadened world with the various sections of the orchestra at odds with each other, both in terms of key and the fragments of themes they use. That hollow world comes to a close as violas infuse a warm, noble light over the frightened darkness, complete with a fanfare. But the themes from the darkness return, building up to a huge fantastical climax, a collage of minutely organised material, the snare-drum, playing ad lib, attempting to stop the progress of the whole symphony. The huge construction moves into a cathartic hymn, G major triumphant, until ending in calm but inconclusive clarity. The second movement opens with a joyous and vital energy. An inconclusive climax leads to a fast fugue, exchanged for a spare landscape (another fugue), moving the symphony to its close, where the key of E flat major finally triumphs in a great outpouring, silencing all the previous conflict. In this marvellous symphony lies the primal opposition of the 20th century, between the propelling thrust to improve the lot of humankind, and the forces of anger and anxiety that seek to constrict it.

The *Symphony No. 6 'Sinfonia semplice'* (1924–25) is the culmination of this cycle. It is anything but simple, except in the paring away of orchestral texture and the remove at times to the most innocent of emotions, and it has baffled many. However, it is first cousin to another sixth symphony, that of **Martinů**, not in terms of construction, but in the instinctive exploration of the opposition of styles and material that the composers had already assimilated in more conventional settings. The first movement, opening with the sound of bells on the celesta, an idea that will recur in the symphony when a calm is needed is full of lean textures (often only one or two instruments), passages of almost deliberate naïvety, such as the march at the opening, sections without any sense of key, or with clashes of key, and a child-like atmosphere. Eventually it moves into a disturbing, thick-textured climax resolved by the bell sounds, only to return to the disturbing, polytonal mood. The extraordinary second movement had no match in the literature of the symphony until **Shostakovich's** fifteenth symphony, a world that suggests the puppet theatre or the toy store. The third movement, with its searching, anguished string ostinati, unfolds a seascape seen from the flat Jutland shoreline with its limitless sky, anticipating **Britten**'s 'Sea Interludes' from *Peter Grimes*. The symphony moves on to a new plane of expression in the fourth movement, from a sardonic, mawkish march to an atmosphere of disjointed ideas and points of colour, together with moments of jovial rhythm, the theme from the more furious passage, and textures of minute delicacy. It is as if the ideas in the symphony had been taken apart into fragments, and left with their essence, with a sense of logic that is haunting and instinctively appropriate, the silence between the fragments of crucial importance.

Nielsen also wrote three concertos. The *Violin Concerto* (1911) shows Nielsen sitting on the cusp of late Romanticism; much of the writing has a Romantic limpidity and beauty of line, reflecting Nielsen's own prowess as a violinist. The first movement is preceded by a slow introduction moving from G major to D minor (the progressive tonality of the whole concerto); the body of the movement is attractive, relatively conventional and, like the finale, not exceptionally inspired. The slow movement is deliberately simple and lyrical, with a Romantic sense of nostalgia, and acts as a slow introduction to the linked finale. The *Flute Concerto* (1926) is a lovely and straightforward work, with a refined delicacy in the solo writing and a small orchestra to give clear textures. Its generally pastoral air covers martial and more ruggedly emphatic elements; a classical dance also appears, with touches of restrained humour. The *Clarinet Concerto* (1928) combines neo-classical orchestral writing with florid, bold solo writing, with some extraordinary effects, such as the combination of clarinet and snare-drum, which sometimes acts as a kind of counter-instrument to the soloist, sometimes as a link between soloist and orchestra. The solo line often has little sense of key, in contrast to the orchestra; like the *Symphony No. 6*, this is not an easy work on first encounter, but a rewarding one.

Nielsen's two operas have remained in the Danish repertoire, but are less well known outside Denmark. *Saul and David* (1898–1901), whose libretto by Einar Christiansen is based on the biblical story, concentrates on the psychological conflict between the two main characters and ends with David's coronation. With a relatively taut four-act plot (the Witch of Endor scene is notably dramatic), it contains fine music in the idiom of the second symphony, especially in the choral writing, which has given it the unjustified reputation of being more an oratorio than an opera. His three-act comic opera *Maskarade* (1904–06) to a libretto by Vihelm Andersen, has recently become much better known. It is based on a classic Danish comedy by Ludvig Holberg (1684–1754). The opera is set in 1723, and opens with the hero Leander discussing his love life with his valet Henrik. The previous night Leander had fallen in love with an unknown woman at the Masquerade, and they exchanged rings. However, Leander's father has promised him to another, whose father reveals that his daughter had a similar experience the previous evening. The second act introduces the people on their way to the Masquerade, which continues that night. Leander and Henrik, locked up by Leander's father to prevent them attending the Masquerade, escape to join in the fun. In the last act, the eventual unmaskings reveal that the unknown woman is actually the person Leander is to marry; but they also reveal the presence of his father, and, unknown to either of them, his mother. In the music for this zestful little comedy, Nielsen reverts to the spirit of the Classical comic opera within the means of the early 20th century, anticipating a similar inspiration for **Strauss** and von Hoffmannsthal in *Der Rosenkavalier*. This inspiration is immediately obvious from the overture and the orchestral interludes, often heard on their own (though the lovely prelude to Act II has its own antecedents in Scandinavian musical tone-painting), while the role of Henrik has parallels with that of Figaro, especially when he has to have the final word. Allied to this was Nielsen's growing interest in folk song, which indirectly colours much of the vocal writing, overtly in such arias as Jeronimus's 'Fordum var der Fred paa Garden'. Those expecting a similar style to the symphonies will be disappointed, but this opera is full of delights, the characters drawn with warmth, humour and understanding, and only the absence of the kind of deeper comic-tragedy that is found in Mozart or **Strauss** prevents a more considerable achievement. The attractive and unassuming little *Aladdin Suite* op. 34, drawn from Nielsen's incidental music (1918) to the play by Adam Ochlenschlager (1779–1850), may also be encountered; it has something of the grace, colour and dancing swirl of Tchaikovsky's ballets, combined with many exotic touches in keeping with its subject.

Of Nielsen's other music, his songs increasingly moved away from the art song to folk forms, and many have become generally popular in Denmark. More serious in content are the *Three Motets* op. 55 (1929) for chorus, Nielsen's last major work, which are settings of the Psalms in Latin. There are also two major late piano works which show how far Nielsen had travelled in the evolution of his idiom. The *Suite* op. 45 (1920) for piano, his finest piano work, has six contrasting sections rather than the formal layout of a conventional suite, and is harmonically restless and experimental, while the *Tre Klaverstykken* (*Three Piano Pieces*, 1928) have

been compared to **Bartók** in their suggestion of atonality and the use of embryonic
tone clusters. His major organ work, *Commotio* (*Movement*, 1931), is an important
contribution to the organ literature, in
toccata form. The genial *Wind Quintet*
(1922) was written for the Copenhagen
Wind Quintet, and the variations that
create the finale reflect the different characters of the quintet's members. In the
prelude to the finale the cor anglais replaces the oboe, and the eleven variations
include discourse and argument between
the instruments, as well as two unaccompanied variations (for bassoon and for
horn).

Nielsen's music is still woefully
neglected outside Scandinavia; he has suffered in the reaction against the post-
Romantics observable from the 1960s
onwards (**Sibelius** has suffered a similar
neglect), and his innovations and highly
individual voice have not yet been fully
recognised. Yet his influence has been
more considerable than is suggested by his
current position, most directly on **Shostakovich** and on **Britten**: those familiar with
the latter's work will find many stylistic
resonances in Nielsen's later music. Similarly, the experience of Nielsen's fifth lies
behind **Vaughan Williams's** sixth symphony. Less directly, **Martinů** extended
the principle of progressive tonality, with
the same goal of the search for hope in any
situation. As the century draws to a close,
it is becoming clear that Nielsen's fifth and
sixth symphonies join those from **Mahler,
Sibelius, Vaughan Williams, Martinů** and
Shostakovich in providing the core 20th-
century works in which an expression of
the human condition has been most fully
realised.

Nielsen was conductor of the Copenhagen Royal Orchestra from 1904–14, assistant conductor at the Royal Opera
(1908–14), and regularly conducted the
Göteborg Symphony Orchestra in Sweden
between 1918 and 1922. He taught at the
Copenhagen Conservatory (1915–19), having joined its governing board in 1914.

RECOMMENDED WORKS
Clarinet Concerto (1928)
Commotio for organ
Flute Concerto (1926)
tone poem *An Imaginary Trip to the
Faroe Islands* (1927)
tone poem *Pan and Syrinx* (1918)
tone poem *Saga Drøm* (1908)
String Quartet No. 4 (1906, revised
1923)
Suite op. 45 (1920) for piano

Symphony No. 1 (1890–92)
Symphony No. 2 *The Four
Temperaments* (1901–02)
Symphony No. 3 *Sinfonia espansiva*
(1910–11)
Symphony No. 4 *Inextinguishable*
(1914–16)
Symphony No. 5 (1921–22)
Symphony No. 6 *Sinfonia semplice*
(1924–25)

BIBLIOGRAPHY
R. Simpson, *Nielsen*, 1979

Nørgård Per *
born 13th July 1932 at Gentofte

Per Nørgård has through his own experimentation and through his teaching, particularly at Århus Conservatory, established himself as the most important and
influential Danish composer of his generation. His early music was in a Scandinavian
nationalist style, influenced by **Sibelius**
(the choral *Aftonland*), and then included
neo-classical features (*Triptychon* for chorus and organ or wind instruments, 1957).
The culmination of this period is *Konstel-
lationer* (*Constellations*, 1958), for twelve
string solo instruments or twelve string
groups, a three-movement concertante
work that still shows the influence of his
teacher Vagn **Holmboe**, but which is
rhythmically organised by serial techniques.

Nørgård became increasingly aware of
developments elsewhere in Europe, and
after a series of pieces entitled *Frag-
menter* (1959–61) he developed what
might be described as a minimalist style.
Most characteristic is the continual contrapuntal and rhythmic transformation of
short motifs, and a concentration on colour
and texture, flexible rhythms, and the
creation of a sense of static repetition. He
had used overlapping layers of different
tempi in the otherwise conventional *Clarinet Trio* (1955). By *Inscape* (1969) for
string quartet, the preoccupation with
texture had been established, and contrasts are provided by different flexible
rhythms. He had also developed the notion
of what he has called 'infinite series' – a
method of establishing hierarchical relationships within a chromatic palette, and
which remains the same for each work
even though the motivic series may vary.
This usually results in the repetition of the
harmonics of a particular note, adding to
the sense of minimalism and creating resonances that are generally more consonant

than dissonant. The basis of the method is to have elements of the series, which is capable of an infinite number of transformations, running in parallel at different tempi. The principle is demonstrated in *Voyage into the Golden Screen* (1968) for chamber orchestra, while in *Arcana* (1970, revised 1975) for electric guitar, amplified accordion and percussion the emphasis is on the timbral merger of the instruments.

The equally minimalist *Symphony No. 2* (1970–71) uses the 'infinite series' principle, in a single movement including the first 4,096 notes of the infinity row. The effect is of a slowly undulating variation of material, gradually evolving more incident, lyrical or interjectory; there is no sense of traditional symphonic development other than by the continuous transformation. The static *Symphony No. 3* (1972–75) for chorus and orchestra is as questionable a 'symphony' as its predecessor, and also concentrates on textures, using the infinity series as well as the Golden Section for rhythmic values.

In the early 1980s Nørgård's music underwent a further change, adding more violent and dramatic elements, following his discovery of the works of the schizophrenic Swiss artist and writer Adolf Wölfli. The major work to reflect this change was the collage-like *Symphony No. 4* (1980–81, subtitled, after Wölfi, *Indischer Roosen Gaarten und Chineesischer Hexensee*). Violent, sometimes brutal juxtapositions of various styles and borrowings (including bird-song) reflect the subject matter. Among his other works of the early 1980s is the unusual *Plutonium Ode* for soprano and cello, a passionate setting of Ginsberg's poem against nuclear power, with a virtuoso cello part.

Nørgård has also written works designed for teaching, in which he attempts to combine modern musical styles with ease of playing or singing. He was music critic for the Copenhagen *Politiken* (1958–62), and taught at the Odense Conservatory (1958–61) and the Copenhagen Conservatory (1960–65) before establishing himself at Århus.

RECOMMENDED WORKS
Symphony No. 2 (1970)
Symphony No. 3 (1972–75) for chorus and orchestra
Symphony No. 4 (1980–81)

Ecuador

Ecuador's main 20th-century composer has been Luis Salgado (born 1903), who developed a nationalistic idiom using native themes and pentatonic scales, and Ecuadorian history and subject matter. His major works include seven symphonies, two ballets (*El Amaño*, 1947, and *El Dios Tumbal*, 1952), a symphonic suite *Atahualpa o El Ocaso de un imperio*, and three operas including *Cumandá* (1940, revised 1954), set in the Amazon with a native theme. He taught at Quito University from 1934 to 1968.

Eire

Introduction

Ireland's major contribution to 20th-century music has been in the field of folk and popular music rather than classical; her folk songs are heard worldwide, and the more recent fusion of Celtic music with rock music has been a major international influence.

Irish classical music was founded on the achievement of John Field (1782–1837) in piano music, and the opera singer and composer Michael Balfe (1808–70). However, two major British figures of the late 19th and early 20th century were actually Irish, Charles **Stanford** (1852–1924) and Hamilton **Harty** (1879–1941), both of whom wrote in a late Romantic idiom. Both were sufficiently aware of their native roots to include Irish elements in their music, and properly belong to any history of Irish music. Irish influences are to be found in the works of a number of English composers of the same period, notably Arnold **Bax** (1883–1953), who wrote Irish nationalist novels under an assumed name.

The composers following this generation, who have worked exclusively in the context of an independent Eire, are virtually unknown outside Ireland. Frederick May (1911–85), who studied in Vienna but whose compositions were curtailed by the onset of deafness, is best known for his articulate *String Quartet in C* (1936), and Brian Boydell (born 1917), active as a teacher and promoter of new music, for his own string quartets. Gerard Victory (1921–95) and John Kinsella (born 1932) both adopted 12-tone techniques; the former is known for his radio and television work, and his output includes *Jonathan Swift – a symphonic portrait*, a descriptive tone poem following the life of the Irish satirist. Seán Ó Riada (1931–71), musical director of the Abbey Theatre from 1955 to 1962, was eclectic in style, ranging from 12-tone to folk song, and is known for his series of works titled *Nomos*. In an Irish context (but not that of Eire) mention should also be made of Howard Ferguson (born 1908), the major Ulster composer of the 20th century. His small, neo-Romantic output concentrated on chamber works, notably the *Octet* (1933), but also includes the choral *The Dream of the Rood* (1958–59). He gave up composing in the early 1960s, feeling he had already said all he wanted to, and concentrated on musicology.

In Eire there is a lively group of younger composers centred on Dublin, but these have yet to be heard widely outside Ireland; they include Roger Doyle (born 1949) whose works sometimes reflect popular influences, and often use electronics. His output includes stage works, notably *The Love of Don Perlimplin and Belisa in the Garden* (1984, revised 1988), based on Lorca, and he has produced one of the first scores for the new technology of virtual reality (1992).

Eire Music Information Centre
Contemporary Music Centre
95 Lower Baggot Street
Dublin 2
Eire
tel: +353 1 661 2105
fax: +353 1 676 2639 in Eire

Harty (Sir Herbert) Hamilton*
born 4th December 1879 at
Hillsborough (Co. Down)
died 19th February 1941 at Hove

Sir Hamilton Harty is probably better remembered as a conductor than a composer, though there has been a recent revival of interest in his music. With Field (1782–1837), Balfe (1808–70) and **Stanford** he remains Ireland's most distinguished composer. Born in an age when all Ireland was part of the UK, he spent much of his professional life in Britain, although he retained a love of Irish folk tradition, which informs his otherwise overtly Romantic idiom, often derivative (from Tchaikovsky to **Sibelius**) and usually traditionally tonal.

Most of Harty's music for orchestra, when not actually quoting Irish material, has Irish legend as a programmatic base. Best known is the tone poem *With the Wild Geese* (1910) – an Irish regiment who fought for the French in 1745 – which is a dramatic and marvellously stirring evocation of the period leading up to a battle. More familiar by name than by performance, *An Irish Symphony* (1904, revised 1915 and 1924) is a compendium of themes based on Irish folk tunes, combining bright warmth and the Irish melancholy that infects all his music. It is well crafted and attractive, if without depth, with some expansive moments. The *Violin Concerto in D minor* (1908) is entirely abstract. The first of many 20th-century compositions especially written for the famous violinist

Josef Szigeti, it is in the Romantic virtuoso tradition, sympathetic and with singing but not especially memorable solo lines. The slow movement is a poetic song with the soloist playing almost continuously. The *Variations on a Dublin Air* (1912) for violin and orchestra are in a similar vein. By far the most impressive of these earlier works is the *Ode to a Nightingale* (1907) for soprano and orchestra. The extended setting of Keats's poem has something of the expressive ecstasy and wide-ranging, high solo lines of late Romantic vocal settings on continental Europe, looking to Wagner and **Mahler** while influenced by **Elgar** rather than Tchaikovsky. His gift for rich orchestration is sharply focused in contrapuntal writing of considerable clarity.

Harty's conducting career limited composition later in his life, but the handful of works include some of his most appealing music. The *Piano Concerto* (1922) is a virtuoso concerto in the tradition of Tchaikovsky and **Rachmaninov** – Harty was himself a concert pianist and an accomplished accompanist. The work combines grandeur and tongue-in-cheek effects with deft touches of orchestration, such as a bell in the attractive slow movement. The opening of the short fantasy for flute, harp and orchestra, *In Ireland* (1935), has a particularly Celtic flavour (heightened by the solo instruments), rhapsodic melodic lines, and is instantly appealing. A Wagnerian influence returns in the opening of the tone poem *The Children of Lir* (1938) for orchestra with wordless soprano solo. It is based on the Irish legend of three children of Lir who were turned into swans for a millennium before returning as ancient humans. In spite of some atmospheric moments, sonorous orchestration, and a fine ending, it ultimately lacks the memorability of a **Sibelius** tone poem or the personal idiom of **Bax**, whose infusion of Irish Celticism is far more interesting, and to whom readers are advised to turn first.

Harty's arrangements were staples of the English orchestral repertoire until eclipsed by the movement for authenticity, notably of Handel's *Water Music*, and *A John Field Suite*, orchestrations of piano music by Field. Harty was principle conductor of the Hallé Orchestra from 1920–33, achieving an international reputation for both himself and the orchestra, and was knighted in 1925.

RECOMMENDED WORKS
Ode to a Nightingale (1907) for
soprano and orchestra
fantasy *In Ireland* (1935) for flute,
harp and orchestra
tone poem *With the Wild Geese* (1910)

BIBLIOGRAPHY
D Greer (ed.), *Hamilton Harty: His
Life and Music*, Dublin (1978)

Stanford (Sir) Charles Villiers*
born 30th September 1852 at Dublin
died 29th March 1924 in London

Charles Stanford and Hubert **Parry** were the major figures in the revival of British music at the turn of the century, and Stanford's role as the teacher of many of the next generation of British composers is historically of greater significance than his music. Stanford studied in Germany, and his own music follows German late Romantic models, notably in his seven symphonies. Following his death, his works fell into complete obscurity except for a handful of liturgical works, still often encountered in Anglican churches. Recently there has been a revival of interest in his music, both out of historical curiosity and for his solid if uninspired technique. His work remains entirely in the Romantic tradition, but with the twin influences of Brahms and Irish mysticism. For all their craftsmanship these works lack an especially distinctive voice, partly through the lack of any sense of inherent tension.

The *Symphony No. 3 'Irish'* (1887) is probably the best known of the symphonies, for its Irish influence in the Brahmsian symphonic cast, and it was the work that brought Stanford an international reputation. The scherzo uses echoes of the jig, and the main theme of the slow movement, often compared to the very similar theme from Brahms's fourth symphony (premièred a year earlier), was actually from a collection of Irish folk songs. Irish melodies are again used in the lively and enjoyable finale. The subtitle of the *Symphony No. 5 'L'Allegro ed il penseroso'* (1894) refers to Milton's two poems. With its vigorous and arresting opening, and atmospheric sections in the slow movement, this is a fine example of the well-constructed, if not especially memorable, late Romantic symphony. The *Symphony No. 6* (1905) was written to honour the memory of the artist George Frederick Watts, who had died in 1904, and though without a specific programme was influenced by various works by Watts; a theme representing death returns in each of the four movements. There is a vigour, too, to the opening of this work, with echoes of Dvořák in its largely lyrical drive. The slow movement opens with a limpid cor anglais tune, representing love, which vies with and is eventually overcome by death in a calm close.

Of his concertante works, the unassuming and Brahmsian *Clarinet Concerto* (1902) is still sometimes heard, while the *Piano Concerto No. 2* (1911) is completely under the spell of **Rachmaninov's** second piano concerto (Stanford had conducted the British première just before writing his own concerto). Of his very large chamber output, the best is to be found in the *Clarinet Sonata* (1911), with an Irish lament for its second movement, and the Brahmsian *Piano Trio No. 1*.

Although the Scot Alexander Mackenzie (1847–1935) had written two *Scottish Rhapsodies* in the 1880s, it was Stanford with his *Irish Rhapsodies* who set the example for subsequent British composers of a rhapsody based on British folk musics. The alternately boisterous and quietly beautiful *Irish Rhapsody No. 1* (1902) is based on the heroic Irish legends of Cuchullin, and uses two traditional Irish tunes, the first a battle song, the second the well-known 'Londonderry Air' (its Irish folk-song title is 'Emer's Farewell to Cuchullin'); Stanford provides an attractive and gentle setting for its appearance. The *Irish Rhapsody No. 3* is for cello and orchestra, while the colourful and expansive *Irish Rhapsody No. 4* (1913), subtitled 'The fisherman of Loch Neagh and what he saw', uses a traditional fisherman's song, as well as an Ulster marching tune and the well-known 'The Death of General Wolfe'. The *Irish Rhapsody No. 6* is another concertante work, for violin and orchestra.

Choral works occupy some fifty of Stanford's 177 opus numbers, but apart from his church services, most have been forgotten. The work most often revived is the song-cycle *Songs of the Sea* (1904) for bass and orchestra to verses by Sir Henry Newbolt, a cross between Victorian salon song and sea shanty. Its success led to a second set, *Songs of the Fleet* (1910), of which the third song, 'The Middle Watch', is an effective piece of nocturnal tone painting. His church music set new English standards, especially the often used Anglican service known as 'Stanford in B'. He was also concerned with reviving English opera, but of his ten operas only

Shamus O'Brien (1896) achieved any success, and all are now forgotten.

Stanford taught at the Royal College of Music from its inception in 1883 until 1924, and at Cambridge from 1887 to 1924. He was notorious for the conservatism of his tastes, his most vitriolic distaste reserved for **Debussy** and **Strauss**, whom he parodied in a choral work *Ode to Discord* (1914). His many pupils included **Bliss**, **Bridge**, **Holst**, **Howells**, **Ireland**, **Moeran** and **Vaugham Williams**. He was active as a conductor (notably of the London Bach Choir, 1885–1902), and was knighted in 1902.

RECOMMENDED WORKS
   Clarinet Concerto (1902)
   Clarinet Sonata (1911)
   Irish Rhapsody No. 1 (1902) for
      orchestra
   Symphony No. 5 *L'Allegro ed il
      penseroso* (1894)
   Three Motets op. 38 (1905)

BIBLIOGRAPHY
   J. F. Porte, *Sir Charles V. Stanford*,
      1921, reissued 1976

Estonia

Introduction

Estonia had an independent, nationalist musical life during the period of the Estonian Republic, between the end of Tsarist domination (1918) and the Soviet takeover (1940), a heritage that has blossomed again since the breakup of the Soviet Union. The natural inclination of this compositional life has been to look to Scandinavian rather than Russian models, with the sense of space and luminous light that is characteristic of northern composers. Now Estonia has again achieved independence, her music should be grouped with the other Scandinavian countries rather than with those of the former USSR, and is likely to give pleasure to those who already enjoy other Scandinavian music.

The origins of modern Estonian music go back to Rudolf Tobias (1873–1918) and Artur Kapp (1878–1952); the latter's best-known work is the overture *Don Carlos* (1889). The first Estonian symphony was written in 1908 by Artur Lemba (1885–1963), and gradually Estonian composers introduced Estonian folk music into their works. The main Estonian composers before the take-over by the USSR were Heino Eller (1887–1970) and Eduard **Tubin** (1905–82). Eller's idiom was Romantic, but with Scandinavian colours, and his output included three symphonies and five string quartets. The late Romantic nationalistic tone poem *Dawn* (1918) and the *Five Pieces for String Orchestra* (1953), with their modal shades and a sense of northern space, provide an attractive introduction to his work. He was also an important teacher of the next generation of Estonian composers. The core of **Tubin's** output is his ten symphonies in a neo-Romantic style that have recently attracted much attention. He left for Sweden in 1944.

Estonian music languished in the later 1940s and 1950s under the dead weight of Soviet Socialist Realism, but a revival came with the work of three composers who came to the fore in the 1960s. Eino Tamberg (born 1930) continued the use of folk music, while Jaan Rääts (born 1932) turned to a neo-classical idiom; his fine *Symphony No. 4* is recommended. The third composer, Arvo **Pärt** (born 1935) has become the best known of all Estonian composers. To the distaste of the Soviet authorities, he turned to 12-tone and serial music in the 1960s, and then during the

1970s developed a spare, neo-tonal style which has connections with the minimalists while retaining an atmosphere still recognisably Scandinavian. There is now a lively group of younger composers in Estonia whose works are starting to be heard elsewhere, often under the influence of Pärt and the minimalists, and Estonian music's long obscurity seems finally over.

Pärt Arvo··
born 11th September 1935 at Paide, Estonia

The Estonian composer Arvo Pärt is, with **Schnittke**, the most interesting and inventive of the younger generation of composers who emerged in the former Soviet Union in the late 1960s. Like Schnittke, his music has had considerable international impact, especially after his temporary emigration in 1988, and he is now the best-known composer from the Baltic countries.

His early works combined the influence of the Soviet tradition with an awareness of the Second Viennese School, as well as the Estonian inheritance exemplified by the more traditional **Tubin**. He was one of the first Soviet composers to make public use of 12-tone techniques, especially in *Obituary* (1960, also known as *Nekrolog*) commemorating the victims of fascism. It was condemned as 'ultra-expressionist', though this did not prevent his music becoming widely known inside the Soviet Union in the 1960s and 1970s. Post-Webern serial techniques lie behind the *Symphony No. 1* (1964, sometimes known, with its canonic writing, as the *Polyphonic Symphony*). The organisation is strict (the tone-rows are numbered in the score), divided into two movements ('Canons' and 'Prelude and Fugue'), themselves each in two sections. It is a lean work, influenced in spite of its serial elements by both neo-classicism in its orchestral layout and clarity and by **Shostakovich**. It was preceded by *Perpetuum mobile* (1963) for orchestra, an angry arch that builds to thick orchestral textures before dying away, and an early indication of Pärt's later concentration on a single idea.

Pärt's music in the 1960s is dark, with an undercurrent of destruction, and it started to quote the music of earlier periods in collage effects – the *Symphony No. 2* (1966), for example, takes apart material by Tchaikovsky. Baroque fragments, tone clusters, and tonal chords juxtapose in the short *Cello Concerto 'Pro et Contra'* (1966), where the slow movement is a thirty-second snatch of pseudo-Baroque music, and the final movement is a sarcastic but catchy comment on other Russian and Soviet composers (notably **Shchedrin**). The severe and discordant *Symphony No. 2* uses a squeaky toy for tone colour, which is otherwise dominated by percussion.

By the stylistically transitional *Symphony No. 3* (1971), in three-movement classical form, that assimilation of the past started to include techniques inspired by the medieval European polyphonists, and by Gregorian chant (by coincidence using in the symphony the same chant as Respighi's *Botticelli Pictures*). With this largely peaceful work his harmonic language evolved into a more lyrical and free harmonic idiom with tonal associations; the anger seems to have dissipated, and a luminosity emerges.

After a compositional pause until 1976, a series of sacred pieces under the spell of this liturgical influence emerged, including *Missa* (1977–79) for vocal ensemble and old instruments, and *Cantate domino canticum novum* (1979, a setting of Psalm 95) for vocal ensemble and instruments. On his departure from the USSR, he developed an association with the English Hilliard Ensemble, a vocal group who specialise in early music and who have championed Pärt's music. Accompanying this change of musical direction is an introverted spiritualism, and (like his historical models) a concentration on purity of internal colour and effect rather than any dramatic or overtly emotional expression. The results have similarities with minimalism, and a sense of contemplative ritual pervades. The basis of his harmonic language has become simple and triadic (although the polyphonic webs set up overlapping areas), classical forms abandoned in favour of slow-moving, long-phrased repetitive structures. Pärt himself has pointed to the mystical significance of the tones he uses, which he has described as 'tintinnabulation' (the sounding or the sounds of bells). Among these works are *Tabula rasa* (1977) for two violins, prepared piano and strings, and *Fratres* (1977) which, like a number of Pärt's later works, exists in more than one version: for violin and piano, for twelve cellos, and arranged for string quartet.

The work that first brought international attention was the short *Cantus in Memory of Benjamin Britten* (1977) for strings and bell. Its deceptively simple waves of polyphonic string-writing are based on the extension of a single falling idea, punctuated by the tolling of one of

Britten's favourite instruments; in its basis of perpetual variation Pärt has reconciled the influences both of **Webern** and of medieval polyphonic models. Early liturgical chant and a monastical contemplation are emulated in the *Passio* (*Passio Domini Nostri Jesu Christi Secundum Joannem*, 1982), a very slow-moving meditative setting of the St John Passion using a countertenor voice. The lovely *Stabat Mater* (1985) for three soloists and string trio, similar in evocation, is a more immediate approach to Pärt's haunting liturgical idiom, built on the simplest of materials, relying on the slightest touch of timbre or colour for its movement. The *Te Deum* (1984–86) for chorus, strings, prepared piano and organ opens with long-breathed swathes of string and vocal sound, with little attempt at dramatic colour. But the mesmerising effects of this idiom belie the intensity that very slowly emerges, building to a grand climax before a sparse close in one of Pärt's finest later works. The *Magnificat* (1989) for chorus has a similar effect. The danger of this religious style is that it is inclined to be repetitive, and the *Berliner Messe* (1990–92) for chorus and strings emerges as a less effective variant of the *Te Deum*, without its passion.

Pärt's recent rarefied style has attracted considerable international acclaim, appealing both to those who have been attracted by minimalism, and those who see in his style elements of a more complex tradition. Whether the extremely sparse nature of his recent works will continue to hold such appeal remains to be seen; but his instinct for compositional metamorphosis suggests that he will remain a composer worthy of attention.

RECOMMENDED WORKS
  *Cantus in Memory of Benjamin
    Britten* (1977) for strings and bell
  Stabat Mater (1985)
  Symphony No. 1 *Polyphonic* (1964)
  Symphony No. 3 (1971)
  Te Deum (1984–85) for chorus, strings,
    prepared piano and organ

Tubin Eduard*
  born 18th June 1905 at Kallaste
  (Estonia)
  died 17th November 1982 at Stockholm

Eduard Tubin was the most eminent composer to have emerged from Estonia before **Pärt**. His current prominence, prompted by the advocacy of his fellow Estonian the conductor Neeme Järvi, has been created by a number of critics who have turned to his conservative oeuvre with a certain amount of relief. The subsequent praise, heightened by the composer's long neglect and his escape from Estonia to Sweden in 1944, has been exaggerated. That said, Tubin's work often has moments of considerable interest, and is always well-wrought and sincere.

His ten symphonies, the centrepiece of his output, have a number of features in common. The harmonic language is conventional, even the moments of polytonality more the result of orchestral blocks than harmonic experiment. Two- or three-movement structures are preferred. The orchestral colours are usually sharp-edged and dark, emphasising the opposition of brass against strings. An almost continual rhythmic vigour is maintained by the prominence of percussion, especially timpani, combined with the use of ostinati. The progress of quiet, building to climax, and back to quiet is a regular structural feature. The strength of these symphonies lies in a kind of Scandinavian inevitability, the earnestness of an exile, and in a generally dark-hued view of the world. Their failings are their unmemorable melodies and moments of banality (e.g. the quasi-jazz rhythms crossed with **Khatchaturian**-like melodic line of the second movement of the sixth symphony); overall they add little to the body of symphonic language or structure.

The *Symphony No. 2* (*Legendary*, 1937), with its impressive and quiet opening and close, its echoes of **Sibelius**, its ruggedness and sense of drama, sets out the main features of his work. The *Symphony No. 4* (*Sinfonia lirica*, 1943, revised 1976) is elegiac, with long spans of softer colours and an unfolding sweep of melodic idea in one unbroken movement, mostly pastoral in feel with strings predominant. The *Symphony No. 5* (1948), Tubin's first work in Sweden and sometimes seen as a political statement, uses an Estonian folk song and chorale in its neo-classical slow movement. Marred by the banality of its opening, there are echoes of **Shostakovich**, but the cumulative vigour of the first movement is compelling. With the *Symphony No. 6* (1954), his symphonies take on a new maturity, integrating more closely the elements that had been introduced in the earlier works. Dramatic, and for large forces, it is exotically rhythmical, the saxophone is prominent, and the middle movement has, as already mentioned, jazz echoes. The *Symphony No. 7* (1956–58) is similarly dark, but for a smaller orchestra, and is perhaps the most impressive of the cycle in its purposeful construction and its scope, with the sombre scherzo placed inside the second movement. The two movement *Symphony No. 9 (Sinfonia Semplice*, 1969) is a rather ineffectual return to a less complex idiom, with echoes of **Janáček** in the use of block orchestration in the climax.

Of the minor orchestral works, the Estonian-inspired *Estonian Dance Suite* (1939) or the *Suite on Estonian Dances* for violin and orchestra (1943, orchestrated 1974) are too trite to merit consideration. The *Sinfonietta on Estonian Motifs* (1939–40) has an anachronistic Sibelian drive, while the totally overblown and unmemorable *Concertino for Piano* (1944–45) has a quasi-romantic virtuoso solo part and grandiose gestures. The *Violin Concerto No. 1* (1943) fails to hold the interest, while the *Balalaika Concerto* (1950–79) is best avoided. Among a number of choral works, the *Requiem for Fallen Soldiers* (1950–79) is simple and affecting, with percussion and timpani to the fore. Its première in 1981 was Tubin's last appearance as conductor.

RECOMMENDED WORKS
Symphony No. 2 (*Legendary*, 1937)
Symphony No. 6 (1954)
Symphony No. 7 (1956–58)

Finland

Introduction

Finnish 19th-century history was dominated by Tsarist Russia, which allowed the Finns autonomy as a Grand Duchy until the end of the century, when a policy of Russification was imposed. However, Finnish cultural roots have always been Scandinavian, while the origins of composition in 19th-century Finland were German; consequently Russian influences on the music of Finland are limited. The major Finnish composers during the 19th century had come from Germany, notably Fredik Pacius (1809–91) and Richard Faltin (1835–1919), both important teachers. But it was not until 1882, when the Helsinki Institute of Music (now the Sibelius Academy) and what was to become the Helsinki Symphony Orchestra were founded, that the grounding for a widespread indigenous composition was established.

Immediately a Finnish composer of international importance emerged. Finnish music at the turn of the century was dominated by the commanding figure of Jean **Sibelius** (1865–1957), who achieved international popularity (especially in Great Britain) with his tone poems and his series of seven symphonies. The sense of the northern landscape and emotions that these symphonies evoked has never been matched; in addition, his development of the symphonic form marked a new evolution of the symphony, and with **Mahler** and **Nielsen** he is the most important symphonist of the first part of the 20th century.

The dominance of Sibelius has obscured the very real merits of other Finnish composers of the same generation. Erkki Melartin (1875–1937), philosopher, mystic, naturalist and painter, produced a huge output (including some 300 songs) in a style that ranged from a lyrical Romanticism to a restrained Expressionism. His most important works are his six symphonies, of which the *Symphony No. 6* (1924), martially turbulent in the first movement, nature-painting in much of the rest, exemplifies his style. He was an influential teacher. Selim Palmgren (1878–1951), perhaps the most conservative of this group, concentrated on piano music and five piano concertos. Leevi **Madetoja** (1887–1947) composed three fine symphonies, as well as the quintessential Finnish opera, *Pohjalaisia* (1924). Yrjö Kilpinen (1892–1952) concentrated on *lieder* of a high quality, with some eight hundred songs and only a few instrumental works in his output. Aarre Merikanto (1893–1958) is not to be confused with his father Oskar Merikanto (1868–1924), who wrote the first Finnish opera (*Pohjan Neiti* [*The Maid of Pohja*]). Aarre is now best known for the opera *Juha* (1922), to a story based on a folk-novel by Juhani Aho, whose vocal lines have a close correspondence with the rise and fall of speech. It is a dark, often turbulent work, leavened by folk-inspired sections; the stormy opening of the second act is especially noteworthy. It was not performed until 1963, in part because Merikanto's idiom had generally been considered too advanced – he had come under the influence of **Schoenberg's** atonalism as early as 1925 – but has taken its place with *Pohjalaisia* as the cornerstone of Finnish opera; it should not to confused with the opera on the same subject by **Madetoja**.

The vitality of Finnish composition was enhanced by four composers born between the two World Wars, three of whom have revived Finnish opera with considerable success. Erik **Bergman** (born 1911), an outstanding composer of choral and vocal works, combines delicacy of texture and effect with sureness of word-setting. Joonas **Kokkonen** (1921–96) has concentrated on orchestral and instrumental writing with a mystical atmosphere, and more recently opera. Einojuhani Rautavaara (born 1928) has written in most genres, and is one of the European mainstream composers who has benefited from the example of **Berg**. Currently, his vocal and choral works, often with a strong visionary element, are most likely to be encountered. They range from the rather disappointing *Suite de Lorca* (1973) for unaccompanied chorus to the wide-ranging choral techniques (including cluster effects and chant) of the very effective *The Cathedral* (1983), also for unaccompanied chorus, which muses on human existence. He has written a number of operas, including *Kaivos* (*The Mine*, 1957–63), *Thomas* (completed 1985), and notably *Vincent* (completed 1990). The literate, Expressionist libretto of *Vincent*, by the composer himself, follows Van Gogh's life through a kind of dream flash-back sequence of scenes. The place of the visionary in both religious and artistic terms, the conflict between reality and illusion, and the satire on the uncomprehending experts in Van Gogh's life, are powerfully realised in dark, Expressionist music. Each of the three

acts is preceded by a very effective orchestral prelude depicting one Van Gogh painting; flowing vocal lines are set against 12-tone orchestral writing, and this difficult but intense opera is recommended. Aulis **Sallinen** (born 1935) started as a 12-tone composer, but moved into a freer idiom, notably in his powerful symphonies and in his operas.

Besides these four composers, there is also an impressive group of less well-known figures of the same generation. Seppo Nummi (1932–81) is remembered for his outstanding song cycles and songs, rooted in folk-music traditions. The neo-classicist Einar Englund (born 1916) came to prominence through the symphonic poem *Epinika* and two large-scale symphonies (the *Symphony No. 2*, 1948 has a notably evocative nocturne). He abandoned symphonic works for many years (with a compositional silence from 1960 to 1966), and suddenly in the 1970s produced three concertos, including the *Concerto for Twelve Cellos*, and three new symphonies. Of these, the *Symphony No. 4* (1976) for strings and percussion is a tribute to **Shostakovich**, using many of the Russian composer's stylistic features. He is best known for his piano music, and for the *Piano Concerto No. 1* (1955). Paavo Heininen (born 1938) has written expressive works in most genres, including the chamber opera *The Silken Drum* (1983), based on a Noh play, but is best known for his handling of very large orchestral forces, with a wide range of colour effects. Of the younger composers, Kalevi Aho (born 1949) has received attention; his output includes a large number of symphonies influenced by **Shostakovich**. The *Symphony No. 4* (1972), whose three movements are based on a triple fugue, is a huge, uneven, overblown but sometimes impressive edifice, a Finnish equivalent to the symphonies of the Swede **Pettersson**. His interesting *String Quartet No. 3* (1971) covers a wide range of neo-Romantic effects, from minimalism to fugue, from the tonal to the harmonically astringent. He has also written a one-man opera, *The Key* (1979). Henrik Otto Donner (born 1939) is the most experimental of his generation of Finnish composers, whose works often have a rebellious sense of humour. Jouni Kaipainen (born 1956), with Kaija Saariaho (born 1952), Olli Kortekangas (born 1955), Magnus Lindberg (born 1958) and Esa-Pekka Salonen (born 1958 and best known as a conductor) founded the 'Ears Open' movement, dedicated to absorbing the avant-garde and elements of rock music into Finnish composition.

Finnish Music Information Centre:
Suomalaisen Musiikin Tiedotuskeskus
Lauttasaarentie 1
FIN – 00200 Helsinki
Finland
tel: +358–9–68101 313
fax: +358–9–682 0770

Bergman Erik Valdemar°°
born 24th November 1911 at Nykarleby

Erik Bergman has a high reputation in Finland for the application of new musical languages to the Finnish choral tradition in an individual, unostentatious voice, and for his orchestral works, which include four concertos. He is less well known outside Finland (this in part stems from the unfamiliarity of singers with the Finnish language), but his choral works are outstanding in their marriage of musical and verbal evocation.

His earliest music was in the Finnish mainstream tradition, and he attracted attention with *Rubaiyat* (1953) for baritone, male chorus and orchestra, setting verses by Omar Khayyam. He adopted 12-tone and serial techniques and in the late 1960s introduced mild improvisatory and aleatoric elements into his work. An interest in the folk music of the Near East has added an exoticism of colour and a sense of the mystical, and he has often preferred a refined instrumental texture, with tuned percussion and woodwind, which Bergman himself has called 'refined primitivism'.

Bergman reached an international audience with his serial *Aubade* (1958) for orchestra, which is evocatively tinged with the colours drawn from his study of folk music in Turkey and Egypt. It was followed by a cantata, *Aton* (1959), for speaker, baritone, chorus and orchestra, whose text is a translation of Pharaoh Akhenaton's *Hymn to the Sun;* the chorus use speaking and whispering effects. Bergman's powers of evocation through the combination of musical landscape and words is exemplified in the outstanding *Fåglarna* (*The Birds*, 1962) for baritone, five solo voices, male chorus, percussion and celesta, a setting of a poem by Bergman's wife, the poetess Solveig von Schoultz. The baritone has the role of the persona of the poem, the soloists the gathering of birds with emotive effects, the chorus an atmospheric backdrop of clusters and other effects such as verbal ostinati, tinted by high, delicate percussion, with lower percussion creating drama. *Nox* (1970) for baritone, chorus, flute, cor anglais and percussion is a setting of four poems about night. The first poem is by Quasimodo; the second (by Arp) an evocation of the noisier sounds of night with clanging percussion and ostinati xylophone; the third (by Eluard) a lover's night with tinkling percussion; and the last (by Eliot) a bonfire dance, opening with the shades of night on flute and cor anglais, and continuing with improvisatory dancing drums.

Colori ed improvvisazioni (1973) for orchestra explored subtle colours and their mutations, exotic percussion prominent. *Noa* (1976) for baritone, chorus and orchestra is based on the manipulation of fifteen Hebrew words from the Biblical story of Noah and the flood, with a wide range of vocal effects. *Bim Bam Bum* (1976) for reciter, tenor, male chorus, flute and varied percussion from prepared piano to conch shell, sets poems by Christian Morgenstern. This is an evocative cycle of considerable power, a sardonic humour lying mainly in the verses. The third song ('Fish's Night Song') is a graphic poem without words, instrumentally recreated entirely with unpitched notes. The delicate variety of the instruments is considerable, their pitches often unsubstantiated, and against this the choral writing is often almost tonally chordal; the overall effect is both appealing and haunting. The last song shows Bergman's predilection for marrying the spoken or half-spoken word with music, a technique he learnt from his Swiss teacher Vladimir Vogel. The *Hathor Suite* (1971) for soprano, baritone, chorus, flute, cor anglais, harp and percussion, returns to ancient Egypt, using texts to the cow-goddess Hat-Hor freely translated into German by Siegfried Schott. There is a stronger sense of ritual about this piece, partly through the instrumental effects and the slow rhythmic progression.

A completely different side of Bergman's interest in sonority and colour is shown in the impressive *String Quartet* (1982) of compelling logic and taut, almost exhausting, emotions. The opening movement is expressive and dramatic, exploiting the full range of string effects, as if the spirit of **Bartók** had been transported into the north of the 1980s; the moods that follow range from the serene and melancholic to grinding violence that turns into anxious breathing effects.

Few composers have used the languages developed in the avant-garde period with such delicacy, nuance, and underlying lyricism in vocal works, and those interested in modern choral music are encouraged to discover the music of Bergman. He taught at the Sibelius Academy (1963–76), and has a wide reputation as a choral director.

RECOMMENDED WORKS

Aubade (1958) for orchestra
Bim Bam Bum (1976) for reciter, tenor, male chorus, flute and percussion
Colori ed Improvvisazioni (1973) for orchestra
Fåglarna (*The Birds*, 1962) for baritone, 5 solo voices, male chorus, percussion and celesta
String Quartet (1982)

Kokkonen Joonas*

born 13th November 1921 at Iisalmi
died 2nd October 1996 at Helsinki

Joonas Kokkonen was one of the best-known of his generation of Finnish composers, and followed a mainstream, mostly orchestral, path. Much of his early work was for chamber forces, including the *String Quartet No. 1* (1949), and in neo-classical style. The work that brought him attention was *Music for Strings* (1957), symphonic in scale and in the layout of the four movements, which shows his predilection for alternating darker, pessimistic passages with brighter, more hopeful ideas. In it he combined neo-classical elements with 12-tone ideas, and for a short period 12-tone principles guided his structures, including those of the *Symphony No. 1* (1958–60)

From the early 1960s this developed into the synthesis common to many European mainstream composers of tonal, chromatic and occasional 12-tone harmonic elements. But in Kokkonen's case structures are often built on one or two initial motifs that provide the basic material for the whole work, combined with rhythmic energy and an increasing command of orchestral colour. Of his other symphonies, the tautly argued *Symphony No. 4* (1971) is the most impressive, while the *Symphony No. 3 'Sinfonia da camera'* (1962) for strings gave Kokkonen an international reputation; it uses the B-A-C-H motto theme (H = German for B natural). The alternations of dark and light shading, the strong influence of neo-classicism, and the synthesis of harmonic systems, as well as the characteristic impression of rugged solidity, are well expressed in ... *durch*

einen Spiegel (*Through a Mirror*, 1977) for twelve strings and cembalo. This effective and extensive work of symphonic proportions has both rhythmic drive and moments of mystical atmosphere, with the strong contrast between cembalo and strings providing continual interest. In Finland, Kokkonen has sometimes been compared to **Britten**, and in many passages of this work, particularly when a long flowing line unfolds over chattering strings, the analogy is apt.

However, it was Kokkonen's opera *Viimeiset kiusaukset* (*The Last Temptations*, 1973–75) that brought his name to a wider audience outside Finland. Based on a play by his cousin, Lauri Kokkonen, its central figure is the early 19th-century evangelical leader Paavo Ruotsalainen, who on his death-bed has a series of flashbacks showing his single-mindedness, his abuse of his family, and his arguments with established dogma. A major flaw of the libretto is that all this is announced in the opening introductory scene, mostly semi-spoken against the orchestra; any sense of dramatic expectation or progression is thus weakened. The plot contains a basic contradiction: the first Act, which is essentially about the strongly-drawn character of his first wife Riitta, shows the dysfunctional result of religious fanaticism on the family, while the second, mainly concerned with Paavo, seems to condone this religious fanaticism. Nonetheless, Kokkonen succeeds in making this ill-considered libretto viable by the sheer energy of his music, which drives the momentum on, notably in the power of the fourth scene, and the folk-dance in scene seven. Certain symbols recur – the images of frost and of opening the gate into heaven, and the use of hymn-tunes – and the music, symphonically laid out, is extraordinarily eclectic, drawing on **Nielsen**, **Janáček** and the **Shostakovich** of *Lady Macbeth of the Mtensk District*, but most successfully welded into a personal idiom. Though the lack of character in the libretto (the secondary characters are all cyphers) inevitably leads to a certain lack of character in the score, this opera is worth encountering.

Of his other vocal works, the beguiling *Requiem* (1981) for soprano, baritone, chorus and orchestra, is surprisingly straightforward and conservative in its harmonic idiom. Composed in memory of his wife, Kokkonen intended it to be positive, and it is indeed uplifting, rhythmically vital, the choral lines tending towards a higher range to create a sense of joy, with touches of bright detail from the orchestra. It would be ideally suited to amateur choral societies.

Kokkonen taught at the Sibelius Academy from 1950 to 1963.

RECOMMENDED WORKS
   . . . durch einen Spiegel (Through a Mirror, 1977) for 12 strings and cembalo
   Symphony No. 4 (1971)
   opera *The Last Temptations (Viimeiset kiusaukset,* 1973–75)

Madetoja Leevi Antti[*]
born 17th February 1887 at Oulu
died 6th October 1947 at Helsinki

The works of Leevi Madetoja have been overshadowed by those of his contemporary **Sibelius**, and his supposed debt to the older composer has been overstated, even if the influence is audible from time to time. His idiom is post-Romantic, but he has an individual voice, sometimes imitating or quoting folk song and often using melodies with a modal cast, combined with a strong Scandinavian instinct for nature of a more pastoral vista than Sibelius – as if surveying the farmed lands rather than the raw coastline.

Madetoja's three symphonies deserve to be better known. The central slow movement of the three-movement *Symphony No. 1* (1914–15) is a marvellous creation, opening with a slow, unsettled, swelling seascape of dark colours, building up to the rumblings of a storm and dying away again. The finale is bold and individual, with a close, surrounded by fanfares, of considerable nobility. The *Symphony No. 2* (1926) has a magical opening of pastoral pleasure, with a dancing woodwind figure over held horns and a string melody; the influence of Sibelius emerges in the subsequent build-up of tension. The slow movement is linked without a break, and uses material based on a shepherdess's song heard by Madetoja. The combination of the two movements, with horn calls and a return of the shepherd song ending the andante, is an exceptionally attractive pastoral evocation. The last two movements are also played without a break; the furious third movement completely changes the tone, while the short fourth acts as an epilogue, returning to the tranquillity of the opening with a mysterious and tonally ambiguous atmosphere that evolves into a beautiful golden light. The symphony is linked thematically (the second theme of the opening, which itself is evolved from

the first, reappears in the third movement). The *Symphony No. 3* (1925–26) has a very different feel. Partly written in France, its lighter textures, at times creating the sound of a chamber orchestra, and its gentle and graceful good humour edge towards a French neo-classicism, combined with darker northern colours.

Of his other orchestral works, the early symphonic poem *Kullervo* (1913) was inspired by a story from the Finnish national epic, the Kalevala, and shows the influence of Tchaikovsky. Much more interesting is the suite from the pantomime-ballet *Okon Fuoko* (1927), based on a work by the Danish symbolist Poul Knudsen and taken from a Japanese tale, which is melodically attractive, atmospheric, and restrained in its use of exotic and percussive colours.

Madetoja's opera *Pohjalaisia (The Ostrobothnians,* completed 1923) occupies an important place in Finnish musical history, as the earliest indigenous opera to enter the repertoire. Based on a famous 1914 play by Artturi Järviluoma, it has a nationalist content (attacking Tsarist control over Finland) and is set in Madetoja's rural home area. It draws on folk melodies, and imitations of folk styles.

Madetoja taught at the Helsinki Conservatory from 1916, and then at Helsinki University from 1926; he was also active as a music critic, and conducted the Helsinki Philharmonic Orchestra from 1912 to 1914. His wife, the poetess L. Onerva, wrote many of the words for his songs.

RECOMMENDED WORKS
   ballet suite *Okon Fuoko* (1927)
   opera *Pohjalaisia (The Ostrobothnians,* completed 1923)
   Symphony No. 1 (1914–15)
   Symphony No. 2 (1926)

Sallinen Aulis[**]
born 9th April 1935 at Salmi

Aulis Sallinen has emerged as a major Finnish composer of orchestral works and operas. He has sometimes been called a 'neo-Romantic', but this is misleading as his idiom is less a conscious return to tonal principles than an individual voice that has developed from a mainstream tradition, ultimately from **Sibelius** and **Nielsen**.

In his earliest music he was attracted to atonal and 12-tone methods, but gradually he worked towards an expansion of his harmonic interests, represented by *Quattro per Quattro* (1964–65) for oboe, violin, cello and harpsichord, whose title simply refers to four movements for four instruments. As his idiom matured he evolved a style that combined some of the mainstream European orchestral developments, notably cluster tones, with a diatonic basis to the harmonic language. Often his music has an undercurrent of expectation (sometimes intentionally not fulfilled), created by an underlying sense of pulse, again perhaps traceable back to **Sibelius**. A strong feel for the northern landscape informs his music, as well as a primary opposition: sombre, dark colours and rhythmic figures set against high, bright, clear vistas often created by tuned percussion or high woodwind. Often the darker elements generate the more positive. From time to time this cast takes on an almost fantastical hue, as if the material were being seen through a prism, most obviously in the *String Quartet No. 3*.

His four symphonies provide an effective introduction to his music. The *Symphony No. 1* (1970–71) is perhaps his finest, a concentrated, fifteen-minute single movement of organic growth. All the material grows out of the opening cells, starting with a haunting, sparse, held chord, F sharp prominent, joined by a string quartet with woodwind and percussion. The effect of this opening is of hushed expectation, and, when merged with darker colours in collusion rather than opposition, of new life pushing up from a dark earthiness. Fertile woodwind figures spring out, joined by dancing ideas against the held F sharp, and a climax leads to bell-like sounds from the percussion (a favourite device) and the suggestion of rain-drops. A more vigorous rhythmic figure emerges, and eventually the organic growth is complete, leaving the held F sharp on the horn, and a strong feeling of fulfilment.

The cyclical one-movement *Symphony No. 2* (1972) is for orchestra with a virtuoso percussion part that emerges from the orchestra at the end of the first and in the last of the three sections. Subtitled a 'symphonic dialogue', the slow middle section is especially effective, dominated by a bassoon against a slow, sparse backdrop. The *Symphony No. 3* (1974–75) occupies a large canvas, in three movements. The first was inspired by the seascape around the Baltic island where it was written, with a sense of the wind, the sea in the surging strings, and the cries of gulls in the woodwind. The central movement is a chaconne, built from material in the coda of the first movement. The final movement

returns to the atmosphere of the first, but here the sea builds up into an engulfing orchestral wave pouring over the landscape. The *Symphony No. 4* (1979) has a more concrete message than its predecessors. The symphony was written just after his *Dies Irae* (1978) for soprano, baritone, male chorus and orchestra, which commented on nuclear destruction, and a sense of that fear and danger underlies the symphony. The opening is arresting: an energetic march juxtaposed with a hushed desolation, an opposition the informs the whole work. Eventually the march turns into the fantastical, felt again in the middle movement (subtitled *'Dona Nobis Pacem'*), which attempts to resolve the undercurrent of menace. Here, tuned percussion, joined by woodwind ostinati, oppose more strident brass and strings, and the final movement is dominated by the sound of bells.

Such an opposition of light and dark is found again in the *Cello Concerto* (1977), which has the unusual form of a dark, tragic twenty-minute opening movement countered by a five-minute second movement of brightness. *Chamber Music I* (1975) for chamber orchestra uses a web of short-phrased sound as its opening, from which themes emerge, the atonal hue being gradually cast off. Again there is a contrast of darkness and light, and a slow ending of considerable beauty that returns to the atmosphere of the opening but with transformed material, now diatonic. The more pastoral *Chamber Music II* (1976) is for alto flute and string orchestra, its colours dominated by the rich tones of the solo instrument.

The work which brought Sallinen international prominence was the haunting *String Quartet No. 3* (1969), subtitled 'Some Aspects of Peltoniemi Hintrik's Funeral March' (and arranged for string orchestra, 1981). Its basis is a famous Finnish funeral folk lament, put through five variations, two intermezzi, and a coda; its power lies in the continual sense of distortion and of the fantastical, created less by manipulation of the basic tune than by the surrounding colours and instrumental effects, and by the broken use of folk-like rhythms. The effect of this attractive, immediate, and unusual quartet is not unlike going to a ruined historical site and imagining the sounds that once occupied it when it was full of life.

In the 1970s Sallinen emerged as an opera composer of considerable powers, with a marvellous instinct for dramatic musical atmosphere and for the pace of a musical–dramatic work. He is especially effective at suggesting barely suppressed tension; often the sound-scapes are layered, with an orchestral mass in the background, individual instruments in the foreground, and voices acting independently. The chorus usually has a prominent role. The subjects of his operas concern Finnish identity and nationalism, but inherent is a duality between the tensions of an individual's life and family – Sallinen's heroes are often reluctant heroes – and the wider context. *Ratsumies* (*The Horseman*, 1972–75) established Sallinen as an opera composer. The Horseman of the title turns into a mystic national leader after his wife is seduced by the Merchant to whom they are both slaves. Ultimately the uprising he leads fails. The basic plot is straightforward, but the libretto by the poet Paavo Haavikko is far more complex: allusive, symbolic, often ambiguous, exploring the nature of mysticism in addition to the political and national allegory. This essentially literary complexity is too dense to be encompassed in an opera, but Sallinen produced a powerful score, probing the main psychological layers. Related to the opera is a song cycle *Neljä laula unesta* (*Four Dream Songs*, 1973) for soprano and piano, also to texts by Paavo Haavikko.

The themes of *The Red Line* (*Punainen viiva*, 1977–78), to a libretto by the composer based on a celebrated 1911 Finnish novel by Ilmari Kiant, are both political and social. The backdrop is the first full suffragette elections in Finland in 1907, and especially the accompanying socialist agitation (hence the red line). The foreground is the extreme poverty of parts of rural Finland at this time. The opera is framed by the presence of a bear, loaded with its own political symbolism, but also representing raw nature, who raids the simple farming household at the opening, and kills the man of the farm at the end, with a slash across the throat (another red line). Underlying this scenario is a sense of hope, symbolized by a young birch tree at the close. This powerful, well-wrought libretto perhaps has more resonances in northern frontier countries, such as Finland, Russia or western Canada, where such conditions pertained at the turn of the century and still have resonance today. The musical style and framework are relatively conventional, dividing the opera into two acts and including a few set solos, and treating the story largely realistically. Sallinen has a very strong sense of musical drama and pace, for vocal lines that express the underlying emotions of the

characters (as in the heroine Riika's powerful solo in Act I, scene 2), and for a clarity of orchestration that creates atmosphere and movement; he uses such effects as children's voices with restraint and emotional effect. *The Red Line* is the most effective opera to have yet emerged from Finland.

Kullervo (1986–88) takes as its subject a central myth of Finnish tradition, to a libretto by the composer drawn from the play of the same name by the 19th-century playwright Alekis Kivi, and from the national epic *Kalevala*. Its plot revolves around a blood-feud. Kullervo, victim of a revenge fire in childhood, becomes an outcast who seduces and kills his own sister; his character explores the position of the outsider changed by family events into a figure in whom both good and evil are magnified, and who struggles with the internal conflict. The touches of the Messianic provide strong affinities with the character of the Horseman. The opera is essentially continuous, divided into two acts for convenience more than contrast, and almost all the characters have strong archetypal elements. Much of the scenario is spent in reporting actions rather than presenting them, so that often the opera takes on the qualities of a staged cantata, in spite of its many powerful musical moments.

Sallinen taught at the Sibelius Academy, Helsinki (1965–73).

RECOMMENDED WORKS
    opera *The Horseman* (*Ratsumies*, 1972–75)
    opera *The Red Line* (*Punainen viiva*, 1977–78)
    String Quartet No. 3 (1969)
    Symphony No. 4 (1979)

Sibelius Jean Johan Julius Christian···
born 8th December 1865 at Tavastehus
died 20th September 1957 at Järvenpää

Jean Sibelius is the most distinguished of all Scandinavian composers, and a major figure in the transition from the late Romantic 19th century to the world of the 20th. His importance to Scandinavian music cannot be underestimated, first (following the example of Greig) for his use of indigenous Finnish legends, connected with the Old Norse myths, which established that Scandinavian composers had their own potent heritage to draw on; and second and more crucial, the development (together with the less influential **Nielsen**) of an orchestral sound that reflected the qualities of the northern landscape and light, with the use of *moto perpetuo* figures providing a structural backdrop. Part of Sibelius's initial impact in Finland was his use of nationalist themes at a time when the country was rediscovering its own heritage in the face of considerable Tsarist oppression (Sibelius's family, like most middle-class Finnish families of the period, spoke Swedish rather than Finnish), and his works, like Verdi's, carried political overtones.

His compositional life is a paradox; between 1881 and 1926 he produced a huge number of works; then, after working on an eighth symphony, he fell completely silent until his death in 1957. Although he wrote in all genres (including an early unpublished opera) the core of his output falls into two categories, the orchestral tone poems built around Finnish myths, and the seven symphonies, which span his mature compositional life.

Behind much of his work lies the inspiration of the great Finnish national epic, the *Kalevala*. This work was compiled in 1835 by Elias Lönnrot (1802–84), who brought together a huge body of Finnish and Karelian folk poetry, shaping it into an epic, leaving the actual poetry virtually untouched. Starting with the creation and ending with the coming of Christianity into Finland, its central theme is the struggle between two groups for the talisman 'Sampo', which brings prosperity to its owner; its central character is an old man who defeats his enemies by wisdom and magic. With such an episodic construction it is a gold mine for a composer of tone poems. It is for this reason that so many apparently unconnected stories in Sibelius's tone poems can be traced to the same source.

His earliest treatment of the Finnish epic was in the huge *Kullervo Symphony* (1891–92), not included in his numbered symphonies, which uses baritone, soprano and male chorus. It is a transitional work in Sibelius's output, showing the influence of Tchaikovsky and Bruckner, but also the development of his own mature voice. At the same time he was writing the first of his more familiar orchestral tone poems, *En Saga* (*A Saga*, 1892), whose title is loosely inspired by the Icelandic *Edda*. Like many of Sibelius's tone poems, there is no programme as such; Sibelius preferred to evoke the atmosphere of the story and to paint the landscape setting rather than retell events. Although the

climactic outburst before the typically quiet ending looks backwards rather than forwards, *En Saga* has many of the hallmarks of Sibelius's mature idiom: shimmering string effects countered by rugged themes stalking through the foreground; the sudden generation of powerful impetus swelling into a climax; the brass striding out over a strong underlying rhythmic pulse; and one theme sliding into or over a very different one, an effect that sometimes verges on the polytonal. Much of the melodic cast has suggestions of folk music, but as is usual with Sibelius, these are of his own invention. Another feature of *En Saga* found throughout Sibelius's work is pedal-points, around which the melodic and harmonic material move, as well as themes that grow and develop out of their initial material.

It was followed by one of Sibelius's most popular works, the invigorating *Karelia Suite* (1893), whose title refers to the area bordering on Russia which was a centre of nationalist sentiment. In three movements, it opens with unforgettable fanfares over shimmering strings, swelling through rising strings to the famous march, trumpets buoyed up by the quiet energy of the accompaniment. The central movement (for chamber forces of wind and strings) is a ballade with melancholic overtones but a throbbing pulse, and the last movement another march with percussion again prominent. The influence of the *Kalevala* then re-emerged with the *Lemminkäinen Suite* (also known as *Four Legends*, 1893–95, revised 1896 and 1900), whose four tone poems, usually heard separately, are based on *Kalevala* stories. The best known of these are the third, *The Swan of Tuonela*, and the fourth, *Lemminkäinen's Return*. *The Swan of Tuonela* describes the singing of the swan that glides on the black flood waters of Tuonela, the mythological land of the dead. The swan is represented by a cor anglais, joined by a cello theme against divided strings, and the entire picture is of a ghostly melancholy, the graceful movement of the swan accompanied by pictorial water effects. It was originally intended as the prelude to an opera project, *The Building of the Boat*. *Lemminkäinen's Return* describes the return of the hero, restored to life by his mother and persuaded to forsake his lover, and is more dramatic, with a driving energy gradually building up in thematic snatches; it foreshadows some of the techniques of later symphonies.

It was the nationalist symphonic poem

Finlandia (1899, revised 1900) that gained Sibelius an international audience. The Tsarist authorities had clamped down on freedom of speech, and in response a number of meetings were held, culminating in an evening at the Swedish Theatre to which Sibelius contributed music for a series of tableaux depicting Finnish history, of which *Finlandia* was the last, (three others were published as *Scènes historiques* op. 25). Its dramatic brass opening, countered by a hymn-like theme, the turbulent allegro with an insistent, demanding rhythmic figure from the trumpets, the famous central tune that has become as endemic to Finland as **Elgar**'s *Pomp and Circumstance No. 1* has to the British, all contribute to one of the most stirring pieces of all music, that manages to avoid both bombast and sentimentality.

In 1903 Sibelius wrote incidental music to *Kuolema* (*Death*), a play by his brother-in-law Arvid Järnefelt, and drew from it the short *Valse Triste*. With subdued melancholy it evokes an ill mother dancing with the shades of the night. The symphonic fantasy *Pohjola's Daughter* (1906, probably earlier) returns to the *Kalevala*; a traveller sees Pohjola's daughter, of the land of the North, sitting on her rainbow, spinning. He woos her, and has to perform three magic tasks; he succeeds in two, but not the third, and so he continues his journey. It is one of the most colourful and graphic of Sibelius's tone poems, making full use of the possibilities of the very large orchestra. *The Bard* (1913, revised 1914), represents Sibelius's increasing refinement of texture and economy of means, in a restrained, almost introverted work. Sibelius's final symphonic poem, and his last completed work, *Tapiola* (1925), is a description of the northern woodlands ruled by Tapio, King of the Forest. Its five sections give it the proportions of a symphony, and there is a suggestion of elemental savagery (especially in the storm section) not found in his early tone poems, as well as a descriptive feeling of true, unpeopled wilderness.

These works represent the best of his large output of tone poems and suites, though many of the others, such as *Nightride and Sunrise* op. 55 (1907), or *The Oceanides* op. 73 (1914), are worth exploring. In them Sibelius, along with his contemporary **Strauss**, was bringing a Romantic tradition to a close. Both had their roots in the same Germanic tradition, and both used tonal harmony. While Strauss described the psychological states of heroes or his own family in an increasingly

chromatically complex and dense idiom, Sibelius took a very different route, thinning out the dense late Romantic textures, seeking harmonic progressions that pared off the superfluous, and describing moods and states that are evoked externally; in this he has parallels with some of the northern landscape painters of the period. These concerns also tend towards the abstract, and it was entirely logical that Sibelius's genius should be turned to the form of the symphony.

In the symphonies Sibelius evolved a completely new path of symphonic development, with the first two symphonies acting as a prelude, the third as the catalyst, and the remaining four the evolution of this development. Especially in the last four symphonies, progression is predicated by the different rates of flow within the overall current of a movement, sometimes with a step-like progression. The thematic material is often chosen to aid that flow, with themes that develop from short figures and are often capable of endless transformations. There are few themes that carry their own recognisable emotional weight; that is gained during the flow and by their orchestration. The harmonic progressions are similarly intertwined with this flow: although Sibelius uses essentially traditional frameworks, the method by which they progress is not. He cuts away much that is superfluous, so that one key may abut another without the traditional bridge. Again, this contributes to the sense of pulse, and movement by steps. Similarly, he often uses a favourite device of a pedal-point as an anchor for that flow, around which movement on a very large scale can hinge and allow evolution without disintegration.

All this has led to confusion and contradiction among those who have tried to analyse the later symphonies in terms of 19th-century theory in which key relationships and their placement are primary. (The opening movement of the sixth has been variously described as having a 'normal sonata form' and as having lost all connection with sonata form!) They really need different methods that would recognise the primacy of pulse, and within that the relationships of key. Sibelius was anticipating methods that have become increasingly familiar through the century, both in terms of thematic transformation from germ cells, but more important, progression through the underlying pulse and changes in the surface movement, found in works as disparate as those of **Martinů** and the minimalists. There is another aspect that removes the later symphonies from the Romantic era; as Neville Cardus originally observed, it is very difficult to imagine these symphonies as being peopled by anyone (which is not true of most late-Romantic symphonists, or of **Mahler** or **Shostakovich**); it is possible to imagine them as landscapes, but ones devoid of people. There is a sense of distancing, yet at the same time they are absorbing and involving. Herein, perhaps, lies the real purpose of that pulse and flow; they match our internal physical pulses, particularly our different types and rates of breathing, and it is this that produces such excitement or simple pleasure, and which can be so triumphantly overwhelming when Sibelius builds up to a great climax. This, again, is a specifically 20th-century idea, formulated and utilised in music in the second half of the century; with Sibelius, it is cloaked in the remnants of the 19th-century orchestra and symphonic layout and therefore often overlooked.

The direct utterance of the first two symphonies has made them the best known to general audiences. The memorable first movement of *Symphony No. 1* (1898–99) immediately announces a symphonist of stature, with the sense of growth and propulsion within the sonata form. The second movement suggests a seascape, with distant echoes of Wagner and Dvořák, a sombre opening leading to a haunting nostalgia. The lithe third movement has been compared with Beethoven's *Pastoral Symphony*, from its general mood and the handing of ideas around the orchestra. The last movement returns to Dvořák in attempts to generate momentum and in the later dance-like passages. At its heart is a big, noble tune; this is the weakest movement of the symphony, for while its episodes are interesting, they fail to gel.

The *Symphony No. 2* (1901–02) has an overall mood of expansive triumph, the opening movement one of fermenting energy, expectation alternating with emotional pause at its start, and the subsequent build-up employing a technique where the expected pedal-point is only occasionally sounded, creating considerable nervous tension. The second movement is perhaps the symphonic movement closest to the tone poems, with its unusual opening pizzicato on the lower strings, its dramatic and lyrical elements, and a big swell reminiscent of *Finlandia*. It is the lovely pastoral trio of the third movement that provides the most lyrical slow passage of the symphony, while the gorgeously expansive finale strives for synthesis through the build-up of material over a long period, often using step movements, and largely succeeds.

The *Symphony No. 3* (1904–07) is in three movements, and in it Sibelius moves musically from the 19th to the 20th century. Sibelius suggested the opening movement represented fog banks off the English coast; if so, these fogs were shot through with sunlight, though the uplifting flow of the movement has the feel of the sea. The middle movement has the gentle air of melancholy being released, as if the Swan of Tuonela had been brought out to a calm lake in the dawn sunlight, while the build-up to the climax of the finale has tremendous power.

The four-movement *Symphony No. 4* (1911) is the darkest of the symphonies, constructed on the interval of the tritone, once considered the interval of the devil and here used both to disrupt through dissonance and to build the harmonic progression. Each movement starts with the end note of its predecessors, and as in the later symphonies of **Nielsen** there is little distinction between major and minor. The opening movement is sad and weary, no blaze in the coda but bleak and sparse textures. The second movement makes an attempt to be more jovial, following images of grey, dancing waves; it fails, and the reprise of its A–B–A form is very short, truncated by the timpani. The desolate slow movement has dark, wandering fragments of different themes that eventually coalesce into a brighter image, and dissolve again into fragments, one of which eventually emerges as the major idea. The final movement, of enormous latent energy, has new features, the colours of the glockenspiel, woodwind snarls and screams, and the kind of melodic shapes also heard in *Luonnotar* (see below); the sense of pulse and surge reverberates through this ending.

The *Symphony No. 5* (1915, revised 1916 and 1917) was originally in four movements, but Sibelius revised it into three. Its core is the final movement, which the rest of the symphony sets up, though this is not apparent during its progress. To all intents and purposes, Sibelius had by now evolved his own principles of organic growth, discarding sonata form and contrasts of 'subjects'; discussion in terms of 19th-century models becomes unfruitful. Its opening, with calling horns and woodwind, suggests the calling to a quest, and the movement, heroic in cast, has one long overall flow within which there are passages of organic fertile growth, surges to a climax, and retreats to a lighter, dancing vein. Granville **Bantock**, a close friend of Sibelius, saw this whole symphony as a description of Sibelius's home landscape. The second movement, essentially a theme and variations, has grace and charm and is a kind of interlude between the pace and tensions of the outer movements. The short and magnificent finale, its mood of rock-solid confidence and joy a complete answer to the desolations of the fourth symphony, simply allows the orchestra to breathe in different ways: the long overall breath that is the momentum of the entire movement, the short breaths of the opening string *moto perpetuo*, the glorious rocking breaths of the idea that follows; the different rates of breathing interact and eventually join together. At the same time it transcribes a huge swing around the key of the symphony, E flat, and with the final tremendous hammer strokes arrives at the home key.

The *Symphony No. 6* (1923) is another departure, being Sibelius's pastoral symphony. The textures are leaner, more astringent, the mood more contemplative, the characteristic pulse much less obvious in the opening movement that evolves into a kind of joyous ride through a sparkling countryside. The second movement, with its overlapping rising lines, has almost neo-classical textures, while the scherzo has a jerky march, as if Sibelius's normal flow had been taken apart and recast. The beautiful last movement, the Sibelian pulse more plastic and less assertive, returns to the gentle and the pastoral with a quiet close.

The *Symphony No. 7* (1924) was originally entitled *Fantastica Sinfonica*. As with three other last symphonies, those of **Nielsen** (*Sinfonia semplice*), **Martinů** (*Fantaises symphoniques*), and **Shostakovich**, the composer had arrived at such an instinctive command of his particular symphonic structure that he had departed far from the traditional norms. The symphony is in one movement, and opens with a marvellous fluidity that resolves into an atmosphere of glowing nostalgia and then a hymn-like string theme tinged with sadness, as if shot with golden sunset colours. It builds with a typical Sibelian walking bass in a passage that is among the noblest music written. Trombones join the texture in Nordic fanfare, and the material on which the symphony is built has now all been presented. The luminous mood then evolves into a more turbulent

dance that leads to the equivalent to a recapitulation, with long swirling string figures and the return of the trombones. However, new ideas are introduced, including a suggestion of the waltz and moments of mawkish woodwind. The trombones herald the final section of the symphony, building to an extraordinary climax in which all Sibelius's favourite moods are overlayered: nobility, tense expectations, the vistas of the dark northern landscapes. A great swelling chord emerging into the light of A major, soon touched by sadness. The fanfares return, now nostalgic, woodwind sing a plaintive song over tremolo strings, and suddenly the orchestra emerges in a great swell to C major. The whole work is one overall phrase, the various events rising and falling within it, less the swells of the ocean than the unending reshaping of clouds, some scurrying, some building into thunderheads, some serene, but all part of the same, still unpeopled, vista, ending in the great glory of the sun. After writing a work so self-contained and so complete it is hardly surprising that Sibelius never completed another symphony.

Sibelius's sole concerto is the *Violin Concerto* (1903, revised 1905), an unforgettable work of passionate intensity, requiring richness of tone from the soloist. It is, though, oddly balanced, the massive first movement (completely reordering the normal events of a sonata-form movement) outweighing the other two. It is a transitional work, the solo writing emerging from the 19th-century tradition, and with overall ideas looking towards the later symphonies. Underneath the intensity there is a mellowness to the whole work, especially in the string colours, emphasised by the low writing for the soloist in the gloriously rich slow movement. Sibelius's only important chamber work is the *String Quartet 'Voces Intimae'* (1908–09). It is a beautiful, often meditative work in five movements, using the generation of themes from initial cells that Sibelius was then developing in the symphonies. However, it gives the impression of a symphonist turning to the form rather than a born composer of string quartets; Sibelius's general avoidance of counterpoint throws the emphasis on chordal progression and long evolving short-note phrases, which minimise the contrasts between the instruments, making the quartet rather monochromatic.

Of his vocal music, *Luonnotar* (1913) is the finest, a marvellous nine-minute tone poem for soprano and orchestra setting the

Finnish myth of the creation that opens the *Kalevala*, with the world emerging from the breaking of a teal's egg. The pent-up excitement of the string opening is Sibelius at his descriptive best. Over this soar imaginative soprano lines of an exceptionally wide range, much very high, with a melodic cast that has something of the shape and spontaneity of an improvisatory folk song. Sibelius wrote nearly a hundred songs, all with piano and mostly to Swedish texts, and their variable quality has masked the very real impact of the best; generally they are more effective when sung by larger, operatic voices. The best are to be found in op. 35, op. 36, op. 37 and op. 38. *Six Songs* op. 36 (1899) includes the famous *Svarta rosor* (*Black Roses*), with its flowing accompaniment to a poem by Ernst Josephson about the black roses of sorrow, and the equally well-known and limpidly beautiful *Säv, säv, susa* (*Sigh, rushes, sigh*) to a poem by Gustaf Fröding telling of the death of Ingalill, drowned in a lake. The last of the *Five Songs* op. 37 (1900), *Flickan kom ifrån sin älsklings möte* (usually known as *The Tryst*), is a passionate short ballad by J. L. Runberg telling of a young woman returning home from her unfaithful lover and hiding the fact from her mother. *Höstkväll* (*Autumn evening*), the first of the *Five Songs* op. 38 (1903–04), is a haunting description of a coastline in the autumn rain watched by a traveller, setting a poem by Viktor Rydberg. The restrained piano part is confined at its climax almost entirely to a repeated note before breaking out with a Sibelian intensity. *Two Songs* op. 35 (1907–08), the last of this group to be written in spite of the opus number, comprises two inventive and almost operatically dramatic songs, the piano writing acting as descriptive commentator. *Jubal* is a poem by Ernst Josephson about Jubal killing a swan at dusk and agreeing to mourn it in song every evening, and *Teodora* a setting of Bertel Gripenberg where the singer tells of his lust for the Byzantine Empress Theodora with an almost Straussian dark eroticism; with *Luonnotar*, this is the most original of Sibelius's vocal output. Of his late songs, the first of the *Six Runeberg Songs* op. 90 (1917), *Norden* (*North*), is a magical evocation of the frozen north, the flying swans of the poem again firing Sibelius's imagination, the piano providing the monochromatic colours of tinkling ice, the whole setting seeming to occupy one long breath.

Sibelius has suffered in the reaction against the late Romantics of the 1940s and 1950s: those who appreciated his earlier music precisely because it belonged to the residue of the 19th century could not understand his later music, as it moved into the 20th. Many who might have appreciated this later music were put off by the Romantic hue of the earlier music, and were denied works that are one of the cornerstones of 20th-century music, and the foundation of almost all Scandinavian composition.

RECOMMENDED WORKS
Symphonic poem *Finlandia* op. 26 (1899)
Karelia Suite op. 11 (1893)
Lemminkäinen's Return op. 22, No. 4 (1895)
symphonic fantasy *Pohjola's Daughter* op. 49 (1906)
tone poem *Luonnotar* (1913) for soprano and orchestra
symphonic poem *En Saga* op. 9 (1892)
The Swan of Tuonela op. 22, No. 3 (1895) for orchestra
Symphony No. 1 (1899)
Symphony No. 2 (1901–02)
Symphony No. 3 (1904–07)
Symphony No. 4 (1911)
Symphony No. 5 (1915)
Symphony No. 6 (1923)
Symphony No. 7 (1924)
symphonic poem *Tapiola* op. 112 (1926)
Two Songs op. 35 (1907–08)
Valse Triste op. 44 (1903) for orchestra
Violin Concerto op. 47 (1903, revised 1905)

BIBLIOGRAPHY
R. Layton, *Sibelius*, London, 1965, 1978

France

Introduction

Although Paris remained one of the chief musical centres of Europe, French classical music during the 19th century was eclipsed by German and Austrian music, and by Italian opera. Throughout the century, France produced composers of interest and sometimes passing fame, but lacking the individuality and spark of lasting genius. The exception was Hector Berlioz (1803–69), arch-Romantic musical visionary, whose example continues to resonate through French music. The French composers of the later 19th century fall into distinct groups. Camille Saint-Saëns (1835–1921) was the major French Romantic composer, often under the spell of Liszt; his sense of technical craftsmanship provided an important example to the next generation of composers. Other Romantics included Emmanuel Chabrier (1841–94), an admirer of Wagner. French opera, mostly on a grand scale, provided a second thread, including those of Charles Gounod (1818–93), Georges Bizet (1838–75) and Jules Massenet (1842–1912), all of whom included an element of realism in depicting relationships between ordinary people in their major works, in contrast to the mythology of Wagner or the characters of power and position in Italian opera before **Puccini**. More notorious than any of these composers was Jacques Offenbach (1819–80), whose small-scale musical comedies stormed Europe, and whose qualities of grace, sparkle, and sheer fun helped establish an important strand in later French music.

The third main group provided the foundations for a renaissance of French music, and were centred around the figure of César Franck (1822–90). The basis of Franck's aesthetic – a preoccupation with musical form and architecture and an admiration for Classical forms and examples – was very different from the German and Austrian ones. Its importance to later French music has been overshadowed by his best-known technique, the use of germ themes that return in different movements in a cyclical principle. Two of his pupils developed and promoted this aesthetic in both their music and their teaching. Vincent **d'Indy** (1851–1931) was the more conservative, and fused the inheritance with an admiration for Wagner while maintaining a French clarity. Gabriel

Fauré (1845–1924) refined the aesthetic, especially in his chamber works, taking it towards Impressionism, and in the final years of his life anticipating neo-classicism. Of Franck's other pupils, Henri Duparc (1848–1933), whose output was curtailed by mental illness, produced perhaps the most perfect collection of songs ever written.

Meanwhile, two composers emerged at the end of the 19th century who were to cement the renaissance of French music initiated by Franck, and place it on an equal footing with German and Austrian composition. Claude **Debussy** (1862–1918) revolutionised the way composers have thought of music, initially through what has become known as Impressionism. Maurice **Ravel** (1857–1937) was both less revolutionary and less influential, but the immense popularity of his music established a vital and colourful alternative to the Germanic tradition. Of their contemporaries, Paul **Dukas** (1865–1935), an important teacher, refined the late Romantic tone poem with incisive orchestration and formal construction. The eccentric Erik **Satie** (1866–1925) developed the miniature form often with dissonant harmonies, and including unusual sound sources later in his career; his particular brand of the absurd, his quirky sense of humour, and his drive towards simplicity were widely influential. Albert **Roussel** (1869–1937) became the classicist of the period in his own individual style, traceable back to Franck and with oriental influences from his own travels.

The potency of French music was confirmed after World War I as Paris became a magnet for writers, visual artists and composers from all over the world. Here were to be found such diverse artists as Picasso and Joyce, Hemingway and Le Corbusier, and among the foreign composers who lived in Paris in this period were **Stravinsky, Martinů,** and **Prokofiev**. French composition followed clearly defined lines, committed to the traditions of tonal music, or their development by **Debussy**, rather than following the harmonic revolution of Schoenberg and his followers.

The interwar period was dominated by a group known as 'Les Six', consisting of Georges Auric (1899–1983), Louis Durey (1888–1979), Darius **Milhaud** (1892–1974), Francis **Poulenc** (1899–1963), Germaine Tailleferre (1892–1983) and perhaps the most outstanding, the Swiss Arthur **Honegger** (1892–1955). Although they together produced a group of piano pieces (*Album des Six*, 1920), and a joint ballet (*Les*

Mariés de la Tour Eiffel, 1921), their common denominator was extra-musical, the influence and leadership of the writer Jean Cocteau (1891–1963), whose ideas of modernity, simplicity and directness were themselves influenced by **Satie**. The six composers quickly went their different ways, and had little in common musically. Auric wrote ballets for Diaghilev, but remained close to Cocteau, writing music for his films. **Milhaud** also followed Cocteau's aesthetic in some of his huge output, especially his collaborations with the writer Paul Claudel, but otherwise pursued neo-classicism and developed polytonality. His idiom became very wide-ranging; the best of his works show what a prodigious talent he had, and the rest what little self-criticism. Durey became politically involved, eventually writing settings of communist writers, including Mao Tsetung and Ho Chi Minh. **Poulenc** is the most interesting of the French composers of this group, shedding his early reputation for flippant gaiety and elegance for a thoughtful and personal idiom characterised by grace and craftsmanship, including many superb songs. Tailleferre remained the most conservative of the group, and is now most often encountered in her harp music. Outside 'Les Six', Florent **Schmitt** (1870–1958) represented a last flowering of late Romanticism in France.

A reaction to what was perceived as the shallowness of this period of French composition, and especially the neo-classicism that became prevalent in Paris in the 1930s, was inevitable, and future historians may see the revolution that followed (partially delayed by World War II) as being as crucial to the development of classical music as **Debussy** or **Schoenberg**. There was already a French composer that had started this revolution, but since his ideas were so far in advance of 'Les Six', and because many of his premières had taken place in the unsympathetic milieu of New York, he had not been as noticed. Edgard **Varèse** (1883–1965) was experimenting with completely new concepts of sound and its organisation, including the use of new instruments, and with **Debussy**, **Schoenberg, Webern** and **Cage** was one of the innovatory musical geniuses of the century. One significant French composer, André **Jolivet** (1905–1974), had studied with Varèse (1930–33); with Olivier **Messiaen** (1908–92), the figure who was to become central to this revolution, he co-founded 'La Jeune France' in 1936. The other members were Yves Baudrier (1906–88), whose output was restricted by ill-health, and Daniel-Lesur (born 1908), who, beside his own compositions, did much to promote contemporary music on French radio after World War I. Jolivet developed an idiom tinged with exoticism, often with an incantatory or mythical impulse, dissonant effects and sometimes complex rhythms, and stood largely apart from developments after 1945. Messiaen, however, became the major French teacher of the period, writing music of astonishing power and spirituality, his mysticism paralleling that of Jolivet but firmly rooted in Christian theology. Messiaen's innovations included the development of modes, the extension of rhythmic patterns, sometimes influenced by Eastern musics, and the exploration of a wide range of new tone colours, often drawing on bird-song.

These innovations paved the way for post-war developments; in particular, the systematisation of rhythm pointed to the possibility of 'total serialism', the extension of 12-tone principles into areas of musical construction other than harmony. This major step was led by one of Messiaen's French pupils, Pierre **Boulez** (born 1925), who consolidated the principles of total serialism in 1951–52. The importance of this step cannot be overestimated. Quite apart from the widespread emulation and development of serialism all over the world (including such French composers as Jean **Barraqué**, 1928–1973, and Gilbert **Amy**, born 1936), it reconciled two divergent strands of musical continuity that had been temperamentally at odds for 150 years and beyond, the French and the German traditions. On the one hand total serialism can be traced back through **Webern** and **Schoenberg** to Wagner and ultimately to Beethoven; on the other, through **Messiaen** to the twin progenitors of **Varèse** and **Debussy**, and beyond them to Franck and his precursors (it is perhaps no coincidence that Boulez is celebrated as a conductor of both Wagner and Debussy). To cement this conjunction, one of Messiaen's other pupils, **Stockhausen**, took serialism back to Germany. This reconciliation is partly responsible for the international embrace of serialism; from the 1950s the major divide in classical music has been not between France and Germany but between Europe and North America, however strong the cross-fertilisation.

At the same time, another musical revolution was taking place in France which may prove even more far-reaching. **Varèse** and **Messiaen** had already used electronic instruments (the ondes martenot), and Varèse completed the first work for orchestra with tape in 1954, but the development of new technology (particularly the tape recorder) gave birth to a completely new medium: electronic music. The pioneers were Pierre **Schaeffer** (1910–95) and Pierre **Henry** (born 1927), who had studied with Messiaen. Schaeffer's first electronic works were composed in 1948, using the technique of *musique concrète*, in which naturally occurring sounds, including those of musical instruments, are electronically manipulated to create completely different sounds. Electronic composition using purely electronic sound sources soon followed. The 'Groupe de Musique Concrète' was established in 1951, and an advanced interest in electronic and then computer technology has informed French music ever since, notably in the Service de la Recherche de O.R.T.F. (French Radio), and then in 1977 with the opening of the Institut de Recherche et de Coordination Acoustique-Musique in the Centre Pompidou in Paris, directed by **Boulez**, which has attracted composers from all over the world interested in advanced technology. Among later French composers of electronic music have been François **Bayle** (born 1932), François-Bernard **Mâche** (born 1935), and Luc Ferrari (born 1929), who increasingly left the sound sources as natural as possible, eventually arriving at 'anecdotal music': *Presque rien no. 1 (Nearly Nothing No. 1,* 1970) is the skilfully edited sounds of a busy beach, anticipating the environmental soundscapes of the 'New Age' movement.

Meanwhile, other French composers have pursued a less radical path. Jean **Françaix** (1912–97) continued the French tradition of grace and charm, while the most interesting of the mainstream composers have been Marcel **Landowski** (born 1915), absorbing some of the new sounds into a more traditional idiom, and Henri **Dutilleux** (born 1916), who has forged a powerful individual idiom emerging from the influence of **Roussel**. Henry Barraud (1900–97) is best-known for the suite *Un saison en enfer (A season in hell,* 1969 after Rimbaud, for orchestra), notable for its sure handling of orchestral colour. His impulse is often religious (*Mystère des Saints Innocents* for soloists, chorus and orchestra, 1942–44; *Te Deum* for chorus and winds, 1955) or humanitarian; works less intense in emotional scale, such as the *Piano Concerto* (1939) or the *Concerto for Flute and String Orchestra* (1963), are characterised by grace and style. Alain Bancquart (born 1934) has

been one of the few composers to use quarter-tones extensively in large-scale orchestral works while keeping relatively traditional structures, including the symphony. His use of quarter-tone writing dates from 1967, works or movements for strings predominate, and where instruments are unsuitable because they cannot play quarter-tones, Bancquart has found alternatives: bassoons, for example, are replaced in the *Symphony No.1* by electric bass guitars. In some cases an instrument can simply be retuned to quarter-tones, as in the effective *Ma Manière de Chat.* (1978) for solo harp, where twelve different notes can be produced in two octaves without pedal changes. His dark *Symphony No. 1* uses opposed orchestral blocks, setting up sonorities not dissimilar to the effects of some electronic music. The slow movement is for strings alone, while the final movement introduces the deep sounds of the electric bass guitar. The music of Henri Tomasi (1901–71), once extremely successful in France, is dominated by his operas and by many concertos, and is noted for its orchestration and use of exotic and Impressionistic colours within a conventional, occasionally dissonant harmonic framework. His exoticism partly reflects his time with colonial radio services in French Indochina from 1930 to 1935 (eg *Chants laotiens,* 1934), but extends to scenes as far apart as the Sahara (*Impressions sahariennes,* 1938, for orchestra) and the South Pacific. Of his concertos, the *Trumpet Concerto* (1949) is probably the best known. It is very direct and undemanding, with a mysterious, nocturne slow movement and transparent orchestration. A number of his operas were conspicuously successful in their time, including *Atlantide* (1954), *Miguel de Mañara* (1956) and *Sampiero Corso* (1956). His later works reflected social issues, and included the *Symphonie du tiers monde (Third World Symphony,* 1969) and the *Chant pour le Vietnam (Song for Vietnam,* 1969) for wind ensemble and percussion. Throughout the century there has been a vigorous tradition that has often been overlooked, but which unexpectedly met the latest developments in the figure of **Messiaen**: that of French organ music. Again with its origins in the figure of Franck (a major organist), it has produced a number of organist-composers who have kept the art of improvisation at the keyboard alive. Charles Widor (1844–1937) wrote ten symphonies for organ in a grand late Romantic style; the thunderous and mercurial toccata from the

Symphony No. 5 (1880) is often heard. Louis **Vierne** (1870–1937) wrote symphonies for the organ that range in mood from thoughtful sensitivity to the full power available from the large cathedral organ. Charles Tournemire (1870–1939) produced influential organ works with a mystical cast; his major accomplishments were the fifty-one organ masses for the liturgical year, *L'orgue mystique* (1927–32). Jean Langlais (1907–91), like **Vierne** blind from birth, followed Tournemire in the influence of old church modes and melodic lines founded on Gregorian chant, but often with a more dramatic content. Besides his organ music, his bold *Salve Regina Mass* (1949) for three choirs, two organs and two brass ensembles, designed for the large spaces of Notre Dame, and the colourful and dramatic *Messe solennelle* (1952) are worthy of note. He also produced a number of works for chamber groups and organ. Maurice **Duruflé** (1902–86) also followed the style established by Tournemire in his own delicate fashion. One of the finest of these organist-composers was Jehan **Alain** (1911–40), whose output of smaller-scale works had less of a strictly liturgical intent, and explored possibilities of the development of the sounds available for the organ, a process taken further by **Messiaen** himself.

Among the most remarkable musical figures working in Paris in the century was the composer and teacher Nadia Boulanger (1887–1979), whose very long teaching career encompassed many famous pupils, and was noted for its principles of craftsmanship and clarity. In particular, her encouragement of American composers in the 1920s and 1930s was instrumental in forging a distinctively American tradition of composition.

French Music Information Centre:
Centre de Documentation de la Musique
Contemporaine
Cité de la Musique
16, Place de la Fontaine aux Lions
75019 Paris
France
tel: +33-1-47-154981
fax: +33-1-47-154989

Alain Jehan Ariste*
born 3rd February 1911 at Saint-Germain-en-Laye
died 20th June 1940 at Saumur

Alain, who was killed in action in the Second World War at the age of 29, is chiefly known for his organ works. Coming from a family of organists (his father was a celebrated organist, and his famous sister, Marie-Claire Alain, has championed his music), he himself became a church organist in Paris in 1936. Almost all of his music is miniature in length but not always in scale, and is largely divorced from liturgical or programmatic connotations. Throughout there is an emphasis on rhythm, sometimes of the most complex nature and often with the presence of dissonant harmonies, and an acute awareness of the possibilities of registration. He was influenced by exotic and oriental colours, as in the sonorous and touching *Deux danses à Agni Yavishta* (1934), or the Moroccan song that comes through the exotic underplay and rhythmic complexities of the atmospheric *Deuxième Fantaisie* (1936), one of his finest pieces. An ethereal, mystical quality imbues such works as the famous *Le jardin suspendu* (1934), evoking the artist's ideal that is perpetually sought but always out of reach. A wistfulness haunts *Aria* (1938), his last composition that almost ignores the use of pedals, and *Lamento* (1938), dissonance typically adding an edge, while there is a dreamy evening reflectiveness in the marvellous *Postlude pour l'office de Complines* (1930), with its sense of plainsong drifting high into the nave.

His two major works are on a grander scale. The *Trois pièces* (1937) includes *Litanies*, his most regularly heard work, and was written after the death of a sister. An ardent but powerful supplication, it repeats the same dance-like pattern in changing colours and settings, a 'tornado' (as Alain described it) of faith. The thematically linked *Trois danses* (1937–39) were designed as a symphonic poem for orchestra, but the manuscript blew out of his sidecar in Flanders during the war, and it exists perfectly successfully as a work for organ. Rhythm dominates, often in complex fashions, especially in the jazz-influenced first dance, where the shifting patterns are laid over a regular beat. The long second dance has an atmosphere of despair or resignation, again with extraordinary shifting rhythmic effects, while the final movement adds grandeur to the rhythmic energy. Alain stands between the French organist-composers of the previous generation and his contemporary **Messiaen,** and if his life was short and the works few, he continued, with his sense of humour and dance as well as devout myticism, the finest traditions of French organ music.

124 **France,** Alain

RECOMMENDED WORKS

The complete organ works, especially:
Trois danses op. 81 (1937–39) for
organ
Trois pièces op. 79 (1937) for organ
Postlude pour l'office de Complines
op. 21 (1930)

Amy Gilbert
born 29th August 1936 at Paris

Amy has achieved prominence both as a conductor and as a composer. Early in his career (1956) he came under the influence of **Boulez,** whom he succeeded as director of the Domaine Musical concerts (1967–73). From his early works (e.g. the *Piano Sonata,* 1960) his music has employed an increasingly broad and Expressionistic canvas, while retaining serial forms. A favourite device has been to use divided forces: *Antiphonies* (1960–63), for example, uses two main orchestras, each with their own conductor, with a concertino group as mediator. This has led to exploration of the timbral and expressive interactions of such forces, exemplified by the contrast of percussion instruments of different character (e.g. pitched versus unpitched) and different sonorities (e.g. wood versus skins) in *Cycles* for six percussionists (1964–66), or the wandering violin opposed to the orchestra (broken into blocks of instruments) in *Trajectoires* (1966) for violin and orchestra, which uses quarter-tones. This exploration has been extended into vocal works: in *Strophe* for soprano and divided orchestra (1964–66, reorchestrated 1977) a short text is broken into enunciation, then vocalisation, and then reduced to phonemes (i.e. individual constituents of sound). There is a similar process in *Récitatif, air et variation* (1970) for twelve voices, admirably clear in its interaction of the linear opposition of voices and the vertical opposition of the structure of words broken up. In *D'un espace déployé* (1972–73), a concertante effect is achieved by using two instrumental groups, a solo soprano part using more extreme writing. The *Sonata pian'e forte* (1974) for two female voices and instrumental group, with antiphonal effects and the soloists singing into a prepared piano, went further along these lines.

Amy is representative of the group of composers who extended **Webern**'s ideas into serialism. Like that of so many of these composers, his music is not always comfortable listening, its complex structures extending over considerable periods rather than on the miniature scale of Webern himself. This very inflation seems destined to condemn his music to a limited audience. In 1973 Amy was appointed musical Adviser to ORTZ; he co-founded and directed the New Philharmonic Orchestra of French Radio (1976–81), and has been director of the Lyons Conservatoire since 1984.

Barraqué Jean*
born 17th January 1928 at Puteaux
died 17th April 1973 at Paris

Jean Barraqué is a figure virtually unknown to all but a few specialists, but in the six acknowledged works that he completed before his early death, he established himself as one of the most imaginative and far-sighted of those composers developing post-**Webern** serialism. In particular, he sought to use serialism to express late Romantic Expressionist concepts, seeing music as 'the complete game, quaking on the edge of suicide'. Consequently he attempted to marry serialism with large-scale works, meticulously arranged and with an astute sense of instrumental colours and their combinations.

He came to notice with the *Piano Sonata* (1950–52), a forty-minute work pitting ideas arising out of rhythmic cells against freer movement, with silences that become longer and longer until denuding the work; and with the related *Séquence* (1950–55) for soprano and instrumental ensemble, both works of turbulence and cold despair. Barraqué then embarked on what was intended as a large series of musical commentaries on the novel *The Death of Virgil* by Hermann Broch. The first to be written, *Le temps restitué* (1957), was revised for soprano or contralto, chorus and instrumental ensemble in 1968, and its texts, in five sections, explore cosmic philosophical questions of the interrelations of the human soul with time, death, and chance. The vocal writing includes extended vocal ranges and techniques, variously allowing the words to emerge and to be subdued in almost hallucinatory textures, the choir sometimes supporting, sometimes opposing the soloist. It is an intensely dramatic work of considerable scope, sometimes lyrical, with the instrumentation in constant metamorphosis.

The second commentary, ... *au delà du*

hasard (... *beyond chance*, 1958–59) for soprano, women's chorus and four instrumental ensembles, pits the vocal forces against sharply differentiated instrumental groups: brass and vibraphone, tuned percussion with piano, non-pitched percussion, and four clarinets. The third, *Chant après chant* (*Song after Song*, 1966) reduces the forces to soprano, piano and a large variety of percussion. The textures of Barraqué's final completed work, the *Concerto* (1968) for clarinet, vibraphone and six instrumental trios, are a collage of sharply differentiated colours, notably the harpsichord, emphasised by the placement into six groups, with the clarinet intervening only after an introduction by strings, and the vibraphone not appearing until considerably later. It is an exceptionally difficult work to assimilate, but nonetheless a rewarding one, its façade a ferris wheel of different events and colours, silence occupying the spaces between the chairs. It has the underlying logic that informs Barraqué's work, weaving a large web in which at any one moment a particular strand may be sounding, starting another in its train. Barraqué's music is not for the faint-hearted, but for an example of the expressive powers of serialism, what one commentator has called the 'combination of Logic and Passion', it is of great fascination.

RECOMMENDED WORKS
    Piano Sonata (1950–52)
    Le temps restitué (1957, revised 1968)
        for soprano or contralo, chorus and
        instrumental ensemble

Bayle François
born 27th April 1932 at Tamatave (Madagascar)

Bayle studied with **Stockhausen**, and in 1960 joined the Groupe de Recherches Musicales (founded in 1950 by Pierre **Schaeffer** and Pierre **Henry**), a major French experimental electronic studio, and became its director in 1964. Using almost entirely electronic means (both electronically generated and *musique concrète*), he has been one of the more successful at creating a suitable indigenous electronic sound, rather than adapting an instrumental language to an electronic palette. Thus, although his earlier works use conventional instruments, such as *L'oiseau, le chanteur* (*The Bird, the Singer*, 1963, from a film score), *Trois portraits pour l'oiseau qui n'existe pas*

(*Three portraits of the bird which does not exist*) for horn, oboe, clavichord and electronic sounds, or *Archipelago*, 1963–67, for string quartet and recorded sounds, these are inclined to provide support for the electronic effects rather than the other way around. Some of his explorations (such as *Solitude, 1969*, mixing rock sounds with street and other noises) were a sonic disaster, but an important and still effective work (especially the sonorous third section, *Hommage à Robur*), which achieved some prominence at the time of its composition, was *Espaces inhabitables* (*Uninhabitable spaces*, 1967) with a formal five-movement structure, a conscious use of the descriptive powers of electronic sounds, and rhythm created by changes of timbre and colour.

Bayle has continued to develop these concerns, especially in the area of what he has called 'the poetics of timbre', in a large series of eight works titled *Propositions* (1972–89). Designed to be heard singly or as a group, they cover a wide range of sound sources: the first four are for strings, wind, percussion and voices respectively, while the last four are for unusual sound sources, without any of the sonorities heard in the first four. The dream-like and sonorously impressive *Proposition I* (1972–73) contrasts a held note with clusters in a mobile form; the strings sounds benefit from Bayle's experience with electronic textures. The foundation of a long held note recurs in *Proposition II* (1979–80), where the wind instruments conduct a lively dialogue using mirror forms before the held note takes over, evolving into a haunting landscape of homogeneous sonorities before ending with a curious, accelerating clicking passage created by unusual usage of the instruments. *Propositions III* (1982–83) for six groups of percussion, is divided into four sections each reflecting different groups of percussion sound, from the primitive, unpitched and strident to the delicacy of tuned metal instruments. *Proposition IV* (1986) for twelve solo voices uses phonemes and a multitude of vocal sounds in a luxuriant and compelling display of vocal sonorities, again with delicate and clicking passages, sometimes recalling **Stockhausen's** *Stimmung*.

The second set of four works moves to sound worlds more distant from traditional experience. *Proposition V* (1986) is for twenty-eight non-European instruments from five continents, *Propositions VI* (1987) was written for older European instruments (i.e. 'original instruments'),

Proposition VII (1987–88) uses computer sound synthesis, and *Propositions VIII* (1988–89) moves away from humanly created sound by utilising recordings of birds and of the elements. Thus the first four of this set can be seen as representing the development of a Western tradition, the second four representing new sources to enliven that tradition, and if none of these pieces is individually remarkable, they are consistently interesting, presenting an unusual overview of the development of post-avant-garde music and an enormous range of sonorities.

Bayle has taught at the University of Paris VIII, and among his writings is a large study, *Schönberg à Cage* (1981).

RECOMMENDED WORKS
 Uninhabitable Spaces for tape (1967)
 Propositions I—VIII (1972–89)

Boulez Pierre***
born 26th March 1925 at Montbrison

Pierre Boulez has been among the most influential of all composers since World War II. However, the considerable effect of his work, his ideas, and incisive intellect is more observable on two generations of composers than in a widespread appreciation of his music by general audiences, to whom he is far better known as a conductor of international renown. This situation has been exacerbated by Boulez's habit of leaving work unfinished, albeit with sections ready for performance, by his reworkings of earlier material, and by the relative paucity of works in recent years.

Following Boulez's discovery of the music of **Schoenberg** in 1945, his studies with René Leibowitz led first to a period fusing 12-tone techniques with the idea of his earlier teacher **Messiaen**, and then, crucially, to his adoption of what has come to be known as 'total serialism' (and which Milton **Babbitt** had independently already formulated). Extending the ideas of the Second Viennese School, and particularly those of **Webern**, the rules of the 12-tone system were developed by equivalents to cover not just pitch but all aspects of music – rhythm, dynamics and instrumentation. Messiaen had already applied such ideas to rhythm (by adding or removing fractional values) but not in a serial context, while **Varèse** and his follower **Jolivet** had added irrational smaller units of rhythm. Having already abandoned time signatures in the *Piano Sonata No. 1* (1946), which is typically built on motivic cells of ideas, Boulez started to apply 12-tone ideas to rhythmic concepts in a serial frame in the *Piano Sonata No. 2* (1948) and then in the rhythmically unsettled *Livre pour quatuor* (*Quartet-Book*, 1948–49), now withdrawn and revised as the haunting, distant and dense *Livre pour cordes* (*Strings-Book*, 1968). But it was with *Polyphonie X* (1951) for eighteen instruments, with its extreme leaps of register, its inexorable logic and its clarity of texture, and with *Structures Ia* (1951–52) for two pianos, that he applied analogous principles to dynamics and timbre as well as rhythm, thus achieving a total systematic control over the material. Among those immediately influenced by these works were **Berio, Cage, Pousseur** and **Stockhausen** – all of whom soon found the strict application of total serialism too restricting, and adapted some of the techniques thus learned to the development of the avant-garde, or combined them with other concepts, particularly, in the case of Cage and Stockhausen, chance happening (the antithesis of total serialism).

Boulez himself relented from such absolute strictures in what has become his best-known work, considered by many to be his masterpiece. *Le marteau sans maître* (*The Hammer Unmastered*, 1953–55) for contralto, alto flute, viola, guitar, vibraphone, xylorimba and percussion, sets three poems by René Char, and intersperses them with musical commentaries on those poems using associated material preceding and succeeding the actual songs. The resultant sense of strong structure, together with the clarity of the instrumental writing, pointillistic in feel (developing the lead of **Varèse** and **Webern**), is arresting and compelling. Its effect is heightened by a basic opposition between the sensuality of the surrealist poetry, supported by a rich and sometimes exotic instrumental timbre, and the intellectual incisiveness of the technique and structure.

Boulez had already set René Char in two works using chorus, both of which have complicated histories in which their current versions reflect the additions and changes in Boulez's style since their original inception. *Le soleil des eaux* (*The Sun of the Waters*, originally incidental music, 1948, versions 1950 and 1958, final version 1965) for soprano, chorus and orchestra sets two allusive poems: a lizard in love, complaining of man's destruction, and the river as a metaphor for nature and life, the soloist predominant in the first, the chorus in the second. The cantata *Le visage nuptial* (*The Nuptial Countenance* for chamber ensemble, 1946, version 1951, current version 1988–89) for soprano, contralto, women's chorus and orchestra is Boulez's choral masterpiece. The poem, in five sections, deals with erotic experience in dense language and imagery, and the antecedents of both text and music are to be found in the rich, allusive, luxuriant styles of Expressionist Vienna. It is a heady work, ceaselessly shifting, effusive were it not for the sense of order weaving through the intensity; Boulez produces restless but sometimes lyrical layers requiring extraordinary virtuosity from all the performers. This web is almost too rich – the moments of respite are brief, but sometimes magical, as in the end of the third song. But every strand of this dense and complex work has purpose and integrity. The cantata stands as the culmination of a line that looks back through the vocal works of **Berg** to the earlier, sensuous **Schoenberg**, but has arrived at the late 20th century.

After *Le marteau sans maître*, Boulez started to apply some of the freedoms he found in the poems of Mallarmé in an effort to develop and broaden the intellectual techniques which power his music. Notable among these was the concept of continual transformation within self-contained forms – all of which contributes to the officially unfinished character of so many of Boulez's works. Boulez initially tried a musical equivalent in the *Piano Sonata No. 3* (1957, discussed below), but it is in *Pli selon pli* (*Fold upon Fold*, 1957–90, some sections existing in different versions and revisions) for soprano and orchestra that the tribute to Mallarmé is overt. Centred on three *Improvisations sur Mallarmé* (which transcribe elements of sonnet form) the potential aridity of serialism is countered by the allusive writing, with constantly changing timbres and colours, some of which are intended to be symbolic. The opposition here is between those inner sections with complete settings of Mallarmé texts for chamber forces, and the outer sections where only fragments are set with complete orchestra, the music contributing the rest of the whole. The transference of poetic structures into music was further explored in *cumming ist der dichter* (unfinished, 1970–) a setting of *birds* (*here invented*) for sixteen voices and twenty-four instruments.

The importance of timbre in Boulez's work, the extension of controlled but durationally undetermined events, as well as the synthesis of different works, was further demonstrated in *Éclat* (meaning both 'burst' and 'glitter', 1964–65) for two keyboards, three strings, four winds and percussion, which exists as an independent piece or as the opening of the unfinished *Éclat-Multiples*. With a polarity between those instruments that have a quick decay of sound (playing in the foreground as soloists), and those that are more sonorous (providing the background), its colours do shimmer in changing textures of light, enhanced when the conductor, at moments of his or her own choosing, requires the orchestra to respond with a burst of sound. The unfinished (but playable) *Multiples* (1974–) exists only in conjunction with the earlier score, adds nine violas and a basset horn, and provides a further opposition, its more continuous lines and sonorous textures retrospectively highlighting what has already been heard.

His most immediate work of the 1960s and 1970s was *Rituel in memoriam Bruno Maderna* (1974–75) for eight groups of instrumentalists and nine percussionists. The sense of ritual, with insistent percussion suggesting the Far-Eastern processional, is paramount, enhanced both by exotic spotlighting of colour and an extremely effective structure. It is divided into fifteen parts, which alternate between very slow (controlled by the conductor over freer percussion) and moderately slow (more improvisatory, with the conductor setting events in motion). At each section (until section 13) the duration gets longer and more forces are added; after section 15, the entire process is reversed. *Rituel* has affinities with the ritualistic insistency of **Varèse**, and in its vivid sense of colour and its instrumental transparency is probably Boulez's most approachable work. Manipulation of short sections is also found in *Domaines* (1968) for clarinet and twenty-one instruments, where the order in which the twelve sections are to be played is first chosen by the conductor, and then by the soloist. *Messagesquisse* (1976) for seven cellos emerged as a more conventional if still compelling work, unfolding with beautiful formal logic from an opening statement of six notes (based on the surname of Paul Sacher, the dedicatee), moving through very fast, eliding variations, to a solo cadenza and a final coda. There is even a suggestion of an underlying key, though the work is in no way tonal. The equally effective *Notations* (1978) for orchestra is a reworking of four pieces from an early piano work, *Twelve Notations* (1945); short but densely packed, they are almost raunchy in feel.

Following the foundations of IRCAM (see below), Boulez has further extended the parameters of his technique. The major work to emerge has been *Répons* (1980–, again incomplete, currently in three sections). Electronics have been added and again there is a basic opposition of textured concept. Six soloists (piano, organ, harp, cimbalom and tuned percussion) are spaced around the hall, electronically modified, both timbrally and spatially, into shimmering sounds. Against them are an ensemble of twenty-four players, their unmodified writing particular and detailed.

The three piano sonatas are regularly encountered (at least in reference if not in performance). The short two-movement *Piano Sonata No. 1* (1946) shows the influence of **Webern**, while the *Piano Sonata No. 2* (1947–48) – which at one point quotes from Beethoven's *Hammerklavier Sonata* – is one of the seminal works of the period. Extremely virtuosic, its material is again developed from melodic cells, its rhythmic complexities regularly precluding a sense of metre, and taking advantage of the sounds of the release and decay (rather than just the playing) of notes. The third movement shows another characteristic of Boulez – the continual presence of a particular interval, here major 2nds. The structure of the *Piano Sonata No. 3* (1956–57) of which two movements of the projected five have been released (it is rumoured that the other three were complete by 1959) derives from a Mallarmé poem designed to look like a constellation. In the poem the reader can move from place to place in the constellation; so in the sonata, whose *Constellation-Mirror* is in two forms (forward and retrograde), while the whole extant piece can also be played in retrograde.

Boulez's particular genius has not just been to emerge as the most prominent and most influential innovator of total serialism, but also to produce music of striking power and effect that goes considerably beyond the intellectual rigour of the theoretical conception. A number of characteristics seem to be responsible. The parameters are almost always controlled, and when aleatory elements appear, they are within the basis of the overall structure.

Crucial to many works is a central contrast, often between instrumental forces, which adds another dimension to the serial structures. Above all, there is an instinct for and preoccupation with timbre and colour. This is a fundamentally sensuous instinct, in opposition to the formidable intellectualism of the form and technique. The idiom is extremely difficult for those unused to serial music; but that clash between content and form, that containment of the sensuous by the intellect, is a late 20th-century version of a basic duality that has imbued all great music. Its absence or imbalance in so many of Boulez's followers is partly responsible for the aridity of so much serial and post-serial music.

Amongst Boulez's many conducting activities have been his appointments as chief conductor of the BBC Symphony Orchestra (1971–74) and the New York Philharmonic (1971–78). Between 1974 and 1977 he set up with government backing the Institut de Recherche et de Coordination Acoustique-Musique (IRCAM) at the Pompidou Centre in Paris. IRCAM has become one of the world centres for new music, and through it Boulez has again influenced or promoted the music of composers of his own generation, including **Berio, Birtwistle** and **Kurtág**, as well as a whole new generation.

RECOMMENDED WORKS
    Éclats-Multiples (1965–)
    Le marteau sans maître (1953–55)
    Piano Sonata No. 2 (1947–48)
    Pli selon pli (1957–90)
    Répons (1981–82)
    Rituel in memoriam Bruno Maderna (1974–75)
    Le visage nuptial (1946–89) for soprano, contralto, women's chorus and orchestra

BIBLIOGRAPHY
    P. Boulez, *Boulez on music today*, trans. S. Bradshaw & R. R. Bennett, 1971
    Conversations with Céleste Deliège, trans. E. Wangermée, 1976
    Orientations: collected writing, trans. J-J. Nattier, 1986
    ed. W. Glock, *Pierre Boulez – A Symposium*, 1986
    P. Griffiths, *Boulez*, 1978
    Joan Peyser, *Composer, Conductor, Enigma*, 1976
    P. F. Stacey, *Boulez and the Modern Concept*, 1987

Canteloube de Malaret, (Marie) Joseph*

born 21st October 1879 at Annonay (Ardèche)
died 4th November 1957 at Grigny

Canteloube is almost entirely known for one set of works, which have become world famous and a staple of the vocal repertoire. They are the *Chants d'Auvergne (Songs of the Auvergne)* published in five sets (1924, 1924, 1927, 1930, 1955), which are arrangements of folk songs collected from 1900 onwards in the region between the Dordogne and the Rhône. The involved and very beautiful orchestration is so extensive that, apart from the melodies and the words, these are essentially original works. He uses a large Romantic orchestra, often pulling out solo groups of instruments and favouring the upper woodwind to give a country feel and as a colour device to point up the expressiveness or the humour of the songs. The results are sometimes delicate, sometimes Impressionistically languid, usually rich in changing colours, careful to echo the modal nature of the original songs, though sometimes, where appropriate, chromatic in harmony. As much as anyone, Canteloube succeeded in reflecting the varying moods of a rural countryside. He also collected songs from other parts of France (the collection *Chants de France* is sometimes heard), and edited French-Canadian songs. His two operas (one on a rural theme, the other a patriotic portrait of the Gaul leader Vercingétorix), were performed at the Paris Opera, but failed to enter the repertoire.

RECOMMENDED WORK
Songs of the Auvergne (1924–55)

Charpentier Gustave

born 25 June 1860 at Dieuze (nr Nancy)
died 18th February 1956 at Paris

Although he lived until the age of 95, Gustave Charpentier is chiefly known for one work completed in 1900. The opera *Louise*, regularly revived and with one very famous aria (*Depuis le jour*) deserves a place in any survey of 20th-century music, for if its musical idiom has shades of Massenet, Wagner, and Italian *verismo*, its plot (which shocked early audiences), its philosophical attitude, and its essentially ordinary story were distinctly modern, making it a transitional work.

The autobiographical story (very rare in opera) is set among the proletariat of Paris (vividly portrayed), and revolves around the generation gap between the seamstress Louise and her parents, and her leaving home to live with (not marry) the poet Julien. The resulting conflicts and morals are those that have preoccupied the century ever since; the almost incestuous love of the father for the daughter is also a contemporary theme. The opera moves from realism to a symbolic fantasy in its central two acts (Alma Mahler called Charpentier 'the first surrealist') and back to naturalism again, and is more effective on stage than in broadcast or recording. If an autobiographical opera was rare, life reflecting opera was even rarer, for in 1902 Charpentier founded the Conservative Populaire Mimi Pinson, which for thirty-five years gave Paris seamstresses the opportunity for (free) musical training. In 1913 *Louise*'s successor, *Julien, ou La vie du poète*, was staged at the Opéra-Comique with some success, but has been neglected ever since. Charpentier produced little else, and eventually became a recluse; his picturesque orchestral suite *Impressions of Italy* (1889–90) was once popular, but has long disappeared from the repertoire.

RECOMMENDED WORK
opera *Louise* (1900)

BIBLIOGRAPHY
F. Andrieux (ed.), *Gustave Charpentier: lettres inédites à ses parents*, 1984

d'Indy (Paul Marie Theodore) Vincent**

born 27th March 1851 at Paris
died 2nd December 1931 at Paris

Although Vincent d'Indy's influence and importance to French music are universally recognised, his works are surprisingly neglected outside France. Part of the reason is that his compositional career (1870–1931) spans a period of great change in European music; the achievements of the Impressionists in the middle of this period, and of the Parisian circle of younger composers at the end, have overshadowed his personal style, rooted in Romanticism.

He was initially influenced by his teacher César Franck, whose ideas were German-orientated rather than French, with emphasis on counterpoint and fugue (and on Franck's instrument, the organ), on Franck's own development of the cyclic principle (a recurring motif or idea that appears throughout a piece, linking it structurally), and an emotional emphasis on the mystical and the luxuriant. Following visits to Bayreuth, d'Indy became interested in Wagner, the immediate outcome of which was the tone poem *La forêt enchantée* (*The Enchanted Forest*, 1878), a happy and dramatically effective musical painting that is occasionally revived, and whose French aspect is clear from a bright orchestration that includes eight harps. Other Wagnerian works included the opera *Fervaal* (conceived 1878, completed 1897). If d'Indy's style had been exclusively on these lines, his music would probably be forgotten. However, an abiding love of the countryside coloured his music, particularly the Vivarais and Cévennes regions (whose folk songs he collected), tempering the Wagnerian leanings with a light freshness. This is the major element in d'Indy's two most popular works. The lovely and lyrical *Symphonie sur un chant montagnard français* (*Symphony on a French Mountain Song*, also known as *Symphonie Cévenole*, 1886) has a major role for the piano (integrated into the orchestra, and creating a new departure for French piano concertos). Its individuality, in spite of the echoes of Liszt and Franck, is created by a folk theme that links all three movements and by the pastoral atmosphere. Its comparative neglect seems entirely due to the absence of virtuosity in the solo piano part. The large-scale orchestral counterpart is the *Jour d'été à la montagne* (*A Summer's Day on the Mountain*, 1905), incorporating Gregorian chant as well as folk themes. The fine *Diptyque méditerranéen* (1925–26) for orchestra continues this idiom but is less well known.

Of his other works, three in particular stand out. The symphonic variations *Istar* (1896, later successful as a ballet score) are, on a purely emotional level, a marvellous evocation of the Assyrian legend – Romantic in feel and sometimes almost Impressionistic in the shimmering delicacy of orchestration. The variations are in reverse, with the statement of the theme occurring only at the end. The *Piano Sonata* (1907) is a summation of the Romantic inheritance. A work on the grand scale, its debt to Liszt and Franck is evident in the germinal (small cells of material gradually expanded) and cyclical (the third movement reworks material from the other two) structure, with a set of variations as the first movement. The *Symphony No. 2* (1902–03) uses similar structural principles, moving in its course from charm to nobility but with an intellectual energy and orchestral clarity that leave Romanticism behind.

The works written after World War I show a continuation of the move away from Wagner, culminating in the *Concerto for piano, flute, cello and string orchestra* (1927), his last orchestral work. There was also much chamber music, notably the *String Sextet* of 1928. Of his choral works, the dramatic legend *Le chant de la cloche* (*The Song of the Bell*, 1883, for soloists, chorus and orchestra) established him as a composer. Once popular, its prologue and seven tableaux hark back to the example of Berlioz as well as Wagner. Of his four operas, *L'étranger* (1898–1903) is a French parallel to **Britten**'s *Peter Grimes*, while his last opera, *La légende de Saint-Christophe* (1908–13), although reportedly containing fine music, was damned for its anti-semitism at its first production in 1920.

It is symptomatic of this paradoxical man that while remaining a fervent champion of his master Franck, his editing of the then little-known operas of Monteverdi and Rameau, and of some of Bach's works, wittingly or unwittingly helped to lay the foundation for neo-classicism. Such older music sometimes influences his own, e.g. *Chansons et danses* for seven wind instruments (1899) or the *Suite dans le style ancien* for two flutes, trumpet and string quartet (1886). His teaching was hugely influential, especially his co-foundation of the Schola Cantorum (1894), the first modern conservatory whose methods were widely copied elsewhere. He was decorated for bravery in the Franco-Prussian War of 1870, and was the prompter at the première of Bizet's *Carmen* (1875).

RECOMMENDED WORKS

Concerto for Piano, Flute and Strings (1926)
La forêt enchanté for orchestra (1878)
symphonic variations *Istar* (1896)
Jour d'été à la montagne for orchestra (1905)
Piano Sonata op. 63 (1907)
Symphony No. 2 (1902–03)
Symphony on a French Mountain Song (1886) for piano and orchestra

BIBLIOGRAPHY
L. Vallas, *Vincent d'Indy*, Paris, vol. 1
1946, vol. 2 1950 (in French)

Debussy (Achille-) Claude•••
born 22nd August 1862 at Saint-
Germain-en-Laye
died 25th March 1918 at Paris

Debussy is perhaps the seminal composer of the 20th century. His influence has been more insidious and less spectacular than that of **Schoenberg**, less clearly traceable than that of **Webern**, more self-effacing than that of **Stravinsky**. But his aesthetic was a more complete break with Romanticism than that of the Second Viennese School, and his harmonic solutions have proved as durable and as relevant as those of the serialists. The style known as Impressionism has continued to recur as a stylistic element; the concept of the movement in stasis obliquely led to the work of such composers as **Cage**, and, eventually, to the minimalists; the ballet *Jeux* is a distant herald of **Boulez** and **Stockhausen**; and the suggestions of neo-classicism in his later works, although he was not alone in using them, helped pave the way for the neo-classical movement. Moreover, and to a greater extent than any of the other major composers of the 20th century, his music appealed to a very wide general audience, and continues to do so.

His compositions can be roughly divided into three periods. In the first he developed his aesthetic and formulated the characteristic colours and idioms, culminating in the opera *Pelléas et Mélisande* (1893–1902). With *La mer* (1903–05) for orchestra, that development reached maturity, and the works of 1894 to 1910 are both the best known and the ones most associated with Impressionism. With the stage mystery *Le martyre de Saint Sébastien* (1911) and *Jeux* (1912–13) he initiated a final, more rarefieid phase. His revolutionary reaction to Romanticism was to free music from the necessity of thematic development as a means of creating forward motion and form. Thematic development had been the basis of all 19th-century music, had impelled the works of such contemporary composers as **Mahler**, and was, in altered form, to continue to underline the practices of the 12-tone composers, surviving, of course, as a major musical element to this day. In its place Debussy evolved more improvisatory forms, often of short duration, in which static elements are overlaid by metamorphosis of detail

and colour. These are less suited to the traditional genres of the symphony or the concerto, which is why neither of these appear in Debussy's canon, apart from a youthful symphony. It is this reconception of the way music may have motion that led eventually to **Cage**, and by another path, to the minimalists; a variant was also adopted in 1911 by **Schoenberg** in his concept of *Klangfarbenmelodie*.

At the same time, the traditional notions of harmony (which during the 19th century had been stretched to the breaking point by ever-increasing chromatism) were unsuited to this conception. His alternative was less radical than atonalism or 12-tone techniques, but no less influential: to turn to the old Gregorian church modes, and to the whole-tone scale, both of which avoid traditional harmonic implications, and which give much of Debussy's music its individual cast. In particular, he adapted from early music the notion of *organum*, two identical parallel lines of music moving together a given interval apart (often thirds or fifths). Part of the popular appeal of Debussy's music is that this did not lead to dissonance, rather to a juxtaposition of constant ideas.

This evolution of ideas also placed more emphasis on orchestral or instrumental colour. In the absence of traditional harmonic development, the interplay of texture and timbre, the details of the entire orchestral palette, the subtle changing shades and inflections, themselves create momentum and change. Consequently Debussy developed the minutiae of orchestration, using the orchestra in a manner comparable to brush strokes in painting, from a broad wash, through the sharpness of a dab of brass, the points of light from the woodwind, a fluttering figuration for the flutes, to the characteristic brightness of harp or tuned percussion. These details, individually often of short duration, are combined and juxtaposed to create the larger orchestral canvas. Similarly, in his piano music he emphasised the subtleties of colour, pedalling, expression and touch.

These methods were influenced by two experiences. The first was Debussy's stay in Russia (1890) as pianist to Madame von Meck (Tchaikovsky's patron), where he discovered in the music of Mussorgsky (1839–81) an earlier attempt to break away from traditional forms. The second was his encounter with oriental culture at the Paris World Fair of 1889, and especially with Balinese gamelan music, which is built on movement through stasis (and was to reappear as an important influence in Western music after 1945), and which showed the possibilities of new textural colours.

The term 'Impressionist' has often been applied to Debussy, and has been the subject of academic (if not popular) controversy. The term is less appropriate in his earlier works, as he was developing his idiom; the expression 'Symbolist' is here more applicable, and works such as *Prélude à l'Après-midi d'un faune'* (1892–94) or *Pelléas et Mélisande* have affinities with such artists as Beardsley. But in the central period of the best-known works, the techniques do parallel those of the Impressionist painters. Points of light and colour, individually insubstantial and without sharp delineation except in the larger context, combine to create light and shade, momentum, the subtleties of impression. Similarly, the overview of a Debussy work or an Impressionist painting is often static; the momentum is created internally and thus self-contained by the interplay of the details.

But much more important than these technical similarities is the perception of the world that Impressionism represents. In place of dramatic, programmatic or symbolic content, or a view of nature that sought to mirror the nature of man, the Impressionists sought to show how a single still view could contain a multitude of impressions that affect the viewer and contain their own momentum. The result is an attempt to reconnect with the natural world from an urban perspective that seemed to have lost the capacity for such contemplation. This is precisely the stance that Debussy, friend of painters and poets as much as musicians, himself adopted. It is profoundly different from the main thrust of music at the time, which was increasingly expressing heightened and more complex conflicts of internal psychology, a trend that was continued in the work of the atonal and 12-tone composers. Thus through this very different response to the world Debussy achieved a break with late Romanticism. Although Debussy's maturity as a composer is often dated from the *Prélude à l'Après-midi d'un faune'* (1892–94) for orchestra, the impulse to express pictorial essence is already observable in the charming and unpretentious *Petite suite* (1889) for two pianos, most familiar in its orchestral version, and which has something in common with the pictorial reveries of the Spaniard Albéniz. It was the *String Quartet* (1893) that first brought Debussy to the attention of the

musical world of Paris. The form still follows the models of the cyclical structure of César Franck, but there is a fluidity of movement, with constant changes of mood, an oriental influence in the scherzo (recalling the contemporary French literary orientalism) and a stillness in the slow movement of this alluring, sometimes yearning, sometimes nervously energetic work. *Prélude à l'Après-midi d'un faune'*, perhaps Debussy's best known work, is based on a poem about the nature of dreams and reality by Mallarmé, though it is more an expression of the moods of the poem – languor, sensuousness – than of its content. The limpid flute, cascades from the harp, a solo violin, are typical Debussy colours, the dreamy stillness a typical Debussy atmosphere. Apart from its atmospheric allure, its appeal lies in its completeness; it seems exactly to contain what it should, no more, no less. The three *Nocturnes* (1897–99) for orchestra hover between Symbolist and Impressionist palettes, with a central dance flanked by first an Impressionist orchestral evocation of clouds and the interplay of light, and second the shifting swells and arabesques of the final 'Sirènes', with its wordless female chorus.

With *La mer* (1903–05) for orchestra the development of *Nocturnes* is fulfilled (it actually quotes a phrase from the earlier work). One of Debussy's best-loved works, and one of the most successful translations of the sea into music, it is built on wisps of harmony and fleeting rhythmic ideas. The main emphasis falls on the vividly detailed orchestration and on a rhythmic heave and flow; momentum without going in any direction, the satisfaction of arriving in much the same place while having experienced the essence of that place. Of the three pieces that form *Images* (1908–12) (not to be confused with the piano sets of the same name) for orchestra, the most popular is the central 'Ibéria', with its Spanish atmosphere again an imaginary evocation of received impressions (for Debussy visited Spain for but a couple of hours). In three parts, it ranges from vivid poster paint colours, Spanish rhythms and melodic ideas to a more nocturnal mood. But in *Images* Debussy is already moving away from the 'Impressionist' style, when layering an independent foreground of lithe woodwind against a background of a slow orchestral swell (a technique brought to fruition by **Britten**); in the sometimes almost mechanistic ostinati of 'Ibéria'; in the unusual rhythmic dance effects of 'Rondes de printemps' (with prominent timpani), and especially in the more open, lean orchestral sound and the use of a folk song in the 'Gigue' which starts the set, but which was written last.

The thinning out of Debussy's idiom was heralded by the incidental music to *Le martyre de Saint Sébastien* (1911), now most often encountered in the piano suite, the suite of symphonic fragments (arranged by André Caplet) or in a concert oratorio version retaining the choruses and songs linked by a connecting text. The influence of church modes is immediately evident, with the use of parallel fifths, but it is combined with a restrained languor, a Mediterranean sensuousness, the thinner orchestral palette that aims for long melodic lines of single colours rather than the detail of earlier works. Debussy had stripped down his aesthetic, and in doing so, made it more direct. In the ballet *Jeux* (1912) the earlier Symbolism seems almost to return, using a construction of contrasting short sections or blocks, whose juxtaposition creates the momentum but which are linked by harmony or common intervals. Its extraordinary opening, with ostinato fragments and bare percussion, seems to leap forward two or more decades; if the subsequent music is not so startling, it nonetheless has a new sense of poise and motion through the use of fragmentary motifs whose logic avoids all traditional progressions. *Jeux* remains a seminal work for the Debussy connoisseur.

Late in his life Debussy returned to chamber music, planning a set of six sonatas, of which only three were completed, in intended imitation of 18th-century French music. The return to traditional structures brings with it not only an element of formality, as in the opening of the *Cello Sonata* (1915), which is tinged with the tragedy of World War I, but also a concentration on the purely abstract qualities of the music, and in particular – and this is the strength of these late works – a leanness in which every note carries weight. In the central slow section of the *Cello Sonata* there is a suggestion of the rhythmic irregularity, the deconstruction and juxtaposition of material that was to be pursued later in the century. The *Violin Sonata* (1916–17), better known because of its brighter and more flowing lyricism, explores the shades of colour of the string instrument. The most appealing of these sonatas is, though, the *Sonata for flute,*

viola and harp (1915), in which some of the Mediterranean nuance of colour achieves a richness of texture through the barest of means. The earlier *Syrinx* (1913) for solo flute has a haunting mixture of Celtic mysticism and Dionysian sensuousness; much 20th-century flute music has been under its shadow.

Of the piano pieces, *L'isle joyeuse* (1904) is the first of Debussy's works for that instrument to embrace the virtuoso expression of light and water, probably influenced by **Ravel**'s *Jeux d'eau*. Most of his piano music is arranged in sets; while individual pieces conjure up some particular atmosphere or scene, usually in an improvisatory way, the careful architecture created by the juxtaposition and order of small pieces is only revealed over the longer span of the sets. The *Suite bergamasque* (1890, revised 1905) anticipates neo-classicism in some of its echoes of the age of Couperin; the third of its four pieces, 'Clair de Lune', dreamy, nebulous, eventually rippling with a nocturnal sparkle, has become one of his most famous works. The two sets of *Images* (1905 and 1907) are perhaps the most obviously Impressionistic of the piano works, with the typical evocation of light and shade on water and its eddying motion ('Reflets dans l'eau' or 'Poisson d'or') or the light of the moon.

The two books of *Préludes* (1909–10, 1912–13, each of twelve preludes) vary from the mysterious atmosphere painting of 'La cathédral engloutie' ('The Sunken Cathedral') to more abstract evocations such as 'Les tierces alternées ('Alternating Thirds'). Showing Debussy's wide range of affinities and pianistic moods, they embrace visual scenes (mists, dead leaves, winds), places (with the Spanish element of the Alhambra, Egypt, the hills of Anacapri), or people and dances (Delphic and Shakespearean), ending with fireworks. Even in the more obviously extrovert works, there is a feeling of the music being garnered from the wind, spun out on the keyboard, and released to the wind again, a triumph of instinct, judgement and technique. Debussy placed the titles at the end of each piece, rather than the beginning, as if to say: gain your own impressions, and then see the source of inspiration.

The *Études* (1915) are the summit of Debussy's pianistic art. Evocative titles are now dropped; instead the twelve pieces divided into two books have titles reflecting technical musical aspects, for example 'Pour les sonorities opposées ('For opposed sonorities'). The intention is by no means solely to provide some practical pianistic manual; rather it is Debussy's own exploration in a series of miniatures of the possibilities he has reached on his favourite instrument. The first book has an almost spartan quality, the studies concentrating on sureness of technique, except for the last flowing fantasy 'Pour les huit doigts' ('For the eight fingers'), while the second set explores shades of touch and colour.

Mention should also be made of the ever-popular *Children's Corner* (1906–08), a suite of six innocent and delightful pieces written for his daughter, including the 'Golliwog's Cake-walk', its rollicking jazz rhythm delighting children, the satire on Wagner (it quotes *Tristan*) entertaining adults. One of his finest late compositions is the three-movement suite *En blanc et noir* (*In White and Black*, 1915) for two pianos. There is enough characteristic phrasing to be instantly recognisable as Debussy, but it is combined with a simplification of colour, a rarefication of idiom (the two pianos provide a spatial atmosphere rather than being used to double the potential), a formality of overall outline, and a willingness to veer into unexpected directions, be they jaunty or tumultuous.

Debussy also contributed to the revival of French song as a genre in its own right rather than following German models. All are for voice and piano, although the *Trois ballades de Villan* (1910) were also arranged for voice and orchestra. Besides many early songs, some of which are only now coming to light and which show the shadow of Massenet, the song-cycle *Cinq poèmes de Charles Baudelaire* (1885–88) still has touches of Wagner in the melodic lines and in the emotions, but also a restraint and close integration between singing line and piano that was to become characteristic. *Ariettes oubliées* (1887–89), to words by Verlaine, one of Debussy's favourite poets, reveals a similar influence in its 'through composition', rather than an internal division in the songs into the traditional three parts. The next Verlaine settings, *Trois mélodies* (1891), are far more lithe, with loose-flowing vocal lines, rippling piano arpeggios, and shifting consonant harmonies. Conventional song structures, based on verse forms, are now almost completely dissolved in favour of following the essence of the words. Verlaine was also the poet for the two sets of

Fêtes galantes (1891 and 1904), which follow similar lines, though the first are more delicate and direct (especially in the piano writing), the second more divergent and confident, especially in the swell and nebulous piano fragmentation of 'La faune'. The *Trois ballades de Villon* (1910) throw the emphasis on the free vocal lines, with restrained and clear-cut piano writing, capturing something of the dichotomy between the outward naïvety and the hidden complexity of Villon's verse, and with a peasant loveliness in the final song extolling the superiority of the Paris women, or rather their nagging tongues. Debussy's last song-cycle, *Trois poèmes de Mallarmé* (1915) is lyrical and restrained, almost pessimistic in tone.

The opera *Pelléas et Mélisande* (1893–1902), a virtual word for word setting of the symbolist play by Maurice Maeterlinck, is spellbinding. It treats what might be described as an episode from an Arthurian legend, not in the grand manner, but as an interior and intimate drama, in which sychronistic action plays more of a role than the inevitability of fate. There is an ethereal quality throughout the score (which discreetly uses recurring motifs), but also an astonishingly close correspondence between the vocal line and the words (a correspondence also found in Debussy's songs), and in particular between the emotional content of the words and music. As a result the vocal lines are spontaneous and natural, and aid the very strong portrayal of the characters. The story itself operates in short scenes on the level of subconscious empathy rather than surface action, in spite of the vivid naturalness of some of its dialogue. It is this subconscious layer, without a wide range of orchestral colour but with a richness and consistency of subdued texture, that Debussy's score so amplifies in slowly evolving detail. The aura of innocence removes it far from Expressionist angst (the anguish and anger of the betrayed husband Golaud is all too directly expressed), and all these qualities made the opera both remarkable and widely influential when it appeared, but almost impossible to imitate, and its tone has since perhaps only been matched by **Bártok**'s *Bluebeard's Castle*. Debussy also worked for many years on a second opera, based on Poe's *The Fall of the House of Usher*; he never completed it, but enough has remained for others to put what remains in performable order, suggesting a dark oppressive drama.

RECOMMENDED WORKS
All Debussy's works are recommended. A sensible introduction is through *Prélude à l'Après-midi d'un faune'* (1892–94), *La mer* (1903–05) and some of the earlier piano music, such as *L'isle joyeuse* (1904) or the *Images* for piano (1905 and 1907). Those familiar with the popular works of Debussy might consider the more rigorous late works, and the opera *Pelléas et Mélisande* (1893–1902)

BIBLIOGRAPHY
C. Debussy, *Debussy on Music*, 1976
M. Dietschy, *A Portrait of Claude Debussy*, 1990
E. Lockspeiser, *Debussy*, 1962–65

Dukas Paul Abraham**
born 1st October 1865 at Paris
died 17th May 1935 at Paris

For many years Dukas has been known by a single work, albeit one of the most popular in the orchestral repertoire. But recently the real value of his very limited output has begun to reach wider audiences. One of the most fastidious and private of composers, he is known to have destroyed much of his unpublished and unperformed work before his death, including three incomplete operas and a symphony.

His first success was *Polyeucte – Ouverture pour la tragédie de Corneille* (1891) whose successful and seamless five-part structure, allied to a general Wagnerian wash with a lovely and nostalgic slow ending, reflects his lengthy studies of Classical composers – pleasant, if unstartling music. The *Symphony in C major* (1896) is more individual, equally skilfully crafted, and indebted to Beethoven.

In 1897 appeared Dukas's most famous work, *L'apprenti sorcier (The Sorcerer's Apprentice)*. This brilliant scherzo, one of the most graphic tone poems ever written, which conjures up both the action of the story and the feelings of the unfortunate apprentice, is based on a monologue by Goethe, describing an apprentice attempting – disastrously – to use magic to do his chores for him. Particularly brilliant is the sharp, rich and yet crystal clear orchestration, with the enchanted broom splitting into two on clarinet and bassoon, and the gripping depiction of movement through rhythm. It was equally brilliantly adapted for a cartoon (with Mickey Mouse as the apprentice) in Walt Disney's *Fantasia*, ensuring its world-wide popularity. It also caught the attention of younger composers at the time of its composition, for its absence of Wagnerian influence (it is much more akin to contemporary Russian tone poems), for its orchestration, and for the harmonic devices.

But *L'apprenti sorcier* is not entirely characteristic of Dukas's concerns, which were more with the problems of large-scale musical architecture, as in his best-known piano work, the wide-ranging *Variations, interlude et final sur un thème de Rameau* (1899–1902). His other major surviving work, the opera *Ariane et Barbe-Bleue*, (1900–1906), seems to be regaining some of the attention it deserves. It also uses variation technique, usually associated with operas later in the century. Maeterlinck's reworking of the traditional story was unusual for the time, though it now has a contemporary ring. The subject is Ariane herself, who not only rescues Bluebeard, but asserts herself and eventually subdues him, emerging as a modern and undominated woman. Dukas provided music that sometimes has a Wagnerian grandeur, but also something of the line and atmosphere of Debussy's *Pelléas et Mélisande* (also to a Maeterlinck text) – at the name of Mélisande (one of Bluebeard's former wives) Dukas quotes Debussy. It is a compelling score and drama, with a massed chorus of villagers outside the castle walls, and a major and difficult role for the mezzo-soprano heroine.

Dukas's last work, apart from one song and *La plainte, au loin, du faune . . .* (1920) for piano, a tribute to Debussy, was the ballet or 'poème-dansé' *La péri* (1911–12) to which he later added an imposing brass fanfare in a ceremonial style **Walton** was to emulate. In contrast to the fanfare, the actual ballet, an eastern fairy tale telling how La péri, guardian of the Lotus of Immortality, wins it back through her dancing when it is taken by King Iskender, is hauntingly atmospheric. Again the orchestration is brilliant and lucid; sections of the orchestra are layered (the flutes and high woodwind sometimes running at a different pace), giving great depth to the rich overall sound in what is perhaps a finer achievement than *L'apprenti sorcier*.

Dukas was active as a critic, and one of the editors of the complete editions of Rameau and François Couperin, and taught at the Paris Conservatoire, **Messiaen** being the most notable of his pupils.

RECOMMENDED WORKS
    opera *Ariane et Barbe-Bleue*
    (1899–1906)
    L'apprenti sorcier (1897) for orchestra
    La péri (1912) for orchestra

BIBLIOGRAPHY
    P. Dukas, *Écrits sur la musique*, 1948
    (in French)
    G. Favre, *L'oeuvre de Paul Dukas*,
    1969 (in French)

Duruflé Maurice*
born 11 January 1902 at Louviers
died 16th June 1986 at Paris

Duruflé, an organist-composer in the French tradition, published only a handful of works. He is known for one in particular, the *Requiem*, op. 9 (completed 1947, for mezzo, bass, organ and orchestra, also version for organ alone), which takes up the spirit of **Fauré's** *Requiem* (both were written in memory of the composer's father), and cloaks it in a late Impressionist hue. It shows the main features of his style – largely gentle, but with more dramatic moments well integrated into the whole. Melodically his idiom is based on Gregorian chants, while employing an orchestral wash of subdued colour, with only limited use of other instrumental touches. The deep sonorities are aided by the use of the organ. The Impressionist harmony uses modal ideas, and aims at a gentle and intimate evocation (the ostinati of the 'Sanctus' seem to stand between Impressionism and the minimalists). A similar combination of Impressionist harmonies and liturgical influence had already surfaced in the *Trois danses* (*Three Dances*, 1936) for orchestra.

His organ music shows the influence of Tournemire, and is distinguished by its meticulous craftsmanship and by the sense of the self-sufficiency of individual pieces. His style, which first attracted notice in the *Prélude, Adagio et Choral varié* (1929), has distinct layers of simultaneous action, usually employing different but related rhythms. In the *Scherzo* op. 2 (1926) the counterpoint leads to a gentle but lively mood, in the chorale variations of *Veni Creator Spiritus* (1930) to multiple strands of idea. The rhythmic emphasis is even more marked in the elliptical opening of the *Prélude et fugue sur le nom Alain* (1943), commemorating the organist-composer **Alain**, and quoting his *Litaines* – the use of plainsong is also overt. This small body of organ works, so finely crafted, is particularly pleasing.

RECOMMENDED WORKS
    complete organ works
    Requiem, op. 9 (1947)

Dutilleux Henri**
born 22nd January 1916 at Angers

The music of Henri Dutilleux has still to reach a wider musical public outside France. His style has a more traditional base than many better-known modern French composers, and has therefore attracted less attention, less of the excitement of the new. He has not subscribed to any 'school', and like another French composer who has been a major influence on his own work, **Roussel,** has been something of an isolated figure. In addition, his output has been limited to a handful of works (nine major scores in forty years), less a reflection of his numerous other activities as teacher and administrator than of his extreme fastidiousness, which led to the suppression of his earlier scores.

Orchestral writing (non-programmatic, but usually with a poetic subtitle) has dominated Dutilleux's output. The most obvious characteristic is the mastery and brilliance of the orchestration, from the glowing textures of the *Symphony No. 1* (1949–51) onwards. Typically he subdivides the orchestra into small units that are either briefly highlighted or act autonomously to generate polyrhythmic and polytonal effects, so that, for example, the strings of *Métaboles* (*Metabolism*, 1962–65) for orchestra are subdivided repeatedly in one of its sections, while the *Symphony No. 2 'Le double'* (*The Double*, 1956–59) pits, in concerto grosso fashion, twelve solo players against the rest of the orchestra. In non-orchestral works there is a similar preoccupation with expressive colour, so that the *String Quartet 'Ainsi le nuit'* (*Thus the Night*, 1975–76) explores every permutation of string colour in seven movements with four 'parentheses'. His harmonic language, which has ranged from the obviously tonal (the *Piano Sonata*, 1947, a well-known piece in France) to a 12-tone idea in one of the sections of *Métaboles*, always has the feel of a tonal base and, thanks to the clarity of orchestral texture, rarely feels dissonant in spite of the polytonal effects.

As a result, much of the emotional and structural preoccupation is with sonority, and in particular a sense of the opposition of two basic concepts, what one might describe as the still point and the turning world. At times this might be between massed sound and silence, at others between low, held chords and fluttering ideas. His preferred method of musical structure emphasises these features. In place of the traditional methods of statement and development, he has developed structures that rely on internal metamorphosis, in which individual ideas almost imperceptibly evolve, and the overall pattern is eventually seen to have slowly undergone consistent change. Shorter linked sections that evolve into each other therefore predominate over traditional movements. The origins of this lie in variation technique (used in the *Piano Sonata*) and allow for a sense of plastic freedom, most clearly seen (as its title would suggest) in *Métaboles*.

Of the individual works, the rather ineffectual extended melodic lines of the passacaglia that starts the *Symphony No. 1*, initially tinged with an almost jazzy feel, should not deter listeners from the rest of the work, which is in one continuous flow from gossamer moments of colour and effect, to more aggressive brass and darker strings, with great rhythmic energy reminiscent of **Roussel** or **Walton**. The *Symphony No. 2 'Le double'* is less assertive until the finale, but equally effective. *Métaboles* is perhaps Dutilleux's most characteristic score, the five sections playing continuously, with the third part ('Obsessional') in the cast of a passacaglia, the emotions ranging from a dark mystery to nobility. The orchestral diptych *Timbres, espaces, mouvement* (1977), subtitled *La nuit étoilée* (*Tone colours, space, movement* or *The starry night*) has brilliant instrumental writing, and is built around the metamorphosis of a single note (G sharp).

These works show Dutilleux's idiom to be essentially poetic, a musical expression of the deep colours and landscapes of our subconscious, in which changing timbre is always more important than melodic line. Both, however, come to the fore in the two concertos which many may find an appealing approach to the composer. However, even in the *Cello Concerto* – titled *Tout un monde lointain* (*A whole distant world*, 1968–70) after Baudelaire – often it is the interaction of the colours of the orchestra and the highly rhapsodic and flowing solo line that is responsible for the effect. It was the cellist Rostropovich's advocacy of this work that introduced Dutilleux to a larger audience, and Isaac Stern has

repeated this with the *Violin Concerto* (1985, subtitled *L'arbre des songes*), a less lyrical, more brittle work with a close dialogue between orchestra and soloist leaping melodic phrases and sharp instrumental colours.

Dutilleux was director of singing at the Paris Opéra in 1942, joined French Radio in 1943, becoming director of music productions 1945–63, and professor of composition, first at the École Normale de Musique in 1961, then at the Paris Conservatoire from 1970.

RECOMMENDED WORKS

> Cello Concerto (*Tout un monde lointain*) (1968–70)
> *Métaboles* (1962–65) for orchestra
> Piano Sonata (1947)
> Symphony No. 1 (1949–51)
> Symphony No. 2 (*Le double*) (1956–59)
> *Timbres, espace, mouvement* (1977) for orchestra
> Violin Concerto (*L'arbre des songes*) (1985)

BIBLIOGRAPHY

> P. Mari, *Henri Dutilleux*, Paris, 1973 (in French)

Fauré Gabriel (Urbain)***
born 12th May 1845 at Pamiers (Ariège)
died 4th November 1924 at Paris

Although Fauré was 54 at the turn of the 20th century, he was a composer who strode both centuries not only temporally, but also musically, being a traditionalist who introduced into his style many elements that were to come to fruition in the following generation. He concentrated on small-scale forms: the song, of which he is one of the great French masters, piano music and above all chamber music. In addition his relatively small output was constrained by financial obligations to his family – throughout his life he could devote time to composition only in the summer. His art is one of understatement, absence of display, and appeals more to those who are prepared to explore and share its intimacy. It is significant that Fauré was one of the few composers of his generation who was immune to the spell of Wagner (apart, perhaps, from the *Ballade* for piano and orchestra, 1881).

His earliest music reflects the Romanticism of his teacher, Saint-Saëns, and the *Violin Sonata No. 1* (1876) has remained popular for its lyricism and the flowing ideas that were to remain a major characteristic. During the last two decades of the 19th century his style matured, adding an assertiveness to the underlying lyricism and introverted grace. The *Requiem* is the outstanding work of this period. But Fauré's summit of achievement did not come until the 20th century, and especially the last two decades of his life – he continued to compose masterpieces until his death at the age of 79. Notably in a series of chamber works, his expression becomes more refined, more ethereal, tauter and more radiant. His characteristic traits remain: the preference for long melodies created from harmonic or rhythmic germ-cells over vividness of colour, for which Fauré seems to have had less feel than almost any other major composer (one reason why there is so little orchestral music and none for wind); a rhythmic sense that is rarely central to his music and which has sometimes been criticised for monotony; three- or four-movement structures that often include scherzos of Gallic impishness and humour; an essentially diatonic harmonic palette that includes modes inherited from the church music Fauré was accustomed to as a professional organist; and a harmonic freedom created by the naturalness of his technique. The bulk of his output puts the piano in a central postion, in the songs, (where Fauré gave the French art song a new importance in relationship to the voice), in the solo piano music, and in the chamber music. His last works extend the harmony to include elements of dissonance, chromaticism, and whole-tone passages, and the kind of introverted serenity that is the province of only a handful of composers in their old age. Fauré, like Beethoven, had the additional handicap of deafness, which had become serious by 1910.

Of his orchestral music, the masterpiece is the lucid suite from his incidental music to *Pelléas et Mélisande* (1898), the first musical work based on Maeterlinck's influential play. Unlike **Schoenberg's** tone poem or **Debussy's** opera, it looks back to classical models, and thus forward to the neoclassical movement. The now little-heard *Prométhée* (1900), originally for three wind bands, 10 strings and twelve harps, together with soloist and choirs, secured Fauré considerable public success. The suite *Masques et bergamasques* (1918–19) for orchestra and based on incidental music and material from as far back as 1869, again has a strong feel of neoclassicism in its series of entertaining dances and in its light scoring. Fauré

destroyed other large-scale works before they were publicly heard or published.

It is in Fauré's chamber music, which spanned his entire compositional life and reflects the evolution of his style, where more rewards are found. The *Piano Quartet No. 1* in C minor, op. 15 (1879), probably his best-known chamber work, is classical in form, essentially lyrical and graceful, as is the frequently heard *Élégie* for cello and piano, op. 24 (1883). But the beautiful *Piano Quartet No. 2* in G minor, op. 45 (1886) is wider ranging in its ideas, more powerful in its impact, with a greater freedom and delight in the manipulation of the material, especially in the sometimes ravishing harmonic changes. There is similar contrast in the two piano quintets. The *Piano Quintet No. 1* in D minor, op. 89 (1887–1905) is more conventional than its successor, the mellow *Piano Quintet No. 2* in C minor, op. 115 (1919–21). Sustained by its extended formal arguments, this latter quintet has a beautifully carefree and graceful atmosphere, as well as breathless and dissonant moments in the scherzo. The two *Cello Sonatas* (1917 and 1922) and the *Piano Trio* in D minor (1923) continue the rarefied and lyrical aesthetic. Fauré left writing a string quartet until the very last, at the age of 79. The *String Quartet* in E minor, op. 121 (1923–24) is strong in melodic line, transparent in construction, and has an ethereal, otherworldly quality. It seems slightly rough-hewn for Fauré, and he did not live to revise it as he wished.

Much of Fauré's distinctive piano music is grouped into forms that evoke the titles of Chopin – *Impromptus, Barcarolles* and *Nocturnes.* The attractive *Theme and Variations* in C sharp minor, op. 73 (1897) is quite often encountered, while the later works, (the last three *Nocturnes,* or the later *Barcarolles*) again show compression of concept. Many commentators have traced some of the ideas of Impressionism back to Fauré's piano music.

His songs were gathered into three collections published in 1879, 1897 and 1908. With the exception of the settings of Verlaine, for whose poetry Fauré had a particular affinity (e.g. the song-cycle *Cinq mélodies de Verlaine,* op. 58, 1890), he often chose poetry devoid of obvious musical content or clear description, allowing the piano a greater (sometimes contrasting) role than had been customary. In his earlier cycles (e.g. *La bonne chanson,* op. 61, 1891–92) also in version for piano, string quartet and double bass) he arranged the poetry into a dramatic progression, emphasising this musically by the use of recurrent themes. His last song-cycles (*Le jardin clos*, op. 106, 1914–45, *Mirages*, op. 113, 1919, and *L'horizon chimérique*, op. 118, 1921) omit this technique, but show the subtlety of thought and detail that mark his other later works.

His opera *Pénélope* (1913) is derived from the techniques of song, the drama introverted, theatrically absent. But his best-loved work is the *Requiem*, op. 48 for soloists, chorus and organ (1877–90, version for small ensemble 1888–92 with soloists and chorus, full orchestration 1899), written in memory of his father. Its simplicity and purity, untroubled by banality or self-consciousness, have exceptional appeal. Of the three versions (with organ, with small instrumental ensemble, with orchestra), that for a small instrumental ensemble (without violins and with divided violas and cellos) perhaps most happily matches the scale, intimacy and lucidity of the writing, from the initial echoes of old church music, the lovely rocking of the 'Sanctus', through to its famous close, with the atmosphere of a gentle carol, the organ weaving its own song above. There is also a version for the smaller orchestral ensemble with two extra movements and two horns added by Fauré in 1893.

Undoubtably, one of Fauré's greatest legacies was his influence through teaching, and the very French example of his own music, effortless, intimate and yet full of clarity, light, grace, and charm, that so contrasted with German models. Among his pupils were **Enesco, Koechlin, Ravel,** Florent **Schmitt,** and the most notable teacher of the succeeding generation, Nadia Boulanger. In addition to his posts as organist, he started teaching at the Conservatoire in 1896, and was its director (introducing major reforms) until 1920. Until his death he was a champion of new music, co-founding the Société Nationale de Musique with **d'Indy,** Lalo, Duparc and Chabrier in 1871, and becoming president of the new Société Musicale Indépendante in 1909. He was music critic for *Le Figaro* (1903–21), fought in the action that raised the siege of Paris in 1870, and was awarded the Grand Croix of the Légion d'Honneur in 1920. He edited the complete piano works of Schumann and the organ works of Bach.

RECOMMENDED WORKS
Barcarolles Nos 1–13 (1880s–1931) for piano
Cello Sonata No. 1 in D minor, op. 109 (1917)

Cello Sonata No. 2 in G minor, op. 117 (1922)
suite *Pelléas and Mélisande*, op. 80 (1898) for orchestra
Piano Quartet No. 1 in C minor, op. 15 (1879)
Piano Quartet No. 2 in G minor, op. 48 (1886)
Piano Quintet No. 2 in C minor, op. 115 (1919–21)
Piano Trio in D minor, op. 120 (1922–23)
Requiem, op. 48 (1887)
Requiem, op. 48 (1893 version with two extra movements and small orchestra)
Quartet in E minor, op. 121 (1923–24)

BIBLIOGRAPHY
ed. J. M. Nectoux, *Gabriel Fauré: his Life through his Letters*, 1984
R. Orledge, *Gabriel Fauré*, London, 1979

Françaix Jean
born 23rd May 1912 at Le Mans
died 25th September 1997 at Paris

Jean Françaix epitomises a particular French brand of musical expression: an amiable, delicate palette in which emotion is played down in favour of wit and elegance tinged with an amused irony. That his works rarely address deeper understandings (coming closest in the oratorio *L'Apocalypse selon St Jean*, 1942) makes him an intrinsically less interesting composer than, for example, his contemporary **Poulenc,** who was equally capable of creating such Gallic pleasures. Some listeners may therefore find Françaix's music too trite; others may enjoy exactly such an idiom.

The *Piano Concerto* (1936) confirmed the promise of the sparkling *Piano Concertino* (1932). The concerto is typical of his style: delicate, chamber in feel (in spite of the large orchestra, its size used for shades of colour), and with more of an amiable dialogue between soloist and orchestra than a confrontation. Similar clarity of line and texture, gentle lyricism, and light-hearted rhythms are found in other concertante works: the *Suite* (1934) for violin and orchestra with piquant Stravinskian elements, the *Rhapsody* (1946) for viola and small wind orchestra with episodes of sardonic humour, the admired *Fantasy* (1955, from earlier material) for cello and orchestra, or the *Concerto for two pianos and orchestra* (1965). Ballet music formed a large proportion of his earlier music, including *Scuola di ballo* (*Ballet School,* 1933) based on themes by Boccherini (1743–1805). His chamber music includes the happy *Wind Quintet* (1948), full of lively and expertly crafted writing, especially for the horn, and the very attractive 'musical game' *Sérénade BEA* (1952) for string sextet, commissioned for a beautiful woman named Beatrice. Françaix was a brilliant pianist, and toured extensively.

RECOMMENDED WORKS
Concertino (1932) for piano and orchestra
Piano Concerto (1936)
'musical game' *Sérénade BEA* (1952) for string sextet
Wind Quintet (1948)

BIBLIOGRAPHY
D. Ewen, *Françaix*

Henry Pierre*
born 9th December 1927 at Paris

Pierre Henry was a pioneer and leading exponent of the *musique concrète* movement, exploring electronic composition through the manipulation of acoustic, non-electronic sounds. After studying with **Messiaen** and Nadia Boulanger, he collaborated in 1949 with Pierre **Schaeffer** in the first *musique concrète* experiments at the Experimental Division of the French Broadcasting Network, becoming the head of the Research Group (1950). He left in 1958 to set up his own studio, the Studio Apsome.

In the earliest pieces (for example, the *Concerto des ambiguïtés,* 1950) atonal techniques were modified by electronic distortions of tempo, pitch, and timbre. With *Bidule en nuit* (1950) and *Symphonie pour un homme seul* (*Symphony for a man alone,* 1950), both developed with **Schaeffer**, this developed into a purely electronic language, in which the material is based either on sounds electronically generated or non-musical sound sources electronically manipulated. The intention was to liberate music from conventional, inherited notions, and to evolve a musical language more in keeping with the realities of contemporary existence. The results were almost totally divorced from the accepted musical sounds or forms (other than the necessity of organising material within time limits), and favoured low-pitched electronic sonorities.

With a series of ballet works for the choreographer Maurice Béjart, following their meeting in 1955, Henry's abstract vocabulary was modified into an almost pictorial expression of clear programmatic content. Some of these ballets use purely electronically generated sounds (*Le voyage,* 1962, concert version 1963), some *concrète* sounds (the creaking door in *Variations pour une porte et un soupir* [*Variations for a door and a sigh*], 1963, other more recognisable musical elements (pop music in the *Messe pour le temps présent* [*Mass for the present time*], 1967). *Le voyage,* based on the Tibetan Book of the Dead, is perhaps the most remarkable of these, following the journey of the soul on the death of a man; the wind that comes with death, the extra-worldly light and darkness, and the fear and the final dissolution described in the text are highly suited to electronic realisation, and Henry's score is vivid, descriptive, and sometimes genuinely frightening. Its construction and metaphysics are perhaps influenced by **Messiaen**.

The slow immobility of *La noire à soixante* (1961), later combined with the extreme quasi-speaking techniques of a manipulated voice of *Granulométrie* (1968), admirably illustrate *concrète* techniques and include a humorous element, but are of limited aural interest when divorced from a visual context. Henry's later music has extended the scale of these programmatic stage-orientated works into larger spectacles, with extensive lighting and stage effects, and includes a re-exploration of the 'noise-makers' invented by the Futurists in the 1920s in *Futuristie I* (1975), and the Béjart ballet *Nijinsky, clown de Dieu* (*Nijinsky, Clown of God,* 1971). But it is Henry's earliest works, pioneers in electronic music, that are of the most interest and of historical importance, while *Le voyage* remains one of the most potent of electronic scores.

RECOMMENDED WORKS
Concerto des ambiguïtués (1950)
Symphonie pour un homme seul (1950) (with Pierre Schaeffer)
electronic ballet *Le voyage* (1962)

Ibert Jacques François Antoine*
born 15th August 1890 at Paris
died 5th February 1962 at Paris

Although for much of his life Jacques Ibert was mainly involved with opera and incidental music, he is best known for a handful of orchestral and chamber works that have endured in the repertoire. Otherwise his music, full of charm and sparkle and utilising both Impressionism and neoclassicism, has been largely too shallow in substance to survive.

His works usually combine classical forms with bright colours, a poster-paint vivacity, sometimes unexpected harmonies, and a piquant imagination (as in the juxtaposition of the sonorous string tone of the cello against wind instruments in the *Concerto for Cello and Wind Instruments*, (1925). In the *Suite Élizabéthaine* (1944) for solo voice, chorus and orchestra, he incorporated music from the English Elizabethan composers, while the ballet *Diane de Poitiers* (1933–34) expands Renaissance dances with primary colours and a lively *joie de vivre*. His best-known work is probably the *Divertissement* (1930) for chamber orchestra, witty, fun and colourful, and originally written to accompany Lebiche's celebrated farce, *The Italian Straw Hat*. It includes musical jokes, from a policeman's whistle and jazz to a parody of Mendelssohn's Wedding March.

There is an element here of the French tradition stemming from the delightful humour of Offenbach, as there is in *Angélique* (1962), the best known of his seven operas, including two written in collaboration with **Honegger**. The symphonic suite *Escales* (*Ports of Call*, 1922), evoking the atmosphere of three Mediterranean ports, was once very popular, while the entertaining *Trois pièces brèves* (1930) are often encountered in wind quintet recitals. The lively *Concertino da camera* (1935) for alto saxophone and eleven instruments makes full use of the potential of the saxophone, but his most successful concerto is the *Flute Concerto* (1934). It typifies much of Ibert's idiom: a classical three-movement structure, a strong lyrical sense made to feel elliptical by the harmonies, a sense of pleasure and fun, and sometimes a feeling at the end of a passage that for all the facility nothing memorable has been said. Nonetheless, this is a warm and charming work, an important contribution to a limited repertoire.

Ibert was director of the French Academy in Rome (1937–55, except for the war years), and director of the Paris Opéra Comique from 1955 to 1957.

RECOMMENDED WORKS
Ballade de la geôle de Reading (1922) for orchestra
Flute Concerto (1934)
Divertissement (1930)

Trois pièces brèves (1930) for wind quintet

BIBLIOGRAPHY
G. Michael, *Jacques Ibert*, 1967 (in French)

Jolivet André **
born 8th August 1905 at Paris
died 20th December 1974 at Paris

In the last few years Jolivet's music made something of a comeback outside his native France, where he has always been highly regarded. In 1936, in reaction to the intellectual experimentation – especially neoclassicism – of contemporary French composers and of **Stravinsky**, he formed La Jeune France with the composers Baudrier, Lesur, and **Messiaen**, to promote their own ideas and compositions. Subsequently his idiom consistently attempted to return music to its antecedents as a reflection of the spirituality of humankind, as ritual and sacrament, through a language that gradually moved further and further away from a tonal base but without strict serial techniques. He achieved this through primitive ritual, incantation, an interest in exotic and ancient musics, and the use of Pythagorean number ratios and the 'golden section'. Prominent in his idiom is the use of percussion (which he learnt from studies with **Varèse**, 1930–33) and a strong melodic interest.

Ritual was not apparent in his earliest works. In the uncompromising *String Quartet* (1934), written under the influence of **Varèse**, dissonances and harmonic conjunctions destroy traditional tonality, and it was followed by the earnest but lovely *Andante* for strings (1934). With *Mana* (1935 – *Mana* refers to the spirit of fetishes), six piano pieces based on objects given to him by **Varèse**, *Cinq incantations* for flute (1936) and the *Danses rituelles* (1939, orchestrated 1940–41) the ritual element was established. The effective *Danses rituelles*, perhaps inevitably, echo the ritualistic works of the Impressionists and of the **Stravinsky** of *Rite of Spring*, but are clothed in thick orchestral textures, primitive dance rhythms, and with the flute prominent, appropriate to a sense of ancient ritual. The heady atmosphere of ancient religious ceremony and music from other cultures is most overt in the *Suite delphique* (1943), whose twelve instruments include the ondes martenot and percussion instruments used to make such sounds as that of baying dogs. Its exoticism, created by unusual rhythms, eastern harmonic effects and melodies, is blended with a sense of traditional tonality and a feel of the convocation of traditions.

With the exhilarating and dissonant *Piano Sonata No. 1* (1945) and the *Ondes Martenot Concerto* (1947), the first of the fourteen concertos that form the core of his music, Jolivet submerged the more overt aspects of ritualism and exoticism into a broader language. Those aspects are retained in a sense of the dance, and especially in a spontaneous expression of the human spirit; one of the results is the increasing violent use of dissonance and unusual percussive/rhythmic effects no longer so clearly connected to exotic borrowings or ancient ritualism. This new direction was reflected in the *Concertino for trumpet, piano and strings* (1948, numbered as the *Trumpet Concerto No. 1*), in which Jolivet tries to merge jazz influences and some dizzy dissonant sections with a neo-classical base in an entertaining if lightweight piece. The *Flute Concerto No. 1* (1949) is also an attractive neo-classical work, with a florid solo part and string orchestra. A third concerto in a popular idiom was the *Trumpet Concerto No. 2* (1954), with echoes of jazz and **Stravinsky**.

Of more substance, and the work that brought Jolivet international prominence, was the large *Piano Concerto* (1950). It opens with an ostinato piano against African-style drumming and Arabic woodwind, progressing to shades of **Bartók** and hints of **Ravel**. Heavily orchestrated sections, emphasising woodwind and percussion in snatched phrases, contrast with passages for piano and single instruments of exposed percussion. The first movement is supposed to evoke Africa, the second the Far East, the third Polynesia. It caused quite a furore when it appeared and is well worth hearing, though its constantly shifting elements, including three separate batteries of percussion, crowd out an overall sense of unity. The eclectic abandon of this work (more commonly associated with young composers than one of 45) is present in the much more effective *Symphony No. 1* (1953), whose four movements develop by the opposition of ideas rather than classically. Again a fusion of the occidental and the oriental, it has a steamy and sensual slow movement followed by an other-worldly allegro full of ostinati.

With the raucous *Symphony No. 2* (1959) Jolivet attempted a synthesis of serial and modal music, and of melodic continuity and restless rhythm, although interrupted by characteristic violent outbursts. The most difficult of the symphonies, *Symphony No. 3*, (1964) is also the finest. There is a battery of twenty-four percussion instruments, and the predominant language is violent and dissonant, with massed timbres. The sense of a tonal base is almost, though not quite, extinguished; underlying it is the elemental pounding of ritual. In the sombre *Cello Concerto No. 1* (1962), the lyric flow and harmonic insecurity are predominant, with a restrained orchestra (that nonetheless employs twenty-two percussion instruments), and a striking second movement of cello against revolving percussion. The similarly rhapsodic *Cello Concerto No. 2* 1966), with a very difficult solo part written for Rostropovich, uses only strings (with a solo quintet).

Of his chamber music, a special place is given to the flute, and his music is often encountered in flute recitals, especially the *Cinq incantations* (1936) and *Ascèses I* (1967, for various flute types played solo). Among his vocal music is the large-scale oratorio *La vérité de Jeanne* (*The Truth of Joan*, 1956), written to commemorate the 500th anniversary of Joan of Arc's death, and the appealing *Epithalame* (1953), a 'vocal symphony' for twelve voices.

Jolivet's place in the music of the 20th century is difficult to establish. Most readers should find merit in the earlier ritual works, and entertainment in the two trumpet and second flute concertos, and a rugged interest in the first cello concerto. Those prepared to accept the violence of the language will find the later works of interest, but lacking that individuality which was always threatening to emerge. His technique of blending other types of music with an essentially tonal base is of interest to an age that is searching for new ways to extend traditional patterns of harmony while rejecting 12-tone techniques and the avant-garde experiments that followed.

Jolivet was director of music at the Comédie Française (1943–59) and his only opera, *Dolores ou Le miracle de la femme laide* (*Dolores or The miracle of the ugly woman*, 1942) is an opera bouffe. He founded the Centre Français d'Humanisme Musical at Aix-en-Provence (1959), and taught at the Paris Conservatoire (1966–70).

RECOMMENDED WORKS
Andante for String Orchestra (1934)
Ascèses for solo flute (1967)
Cello Concerto No. 1 (1962)

Cello Concerto No. 2 (1966)
Danses rituelles (1939, orch. 1940–41)
    for orchestra
vocal symphony *Epithalame* (1953)
Flute concerto (1949)
Cinq incantations for solo flute (1936)
Piano Sonata No. 1 (1945)
Suite delphique (1942) for chamber
    ensemble
Symphony No. 3 (1964)
Trumpet Concerto No. 2 (1954)

BIBLIOGRAPHY
H. Jolivet, *Avec André Jolivet*, 1978

Koechlin Charles*

born 27th November 1867 at Paris
died 31st December 1950 at Le Canadel

The music of Charles Koechlin is currently something of an enigma. His very large output (some 350 works, and over 225 opus numbers) includes almost every idiom except stage works (with one exception), but he is chiefly remembered as a famous teacher (his pupils included **Milhaud** and **Poulenc**), and as a considerable theorist and writer on music. The neglect of his music was partly due to his reluctance to publish or perform his compositions. However, there are signs that his work is currently undergoing a re-evaluation.

Like his teacher and mentor **Fauré**, his early reputation was based on his songs and his choral music, and of all Koechlin's output it is the songs that are the most likely to be heard. The earliest songs belong to Romanticism, but the precise clarity of the first two sets of *Rondels* (op. 1 and op. 8, 1890–95) herald later developments in French music. These settings of nature poems by Théodore de Banville are very attractive and direct, from the metronomic regularity of the accompaniment to *L'hiver* (*Winter*) that is merely an icicle phrase running up and down, to the lyric freedom of *Le thé* with its delicate rippling accompaniments. By 1905 he had started to use a subdued polytonality in his songs (influencing such French composers as **Milhaud**).

Koechlin's harmonic idioms are as eclectic as the inspiration for his works, which is almost invariably extra-musical. They range from elements of Impressionism to polytonality, atonality and the use of modes or polymodality that, in conjunction with counterpoint, give an archaic feel to a modern idiom. Often there is a tint of exoticism to the melodic line. Similarly his aesthetic ranges from the subdued Germanic Romanticism and modal scales of the rather attractive *Ballade* op. 50 (1919) for piano and orchestra, to the neo-classicism of the pleasant *Partita* (1945) for chamber orchestra, echoing the stately dances of the time of Louis XIV. Koechlin had a reputation for mastery of orchestration. Of the orchestral works, the most widely known is the cycle of symphonic poems on Kipling's *Jungle Book* (1899–1940). Of these, *Les Bandar-Log* parodies the techniques of **Debussy**, **Schoenberg** and **Stravinsky**, but transforms each parody into personal music. Koechlin was also noted in France for his choral music, which left behind the choral conventions of the 19th century; here his use of modal ideas and chant-like melodies is most marked. Among these is the large-scale *L'Abbaye* (*The Abbey*, 1899–1908), a 'religious suite' in two parts. The chamber music most often encountered includes an attractive but lugubrious six-movement *Wind Quintet* (1943), and cello, violin and viola sonatas. Apart from his own film music, Koechlin was also fascinated by film stars, reflected in another work occasionally encountered, the *Seven Stars Symphony* (1933) – less a symphony than seven unrelated tone portraits of seven film stars, in a contemplative style using a wide range of harmonic devices as well as the ondes martenot, of which Koechlin was one of the early exponents. It is a strange work, from the Impressionistic and oriental sinuousness of 'Douglas Fairbanks' to the lengthy final portrait of Chaplin, integrating jerky ideas reminiscent of piano accompaniments to silent films. But again, if there are some pleasant touches the *Seven Stars Symphony* seems uninspired and uninspiring, its gestures conventional and unmemorable.

Even more curious is the final song-cycle *Sept chansons pour Gladys* (1935), which celebrates the film star Lilian Harvey (he also wrote 113 short piano pieces in her honour). A strange juxtaposition of contemplative music and semi-serious words (undifferentiating between real and screen presence), it features long vocal lines with an archaic quality that recalls sad southern troubadour's songs. Quite apart from the curiosity of the subject matter and the words, this is a tender, gentle and very French song-cycle, rhythmically almost improvisatory, its tone that of contemplative love songs, albeit in an idiom of two decades earlier. Indeed, much of Koechlin's music seems to have had a luminous and contemplative feel, combined with what a number of commentators have suggested are moments of brilliant academicism. There have recently been strong claims for the quality of Koechlin's works; perhaps as more of them emerge from obscurity those claims will be justified. Koechlin was co-founder of the Société Musicale Indépendante in 1909, and, as a supporter of communism, president of the Fédération Musicale Populaire from 1937.

RECOMMENDED WORKS

song-cycle *Sept chansons pour Gladys* (1935)

song-cycles *Rondels* op. 1 and 8 (1890/ 1895)

symphonic cycle *Jungle Book* (1926–40)

BIBLIOGRAPHY

R. Orledge, *Charles Koechlin (1867–1950): His Life and Works,* London, 1990

Landowski Marcel··

born 18th February 1915 at Pont L'Abbé (Finistère)

The grandson of the French violinist–composer Henri Vieuxtemps (1820–1881), and the son of sculptor Paul Landowski, Marcel Landowski has been an important figure in French administrative musical circles, but his own work, essentially conservative in idiom, has suffered from the French vogue for the avant-garde and for serialism. He was involved for many years in academic arguments over the merits of respective schools, and later supported all forms of contemporary music when appointed music director at the French Ministry of Cultural Affairs in 1966. He once gave his music the tongue-in-cheek description 'Centre-Right'.

Within conventional forms, Landowski's music is characterised by a strict, sometimes over-meticulous sense of logic supported by powerful rhythmic momentum. In the symphonies and concertos the intention is the disciplined depiction of powerful human emotions; there is little improvisatory feel, the harmonic language is rarely dissonant, and slow movements are lyrical. His orchestration creates dense soundscapes with broad changes of sometimes unusual colour; a favourite device is a strong contrast between themes that involve brighter, fast-moving material against slower, grander ideas. His symphonies display a powerful sense of purpose,

with philosophical inspirations. The most immediate is perhaps the *Symphony No. 1 'Jean de la peur'* (1949), with an atmostpheric opening where bright, twittering and insistent ostinati are pitted against broader ideas. The final movement is dominated by a dark chorale, and eventually the opening ostinati return at a slower pace to close a most effective work. The *Symphony No. 3 'Des espaces'* (1965) is in two movements, less arresting than the first symphony, somewhat turbulent, but the progression equally vital as it works towards a joyous close. The *Symphony No. 4* (1988) in five movements emerges as a deliberate return to the large post-Romantic symphony (there are moments reminiscent of the **Vaughan Williams** of the early 1950s, and of **Honegger**), and the elements of a more modern sound world (such as the percussion in the furious second movement) are integrated into this general cast. It has another magical opening, contrasting the hushed and the grand, the former picked up and elaborated in the third movement. The fourth movement is full of bell sounds (it is titled 'Les cloches de Bruges'); the broad final movement is the weakest part of the symphony until a turbulent passage evolves into calm and then triumph and calm again. The urgent vitality of this symphony, its beautifully layered orchestration, and its ability to change focus or open out into broad melody, make it much more effective than similar works from such composers as **Tubin** or **Lloyd**.

These orchestral works have a strong sense of atmosphere, but it is as a vocal composer that Landowski has shown a particularly powerful voice. His masterpiece is the three-act opera *Le Fou (The Madman,* 1955–56), which as music drama was ahead of its time, and today seems more apposite than when it was written. The libretto by the composer combines the kind of half-mythical, half-imaginary setting at which opera excels: a state of war, the country in ruins, and about to be defeated. The central character, the scientist Peter Bel, has invented a nuclear device. He knows that it can save his country. He also knows what it will do to humankind, and the opera is the story of his internal struggle between these two pulls. He dies in his refusal to divulge his invention. The intentionally abstract background is divided into a number of layers, including Paul's internal torment reflected in voices and distant chorus, the wasteland and depravity of the ruined town and its despairing people, and between them the

archetypal figures of those who organise
and rule: the Prince, Paul's wife, and the
Prince's hard-line official. The musical
idiom is founded on a spartan tonal lyricism, dark but attenuated by colouristic
and expressive effects: percussion, vocal
techniques from *Sprechgesang* to high,
flowing anguished lines, and especially
electronic effects (one of the first operas to
use them). All these musical devices, from
the conventional to the more unusual, are
used to underline and expand the actual
text, to considerable effect. With its central moral messages and its exploration of
loyalty and betrayal and the responsibility
of the scientist, it seems surprising that
this powerful piece of music theatre is not
better known.

The *Messe de l'aurore* (*Dawn Mass*,
1977) for tenor, soprano, bass, chorus and
orchestra, was written for the tenth anniversary of the founding of the Orchestre
de Paris, for which Landowski was responsible. It sets poems by Pierre Emmanuel
that parallel the Catholic Mass. Landowski's dense settings make the work seem
over-heavy, but it has an insistent fervour,
with the ondes martenot adding other-
worldly effects at important moments.

Among his more recent works are a pair
of effective song-cycles written for singer
Galina Vishnievskaya and her husband,
the cellist Mstislav Rostropovich. *Un
enfant appelle* (*A Child is Calling*, 1979)
for soprano, cello and orchestra, is subtitled a 'concerto-cantata', and in it the
cello solo parts comment and add another
emotional layer. Landowski had attempted such a fusion of genres earlier, in *Le
rire de Nils Halerius* (1944–48), whose
first act is an opera, the second a ballet, and
the third an oratorio. In *Un enfant appelle*
the sense of orchestral layers, observable
in Landowski's earlier music, is extended:
tense string clusters and double layers of
the rhythmic ostinati (moving at different
speeds) are added to the approachable but
dark idiom, matching the expression of
anguish and experience, innocence and its
renewal, in the texts. *La prison* (1981),
subtitled an 'opera-concerto', is a music-
theatre piece for soprano, cello and orchestra to a text by the composer. The protagonists are the singer, representing a victim
of political oppression waiting for arrest
and undergoing interrogation in prison;
the cello, lyrically associated with her
happier memories and hopes; and the percussive small orchestra representing
Force. It is starkly naturalistic, a portrait
of internal aloneness, and most effective,
suggesting that his idiom has responded to

some of the mainstream developments in
European symphonic music.

Landowski was director of the conservatory at Boulogne-sur-Seine (1959–62),
music director at the Comédie Française
(1962–65), and was appointed inspector-
general for music education in 1965. His
own writings include a book on **Honegger**
(1957).

RECOMMENDED WORKS
   opera *Le Fou* (1955–56)
   'opera-concerto' *La prison* (1981)
   Symphony No. 1 (*Jean de la peur*)
    (1949)
   Symphony No. 4 (1988)
   'cantata-concerto' *L'enfant appelle*
    (1978) for soprano, cello and
    orchestra

BIBLIOGRAPHY
   A. Gola, *Marcel Landowski*, Paris,
   1969 (in French)

Mâche François-Bernard*
born 4th April 1935 at Clermont-
Ferrand

François-Bernard Mâche has concentrated on the mixing of natural sounds
from a wide variety of sources, often
including speech, with electronic sounds.
From his earliest works, such as *Volumes*
(1960) for chamber orchestra and 12-track
tape, he has used electronic means.

A series of works in the 1960s (*La peau
du silence*, 1962–66, for orchestra; *le son
d'une voix*, 1964; and *Nuit blanche*, 1966,
for speaker and two-track tape) used written text by breaking it down into phonemes, and using them as the base material. In the late 1960s he was involved with
the Groupe de Recherches Musicales of
French Radio, producing the effective
Synergies (1968) for orchestra with tape
for the 'concert collectif', with low shifting
waves of electronic sonorities, that turn to
percussive effects, the piece drawing on
themes and ideas provided by the collective of composers.

In 1972 he started a cycle of works
entitled *Melanesia*, reflecting the rituals
and myths of Melanesia. The first of these
was a tape composition, *Agiba* (1972),
made up entirely of natural sounds, from
the elements to animals, and including the
sounds of the southern African Xhosa
language, which is full of rhythmic clicking.
The second, *Kowar* (1972) for harpsichord
and tape, starts with the Xhosa language,

overlaid with electronic sounds and joined by the harpsichord, the rhythms of the accompanying sounds matching and emphasising those of the speech. Gradually the voice falls away, to be replaced by other natural sounds, bird-calls and the noises of pigs, manipulated to maintain the same basic rhythmic feel, eventually leading to a dramatic climax. A kowar is a New Guinean container for a skull covered in clay; subsequent works in the cycle referred to other cult skull-objects, including *Rambaramb* (1972–73) for piano, orchestra and tape, and *Temes Nevinbür* (1973) for two pianos, two percussionists and tape. The latter utilises the deeper sonorities of the two pianos and delicate percussive touches and piano cluster swirls; the natural sounds are allowed to stand alone, the piano and percussion providing a contrasting layer rather than pointing up the natural rhythms. In all these works the basis of the tape was drawn from *Agiba*, and thus they become a kind of variation on a sound-source. Of the further works in the cycle, *Le jonc à trois glumes* (1974) is for orchestra alone, while *Naluan* (1974) for piano, chamber ensemble and tape and *Maraé* (1974) for six percussionists and tape used new taped material.

Of his works without electronics, *Canzone II* (1963) for brass quintet is Mâche's only serial work, a virtuoso piece of very short contrasting sections that explores various acoustical and mute effects, including the first use of the percussive effect of striking the mouthpiece of the brass instrument. *Kemit* (1970) for darbouka or zarb solo is a virtuoso percussion transcription of material recorded in Nubia. Of his more recent works, *Styx* (1984) for two pianos, eight hands, is an especially effective piece of tone-painting, featuring the addition of sonorities to a rippling climax (material then being thrown around between the pianists), tone clusters, suggestions of minimalist influence and pedal effects.

Mâche graduated in classical literature and Greek archaeology, and has taught contemporary poetry and Greek as well as musical theory.

RECOMMENDED WORKS
   Canzone II (1963) for brass quintet
   Temes Nevinbür (1973) for two pianos, two percussionists and tape
   Styx (1984) for two pianos, eight hands

Messiaen Olivier Eugène Prosper Charles***

born 10th December 1908 at Avignon
died 28th April 1992 at Paris

When the 20th century is long gone, it may well be that **Mahler** and Olivier Messiaen will be seen as the colossi of the century, in the same way as Beethoven and Wagner stand out in the 19th century. Often vilified and misunderstood, Messiaen's music occupies a different plane from every other major 20th-century composer. Its purpose is to express the glory of creation, and through the creation the glory of God; its theme is the cosmos, and the mysteries of the cosmos, life and death, creation and destruction, the wonder of nature. For Messiaen the foundation for that expression was the Catholic church, not the church of social rules and behaviour, but that of the Christian mystic. In the interrelation of man, the cosmos, and God he comes close to Eastern religions, particularly Hindu and Buddhist (as do the Christian mystics).

Messiaen is one of the most profound spiritual contemplators of any age. His roots in the Catholic church reflect his own geographical background, and are in one sense incidental to appreciating his work, for the subjects of his spiritual contemplation are universal. Necessarily, many of his works are vast in duration and scale, the more so because a major component of that cosmic contemplation is the realisation that time as we experience it is an illusion of the material word (again, in common with much Eastern philosophy), and consequently Messiaen's music increasingly operates on different time-scales than those normally associated with music. This is most obvious in the sense of the static in his music (though it is an inadequate word), without development, for in such a time-scale the ending is contained in the beginning and vice versa.

At the same time, Messiaen was one of the major technical innovators of the 20th century, in part to find the means of expression for this meditation on the cosmos. In this, following **Varèse** and initially in common with **Jolivet** (who with Messiaen and others founded 'La Jeune France' in 1936), Messiaen was the chief figure in turning French music radically away from the neo-classicism and tradition of charm and flippancy that had dominated between the World Wars. The first innovation was harmonic, in what he termed 'modes of limited transposition'. The mode referred to is a scale of notes, in which the

intervals between the notes are so
designed that there are only a limited
number of times that the scale can be
transposed, maintaining those intervals,
before the pitches of notes are repeated.
The obvious example of this is the whole-
tone scale, utilised by **Debussy** but not
overtly by Messiaen, of a scale of seven
notes, which has an interval of a major
second between each note. This Messiaen
designated as the 'first mode'. Messiaen
designated seven of these modes (the
'second mode' could be transposed twice,
the third three times, and so on), and they
each have the characteristic that they
divide the octave symmetrically, but in
different places. Harmonic progression
using these limited transpositions and
symmetrical shapes creates a very static
feel, often moving in block-like fashion;
Messiaen used these modes vertically as
well as horizontally (i.e. in chord construction as well as melodic series) and they
influence his distinctive melodic shapes.
Chords derived from the modes create
'added resonance' (Messiaen's 'chord of
resonance', taken from mode 3, creates a
fundamental note and a tower of natural
harmonics). When used quietly over
another chord or note, or emphatically
below, this creates the sense of depth and
resonance endemic to Messiaen's style.
The soundscapes that such harmonic devices created have become a normal currency of subsequent 20th-century composition for composers of a wide range of
styles and procedures, even though they
are rarely arrived at with the systematic
technical means used by Messiaen.

The second innovation was rhythmic.
Messiaen introduced the widespread use
of rhythmic patterns based on Eastern
musical traditions, particularly those of
Indian classical music, where rhythmic
events unfold on two simultaneous time-
scales, that of a pattern or phrase of beats
which is itself repeated in a larger pattern,
and those of Balinese gamelan music, with
its regular repetitive patterns of irregular
rhythms. To this he added the influence of
ancient Greek and medieval metres. He
also utilised two important rhythmic concepts drawn from the Western tradition.
The first was 'additive rhythms', in which a
rhythmic note or pattern is lengthened by
the addition of half its value, and the
second 'non-retrogradable rhythms' in
which a rhythmic idea is symmetrical, and
therefore its retrograde is identical. The
effect of these techniques is to create
continuity of patterns, within which the

additive rhythms allow proportional irregularities. Rhythms thus become a systematic element, and Messiaen used them
much as he used his harmonic modes. This
was of crucial importance to the development of music, for it showed such composers as **Boulez** that the other elements of
music could be systematised in the same
fashion as harmony, and when this principle was applied using analogies to the 12-
tone inheritance of **Webern** it produced
'total serialism'. Messiaen treated colours
with the same kind of systematic
approach, for of all the musical elements
colour was perhaps the most important to
Messiaen, and changes of colour take on
added significance in musical progression
when the harmonic structures are largely
static; in this Messiaen had the example of
Varèse. Messiaen 'saw' colours when he
was composing, and timbre and tone-
colour, and their combinations, were as
crucial as pitch or duration to his idiom.

A major characteristic of Messiaen's
music, one so thoroughly explored that it
has become virtually impossible for any
other composer to emulate it, was the
influence and inspiration of bird-song. It
fascinated Messiaen from an early age, and
provides the basis for many of his melodic
ideas throughout his career, especially in
the early 1950s. On a philosophical level,
bird-song represents the aspect of the
natural in the cosmos, the musical representation of nature around us. He remains
generally true to the originals, transposing
them into the range of the instrument
sounding them, and mixing their rhythmic
patterns with his own rhythmic idiom.
Equally important to his overall aesthetic,
the organ occupies a central place in Messiaen's output, and he elevated writing for
the organ to a position it had not held since
the 18th century. It is impossible to
divorce the experience of the organ from
Messiaen's entire oeuvre, as they mutually
interact. In the organ the spiritual, the
religious and the earthly combine on a
symbolic as well as musical level. The
acoustic of the buildings that house the
large instruments Messiaen played tends
towards the large-scale expression of the
vastness of the cosmos, and the tradition of
improvisation (continued by Messiaen)
influences the element of spontaneity
within strict technical parameters that is
part of Messiaen's idiom.

All the technical devices, fascinating and
influential though they are, are strictly
means to an end, and knowledge of Messiaen's technique is not necessary to feel
the impact of his music. Indeed, there is a

completely different way of considering Messiaen's idiom. Messiaen himself said that all his music was influenced by the landscape of the French Alps, and there is a sense that his music is an evocation of the vastness of the cosmos that many experience when visiting mountains.

His output can be divided into fairly distinct periods, though there is a strong continuity of voice throughout. In his works to around 1935 Messiaen forged his idiom, and this period shows lingering traces of his early influences. From 1935 to 1950 he developed the spiritual and religious content, the rhythmic aspects of his music, and the use of large-scale cycles. This period includes a trilogy of works – the song-cycle *Harawi*, *Cinq rechants* for chorus, and the *Turangalîla-Symphonie*; Messiaen called them his 'Tristan' triptych, though they were not planned as a trilogy – where the subject is love within the theological cosmos. From 1950 to 1960 he developed the technical aspects of his music, including a foray into electronic music in a collaboration with Pierre **Henry** (*Timbres-durées* 1952). Here are also to be found the three works that thoroughly explore the possibilities of bird-song – *Réveil des oiseaux* and *Oiseaux exotiques*, for both piano and orchestral forces, and *Catalogue d'oiseaux* for piano. The works of the 1960s consolidated these technical advances, culminating in *La Transfiguration de notre Seigneur Jésus-Christ* for chorus and orchestra, which heralds his last works. Then from 1970 to his death he wrote four huge works (*Des canyons aux étoiles* for piano, horn and orchestra, the opera *Saint François d'Assise*, and the two organ cycles *Méditations sur le mystère de la Sainte-Trinité* and *Livre du Saint Sacrement*) in which he utilised all his experience in a language often more luminous and simplified. Combined with this is a spiritual understanding that is both more rarefied and more profound in its unity.

Messiaen became organist of L'Eglise de la Trinité in Paris in 1930, and remained there for over forty years. At this time he had already written the set of eight *Préludes* (1928–29) for piano. These lovely, sometimes mysterious pieces owe something to the piano music of **Debussy** but also show unmistakable Messiaen mannerisms. Bird-song is not used directly, but there is a definite suggestion of it in the trills and answering calls, and much of the impact of the pieces is achieved through an emphasis on changing colours and sonorities. Hints of exoticism are in part created by the 'modes of limited transposition', which Messiaen here specifically associated with actual colours, building the juxtapositions of the pieces accordingly. The *Préludes* make a suitable introduction for those new to Messiaen's music.

Messiaen's development is most easily followed in the organ works. The *Le banquet céleste* (1928) occupies a similar place in Messiaen's orgen output to that of the *Préludes* in his piano music, and is an equally good starting point for new listeners, rather than the more conventional *Diptyque* (1930) for organ. It is a meditation on the Holy Communion; the slow, subtly unfolding swathes of colours, and the addition of a high voice as if suspended over the general sound, were retained throughout Messiaen's organ music. *Apparition de l'Eglise éternelle* (*Vision of the Church Eternal*, 1932) initiates the strand of the revelation of the glorious in Messiaen's organ music. *L'Ascension* (1932–33), in four movements, each a meditation on biblical quotations, was originally written for orchestra, but is much better known in its organ version. The slow, vast textures of its first movement show a typical Messiaen trait, lifting moments of light (by use of a major chord) from the darkness, and the transcendental last movement (sometimes played on its own, as is the third) has a lucid, magical beauty. It is still a transitional work, the rhythms relatively conventional); the mighty opening of the third movement recalls an earlier French Romantic tradition.

In *La Nativité du Seigneur* (*The Birth of Our Lord*, 1935) these more conventional elements are discarded. It is cast in nine sections meditating on the Word of God among humans and the maternity of the Blessed Virgin. Modes of limited transposition and irregular additive rhythms are used, and the rhythms are influenced by classical Indian models. The effect is more ethereal, more haunted than *L'Ascension*, and this cycle is one of Messiaen's best-known works, although not as fine as some of his later organ music. Messiaen's third organ cycle, *Les corps glorieux* (*The Glorious Hosts*, 1939), subtitled 'Seven Short Visions of the Life of the Resurrected', is very wide-ranging in mood, from the delicate wraiths of 'L'Ange aux parfums' ('The Angel of the Perfumes') to the titanic 'Combat de la mort et la vie' ('The Combat between Life and Death'), a section sometimes heard on its own, divided into two moods, the first the gigantic struggle, the second densely meditative.

The war intervened, and Messiaen's

next organ work did not appear until 1950. The *Messe de la Pentecôte* (1949–50), divided into five sections, started a phase in Messiaen's output where the technical developments were joined with more exotic and programmatic elements. In it Messiaen uses unusually proportioned rhythms (3:2, 5:4) and Hindu modes and colours. The moods are restrained, exploratory, and throughout emulate external, natural sounds: bird-calls, drops of water, the fierce wind and the songs of the lark in the closing 'sortie'. In the *Livre d'orgue* (*Organ Book*, 1951), perhaps Messiaen's most difficult organ work, he concentrated on the technical aspects of his music rather than the spiritual goal which informs the other organ works. The largely abstract sections are the closest Messiaen came to serialism, and only the fourth piece, 'Chant d'oiseaux' ('Bird-calls') is deliberately evocative.

Apart from the *Verset pour la fête de la dédicace* (1960), Messiaen wrote no more organ music until the huge *Méditations sur le mystère de la Sainte-Trinité* (1969). The thematic basis of this cycle is created by assigning a sound, a pitch, and a duration to each letter of the alphabet, and then building themes from the texts chosen, omitting minor words but using other themes to indicate grammatical contexts. There is a different sense of the overall progression of time to this work, as if working in a different spiritual dimension (most obviously realised in the long-held sonorities and chords), and a refinement of his language. The contrasts of the colour associations, rhythms and dynamics of the different bird-calls in the fourth section represent a summation of this strand in Messiaen's work.

Liturgy and bird-song were also to coalesce in Messiaen's last and perhaps finest organ work, the *Livre du Saint-Sacrément* (1984). This huge set of eighteen pieces for organ is divided into three groups – acts of adoration, the Mysteries from Christ's Life, and the Blessed Sacraments – and is a major simplification of Messiaen's language, tonally direct, mostly in slow tempi, stunning in its spare unfolding of the spiritual landscape, from the delicacy of the peace of the desert, through the extraordinary series of great stepping-stone chords to Christ's Resurrection, to the gigantic depiction of the walls of water in the crossing of the Red Sea.

Messiaen's orchestral works show the same development and stylistic traits as the organ music, and many include the piano as a solo instrument (his second wife was the celebrated pianist Yvonne Loriod). The first orchestral work to achieve international recognition (and controversy) was the massive *Turangalîla-Symphonie* for piano, ondes martenot and orchestra (1946–48). The title is a compound Sanskrit word referring to motion and action, in terms of all the actions of the cosmos from creation to destruction. The symphony is divided into ten sections, united by four themes that recur; the orchestration gives prominence to the two instruments acting as soloists, the ethereal colours and long lines of the ondes martenot contrasting with the more brittle piano writing, revolving around clusters and bird-song. A large percussion section emphasises the varied rhythmic effects, influenced by Balinese gamelan music. It presents a sound world unlike any other large-scale orchestral work (though its antecedents come from **Varèse**), sometimes on a vast scale, more often with individual orchestral components, creating a chamber-like atmosphere, ranging in mood from the mystical to the violent. Its rhythms are invariably untraditional and dynamic, pointed by the instrumentation; the ondes martenot weaves a thread of the ethereal qualities of love, the brass expresses its physical excitement, and the piano weaves a web between both these extremes. It is music that seems to have lifted away from the earth to occupy some space in the heavens, and it is one of those works to which it is very difficult to remain neutral: it usually provokes either a transcendental experience or deep loathing in its audience.

Réveil des oiseaux (*Dawn Chorus*, 1953) for piano and orchestra, and *Oiseaux exotiques* (1955–56) for piano, eleven wind and six percussionists, turned to detailed exploration of the musical possibilities of bird-song. *Réveil des oiseaux* opens with lean textures, the different bird-calls given to the different instruments in almost pointillistic fashion, the colours sharply contrasted. It then builds into a climatic overlay of calls, a babble of birdsong where the musical continuity is created by complex rhythms with an underlying progression: this matches the progression of events in the dawn chorus, and is highly evocative. The dawn having arrived, solo birds take over again, initially in a long piano cadenza, and then with less harsh colours from the orchestra. *Oiseaux exotiques* includes the calls of forty different birds metamorphosed into Messiaen's idiom, overlapping and cross-calling in brilliant dense textures of sparkling plumage, the complex kaleidoscope of rhythms creating a jungle of patterns.

The title of *Chronochromie* (1960) for large orchestra is drawn from the Greek words for time and colour. Messiaen used an ordered scale of thirty-two 'durations' from a demisemiquaver to a semibreve (whole note) to systematise the rhythmic elements; bird-song is again included, as well as the sound of Alpine rivers. With *Couleurs de la cité céleste* (1963) for piano, thirteen wind and six percussionists, Messiaen placed the spiritual meditation in an orchestral context, based on five quotations from Revelation. The musical elements, notably bird-song and Indian and Greek rhythms, are designed to evoke the colours of the title. *Et exspecto resurrectionem mortuorum* (*And I Await the Raising of the Dead*, 1964) for thirty-four wind and three percussionists, was designed for large open-air spaces or churches, its five sections headed by biblical quotations. It is slow-moving (to suit the acoustics of large spaces), but ritualistically dramatic; the gamelan influence, and that of temple gongs, is to the fore. The huge *Des canyons aux étoiles* (*From Canyons to the Stars*, 1971–75) for piano and forty-three instruments was inspired by the Grand Canyon, and is in three parts with a total of twelve sections. Its subjects are both the natural landscape and its religious associations, encompassing the vastness of the Canyon landscape and that of the night sky. Birdsong, using birds of the American West, is extensively used, and the wide range of colours is reinforced by the addition of desert sounds created by a wind machine and a sand machine. This enormous work has a transparency and fluidity that is characteristic of Messiaen's late works, and is the summation of his orchestral writing.

Messiaen wrote very little chamber music, but his major chamber work is one of the masterpieces of the 20th century. *Quatuor pour la fin du temps* (*Quartet for the End of Time*, 1940–41) for clarinet, violin, cello and piano was written for his fellow inmates in a German prisoner of war camp; it was first played complete to an audience of 5,000 prisoners. The inspiration for the eight sections is from the Apocalypse in the biblical Revelation, and the different sections use different instrumental combinations; the third, 'Abyss of the birds', one of the earlier extended appearances of bird-song in Messiaen's music, is for clarinet alone. Much of the work is slow-moving and meditative, the

traditional progress of musical time dissolved by long periods of held colours. It combines Messiaen's technically advanced language with echoes of a more conventional sound: the fourth section, 'Interlude', is a little dance connecting Messiaen to earlier French music, and the following 'praise to the eternity of Jesus' a beautifully limpid cello solo over piano chorus, whose simplicity and harmonic cast has been echoed in some of the chamber works of **Pärt**.

Of his piano music, after the *Préludes*, the major works are *Visions de l'Amen* for two pianos, *Vingt regards sur l'Enfant Jésus, Quatre études de rythme*, and *Catalogue d'oiseaux*. *Visions de l'Amen* (1943) is in seven sections, each contemplating an amen connected with a religious theme. *Vingt regards sur l'Enfant-Jésus* (*Twenty Looks at the Infant Jesus*, 1944) is an enormous cycle of works, each descriptive of a contemplation of the holy child through the concrete, such as the Virgin, the theological, such as the angels, the symbolic, such as the cross, or the abstract, such as the Spirit of Joy. Although one of Messiaen's lesser-known works, it is one of the finest, with its clearly focused but visionary philosophical base and magical piano effects, often expressing qualities of light, and best summed up by Messiaen himself: 'I have looked here for a language of mystical love, to be varied, powerful and tender, sometimes brutal, responding to multi-coloured commands.' *Quatre études de rythme* (*Four Studies of Rhythm*, 1949) includes the *Modes de valeurs et d'intensités*, a seminal work in the history of 20th-century music. Each aspect of the music is governed by a 'mode': one containing thirty-six pitches, one twenty-four durations, one twelve types of attack, and one with seven types of intensity (volume); the independent use of these modes, integrated into a larger structure, paved the way in particular for 'total serialism' by showing the possibilities of simultaneous structurings of parameters. It deeply influenced **Stockhausen** and **Xenakis**. *Catalogue d'oiseaux* (*Bird Catalogue*, 1956–58) is a large musical catalogue in a cycle of thirteen pieces in seven books of the songs of French birds, the musical background including an evocation of the appropriate habitat and the sounds of other birds of the area. Messiaen included detailed written introductions to the sounds, the context, and the musical constructions. This marvellous collection is best dipped into, as one would a visual catalogue.

Messiaen wrote three major song-cycles, all to his own texts, utilising his idiomatic techniques, but without bird-song. The two books of *Poèmes pour Mi* (1936, orchestrated 1937) for soprano and piano or orchestra combined earthly love, in the sacrament of marriage ('Mi' refer-ring to his first wife, the composer Claire Delbois), with its heavenly counterpart. *Chants de terre et de ciel* (1938) for soprano and orchestra turn to fatherhood (both earthly and heavenly) and to resurrection. More unusual than either is *Harawi* (1945) for soprano and piano, part of Messiaen's 'Tristan triptych'. Its title is a Peruvian Quecha word describing a lovers' song that ends in death, and the cycle of twelve songs is subtitled 'songs of love and death'. Love becomes related to the cosmos in the symbolic association of love and death and the ecstatic ascent to heaven, and it ends with the image of a sleeping town unaware of the personal-cosmos drama that it has witnessed. The piano writing, largely inde-pendent of the vocal line, is especially vivid; the intense, almost surrealistic cycle abounds in rhythmic and onomatopoeic effects.

Messiaen's major work for chorus is *La Transfiguration de Notre Seigneur Jésus-Christ* (1965–69) for piano, flute, clarinet, cello, vibraphone, marimba, xylorimba, large choir and large orchestra. It is divided into two parts, each of seven movements, with texts drawn from the Bible, St Thomas Aquinas, and from Cath-olic rites. The first part of this vast work, over an hour-and-a-half long, is concerned with the Transfiguration. In many respects it is an equivalent of the *Turangalîla-symphonie* in verbal and reli-gious form, with similar use of ritualistic percussion and sudden vast vistas. The choral lines have the gravity of Gregorian chant or expand into dense textures, and to this are added chorales of the kind of luminosity and simplicity found in the *Livre du Saint-Sacrément*.

Messiaen's only opera was one of his last works, and characteristically it pays little heed to traditional theatrical or operatic parameters. *Saint François d'Assise* (1975–83) is a huge meditation on the life of St Francis of Assisi, in three acts and eight scenes lasting some three hours, not including intermissions. To approach it with any kind of conventional theatrical expectation is doomed to failure; with only seven characters (St Francis, his fellow monks, and an Angel), each of whom is assigned a theme and a bird-song, and a chorus which is used to symbolise the voice of Christ, it is virtually devoid of action

other than the curing of the leper, the appearance of that angel, and St Francis's death. The simplification of Messiaen's later style is evident, as is the fluidity of his idiom, often with haunting or startling musical effects (such as the other-worldly sounds accompanying the knocking of the Angel at the door and at the receiving of the Stigmata) and an extraordinary lumi-nosity and spirituality that suspends the sense of time. Messiaen's lifelong love affair with bird-song is encapsulated in the sermon to the birds that forms the sixth scene. It is a remarkable, transcendentally beautiful work which has to be approached on its own terms.

The importance of Messiaen as a teacher, and the very high calibre of his students, has already been indicated. He taught at the École Normale de Musique and at the Schola Cantorum in Paris, and widely outside Europe in the late 1940s. He was appointed professor of harmony at the Paris Conservatoire on his release from a prisoner of war camp in 1941, and a class for analysis was specially created for him there.

RECOMMENDED WORKS
All of Messiaen's works are recommended. Those new to his music could start at the beginning and the end of his output, with the *Préludes pour piano* (1928–29) and the earlier organ works, and the *Livre du Sainte-Sacrément* (1984). The *Quatuor pour le fin de temps* is an excellent introduction to Messiaen's mature sound world.

BIBLIOGRAPHY
O. Messiaen, *Technique of my Musical Language*, 1944, English translation 1957
P. Griffiths, *Olivier Messiaen and the Music of Time*, 1985
R. S. Johnson, *Messiaen*, 1975
R. Nichols, *Messiaen*, 1975

Milhaud Darius**
born 4th September 1892 at Aix-en-Provence
died 22nd June 1974 at Geneva

The works of Darius Milhaud still remain one of the unassessed quantities of 20th-century music. As one of its most prolific composers (around 450 works), he wrote music whose quality is so uneven that the reputation for the banal and the shallow has masked what is both inspired and fascinating. He was one of the members of Les Six, the group active between 1917 and the early 1920s, that was dominated by the aesthetic of Jean Cocteau.

Milhaud's reputation was secured by his early music, where he showed both a typically French sense of wit and elegance, and a predilection for the ultra-modern. His incidental music to *Les choëphores* (*The Libation Bearers*, 1915) includes chorus whistling and hissing, and shows an early fascination with percussion and bitonality. A period in Brazil (1917–18) with Paul Claudel, diplomat, poet, and the composer's close collaborator, led to the addition of South American colour and influences to his innovative effects. The evocative opening of the ballet *L'homme et son désir* (*Man and his Desire*, 1917) for wordless voices and including a large percussion section, was inspired by the Brazilian forest. *Saudades do Brasil* (1920, originally for piano, and then extended and orchestrated) is a set of dances picturing Rio de Janeiro and inspired by folk music. The ballet *Le boeuf sur le toit* (1919) again uses Spanish-American dance rhythms, combined with experimental dissonant effects, and is one of Milhaud's most often heard works. Most of these pieces caused furores when they were first performed.

With the addition of jazz (which Milhaud had heard in Harlem in 1922) in the ballet *La création du monde* (1923, see below) and the bitonality of *Le carnaval d'Aix* (1926) for piano and orchestra (based on ballet music *Salade*, 1924), the major features of Milhaud's style had appeared, and if added to, were to remain largely unchanged through the course of his life. Aside from his extraordinary facility, chief among these was bitonality: the use of two keys simultaneously. Although his teacher **Koechlin** had already developed its use before Milhaud, it was the latter who conspicuously developed and extended it to polytonality, in the simultaneous sounding of melodies, with considerable influence on his generation. His rhythms, emphasised by extensive use of percussion (of which he was an early large-scale exponent, including such works as the *Percussion Concerto*, 1929), owe much to jazz and Spanish-American music, both novel influences in the 1920s. The *Six Little Symphonies* (1917–23) for different chamber ensembles, added neo-classicism and a mastery of counterpoint to his palette.

This period also saw Milhaud explore brevity, not only in the *Six Little Symphonies*, but in such works as the three *opéras*

minutes (*L'abandon d'Ariane*; *L'enlèvement d'Europa*; and *La délivrance de Thésée*, 1927), each lasting under ten minutes. The *Suite provençale* (1936), based on themes from his own region, confirmed another aspect of Milhaud's character, the lyrically pastoral, which had appeared in the middle movements of such works as the *Little Symphony No. 2* or, flanked by the influence of jazz, in the neo-classical *Viola Concerto* (1929) written for **Hindemith**. Similar moods recur throughout Milhaud's works, from the melodic *Clarinet Concerto* (1941) to the *Sonatine pastorale* (1960), the opening of the *Symphony No. 6* (1955) or the *Violin Sonata No. 2*. The presence of the Mediterranean sun has been repeatedly noted by both critics and admirers, and is evident in such works as the baroque-inspired *Sonata for Violin and Harpischord* (1945), the twelve-minute *Piano Concerto No. 2* (1941), with its brilliant colours, bouncy good humour and languid slow movement, or the *Suite française* (1944). This sunny quality became more evident after Milhaud's move to the USA (1940), with the development of a more abstract language in which the various disparate elements become more integrated, and, generally, less inventive and interesting.

His chamber music includes eighteen string quartets (Milhaud was determined to write one more than Beethoven), many of which are on a small scale, and which show Milhaud's strengths (his great command as a technician) and his weaknesses (a lack of distinctiveness). They range from neo-classicism (including the tuneful *No. 6*, 1922), through the lyricism of the opening of *No. 9* (1935), the overt polytonality of *No. 10* (1940, subtitled *Birthday Quartet*), the Mexican evocation of the finale of No. 13 (1946), to *Nos. 14* and *15* (1949) which can be played together to form a rather brutish octet. The rest of Milhaud's extensive chamber output covers the range of his styles, including elements of controlled chance in the late *Septet for Strings* (1964).

Among the considerable number of choral works are liturgical works that reflect Milhaud's Jewish faith and generally show a more diatonic harmonic language. Chief among these is the *Sacred Service*; music inspired by his faith also includes such stylistic mishmashes as the large-scale orchestral *Opus Americanum No. 2* '*Moses*', and the opera *David* (1953). The intense *Christophe Colomb* (*Christopher Columbus*, 1929), considered by some to be

Milhaud's masterpiece, is the most important of his six large-scale operas, and is now receiving wider attention. Cast in twenty-seven tableaux, it uses film projection and rhythmically spoken narration set against percussion to mix reality, symbolism and dreams. The libretto is by Paul Claudel, who collaborated on nearly thirty works with Milhaud between 1912 and 1970. The story of Columbus discovering America serves as a backdrop to the psychological exploration of the character of Columbus (especially as an old man) and those around him, and the moral, social and political ramifications of his actions and discoveries, including the destructive effects on native Americans. With its short sections, and extensive use of chorus, its dry orchestration and lively rhythmical power, this highly effective work has also been performed as an oratorio. In Milhaud's lifetime, the most successful of his operas was the half-hour *Le pauvre matelot* (*The Poor Sailor*, 1927) to a Cocteau text, that mixes music hall with sea shanties (including *Blow the Man Down* as the wife kills her sailor husband).

This very wide disparity of quality and styles creates problems for those wishing to explore Milhaud's music. The vacuousness of which Milhaud was all too easily capable is exemplified in the appalling *Kentuckiana* for orchestra, where he tries to add spice to folk tunes by playing them simultaneously, or in the even worse *Globetrotter Suite*. His best works probably come from the 1920s, when his invention was fresh, and the small scale of both instrumental forces and musical forms most suited his imagination. Among the most successful works is the delightful suite for two pianos, *Scaramouche* (1937, reworked like a number of Milhaud scores from earlier material). Its brilliant first movement has an infectious precociousness and gentle polytonal colours, matched by the Latin American influences of the boisterous 'Brazileira' finale. The middle movement exemplifies Milhaud's lyricism and capacity for classical feel. *Les quatres saisons* (*The Four Seasons*), cast like those of Vivaldi as a series of four concertos, are sometimes revived, especially the first (*Printemps* [*Spring*]). The *Suite for violin, clarinet and piano* (1936, again drawn from earlier incidental music) exemplifies Milhaud's sense of fantasy and his various influences, from Brazilian dance rhythms to jazz. Among his later works the *Second Concerto for two pianos* (1961), with its sparse orchestration and a slow movement that combines a classical delicacy with a stubborn harmonic restlessness, is an interesting example of his later style, where the Gallic wit is sometimes made more acid by the harmonies and the polytonality.

However, Milhaud's masterpiece is the music for the ballet *La création du monde* (*The Creation of the World*, 1923), the first major score to use jazz (and still one of the most successful), which entirely succeeds in the composer's stated intention to combine a jazz style with a purely classical feel. It has the brilliance and spontaneity of jazz, but creates a larger impression through the clarity of instrumentation, the simultaneous use of major and minor keys, and the counterpoint. There is a version for large orchestra; that for the original ensemble is much more effective.

As important as Milhaud's compositions was his influence as a teacher, at Mills College, Oakland, California (from 1940) and then from 1947 to 1971 at the Paris Conservatoire. Among his pupils were **Bolcom, Reich,** and the jazz composer and player Dave Brubeck. Milhaud himself was an accomplished violist who took part in the first performance of Debussy's *Sonata for flute, viola and harp*. He was made a Chevalier de la Légion d'Honneur in 1933.

RECOMMENDED WORKS
 ballet *Le boeuf sur le toit* (1919)
 opera *Christophe Colomb* (1929)
 ballet *Le création du monde* (1923)
 Scaramouche (1937) for two pianos
 Saudades do Brasil (1920–21) for
  orchestra
 Suite for violin, clarinet and piano
  (1936)

BIBLIOGRAPHY
 D. Milhaud, *Notes without Music*, 1952
 P. Collaer, *Darius Milhaud*, trans. J.
  H. Galante, 1988

Poulenc Francis**
born 7th January 1899 at Paris
died 30th January 1963 at Paris

The French composer who above all others took the tradition of French charm, wit, delicacy and colourful fun, and imbued it with genius and restrained passion that lifts it above the merely entertaining, is Francis Poulenc. Poulenc's style is elusive, using the commonplace, the gauche, and the ingenuous as the basis for a deeper reflection on the human spirit. In addition,

Poulenc subscribed to no systems or theoretical models; he took whatever was suitable to the task in hand, integrating many stylistic borrowings into his distinctive and self-deprecating voice that often seems to be standing apart from its subject and commenting on it. A more serious and personal side to Poulenc's musical character surfaced in the concertos and some of the song-cycles, and culminated in the religious works, in which a meditative, simple voice emerges from behind the mask, looking at the world with a kind of celebratory innocence. These works often include a very recognisable orchestral combination of strings, brass punctuation, and timpani with a favourite figure of a rising major third.

Poulenc first came to prominence with his songs, and the song remained a major factor in his output, fostered by his deep love of poetry. His vocal music constitutes perhaps the finest body of French songs since **Fauré**. He is particularly associated with the poetry of Apollinaire and Max Jacob. His first setting of Apollinaire was a cycle of six songs describing animals with different human characteristics, *Le bestiare* (1917) for baritone and chamber orchestra, typically light in orchestration, and with a deft and physical sense of humour. But it was the *Rhapsodie négre* (1917) for baritone, piano and chamber ensemble in five movements (only one of which is sung) that brought Poulenc notoriety; the vocal setting was of a nonsense hoax poet, purportedly a Liberian. It has an undercurrent of primitivism and exoticism, especially in the rhythms and in the artless baritone song, with shades of **Satie** and **Stravinsky**.

The same year saw the establishment with Aurie, Durey, **Honegger, Milhaud** and Tailleferre of the group (more a collection of friends than like-minded composers), active between 1917 and the early 1920s, which became known as 'Les Six'. The aesthetic domination of Jean Cocteau on Les Six is reflected in Poulenc's setting of Cocteau texts, *Cocardes* (1919), evoking the Paris of street musicians and recalling **Satie**. Much more personal are the *Chansons gaillardes* (*Bawdy songs*, 1925–26), to 17th-century texts, full of a piquant combination of the delicate and the coarse. The intentional artlessness that Poulenc could sometimes employ surfaces in the 1930s settings of Apollinaire and Max Jacob. The *Trois poèmes de Louise Lalanne* (1931) are settings of three Apollinaire poems ostensibly by the fictitious Louise Lalanne, the first sung very fast with no change of tempo, and the second based on the rhythms of children's patter. Artlessness of a different kind is incorporated into the *Quatre poèmes d'Apollinaire* (1931): the first is a rollicking drinking song celebrating the seedier side of one of Poulenc's favourite subjects, Paris; the third makes fun of fashionable word snobbery. The *Cinq poèmes de Max Jacob* (1931), drawn from the poetry collection *Chants bretons*, reflect the artless simplicity of the peasant girl who sings them, with a certain amused but kindly comment in the piano accompaniment; in the second song she has lost her lover, in the third she superstitiously prays to ward off devils, the fourth is a cradle song, and the last is a nonsense song.

Max Jacob was also the inspiration behind the secular cantata *Le bal masqué* (1932) for baritone or mezzo-soprano, oboe, clarinet, bassoon, violin, cello, percussion and a prominent piano. The three poems, divided by two instrumental interludes, evoke carnival time in the Paris suburbs; they contain a kind of sophisticated naïvety, with incongruous images and word play with surrealist overtones. The musical setting is Poulenc in what might be described as his 'Mickey Mouse' mood, since the idiom was picked up by the Hollywood short cartoon, and the humour is not dissimilar; 'wrong' notes, silly tunes and perky humour abound. The instrumental contribution is as important as the vocal, and the cycle is light, humorous and fun, sometimes with a jazzy feel, sometimes with exotic touches.

Around 1935 there was a discernible change in Poulenc's vocal output, though its seeds are to be found in many earlier works. In place of the overtly ironic or satirical there appears a subdued lyricism, an increasing sense of the spiritual. The immediate catalysts were the death of a close friend in 1935, Poulenc's discovery of the poetry of Paul Éluard, celebrating love and liberty, and his rediscovery of Monteverdi and the Renaissance polyphonists. The change is reflected in the *Sept chansons* (1936) for unaccompanied choir, setting five poems by Éluard and two by Apollinaire. Inspired by Monteverdi, their effective polyphonic writing has a mystical quality. In one of his finest song-cycles, *Tel jour, telle nuit* (1936–37), Poulenc found the combination of refined delicacy, restrained lyricism, transparent textures, and easy flow that exactly suited Éluard's poems of love. The *Trois poèmes de Louise Vilmorin* (1937) continues this idiom, but with a more forward liveliness.

The delicate writing of *Fiançailles pour rire* (1939), another setting of Vilmorin, covers a wide range of poetic subjects, including the lament of one who has died for love, a self-portrait of a statue, and flowers in winter.

During World War II Poulenc expressed his political awareness both by joining the French resistance and through a number of musical works, including the moving *Violin Sonata* (1943), dedicated to the memory of Lorca. The secular cantata *Figure humaine* (*The Human Face*, 1943) for double unaccompanied chorus sets eight poems by Éluard expressing the horrors of wars and passionately extolling liberty, certain that the human spirit will ultimately triumph: the poetry collection had been circulated among the underground, and dropped by the RAF. The chamber cantata *Un soir de neige* (1944) for unaccompanied choir sets four poems by Éluard describing nature in the grip of winter, symbolic of the occupation of the Nazis. The song-cycle *Calligrammes* (1948), based on seven poems by Apollinaire, recounts the poet's experience in World War I, and includes the famous poem *Rain*, written in vertical falling lines. There is a poignancy and surface simplicity to this affecting cycle, a more flexible rhythmic variety and change of mood, especially in the piano writing, and more plastic vocal lines, that makes it one of the most effective of Poulenc's song-cycles.

The strength of feeling combined with a simplicity and luminosity that emerged in *Figure humaine* came to fruition in the late religious works, combining joyous affection, a sense of personal supplication, and dramatic elements, especially in driving rhythms and the punctuation of brass. The *Stabat Mater* (1950) for soprano, chorus and orchestra is built on slowly evolving sonorities emphasised by the largely homophonic choral writing, the flow often driven by plucked string basses and its warm but limited range of colours dominated by the strings. The overall mood is of a restrained and joyful ecstasy. The wonderful *Gloria* (1959) for soprano, chorus and orchestra continues this general framework, but in a less restrained fashion.

Orchestral music forms only a small portion of Poulenc's output. His first major orchestral success (and one of his most familiar scores) was the high-spirited ballet *Les biches* (1924, later orchestral suite) which pits a gently lyrical innocence against the sexual atmosphere of the music of Parisan nightlife. The mood of the melodic line is infectious, and a Poulenc hallmark makes its appearance in falling and rising brass fanfare phrases answered by strings alone. The *Suite française* (1935) for small orchestra, originally written as incidental music, is an odd combination of the style of medieval dances with a modern gloss: each section is initially presented in quasi-authentic fashion and then in both Poulenc's ironic, semi-farcical style and his more lyrical, pastoral vein. The ballet *Les animaux modèles* (1942) was designed to lift the French spirit during the war, and is based on La Fontaine fables; it contains enjoyable music in a lighter vein. The *Sinfonietta* (1947) is a work of charm and grace, and lightweight, leaning more towards a *divertissement* than its four-movement symphonic form would suggest.

Poulenc wrote three important concertos. The *Concerto champêtre* (1927–28) for harpsichord and orchestra came from a period when he was much better known for his more daring and farcical idioms, and its considerable value has been rather overlooked. Pastoral moments creep into all three movements, the first being Poulenc in extrovert mood, but with the orchestral colours muted to match the scale of the harpsichord, the second a graceful slow dance, the third largely neoclassical. Perhaps the most extraordinary of the concertos is the *Concerto for Two Pianos and Orchestra* (1932), combining a riot of themes and ideas, a very French piquancy, a strong melodic element, and a classical sense of proportion and grace. The middle movement is an exceptionally delicate, beautiful and sometimes quirky pastiche of Mozart, while the outer ones display sparkling brilliance, drama, gentle lyricism and a humorous delight in the trite.

The *Concerto for Organ, Timpani and Strings* (1938) is one of Poulenc's masterpieces, and on the face of it an unlikely one. It seems composed of borrowings, the emphatic organ opening (the work opens and closes with the same G major chord) from Bach and much of the dancing sections from Mozart, although the rhythmic exuberance is entirely Poulenc's. Part of the secret is the scoring, which is anything but traditional and shows three facets of Poulenc's personality; the organ is bold and near-violent, the timpani rhythmically emphatic, almost brash, the strings more graceful and luminous. In addition, the atmosphere of the work evokes the combination of the spiritual and secular that marks Poulenc's later works. On the surface the work seems deceptively simple, its stylistic borrowings too obvious, but underneath, the proportions between the sections, between the moods of eruptive violence and graceful withdrawal, are near perfectly balanced. The styles have become blended into Poulenc's voice, and because the sense of uplifting joy and praise is so memorable and so triumphant, it entirely succeeds.

Poulenc also wrote three major operas that perhaps best demonstrate his abilities. *Les mamelles de Tirésias* (1944) is based on a surrealist play by Apollinaire whose semi-farcical subject brought out that side of Poulenc that delighted in the satirically absurd. The underlying theme is that the French must have more children: in Zanzibar, Thérèse and her husband change sex, Thérèse becoming Tirésias. In the second of two scenes their progeny are scattered around the stage; gendarmes, a journalist, the people of Zanzibar, with various minor characters providing the backdrop. Poulenc takes full advantage of this slim plot, drawing on dance forms, creating a tension between humour and lyricism that takes the comic opera beyond mere farce.

La voix humaine (1958) is a more daring and more satisfying work. Its basis is a play by Cocteau; there is only one character, a woman who has been jilted by her lover, who is about to marry another. The entire action takes place in her room, as a telephone conversation with that lover. As a capsule of the kaleidoscope of emotions that the woman traverses, from denial to acceptance, from pain to anger, from hope to resignation, the text is brilliant; throughout we understand the twin tugs of her love and her rejection. Poulenc wisely decided to create a largely declamatory style for this text, the music often subtly pointing up the emotions, and maintaining its own layer of psychological progress. The result is unusual for an opera (much of its effect is dependent on the skills of the singer) but almost perfectly captures one aspect of the human emotional experience.

Poulenc's only full-scale opera is also perhaps his finest work. *Les dialogues des carmélites* (1953–56), based on a play by Georges Bernanos, itself taken from a novel by Gertrud von Le Fort, is set against the backdrop of the French Revolution, but as context rather than stage action. Its central character, Blanche, becomes a Carmelite nun; her convent is disbanded, and eventually the nuns choose martyrdom at the guillotine. The opera concentrates on the psychology and spirituality of Blanche and the nuns; its underlying theme is fear (and the fear of death) and its relationship with spirituality and faith. Consequently it is a largely abstract opera, its focus on metaphysical questions and their relationship to the psyche rather than on the plot. Poulenc's score is restrained but luminous, the clarity of the vocal line paramount; the style is arioso, with no doubling of voices unless multiple voices would occur naturally. The opera has been criticised for its lack of dramatic variety, but this suits its subject matter, and follows a French tradition of meditative opera.

Poulenc's chamber music is often encountered, in part because it is so enjoyable to play, though he is more successful in writing for wind, where he has a happy nonchalance, than for strings. His nine sonatas for various instrumental ensembles range from the sinuous *Sonata for two clarinets* (1918, revised 1945) to the jovial wit of the *Sonata for horn, trombone and trumpet* (1922), and include Poulenc's chamber masterpiece, the very lyrical *Flute Sonata* (1956), with an unforgettable haunting opening. The *Sextet* (1932–39) for piano and wind contrasts the more lyrical piano with boisterous winds, dripping with a sorrowful charm in the slow movement, while the attractive *Trio* (1926) for oboe, bassoon and piano has a charming simplicity, its avowed models Haydn, Mozart and Saint-Saëns in the three movements. The best of his piano writing is to be found in the songs, but the *Mouvements perpétuels* (1918) brought Poulenc notoriety and has remained one of his most popular works, for its acid opening harmonies, rhythms that keep unravelling like a kitten playing with a ball of wool, and its lyrical humour.

RECOMMENDED WORKS

Le bal masqué (1932) for baritone or mezzo-soprano and chamber ensemble
ballet suite *Les biches* (1923)
song-cycle *Calligrammes* (1948)
opera *Les dialogues des carmélites* (1953–56)
song-cycle *Fiançailles pour rire* (1939)
Flute Sonata (1956)
Gloria (1959) for soprano, chorus and orchestra
opera *Les mamelles de Tirésias* (1944)
Mouvements Perpétuels (1918) for piano
Rhapsodie négre (1917) for baritone,

piano and chamber ensemble
Stabat Mater (1950) for soprano,
chorus and orchestra
Trio (1926) for oboe, bassoon and
piano
opera *La voix humaine* (1958)

BIBLIOGRAPHY
P. Bernac, *Francis Poulenc: the Man
and his Songs*, 1978
W. Mellers, *Francis Poulenc*, 1993

Ravel (Joseph) Maurice***

born 7th March 1875 at Ciboure
(Basses-Pyrénées)
died 28th December 1937 at Paris

Maurice Ravel, so clearly a composer of the 20th century, nonetheless occupies a personal no man's land between the Romanticism that his age was leaving behind, and the neo-classicism it was about to adopt. As a pupil of **Fauré** he was trained in a French school that was seen as an alternative to the Germanic post-Wagnerian tradition. With **Debussy**, he was one of the first composers whose rejection of a 19th-century aesthetic met with approval beyond a limited audience of composers, critics, or other musicians, to reach a wide public popularity that his music retains to this day. In parallel with Debussy, he also initiated a musical style that was a counterpart to the Impressionism that had taken the artistic world by storm at the end of the 19th and the beginning of the 20th centuries. Unfortunately that association with **Debussy**, originally perpetrated by critics antagonistic to the music of both composers and who could not understand the work of either, has persisted. For Ravel's is a very different musical temperament, attracted on the one hand to music that works on the emotions rather than the intellect, and on the other, through a paradoxical personal reluctance to express feelings, to forms that would contain such tendencies, mainly Classical in origin. It is the fusion of these two opposing pulls that gives Ravel's music its impact, and sets it aside from the main lines of development in modern music. He was of mixed Swiss and Basque parentage, and his music is a rare example of cultural stereotypes (the one mechanical, ordered, the other hot-blooded, expressive) having a metaphorical validity.

Now most celebrated as a supreme handler of the orchestra, Ravel was first known for his piano works. He preferred miniature forms and favoured dance structures drawn from many different traditions; longer works are usually the judicious arrangement of a series of these shorter forms rather than based on an overall harmonic or thematic development. One of the consequences is that individual items are often unfortunately taken out of context and performed on their own. Within these forms, Ravel drew inspiration from a wide variety of sources, notably Spanish popular music and Classical and pre-Classical styles; the twin shadows of Mozart and Liszt also stand behind much of his music. Such anachronistic influences are not used directly, but assimilated into a modern idiom and transformed into Ravel's unique personal language. Ravel anticipates the neo-classicists rather than being counted among them.

The oblique use of influences is further tempered by the melodic and harmonic language. Melody predominates, but often built on irregular metrical schemes, and accompanied by ostinati or single repeated notes. Ravel's harmonies are firmly rooted in the traditional diatonic system, based on the use of Phrygian and Dorian modes (the latter a major element of Basque music), and delighting in the use of 7ths, 9ths, and 11ths, and the movement in parallel motion that was a signature of the Impressionists but anathema to the Classicists. To further disguise the traditional foundation, cadences often remain unresolved, and the frequent dissonances are created by the calculated and momentary application of unsympathetic notes to the underlying harmony.

Such is the craftsmanship of Ravel. He saw the major purpose of his music as one of 'divertissement', and it rarely explores profound emotions and intentionally disguises any manifestation of Ravel's inner personality. Instead its characteristics are intellectual wit, clarity, the elegant evocation of idea or place, humour – often ironic – and occasional fantasy accompanied by tenderness. Yet from time to time a passion will elude the emotional control, the Basque heritage seeking expression.

That Ravel's music does not remain merely the art of the miniature is due to two principal factors. The first is his orchestration, indulging in large forces and exotic colours, exploring with great precision the extreme potential of instruments, sometimes with mawkish effects. It achieves individual clarity within complex densities, and creates momentum by changes of timbre. Most of the longer pieces were first written for piano, and most of the piano music and songs have orchestral equivalents. The second factor is the intrusion of sympathies that are less intellectual than sentimental: not only the exotic, or the evocation of the 18th century, but also affection for children and animals. It is these that have appealed to a general public, while it is the intellectual fastidiousness and craftsmanship that have continued to fascinate musicians.

The earliest works are dominated by Impressionism. Ravel came into prominence with a piano piece that is the first Impressionist work for the piano, preceding **Debussy's** earliest Impressionistic piano works. *Jeux d'eau (Fountains,* 1901) was inspired by the 'sound of water and the music of fountains, waterfalls and streams'. Those images are conjured up by extended arpeggios pitted against dreamy harmonies, by a cascade of sixteenth and thirty-second notes, and at the end a veritable waterfall of sixty-fourths, all laid out in a loose sonata form. Of all musical Impressionistic pieces, *Jeux d'eau* most echoes the interplay of light and water so beloved of the Impressionist painters, the keyboard transformed into a palette. It had been preceded by *Pavane pour une infante défunte* (1899), best known in its 1910 orchestration, an evocation of old Spain that has a Debussian sensuous flow imposed on an old dance form.

It was succeeded by the famous *String Quartet* (1902–03), in which Ravel, in his own individual fashion, combined the colours and tone of Debussy's quartet with the more formal structures derived from his teacher **Fauré.** There is a hazy tenderness, a nostalgia inherent in much of this string quartet, combined with shimmering changes of colour and vista, countered by a more incisive precision in faster passages, often played pizzicato to emphasise the contrast. The ravishingly beautiful song-cycle *Shéhérazade* (1903) for mezzo-soprano and orchestra to verses by Tristan Klingsor adds an exoticism to the Debussian sensuousness. The heady vocal line has considerable independence from the orchestra, floating over the luxuriant and warm orchestral textures.

The cycle of five piano pieces, *Miroirs* (1904–05) continues the Impressionistic pianism, the mirrors of the title conjuring up lazily moving waters, or the ripples, swells, and breaking waves of 'Une barque sur océan'. However, into this favourite imagery of the Impressionists is injected a new pictorial imagery in the fourth piece. Still glittering but much more direct, the brilliant *Alborado del gracioso* (The jester's morning'), best known in an orchestral version (1919), launches into a bright, sharp, extrovert Spain, complete with castanets and pinpoints of sharply etched colours from all over the orchestra, with sudden emotive surges of climax. With this piece, the shifting, hazy mystery inherent in the Impressionistic style is brought into sharp focus, still using the same techniques, but to a different, incisive end. The mysterious, atmospheric opening of the celebrated *Introduction and Allegro* (1905) for harp, flute, clarinet and string quartet, with its pastoral shepherd flute moving into the rippling waves of the harp, immediately announces an Impressionistic piece, but this gentle and beautiful work, a kind of Arcadian dialogue between the instruments, has a purposeful Impressionism created in part by the Classical organisation of the work. The little *Sonatine* (1903–05) for piano moves towards a different direction, for it harks back to the world of Mozart and Couperin, light in the opening movement, serene and reflective in the central minuet, bright-coloured, pianistic and joyful in the finale.

The evocation of Spanish colour, and the movement away from Impressionism, was taken a stage further in Ravel's first piece originally written (except for one section) for orchestra. The *Rapsodie espagnole* (1907–08) for orchestra is in four sections, opening with the murmurings of dusk, with motoric elements and marvellous counter-movements in the 'Malagueña', and with the use of instrumental lines with vocal overtones in the final 'Feria'. At the same time, Ravel embraced the Spanish idiom more specifically in the short one-act opera *L'heure espagnole* (*The Spanish Hour,* 1907–09) which tells, in farcical style, the adventures of a would-be adulterous clockmaker's wife. *Ma mère l'oye* (*Mother Goose,* 1908, orchestrated 1911, expanded into full ballet 1912) was originally a suite of pieces for piano duet written for children (rather than to be played by children), but is much better known in its orchestral, ballet form. The child-like aspect emerges in the fantasy of the pieces, drawing together various well-known fairy-tales, dressed in gorgeous orchestral colours.

The pianistic culmination of this period is the triptych *Gaspard de la nuit* (1908), inspired by the fantasy prose poems of the 19th-century poet Aloysius Bertrand. The spirit behind this work is the virtuosity and fantastical imagination of Liszt; the first of the nocturnal visions is that of the water-nymph Ondine, who unhappily falls in love with a mortal; the second of a gibbet with a hanging skeleton; the third of a goblin, darting and shifting in Ravel's portrait. The writing has an uncanny ability to get behind these visions, almost as if they were archetypes of Ravel's own psyche. The pieces have a spontaneous, improvisatory feel (in fact they are meticulously calculated) that adds a haunting and harrowing immediacy. *Gaspard de la nuit* makes great expressive and technical demands on the pianist, and has become one of the touchstones of the great pianist's art.

The orchestral culmination of this period is very different. Ravel called the ballet *Daphnis et Chloé* (1909–12) a 'choreographic symphony'; it is based on the Greek legend, and was the longest work he wrote. The Greece he conjured up was that seen through the arcadian eyes of the late 18th-century French artists. The result is electrifying music steeped in pagan sensuousness. For the magic of the orchestration and for sheer evocation, nothing has yet rivalled the music of 'Lever du jour' ('Daybreak'), with its rippling flutes over the tinkling of the harp, its hush of a new dawn, the eddies of water, the calls of birds, the great swell of the rising sun into the dawn. Ravel made two suites (1911, 1913) from the ballet. The first suite uses the first third of the ballet score, and the second suite, which has become the form in which the music is most often heard, the last third.

The works immediately following *Daphnis et Chloé* are smaller in scale, and concentrate on clearer textures and a more idiomatic melodic line. The shades of Schubert's Vienna stand at the shoulder of the suite of waltzes, *Valses nobles et sentimentales* (1911, orchestrated 1912); the suite is often heard in both the original piano and later orchestral settings. The *Piano Trio* (1914), with its suggestion of Spanish themes, hauntingly explores the contrasts of sonorities between the piano and the strings. The tendency to distil images of bygone eras reached its fulfilment in *Le tombeau de Couperin* (1914–17), a set of six piano pieces, four of which were orchestrated and reordered in 1919, each with a dedication to a friend who had died in the war. In spite of the title, Ravel does not summon up the style of Couperin, but rather that of French 18th-century court dance music, creating what is to all intents and purposes a neo-classical work, with restrained, clean orchestration. It displays all Ravel's powers of charm and grace and

meticulous craftsmanship. The short ballet *La Valse* (1919–20), now a regular orchestral piece in the concert hall, veers in a completely different direction, taking the world of Richard Strauss's Viennese waltz head on, outscoring the German as it does so. The scale is huge – this is a waltz in a gigantic, glittering palace ballroom – but there is a disturbed ghostly undercurrent to the whole thing, (partly created by the swooping middle ground voices of the orchestra), as if Ravel was looking back on pre-war Imperial Vienna through the horror of the trenches. The *Sonata for Violin and Cello* (1920–22), dedicated to the memory of **Debussy**, is a strange and under-appreciated work, one of the most intellectual Ravel wrote. The dialogue between the unusual instrumental combination is spartan and discursive, and may appeal to those who find Ravel's major works too sumptuous. In the *Violin Sonata* (1923–27) – actually his second in the genre – the rather uneasy juxtaposition of the sparse lines and textures of the first movement and the bitter blues of the middle movement have perhaps inhibited wide popularity.

The highpoint of this period is the one-act opera *L'enfant et les sortilèges* (*The Child and the Spells*, 1920–25). The brilliant, perfectly proportioned libretto by Colette tells of a boy who ignores his mother's warnings, maltreats a pet squirrel, is then tormented by the coming to life of all his toys (and the furnishings of his room), is transported into the nocturnal garden, and is then redeemed by all the animals of the garden. It is one of those rare works which appeal to both children and adults, and its episodic nature allows Ravel a wide range of styles, from the jazz spoof of the teapot and teacup to the glittering lyricism of the Princess. The range of orchestration is considerable and highly refined, and the moment when the room dissolves and the garden appears, complete with owls hooting and frogs croaking, is as magically evocative as anything in *Daphnis et Chloé*. Stylistically, the opera is a kind of summary of the different facets of Ravel's compositional idioms.

Ravel's tendency to find inspiration in other musics is exemplified in the short but virtuoso *Tzigane* (1924), which exists in versions for violin and piano and violin and orchestra, though the latter is much more effective. In it he invokes the spirit of Hungary, and especially of the Hungarian gypsy fiddlers. It opens with a long quasi-improvisatory extended solo, countered by an orchestral introduction that is a web of sounds dominated by a prominent harp. Thereafter Ravel darts around his various visions of the Hungarian spirit, including a spoof of the refined Hungarian orchestral dances that is surely a tribute to Liszt. There is humour in this work, as well as mystery in the high orchestral and solo moments that employ harmonics.

Ravel's best-known work started as a request for a short ballet. *Boléro* (1928) for orchestra marries the Spanish influence, and a Spanish 3/4 dance rhythm, with the rigidity of modernity. It is a continuous ostinato, a reiterated linear repetition, a progression of awesome power and control. The propulsive force is a sidedrum remorselessly beating out the rhythm, echoed by brass. Transformation is achieved by subtle orchestral colours that are piled up, iron-fisted, element by element. Yet the main theme is sensuous, Moorish, sinuous, and when nothing else could possibly seem to happen in this remorseless progression, the whole orchestra shifts from C major to E major, and on towards a blaze of triumph in C major.

Irony conflicts with lyricism and virtuosity in the two piano concertos. Ravel worked on them simultaneously, and there could scarcely be more of a contrast between the two. The better-known *Piano Concerto in G* (1929–31) is the more traditional, cast in three movements, and is of almost chamber proportions. The example of Mozart is most prominent in the delicate and beautiful neo-classical slow movement, where the piano is gradually joined by other instruments until an almost bluesy tone is reached. The first movement opens with a clapper, which, it has been pointed out, sounds like the composer's ring-master whip as he is about to put the pianist through his or her paces. The last movement has strong jazz influences in the orchestration (notably the trombone slides and the scrawling clarinet) and in the rhythms.

The dramatic *Piano Concerto for the Left Hand* (1929–30) is perhaps the finer work, for it explores greater depths, and in it Ravel set himself a far harder task. It was written for the one-armed pianist Paul Wittgenstein and is the best of the many works written for him. Ravel returns to the sensuous ecstasy of *Daphnis et Chloé*, though tempered by a more direct and cogent drive. Something of the horror of the First World War (in which Wittgenstein lost his arm) lies behind this work. Cast in one movement, it is propelled inevitably from its extraordinary opening, the bassoon rising out of hushed lower strings, to its bitter-sweet end. Within the overall progression are a series of almost episodic emotional surges, driven by the orchestra and pianist alternately, including a sardonic march as menacing as anything by **Prokofiev**. Not the least remarkable aspect of this concerto is the piano writing: never once does it sound as if it is the left hand alone playing.

Ravel was also important as a writer of songs notable for the freedom of their vocal lines. Among his works in this genre the *Trois poèmes de Stéphane Mallarmé* (1913) for soprano and nine instruments are unusual in that Ravel intentionally used the same instrumental forces as **Schoenberg's** *Pierrot Lunaire*, although at the time he had not heard it nor seen a score. There are two sets of songs based on existing material, the *Cinq mélodies populaires grecques* and the *Deux mélodies hébraïques* (1914), the former based on ancient and recent Greek folk songs, the latter on two Hebrew melodies. In both cases the independence of the piano writing takes them out of their folk origins into the area of *lieder*, and the Greek set, with its illustrative, often sharp-coloured piano writing and natural vocal lines, is especially effective. There is a combination of melancholy, sensuousness and (in the central song), bitterness in the three songs that make up *Chansons madécasses* (1925–26) for high voice, flute, cello and piano, to poetry by the 18th-century Creole poet Evariste Parny. There is little of Impressionism left here; instead the three instruments and the voice make a quartet. The writing is linear, the edges of the textures clear-cut, the repetitions adding a touch of primitivism, with a restrained eroticism in the interweaving of the four lines. Ravel's last work, the three songs of *Don Quichotte à Dulcinée* (1932–33) for baritone and piano or orchestra, combines the Spanish influence (with words by Paul Morand drawn from Cervantes) with a carefully poised and perfectly calculated sense of the character who is singing the songs. The first has piano writing that imitates the guitar, the second (the Knight's epic prayer) a modal feel recalling Spain's ancient noble past, the third a drinking song whose rollicking, semi-flamenco nature hides an undercurrent of sadness appropriate to the character.

Ravel's art was too precise for easy emulation, though among his few pupils was the unlikely figure of the older **Vaughan Williams**, and the influence of the post-Impressionist Ravel is evident in the latter's work. Ravel's failure to receive the Prix de Rome at his fourth attempt led to a scandal and extensive changes at the Conservatoire; because of that snub, he also later refused the Légion d'Honneur that was offered to him. He served in World War I as a driver, and was afflicted by a brain disease (Pick's disease) in the last years of his life.

Ravel has sometimes been criticised for being too shallow: those unsympathetic to his aesthetic have seen in his music not an original approach, but the aimless manifestation of cultural decadence. Certainly in some of his music he created a filter between his own inner feelings and the outward expression, but such a criticism is difficult to apply to works such as *Daphnis et Chloé* or the *Piano Concerto for the Left Hand*. There is certainly a paradox in Ravel's musical personality, between the sumptuous but refined sensuousness of some of the scores, and the equally refined but much drier technicality of others, notably the later chamber works. It is perhaps ironic that many unsympathetic to the former are unaware of the latter, but the sheer pleasure that Ravel provides in so many of the orchestral works is unlikely to be dimmed.

RECOMMENDED WORKS
  Alborada del gracioso (1918) for orchestra
  ballet *Boléro* (1928) for orchestra
  song-cycle *Chansons madécasses* (1925–26)
  ballet *Daphnis et Chloé* (1909–12)
  song-cycle *Don Quichotte à Dulcinée* (1932–33)
  opera *L'enfant et les sortilèges* (1920–25)
  Gaspard de la nuit (1908) for piano
  Introduction and Allegro (1905) for harp, flute, clarinet and string quartet
  opera *L'heure espagnole* (1907–09)
  Jeux d'eau (1901) for piano
  Miroirs (1904–05) for piano
  Pavane pour une infante défunte (1899) for piano or for orchestra
  Piano Concerto in G (1929–31)
  Piano Concerto for the Left Hand (1929–30)
  song-cycle *Shéhérazade* (1903)
  String Quartet (1902–03)
  Le tombeau de Couperin for piano or for orchestra
  Tzigane (1924) for violin and piano or violin and orchestra
  (ballet) *La valse* (1919–20) for orchestra

BIBLIOGRAPHY
  R. Manuel, *Maurice Ravel* (Eng. trans.), 1972
  R. Nichols, *Ravel*, 1977
  – *Ravel Remembered*, 1987
  A. Orenstein, *Ravel, Man and Music*, 1975

Roussel Albert**

born 5th April 1869 at Tourcoing
died 23rd August 1937 at Royan

Roussel pursued a career as a naval officer before devoting himself to music. He occupies an important, if tangential, place in French music. Although his earlier works were influenced by Debussy's Impressionism (the opening of the symphonic suite from the ballet *Le festin de l'araignée* [*The Spider's Feast*], 1913, is an obvious example), he developed a very individual style of neo-classicism that was quite at odds with the mainstream of French music of the 1920s and 1930s.

His classicism is expressed in an adherence to the logic of traditional structures and in fastidious craftsmanship, both legacies from his teacher **d'Indy**, which give his mature works a sense of rugged order. This is reinforced by his emphasis on counterpoint, and by the occasional use of a cyclical structure (a motto or idea that recurs throughout a work) – a French tradition, from Berlioz via Franck and d'Indy. The personal brand of modernism arises from his harmonies, which are rooted in tonality, but branch out into unexpected directions and dissonances. In addition, a modern element is injected by the influence of Eastern musics and their exotic colours, particularly Indian, which Roussel assimilated on his naval travels and on his honeymoon in 1908. This also influenced his melodies, often modal and often using the tritone. If these melodies are usually not very striking (and sometimes downright weak), this is entirely counterbalanced by the chief characteristic of his music: his driving sense of rhythm, a motivating element that is similar to that of **Prokofiev**, and which combines with the counterpoint to produce a strong sense of impulse, energy and grandeur. His orchestration has sometimes been described as thin, but although it is used sparingly and with great clarity, the effect is often rich and sensuous.

Central to his output are the four symphonies. The *Symphony No. 1*, subtitled *Le poème de la forêt* (*The Poem of the*

Forest, 1904–06) is essentially a descriptive work, in spite of its classical forms, but the *Symphony No. 2* (1919–21) firmly established his classical style. *The Symphony No. 3* (1929–30) and the *Symphony No. 4* (1934) are the most commonly encountered. The former shows all Roussel's personal style, from the vigorous rhythms of the opening, the classical logic, the use of a motif phrase, the acerbic harmonies countered by the sensuousness of the violin solo part, the lilting rhythms of the slow movement (with strong similarities to **Prokofiev**), to the energetic scherzo and echoes of Berlioz in the finale. In the fourth symphony, with its complex and impassioned slow movement, a mock-martial scherzo, and a very fine and concise finale, the element of the melancholic that is latent in Roussel's work is more obvious.

Of his other works, the *Suite in F* (1926) for orchestra heralded the move away from Impressionism, while the most overtly neo-classical work is the fine *Sinfonietta* (1934) for strings, austere in its discipline and rugged in its drive. The *Piano Concerto* (1927) successfully integrates the soloist with the orchestra, while the little *Concertino for Cello and Orchestra* (1936), his last orchestral work, is neo-classical in feel, rather melancholy in sentiment. Of the chamber music, the finest works are the *String Quartet* (1932) and the spare *String Trio* (1937), though the *Sérénade* (1925) for flute, violin, viola, cello and harp is delightful, quickly moving away from any suggestion of Impressionism at its opening to a laughing neo-classicism, with cello rhythmic lines reminiscent of **Stravinsky**.

An unsympathetic libretto (based on an Indian story) has probably prevented any revival of his 'opera-ballet', *Padmâvatî,* (1914–18), musically interesting for its rhythmic invention, the formality of its design and its use of Indian rāg and Near Eastern melody. The works which those unfamiliar with Roussel's music will find most immediately appealing are the ballet scores *Le festin de l'araignée* (1912), with its Impressionist feel, happy tunes, rhythmic felicity, and marvellously pointed small orchestra, and *Bacchus et Ariane* (1930). In the latter (turned into two orchestral suites) the voluptuousness is contained by the incisiveness of the writing and the flow of rhythmic dance, its suggestion of barbarity curbed by the control of musical thought and the deft precision of its often vivid orchestration. A third ballet, *Aenéas* (1935), sung as well as danced, is more sparse.

Although he taught at the Schola Cantorum (1902–14), Roussel has no obvious French followers, even if there are echoes of his aesthetic in the concertos and symphonies of **Dutilleux** and **Jolivet**. On one major composer, however, he did leave his mark. The later works of **Martinů** (Roussel's pupil from 1923–24) have the clear imprint of the neo-classical form enlivened by a generating sense of rhythm exemplified in Roussel's *Sinfonietta.*

It is not difficult to see why Roussel's music has been relatively unpopular. Apart from its divergence from the general progression of French music, the balance between expressive tendencies countered by intellectual rigour is a particularly personal one. His many admirers attest to the success of that balance.

RECOMMENDED WORKS
> ballet *Bacchus et Ariane* (1930)
> ballet *Le festin de l'araignée* (1913)
> *Sinfonietta for string orchestra* (1934)
> String Quartet (1932)
> Symphony No. 3 (1930)
> Symphony No. 4 (1934)

BIBLIOGRAPHY
> B. Deane, *Albert Roussel,* 1961

Satie Erik Alfred Leslie**
born 17th May 1866 at Honfleur
died 1st July 1925 at Paris

The place of Erik Satie's music has perhaps been exaggerated, in part because it enjoyed a vogue during the hippie period of the late 1960s and early 1970s when Satie's unusual life-style and rebellious brand of anti-establishment humour found a ready audience. His ideas, though, have been of importance to later composers, and he has been described, with some justification, as a minor composer of major significance.

Satie's personal reaction against Wagnerian late Romanticism, and against the studied symbolism often present in Impressionism, was to deride and undermine the mantle of seriousness with which classical music has so often cloaked itself. One part of that response came from Satie's own eccentric sense of humour that mocked pretentiousness – it was typical that he numbered his first published pieces (*Valse-Ballet* and *Fantaisie-Valse,* 1885, both for piano) opus 62. A second response was to seek inspiration and images, and, later in his career, sound sources, outside those then associated with serious music.

A third was to rebel against accepted forms and harmonic progressions, and to evolve his own plastic solutions to each piece. His major influences were unusual, those of Gregorian chant and medieval music and Gothic art, all of which he studied. To this was added from 1890 an interest in the mystical and the occult.

The problem for all composers abandoning traditional forms is inventing new ones, and these often emerge initially in small-scale works. Satie was no exception, and all his earlier works were short piano pieces; however, for Satie these small forms were temperamentally conducive, for he had the instincts of the miniaturist for making precise, cogent and self-contained statements in small-scale forms. *Ogives* (1886), a set of four piano pieces, was imbued with the Gothic, and was followed by the three *Sarabandes* (1887) for piano, but it was the *Gymnopédies* (1888), a set of three slow dances for piano, that have become Satie's best-known works, especially after **Debussy** orchestrated two of them. The title refers to ancient Greek ritual dances by naked boys, and the music has a limpid simplicity and beauty with haunting melodies which, together with the sense of progression or time hung in suspension, influenced musical Impressionism. The technique of imposing a long melody over chord progressions creates an extraordinary sense of relaxation which has endeared these pieces to later generations. The three *Gnossiennes* (1890) have a similar limpid feel, but with more abrupt harmonic shifts and right-hand melodies that wander in flights of delightful fancy. In these sets Satie was exploring new ideas; they are in groups of three because each piece of a set essentially explores the same melodic and harmonic idea from a different angle (hence the surface similarities of the three *Gymnopédies*). Harmonically, there is a strong modal cast (a reflection of Satie's medieval studies), which involves the use of unresolved 7ths and 9ths. In *Gnossiennes* Satie removed bar lines, emphasising the free, plastic flow. There is often little sense of closure – these pieces emerge and fade away rather than having strong openings and endings. There is a conscious simplicity, a paring away of unnecessary content, that is one of the hallmarks of the miniaturist.

Gnossiennes marked the end of this period in Satie's output, for from *Première pensée Rose + Croix* (1891) until the *Prélude de la porte héroïque du ciel* of 1894 Satie wrote a series of piano pieces that reflected his involvement with the mystical Christian Rosicrucian movement, all written for imaginary ritual ceremonies. This period ended with the *Messe des pauvres* (1895) for chorus with organ or piano, and was followed by two years of silence, broken by the *Pièces froides* (1897) for piano, where the sense of suspension of the pre-Rosicrucian works has become a musing wandering, regularly returning to the main melodic idea. Then, developing this idiom, his piano miniatures take on a new cast, still whimsical, but with the influence of popular French music-hall tunes, outrageous and sometimes misleading titles, such as *Trois morceaux en forme de poire (Three pieces in the shape of a pear*, 1890–1903) for two pianos – there are actually seven pieces – and with equally quirky instructions in the score, such as suggesting the sound should be 'like a nightingale with toothache.' Behind these eccentricities lay a serious intent. He continued to experiment with unusual harmonies in these piano pieces, his output reaching its zenith in 1913, after he had been championed by the famous pianist Ricardo Viñes. Within the miniature forms and the deliberate simplicity Satie was using humour to cock a snook at the received wisdom of the establishment; at the same time he was trying to forge an idiom that would find a wider popularity (hence the music-hall influence; Satie supported himself by playing popular piano). Satie called this 'musique de tous les jours' ('everyday music').

Meanwhile, recognising that his training and development had confined him to the miniature, Satie enrolled in the Schola Cantorum in 1905, studying with **d'Indy** and **Roussel** until 1908. Satie then felt he had the training for larger works with orchestra or instrumentation other than piano, and these are of more substance and of more lasting interest than his better-known piano works. He lost none of his quirkiness or his deliberately unconventional way of looking at the world: the first, the satirical stage work *Le piège de Méduse* (1913) for actors and eight instruments, has an absurdist text, including a stuffed monkey that dances between the scenes. Then in 1916 Satie produced for Diaghilev the ballet *Parade*, with a scenario by Jean Cocteau, choreography by Massine and costumes by Picasso. It created a sensation (Satie so insulted one of the critics that he was prosecuted for defamation of character, and received a suspended jail sentence), for in many ways it was a revolutionary work. In form it is a suite of small pieces (the favourite technique of the miniaturist seeking a larger form). It included such influences as ragtime, and used unusual sound sources: sirens, typewriters, revolvers, motors. The title refers to the excerpts that showmen at the fair display outside the performance tent in an attempt to attract an audience, and allowed Satie to parade such diverse characters as a Chinese Conjurer and the Little American Girl in brief appearances; ultimately the Manager fails to gain an audience, as the audience are quite satisfied by the snippets they have seen outside the tent. The vivid, down to earth, and completely unsentimental score has been compared to Cubism in its juxtaposition of blocks of ideas, themselves parodies of a multitude of sound sources from the two-step, through Oriental exoticism and the rhythms of the typewriter, to the fugue that opens and closes the ballet.

Parade was followed by Satie's masterpiece, the symphonic drama *Socrate* (1918) for four voices and orchestra. Based on Plato's *Dialogues*, it is divided into three parts: a portrait of Socrates by Alcibiades, the conversation between Socrates and Phaedrus on the pleasant banks of the Ilissus, and the death of Socrates related by Phaedo. Satie's idiom had always tended to the simple, but in *Socrate* it becomes deliberately spare, almost artless. The vocal lines follow the inflections of the reported speech, and are without any sense of bar line; the subdued pulse is mostly provided by the orchestra, drained of most colours except those around the middle register; the harmonies and melodic lines have the simplicity and the modality of plainchant. The critics at the first performance were baffled, thinking it another of Satie's jokes, but this sparse setting is gently mesmerising, creating an atmosphere that presents an individual and convincing interpretation of Socrates, conviction combining with a completely unaggressive sense of pleasure and acceptance. *Socrate* is the least immediate and the most serious of Satie's works, but the courage to provide such a simplistic setting for such potent words was justified; each of the three sections uses the same harmonic and melodic idiom from a different angle, as in his early piano works, and the whole piece has the precise focus of an expanded miniature.

In 1920 Satie extended his concept of 'everyday music' by creating 'furniture music' (Matisse's term) designed to accompany a gallery exhibition and to be completely unobtrusive; Satie was annoyed when the gallery visitors stopped to listen to the result, entitled *Musique d'ameublement* for three clarinets, trombone and piano, and written in collaboration with **Milhaud**. Following this experiment of context, he wrote two further large-scale works of importance. The ballet *Mercure* (1924), in thirteen very compressed sections, caused another scandal, as the surrealists in the audience supported the designer Picasso, but not the composer; the choreography was again by Massine. (At a later performance the wife of the Count who commissioned the ballet bought all of the seats to give her friends, but forgot to do so, and the theatre was virtually empty.) The plot is based on Mercury's meeting with the Graces, but the idiom is drawn from country-fair music, bright and sometimes brash, again with a deliberately artless element, but constructed with Satie's customary care for self-containment and detail. The ballet *Relâche* (referring to a theatre that is 'dark' or closed, 1924) was both a return to the absurd in Satie's aesthetic and experimentally daring, with elements of Dadaism and surrealism: it includes a striptease, dances with objects (such as wheelbarrows), and a film section with an unrelated musical accompaniment.

Satie's main accomplishment was to broaden the parameters within which serious music could take place, elevating parody and the absurd to a serious context. He was a pioneer of the aesthetic of the humorous, the quirky, and the rebelliously surreal in music, idioms unthinkable in the 19th century but now commonplace. His concepts of simplicity and an assumed naïvety or direct artlessness that would appeal to a wider audience greatly influenced Jean Cocteau, both in his own writings and also in the aesthetic he transmitted to such composers as **Milhaud, Honegger**, and, briefly, **Stravinsky**. The modal shades of his harmonies and the lack of traditional resolution also had a subtle influence on later composers, even, distantly, such composers as **Britten** (audible in a comparison between the harmonic cast and decorative piano line of the *Gnossiennes* and such songs as *Winter Words*, No. 6).

RECOMMENDED WORKS
In addition to the works listed below, all of Satie's later piano music is of interest.
ballet *Mercure* (1924)
ballet *Parade* (1917)
ballet *Relâche* (1924)

symphonic drama *Socrate* (1918) for
four voices and orchestra
Trois gnossiennes (1890) for piano
Trois gymnopédies (1888) for piano

BIBLIOGRAPHY
E. Satie, *The Writings of Erik Satie*
(ed. N. Wilkins), 1976
A. M. Gillmor, *Erik Satie*, 1988
R. Mayers, *Erik Satie*, 1948

Sauguet Henri

born 18th May 1901 at Bordeaux
died 22nd June 1989 at Paris

Much better known inside France than
outside, Sauguet's large output initially
came under the influence of **Satie**, and he
was a member of the group known as École
d'Arceuil (1923–25), the name of the district where Satie lived. That influence is
(intentionally) obvious in Sauguet's best-
known score, the ballet *Les Forains* (*The
Strolling Players*, 1945), a watered-down
imitation of Satie's *Parade*, the idiosyn-
crasy if not the vivacity smoothed out. It is
colourful, but more appropriate to the
ballet stage than the concert platform. His
earlier music is characterised by an effortless free-flowing lyricism and transparency of colour, richer in charm than strong
individuality. Wistfulness is apparent
even in more public works, such as the
extended suite *Tableaux de Paris* (1950)
for orchestra, describing sections of the
French city, from a dreamy mystical view
to touches of jazz. Sauguet's idiom then
gradually evolved to include more complex
harmonic ideas, and by the 1960s became
less tied to a tonal base.

Of his earlier works, the *Piano Concerto
No. 1* (1933–34) is Romantic in feel and
deserves hearing for its beautiful and
effective slow movement in which the
echoes of **Debussy** stimulate a more direct
and precise utterance. Of his later music,
12-note melodies (though not following
any system) are used in the attractive
cantata *L'oiseau a vu tout cela* (*The Bird
Saw All That*, 1960) for baritone and string
orchestra, with a haunting slow-moving
atmosphere sometimes countered by busy
instrumental textures. His typical wistful
charm is retained in such works as the
Mélodie concertante (1964) for cello and
orchestra and the *Garden Concerto* (1969)
for harmonica and orchestra (also version
for oboe and orchestra).

Of his chamber music, the *String Quartet No. 2* (1947–48) and the *String Quartet
No. 3* (1978) exemplify his preference for
clothing a kind of lyrically sad serenity in
more direct, conversational utterance. A
large part of his output consists of works
for the stage, and his first large success
was the ballet *La chatte* (*The Cat*, 1927) for
Diaghilev, based on an Aesop tale of a man
who falls in love with a cat, obligingly
turned into a woman by the goddess Aphrodite, until she sees a mouse, and reverts.
The lively music is entertaining, with a
Parisian *joie de vivre* touched with dreamy
lyricism. Among his operas, *Les caprices
de Marianne*, with Bizet a distant model,
was much admired when it appeared in
1954. The most ambitious is *La chartreuse
de Parme* (*The Charterhouse of Parma*,
1927–36, revised 1968).

RECOMMENDED WORKS
ballet *La chatte* (1927)
ballet *Les Forains* (1945)
cantata *L'oiseau a vu tout cela* (1960)
Piano Concerto No. 1 (1933–34)

BIBLIOGRAPHY
F. Y. Bril, *Henri Sauguet*, Paris 1967
(in French)
M. Schneider, *Henri Sauguet*, Paris
1959 (in French)

Schaeffer Pierre*

born 14th August 1910 at Nancy
died 19th August 1995 at Aix-en-
Provence

Pierre Schaeffer's name would probably
be much better known had he not given up
composing at the end of the 1950s to
concentrate on writing. Nonetheless, in
the history of 20th century music his
innovations occupy an important place.
After studying electrical engineering and
working as a radio technician (as well as
becoming a novelist), he founded 'Jeune
France' (not to be confused with the group
'La Jeune France') devoted to inter-arts
experiments. These were extended when
he co-founded the Studio d'Essai (Experimental Studio) in 1942, as part of French
Radio. Then in 1948, taking up the theoretical ideas of **Varèse**, he started experimenting with the manipulation and editing of
natural sounds, first on disc and then on
tape, thus arriving at the concept of *musique concrète*. This led to the formation of
the Groupe de Recherche de Musique
Concrète (1951) with Jacques Poulin and
Pierre **Henry**, and then, with François-
Bernard **Mâche** and Luc Ferrari, to the
creation of the Groupe de Recherches
Musicales (Group for Musical Research).
His particular interest has been collecting
sounds and their classification, and it is in

the distinguishing between the qualities of different sounds and their subsequent manipulation and juxtaposition that Schaeffer has been particularly influential. Chief among his own works is the series of *Études* (*Studies*, 1948–59) for tape, noteworthy for their clean, simple, sparse textures, and their sounds based on a wide variety of sources, instruments and voices, as in the *Étude aux sons animés*, 1958. From 1953 to 1958 Shaeffer was active in the creation of the overseas services of French Radio, and from 1958 he concentrated on theory, teaching electronic composition at the Paris Conservatoire from 1968. His novels include *Prelude, Chorale et Fugue* (1983).

RECOMMENDED WORKS
    Symphonie pour un homme seul (with
      Pierre **Henry**) (1950)
    Étude aux objets (1959)
    Étude de bruits 1958)
    Études aux allures (1958)
    Études aux sons animés (1958)
    L'oiseau RAI (1950)

BIBLIOGRAPHY
    P. Schaeffer, *À la recherche de la
      musique concrète*, 1952
    La musique concrète, 1967
    S. Brunet, *Pierre Schaeffer*, 1970 (in
      French)

Schmitt Florent[*]
born 28th September 1870 at Blâmont
(Meuthe-et-Moselle)
died 17th August 1958 at Neuilly-sur-Seine

Florent Schmitt was as well known as an influential and perceptive music critic (for *Le Temps* from 1929 to 1939) as a composer. His music shows the formal inheritance of his teacher **Fauré**, but against this is set a dreamy lyricism that has affinities with the Impressionist music of **Debussy**, combined with moments of powerful utterance, dynamic orchestration, and rhythmic power that place his style in the 20th century rather than in the period of Romanticism. Once he had established these elements of his style, it changed little apart from a gradually increasing use of chromaticism.

His idiom is well represented by the three works from just after the turn of the century that remain the best known of his large output (138 opus numbers). *Psalm 47* (1904) for soprano, chorus, organ and orchestra is a huge and passionate setting,

ranging from exultation and jubilation to a sensuous celebration of the mystery of the passion for God. The ballet *La tragédie de Salomé* (1907, revised as symphonic poem, 1910), a symbolist version of the Salome story, combines the languorousness of Impressionism (notably in the opening melodic lines, the central mysterious seascape, and the wordless female chorus, all reminiscent of **Debussy**) with grander, more powerful emotions in marvellous orchestral colours. At times, its atmosphere of heady sensuousness, rich orchestration, and powerful rhythms provides something of a foretaste of **Stravinsky's** early ballets (Stravinsky himself greatly admired this work), especially in the violence of the final dance. The long three-movement *Piano Quintet* in B minor (1902–08, revised 1919) is less immediately impressive than these two works, more clearly under the influence of **Fauré**. The writing is mostly dense and passionate, with the impression of extended, seamless lyrical melodic flow in the strings, either in consort with the piano or against a more decorated piano backcloth.

Schmitt was director of the Lyons Conservatory (1922–24).

RECOMMENDED WORKS
    Psalm 47 (1904) for soprano, chorus,
      organ and orchestra
    ballet *La tragédie de Salomé* (1907)

BIBLIOGRAPHY
    Y. Hucher, *Florent Schmitt*, 1953 (in
      French)

Varèse Edgard[***]
born 22nd December 1883 at Paris
died 6th November 1965 at New York

It has been said, with some justification, that the only two truly revolutionary composers producing an entirely new world of sound since World War I have been **Webern** and Edgard Varèse (by coincidence, both their fathers were engineers). Certainly the most experimental composers since 1945 have been deeply indebted to one or the other, and Varèse counts as one of the innovative geniuses of the modern age. His output consists of only fourteen complete surviving works, and it is extraordinary that, in comparison to similar figures in other artistic fields Varèse's name, let alone his music, is still known only to relatively few.

Varèse was constantly looking for new sounds, ones that would of themselves be able to keep up with and reflect new thought and a new age. For it was the qualities of individual sounds that were central to his aesthetic: their colour, depth, resonance, emotional effect. His orchestration and instrumentation were a reflection of the interaction and combinations of the sounds he was using, hence his constant search for new instruments or instrumental combinations. He preferred instruments that could create distinct and harsh sounds, especially percussion, wind and brass, and avoided those with vibrato, such as strings. Harmony becomes secondary, the tone qualities producing harmonic combinations; as Giles **Tremblay** has pointed out, this returns harmony to a primitive quality of resonance and timbre, and is often aggressively dissonant.

Such a concentration on the qualities of sounds throws two musical elements into sharper relief. First rhythm becomes important as a structural basis for the composition, and Varèse greatly developed the use of rhythm, in particular irregular and swiftly changing pulses and metres, and the interaction of different rhythms. Second, dynamics take on new importance, because the individual dynamics of an instrument change its sound, and the interaction of different dynamics alters the overall sound. This also becomes interrelated with rhythm, since the rhythm of changing dynamics can help shape the overall progression of a Varèse work. Varèse's plastic forms, as he himself observed, are a consequence of these concerns rather than following any traditional patterns; and the logic and seeming inevitability with which his works unfold is one of their remarkable features. The different sound-blocks or masses, often using silence as a component and often associated with different rhythms, overlap and interlink to create this flow.

Among his earliest works, all subsequently destroyed or lost, was a Straussian tone poem *Bourgogne*, which created a scandal when first performed in 1910, and a *Prélude à la fin d'un jour* for an orchestra of 120. He also worked on an opera, *Oedipus and the Sphinx*, with Hugo von Hofmannsthal. With his move to New York in 1915 he found a society filled with the excitement of the new, largely untrammelled by the weight of European tradition, that entirely suited his aesthetic. That break with Europe was expressed in his earliest surviving work, *Amériques* (1921, revised 1929). In its original version it was for a huge orchestra of 142 instruments, but he revised it for a still larger

orchestra, whose most remarkable feature was a battery of twenty-one percussion instruments with ten players. This massive work, generating excitement through its massed forces, the percussion permeating the orchestral sound as a separate block, is prophetic of Varèse's later work and of more recent orchestral developments. Ranging through the ritualistic, the mechanical, the primitive, it maintains a constant ferment of emotional expression through changes of colour and dynamics; the sound of the siren, capturing the momentum he found in America, became a feature of Varèse's style. More transitional is *Offrandes* (1921) for soprano and small orchestra, setting poems by the Chilean Vicente Huidobiro and the Mexican José Juan Tablada. The orchestra provide the block effects, with rocking rhythms and clockwork percussion, against the lyrical long lines of the soloist.

But it was *Hyperprism* (1922–23) for flute, clarinet, three horns, two trumpets, two trombones and sixteen percussion instruments that wrought the revolution. Its colours and its construction by blocks and rhythmic change were completely new, and it too caused a scandal on its first performance. Much of the writing is for unpitched percussion sounding and clashing against each other; in between, the pitched instruments create blocks of sound, in contrasting rhythms to the percussion, with an insistence on a repeated note that is another feature of Varèse's style. It is a short work, saying all it needs, no more and no less, evoking the power and rhythm, and aggressive sounds of the urban jungle. *Octandre* (1923) for seven wind and double-bass, is actually in three linked movements, a different wind instrument introducing each. Its a kind of natural equivalent to the urban *Hyperprism*, a raw primitive landscape or jungle, equally populated by blocks of sound, but with the textures of wind rather than the raucousness of percussion. *Intégrales* (1924–1925) for eleven wind and four percussion completes what amounts to a trilogy. With its different blocks moving at different speeds, its repetition of single notes and the impulse of the percussion, it has a primitive energy and gave rise to the expression 'spatial music'.

Varèse then turned back to a large-scale work for orchestra, *Arcana* (1925–27), which has a quotation from Paracletus at the head of the score, referring to the order of stars. It is based on a single idea of eleven notes, which provides the material for many different shapes, moods and sound-blocks conflicting with each other, but with a quiet close added in 1960. He followed it with his most famous work, *Ionisation* (1929–31) for thirteen percussion, written during a period in Paris (1928–33). It took the earlier trilogy of short chamber works to its logical conclusion: the complete absence of any instruments other than percussion, and, until the use of tuned percussion, the absence of any pitched sound apart from the variable wail of the siren, which opens the work and regularly returns. It has an extraordinary sense of forward motion, created by the rhythms and by the movement of percussive sounds and colours, and a mesmerising sound world of hard, sharp, incisive percussion. It is believed to be the first Western piece for percussion alone, and its demonstration of how unpitched material could create a musical piece has been extremely influential.

With *Ecuatorial* (1932–34) for bass soloist or bass chorus, eight brass, piano, organ, two ondes martonets, and percussion, Varèse extended his available sounds by using voice and the then new ondes martenot, an early electronic instrument whose haunting sound has permeated much French music since *Ecuatorial*. Influenced by pre-Columbian art and setting a Mayan poem (in Spanish), it has an ethereal, incantatory ritualistic quality. A similar mood permeates *Density 21.5* (1936) for flute, commissioned for a flute made of platinum (whose density is 21.5). Its precursor, like so many 20th-century solo flute works, is **Debussy's** *Syrinx*, and it opens with a plaintive, pastoral flute unravelling a climbing melody, but quickly moves into more ecstatic regions with wide leaps, regularly touching base with the pastoral source.

Apart from *Étude pour espace* (1947) for chorus, two percussion and tape, Varèse remained silent until the gift of a tape recorder (then recently invented) opened up new possibilities of sound and sound patterns. The result was his masterpiece, *Déserts* (1950–54) for fourteen wind, piano, five percussion and tape, originally intended for a projected film showing the deserts in the landscape and the deserts in the mind, and the first work anywhere for orchestra and tape. The tape segments are inserted at three points in the score, and are of *musique concrète* sounds, including modified instruments with colours quite unlike anything possible from an orchestra. The piece progresses through opposing planes in an overall tone of suffering and desolation. The first tape entry creates a moment of shock, its frightening, threatening sounds like distorted screams of cries, before the piece ends with the deserts in quiet repose.

Nocturnal (1961) for soprano, bass chorus and orchestra is a bleak setting of a few phrases from Anaïs Nin's *The House of Incest*, the orchestra including two ondes martenots. Varèse started two companion works, *Nocturnal II* and *Nuit* for soprano and nine or ten instruments, both based on texts from the same source, but neither were completed. His final two completed works were both for tape, the short *La procession de Vergès* (1955), and the major *Poème electronique* (1957–58). Commissioned for the Le Corbusier Philips pavilion at the 1958 Brussels Exposition (in which **Xenakis** was also involved), the latter used 400 loudspeakers sweeping the sound through the building. It is based on a wide variety of *concrète* and electronic sounds, including transformations of percussion instruments, natural sounds, and a voice. Varèse said he wanted it to express tragedy or an inquisition, and with its extraordinary spatial effects, and elements of fury and loneliness, it remains one of the most powerful of all electronic works, heard at the Exposition by more than two million people.

RECOMMENDED WORKS
All of Varèse's surviving works are recommended. *Ionisation* (1929–31) makes a sensible place to start.

BIBLIOGRAPHY
H. Jolivet, *Varèse*, 1973 (in French)
F. Oulette, *Edgard Varèse*, 1966, English trans. 1968
L. Varèse, *A Looking-glass Diary*, 1972
O. Vivier, *Varèse*, 1973

Vierne Louis*
born 8th October 1870 at Poitiers
died 2nd June 1937 at Paris

Louis Vierne was one of the last major exponents of highly chromatic late Romanticism, expressed in a series of symphonies for organ. The style of these works is partly predicted by the huge, powerful and sonorous late 19th-century organs for which he was writing, such as that at Notre Dame, where Vierne was organist from 1900 to his death. In these symphonies Vierne followed the cyclic principles of his teacher César Franck, where initial ideas permeate and unify an entire work through transformation. They are more obviously symphonically constructed than those of Widor, and most of them are cast in five movements, each representing a contrasting mood. They are vivid works entirely married to the potential of the instrument, sometimes with power and sonority, often with a delicate playfulness. The *Symphony No. 3* (1912) is perhaps the most popular, the regal opening movement balanced by the fiery finale; the second and fourth movements are reflective, the former with a lyrical pastoral mood ending in a gentle murmur, the latter more ruminative. At the centre of this mirror structure is a lithe, angular little dance with quirky harmonic colours. The *Symphony No. 1* (1899) includes a thunderous toccata as its finale. The *Symphony No. 5* (1924) is the most introspective, and the most chromatically extreme; the *Symphony No. 6* (1930) the most difficult to play.

His other organ works include the *24 pièces en style libre* (1913), which follow Bach in using all twenty-four major and minor keys. Of his choral music, the *Messe solennelle* (1900) for chorus and two organs is an antiphonal mass with an organ and divided choir at opposite ends of church.

Vierne was nearly blind from birth, and was celebrated for his playing and in particular for his improvisation. He died while actually playing in Notre-Dame. Organ-lovers will need no introduction to his work, but for others his symphonies are a major contribution to a genre of music often overlooked, and opportunities to experience one of these works in the large-scale settings for which they were intended are rare but should not be missed.

RECOMMENDED WORKS
Organ Symphony No. 3 (1912)
Pièces en style libre (1913) for organ

Georgia

Introduction

Most of Georgia's 20th-century compositional life followed the pattern of Soviet republics, with any experimentation that took place in the 1920s eradicated in favour of music that glorified Soviet subjects. However, the rich legacy of Georgian folk-music had already been explored before this time, and its inclusion in works of Soviet socialist realism was actively encouraged. The father figure of 20th-century Georgian classical music was Zakhary Petrovich **Paliashvili** (1872–1933). One of the first collectors of Georgian folk music, he used the influence of folk idioms to colourful and powerful effect in three operas, *Abessalom and Eteri* (1909–18), *Daici* (*Twilight*, 1923) and *Latavra* (1930).

Lev Knipper (1898–1974) had a reputation as a modernist in the 1920s, notably for the satirical operas *The Legend of the Plaster God* (1925) and *The North Wind* (1929–30), the latter incurring official displeasure. After studying Tajikistan folk music, he produced a symphonic suite *Vatch* (1932) incorporating folk themes, which had a high reputation for its orchestral skill. He then embarked on a series of symphonies (he eventually produced twenty) with a strong Soviet content, of which the *Symphony No. 3 'Far Eastern'* (1933) uses huge forces to reflect life in the Red Army. Many of his songs have been popularised by the Red Army, and one of the best known occurs in the *Symphony No. 4 'Poem about the Komsomol Fighter'* (1934), a combination of full-blooded and often effective orchestral writing and patriotic tunes. The music of Vano Muradeli (1908–71) is rooted in Georgian folk music without direct usage of folksong, exemplified in his two symphonies (No. 1 1938 and No. 2 *The War of Liberation*, 1942). His opera *The Great Friendship* (1947) was the catalyst for the Zdhanov crackdown on 'formalism' in 1948. Otar Taktakishvili (1924–89) was probably the best known name outside Georgia during the Soviet period; he served as Georgia's minister of culture. His tonal idiom was well within the approved Soviet style, and quite highly regarded. Of the succeeding generation, Giya **Kancheli** (born 1935) has established himself as a powerful international voice, and the most interesting of all Georgian composers.

Georgian Music Information Centre:
David Agmashenebeli Ave. 123
380064 Tbilisi
Republic of Georgia
tel: +995 8832 95 48 61
fax: +995 8832 96 86 78

Kancheli Giya*
born 10th August 1935 at Tiflis

Giya Kancheli's name was virtually unknown outside the former USSR until the late 1970s, but since his move to Berlin in 1992 he has become internationally established as a symphonist of stature. His idiom prefers slow atmospheric progressions of changing dynamics and ideas, sometimes violent, often with a sense of churning immobility, and with delicate groupings of instruments being contrasted with the mass orchestra. In tone, it often reflects the emotional effects of Stalinist oppression, in darker feelings of fear and protest; in this he is the heir to **Shostakovich**. At the same time there is an intensity that suggests a more spiritual dimension, a striving for what Kancheli has described as a 'deeper continuity'. Georgian folk music has influenced his orchestral colours (notably in the use of alto flute and viola, and in drone effects), and his later orchestration often includes the electric bass guitar.

Stravinsky and **Shostakovich** both influence the *Symphony No. 2* and the *Symphony No. 3* (1973), which frames the aggressive with passages using a wordless tenor. The *Symphony No. 4 'In memoria di Michelangelo'* (1975) opens with the slow tolling of a bell, with something of the gentle unfolding of **Gorecki's** celebrated third symphony, but is musically far more interesting. With a riotous, tormented scherzo section, this monumental work traverses great swells of climax, vast vistas of texture, and moments of delicacy. The sometimes violent *Symphony No. 5* (1977) again has very sharp contrasts of dynamics, incidents exploding out of near silence, and a generally slow progression, with vivid colours in climactic moments. Similar outbursts are found in the *Symphony No. 6* (1981), which exemplifies the contrasts of tragic sadness and brute force; it includes two violas placed behind screens to either side of the orchestra. He has written a multi-media opera, *Music for the Living* (1984), and a number of vocal works, often including a boys' choir.

RECOMMENDED WORKS
Symphony No. 4 *In memoria di Michelangelo* (1975)
Symphony No. 5 (1977)
Symphony No. 6 (1981)

Paliashvili Zakhary Petrovich
born 16th August 1871 at Kutaisi
died 6th October 1933 at Tbilisi

Paliashvili was the foremost Georgian composer of his generation, who studied and collected Georgian folk songs, recording over 300 of them and publishing his researches in 1910. Wishing to see an indigenous Georgian operatic tradition, he co-founded the Fraternity for the Creation of Opera in the Georgian Language (1906), and his best-known work is the Georgian opera *Abessalom and Eteri* (1909–18). Based on a Greek legend, it is strongly pervaded by the exotic colours, modal harmonies and sinuous melodic style of Georgian folk music (with the influence of Near Eastern music). It is the combination of folk styles and Western techniques that gives the opera its vivid colours and at times an unusual and evocative idiom, although the formal epic construction is conventional (arioso and recitative). The opera *Daici* (*Twilight*, 1923) is in the 19th-century operatic tradition, laced with folk dances and choruses, patriotism and a final rousing Soviet-style chorus. The story is one of jealousy, the heroine being betrothed to a warrior but loving another, who is killed by the warrior in a duel. In penance, he decides to give his life in the next battle; the opera ends with the departure of the soldiers.

Paliashvili taught and conducted in Georgia. His brother was a well-known conductor; of his eleven children, five were professional musicians.

RECOMMENDED WORK
opera *Abessalom and Eteri* (1909–18)

BIBLIOGRAPHY
A. Tsulukidze, *Zakarja Paliashvili*
Tbilisi, 1971 (Georgian, Russian and French editions)

Germany

Introduction

It is almost impossible to give a satisfactory history of German music in the 20th century in a few pages, so complex and full has that history been. In the 19th century, Germany, together with Austria (whose musical activity has been closely allied with that of Germany), was the pre-eminent powerhouse of classical music, and has retained something of that position in the 20th.

Towards the end of the 19th century one figure dominated German music: Richard Wagner (1813–83). In his operas he had stretched traditional concepts of tonality, and the size, complexity, and power of the orchestra almost to their limits. His specially constructed opera house at Bayreuth has continued to present his operas annually, and remains a major attraction for lovers of opera. His legacy dominated European music at the turn of the century. To his contemporaries, another branch of German music, tracing its roots back to Beethoven and the music of the Classical period, was represented by Brahms (1833–97) but Brahms's influence was felt more in Vienna, notably in the early work of Schoenberg. An exception is the German Max Reger (1873–1916), who developed the classical heritage of Brahms by turning back to the model of Bach, adopting such forms as canons, fugues and chorales, and combining them with late Romantic harmonies. The intellectual dryness of much of his music has perhaps hindered a wider appreciation of this prolific composer.

At the turn of the century the pre-eminent German composer was undoubtably Richard Strauss (1864–1949), who in his tone poems built on the example of Wagner in the use of huge orchestral colours and effects, and in the restless extremes of chromatic writing. After the turn of the century his output consisted largely of operas, where similar means were turned to subjects more psychologically complex and anguished than those of the more consciously nationalist and mythological Wagner operas, and to almost Mozartian domestic hue filtered through a huge late Romantic palette. Similarly, composers such as Hans Pfitzner (1869–1949) continued the Wagnerian tradition both in orchestral and operatic works. At the same time, the busy musical life of Berlin had attracted such experimenters as the Italian Busoni, and later the Austrians Schoenberg and Schreker, all three of whom became important teachers.

The subsequent history of German music is inextricably bound up with political events within Germany, and is in part a cultural reflection of those events. The turbulent years between the end of World War I and the assumption of power by the Nazis in 1933 saw the emergence of a new direction in music, that of politically conscious music that reflected proletariat concerns, a capitalist parallel to the socialist music of Soviet Russia. This music was influenced by the emergence in Berlin of a style of cabaret that was satirical in content, influenced by jazz, but with a Teutonic rigidity of rhythm. Such non-musical objectives inevitably involved the use of text, and central to this development was the fiercely political playwright Bertolt Brecht (1898–1956). The cabaret style and Brecht's texts combined in the music theatre works of Kurt Weill (1900–50), whose works employ small-scale bands, unextravagant staging, and set numbers; his song 'Mack the Knife' from *The Threepenny Opera* has become one of the best known of all tunes. The continuing popularity of Weill's works has obscured those other composers working with political subjects in Berlin, such as Hanns Eisler (1898–1962), the Austrian Krenek, the Polish-born composer Max Brand (1896–1980), best known for his opera *Machinist Hopkins* (1929), in which surrealistic elements appear (the machines sing), and which remains a powerful political statement, or the earlier works of Paul Dessau (1894–1979). The operas of these politically conscious composers became known as 'Zeitoper' ('opera of the times'). Similarly, the cabaret style spilled over into purely abstract music, such as the dance suites of Eduard Kunneke (1885–1953), better known for his operettas. Stefan Wolpe (1902–72), who settled in the USA in 1938, initially incorporated jazz elements into his music, but then turned to a more experimental style, eventually leading to a personal brand of serialism developed after he left Germany.

Among those composers who worked with Brecht was Paul Hindemith (1895–1963), a major force in German music who developed in directions that departed from both the Wagnerian and socialist musical traditions, although his earlier work includes Zeitoper. Intellectually he is a counterbalance to the 12-tone system developed by Schoenberg. His social awareness was expressed in the concept of 'Gebrauchsmusik' (a term coined by Besseler in 1925): music that would be socially useful. This included music for films and radio, but is especially associated with Hindemith's numerous works for amateur musicians and choirs, music that was both contemporary, and yet of a simplicity appropriate for relatively untrained musicians. A composer of rigorous intellect and formidable energy, he became the chief German exponent of neo-classicism in the 1920s and 1930s, turning back to the Baroque for inspiration and re-exploring the skills of counterpoint and polyphonic writing. As a composer he was of immense influence between the World Wars; as a theorist his treatises on harmony continue to be respected. Among those German composers directly influenced by Hindemith were Boris **Blacher** (1903–75), Karl **Hartmann** (1905–63), and later Hans Werner **Henze** (born 1926); outside Germany notably the Russian **Shostakovich**. His other German pupils included Harald Genzmer (born 1909), who pursued a Hindemithian idiom in three symphonies and a number of concertos.

In complete contrast, Carl **Orff** (1895–1982) developed a very personal brand of music founded on rhythm, ostinati, and percussive effects, usually in vocal genres. The full impact of his work has been masked by the popular reaction to his cantata *Carmina Burana* and is only now becoming apparent as minimalism gains acceptance. His masterpiece, *Antigonae*, is the only 20th-century German opera besides those of **Strauss** to rank with those of **Berg**, **Janáček** and **Britten**. Another composer who followed his own, if more traditional, path was Werner **Egk** (1901–83), who brought a Gallic sensitivity to the Germanic tradition, and is best known for his operas. Joseph Suder (1892–1980) remained firmly in the 19th-century tradition while developing a personal use of 'thematic synthesis', in which themes that had appeared contrasting combine harmoniously at the end of a movement, a technique developed in the *Chamber Symphony* (1924). His opera *Kleider machen Leute* (*Clothes make the man* 1926–34) is of passing interest for its sumptuous late-Romantic idiom (the orchestral writing is more interesting than the vocal). The libretto, by the composer, is fairly preposterous, telling of a tailor, expert on the violin, who is mistaken for a gentleman, falls in love with the most eligible young woman, is unmasked, and is eventually persuaded by the young

woman to follow his true calling, violin playing; she joins him in the happy ending. Karl **Hartmann** (1905–63), while assimilating ideas from the neo-classicists, provided a link between the Expressionist idiom of **Berg** and the more modern mainstream, especially in his eight symphonies, the finest German symphonies of the century.

Before the rise of the Nazis, there were then essentially three trends in German composition: the legacy of the large-scale late-Romantic idiom, typified by **Strauss**: the politically aware socialist works of **Weill**; and a neo-classical trend, abstract and intellectual, represented by **Hindemith**. Under Nazism Germany's musical experimentalism came to a halt; works that hinted at socialism or 'decadence' were banned and Wagner and late Romanticism were restored as the nation's music. Those composers and musicians that stayed in Germany, such as the conductor Furtwängler or **Strauss**, became inextricably enmeshed in the demands and constrictions of the Nazi system, with the notable exception of **Hartmann**.

Contemporary music of any value, apart from the works of **Orff**, **Egk**, and **Hartmann**, ceased during the Nazi domination, but after 1945 a new phase of German music accompanied the emergence of the country from its war-time devastation. The impetus for the revival was twofold. First, the International Summer Music Courses at Darmstadt, founded in 1946 by Wolfgang Steinecke, became a centre for the very latest music ideas, and thus a major factor in the emergence of the avant-garde movement of the 1950s and 1960s. Among those who taught there were **Messiaen**, **Berio**, **Boulez**, **Maderna**, **Nono** and **Pousseur**. Second, Karlheinz **Stockhausen** (born 1928) himself a student at Darmstadt, emerged as a major force in modern music, initially as a serialist, then as a composer of electronic music and explorer of new sound worlds, and more recently as a composer of a huge cycle of operas using unusual venues. His co-direction (from 1963) of West German Radio's electronic studio in Cologne attracted composers to the city. The prolific Hans Werner **Henze** (born 1926) emerged in the same period, less experimental than **Stockhausen**, but attracting international attention and political controversy with the socialist subject-matters of his operas. Giselher Klebe (born 1925), has followed a similar path to that of Henze, adopting serial ideas in the 1950s, but then developing a more Romantic style in which 12-tone methods have formed only a part. He has used the variable metres developed by **Blacher**, and his output, little known outside Germany, has been dominated by eleven operas and five symphonies. An important avant-garde individualist was Bernd Alois **Zimmermann** (1918–1970), whose celebrated opera *Die Soldaten* (1956–60) was the culmination of Expressionist extremes.

Other figures to emerge from the explosion of activity after 1945 included Herbert Eimert (1897–1972) who utilized an atonal idiom in the 1920s before turning to 12-tone principles. His *Four Pieces* (1952–53) was one of the earliest purely electronic German works, influencing Stockhausen. Goetfried Michael Koenig (born 1926), who has lived in Holland since 1964, briefly attracted attention in the 1960s with his electronic works, such as the aggressive *Terminus II* (1966–67) and a series of *Functions*, each based on a different colour. His pieces are more interesting for the early use of computers in determining construction than in aural effect. In a completely different field, Ernst Pepping (1901–81) continued the German tradition of Lutheran liturgical and organ music.

During the 1950s and 1960s Germany led the European avant-garde movement, together with the Frenchman **Boulez**. With the collapse of the swift-moving experimentation of those decades in the 1970s, German composition has fallen into comparative obscurity. Among the younger generation of German composers, the best known internationally is probably Aribert **Reimann** (born 1936), whose opera *Lear* is a successful setting of the Shakespeare play. The major work of Konrad Beohmer (born 1941) has been the opera *Docteur Faustus* (1985). York Höller (born 1944), a pupil of **Boulez** and **Zimmermann**, has concentrated on combining electronics with live instruments. The influence of Zimmermann emerged in the large-scale, sometimes fantastical, opera *Der Meister und Margarita* (*The Master and Margarita*), based on the novel by Mikhail Bulgakov. He is perhaps best known for a work without electronics, the *Piano Concerto* (1985). Snatches of Berlin cabaret jazz, the blues, the neo-classical and the neo-baroque join stylistic fragmentation and other elements in the work of Hans-Järgen von Bose (born 1953), as, for example, in the 'kinetic action' (ballet) *Die Nacht aus Blei* (*The Night of Lead*, 1981). The limited output of Marc Neikrug (born 1946) has included an effective music-theatre work, *Through Roses* (1979–80) for an actor and eight instruments to a text inspired by the prisoner-musicians who played in Nazi concentration camps.

Paul **Dessau** and Hanns **Eisler** remain the outstanding figures who remained in or moved to the former East Germany after the World War II. Of other East German composers, Ottmar Gerster (1897–1969) is perhaps best known for his opera after Tennyson, *Enoch Arden* (1936), about a sea-captain who returns home after an absence of twelve years to find his wife remarried to one of his friends. It is a combination of sumptuous late-Romanticism with neo-classical elements. Of the younger composers, Udo Zimmermann (born 1943) is best known for his outstanding chamber opera *White Rose* (1986), his second work on the same subject. Based on texts by Wolfgang Willaschek, it explores the psychological states of members of the anti-Nazi resistance group, the 'White Rose', as they languish in prison, expressing the horror not only of their incarceration as they wait for death, but also of their times. The musical means are deceptively simple, with two soloists and fourteen instrumentalists dominated by wind and brass and including harp and piano. The range of effect is considerable, sometimes harking back to **Stravinsky** or **Weill**, but for the most part demonstrating an astringent sense of clarity, with spare and often very high vocal writing interspersed with outbursts that include near-speech. It is essentially an extended song cycle in sixteen sections that can also be staged, and this work, exceptional in both the impact of its text and its affecting score, works especially well in recording. Zimmermann's other works include a further three operas, and a number of concertos.

Germany's vigorous compositional life is matched by the strength of its music-making, strongly supported by federal and local governments who have long recognised the importance of the arts to the overall pulse of the country. Outstanding have been the contributions of German radio stations in encouraging new music, and the widespread commitment to opera reflected by the large number of smaller opera houses.

German Music Information Centre:
International Musikinstitut Darmstadt
Nieder-Ramstädter Strasse 190
D-64285 Darmstadt
tel: +49 6151 132416/7
fax: +49 6151 132405

Blacher Boris*

born 19th January 1903 at Niu-chang,
China
died 30th January 1975 at Berlin
(birth date sometimes given as 6th
January, according to Russian old-style
calendar)

An important teacher as well as composer,
Boris Blacher in many ways sidestepped
the German musical traditions, both old
and new. Unusually for someone working
in Germany, his music has its antecedents
in French examples, particularly the lyrical ideas of **Satie** and the verve of **Milhaud**,
combined with the rhythmic vitality of
Stravinsky. That his music is not wider
known is explained partly by this individual approach, and partly by its generally
witty and playful nature.

Blacher's earliest work to receive widespread attention (and still one of his best
known) was the neo-classical *Concertante
Musik* (1937) for orchestra, a lithe and
witty score that shows many of his later
hallmarks: a construction based on the
expansion of a germ idea, lucid and clear
orchestration, a delight in varied rhythmic
play, and echoes of the German cabaret
jazz of the time. It is an object lesson in
how music with a light character can at the
same time be intellectually entertaining,
and never appear trite. Its success was
followed by the set of sixteen *Variations
on a Theme of Paganini* (1947), based on
the same theme used by Rachmaninov,
and others, which displayed a similar sense
of delight in large orchestral colours.

By the 1940s Blacher had begun to
systematise his rhythmic exploration,
which led to the adoption of 'variable
metres' – a system for altering the metre in
each bar, first used in *Ornamente* (1958)
for piano. At the same time he embraced
12-tone techniques (as in the ballet *Lysis-
trata*, 1950), eventually serialising rhythmic as well as harmonic elements.

Blacher's stage works, both ballet and
opera, were a significant part of his output
throughout his career. The 'dance drama'
Fest im Süden (*Festival in the South*,
1935) was an international success. His
twelve operas (of which seven are full-
length, the rest chamber) usually deal with
crime in some respect, and, apart from two
comedies, combine tragic elements with a
sense of the grotesque. Within this overall
approach, the variety of means is considerable, but usually leavened with lighter
numbers or sections. Of the two comedies,
the ballet-opera *Preussiches Märchen*
(*Prussian Fairytale*, 1949) sent up the

German military tradition, while *Zwei-
hunderttausend Taler* (usually known as
200,000 Taler, 1969) has a Jewish story in
the same genre as *Fiddler on the Roof*, and
employs eclectic musical means, from tone-
clusters to the development of small
motivic cells. With its singspiel vocal writing, and a folk feeling in its happy ending, it
scored something of a success. Of his more
serious works, the 90-minute *Yvonne,
Prinzessin von Burgund* (1972), with a
tragic folk-like tale in which the ordinary
girl the Prince has married is murdered by
the court, was highly regarded, incorporating popular elements (including a solo
violin tango) into Blacher's characteristic
style. *Zwischenfälle bei einer Notlandung*
(*Crash Landing*, 1965) used predominantly electronic sounds. Many of Blacher's ideas come together in the short
Abstrakte Oper No. 1 (1953), whose text by
fellow-composer Werner **Egk** is largely
composed of abstract phonemes expressing the notions of love, fear, pain, and
panic. It is a work full of humour, musically
combining variable metres with stricter
serial procedures, with hints of jazz and
clear, spare orchestration. The vocal lines
are lyrical, sometimes ecstatic, sometimes
close to parody with echoes of **Orff** and
Weill.

Concertos form a significant part of
Blacher's orchestral output, including the
Piano Concerto No. 2 (1952), which uses
variable metres, and the *Cello Concerto*
(1964), which uses extended instrumental
techniques and extremely sparse orchestration in a structure consisting of a central allegro movement framed by two
adagios. Of his piano music, tongue-in-
cheek wit is combined with neo-classicism
and jazz in the amusing three studies *What
about this, Mr Clementi?* (1943). In a more
serious vein, though still with a dominant
sense of *joie de vivre*, the *Piano Sonata*
(1951) concentrates on rhythmic play, and
combines French-influenced piano writing
with post-Schoenbergian harmony. In the
1960s Blacher also produced a number of
electronic scores.

Blacher taught at Dresden University
in 1938, but resigned after Nazi pressure.
After the war he taught in Berlin, becoming director of the Berlin Hochschule für
Musik (1953–70). Among his many distinguished pupils were **von Einem** and **Reimann**.

RECOMMENDED WORKS
  Concertante Musik, op. 37 (1937) for
    orchestra
  Variations on a Theme by Paganini,
    op. 26 (1947)

BIBLIOGRAPHY
A. Stuckenschmidt, *Boris Blacher*,
1985 (in German)

Dessau Paul*

born 19th December 1894 at Hamburg
died 28th June 1979 at East Berlin

The communist composer Dessau is, with
Eisler, the best known of the composers
who spent much of their working career in
what was East Germany. He fled Nazi
Germany in 1933, spending periods in
Paris and Palestine before moving to the
USA in 1939.

His earliest works, including a *Concertino* (1924) and the *Symphony No. 1* (1926),
were Expressionist in style, but his individual voice did not mature until his studies of 12-tone music with Leibowitz in
Paris, and then his meeting with Brecht in
the USA in 1946. It is for his collaborations
with Brecht that Dessau is best remembered. Although he had composed songs
for a Brecht production in 1938, it was with
the music for the Brecht plays *Mutter
Courage und ihre Kinder* (*Mother Courage and her Children*, 1946, revised
1947–48) and *Der gute Mensch von Sezuan*
(The Good Person of Setzuan) (1947) that
Dessau achieved prominence, and his
music is still most likely to be encountered
in productions of these plays. In keeping
with Brecht's philosophy that music
should be the servant of the text, the songs
are self-contained and point up the political
content of the plays in an idiom descended
from the satirical cabaret songs of pre-war
Berlin.

Though less well known, Dessau's most
important works are two operas, *Die Verurteilung des Lukullus* (*The Condemnation of Lucullus*, 1949) and *Puntila*
(1957–59), both to Brecht texts, and written after Dessau and Brecht had returned
to East Germany. The first, originally
titled *The Trial of Lucullus*, but revised in
1951 to satisfy the East German authorities, has for its libretto an unusual interpretation of the life of the Roman soldier
and philosopher Lucullus. Lucullus has
died, and the opera opens with his funeral
march; it then, through the device of a trial
after his death, examines his life, concluding that he was a mass murderer, assessing his warfare methods and the social
purpose of his life. The music is intense,
busy, swift-moving, and with a spontaneous, rough-edged feel. The repetitive

rhythmic ideas, the orchestration (especially in the solo woodwind figures and
percussion) and choral writing, the often
declamatory vocal lines, recall the dramatic works of **Orff**. Its satirical tone is
heightened through the interweaving of
sections influenced by cabaret styles and
by jazz. If the Marxist imprint, in which
the music as much as the text is designed
to promote social and political responses in
the audience, can be accepted, it remains a
powerful dramatic work.

Puntila (1957–59) was written after
Brecht's death, and was based on a 1949
Brecht play for which Dessau had written
the original incidental music. More sophisticated in its construction and flow than
Lukullus, its plot is a variant on the age-old theme of a dominating father (Puntila)
attempting to marry off his daughter. The
story, which originated in a Finnish folk
tale, has the added twist that the alcoholic
Puntila oscillates between being a normal,
caring father and a ruthless schemer; the
political content lies in this dichotomy and
in its wider applications. The music is
essentially Expressionist, recalling **Berg**,
with heightened, anguished vocal lines
that echo the variations of human speech
in extreme emotion. Its very large cast and
its Marxist subject-matter have perhaps
prevented the wider dissemination of this
dark and aggressive work. Dessau's last
opera, *Einstein* (1971–73) is a Marxist
view of the physicist's life, concentrating
on the social responsibilities of the scientist. It draws on contemporary developments (tone-clusters, and the use of tape),
on Dessau's earlier experience (jazz, 12-tone techniques), and incorporates quotations from Bach.

Dessau's songs encompass works with
less populist musical elements, such as the
gritty and wispish song-cycle *Fünf Tierverse* (verses by Brecht, 1972) for soprano
and guitar. He also wrote a considerable
amount of communist propaganda music,
notably popular mass songs, but including
such works as the *Orchestermusik No. 3
'Lenin'* (1970) for chorus and orchestra.
Apart from his two symphonies (1924,
1936, revised 1962), his orchestral output
was written entirely in East Germany,
where it was highly regarded. *In Memoriam Bertolt Brecht* (1957) incorporates
themes from the incidental music to
Mother Courage, and is a powerful orchestral reflection in three linked sections. Its
writing (especially in the use of high woodwind and scurrying lower string phrases)
is sometimes reminiscent of **Britten**. The

large scale *Bach-Variationen* (*Bach Variations*, 1963) for orchestra are also of interest, ambitious in their scope, drawing on themes by J.S. and C.P.E. Bach, and adding two further motives developed from the letters of the names of Bach and Arnold **Schoenberg**, thus creating a link between the two periods, in a considerable range of idiom and mood.

Dessau's large output awaits a fuller evaluation, and it may be that with the collapse of East Germany, the political content of so many of his works will assume historical interest rather than a dialectical intent, and a purely musical assessment may emerge. Dessau was assistant conductor to Klemperer at the Cologne Opera (1912–23), and conductor of the Städtische Oper in Berlin from 1925 to 1933.

RECOMMENDED WORKS
  Bach Variations (1963) for orchestra
  opera *Puntila* (1957–59)
  In Memorian Bertolt Brecht (1957) for
    orchestra
  opera *Die Verurteilung des Lukullus*
    (1949)

BIBLIOGRAPHY
  P. Dessau, *Aus Gesprächen*, Leipzig,
  1975 (in German)

Egk Werner (born Werner Mayer)**

born May 17th 1901 at Auchsesheim, Bavaria
died July 10th 1983 at Inning

Werner Egk, once renowned as an opera composer, has fallen into undeserved neglected in recent years. His idiom is an unusual combination of sophisticated earthiness, Bavarian vitality and French charm, often infected by the dance, and notable for the clarity of vocal lines.

Typical of this combination is the short oratorio *La Tentation de Saint Antoine* (1945, revised 1952) for contralto, string quartet and string orchestra, which forms an attractive introduction to his work. Built on French tunes and verses of the 18th century, it has an infectious charm, earthiness, and gentle humour – the pious narrative is presented in an amusing, even frivolous way. But it also contains delicate and thoughtful writing for the string quartet, dissonant harmonies adding a weighty undercurrent to the surface whimsy. With its flexible rhythmic vitality, it is a particularly fine example of the chamber oratorio.

Folk-like earthy rhythms are found in another and better-known early work, *Geigenmusik mit Orchester* (*Violin Music with Orchestra*, 1936), while the closest parallel to the *Quattro Canzoni* (*Four Italian Songs*, 1932, revised 1955) for high voice and orchestra are probably **Canteloube's** *Songs of the Auvergne*.

It is, though, as a composer of ballets and operas that Egk achieved prominence. Of the former, the best known is *Die chinesische Nachitgall* (*The Chinese Nightingale*, 1953), full of brilliant orchestral colours, and ranging from an exuberance touched with oriental colours and percussive vitality to a passionate lyricism (one of its sections is a miniature violin concertino). *Abraxas* (1948), based on the poet Heine's version of the Faust legend, was banned in Germany following its première due to its sexual explicitness; but there is little suggestion of such lasciviousness in the pleasant but innocuous suite drawn from the ballet.

Egk's first opera, *Columbus* (1933), was written for radio rather than the theatre, and is one of the earliest examples of such (it was revised in 1942 for stage production). His first major operatic success, however, was *Die Zaubergeige* (*The Magic Fiddle*, 1935), an unsophisticated work full of German folk tunes that suited the political and cultural climate emerging under the Nazi regime. It was followed by his major work, the satirical *Peer Gynt* (1938, minor revisions 1969), which the authorities attempted to ban for its obvious political alligony (ritual is parodied, and Mussolini actually quoted); they failed only through the insistence of the general manager of the Staatsoper Berlin. Based on the Ibsen play, Egk's libretto plays down the Norwegian folk antecedents and amplifies the elements of dream and fantasy world. It emerges as a parallel to the Faust legend, focussing on the internal wandering drive of Peer as he is pursued by his daemons the trolls. Ranging from Norway to a Latin American seaport (a scene that includes a ship blowing up) its atmosphere is surrealistic, Egk dividing the action into nine self-contained scenes and a prologue, arranged in three acts. The music is eclectic and wide-ranging, sometimes with deliberate echoes of Wagner, **Strauss**, Offenbach and **Orff**. Moods range from savage black humour (the hall of the trolls is populated by the aggressive parasites and misfits of mankind) to delicate lyricism. The musical ethos of German cabaret, exemplified by **Weill**, is never far removed. Egk's achievement is to weld these divergent materials into a convincing synthesis. The depth of emotional presentation makes it more than mere satire and a parallel to **Shostakovich's** *Lady Macbeth of Mtsensk*: it is a version of the hero-myth, drawing on the phantasmagorical internal paranoias of the hero and ending on that most German of themes, redemption through love. This is an opera of many complex layers; probably only its large cast and staging requirements have prevented its wider dissemination.

Egk's other operas were based on similarly distinguished and powerful literary material: Kleist, Yeats, and in *Der Revisor* (*The Inspector General*, 1957), Gogol.

Egk was conductor of the Prussian State Opera, Berlin (1936–40), and, among other administrative positions, director of the Berlin Hochschule (1950–53). Boris **Blacher** was one of his pupils.

RECOMMENDED WORKS
> ballet suite *Die chinesische Nachtigall* (1953)
> *Quattro Canzoni* (*Four Italian Songs*) (1932 revised 1955) for soprano and orchestra
> opera *Peer Gynt* (1938)
> *La Tentation de Saint Antoine* (1945) for alto, string quartet and string orchestra
> *Geigenmusik mit Orchester* (*Violin Music with Orchestra*) (1936)

BIBLIOGRAPHY
> W. Egk, *Musik, Wort, Bild* (in German), Munich, 1960

Eisler Hanns**
born 6th July 1898 at Leipzig
died 6th September 1962 at Berlin

The career of Hanns Eisler was so circumscribed by political events that he stands as an exemplar of the effects of politics on art in the 20th century. His earlier work shows the influence of his teacher **Schoenberg**; among the lesser of **Schoenberg's** pupils (when compared with **Berg** or **Webern**), he embraced 12-tone techniques with particular enthusiasm. In 1926 he joined the Communist party, and started to write mainly vocal works and film scores with a left-wing tendency, reducing 12-tone experimentation in favour of what he considered a more universal and direct musical language; among his collaborators was Bertolt Brecht. Banned by the Nazis, he left Germany in 1933 and settled in the

USA. Among his works there were a number of film scores (notably *None but the Lonely Heart*, 1944). In America he came to the notice of McCarthy's Un-American Activities Committee. The subsequent deportation order caused such a storm of protest that it was revoked, but Eisler left anyway, eventually settling in East Germany, where he continued to write vocal works and film scores with a socialist slant, as well as the DDR national anthem. His output is stylistically diverse, ranging from 12-tone to socialist realist.

Although the *Duo*, op. 7 (1924) for violin and cello has a stern Schoenbergian expressiveness, the contribution that Eisler made to the **Schoenberg** circle was a wry humour that is not often found in the works of its three most famous members, and which informs much of Eisler's subsequent music, whatever the style. The combination of 12-tone techniques and a satirical bent emerges in the song cycle *Palmström* (*Studien über Zwölfton Reihen*), (1926) for soprano, flute (doubling piccolo), clarinet and string quartet – the same forces, less the piano, as Schoenberg's *Pierrot lunaire*. Typical of the early followers of Schoenberg are the extreme leaps in the vocal writing, the care in the interaction of instrumental colours, and the sense of short phrases carrying large weight. By the *Kleine Sinfonie* (*Little Symphony*, 1931), there is an uneasy mixture of expressive formality and the creeping influence of jazz and Berlin cabaret, angular themes betraying the Schoenbergian influence but allied to conventional rather than 12-tone harmonic structures. The marriage is unusual, and the vivacious work is more than an interesting curiosity. There are similar echoes of such melodic lines in the short *Nonet No. 1* (1939), combined with a pastoral, outdoor mood and cast in a set of variations, while the rather self-effacing *Nonet No. 2* (1940–41), based on music for a socialist documentary film, covers a range of styles, with wisps of folk themes and a march. None of these works are especially profound, but all are attractive; the *Vierzehn Arten den Regen zu beschreiben* (*Fourteen ways of describing the rain*, 1941) for flute, clarinet, violin, viola, cello and piano is more than that. Written for **Schoenberg's** 70th birthday (and thus given the spurious opus number 70), one idea uses Schoenberg's initials, while the structure of the seventh variation plays on his birthdate. Such technical tricks are cleverly combined with descriptive music (whose origins are in a documentary film score of the same date) to create a piece of intellectual wit and pictorial interest, if lacking the immediacy associated with Eisler's works for a wider audience.

Some of Eisler's most entertaining music consists of arrangements he made of some of his film music of the 1930s for concert use. The *Suite No. 2 'Niemandslied'*, op. 24 (1931), for example, has the kind of jazzy bounce and verve that eluded **Weill** (whose music it resembles) outside the actual theatre, and a similar style is found in its companions. Popular in their appeal and yet sophisticated in their small-orchestral means, these are exactly the kind of 1930s Berlin works that would entertain a wide audience if they were better known.

However, it is for his songs that Eisler is best remembered, especially those written with Brecht. They range from 12-tone works, through a large corpus of Brecht songs, to works written in East Germany. Throughout, the emphasis is on the words, the music pointing and commenting rather than acting an emotional reflection of the verbal content. A number are combined into a series of chamber cantatas (*Kammerkantaten Nos 1–9*, 1937, texts by Brecht, Eisler and Silone), which show the simpler means and more traditional harmonies that Eisler was aiming for at the time, as well as the influence of Berlin cabaret music. Brecht's text are usually left-wing, some of them rather naïvely. The earliest collaborations between the two were *Das Massnahme* (1930) for tenor, three speakers, male chorus, small chorus and orchestra, and an adaptation of Gorki, *Die Mutter* (1931), both using tonal harmonies. The large-scale *Deutsche Sinfonie* (1935–39) for soloists, chorus and orchestra, is an attack on fascism, and *Swieyk im zweiten Weltkrieg* (1957), their last collaboration, contrasts Nazi leaders with the working class; true to the origins of the Czech satire that inspired Brecht's play, Eisler turns a quotation from Smetana into a political song. All these works were designed to use self-contained musical numbers; many of the songs and song-cycles, such as the gentle *Legend von der Enstehung des Buches* (verses by Brecht) display a wistful lyricism in addition to echoes of an earlier Berlin. In the same category belongs the beautiful little dramatic *Zuchthaus-Kantate* for soprano and chamber ensemble. Among his output are also a number of marching songs that became popular with socialist groups.

It is difficult to assess the value of the huge body of Eisler songs, as their usually socialist message has almost totally banished them from the Western concert platform and recording studio. Certainly those that have emerged show a sureness of touch and intent that suggest that many more may merit rediscovery.

RECOMMENDED WORKS
Deutsche Sinfonie
Duo (1924) for violin and cello
Kammerkantate No. 3 'Die römanische Kantate' (1937) for lower voice, 2 clarinets, viola and cello
Nonet No. 1 (1939)
Nonet No. 2 (1940–41)
Palmström (1926) for voice, flute, clarinet and strings
Piano Sonata No. 1 (1923)
Piano Sonata No. 3 (1943)
Violin Sonata (1937–38)
Vierzehn Arten den Regen zu beschreiben (1941) for six instruments
Zuchthaus-Kantate for soprano and instrumental ensemble

BIBLIOGRAPHY
H. Eisler, *Hanns Eisler, A Rebel in Music*, ed. M Grabs, 1978
A. Betz, *Hanns Eisler Political Musician*, 1982

Fortner Wolfgang*
born 12th October 1907 at Leipzig
died 5th August 1987 at Heidelberg

Wolfgang Fortner occupied a more important place in modern German music than his current reputation outside Germany would suggest. His influence as a teacher has been considerable, especially in the years following World War II at the Darmstadt summer school (Hans Werner **Henze** is his most distinguished pupil), and his compositions cover a broad span of mid-20th-century German musical thought.

His music before World War II was neo-classical in style, exemplified by a series of concertante works influenced by **Hindemith** and, in their rhythmic insistence, by **Stravinsky**. His preoccupation with polyphony followed German tradition, and throughout his output the inspiration of Bach was paramount, overtly in the neo-classical works and as a background in his later music. At the same time he continued the German Lutheran tradition of writing religious works, which are an important part of his output. After 1945 he was exposed to the developments of the Second Viennese School (suppressed in Germany by the Nazis), and they attracted his natural propensity for intellectual technical means. After a freely atonal period, in which the *Symphony* (1947) was an important landmark in post-war German music, he developed an individual use of 12-note technique in which he created 'modes' from the 12-tone row that could be subjected to non-serial manipulation. These first appeared in the *String Quartet No. 3* (1948), and led to his most internationally celebrated work, the opera *Die Bluthochzeit* (*Blood Wedding*, 1957), based on Lorca's play. This dramatic opera, closely following Lorca's text, contrasts the influence of Spanish folk music with 12-tone ideas, and includes spoken dialogue. The story revolves around a family feud; a young bride runs away with a rival on her wedding day and both her lover and fiancé are killed in an ensuing fight; her mother remembers how her husband and father had also been killed by an earlier generation of the fiancé's family. Fortner returned to Lorca in the chamber opera *In seinem Garten liebt Don Perlimplin Berlisa* (1962, usually known as *Don Perlimplin*), which combines magical elements with the comic and the grotesque, in following the age old theme of January marrying May, with betrayal by the young woman, though here the old man kills himself to present to her his soul. An initial 12-note series provides the base material for each of the four scenes. His most ambitious opera was a large-scale depiction of the struggles between Elizabeth I and Mary Queen of Scots, *Elisabeth Tudor* (1972).

Religious subjects occupied an important place in Fortner's output. The dramatic *Isaaks Opferung* (*The Sacrifice of Isaac*, 1952) for three soloists and 40 instruments includes jazz influences in the brass writing. His major religious work is *Die Pfingstgeschichte nach Lukas* (*The Gospel according to Luke*, 1963), a stern, dark work for tenor, chorus, chamber orchestra and organ, in which the choral writing reflects the avant-garde developments of its time. The impression is that of an intense sincerity, the overall effect curiously unmemorable.

Fortner founded the Heidelberg Chamber Orchestra (1935) and the Musica Viva concerts in Heidelberg (1947), and directed the Munich Musica Viva concert series from 1964. He taught theory at the Heidelberg Institute of Church Music, composition at Darmstadt, and was professor at

the North-Western German Music Academy (1954–57) and at the Freiburg Musikhochschule (1957–72).

RECOMMENDED WORKS
  opera *Blood Wedding* (1957)
  opera *In seinem Garten liebt Don Perlimplin Berlisa* (1962)

BIBLIOGRAPHY
  ed. H. Lindlar, *Wolfgang Fortner*, 1960 (in German)

Hartmann Karl Amadeus**
born 2nd August 1905 at Munich
died 5th December 1963 at Munich

Hartmann is primarily remembered as the main German representative of that generation of symphonists who were influenced by the neo-classicists, maintained the symphonic tradition through the rigour of their formal procedures (often influenced by **Hindemith**), and yet were ultimately more concerned with the expressive content of their symphonies than the means which propelled them; **Rosenberg** in Sweden and **Piston** in the USA, to name but two, belong to this movement that married the neo-classical and the Romantic heritages.

Hartmann disowned all the works he had written prior to studying with **Webern** (1941–42), though some of it reappeared after World War II, usually in revised form. His music, however, is far from the style of the 12-tone composers, and his symphonic origins have something of the Romantic fervour and breadth of **Mahler**, the procedural rigour of Reger and **Hindemith**, and sometimes an expressive acidity that recalls **Berg** and **Bartók**. He thus followed a particular German symphonic tradition, to which he added his own vigorous and intense voice. Formally, he employed a number of favourite devices, including combining variation form and the fugue (successive fugues are variations of the first), mirror forms (the inversions or retrogrades of theme, a central device of **Webern**), and the 'variable metres' devised by **Blacher**. These all give his music a sense of ordered, rugged formality. His harmonic style is essentially traditional, though considerably extended beyond formal tonality, and his rhythms are vigorous, usually intensely purposeful, and sometimes complex, including polyrhythmic passages.

The core of Hartmann's output is eight symphonies, and their relative obscurity is completely inexplicable. For as a cycle they are one of the most assured of the 20th century, consistently interesting in formal structure and powerful and often complex in their emotions. Their lack of instantly identifiable popular features (such as the scherzos of **Shostakovich,** or the haunting soundscapes of **Vaughan Williams**) may limit their general appeal, but they should be much wider known by informed and knowledgeable audiences. Their general characteristics are a nervous energy, memorable and vivid orchestral colours, with masterful use of piano, tuned percussion and brass, and the use of Classical formal structures such as the ricercare, passacaglia, and especially fugues. The emotional range is wide, though inclining to the melancholic and the turbulent, and while there are many passages of great atmospheric beauty, Romantic lyricism and lyrical melodic lines are avoided. There is a basic duality between these turbulent emotions and their containment in stricter procedures based on Classical or Baroque models; the former are often found in more vertical writing, the latter in a purposeful horizontal drive. This duality is often expressed in contrasting movements, especially in the symphonies with a two-part structure.

The *Symphony No. 1* (1935–36, revised 1947–48) for alto and orchestra is based on poems by Walt Whitman (sung in German), and was subtitled 'Study for a Requiem'. It is in five movements, the second of which is a setting of the famous 'When Lilacs in the Dooryard Bloom'd', later set by **Hindemith** (among others). The opening, with the colours of timpani, brass, harp, followed by the entry of the vocalist, is savagely exciting, tension maintained through dense and arresting orchestral writing. Its sweep of Expressionist emotions, and flow of sometimes violent contrasts, has its closest parallel in the orchestral writing of **Berg**; like the Austrian's music, this moving and consistently fascinating symphony provides a link between the late Romantic song-cycles of **Mahler** and later mainstream European writing.

The *Symphony No. 2* (1946) is a single-movement adagio, cast in the form of variations with an arch structure. It builds from solo lines contrasted with denser material, the similarity to **Shostakovich** probably deriving from the common influence of **Hindemith.** The denser material is richly exotic, with the luxuriance of the central climax evolving into a much grittier utterance, as if remembering the war

that had just ended. The *Symphony No. 3* (1948–49) draws on material from two earlier unnumbered and withdrawn symphonies, the *Sinfonia tragica* (1940) and the symphony *Klagegesang* (1944). Written in two movements, it has a major change of mood in the first, resulting in two distinct sections. After the opening, where a solo double-bass slowly unfolds a lament over timpani, the first half of the first movement is for strings alone. A sparse landscape of ethereal lamentation is slowly drawn, an equivalent to the contemporary epilogue to **Vaughan Williams's** *Symphony No. 6*, if not as intense. Into this bursts a bold, aggressive counter-mood, propelled by timpani, evolving into an energetic fugue, and eventually arriving at an exotic section of tuned percussion, momentarily halting the flow before letting it resume, its colours affected by the interruption. The second movement opens with a funeral march, leading to a turbulent climax of triumph and hope whose energy is dissipated around the orchestra. The work's close is one of ghostly beauty, the rhythm of the timpani at the opening symphony now transferred to the wood-block.

The tendency towards tonality emphasised by contrapuntal flow that had gradually emerged in the preceding symphonies became more overt in the *Symphony No. 4* (1946–47) for strings alone, though the melodic material still has an angular or modal cast. It has a very beautiful and atmospheric first movement, opening with a firm theme contrasted with distant atmospheric colour that combines melancholy with ecstasy. The second movement is the culmination of Hartmann's neo-classical leanings, contrasting in style with the first movement while maintaining its colours. The *Symphony No. 5* (1950) shows a very different side to Hartmann's temperament. It is aptly subtitled 'Symphonie concertante for orchestra'. It was a second rewrite of a trumpet concertino (*c.* 1933) and was intended as a homage (sometimes tongue in cheek) to **Stravinsky**. Gone are the dense textures and atmospheric writing. In their place is a bouncing, dance-like idiom, with thinner orchestration, prominent trumpet, a homage to the *Rite of Spring* in the second movement, and a roisterous ending. The reference to the bassoon melody of the *Rite of Spring* had special significance for Hartmann, as he also used it to open the piano sonata *27 April 1945* (1945), describing the prisoners leaving Dachau concentration camp.

With the *Symphony No. 6* (1951–53),

Hartmann reverted to a larger orchestra and denser textures, with few neo-classical traces. Each of the two movements attempts to resolve the agitation of its opening. In the first the energy of the muted drama, with unusual colours, dense textures, and swirling ideas, reaches a tormented climax before emerging into a more serene contemplation. In the second, the turbulent opening resolves into a complex but potent structure combining the fugue variation form; three fugues are used, the second two varying the theme of the first. The result is music with an urgency of momentum and expression.

The *Symphony No. 7* (1956–58) is ostensibly in two parts, but the division of the second into an adagio and a finale creates a three-movement work. The first uses complex alternations of fugues, concerto episodes and codas, and ends in a motoric fashion. The adagio is built in an arch, troubled and angry, and the finale is a headlong drive led by the strings. The *Symphony No. 8* (1960–62) carries the inscription 'per aspera ad astra' ('through hope to the stars'), and is in two linked parts. The first is more personal and intimate in character, the customary drive fragmented, but coloured by solo melodic ideas and featuring high percussion, suggesting a return to the idiom of the first symphony. The second creates a kind of clockwork world of precise movement, as if a Baroque concerto grosso had been turned into an inexorable machine; this suddenly emerges into a short coda, promising glimpses of the stars, if no more.

The entire series of Hartmann symphonies is unquestionably the major German contribution to the genre in the 20th century, and they transcribe a kind of arch, with the most lucid and straightforward symphonies at its centre, and the emotionally most complex at the beginning and the end. Those who enjoy **Berg** might try the first and last as an introduction to these symphonies; those who respond to the later **Shostakovich** might consider the third or the fourth.

Of Hartmann's four concertos, the best known is the *Concerto funebre* (1939, revised 1959) for violin and string orchestra. Its dark hues match its title, opening with a beautiful and dolorous lament that favours the lowest registers of the solo instrument, then bringing heightened emotion by reaching up to the highest. Its suggestions of modal scales (it uses a Hussite chorale) and the song-like role for soloist, recall **Vaughan Williams** in a similar

mood. The counterbalancing second movement builds on vigorous contrapuntal writing in a more equal distribution of roles, and with a considerably more angular and chromatic cast to the ideas, before returning to the opening mood of the concerto. In contrast, the entertaining, jazz-influenced *Concerto for Winds, Piano and Percussion* (1956) has moments that almost seem to revert to the Berlin jazz of the 1930s.

Hartmann opposed the Nazi regime while remaining in Germany at great personal risk. He forbade public performance of his music in Nazi Germany and helped those in danger to escape. He studied with **Webern** from 1941–42 and in 1945 founded in Munich the important Musica Viva series of concerts concentrating on new music.

RECOMMENDED WORKS

> *Concerto funebre* (1939, revised 1959) for violin and string orchestra
> *Concerto for Piano, Winds and Percussion* (1956)
> complete symphonies (Nos 1–8) (1935–62)

Henze Hans Werner•••
born 1st July 1926 at Gütersloh

One of the most successful – and eclectic – German composers since World War II, Henze's rather isolated position as a composer who appeals to both a specialist and a more general audience has generated social and political rather than musical controversy. His large output has been based on three rather divergent strands. His first successes during the 1950s were with opera and stage works; then during the late 1960s and 1970s he developed an overtly left-wing stance in his more polemical works, especially after his stay in Cuba (1969–70); and throughout he has written purely abstract works, particularly symphonies, concertos, and chamber music. His idiom is a fusion of many different trends, especially neo-classicism, an easy-going and lyrical serialism, and jazz. It also reflects the duality of the German tradition of his country of origin, and the Italian landscape of his adopted home. The rather diffuse nature of his output, with its rapid changes of style, political stance, and the absence of any particular work of obvious repertoire popularity, has perhaps hindered an overall appreciation of his contribution.

In many ways Henze continues the

example of **Hindemith**, particularly in his predilection for the remoulding of classical forms, from the symphony and the sonata to the ricercare and chaconne, in his incorporation of older German musical traditions (renaissance music, cantatas), in his lyricism, and in his harmonic preferences, which are to marry the use of 12-tone series with a sense of tonality, although his works in the later 1970s are harmonically more acerbic. His harmonic concerns were heralded by the *Violin Concerto No. 1* (1947), whose opening melody uses a series against a related theme in a Lydian mode. Subsequent works have used series that allow tonal influences, following the example of **Berg**. His use of orchestral colour, and the importance of timbre, also recall **Hindemith**: when not writing for very large orchestras, Henze often prefers ensembles that include delicate instruments such as tuned percussion or the mandolin, the lute, or the harp, and especially the guitar, which has featured prominently in his work and which Henze sees as the 'echo-sounder of history'. Thus, for example, all of Orpheus's arias in the ballet *Orpheus* (1979) begin with the instrument.

Another trait has been the combination of genres within a single work. The early and rather gritty ballet *Apollo et Hyazinthus* (1948) combines elements of a concerto (for harpsichord) with voice setting (of Trakl verses) and a symphonic poem (for the instrumental forces of a string quartet and a wind quartet). Similarly, Henze has drawn on a very extensive canon of extra-musical inspirations, especially literary influences. In the vocal works, these range from Expressionists (Trakl), through classical poets (Virgil in *Muses of Sicily* for mixed chorus, wind band, two concertante pianos and timpani) to contemporary left-wing or revolutionary poets in his more political works. Literary influences also appear in non-vocal works, (such as the Shakespearean characters in the popular and expressive *Royal Winter Music I & II* for guitar (1975–76).

Throughout his career, Henze has written a series of symphonies, the earlier ones for small orchestral forces. Dissatisfied with the *Symphony No. 1* (1947), he rewrote it in a new version for chamber orchestra in 1963. Its opening slow movement has a gentle Italianate light, its modal harmonies reminiscent of **Respighi** or those of **Hartmann's** *Concerto funebre*. To these are added melodic lines and more emphatic moments tinged with angular ideas, culminating in an incisive and percussive final movement (with a piano prominent). The atmosphere remains descriptive throughout. The *Symphony No. 2* (1948), in three movements, continues this mood, the dark pines of Respighi's Appian Way transported to a more dissonant Teutonic destination. Direct contrapuntal writing emerges in the short, second movement, while the final adagio returns to a misty, half-light atmosphere, before building into a bolder climax (which uses the opening of the chorale 'How brightly shines the morning star').

The titles of the three movements of the *Symphony No.3* (1949) – 'Invocation of Apollo', 'Dithyramb' and 'Conjuring Dance' – suggest a more overtly Mediterranean focus, and a connection with dance that is obvious throughout the work. A mixture of chamber ideas concentrating on wind instruments (and including the colours of the saxophone) combine with much grander climactic gestures, in a musical idiom gradually becoming infiltrated by more modern ideas. None of these symphonies quite matches the grandeur of their intent, as if Henze had been reaching for a conception – the mixture of a web of sound on a Classical base – that did not match his musical persona. However, for anyone who has avoided the later Henze, they are an attractive semi-abstract introduction.

By the *Symphony No. 4* (1955) Henze had been influenced by post-**Schoenberg** ideas. Cast in a single movement in five sections, the material had originally appeared as the second act finale of the opera *König Hirsch*. In his revision of the opera, Henze reworked the vocal material into the orchestral weave to form the symphony. The scenario of the original, a conversation between the Stag-King and the forest and its inhabitants, gives a key to the web of descriptive and discursive sounds of the symphony. The *Symphony No. 5* (1962) is more purposeful than any of the earlier symphonies; its classical layout, with an opening sonata movement that contrasts an energetic brass theme with an introverted one, is taken up in the still Mediterranean slow movement. The *Symphony No. 6* (1969), is a radical departure from the progression of Henze's symphonies. It has an overtly political base, using the opening notes of a communist Vietnamese liberation song, a concept of light into darkness derived from the Cuban poet Miguel Barnet, and a quotation from Theodorakis's 'Hymn to Freedom'. Written for two chamber orchestras (with electric amplification), which have correspondences, instrumental associations and contrasts with each other (an idea pioneered by **Stockhausen**), it is in three parts played without a break. The first is based on sonata form, the second on a series of transformations, and the third a fugue with interludes. The rhythmic inspiration is from traditional Latin American music. Henze's idiom is on the one hand brutal, full of massive contrasts, on the other fascinated by the multiplicity of sounds (including varied percussion and banjo). It is the most difficult of Henze's symphonies to penetrate, but the contrasts of mood and orchestral colours make it both experimental and aurally interesting.

The very large *Symphony No. 7* (1983–84) is Henze's finest symphony, and perhaps his finest work. Commissioned for the 100th anniversary of the Berlin Philharmonic, who have had a long association with Henze's orchestral music, the impulse is less the tradition of the classical symphony than that of German Romantic symphonic expression, intentionally alluding to Wagner and **Mahler**. The orchestration incorporates a number of unusual instruments (including the heckelphone) designed to reinforce bass colours, and there is an unstated programme that the composer hopes audiences will guess through the emotional expression. The opening movement is a *tour de force* of motoric rhythms combined with a memorably bouncy verve that harks back to the example of **Hindemith**. Fluttering glissandi conjure up Henze's sense of Italian light, with thick textures in constant motion. The slow movement concentrates on dark string colours, again evoking a mysterious atmosphere of swirling mists, expanding to include brass in its colours. A third movement of driving purposefulness follows, still texturally composed of fragments launching off into different directions, like a churning star constantly emitting matter. It is counterpoised by a slow, complex, neo-Romantic finale – an exceptionally beautiful epilogue that seems to evoke the wonder of the night sky, before swelling in chromatic complexity to a large climax that dies away. Indeed, the entire symphony is a huge aural landscape of illumination and power, a sparkling web of subtle and dense orchestration always underpinned by an underlying energy and sense of purpose.

Henze has written a considerable number of concertante works. The *Piano Concerto No. 1* (1950) is imbued with the spirit of the dance that has so often emerged in his work. Typical of Henze's use of a combination of elements is the *Double Concerto* (1966) for oboe, harp and eighteen strings, which in a rather unsettled fashion uses 12-tone elements and an underlying lyrical flow in an 18th-century orchestral context. The *Piano Concerto No. 2* (1967) is a work huge in length and complex in conception, with one forty-five-minute movement divided into three main sections. The tone of the concerto is often rich and sensuous, its thick tapestry flecked with delicate colours. The piano is in intimate connection with the orchestra, sometimes as antagonists, sometimes as part of the fabric. There is a sombre side to this demanding but forceful work, exemplified in the opening and the dark core at the centre of the piece.

The *Violin Concerto No. 2* (1971) for violin, tape, voices and thirty-three instruments is intensely dramatic, with various independent textures including tape and fragments of Elizabethan and Romantic music – Henze perhaps attempting, in this convoluted work, to come closer to the sound world of the avant-garde. *The Miracle of the Rose* (1981) combines the concepts of a clarinet concerto, a suite of seven dances, and a tone poem (based on Genet). Of his purely orchestral works, *In memoriam: Die weisse Rose* (1965) for chamber orchestra is a commemoration of an anti-Nazi resistance movement, its double fugue inspired by Bach. *Barcarola* (1980) is an elegy on the death of **Dessau**, the Styx represented by the flow of the orchestra, Charon by fanfares. The *Requiem* is not a vocal-choral work, but a series of nine spiritual concertos influenced by the Baroque concept of the sacred concerto.

Henze's string quartets illustrate the developments of his style, and are the most abstract of his works: there is no quartet that represents his overtly political period. The four-movement *String Quartet No. 1* (1947) was heavily influenced, as Henze has acknowledged, by **Hindemith** and **Fortner** – a likeable, well-wrought but unremarkable work. The *String Quartet No. 2* (1952) is dense and rhythmically complex, reflecting Henze's discovery of 12-tone techniques. The next three string quartets are all memorial pieces. The *String Quartet No. 3* (1975) is cast in a single movement, with tense, eloquent counterpoint and a beautiful solo viola ending. In the *String Quartet No. 4* (1976) a different instrument takes the lead in each of the four movements in a work of dramatic intensity, whose adagio is based on a Byrd pavane, contrasted by haunting dissonances. The *String Quartet No. 5* (1977) is more introverted, but the three make up a group of powerful works, albeit among the most difficult of all Henze's works to assimilate. The intense emotions, the often rich sonorities and sometimes extraordinary string effects have an immediate impact; but the density of much of the language and the clearly personal nature of some of the expression require repeated listening and familiarity to be appeciated.

Much of Henze's output has been for voices. His oratorios follow the general outlines of his musical and political development. *Whispers from Heavenly Death* (1948) is a setting of Walt Whitman, for high voice and an instrumental ensemble that anticipates colours favoured by **Boulez** and his followers (trumpet, celesta, harp, cello, and tuned and small untuned percussion). Written as Henze was exploring 12-tone techniques, it sets a wide-ranging but flowing vocal line against delicate instrumental colours. The title of *Kammermusik* (1958, epilogue added 1963) for tenor, guitar and eight instruments recalls **Hindemith's** series of works of the same name; setting fragments of Hölderlin texts, it utilises long flowing vocal lines, with the guitar prominent against thick instrumental textures. The influence of Italian thought and landscape is evident in a series of shorter oratorios written in the early 1960s, with rapturous love as their basis. *Ariosi* (1963) is a five-movement work for soprano, solo violin and orchestra, setting verses by Tasso. The violin is itself a symbolic protagonist, and the soprano is silent in the second and fourth movements. The overall effect is of a sensuous ecstasy tempered by a sense of nostalgia. *Muses of Sicily* (1966) for chorus, two pianos, wind and timpani, was a deliberate attempt at a simpler language, revolving around obvious tonal centres, and using texts from Virgil's *Eclogues* that invoke the ordinary people of Sicily, their dances and their lives (the sound of bells is prominent); the last of three sections sets Silenus's famous tale of the Creation.

The almost operatic seventy-five-minute oratorio *Das Floss der Medusa* (*The Raft of Medusa*, 1968, text by Ernst Schnabel) belongs to Henze's political output; its first performance had to be cancelled due to a near riot. However, the allegorical nature of the text and its dramatic power extend beyond polemics. Based on a true story, it tells of the shipwreck of a French ship in 1816, the escape of the officers, nobility and priests on the life-boats, and the subsequent trials of the ordinary people, saving themselves on a large raft; fifteen out of 154 survived. The three main protagonists are Charon, a central role for a narrator, a mulatto on the raft, and Death (soprano). These provide a foreground to a large chorus, including children. The vocal lines are often declamatory, the chorus heavily textured and often ghostly (the dead singing lines from Dante), the orchestral colours dark. The work's revolutionary message is summarised in the lines 'But the men who did survive ... returned to the world again, eager to overthrow it.' Its serialist idiom, anguished and impassioned but often lyrical, is applied to the half-fantastical, half-real depiction of purely human suffering to give substance to the political message. On an equally large scale is *Voices* (1973) for two voices and fifteen instruments, in which Henze utilises many styles and idioms in the service of an expressive and eclectic series of texts, with the general theme of the political and social responsibility of the artist. The twenty-two songs include post-serial ideas, jazz, aleatoric elements, folk styles, and the German tradition of **Weill, Eisler** and **Dessau.** Tape is used, and only three of the songs use both solo voices. The instrumental scoring, drawn from the pool of fifteen players, is constantly changing for each song, providing a wide range of colour, and in one song the instrumentalists themselves are required to sing. Henze makes full use of the opportunities such diversity affords, providing cohesion through the common themes of the texts in one of Henze's most effective political scores.

Henze has perhaps reached the widest public with his operas, sufficient in number and quality to make him a leading 20th-century operatic composer. They cover widely diverse subjects. His first full-scale opera, *Boulevard Solitude* (1951), was based on the story of Manon (essentially following the sequence used by Puccini in *Manon Lescaut*, without the last act), updated to more modern times (it opens in a railway station). However, the surface gentility of Puccini's treatment is replaced by much more open passions and a more seamy world, including drugs and prostitution. The idiom mixes opera and ballet for a work whose pre-Romantic structure is a kind of suite, incorporating seven tableaux and five orchestral intermezzi, and using classical recitatives and arias. Its style is eclectic, often jazzy, but entirely based on a single 12-note series. His next full-length opera was similarly successful: *König Hirsch* (*King Stag*, 1952–55, revised as *Il re cervo*, or *The Errantries of Truth*, 1963) is based on the Gozzi tale of a king who takes the form of a stag, to a libretto by H. von Cramer. It moved away from strict 12-tone usage, and in its original version ran for over five hours. *Der Prinz von Homburg* (1958, libretto by Ingeborg Bachmann) emulated 19th-century Italian opera, especially Verdi. A second collaboration with Bachmann, *Der junge Lord* (*The Young Lord*, 1965) is an attack on the German bourgeoisie, but one whose humorous plot goes deeper than mere political satire, examining the nature of human illusions and disillusions. An eccentric Englishman stays in a small German town whose inhabitants fawn on him. He introduces his nephew, who eventually turns out to be an ape, to the consternation of the young woman who has fallen for him. The entertaining score encompasses a variety of associations, including Classical opera buffa, Straussian vocal lines, and Henze's lyrical idiom.

A collaboration with W. H. Auden and Chester Kallman, *Elegy for Young Lovers* (1959–61), is set in the Austrian Alps, a claustrophobic story of tense psychological relationships within a family torn between reality and pretence, and dominated by the figure of an elderly, world-famous poet. The libretto is stylised and stylish, and Henze responded with a score using chamber forces, assigning different instruments to each character. The success of this collaboration was exceeded in their next work, *The Bassarids* (1964–66), based on four episodes from Euripides' *The Bacchae*. The libretto is exceptional in terms of literary quality, dramatic power, and musical understanding. The main character is Pentheus, king of Thebes, beset by the arrival of Dionysus and his hold over the populace. The central theme is of the conflict between the intellect and the sensuously physical; the king is unable to find a balance, and is torn to pieces in a Bacchanalian rite. Continuing the exploration of forms that might be suited to modern opera, Henze employed a structure quite different from his earlier operas: a four-movement symphonic form in which the music and action flow continuously, and which takes full advantage of the opportunities that the libretto offered for scenes for multiple voices. The work's texture is often stark and brittle; the colours sometimes transparent and delicate. Underneath the largely lyrical vocal writing is a fluid, plastic orchestra, acting as the equivalent of a Greek chorus, sometimes crashing in, always imbued with rhythmic variety and flow, as if it was itself following a Bacchanalian dance. The result is a musical drama of singular power, doing what opera does best: presenting the psychology of archetypes and archetypal conflicts. The dance of the Maenads in the hunt for Pentheus at the end of the third movement has become celebrated for its frenzied power, and the opera closes with Pentheus's palace going up in flames as Dionysus triumphs.

Henze's next opera came from his most political period. *We Come to the River* (1974–76), described as 'actions for music', used an allegorical libretto by the English playwright Edward Bond, and is an anti-bourgeois and anti-militaristic work that did not have the success of his previous operas. Bond was also the librettist for *The English Cat* (1980–82), a political satire based on a Balzac short story. *Das verratene Meer* (1990) was unexpectedly based on a novel by a right-wing author, Yukio Mishima's *The Sailor Who Fell from Grace with the Sea*; its study of internal and torrid family tensions (including voyeurism and murder) was nevertheless well suited to Henze's idiom. It is constructed in a sequence of tableaux and orchestral interludes, richly scored, with a huge percussion section devoted to the expression of neurosis, and created a considerable impact on its première. Mention should be also made of two music-theatre works. *Moralities* (1967) is a set of very short and simple morality tales, designed for schools and colleges, with miniature arias, chorus sections, and roles for a speaker, and deliberately leaving any stage ideas to the performers. *El Cimarrón* (1969–70) for baritone, flute, guitar and percussion, is about a revolutionary Cuban fighter, and also includes an element of performer choice.

The position of Henze is difficult to assess. He has not led with innovation, but attempted a synthesis of a wide range of styles into a personal idiom, from the Renaissance to the avant-garde. His fertile musical imagination, his craftsmanship, and his prolificacy have assured him a widespread reputation. Against that, he is a composer whose music, though well known, is not instantly remembered; a kind of Telemann of the 20th century. His fecundity and his involvement in extreme left-wing politics in the late 1960s has perhaps masked the real impact of his best works, such as the *Symphony No. 7* and *The Bassarids*.

RECOMMENDED WORKS
opera *The Bassarids* (1964–65)
opera *Boulevard Solitude* (1951)
opera *Elegy for Young Lovers*
(1959–61)
oratorio *Das Floss der Medusa* (*The
Raft of Medusa*, 1968)
Royal Winter Music I & II (1975–76)
for guitar
Symphonies Nos 1–3 (1947, 1948, 1949)
Symphonies Nos 5–7 (1962, 1969,
1983–84)
String Quartets Nos 3–5 (1975, 1976,
1977)
Voices (1973) for two voices and
fifteen instruments

BIBLIOGRAPHY
H. W. Henze, *Music and Politics:
Collected Writings 1953–1981*,
trans. P Labanyi, 1982
E. Restagno, *Henze*, 1986 (in Italian)

Hindemith Paul***
born 16th November 1895 at Hanau
died 28th December 1963 at Frankfurt

Of all the major composers of the 20th century, Hindemith remains the most enigmatic: universally considered of major stature, of unquestionable musical integrity, and yet nowadays heard far less than his reputation would suggest, in spite of his prodigious output. A viola virtuoso who played with the Amar Quartet in the 1920s, famous for its contemporary performances, Hindemith pursued an active solo career (premièring, for example, the **Walton** *Viola Concerto*) and could play virtually every instrument he ever wrote for. His compositional art is on the one hand intellectually rigorous, and yet on the other often concerned with music for amateur players. It is founded on the reaction to the end of the Romantic period, and the problems presented to composers by the collapse of the Romantic aesthetic. He stands in contrast to the (earlier) Impressionist reaction, or the contemporary trends of the Second Viennese School. Essentially his is a neo-classical oeuvre, but one which presents a particularly German solution, and which especially embraces an individual approach to harmony. With its disavowal of sentimentality, it has often been referred to as 'humanist'. His output was very large, and to avoid confusion when identifying works it should be noted that Hindemith ceased assigning opus numbers once he had reached op. 50 (when he was 35).

Hindemith's music falls loosely into four overlapping periods that show more of an evolution than any sudden change. After abandoning youthful Romanticism, his earliest, dissonant works were influenced by **Stravinsky** and jazz. In the early 1920s he also adopted a neo-Baroque style characterised by compelling rhythmic drive, and still dissonant harmonies now created by the conjunction of linear lines of counterpoint. Such pieces were mostly written for chamber forces. By the beginning of the 1930s the acerbic harmonies had mellowed, with the development of Hindemith's particular harmonic theories, and the use of larger-scale forces. Finally, there was a general easing of the severer side of his idiom (particularly the driving rhythms), following his move to Switzerland in 1937, and to the USA in 1940, where he became a citizen in 1946. Throughout, the influence of Bach is present, in both the delight in technique (especially the panoply of linear counterpoint) and in the intellectual aesthetic. Hindemith's concept of harmony, developed and refined by the mid-1930s, allowed a freeing of the constraints of traditional tonality without losing the sense of tonality itself. It is based in part on the relationship between the overtones of different notes, and the result is a concern more with the tensions inherent within a chord, and thus a movement between different tensions, than the relation of tension and resolution between two or more different chords. The system, which allows a series of chordal relationships covering the whole chromatic scale (readers further interested in this system are advised to explore the *Ludus Tonalis*, discussed below), suits the linear counterpoint that is such a feature of Hindemith's writing, but has had little effect on subsequent music theory.

Throughout Hindemith's output a number of features remain consistent. His harmonic palette was founded on a desire to continue and develop the tonal tradition, rather than to construct an alternative; consequently there is always a tonal base or centre to his work, often moving underneath the surface, even in the more dissonant earlier works where the dissonance is used more for effect than for harmonic progression. In this pattern keys become diffused, and melodies sometimes have a modal cast, but the traditional triad remains a point of resolution and centre. Counterpoint remained the foundation of his art, which looks back to pre-Classical models while avoiding some of the sheer emotional effect achieved by those of his contemporaries less consistently dependent on counterpoint. His rhythms are often vital and driving, but usually serve the needs of propelling the counterpoint rather than becoming a motivating force in the construction. Perhaps the most interesting feature of his style is his sense of orchestration and instrumentation: he delighted in careful blending of instruments and their colours (sometimes creating unexpected combinations), and was more concerned with the texture than with the effect of individual colour or stark contrast. Middle voices, as opposed to extremes, are usually favoured, especially woodwind and the sound of the viola. The resulting sound does not have the startling impact of more contrasting or emphatic use of instruments, as was becoming common among his contemporaries, but is immensely satisfying.

Hindemith's early music is eclectic in influence, from Reger to **Strauss**, but developed into an anti-Romantic rebelliousness permeated by jazz. This reflection of the carefree nihilism of the Germany of the 1920s is clearly apparent in his earlier piano music, which combines Romantic echoes with a rather weighty sentiment leavened by strong jazz influences. The opera *Mörder, Hoffnung der Frauen* (*Murderer, Hope of Women*, 1919), sets a semi-intelligible, symbolic text by the painter Oskar Kokoschka on the relationship between the sexes. Taken literally (which was not intended), its message of woman achieving actuality only through men expressing their sexuality and turning away from the eternal, would be unacceptable today, which probably explains its virtual disappearance, in spite of its dramatic and immediate music. Similarly, the highly satirical opera *Das Nusch-Nuschi* (1920), to a libretto by Franz Blei, is intentionally irreverent, quoting from Wagner's *Tristan und Isolde* when the Burmese king (who judges a dance contest) realises that his four wives have been seduced by his favourite general.

The end of this apprenticeship of idiom came with two arresting string quartets, which combine that rebelliousness with pre-echoes of his mature style. Hindemith came to prominence with the *String Quartet No. 2*, op. 16 (1921), played at the Donaueschingen music festival, which specialised in contemporary chamber music and with which Hindemith had become closely associated. Its lively, thrusting first movement was seen at the time as almost primeval, while the magical effects and melodic counterpoint of the second

and the drama of the third movement of this arresting work foreshadow **Shostako-vich**. The atonal *String Quartet No. 3*, op 22 (1922) has a memorable slow movement, and overall stands between Expressionism and Hindemith's move towards neoclassicism.

The germinal work of his maturity is the extensive, sensitive and contemplative song-cycle *Das Marienleben*, op. 27 (1922–23, revised 1936–48 in a version many consider inferior to the original, and orchestrated 1938–59) for soprano and piano. The formal scheme of the four groups of songs, from the lyrical to the philosophical, reflects Baroque models. The preoccupation with linear counterpoint and repetitive patterns of rhythms is clear, while the harmonic patterns reflect the inner chordal tensions already outlined. The first series of works to reflect Hindemith's individual aesthetic is *Kammermusik* (*Chamber Music*, 1922–27), which consists of seven concertos for various chamber orchestra ensembles. In these he developed a neo-classical idiom that contrasted with the jazziness of the earlier rebellious works, and saw an anti-Romantic return to Classical models. The forms are neo-Baroque, and the use of the orchestra quite antithetical to any 19th-century model; the chamber orchestra is essentially a collection of soloists (even when there is an actual solo instrument). The strong sense of linear polyphony is another neo-Baroque element; it is the harmonies (tonal, but with strong dissonances set up by the polyphony) and the rhythmic impulse (driving the energy forward) that are individual and modern. These works breathe vitality, wit, the joy of pure construction, and combine them with energy, rather than any overt display of emotions or Romantic evocations. The ostinati, the bitonality and the tuned percussion of the lithe and supple *Kammermusik No. 1*, op. 24, No. 1 (1922) anticipate **Orff**, and still have echoes of the rebel in the closing whistle and the instruction that the performers were not to be seen from the audience. *Kammermusik No. 2*, op. 36, No. 1 (1924) is a linear piano concerto, with shades of Bach in the slow movement; *Kammermusik No. 3*, op. 36, No. 3 (1925), a cello concerto alternating *joie de vivre* with a grander forms of expression; and *Kammermusik No. 4*, op. 36, No. 3 (1925), a more declamatory violin concerto, whose use of drums was developed from jazz influences, and which includes a lovely and typically purposeful nocturne. The best known is *Kammermusik No. 5*, op. 36, No.

4 (1927), a viola concerto with a strong concertante spirit, which ends with a boisterous Bavarian dance parody. *Kammermusik No. 6*, op. 46, No. 1 (1927) is a viola d'amore concerto, unusual for its solo instrument, but less interesting than its predecessor. *Kammermusik No. 7*, op. 46, No. 2 (1927) is an organ concerto, its linear polyphony conspicuous. In all these works, Hindemith explores unusual forces, not for the effect of swathes of orchestral colour, but for the intrinsic qualities of colour peculiar to each instrument.

The considered instrumental combinations of the *Kammermusiks*, often notable for their clarity and sometimes consistency of timbre, are found throughout Hindemith's work. A similar neo-Baroque aesthetic underlies the *Concerto for Orchestra* (1925) and the opera *Cardillac* (1926), which combines an Expressionist plot with Baroque forms. The central character is a psychopathic goldsmith who prefers murdering his clients to parting with his creations; he is eventually lynched by a crowd outside the opera house. The delight in unusual but logical structure continued in the opera *Hin und zurück* (*There and Back*, 1927), where the action and the music of the second half mirrors in reverse that of the first. To a libretto by Marcellus Schiffer, this one-act 'sketch with music' revolves around the shooting of a woman when a letter, purported to be from her tailoress, seems to be from an illicit lover; the frenetic score, piano prominent, catches the absurdity of the story with a music-hall flavour. The culmination of Hindemith's sense of burlesque humour was the highly satirical, jazzy three-act opera *Neues vom Tage* (*News of the Day*, 1928–29), in which operatic conventions are reversed, so in place of a love-duet there is a hate-duet, and instead of a wedding a divorce. In the original version the heroine at one point sits naked in her bath surrounded by the hotel staff; the couple regret their divorce and want to reconcile, but the publicity surrounding their separation (including film offers) is so great that such an action is impossible. There is a fine suite from the opera.

Gradually Hindemith expanded his abstract conceptions (while usually maintaining chamber-sized forces), retaining his neo-classical approach and extending lyrical content, the harmonies often becoming more obviously consonant. The result was the three works that make up *Konzertmusik* (*Concerto Music*, 1930), the first of which is less a concerto than a divertimento for viola and orchestra. The

Konzertmusik, op. 49 (1930) for piano, brass and two harps and the *Konzertmusik*, op. 50 (1930) for strings and bass have two distinct movements that are themselves divided into contrasting sections. The former matches the brass to the more aggressive part of the piano's character, and the harps to the more reflective. The formality and grandeur of the *Konzertmusik* for strings and bass, with (until the close) opposing orchestral forces, reflects a larger conception, while Hindemith's vivaciousness emerged in the *Philharmonisches Konzert* (*Philharmonic Concerto*, 1932). *Der Schwanendreher* (*The Swan Catcher*, 1935) for viola and orchestra was based on traditional folk songs. Particularly beautiful (its modality sometimes similar to that of **Vaughan Williams**) is the *Trauermusik* (*Funeral Music*) for viola and strings, written in one night in 1936 at the request of the BBC on the death of George V. At the same time, Hindemith had not turned his back on experimentation. In 1935 he wrote one of the earliest works for an electronic instrument, *Langsames Stück und Rondo* for trautonium; initially haunting, and then cheekily bouncy, but throughout taking advantage of the resonant timbres and ethereal sonorities of the instrument.

Meanwhile, Hindemith had embarked on a different aspect of music-making: works for amateur performers, generally known as *Gebrauchsmusik* (literally 'utility-music'). These works range from *Lehrstück* for any combination of instrumentalists, with soloists, chorus, clowns and audience participation, and many works for piano and wind combinations, to cantatas and vocal works, as well as a musical play for children. Part of the impulse was to restore the place of the composer within the more ordinary activities of a society. The influence of such ideals was not immediately apparent in the next generation of composers, but it has lingered: minimalist composers Philip **Glass** and Steve **Reich**, leading their own instrumental ensembles, have returned to such a relationship with audiences, and a number of composers have more recently attempted music-theatre works that restore a kind of travelling-players relationship with the audience.

With the opera *Mathis der Maler* (*Mathis the Painter*, 1933–34), Hindemith created what many consider his masterpiece (it brought him to the attention of a much wider international public), and initiated a new direction in his work. Based on the life of the painter Mathis Grünewald, *Mathis der Maler* confronts an issue central to Hindemith's own artistic outlook and to the times in which it was written: should an artist continue his art in the face of human misery and upheaval? Inspired by Grünewald's famous altarpiece of the Crucifixion in Isenheim, the opera is set in 1525, the period of the Peasants' Revolt, with the painter caught up in the political violence of the times. The symphony *Mathis der Maler* (1934) is essentially a suite of three excepts from the opera, but it is an indication of the formal security of the opera that the symphony has genuine symphonic structure, with the first two movements in sonata form. Echoes of old German music are woven into a contrapuntal tapestry of vigour and dark-hued beauty, typically earnest in texture, powerful in effect. The juxtaposition of concentrated moods give a seriousness to a work which is perhaps the finest introduction to Hindemith's genius.

During the 1930s Hindemith developed his harmonic ideas in a number of influential publications; he came under attack from the Nazis, and emigrated to the United States in 1937. The most complex work of the period, and the summation of his harmonic ideas, is the extended piano work *Ludus Tonalis* (1942), which, although designed to illustrate his theories, is an extraordinary if severe *tour de force* of musical idea and pianistic expression through intellectual rigour. Framed by a prelude and a postlude that are mirrors of each other, the body of the work consists of twelve fascinating and never drily academic fugues, divided by eleven interludes that modulate the keys, arranged according to Hindemith's concept of the harmonic series.

In general Hindemith's later works are larger in scale and less uncompromising than those written before his emigration. Although they maintain a neo-classical sense of organisation and instrumentation, these works are more obviously tonal. At the same time, they perhaps have less character. They include a series of sixteen sonatas for solo instrument and piano (1935–55) and, starting with the best known, the *Violin Concerto*, eight concertos (1935–62). The outstanding works of this later period are all large in scale. The ballet *Nobilissima Visione* (1938), best known in its orchestral suite form, is one of Hindemith's most immediate scores, rich and sonorous, the mellower tones of

strings and brass opposed to high woodwind. The austerity and nobility of the *Symphony in E flat* (1940) give a wartime feel, with solid but limited orchestral colours, and large-scale dramatic effect. The equally often encountered *Symphonic Metamorphosis on Themes of Carl Maria Weber* (1943) never quite lives up to its aspirations as a concerto for orchestra. The requiem *When Lilacs Last in the Dooryard Bloom'd* (1945–46) for mezzo-soprano, baritone, chorus and orchestra is a lyrical and sometimes earnest setting of Whitman's valedictory poem, harking back to Bachian models. But the major work of his later years is the opera *Die Harmonie der Welt* (*The Harmony of the World*, 1956–57), conceived as early as 1930; the accompanying symphony, *Harmonie der Welt*, containing the final scene complete except for voices, was finished in 1951, and is much more likely to be encountered. The opera depicts the attempts of the astronomer Kepler to discover the music of the spheres, with an obvious relationship to Hindemith's own ideas.

Hindemith remains a difficult composer to assess. Those familiar with his later music will be surprised at the polish, humour and outrageousness of his earlier works, which, as much as those of **Weill**, reflect the atmosphere of the Berlin of the 1920s. Many of these early scores, especially the satirical operas, are worth exploring: their sense of fun completely belies Hindemith's reputation for dryness. His middle-period works, notably the series of chamber works and concertos, are consistently appealing, without the startling individuality of his major contemporaries but beautifully crafted. The later, post-war works are generally drier and less interesting for those starting to explore Hindemith's music. The three major operas, and the symphonies derived from two of them, remain the central works of his genius.

Hindemith was professor of composition at the Berlin Hochschule from 1927. He attempted to encourage musical knowledge and skills at a basic as well as virtuoso level (an approach now almost universally adopted). With these principles he organised systematic music activities in Turkey (1935 and 1936), from school teaching to symphony orchestras. He taught at Yale during his stay in the USA (1939–53), became an American citizen in 1945 and in 1953 settled in Switzerland. He was said to be one of the worst conductors of his own music.

RECOMMENDED WORKS
    opera *Cardillac* (1926)
    opera *Harmonie der Welt* (1956–57)
    sketch with music *Hin und zurück*
       (1927)
    series *Kammermusik* (1920–27) for
       various forces
    Ludus Tonalis (1942) for piano
    song-cycle *Das Marienleben* (1922–23)
       for soprano and piano
    opera *Mathis der Maler* (1932–34)
    String Quartet No. 2 (1921)
    String Quartet No. 3 (1922)
    *Symphonic Metamorphosis on
       Themes of Weber* (1944) for
       orchestra
    Symphony *Harmonie der Welt* (1951)
    Symphony *Mathis der Maler* (1934)
    Trauermusik (1936) for viola and
       strings

BIBLIOGRAPHY
    P. Hindemith, *Composer's World*, 1952
    *A Concentrated Course in Traditional
       Harmony* (2 vols), 1943, 1953
    The Craft of Musical Composition,
       1941
    Elementary Training for Musicians,
       1946
    I. Kemp, *Hindemith*, 1970
    G. Skelton, *Hindemith: The man and
       his music*, 1975

Killmayer Wilhelm *
born 21st August 1927 at Munich

Under the influence of his teacher Carl
Orff, Killmayer first came to notice with
the opera-ballet *La buffonata* (1959–60; he
himself was ballet conductor at the Bavarian State Opera from 1961 to 1965), and
then with light music-theatre pieces,
before adopting a quasi-serial idiom. By
the late 1960s he had developed a very
personal style, with works containing a
minimum of musical ideas that rely on the
contrasts of silence and rhythm. The music
is distantly grounded in models from older
music though totally assimilated into his
modern idiom.

The essential features of Killmayer's
spare style are the building of long strands
of ideas (usually in long unbroken
phrases); small orchestral forces with a
preference for a single instrument or
instruments of a similar colour playing at
any particular moment; a harmonic
emphasis on one particular note; and inter-
ruptions or dissonant climaxes contrasted
through the emphatic use of ostinati figures (derived from **Orff**) or a sudden

change of colour or timbre. This style
combines a purity with a sense of underlying tension, sometimes nervous in character, which is clearly meant to express
various states of the human soul. At times
the music is reduced to virtually nothing,
as in *The woods so' wilde* (1970) for chamber ensemble, where eventually a broken
chord on the guitar sounds like an intrusion on the simplest of musical ideas that
precede it. Sometimes an underlying drive
breaks out, as in the central section of the
Piano Quartet (1975). But in the three
symphonies there is a very effective
expressive power based on the careful
control of minimal material, though the
symphonic developments are more in the
nature of tone poems than symphonies.
The *Symphony No. 1 'Folgi' (Leaves,* 1968)
sets the style. A long tense sigh of high
strings is contrasted first with minimal
points of instrumental colour on woodwind
with Mahlerian references, and then, in a
slow progression, with darker sonorities
(mainly percussive). The construction is of
one long slow span lying over the three-
movement structure, with moments of
silence playing an important role. The
Symphony No. 2 'Ricordanze' (Memory,
1968–69) for thirteen instruments opens
with the emergence and fading of string
timbres on various held notes. The gradual
extension of this stillness into underlying
movement, eventually introducing harpsichord chords, becomes the expressive purpose of the work. It was followed by the
static *String Quartet* (1969). The *Symphony No. 3 'Menschen-Los' (Human Destiny,* 1972–73), longer and more clearly
symphonic, combines these elements of
stripped-down orchestral writing with
much more extrovert music that recalls
many past symphonic styles (again, especially **Mahler**). In the late 1970s Killmayer
produced a group of short tone poems that
extend this milieu, including *Überstehen
und Hoffen (Survival and Hope)* and *Im
'Freien (In the Open Air).* Quotations from
past music are more overt in the *Five
Romances for Violin and Piano 'Vanitas
Vanitatum',* the subtitle a reference to
Schumann, in a work of eclectic moods that
is intended to create a spiritual connection
with early German Romanticism.

The allusive nostalgia of Killmayer's
music can be irritating when not combined
with his innate sense of internal stillness
and movement (as in, for example, *Para-
dies,* 1972, for pianos). But with a harmonic
outlook firmly rooted in traditional tonality, it may attract as an unusual alternative to other trends, such as minimalism,

that have attempted a return to tonality. Killmayer has been professor of composition at the Staatliche Musikhochschule in Munich since 1974.

RECOMMENDED WORKS

Five Romances 'Vanitas Vanitatum' (1988) for violin and piano
Symphony No. 1 *Fogli* (1968)
Symphony No. 2 *Ricordanze* (1968–69)
Symphony No. 3 *Menschen-Los* (1972–73)
tone poem *Überstehen und Hoffen*

Orff Carl•••
born 10th July 1895 at Munich
died 29th March 1982 at Munich

The achievement of Carl Orff has been totally obscured by the phenomenal success of his cantata *Carmina Burana* (1935–36), one of the few serious pieces of classical music written since World War I to have achieved genuine popular appeal. Partly because of that very success, and partly because of its aesthetic and musical content, he has been vilified by critics and intellectual commentators. Yet his position in 20th-century music is slowly emerging in a different light. The success of his educational methods (the Orff Method, discussed below) has rarely been questioned. What is less acknowledged is his status as the father of 'minimalist' music. Many minimalist techniques – the predominance of ostinati and interweaving patterns, the use of tonal harmonic colours, the impulse of rhythm, the particular use of percussion or percussive effects, the exploration of the combination of dance or movement and music – owe their origins to Orff. Even less acknowledged is Orff's power as an opera composer, who forged the first genuinely new approach to the medium since **Berg** and **Weill**. The lack of good performing versions in English, combined with critical and musicological disapproval, has hampered their dissemination outside Germany. As audiences become increasingly familiar with minimalist operas, notably those of Philip **Glass**, it seems inevitable that there will be a renewed interest in Orff's operas, especially *Antigonae* (1947–48), whose impact, depth of emotion, intellectual integrity, and dramatic excitement have yet to be matched by any minimalist composer.

Orff's output, exclusively vocal after 1936, falls into three general areas. A number of works, mostly staged but including some choral pieces, explore various aspects of human life, from love and pleasure to elemental spiritual themes. Four of the 'operas' (*Der Mond, Die Kluge, Die Bernauerin* and *Astutuli*) are more in the nature of music-theatre works, drawing on a variety of popular idioms and including spoken dialogue; two religious music-theatre pieces have a similar folk base. Finally, there is a trilogy of operas based on Greek tragedies. Overall, these three areas have a common purpose and theme: the expression of the archetypal and elemental emotions of the human psyche, explored from a humanist and intentionally uncritical angle: consistently, Orff intends to release those emotions in his audience, not to persuade intellectually. Thus he draws on the heritage of Western art, seeking texts to match this vision: the choral works often use Latin or medieval sources; two of the music-theatre pieces are based on Grimm's folk tales, two on Bavarian stories; and the Greek tragedies are as archetypal as any source.

The foundation of Orff's style is movement; rhythm becomes the primary organisation of the music, usually through ostinato phrases. Tension and release are created less through harmonic resolution than by shifts in the underlying pulse, or stopping it completely before resuming it (a favourite device). If the origins of this are to be found in **Stravinsky**, Orff's development of a rhythmic base essentially pioneered a reversal of the usual methods of constructing music that has become assimilated only in the last two decades of the 20th century. The other elements of the music are designed to reinforce this primacy of rhythm. The changes in rhythm and pulse, or the juxtaposition of blocks of different movement, are heavily emphasised by the orchestration, so that whereas the rhythmic elements provide a linear flow, the changes of colour create a vertical expansion or contraction of the overall sound. The orchestrations are unusual, relying on instruments capable of percussive emphasis but a wide variety of colour, so that in many of Orff's works there is a huge battery of percussion, and usually more than one piano, used as tuned percussion. Orff was a master of such orchestration, and some of the resulting sonorities, often countered by bright single notes or small ostinato phrases, are remarkable. The role of harmony occupies a much reduced role in this scheme (analogous to the role of rhythm in pre-20th-century music), generally relying on the traditional triad, often moving in repeated small steps (such as major seconds) that reinforce the rhythm; consequently the dissonant moments become all the more marked. Vocal or melodic lines are long and flowing, often harking back to models of chant or more popular song, and sometimes emerge into beautiful and ecstatic free-flowing melodies where the rhythmic pulse is generally suspended.

This reversal of the more traditional construction of serious music has been one reason why critics have so little understood Orff's music. In fact, the interactions of movement in Orff's music (the primary elements) are often extremely complex and subtle, and the interactions of colour (the second element), sounding so spontaneous, are equally meticulously arranged. This sound world also interacts with the audience in a different manner to most other classical musics: its rhythmic elements elicit an earthy, non-cerebral response akin to ritual. Orff understood the importance of movement in this reaction, for it might be described as a body response, and is connected to the archetypal elements in his thinking. Again, such responses have been traditionally seen as belonging to 'primitive' or popular musics, but Orff allies them to intellectual concepts through the texts, which is why words are so important in his output. The necessity to the human psyche of such an integration between the elemental and the intellectual is a concept coming into the fore only at the close of the 20th century, in reaction to the suppression of the former; in this Orff was considerably ahead of his time. It is a concept to which audiences, until recently unaccustomed to such elemental music, easily respond, and it is no surprise that the area in which this cast of movement and rhythm was first generally accepted was in Orff's music for schools. In asking audiences to respond in such a way, Orff was close to the changed relationship between composer and audience that **Hindemith** had been attempting in the concept of *Gebrauchsmusik*.

Orff withdrew almost all his music that preceded the composition of *Carmina Burana*. A precocious composer (his first songs were published when he was 17), his earliest works were almost all songs or vocal music, influenced by **Debussy**; though in his first opera, *Gisei, das Opfer* op. 20 (1913), an emphasis on gradations of tonal colour was reportedly evident, with a very large percussion section for the time, including tuned, bright colours, such as the glockenspiel and glass harmonica. At this time he was influenced by **Strauss** and **Pfitzner**, especially the latter's opera *Palestrina*, and by Expressionist writing. By the time of the cantata *Des Turmes Auferstehung* (1920, never performed), Orff's orchestration had developed into the colours that were to become familiar in his mature works: strings, six each of flutes, oboes, and bassoons, four each of trumpets and trombones, percussion, four harps and four pianos. During the 1920s his work on children's music extended his experience with ostinato percussion effects and instruments. To this were added two major influences, that of folk stories, and especially the music of the early Baroque, represented by Monteverdi; Orff made performing versions of a number of his works. With practical experience writing incidental music for the theatre, these sources converged into a personal style, evident in the works immediately preceding *Carmina Burana*, and reaching its maturity in that work.

The immediate precursors of *Carmina Burana* were a series of short cantatas collected in two *Werkbücher* (*Workbooks*). The first (1929–30) consists of reworkings of songs to words by Werfel (originally written in 1920–21) into a set of three cantatas (*Veni creator spiritus, Der gute Mensch,* and *Fremde sind wir*) for chorus and instruments. The deliberate simplicity, sacrificing complexity for intensity, the ostinato rhythms, the echoes of plainchant in the melodic lines, and sense of ritual anticipate *Carmina Burana*. The orchestration of the first two cantatas (pianos and percussion) anticipates *Antigonae*; the first part of *Der Gute Mensch* (*The Noble Man*) is especially delightful. The second *Werkbuch* (1931) consists of two cantatas, of which the first remains unpublished. The second, *Vom Frühjar, Öltank und vom Fliegen* (*On Spring, Oiltank, and on Flying*) for chorus, three pianos and percussion, rather unexpectedly sets bitter texts by Brecht contrasting man's technological aspirations with Nature. The influence of ancient classical texts surfaced in *Catulli Carmina I & II* (1930 and 1931) for unaccompanied choir, the first discussed below under its revision and expansion of 1943.

Carmina Burana (1936) for soprano, tenor, baritone, chorus, children's chorus and orchestra, is a secular 'scenic cantata', most effective when staged. The texts, some in German and some in medieval Latin, are from a collection of 13th-century songs known as the 'Songs of Benediktbeuern' and associated with wandering monks called Goliards. These songs are concerned with love, drinking, joys and sorrows, often with religious references but far from reverent, as if Christianity had been merged with a Bacchanalian paganism. Orff's setting opens and closes with a Latin hymn of the wheel of fortune, the theme of the whole work; within this, the twenty-three songs are divided into three parts, the first 'On Spring', the second 'On the Green' concerned with dance and joy, the third 'The Court of Love', ending with the love story of Blanchefleur and Helen. The range of tone is considerable, from the driving force of the opening and closing chorus, through the haunting, disembodied song of the swan and the dancing orchestral pastoralism on the green, to the high, ecstatic love song at the end. The energy is earthy, the colours vivid, the primary emotions joy, a delight in the cornucopia of life.

The last vestiges of a Romantic idiom with large-scale orchestral effect linger in *Carmina Burana*, and were increasingly pared away in Orff's later works. He later made it the first part of a trilogy, *Trionfi*, of which the second part is *Catulli Carmina* (*The Songs of Catullus*, 1943), which, while not so immediate, is a more representative and a finer work. In an opening and closing frame, two choral groups, representing youth and age, backed by percussion and four pianos, argue about the importance of love. The main body of the work is a moral tale about love told by the old to the young: the songs of Catullus describing the love between Catullus and Lesbia, almost entirely sung by a cappella chorus but including some beautiful solo songs (it has been aptly described as almost a madrigal opera). At the end the young start up their driving rhythms again, totally ignoring the tale and its moral. Those used to *Carmina Burana* may be initially disappointed by its sparseness, but familiarity reveals a work more tautly laid out, more single-minded in its theme and message, and of considerable impact. The third work in the trilogy, *Trionfo di Afrodite* (*The Triumph of Aphrodite*, 1952), follows a wedding in which the couple give themselves to the laws of the goddess of sensual love. Using texts in the original languages by Sappho, Euripides and Catullus, it combines some of the more ascetic idiom of the Catullus songs with the richer colours of *Carmina Burana*. It is the most sensual and lyrical of Orff's works, with a kind of Mediterranean warmth: the rocking chorus of the 'Epitalamo', gradually building to a climax with the solo voice of Corifeo exclaiming over the chorus, is one of Orff's most alluring passages, leading into an ecstatic duet for the lovers, written high over a held note.

Orff's first two mature operas set allegorical fairy-tale subjects based on Grimm. *Der Mond* (*The Moon*, 1937–38, revised 1970) tells of a land without a moon; instead a soft globe was hung in a tree for night illumination. Four travellers took it, and lit their own land, but when one died, a quarter of the moon was cut out and laid in the grave with him. Eventually the whole moon was in the land of the dead, waking them up. They made such a noise, that it reached the heavens, and the moon was restored to the land of the living. In some aspects an obvious successor to *Carmina Burana*, it is his most lyrical opera, announcing from the very opening a melodic flow and a folk idiom, with elements drawn from such diverse sources as drinking songs and chorales. Dance rhythms inject virtually every moment with an earthy energy, but there is sophistication too in the flow, tension and release of rhythms.

Die Kluge (*The Clever Woman*, 1941–42) is in twelve scenes, using a stage divided into two sections that act in counterpoint, the first telling the story of the clever woman, the second a sub-plot involving three thieves. A peasant, now in a dungeon, had found a golden mortar, and was correctly advised by his clever daughter that he would be accused of stealing the pestle. The king, hearing of this, meets the daughter and marries her. Meanwhile, the thieves are joined by a man with a mule and a man with a donkey, who asks the king to rule that a new foal has to be his, since a mule cannot reproduce. The thieves so muddle up the facts that the king rules in the mule's favour, whereupon his wife shows her husband a moral trick to demonstrate his capriciousness, and is told to leave the next day, with just one favourite possession. She chooses to take the king, and the tale ends happily. It is a more grotesque work than *Der Mond*, in which percussion makes its appearance in blocks, with deliberately exotic quasi-eastern melodic ideas, especially beautiful towards the end. An indication of the universality of the story and the music has been its success in many different languages across the world.

Die Bernauerin (1947, revised 1956 and 1979–80) is based on a Bavarian ballad and adopts the same idiom as *Der Mond* and *Die Kluge*. In spite of some arresting passages, it is overall not as interesting as either, although the bareness of some of the writing, reducing colours to a minimum before expanding them, looks forward to *Antigonae*.

Antigonae (1949) is a setting (virtually word for word) of the Sophocles tragedy in a German translation by Hölderlin. In it Orff makes no attempt to use music to comment on the action, or to provide an additional emotional layer, as is customary in opera. Instead, the text is paramount; the music amplifies emotions of the words so that they are felt as well as understood. The effect is to dissolve the distancing effect that a conventional staging of the tragedy is inclined to create. The extraordinary orchestration, almost entirely a huge percussion section, including those capable of low sounds (large gongs, bass drum) and eight pianos, is designed to create a panoply of very particular colours and a large variety of timbres, while being capable of consistent rhythmic attack. The aim is to set the text as a kind of incantatory recitative that closely follows the rhythms and patterns of speech while formalizing them. This then widens, a lengthened syllable or small variations in pitch reflecting small changes of emotion, and then expanding considerably into rhythmic melody for the more heightened emotions. The basic rhythms of the words are underlined, expanded, or complemented by massed orchestral interjections. Typical of the technique is Antigonae's intensely dramatic solo in Scene IV, where declamatory vocal writing broadens into wide leaps, mostly accompanied by a muted tango rhythm but interrupted by dramatic interjections from the orchestra, resounding with lower reasonances and energised by cymbals and high bells. It is followed by a chorus where the subtlety of the changes in orchestral rhythm and colour is hardly noticed in the dramatic pulse, but is crucial to the overall effect. Sophocles's Greek chorus is treated as a chorus, but with a solo voice singing certain passages. The ending, to a relentless but warm-coloured ostinato that turns into a funeral drum, as Creon realises what he has done, is gripping in its anguish. If the idiom sometimes superficially resembles that of the **Stravinsky** of *Les Noces* or *Oedipus Rex*, its application is very different, its intent to draw in the audience rather than distance them. The closest parallels to this seminal 20th-century opera are those of Philip **Glass**; but *Antigonae*, with its consistently detailed and subtle movement of effect and its deep understanding of elemental human emotions, emerges as a much more sophisticated and powerful musical creation. It goes far in helping one understand exactly why the Greek tragedies were semi-sung to music. Orff subsequently added two more operas based on Greek tragedy to create a trilogy. *Oedipus der Tyrann* (*Oedipus the Tyrant*, 1959) follows a similar idiom to *Antigonae*, with brass fanfares adding a menacing element, but the musical content is yet further pared down. *Promtheus* (1969) takes this process a stage further: whereas *Antigonae* hovers on the edge of theatre-with-music while emerging triumphantly as an opera, *Prometheus* comes closer to drama with highly effective music.

Orff's last stage work took the most elemental subject of all: how the world began, and how it might end. Much of the impulse behind *De temporum fine comoedia* (1960–71, revised 1979), is gnostic: Lucifer is transformed back into an archangel, and the guilt that came from original sin disappears. The forces are large; the orchestra (a viola quartet, lower strings, woodwind brass, harps, three pianos, two organ, wind machine and various percussion) is augmented by tape. Besides nine Sibyls, nine Anchorites, and a Chorus Leader, there are two singing solo roles, and a speaker as Lucifer, with a boys' choir in addition to a main choir. The work, full of textual symbolism, is divided into three parts, 'The Sibyls' (for women's voices), 'The Anchorites' (for men's voices), and 'Dies Illa'. The first two often hark back to the spare idiom of *Catulli Carmina*, but it is the 'Dies Illa' that is the finest section of the work, using the full forces. It opens in an angry wasteland, with declamatory chorus and bare low percussion, when any sense of pitch is often lost. It ends with the appearance of Lucifer at the words 'Pater peccavi' ('Father, I have sinned'), a celestial choir sounding a perfect fifth as a symbol of purity, followed by hauntingly beautiful viola quartet, based on a Bach chorale, which reverts to its opening to symbolise the world turning full circle that pervades so much of Orff's thinking.

Orff's methods of teaching music in school were developed with Dorothee Günther at the Günther School of Music (founded 1924) and elaborated in the five-volume *Schulwerk* (1930–33). It starts in the first year of school; children are taught first the elements of rhythm using percussion instruments, and to express that rhythmic sense with their bodies. This is then applied to melody, including singing, with an element of improvisation and musical self-expression, and to the application of simple formal structures to those melodies. It has been very successful and widely adopted; it teaches children to live and breathe music, rather than to learn an external system. There is a large body of educational music by Orff following these principles; a good example of its more sophisticated school application is the delightful Christmas work *Weihnachtsgeschichte*, with text by Orff and very Orffian music by Gunild Keetman.

Orff was a pioneer; his small output is variable, but the major works, where all the elements of his art come together triumphantly, are extraordinarily powerful. An exceptionally private man, his concern with the expression of contemporary events and concerns was minimal (though the allegory in *Die Kluge* must have been dangerously close to subversion in Nazi Germany), but his understanding of elemental, archetypal human motivations remained paramount. His philosophy is inclined to be misunderstood on acquaintance with one or two works, but becomes clear when a larger number are known. He is a composer who, as minimalism is assimilated into the mainstream of modern composition, may prove far more seminal to the 20th century than his current position would suggest. Those who respond to *Carmina Burana* will need no encouragement to explore his music further, though later works are both intellectually and musically tougher. Those hostile to Orff's idiom might attempt to accept that the harmonies are predictable and straightforward, and instead listen for and analyse the marvellous webs that are the rhythmic constructions and the accompanying orchestral colours.

RECOMMENDED WORKS
opera *Antigonae* (1949)
secular staged cantata *Carmina Burana* (1936)
secular staged cantata *Catulli Carmina* (1943)
cantata *Der gute Mensch* (1930)
opera *Die Kluge* (1943)
opera *Der Mond* (1937–38), revised 1970)
opera *Oedipus der Tyrann* (1959)
staged cantata *De temporum fine comoedia* (1960–71, revised 1979)
secular staged cantata *Trionfo di Afrodite* (1952)

BIBLIOGRAPHY
A. Liess, *Carl Orff* (trans. A and H Parkin), 1966

Pfitzner Hans**
born 23rd April 1869 at Moscow
died 22nd May 1949 at Salzburg

Hans Pfitzner was a senior figure among those composers who continued to develop the late Romantic Germanic idiom well into the 20th century. While not achieving the same technical individuality or emotional depth as **Mahler** or **Strauss**, his is still a powerful voice, and with **Zemlinsky** and **Schoeck** he is the most important of the secondary composers working with the embers of Romanticism. That his music is not better known is due to two factors: the reaction against Romanticism that has prevailed until recently; and Pfitzner's German nationalism, evident in both World Wars, that has inextricably, though somewhat unfairly, associated his name with Nazism. In his lifetime he was famous as an exceptional conductor, following his motto of 'Werktreue', strict adherence to the score of the work he was conducting. He was also an accomplished piano accompanist. It is a measure of his musicality that once, when he was conducting Wagner's *Die Meistersinger*, he handed the baton to his young assistant Klemperer for the second act and himself replaced the sick Beckmesser on stage.

A paradox in Pfitzner's output is his interest in medieval thought and music: when he handles such material, it is not in the neo-classical or neo-madrigal idioms that were developing elsewhere, but strictly within the framework of his late Romantic style. Like Wagner, such concepts from the past were primarily material for his German nationalism. His major work is firmly set in the Renaissance period, and equally firmly employs all the techniques of post-Wagnerian opera. The mystical and massive opera *Palestrina* (1912–15) is one of those works that has gathered strong adherents while baffling or boring others. Huge in scale, daunting in the sheer enormity of its staging demands, its theme – powerfully and honestly argued, and influenced by Schopenhauer – is that of the creative artist in a materialist society, represented by the Italian Renaissance composer Palestrina (1525/6–94). Pfitzner, emphasising the influence of Wagner, subtitled the work a 'musical legend', 'legend' also being the generic word for the lives of saints. He himself wrote the libretto, itself of considerable merit, though the dramatic possibilities are curtailed by the absence of Palestrina himself in Act II, and each act is almost a complete work in itself. Leitmotifs are used for the major characters and for places and moods they are associated with, but more sparingly than in a Wagner opera. The influence of the music of Palestrina's era is principally in thematic ideas, with moments of deliberate pastiche woven into a Romantic musical fabric. Structurally, the outer two acts are concerned with Palestrina's personal drama, and his decision to write a polyphonic mass that would dissuade Church critics from banning polyphony, the central act nothing less than the Council of Trent, hotly debating those very issues. The long, inspired first act consists of extended outpourings of sublime music, visionary in appeal, rich in uplifting sonority, framing a central, impassioned argument between Palestrina and Cardinal Borromeo. In *Palestrina* Pfitzner's powers and depth of philosophical thought reached a creative plane he never otherwise matched. However limited its appeal, it remains one of the masterpieces of the 20th-century operatic repertoire.

Of his other operas, *Der arme Heinrich*, described as a 'music drama' (1891–93, libretto by the philosopher James Grun), is based on a medieval variant on the biblical Abraham and Isaac story but with the Germanic-Wagnerian theme of redemption by beauty and purity. Its hero is a knight whose mysterious sickness can only be cured by the sacrifice of a willing girl. The 14-year-old Agnes offers herself. As she is about to die a miracle occurs: the knight, Heinrich, recovers and prevents the death. The music is predominately meditative and slow moving, influenced by Wagner's *Parsifal*.

Die Rose vom Liebesgarten (*The Rose from the Garden of Love*, 1897–1901) is marred by its symbolist libretto (also written by James Grun), inspired by a painting. *Christelflein* (*The Little Christmas-Elf*, 1906), is, as its name indicates, a Christmas story.

It is Pfitzner's incidental or excerpted orchestral music that is most likely to be encountered in the concert hall. Chief among these are the preludes to the three acts of *Palestrina*, which stand magnificently on their own. The first, influenced by old church modes, has a drawn-out visionary beauty built on long string lines. The second is vitally exciting, the brass predominating, the strings looking back to

Wagner, the rhythmic counterpoint to **Hindemith**. The third combines both moods. The overture *Das Käthchen von Heilbronn* (1905) is a tone poem clearly influenced by **Strauss**, complete with a fanfare/bird-call passage that uncannily anticipates that in Strauss's *Die Frau ohne Schatten* (1919). Its long smooth melodies, usually constructed to avoid the chromaticism that permeates the rest of the scoring, are typical of Pfitzner. The *Blütenwunder* (*Miracle of the Blossoms*) from *Die Rose von Liebesgarten* is exceptionally beautiful, the musical palette dotted with fluttering colours behind string melodies. It has so many of the qualities of a standard orchestral encore work that it is surprising it is so little known. Of his other orchestral music, the *Symphony in C sharp minor* op. 36a (1932) is a reworking of the *String Quartet* No. 2. The late one-movement *Symphony in C* op. 46 (1940) is in the bright and optimistic key of C major. Attractively constructed, with late Romantic emotions subdued in favour of a Classical clarity of texture and line, the end result does not match its promise.

The *Violin Concerto in B minor*, op. 34 (1925) is the best known of Pfitzner's concertante works. Firmly cast in the Romantic tradition, the solo line is especially rhapsodic, and its melodic line harmonically straightforward. The atmosphere of the concerto is intimate. Violin and orchestra are treated as equals, the solo writing demanding purity of tone and timbre rather than obvious virtuoso display; indeed the soloist is silent in the atmospherically beautiful second of three linked movements. The late *Duo* op. 43, for violin, cello and orchestra, is a rhapsodic and lyrical single movement, richly textured and wistful in its interplay between the two soloists. It has something of the mood of **Strauss's** late works, but with sad rather than sublime introspective intensity, as do the *Five Piano Pieces* op. 47 (1941). The emphasis is still on melody, but with moments of complex chromatic interplay in the writing that look back to Brahms.

Songs form an important portion of Pfitzner's output. The early songs – the first seven sets were written by his early twenties – range from the lighthearted, almost populist ('Über ein Stüdlein' from *5 Lieder*, op. 11) to more intense works. The straightforward harmonies and plain textures throw the weight on the vocal line, and the emotion is confined to a narrow focus. These characteristics are essentially unchanged in subsequent works, where Eichendorff is often the preferred poet, the heart of the texts is worn on the sleeve, and the resultant feeling of simplicity has its own attractions. The conventional Romantic accompaniment against a slightly dissociated solo line that appears in the song-cycle *Sechs Liebeslieder*, op. 35 (1924, to verses by Huch) is converted into an unsettling and heavy chromaticism. The emotional intensity is heightened in such late songs as the gentle *Das Alter* of 1931, a contemplation of old age. The slow-moving, beautiful *An den Mond*, op. 18 (1906) for baritone and orchestra, on the other hand, epitomises German late Romanticism. For larger forces, *Von deutscher Seele*, op. 28 (*The German Soul*, 1921) for soloists, chorus, organ and orchestra, is one of Pfitzner's most expansive and effective works. Based on poems by Eichendorff, it is divided into three parts and includes four orchestral interludes that are tone poems in themselves. It is a work in the tradition of Brahms's *German Requiem*, with chorales a major element of the choral writing. The overall mood remains relatively sombre until the huge soaring finale.

Pfitzner wrote four string quartets, the first unnumbered. The *String Quartet No. 1 in D major*, op. 13 (1903) was admired by **Mahler** but now seems somewhat dry and long-winded. The austere *String Quartet No. 2*, op. 36 (1925) was reworked as the *Symphony in C sharp minor*, op. 36a. The late *Sextet in G minor*, op. 55 (1945) for clarinet, strings and piano, while retaining an idiom that recalls the first decade of the century, has a lightly spun lilt, a sense of the sophisticated salon, that makes it worth the occasional revival, especially as the sextet repertoire is limited.

Pfitzner was one of the first composers to record his own works on tape (the overture *Das Käthchen von Heilbronn*, recorded in Berlin in 1944). He was also a noted essayist and writer, defending his musical views with verve and conviction.

RECOMMENDED WORKS

Blütenwunder from the opera *Die Rose vom Liebesgarten* (1897–1900)
overture *Das Käthchen von Heilbronn* (1905)
opera *Palestrina* (1912–15)
Preludes to *Palestrina* (1912–15)
Violin Concerto, op. 34 (1925)
cantata *Von deutscher Seele*, op. 28 (1921)

BIBLIOGRAPHY
J. Müller-Blattau, *Hans Pfitzner*, Frankfurt, 1969 (in German)

Reimann Aribert*

born 4th March 1936 at Berlin

Aribert Reimann is as well known as an accompanist to many famous contemporary singers especially in 20th-century repertoire. As a composer, he achieved international prominence with the opera *Lear* (1978). Vocal works have dominated his output, although his canon includes two piano concertos.

Most of his works use sparse orchestration to achieve a clear texture, the earlier ones employing 12-tone or serial principles, which were soon joined by cluster and massed dissonant effects. Subjects chosen usually reflect some manifestation of the extremes of human character or behaviour, expressionistic or surrealistic, as in the nuns, the knights in armour, the Prussian grenadiers, and the World War II soldiers of the ballet *Vogelscheuchen* (*Scarecrows*, 1970, after Günter Grass). The sparse feel is evident in *Entführung* (1967) for tenor and piano, the piano often having a line of single notes, the solo line preferring lines of longer notes. In the *Concerto for Piano and Nineteen Players* (*Piano Concerto No. 2*, 1972) the textures are deliberately chosen to give a chamber feel, and the appearance of the alto flute adds an unexpected colour. Otherwise the work is infectious rather than individual, a loping torrent of serially organised notes from the piano, a bouncing sense of rhythmic impulse, and a deceptively careful structure, as if the various folds of an origami construct were lapping over each other from the **Messiaen**-like opening.

Reimann's first opera, *Ein Traumspiel* (*Dream Play*, 1963–1965, after Strindberg) uses 12-tone techniques and the contrast of slow massed chords against extreme sounds, often organised in traditional forms (such as the passacaglia), or (in a section for piano fugue with bongos) jazz-influenced. The vocal lines are wide-ranging, the characterisation extreme. His *Symphony* (1976) is based on material from the opera. His fourth opera, *Die Gespenstersonate* (*Ghost Sonata*, 1984), was also based on a Strindberg play. The atonal opera *Melusine* (1970) combined reality and fantasy in the story of a woman who is a woman for six days of the week, and a mermaid for the seventh. Spoken text is combined with aria and duets, with a vocally extreme and difficult title role for coloratura soprano. The orchestra is of chamber size, and clusters and static layers combine with atmospheric and nature effects.

Lear (1978), Reimann's third opera, is a powerful, dark and tortured operatic version of Shakespeare's play, using a German text. From the opening scene the atmosphere of Expressionist extremity is established. Lear and his court are on the edge of neurosis, a fact reflected in the vocal lines, in orchestral colours that combine brooding darkness with high effects that slice and cut (such as the extreme ranges of woodwind), and in the constantly dissonant, angry or unsettled harmonic combinations. The vocal lines predominate throughout the opera, their inflections following those of the spoken line, sometimes falling into near-speech, and regularly set in alternation with the orchestra, accompanied by silence, a held note, or subdued repeated patterns. The orchestra thus emerges as a kind of chorus, commentating on the vocal lines, and the effect is to recast the play as a huge Greek tragedy. All these techniques had already been developed by **Orff** in his operas based on actual Greek tragedies, and when Reimann uses pseudo-archaic melodies for the vocal lines the similarity to Orff, and the continuation of this particular branch of German opera, is clear. The major difference is that whereas Orff uses his orchestra in changing repeated patterns that remain wedded to traditional harmonic patterns, Reimann uses the full force of the Expressionist orchestral effect and line developed by **Berg**, while retaining the sense of inevitability of ritual. The primacy of the drama predominates; the musical and vocal material act as supporting elements to the presentation of characters *in extremis*. It is perhaps inevitable that only one side of Shakespeare's complex drama emerges, that of the dark human nature near madness. But as drama it is extremely powerful, with musical moments of huge force, especially when Reimann uses the orchestra as a giant aural landscape, and it has a compelling inevitability.

The hour-long *Requiem* (1982) for soloists, chorus and orchestra, includes dramatic passages which recall *Lear*. The text is drawn from the Latin Requiem mass, interleaved with quotations from the Book of Job that are sung in a number of languages (German, English, French, Hungarian, Latin, Greek and Hebrew) in an attempt to achieve a wider relevance. Intense and earnest, it is often a bullish

work, the darkness of the subject matter reflected in the typically unusual scoring, omitting higher strings and horns but adding lower woodwind. Using a wide range of contemporary effects, the idiom slides from the harshly atonal – used for dramatic effect, and always suggesting some distant goal of a key – through cluster effects (particularly in the choral writing) to the melancholically lyrical. A sense of space and airiness is created by the juxtaposition of unaccompanied voices (both choral and solo) with blocks of instrumental colour and idea, or accompanied passages. At times the shadow of **Britten's** *War Requiem* stands behind the writing (especially in the opening of 'Domine Jesu Christe', complete with prominent harp) but the overall effect is quite different from the earlier work. There is a feeling of dark, impassioned monastic ritual, of a Gregorian chant reconstituted. Its sincerity is undoubted, and some of its dramatic effects and moments of light are compelling, with long, high, floating solo lines. But overall it lacks the variety of character and emotion to sustain such a long work.

RECOMMENDED WORKS
  opera *Lear* (1978)
  Requiem (1982)
  Concerto for Piano and Nineteen
    Players (1972)

Rihm Wolfgang Michael*
born 13th March, 1952 at Karlsruhe

Wolfgang Rihm has attracted considerable attention as a post-avant-garde composer who continues the Expressionist inheritance of earlier German composers, combining it with more recent techniques. His orchestral works include the *Symphony No. 3* (1977), which uses texts by Nietzsche and Rimbaud, but it is the forms of the opera and the string quartet, of which he has now written eight, that have dominated his output. His best-known work is probably his second chamber opera, *Jakob Lenz* (1978), to a libretto by Michael Fröling based on a fragment by Büchner that tells the story of the madness and death of the late 18th-century poet Jakob Lenz. The dark, starkly Expressionist opera contains twelve scenes, the poet eventually coming across the corpse of a young woman, which in his madness he thinks is the body of his lost beloved that he has killed. He ends up in a strait-jacket in a mental asylum. Throughout, he hears voices represented by a sextet of solo voices and a boys' choir; harpsichord and percussion play a prominent part in the instrumental forces. It is a harrowing but powerful work, the eclecticism of the style (ranging from the violently dissonant to the tonal) designed to represent the extremes of mental confusion and anguish. Among Rihm's more recent operas have been *Hamlet-maschine* (1986) and *Oedipus* (1987). The *Conquest of Mexico, (Die Eroberung von Mexiko,* 1992) is based on Antonin Artaud's theatrical outlines, old Mexican texts, and the writings of Octavio Paz; it concerns the arrival of Cortez in Montezuma's court. The central opposition is between the static contemplation of the indigenous Indians and the dynamism of the Christians; Montezuma himself is afflicted by this duality, and splits into a male and female role. It is a strongly ritualistic work, the music for the natives primitive, that for the unfolding story bleakly Expressionist. The instrumental writing is often spare in the extreme, otherwise using blocks of sound or colour, but there are powerful and, in the end, lyrical moments. A number of Rihm's other vocal works set texts by mentally disturbed authors.

Rihm has taught at the Karlsruhe Musikhochschule since 1973.

RECOMMENDED WORKS

opera *The Conquest of Mexico* (1992)
opera *Jacob Lenz* (1978)

Schnebel Dieter*
born 14th March, 1930 at Lahr, Baden

Dieter Schnebel has combined the unusual callings of religion and avant-garde composer (he was a minister in Kaiserslautern, 1955–63, and has taught religious studies in Frankfurt, 1963–70, and since 1970 in Munich). He belongs to that generation of composers who took up the serial developments of **Stockhausen** and explored their potentialities, but in the 1970s completely changed his style into one of the most effective examples of neo-Romanticism.

Deuteronomium 31,6 (1956–58, the formal title is *dt 316*) for twelve or more unaccompanied singers, was one of the earliest works to explore the possibilities of phonemes, and is the first of a cycle of three sacred works. The text – in various translations as well as the original Hebrew – is deconstructed into phonemes, and these are rearranged to form musical chains of verbal sound. To match this,

musical events overlap each other in layered succession, emphasised by spatial distancing of the voices, by the addition of speech, hissing and clicking elements which give timbral variety, and by vocal lines being stretched into unusual regions – all typical of the choral techniques being explored during the late 1950s and 1960s. The interest in the verbal was extended in a number of works, including *Glossolalie (Speaking with Tongues, 1959–60)* for speakers and instrumentalists, written on twenty-six pages and playable in almost any form. Snatches of words or phonemes are predominant; the composer's own realisation includes instrumental gleanings from well-known works, and is a montage of verbal sounds and events worthy of Babel.

After a number of such works in the avant-garde period of the 1960s, Schnebel started a series of works under the general title *Bearbeitungen (Arrangements),* in which he sifted through music of older composers, including Bach, Weber, Beethoven, and Wagner. The best of these works assimilating the past is perhaps the *Schubert-Phantasie* (1978) for orchestra. The basic material is from the first movement of Schubert's *Piano Sonata in G major,* D894, but the filtering of this material is far from the fragmentary, mosaic structures of the avant-garde 1960s. Instead the basis is a massive timbral layering of sound, based on the darker colours of strings, moving like the waters of the deep, out of which swell changes and larger waves, sliding back into the surface. This accumulation of layers, as uncertain of its direction as an ocean, starts to reshape itself into a cast that is unmistakably Mahlerian, building up in small accretions, eventually reaching a massive sonorous climax before subsiding. The effect is to draw a continuum between the Vienna of Schubert, the Vienna of **Mahler**, and today, and in a musical soundscape to present the indivisibility of the past in the present.

In a counter-series, *Tradition,* Schnebel's intention is the reverse: to filter the sounds of contemporary composition through the forms of the past. Thus *In motu proprio* (1975) and *Diapason* (1976–77), both for chamber ensemble, are both canons, though the thinness of textures, the sparseness of idiom, and the fragmentary nature of the material of the former bring it closer to the invective of the 1960s avant-garde than the sumptuous dream-world of the *Schubert-Phantasie. Diapason,* within a similar framework, has more obvious references to the techniques of the past, as well as an eerie, neo-Impressionist section, but the enfolding of historical continuity remains most powerful in the *Schubert-Phantasie*, which should be sought out by anyone interested in contemporary music.

RECOMMENDED WORKS
> *Schubert-Phantasie* (1978) for
> orchestra
> *Diapason* (1976–77) (*Tradition* I, No.
> 2) for chamber ensemble

Stockhausen Karlheinz***
born 22nd August 1928 at Mödrath
(Cologne)

Perhaps no composer in the second half of the 20th century has inspired such anger and bewilderment in those unfamiliar with new music as Stockhausen, unless it be John **Cage**. By the same token, perhaps no other composer has been so influential in the development of new musical ideas in Europe in the 1950s and 1960s, analogous to the dominance of **Cage** in the United States. His position in the 20th century has been compared to that of Wagner in the 19th, and there is some of validity in this comparison. As with Wagner, once the unaccustomed and novel languages that Stockhausen employs become more understood, the eminence of his position is fully justified.

His musical maturity dates from his discovery in 1951 of the potential for serialism opened up by **Messiaen**, and his subsequent studies with the French composer. The essence of such serialism, sometimes known as 'total serialism', is that not only could the pitches of the notes be organised along rational, preordained structural lines or systems – as established by the 12-tone composers – but also that the other parameters of music, rhythm, duration, timbre, dynamics, could be subjected to similar procedures, thus creating a total cerebral control over the material. Fellow composers such as **Boulez** and **Nono**, mostly associated with Stockhausen through the summer courses at Darmstadt, were following similar directions.

What distinguished Stockhausen were two things. First, he realised that such serial developments had much more potential than the mere structured organisation of musical parameters. They could allow music to break away from the traditional means of taking music from the written page and bringing it to life, such as the symphony orchestra or the human voice,

either by inventing totally new media, or by extending the traditional parameters of such bodies out of recognition. Such ideas had often been mooted or attempted, but threatened to disintegrate into chaos because the forms had not been developed to contain them; total serialism provided such forms, by relating each element to rational rules and structures. Eventually such new musical sounds became established in themselves, and no longer needed the formal structures of serialism to maintain them. That process, in which Stockhausen himself has had a hand, is still too young and too little assimilated to be evaluated. Conversely, these new musical carriers could free serialism from being another method of arranging traditional musical ideas, and extend it into genuinely new musical horizons. Of course, other composers came to similar conclusions, but Stockhausen's extraordinarily fertile and energetic imagination was capable of seizing on and exploiting a wide range of such possibilities, pioneering many of them in the process, whereas many of his fellow composers were content to use inherited traditional means to express their serialism, or concentrated on one branch of the new media.

The second factor has been Stockhausen's single-minded concentration on the structures that contain his music, rather than the details of the music contained within them. The conception and the comprehensiveness of the former must be complete before the latter are tackled. This is the antithesis of the concept of organic growth, in which the outlines of the overall form are partly determined by the growth of the internal musical ideas. However contained, it is such linear organic growth that listeners are most used to in our Western tradition, and whose apparent absence in much avant-garde music can be so disconcerting to newcomers. Thus those coming to Stockhausen's music for the first time will derive real benefit and considerably more understanding and pleasure if they can grasp the overall structures and principles of one of his pieces first, before listening to the realisation. This is the reason that so much modern music is accompanied by detailed programme or sleeve notes. Unfortunately, they are often couched in such perverse, obscure and complex terms as to be rendered meaningless, but it is still worth searching out or demanding good ones. Stockhausen's own are often models of lucidity, unlike some of his other pronouncements.

Of course, this does not mean that Stockhausen is unconcerned with the internal details of his works – far from it, for he can be a meticulous craftsman – only that they are a secondary process, and indeed, have often been left to the performers, to chance, or to completion by others. His imagination prefers the broader implication, and in recent years has developed a huge spiritual dimension, that had indeed always been a factor in his music. Since the mid-1970s he has concentrated on a gigantic cycle of seven operas or musical ceremonies designed to coalesce mythologies and ideas from all over the world in one super-synthesis, and to utilise all the different musical innovations and experiences that Stockhausen had developed over his previous musical career. In such a combination of all-embracing vision and the implant of new musical ideas, the comparison with Wagner is most apt. No other contemporary composer has had such breadth and single-mindedness.

After *Kreuzspiel (Crossplay*, 1951) for piano, oboe, bass clarinet and three percussionists, in which Stockhausen applied serial methods to duration as well as pitch, the work that firmly established a new voice was *Kontra-Punkte* (1952, revised 1962–66) for ten instruments. This utilised **Webern's** conception of what became known as 'pointillism', the importance of each and every note. It was followed by a series of influential piano pieces, *Klavierstücke* I–X, 1952–55, IX and X, revised 1961, that continued the exploration of serial possibilities. *Klavierstücke* XI (1956) extended these developments beyond the traditional parameters of the instrument, along the lines Stockhausen was simultaneously exploring elsewhere. It is made of nineteen written fragments. In addition, there are six different tempi, dynamics, and types of pianistic touch available to the performer, who can make his or her own choice. The pianist also chooses which order to play the fragments. When any one fragment has been repeated three times, the piece ends. This process exactly describes Stockhausen's concern with the precise parameters of the overall structure and his willingness to allow musical events to have more freedom (and the performer to have a larger role in the execution of a piece) within those parameters. In addition, the piece is available in the form of a roll packed in a cardboard carton, in the form of a piece of board, or as a roll complete with a little wooden stand to put on the piano.

The influential *Zeitmasze (Tempi,*

1955–56) for five woodwind instruments makes use of the excellent expedient of writing out all accidentals as sharp signs, and not using naturals or flats, which performers have found much easier to read in such complex music. The score is a serial extension of **Webern**, but the chief innovation is the freedom of rhythmic impulse. Some sections use traditional pulse and bar lines as points of reference, but others go completely beyond these bounds. Almost every note carries its own dynamic marking; at times the different instruments play at different metronome markings. The effect is fascinating, but potential listeners should be warned that (unlike most of Stockhausen's later works), familiarity with the 12-tone sound pioneered by **Webern** is really essential before listening to *Zeitmasze.*

The opposite of allowing performer freedom is the complete control by the composer of every aspect of a performance. *Zeitmasze* was one way of achieving this. However, Stockhausen found more fertile directions in the new medium of electronic music, where every parameter is controlled by the creator and not left to the caprice of a performer. He started working with electronic equipment in 1953 (*Studien I* and *II*), and with such means started to achieve another musical ambition. The realisation of traditional music has involved one area of sound source (the concert platform), albeit a broad one in the case of a symphony orchestra. Attempts had been made to free that constriction in the past but nothing on the scale that Stockhausen envisaged. If pitch, duration and dynamics could be organised by rational rules and patterns, then so could the spatial sources from which music emerged: one element from one direction, another from another, and so on. Ideally these would be chosen from a 360° circle around the audience, and not merely from in front of them. Such conceptions had problems of co-ordination and control with live performers, but electronic tape avoided such difficulties. *Gesang der Jünglinge* (*Song of Youth*, 1955–56) was the first such product. The tape is composed partly of sung sounds, recorded and then transformed, the words sometimes audibly emerging as a praise to God from the Book of Daniel and partly of electronically created noises that mimic vowels, consonants, and the tone mixtures between. It was designed for five banks of speakers that surround the audience. Strands of children's voices emerge and fall away in different spatial areas, against which purely electronic elements lend sonority and colour. Overall, it is as if fragmentary aural memories of childhood join up, re-emerge in the adult consciousness, and then fade away.

Stockhausen applied these spatial concepts to live orchestral music in *Gruppen* (*Groups*, 1955) for three orchestras, each with its own conductor. One orchestra of thirty-seven players is placed in front of the audience, the other two, each of thirty-six players, to either side. The intention was not merely to create spatial effects, with interaction and opposition between the three orchestras, but also to allow layers of different tempi to exist simultaneously, clarified by their emergence from different directions. In addition, the colours of the orchestras, similar in each group, were chosen by a serial structure of timbral colour (the 'scale of timbres'). It is an iron-edged, sometimes brutal score, of short isolated events whose serial melodic base is easy to discern and identify aurally. These pointillistic elements overlap or conjoin in serial fashion. The three-dimensional effect gives a clarity to their conjunction that is on a different scale from the usual post-**Webern** score. It allows an uncommon sense of freedom to the material, and a new layer of momentum when the colours and material of one snatch are taken up by one of the other orchestras. In this spatial relationship, colour and sonority, whether in conjunction or in opposition, emerge as principal concerns. It is a score that may seem bewildering at first, but whose vision becomes clear with familiarity.

Such spatial conceptions were taken further in *Carré* (1958–59) for four orchestras and four choirs, whose complete conception was worked out by Stockhausen, but whose details were realised by his pupil, Cornelius Cardew, under the composer's supervision. Again, the four groups of performers each have their own conductor, and the audience is arranged in a circle, each quadrant facing a different direction. The text is entirely phonetic, apart from a few names of friends. From its opening, a deep ritualistic chant emphasised by the use of brass, timbre is dominant. The events are much more slow-moving than in *Gruppen*, the textures far thicker, the voices fused into the orchestral density of sound, with the occasional interjection of a single cry or note. Again the spatial elements give clarity, unravelling what would otherwise be a dense wall of notes built up on each other in chords

whose composition relies little on traditional methods. The piece becomes increasingly frenetic, underpinned by held vocal notes. The sequential succession of events that has become traditional in Western music has less relevance to the piece than eastern musics, in which there is no overt direction towards an end, but rather patterns of sounds designed for contemplation rather than linear progression. This departure has become increasingly common in modern music, but requires a shift of perception and expectation on the part of listeners unused to such idioms.

The next development, again using spatial elements, was to combine the electronic and the instrumental. This Stockhausen explored in *Kontakte* (1958–60), whose title (*Contact*) refers in part to the contact between live instrumental sound groups and pre-recorded tape, though there is also a purely electronic version. In this electronic version the distancing of reality felt in *Gesang der Jünglinge* is taken considerably further. There is little connection with any sounds or techniques recognisable from conventional experience. A completely new sound world has emerged, one again primarily concerned with successive swathes of timbre, in dense, dark-coloured sounds, often of a metallic nature. *Momente* (1961–62) for soprano, four choral groups, and thirteen instrumentalists, combined all these techniques, including two electronic keyboard instruments. It added (to an orchestra that already included a very large variety of percussion instruments) other unconventional sounds to be performed by the chorus: boxes with lead shot, cardboard tubes hit with rubber mallets, and steel tubing – an early example of the use of 'found objects'. With sounds also produced by such things as clapping, knee-slapping and clicking, Stockhausen was intent on increasing still further the available range of timbral colour. The 'moments' of the title are arranged in three groups: melody-orientated moments, sound-event moments, and polyphonic moments, which influence each other during its performance. The arrangement of these moments is variable, and depends on the forces and time available; they are prearranged for performance. Against the multiplicity of sound-sources available, there are regular periods when the choral writing sounds like some distorted grand oratorio, and overall there is an element of self-consciousness in both the means and the content of *Momente* when compared to other works of the period, for all its moments of fascination and power.

Stockhausen further developed the possibilities of free, performer-controlled elements within a formal structure in *Zyklus* (*Cycle*, 1959) for one percussionist, in which an element of visual drama was added. The title refers to a number of cycles: the first a general plan of seventeen periods, whose order is chosen by the performer; the second nine cycles, each further sub-divided and characterised by a particular rate of strokes; and lastly, the cycle which the performer transcribes by moving slowly around his battery of percussion instruments, playing each in turn or in conjunction. The philosophical intent was the closing of an open form within a circle. Within these parameters the player has considerable freedom and the results very much depend on the choices of the performer.

In the early 1960s, developments in electronic technology gave Stockhausen more freedom to explore. Electronic manipulation of instruments could now be achieved while the instruments were playing, and not just afterwards through the manipulation of a recording in the studio. Stockhausen formed his own ensemble to perform such works. *Mikrophonie I* (1964) electronically manipulated the sounds of the tam-tam, *Mikrophonie II* (1965) the human voice against an organ, with taped moments ('windows') recalling earlier Stockhausen works. *Mixtur* (1964) for orchestra, sine-wave generators, and ring-modulators, extended this interplay to the orchestra, using four technicians to modify the sounds of an orchestra divided into four groups (woodwind, brass, two string groups) and relay them through four banks of loudspeakers, interweaving the results with the live playing – hence the 'mixture' of the title. A fifth orchestral group of three percussionists is amplified over a further three loudspeakers. Stockhausen used the electronics to transform timbre, pitch and rhythm, and recreate in live performance timbres that had previously been possible only in electronic music. This interaction on such a large scale was pioneering: it is only in the 1990s that such techniques are becoming more widely used, as small portable computers make the task of simultaneous transformation considerably easier. The chief interest of *Mixtur* remains the colour effects produced by the interaction.

The purely electronic *Telemusik* (1966) was the summit of these experiments; it introduced a new philosophical direction into Stockhausen's canon, and remains one of the most successful and satisfying electronic scores ever written. Stockhausen was attempting to fulfil a desire he had long held, to integrate the essence of musics from all over the world (of which his knowledge and experience were considerable), including Balinese, Gagaku (Japanese), Spanish, Saharan, Amazonian, Chinese, into a kind of supra-world music. Even Stockhausen himself was not sure how he did it, allowing these influences to infiltrate by instinct. *Telemusik* is composed of a multitude of electronic sounds whose origins are in the kind of sounds heard as radio interference. These are carefully layered from the very lowest to a regular background of extreme high frequency, acting as a sort of constant firmament, an Ariel moving around the rigging of Prospero's ship. Within this extreme clarity of vertical texture, there is considerable drama that unfolds with an inexorable if unanalysable momentum; into this framework are dispersed the distorted echoes, sometimes distantly recognisable, of the various world musics. There are few electronic scores whose elements emerge so cleanly or so clearly, that so constantly hold the attention, and are so persuasive in their creation of a sound world that it is impossible to create or imagine through normal methods of sound production. It also has the inestimable virtue, uncommon in electronic scores, of being exactly the right length for its material.

This philosophical bent was put in more concrete form in *Hymnen* (1967), a tape based on national anthems, which can be supplemented by four musicians who comment on the proceedings, or even an orchestra. Its intent and execution are clear, though its length (two hours) is daunting. *Spiral* (1968), for one soloist with short-wave radio, paid homage to one of the early inspirations for electronic music, the electronic noise generated by radio signals, while extending the parameters of control and improvisation into areas that everyone can experiment with (as Stockhausen points out, most people have a short-wave radio and a voice). The basic concept is that the soloist, using whatever instrumental means are appropriate, imitates, transforms, and interacts with the sounds from the radio. The composed parameters are the alternation between periods of action and silence, and detailed signals of how material already played is to be transformed in the next section (such as dynamics, pitch range, as decoration and chordal accumulations). Within those 'transformation signs' all the other parameters are determined by the material issuing from the short-wave radio and the player's choice. Thus an infinite number of possibilities is available in one of Stockhausen's most aleatoric scores, though the element of chance is controlled by what is on the radio during performance. Precisely the same techniques were then extended to a number of players in *Kurzwellen* (1968), and the two pieces are essentially variants of one idea. Such techniques were then used in *Opus 1970*, commissioned by Deutsche Grammophon to celebrate the 200th anniversary of Beethoven's death, except that the material for live transformation is fragments of Beethoven's music.

Such aleatoric procedures, for all their potential, become redundant when any reaction to anything that is happening becomes valid. For many, that is exactly what seemed to be happening in Stockhausen's work. Then in the same year (1968) he unveiled a work that, like *Telemusik*, proved to be seminal in his output: *Stimmung* ('tuning' but also 'mood' in both the atmospheric sense and that of 'world-harmony', a German equivalent to 'karma' – the title is deliberately ambiguous) for a group of six a cappella singers. It appeared to be a complete volte-face; it was an instant sensation, and its influence continues to reverberate through modern composition. Its basis is a series of magic names (drawn from anthropological sources, and representing magic talismans from all over the world), days of the week (themselves full of mythical symbolism) and phonetic vowels, set out in a formal scheme whose order is partly determined by the drawing of cards. The calling of a magic name signals a change of mood, during which the name is repeated and gradually clarified until another magic name is called, and the process repeats. Much of this had been heralded by earlier Stockhausen works: but what made *Stimmung* so revolutionary, and such a contrast to his preceding works, was its basis in a harmonic structure that is instantly audible and has connections, however distant, with the Western tradition. The basis is a held low B fundamental, on which are built conglomerations of the 2nd, 3rd, 4th, 5th, 7th, and 9th intervals – pure tones of the harmonic overtone sequence – and this fundamental chord is softly played on an electronic tape in the background of a performance. Vocally it is the interval of the (pure) seventh that is most prominent, but because of the sequence of overtones,

it has absolutely no conventional connotations (in which it would edge to the octave). Also important was Stockhausen's insistence on very specific vocal techniques – long breaths, no vibrato, and a concentration on the overtones built on the fundamental B.

In performances the vocalists are amplified to allow them to produce sounds of a low level. There is no conductor, but one voice emerges as dominant; when the moment is felt to be appropriate, he or she hands over to another. The whole atmosphere of the piece is gentle, quiet, meditative – purring might be an apt description – overlaid with occasional calls reminiscent of bird-cries. The effect is of a nocturne, but it is also intentionally meditative, timeless in that the progression of time, and any linear association of musical events is irrelevant. Indeed, it is best listened to in mediative mood, to achieve what Stockhausen calls 'inner quietness'. All these elements have their basis in Eastern musics, not only the meditative philosophy, but also the specific vocal techniques, which were based on Asian models. *Stimmung* demonstrated to contemporary composers that eastern techniques and approaches could be assimilated into an entirely original Western composition. It also demonstrated the possibilities of a return to recognisable, if unconventional, harmonic structures without the need for either a serial or a traditional base. Its influence has touched the minimalists, who employed similar means for their own ends. It is a deeply alluring score, with a ritualistic atmosphere that is elemental, sensual and yet complex, transporting the listener into some musical realisation of the collective unconscious.

The succeeding works consolidated the musical and philosophical ground already covered. *Mantra* (1970) for two pianos, uses transformations of material and electronic modulation (operated by the pianists), and is built on a sequence of thirteen notes arranged into the Eastern symbol of the mantra of the title. The work is a series of sequence of this mantra, and emerges like an old man taking a gentle perambulation, occasionally rattling the railing with his walking stick, or becoming briefly annoyed at some event in his path. *Sternlag (Starsound*, 1971) is for five electronic ensembles in a park, communicating through music and by human messenger. *Trans* (1971) for string orchestra arose from a dream, the players bathed in light, gentle chords backed by wind sounds and percussion changing in reaction to a tape.

Tierkris (*Zodiac*, 1975) explored the signs of the zodiac. *Der Jahrelauf* (*The Course of the Year*, 1977) is for Japanese gagaku ensemble, or its Western counterpart. *Jubilum* (1977, later revised) for an orchestra divided into four groups from bass to treble, each running at different tempi, is derived from fifteen harmonised notes divided into five phrases. In the revision, a number of amplified solo lines were added, linking the different layers. Written for a festive occasion, it is a sonorous showpiece for orchestra, one of Stockhausen's most approachable works. When its fanfare-like block chords move against a twittering, middle-voice background it is reminiscent of mainstream European orchestral developments, but is otherwise full of touches that are typical of Stockhausen's canon. None of these works had quite the influence or impact of Stockhausen's earlier music, but the stage was set for his most ambitious project.

The first of the projected cycle of seven operas or ceremonies, one for each day of the week and collectively titled *Licht* (*Light*), was *Donnerstag* (*Thursday*, 1977–80). The subject of this cycle (planned for completion in 2002) is an invented primordial ur-myth, heavily dependent on symbolic elements from the lives of Stockhausen and his family. His scope is indicated by its prelude (*Michael's Greeting*, including gamelan), played in the foyer, and its postlude (*Michael's Farewell*) played by five trumpeters dispersed around the roof or balconies of the building concerned. Behind the scenario are 'invisible choirs' on tape; the central character is a trumpeter, Michael. The first of three acts is entitled 'Michael's Youth', and describes his childhood, first love, and examination to enter music school. The second is 'Michael's Journey around the Earth', in which he is seduced by Eve disguised as a basset-horn player, and the third 'Michael's Return Home' to his heavenly residence, united with Eve. The whole of this extraordinary scenario bursts with symbol, allusion, and stylised characters, from Lucifer-as-Father to Eve-as-Moon, to a visual artist with three 'compositions of light'. Such a scenario attempts through text and staging the distancing from common reality that Stockhausen had earlier sought entirely through musical means. It is difficult to divorce the intellectual conception from the total spectacle Stockhausen intends, in which these symbols are reinforced by the perception of the staging and design. Musically, the whole gamut of Stockhausen's

skills are employed, often to eerie and magical effect.

The second in the cycle, *Samstag* (*Saturday*, 1981–83) follows similar lines. The chief protagonist is Lucifer, and it opens with his greeting for twenty-six brass and two percussionists. They appear at four high cardinal points in the auditorium, and this structure of points, lines and diagonals is used formally for the subsequent events. The first is 'Lucifer's Dream', for bass voice and piano, designed with projections and colour bands of light notated in a formal scheme. The second is 'Lucifer's Requiem', for flute and six percussionists, which is in the form of musical exercises listened to by the soul for forty-nine days after death. In 'Lucifer's Dance', the third scene, the whole orchestra is arranged in the shape of a human face, with different dances for each feature, each with its own rhythmic pattern. Scene Four, 'Lucifer's Farewell', is for male choir, organ and seven trombones, and is designed to be performed not in the opera house, but in the quiet surroundings of a nearby church, and uses St Francis of Assisi's 'Hymn to the Virtues'. Typical of the obscure symbolism is the birdcage carried by one of the singers (who are all dressed as monks) containing a blackbird, eventually set free outside to form the end of the performance. The most recent in the cycle, *Montag* (*Monday*, 1984–1988) extended the element of spectacle considerably further by being designed not for the confines of the opera house but for an outdoor stadium.

At this stage, it is too early to assess the success of such a gigantic enterprise, or indeed to decide whether Stockhausen's vision has now become so complex and so intertwined with personal symbolism that it is impossible to get behind the references and understand the drive of the work. In other words, *Licht* may operate only through the perceptions and emotional reactions of the audience, bombarded with the visual spectacle and the undoubted moments of musical beauty or force. If so, the symbolism merely stirs individual resonances within each audience member's own psyche, and is thus ultimately unanalysable. Fortunately, Stockhausen has designed many of the sections of the cycle to be capable of existing in their own right, and these individual compositions are easier to assimilate. Thus *Unsichtbare Chöre* (1979) – the *Invisible Choirs* tape of *Donnerstag* – works very successfully on its own, featuring dense layers of choral sound influenced by chant, and a starry firmament projected on the ceiling of the hall.

Lucifer's Dream is also *Klavierstück XIII* in the long-running series of piano works, and the whole enterprise was preceded by a series of fifteen works ('texts') *Aus den Sieben Tagen* (*From the Seven Days*, 1968). Of these the raucous and ugly *Kommunion* follows Stockhausen's interests of the time in its disposition of voice, short-wave receiver, glass and stones, and electronic transformation, while *Intensitt* uses electronics and found objects, including nails, hammers, and four car horns. *Fais voile vers le soleil* creates a particularly effective sonorous atmosphere, with live instruments and electronics, and a slow-moving, regular pulse.

Not all Stockhausen's music is successful, or fulfils the expectations aroused by his fertile imagination. *Momente* can emerge as academic, *Hymnen* or *Opus 1970* become wearisome after the initial conceit is enjoyed, works such as *Kurtzwellen* or *Spiral* must be much more fun to play than to listen to, and parts of *Licht*, divorced from their visual accompaniment, are stupefyingly boring – though in all these works there are moments of surprise. However, at his best, Stockhausen is extraordinarily successful, and the progression of events emerges completely naturally. The reasons seem to be beyond current methods of analysis, and perhaps not even Stockhausen can provide the answer. For all his formal structures, there is a large element of instinct, as Stockhausen has himself admitted, and it is that surety of instinct that marks Stockhausen out as a remarkable composer.

Those coming to Stockhausen's music for the first time invariably encounter difficulties. Perhaps the easiest approach is first to luxuriate in the colours and textures, and ignore everything else that is going on. Once such textures and events have become familiar, as with a new language, it is considerably easier to start identifying and understanding the processes and structures behind the emotional layer. This process is slow, but the results are worth it, and once such familiarity is achieved, new Stockhausen scores become much easier to appreciate on a first hearing.

It is worth pointing out that the spatial effects in many of Stockhausen's works are difficult to reproduce in recordings, which are still the means by which most people will have the opportunity to encounter or explore his music: the sound stage remains largely on one plane. But Stockhausen, with a typical attention to detail and a desire to retain control of every aspect of his music, has used his considerable knowledge of acoustical principles to reduce multidirectional recordings to stereo tapes, with often remarkable success. Stockhausen was one of the editors of the magazine *Die Reihe* (*The Row*), a quarterly review of serial music, and has lectured extensively on his own music.

RECOMMENDED WORKS
from *Aus den sieben Tagen* (*The Seven Days*): *Fais voile vers le soleil* (1968)
Gruppen (1955–57) for three orchestras
electronic *Gesang der Jünglinge* (1955–56)
Jubilum (1977) for orchestra
Klavierstücke I–XI (1952–56, revisions 1961) for piano
Klavierstücke XII–XIV (1977, 1981, 1988) for piano
electronic *Telemusik* (1966)
Stimmung (1968) for voices
electronic *Unsichtbare Chöre* (*Invisible Choirs*, 1979)
Zeitmasze (1955–56) for five woodwind

BIBLIOGRAPHY
ed. J. Colt, *Stockhausen: Conversations with the Composer*, London, 1973
J. Harvey, *The Music of Stockhausen*, London, 1975
M. Kurtz, *Stockhausen: A Biography*, London, 1992
R. Maconie, *The Works of Karlheinz Stockhausen*, 1976
K. H. Wörner, *Karlheinz Stockhausen*, 1973

Strauss Richard Georg***
born 11th June 1864 at Munich
died 8th September 1949 at Garmisch-Partenkirchen

Richard Strauss strides two centuries, a colossus who is typically seen as a giant in the end of the 19th and a tottering anachronism through the first half of the 20th, when his essentially Romantic idiom seemed increasingly out of place. Recently this view has changed. The works of his later life are becoming better known, and the overall achievement of this fertile, often flawed, regularly bombastic, but above all exuberant composer of the richness of emotional life is becoming more appreciated.

Strauss's most important works divide fairly straightforwardly into ten tone poems, mostly written before the turn of the century, and fifteen operas, all but two written between 1903 and 1941. The former represent the summit of the form, of the 19th century tone poem, and the most significant and enduring achievement by any composer of the genre. The latter, together with operas by **Berg**, **Britten** and **Janáček**, form the basis of the 20th-century repertoire, a situation that seems unlikely to change as the century moves to its close.

Strauss's earliest works were heavily influenced by Brahms and Mendelssohn, and include the *Symphony in D minor* (1881), the product of an immature but gifted composer. The *Symphony in F minor*, op. 12 (1883–84), conceived on a large scale, shows more Wagnerian influence and characteristic Straussian turns of musical phrase; its stirring moments make it more than just a curiosity. With *Aus Italien* op. 16 (1886), a four-movement programmatic symphony, and the now little-heard *Macbeth* op. 23 (1886–89), Strauss created his own development of the Wagnerian idiom. *Don Juan* op. 20 (1888–89) and *Tod und Verklärung*, op. 24 (*Death and Transfiguration*, 1888–89) saw his emerging voice achieve musical maturity, and established the basis of his style in the major tone poems and the earlier operas.

Strauss's orchestration is dense and intricate, all sections having an equal importance in the overall sound, a lush and sinuous interweaving of colour and line. Against this an individual instrument will emerge for a sensuous melody, ripe with beauty, usually conceived at great length so that it can soar and develop over time. Brass fanfares or passages that seem to be bursting their restrains provide interjections. The appeal, by almost overwhelming the senses, is entirely to the emotions; the post-Wagnerian harmonic palette is essentially tonal, but supercharged by a mass of often unresolved chromaticism created by the profusion of instrumental activity. All this is underpinned by the energy, flurry and constant restlessness of the rhythmic activity. Phrases launch out, soar up, twirl away, are overtaken by others, generating still more, often fragmented. The effect is heightened by the diversity and volume of the large orchestras he employs, often extending instruments to extreme ranges and employing unusual instruments.

Don Juan, the story of the famous lover, immediately establishes the voluptuousness that is elemental in Strauss's fabric. *Tod und Verklärung* is one of Strauss's finest creations, perhaps because the development of the two principal ideas is so directly geared towards the final end, each being gradually extended, restrained and stretched again, reaching their apotheosis in the final pages. It also introduces many philosophical themes that were to occur throughout Strauss's output. The programmatic basis of the work is a dying person, remembering the events of his childhood, finally expiring and achieving transfiguration. When its luminosity is considered together with the late meditation on death, the *Four Last Songs*, which quote the earlier work, the two works form the arch within which all Strauss's major works are contained. The tendency to take an individual's life and make a hero of an ordinary mortal, which infects much of Strauss's work and has often been misunderstood, is here seen in embryonic form.

The best-known and most popular of Strauss's tone poems is also his shortest, *Till Eulenspiegels lustige Streiche* op. 28 (1894–95, difficult to translate, but usually and horribly known as *Eulenspiegel's Merry Pranks*). Originally conceived as an opera, it tells of a trickster whose antics finally lead him to the gallows. As in *Don Juan*, the hero has two themes associated with him. It opens with a famous theme that aims at nobility, but, in keeping with Till's character, doesn't quite make it. In its short span are stirring noble drama, the constant injection of perky humour, an unforgettable march, a swirling, slightly macabre waltz, and the full dire majesty of the law at the end. It is an indication of how a novel musical language can be considered so difficult by the first generation to encounter it, and yet can be accepted so naturally by the next, that when this now universally popular work was first given in England in 1896, it was considered so complex it was played twice.

Strauss turned to a philosophical programme for his next tone poem. *Also sprach Zarathustra* (*Thus Spoke Zarathustra*, 1896) is based on the prose poem by Nietzsche, which seeks to portray the development of the human race from its origins to Nietzsche's idea of the Superman. To this extent it continues Strauss's theme of the hero, though here in a more abstract form. It is divided into nine sections strongly differentiated in mood, from 'Von den Hinterweltern', using a Gregorian chant as its melodic base, through the fugue of 'Von der Wissenchaft' ('Of Science') to the tolling bells of 'Nachtwanderlied' ('The Song of the Night Wanderer'). Its opening is one of the most impressive in music, a slow stirring fanfare announcing the motto of the 'World-Riddle' against the huge thunder of organ and timpani. For all its moments of sheer size and sonic power, it is a more contemplative, illusive and intricate score than the other Strauss poems, with sections of visionary beauty, and an ending in two different keys.

A more tangible hero was the subject of Strauss's next tone poem, *Don Quixote*, op. 35 (1897), based on the novel by Cervantes. This is a hero of a different kind, the common man who not only has the delusion of being a hero, but actually lives that delusion. Strauss has considerable musical sympathy for him, as if saying that the very attempt is worthy of our respect. A solo, concerto instrument – the cello – is used to portray Don Quixote himself. The work's descriptive content is vital and vivid, allowing moments of a quasi-Eulenspiegel mischief and bombast as well as of tenderness and seriousness. The choice of the cello, with its mellow tones, appropriately gives Quixote something of the character of a Falstaff. Two passages have become particularly well-known: the tilting at the windmills, a furioso of discordant, giddy dissonances, and the battle with the sheep.

From the depiction of historical or philosophical heros, Strauss turned to the artistic hero in *Ein Heldenleben*, op. 40 (*A Hero's Life*, 1897–98). This work has sometimes been held at a critical arm's length because of the autobiographical content, yet the concept of personal internal exploration reflects the new Freudian view of the world. The unusual feature is that it is cloaked in Romantic hues, not Expressionistic ones. Personal depiction remained a theme throughout Strauss's life, and his portrait of the artist-self as a type of hero, with its origins in Nietzsche, has been more easily understood in recent years. *Ein Heldenleben* is one of Strauss's noblest scores, full of beauty and rich delights – from the tubas that describe the critics and self-doubts, through the glorious theme, worthy of **Elgar**, that intertwines with the theme of the hero's Companion, to the marvellous juxtaposition of themes from Strauss's earlier works as he struggles between his self-doubts and achievements.

The criticism meted out to *Ein Heldenleben* was nothing compared with the vilification heaped on the *Sinfonia Domestica*, op. 53 (1902–03), which depicts Strauss's own household and prompted a famous American conductor to tell Strauss he should never intrude his own personality or his domestic life on the public. But such a portrait was only an extension of Strauss's subject matter. Much of the scorn can be traced to attitudes towards women and domestic life that considered that the former should be seen and not heard, and the latter kept behind closed doors. This attitude still prevails in some musical quarters, which consider the work unsavoury. Again, Strauss seems to have been ahead of his time, and was to returned to the subject in the opera *Intermezzo*. Although there is a certain musical contradiction between the intimate depiction and the large forces employed, the score is full of perky wit and humour, from the picture of the baby having a bath, to the musical grumblings of the composer-father. Perhaps of all Strauss's tone poems, this is the one most enjoyed if the details of the programme are followed while listening.

Strauss wrote one final tone poem, *Eine Alpensymphonie* (*An Alpine Symphony*, 1911–15), describing a walk in the Alps. For all its nature mysticism, here Strauss does perhaps overreach himself in deploying forces including at least sixty-four strings, an offstage band, and cow-bells. Some of the work emerges as bombastic and it does not sustain its material. However, there are glorious moments of sonic splendour, power, and sheer visual depiction which make the symphony (actually in twenty-two clearly defined sections) well worth hearing. In it Strauss reached the summit of his powers of descriptive orchestration, as he himself recognised – from then on, his scoring is gradually and artfully reduced.

At the turn of the century, the main thrust of Strauss's output turned from the tone poem to opera, from the depiction of male to female protagonists. If the musical means of these stage works belong to the end of the Romantic era (large-scale forces and chromatic harmonies), it is difficult so easily to pigeon-hole their subject matters. The vivid characterisations of Salome and Elektra in the first two major operas, agonisingly laying bare the raw flesh of desire which the 19th century was at pains to suppress, are the erupting recognition of a Freudian world. The masterpieces written with librettist Hugo von Hofmannsthal developed that understanding of the human subconscious by adding layers of symbolism designed to express the complex interplay of the unconscious and the real world, even in the least symbolic of their operas, *Der Rosenkavalier*. In doing so they created an ethos best explained in Jungian terms, which combined with a delight in the illusion of time and reality to give a sheen of elegance and wit. By no stretch of the imagination can this be called a 19th-century view of human nature: the Pandora's box of the subconscious had been opened, and cannot be closed again. That Strauss still used late Romantic methods to express this in part reflects his own place in such a transition of human thinking, and it may be they have more force because they are placed in a more familiar musical context.

There may be another factor that has made it difficult for some to accept such new wine in old bottles. For all his understanding of the depths of the human psyche (and it is difficult to see how Strauss could have achieved such characterisation without such a personal understanding), there is a sense in which the expression of Strauss's personal psyche is always at one remove from his scores, as if he is not going to reveal himself directly in his operas, unlike **Berg** or **Britten**. Such an impression emerges most directly in *Intermezzo*, that clearly describes one of Strauss's own marital arguments, but in which the very presentation of such a scene is a kind of mask to divert reality, held up to diffuse reality through operatic presentation and convention. All the most beguiling and most psychologically complex portraits in Strauss operas are of women, as if Strauss needed the removal of gender to allow such expression. There are some marvellous male roles, but perhaps the most memorable, that of Octavian in *Der Rosenkavalier*, is sung by a woman, and it is perhaps significant that when Strauss revised *Ariadne auf Naxos*, adding the role of the composer, he insisted that it should be sung by a woman, somewhat to Hofmannsthal's disgust. The use of symbol, so prevalent in the Hofmannsthal operas, is another method for the expression of unconscious human motivations and emotions without a direct, personal involvement.

Strauss's first opera, the Wagnerian *Guntram* (1892–94), is spoiled by its poor libretto, as is its successor *Feuersnot* (*Fire-Famine*, 1900–01), although the love scene of the latter between the heroine Diemut and the young magician Kunrad is worth reviving; during its climax every fire in the village, extinguished by his

magic, flares up again. But with *Salome* (1903–05), Strauss found in Oscar Wilde's treatment of the biblical story of Herod, Salome and John the Baptist, a libretto whose dramatic structure could serve as a taut container for the sumptuousness of his musical idiom, and whose hedonistic and sensual milieu, clashing with the morality and stern dignity of John the Baptist, matched his own musical inclinations and philosophical curiosity. Its sensuousness, its undercurrent of sudden violence, its incestuous implications, and its heady atmosphere in which the nightscape itself becomes cloying, shocked contemporary audiences and remains massively potent. The 'Dance of the Seven Veils', danced by Salome to seduce and sexually infuriate both John the Baptist and Herod, is often heard on its own; it is a variant on a recurrent theme of Strauss's work, the waltz, in which the formalities of the Viennese waltz tradition have been totally subverted to the ends of pure eroticism.

Strauss turned to classical Greek tragedy for his next opera, *Elektra* (1906–08). He discovered the perfect verbal match for his musical instincts in a free modern version of the Sophocles drama by the young playwright Hugo von Hofmannsthal. The story begins after Agamemnon's murder by his wife Clytemnestra and her subsequent marriage to Aegisthus. Elektra is determined to murder them and their whole household in revenge for her father's death. In the event, the deed is carried out by her brother Orestes, but the entire opera is a study of her obsession, the most extreme characterisation ever attempted by Strauss, a terrifying realisation of a human being whose every emotion is subservient to a single ghastly aim. It is a study of psychosis, and Hofmannsthal read Freud and Breuer's study of hysteria before writing it. Strauss's music entirely matches this portrait, with a title role of such stunning proportions that it has limited performance of the opera (Elektra is on stage virtually the entire time). Strauss used a huge orchestra (around 115 players) to provide force and a welter of colour, and seemed to have taken Expressionist opera in its post-Wagnerian garb to the limits of possibility.

Hofmannsthal collaborated directly on Strauss's next opera, starting one of the most fruitful and brilliant opera partnerships in history. In *Der Rosenkavalier* (*The Knight of the Rose*, 1909–10) Strauss seemed to renounce all the tortured Expressionism of his previous two operas.

In its place composer and librettist con-
cocted a comedy that intentionally echoes
the humorous, flirtatious, innuendo-laden
world of Mozart's *Marriage of Figaro*. It
was an instant success, and has remained
so ever since. Hofmannsthal's libretto creates a Vienna that has no direct authenticity, but is the world of our historical
fantasies. It weaves misunderstandings
and amorous situations that, as in the
greatest comedies, both threaten to turn
to tragedy and allow depths of genuine
human feelings, be they the musings of the
Marschallin on the autumnal years of a
woman's life, or the outpouring of love by
the young Sophie. Strauss responded with
a score of Mozartian delight and airiness,
but did so entirely within the terms of his
own musical fantasy, without any suggestion of neo-classicism. The orchestra is
huge, but used almost throughout with a
deft touch. Behind the entire opera lies the
spirit of the Viennese waltz, sometimes
overtly (as when Baron Ochs inspects his
proposed fiancée Sophie), but otherwise as
a kind of blueprint. Within the characteristic general method of drawing out and
extending melodic ideas, and using themes
as leitmotifs, time and time again phrases
occur that might be developed into a
classic Viennese waltz, or might belong to
part of one but instead immediately launch
off into different directions. Above all, this
is an opera of happiness, its characterisation, both in text and music, brilliant
within its limitations, and its climax – the
Act III trio for three women's voices – one
of the supreme operatic moments. If it
does not have the psychological power and
depth of *Salome* or *Elektra*, it instead
suggests another aspect to the human
condition that does not negate those earlier explorations: the delight in diversion
and love, and in particular the pleasure and
warmth, both emotional and, by implication, sexual, of the women caught up in its
intrigues.

Strauss and Hofmannsthal's next opera
was on a chamber scale, with an orchestra
of only thirty-seven players. *Ariadne auf
Naxos* (1911–12) was originally designed
as an ending for a Max Reinhardt production of a condensed version of Molière's *Le
bourgeois gentilhomme*. The play and the
opera proved a clumsy and lengthy combination, however, so for a 1916 performance
Strauss replaced the play with a prologue
set in a house in Vienna; the opera then
becomes the evening entertainment. In
doing so, he added the character of the
composer, sung by a soprano, which has
since become a coveted role for aspiring
singers. The opera itself is the classical
story of Ariadne and Bacchus, in the style
of 'opera seria'; but to make life more
complicated, *a commedia dell' arte* troupe
has arrived to present a buffo-style farce,
and is ordered to do so simultaneously. In
the event, they take part in the other
opera, too, rather like the critics in **Prokofiev's** *Love of Three Oranges*. The entire
work develops a theme that Strauss was to
return to in *Capriccio*, the multiple illusions of art, with a delightful and delicate
musical wit, full of neo-classical references,
humour, pomposity, and parody. Both the
original and the revised version are still
presented, though the latter is more common.

Strauss and Hofmannsthal produced a
much more serious and lengthy work in
*Die Frau ohne Schatten (The Woman
without a Shadow*, 1914–18), the grandest
of Strauss's works, considered by many
(including this writer) to be both Strauss's
and Hofmannsthal's greatest achievement. It is an opera of genuine difficulties,
its extremely large stage and vocal
demands ensuring that its presentation is
a rare and major occasion. In it Hofmannsthal plunged into a story that combines
myth, folk tale and complex layers of
symbolism. The Emperor has married the
daughter of Keikobad, king of the spirits,
but unless their union produces children
(their childlessness is symbolised by the
Empress throwing no shadow, hence the
title) the Emperor will be turned to stone.
The Empress and her nurse go down to a
different level of humanity, that of ordinary mortals, and there persuade the dyer
Barak's wife to sell her right to have
children to the Empress. At the last
moment, threatened by her dignified and
noble husband, the woman refuses, and the
ground swallows Barak and his wife into
an underworld. In the final Act, the
Empress is told to drink the Waters of Life
to gain her shadow, and deprive Barak's
wife of hers, or else the Emperor, who now
has turned completely to stone except for
his eyes, will be totally petrified. Torn
between her desire to save her husband
and to spare the innocent Barak and his
wife, she refuses, and in her refusal finds
redemption. The opera ends with the voices of the unborn children of both couples.

Such are the bare outlines of the opera,
but they scarcely do justice to the multiple
layers of allusion and symbolism that Hofmannsthal creates. The work has often
been described as Freudian, but it is much
more accurately termed Jungian. For, as in

the great fairy tales and myths, Hofmannsthal has succeeded through symbolism in penetrating the archetypal truths of the human condition, from the central question of the opera – the balance between earthy materialism and esoteric spiritualism, and the necessity for both – to that of the innate desire for the continuation of humanity through having children. All the characters, from the Emperor to the Keeper of the Temple, are archetypes, and like all myths the work yields more the more one is familiar with it. Strauss was exactly the right composer to set such a libretto, with his understanding and command of the use of themes and musical symbolism, his sympathy with many different sides of human nature – Barak is one of his most sympathetic musical portraits – and his ability to reach into the subconscious of the audience. Nor is this confined to the larger moments, for Strauss often turns his huge forces into a chamber delicacy; the theme of the spirit-messenger, represented by a falcon, is as haunting as any Strauss wrote. *Die Frau ohne Schatten* is the last great opera written using all the panoply of Romantic means; the Expressionism of earlier works (or indeed, of its contemporary, **Berg's** *Wozzeck*) is absent; in its place is something just as modern, an archetypal myth. In the opera house where the symbolism can be matched and clarified by the visual staging, it is an overwhelming musical experience.

For his next opera Strauss himself wrote the libretto. *Intermezzo* (1918–23) is an autobiographical opera, with the two central characters, Robert and Christine, representing Strauss and his wife Pauline. While Robert is away, Christine takes under her wing the young Baron Lummer, whom she has met on the ski slopes. Her patronage has elements of flirtation, but she is horrified when he turns out simply to want money, and then when she intercepts a letter apparently from some lover to Robert (based on an actual incident in the Strauss marriage). Robert is equally horrified when telegrammed by Christine, for he knows nothing about the supposed affair. Eventually it turns out that the letter was sent to Robert in error, being intended for someone else, and the couple are reconciled. Among other things, the opera reveals the chaotic disorder of the Strauss household, Strauss's love of the game of skat, the multiple sides of Pauline's character, and the awareness that both of them were stimulated by their arguments and rows, underneath which

was a strong romantic love. The orchestral forces are small (strings, three horns and two trombones), Strauss aiming for the lightness of *Der Rosenkavalier*, at which he sometimes succeeds. The opera is unified by a host of leitmotifs and personal references to Strauss's own music and works by other composers. Reactions to this work have varied, some finding the sentimentality overpowering (especially in the final duet). Family life is not so clothed in secrecy as it was in the 1920s, and *Intermezzo* is perhaps now easier to assimilate. Certainly the importance of quarrelling in successful relationships (and Strauss's marriage seems to have been that) is something that has only recently been appreciated psychologically. The orchestral interludes are marvellous, and were reworked into an orchestral suite.

Hofmannsthal returned as librettist for the next opera, *Die Ägyptische Helena (The Egyptian Helen*, 1923–27, revised 1932), the most problematic and least heard of their collaborations. The basis of the story is an old legend that the real Helen of the Greek Trojan story did not go to Troy, but remained on an island until reunited with Menelaus, while a spirit double took her place. Hofmannsthal complicates this idea with potions, the introduction of an African chieftan who falls in love with Helen, and the concept that the real and spirit Helen are one and the same person. Menelaus eventually realizes he has found the whole Helen, her history included, and embraces her rather than killing her. Hofmannsthal did not seem to have realized what he had written, imagining it to be a light comedy. What he produced was equivalent to a dream, with similar patterns of action, symbolism, and multiple illusions. It awaits a major production that would single-mindedly present it as such, when its strange action may then match the power and beauty of some of the music, especially Helen's 'Zweite Brautnacht' from Act II. This is the Strauss opera that most glorifies the singing voice, and is worth hearing for that alone.

The last collaboration between Strauss and Hofmannsthal was also one of their most successful. *Arabella* (1930–32) was once ignored as being a reworking of the milieu of *Der Rosenkavalier*, but the similarities are confined to the Viennese setting and the return to naturalism. The scoring is lighter, more direct, and warmer than the earlier opera, and the story, on the surface light and entertaining, has the darker undercurrent of the best comedies (it has been pointed out that it is an accurate portrait of an addictive family). Count Waldner, an inveterate gambler, is living in a hotel with his family, trying to keep up noble appearances. His elder daughter, Arabella, has to find a wealthy husband; to save money the younger, Zdenka, is dressed up as a boy. The penniless Matteo is in love with Arabella, but she sees a Croatian stranger Mandryka, who has fallen for the photograph of Arabella that her father had sent his father. They meet at a ball, and agree to marry each other. Matteo is heart-broken, and threatens to commit suicide. Zdenka, who is in love with him, sets up a deception where he will think he is visiting Arabella's room that night, but will actually encounter Zdenka in the darkness. Mandryka overhears this, and thinks he is being duped. In the last act, Matteo is astounded to encounter Arabella, whom he thinks he has just left in the darkened room; Mandryka further compounds the misunderstandings, and is left alone, thinking he has lost Arabella, until she enters the room and all ends happily.

The next two operas, written after Hofmannsthal's death in 1929, have all but disappeared from the repertoire. *Die schweigsame Frau* (1933–34), to a libretto by Stefan Zweig based on Jonson's *The Silent Woman*, is a lighthearted comedy in which Strauss, not altogether successfully, tried to emulate his 19th-century predecessors, with division into set pieces and spoken dialogue. *Friedenstag* (1935–36), to a libretto by Joseph Gregor, is a short one-act anti-war opera, opening in the middle of a war, the countryside and its people devastated. This setting is interrupted by a folk-song from a Piedmontese youth, in Italian style, and at the end the desperate, starved people storm the fortress. The town officials and the officers debate whether to surrender the town to the enemy. The Commandant is set on resistance, despite all the odds, but seems to relent; in fact he plans to blow up the town and all in it. The central section of the opera concerns the Commandant's wife, and her love and support for her husband. He tries to persuade her to leave, showing his fondness for her, but she elects to stay with him. The last section is a melée of preparations and remonstrations as the enemy advance, joined by the sound of bells, with the arrival of peace, and a setpiece choral ending. It is the strangest opera in Strauss's output, dark and harsh, with more choral writing than usual, some violent, satirical marches, and social-political subject matter which shows a very different side to the composer.

The next Strauss–Gregor collaboration is one of Strauss's most lyrical, beautiful and happily proportioned works, but again is very little known. *Daphne* (1936–37) is based on a story from Ovid's *Metamorphoses*. Daphne regrets being attracted to the disguised Apollo, who kills her mortal admirer Leukippos. Apollo, admitting his error, transforms her into a laurel tree. The undercurrent to the plot is the opposition between the Apollonian and the Dionysian (Leukippos tries to persuade Daphne to join in the Dionysian rites). The one-act opera is built in an arch, from the magical pastoral opening, with its evocation of nature, through the central turbulence of the Dionysian rite, to the transformation of Daphne, her words turning to sounds as she reaches to the Apollonian light. Although Gregor's poetry is pedestrian (one longs for Hofmannsthal's skills), it does not hamper the flow of the story or Strauss's marvellous music, dramatically intense but on a chamber scale; the final transformation scene is inspired, approaching the kind of luminosity he achieved in his final works.

The full-length *Die Liebe der Danae* (1938–40) was intended as a witty mythological opera. The original inspiration is from Hofmannsthal, who had produced a viable and interesting outline joining the legend of Danae with that of Midas (the love of gold being the common factor). Unfortunately, Gregor so adulterated and complicated the basic idea that it is virtually unmanageable as a theatrical work, though it contains fine music: the *Symphonic Fragment* for orchestra, arranged by Clemens Krauss and mostly drawn from the first scene (which contains the finest music of the opera), is sometimes heard on its own.

Strauss's final opera is among the finest of his creations. For *Capriccio* (1940–41) he eventually found in Clemens Krauss a librettist who could again match his particular genius, and help achieve the kind of synthesis of idea, word and music that he had experienced with Hofmannsthal. It is the most personal of all his operas, completely breaking the operatic rules and conventions, and assumes a knowledgeable and sophisticated audience that can respond to its intellectual wit, emotional mellowness and its myriad of detailed allusion. It will never be popular and has often been considerably misunderstood, but such gems are so rare that it will always be cherished. On the surface *Capriccio* is a series of conversations that explore the relationship between music and words, the very nature of the operatic conceit. The setting, recalling *Der Rosenkavalier* and *Arabella*, is a notional Paris towards the end of the 18th century, but is deliberately timeless. In the Countess's house music and drama is performed and discussed, some of it from previous eras. The works under consideration turn out to share the subject matter of earlier Strauss operas. We therefore look in on a series of windows looking in on windows, starting from our own time, and moving backwards. Its completely unconventional aspects include a long opening consisting entirely of the movement of a string sextet, in a style that manages to be both of the period and unmistakably Strauss. Underneath is a gentle undercurrent of love and emotion in different guises, presented with affection but without moral or physical certainties. The characters – including the countess, a poet-librettist, the composer, a sleepy prompter, and the theatre director, a study based on Max Reinhardt – are drawn with marvellously subtle detail, and totally without censure or appraisal. It evolves into one of most satisfying theatrical twists in all opera: the Countess and the house-guests decide to write an opera, one that will reflect the everyday concerns and life that they experience by relating the events they have gone through. We realise that what we are listening to is that very opera, having reached the point at which they are discussing writing it. It ends equally brilliantly with the Countess undecided about which of her admirers she is going to choose, and waiting to hear how the proposed opera is to end. What Strauss seems to suggest is the illusory nature of reality, neatly underscored by a glimpse of the servants, presenting quite a different picture of the proceedings. There ultimately are no answers to the debate about primacy of words or music, or to the permanence of the Countess's choice. In *Capriccio* Strauss suggests that in that very lack of firm and definite answers lies the secret of life – in being able to love, live and argue and then take pleasure in the ambiguities. He himself does this in the music, a luminous score of wonderful assuredness, a seamless flow of natural song, building into a great central octet, and culminating in the translucent mirage of the Countess's final song. The opera glows with the gentle warmth of the wisdom of a composer in his old age, one

who has reached the stage of artistic enlightenment when there are no longer any musical axes to grind. Both libretto and score are masterpieces.

Strauss did not expect to live to see the première of *Capriccio*; not only did he do so, but he then produced a number of works of extraordinary luminosity, in which he bathed in the setting Apollonian sun to which his music had so often reached. Behind so many of Strauss's earlier works lies a restlessness exemplified in rhythmic fragmentation, however much it was submerged in sumptuousness or lyricism. In these last works, that restlessness fades away.

The *Horn Concerto No. 2* (1942) initiated this period, combining Romantic writing for the soloist with a somewhat neo-classical cast to the orchestra. But it is *Metamorphosen* (1945) for twenty-three solo strings that is, with the *Four Last Songs*, the most remarkable of the late works. It unfolds as a continuous sonorous web of interlinking string lines and changing textures, completely seamless, its rich glowing colours like amber or burnished walnut. Initially restrained, it builds slowly to impassioned moments, sometimes with the warmth of old age, sometimes with intense tragedy, referring along the way to Wagner's *Tristan und Isolde* and to Beethoven's *Eroica* symphony. *The Oboe Concerto* (1945–46) is a captivating little work, a rumination upon old age with a Mozartian lightness, a lovely slow movement, and constant suggestions of earlier Strauss works, especially in the orchestra.

The *Vier letzte Lieder (Four Last Songs*, 1948; the title was the publisher's) contains perhaps the most perfect music Strauss ever wrote. The settings of Eichendorff and Hesse are autumnal, with the warmest glow of sunset colours; with all the wisdom and serenity of his old age, Strauss looks back over his life with equanimity and understanding, and at the same time forward, beyond death. The songs are suffused with nostalgia, and sometimes sadness at the coming parting, but never with sentimentality. The music ranges from the rich textural tapestries of 'September' to the luminosity of 'Im Abendrot'; rather than the neo-classicism of his other late works, Strauss returned here to the rich sonorities of the late Romantic orchestra. Only warm colours are used, strings predominant, the harmonies moving with astonishing fluidity; to this base are added luminous flute figures, the mellowness of the horn, and floating vocal lines so ethereal they are almost disembodied. In the final song 'Im Abendrot' (actually the first to be written) there is a quotation from *Tod und Verklärung* and a return to the atmosphere and colours of the end of *Der Rosenkavalier*, tinged with the radiance of nostalgic peace.

Strauss wrote songs throughout his life (though the majority were written before the period of the operas), and many of them have become staples of the *lieder* repertoire. He generally chose poems that had a personal significance for himself and his wife Pauline, herself a fine singer. Consequently they are most commonly heard sung by women. The characteristics of Strauss's songs are an emphasis on melody, often extended and developed freely throughout the song, strict formal structures, and rich piano accompaniments to support the melody and flow, and delineate the formal structure. They lend themselves to orchestration, and Strauss orchestrated many of the better-known songs, sometimes years later (*Zueignung*, for example, was written in 1885 and not orchestrated until 1940). Among the finest are the sensuous, undulating and ecstatic *Cäcile* (1894, orchestrated 1897), the limpid, heart-rending *Morgen* (1894, orchestrated 1897), *Ständchen (Serenade*, 1886), the lovely, rocking nocturne *Traum durch die Dämmerung* (1895), and the gossamerlike, exceptionally beautiful *Wiegenlied* (1899, orchestrated c.1916).

Strauss's first opus number is dated 1876, the year of the première of Wagner's *Siegfried*, his last work 1948, the year of the first pieces of *musique concrète*. To cover such a span, in which music and the Western world so massively changed, with a continuous creative output, is scarcely imaginable. But this Strauss achieved, and, in spite of his unevenness, produced masterpieces throughout this huge period of history. He held conducting posts at Meiningen (1889–94), Munich (1886–89), Weimar (1889–94) and Berlin (1898–1908), before devoting himself entirely to composing, though he often appeared as guest conductor and recorded a number of his own works. In 1933 he was made president of the Nazi *Reichsmusikkammer* but subsequently resigned. He remained relatively secure in his reputation as Germany's greatest composer but out of official favour, spending much of the war in relative obscurity in Austria.

RECOMMENDED WORKS
> tone poem *Also sprach Zarathustra*, op. 38 (1896)
> opera *Arabella*, op. 79 (1930–32)
> opera *Capriccio*, op. 85 (1940–41)
> opera *Daphne*, op. 82 (1936–37)
> tone poem *Tod und Verklärung*, op. 24 (1889)
> tone poem *Don Juan*, op. 20 (1888–89)
> tone poem *Don Quixote*, op. 35 (1897)
> opera *Elektra*, op. 58 (1906–08)
> opera *Die Frau ohne Schatten*, op. 65 (1914–18)
> tone poem *Ein Heldenleben*, op. 40 (1897–98)
> Horn Concerto No. 2 (1942)
> *Metamorphosen* (1945) for 23 strings
> opera *Der Rosenkavalier*, op. 59 (1909–10)
> opera *Salome*, op. 54 (1904–05)
> songs (see text)
> tone poem *Till Eulenspiegels lustige Streiche* op. 28 (1894–95)

BIBLIOGRAPHY
> N. Del Mar, *Richard Struass* (3 vols), 1962–72
> K. Wilhelm, *Richard Strauss: an intimate portrait*, 1989

Weill Kurt
born 2nd March 1900 at Dessau
died 3rd April 1950 at New York

Kurt Weill was the 20th-century composer most successful in fusing the classical tradition with populist elements, especially those drawn from Berlin cabaret jazz and vaudeville. Although others such as **Eisler** used a similar idiom, it has become inextricably linked with Weill, and widely emulated. His output, influenced philosophically by his teacher **Busoni**, is almost entirely vocal and for the stage, and, after his early works, falls into three periods: the development of his mature idiom (1925–28); the period of his most famous works (1928–36); and his time in the United States, a period dominated by his production of Broadway musicals. Weill worked best when using material with strong social comment and satire, exemplified in his collaborations with Bertolt Brecht. The marks of his maturity are, firstly a genius for hauntingly memorable melodies, often bitter-sweet, the sentimentality of a beautiful line instantly destroyed by the harmonies of the musical context and by dramatic situation. Many modern, especially North American, renditions of his more popular songs entirely destroy this undercurrent of irony. Second, his orchestrations, almost invariably for small ensembles, set up an often jerky, raucous layer derived from jazz, with emphasis on the beat, either regular or syncopated, and on rhythm. The tango often appears, associated with sexual expression, usually ambivalent, illicit or betrayed. The combination of basic elements is sometimes deliberately vulgar as part of the satire. There is also a kind of *ur*-song that permeates Weill's work, appearing in various guises in *The Threepenny Opera, Happy End* and *Johnny Johnson*. In *The Threepenny Opera* and *The Rise and Fall of the City of Mahagonny* Weill forged a new kind of opera (or in the case of the former, music theatre) that confirmed the general acceptance of drawing on popular elements and fusing them into a more serious tradition.

Weill's *Symphony No. 1* (1921) is of interest mainly as an assured example of his early style, before he acquired a personal voice and turned to the stage. The *Symphony No. 2* (1933–34) has a classical construction and feel, built to support melodic and sometimes lightly ironic march tunes. The slow movement recalls the **Prokofiev** of the ballets, in its melodic ideas, phrasing, and orchestral colours. As a whole the symphony fails; too many passages seem just note-spinning, without constructive or emotional weight. Throughout Weill the song-writer seems to be straining to be released from the symphonic form, which was a response to a commission rather than an artistic goal, but it is worth discovering for the slow movement.

Royal Palace (1925–26), now largely forgotten, was the first work in which Weill used jazz overtly, notably in the orchestral tango accompaniment to the suicide of the bored socialite whose life forms the main theme of the opera. The one-act *Der Zar lässt sich photographieren* (*The Tsar has his photograph taken*, 1927), is much more successful, in part due to its libretto by Georg Kaiser. The unidentified Tsar of the title is to have his photograph taken, but three terrorists take the place of the actual photographers. They are captured before they can carry out their assassination, and the real photographers finish the work. In this fast-moving comedy, Weill used a male chorus commenting on the action, a generally Expressionist tone, and again a tango at the climax of the work.

These works were essentially Weill's operatic apprenticeship. It was through his collaboration with Bertolt Brecht, starting with the *Mahagonny Songspiel* (1927), that the particular elements which Weill had been seeking in stage works came to fruition. Brecht had published the texts of *Mahagonny Songspiel* (often known as *Kleine Mahagonny*) in 1926, writing music for them himself (Weill reused one of the tunes). Brecht's text is a biting, semi-grotesque, semi-surrealistic satire on the results of capitalism. Both music and text are a deliberate mixture of the sophisticated and the coarse, with echoes of the chamber stage works of **Stravinsky**, but combined with elements of jazz and Berlin cabaret. Above all, the work, originally staged in a boxing ring with Expressionist back projections, relies on formal songs (hence the title) in the tradition of the popular ballad, with instantly appealing melodies repeated with each verse. The skill of Weill's writing, the infectiousness of his tunes, the brash colours, and feverish rhythms have gained the work an audience with the musically knowledgeable and novices alike.

Brecht and Weill's next collaboration has become the most celebrated work by either artist, and its best-known song, 'Mack's Ballad', under its more popular title of 'Mack the Knife', is probably the most widely-known piece of music by any composer in this guide. *Die Dreigroschenoper* (*The Threepenny Opera*, 1928) redefined the boundary between music and words, being a combination of theatre, opera, vaudeville, and cabaret entertainment, without being obviously any one of those. Consequently it has become one of the cornerstones of music theatre, its music designed to be sung by actors with a strong musical ability rather than by trained opera singers. The story is based on Gay's 18th-century *The Beggar's Opera*, itself a parody of the Handelian opera of the day. Elizabeth Hauptmann (who apparently laid the groundwork for a number of Brecht's works) translated the original for Brecht. Polly, daughter of Peacham, king of the London beggars, is in love with, and marries (in a scene added by Brecht) Peacham's younger rival, Mack, who protects beggars through his friendship with the Police Chief. Strongly disapproving of his daughter's match, Peacham persuades the Police Chief to arrest Mack, who is betrayed by a prostitute, Jenny, in a brothel. Mack escapes from prison, is recaptured and is about to be hanged when an emissary from the King pardons him and raises him to the peerage, a deliberately farcical ending intended to prevent anyone taking the earlier events too seriously. Weill's music works on two levels: its bitter-sweet melodies and jazz rhythms are immediately entertaining; and through parodying, in some fashion or another, the conventions of traditional opera, not the least in the orchestral forces (saxophones, trombones, trumpets, timpani, banjo and harmonium). This combination of biting social satire, popular entertainment, and artistic parody has ensured the continuing popularity of this marvellously outrageous work.

If *The Threepenny Opera* was intended to parody operatic convention, the next collaboration was intended, at least on Weill's part, to forge a new operatic style. *Aufsteig und Fall der Stadt Mahagonny (The Rise and Fall of the City of Mahagonny*, 1927–29) was a development of the *Mahagonny Songspiel*, and includes the music of the earlier work. Set in a fantastical America in the city of the title, designed by Alaskan trappers as a place of pleasure, it attacks the pretensions of the bourgeoisie and the false allure of capitalism. The dream city is advertised and attracts customers with its promise of easy women and riches. But after a boom a series of scenes shows the degradation the city has come to, from gluttony to violence and alcoholism, seen through the story of Jimmy, whose main crime is not being able to pay his debts. The city burns as the inhabitants march carrying placards for and against capitalism; a chorus from hell accompanies them (the inhabitants, we have already learnt, can't be sent to hell by God since they are already there). *Mahagonny* develops the jazz influences in *The Threepenny Opera*, while adding strings and woodwind that completely alter the overall sound, taking it from the music-theatre to the opera stage. Weill's music opts for a more consistent, flowing and less populist idiom, far less sentimental and more biting in its social comment, to create his finest work. It should be noted that different versions with a large number of small alterations or changes of order exist for both *The Threepenny Opera* and *Mahagonny* (as they are usually known), including a completely different alternative set of names for the latter in the printed score.

The next collaboration between Brecht and Weill was a work that in many respects is *The Threepenny Opera* revisited. *Happy End* (1929) has a story of American gangsters and a Salvation Army worker that bears an uncanny resemblance to the short story by Damon Runyon which became the basis of the hit musical *Guys and Dolls*. Brecht disguised the origins of his work with fictitious sources (he could not have seen the short story, which appeared in 1932), and the two may have had a common, earlier American source. It is excellent, tongue-in-cheek drama, and the music contains, besides parodies of Salvation Army music, three of Weill's most famous songs, 'Surabaya Johnny', 'The Bilbao Song' and the 'Sailor's Song'.

Their next work was a school opera based on a Japanese Noh play, *Der Jasager (The Yes-Sayer*, 1930). With hindsight, the text can be regarded as unwittingly marred by a fatal flaw, in which the moral, intended to show the importance of steadfastness to Marxist principles, could all too easily be interpreted as condoning Nazi and Stalinist brutality. (Brecht tried, somewhat unsuccessfully, to change it, turning the yes-sayer into a no-sayer). The music is entirely successful, tailored for school ensembles yet showing Weill's characteristics, while being devoid of parody.

Brecht and Weill collaborated on concert as well as stage works. *Berliner Requiem* (1929) commemorates Rosa Luxembourg and the end of World War I. To the characteristic melodies and rhythms of their stage works is added a denser polyphony in rather this stern work. More effective is the short *Zu Potsdam unter den Eichen* (1929) for unaccompanied male choir, again marrying vintage Weill with traditional polyphony. Their final collaboration was the sung ballet *Die sieben Todsünden der Kleinbürger (The Seven Deadly Sins of the Petty Bourgeois*, 1933), written in Paris after Weill had fled the Nazis. The protagonists are two Annas, one the narrator of the story and the other her representation in dance; they leave their bourgeois home in Louisiana for seven sleazy but lucrative episodes each illustrating one of the deadly sins. The moral is of the hypocrisy of bourgeois values when set against bourgeois actions, reinforced by their occasional desire to return to virtue and Louisiana. Now rich, this they do, to the house built by their relatives (who call them back throughout the work). Musically the idiom is a less biting version of The *Threepenny Opera*.

Weill produced two operas without Brecht, now largely forgotten. Both *Die Bürgschaft (The Pledge*, 1931), to a complex and unsuccessful libretto by Caspar Neher, and *Der Silbersee (The Silver Lake,*

1932), to a libretto by Georg Kaiser, have Brechtian overtones and fantastical allegorical plots, and both contain some fine music. After Weill left for the United States in 1935, he turned increasingly to the medium of the Broadway musical, which lies outside the scope of this guide. In these he produced a number of songs that are now part of the American heritage. Two works are worthy of note here: *Johnny Johnson* (1936) is a biting anti-war satire to a libretto by the left-wing American folk playwright Paul Green, and includes the haunting 'Johnny's Song'; *Street Scene* (1947), has a libretto by Elmer Rice, based on his 1929 play, and was an attempt to write an American popular opera.

RECOMMENDED WORKS
> opera *Aufsteig und Fall der Stadt Mahagonny* (*The Rise and Fall of the City of Mahagonny*, 1930)
> school opera *Der Jasager* (1930)
> opera *Die Dreigroschenoper* (1928)
> opera *Happy End* (1929)
> musical play *Johnny Johnson* (1936)
> *Kleine Dreigroschenmusik* (1929)
> *Mahagonny Songspiel* (1927)
> Symphony No. 2 (1934)
> *Zu Potsdam unter den Eichen* (1929) for unaccompanied male choir

BIBLIOGRAPHY
> D. Drew, *Kurt Weill: A Handbook*, 1987
> R. Sanders, *The Days Grow Short*, 1980

Wolpe Stefan *
born 25th August 1902 at Berlin
died 4th April 1972 at New York

Stefan Wolpe has attracted attention as a composer of structurally rigorous works that developed a personal 12-tone and serial idiom. This interest has come more from musicologists (he has been seen as a link between **Busoni** and the avant-garde) than performers, and it is still difficult to encounter his music or get an overall view of his relatively large output.

In the 1920s and 1930s Wolpe was influenced by jazz and by left-wing German politics and its associated music. The *Tango* (1927) and short *Rag-Caprice* (1927), both for piano, show the former influence, and the series of piano marches *Cinq marches caractéristiques* (1928–34) the latter. The motoric *Stehende Musik* (*Stationary Music*, 1927), derived from a lost piano sonata, shows an early preoccupation with form in its contrasts of tension and release. In 1933 Wolpe fled Berlin, and studied briefly with **Webern** before moving to Palestine. Most of his works from this date avoid any descriptive title, preferring to indicate their form. One fine work is the *Passacaglia* (1936) for piano, relentlessly logical in its construction, building through increased density in its overall structure. In this period Wolpe also wrote some less severe works, especially songs and choruses for the Kibbutz movement (some of which have become accepted as folk songs in Israel), including the *Songs from the Hebrew* (1938) for soprano and piano.

In 1938 he moved to the United States, where he adopted a style that has been described as abstract expressionism, and connected with such painters as Klee. Structures are usually built from small cells, which then are subject to highly detailed changes, using asymmetrical metres and rhythms, variations of instrumentation and colour, and expressive contrasts of density and complexity. Though some of the techniques are derived from serial procedures, the basic structures often hark back to Classical models; the concentration on the detail of each element is traceable to the influence of **Webern**. These techniques are essentially personal rather than closely following any formal system, and the resulting idiom emerges as formal, rugged, capable of a sense of instinctive freedom through the contrasts and consequently often more lucid than much of the writing of the avant-garde. The concentration on vertical detail, and on activities with short time-frames, militates against any sense of linear development, and it is this which has perhaps hampered a wider appreciation of his music. Its virtues are the combination of meticulous detail with the capacity for emotional expression, but the results are rather astringent.

These techniques are exemplified in the one-movement *Form* (1959) for piano. It opens with a short, light, toying phrase made up of the first six notes of the 12-note row used. The next bar uses the same notes in a completely different arrangement and register, imposing a dark, and more complex mood. The third bar superimposes the two moods, before a trill then introduces the next six notes of the row. This basic material is used for a free interaction of lucid, airy textures, before the notes of the opening return. There is an analogy to classical sonata form here, with the two opening bars representing two themes, the main body of the work the development, and the return of the opening notes the recapitulation. The abrupt contrast of mood at the opening is typical of Wolpe's abstract Expressionist contrasts. It is a fascinating work, but it remains dry, as if Wolpe were using form to suppress emotional expression. It was joined by a later companion piece, *Form IV: Broken Sequences* (1969) for piano.

Of the other better-known works, *Battle Music* (1943–47) for piano is one of his more expressive pieces (and one of the few with a descriptive title) and exemplifies the combination of a classical formal base and abstract expressionist procedures. The half-hour *Enactments* (1950–53) for three pianos displays a fragmentary style and fertile complexity with expressive possibilities. Two of its five movements require strings to be plucked. The serial *Symphony* (1955–56, revised 1962) is a difficult work with little linear development. Wolpe subsequently compressed his idiom into shorter and more succinct works, such as *Form*, discussed above, that lost none of the complexity of construction while exploring the possibilities of changing shapes. Dominating these were a series of complex works for chamber ensemble, usually constructed by initially stating a small number of notes that then undergo constant changes whose strong contrasts between close groupings and extreme registers give an expanding and contracting effect. Longer term movement is created by the removal of certain pitches and the addition of others, thus slowly changing the overall harmonic cast. Typical of these later works is the effective *Chamber Piece No.1* (1964) for fourteen instruments, with pointillistic instrumental writing.

Wolpe was an important teacher in the United States, and this influence has probably been of more significance than his music. He taught privately in New York (1938–52), at Black Mountain College in North Carolina (1952–56) and at Long Island University (1957–68). Among his pupils were Morton Feldman and Charles **Wuorinen**.

RECOMMENDED WORKS
Battle Music (1943–47) for piano
Chamber Piece No. 1 (1964) for
    fourteen instruments
Enactments (1950–53) for three pianos
Form (1959) for piano
Passacaglia (1936) for piano

Zimmermann Bernd Alois**
born 20th April 1918 at Bliesheim
(near Cologne)
died 10th August 1970 at
Grosskönigsdorf (near Cologne)

Bernd Alois Zimmermann is best known for a single work, the opera *Die Soldaten*, whose reputation and influence secured him an important position in post-1945 German composition. His earlier works are emotionally Expressionist, using an essentially tonal base. From the middle 1950s he turned to strict formal structures and serial procedures, but from around 1960 he forged a synthesis of various avant-garde styles in an idiom he called 'pluralistic', which could range from the avant-garde jazz of such works as the instrumental *Die Befristenten (The Numbered)*, through electronic works, to the extreme Expressionism of *Die Soldaten*. These works often quoted earlier music: *Dialogues* for two pianos and orchestra, (reworked as *Monologue*, 1964, for two pianos) quotes, for example, from Bach, Beethoven and **Messiaen**. Central to his aesthetic was the idea that time as a concept includes the simultaneous confluence of past and future as well as present (partly explaining his use of quotation); in this he was influenced by such writers as James Joyce. Although he only wrote one opera, the basic impulse of most of his music is dramatic effect.

The *Symphony* (1951) in one movement illustrates Zimmermann's earliest phase. The composer himself pointed out the symphony was not a compression of the customary movements into one, but a single evolutionary event, an arc reaching from chaos to organisation with the full statement of thematic material at the end. However, no such explanation is needed, for this tremendously vital symphony has a clear logic of its own, a kind of compression into a single concise movement of Mahlerian events turned wild, with impressive clarity of orchestration and essentially tonal points of reference. The *Oboe Concerto 'Homage à Stravinsky'* (1952) is a tribute to the older composer, emulating his small blocks of orchestral sound. The flowing solo line is supported rather than opposed by the orchestra, and gives the work a neo-classical hue.

Zimmermann's most important work is *Die Soldaten* (1958–60, staged in revised form in 1965). This huge opera, building on the Expressionist legacy of **Berg**, is based on a 1771 play by Jakob Lenz about Marie, a respectable woman who becomes the regimental whore, after being thrown aside by her officer lover. Dense in both dramatic and musical texture (action happens simultaneously on a number of stages), and requiring huge forces, including 26 singers and a very large orchestra, it is an unremittingly harrowing work that draws on a number of different styles, from jazz and dance to pantomime and the use of tape. Its study of the military and of sexual repression is overwhelming in its visual and musical complexity, in its harshness, in the difficulty of much of the vocal writing, in the extremes of the emotions, and in its assault on the musical and dramatic senses. Whereas **Berg** in *Wozzeck* carefully controls his material, in *Die Soldaten* Zimmermann seems to be directly expressing, and at times barely mastering, his own inner fervour; as such it is the culmination of Expressionism in music. Ultimately, it does not stand comparison with Berg's opera, but it is an extraordinary experience, not to be missed.

In common with a number of Zimmermann works, the piano trio *Présence* (1961) was envisaged (and has been staged) as a ballet. It veers abruptly but smoothly from avant-garde writing to quotation (**Debussy, Strauss, Prokofiev** and **Stockhausen**) and pastiche and back again. Each of the three characters is represented by an instrument, Don Quixote by the violin, Molly Bloom (from Joyce's *Ulysses*) by the cello, and King Ubu (from Alfred Jarret's black comedy *Roi Ubu*) by the piano. King Ubu reappeared in his own 'ballet noir' *Musique pour les soupers du Roi Ubu* (1966).

The cello was a favourite instrument for Zimmermann, who used a panoply of extended instrumental techniques in his writing for the instrument; his last work was the *Vier kurze Studien* (*Four Short Studies*, 1970) for solo cello. Don Quixote reappeared in the *Cello Concerto 'en forme de "pas de trois"'* (1965–66), which was originally envisaged as a ballet and whose subtitle refers to a union of soloist, orchestra and ballet. This colourful and dramatic work is divided into five sections, reflecting various visions of imaginary ballet figures; in the final section the various characters come together. Against the virtuosic solo writing, the unusual orchestration includes a concertante group of mainly plucked instruments (mandolin, guitar, dulcimer, celesta, harp, piano, harpsichord), giving a distinctive and unusual overall colour. There are jazz and blues influences, but the predominating sense is that of the dance, overt in a section for cello against castanets and clockwork

percussion. An earlier cello concerto was titled *Canto di speranza* (*Song of Hope*, 1953, revised 1957). *Intercomunicazione* (1967) for cello and piano opens with solo cello sounds reminiscent of electronic effects, and throughout the two instruments are kept as distinct layers. Dark, sonorous, and austere expression from the solo cello dominates, often in two voices and with quarter-tone intervals. The piano provides counter-chords or snatches of repetitive phrases, before taking up the deep timbres of the cello, until towards the end both instruments become more agitated and take on new colours. The more tragic, pessimistic aspects of this sonorous, slow-moving and effective work reflected an increasing grimness in Zimmermann's output – *Requiem für einen jungen Dichter* (*Requiem for a Young Poet*, 1967–69) for soloists, choruses, orchestra, jazz group, organ and tape sets verses from three poets who committed suicide – leading to Zimmermann's own suicide in 1970.

In 1966 Zimmermann created one of the finest of all purely electronic works, *Tratto I*. In it he avoided the synthesised sounds that were just becoming available and which have become the staple of recent electronic music, and turned to pure electronically created sine vibration ('simple tones'). A basic interval, the tritone (with its overtones) dominates the work. The Italian title refers to both a stretch of time and a place in a written work, and was used in *Die Soldaten* to title the interludes. The fifteen-minute piece is a slow-moving vista of shifting sonorities, its internal pacing bearing little relationship to conventional music. Its timbral qualities and its sense of perfect proportion as it gradually builds to a climax are unforgettable.

Zimmermann taught at the Cologne University (1950–52) and at the Musikhochschule at Cologne (1957–70).

RECOMMENDED WORKS

Cello Concerto *en forme de 'pas de trois'* (1965–66)

opera *Die Soldaten* (1958–60, revisions to 1964)

Intercomunicazione (1967) for cello and piano

Symphony in One Movement (1947–51)

electronic *Tratto I* (1966)

Greece

Introduction

Greece has not been a major factor in European music, though it has produced one major conductor, Dimitri Mitropoulos (1896–1960), who himself wrote the first modern Greek opera, *Soeur Béatrice* (1919), as well as a string quartet and other works, and perhaps the most outstanding soprano of the century, Maria Callas (1923–1977), whose ability to instil the expression of character into a vocal line has never been equalled. The dearth of performing bodies of sufficient calibre (apart from a period in the 1920s and 1930s when Mitropoulos conducted the Athens Symphony Orchestra), and of companies interested in recording and disseminating modern Greek music, has greatly hampered Greek composers, and limited outside knowledge of their work.

Nikos **Skalkottas** (1904–1949) has particularly suffered, and his large body of works that developed an expressive version of 12-tone techniques needs to be more widely heard and explored. The elder statesman of modern Greek music was Manolis Kalomiris (1883–1962), who attempted to create a Greek nationalism with Romantic means, most obviously in his sumptuous but rather pedantic *Symphony No. 1 'Leventia'* (1918–20), influenced by his stay in Russia (1906–10). A prolific composer, his activities as a teacher were perhaps more important: he founded two conservatories. Mikis Theodorakis (born 1925) became instantly famous for his colourful score for the film *Zorba the Greek* (released 1964); his concert works, after early orchestral and ballet suites on Greek subjects, have attempted to fuse popular elements drawn from pop music and Greek and North African folk sources. He has been politically active, was imprisoned from 1967–70 by the 'colonel's regime', and more recently served as a member of the Greek Parliament and Minister without Portfolio. The works of Jani Christou (1926–70) include large-scale religious pieces with ritualistic tendencies.

Greece can claim one composer who has had a profound influence on European music through his intellectually rigorous and arresting avant-garde works. Iannis **Xenakis** (born 1922) has lived in France since 1947, in addition to his compositional activities working as an architect with Le Corbusier until 1960. His major intellectual contribution has been to demonstrate that modern mathematical principles could be the foundation of a plastic and immediate musical idiom; his major musical contribution a personal vision of the avant-garde that has an immediate physical impact on more general, rather than specialist, audiences.

Skalkottas Nikos*

born 8th March 1904 at Chalkis (Halkis), Euboea
died 19th August 1949 at Athens

It is still very difficult to gain a full idea of the worth of the music of Nikos Skalkottas. His obscurity is partly due to the strange circumstances of his life. Having already produced atonal works in the early 1920s, he then from 1927 to 1931 studied with **Schoenberg**, who considered him one of his most talented pupils. In 1933 he returned to Athens, and there played violin in various orchestras, completely cut off from any subsequent developments in European music. During this time his own works were unheard, but after his death a large number of compositions were found (his output totals over 150 works). Taking their point of departure from his studies with Schoenberg, they developed a personal technique derived from 12-tone methods, managing to combine it with a sense of tradition (he also wrote a number of more traditional works, such as the *Thirty-Six Greek Dances*, 1936, for orchestra, that echo Greek folk music).

After his study with Schoenberg, his output falls into distinct periods. From 1928 to 1938 his works follow a strict 12-tone system, though those written after his return to Athens are more spacious. From 1938 he started to vary the strict techniques and add modifications of his own, and his works became longer. In place of a single row he developed multiple rows, as many as four interacting at any given moment, creating a rich polyphonic counterpoint and luxurious sonorities. These rows are often subdivided, producing considerable possibilities of variation, though Skalkottas avoided those that would be aurally too complex (such as inversion and transposition). His overall structures are often developed from traditional sonata form; the use of flowing melodies drawn from the rows (as opposed to more jagged or pointillistic lines) and the sense of a tonal centre in writing that is never tonal, are two elements that create a link with tradition. In his final period (1946–49), when he concentrated on a small number of chamber pieces, his idiom became freer, without obvious tone-rows, and the emotional colours darker. Energetic rhythms play an important role, and are not systematised. The overall idiom has often been described as having a Mediterranean sense of colour and lucidity, and the richness of sound and use of more flowing melodic lines has led to a comparison with **Berg**.

Of a number of major orchestral works, *The Return of Ulysses* (1942–43), intended as an overture to an opera on the same subject, has a high reputation, while the *Symphonic Suite No. 2* (1944–49) is on a monumental scale, in six movements and lasting an hour and a half. These orchestral works are almost impossible to hear performed and badly need to be recorded. *Thirty-Six Greek Dances* (1936) is the best-known orchestral work, but, though delightful, is not representative of Skalkottas's main concerns. More likely to be heard are his more than fifty chamber works, or piano pieces that follow the general changes of style outlined above. The graceful *Octet* (1931) for four winds and four strings was discovered in the shop of a Berlin music dealer, while the *String Quartet No. 3* (1935) follows the strict organisation and methods of **Schoenberg**.

A Skalkottas Society in Athens has published some of his works.

RECOMMENDED WORKS
So rare is Skalkottas's music that any works can be recommended as a sample of the music of this unusual composer.

BIBLIOGRAPHY
N. Skalkottas, *The Technique of Orchestration*, 1940 (in Greek)

Xenakis Iannis***

born 29th May 1922 at Braïla, Romania

Of all the avant-garde composers who came to prominence in the 1950s and 1960s, Xenakis has been one of the most difficult to grasp intellectually (unless one is a mathematician), but at the same time one who makes an immediate appeal to a non-specialist audience. He was born in Romania of Greek parents, moved to Greece in 1932, and has lived in France since 1947, becoming a French citizen in 1965.

Xenakis's methods have been his own, and partly reflect his prominent parallel career as an architect. Many of the initiating ideas and subsequent construction of his works have been based on mathematical or physical models not normally associated with music (from Boolean algebra to the Kinetic Theory of Gases), which he has applied to music often through use of a computer. The details of these methods, excepting the area of probability theory, are not necessary for an immediate appreciation of the music, fascinating though they are and recommended to anyone who has already enjoyed Xenakis's individual approach.

An important concept is that in a random and chaotic set of elements the laws of probability allow for a combination of elements that is neither random nor chaotic (the most famous and extreme example is that a monkey, randomly playing at a typewriter, will eventually type a combination of letters that are a Shakespeare sonnet). Xenakis has consistently used these stochastic principles, especially after the advent of the computer, but it must be stressed that (unlike some of his contemporaries) his music is not aleatoric in the sense of chance being admitted, randomly and uncontrolled, into performance.

The connection between architecture and music surfaced in *Metastasis* (1953–54), written for sixty-one instrumentalists in sixty-one parts, and the only Xenakis work with serial elements. It is primarily composed of glissandi, whose continual divergence in many parts sets up a constantly shifting weave of sound; that divergence from the horizontal inspired Xenakis's design for Le Corbusier's Brussels Pavilion in 1958 (see also the entry on **Varèse**, who wrote the music for the pavilion). The work resembles in its sounds an electronic score – intentionally, as Xenakis wanted to show that the same sound world could be produced by an orchestra. The effects of sonorities, with clusters and very high string effects, were further explored in *Pithoprakta* (translatable as 'actions by probabilities', 1955–56) for 46 strings, two trombones, xylophone and wood block, with interesting percussion sounds that look forward to his later work, and an inherent contrast between glissandi and pizzicati. *Achorripsis* ('jets of sound', 1956–57), for twenty-one instruments, further developed composition using stochastic techniques; but the refinement of the idea came with the use of an IBM computer in the composition of *ST/10* (1956–63) for ten instruments (ST standing for 'stochastic', 10 for the number of instruments), more likely to be encountered in its version

for string quartet, *ST/4*. The rich sonorities and potent energy of *Syrmos* (1959)
for eighteen strings are based on transformations of eight base textures, including
glissandi and 'clouds of pizzicati', with a
mathematical structure and swooping and
gliding effects.

At the end of this period Xenakis wrote
a number of purely electronic scores, of
importance mainly for indicating the kinds
of sounds Xenakis wished to emulate with
purely orchestral forces. Indeed, *Bohor I*
(1962) sounds like his orchestral scores of
the period, with the same sense of teeming
life, the sound of a huge bell engulfing all
else, and closing with roars of a 100,000
voices, that resemble the sound of a storm.
The earlier *Diamorphoses II* (1957) shares
these storm-like sonorities, but they are
offset by delicate sounds and glissandi in a
memorable combination that makes this
short piece one of the more effective examples of the genre in the period. *Concert
P-H II* (1958) was written for the Le
Corbusier Philips Pavilion at the Brussels
Expo, acting as a prelude to music by
Varèse, and is composed of delicate sounds,
like the tinkling of hundreds of shards of
glass.

From 1959 Xenakis increasingly concentrated on composition (as opposed to architectural activities), notably in a number of
large-scale orchestral works in which the
exploration of sonority is the must obvious
element. In *Terretektorh* (1965–66) each of
the eighty-eight musicians (dispersed in
the audience) has three percussion instruments in addition to their own instrument.
With its wonderful opening, long held
strands of sounds, percussive clickings,
whistles, and sonorities like the croaking
of massed frogs, it has a powerful earthy
energy. *Nomos gamma* (1967–68), for an
orchestra of musicians again dispersed in
the audience, creates layers of event, using
overlapping swathes of brass strands
against other instruments, and held periods of a given colour, often with high
harmonics against the crash of percussion.
The summit of these orchestral works,
Kraanerg (1968–69) for orchestra and
tape, is a huge piece, whose title signifies
accomplishment combined with energy,
and reflects the biological and cultural
diversity, as well as the potential for
conflict, that the population explosion
implies. With its swathes of sonorities
ranging from deep sounds to extreme
woodwind, and the orchestra supporting
the huge soundscape of the electronic tape,
this monumental work teems with harsh
life, like an industrial landscape that

threatens to overwhelm with grinding
inevitability.

Meanwhile Xenakis had written two
works for voices on classical Greek subjects that form an effective pair, and whose
immediate idiom make them a possible
introduction to his music. *Oresteia*
(1965–66) for chorus, children's chorus and
twelve instruments, opens as a kind of
primitive ritual. Clashing elemental
sounds and reedy woodwind give way to
chant-like vocal writing, becoming more
complex and more brittle through the four
sections. It ends with rich vocal textures
that recall the immediately preceding
orchestral works. It includes the use of a
percussion instrument (either wooden or
metal) of Xenakis's own invention, the
simantra. *Medea* (1967) for male voice
choir, pebbles and orchestra is equally
ritualistic. Heavy, pounding drums,
orchestral strands, fanfares, and ritualistic
declamatory vocal lines eventually give
way to a primitive dance.

The ritualistic was combined with spectacle in a number of monumental and
arresting works designed for performance
at specific sites, some out of doors. The
raucous and short *Le Polytope de Montréal* (1967) for four orchestras spread
around the audience was written for the
Montréal Expo. *Hibiki Hana Ma* (1970)
for 12 tape channels was designed for a
laser beam spectacle at the Osaka Expo.
Polytope de Cluny (1971) for six hundred
flashes, three laser beams and seven tape
channels was commissioned for the Paris
Autumn Festival. The most spectacular
were two site-specific works written for
the Persepolis Festival in Iran. *Persephassa* (1969) for six percussionists is a
monumental *tour de force* requiring great
virtuosity. Deep drum sounds, usually
struck with slight overlaps, dominate the
opening and close of the work. These are
taken over by very delicate high tinklings,
wood-blocks, high siren-whistles, and the
metallic sounds of the simantra. By the end
all coalesce into a long and exciting accelerando. With its clear unfolding of event,
combining a primitive, elemental sound
world with sophisticated utterance, it is
one of Xenakis's most arresting works.
Persépolis (1971), subtitled 'We bear the
light of the earth', is electronic, and was
originally combined with staged and lighting effects in the ruins of the palace of
Darius in the city of the title. It is not
difficult to imagine the effect of this dense
and often harsh work in its original setting,
but too much is lost taking it out of context.

The possibilities of purely percussive

works were further explored in the catchy *Psappha* (1975) for solo percussion, with effects similar to the opening and to the accelerando dance of *Persephassa*, except that a gamelan-like section of tuned percussion bursts in to end the work. The attractive and colourful *Pleïades* (1978–79) for six percussionists has proved one of Xenakis's most enduring works, with unexpectedly jazzy sounds emerging briefly in a third movement that concentrates on keyboard percussion. The frenetic *Khoaï-Xoai* (1976) for amplified harpsichord, one of the most difficult of all harpsichord pieces, demands complex polyrhythms (7/8 against 9/8) and one hand to play both keyboards simultaneously.

More recently, Xenakis has played down complex vertical textures and sonorities in favour of a more linear flow that many may find more approachable than his earlier works. The title of *Aïs* (1981) for baritone, percussion and orchestra is the classical Greek word for Hades, and the work is a setting of fragments of Homer (Ulysses visiting the land of the dead, and the death of Patrocles) and Sappho (longing for death). The writing for the baritone, often in falsetto, suggests an equation between the ecstasies of love and those of death; it is supported by the linear rhythms of the percussion, and by the flow of the orchestra. The result is a work whose antecedents are the ritualistic elements of the classical Greek vocal works of the 1960s and the rhythmic patterns from the percussion works. *Keqrops* (1985) for piano and orchestra includes the rich, complex and dense orchestral sonorities so typical of Xenakis, but also a strong linear pulse, and a kind of linear lyricism in some of the melodic patterns. There are suggestions of more traditional harmonies, and this powerful music has an immediate impact. Sections of *Exchange* (1989) for bass clarinet and wind, brass and string announced a further departure in Xenakis's style. Although informed by the occasional extreme effect from the soloist, mathematical construction and complex rhythms are abandoned for music rich in swathes of sonority. There are passages with diatonic harmonies and recognisable tunes, and a slow progression and general simplicity in its opening, although it builds up to more dissonant and complex material.

Xenakis's particular achievement is to introduce new possibilities of sonorities and sound combinations into 20th-century music. His music has a sculptural quality, and this may come from the strong visual sense of the architect. More than most avant-garde composers, his sound world can be appreciated simply for these qualities, for the often harsh but usually exciting physical impact of the sound, based on unusual but secure methods of construction. Xenakis founded the School of Mathematical and Automated Music in Paris in 1966, and a similar department at the University of Indiana in 1967.

RECOMMENDED WORKS
Aïs (1981) for baritone, percussion and orchestra
electronic *Diamorphoses II* (1957)
Keqrops (1985) for piano and orchestra
Kraanerg (1968–69) for orchestra and tape
Medea (1967) for male voice choir, pebbles and orchestra
Nomos gamma (1967–68) for orchestra
Oresteia (1965–66) for chorus, children's chorus and twelve instruments
Pleïedes (1978–79) for six percussionists
Psappha (1975) for solo percussion
Persephassa (1969) for six percussionists
Syrmos (1959) for eighteen strings
Terretektorh (1965–66) for orchestra

BIBLIOGRAPHY
I. Xenakis, *Formalized Music*, 1971

Holland

Introduction

The music of the Netherlands had a glorious history during the Renaissance but faded into obscurity until the end of the 19th century, when a revival laid the groundwork for Holland's vigorous 20th-century compositional life. Bernard Zweers (1854–1924) sought nationalistic subjects for his German-Romantic idiom, notably in the *Symphony No. 3 'To My Country'* (1890), but it was Alphons Diepenbrock (1862–1921) who was the major figure in this revival. Initially influenced by Wagner, his music became increasingly Impressionistic following his discovery of the music of **Debussy** in 1910. His main achievements were in the field of *lieder*, setting a number of German Romantic poets, often with orchestral accompaniment, and French poets mainly with piano. Johan Wagenaar (1862–1941) produced a number of late Romantic tone poems, mostly on lighter subjects.

The main figures of the following generation were Matthijs **Vermeulen** (1888–1967), whose achievement was not fully appreciated until the last decade of his life, and Willem **Pijper** (1894–1947), whose influence on Dutch music through both his music and his teaching was considerable. Three figures, all pupils of Pijper, stand out from among the following generation. Guillaume Landré (1905–68) used monothematic procedures are then 12-tone techniques in a generally elegiac idiom; his major works include four symphonies, four string quartets, and a number of orchestral works. Henk **Badings** (1907–82) initially came to prominence with powerful symphonies, and then from the 1950s with an exploration of electronics, notably in stage works. Kees van Baaren (1906–70) was a major teacher, and the pioneer of 12-tone techniques in Holland in the *Wind Trio* of 1936; his *Septet* (1952) for violin, double-bass and wind quintet was the first major Dutch work to follow strict 12-tone procedures throughout.

His later works include a 12-tone symphony. Ton de **Leeuw** (1926–96) was a pioneer of Dutch electronic music; his brother Reinbert de Leeuw (born 1939) has been influenced by **Cage** and by minimalism. Otto Ketting (born 1935), best known for *Time Machine* (1972) for wind and percussion, uses a direct and lyrical idiom that draws on **Berg** and **Stravinsky**.

His style has a sense of precision and muted effect, with clean instrumentation. His opera *Ithaka* (1986) has an unusual surrealist text (in English) that follows the fantasies of a journalist, a poet and an ex-model. It shows his sense of muted dramatic effect to good advantage. The song-cycle on ancient Egyptian texts, *The Light of the Sun* (1978, revised 1983) for soprano and orchestra, is also recommended. Peter Schat (born 1935) was initially influenced by **Boulez**, and explored aleatory elements in such works as the *Improvisations and Symphonies* (1962). His spectacular opera *Labyrinth* (1966) used electronics, a chorus in the audience, a counter-plot sung in Latin, film and dance. In the 1960s, following a visit to Cuba, his music became overtly political. He was one of the composers involved in the major Dutch avant-garde event of the late 1960s, the anti-American collectivist opera *Reconstructione* (1969, with Louis **Andriessen** and Ton de Leeuw, among others). In the 1980s his idiom moved towards the mainstream, including two symphonies.

One family has played a major role in 20th-century Dutch music. Hendrik Andriessen (1892–1981) was especially known for his clean-textured liturgical music, but his concert works include four symphonies and the *Ricercare* (1950) for orchestra, which commemorated the 200th anniversary of the death of JS Bach and is perhaps his best-known work. Its combination of a neo-classical rhythmic impulse and broad, clear colours is reminiscent of **Martinů**, and is recommended. His brother Willem Andriessen (1887–1964) was also a composer and a concerto pianist. Hendrik's sons, Jurriaan Andriessen (1925–96) and Louis **Andriessen** (born 1939) are both composers; the latter has been the most influential Dutch composer of the 1970s and 1980s, evolving a minimalist style with features similar to that of Philip **Glass** in the USA. His works have been widely influential on a younger generation of composers in Europe and New York.

Netherlands Music Information Centre:
Gaudeamus Foundation
Swammerdamstraat 38
1091 RV Amsterdam
tel: +31 20 6947349
fax: +31 20 6947258

Andriessen Louis *
born 6th June 1939 at Utrecht

Louis Andriessen has become one of the better-known of the younger Dutch composers through his minimalist works of the 1970s, widely heard in Europe and the United States, which have influenced a younger generation of composers on both sides of the Atlantic. His earlier music utilised a free 12-tone style, often hinting at tonality and earlier musics, as in *Anachrony I* (1967) for orchestra, which includes sections following strict 12-tone principles, but also quotations from Bach's *St. Matthew Passion* and **Roussel's** *Symphony No. 3*. By 1970 his music had become overtly experimental and political in such works as *Volkslied* (*National Hymn*, 1971) and *Workers' Union* (1975). He also founded a wind ensemble, 'De Volharding' ('Perseverance'), its name drawn from a piece of the same title (1972). But it was with *Hoketus* (1977) that Andriessen established his minimalist style and his international reputation, especially through performances by the group Hoketus that was subsequently formed with Andriessen as pianist.

Andriessen's minimalist style has affinities with **Glass**, especially in its sudden harmonic gear-shifts, and with **Reich** in some of its rhythmic features. It is distinguished by his willingness to let dissonant elements intrude, as well as elements of performer choice. Generally, his instrumentation has favoured wind and brass instruments over strings. A particular feature of his minimalism has been a development of the 14th-century concept of 'hoquetus' (hocket) in which a phrase is sung by two voices in fast alternation. In Andriessen's minimalism these alternations overlap in a technique similar to that used in Peruvian pipe-playing. In *Hoketus* for small ensemble electronically amplified, a repetitive phrase, based on two notes, is started alternately by two groups. Additions are gradually made to the basic length of the phrase, thus building a sense of acceleration while maintaining the basic tempo. Changes are created by altering the two notes and gradually adding other rhythmic ideas. The effect is a mesmerising, almost motoric insistence, unrelieved by the kind of diatonic harmonies found in the works of **Glass**. Its length is determined by the players, who choose the number of repetitions.

Some of these minimalist techniques had been used earlier in *De Staat* (*The Republic*, 1973–76), a discussion of the place of music in politics with a text from Plato. Its basis in tetrachords (groups of four notes) is paralleled by the forces: four of women's voices, horns, trumpets, trombones, and violas, with two electric guitars, bass guitar, two pianos and two harps. Initial repetitive phrases give way to a more diverse and complex use of repetitive ideas, swelling and falling counterphrases, hoketus effects, subtle changes of colour and allusions to **Stravinsky's** *The Rite of Spring* that make *De Staat* one of the most vital and varied of all minimalist works.

Mausoleum (1979), for two baritones and large wind ensemble with piano and percussion, combined some of the insistence of *Hoketus* and the variety of *De Staat* with chant-like vocal writing. Repetitive minimalist effects are merged with other orchestral effects to create a more obviously mainstream idiom, especially in the slow dirge that ends the work. The texts are drawn from Bakunin, setting out his anarchist beliefs (shared by the composer) and from a poem about Bakunin by Arthur Arnould. The dry *De Snelheid* (*Velocity*, 1983) for orchestra explores different tempi and pulses, using high percussion as a metronome and dividing the orchestra into three groups. It is a sterile work, showing the pitfalls of a preoccupation with minimalist means rather than content. *M is for Man, Music, Mozart* (1991) for two voices and ensemble was commissioned for a Mozart television film, with four songs and three instrumental sections. The opera *Rosa* (1994) centres on the story of the wife of the Uraguayan film composer Juan Manuel de Rosa, with a libretto by film-maker Peter Greenaway in which she attempts to turn herself into a horse to match her husband's first love.

Andriessen has taught at the Royal Conservatory of the Hague since 1974, and co-authored a book on **Stravinsky** (1983).

RECOMMENDED WORKS
> *Hoketus* (1977) for small ensemble
> *De Staat* (1973–76) for four women's
> voices and ensemble

Badings Henk*
born 17th January 1907 at Bandung, Java
died 26th June 1987 at Maarheeze

With **Pijper**, Henk Badings was the major figure of Dutch music in the 20th century, once well known internationally, but now virtually forgotten outside Holland. His output was vast: nearly 500 compositions in virtually all the musical genres. He made his reputation with a series of rugged and rather stern symphonies, their emphasis on counterpoint following the tradition of **Hindemith**. Their use of a tonal base with scales built from six or eight notes creates suggestions of modality, and there are often polytonal passages. His formal structures emphasise taut integration, so that in the *Symphony No. 2* (1932) the finale uses varied themes from the earlier movements; the five subjects of the fugue finale of the choral *Symphony No. 6* (1953) also use motifs from preceding movements, capped by a finale in which the chorus sings four of the themes, and the orchestra play the fifth, evolving into a full theme that contains the smaller motifs heard earlier. Elsewhere Badings employed his teacher **Pijper's** technique of building material from 'germ-cells', as in the *Symphony No. 4* (1943).

The best known of the symphonies is the *Symphony No. 3* (1934). Dense swirling textures in the rugged opening contrast with an elegiac theme, itself multi-stranded and contrapuntal. This contrast, between the tough, turbulent, almost martial, and the more reflective, permeates the symphony. Its restless, almost nervous energy is tautly contained in the overall construction. The scherzo is almost mawkish; its tragic and sparse slow movement seems to herald the coming war in a similar fashion to **Vaughan Willams's** *Symphony No. 4* of the same year. From the same period comes the first of four works titled *Symphonic Variations* (1936), using two contrasting themes in nine variations laid out symphonically.

In the 1940s Badings lightened the tone of his music with more lyrical thematic ideas, though the darker hue could return in such works as the powerful *String Quartet No. 3* (1944). The major work of this period, besides the third, fourth, fifth and sixth symphonies, was the ballet *Orpheus en Euridike* (1941) for baritone, chorus and orchestra, in which Orpheus is played by an actor rather than a dancer. The flowing writing of the extended *Ballade* (1950) for flute and harp reflects this lighter touch, and demonstrates a technique of building scales from alternate major and minor seconds. The culmination of this period was the *Concerto for Two Violins No. 1* (1954).

From 1952 Badings became interested in electronic music, while continuing to write more conventional works, and he helped create the Philips electronic studio in Eindhoven. The radio opera *Orestes* (1954) used a *musique concrète* score, including the speeding up of a taped male chorus. Another radio opera, *Asterion*, employed a similar technique in the electronic manipulation of musical or natural

sounds, while the television opera *Salto mortale* (1957) had a purely electronic-generated accompanying tape.

The kind of sounds that Badings was able to create in his electronic scores influenced some of his later orchestral works, which have equivalent sounds produced by purely orchestral means. In these later works he sometimes combined instruments with electronics and experimented with more complex scales, developing a microtonal scale of thirty-one notes. This was used in such works as the *Concerto for Two Violins No. 2* (1969) and in the *Sonata for Two Violins No. 3* (1967). His later operas included *Martin Korda D.P.* (1960), which denounced Soviet gulag camps.

Badings' later career was haunted by his wartime activities; the Nazis described him as 'the very model of a Nationalist Socialist artist', and until the end of his life protests met the premières of a number of his works. He gradually reestablished his reputation, notably through his teaching activities at Utrecht University (1961–72) and the Stuttgart Musikhochschule (1962–72), but the lingering memory of his collaboration may have hampered a wider dissemination of his music outside Holland.

RECOMMENDED WORKS
   Symphony No. 3 (1934)
   Concerto for 2 Violins and Orchestra
      No. 1 (1954)

BIBLIOGRAPHY
   J. Wouters, *Henk Badings*, 1971 (in
      Dutch)

de Leeuw Ton[*]
born 16th November 1926 at
Rotterdam
died 30th May 1996 at Paris

Ton de Leeuw was one of the first Dutch composers to make extensive use of electronics in his music, and has a special interest in the spatial structure of slow changes in sound that not only reflect electronic possibilities, but also the influence of the Asian music traditions that he has studied. Much of his work uses a favourite device, the octave divided by its fourth/fifth. Obvious spatial effects are found in such works as *Spatial Music I* (1965–66) for thirty-two to forty-eight instruments, but also in such structural devices as the repetition of a movement within another movement (*Mouvements rétrogrades*, 1957, for orchestra) or the Hindu technique of dividing larger time units into three smaller ones. Gamelan music is an influence in *Haiku II* (1968) for soprano and orchestra, *Lamento Pacis II* (1969) for choir and instruments, and *Gending* (1975) for gamelan orchestra. Many of these traits were drawn together in a triptych on Biblical texts, of which *Car nos vignes sont en fleur* (1980) for a cappella choir uses a kind of vocal tuning system before the texts begin.

His electronic music falls into two periods. The early period includes *Study* (1957), which used serial procedures and microtones, and *Antiphonie* (1960) for wind quintet and four tape tracks. Then until 1977 (by which time development of electronics had opened new possibilities) de Leeuw wrote little electronic music. But in *Mountains* (1977) for bass clarinet and tape, he applied Hindustani vocal techniques to the material, while in the *Magic of Music II* (1978) for voices, speaker and tape, the singer's first realisation of the score is taped and replayed while the layers improvise. This in turn is taped, and the process repeated four times, gradually building the sonorities. European folk music, including drones, has influenced two purely electronic works, *Chronos* (*Time*, 1980) and *Clair-Obscur* (1982). An interesting introduction to his music is through the *String Quartet No. 2*, which exists in two versions, for quartet alone (1964) and with tape (1965).

De Leeuw initiated and directed the electronic studio in the Sweelinck Conservatory, Amsterdam.

RECOMMENDED WORK
String Quartet No. 2 (1964) for quartet alone or (1965) with tape

Pijper Willem**
born 8th September 1894 at Zeist
died 18th March 1947 at Leidschendam

Willem Pijper is the best-known Dutch composer of the century, whose influence was considerably extended by his activities as a teacher (at the Amsterdam College of Music, 1920–22, the Amsterdam Conservatory, 1925–30, and as director of the Rotterdam Conservatory, 1930–47). His pupils included many of the major Dutch composers of the following generation.

The core of Pijper's output are the three symphonies and his chamber music. His earliest works came under the influence of **Debussy**, although the *Symphony No. 1* (1917–18, known as *Pan*) has shades of

Mahler. With the two-movement *Symphony No. 2* (1921) and its very unusual instrumentation (116 instruments including organ, three pianos, six mandolins, celesta and tuned steel plate), Pijper matured into a more individual voice. This led to a period of fruitful individualisation (1920–30) followed by a gradual simplification of his established style, aimed at a more direct clarity.

The material of the *Symphony No. 2* is, as in most of his works, built up from cells of ideas, rhythmic, melodic and harmonic (Pijper, an exceptionally erudite man, especially in biology, used the term 'germ-cells'), and suggests bitonality in much of its treatment. A residue of **Mahler** remains in the use of mandolins and horn-calls, though not in the tango/habanera rhythms that were to become a particular favourite and whose juxtaposition with declamatory material is the chief feature of this symphony. It is an enigmatic work, full of unusual instrumental colours and quasi-popular rhythms, purposeful in passing yet seemingly without a goal.

The one-movement *Symphony No. 3* (1926), again with piano and mandolin in the orchestra, remains his best-known work, but it does not seem as inventive as its predecessor, in spite of the touches of jazz and the mysterious atmosphere of the slow second section, hauntingly pointed up by a tango rhythm. Polymeters (more than one rhythm occurring simultaneously) join polytonality in these works, and are heard again in the *Piano Concerto* (1927), which alternates solo and orchestral music, again with touches of jazz and blues, in a seven-section single-movement structure.

Of the chamber music, an embryonic bitonal technique appears in some passages of the *Violin Sonata No. 1* (1919), otherwise lyrical and conventional. Poly-rhythms and unusual instrumental effects are found in the *Cello Sonata No. 1* of the same year. The *Septet* (1920) initiated Pijper's use of the 'germ-cell' principle, while the gentle *Flute Sonata* (1925), if unmemorable, has a certain Gallic charm. The *Wind Quintet* (1928–29) is equally ingenuous, wearing its contrapuntal complexities on its sleeve. Of the string quartets, *String Quartet No. 4* (1940) is astringent and abstract, utilising all Pijper's characteristic devices: in the first movement the first violin has 133 bars, the cello 170, such is the effect of the polyrhythms. With its totally inconclusive ending, it emerges as one of his most interesting works. The freer *String Quartet No. 5* (1946), which shares some devices with its predecessor (for example, rhythms of two against three), promised to be even finer, but was left unfinished. Of the piano music, the short and dense *Sonatina No. 2* and *Sonatina No. 3* of 1925 are infected by blues and jazz, while the *Old-Dutch Dances* reflect an interest in Dutch folk music, particularly ballads. Pijper edited several collections of folk songs, and the influence appears in his choral and vocal settings, notably *Herr Halewijn* (1920) for eight-part unaccompanied choir. Folk songs also formed the catalyst for the opera *Halewijn* (1933–34). His incidental music shows a fascination with Greek drama, including three scores for *Antigone* (1920, 1922, 1926) and others for *The Baccantes* (1924) and *Cyclops* (1925).

Sharing some features with his contemporary **Vermeulen** (polyrhythms, polytonality), Pijper's music is technically superior, though its lack of an individual voice, of clear-cut purpose, makes it seem less intrinsically rewarding. His use of a scale of alternating whole-tones and semitones has become known in Holland as the 'Pijper scale' (although he was not the first to use it – in Russia it is known as the Rimsky-Korsakov scale).

RECOMMENDED WORKS
    Symphony No. 2 (1921–29)
    Symphony No. 3 (1926)
    String Quartet No. 4 (1928)
    String Quartet No. 5 (1946)
        (incomplete)

BIBLIOGRAPHY
    W. Pijper, *De quintencircel*, 1929 (in Dutch)
    De stemvork, 1930 (in Dutch)

Vermeulen Matthijs*
born 8th February 1888 at Helmond
died 26th July 1967 at Laren

Until recently, Matthijs Vermeulen was recognised in Holland chiefly as a forceful and provocative music critic who strove to wrest Dutch music away from the dominance of German models, and steer it towards those of the French. But in the last years of his life, his own music, hitherto hardly performed, began to be heard and appreciated, and he is now considered by many in Holland to be a major composer, an individual voice whose unheard vision was ahead of its time. His music is slowly becoming known outside Holland.

As with many such figures, the claims made for his music can seem exaggerated outside a Dutch context, but he is certainly a composer of more than passing interest whose music is rarely dull. His output, dominated by seven symphonies, is little influenced by the French whose cause he espoused (except shades of **Debussy** in the early songs, and an hedonism that has as many Russian as French parallels). The earliest extant work, the *Symphony No. 1 'Symphonia carminum'* (*Symphony of songs*, 1912–14) is Mahlerian, with juxtaposition of martial and pastoral ideas, but is too untamed to be of real worth. It includes the hallmarks of Vermeulen's music: a tumultuous sense of ecstasy (the closest parallel is perhaps **Scriabin**) and largely optimistic conclusions expressed by a large orchestra.

With the *Symphony No. 2 'Prélude à la nouvelle journée'* (1919–20) these concerns were dressed in a radically different language. Here there is a continual flow of long irregular melodic ideas, swapped from instrument to instrument and often using extreme registers. The different melodic strands progress independently, intersecting in unusual chordal combinations. As a result, although individual melodies may be grounded in one mode or key, the combination of them goes beyond tonality. Polyrhythms contribute to wild moments of ecstatic climax. Dense, vibrant, and sometimes as wild as a tropical jungle, it is too flawed to be a masterpiece; but its narrow insistence and its lack of emotional contrasts make it a fascinating battering-ram of a work. It was not performed until 1953, when it won a prize at the Queen Elizabeth Competition in Brussels.

The subsequent symphonies take these methods as their point of departure, with *Symphony No. 5 'Les lendemains chantants'* (1941–45) being the longest and most concentrated. The final *Symphony No. 7 'Dithyrambes pour le temps à venir'* (*Dithyrambs for the times to come*, 1963–65) simplifies the language into an almost neoclassical clarity of instrumental flow, motoric in some of its rhythmic and instrumental effects. All these works are worth exploring, though ultimately the improvisatory feel fails to mask the lack of symphonic argument or development. The *String Trio* (1923) and *Violin Sonata* (1924) reflect Vermeulen's characteristic extravagance of mood, while the *String Quartet* (1923) translates the density of texture to the chamber medium.

Vermeulen lived near Paris from 1921 to 1946, but returned to Holland to edit the newspaper *De Groene Amsterdammer*.

His writings include a psychoanalytical view of music (*Princiepen der Europese Muziek*, 1949). There is now a Matthijs Vermeulen Foundation in The Hague.

RECOMMENDED WORKS

Symphony No. 2 *Prélude à la nouvelle journée* (1919–20)
Symphony No. 7 *Dithyrambes pour les temps à venir* (1963–65)

Hungary

Introduction

Hungary has had a long and fertile history of classical music, reflecting the location of the country within the Austro-Hungarian Empire. Like the Czech lands, its position of subservience within German-speaking political dominance led to the rise of nationalism in the latter half of the 19th century, a process in which composers were involved. Ferenc Erkel (1810–93) founded a national operatic style, while the major international figure, the composer and pianist Franz (Ferenc) Liszt (1811–86), wrote some works with a nationalist flavour (such as the *Hungarian Rhapsodies*), even if his major legacies were an extension of tonality (that makes him a precursor of Impressionism), new structural principles, the development of pianistic techniques, and a sense of the visionary. The major Hungarian representative of Romanticism in the 20th century, who combined the influence of Brahms with nationalism was Ernö **Dohnányi** (1877–1960).

Two major international figures freed nationalist musical elements from Romanticism. Starting in 1905, Béla **Bartók** (1881–1945) and Zoltán **Kodály** (1882–1967) together collected folk songs from Hungary, Slovakia and Romania, making some 16,000 recordings in the process. They realised that the elemental power and unusual scales and colours of folk music could be the catalyst for their own music, rather than being a colour element within a traditional framework. Bartók, in his expressive and sometimes barbaric idiom took this process further, evolving a system of harmony that was influenced by the scales of folk music, and has been deeply influential on later composers. Kodály's most important achievements are in vocal and choral music, drawing on that folk heritage, and in his teaching system (the 'Kodály method'). The third figure of this generation, Leó Weiner (1885–1960), was an important teacher, but his own compositions, such as the *String Quartet No. 2* (1921) or the *String Quartet No. 3* (1938) are bland, if well constructed.

The influence of **Bartók** and **Kodály** was paramount on subsequent Hungarian composers until the 1960s. They dominated Hungarian composition until World War II, when the invasion of Hungary by the

Nazis (1944), and the rise of communism (1947, with full communist control in 1949), effectively cut off Hungarian composers from any further developments in Western music. However, from 1959 Hungarian composers were more open to Western influences, discovered 12-tone and serial music, and very rapidly absorbed both the musical legacy of the previous two decades and the latest techniques and developments. Some had fled, especially during or after the Soviet invasion in 1956. The most prominent of these was György **Ligeti** (born 1923); the chief figure that stayed, György **Kurtág** (born 1926), remained silent through the more repressive years of the communist regime, but from 1959 has produced a series of works of remarkable sensitivity.

Hungarian composers quickly absorbed new ideas from 1960, in spite of restrictions behind the Iron Curtain. Of all the ex-communist countries, Hungary was the least affected by Soviet Socialist Realism, and virtually none of the composers in this section have written anything in that banal idiom. Instead, composers turned to an increasing refinement of idioms often derived from **Bartók** or **Kodály**, and a development of expressive possibilities within that refinement. This has continued in a rapid development of techniques since the 1960s: Hungary has continued to produce a remarkably large number of composers of a consistently high standard in addition to the internationally known figures. As Hungary emerges from communism, this has created an exciting base for the future of composition in the country, as well as providing the opportunity for some of these composers to receive the wider exposure that they deserve.

Besides the major figures already noted, the best known of the interwar generation of Hungarian composers is probably Miklós Rózsa (1907–95), creator of some of the most famous Hollywood film scores. His concert work concentrated on chamber music for smaller forces and concertos. It is primarily motivated by the integration into the Austro-Germanic tradition of the Hungarian folk music of his childhood. The folk influence includes characteristic Magyar intervals and inflections rather than direct quotation. Of his concertos, the *Piano Concerto* (1966) is, in spite of its driving opening, typically Romantic in tone and feel, with virtuoso solo writing. More effective and individual is the *Cello Concerto* of 1969, while the *Violin Concerto* (1953) is considered by many to be his finest work. His more opulent film music,

which numbers over eighty scores, has included glittering epic scores of enormous panache that employ the modal melodies characteristic of his lyricism (*Quo Vadis?*, 1951, *Ben-Hur*, 1959) as well as tense and gripping scores for directors such as Alfred Hitchcock. He received three Oscars (for *Ben-Hur*, *A Double Life*, and *Spellbound*).

More important to Hungarian music is the conservative but assured Ferenc **Farkas** (born 1905). György Ránki (1907–92) achieved recognition for the orchestral suites (1954) from the opera *Pomád kirly uj ruhja* (*King Pomade's New Clothes*, 1953), a colourful but very conventional score. Its sense of folk-inspired humour and grotesqueness was a feature of his earlier music, as well as oriental touches derived from his studies of Eastern music. However, in the 1960s he turned to large-scale 'historical tableaux' reflecting historical events with a strong dramatic content (*1514* for piano and orchestra, 1961, or the oratorio *1944*, 1966). These rather portentious works have strong dramatic gestures and more contemporary elements. Gyula Dávid (1913–77) collected folk music (at his teacher **Kodály's** suggestion), and his earlier music shows folk influences. Although he later turned to 12-tone technique, his idiom remained rooted in a more conservative Hungarian tradition: in the *String Quartet* (1962) in honour of Kodály's 80th birthday, the timbres, line and rhythms of Hungarian folk music are more in evidence than the dodecaphonic elements. His unassuming but attractive *Viola Concerto* (1951), has echoes of a folk idiom. The music of Rudolf Maros (1917–82, not to be confused with his son, Milkos, born 1943, who works in Sweden) concentrated on folk and nationalist idioms, though the discovery of serialism at the beginning of the 1960s led to a more individual position using serial elements without any strict adherence. Frank **Martin** was an influence on the *Ricercare (In Memoriam, 1919)* (1959) for orchestra, which incorporates elements of 12-tone technique. A concern with delicacy of changing orchestral colours and clarity of sound was expanded in such works as *Three Eufonias* (1963–65) for orchestra, using tone-clusters and micro-tones. In his later music the scoring became simpler, while still concentrating on colour effects. András Mihály (1917–93) initially followed the example of **Bartók** and **Kodály** (for example, the *Cello Concerto*, 1953), though the *Violin Concerto* (1959) has echoes of the Baroque. From the late 1950s his idiom became increasingly complex, in an attempt to combine some of the idiom of Bartók with the ideas of the Second Viennese School. The Bartókian *Dalok József Attila verseire* (*Songs on poems by Attila József*, 1961) is recommended, while the influence of **Berg** is overt in the opera *Egylt es egyedl* (*Together and Alone*, 1964–65) and that of **Webern** covert in the *Symphony No. 3* (1962). By the middle 1960s he started to incorporate some of the ideas of the avant-garde, including clusters and aleatory methods.

The next generation of Hungarian composers was the first to come to artistic maturity during the communist period. István **Sárközy** (born 1920) is discussed under his entry below. The earlier works of Kamilló Lendvay (born 1928) were influenced by **Bartók**, but from the 1960s his generally expressive style showed a clear awareness of the main currents elsewhere in Europe. The dark and sometimes violent oratorio *Orogenesis* ('mountain slide' or 'birth', 1969–70) has some effective moments, and the cantata *Jelenetek* (*Scenes*, 1979–81), based on texts by Thomas Mann, is recommended. The powerfully characterised vocal lines are set against restrained orchestration, developed from the resonant orchestral palette of *A csend harmnija* (*The Harmony of Silence* for orchestra, 1980) and favouring higher registers, with a crumhorn in the final scene. His television opera *A tisztességtudó utcalány* (*The Respectful Prostitute*, 1976–79) is also worthy of note, its music an effective foil to a strong drama based on a Sartre play. András Szöllösy (born 1921) has written works of impressive sonorities and massed sound effects. István **Láng** (born 1933) has been one of the leading Hungarian composers to embrace serial ideas. The music of Zsolt Durkó (1934–97) has attracted attention in Britain, and perhaps deserves wider notice. Always meticulously crafted, his style is expressive, concentrating on rich textures and episodic structures (exemplifed by the nine sections of *Organismi*, 1964, for violin and orchestra) and using an unextreme serial technique. Much of his output is vocal, including a setting of the first extant Hungarian text (the oratorio *Burial Prayer*, 1967–72) and a large-scale opera, *Moses* (1973–76). His sense of colour, which is almost Impressionist in the *Turner Illustrations* (1976) for solo violin and fourteen instruments, is evident in the use of wordless chorus in such works as *Altamira* (1968) for chamber choir and orchestra. Sándor Balassa (born 1935) has used 12-tone (but not serial) elements in his expressive idiom, often with a sense of fantasy, using contrasts of light and dark. *Tabulae* (1972) for chamber orchestra and *Calls and Cries* (1982) for orchestra are a good introduction. His expressive opera *The Man Outside* (1973–78), based on a drama by Wolfgang Borchert, echoes **Berg's** *Wozzeck* in its story of a soldier returning from the war to find his wife has left him. János Decsényi (born 1927) has developed a Hungarian minimalism that combines 12-tone elements with minimalist ostinati and repetition. These are handled with delicate textures, a strong sense of colour, and a structure that usually starts very simply but moves to the more complex. The results are far removed from the stifling harmonic sequences of so many minimalists. A prime example is the engaging *Epitaph from Aquincum* (1979) for soprano, electric organ and strings, whose haunting simplicity is perfectly judged. In such less obviously minimalist works as the *String Quartet* (1978), there is still the same concentration on the relationship between simplicity and complexity – here the first movement is based on seven tones, the second on twelve, and the sparse and beautiful third on four.

Of the younger generation, Attila **Bozay** (born 1939) and László **Dubrovay** (born 1943), a pioneer of Hungarian electronic music, are discussed under their own entries. The Budapest New Music Studio (Üj Zenei Stúdió), founded in 1970, was influenced by the ideas of **Cage** before developing a more minimalist approach, experimenting with extended instrumental techniques in the process. Its co-founders and leading figures are Zoltán Jeney (born 1943), László Sáry (born 1940) and László Vidovsky (born 1944). Jeney's austere music is often slow-moving and meditative, with shades of **Reich** in such works as *OM* (1979) for two electric organs, and an emphasis on rhythm and melody in *To Apollo* for chorus, electric organ, cor anglais and twelve crotales (a type of castanet). *Laudes* (1976) for orchestra took the adagio of **Mahler's** *Symphony No. 10*, maintained all the pitches, dynamics and rhythms, but completely redistributed the order of notes and rests. Sáry has also concentrated on the continuous variation of pitches, rhythms and dynamics, and has used hocket effects (see under **Andriessen**, Holland). Vidovsky's music has often included a strong visual or theatrical element. In *Schroeder haláda* (1975) for piano and three assistants, the piano writing consists of repeated scales; in the middle of the performance the assistants prepare the piano, changing the sound until eventually the strings themselves cease to sound. The 'musical farce' *Narcissus and Echo* (1981) for four soloists, girls' chorus and five amplified instruments, parodied the styles of Wagner, Liszt, **Mahler** and **Weill. Kurtág's** son, also called György Kurtág (born 1954), has also worked in the studio.

Many new Hungarian works have been heard in the Budapest Music Weeks, which since 1974 has included two weeks devoted to new music. Readers should note that the normal Hungarian practice is to place the Christian name after the surname, which can cause some confusion if dealing with material of Hungarian origin – thus Franz Liszt is written as Liszt Ferenc. Such an error has caused Kodály's opera to be known in English as *Háry János*, whereas the second word is actually the Christian name.

Hungarian Music Information Centre:
Hungarian Music Council
Vörösmarty tér 1. I. 105
H-1364 Budapest P.O. Box 47
Hungary
tel: + 36 1 317 9598
fax: + 36 1 317 8267

Bartók Béla•••
born 25th March 1881 at
Nagyszentmiklós
died 26th September 1945 at New York

Béla Bartók is Hungary's greatest composer, and one of the most important of all 20th-century figures. His achievement was to show how completely the influence of folk musics, with rhythmic and harmonic traditions quite different from those of the classical tradition, could be absorbed into a distinctive and emotive modern idiom. He worked largely outside any school of 20th-century music, preferring to utilise those elements of his style that were appropriate to a particular work. This is in general contrast to those composers, such as **Schoenberg** or **Stravinsky**, whose individual works fit into a particular system or pattern. It is difficult to ascribe any 'method' to Bartók; and those he has influenced have responded to the intensity and integrity of emotion that is a primary motivation of his music rather than the intellectual conceptualisation or abstraction of any 'system'.

That being said, Bartók's mature works show a stylistic evolution rather than any abrupt separation into periods. Initially he left behind the vestiges of Romanticism, and began to assimilate folk music into his idiom. Next the impetus of the elemental inherent in that folk music became fully absorbed, controlled by brilliantly engineered interlocking constructions. The harmonic structures moved far from tonality, evolving new harmonic applications without ever completely losing touch with tradition. Finally Bartók moved back to a more obvious tonal base and to the Romanticism of its origins, but in an idiom that had absorbed the constructional experience and which had refined the harmonic colours of the folk inspiration. As a rough guide, the dates of these three phases are from 1905 to 1917, 1918 to 1927, and from 1937 to his death. Some critics have attempted to postulate different stylistic periods based on these dates, but there is a considerable overlap that makes such chronological pigeonholing unreliable.

Bartók's youthful music included the ballet *Kossuth* (1903), a response to his discovery of Richard **Strauss**, and the *Rhapsody*, op. 1 (1904) for piano and orchestra, which owes a debt to Liszt in the grand manner of the virtuoso solo part. In 1905, Bartók, in company with **Kodály** and a recording gramophone, started the systematic investigation of folk music that was to form the basis of his idiom. In many countries (including Hungary), folk music had already formed the basis of nationalism in music, but only insofar as a folk idea or melody was modified to the demands of a late Romantic idiom as a kind of exoticism. What Bartók discovered was that he could use the unmodified structural characteristics of folk music as the foundations of a personal language that would be free from the controls of that late Romantic idiom. This paralleled other means of musical emancipation, notably the neoclassicism of **Stravinsky** and his followers, and the 12-tone system of **Schoenberg** and the Second Viennese School. The difference was that these systems were founded on intellectual concepts. The very nature of folk music, a form both instinctive and elemental, meant that Bartók's evolution could proceed as his temperament required.

Initially these folk influences were more obvious in smaller-scale piano works (from the *For Children* collection of 1909 to the *Fifteen Hungarian Peasant Songs* of 1917). A series of stunning and sometimes savage stage works translated the new freedom supplied by folk music into large-scale works of striking versatility. This aggressive tone was heralded by the *Allegro barbaro* (1911) for piano, and led to such works as the *Piano Concerto No. 1* (1926). The climax of this period was the *String Quartet No. 3* (1927). In such works, however experimental the harmonies, the influence of folk music is often apparent in the melody or rhythm at the start of a movement. In the late works, where the melodic lines become more Romantic and flowing and a clear sense of tonality returns, the modalities and scales are still often derived from folk music. Throughout his career Bartók wrote pieces in more direct folk-song style, such as many of the *Mikrokosmos* (1926–39) for piano, or the marvellous two- and three-part choruses for children's or women's choir (1935); this aspect of Bartók's output is perhaps the least known outside Hungary.

In the bulk of Bartók's work, folk influences are absorbed into an idiom that shows a number of clear characteristics. Harmonically, the sense of tonal base is established, but the constraints of tonality are overthrown by movement around an axis that provides a basic pitch, often swinging around the interval of the tritone (augmented fourth). Chords are often built in fourths, rather than the traditional thirds, and piled on one another; movement is often in steps of more unusual intervals (2nds, 7ths). Scales derived from folk music add to the unusual harmonies, but the use of drone effects or reiterated bass notes reinforces a basic point of harmonic departure and return. Works are usually monothematic, subsequent material being derived from the opening idea; counterpoint became more important as his idiom developed, creating linear flow and dense textures. Rhythms often employ unusual and irregular metres, the combination of tempi within a pulse (for example 3+3+2), and alternating rhythmic ideas; ostinati abound. Percussion becomes an important element of larger-scale works, and in the piano music one notices the use of percussive effects. One recurring feature has become known as 'night-music': movements or sections that have a nocturnal character, whose evocation is often achieved through unusual orchestration or instrumental colours. In the string quartets, which form the heart of Bartók's achievement, string techniques are extended to encompass a very wide range of effects.

If Bartók's gradual development is best heard in the string quartets, it is most often encountered in the concertos. His earliest musical influences are clearly heard in the *Rhapsody for Piano and Orchestra* (1904), modelled on Liszt's *Hungarian Rhapsodies* and in the grand Romantic virtuoso vein. The two movements of the Romantic *Violin Concerto No. 1* (1907–1908, though not performed until 1958) are a portrait of a violinist Bartók was briefly in love with. The first is full of a sad, limpid beauty, the second more lively; again, this work reflects his antecedents, not his mature voice. The *Piano Concerto No. 1* (1926) occupies a totally different musical world, percussive, aggressive, mysterious, elemental, and with just enough echoes of the traditional virtuoso concerto to emphasize how the tradition is being subverted. In this, and in some of the melodic shapes and harmonies, it recalls **Prokofiev**. The frenetic opening movement remoulds Romanticism into Constructivism, but it is the slow movement that takes the concerto into uncharted regions. Much of it is mysterious and dramatic and written only for the piano and percussion. A percussion outburst leads into the finale, which rushes forward with the piano caught in the mêlée. The excitement and elemental emotions of this concerto, exceptionally difficult to play, make it one of the most potent of the 20th century, arguably finer than its two successors. Two *Rhapsodies for Violin and Orchestra* (1928) reflect the influence of folk music, both using actual folk tunes. The first, with the colour of the cimbalom prominent, is more obviously a folkish rhapsody; the second is musically more adventurous. In both works the soloist is prominent.

In the *Piano Concerto No. 2* (1930–31), as in the first, the soloist is a more equal partner with the orchestra. Here the aggressive intensity of its predecessor is toned down. The opening movement, featuring wind and percussion, is helter-skelter, but leads into the slow movement, opening with an adagio nocturne using timpani and muted strings. A swirling scherzo follows (using strings, wind and percussion) dominated by piano arpeggios. The finale, bringing in the full orchestra, is buoyant, but if the overall progress and construction is more assured than that of the first concerto, the impact is lessened.

The *Violin Concerto No. 2* (1937–38) heralded a mellowing in Bartók's writing. Each of the three movements uses variation form, with the last a free variation of the first; solo writing is dominant, in the Romantic tradition. The first movement has a rhapsodic quality, harsher interjections from the orchestra constantly answered by a singing solo line. Compared with Bartók's earlier concertos, the harmonies are more traditional, the folk influence mainly audible in the melodic cast of the solo line. The central movement is a theme with six variations covering a wide range of expression, from dance to the atmospheric Impressionist painting of the second variation, the soloist set against woodwind, harp and celesta. In the finale the soloist reaches a moment of ecstatic repose among the rhythmic energy; towards the end the orchestra alters its character, enlarging its sound to give a feeling of completion and satisfaction (Bartók provided an alternative ending that is shorter and with the soloist silent). The assured construction and the direct, almost Romantic voice makes this the most popular of Bartók's concertos. The *Double Piano Concerto* (1940) is a version of the *Sonata for Pianos and Percussion*, discussed below.

The heart of the *Piano Concerto No. 3* (1945), its last 17 bars finished by Tibór Sérly, is the central adagio, a nocturne of great beauty populated by the sounds of the night. Neither of the outer movements are as interesting, although this remains the best known of Bartók's piano concertos, partly because those outer movements are in a more easy-going style. The *Viola Concerto* (1945) was reconstructed by Tibór Sérly: the notes and rhythms are Bartók's, the rather sparse orchestration Serly's. A melancholy introductory song for the soloist contrasts with passages of restlessness and agitation, leavened by lighter dance moods, from which soloist and orchestra emerge into an epilogue of beauty and resignation to end the first movement. In the slow movement an air of poignant rhapsody dominates. The finale takes up the mood of the dance, initially as almost pure folk music, ending with an air of confidence that the rest of the concerto has not entirely confirmed.

Bartók's two important orchestral works both come from late in his life. Of the earlier works, the picturesque five-movement *Suite No. 1* (1905) is late Romantic in its harmonies and colours, chiefly interesting for its echoes of urbanised Hungarian gypsy music. The first of the *Two Portraits* (1907–11) is actually the first movement of the *Violin Concerto No. 1*, the second an arrangement of a short bagatelle for piano. The first of the *Two Pictures* (1910) is a hazy Impressionistic painting, the second a refined rustic portrayal of the 'Village Dance'. The *Dance Suite* (1923), drawing very widely for its folk-derived material, summarises many of Bartók's folk assimilations.

But with the *Music for Strings, Percussion and Celesta* (1936) Bartók produced an orchestral masterpiece. Its four movements approximate the traditional symphonic layout; its tone creates the grandest scale out of the chamber textures. The strings are divided into two bodies, with the percussion, piano, harp and double-bass in the centre. Much of the material of the four movements is derived from the fugue of the opening movement, which is brooding, dark, and dense, articulated by the strings. The movement builds into an arch, each entry of the fugue theme appearing a fifth higher or lower, and then reversing from the central climax; in parallel, the dynamics slowly grow and then die down. The second movement has a pounding rhythmic intensity, a vital excitement accentuated by pizzicato effects. The third is an example of Bartók's 'night music', the xylophone ushering in an eerie percussive atmosphere that is half Impressionistic, half charged with ghostly tension. Its taut five-part structure includes the use of retrograde, where the material is heard again in reverse. The finale combines antiphonal effects, exuberance, and Bulgarian rhythms, kept under a taut rein. The *Concerto for Orchestra* (1942–43) is probably the Bartók work best known to a general public. In its five movements are found the darkness of the opening of his opera *Bluebeard's Castle*, Impressionistic hazes, vigorous rhythms, a chorale-like nobility, perky interjections, a parody of the reiterated theme from the first movement of **Shostakovich's** *Symphony No. 7*, and touches of 'night music'. There is also a pastoral simplicity, and a constant movement around the orchestra as various sections are highlighted.

Stage works form a small but important part of Bartók's output. The one-act opera *Bluebeard's Castle (A kékszakállù herceg vára*, 1911), Bartók's first undoubted masterpiece and one of the most unforgettable contributions to the 20th-century music stage, is a powerful allegory with haunting vocal lines. Its poetic libretto by Béla Balázs describes Bluebeard introducing Judith, his fourth wife, to his castle, whose main hall has seven doors. One by one she opens the doors, each showing a different aspect of the castle, but more important, of Bluebeard's subconscious. The final door, which he tries to persuade her not to open, reveals his previous wives, whom Judith joins, leaving Bluebeard alone in darkness. The opera demands to be seen as an allegory: every element in the castle, from the haunting sounds to the vision of light, represents some aspect of Bluebeard, suppressed or otherwise. The opera emerges as a brilliant symbolic study of the unconscious forces at work on a complex personality. Balázs and Bartók succeeded in making Judith completely convincing in her curiosity and steadfastness, showing those elements of human personalities that remain (or should remain) separate in partnership. Musically, its opening is Gothic, with dark lower strings and an assertive figure that is passed around the large orchestra. This leads the way out of late Romanticism into the recess of the subconscious, and the slow, brooding atmosphere of this opening reverberates throughout Bartók's later music. As the opera progresses, dark hues predominate, the tension of the vocal lines only momentarily relieved by tender moments of great beauty, such as the delicacy of the shining jewels of the third door. The point where Judith opens the door to survey Bluebeard's domains, the orchestra bursting in to create a vast vista, is one of the most climactic moments in all opera.

The ballet *The Wooden Prince* (*A fából fargott királyfi*, 1914–17, suites 1921 and 1931), to a scenario by Béla Balázs, is an allegory of individual maturation. A prince with a guardian fairy makes a wooden puppet to attract a princess, but she is more affected by it than him, until he renounces the fairy's magic. The score has echoes of **Strauss** and Impressionism, including a beautiful prelude evoking the landscape. The work is dramatically descriptive, and written on a grand scale – Bartók uses a huge orchestra to create a 'big' sound, though with sharp detail.

The vivid ballet-pantomime *The Miraculous Mandarin* (1918–23, best known as an orchestral suite) is the culmination of the barbaric (but not overtly violent) side of Bartók's earlier output. Its extraordinary symbolic story, where the wounds of a mandarin beaten up by thugs refuse to bleed until the whore who enticed him into the situation embraces him, was considered by many immoral. Its powerful expressiveness is built from rhythmic, motoric impulses, with a particularly barbaric opening; the tense, erotic music shows little trace of folk influence.

In the same vein as these stage works, but written for the concert hall rather than the stage, is Bartók's vocal masterpiece, the *Cantata Profana 'The Giant Stags'* (1930) for tenor, baritone, double choir and orchestra. Based on a Romanian folk ballad, it tells of nine sons who have been brought up to hunt stags, but are themselves turned into stags. The father sets out to find his sons, and is about to shoot one of a group of stags when it calls out to him. The father recognises his sons, and urges them to return; but their metamorphosis is too complete. In this simple story lies a web of symbolism, of the universality of nature, of the need to leave behind each stage of life, of the apartness of the artist, of freedom of choice. Bartók responded with music consumed by a passion more intense than almost any other of his works. It has an intricate symmetrical structure with a clear tonal centre, using one of Bartók's characteristic scales (the augmented 4th and diminished 7th prominent). The choral writing is clearly derived from folk-music, and the cantata contains moments of melodic beauty and pounding rhythms in Bartók's dark, brooding vein.

Bartók's chamber music is dominated by the six string quartets, generally considered to be the most important cycle since that of Beethoven. This reputation is based on three main factors. The first is the exceptional technical interest: the development of interlocking, sometimes symmetrical, structures, the increasing use of a central axis around which the harmonies evolve, and the motivic development from germ-cells. The second is emotional intensity, often on an almost symphonic scale, both in overall impact and in breadth of sound. Thirdly, they introduced new features into the medium: the assimilation of folk music and an extraordinary range of instrumental effects, some of which are akin to the effects found in folk string playing.

The *String Quartet No. 1* (1908) is the most conservative, although the first movement with its suggestion of a drone is tonally ambiguous. The rhythmic urgency of the final movement, derived from Magyar folk music, is characteristic. The *String Quartet No. 2* (1915–17) is perhaps the best introduction for those new to Bartók's string quartets. It has thematically linked first and last movements, and shows the influence of Arab folk musics. The unsettled start germinates like flowers emerging in time-lapse photography, an effect matched by the wonderful muted dissonant chords of the opening of the third movement. A feeling of ambiguity, both emotional and technical, pervades the close. The *String Quartet No. 3* (1927) has two parts, to which are added a recapitulation of the first part and a coda, all performed without a break. It is the most compressed of the quartets, and harmonically far more astringent than its predecessors, often without a sense of key or tonal base. It also has an urgent linear flow, audibly derived from the rhythmic drive of folk music, massive contrasts, and a panoply of instrumental effects. At the same time there is an emotional ambiguity, as if we had dropped in on a dialogue of great passion and ended up uncertain of its nature. The *String Quartet No. 4* (1928) further develops both the instrumental effects and the harmonic acerbity of *No. 3*, almost approaching atonality. Its contrapuntal flow entirely offsets the lack of obvious themes (the material is developed from germ-cells). Its wider range of expression partly derives from a symmetrical five movement archform, with the slow third movement forming the heart of the work, and violent pizzicato writing in the fourth. This quartet approaches the ideal of the form. On the one hand, the fascinating technical construction allows the quartet to be appreciated entirely for its abstract musical solutions. On the other, the impact of the emotional expression is vivid without any knowledge of that construction. The *String Quartet No. 5* (1934) also has a five-movement arch form, though the symmetry is even more marked. The second and fourth movements are slow, in Bartók's 'night music' style, and the overall tone is more airy and graphic (with a barrel-organ parody in the final movement). Its thematic material is more obviously melodic, and the lovely second movement has a neo-Romantic hue. The atmosphere of the *String Quartet No. 6* (1939) is rather different from its predecessors, with an aura of the other-worldly, and a streak of the sardonic and the bitter. It is difficult not to equate the work with the political events in 1939, and it was the last work Bartók wrote in Europe. Each of its four movements is preceded by a gradually modified ritornello, which furnishes the material for the rather resigned final movement.

Of his other chamber music, the two fine violin sonatas (1921 and 1922) represent Bartók at his most harmonically radical. The *Violin Sonata No. 2* opens with a lament obviously derived from folk music. It quickly becomes merged with atonal Expressionism, but folk music remains a distant point of reference throughout the work. In the marvellous *Sonata for Two Pianos and Percussion* (1937), turned into

the *Concerto for Two Pianos and Orchestra* in 1940, Bartók allied his sense of rhythmic drive to more directly tonal ideas than in his earlier chamber works. The slow movement is a night scene, rustling with the sounds of insects. The Impressionistic touches, and the ebullient, sometimes perky finale (percussion predominating) make this one of Bartók's most immediate works. The colours and effects are perhaps more remarkable in the chamber version.

Bartók's piano music ranges from the savage bite of the *Allegro barbaro* (1911), which predates Stravinsky's *Rite of Spring* (usually cited as the progenitor of such 'barbaric' idioms), to many works based directly on folk music. These are attractive and well worth exploring. The piano music is dominated by the six books of *Mikrokosmos* (1926–39), a huge series of miniatures ranging from folk ditties to more complex pieces, designed to explore the range of piano technique. They are more interesting to play than to listen to. They were preceded by a series of eighty-five miniatures *For Children* (*Gyermekeknek*, 1909–10), which make more attractive and direct listening.

Bartók's mature output might be said to describe a huge arch. Underlying the entire structure is folk music, supplying a secure foundation to Bartók's music from 1905 until his death. The start of the arch is rugged, Impressionism colouring it, a village face peering out in places, figures of melancholy lovers in others. At its apex, it has transformed into intricate architectural patterns, as if a Roman architect had conspired with the builder of a Moorish mosque; within these patterns are fantastical images, some mysterious, some brutish and aggressive, some of archetypal figures from the subconscious. At its end, it assumes graceful Classical proportions, less adorned, more assured, but from time to time carved into mournful lilies; but in those proportions the Classical architecture has been modified to provide new solutions with traditional structures.

In the development of new harmonic ideas that maintain their links with tonality, and in the absorption of new scales and intervallic progressions, Bartók has no 20th-century peer, and it is this example that has been so influential on later composers. His structures derived from classical principles and forged with such surety of proportion and unity, demonstrated that traditional forms were capable of renewal. There is scarcely a mature Bartók work where these elements are not the source of endless fascination; that alone makes him a great master. However, the success of the emotional content is more questionable. Time and again in Bartók's music emotions seem to be driven by the kind of fervour he found in folk music, but as they are about to make an expressive statement they become constrained by the very technical processes designed to provide their framework. The effect is more marked when compared with those works where Bartók does allow full reign to the emotive content, with such stunning impact – in the slow movement of the *Piano Concerto No. 1*, or in the *String Quartet No. 4*, the *Cantata Profana* or the *Violin Sonata No. 2*. But these moments are relatively rare, and *Bluebeard's Castle*, that seminal Bartók work, remains perhaps the most complete expression of his emotional concerns. This reticence may explain why, for such a major composer, only a handful of works are known to a wider public. It may be that, after the excesses of Expressionism, the experience of World War I, and the turmoil of central Europe between the wars, the containment of emotions in technical strait-jacket became a psychological necessity for such composers.

Bartók became professor of piano at the Budapest Royal Academy in 1907, and toured widely as a pianist. With **Kodály** he founded the New Hungarian Musical Society in 1911. A strong opponent of Nazism, he left Hungary in 1939 and moved to the USA in 1940.

RECOMMENDED WORKS
opera *Bluebeard's Castle* (1911)
Cantata Profana (*The Giant Stags*, 1930)
Concerto for Orchestra (1943)
Music for Strings, Percussion and Celesta (1936)
Piano Concerto No. 1 (1926)
Piano Concerto No. 2 (1930–31)
Sonata for Two Pianos and Percussion (1937)
String Quartet No. 1 (1908)
String Quartet No. 2 (1915–17)
String Quartet No. 3 (1927)
String Quartet No. 4 (1928)
String Quartet No. 5 (1934)
String Quartet No. 6 in D (1939)
ballet *The Miraculous Mandarin* (1919)
Viola Concerto (1945)
Violin Concerto No. 2 (1939)
Violin Sonata No. 1 (1921)
Violin Sonata No. 2 (1922)

BIBLIOGRAPHY
Bartók, *Letters*, 1971
Essays, 1976
P. Griffiths, *Bartók*, 1984
H. Stevens, *The Life and Music of Béla Bartók*, 1953, 1964

Bozay Attila *
born August 11th 1939 at Balatonfüzfö

One of the more interesting Hungarian composers of his generation, Bozay's talent was shown in the four lilting and haunting miniatures of the song-cycle *Papírszeletek* (*Paper Slips*, 1962) for soprano, clarinet and cello. His subsequent output has been limited in quantity but thoughtful in tone. In the middle 1960s he combined a preference for the lyrical with a not particularly rigid serial technique in works of short duration. This led to the expressive and rather sad *String Quartet No. 1* (1964), which has echoes of **Bartók**; the overall form is that of a sonata, whose sections act as movements. Other works of this period include the *Piano Variations* (1964), filtering folk material through serial technique, and the well-sustained *Pezzo concertato No. 1*, (1965) for viola and orchestra, which is built in a 12-tone row, and whose single movement is divided into a large number of small units with a homogeneous but transparent orchestration whose colours aim to match the viola. A similar structure is the basis of *Pezzo sinfonico No. 1* (1967), which extends the colour effects by the use of clusters.

Bozay acknowledged a change of direction in 1969, when his works became longer and attempted to utilise both rigid pre-planning and organic development, as in the third and second movements of the severe *String Quartet No. 2* (1971), or *Malom* (*The Mill*) for chamber ensemble. One of the most imaginative and attractive pieces of this period is *Improvisations No. 2* (1976) for recorders, violin, viola and cello, an unusual addition to the recorder repertoire with the South American influenced bird-calls of the recorders hovering over a string trio.

Bozay's uncompromising idiom was extended and popularised in his major work of recent years, the large-scale opera *Csongor es Tünde* (1979–84), based on the classic Hungarian fairy-tale play of the same name (1836) by Milhály Vörösmarty. It is a powerful work, down to earth and beautiful, with strong musical characterisation (especially of the seedier characters), the relative meagreness of the story redeemed by a panoply of Jungian archetypes. Bozay convincingly blends a number of styles, echoing **Bartók** and including his own 12-tone technique. The basis of the parts of the lead characters is a stock of nine notes in two clusters to which can be added a tenth, creating a number of internal possibilities, often very lyrical. Particular combinations of instruments and recurring motifs are allocated to characters, as well as to a hauntingly ethereal chorus. This operatic debut suggests the possibility of exciting work to come. Bozay has taught at the Liszt Academy since 1979.

RECOMMENDED WORKS

opera *Csongor es Tünde* (1979–84)
Improvisations No. 2 (1976) for
    recorders, violin, viola and cello
song-cycle *Papírszeletek* (1962)
*Pezzo concertato No. 1 for viola and
    orchestra (1965)*

Dohnányi Ernö (Ernst von)•
born 27th July 1877 at Pozsony
died 9th February 1960 at New York

The works of Dohnányi might be better known were it not for lack of support from his native Hungary, based on accusations of collaboration with the Nazis during World War II (his music has now been rehabilitated). As a virtuoso pianist, his reputation was worldwide, and most of his compositions now heard include that instrument. He ceased touring as a pianist in the 1920s, but continued to conduct. As a composer, he was once rated with **Bartók** and **Kodály** as the most important Hungarian figure of his generation. However, while his two fellow composers represent a 20th-century awareness of Hungarian folk music, Dohnányi's music represents a last flowering of a Romantic Hungarian nationalism, rooted in the 19th century. His totally traditional idiom is influenced by Brahms, and combines respect for the classical masters with a happy lyricism and humour.

Indeed, Dohnányi's best-known work not only illustrates his favourite form – variations – but also his sense of humour: the *Variations on a Nursery Song* (1913) for orchestra and piano concertante. Once extremely popular, this entertaining work built around the tune 'Baa, baa Black Sheep' ('Twinkle, Twinkle, Little Star' or 'Ah, vous dirai-je, maman') is still often heard and has lost little of its sparkle. Its

portentous opening is spiked by the triteness of the tune, and it is full of lyrical interest and moments of understated pianistic virtuosity. The best-known purely orchestral work is perhaps the *Suite in F sharp minor* (1908–09), which also uses a set of variations in its opening movement. The early *Piano Concerto No. 1* (1898) is an unoriginal work of pianistic brilliance in the tradition of Liszt; the second has entirely disappeared from the repertoire. The solo piano music, surprisingly, is relatively uninteresting, with those works that stray most from pianistic convention (e.g. *Ruralia Hungariaca*, 1923), the most worth hearing. Of his chamber music, the influence of Brahms is overt in the *Piano Quintet No. 1* (1895), and latent in the darker *Piano Quintet No. 2* (1914) and in the *Piano Sextet*. The *String Quartet No. 2* (1906) and the *String Quartet No. 3* (1926, again using variation form) once enjoyed wide popularity. His major serious opera, *The Tower of the Voivod* (1922), which enjoyed some success at its première, is based on a Hungarian folk ballad, but the music remains in the Romantic tradition.

Dohnányi's teaching and administrative activities were considerable. He was a professor of piano in Berlin (1908–15), director of the Budapest Royal Academy during the year of the communist regime (1919), continued as conductor of the Budapest Philharmonic, and returned to the Academy (1928) and became its director again (1934). He fled Hungary in late 1944 (his two sons were killed during the war) and was eventually to join the faculty of Florida State University, Tallahassee (1949). He also taught at Ohio University and was active until his death at the age of 82.

RECOMMENDED WORKS

Suite in F sharp minor (1908–09)
Variations on a Nursery Song (1913)
    for orchestra and piano obligato

Dubrovay László
born 23rd March 1943 at Budapest

An interesting composer who studied with **Stockhausen** (1972–74), Dubrovay has applied techniques and acoustical effects developed in electronic music to conventional instruments and orchestral scores. He is also interested in natural acoustics, and both areas find expression in a series of concertos begun in 1979. The effective *Concerto No. 1* (1979) for eleven strings explores sonorities and string effects akin to the singing sounds of whales but with an echo of Hungarian folk music, evolving them in slow-moving underlying patterns with a strong structural feel and a sense of tonal centre. A similar preoccupation with ethereal and natural sounds, with the addition of a trumpet part that borrows the effects of avant-garde jazz, is evident in the more aggressive *Concerto No. 2* (1981) for trumpet and fifteen strings. The more extensive and extraordinary *Concerto No. 4* (1982) for piano, synthesizer and orchestra pits this exploration of sonorities against a full-blown and eventually distorted Romantic orchestral sound.

Dubrovay's recent electronic music, which has included computer-aided composition, has seen a return to the structures of conventional sound production. *Felhangok II* (*Harmonics II*, 1983) is an electronic version of a piano piece (*Harmonics I*, in which played notes were overlaid on other, mute, depressed keys, setting up harmonic effects). The electronic *Szonáta számítágépre* (*Sonata for Computer*, 1984) has a genuine sonata structure, while *Parte con moto* (1984) aims at orchestral effects through electronic means. Other works have explored acoustical techniques.

Dubrovay has been a professor at the Budapest Academy since 1976.

RECOMMENDED WORKS
  Concerto No. 1 (1979) for 11 strings
  Concerto No. 2 (1981) for trumpet and strings

Farkas Ferenc*
born 15th December 1905 at Nagykanizsa

A senior figure in Hungarian music, Farkas's conservative but effective works have been heard widely outside Hungary, particularly his chamber scores. Although his early music reflected an interest in folk music (he collected folk songs in the 1930s), his output includes everything from symphonies to opera. His idiom ranges from the neo-classicism of such works as the cheerful but unmemorable *Piccola musica di concerto* (1961) or the more biting *Trittico concertato* (1964) for cello and orchestra, through Russian intensity and the shadows of **Prokofiev** and **Shostakovich**, the orchestral drive of **Bartók**, and the symphonic painting of his teacher **Respighi** (all these influences are clear in, for example, *Planctus et consolationes* for orchestra, 1965).

Farkas's major compositional arena is the large series of cantatas, starting with the *Cantata lirica* (also known as *The Well of St John*, 1945). Some are on relatively modern texts, such as the *Tavaszárás* (*Waiting for the Spring*, 1965) for baritone, chorus, children's choir and orchestra, relatively uninteresting except for a dark section of Bartókian line and colour. However, Farkas is more inspired when setting older writings. Thus *Aspirationes principis* (*Aspirations of the Prince*, 1974–75) is a powerful cantata mixing Latin and Magyar, and combining 12-note effects with a tonal base. Its portrayal of the contrast between the inner desire for peace and the necessities of kingship is both human and moving. The *Vivit Dominus* (1981–82) for choir and orchestra is similarly assured, with conventional harmonies but beautiful and sometimes triumphant writing for choir. An interest in history also surfaces in some of the instrumental music, as in the neo-Baroque structures of such works as the attractive *Concertino No. 4* (1984) for oboe and strings, alternately playful and lyrically beautiful.

Farkas lived for a time in Copenhagen and Vienna (1933–35), writing film scores, and then taught in Hungary before being appointed professor at the Liszt Academy of Music in 1949, a post he retained until his retirement.

RECOMMENDED WORKS
  cantata *Aspirationes principis* (1974–75) for tenor, baritone and orchestra
  Concertino No. 4 (1983) for oboe and strings

Kodály Zoltán**
born 16th December 1882 at Kecskemét
died 6th March 1967 at Budapest

The music of Zoltán Kodály has been completely overshadowed by that of his contemporary **Bartók**. For many music lovers his name will be far more familiar than his music, apart from the immensely popular suite from the quasi-opera *Háry János*. Like Bartók, the starting point of his music was the influence of Hungarian folk music, which they collected together from 1905. But whereas Bartók used Hungarian folk music as a major element in a process of individual development, Kodály's idiom is far more concerned with a marriage of folk music and traditional classical music. His style – straightforward, incorporating Romantic and Impressionist elements, with energetic rhythms and colourful orchestrations, and always tonal – remained largely the same, apart from a gradual move to leaner textures. He is the major representative of Hungarian nationalism in music.

Until 1918 Kodály's output consisted mainly of chamber pieces, but the following decade saw the appearance of the vocal and choral works that established his name. His literary knowledge was considerable, his understanding of Hungarian folk lyrics expert, and in setting words he found the medium that most suited his idiom and his interest in folk music. The major orchestral works date from the 1930s. After World War I, when the communist authorities in Hungary treated him as a musical elder statesman, his compositions became less frequent, and include little that is regularly encountered.

The first work to bring Kodály widespread recognition was the *Psalmus Hungaricus* (1923). A direct and dramatic work in moods ranging from lament to exuberance, it is based on a 16th-century version of Psalm 55. This achievement was confirmed by two other outstanding works for vocal forces and orchestra. The powerful *Budavari Te Deum* (1936) for soloists, choir, organ and orchestra has the atmospheres of ancient church music and triumphant occasions with a strong flavour of Hungarian folk-music (with 'towers of fourths'). The more solemn *Missa brevis* (1944, orchestrated 1951) has similarly colourful orchestration, and while the influence of old liturgical music remains strong, the nationalist element is less overt. These three pieces are perhaps the works in which Kodály most successfully integrates a powerful idiomatic style with an emotional feel for material of Hungarian origin.

Of his orchestral music, the two dance scores – the boisterous *Dances of Marosszék* (1923–27 in a piano version, orchestrated 1930), and the *Dances of Galánta* (1933), based on music remembered from his childhood in the town of Galánta – are brilliantly colourful expressions of orchestrated folk music. More intense are the *Peacock Variations* (1938–39) for orchestra, with some hauntingly beautiful music. The score was banned by the authorities in Hungary in 1940. The *Concerto for Orchestra* (1939–40), still using Hungarian dance material while loosely recalling Baroque

concerti grossi and designed to show off the orchestra, is less obviously successful; the later *Symphony* (1961), in memory of Arturo Toscanini, continues a similar style.

Kodály's chamber music dates from the first two decades of the century; its basic material is almost always derived from folk music. The masterpiece is the rhapsodic *Sonata for solo cello* (1915) – Kodály was himself a cellist. His string quartets, the first (1909) yearning and dramatic, the second (1918) lighter in feel, deserve to be better known.

Of his three operas, the comic *Háry János* (1925–27) is in the idiom of folk theatre, a play with music (and therefore long stretches of dialogue). It is totally delightful, using virtually unchanged folk music as well as original material. Some of its music was extracted with great success for a suite in which Kodály's facility for long melodic lines and happy and memorable tunes, as well as a sense of piquant and pictorial fun, are shown at their best. The orchestration is colourful, sometimes exotic, and includes a celebrated part for cimbalom. Steeped in a Hungarian identity whose delight becomes universal, it is one of the most accomplished and satisfying showpiece orchestral suites of the 20th century.

Perhaps even more important than his achievement as a composer was Kodály's work as a collector of Hungarian folk songs and as an educator. His music teaching method for children (the 'Kodály Method'), based on singing, has been widely influential and is used throughout Hungary as well as in many other countries. He taught from 1907 to 1941 at the Academy of Music in Budapest (being suspended, 1919–22, by the short-lived communist regime), and later became its director.

An encounter with Kodály's music is almost always a vivid experience, if rarely intellectually stimulating. Above all, it is music designed to convey the pleasure inherent in its folk-based material.

RECOMMENDED WORKS
  Budavari Te Deum (1936) for soloists, chorus, organ and orchestra
  Dances of Galánta (1933) for orchestra
  Háry János Suite (1926) for orchestra
  Peacock Variations (1938–39) for orchestra
  Missa brevis (1948, orchestrated 1951)
  Sonata for solo cello (1915)

BIBLIOGRAPHY

L. Choksy, *The Kodály Method*, 1974
L. Esze, *Zoltán Kodály: his Life in Pictures*, 1971, reprinted 1982
P. Young, *Zoltán Kodály*, 1964

Kurtág György··
born February 19th 1926 at Lugoj (Rumania)

The music of György Kurtág came to international prominence in the middle of the 1980s, and seemed to herald a major new discovery in European music. So far that prominence has been among critics and specialists rather than a wider public. It seems likely to remain that way, for his highly condensed, deeply thoughtful idiom is intellectually rigorous and uncompromising. In addition, after earlier works that included a *Viola Concerto* (1954) and a *Korei Kantáta* (1953), his music from the *Strings Quartet* op. 1 (1959) onwards has been confined to a small number of works for chamber forces on miniature scale, either purely instrumental or with voice.

That string quartet, written after studies in Paris (1957), is a suitable introduction to his music. A taut and powerful work in six very short sections, it illustrates Kurtág's especial achievement to date: the combination of the serial techniques of the Second Viennese School and **Webern** in particular, and an emotional expressiveness that derives from **Bartók**, notably an intensity of rhythmic logic, structural continuity, and sureness of sonority and texture. Colouristic instrumental effects, used in short snatches of phrases as structural elements, are developed in his later works, a technique that may derive from his studies with **Messiaen**. Kurtág developed different aspects of this string quartet in his next three works: the use of instrumental colour in the *Wind Quintet* op. 2 (1959); the expressiveness in the *Eight Piano Pieces* op. 3 (1959); and the sense of the miniature, created by very short internal units, in the five-minute *Eight Duets for Violin and Cimbalom* op. 4 (1960–61).

Kurtág's harmonic language is largely 12-tone, with an occasional tonal base as deliberate contrast. Often a work or movement is strongly identified with a dedicatee, sometimes a performer (Márta Kurtág or the conductor András Mihály), more often another composer (for example **Sárközy**, or a composer of the past, Scarlatti or Paganini). This allows him to take elements of those composers' styles and fuse them into his own idiom, with a remarkable lack of straight derivation or obvious pastiche. At the same time he has extended the miniature into extended sets. Thus the remarkably consistent series *Játékok* (*Plays and Games*, 1973 onwards) for piano or two pianos, now runs to over 200 works in five volumes. It includes the serial deconstruction of Scarlatti's stylistic ideas in *Hommage à Domenico Scarlatti*, shades of **Messiaen** (particularly bird song), and such instrumental effects as imitating the cimbalom, in a series of sparkling miniatures. Similarly the *Twelve Microludes* for string quartet (1977–78, titled *Homage à Mihály András*) each contain elements of music by other composers, with **Bartók** especially prominent.

However, Kurtág's especial genius is the combination of this miniaturised idiom with the expressive power of words. His output since the middle 1970s has almost exclusively included voice, apart from two concertante works, ... *quasi una fantasia* ... (1988) for piano and orchestra and the *Double Concerto for Piano and Cello 'Requiem for a Friend'* (1990). He has an uncanny knack for selecting poetry of a high literary value that also interacts well with music; often the poetry has strong visual imagery but a restrained emotional expression which can be amplified in the setting. It is almost invariably dramatic, with a powerful persona in the poetry that creates an almost operatic impact. The vocal and the instrumental lines usually have sharply individual characters. His first song-cycle, *The Sayings of Péter Bornemisza* (*Bornemisza Péter Mondásai* 1963–68) for soprano and piano, based on the sermons of a 16th-century Lutheran poet-preacher, is a large-scale work in four parts. It ranges from the contemplation of death to the hope of spring and nature, with the central sections divided by 'sinfonias'. The individual songs have the feel of miniatures welded into a larger conception by an overall scheme that distantly corresponds to sonata form. The piano's range is considerable, from musical description to spartan, **Webern**-like delicacy, using such techniques as the held middle pedal for cimbalom-like resonance. Vocal lines have wide leaps and markings designed to increase the emotional intensity (such as 'barking or gasping').

A less monumental introduction to Kurtág's vocal music is the *Four Songs to Poems by János Pilinszky* (*Négy dal Pilinszky János verserie* 1973–75) for baritone and piano or chamber ensemble,

whose texts typify the poetic features that
attract Kurtág. It was the song-cycle *Messages of the Late Miss R.V. Troussova*
(1976–80) for soprano and small orchestra
that gave Kurtág an international prominence. The verses, by the Russian poetess
Rimma Dalos, treat the theme of a woman
reflecting on her life and loves, with sometimes graphic erotic imagery: The number
of songs (twenty-one), the use of *Sprechgesang* and the changes of instrumentation
suggest a tribute to **Schoenberg's** *Pierrot
lunaire*. The vocal writing is again very
wide-ranging, with the sense of the miniature (many of the poems are of only three
lines) to the force. The gigantic and austere cycle *Fragments* (1987) for soprano
and orchestra uses passages of Kafka's
letters and diaries. *Homaggio a Luigi
Nono* (1979) for unaccompanied chorus is a
six-movement setting of Russian texts by
Akhmatova and Dalos, the chorus using up
to twelve parts and dividing into two
groups. Kurtág's sensitivity to the nuances and sounds of words, his ability to
create startling instrumental sounds and
patterns that amplify and match psychological emotions, and his combination of
the miniature in individual songs and the
large-scale in the overall conception, suggest he will emerge, with **Mahler** and
Britten, as the finest song-cycle composer
of the century.

Kurtág has taught at the Budapest
Academy since 1968. His son György (born
1954) is also a composer.

RECOMMENDED WORKS
Kurtág's small output is of a
consistently high quality, and all his
mature works are recommended.

Láng István*
born March 1st 1933 at Budapest

István Láng is emerging as one of the most
interesting Hungarian composers of his
generation, who has fused the heritage of
Bartók with techniques and instrumental
effects drawn from 12-tone and serial
music. His music in the 1960s included
microelements (short motivitic ideas), the
use of mathematical series, and aleatory
techniques, often in cyclic forms. From this
he has developed a sound world concerned
with the shape of musical sounds and their
emotional effect, generally built on a duality between short events and long time-
spans. This has showed how some of the
techniques of the avant-garde can be
moulded into a more direct and immediate

idiom with a wider appeal. The short
events, carefully related, occupy the foreground and dominate the attention
through their highly charged emotional
content, and are emphasised by a feeling of
space around them, created by silences or
by the orchestration. The longer structures are not immediately apparent, but it
is one of the achievements of Láng's music
that during or towards the end of a piece
one apprehends a coherent and satisfying
overall pattern. An analogy might be with
a busy but unstructured week full of
varied events: one is aware of those events
as the week passes, but only at the end of
the week does the overall period, and its
sense of actual structure, become apparent.

Both Láng's musical antecedents and
some of his later characteristics are found
in the *Variations and Allegro* (1965) for
orchestra, rearranged from an earlier symphony. The variations use two themes, the
first Bartókian, melodic and nocturnal, the
second a more fragmented idea drawn
from 12-tone techniques. The variations
are dramatic, with short events contrasting light and density and incisive and
smooth sounds, and a covert sense of
underlying cohesion. The allegro employs
driving percussive rhythms clearly
derived from **Bartók**.

The dramatic has always been a feature
of Láng's music. A sense of theatre pervades such works as *Three Sentences from
Romeo and Juliet* (1969–70) for string
orchestra, where each movement explores
the possibilities of a Shakespeare quotation. In the *Concerto bucolico* (1969–70) for
horn and orchestra, the horn part is less
that of a virtuoso conflict with the orchestra than a character with sometimes wild
moods wandering among them. In the dark
Violin Concerto (1976–77) the drama is a
submersion and stripping away of the
lyrical melody of the opening movement.
The second movement has three distinct
characteristics (scherzo, dialogue and burlesque), and the finale resolves an harmonic tension set up in the first movement
by its opening and closing note. The *Double Concerto for Clarinet and Harp*
(1979–80) is perhaps the best introduction
to his idiom, a wondrous work that manages to appear both static and in motion. It
is as much a concerto for the whole orchestra, since various instruments emerge
with a phrase and step back again, each as
a sharply drawn personality. The harp is
generally sober, the clarinet much more
wild (at one point teasingly swooping into
the opening of Gershwin's *Rhapsody in*

Blue), and the five movements, played without a break, are more changes of density of texture than sharp divisions of mood.

Láng's idiom is less immediate in smaller-scale works. *Villanások* (*Flashes*, 1973) for solo violin, for example, seems ordinary, even if the first of its nine aphorisms uses only the note A played in various registers. However, the short single-movement *String Quartet No. 3* (1978), bears repeated hearing for its sharp contrasts and emotive tension. Typical of his expressive style is the intriguing TV opera *Álom a Szinházról* (*A Dream About the Theatre*, 1977–81), in which the instrumental forces (often fluttering high wind) are opposed by a battery of twenty-eight sometimes brutish percussion instruments. The lyrical line is developed from micro units in a modified serial technique. Dramatically the style is surrealist; the libretto by Láng after three works by Iván Mándy revolves around a writer who dreams of the première of one of his plays. The illogicality of dream events, images, and actions is brilliantly caught. The surrealist possibilities of video effects are cleverly utilised, from an umbrella chasing the writer down the street to his apartment turning into a whirlpool. The zaniness of images forms one of the work's main threads, and Láng's musical style, with its bursts of idea and wide-ranging, often humorous instrumental effects, is entirely suited to this unusual work.

Láng was the musical director of the Budapest Puppet Theatre (1966–84), and since 1973 has been a lecturer at the Budapest Academy.

RECOMMENDED WORKS
Double Concerto for Clarinet and Harp (1979–80)
opera *A Dream about the Theatre* (1977–81)
Violin Concerto (1976–77)

Ligeti György Sándor***
born 28th May 1923 at Dicsöszentmáron

One of the major figures of the avantgarde, Ligeti (whose birthplace is now in Romania) left Hungary after the abortive uprising of 1956 to live in Vienna, and is now an Austrian citizen. His early music showed the influence of **Kodály**, although privately (as they could not be performed in the Hungary of the time) such works as the *String Quartet No. 1* (1953–54) showed

an awareness of more modern ideas, including the Second Viennese School. Since his departure from Hungary, his major achievement has been the establishment of a kind of aural structure in which the normal parameters – rhythm, vertical harmony, horizontal progression – are so blurred that they become almost static, creating a dense swathe of slowly evolving sound. He himself termed this style 'mikropolyphonie'. On the one hand the effect is almost that of the folding and refolding of pure sonority; on the other, the multifarious vertical strands and the sense of the ethereal they create make this language a kind of 20th-century equivalent to the great polyphonic motets of the 16th and 17th centuries. The basic unit of this structure is the tone cluster, a swathe of adjacent notes that can have elements of a centre but also blurred outlines. With little sense of rhythmic drive or motivation, the contrast of cluster events creates tension, their various oppositions movement. The juxtaposition of many clusters, the simultaneous use of opposing dynamic changes, and the detailed use of more conventional devices that are felt rather than individually heard give the unexpected sense of one underlying tonal area shifting into another.

The orchestral *Apparitions* (1959) introduced this style, while the aptly titled *Atmosphères* (1961) for orchestra, which includes a basic 12-tone language, and a final section of nineteen seconds of reverberation time and silence, established it. *Volumnia* for organ (1961–62) brilliantly applied many of these ideas to the organ, creating dense sound possibilities through new techniques, for example changing organ breathing and thus tonal colour by switching the organ off and on. A similar submergence of individual components into the overall atmosphere of sound was apparent in the other-worldly *Lux aeterna* (1966) for a cappella mixed chorus. The summit of this style is the extraordinary *Requiem* (1965) for soprano, mezzo-soprano, chorus and orchestra, where the technique of changing overtones produced by shifting clusters from the chorus creates haunting effects and huge resources. To this are added violent changes of dynamics, and wide leaping solo vocal lines. These preoccupations were continued in the beautiful *Lontano* (1967) for orchestra. The fusion of microtonal intervals adds a haunting, ghost-like quality to the atmospheric *Ramifications* (1968–69) for twelve string players or string orchestra, where the players are divided into two, tuned a quarter-tone apart. In the opening of the *Chamber Concerto* (1969), the clusters are elongated into wisps of linear idea. This language has had a very wide appeal, the dense swathes of sound proving attractive to those who feel threatened by avant-garde ideas. Its popularity was enhanced by the use of Ligeti's music in the film *2001: A Space Odyssey.*

A different aspect of Ligeti emerged in *Aventures* (1962) for three singers and seven players. With its staccato phrases, extended vocal techniques, sense of humour and parody, it concentrates on foreground events, notably a metronomic sense of rhythmic regularity, although there is a magical transformation into swathes of cluster colours sounds and back again. It was followed by a sequel, *Nou-velles aventures* (*New Adventures,* 1962–65). Increasingly these two sides of Ligeti's musical character have been juxtaposed (as in the *Cello Concerto,* 1966), or used in combination, the one emerging from the other, summed up in the title of a work for twelve female voices and orchestra, *Clocks and Clouds* (1972–73). Its style is a kind of neo-Impressionism, the orchestra scurrying like clouds across the aural sky, joined by the bright sunlight of the voices, who move towards clock-like sounds and back to the clouds. The undulating linear flow makes this work one of the most effective introductions to Ligeti's music. A similar convergence of methods of expression is apparent in the marvellous *String Quartet No. 2* (1968–69), with its very wide range of string techniques. Its overall sense of traditional structure is created more by the contrast and development of sound ideas and particular colour combinations than by conventional themes. Its third movement has elements of the then emerging minimalism, a fact recognised in the two-piano triptych *Selbstportrait mit Reich und Riley (und Chopin ist auch dabei)* (1976).

Melodien (1971) for orchestra signalled a new interest in melody, and gradually the more static elements of Ligeti's idiom were toned down in favour of harmonic and rhythmic exploration, tending on the one hand towards a delicate luminosity, on the other to a precisely calculated biting instrumental effect. This is most obvious in the harsh opening to the opera *Le Grand Macabre* (1974–77), to a libretto by Michael Meschke based on Ghelderode. The macabre of the title is fully realised by the opera's grotesque story – centred on the supposed end of the world, and combining erotic and surrealistic images – in a

dark satirical quasi-comedy of singular theatrical effect. The more melodic and luminous trend surfaced in the *Double Concerto* (1972) for flute, oboe and orchestra and in *San Francisco Polyphony* (1975) for orchestra. The *Horn Trio* (1982) paid clear homage to the trio of Brahms, while also parodying a motif from Beethoven's *Les Adieux* piano sonata. Its instrumental sound gained from the experience of *Le Grand Macabre,* and it is light years away from the cluster choral works of the 1960s. But interesting though it is, (especially its melancholy and beautiful final movement) one can't help feeling the extraordinary had been lost in favour of the curious. The humour apparent in the *Horn Trio* has been a thread throughout Ligeti's output, erupting in the rather tedious *Poème symphonique pour cent metronomes* (1962) for 100 metronomes, and more effectively in such works as *Hungarian Rock* (1978), one of a number of Ligeti works for harpsichord.

RECOMMENDED WORKS
  Atmosphères (1961)
  Aventures (1963)
  Chamber Concerto (1970)
  Clocks and Clouds (1972–73) for
    female voices and orchestra
  Double Concerto (1972) for flute, oboe
    and orchestra
  opera *Le Grand Macabre* (1974–77)
  Lontano (1967) for orchestra
  Nouvelles aventures (1965)
  Requiem (1965)
  String Quartet No. 1 (1953–54)
  String Quartet No. 2 (1968–69)
  San Francisco Polyphony (1975) for
    orchestra
  Volumnia (1961–62)

BIBLIOGRAPHY
  P. Griffiths, *György Ligeti,* 1983

Sárközy István*
born 26th November 1920 at Pesterzsébet

If never especially demanding, the consistently attractive and interesting oeuvre of István Sárközy well repays those interested in exploring the byways of European music. His earliest works were mostly choral, and he attracted attention with the long-running musical play *Szelistyei asszonyok* (*The Women of Szelisthe,* 1952). Much of his subsequent work has intentionally explored older musical forms and ideas, from the *Concerto grosso* (subtitled

Ricordanze I, 1943–44, revised 1969) which is a neo-classical work, distorting Baroque ideas through a grotesquerie of harmonies as if through a distorting lens, to the *Concerto semplice* (*Ricordanze II*, 1974) for violin and orchestra, whose solo part looks back to Romantic virtuoso writing.

At the same time his orchestration and harmonic language owe much to **Bartók**, whose influence is clear in the night-music writing of the slow movement of the *Concerto grosso*, or in the *Sinfonia concertante* (1963) for clarinet and strings. The character of earlier periods is constantly subject to more modern reconstruction (as in the passage for violin and percussion alone in the *Concerto semplice*). Characteristic of his style is a lyrical line that is rather haunting and waif-like. This is particularly expressed in his writing for voice. Thus the haunting and beautiful cantata *Júlia nekek* (*Julia Songs*, 1958) has a deliberately archaic tone reflecting the 16th-century verses, and an ecstatic sensual element reflected in the instrumentation of flute, harp and harpsichord. More recent works include a third *Ricordanze* (1977) for string quartet, and a rather brash piano concerto titled *Confessioni ('Anno 1853')* (1978), which, like the *Sinfonia concertante*, are at moments reminiscent of **Prokofiev**.

Sárközy taught at the Budapest Academy from 1959.

RECOMMENDED WORKS
  Concerto grosso (1943–44, rev. 1969)
  cantata *Julia Songs* (1958)

Iceland

Introduction

For such a small country, with a total population smaller than most cities, Iceland has a lively compositional life. This has been entirely a 20th-century phenomenon, part of the resurgence of Icelandic cultural life following independence in 1918, and full separation from the Danish crown in 1944. The musical resurgence has drawn for inspiration on modern Icelandic literature and the roots of the great period of Icelandic sagas in the 12th and 13th centuries, as well as Icelandic folk music, of which the first substantial collections and recordings were made in the late 1920s.

The first Icelandic composer of note was Sveinbjörn Sveinbjörnsson (1847–27), who spent most of his working life in Edinburgh. The work of Jon Leifs (1899–68) included the graphic *Symphony No. 1* (1941–42), in which each of the movements is inspired by a Icelandic saga. Perhaps the most interesting Icelandic composer is Atli Heimir **Sveinsson** (born 1938), who is discussed under his own entry. Among the founding generation of Icelandic composition, Jón Nordal (born 1926) is primarily a composer of orchestral and concertante works, whose music has been heard in both Europe and North America. He evolved from a nationalistic style to an expressive lyricism whose atonality follows the mainstream of European ideas, as in the meditative and atmospheric *Choralis* (1982) for orchestra, which uses material from old Icelandic songs. Leifur Thórarinsson (born 1934, not to be confused with the composer Jón Thórarinsson, born 1913) was the major Icelandic advocate of serialism during the 1950s and 1960s, being influenced by **Webern** and pointillism in such works as the *Symphony* (1963). This culminated in the thick-textured *Violin Concerto* (1969 revised 1976), in which the solo instrument rather violently fights its way through the orchestral textures. In the equally unconventional one-movement *Oboe Concerto* (1982), the oboe regularly emerges from the large aggressive orchestration, with little sense of the more mellow writing of other recent works.

Perhaps the most prolific of Icelandic composers is Thorkall Sigurbjörnsson (born 1938). He has written works in all genres, including chamber opera and electronic and computer music. Primarily a tonal composer, much of his music belongs to the Icelandic story-telling tradition, utilising Icelandic mythology or lore, exemplified in his suite of folk-song arrangements for wind quintet, *Hraera* (1985). The orchestral *Mistur* (*Mist*, 1972) shows his descriptive and dramatic preference, with lucid orchestration and rhythmic drive, and a broad pictorial canvass. The bleak song cycle *Níu lög úr porpinueftur Jón úr Vör* (*Nine Songs from 'The Village' by Jón úr Vör*, 1978) for soprano and piano is particularly effective, reflecting a specifically Icelandic aesthetic. Of his instrumental music, *G-Sweet* (1975) for violin and piano is a pun on the string (Gee) and the form (one-movement suite), whose insistent drama belies its title.

Of the younger Icelandic composers, the flautist and composer Jónas Tómasson (born 1946) has followed unconventional patterns. In his considerable output he prefers series with abstract titles (notably a series of fifteen sonatas for various instruments, 1965–85), and webs of textured sounds, formally free and often slow moving and introspective. The atonal *Orgia* (1973) for orchestra is ritualistic, with layers of rhythmic activity and dark-hued rugged orchestral textures. The expressive and severe *Vetrartre* (*Winter Trees*, 1982–83) for violin and piano is an effective work.

Iceland Music Information Centre:
Islensk Tónverkamidstöd/Iceland MIC
Sídumúli 34
IS – 108 Reykjavík
tel: +354 5 68 31 22
fax: +354 5 68 31 24

Sveinsson Atli Heimir*
born 21st September 1938 at Reykjavik

Atli Heimir Sveinsson (born 1938, not to be confused with the composer Gunnar Reynir Sveinsson, born 1933) is the most interesting of the Icelandic composers. He has embraced a variety of styles, including a popular musical, *Land mins föður* (*My Father's Country*, 1985), though his idiom largely follows the European mainstream of the post-avant-garde. The dramatic and intense *Flute Concerto* (1973) is one of the finest written since World War II. It pitches a percussive opening influenced by African rhythms against a haunting flute, followed by atmospheric and often complex virtuoso writing. His orchestral music includes the existential *Hreinn: Súm: 74* (1974) for a variable ensemble of two pianos, one to ten violins, electric guitar and obbligato winds and percussion. Inspired by the painting of Hreinn Friofinnsson, it uses the minimum of means to express the white minimalism of the Icelandic landscape. The improvisatory *Gloria* (1981) for piano is a meditation (influenced by **Messiaen**) on the Nativity story, using extremes of register and washes of effect, before moving to a melodic sense of tonality and dramatic outbursts. Sveinsson currently teaches composition at the Reykjavík College of Music.

RECOMMENDED WORKS
Flute Concerto (1973)
Hreinn: Súm: 74 (1974) for various forces

Israel

Israeli classical music has inevitably been founded on the traditions and cultural origins of those composers and performers who left Europe in mid-century to emigrate to the new country, and Israel's orchestras quickly established themselves as venues for international performers and conductors. Polish-born Joseph Tal (born 1910) has been the main Israeli composer to use 12-tone techniques and electronic music. Yohanan Boehm (born 1913 in Silesia, died 1986) has used neo-classicism with shades of **Mahler**, especially in the *Symphony No. 1* There are touches of eastern exoticism in the *Concerto for English Horn and Orchestra* (1956–58), while the *Oboe Concertino* (1953) has an equally unassuming cheerfulness.

The early works of Israel's most celebrated composer, Paul Ben-Haim (1897–1984, born Paul Frankenburger in Munich), were in a late Romantic vein, exemplified by the oratorio *Yoram* (1931). In 1933 he emigrated to Palestine, and following his meeting with the folk-song collector and singer Braha Zefira, developed in the 1940s an idiom that combined the European heritage with the influence of Near Eastern folk musics, adding an exotic hue to an otherwise conventional idiom. His best-known work is probably the *Symphony No. 2* (1942–45), Romantic in scale and conception, but shot through with colourful exoticism created by the use of modal keys and the occasional exotic rhythmic percussive passage. Emotionally and intellectually undemanding, it is nonetheless attractive music. His *Violin Concerto* (1960) is also well known in Israel.

The merging of a European tradition with Near Eastern colours has become known as the Eastern Mediterranean School, and was used by such composers as Alexander Boscovich (born 1907 in Transylvania, died 1964), and Tzvi Avni (born 1927 in Germany); both these composers were influenced by the European avantgarde in the 1960s. A third composer of some prominence who started in the 'Eastern Mediterranean' style was Noam Sheriff (born 1935). In the late 1950s he developed a personal, vital form of neo-classicism, and then a more advanced style, sometimes combining various stylistic elements, as in the orchestral *'La Folia' Variations* (1985). The symphony *Mechayae Hametim* (1987), synthesising a wide range of musical sources, follows Jewish life from the diaspora to the holocaust and the post-war resurgence.

Israel Music Information Centre:
Israel Music Institute
144, Hayarkon St
63451 Tel Aviv
Israel
tel: + 972 3 527 0219/972 3 524 6475
fax: + 972 3 524 5276

Italy

Introduction

As the 20th century dawned, music in Italy was dominated by opera, by opera houses of widely varying standards but enthusiastic audiences, and by opera composers, as it had been for the previous century. Guiseppe Verdi, with Richard Wagner the most important opera composer of his age, died in 1901, while Giacomo **Puccini** (1858–1924) adapted the typical Italian melodic emphasis and expressive orchestration to more realistic psychological scenarios in a style known as *verismo*. His last opera, *Turandot*, has a musical language that belongs to the 20th century, but many of his followers wrote in an idiom that harked back to the 19th century. Franco **Alfano** (1876–1954) is discussed below; of the other major *verismo* composers, Umberto Giordano (1867–1948) had his greatest success with *Andrea Chenier* (1896) and *Fedora* (1898), although he continued with seven more operas, notably *II Re* (1929). Pietro Mascagni (1863–1945) had similar early success with *Cavalleria rusticana* (1890), one of the staples of the operatic repertoire, and with *L'Amico Fritz* (1891). The only opera of Riccardo Zandonai (1883–1944) to survive in the regular repertoire is *Francesca da Rimini* (1913–14). Ermanno Wolf-Ferrari (1876–1948) continued this Italian tradition, but with comic operas often drawing on 18th century music: his enduring work is *II segreto di Susanna* (1909). The move towards a more modern language was led by such figures as the neo-classicist Giorgio Ghedini (1892–1965), who used *Billy Budd* as the basis of an opera in 1949, two years before **Britten**, and Ildebrando **Pizzetti** (1880–1968), who was influenced by **Debussy** and Mussorgsky.

Noted composers of orchestral and instrumental music had disappeared from 19th century Italy, and it was not until World War I that a generation of Italian composers emerged who were less single-mindedly interested in the operatic stage. Two features in particular emerged: the influence of Impressionism, and a renewed interest in Gregorian chant. Both are found in the music of the best-known Italian composer of this period, Ottorino **Respighi** (1879–1936). The revival of interest in older music centred on plainsong, on the Italian madrigal (with a revival of interest in Monteverdi), and on Italian baroque music.

Meanwhile the one innovative genius that Italy produced, Ferruccio **Busoni** (1866–1924), preferred to live in Germany, where his ideas on the movement away from Romanticism were enormously influential. In Italy, it was left to Alfredo **Casella** (1883–1947) to espouse the cause of the modern. He introduced the latest European music into Italy, and from 1913 the newest techniques into his own compositions, with an awareness of **Bartók**, **Schoenberg** and **Stravinsky**. With Mario **Castelnuovo-Tedesco** (1895–1968), Vittorio Gui (1885–1975), Gian Francesco **Malipiero** (1882–1973), **Respighi** and Vincenzo Tommasini (1878–1950), Casella founded the Società Italiana di Musica Moderna (SIMM) that promoted new works between 1917 and 1919 through concerts and the magazine *Ars Nova*. In 1923 the poet D'Annunzio, Casella, Malipiero and Labroca inaugurated a successor, the Corporazione delle Nuovo Musiche (later incorporated into Italy's ISCM), which introduced new European as well as Italian works. After 1920 Casella's own style mellowed, and the gauntlet of the new was taken up by Goffredo **Petrassi** (born 1904), whose style has followed modern developments right up until the present age, and Luigi **Dallapiccola** (1904–75), who emerged as the most original and fascinating Italian composer of his generation. The imposition of Fascism from 1922 to 1945 gradually stifled both innovation and contact with developments outside Italy, and composers of this generation turned to earlier Italian music. The development of contemporary Italian music was also hampered by a famous attack on modernity led by **Respighi**, Zandoni, and **Pizzetti**, published in 1932. Vittorio Rieti (1898–1994) moved to Paris and in 1940 to the USA. Initially known for his ballets for Diaghilev (*Barabeau*, 1925, and *Le Bal*, 1928), he is now most likely to be encountered in such refined and neo-classical chamber works as the *Sonata for piano flute, oboe and bassoon* (1924) or the *Partita* (1945) for flute, oboe, string quartet and piano obbligato. His opera *Don Perlimplin* (1952), based on Lorca, combined commedia dell'arte and Romantic elements.

Malipiero, with his clear architecture and direct language founded on neo-classicism and the neo-madrigal style that looked back to the Renaissance continued to be the leading composer after 1945. Modernity in Italian music swiftly revived, led by **Petrassi** and **Dallapiccola**. Of the older generation, Riccardo Nielsen (1908–82), experimented with 12-tone rows in 1927 but abandoned the technique until 1942: Mario Peragallo (1910–96) was initially a *verismo* opera writer, but embraced 12-tone techniques in such works as the opera *La gita in campagna*, and in the serial but lyrical *Violin Concerto*. The Romanian Roman Vlad (born 1919), who settled in Italy in 1938 and became a citizen in 1951, produced non-dodecaphonic works in a fusion of tonal and atonal elements. The following generation was influenced by the avant-garde represented by **Boulez** and **Stockhausen**, and three important Italian composers made major contributions to the avant-garde. Luciano **Berio** (born 1925) has been the most accessible, moving to the use of folk music in the 1970s, and Luigi **Nono** (1924–90) the most extreme, with a deep commitment to left-wing politics. Bruno **Maderna** (1920–73) became celebrated as a conductor of contemporary music; with Berio he founded the Italian Radio electronic music studio in Milan in 1955. The oldest of these post-modernists, Giacinto **Scelsi** (1904–88), is just beginning to become known for his often spartan works combining a spiritualism drawn from eastern philosophies with unusual harmonic concepts. Sylvano **Bussotti** (born 1931) took the avant-garde firmly into Italian opera in often outrageous works.

Italian music of the 20th century is still far too little known outside Italy: **Casella**, **Dallapiccola**, **Malipiero** and **Petrassi** in particular deserve wider appreciation. One of the reasons is that music in Italy has remained committed to opera, with no outstanding symphony orchestra of international fame. Another is the lack of Italian recording companies that might have disseminated Italian music with the enthusiasm and dedication of those in other countries. Symptomatic of this is the lack of an Italian Music Information Centre.

Alfano Franco
born 8th March 1876 at Posillipo (Naples)
died 26th October 1954 at San Remo

Alfano is chiefly remembered outside Italy for his completion of **Puccini's** *Turandot* (1925, although Alfano's uncut ending, considerably longer, has only recently been rediscovered). However, his own *Risurrezione (Resurrection*, after Tolstoy, 1902–03), his third opera and the second to be performed, followed Puccini's *verismo*

example and has had great success in Italy. At the same time his orchestral music (for example, the *Suite romantica*, 1907–08, revised as *Eliana*) followed a Romantic vein. With his eighth opera, *L'ombra di Don Giovanni (The Ghost of Don Giovanni*, 1913, revised 1941), Alfano started to move away from the still current and popular Italian operatic tradition to include the influence of **Debussy** and **Strauss**. This awareness of more modern ideas resulted in his co-founding of Musica Nova in Bologna (1920). The culmination of this development was the opera *La leggenda di Sakuntala (The legend of Sakuntala*, 1914–20), considered to be his major work. Based on a Sanskrit play, it combines an Italian lyricism with luxuriant orchestration and exotic colours. Such works were less to Italian tastes than *verismo* operas. He wrote some admired chamber music (*Cello Sonata*, 1925, *Violin Sonata*, 1922–23, revised 1933) and songs that have remained in the Italian repertoire (four settings of Tagore, 1918, 1928, 1934, 1947). His later operas, of which the best known is probably *Cyrano de Bergerac* (1936), became more conventional, while a neo-classical idiom emerges in his later orchestral works (as in the *Divertimento*, 1934, for small orchestra with piano obbligato).

Alfano's main teaching posts were at the Liceo Musicale Bologna (1916–23, director 1918), as director of the Liceo Musicale Turin (1939), and at the Liceo Musicale Pesaro (1947–50).

RECOMMENDED WORKS
    opera *La leggenda di Sakùntala* (1914–20)
    opera *Cyrano de Bergerac* (1936)

Berio Luciano**
born 24th October 1925 at Oneglia

Luciano Berio was considered in the early 1960s to be one of the major Italian exponents of total serialism, a reputation which hampered a wider appreciation of his music. As his idiom has developed, it has proved to be one of the most accessible of the post-war avant-garde, and he has emerged as the leading Italian composer of his generation.

Berio's earliest works show an explosion of interest in the new ideas of the day which he encountered after the end of the Fascist regime, and which are exemplified in the angrily energetic *Concertino* (1951) for clarinet, violin and orchestra. The

Three Poems from James Joyce's 'Chamber Music' (1953) for soprano range from a strict pointillism to a sensual array of rich colours and expressive effects. At the end of the 1950s Berio had developed a set of personal preoccupations that gave his music individuality. The first was an increasing interest in the voice, influenced by three contemporary Italian writers, Italo Calvino, Umberto Eco, and Edoardo Sanguineti, and by the emerging discipline of semiotics. The voice was of interest to Berio not just for the musical production of word-texts, but also for its colours and sounds, both of the imitation of nature and of elemental language structures without concrete meanings. The second was a love of theatrical content and effect, in concert as well as stage works, where dramatic events could take place again without the necessity of concrete language. The third was a concern with creating a musical commentary on, and merger with, other musics (including his own) and other art forms. In these, Berio proved to be the main composer of a post-modernism that paralleled that of the literary arts.

With the *Sequenza I* (1958) for flute, Berio embarked on a series of *Sequenzas* for solo instruments virtuoso works using extremes of register and new techniques, and often (as in the clown/performer analogy of the *Sequenza V*, 1966, for trombone) involving a large measure of theatrics in performance. The works aim to investigate the relationship between the performer and the instrument, and if the extreme nature of some of the writing is accepted, this series is a fascinating commentary on music and its performance. The best known is probably *Sequenza III* (1966) for female voice, a work that had been heralded by the seminal electronic piece *Ommagio a Joyce* (1959), in which Berio took recordings of his wife, the soprano Cathy Berberian, reading excepts from James Joyce's *Ulysses* in English, French and Italian, and made an electronic construct out of them that musically echoed Joyce's own reworking of language. Even in the purely electronic *Momenti* (1960) much of the work sounds like the chattering of hundreds of voices, while *Visage* (1961) is an imaginary drama using Berberian's voice mixed with electronics, full of allusions to dramatic incident and extreme emotions and reactions. *Epifanie (Epiphanies,* 1959–1961) for soprano and orchestra is a kind of mobile showing alternative ways of setting text to music, while *Circles* (1960) for female singer, harp and percussion transcribes a musical circle

from understandable language to disconnected vocal sound and back again. The singer physically circles on stage, joining different instrumentalists and blending her voice with that particular sound. The commentary on Berio's own work came in a series of pieces in which one arises out of the other. *Sequenza II* (1963) for harp led to *Chemin II* (1965) for harp and orchestra, *Sequenza VI* for viola to *Chemin II* and *Chemin III* for viola and orchestra (all 1967), while *Chemin II* itself became *Chemin IIb* (1969) for small orchestra, and *Chemin IIc* (1972) for bass clarinet and small orchestra. Berio himself has described this process as similar to covering an onion core with new layers. *Chemin IV* (1975) for oboe and thirteen strings is a commentary on *Sequenza VII* (1969) for oboe.

The first of Berio's stage works also dates from this period. *Passaggio* (1961–62) is a protest music-theatre work, and the exhilarating *Laborintus II* (1965) for speaking voice, female soloists and ensemble is a music-theatre piece whose texts were compiled by Edoardo Sanguineti from works by Dante, Eliot, Pound and Sanguineti himself in homage to Dante. With the concert work *Sinfonia* (1968, fifth movement added in 1969), Berio produced one of the choral masterpieces of our age, that seemed to reflect exactly an aspect of modern western culture, being fragmentary in appearance but with a continuous undercurrent of anguished joy. Its third movement takes quotations from the scherzo of **Mahler's** *Symphony No. 2,* and places them in a complex web of vocal dialogue. It was followed by his first large-scale opera *Opera* (1969–70), which drew an analogy between the outmoded form and outmoded capitalism. Berio's subsequent operas, *La vera storia* (first performed 1982) and *Un re in ascolto* (first performed 1984) have been musical responses to the new literature examining the process of literature, using the kind of fantastical ideas beloved by the novelist Calvino, the librettist of *La vera storia. Un re in ascolto* (*A King Listens*) uses texts by Calvino, W. H. Auden, and a play by the 18th-century Friedrich Gotter. It explores the world of dreams and fantasies, both of life and of the theatre, through a theatre impresario who is auditioning for a play. Layered on this is a wealth of Shakespearean allusion; the impresario is named Prospero, and various characters have reference to *The Tempest.* The various layers of the stage action are matched by differentiated layers of music.

Classical in their cast, such as the formal
out and harmonies in the *Elegie* (1920)
clarinet and piano, or the shadow of
ch in the *Divertimento* op. 52 (1920) for
te and piano, that they seem to have lost
uch with the century they are written in.
His major works for orchestra are
omantic in scale, scope, and execution,
owever much individual procedures
eflect his study of Classical musics, and
owever much commentators have tried
o claim otherwise. The *Piano Concerto*
1903–04) for piano, male chorus and
orchestra is a gigantic work for huge forces
hat requires great stamina from the solo-
st. It opens in the grand virtuoso manner,
a long orchestral introduction leading to
the entry of the soloist pounding out
arpeggios in one of the noblest and most
exciting introductions to any concerto.
After the first movement, the soloist
becomes first among equals; the impulse
remains purely late Romantic. It depicts
the struggle of the soul, symbolised by the
illustrations of temples that Busoni
requested for the frontispiece of the score,
and ends with the male chorus singing a
song of triumph from *Aladdin* by the
Danish poet Oelenschlaeger. The five
movements were to be played without a
break, though performances inevitably
have a pause, simply to get breath back.
Beethoven and sometimes Berlioz lie
behind this concerto, in both temperament
and actual sound. In the second movement
there is a resemblance to d'Indy's *Symphony on a French Mountain Air* of 1886
so marked that one wonders whether
Busoni had unconsciously borrowed. By
leading back to Beethoven and using the
scale of **Mahler**, Busoni marked the apogee
of the Romantic piano concerto. The *Violin
Concerto* (1897) has almost completely
disappeared; it is a lyrically rich work with
much of the solo part in a low register. The
slow movement is gorgeously sensuous,
with echoes of Gregorian chant, and the
entertaining finale makes mischievous
allusion to Dvořák's *New World
Symphony* and sets up a fantastical and
humorous interplay between trumpets
and soloists. It deserves to be better
known.

Busoni's major works for solo piano are
the huge *Fantasia contrappuntistica*
(1910) and the six piano sonatinas. The
Fantasia derives some of its material from
the last, unfinished, fugue in Bach's *The
Art of Fugue*, and combines its contrapuntal creations with intermezzos and variations. The sonatinas show the range of

Busoni's stylistic interests and the incisiveness of his piano writing. The procedural formality of Bach is never far away,
but mixed with echoes of **Debussy** (notably
in the fourth sonatina) and (in the second)
of **Schoenberg**. They make fascinating if
not immediately alluring listening. The
Sonatina No. 1 (1910) oscillates between
the thinnest of austere textures and contrapuntal layering or Impressionistic
strokes. *Sonatina No. 2* (1912) is stormy,
thunderous, with dense textures and harmonies verging on the atonal. *Sonatina
No. 3* (1915) is much more lightly textured,
being subtitled (in Latin) 'Sonatina for the
Use of the American Child Madeline M.
Composed for the Harpsichord', though it
would require a child of prodigious talents
to play it, and is clearly written with the
piano in mind. The opening of the *Sonatina
No. 4* (1917), subtitled 'In diem nativitas
Christi MCMXVII' seems like Bach in
modern guise; its ending was also used in
the opera *Arlecchino*. The homage to Bach
is direct in *Sonatina No. 5* (1918), which
reworks Bach's *Fantasy and Fugue in D*,
BWV 905. *Sonatina No. 6* (1920) is different in tone and content, a wild and brilliant
fantasy on themes from Bizet's opera *Carmen*, full of Lisztian touches of pianistic
colour and surprise.

Busoni's earliest opera to maintain a
precarious foothold in the repertoire, the
'theatrical capriccio' *Arlecchino* (1914–16),
is a comic satire in the style of commedia
dell'arte, telling the story of a cuckolded
tailor and the jealousies and loves of the
cast, including the successfully adulterous
hero and a caricature of the operatic tenor
in the person of a knight. Its entertaining,
tuneful style anticipates **Weill**, who was
deeply influenced by the work. It is perhaps the first neo-classical opera, harking
back to the buffa style of Rossini. *Turandot* (1917) was a comic companion piece to
Arlecchino, but has been completely
eclipsed by **Puccini**'s opera on the same
subject. Full of exotic melodies and colours, some of the music was turned into an
entertaining orchestral suite. Busoni's
masterpiece is generally agreed to be his
final opera, *Doktor Faust* (1910–24), with a
libretto by the composer, and completed
after his death by Philipp Jarnach; a more
effective version by Anthony Beaumont
appeared in 1986. In reaction to the prevailing fashion of *verismo*, exemplified by
Puccini, Busoni decided that a naturalistic
opera plot told by singing was inherently
absurd; opera should show the fantastical
and the symbolic, and thus the Faust story

Recital I (1972), a theatrical piece for a virtuoso performer, shows a singer on the edge of breakdown, psychologically and linguistically. The correlation between singer and instrument, evident in *Circles*, is also seen in *Coro* (1975–76) for forty voices and orchestra, where each singer is placed next to an instrument of similar range. This epic work juxtaposes small groups or solos based on folk texts (often with unusual effects, such as the murmurings of an African Gabon song) and massive chordal, cluster-filled swathes of orchestral chords in which the tutti choir merge with fragments from the poetry of Pablo Neruda. *A-ronne* (1974–75) for eight voices explored the relationship between speech and music, using a poem by Edoardo Sanguineti that itself draws on fragments by other writers, from Dante to Eliot and Barthes. It concentrates on the inflections of speech in various settings and with a wide range of emotions, in what Berio has described as documentary style. The quasi-speech sounds eventually emerge into a neo-madrigal idiom. Its documentary nature distances the listener, but it is nonetheless fascinating, and not without moments of humour.

Coro had also demonstrated the integration of folk music into Berio's idiom. This has been of importance since the early 1970s; he had already arranged folk songs in *Folksongs* (1964) for soprano and seven instruments, orchestrated in 1973, which with its hues of modernism has proved widely popular. *Cries of London* (1974, later revised) uses street cries as the basis for a varied series of a cappella miniatures, applying modern textures to a traditional base. In the rather introverted and essentially lyrical *Voci* (1984) for viola and orchestra, the Sicilian folk melodies on which it is based have merged with the colours of the orchestra. Folk music is totally assimilated into the overall means of expression through a distorting filter.

Berio's voice has been less prominent since the 1980s, partly because the post-modernist movement which his music embodied has passed the peak of its intellectual incisiveness. He lived and taught in the USA from 1962 to 1971.

RECOMMENDED WORKS
Circles (1960) for female voice, harp and two percussionists
Coro (1975–76) for chorus and orchestra
Epifanie (1959–61, rev. 1965) for soprano and orchestra
electronic *Omaggio a Joyce* (1959)

opera *Un rè in asc...*
Sequenza III (1966...
Sequenza IV (1966)...
Sequenza V (1966) f...
Sinfonia (1968) for ...
orchestra
Three Poems from J...
'Chamber Music'...
Voci (1984) for viola a...

Busoni Ferruccio (
Michelangiolo Ben...
born 1st April 1866 at E...
died 27th July 1924 at B...

Ferruccio Busoni is one o...
thinkers who influenced m...
tury more by his concepts...
pioning of other composer...
own compositions, which ...
known to a wider public. He ...
the greatest pianists of his da...
as well as Italian ancestry, h...
of his life working in German...
Berlin in 1894), as h...
characteristics reflected, a...
thought of himself as Italian...

It was Busoni who, react...
Romanticism in general and ...
particular, advocated an ...
approach to that of the Fren...
sionists. In doing so, he an...
number of trends that were t...
fruition in the second and third...
the 20th century. His early r...
influenced by Mendelssohn an...
culminating in the 1890s in an...
that harked back past the develo...
the 19th century to the Classi...
and beyond (in particular to ...
interest in whom he did much t...
He sought a return to the grace, ...
and formal structures of the Bar...
Classical periods within a mode...
Harmonically, he tried to remov...
from the 'tyranny of minor and ma...
experimented with new scales (i...
113 possible ways of arranging w...
half steps within a seven-note ...
occasionally coming close to atona...
generally not straying far from ...
base. Counterpoint also plays a ma...
in his art. At the same time his in...
inquisitiveness could equally adopt ...
that sounds totally Romantic, or ...
Impressionism. He is, though, as n...
any composer the founder or at le...
precursor of neo-classicism, incorp...
what he termed 'junge Klassizität' f...
early as the *Konzertstück* (1890) for...
and orchestra. Some of his later wor...

was a suitable text. While including the main elements of the story (Faust summoning Mephistopheles, Faust's death), Busoni chose essentially unlinked episodes from the story, creating an overall character portrait in a number of scenes, initiating (with, to a lesser degree, **Berg's** *Wozzeck*) a technique widely employed in later 20th-century operas. Instead of the conventional Christian ending, as Faust dies he passes his personality to his dead child, who springs up as a youth. However, Christian imagery lies behind much of the work, as in the memorable scene where Faust signs the pact with Mephistopheles and wonders what he has done to the backdrop of a distant Easter chorus, the orchestra quietly undulating as a third layer; all three build to a powerful climax as Faust becomes more and more agitated. Musically, the idiom is late Romantic, though permeated with Busoni's knowledge of earlier musics and with an often lean clarity of texture.

Doktor Faust occupies a similar position to Pfitzner's masterpiece, *Palestrina*, both more familiar by name than in performance, yet offering an earnest sincerity and convincing portraits of their main characters. There are many sections of memorable power, including the intermezzo introduction to the main action (starting with a soldier's prayer against the organ), and the arguments between the Catholic and Protestant students (with the intolerant Protestants prophetically marching off to a goose-step, right arm raised). The purely symphonic passages are especially effective, notably the very beautiful and subdued opening Easter Sinfonia.

The works of Busoni most likely to be encountered are unfortunately not his original compositions, but the extraordinary transcriptions he made of earlier music, notably that of Bach. They are often used as encores by virtuoso pianists, and can be terrifically exciting. As enduring was Busoni's influence as a teacher (his most notable pupil was **Weill**) and as musical thinker; his *Sketch for a New Aesthetic of Music* was published in 1907.

RECOMMENDED WORKS
    opera *Arlecchino* (1914–16)
    opera *Doktor Faust* (1916–24)
    Fantasia contrappuntistica (1910–12)
        for piano
    Piano Concerto (1904)
    Piano Sonatinas Nos 1–6 (1910–20)

Violin Concerto (1897)

BIBLIOGRAPHY
  A. Beaumont, *Busoni, the Composer*, 1986
  E. J. Dent, *Ferruccio Busoni*, 1933, revised 1974

Bussotti Sylvano*
born 1st October 1931 at Florence

Bussotti is a polymath: composer, successful painter, set designer, stage, film, and opera director (and not merely of modern works), and experimenter in all multimedia forms. He established his reputation for multimedia stage presentations with *La Passion selon Sade* (1965–66), which, although based on a 16th-century French sonnet, incorporates Sade's two heroines, Justine and Juliette, as well as O from *The Story of O*, in a staging that includes gestural, sound and lighting effects, mime, and dance; Bussotti termed it a 'chamber mystery play'. In it are a number of features, discernible in earlier works, which together become characteristic of his music. The multi-roles of musicians and actors and the sense of theatrical fantasy provide the stage structure for free and fragmentary musical ideas evolving from a 12-tone idea, unified by the use of the combination of two mottos, D-Es-A-D-E (De Sade) and BACH (Es=E flat, H=B natural). The theatrical elements include the multi-layering of time and characters: the 20th century mirrors the Romantic writer Alfred de Musset, who is mirroring the Italian Renaissance. The strong erotic themes were evident in the homoerotic texts of *Pièces de chair II* (*Flesh Plays*, 1958–60), a set of fourteen pieces for low voice, piano and ensemble. Five of these became the best known of his earlier works, *Five Piano Pieces for David Tudor* (1959), with graphic pictorial notation and unpredictable elements that reflected the influence of **Cage**.

The element of fantasy (or the fantastical) often emerges in Bussotti's music in sound combinations moving in and out of focus with insubstantial rhythms, as in *Cinque frammenti all'Italia* (1967–68) for six soloists and chorus. Characteristically, it assimilates Renaissance madrigals in setting fragments from a number of poets, with brief contributions from piano and tubular bells in the second of five sections, the last opening with the title-words of all the previous sections. Bussotti developed this method of quotation and incorporation to include his own works, a concept initiated in the opera *Lorenzaccio* (1968–72) in twenty-three scenes, 250 costume changes (all the costumes originally designed by the composer), and multimedia elements (film, spoken sections, offstage happenings). It is based on a play by Alfred de Musset about the assassination of the Florentine Alessandro de'Medici by his brother Lorenzo in 1537. The musical sources range from Monteverdi to Webern, from Verdi to Tosti (Bussotti's teacher), and finally, to end the work, the inclusion complete of his own *Rara Requiem* (1969–70) for voices (in several languages) and orchestra. The complex web of allusion cannot, of course, be appreciated in totality by the audience, but this is not Bussotti's intent. Rather it is a kind of autobiographical self-creation in which the memory becomes the motivation of the piece, which in turn reworks memory. Sections of the opera were used for the rather raucous '*Lorenzzaccio' Symphony* for orchestra.

The process was developed further in *Bussottioperaballet* (1975), in which the theme of the whole piece – the position of the artist – is expressed by two parts, the first a ballet on an Egyptian myth incorporating fragments of *Pièces de chair* on tape, the second, *Nottetempo (Nighttime)* for soloists and chorus, weaving two plots, the one Greek mythology, the other an episode from Michelangelo's life. The element of the fantastical is to the fore in an earlier ballet, *Bergkristall* (1972–73), based on a novel by Adalbert Stifter in which two children have dream-like visions after getting lost in the snow at Christmas; they are eventually rescued. Bussotti's score abounds in shifts of focus and in the insubstantial, sometimes with glittering cold effects, and verging on the Expressionist. Bussotti's own experiences in Paris in the 1950s surface in *La racine* (1980–81), with a 12-note idea based on the 12 syllables of Racine's iambic hexameters. Autobiographical and erotic elements, as well as vocal influences from the madrigal to *Sprechgesang*, recur in *La Rarit, Potente* (1980). These essentially theatrical concerns, designed to weave a complex series of dramatic reactions rather than intellectual responses, parallel the recasting of process evident in other Italian media (for example, the writing of Calvino) with their elements of fantasy, reworking of the past and complex allusion, and have provoked strong audience reactions.

Bussotti was professor of the history of music drama at L'Aquila Academy of Fine Arts (1971–74), and from 1975 artistic director of the Teatro la Fenice, Venice.

RECOMMENDED WORKS
    ballet *Bergkristall* (1972–73)
    opera *La Passion selon Sade*
        (1965–66)
    Five Piano Pieces for David Tudor
        (1959)

Casella Alfredo**
born 25th July 1883 at Turin
died 5th March 1947 at Rome

Alfredo Casella was the major personality in Italian new music between World Wars I and II through his promotion of new music as organiser, pianist and conductor and through the example of his own compositions. Although the music of **Respighi** or **Malipiero** is more likely to be encountered, Casella's knowledge of contemporary trends in both music and the visual arts had more effect on the development of Italian music than these better-known composers. He spent 1896 to 1905 in Paris, thus being immersed in concert music rather than opera. His early works show an eclectic range of influences, from **Mahler** (in the two symphonies, 1905–06 and 1908–09) to **Fauré**. The best-known work of this period is probably the *Sicilienne and Burlesque* (1913) for flute and piano or piano trio (many Casella works exist in more than one arrangement), in an Impressionist style similar to **Respighi**. The use of Italian folk song, uncommon among Italian composers, is most overt in the Sicilian and Neapolitan tunes of *Italia* for orchestra (an Italian response to the music of the Spaniard Isaac Albéniz, 1860–1909).

With the song-cycles *Notte di maggio* (1913) for low voice and orchestra, and *L'adieu à la vie* (1915, to words by Tagore translated by Gide) for low voice and piano (instrumental arrangement, 1926) Casella embraced the latest ideas, having discovered the music of **Stravinsky** and **Bartók**. The works of this period experiment harmonically through extreme chromaticism and polytonality, but still include a wide range of emotions, from reflections on the war (*Pagine di guerra*, 1918, for piano duet, later orchestrated, and *Elegia eroica*), to the sarcasm and dissonance of the *Piano Sonatina* (1916). This modern stance mellowed in the 1920s, as he returned to Italian folk song, in the lively ballet *La giara (The Jar)*, 1924, based on Pirandello, and added an interest in pre-

Classical Italian music, in an attempt to parallel what he saw as the lucidity of landscape in Italian art. It is the music from this period, sometimes infected with a pleasurable sense of humour, that is likely to be encountered. The *Scarlattiana* (1926) for piano and small orchestra is an Italian equivalent of **Stravinsky's** *Pulcinella*, based on Scarlatti keyboard sonata themes, entertaining in its colourful instrumentation and neo-classical combination of the antique and modern, if not as individual or as piquant as Stravinsky's score. The craftsmanship and timing in *Serenata* for clarinet, bassoon, trumpet, violin and cello (1927, also version for small orchestra), is delightful. With its sinuous melodic flow, and a mysterious nocturne that includes an almost Mexican solo trumpet, it is not surprising that it shared (with a work by **Bartók**) a major composition prize in Philadelphia. The Italian neo-classical is at its grandest in the *Concerto romano* (1926) for organ, brass, timpani and strings, which is purely baroque in musical (and architectural) inspiration.

Neo-classicism is also evident in Casella's first opera, *La donna serpente* (1931), inspired by 18th-century commedia dell'arte. The political climate in Italy was reflected in the opera *Il deserto tenato* (1936–37), which praises Mussolini's Ethiopian war, but in Casella's last works (such as the *Concerto* for piano, timpani, percussion and strings) there is a suggestion that Casella was moving towards the adoption of a 12-tone system.

Casella founded (with **Castelnuovo-Tedesco**, Gui, **Malipiero, Respighi** and Tommasini) the Società Italiana di Musica Moderna (SIMM) which, with its magazine *Ars Nova*, was enormously influential in its two years of activity (1917–19). In 1923, with the backing of D'Annunzio and with Malipiero and Labroca, he set up the Corporazione delle Nuovo Musiche (later incorporated into Italy's ISCM). He continued his promotion of new music at the Venice Festival of Contemporary Music (1930–34), while his interest in Italian Baroque music was reflected in his founding of the Siena Weeks music festival, which still runs.

RECOMMENDED WORKS
Concerto romano (1926) for organ, brass, timpani and strings
ballet *La giara* (1924)
Scarlattiana (1926) for piano and small orchestra

Serenata (1927) for clarinet, bassoon, trumpet, violin and cello

BIBLIOGRAPHY
A Casella, *Music in My Time*, 1941, trans. S Norton, 1955

Castelnuovo-Tedesco Mario*
born 3rd April 1895 at Florence
died 16th March 1968 at Hollywood

Castelnuovo-Tedesco's life was divided between Italy and the USA, as he left Italy in the face of anti-Semitic pogroms in 1939 and became an American citizen in 1946. His output is huge, much of it unpublished and rarely heard, especially (as was the fate of many émigrés of the time) that written in the USA. As far as one can judge, his works are uneven; those now most often heard involve the guitar, for which he showed a particular sensitivity. The basis of his idiom is Impressionism, and the core of his output loosely divides into concertos, works based on Shakespeare, music with Jewish influences, and, in the 1940s and 1950s, a considerable amount of film music.

Of his concertos, the *Concertino* (1934) for harp and chamber orchestra demonstrates both his virtues and the unevenness. The Mediterranean colours, the sparkling Impressionism and the unusual effects are particularly attractive, but too often the music is trite and unmemorable. Much more consistent, and his most frequently played work, is the *Guitar Concerto* (1939). The felicitous opening movement has a memorable main theme and a pastoral atmosphere set up by the guitar's answers to a lovely passage of horn calls. The slow movement is gentle and melodic, the finale rumbustious; throughout the work, the emphasis is on delightful melodies in one of the most attractive of all guitar concertos. Castelnuovo-Tedesco's solo guitar music is extensive, often written for the Spaniard Andrés Segovia; the series *Les guitares bien tempérées* for two guitars is especially effective, combining the formality of the prelude and fugue, some of the spontaneity and earthiness of the folk origins of the instrument, and the resonating colours available from two guitars.

The music inspired by Shakespeare includes eleven concert overtures, song-cycles, duets, and two operas, of which *The Merchant of Venice* was a success on its appearance in 1956. The most important are the thirty-three *Shakespeare Songs*, (1921–25), whose wide range of styles includes the tango. Often in his songs one encounters works of telling effect, as in the simple settings of *Sei odi di Orazio (Six Horatian Odes*, 1930), Impressionistic in their accompaniment, but with long canta- bile vocal lines. The works with a Jewish influence include the *Jewish Rhapsody* for piano, using Hebrew themes, and the *Vio- lin Concerto No. 2* (titled *The Prophets*, 1933). *Le danze del Re David* (1925), one of three *Rhapsodies* (opp. 30, 32, and 37), combines overt Impressionism with Liszt- ian echoes, a Hebrew linking motif, and, towards the end, the kind of modal harmo- nies associated with **Respighi**.

Castelnuovo-Tedesco taught at the Los Angeles Conservatory from 1946 to 1968, and among his many distinguished pupils were band leaders Henry Mancini and Nelson Riddle, the conductor André Pre- vin and the film composer John Williams.

RECOMMENDED WORKS
  Guitar Concerto in D (1939)
  song-cycle *Sei odi di Orazio* (1930)

Dallapiccola Luigi**
born 3rd February 1904 at Pisino (Istria)
died 18th February 1975 at Florence

Dallapiccola was one of the first major composers outside **Schoenberg's** circle to adopt 12-tone techniques, and with **Berg** he was the main composer to show that 12- tone ideas could produce sounds that had audible connections with the tonal tradi- tion. He fused the lyrical, and especially vocal, Italian tradition with the new proce- dures, suffusing them with the northern Italian light that gives the wonderful illu- sion of being both sharply focused and hazy at the same time. His sense of orches- tral or instrumental drama has much in common with **Berg**: surges suddenly swel- ling up from underneath the music or tense rhythmic phrases injected to turn the progress in a new direction. His textures are generally much lighter than those of the Austrian composer, his colours far more monochromatic. Much of his output is vocal music, and his adoption of 12-tone techniques seems to have been an organic recognition that they answered his needs for word setting, rather than a reaction to the tonality of his contemporaries; conse- quently his music has a naturalness and

fluidity often lacking in those contempora- ries. A kernel four-note idea, first heard in the *Divertimento* (1934) for voice and five instruments, recurs through his music, as well as the use of quintuplets symbolising the five syllables of his name.

His earliest music had neo-classical and neo-madrigal elements (in such works as the *Cori di Michelangelo*, 1933, for chorus and boy's or women's voices and seventeen instruments), but the *Sei cori di Michelan- gelo Buonarroti il Giovane* (1936) for cho- rus and orchestra takes chromaticism to its limits for atmospheric effect, and uses an 11-note series at the end. The intense *Tre laudi* (1936–37) for soprano or tenor and thirteen instruments explores 12-tone ideas, using a series in retrograde and inversion, and was the study for Dallapic- cola's first opera, the one-act *Volo di notte* (1937–39), based on Antoine de Saint- Exupéry's *Night Flight*, which contrasts the freedom and adventure of flight against the regularity and security of the earth-bound world.

The seminal works that established Dal- lapiccola's combination of Italian lyricism and 12-tone techniques are the three sets of *Liriche greche (Greek Lyrics*, 1942–45), using translations by the Italian poet Qua- simodo. The *Cinque frammenti di Saffo* (1942) for voice and fifteen instruments combine a different 12-tone row with tonal elements in each song, whereas the *Sei carmina Alcei* (1943) for voice and eleven instruments are based on a single row, manipulated canonically. A sense of com- plete technical freedom is achieved in the *Due liriche di Anacreonte* (1946) for voice and four instruments. The *Due studi* (1947) for violin and piano have something of the extreme reduction to basic elements of **Webern**, while maintaining a melodious atonal flow. *Job* (1950), a *sacra rappresen- tazione* or staged cantata inspired by an Epstein sculpture, uses a single 12-note series as the basis of the music. In the *Quaderno musicale di Annalibera (Musi- cal Notebook for Annalibera*, the compos- er's daughter, 1952) for piano, some of the eleven brief, canonic, and often delicate pieces, alternating fast and slow, make references to the past, the first using the B-A-C-H motto.

During the 1950s Dallapiccola's style became increasingly refined and lean, the emotional effects more calculated, as in the *Goethe Lieder* (1953) for soprano and three clarinets, with its complex rhythmic poly- phony, or the intense and dramatic cantata

An Mathilde (1955) for soprano and chamber orchestra, based on Heine. But at the same time he also returned to a kind of neoclassicism, retaining the economy of statement and lucidity of texture, in the *Tartiniana seconda* (1955–56) for violin and piano (also orchestrated) which uses a theme by Tartini in a melodious and delicate four-movement suite. This was a passing aside; Dallapiccola then maintained the rarefied atmospheres and strict procedures reminiscent of **Webern** through the rest of his output. Yet there remained that implicit lyricism, evident in such works as the *Parole di San Paolo* (1964) for soprano and eleven instruments and based on St Paul's *First Epistle to the Corinthians*, where the wide-leaping solo voice and the delicate tracery of the instrumentation creates a radiant atmosphere, or his final opera, *Ulisse* (1960–68), which explores the hero's psychological search.

Throughout his life, Dallapiccola explored the concept of freedom in his works. Many have the theme of freedom denied or freedom regained, in part reflecting his own experiences during childhood and during the period of Fascism and Nazi occupation. The *Canti di prigionia* (*Songs of Captivity*, 1938–41) for chorus, two pianos, two harps and percussion uses texts by three imprisoned writers, Boethius, Mary Queen of Scots, and Savonarola, and offsets the tonal plainchant *Dies irae* against 12-tone harmonies. Persecution, the promise of liberation and psychological torture are the themes of Dallapiccola's one-act masterpiece, the opera *Il prigioniero* (*The Prisoner*, 1938–48), which quotes from the captivity songs. Its central character is imprisoned by the Spanish Inquisition during the Flemish struggles of independence from Spain. He is given hope both for the success of his cause and his personal freedom by his jailor, who helps him escape. But his freedom is short-lived: in the garden outside the prison the jailor is waiting for him, is revealed as the Grand Inquisitor, and leads him to the gallows. This beautiful and dramatically tense work is based on 12-tone principles but with a series that sets up resonances of tonal themes. Lucid orchestral writing carries much of the dramatic impetus, together with passages of polytonality and tonal choral writing. It is difficult to convey the singular atmosphere of this work; it is as if the lyrical urgency of **Puccini**, the dramatic understanding and orchestral punch of

Berg, the instrumental touches of **Orff**, and elements of **Bartók** had been fused into a completely individual, totally modern, and indisputably Italian idiom, of delicacy, power, anguish and urgency. Anyone who is convinced that 12-tone music has to be harsh on the ear should hear this opera.

The end of World War II is reflected in the *Ciaccona, intermezzo e adagio* (1945) for solo cello, moving from the unsettled writing of the opening chaconne and the dramatic effects of the intermezzo to a feeling of desolation in the opening of the adagio that transforms into a gentle song of peace. Freedom is again the central theme of Dallapiccola's major choral work, *Canti di liberazione* (1951–55) for chorus and orchestra, using texts from Sebastianus Castellio and St Augustine's *Confessions*. In the radiantly beautiful *Sicut umbra* (1970) for mezzo-soprano and instrumental ensemble, it is death that is the liberator, in settings of poems by Juan Ramón Jiménez; the final song uses instrumental figures based on the shapes of the constellations, with harp, celesta and vibraphone added to the flutes, clarinets and strings. The Dallapiccola theme of reconstruction after destruction found its final outlet in *Tempus destruendi, tempus aedificandi* (1971) for unaccompanied chorus, centred on the rebuilding of Jerusalem.

Dallapiccola and the Hungarian **Kurtág** are the two composers who have demonstrated that 12-tone principles could be used to create a lyrical idiom that those coming from a tonal tradition can readily appreciate. Nowhere is that better demonstrated than in the opera *Il prigionerio*, which shatters the commonly held illusion that there is no Italian opera after the *verismo* composers that continues the Italian tradition of lyricism and dramatic intensity. Dallapiccola taught at the Florence Conservatory (1930–67).

RECOMMENDED WORKS

Canti di liberazione (1951–55) for
  chorus and orchestra
Canti di prigionia (1938–41) for
  chorus, two pianos, two harps and
  percussion
Liriche greche (*Greek Lyrics*, 1942–45)
  for voice and instruments
opera *Il prigioniero* (1938–48)
Quaderno musicale di Annalibera
  (1952) for piano
Sicut umbra (1970) for mezzo-soprano
  and instrumental ensemble

BIBLIOGRAPHY
  L. Dallapiccola, *Dallapiccola on
  Opera*, Eng. trans. 1987

Maderna Bruno*

born 21st April 1920 at Venice
died 13th November 1973 at Darmstadt

Bruno Maderna was a major figure in the avant-garde movement of the 1950s and 1960s, both for his compositions and his sympathetic and authoritative conducting of works by avant-garde composers.

Maderna's earliest works were neo-classical in style, but he quickly embraced 12-tone music after World War II. Works such as the *Introduzione e passacaglia* (1947) for orchestra, the *Concerto for Two Pianos* (1948) and the Expressionist *Studi per 'Il Processo' di Kafka* (*Studies for 'The Trial' of Kafka*, 1950) for reciter, soprano and small orchestra were influenced by the example of **Webern**, but Maderna then turned to 'total serialism', systematising especially the overall form and rhythm. The *String Quartet* (1956) uses a complex rhythmic structure, with the second movement a retrograde of the first. The *Piano Concerto* (1959) shows the influence of Webern and is notable for its unconventional handling of solo instrument.

Maderna then became primarily concerned with sound events that alternate tension and relaxation, constructing works by mathematical principles, sometimes with performer choices in performance; the effect is a kind of expressive avant-garde Impressionism, where the quality of dense sonorities and textural colours is paramount. The division of forces is responsible for much of the spatial effect of Maderna's sonorities; his works are better appreciated for the sensuous colours and interjectory events than for any understanding of formal procedures, which are anyway often determined by the performers. The stage work *Hyperion* (1964) opposes a tightly controlled system with sections in which the musicians are given wide freedom of choice; it is divided into three sections, an aria for soprano and orchestra to texts by Hölderlin, an orchestral section, and a section for flute and orchestra, containing material from the earlier parts. In *Quadrivium* (*Crossroads*, 1969) for orchestra divided into four orchestral groups and four percussionists, the entire score is precisely notated, but organisation is determined by the conductor. The result is a swathe of different spatial sonorities and events, with much delicate percussion

writing using a battery of tuned instruments in addition to struck percussion. In *Aura* (1971), the fifty-four strings are divided into distinct groups, and interjections provided by blocks of brass. A tapestry of string writing, sometimes undulating, sometimes in swathes, and punctuated by bright percussion, gives the work impetus. The first movement of *Biogramma* (1972) for orchestra is perhaps the most Impressionistic of these works; the last of the three movements is a kaleidoscope of clicking and revolving orchestral sounds. His last work, the opera *Satyricon* (first performed 1973), suggested he was moving in a new direction away from the avant-garde sound world he had done so much to promote.

Maderna became a West German citizen in 1963, and after many conducting posts in Germany he became chief orchestral conductor of Radio Milan in 1971. With **Berio** he co-founded the electronic studio of Italian Radio in Milan.

RECOMMENDED WORKS
  Aura (1972) for orchestra
  Biogramma (1972) for orchestra

Malipiero Gian Francesco**

born 18th March 1882 at Venice
died 1st August 1973 at Treviso

Gian Francesco Malipiero was the major interwar Italian composer who rediscovered the pre-19th-century Italian heritage and created a 'neo-madrigale' form of neo-classicism. Exceptionally prolific, he deserves wider recognition.

In reacting against the Romantic sentimentality of such composers as **Puccini**, Malipiero looked back to the pre-Classical Italian masters, whom he discovered around 1902. He evolved a neo-classical style, incorporating Baroque elements and ideas drawn from the period of Monteverdi ('neo-madrigale'), with sometimes astringent harmonies created by the play of counterpoint and by modal shades. But he was essentially a lyrical composer, his melodic lines often looking back to 16th-century examples or to Gregorian chant; his music is generally good-humoured, with a lightness of touch and texture. It is also usually athematic, with little sense of the formal structures that had been developed out of the Classical period; often his works use what has been described as a 'panel' construction, a series of episodes related in mood or colour. His output falls into recognisable periods. Until 1918 he was primarily concerned with orchestral works, from 1918 to 1930 with operas, from 1931 to 1944 with operas and concertos, from 1944 to 1950 with symphonies, and from 1950 with a variety of genres. Stylistically, Malipiero remained remarkably consistent, with more turbulence and chromaticism in the works until the mid-1920s, a more lyrical, diatonic style until the 1950s, and then a return to heavy chromaticism.

Malipiero's three early symphonies (*Sinfonia degli Eroi*, 1905, *Sinfonia del Mare*, 1906, and *Sinfonia del Silenzio e della Morte*, 1908) were heavily influenced by early Italian music. His first major work was *Impressioni dal Vero II* (1914–15), the second of three orchestral pieces, which included imitations of birds in an Impressionistic style. He attracted wider attention with *Pause del Silenzio* (*Silence Interrupted*, 1917), which expressed the horrors of war. *Grottesco* (1917) for small orchestra, influenced by **Stravinsky**, is an entertaining short ballet scene written for a Futurist puppet ballet event, suitably grotesque and with pungent sonorities. His major orchestral works are the seven symphonies ('sinfonia') composed between 1933 and 1955, which are less symphonies in structure than a series of episodes, and all of which (except for No. 7) carry descriptive subtitles. The *Symphony No. 3 'delle campane'* (1944–45) reflects the wartime circumstances of its composition, and is highly regarded. The *Symphony No. 4 'In Memoriam Natalie Koussevitzky'* has a fast-slow-fast-slow structure, with a poetic, funereal second movement. The *Symphony No. 6* (1947) is for strings, and was reworked as a string quintet in 1953. To these Malipiero added a further four from 1964 to 1969. But the orchestral work most likely to be encountered is the *Violin Concerto No. 1* (1932), an attractive work that belies its surface blandness with warmth of detail and a pastoral slow movement of considerable lyrical beauty. The pastoral lyricism returns in the *Cello Concerto* (1937), an attractive work in which woodwind intertwine with the colours of the cello in the sonorous slow-movement. The eight numbered string quartets also react against 19th-century models, with a freer sense of fantasy in their construction and with a general good humour. The *String Quartet No. 1 'Rispetti e strambotti'* (1920) uses popular forms, while the *String Quartet No. 1 'Stornelli et ballate'* (1923) reflects its title ('Refrains and Ballads'). The *String Quartet No. 5*

'Dei capricci' (1950) reuses music from the opera *I capricci di Callot.*

During World War I Malipiero embarked on a series of experimental stage works, often with elements of fantasy or of a dream-world. The single dancer in the symbolist ballet *Pantea* (1917–19) is an hallucinating woman who is eventually confronted with an apparition of Death. The vocal lines are sung off-stage. *Sette canzoni (Seven Songs*, 1918–19) is a series of seven miniature operas, each woven around a different song, and each with a story that presents a basic twist or opposition, from a blind man who is helpless when deserted by his girlfriend to a mother obsessed by the memory of her son, apparently dead in the war. She does not recognise him on his return, and finally goes mad. *Sette canzoni* formed the centrepiece of a triptych entitled *L'Orfeide*, of which the third opera, *Orfeo* (1919–20) revolves around Nero's sadisms in a conflux of fantasy and reality, and includes reactions from a stage audience. *Tre commedie Goldoniane* (1920–22) was another triptych, based on Goldoni, with a rapid style strong on recitative. The symbolic atmosphere of a dream was most fully realised in *Torneo notturno* (*Nocturnal Tournament* 1929), whose seven episodes portray two characters in various situations that eventually lead to one killing the other in prison. Each scene is to all intents and purposes a tableau; the characters are symbolic (with such names as 'Il disperato', the Desperate), and there are dream-like themes of doors and time passing. The work is essentially a series of arias; the vocal lines draw on the Italian singing tradition, but are combined with a strong neo-madrigale flavour to create an unusual and effective piece of music theatre.

None of the many Malipiero operas from the 1930s to the 1960s had the inventiveness and individuality of these earlier works; the major operas are *I capricci di Callot* (1941–42), based on E.T.A. Hoffmann, whose mixture of vocal writing, dance and mime recalled some of the experimental verve of the early works, and two based on Shakespeare, *Giulio Cesare* (1934–35) and *Antonio e Cleopatra* (1936–37). The major success of this period was *La favola del figlio cambiato* (*The Fable of the Changed Son*, 1933), based on Pirandello. His operas during the 1950s reflect a more chromatic language, and in 1968 he wrote an unusual work, *Gli eroi di Bonaventura*, that was a compendium of scenes from his other operas. His penultimate opera was a sixteen-minute miniature, *Uno dei dieci* (*One of the Ten*), in which an aging member of the Venetian Council of Ten in the Napoleonic period fails to accept that the Venetian Republic is no more, has to face reality, and looks forward to death.

Malipiero's edition of all Monteverdi's works (1926–42), though scholarly suspect, were of immense importance in the revival of interest in Monteverdi and the late Italian Renaissance. He taught at the Parma Conservatory (1921–24) and at the Venice Liceo Musicale (later Conservatory) from 1932 to 1952, becoming its director in 1939. He published a number of books, including one on Monteverdi (1930).

RECOMMENDED WORKS
opera *Torneo notturno* (1929)
opera *Sette canzoni* (1918–19)
String Quartet No. 7 (1950)
Symphony No. 3 '*delle campane*'
(1944–45)
Violin Concerto No. 1 (1932)

BIBLIOGRAPHY
A. Gianuario, *Gian Francesco Malipiero e l'arte monteverdiana*, 1973 (in Italian)
M. Messinis (ed.), *Ommagio a Malipiero*, 1977 (in Italian)

Nono Luigi**

born 29th January 1924 at Venice
died 9th May 1990 at Venice

Luigi Nono was one of the leading Italian figures of the avant-garde, although for many years he was recognised more in Germany than in his home country. He was also one of the few composers in the Western European tradition to devote much of his output to overtly political ends, in Nono's case left-wing, Communist, and social causes. A composer at his best when setting texts, Nono's combination of music and politics itself shaped his approach to music; his uncompromising idiom is inextricably bound up with the message that in part shapes it. He evolved techniques of breaking down text into fragments, and fragments into individual syllables and phonemes using his bold and considerable aural imagination. He was less prominent during the later 1970s and 1980s, probably because his left-wing stances failed to find a ready response in western audiences. However, few have so captured the sense of the brutal disjunction of the modern age,

with a strong sense of drama, of contrasts of texture and tone, and an expressive stance, unpopular and disconcerting though the results may be. Nono disliked conventional concert halls (seeing them as the property of the bourgeoisie), and used such venues as the factory.

Nono's earliest works used 12-tone techniques, as in the *Variazioni canoniche* (1950) for chamber orchestra, which has the same tone-row as **Schoenberg's** *Ode to Napoleon*. Such works are characterised by the use of mirror forms, pointillistic instrumentation (as in *Incontri*, 1955, for 24 instruments) and an abiding sense of colour (as in the percussion, arranged serially by pitch, in *Uno Espressione*, 1953, for orchestra). But he quickly turned to the voice, usually setting subjects of social significance, or with overtly revolutionary texts. In spite of often complex textures, his innate lyricism is inclined to surface even in solo lines with wide intervals.

The major stage work of this period was *Intolleranza 1960* (1960, revised as *Intolleranza 1970*). An examination of the effects of bourgeois capitalism on a poor immigrant, its action is divided into a series of sketches in sharply different styles, with an important role for the chorus. In the late 1950s, after a number of vocal works including *Epitaffio per Federico García Lorca* (1950–53) for various forces, and *La victoire de Guernica* (1954) for voices and orchestra, he developed a serial structure whose elements are the vowels of the text itself. This was initiated in the neo-madrigal cantata *Il canto sospeso* (*The Suspended Song*, 1955–56) for soloists, chorus and orchestra, based on letters from resistance fighters written just before their execution, and developed in *Coro di Didone* (1958) for chorus and percussion to texts by Ungaretti, whose words are broken up into different syllables and into consonant and vowel sounds passing continually from one part to another, involving great difficulty for the singers. A pair of unaccompanied works followed: *Sarà dolce tacere* (*To be silent will be sweet* 1960) for eight solo voices uses both sibilant, hissing, percussive sounds, and longer, floating, held single notes, with elements of each word given to different singers so that only when all are singing is the text by Cesare Pavese reconstructed. Similar techniques are found in *Ha venido, canciones para Silvia* (1960) for solo soprano and six chorus sopranos, in which by elements of the words by Antonio Machado again switch between solo and chorus. Unusually, there is a **Webern**-like delicacy in the orchestration of *Canciones a Guiomar* (1962–63), also on verses by Machado, for soprano, six female voices and instruments including celesta, lute and tinkling percussion, with a very expressive and lyrical solo vocal line, and an ethereal use of the chorus that recalls **Ligeti**. This is one of Nono's most effective scores; its textured fragility heralds the apparent simplicity of later works. There is a similar lyricism in the solo lines of *Canti di vita e d'amore* (*Songs of Life and Love*, 1962, subtitled *Sul ponte di Hiroshima*) for soprano, tenor and orchestra; it also uses the spatial blocks Nono was later to develop.

During the middle 1960s, after his first rather unindividual and pointillistic all-electronic work, *Omaggio a Emilio Vedova* (1960), Nono started to experiment with the combination of electronic sounds and voice. Gradually blocks of sound predominated over serial developments and combined with sound elements derived entirely from the timbral and textural possibilities of the electronics. Nono saw electronics as inappropriate for the concert hall, and the dense sound picture of *La fabbrica illuminata* (*The Product Factory*, 1964) uses concrete sounds recorded in a factory, purely electronic sounds, a chorus singing or rhythmically speaking material connected with the factory, and a solo voice commenting above this.

Even more complex and boldly presented effects, again combining live material and tape, occur in *A floresta è jovem e cheja de vida* (1965–1966) for soprano, three speakers, clarinet, copper plates and tape, which pits 'live' revolutionary slogans against taped texts using American technical war jargon in a work dedicated to the National Liberation Front in South Vietnam. *Ricorda cosa ti hanno fatto in Auschwitz* (*Remember what you have done in Auschwitz*, 1965) for solo voices and tape is a harrowing collage of grating, crying sounds, unrelenting in its appeal for the sanctity of the individual. Collage effects dominate in the phonetic experimentation, the modified street-cries of fish sellers on Venice's Rialto and the noises of water and the bells of St Mark's that are combined in *Contrappunto dialettico alla mente* (1968), for soloists, chorus and tape; two of the sections have overt political references. The range of colour and effect that Nono can command is exemplified in the ice-cold, staccato textures of the first section; a sense of violence is at its most obvious in this powerful soundscape. *Y entonces comprendio* (*And then he understood*, 1969–70) for six female voices, chorus and tape, dedicated to the guerilla leader Che Guevara, uses similar techniques.

Later works continued the combination of electronic and live material, and the use of fragments of revolutionary or political texts, including slogans from the revolutionary Paris of May 1968 in *Musica-Manifesto no. 1* (1968–69) for voices and tape. His second opera, *Al gran sole carico d'amore* (To the great sun leader with love, 1972–75), with a text of Marxist quotations and anonymous workers' comments, celebrates the Paris Commune of 1871.

In the middle of this period of complex and extensive vocal works came one powerful score for orchestra and tape, *Per Bastiana Tai-Yang Cheng* (1967), which treats serially elements from the Chinese revolutionary song 'The East is Red', although the predominant feature is the large-scale swathes of slow-moving spatial effects. *Como una ola de feurza y luz* (*Like a wave of strength and light*, 1971–72) for soprano, piano, orchestra and tape, extends the long swathes of earlier works, using transformed material of the piano and voice on tape behind the live forces in a particularly natural combination of the two media. The piano is used as an instrument of expressive sonority; the voice as a floating lament. Sections of voice/tape alternate with unsettled and powerful writing for piano and orchestra.

A new departure came with *Fragmente-Stille, an Diotima* (*Fragments-Stillness, for Diotima*, 1979–80) for string quartet, inspired by Hölderlin, quotations from whose poetry litter the score, and using material derived (though not audibly) from Verdi and Ockeghem. As its title suggests, this is a score of minute refinement and quietness, rarely rising above the lowest dynamics. This ritualistic style, slow in movement, largely quiet and contemplative, with silence playing a prominent part characterised Nono's latter scores, as if he had moved from the expression of exterior events to an internal poeticism.

RECOMMENDED WORKS
  A floresta è jovem e cheja de vida
    (1965–66) for soprano, three
    speakers, clarinet, copper plates
    and tape

Canciones a Guiomar (1962–63) for
soprano, six female voices and
instruments
Como una ola de fuerza y luz
(1971–72) for soprano, piano,
orchestra and tape
Contrappunto dialettico alla mente
(1968) for soloists, chorus and tape
Fragmente-Stille, an Diotima
(1979–80) for string quartet
Per Bastiana Tai-Yang Cheng (1967)
for orchestra and tape
*Ricorda cosa ti hanno fatto in
Auschwitz* (1965) for solo voices
and tape
Sarà dolce tacere (1960) for eight solo
voices

Petrassi Goffredo ••
born 16th July 1904 at Zagarolo (near
Palestrina)

With **Dallapiccola**, Petrassi is the most
important Italian composer of his generation, and one of those who helped move
Italian music away from purely operatic
concerns. If sometimes derivative, his
music is replete with a strong personality
and sense of purpose in all the three fairly
distinctive periods into which it falls. The
core of his output, a series of eight *Concerti*
for orchestra, spans his compositional
career.

Petrassi's music during the 1930s was in
part neo-Baroque, looking back to pre-
Classical Italian music and beyond, but
possessed of a particularly strident, sometimes harsh, orchestral texture, with brass
prominent. Tonal harmonies were opposed
to dissonant elements, and bound by a
strong sense of rhythm and underlying
optimism. His first success, the violent
Partita (1933) for orchestra, has jazz elements in its three dance movements. In
the brash and especially effective *First
Concerto for Orchestra* (1933–34), the noc-
turne-like slow movement is strikingly
prophetic of that in **Shostakovich's** *Symphony No. 5*.

His second period, coinciding with the
entry of Italy into the war, was ushered in
by the 'dramatic madrigal' *Coro di Morti
(Chorus of the Dead,* 1940) for four-part
male chorus and three pianos, brass, percussion and double-bass. This much more
pessimistic work, with elements of Renaissance polyphony (thus placing it in what
has been called the 'neo-madrigale' movement), also has the suggestion of a tone-
row, and an intentionally strong opposition

between chromatic instrumental writing
and modal choral writing. This period also
saw a number of ballets and operas, often
neo-classical in style but with an increasingly chromatic language; *Sprechstimme*
featured in the philosophical opera *La
morte dell'Aria* (1950), and a buffa comic
style in *Il cordovano* (1949). The elements
of the Baroque were continued in such
works as the *Invenzioni* for piano. But the
masterpiece of this period is the haunting
and moving *Noche oscura (The Dark Night
of the Soul,* 1950–51) for chorus and orchestra, a setting of the poem by St John of the
Cross that reflects an increasing element
of contemplation in Petrassi's music.
Based on a four-note fragment, it creates
out of the dark landscape of its opening
large masses of slowly moving sound, the
chorus always apparently rising over folds
of orchestral texture out of which eventually come individual strands, weaving choral lines, and a vision of light. With the
Third Concerto for Orchestra (1953), which
quotes *Noche oscura,* Petrassi moved
firmly towards atonality and 12-tone techniques, which become much freer in the
Fourth Concerto for Orchestra (1954), for
strings alone. Both works divide a single
movement into sections, and lead to the
stark *Sixth Concerto for Orchestra*
(1956–57), for brass, strings and percussion. The relaxation of strict 12-tone application gives an improvisatory feel to works
of this period, emphasised by the use of
cadenzas for individual instruments, a
pointillistic style of instrumental writing,
and small forces (for example, *Serenata,*
1958, for flute, viola, double-bass, harpsichord and percussion, or the *String Trio,*
1959). Pointillism was also evident in the
orchestration of the *Flute Concerto* (1960),
where opposition comes from the free-
flowing style of the solo lines against serial
orchestral writing. A similar opposition is
found in *Propos d'Alain* (1960) for bass-
baritone and twelve instruments. In the
*Seventh Concerto for Orchestra (Prologo e
cinque invenzioni,* 1961–62) structural
blocks of colour emerge in the clashes of
brass and percussion. The *Eighth Concerto for Orchestra* (1970–72), with a martial third section, is another effective work,
if not so immediate as its predecessor.

Petrassi taught at the Accademia di
Santa Cecilia (1934–36, 1959–75) and at the
Conservatorio di Santa Cecilia, Rome
(1939–59), and gained a considerable reputation as a teacher. His many pupils have
included Cornelius Cardew and Peter

Maxwell Davies, as well as a number of Hungarian composers.

RECOMMENDED WORKS
> *First Concerto for Orchestra* (1933–34)
> *Noche oscura* (1950–51) for chorus and orchestra
> *Seventh Concerto for Orchestra*
> (*Prologo e cinque invenzioni*, 1961–62)

Pizzetti Ildebrando*
born 20th September 1880 at Borgo Strinato (Parma)
died 13th February 1968 at Rome

Ildebrando Pizzetti was one of the major Italian composers to react against the prevalent *verismo* tradition of Italian opera, and attempted to recapture the clarity of Italian Renaissance music in the face of a reliance on the 19th-century Romantic melodic tradition. He is now chiefly remembered for his operas and choral works.

The features of Pizzetti's operatic style are a close correspondence between vocal lines and the patterns of Italian speech, in contrast to the long lyrical lines of the *verismo* composers, and the prevalence of choral writing. His first major opera has remained his best known. *Fedra* (1909–12) was written to a libretto by D'Annunzio, who shared Pizzetti's artistic aims and outlook, and based on the ancient Greek myth of Phaedra. Its central character is obsessed with her stepson Ippolito, and when rejected by him falsely accuses the stepson of having raped her. Her husband, Teseo (Theseus), calls on the sea-god for revenge, and Ippolito is thrown from his horse and killed. Fedra takes poison and confesses, but with the hope that her love will survive beyond the grave. The score combines chromaticism and neo-madrigale elements (especially in the opening chorus of act three, sometimes heard on its own as *Trenodia*), with a powerful characterisation of Fedra herself.

Debora e Jaele (1915–21), to Pizzetti's own libretto, is based on the Biblical story of Deborah, but with considerable departures of motivation and character from the source; one of its themes is the possibility of other modes of thinking (represented by Sisera) than those prescribed by rigid religious law, here represented by Deborah. The chorus again plays a major role and the opera was long considered one of the masterpieces of 20th-century Italian

music before inexplicably falling into complete obscurity.

Most of Pizzetti's late operas were criticised for following the pattern of these two earlier works, but *Assassinio nella cattedrale* (1957), based on T. S. Eliot's *Murder in the Cathedral*, attracted attention; with its extensive choral opportunities and a strong central characterisation it also deserves to be more widely known. Its central moral dilemma is whether Thomas à Becket should obey the King or his own religious conscience. In all these operas the close marriage between spoken Italian and sung line has hampered their dissemination, since their moral and philosophical content requires a full understanding of the texts, and translation destroys the textual qualities of the vocal lines; the advent of surtitles may lead to their reappraisal.

Pizzetti's choral works, often unaccompanied, are deeply imbued with the clarity of polyphonic texture and the procedures and pacing of Italian Renaissance music. Within the limitations these archaic elements impose, the works are exceptionally beautiful, with a feeling or airiness and lightness giving the impression of the spaciousness of a church setting. There is little obvious stylistic change from the earlier choruses, through the purity of the *Tre composizioni corali* (1942–43) to the contrapuntal luminosity and gentle ecstatic motion of the settings of Sappho in *Due composizioni corali* (1961). *I pastori* (1908) for lower voice and piano (later orchestrated), is the best known of his songs, to words by D'Annunzio, and of his non-vocal music the colourful suite from the incidental music to D'Annunzio's play *La pisanelle* (1913) was once popular. His chamber music usually follows vocal models and the slow movement of the *Violin Sonata* (1919) is highly regarded for its expressive qualities.

Pizzetti taught at the Parma Academy (1907–08), the L. Cherubini Institute, Florence (1908–17), was the director of the Milan Conservatory (1924–36), and taught at the Accademia di Santa Cecilia, Rome, from 1936.

RECOMMENDED WORKS
> opera *Debora e Jaele* (1915–21)
> *Due composizioni corali* (1961) for chorus
> opera *Fedra* (1909–12)
> *Tre composizioni corali* (1942–43) for chorus

BIBLIOGRAPHY
G. Tebaldini, *Ildebrando Pizzetti*, 1934, Eng. trans. 1951

Puccini Giacomo***

born 22nd December 1858 at Lucca
died 29th November 1924 at Brussels

Apart from the claims of his less well-known trilogy *Il Trittico* and his last opera, *Turandot*, it is really debatable whether Puccini has any place in a book on 20th-century music. His operas, straddling the 19th and 20th centuries, were seen as a new departure for Italian opera, but with the hindsight of a century they emerge as the culmination of the Romantic 19th-century Italian operatic tradition. Their structures conform to late Romantic requirements, and they are awash with heightened emotions and psychological choices for the central characters that conform to Victorian rather than 20th-century mores. His chief innovation was the development (with Mascagni and others) of a style known as *verismo*, which often used not the historical settings common to earlier Italian opera, but representations of the present or near-past, usually with characters with whom the audience could identify rather than those drawn from noble or powerful classes. This required more accurate psychological characterisation, but by and large Puccini's is a pre-Freudian psychology, relying more on accuracy of observation of human interaction than any understanding of subconscious motivations. Nor do Puccini's operas make use of the kind of psychological symbolism that was being adopted elsewhere: the Louisiana desert in the last act of *Manon Lescaut*, for example, is symbolic of very little, other than to provide a setting for a love-death scene, and the symbolic possibilities of *Turandot* are countered by the sumptuous direct musical treatment. Similarly, his sometimes exotic settings (the wild West, Japan, the China of the past) mainly provide a mask through which *verismo* can induce the tear-jerking sentimentality beloved of the 19th-century. At the same time, he was a master of theatrical effect and of the integration of musical idea and stage action: the orchestra very rarely acts as a mere accompaniment to the vocal line. Well aware of **Debussy**, he responded to his age through daring harmonies and pentatonic melodies, but these orchestral innovations emerge less as a new departure than as exoticism, still part of the Italian lyrical melodic tradition. Notwithstanding a few imitators, whose success was short-lived (see Introduction, above), he drew a period of Italian opera to a close, without the possibility of further development of that particular tradition.

After the one-act *Le villi* (1884), and the failure (through an appalling libretto) of his second opera, *Edgar* (1889), Puccini reached maturity with *Manon Lescaut* (1893), based on the novel by Abbé Prévost already used as an opera by Massenet. All Puccini's mastery of orchestral colour, symphonic construction, and ebullient energy are contained in the first act, and the opera abounds in glorious melodies. There then followed three works that have remained the staples of all opera companies. *La Bohème* (1896) is set in the Latin quarter of Paris, populated by poets, painters, philosophers and musicians, and based on a novel by Henri Murger. It tells, amid scenes of domestic realism, of the love of Mimì for Rodolfo, their parting, and her death by consumption. The meltingly beautiful duet 'Che gelida manina' ('Your tiny hand is frozen') is one of the best known of all duets. *Tosca* (1900) has one of the most celebrated heroines in all opera, a woman who will sacrifice herself and commit murder for her revolutionary lover, and who commits suicide when she realises her rescue attempt has failed. It also has one of the most fascinating portraits of malevolent power in the figure of the police chief, Scarpia, who dominates the second act. *Madama Butterfly* (1904), based on a play by David Belasco, tells of the clash of cultural understanding as an American naval officer marries a Japanese woman, primarily out of sexual infatuation, leaves her, and returns years later with his American wife to find his Japanese woman patiently waiting for him and committing suicide when she learns the truth. All these three operas have a streak of cruelty against women which is disguised by the rich orchestration and the sentimentality of the endings.

La Fanciulla del West (*The Girl of the Golden West*, 1910) took as its basis another play by Belasco. Here the setting is a mining camp at the foot of the 'Cloudy Mountains' of California, with a somewhat melodramatic plot. Although the music successfully integrates genuine folk songs as well as Puccini's own versions, the characterisation emerges as too one-dimensional to achieve the success of the preceding operas, although the work is occasionally revived. Puccini's next opera did not appear for seven years, and with it he changed stylistic direction. *La Rondine* (*The Swallow*, 1917) was an attempt to write a lighter opera in the Viennese style, full of waltzes, and has never been popular. Far more interesting, but almost as neglected, is the trilogy *Il Trittico* (*The Triptych*), in which three operas were combined to follow an old Italian traditional pattern of a tragedy, a morally uplifting work and a farce, all presented in one evening. The actual plots of the three operas have no connection, and they are now generally presented on their own, though those fortunate enough to see all three in one evening have attested to the powerful effect of the juxtaposition of moods. *Il Tabarro* (*The Cloak*, 1913–16) is perhaps the most interesting of the trilogy. Its libretto, based on a play by Didier Gold, has an atmosphere strongly reminiscent of Zola, examining the social conditions of the bargemen on the Seine. The one act is built in an arch, whose first half has a seamless orchestral flow evoking the river, and an interplay between the characters that is one of Puccini's finest achievements. The second half concentrates on the evolving drama between an adulterous wife and a jealous husband. The ending is the one place where Puccini achieves genuine horror rather than sentiment: the husband invites the shivering wife to nestle under his cloak; she does so, only to find there the body of her murdered lover. Puccini's major weakness, his inability to produce a truly spiritual operatic passage, mars the second part of the trilogy, *Suor Angelica* (1916–17), the story of a woman who has become a nun because of an illegitimate child. The most popular of the trilogy is *Gianni Schicchi* (1917–18), based on a fragment from Dante. Firmly in the opera buffa tradition, with touches of commedia dell'arte, it is Puccini's one truly comic opera, stronger on stage action and the twists of the plot than on characterisation.

Puccini's finest opera is *Turandot* (1920–24), based on a Gozzi fairy tale in the commedia dell'arte tradition, and already set with a very different tone by **Busoni**. The story concerns a Princess who refuses to marry unless the potential suitor can answer three riddles; the penalty for failure is death. The latest suitor, Calaf (a prince in disguise) succeeds, but agrees to let Turandot out of the obligation to marry him if she can guess his real name by the next dawn. Calaf's faithful slave, Liù, who is herself in love with him, is about to be tortured to reveal the name of her master, but commits suicide. In a complete turnabout, Turandot realises she is in love with Calaf; he himself, before dawn, tells her his name. At this point the opera was unfinished, apart from a few sketches, although Puccini expressed his intention that Turandot should declare her love for the Prince in the morning. Act III was completed on these lines by Puccini's pupil Franco Alfano, and is usually seen in a curtailed version, although Alfano's longer and dramatically more effective ending has recently been restored in some productions. The opera's ending is problematic: Prince Calaf's love is a kind of blind infatuation, and the 'happy' ending, if ecstatic, raises difficult moral questions about the torture and suicide of Liù, the complete reversal of Turandot's position without any plausible psychological anticipation, and the implied message of the complete submission of women to men. But the musical portrait of the ice-cold and passionate Turandot is brilliant, and Puccini succeeded in combining very different theatrical moods into an operatic whole: the ecstatic passion of the love-music, the tragedy of Liù, and the comedy of the three courtiers, Ping, Pang and Pong, who play a role similar to Shakespeare's 'rustics'. The music, sensuous, ecstatic, sometimes extraordinarily beautiful, moving in blocks of sound with a richness of orchestration that impels the whole drama, marked a new evolution for Puccini. The chorus is far more prominent than in his earlier operas, taking a dramatic rather than a passive role, and the harmonies abound in pentatonic and whole-tone scales, with bitonal moments and an exoticism that is not merely colouristic but an integral part of the harmonic conception. This deeply ambiguous drama produced a score of richness, musical integration, and sheer aural effect unmatched in any of his earlier works.

Not everyone will share the view of this writer that there is a profoundly disturbing aspect to Puccini's output. A streak of cruelty and sadism in his plots is masked, and in a sense condoned, by the sumptuous and lyrical beauty of the musical treatment, so that events that should be tragic all too easily emerge as sentimental. However there is no denying the brilliance of his musical genius and the extraordinary depth of his theatrical understanding. He concentrated entirely on opera; most of his handful of other works are early, and almost never heard.

RECOMMENDED WORKS
  opera *La Bohème* (1896)
  opera *Tosca* (1900)
  opera *Gianni Schicchi* (1917–18)
  opera *Madama Butterfly* (1904)
  opera *Manon Lescaut* (1893)
  opera *Il tabarro* (1913–16)
  opera *Turandot* (1920–24)

BIBLIOGRAPHY
  M. Carner, *Puccini*, 1958, 1974
  H. Greenfeld, *Puccini*, 1980

Respighi Ottorino **··**
born 9th July 1879 at Bologna
died 18th April 1936 at Rome

More than any other Italian composer, Ottorino Respighi restored orchestral and instrumental music to a tradition that had been entirely dominated by opera. His overall achievement has been obscured by the popularity of a trilogy of tone poems about the historical heritage of Rome, *Fontane di Roma* (*The Fountains of Rome*, 1916), *Pini di Roma* (*The Pines of Rome*, 1924), and *Feste romane* (*Roman Festivals*, 1929). The first two have retained their considerable popularity on the concert stage, beloved of audiences but denigrated by the critics, in part because their idiom all too successfully foreshadowed the musical style that Hollywood was to adopt for its epic and heroic films. Respighi's idiom is much more than these atmospheric late Romantic scene paintings; over recent years the rest of his output has been gradually re-examined, and some interesting and attractive music has emerged.

Respighi is the best known of the 'Generazione dell'ottanta' (the 'Generation of the 80s') who revived orchestral and chamber music in Italy, hitherto dominated by opera to the virtual exclusion of other forms of indigenous music. Part of that revival was a re-examination of Italian Renaissance and Baroque music, and Respighi was steeped in those traditions. As a result, his late Romantic idiom, founded on the most masterful sense of orchestral colour of any Italian composer, is not only tinged with the influence of French Impressionism, but also with the modes and styles of early musics.

His early influences included Rimsky-Korsakov, who taught him composition (1901–1903) and the grounding of his brilliant orchestration, and contemporary Germanic models. Among the earlier works is the large-scale *Sinfonia Drammatica* (1913), showing the influence of **Mahler** and of **Strauss** in the extravagance of scale and orchestration. It foreshadows *The Fountains of Rome* in the first movement, and Respighi's later use of the medieval in the material. If the overall structure of the symphony is too diffuse, it nonetheless has appeal both as a late Romantic work and as a very rare example of an Italian symphony of the period. Respighi's subsequent orchestral works, all inspired by visual imagery, fall into two general categories, those descriptive of places, and those with a strong spiritual element, both categories combining Impressionistic writing with elements of old modal chants, lyricism, and Renaissance influences. Of the former, *Fontane di Roma* (*The Fountains of Rome*, 1916) itself is a masterful piece of orchestral tone-painting, direct and appealing and suffused with a love of the subject-matter. *Pini di Roma* (*The Pines of Rome*, 1924), looking back in particular to the Rome of Classical times and the pines that line the Appian way, is almost as fine, with an uncanny sense of the ghostly past in the sound of the nightingale over nocturnal mists and the march of a spectral legion. These works have sometimes been criticised for their limited artistic aims, but such criticism is churlish, as they have no other intent than their mood-evocation, in which they succeed brilliantly. *Feste romane* (1929) is less successful and less often heard; more interesting is the *Impressioni brasiliane* (*Brazilian Impressions*, 1928), which follows a similar formula and in which the plainchant *Dies irae* is prominent, as well as marvellous aural suggestions of the Brazilian wildlife. The element of the spiritual in Respighi's temperament is represented by the *Vetrate di chiesa* (*Church Windows*, 1925, from an earlier piano piece) and by Respighi's loveliest work, *Trittico Botticelliano* (*Three Botticelli Pictures*, 1927), full of luminous light and joy in its aural evocations of *Spring, The Adoration of the Magi* and *The Birth of Venus*.

Respighi's interest in earlier music is exemplified in his arrangements of lute music for orchestra, the *Antiche arie e danze per liuto* (*Ancient Airs and Dances*, set 1 for orchestra, 1917, set 2 for small orchestra, 1923, set 3 for strings, 1931), brought to a wide public by a famous recording conducted by Dorati in the early 1960s, and popular ever since. *Gli uccelli*

(*The Birds*, 1927) for orchestra is a delightful five-movement suite for small orchestra, each movement based on a work by a 17th-century composer. *La boutique fantasque* (1919) arranged the music of Rossini for a ballet. Respighi also produced three major abstract works of considerable interest. Both the *Concerto gregoriano* (1921) for violin and orchestra and the *Concerto in modo misolidio* (1925) for piano and orchestra are examples of works that succeed in spite of obvious faults, here of overall form and contrast of emotional weight. Such overt use of Gregorian plainsong and old modes is rare in 20th century concertos, and the effect is attractive. The best of these abstract works is also the least known, the *Quartetto dorico* (1924) for string quartet (sometimes misleadingly referred to as the *String Quartet No. 3*). It is in one movement, with episodes grouped into contrasting sections that assimilate both folk music and modal and Gregorian influences. Its interesting construction and felicitous quartet colours make it immensely attractive.

Respighi did not neglect the dominant Italian art form: he wrote nine operas, which while not among the masterpieces of Italian opera, are among the second rank of works that can be a pleasure to encounter. *Semirama* (1910) shows the influence of Strauss, while *La bella dormente nel bosco* (*Sleeping Beauty*, 1916–21, reorchestration and version for children's mimes, 1934), originally written as a puppet opera, is generally considered the best of his stage works. The well-known story has some added twists, chiefly that the Princess wakes up in the 20th century. The opera ends with a foxtrot. Respighi's fourth opera, *Belfagor* (1919–22), is a dark-hued romantic comedy, influenced by Verdi's *Falstaff* and especially **Puccini** in the conversational style and the use of one major recurring theme and repeated melodic ideas. The libretto by Claudio Guastalla (the librettist of all his subsequent operas), is based on a comic novel by Ercole Morselli. It tells of a senior devil who comes to earth to see whether, as it is said, all the world's woes are caused by marriage; he is outwitted by his intended bride. There is much attractive music, beautifully and delicately scored, but the character possibilities of the story are not fully realised in the libretto.

La campana sommersa (*The Sunken Bell*, 1923–27) is based on the symbolist fairy tale by Gerhart Hauptmann. A bell-maker is inveigled into the world of the fairies, leading to the betterment of his art but to the suicide of his wife, in a clear allegory of the creative process. In *La fiamma* (1931–33) Respighi seems to have been inspired as much by the sumptuous settings of Byzantine art as by the plot. The story is based on a play by the Norwegian Jenssen, transferred from the Nordic north to 7th-century Ravenna. Respighi responded to the settings with a sumptuous lyrical score, although the symbolic plot, about Exarch's wife who suffers for her adultery by being convicted of witchcraft, is not steeped enough in psychological dilemma to be completely convincing. In the marvellous last act the vocal lines have the sensuality and flow of **Puccini**, at times overidden to great effect by echoes of Monteverdi and Byzantine church music. The general tone is very different, and the symbolism more cogent if less exotic, in *Maria Egiziaca* (1929–31), a triptych that looks back to medieval theatrical models. It recounts three incidents of the life of Mary of Alexandria, with her conversion from a prostitute to a religious believer as the centrepiece. The first has archaic elements, the second the most impassioned vocal writing, and the third the most ecstatic music. The vein of spirituality makes this one of the more interesting Respighi operas, although the Christian fundamentalist concept of women as fallen and sullied may be difficult for many listeners to accept. Respighi's last opera *Lucrezia* (1935–36) was virtually complete when he died, and was finished by his wife, Elsa Olivieri-Sangiacomo (1894–96), herself a composer of two operas. The story is that of the Roman Lucretia (also turned into an opera by **Britten**), and is notable for Respighi's use of a single soloist placed in the orchestra for the role of Greek chorus. Of his other vocal music, the *Lauda per la natività del Signore* (1928–30) for soprano, mezzo-soprano, tenor, chorus, and wind and two-piano ensemble, looking back to music of the late-Renaissance period, is held in high regard.

Respighi was active as a string player and pianist, and taught at the Liceo (later Conservatorio) di Santa Cecilia in Rome, and was its director from 1924 to 1926.

RECOMMENDED WORKS
(English titles when in common use):
Belfagor (1919–22)
opera *La bella dormente nel bosco* (1916–21)
orchestral arrangements *Ancient Airs and Dances* (3 suites, 1917, 1924, 1932)

Concerto gregoriano (1921) for violin
and orchestra
opera *La fiamma* (1931–33)
Fountains of Rome (1917) for
orchestra
opera *Maria Egiziaca* (1932)
Quartetto dorico (1924) for string
quartet
Three Botticelli Pictures (1927) for
orchestra

BIBLIOGRAPHY
E. Respighi *Ottorino Respighi*, 1954,
in Italian, abridged English trans.
1962

Scelsi Giacinto (Count Dayla Valva)*

born 8th January 1905 at La Spezia
died 9th August 1988 at Rome

Giacinto Scelsi spent most of his life outside the limelight, but late in life became
recognised as a major figure. Born a Count
with private means, he travelled extensively, and, without the need for an income
for his music, shunned publicity. He has
been called a minimalist – misleadingly, for
his minimalism bears little relation to the
minimalist school, but rather reflects a
careful use of the spare musical means
where each sound or sonority, however
simple, carries considerable weight. His
musical world, often of luminous beauty,
consists of slow-moving swathes of sound
in which minute changes are continually
occurring, usually around a fundamental
note and often covering a very wide range
of instrumental or vocal colour. Rhythm in
the traditional sense is virtually absent,
though rhythmic events form part of those
microcosmic changes, sometimes using
percussive (or with string instruments,
plucking) contrasts against the general
sonorous flow.

Scelsi studied with a student of **Schoenberg** in Vienna in 1935 and 1936, but
rejected strict 12-tone principles. Following a visit to Tibet and a personal crisis in
the 1940s, which included a psychological
breakdown and hospitalisation, his music
was deeply influenced by oriental philosophies. The most obvious example is *Canti
del Capricorno* (1962–72), a long cycle of
songs for soprano with thai-gong, percussion, saxophone and bass recorder, that
are spare in the extreme, and often sound
as if written by a composer from an eastern
musical tradition. There are no texts, but
rather shifts of phonetic sounds, sometimes incantatory chants, glissandi, and

minute changes of vocal colour or pitch.
Harmonically the microtonal deviations
create a non-tonal soundscape that has
much in common with Eastern folk musics,
though regularly Scelsi will bend them
back again to create moments of uplifting
harmonious concord.

Five string quartets form the basis of
Scelsi's reputation. The four-movement
String Quartet No. 1 (1944) was written
before the development of Scelsi's individual style in the early 1950s, but is still a
distinctive and unusual work, with a jerky,
expressive rhythmic feel, a harmonic language that borders on the atonal, and
propulsive counterpoint. It maintains an
extraordinary tension until the luminous
and final pages. The *String Quartet No. 2*
(1961) belongs to a completely different
sound world. Its five short movements
centre on kernel notes, creating a drone
axis around which minute variations of
colour evolve; sparse, reticent events
emerge and dissolve. The extraordinary
String Quartet No. 3 (1963) describes in
five movements the mystical journey of a
soul toward liberation and catharsis. More
varied than its predecessor, much of it
sounds like *musique concrète*, so varied is
the range of string sounds, which often
appear like disembodied human voices,
torn with anguish in the second movement,
with luminous moments of chordal harmonies in the first and fourth. Both the *String
Quartet No. 4* (1964) and the *String Quartet No. 5* (1985) are more condensed,
covering a wider range than their short
durations would suggest. The former
treats the individual strings of the instruments as separate voices, and has some of
the tension of the first quartet. The latter
is a seven-minute series of forty-three
events, each superficially similar and consisting of an initial attack followed by
decay. Yet each of these cells has a different content, often subtly varying the colours and timbres, and creating longer
changes of emotional content.

The *String Trio* (1958) introduced
microtonal intervals to Scelsi's work, with
a continuous drone of sonority, overlaid
with events (like undulations in a wave),
and minute changes of pitch, colour and
timbre. There is more obvious activity in
Khoom (1962) for soprano, string quartet,
horn and percussion, but the overall mood
is still meditative in one of Scelsi's most
effective pieces. Setting syllables of the
composer's own invention, the seven sections use different instrumental forces,
constantly changing tone and colour, and
the vocal lines have the effect of a lyrical

introverted improvisation. *Natura Renovatur* (1967) is a version of the fourth quartet for eleven strings.

The idiom that Scelsi developed in these chamber works combines the rarefied aural landscape of **Pärt, Górecki** and **Tavener** (predating all of them) with experimental procedures. Anyone who enjoys those composers should sample at least Scelsi's *String Quartet No. 3* as an example of this unusual, prescient, and spiritually affecting composer.

In the 1930s Scelsi organised concerts of new music with **Petrassi**, and joined the Nuova Consonanza group of avant-garde composers in the 1950s. The dating of his works has been hampered by his habit of redating manuscripts to confuse scholars.

RECOMMENDED WORKS

Khoom (1962) for soprano, string
    quartet, horn and percussion
String Quartet No. 3 (1963)
String Quartet No. 4 (1964)
String Quartet No. 5 (1985)

Japan

Introduction

Japan has a long and highly developed tradition of classical music, from the music for Noh and kabuki theatre to the art of the koto. After the restoration of the monarchy (1868) and the increased contacts with the West in the latter part of the 19th century, Japan became exposed to the western classical tradition. Kosaku Yamada (1886–1965) studied in Berlin, founded the Tokyo Philharmonic Orchestra in 1915, and composed symphonic poems, five operas and songs. Yasuji Kiyose (1900–81) combined western influences with a Japanese nationalistic style that used folk subjects (but not tunes). But it was not until after World War II that Japan fully embraced and assimilated the western tradition, becoming a major venue for visiting orchestras and artists, and itself producing orchestras and performers of international repute (of whom the best known is probably the conductor Seiji Ozawa, born 1935); this process has been aided by the growth and domination of the Japanese electronics industry, so that by the 1990s the Japanese Sony Corporation owned a major American classical recording label (CBS).

Japanese classical music has influenced western composers from **Debussy** to **Cage** and **Stockhausen**, and Japan's own composers working in a western tradition (most of whom studied in the West) have been caught between the twin tugs of the two traditions. At its most positive, this has led to a fusion in which new colours and ideas have informed a modern western framework. In the music of Tōru **Takemitsu** (1930–96), the major Japanese composer and the only one encountered with regularity, the infusion has been of a particular Japanese sensibility, delicacy, and a delight in nature; the works of Toshirō **Mayuzumi** (born 1929) have drawn on the Buddhist tradition. Both were influenced by **Messiaen**, and in 1951 Takemitsu and other artists founded 'Jikken-kobo' (Experimental Studio). Shin-ichi Matsushita (born 1922) was the pioneer of electronic music in Japan, while Kan Ishii (born 1921) has worked mainly in modern Japanese dance and opera; works by his younger brother Maki Ishii (born 1936) have included the combination of the traditional gagaku and symphony orchestra in *Sogu II* (1971). Toshi Ichiyangi (born 1933) was influenced by **Cage,** and Yuji Takahashi (born 1938) has become internationally known as a pianist specialising in new music, in addition to his work as a composer.

Japanese Music Information Centre:
Nippon Kindai Ongakukan/Japan Music Information Centre
8–14, 1-chome, Azabudai
Minato-ku, Tokyo 106
tel: 81 1 3224 1584
fax: 81 3 3224 1654

Mayuzumi Toshirō*
born 20th February 1929 at Yokohama
died 10th April 1997 at Kawasaki

Toshirō Mayuzumi has combined dense orchestral textures, influenced by **Varèse** and **Messiaen,** with influences from Buddhist chant and campanology, often with an abstract intent inspired by Buddhism. In his works sonorous tone clusters are countered by rapid leaps from one section of the orchestra to the other. Behind these textures lies a harmonic base with tonal and Romantic substrata, creating an appealing combination of the contemporary and the 'accessible'.

Of his earlier works, the rather brash and rhythmically intense *Bacchanale* (1953) for orchestra suggests a jazzy, harsh form of Bacchanalian rite. *Phonologie symphonique* (1957) for orchestra is even more motorically insistent, influenced by **Varèse** in its rhythms, orchestral colours and blocks of sound. Such works were western in idiom, without Japanese influence, but in the late 1950s Mayuzumi became interested in Japanese temple bells and the combinations of overtones they produced. The resulting *Nirvana Symphony* (1958) for male chorus and orchestra initiated a number of works exploring the ideas and traditions of Buddhism through use of the slow-changing overlay of tones, and employing the intonations and rhythms of Sutra recitations of Buddhist priests. The six-movement work is a highly atmospheric and effective fusion of western and eastern ideas, with a strong impression of ritual and large aural spaces, opposing low sonorities with bright high sounds. The sounds of bells impel the odd numbered movements, alternating and combining with elemental chant, musically basic but nonetheless effective.

The more abstract *Mandala Symphony* (1960), its title drawn from circular paintings that symbolise unity and absoluteness of the universe, is divided into two parts. It

has moments of exotic eastern colour and rhythmic intensity, allied to dense Impressionistic orchestral swirls, a Romantically lyrical violin solo, and a slow-moving close heavily influenced by **Messiaen.** It was followed by *Prelude* (1961), which utilised repetitive chants and bells in the medium of the string quartet. The symphonic poem *Samsara* (1962) addressed the cycle of existence in birth and rebirth through reincarnation. It is a more linear work, the dense textures pared away for individual lines and purer sonorities, and is less interesting than either of the two symphonies.

His later works have included the opera *Kinkakuji* (*The Temple of the Golden Pavilion,* 1976), based on a novel by Yukio Mishima, with whom he collaborated on a number of other works. In 1957 he founded the Karuisawa contemporary music festival, and in 1965 wrote the film score for the Hollywood epic *The Bible.*

RECOMMENDED WORKS
  Nirvana Symphony (1958) for male chorus and orchestra
  Mandala Symphony (1960) for orchestra

Takemitsu Tōru**
born 8th October 1930 at Tokyo
died 20th February 1996

The prolific Tōru Takemitsu was the most important Japanese composer working within the framework of contemporary western classical music. His achievements were twofold: first, to introduce to western audiences a Japanese view of the natural world, an appreciation of detail and a love of what might be called the soul of nature and of the nature of sounds. Secondly, he informed the western classical tradition with such principles. Working in an aesthetic in which humankind is seen as indivisible from the totality of nature, Takemitsu suggested that composition is a process that gives meaning to the sounds that exist all around us. The salient characteristic of his music is concentration on individual sound events, colours and sonorities, sometimes through pointillistic effects, sometimes through denser tonepainting. The overall impression is of contemplation, even in his more turbulent writing. Almost all his music employs extra-musical material, not so much in a programmatic sense, but more to reflect the indivisibility of the natural world. He favoured instruments whose colours aid the aesthetic or are capable of delicate sounds of a wide range of timbres, such as the flute, clarinet, guitar and piano, and much of his orchestral writing includes a solo instrument as the first among equals.

Takemitsu's compositional development was profoundly influenced by his teenage experiences at the end of World War II, which left him with an aversion to traditional Japanese culture and music. Entirely self-taught, his earliest influences were **Debussy**, especially the French composer's sense of light and shade and movement, and **Messiaen**: Takemitsu's *Lento in due movimenti* (1950) for piano includes the use of Messiaen's 'modes of limited transposition'. The influence of the Second Viennese School appeared in such works as *Le son calligraphie* (1958–60) for double string quartet. In 1961 Takemitsu encountered the music of **Cage**, and embarked on a trilogy of works with aleatory elements that mark his maturity as a composer and a new phase in his output. *Ring* (1961) for flute, guitar and lute is in four parts, each representing one letter of the title (retrograde, inversion, noise, and general theme), has no tempo or dynamic markings, and can be played in any order. *Sacrifice* (1962) for alto flute, lute and vibraphone is in two movements, in which the pulse is constant but the actual note durations left to the performer. *Valeria* (originally *Sonant*, 1965, revised as *Valeria*, 1969) for small ensemble is in four sections with varying use of the forces and strong changes of emotional tone. All three works are elusive, sometimes delicate, sometimes harsh, concentrating on the colours of individual events with marked contrasts of tone and dynamics. They fall clearly within the orbit of contemporary post-**Webern** trends, but with a Romantic lyricism in the last section of *Valeria* that looks back to Takemitsu's earliest style and forward to his last works. From the same period came *Coral Island* (1962) for soprano and orchestra, in which (in the words of the text's author, Makoto Ooka) 'words are crystals made of sounds'. Takemitsu continued this idiom in such works as *Stanza I* (1969, later incorporated into the orchestral *Crossing*) for female voice, guitar, harp, piano or celesta, and vibraphone, with texts from the painter Jasper Johns and from Wittgenstein.

Having built on a western foundation, Takemitsu then started to incorporate traditional Japanese instruments, first in film music and then in *Eclipse* (1966) for biwa, a form of Chinese lute, and shakuhachi, a bamboo woodwind instrument; the work is a gentle and beautiful introduction to these Eastern sounds. He then combined these instruments with a Western orchestra in the influential *November Steps* (1967), loosely divided into eleven sections and with improvisatory elements. The microtonal inflections and slides of the biwa and the plucking effects of the shakuhachi (producing multiple and complex tones) create haunting, slow-moving sounds alien to the western tradition. Takemitsu pits them against tense orchestral blocks of varying tone-colours, creating a meeting point between two disparate musics. This seminal work introduced many western musicians to Takemitsu's music. In *November Steps* the two cultures abut; in *Autumn* (1973), also for biwa, shakuhachi and orchestra, they merge. The pattern was continued in the pointillistic, mood-painting *In an Autumn Garden* (1973, expanded version 1979), written for gagaku orchestra (the traditional Japanese court orchestra of wind, plucked instruments and drums).

Takemitsu continued within these general parameters. *Green* (1967) for orchestra presents an Impressionistic view of nature, influenced by **Debussy**. The fine *Quatrain II* (1975) for clarinet, violin, cello and piano, is modelled on **Messiaen's** *Quatuor pour la fin du temps*. Gradually it emerged that Takemitsu's output could be grouped by subject-matter as much as by stylistic development. Water, especially its slow motion and change, is a favourite metaphor, in such works as the early *musique concrète Water Music* (1960), *Waves* (1976) for clarinet with horn, two trombones and bass drum, undulating between stillness and motion and the neo-Impressionist *Waterways* (1978) for clarinet, violin, cello, piano, two harps and two vibraphones, which appears to depict the varying colours of eddies and currents.

In Takemitsu's iconography, gardens reflect the refinement and loving attention to harmony, balance and detail which Japanese tradition has brought to the art. *Arc* (1963–66, revised 1976) for piano and orchestra, is an imaginary plan of a garden in music, where different instrumental groups represent different elements such as flowers and trees. Transformation occurs at different rates in these groups, and the piano appears to be strolling through the garden. Takemitsu described *Dorian Horizon* (1966) for seventeen strings as a 'musical garden'. Trees symbolise time (through tree rings) and idealism, appearing in *Music of Trees*, 1961, for orchestra, in the arboreal tapestry of *Tree*

Line (1988) for chamber orchestra, and in *Eucalypts I* (1970) for flute, oboe and harp and string orchestra and *Eucalypts II* (1970) for flute, oboe and harp. More recently images of the heavens have appeared, in such works as *Cassiopeia* (1971) for percussion, *Star-Isle* (1982) for orchestra, and *Orion and Pleiades* (1984) for cello and orchestra. Rain and trees have been evoked in combination in a number of works.

From the mid-1970s, Takemitsu combined dream, number symbolism and water motives – dream representing indeterminate form, number defined form, and water the symbolic mediator between dream and number. One of the more complex developments of these relationships emerged in one of Takemitsu's finest works, *A Flock Descends into the Pentagonal Garden* (1977) for orchestra, following a real dream inspired by a photograph by Man Ray of Marcel Duchamp. Its harmonies are based on a 'magic square' of five by five units each representing a different pitch, and itself developed from a pentatonic scale used to represent the garden. Numerology as a structural tool appears in a number of other works, as do dreams, in such works as *Dreamtime* (1981) for orchestra, inspired by the Australian Aboriginal creation myth, or *To the Edge of Dream* (1983) for guitar and orchestra.

In 1989 Takemitsu appeared to enter a new phase in a work of gorgeous richness and neo-Romantic luxuriance, the *Viola Concerto 'A String around Autumn'*, its title taken from a poem by Ooka. Described by Takemitsu as an 'imaginary landscape', it progresses in a series of wave-like swells, the cantabile solo line riding the crest, saturated in autumnal colours with a tint of nostalgia.

Not everyone will respond to Takemitsu's musical language. The relative lack of traditional formal structures can present difficulties, and the focus on the contemplation of individual sound objects and sonorities will be unfamiliar to those who have not assimilated western avant-garde developments. As is usual with such a prolific composer, Takemitsu's output is varied in impact, though any one of the works mentioned above will give an idea of his general approach. He undoubtedly enriched the palette of western music, and few will fail to be swayed by the *Viola Concerto*. He was also a composer of film music of high quality, including a number for the famous Japanese film director Akira Kurosawa.

RECOMMENDED WORKS
A Flock Descends into the Pentagonal Garden (1977) for orchestra
In an Autumn Garden (1973, complete version 1979) for gagaku orchestra
November Steps (1967) for biwa, shakuhachi and orchestra
Quatrain II (1975) for clarinet, violin, cello and piano
Valeria (1965, revised 1969) for small ensemble
Viola Concerto '*A String around Autumn*' (1989)

BIBLIOGRAPHY
N. Ohtake, *Creative Sources for the Music of Tōru Takemitsu*, 1993

Korea

Yun Isang (Ysang)*
born 17th September 1917 at Tongyong
died 3rd November 1995 at Berlin

The major Korean composer Isang Yun,
the son of a well-known Korean poet,
had a prolific compositional life, dogged by
political oppression and controversy. He
was jailed in 1943 by the Japanese authorities in Korea, and in 1956, while professor
at Seoul University, he left Korea for Paris
and then Germany. In Berlin in 1967 Yun
and his wife Sooja Lee were kidnapped by
South Korean agents and imprisoned for
treason (for failing to return to South
Korea), but they were released in 1969,
following international pressure. The
South Koreans made another failed kidnap
attempt in 1976. Yun became a German
citizen in 1971.

Some of this experience found its
way into Yun's music: the *Cello Concerto*
(1975–76) reflects his imprisonment; the
cantata *On the Threshold* (1975) was based
on the poetry of Nazi victim Albrecht
Haushofer; and *Exemplum in memoriam
Kwang ju* (1981) for orchestra was a musical reaction to the suppression of a South
Korean popular uprising. However, much
of Yun's music has been essentially
abstract, if permeated by Taoist philosophy; broadly, it has been a blend of the
European avant-garde and orchestral
mainstream, with influences of Korean
music, particularly court music, but with
no direct quotation of Korean folk music
and only the occasional use of a Korean
instrument.

Yun disowned his earlier music, reportedly conservative in style; his earliest
acknowledged works, dating from the late
1950s, reflect the avant-garde developments he encountered in Europe. A number of stylistic features emerged that have
permeated his output. An overall duality
contrasts slow-moving, generally meditative but often tense ideas (whose pace and
tone are influenced by Korean court music)
with shorter bursts of more intense activity. Harmonically, Yun uses 'principal
tones' that provide an aural harmonic
foundation. A streak of lyricism often
surfaces, with inflections of Eastern music
(especially flute music). Orchestral textures are usually dense, but with brighter
percussive sounds again drawn from the
heritage of Eastern musics.

Yun's works in the 1960s concentrated
on tone colours, often used in overlapping
swathes, as in the long phrases and overlapping events of *Loyang* (1962, revised
1964) for chamber orchestra. *Gasa* (1963)
for violin and piano, and *Garak* (1963), for
flute and piano, illustrate the basic duality,
the soloists generally having longer lyrical
lines against the nervous restlessness of
the piano writing. *Réak* (1966) for orchestra, which includes a sharp-sounding
Korean instrument (the 'bak') among the
percussion, is perhaps the most effective of
the tone-colour works.

In the 1970s Yun produced a number of
instrumental concertos and works based
on Western texts. At the same time the
more avant-garde aspects of his idiom
became diluted into a more direct style,
the tone-colour emphasis being partially
replaced by less dense textures and an
emphasis on solo lyricism, which has since
been further developed in such works as
the *Chamber Symphony No. 1* (1987). The
dramatically varied and fervent *Flute
Concerto* (1977), which uses a small orchestra, has a programmatic content based on
an old Taoist tale of a young Buddhist
neophyte who casts off her training to
dance naked in front of the statue of the
Buddha before returning to her original
state. Much of the writing has the spirit of
the dance, from the throbbing rhythm of
the opening, which is unusual in Yun's
output for its regularity. The abstract
Octuor (1978) for three wind and five
strings is one of Yun's most effective
works, the two instrumental groups sometimes opposing each other, and coming
together for the more solemn and subdued
central section. With its colour effects
(such as the series of delicate upward
string slides), its clear structure, and its
sure sense of instrumental emphasis, this
octet provides an interesting and appealing modern contrast to those octets (such
as Schubert's) written for the same forces.

In the 1980s Yun embarked on a series
of five symphonies that draw on the experience of both the tone-colour works and
the instrumental concertos. The basic
duality between the turbulent and the
ruminative remains, but the structure of
the 'principal tone' has broadened into a
harmonic palette closer to traditional harmony. Here dissonance is caused as much
by contrasts of orchestral colour as by the
clash of harmonies. Compared with *Réak*,
the overall impression is of a reversion to a
more conventional idiom, as if Yun had
absorbed **Mahler** and **Shostakovich** (and, in
the third symphony, **Strauss**) along the
way. Although they vary considerably in

structure and instrumentation, the general tone and idiom of the symphonies is consistent; the particular virtues of these symphonies are the detailed sound images that Yun invokes, the potency coming from the local focus rather than the overall impression. The dramatic *Symphony No. 1* (1982–83) warns against the horrors of nuclear disaster (especially in the first movement), though it works perfectly successfully as abstract music, if marred by a tendency for the strings to produce Hollywood-like figures. The more effective *Symphony No. 2* (1984) contrasts two oppositional forces, the positive represented by the strings, the destructive by the brass, with the woodwind acting as intermediaries; the whole work is characterised by a restless lyricism and regular shifting around the orchestral blocks.

The *Symphony No. 3* (1985) is the most inspired and effective of these symphonies, cast in one movement with three sections. Following the Taoist precept of the unity of heaven, earth and humanity, there are three musical entities: the strings (heavenly purity), the brass and timpani (earth) and the woodwinds (humanity), each of which are assigned different tempi and pulses, while being drawn into an overall cohesion. The effect is of constant shifts of overlapping emotional swathes and areas of orchestral colour, sometimes turbulent, sometimes delicate, sometimes almost triumphant, in a structurally interesting and emotionally beautiful work. The harsher *Symphony No. 4 'Singing in the Dark'* (1986) was accompanied by a programmatic commentary, the first of two movements representing the conflicts of human society, the second a song for and by the oppressed; the first movement is influenced by Korean art song, and the second has a quiet beauty before a traditional climactic close. The lengthy, five-movement *Symphony No. 5* (1987) for baritone and orchestra sets poems by Nelly Sachs.

After his release from prison in South Korea in 1969, Yun taught in Hanover (1969–70) and at the Berlin Academy of the Arts (1970–85).

RECOMMENDED WORKS
Octuor (1978) for octet
Réak (1966) for orchestra
Symphony No. 3 (1985)

Mexico

Introduction

Mexican music had been dominated in the 19th century by opera, its indigenous composition consisting largely of operas based on Italian or French models. The Mexican Revolution of 1910 brought massive social and cultural change, and gave the impetus to composers to draw on their country's own folk and popular traditions, and create a nationalist music. The most influential figure of this movement was Manuel **Ponce** (1882–1948), who collected popular and folk ideas, and integrated them into his own essentially European idiom. It was not until the 1930s, however, that the next generation, in particular Carlos **Chávez** (1899–1978) and his exact contemporary, Silvestre **Revueltas** (1899–1940), used indigenous music as the starting-point of composition, the former looking to ancient Indian models, the latter to contemporary popular cultures. Their lead was taken up by other composers, many of whom were pupils of Chávez, and Chávez's contacts in the USA ensured that this music was heard and appreciated outside Mexico.

The reaction to nationalism was led by Rodolfo **Halffter** (1900–87), a Spanish composer who had left Spain at the end of the Spanish Civil War, and by his pupils, influenced in the 1950s by neo-classicism, and since the 1960s increasingly by 12-tone, serial, and European avant-garde techniques. Mexico had already produced a herald of these movements, and a figure of innovative interest and influence. Starting his experiments in the late 1890s, Julian Carillo (1875–1965) developed by about 1920 a system of microtonality he called 'sonido trece' ('13th tone'). He had microtonal instruments made, and continued to write microtonal works until his death. While it is invidious to single out one figure in the development of modern Mexican music, the part that Chávez played was extraordinary, whether through teaching, founding the Orquesta Sinfónica de México, or encouraging other composers. His influence also extended north beyond the border. The similarities between the music of the Mexican nationalists and that of Aaron **Copland** has often been noted. But it was only *after* Copland had conducted Chávez's nationalist music in Mexico that Copland turned from experimental and jazz-orientated works to the style that has become so quintessentially American. It can be argued that Mexican music was the progenitor of that style.

Mexican Music Information Centre:
Centro Nacional de Investigación, Documentación e Información Musical (CENIDIM)
Liverpool 16, Colonia Juárez
06600 Mexico DF
Mexico

Chávez Carlos (Antonio de Padua)**

born 13th June 1899 at Calzada de Tacuba, near Mexico City
died 2nd August 1978 at Mexico City

If Manuel **Ponce** was the father of modern music in Mexico, it was Carlos Chávez who developed in his compositions a truly nationalistic musical language. As a conductor, writer and organiser as well as composer, he was instrumental in bringing Mexican musical life firmly into the 20th century. His best-known works incorporate popular Mexican and Mexican Indian traditions, but these only form about a third of his output. The rest (written in parallel with the nationalistic music) is the product of an exceptionally inquisitive musical mind, keenly aware of contemporary musical developments in Europe and North America, and always ready to explore and to invent.

Chávez was an accomplished concert pianist, and his earliest works are mainly for piano. They look back to the previous century, although an early interest in Mexican folk song is evident in his arrangements. But in 1921 (by when a decade of revolution in Mexico had led to a period of national fervour) Chávez produced a ballet, *El fuego nuevo*, that used Mexican Indian themes recalled from his childhood, and Aztec percussion instruments and story-line. It was followed by two other ballets, (*Los cuatro soles*, 1925), also based on an Aztec story, and the much more successful *Caballos de vapor* (*Horsepower*, usually known as *HP*, 1926–31) that startlingly combined popular Spanish-Mexican folk elements and dances (including a tango) with the latest in motoric and mechanistic music. Characteristic of these nationalist works is the *Sinfonia India* (1935–36). Typically, the indigenous elements (here including actual quotations from Indian folk music) are not used merely as colour effects, but integrated into a more contemporary idiom, with complex rhythms. The orchestration contains a large number of primitive instruments (including a deer-hoof rattle), with a strong sense of hard and contrasting colours, and characteristic use of solo woodwind. The structure is based on variations of repetitive patterns, and the effect of the work is far from a mere colourful pictorial representation – it is often lean and thoughtful, and only occasionally flamboyant. Similar traits are found in the dense-textured *Piano Concerto* (1938), a colourful, but generally uninteresting work, and in the colourful 'imagined Aztec music' *Xochipilli-Macuilxóchtil*, in which a poetic (rather than ethno-musical) realisation of Aztec music is accomplished with copies of ancient instruments. More overtly political were the *Sinfonia proletaria (Llamadas)* for chorus and orchestra (1934) and *Obertura republicana* (1935), drawing on Mexican revolutionary songs and popular Mexican music respectively. In all these works the harmony is based less on a Romantic tradition than on contemporary trends and indigenous effects, with three-note chords that avoid the traditional triad, 7ths, 9ths and octaves, thus adding to the exotic feel.

Many of Chávez's works do not include nationalist elements. Neo-classicism is heard in the *Sinfonia de Antigona* (1933), an austere and nobly beautiful work using Greek modes and based on incidental music to Sophocles' play, and in the ballet *La hija de Cólquide (Daughter of Colchis*, 1943, revised as a suite 1947). The latter is characteristic in its moments of disjointed rhythmic effects, but also includes the uncharacteristically lyrical flow of the *Zarabande* for strings alone, often heard on its own. The *Violin Concerto* (1948–50) displays Chávez's wish to recast traditional structures. The overall structure of its nine movements is palindromic, and it is an exceptionally virtuoso work, with an orchestra whose role is essentially to accompany, although with some unusual colour effects.

The series of *Three Inventions* (for piano, 1958, for string trio, 1965, for harp, 1967) are constructed on a system of non-repetition: successive ideas are generated by the previous one in a constant stream of linear change. The same concept is an element of the striking and emphatic series of *Soli* (1933, 1961, 1965, 1966) for various wind ensembles (*No. IV* with orchestra) in which a different wind instrument takes the solo in each movement. The *Toccata* for percussion instruments (1942,

written for **Cage**'s ensemble, who could not perform the difficult rolls required) is purely abstract, with contrapuntal writing and an exploration of different timbres in its three movements. Its clarity of tone and colour set against a formal structure has made it one of the most successful pieces of its type. The later symphonies are also abstract: *Symphony No. 3* (1953) is dissonant and forceful; *Symphony No. 5* (1953) is for strings, with neo-classical outer movements; and *Symphony No. 6* (1964), using polytonality and atonality, has a passacaglia finale with forty-four variations of the theme. The lighter *Symphony No. 4* (1953 and extensively revised) is aptly subtitled *Sinfonia romantica*. In all these works Chávez shows a consistency of invention that is allied to a truly musical appeal.

Chávez was director of the National Conservatory (1928–33 and 1934), director of the National Institute of Fine Arts (1947–52), and taught at Harvard (1958–59). He directed the Mexican Symphony Orchestra (1928–48). His influence on music in the USA, through his contacts and his conducting activities, was considerable.

RECOMMENDED WORKS
> ballet suite *H.P.*
> (*Horsepower*) (1926–31)
> *Sinfonia de Antigona* (Symphony No. 1) (1933)
> *Sinfonia India* (Symphony No. 2) (1933–36)
> *Soli I* (1933) for oboe, clarinet, bassoon and trumpet
> *Toccata* (1942) for percussion
> *Zarabande* (1943) for strings from ballet *La hija de Colquide*

BIBLIOGRAPHY
> C. Chávez, *Musical Thought*, 1961
> R. Parker, *Carlos Chávez*, 1983

Enriques Manuel*
born 17th June 1926 at Ocotlán
died 26th April 1994 at Mexico City

Enriques was the leading Mexican composer of the avant-garde movement. A violinist as well as a composer, he encountered serialism at the Juilliard School (1955–57), and decided that the relative paucity of national Mexican folk music meant that Mexican nationalism in music was no longer appropriate. His first serial work was the orchestral *Préambulo* (1961), but after a period in which musical materials are reduced to their smallest essentials, notably in *Tres invenciones* for flute and viola (1964), he extended his style beyond 12-tone techniques.

He turned to aleatory devices in *Reflexiones* for violin (1964) and the *Sonata for Violin and Piano* (1964), and in a series of mainly chamber works, notably *Ambivalencia* for violin and cello (1967), *Movil I (Mobile I)* for piano (1969), and in the *String Quartet No. 2* (1967) and the *String Quartet No. 3* (1974), he developed a mixture of predetermined music and carefully arranged periods of aleatoric choice, random chance, or free improvisation. *Viols* (1969) explored the timbral possibilities of combining strings with electro-acoustical effects. At the same time he increasingly relied on complex graphic notation (in itself visually attractive). Following the *String Quartet No. 2*, the manipulation of timbre and aleatoric techniques, were as important as the more determined aspects (pitch, rhythm, etc.). Sonorities pervade the effective septet *Tlachtli* (1978), in which slow-moving, ritualistic layers of colour are punctuated by wild percussive outbursts and disembodied fragments of more lyrical melody. There is a similar sense of short, sharp events and lyrical moments punctuating denser textures in the atmospheric *Piano Trio* (1983).

He applied similar techniques to orchestral music: in *Ritual* (1973) the conductor chooses different sonorous units at random; in the virtuoso *Él y ellos (He and Them)*, for violin and chamber orchestra (1975), the soloist randomly selects segments for himself and for the other players. In 1971 he studied electronic music in the USA and Europe. Enriques was director of the National Conservatory.

RECOMMENDED WORK
Piano Trio (1983)

Galindo (Dimas) Blas
born 3rd February 1910 at San Gabriel (now Venistiano Carranza)
died 19th April 1993

Blas Galindo is of Huichol Indian descent, and his earlier music reflects the nationalist idiom of his teacher **Chávez** and the principles of the 'Grupo de los Cuatro' (Galindo, Ayala, Contreras, and **Moncayo**), formed to promote nationalist Mexican music. *Obra para orquesta mexicana* (1938) used only indigenous instruments, but the Mexican evocation is most brilliantly expressed in the *Sones de mariachi* (1940), a highly colourful and attractive

orchestral work based on the *mestizo* folk music of the traditional Mexican *mariachi* bands. In the 1940s and 1950s, following a period of study with **Copland** in 1941–42, he increasingly combined Mexican folk elements (especially rhythms) with a neo-classical style, exemplified in the suite *Homenaje a Cervantes* (1947), in which baroque dance forms are filtered through Mexican colour. He extended his style into music of all types, continuing to use indigenous instruments at the same time as exploring new media (*Triptico Teotihuacán* for soloists, chorus, wind orchestra and Mexican instruments, 1964, and *Letania erótica para la paz* for narrator, soloists, chorus, organ, orchestra, and tape, 1963–65).

Galindo was professor at, and then director of, the National Conservatory, 1947–61.

RECOMMENDED WORK
Sones de mariachi (1940) for orchestra

Halffter Rodolfo*
born 30th October 1900 at Madrid
died 14th October 1987 at Mexico City

Rodolfo Halffter, whose father came from Germany, was born in Spain but left for Mexico at the end of the Spanish Civil War in 1939. He quickly became both a Mexican citizen and the leading figure in Mexican music after **Chávez**. Although from a musical family (his brother Ernesto Halffter and his nephew Cristóbal Halffter are composers), he received no formal training, and only began to write music in 1924, becoming a member of the 'Grupo de los Ocho' in Madrid.

His earlier music is restrained in style, neo-classical in feel, and influenced by **de Falla**, using the latter's form of polytonality created by the natural overtones of a given chord. Mexican folk idioms are not an element in his music, but the complex rhythms and sometimes the melodic devices of Spanish folk music continued to be an influence after his move to Mexico, as in the otherwise neo-classical and rather colourless comic ballet *La madrugada del panadero (The Awakening of the Baker,* 1940). Halffter's interest in the baroque was evident in the influence of Scarlatti in *Homenaje a Antonio Machado* (1944) for piano, and in the major work of this period, the *Violin Concerto* (1939–41), revised with the violinist Henryk Szeryng, 1953). It is a rather flighty but engaging sunlit work, full of interesting ideas, with a virtuoso solo part fully integrated into the overall sound, and with the occasional shadow of a Spanish melodic feel behind it. The first movement includes a series of variations using Baroque devices.

With *Tres hojas de album* for piano (1953), Halffter changed his style to embrace 12-tone technique (the first Mexican to do so), suggesting that **de Falla's** version of polytonality was not suited to further development. Through his teaching, he encouraged a number of other Mexican composers to follow suit. However, the 12-tone influence is very tame, and melodic ideas still have the feel of a tonal centre, exemplified in *Tripartita* for orchestra (1959), a wiry and rugged piece, sparse in feel in spite of a large orchestra. A similar economy of language is to be found in subsequent works such as the *Piano Sonata No. 3* (1967) and *Pregon para una pascua pobre* for chorus, brass and percussion (1968).

Halffter's influence on musical activity in Mexico is considerable. He was a professor at the National Conservatory, teaching many of the next generation of Mexican composers, and was critic and editor of *Nuestra Musica*. He was manager of *Ediciones Mexicanas de Musica*, and in 1940 he founded the first Mexican ballet company committed to contemporary music.

RECOMMENDED WORKS
Tripartita (1959) for orchestra
Violin Concerto (1939–41)

Lavista Mario
born 3rd April 1943 at Mexico City

Lavista represents the most extreme of the Mexican avant-garde composers. Following his studies with such experimentalists as Henri **Pousseur, Stockhausen** and **Xenakis,** his music has been notable for its comprehensive elements of improvisation and chance. He has also combined visual activity with electro-acoustic effects, collaborating on musical-graphic works with the painter Arnaldo Coen. International duality has appeared in some of his work: *Divertimento* (1968) exists in versions for both unconventional and conventional instruments, and for the same instruments with the addition of noise makers supplied to the audience. The famous concept of silence initiated by **Cage** was taken a stage further in *Pieza para dos pianistas y dos pianos* (1970) which adds a second piano and pianist, both silent, to *Pieza para un(a) pianista y un piano,* thus contrasting the received notions of music and silence. The elasticity of concept, and the use of unconventional sound sources, was extended in *Kronos* (1969), which includes fifteen alarm clocks, and lasts anywhere between five minutes and twenty-four hours. However, his recent output includes the atmospheric and haunting *Ficciones* (*Fictions,* 1980) for orchestra, based (via the writer Jorge Luis Borges) on the legendary bird Simurg (which also inspired a piano piece), and suggesting the textural space of **Ligeti** and the instrumental resources of **Lutosɫawski** rather than continuing the experiments of the avant-garde.

Lavista founded the improvisation group Quanta in 1970, and teaches at the National Conservatory. He has been editor of *Pauta* since 1982.

RECOMMENDED WORK
Ficciones (1980) for orchestra

Moncayo (Garcia) José Pablo *
born 29th June 1912 at Guadalajara
died 16th June 1958 at Mexico City

Moncayo is best known outside Mexico for the colourful and exuberant orchestral *Huapango* (1941), and within Mexico for the opera *La mulata de Córdoba* (first performed in 1948). With Ayala, Contreras and **Galindo,** he was one of the 'Group of Four', formed to promote Mexican nationalism in music and the composers' own works. *Huapango* is a prime example of Mexican nationalist music, based on genuine *sones* folk dances, and using characteristic rhythms (3 set against 2). It is very infectious music, colourfully orchestrated in the rhythmic drive of the opening dance (the brass much in evidence), in the harp tones of the lyrical central section, and the whip-like percussion of the close – one of the 20th century's most successful lighter descriptive pieces, guaranteed to give pleasure to almost anyone. The orchestral *Zapata – Tierra de temporal* (*Land of the Storm,* 1949) harks back to the Impressionists (it quotes **Ravel**), while adding Mexican inflections; it was followed by two other descriptive orchestral works, *Cumbres* (1953) and *Bosques* (1954). The opera *La mulata de Córdoba* uses a Mexican legend of the black sorceress who was brought before the Inquisition but disappeared before their eyes in a puff of smoke.

Moncayo was a member of the Mexico

Symphony Orchestra (1932–46), its director (1946–47), and conductor of the National Symphony Orchestra of Mexico (1949–52).

RECOMMENDED WORK
  Huapango (1941)

Ponce Manuel María*
born 8th December 1882 at Fresnillo
died 24th April 1948 at Mexico City

Manuel Ponce was the first Mexican composer to compose in a recognisable national style, and the concert of his works in 1912 (which included the *Piano Concerto*, with Mexican themes in the second movement) is generally considered the start of Mexican musical nationalism. By this time he had already started to utilise Mexican folk tunes (*Canciones mexicanas* for piano, 1912 onwards), following extensive research into the music of his native land; but until 1926, when at the age of forty-four he went to Paris and studied under **Dukas**, his music concentrated mainly on Romantic and salon piano pieces. His experiences in Paris, particularly Dukas's ideas of free thematic development, were immediately reflected in the symphonic *Chapultec* (1929, revised 1934), which combines French Impressionist orchestral colours and themes with a Mexican flavour. Subsequent works followed a similar pattern. A Romantic and Impressionist base is used for themes that imitate (rather than quote) Mexican folk ideas, while the inspiration itself is often Spanish Mexican (*Cuatro danzas mexicanas* for piano, 1941) or Mexican Indian (*Canto y danza de los antiguos mexicanos* for orchestra, 1933). Both orchestra and orchestration, however, remain European, with increasing tonal ambiguity and occasional dissonant effects that introduced a modernity into Mexican music. An exception is the tone poem *Ferial* (1940), which uses actual folk songs and Mexican folk instruments.

The *Suite en estilo antiguo* (1935) introduced a neo-classical interest, taking its fugue subject from Bach. This influence was developed in the *Sonata en Duo* (1938) for violin and viola, and is marked in his last major orchestral work, the *Violin Concerto* (1942), written for Henryk Szeryng. This work, with its neo-classical use of counterpoint pitted against more modern harmonies, and its somewhat severe first movement, exemplifies the European origin of Ponce's style. Even if the theme of the elusive slow movement is based on his immensely popular song *Estrilla* (1914), itself long mistaken for a genuine folk melody, and the thoroughly neo-classical finale has a Mexican feel to its rhythms, both seem firmly in the contemporary European tradition.

Ponce was also an outstanding composer for the guitar, partly through his friendship with the Spanish guitarist Andrés Segovia. His name is most often to be encountered in guitar recitals, where his music follows a Spanish or neo-classical tradition. The *Sonata III* is the finest of his five solo guitar sonatas, but this is excelled by the *Twenty Variations and Fugure on 'La Folia de España'* (1929), which covers the whole conventional potential of the instrument in music that is thoughtful and intimate, occasionally more flamboyant, harmonically unconventional and consistently rewarding. His aptitude for pastiche and command of early styles were brilliantly realised in the *Suite in A* for guitar, which many long believed to be the work of the 18th-century lutenist Sylvius Leopold Weiss.

Perhaps his most immediately appealing work is one which combines the European orchestral influence with the guitar – the guitar concerto *Concierto del sur*, begun in 1929 but not completed until 1940. Entirely Spanish in flavour, with southern Spanish rhythms, it is light and happy rather than profound in tone (and orchestration). Its far from conventional middle movement is instantly attractive, with its touches of Moorish colour, while its finale is tinged with Flamenco influence – this is the kind of work that critics are wary of, and general audiences thoroughly enjoy.

Ponce taught folklore at the Universidad Nacional Autónoma in the 1930s, and music at the National Conservatory in Mexico, where **Chávez** was among his piano pupils. For a brief period he conducted the National Symphony Orchestra. He was active as a critic, and had a concert hall renamed after him.

RECOMMENDED WORKS
  Concierto del sur (1940) for guitar and
    orchestra
  *Twenty Variations and Fugue on 'La
    Folia de España'* (1929) for guitar

Revueltas Silvestre**

born 31st December 1899 at Santiago
Papasquiaro
died 5th October 1940 at Mexico City

In a short life and an even shorter compositional career (largely 1930–40), Revueltas
established himself, together with **Chávez**,
as the most representative of all Mexico's
composers. He studied violin in the USA
as well as Mexico, and worked as a violinist
in a Texan theatre orchestra and as conductor of an Alabama orchestra (1926–28)
before becoming assistant conductor of the
Mexican Symphony Orchestra under Chávez (1929–35). He also taught violin and
chamber music at the Conservatory in
Mexico City. Politically left-wing, he went
to Spain in 1937 to work in the music
section of the Loyalist government. Three
years later he died of pneumonia complicated by alcoholism, aged forty.

Without drawing directly on Mexican
folk and popular music, Revueltas assimilated their general characteristics (notably
polyrhythms, strong rhythmic drives, and
the 'irregular' quintuple and septuple
metres) into an essentially Romantic personal style that is usually full of warmth,
humour and vigour, as well as clashing
dissonance. His bright, strongly colourful
orchestration has often been compared to
the sharp outlines and bold colours of
contemporary Mexican painters, especially Diego Rivera, with their parallel
nationalist subject matters. His characteristic structure (as with many Mexican
descriptive pieces) is tripartite, using traditional forms.

His first orchestral piece, *Cuauhnahuac*
(1930) described (under its Indian name)
the town of Cuernavaca. It established his
style (later largely unchanged except for
an increasing use of polytonality) and
initiated a series of orchestral pieces
reflecting different aspects of Mexican life.
The symphonic poem *Janitzio* (1933), with
its folk-like melodies, pictured the resort
island of Lake Patzcuaro (Revueltas
described it as his contribution to 'national
tourism'), first as a gentle haven, then in
the rather pompous abandon of its nightlife, complete with an out-of-tune *mariachi* band competing with the street noise.
Caminos (*Roads*, 1934), with its *mariachi*-
style tunes, bouncing feel and rich palette
(including orchestral imitations of car-
horns and a carnival atmosphere), is only
one of a number of works evoking some
particular material item in the Mexican
landscape. Others include *Esquinas*
(*Street-corners*, 1930), *Ventanas* (*Windows*, 1931) and *Colorines* (a Mexican tree,

1932). This series culminated in the very
fine but incomplete *Itinerarios* (*Routes*,
1939–40), which has some of the sweep and
grandeur of the music of **Copland**, episodes
of polytonality that weave multiple layers
in different sections of the orchestra, and a
haunting slow section. His humour and
sense of fun are obvious in such works as
the four-minute children's ballet *El Rena-
cuajo Paseador* (*The Strolling Golliwog*,
1936). His left-wing sympathies are evident in the score to the Mexican social
protest film *Redes* (*Nets*), whose suite
(arranged by Erich Kleiber) was first
heard in Barcelona in 1937. It has a more
serious tone and a broader sweep than the
Mexican orchestral works, including a
relentless and dark ostinato section.

Two of Revueltas's finest pieces are not
Mexican reflections. *Ocho por radio* (*8 x
Radio*, an ambiguous title suggesting both
8 minutes of radio and *8 musicians on the
radio*, 1933), for an octet of strings, wind, a
trumpet and Indian drum, laughingly distils *mestizo* folk-like materials through a
chamber medium, a Mexican parallel to the
filtration of jazz in *La création du monde* of
Milhaud or similar chamber works of **Stravinsky**. Similarly *Homage to Federico Garcia Lorca* (1935 – just a year before the
poet was killed) uses a chamber ensemble
of varied colours with verve and clarity.
Again an essentially Mexican idiom is
transformed as if by a distorting mirror
into rigorous and very dissonant ostinati,
transparent ensemble climaxes, haunting
crystal textures, and the use of a mournful
solo trumpet, before a joyous, rumbustious
and intentionally off-key finale. But his
best-known work, and the most effective
of the scores for full orchestra, is *Sensemayá* (1938), a work of primitivism and
ritual, originally a vocal and orchestral
setting of a poem by the Cuban poet
Nicholás Guillén, describing the ritual killing of a snake, but reworked in purely
orchestral form. Reminiscent of **Stravinsky's** *The Rite of Spring*, in its relentless
drive and repetitive blocks working
towards a great climax, it musically
reflects the onomatopoeic nature of the
original poem, gradually thickening in texture, its polyrhythms getting more complex, its dissonances piling up.

It was the genius of Revueltas not only
to reflect so accurately in music the colourful life of the Mexico around him, but to do
it in an idiom that is unmistakably personal
while also firmly rooted in the traditions of
his country's folk and popular music. This
fusion is so complete that, even more than

Chávez, he is Mexico's national composer. If, unlike Chávez, he did not write music of a deep emotional humanity, his verve, his vivid colours, and above all the surety of his complex rhythms, take his music far beyond purely local confines.

RECOMMENDED WORKS
Homage to Frederico Garcia Lorca
    (1935) for chamber orchestra
Itinerarios (1948) for orchestra
Ocho por radio (1933)
Sensemayá (1938) for orchestra

BIBLIOGRAPHY
G. Contreras, *S Revueltas: genio atormentado*, 1954

Morocco

Introduction

Morocco has been included in this *Guide* through the music of one composer, Maurice **Ohana** (1914–92). Although he could as legitimately have been included under Spain or France, it seems appropriate to place him under his country of birth (then under the control of Spain), as he is a modern example of the cultural forces that have for centuries existed in a crescent from southern France, through Spain, to the north-west corner of Africa.

Ohana Maurice**
    born 12th June 1914 at Casablanca
    died 13th November 1992 at Paris

Maurice Ohana brought to a modern idiom an unusual mixture of musical influences that reflect the circumstances of his upbringing. From his parents, both of Andalusian descent (his father was a British citizen of Gibraltar, and the composer himself fought in the British army), comes a strong Spanish element. From the country of his birth there are reflections of the atmosphere and bright light of North Africa, the music of the Berbers, and other African influences. From the country of his later childhood, France (where he eventually settled in 1945), come elements as diverse as echoes of Impressionism and the residue of his electronic studies with Pierre **Schaeffer**. In 1947 he became one of the Paris 'Zodiaque' group, reacting both against the new serialism and against neoclassicism.

The major work to show Spanish influence is the song-cycle *Llanto por Ignacio Sánchez Mejias* (*Lament for Ignacio Sánchez Mejias*, 1950), for reciter, baritone, female chorus and small orchestra. This powerful score, one of the major Spanish song-cycles of the century, extends the idiom of **Falla** in a style that is both modern and yet unmistakably follows a Spanish tradition. With its direct setting, considerable dramatic colour, and sometimes tense, sometimes broodingly dolorous emotions, it underlines the impact of Lorca's famous cycle of poems, and it deserves to be much more widely known. The instrumentation includes the harpsichord, which remained an important instrument for Ohana, in such works as the atmospheric and funereal *Sarabande* for harpsichord and orchestra. Spanish influences are also to be found in the *Guitar Concerto* (1950–57), properly known as *Tre gráficos* (*Three Designs*), which uses microtones in its slow movement. In this often austere but effective work, which has some of the drama of the Lorca song-cycle, a wide, sometimes brutal orchestral soundscape contrasts with the intimacy of the guitar writing, often unaccompanied, which has distant echos of Andalusian folk roots. The inspiration of Lorca emerged again in the cello concerto *Anneau du Tamarit* (1977).

In the 1960s Ohana's music started to reflect many of the avant-garde trends then current: the rather defracted *Synaxis* (1965–66), for two pianos, percussion and orchestra, for example, is a post-serial score, some of whose phrase lines and orchestral effects recall **Messiaen**. At the same time atmosphere remained the most important characteristic, reflected not just in orchestral colour and effect, but in his interest in ancient musical forms, myths and symbols. Thus *Synaxis* has elements of ancient calls and cries as well as early liturgical hymns. The chamber opera *Syllabaire pour Phèdre* (*Spelling Book for Phaedra*) is based on Greek myth, and *Signes* (1965), for wind instruments, zither in third tones, flute, piano and percussion, considers archetypal symbols, as does *Chiffres de clavecin* (*Ciphers of the Harpsichord*, 1967–68). In this harpsichord concerto there is a considerable range of string colours, from string instruments, through the harp, to the solo intrument; these are set within the larger orchestra, although the overall structure (five linked sections further subdivided) emerges as rather diffuse. The *Twenty-Four Preludes* for piano are conceptually derived from Chopin, and are miniatures of shades of pianistic light, sometimes with an ethereal language that recalls **Messiaen**, sometimes with Impressionistic washes, and discreetly using prepared-piano effects for colour.

The works of the 1970s continued the preoccupation with atmosphere and with ancient forms and symbols, but within less frenetic structures. These include the *Lys de madrigaux* (*Lily of Madrigals*, 1976), for chorus and instrumental ensemble, and the atmospheric *Mass* (1970), with early Christian elements. Especially effective are the *Livres des prodiges* (*Books of Prodigies*, 1978–79), a kind of concerto for orchestra that evokes early mythical images, from the opposition of sun and moon, through the winged bull and the Hydra, to Afro-Cuban rhythmic ideas couched in a more international language.

In all these works, the orchestra is used to shape colour above everything else, with prominent brass, often harsh-sounding percussion, colour blocks, and atmospheric effects, sometimes with a sense of rather brutal or rigid underlying rhythms. Among his more later works is a chamber opera triptych, *Trois contes de l'honorable fleur* (*Three Tales of the Honorable Flower,* first performed 1978), in which electronic sounds are used, and the opera *La Célestine* (first performed 1988).

Ohana's music emerges as a modern, sometimes derivative and often complex idiom that demands concentration. Through the atmospheric and colour-conscious use of that idiom, it evokes symbols or images on an emotional, subconscious level in a manner that withstands purely abstract consideration. In this his aims are not unlike those of his contemporary **Dutilleux**, and if he does not have the French composer's clarity of musical imagination, those who respond to Dutilleux's music – or indeed to the orchestral works of **Messiaen** – may well find Ohana's music an interesting experience. Anyone interested in the 20th-century song-cycle should include *Llanto por Ignacio Sánchez Mejias* among their list of core works.

RECOMMENDED WORKS

Guitar Concerto *Tre gráficos* (1950–57)
Livres des prodiges (1978–79) for
    orchestra
song-cycle *Llanto por Ignacio Sánchez
    Mejias* (1950)
Twenty-Four Preludes for piano

New Zealand

New Zealand's best-known composer, Douglas Lilburn (born 1915), studied in England with **Vaughan Williams**, and he was initially influenced by his teacher's style. Shades of it can be traced in his major early work, the fine and rather brazen *Aotearoa Overture* (1940) – the title is Maori for 'Land of the Long White Cloud', or New Zealand itself. Even more obvious, though, are the echoes of **Sibelius**, in a tone painting describing the antipodean counterpart to the Finnish composer's sunlit Finnish scenes. The influence of Vaughan Williams is more apparent in the *Symphony No. 2* (1951), while the *Symphony No. 3* (1960–61) has much leaner textures of an almost chamber scale. However, Lilburn subsequently adopted many of the developments of 20th-century music, including neo-classicism and serialism, and in 1965 founded the first electronic studio in New Zealand, at Victoria University in Wellington. His electronic pieces mix created and natural sounds.
New Zealand Music Information Centre:

New Zealand Music Centre (SOUNZ)
Level 3
15 Brandon Street
Wellington
New Zealand
tel: +64 4 495 2520
fax: + 64 4 495 2522

Norway

Introduction

20th-century Norwegian music has not yet received the attention paid to that of Sweden or Finland, but shares the general development and characteristics of the musics of those countries. Norway saw a nationalist resurgence and a renewal of interest in her folk heritage in the 19th century, reflected in music in the virtuoso violin transcriptions of Ole Bull (1810–80) and in the symphonies and orchestral music of Johan Svendsen (1840–1911). At the turn of the century Norwegian music was dominated by the most famous of all Norwegian composers, Edvard Grieg (1843–1907), a kind of Mendelssohn of his day (and equally loved in England). Although best known for the beautiful *Piano Concerto* (1869) and the colourful suites from incidental music to Ibsen's *Peer Gynt* (1875), his genius lay in smaller forms, particularly his almost Impressionistic later piano music and his songs, which use folk-like original melodies.

The main figure after the death of Grieg was Christian Sinding (1856–1941). His music, influenced by Wagner, was once popular, but has fallen into relative neglect, in part because of his pro-Nazi sympathies. His piano music travelled widely, especially *Frühlingsrauschen* op. 32, No. 3 (*Rustle of Spring*, 1887), and his heroic late-Romantic symphonies and orchestral works were heard on both sides of the Atlantic. Few of the composers of the next generation left any mark, but Harald **Saeverud** (1897–1992) continued the Romantic tradition in his rugged symphonies. A number of composers persevered with a nationalistic idiom, notably Eivind Groven (1901–77) and Nils Geirr Tveitt (1908–81), who produced five colourful suites with the title *Hundrad Folktonar frå Hardander* as well as concertos and such emotive tone poems as *Nykken* (*Water Sprite*). Knut Nystedt (born 1915) is best known for his choral works, and uses both Biblical and Norwegian folk sources. His one-movement *String Quartet No. 4* (1966) is highly regarded.

One Norwegian composer initiated a more experimental style in the 1920s and 1930s. The reclusive Fartein **Valen** (1887–1952) was one of the first composers outside **Schoenberg's** circle to adopt atonal harmonies (in 1924), and then a personal use of tone-rows, though the descriptive influence of the sea and the Norwegian landscape is rarely absent from his works. His music was little known until after World War II, when he became recognised as a pioneer of contemporary music in Norway. Klaus **Egge** (1906–79) eventually evolved a forceful idiom, founded on counterpoint, that managed to link elements of Norwegian nationalism and the modernism of 12- tone techniques. Finn Mortensen (1922–83), after early works with neo-classical features (including the neo-Baroque *Wind Quintet*, 1951), was the first Norwegian composer after **Valen** to embrace 12-tone technique, later using more experimental techniques such as the elements of choice and improvisation in the *Sonata for Two Pianos* (1964). Bjørn Fongaard (1919–80) developed a microtonal idiom, influenced by the Czech **Hába**. But the finest Norwegian composer since Grieg is Arne **Nordheim** (born 1931), who has used electronics extensively, both in purely electronic pieces, in which he has bridged the structural and stylistic gaps between conventional music and the electronic medium, and in works for conventional instruments with tape.

Norwegian Music Information Centre:
Norsk Musikkinformasjon
Tollbugt. 28
N–0157 Oslo
Norway
tel: +47 2242 90 90
fax: +47 2242 90 95

Egge Klaus
born 19th July 1906 at Gransherad
died 7th March 1979 at Oslo

The music of Klaus Egge stands between the early atonalism of **Valen** and the more cosmopolitan younger Norwegian composers. After a period of Norwegian nationalism, he developed an idiom drawing on 12-tone technique in a free manner which usually has suggestions of a more traditional base, and which creates a polyphonic counterpoint of lean textures, with the focus on the linear flow. He combined this with elements drawn from the Norwegian folk tradition, especially in the rhythms and in the use of old modes and tetrachords that constantly change in support of the melodic line, scale, or row chosen.

His earlier works were influenced by folk music in their rhythms and harmonies; the *Piano Sonata No. 1 'Draumkvede-Sonate'* (*Dream Vision*, 1934) uses modal material drawn from the chants of an early 14th-century folk ballad of the same title.

The *String Quartet No. 1* (1933, revised 1963) is a funeral tribute to the poet Hans Reynolds and includes an Inuit lament in the third movement. A set of three piano fantasies (1939) took as their starting-point the rhythmic structure of Norwegian folk dances. *Fantasi i halling* (*Fantasy in Halling Rhythm*) is a kind of neo-Bach with Nordic overtones, and the *Fantasi i slåtter* (*Fantasy in Slåtter Rhythm*) adds to this unusual combination the lilt of a dance. During the 1940s Egge developed a technique of strict thematic development and complex counterpoint that gives his music an element of sinuous astringency. This period included the epic *Symphony No. 1 'Lagnadstonar'* (*The Sounds of Destiny*, 1942), and the *Piano Concërto No. 2* (1944), for piano and strings, built in the form of seven variations on an old Norwegian tune, 'Sunfair and the Dragon King', with a closing fugue. The one-movement *Symphony No. 2 'Sinfonia Giocosa'* (1947) has echoes of **Bartók** and **Stravinsky**, and rhythms again drawn from Norwegian folk music. The *Violin Concerto* (1952), well regarded in Norway, is a subdued work, with rhapsodic and angular solo lines, and a feeling of restraint or distance that limits its appeal, though the slow movement has a hazy beauty. In the *Symphony No. 3 'Louisville'* (1957), again in one movement, Egge refined his orchestral clarity, and by the *Symphony No. 4 'Sinfonia sopra B.A.C.H. – E.G.G.E.'* (1967) he had turned to 12-tone technique: the symphony uses the letters of the title as the first eight notes of the 12-note row. Perhaps the most interesting of these later works is the *Piano Sonata No. 2 'Sonata patetica'* (1955). This sinuous, writhing sonata, with its clear linear textures and few moments of vertical repose, its sometimes aggressive emotions and contrasts, its angular melodic lines and jerky rhythmic effects, exemplifies Egge's craftsmanship, while having a wistful appeal of its own.

Egge was music critic of the journal *Tonekunst* from 1935 to 1938. He sometimes signed his scores with the musical notation of e–g–g–e.

RECOMMENDED WORKS
Piano Sonata No. 2 *Sonata patetica* (1955)
Piano Concerto No. 2 (1944)

Nordheim Arne**
born 20th June 1931 at Larvik

Arne Nordheim is among the most interesting of his generation of Scandinavian composers, on the one hand firmly within the tradition of northern music, particularly in the atmospheric sonorities of larger-scale works, and on the other an individualistic experimenter. He has owed little to the contemporary avant-garde (though closest to his Polish contemporaries), but rather sought to extend his range in new contexts. Chief among these has been the use of electronics, both in purely electronic pieces and in works with tape or electronics. His understanding of how electronic works could maintain contact with the more traditional developments of instrumental music, while at the same time informing more conventional modes, is perhaps the most developed of any composer working in this field.

His output can be divided into two main areas, besides his considerable number of scores for films: larger-scale works, both for orchestra (with or without voice or electronics) and purely electronic, and works for individual instruments or small groups. The latter are on the whole less interesting and more ephemeral, sometimes influenced by jazz or popular music, sometimes infused with a sense of humour (the exploratory doodlings of *Dinosaurus*, 1971, for accordion and tape, or *The Hunting of the Snark*, 1975, for trombone), and only occasionally with weightier material (*Clamavi*, 1980, for solo cello).

Nordheim was influenced at first by **Bartók**, notably in three works for string quartet (*Essay*, 1954, *Epigram*, 1955, and the *String Quartet*, 1956), but with the song-cycle *Aftonland* (*Evening Country*, 1957), for soprano and string quintet, harp, celesta and percussion (also chamber orchestra version), he started to develop his individual style. Based on verses by Pär Lagerqvist, the song-cycle explores delicate colours, mood becoming more important than melodic line, in a freely atonal harmonic idiom. His next major work, *Canzona* (1961) for orchestra, was heavily atmospheric, built on themes articulated by individual instruments and then merged into the orchestral texture. The death of the flautist Alf Andersen in 1962 inspired *Epitaffio* (1963, revised 1978) for orchestra and tape, in which Nordheim established his mature idiom. The work moves in great sonorous blocks of different atmospheric colour and tone, overlapping and swelling, with long held chords or notes, the tinkling of percussion, mostly on metal instruments, deep sonorities, and towards the end the disembodied, ghostly voices of the tape intoning three words from Salvatore Quasimodo's

exquisite little poem 'Ed è subito sera'. The atmospheric effect of these vocal sounds could only be produced by electronic means, and they are completely merged into the orchestral texture, and sometimes opposed by orchestral events. The genius of the work, and the chief characteristic that marks Nordheim out as a major composer, is the extraordinary sureness of movement and space, that owes little to traditional methods. The points at which the blocks of tone and colour alter into new events or give way to different instrumental colours have a slow pace that seems to be founded mainly on a certainty of instinct. It is a process that has little to do with rhythm (for rhythmic events may occupy only the space of one of the blocks), and has more in common with the underlying pacing of some Eastern musics.

This sense of pace was brought to complete fruition in one of the finest of all electronic compositions, *Solitaire* (1968). It is built in an arch, opening with broad electronic sonorities centred around a chord of A major that swells in a huge crescendo, like a Nordic version of the opening of *Das Rheingold*, offset by high tinkling ideas. This is completed by deep, gong-like sonorities, joined by distant distorted voices reciting from Baudelaire's *Les fleurs du mal*, stopped by aural echoes of rain and thunder, and then replaced by quiet strands of electronic solitudes that are the apex of the arch. The process is then reversed, only with variations on the electronic colours, until the crescendo is repeated to close the work. No one has yet devised such a satisfying and concise musical structure for an electronic piece, not only in the general arch form, but in the use of colour themes, whereby the electronic tinkling sounds that pervade the work undergo metamorphoses while retaining enough of their original sound to remain recognisable. Again, the sense of pace is deeply satisfying, the length perfect, and yet none of the colours and hauntingly atmospheric effect of this seminal work could have been achieved by conventional instruments.

A completely different atmosphere is conjured up in the electronic *Warszawa* (*Warsaw*, 1968), a response to Nordheim's stay in that city. It creates an aural city soundscape that evokes mood and history as well as place, as if we were moving from street to street, each with its own aural signature, from massed crowds to machinery, from individual voices to dripping gutters, many with their own tales of horror and fear, some of beauty, but all haunted by the past and the tension of contemporary Poland. Less effective, but still of interest, is *Pace* (*Peace*, 1970), transforming (out of all recognition) the sound of three voices reading the United Nations Declaration of Human Rights, and turning them into delicate bell-like sounds. The Declaration formed the basis of another work, *Forbindelser* (*Connections*, 1975), which linked three hundred performers in five cities through broadcast media. *Lux et tenebrae* (*Light and Shadows*, 1970) is drawn from the tapes for *Poly Poly: Music for Osaka 1970*, commissioned for the Osaka World's Fair, which combined six cassette tapes, each with different sounds, from pure electronic sounds to everyday household noises to more obviously musical ones. These were so arranged that the interaction of the tapes would never produce a repeat during the six months of the exhibition (the total theoretical length before repeat is 102 years).

In the same period Nordheim produced two major works without electronics. The expressive *Eco* (1968), for soprano, chorus, children's chorus and an orchestra without strings, again sets Quasimodo – here two darker poems laden with images of sorrow and death, observed as if by witnesses, opening with atmospheric shards and a pain-laden chorus. *Greening* (1973) for orchestra opens with an orchestral scream or siren that returns later in the work, and juxtaposes quieter sections, with the strings heavily divided for dense textures, and passages where the orchestral textures flare up, layering the overall sounds. Tinkling bells are prominent, the ebb and flow has at one point an almost Mahlerian expressiveness, and the closing passages seem influenced by Nordheim's experience with electronic sounds.

With *Dorian* (1975), for tenor and orchestra, Nordheim started to incorporate more obviously melodic lines into his idiom, not only in the vocal but also in some of the instrumental writing, within a general atmosphere of long vocal lines against a twittering orchestra or hard glissandi. The work is based on a poem by Ezra Pound, redolent of the imagery of the northern landscape and the theme of transience, and the setting has echoes of **Britten**. In the ballet *Stormen* (*The Tempest*, 1979), for soloists, chorus, orchestra and tape, based on Shakespeare, much of the vocal writing is for wordless voice or voices. The integration of the different layers of sound sources is magically atmospheric, often centred on a single note to which are added layers of colour and timbre for dream-like effects. Sometimes single voices, both vocal and instrumental, emerge and soar, and Nordheim conjures up not only images – the storm, Ariel in the rigging – but also, through the colours of the forces, the various characters, in one of his most beguiling works. In *Wirklicher Wald* (*Real Forest*, 1983), for soprano, chorus, cello and orchestra, drawing on Rilke and the Book of Job, the cello emerges as a counter to the soloist and chorus. *Aurora* (1984), for soloists, crotales and tape (or soloists, chorus, two percussionists and tape), has been well described by the composer as a 'self-generated sunrise', setting Psalm 139 (in Latin and Hebrew) and Dante. It moves from constant motion, with multi-layered fragments and ritualistic elements (chants and bells) to calmer layers with heavy electronic modification of voices: a meditative and effective work requiring virtuoso performers. During the 1980s Nordheim continued to develop this combination of increased lyricism and expressiveness in a number of vocal works, including *Music to Two Fragments by Shelley* (1986) for chorus, and in orchestral works with solo instruments, such as *Boomerang* (1984), for oboe and orchestra.

Nordheim's works for smaller voices rarely answer his requirements for the play of sonorities and rich multiple sounds, but he has often used them to try out interesting concepts. *Signals* (1967), for accordion, electric guitar and percussion, is a kind of musical game in which the instruments build variations on each other's playing. *Colorazione* (1968), for Hammond organ, percussion and electronics, was one of the earliest pieces in which live instruments were modified electronically, with a small delay, to produce an interplay of live and electronic sounds created in real time, as opposed to pre-recorded.

Nordheim's atmospheric idiom suggests the art of story-telling, as if each work has some unstated drama propelling the music. In part this is created by the interplay of sonorities and blocks, and by the favourite contrasts of deep colours and high tinkling sounds. But it is also impelled by Nordheim's distinctive pacing, which has more in common with the long poem than conventional music. When he uses words, the emotions and the tone behind the words are often as important as the words themselves (which in the earlier works are anyway transformed out of recognition). The underlying themes of these unstated dramas are the transience of life and protest at some of its horrors, but also a stark beauty and the emotional symbolism of nature. These emotive suggestions in the abstract works are often confirmed by Nordheim's choice of text in vocal works; but they are also the themes of Old Norse poetry and saga, and Nordheim emerges as a musical heir to that tradition, within the medium of his own, ostensibly abstract, art.

RECOMMENDED WORKS

Aurora (1984) for soloists, crotales and tape, or soloists, chorus, 2 percussionists and tape
Clamavi (1980) for cello
Eco (1968) for soprano, chorus, children's chorus and orchestra
Epitaffio (1963) for orchestra and tape
Greening (1973) for orchestra
electronic *Solitaire* (1968)
electronic *Warszawa* (1968)

Saeverud Harald Sigurd Johan*

born 17th April 1897 at Bergen
died 27th March 1992 at Bergen

Harald Saeverud (not to be confused with his son Ketil Saeverud, born 1939) continued the Norwegian Romantic tradition, notably in a series of nine rugged symphonies that reflect the Norwegian landscape, mostly driven by polyphony and often using repetitive phrases that build in power to huge climaxes, sometimes under the spell of **Sibelius**.

His earliest works were influenced by Brahms, but his *Symphony No. 2* (1923, revised 1924) and the *Symphony No. 3* (1926) introduced a more dissonant idiom, with harmonies verging on the atonal and with strong rhythmic momentum. However, in the 1930s he returned to an extension of tonal harmony, in such works as the *Symphony No. 4* (1937) and the *Cantata ostinato* (1943), which uses old Norwegian church modes. The events of World War II and the Nazi occupation of Norway affected Saeverud deeply, and resulted in a number of powerful and concise works. The one-movement *Symphony No. 5 'Resistance'* (1941) and the *Symphony No. 6 'Sinfonia doloroso'* (1942) are both in single taut movements; the latter reflects his sorrow, and, in the movement towards an heroic climax, continued resistance. The final wartime symphony, *Symphony No. 7 'Salmesymfonin'* (*Psalm*

Symphony, 1945), celebrates the end of the war and those who suffered during it, in a one-movement form in five sections drawing on the Norwegian church tradition. By the *Symphony No. 9* (1966) Saeverud had relaxed the repetitive motifs in favour of more fragmentation and more angular melodic lines and leaner orchestration; the finale uses Norwegian folk dances. His best-known works are probably the two *Peer Gynt Suites* taken from incidental music (1947) to Ibsen's play, full of sharp-edged wit and without the Romantic lushness of Grieg's more celebrated score. Of his piano music, the *Rondo Amoroso*, the seventh of the *Lette Stykker for Klavier* (*Easy Pieces for Piano*, 1939), is a delicate, nostalgic miniature, also orchestrated for oboe, bassoon and strings. The five books of *Slåtter og Stev fra 'Siljustöl'* (*Dances and Country Tunes from Siljustöl*, 1943) for piano, whose title refers to the composer's home, draw on Norwegian folk tunes. Of these, the scherzo *Kjempeviseslåtten* (*Ballad of Revolt*, op. 22 No. 5) has achieved independent life in orchestral form, with a new introduction.

RECOMMENDED WORKS

Symphony No. 6 *Sinfonia Dolorosa* (1942)
Symphony No. 7 *Salmesymfonin* (1945)
Symphony No. 9 (1966)
Peer Gynt Suites Nos. 1 and 2 (1950) for orchestra
Rondo Amoroso (*Lette Stykker for Klavier* No. 7, 1939) for piano

Valen Fartein*

born 25th August 1887 at Stavanger
died 14th December 1952 at Haugesund

Fartein Valen belongs to that group of composers who pursued innovations largely in isolation, little recognised for much of their lives, and about whom exaggerated claims are inclined to be made. His output is small – forty-four opus numbers (and three further incomplete works) – and his personal idiom dates from 1924, when he adopted an atonal harmonic language in the *Piano Trio*. He then developed an interesting combination of atonality, with polyphonic use of tonerows, and an emotional cast heavily influenced by his love for the Norwegian fjord landscape and the sea and by a deep spirituality and religious sensibility. Overall, his idiom is lyrical, often sparse or austere, usually concise, and uninfluenced by Norwegian folk music.

The core of Valen's output are nine short tone poems for orchestra, of which the best known is *Le cimetière marin* (*The Graveyard by the Sea*, 1934), inspired by a poem by Paul Valéry and memories of a Norwegian cholera cemetery; the desolation of the cemetery is contrasted with the surging ocean. *La Isla de las Calmas* (*The Silent Island*, 1934) was inspired by seeing a flock of white doves returning to an island, and has a religious motivation in the contrast of hope and emotions of longing engendered by the sea. The *Symphony No. 1* (1937, first heard 1956) used material from an atonal piano sonata, while the *Symphony No. 2* (1941–44) and the *Symphony No. 3* (1944–46) are both cast with two long movements followed by two shorter ones. The former was partly inspired by the composer hearing cries of wounded in a bombed ship. All are scored for a small orchestra, used most sparely in the *Symphony No. 4* (1947–49).

Two concertos occupy an important place in Valen's output. The *Violin Concerto* (1947), inspired by the death of a child, is a compressed, single-movement work, ending with a chorale. His last major work was the brittle and acerbic *Piano Concerto* (1952), using a chamber orchestra and cast in three concise, linked movements suggesting one overall span. Dry and introverted, but with an interesting insidiousness, it has echoes of **Prokofiev** at his most severe.

Valen was director of the Norwegian music collection at Oslo University from 1927 to 1939.

RECOMMENDED WORKS
Le cimetière marin (1934) for
    orchestra
La Isla de las Calmas (1934)
Piano Concerto (1952)
Symphony No. 3 (1944–46)
Die Dunkle Nacht der Seele (1939) for
    soprano and orchestra
Violin Concerto (1947)

Poland

Introduction

Polish musical achievement in the 19th century was dominated by Frédéric Chopin (1810–49), together with the lesser-known figures of Stanislaw Moniuszko (1819–72), whose most important work is the opera *Halka*, and the violinist Henryk Wieniawski (1835–80). By the turn of the century, Polish composition was distinctly conservative, culturally and politically dominated by Germany, and represented by such composers as Wladyslaw Zelenski (1837–1921) and Feliks Nowowiejski (1877–1946). The outstanding Polish musician of the period was Ignacy Jan Paderewski (1860–1941), a pianist of charismatic success who became the first President of the new state of Poland in 1919; his best-known composition is the opera *Manru* (first performed 1901).

To counter the conservative tendencies of Polish music at the turn of the century, a number of composers formed the 'Young Poland' group. Its short-lived activities attracted writers and artists, and the most important of Polish composers since Chopin, Karol Szymanowski (1882–1937). Initially influenced by Reger and Strauss, he developed, after encounters with the music of Debussy and North Africa, a sensuous, exotic idiom that includes some of the richest and headiest music ever written. From the late 1920s he studied the music of the Tatra mountains, incorporating folk influences into a leaner but still meltingly beautiful style. Few other Polish composers made any strong impression before the 1950s, though the works of Alexandre (Aleksander) Tansman (1897–1986) are sometimes heard, eclectically modernist in the 1920s (when he lived in Paris), neo-classical following his return to Poland in 1946.

A number of younger composers were starting to emerge, suggesting a revival of Polish composition – albeit largely following French neo-classical models – when the Nazis invaded Poland in 1939. Nazi repression stifled cultural activity, and although such composers as Andrej Panufnik (1914–91) continued with considerable courage to compose and arrange concerts, this younger generation of composers made little impression internationally until the late 1950s. For the imposition of communism after World War II continued the repression of the arts, establishing socialist realism and cutting off Polish composers from developments elsewhere in Europe. Tadeusz Baird (1928–81), Jan Krenz (born 1926), and Kazimierz Serocki (1922–81) founded the 'Group 49', ostensibly to promote music that would be 'anti-élitist' and in contact with the listener, but pointing out that they did not want to eschew modern harmonies. Many composers continued in a neo-classical style, notably Grażyna Bacewicz (1909–69), but also lesser-known composers such as Michał Spisak (1914–65), whose *Symphonie Concertante No. 2* (1956) and *Concerto Grosso* (1957) are both lucidly constructed, the former colourful and entertaining, the latter more serious. One of the consequences of the clamp-down was a renewed interest in the folk songs of the various regions of Poland, not only in choral works (such as Serocki's *Mazowsze*, or Lutosławski's *Tryptykśląski*, 1951, for soprano and orchestra, which uses folk-like melodies), but also, for example, in the concertos of Bacewicz. Socialist realism appeared in such operas as *Buntžakow (The Student's Rebellion*, 1951) by Tadeusz Szeligowski (1896–1963).

Most composers stayed in Poland, but one of the finest, Panufnik, left Poland in 1954 and settled in Britain, while Roman Haubenstock-Ramati (born 1919) moved to Israel in 1950 and to Vienna in 1957. However, the foundation in 1956 of the Warsaw Autumn Festival (still one of the major European new music festivals) led to increased contacts with the rest of Europe. The immediate result was the rediscovery of the music of such composers as Bartók (whose harmonic ideas then influenced Bacewicz), but at the 1958 festival Boulez, Cage, Messiaen and Stockhausen were heard too, as well as works by such young Polish experimenters as Henryk Górecki (born 1933). Once the dykes had been breached the floods could not be held back, and the authorities relaxed their control over styles of music. As a result, in the early 1960s, there was an explosion of Polish avant-garde music.

One consequence of the almost two-decade isolation of Polish music was the lack of knowledge of Schoenberg and 12-tone techniques. Jósef Koffler (1896–1943), who had studied with Schoenberg, wrote 12-tone works with a neo-classical base, but died during the Nazi occupation. Baird, among others, wrote 12-tone works in the late 1950s, but generally strict 12-tone or post-Webern serialism was not a feature of the Polish avant-garde. Instead their elements were absorbed into a general style that managed to avoid some of the sterile intellectualism of Western academic composition. A chief characteristic has been what one Polish commentator called 'sonorism', in which sonorities, colour-changes and unusual timbres become the chief features. Consequently, Polish music since 1960 has been among the most vital in Europe, led by Witold **Lutosławski** (1913–94) and Krysztof **Penderecki** (born 1933), both among the best known of all modern composers. The former combined elements of the avant-garde with a more traditional, mainstream approach; the latter was more self-consciously experimental.

Kazimierz Serocki followed a similar path; his earlier works had included two symphonies influenced by Soviet composers, but he started experimenting with 12-tone compositions in the early 1950s, while simultaneously producing more publicly acceptable works. In 1958, he came under the influence of **Boulez**, particularly in the instrumental colouring, and then concentrated on colour effects. *Musica concertante* (1958) for orchestra, Serocki's strictest serial composition, *Segmenti* (1960–61) for chamber orchestra, and *Episodes* (1959), for strings and three percussion groups, all use step-like or block construction with pointillistic effects. With considerable energy in their forward momentum, they have a catchy quality, well worth investigating. By *Symphonic Frescos* (1963–64) for orchestra the formal construction became more fluid; by *Ad libitum* (1977) for orchestra it included aleatoric elements. Such established composers as **Bacewicz** and **Baird** quickly found a new freedom; others, such as Spisek, faded away. Henryk **Górecki**, after being a major figure in the Polish explosion of the avant-garde, turned to a minimalist and spiritual style with affinities to **Pärt** and **Tavener**, and achieved a similar widespread popular success.

A number of lesser-known Polish composers of this period were also producing work of interest and value. Haubenstock-Ramati drew from the dense textures of the opera *America* (1966, based on Kafka) an acid, multi-layered but powerful *Symphony* (1967). The otherwise little-known Andrzej Dobrowolski (1921–90), one of the major Polish electronic experimenters, produced in *Music for Magnetic Tape and Oboe Solo* (1965) an effective combination of solo instrument and electronic material, the solo sometimes going off into ruminative fantasies, sometimes attempting a dialogue with the underlying sounds.

In the 1970s and 1980s the Polish avant-garde gave way to a retrenchment and the development of a neo-Romanticism. **Penderecki** unexpectedly looked back to the scale and harmonic qualities of Bruckner. Haubenstock-Ramati produced an emotive *String Quartet No. 2* (1977). Typical of this trend was the change in the idiom of Marek Stachowski (born 1936): his *String Quartet No. 2* (1972) presents the avant-garde idiom of the time, with aleatoric elements; *Music de camera* (1965) for chamber ensemble has an obsessive, almost minimalist image, and the *Divertimento* (1978) for string orchestra a characteristic Polish richness of sonority. But by the *Sapphic Odes* (1985), for mezzo-soprano and orchestra, Stachowski returned to the influence of the rich sensuous idiom of **Szymanowski**, with grand lyrical vocal lines and intense colour effects in the exotic orchestration in a powerful work. Krisztof Meyer (born 1943) has concentrated on traditional forms (symphonies, concertos and string quartets), his antecedents being **Mahler** and **Shostakovich**, while developing his own brand of spare simplicity.

Polish Music Information Centre:
Polskie Centrum Muzyczne
Fredry 8, 00–097
Warszawa
tel: +48 002 6352230

Bacewicz Grażyna**
born 5th February 1909 at Lodz
died 17th January 1969 at Warsaw

A virtuoso violinist as well as a composer, Grażyna Bacewicz was one of the most distinguished woman composers of the 20th century. Her idiom was founded on neo-classicism, but in the later 1950s, influenced by **Bartók**, she sought to combine his expressiveness and sense of drama with the 12-tone techniques that were being rediscovered in Poland. From 1960 she developed a more avant-garde idiom, still expressive, often dramatic, and sometimes with almost Impressionistic effects. However, she retained the classical outlook of her earlier years, creating an unusual idiom in which the colouristic effects, rhythmic variation and subtleties, and the tendency for the accumulation of short events are encased in a classical formality, flowing with precision and ordered momentum.

The early works such as the *Wind Quintet* (1933) and the *Overture for Orchestra* (1943) reflected her French training (she studied with Nadia Boulanger). Her works of the late 1940s and 1950s combined the neo-classical idiom she had learnt in Paris with rhythmic and harmonic elements drawn from Polish folk music; the *Violin Concerto No. 3* (1948) uses folk themes and the ballet *Z chlopa król* (*From Peasant to King*, 1954) interweaves folk tunes and neo-classical courtly dances in a colourful story of a drunk dressed up to be a king. The neo-Baroque *Concerto for String Orchestra* (1948) employed ostinato motoric rhythms, rhythmic variations, and rich colours combined with lyricism. This period also includes her four dramatic symphonies (*No. 1* 1945, *No. 2* 1951, *No. 3* 1952, *No. 4* 1953).

Gradually Bacewicz started using 12-tone techniques in a free manner, with sharp sonorities, atonal motives, and the stress on tone colour. *Music for Strings, Trumpets and Percussion* (1958) serialises rhythm and dynamics as well as harmony. The seminal work that signalled Bacewicz's break from neo-classicism and the adoption of the avant-garde was *Pensieri notturni* (*Nocturnal Thoughts*, 1961) for orchestra, a fantastical evocation of dream-like images, giving the impression of a world teeming with life that has been contained and is ready to burst out. Slides, glissandi, fragmented effects and sharply contrasting focuses abound, sometimes in the mood of a **Bartók** nocturnal scene, but with the expressive precision and delicacy drawn from the Polish discovery of **Webern**. The combination of a classical layout and avant-garde means of expression is exemplified in the four-movement *Concerto for Orchestra* (1962), of which the expressive, troubled slow movement opens with Webernesque pointillistic effects. Her later works continued the classical formality, in a number of concertos and three orchestral works, including the *Musica sinfonica in tre movimenti* (1965).

The last four of Bacewicz's seven string quartets are very highly regarded in Poland, and in them she sought new means of expression within generally traditional forms. The *String Quartet No. 4* (1951) is lyrical and yet highly charged, with a distant beauty and rich, warm colours, using a Polish dance in the rondo; the overall tone has affinities with **Bartók**, but the strong sense of organised rhythmic momentum shows the neo-classical pedigree, especially in the bouncing opening of the finale. The *String Quartet No. 6* (1960) loosely uses 12-tone principles, but with the sense of fundamental notes, and a wide range of string effects. The *String Quartet No. 7* (1965) covers a broad scope of emotion and incident, with expressive and dramatic effects (including repetitive, clockwork-like moments, sonorous drones, swoops and glissandi), all encased in a classical logic, with a driving rhythmic energy. Of her other chamber music, the *Piano Quintet No. 1* (1952) alternates the dramatic and the intense, as in the brooding opening and sections of the finale, with the bouncingly entertaining, the march of the first movement having the flavour of **Weill**. The slow movement is rich and sonorous, the piano playing a mostly textural role, and this weighty and extended work is worth encountering.

Bacewicz taught at the Warsaw Conservatory. Her music should be known by anyone interested in women composers, for she is one of the finest to have emerged this century.

RECOMMENDED WORKS
> *Music for Strings, Trumpets and Percussion* (1958)
> *Pensieri notturni* (1961) for orchestra
> String Quartet No. 4 (1951)
> String Quartet No. 7 (1965)
> Piano Quintet No. 1 (1952)

BIBLIOGRAPHY
> J. Rosen, *Grażyna Bacewicz – her life and works*, 1984

Baird Tadeusz**
born 26th July 1928 at Grodzisk Masowiecki
died 2nd September 1981 at Warsaw

The music of Tadeusz Baird is still little known outside Poland. It is more self-effacing than that of **Penderecki** or **Lutosławski**, but Baird is a major figure in the history of modern Polish music, and his idiom always has the capacity to appeal, and often to surprise.

His earlier music after World War II, during which he was incarcerated in a concentration camp and was condemned to death by the Gestapo, contained both an awareness of a European mainstream represented by **Shostakovich** and **Prokofiev**, and a neo-classicism influenced by French models. He was one of the founders of 'Group 49', whose aim was to accommodate some of the strictures of the communist regime, and his *Symphony No. 1* (1950) is a monumental, five-movement Mahlerian work. So too, reportedly, was the *Symphony No. 2 'Quasi una fantasia'* (1952). (He destroyed this, but a recording of the first performance survives.) At the same time he looked back to earlier musics: the suite *Colas Breugnon* (1951) uses 16th-century galliards, and the intense, virtuoso *Concerto for Orchestra* (1953) employs Baroque forms, Renaissance procedures and Greek modes, opening with a Gregorian chant. Archaic effects (notably the use of the harpsichord) appear in a lovely song-cycle *Four Shakespeare Love Sonnets* (1955, orchestrated 1965) for baritone and orchestra. The vocal lines have a strong lyrical flow, and the second song (with strings alone) has affinities with **Shostakovich's** later song-cycles.

In the middle 1950s Baird started to adopt 12-tone techniques, initially in the *Cassazione* (1956) for orchestra, the *Divertimento* (1956) for wind quartet, and the *String Quartet* (1957). The last has Webernesque elements, but Baird retained his feel for expressive lyricism and his sense of sonority (as opposed to pointillism). The resulting idiom uses 12-tone techniques very freely, often retaining the sense of a more traditional harmonic foundation. The work that brought him wider attention was the *Four Essays* (1958) for orchestra, largely mournful and meditative, and beautifully orchestrated, each of the four movements using different forces. *Espressioni* (1959), for violin and orchestra, maintains the idiom, but adds an intense passion closer to **Berg**, with soaring declamatory solo lines. *Variations without a Theme* (1962) for violin and orchestra is more fragmented, but concise and orchestrally lucid. *Elegeia* (1973) for cello and orchestra explores more avant-garde textures; compact in size, it is large and dramatic in scale.

By the *Four Novelettes* (1967) for chamber orchestra Baird's material is the closest to the post-**Webern** avant-garde: mostly delicate and ethereal until the raucous close, fragmentary, and sometimes pointillistic. Then in two of his finest late works these more advanced techniques and refined timbres were combined with intense emotional drama. The cantata *Goethe-Briefe* (Goethe Correspondence 1970), for baritone, chorus and orchestra, is based on correspondence between Goethe and Frau von Stein. This powerful, disturbing and concise work opens with musical anger, from the heavily declamatory and brittle chorus-writing to the crashes of the orchestra, the flow held by the solo line, whose emotions range from the angry

to the vocally lyrical. The *Concerto lugubre* (1975), for viola and orchestra, was written following the death of his mother; it has a passionate, highly charged opening movement with an angry, lamenting solo line, a mournful middle movement and a final movement of quiet acceptance. This moving work, with its suggestions of tonal centres, expressive writing, and rich sonorities, is perhaps the most effective introduction to Baird's music.

Baird's development, once he had left behind the Mahlerian influence, is consistent and evolutionary. At the same time, he could revert to a simpler, direct and more archaic idiom, as in the gently lyrical *Chansons des trouvères* (*Songs of the Troubadours*, 1963), for mezzo-soprano, cello and two flutes. The *Four Songs* (1966), for mezzo-soprano and orchestra, on poems by Vesny Parun, combine that lyrical, archaic feel with more modern harmonies and procedures. Baird's contribution to music theatre is the one-act *Jutro* (*Tomorrow*, 1966), based on a short story by Joseph Conrad, in which an old man is disillusioned by the return of his son after an absence of many years; the father has hoped the son will marry the young woman who has kept house for him, but when the son tries to molest her, the father kills him. The setting of this dramatic, psychologically intense story concentrates on the psychology, with orchestral colours developing character, and the alienation emphasised by the role of the son being given to a speaking actor.

RECOMMENDED WORKS
> *Chansons des trouvères* (1963) for
> contralto, 2 flutes and cello
> *Elegeia* (1973) for orchestra
> *Espressioni* (1959) for violin and
> orchestra
> *Four Essays* (1958) for orchestra
> *Four Shakespearean Love Sonnets*
> (1955, orchestrated 1965) for
> baritone and orchestra
> cantata *Goethe-Briefe* (1970) for
> baritone, chorus and orchestra
> *Concerto lugubre* (1974–77) for viola
> and orchestra

Górecki Henryk Mikołai*
born 6th December 1933 at Czernica

Henryk Górecki was catapulted into international prominence in the early 1990s by the astonishing success of the recording of his *Symphony No. 3* (1976), which reached a vast audience. Before that success, his consistently experimental idiom was well known in Poland, but only familiar to specialists outside: he was one of the first Polish composers to mature without the necessity of a degree of socialist realism. He has evolved an idiom of meditative contemplation and slow-moving simplicity, founded on the repetition and slow metamorphosis of a limited range of rich sonorities and restricted harmonies (often employing the alternation of just two notes against a dense background). In its general style and religious impulse his music has affinities with **Pärt** and **Tavener**, but remains distinctively Polish through the use of old Polish chants and modes. A distinctive features of almost all except his earlier works is to end in a mood of uplifting brightness.

His earliest works employed 12-tone techniques, as in the *String Quartet* (1957), or the *Concerto for Five Instruments and String Quartet* (1957), though the latter shows the influence of **Boulez** in its colours (flute, clarinet, trumpet, xylophone, mandolin). In the *Symphony No. 1, '1959'* (1959) he combined the linear serial techniques with ostinato and cluster effects, but with *Scontri* (*Collisions*, 1960) for orchestra Górecki arrived at a personal preoccupation with sonority. Written for a huge orchestra with a battery of percussion instruments, the work caused a considerable stir at its première. Its marvellous semi-motoric opening textures, initially pianissimo and then with violent contrasts, are like a giant saw-mill coming to life. It proceeds with resonating textures, swoops, *sotto voce* held textures, massive dynamic collisions and extreme instrumental ranges. Almost without rhythmic progression in the conventional sense, it is propelled by step-like blocks of differing textures, all the movement in the contrast or changes of colour and timbre, ranging from bell-like delicacies to violent interjections. *Scontri* has a spontaneous, almost naïve, quality in its ferocity, as if Górecki had suddenly found the techniques and the emotions that would unleash Polish music from all its former suppression.

Genesis (1963), a cycle of three works for ensemble, is written in blocks rather than notes, showing the movement of the resulting sonorities; *Refrain* (1965) for orchestra concentrated on tone-clusters. Then Górecki's preoccupation with texture and sonority started to include old sources, such as the chants used in a number of chamber works of the late 1960s. A 14th-century organum and a 16th-century cantus firmus provide the foundation for *Muzyka Staropolska* (*Old Polish Music*, 1969), for strings and brass, contrasting slow-moving hushed string colours with martial brass calls, increasingly fragmented until the resolution of the close. The aesthetic of bare simplicity is predominant, and the overall idiom has affinities with **Panufnik's** works of the same period. At the same time, a religious impulse (Polish Catholic) started informing the music, initially in works such as *Ad matrem* (1971), for soprano, chorus and orchestra. The paring down of means, to concentrate on the movement of sonority and texture (as in the contemplative final section of *Ad matrem*), was matched by a minimal use of words, as Górecki took to extracting just the pertinent phrase for a vocal passage or work.

The *Symphony No. 2 'Kopernikowska'* (*'Copernican'*, 1972), written for the 500th anniversary of the Polish astronomer's birth, heralds some of the techniques of the better-known third, in the apparent simplicity and economy of means, repetitive block chords, minimal intervals, and a continuity of momentum combined with irregular rhythms. The first movement has elements of sonata form, with two contrasting 'themes' created by contrasts of textures and dynamics, and uses a psalm text. The second moves towards luminosity, with another psalm and a setting of text from Copernicus's *De Revolutionibus orbium celestium*, using a 15th-century chorale.

Whereas the second symphony has elements of the monumental, the *Symphony No. 3 'Symfonia Pieśni Żałosnych'* (*'Symphony of Sorrowful Songs'*, 1976) maintains a mood of ethereal luminosity throughout its considerable length (just under an hour). All three movements have verses concerning mothers weeping for their children: in the first movement a 15th-century Polish prayer, in the second a prayer carved on a Gestapo prison wall, in the third a folk song. The first movement is a slowly unfolding, sad and limpid canon (a new departure for the composer), interrupted by the soprano, and eventually building to a climax. Throughout the work the limited range of sonorities is maintained, with just the occasional counteridea of a piano note, like a fish rising on a pond; the third movement, the most beautiful and the simplest, reaches towards a heavenly bright light. It is undeniably a beautiful work, eliciting a sense of meditative bliss (hence its popularity), but it is debatable whether it is a challenging one;

the complexities of the canon do not inter-
fere with the overall impression of simplicity, and its limited range of expression
palls. The more one hears it, the more one
recognises the strong influence of **Szymanowski**. Even more direct, and in a very
similar idiom, is the *Beatus vir* (1979), for
bass-baritone, chorus and orchestra, which
will appeal to those who respond to the
third symphony, while providing confirma-
tion for those who have reservations about
such monochromatic and emotionally
monothematic musical expression.

Some of Górecki's more recent music has
suggested a movement away from such
ecstatic meditations to a more varied
idiom: *'Lerchenmusic', Recitatives and
Ariosos* (1984), for clarinet, cello and piano,
while opening with a plain-chant and
limited colours, includes aggressive ideas,
moments of a wild folk dance in the piano
writing, anger in the middle movement,
and strong echoes of **Messiaen** in the last,
while the dissonant harmonies of the
String Quartet No. 1 'Already it is Dusk'
(1988) almost seem evolved from a **Shostakovich** scherzo.

RECOMMENDED WORKS
  Beatus vir (1979) for bass-baritone,
    chorus and orchestra
  *'Lerchenmusic', Recitatives and
    Ariosos* (1984) for clarinet, cello
    and piano
  Scontri (1960) for orchestra
  Symphony No. 2 *Kopernikowska*
    (1972)
  Symphony No. 3 *Symfonia Pieśni
    Żałosnych (1976)*

Lutosławski Witold•••
born 25th January 1913 at Warsaw
died 7th February 1994 at Warsaw

Witold Lutosławski is the best known
internationally of all 20th-century Polish
composers, and a major figure in the classical music of the latter part of the 20th
century. Although he adopted avant-
garde techniques in the late 1950s, his
development has been consistent throughout his compositional career, and he has
created a synthesis of various modern
techniques within a fairly traditional
framework and through traditional instrumental means, combined with emotionally
expressive qualities. This synthesis has
become the main feature of Lutosławski's
idiom and placed him at the centre of what
has become known as 'mainstream' composition.

Lutosławski's primary musical concern
was with form, and in particular the creation of large-scale forms that would have
connections with tradition while providing
the framework for the new sonorities and
methods. One of his solutions was the use
of aleatoric elements within a 'closed' (self-
contained, strictly controlled) form. In
this, the players are given elements of
rhythmic freedom, so the overlap of lines is
not pre-ordained; but at the same time the
material is chosen to take into account the
harmonic possibilities of the potential
overlaps and combinations. This has given
a sculptural quality to his music, enhanced
by other solutions to the problems of form,
such as interconnections or contrasts
between movements that become resolved
in final sections or movements, and the
linking of material in a 'chain' form. Harmonies, at least in the works after the late
1950s, have little connection with traditional tonality, but the chosen harmonic
combinations often suggest centres that,
combined with a formal clarity that usually
suggests recognisable motion within a formal progression, make Lutosławski's
idiom more approachable than some of his
contemporaries'.

A suggestion of Lutosławski's early
influences is provided by the *Two Fragments* (1963), for flute and harp, which are
reworkings of music written for radio in
the late 1940s and early 1950s. They will
come as something of a surprise to anyone
familiar with Lutosławski's later music, for
the first piece, *Magia (Magic)*, with its
harp arpeggios, seems to come straight out
of **Ravel**, while the second, *Odysseus in
Ithaca*, is warmed by a Mediterranean sun.
In contrast, the roistering *Symphony No.
1* (1948) combines shades of the neo-
classical **Stravinsky** with an element of wild
abandon heavily influenced by **Prokofiev**.
It is, if derivative, nevertheless compelling
for its verve and clarity, and for the
mawkish march which emerges out of the
nocturne textures of the second movement. The bubbling self-confidence of the
symphony was echoed in the equally infectious neo-classical *Overture* (1949).

During the 1950s Lutosławski continued
the exploration of folk music initiated in
such early works as *Twenty Polish Christmas Carols* (1946) for voice and piano.
Now, however, it was combined with the
obvious and beneficial influence of **Bartók**,
in the delightful little suite of four miniature folk dances *Mala Suite (Little Suite,
1950–51)* for orchestra, and in the undemanding but pretty *Tanzpraeludien
(Dance Preludes, 1955)*, for clarinet and

chamber orchestra. *Stronkette* (*Chain of Straw*) for soprano, mezzo-soprano and wind quintet, is perhaps the most beneficial of these works, a cycle of arrangements of miniature folk poems with rocking rhythms and a wind accompaniment that points, juxtaposes and cajoles.

The major work of this period is the outstanding *Concerto for Orchestra* (1950–54), which seeks to combine the neo-classical and the folk, largely confining the latter to thematic fragments drawn from folk music, and which explores the sometimes complex interaction of linear textures and melodic lines. It is both attractive and weighty, the last three of its five movements played continuously to create a quasi-symphonic structure. With its driving rhythmic vitality (again harking back to **Bartók**) and its sharply focused instrumental colours, it has moments of solemnity, and also aural magic, such as the dancing revolutions of soloists handing ideas to each other over held strings and a tingling bell at the end of the first movement, or the passacaglia theme that starts the third movement in the deep double basses and harp, like a slow stamping folk dance, before the whole edifice rises up with the additions of other instruments, ideas eventually flying off with a tremendous sense of impulse and excitement. There are echoes of **Martinů** towards the close, in the step-like construction of momentum and the touch of the chorale against a huge swirling orchestral background, but this is the work in which one can feel Lutosławski developing his personal voice.

Throughout these earlier works, Lutosławski's harmonies had been traditional, leavened by inflections derived from **Bartók**. In the outer movements of *Musique funèbre* (1958) for string orchestra, dedicated to the memory of Bartók, he turned to 12-tone technique. The rows chosen for these sombre and austere movements create a harmonic world akin to the dedicatee rather than anything more astringent, combined with a neo-classical sense of momentum. The middle sections are freer, and the work marks the beginning of the style of synthesis within generally traditional parameters. Then, in the period of the explosion of new musical ideas in Poland, he turned to exploring personal ways of introducing new ideas into large-scale forms. The prelude to this was *Three Postludes* (1958–60) for orchestra, in which each of the three parts would have its own tone and textures, while being dependent in the overall form on the others, to be

drawn together in a final, fourth, postlude; textures and colours were themselves to become a type of theme. The fourth was never written, but the best known of the *Postludes*, the first, is an interesting work in its own right; it has the feel of an arch form and a magical opening with little fragments spinning off from the general texture into space.

Venetian Games (1961) for orchestra, a four-movement instrumental concerto, introduced Lutosławski's crucial concept of controlled aleatoric elements. These were developed in the *String Quartet* (1964), cast in a duality between the slow prelude and a faster movement; most of the score allows the performers freedom in the timing of the actual events played, so their overlaps are not predetermined. But the harmonic results produced by those overlaps *are* determined: filigree effects are created in the opening which lead to a feeling of fluidity, sometimes more dense, sometimes branching out, like a lava flow that eventually peters out. Throughout events seem to be poised to develop in a recognisable fashion, only to turn out to be preludes to other events, and the unusual aural world of this string quartet has an unexpected coherence. In the *Symphony No. 2* (1967) the rhythmic and colour textures created by the aleatoric devices are contrasted with more direct, concerted material, again in a two-movement form. In *Paroles tissées* (*Woven Words*, 1965), for tenor and chamber orchestra, the sense of the mobile is created by a revolving tapestry of note patterns in the orchestra against the floating solo lines. The song-cycle is based on Jean-François Chabrun's *Quatre tapisseries pour la châtelaine de Virgil*, symbolist poetry in four 'tapestries' connected by repeated phrases. Lutosławski's setting, with constantly changing colours and sonorities, ranging from the delicate, with harp and high piano, to the highly charged in the third section, is both compelling and constantly inventive. It was written for Peter Pears, and there is not a huge stylistic leap from the **Britten** song-cycles to the Pole's more contemporary idiom. The expressive and dramatic *Livre pour orchestre* (*Book for Orchestra*, 1968) is divided into four movements (called 'chapters'), with aleatoric elements at pivotal moments; the whole work thrusts towards the large finale.

The culmination of this period was reached in the *Cello Concerto* (1969–70), in four linked movements, with exceptionally difficult solo writing, controlled aleatoric sections, and powerfully expressive emotional content, and in the *Preludi e fuge* (*Preludes and Fugue*, 1970–72), for thirteen solo strings. Here the search for large-scale form moulds one of the central musical structures into an unusual whole: seven linked preludes, each with its own character, culminate in a fugue with aleatory elements that uses six 'bundles' of colour and melodic strands as themes, drawn from the earlier preludes. The sighing, lamenting textures of swooping cries and a nervous intense stutter that form the duality of this work are most effective. In the rather strange *Novelette* (1978) for orchestra, Lutosławski opposes the brash idea of the opening with quietly sonorous material; its five sections are interrelated but distinct in character; its closing bars are pure **Bartók**. *Mi-parti* (1976), which could be called atmospheres and sonorities, returns to the concept of duality, using a technique where the second of two elements acquires new forms in repetition. Here the form is aurally elusive, suggesting fragments flowing together in one flux; but the work is often atmospherically dramatic, with fanfare elements, driving rhythmic energy, and haunting quieter moments, such as the opening, where images seem to be emerging out of mist. The *Double Concerto* (1980), for oboe, harp and orchestra, is more arresting in texture and tone than the *Cello Concerto*, the basic opposition of the densely charged opening countermanded by a pastoral oboe dominating the work. It is rather frenetic in nature in spite of the boisterous close, as if straining after a general character outside Lutosławski's sensibilities.

In these works the basis of Lutosławski's solutions to form had been moving from an essential duality to a more linear linked progression, heralded but left latent in the *Three Preludes* and *Venetian Games*, more overt in the passacaglia of the *Concerto for Orchestra*. Like the passacaglia, the *Preludes and Fugue* and *Novelette* suggested a chain form, in which each section is linked to the next in a linear flow, and this was made explicit in *Chain I* (1983) for chamber orchestra. Here the music is divided into two strands, each beginning or ending simultaneously; the inherent duality of mood of the earlier works has become smoothed out into a more interrelated expressiveness. An element of the cantabile appeared in Lutosławski's last works, *Chain 3* (1986) for orchestra concentrated on shape and instrumental effect, while the *Piano Concerto* (1988) married some of Lutosławski's

idiom with more traditional four-movement form and content. The *Symphony No. 3* (1972–83) moves from a terse, sometimes nebulous sound world to a more lyrical and self-confident mood. Like its predecessor, it is cast in two movements, the first a preparatory movement to the second; here the work is framed by an introduction (including a tense fanfare motif that recurs through the work) and a coda, with the first movement divided into three sections and the whole played without a break. The *Symphony No. 4* (1993) has a form similar to that of the second and third symphonies; once again, and to a greater extent, expectations prepared in the first movement are fulfilled by a lyrical outpouring on strings and horns.

Lutosławski's influence has been considerable; his synthesis of traditions and experimentation in the 1960s and 1970s heralded a movement general in Western classical music. His particular achievement has been to create new ways of setting up expectation and fulfilment for the listener, whether on a small scale (as in the links of his 'chains'), or a large one (as in the last three symphonies). Although its emotional range is somewhat limited, if leavened by a more lyrical flow in his later works, at its best his music is a powerful experience.

RECOMMENDED WORKS

Cello Concerto (1970)
Concerto for Orchestra (1954)
Les espaces du sommeil (1975)
Mi-parti (1976) for orchestra
Paroles tissées (1965) for tenor and orchestra
Preludes and Fugue (1970–72) for thirteen instruments
Symphony No. 1 (1948)
Symphony No. 2 (1967)
Symphony No. 3 (1972–83)

BIBLIOGRAPHY
S. Stucky, *Lutosławski and his Music*, 1981
B. A. Varga, *Lutosławski Profile*, 1976

Panufnik Andrzej*

born 24th September 1914 at Warsaw
died 27th October 1991 at London

Andrzej Panufnik developed an idiom with the inherent sculptural quality that is now recognisable as a hallmark of modern Polish music, albeit in a more traditional setting than either of his better-known contemporaries, **Lutosławski** and **Pender-ecki**. He retained this Polish flavour in his relatively small output in spite of leaving Poland in 1954 and settling in Britain (his mother was English). His earlier compositions were lost in the Warsaw uprising of 1944, and all his works, apart from three that he reconstructed, date from after the end of World War II.

The sculptural quality of Panufnik's music is created firstly by the use of sound-blocks – one block of sound is maintained for a considerable period, to be replaced by another, each with a distinct and homogeneous tone and texture – and secondly by the layering of distinctively shaped material. It has a mathematical basis which, although present even in his earlier works, is overt only in the later ones. Mathematical symmetries and their permutations abound – especially the palindrome, where the second half of a work or movement mirrors the first – and much of his music is founded on the mathematical manipulation of three-note cells. This is allied to an emotional feel of the spiritual or visionary, which, together with the intentionally limited harmonic range and colours, has affinities with the music of **Górecki**, **Pärt** and **Tavener**. But where these composers have turned to older musics and elements drawn from the avant-garde, Panufnik's idiom ultimately derives from neo-classical antecedents. As a result, the mathematical techniques are aurally in the background; at their best, they provide a feeling of great cohesion or impelling force, like some great geared machine at times hardly ticking over, at others pounding in high gear. At their worst – and Panufnik's output is variable – this highly organised simplicity can sound as if the music is a formula. When it is compounded by the often restrained orchestration, and the intentionally limited harmonic or melodic palette for any given piece, the results can be insipid and sometimes tedious. His emotional range is inclined to hover between two states (reflected in the bipartite construction of many of his works): a quiet, atmospheric sense of the visionary, and a controlled anger expressed in the precision of percussion and strings. These are exemplified in his finest work, the *Sinfonia sacra*, in which, it could be claimed, all Panufnik's musical concerns are summated.

Of his early pieces to survive, the *Heroic Overture* (begun 1939, completed 1952) and the *Tragic Overture* (1942, restored 1945, revised 1955) reflect the martial and turbulent events of the times; of the two,

the latter is the more interesting, its material built on a four-note cell that becomes more obsessive in tone as the whole piece evolves from an almost pastoral rumination to a grinding remorselessness. More characteristic of Panufnik's later musical concerns is the beautiful *Nocturne* (1947, revised 1955) for orchestra, arranged in a slow-moving arch and coloured by the use of piano. A martial dissonance invades the tranquillity at close, but is laid to rest by the nocturnal, as if Panufnik was himself laying to rest his wartime experiences. The *Old Polish Suite* (1950, revised 1955) for string orchestra reflects the contemporary Polish interest in older music, and is archaic in feel.

Panufnik had already embarked on the series of ten 'sinfonias' (often referred to as symphonies), each titled, that form the core of his output. His earliest was destroyed in the Warsaw uprising, and the first of the extant works, the *Sinfonia rustica* (*Symphony No. 1*, 1948, revised 1955) is a delightful, lucidly orchestrated, and fresh neo-classical sinfonia – certainly not weighty enough for a symphony – using fragments of Polish folk themes. The symphonic construction is symmetrical in its four movements, and the strings are divided antiphonally between the wind and brass. The harmonies have rustic touches and dissonances, but the ingenuous, vigorous idiom, with no trace of sentimentality in the ruminative slow movement, will appeal to those who enjoy **Vaughan Williams**. It seems astonishing that the Stalinist Polish government banned it in 1949, declaring, 'the *Sinfonia rustica* ceases to exist'. The *Symphony of Peace* (*Symphony No. 2*, 1951) for chorus and orchestra, in which two choral movements frame a purely orchestral one.

The *Sinfonia sacra* (*Symphony No. 3*, 1963), celebrating the millennium of Polish statehood and Christianity, is a much weightier work. It is not only Panufnik's finest creation, but one of the finest 20th-century Polish orchestral works. Cast in two movements, the first divided into three sharply distinct sections or 'visions', it opens with a long series of trumpet fanfares rolling over each other, the trumpeters placed at the four corners of the orchestra. As they reach a climax, there is a sudden hush from held strings, a beautiful vision recalling the *Nocturne*. Against this, percussion breaks out to announce the third vision, a creation of extraordinary power and momentum using relatively simple means. The hymn that forms the second movement is based on a medieval Polish hymn, and opens in disembodied woodwind harmonics. The whole movement organically grows from this opening, predominantly in the strings, but joined by trumpet fanfares that had opened the work, answered by the horns, ending in a triumphant clarion climax. There are affinities in this movement with **Górecki's** later work, but the work with which the symphony as a whole invites comparison is **Janáček's** *Sinfonietta*, which is similar in tone and construction, though here the textures are leaner and more direct.

The meditative and visionary tone of the second section of the *Sinfonia sacra* had been heralded in the opening of the lovely, tragic *Autumn Music* (1962), for orchestra, without violins or brass. These simplest of means (a three-note cell, and a limited series of chords) are used to create a piece containing complex transformations, colours divided between the mellowness and the sharpness of autumn air, and heartfelt sadness. Less successful is the cantata *Universal Prayer* (1969), for four soloists, chorus, three harps and organ, setting a poem by Alexander Pope and musically arranged in a symmetrical arch. The writing for chorus and organ includes aleatoric elements, there being no rhythmical indications. While there are some beautiful moments (especially for the harp), Panufnik's vocal writing lacks the emotional impact or conviction achieved by some of his Polish contemporaries.

The fourth symphony was a concertante work, the *Sinfonia concertante* (1973) for flute, harp and strings, which followed the palindromic and not especially interesting *Violin Concerto* (1971). Both the following two symphonies are more beguiling works than their apparent bareness would at first suggest. In the *Sinfonia di sfere* (*Symphony of Spheres, Symphony No. 5*, 1975) a seemingly barren landscape is contrasted with percussion of pounding rhythmic energy, with an almost jazzy bounce and fluid rhythmic ideas folding over one another. The piano has an important colour role in the otherwise limited colour range, in a work in which the aspect of the suppressed and controlled in Panufnik's musical character is to the fore. The *Sinfonia mistica* (*Symphony No. 6*, 1977) has a long, lugubrious opening, setting the mood of the title, followed by a series of orchestral calls and fanfares thrown around the orchestra, as if the first 'vision' of the *Sinfonia sacra* had been broken up. Just when the varying shades of a similarly meditative mood seem to have outstayed

their welcome, it suddenly expands into a passage of inner movement and greater energy, to magical mysterious effect. Formally, the work revolves around the mystical number six, using six sections and combinations of six in the various construction parameters.

Metasinfonia (*Symphony No. 7*, 1978), for organ, strings and timpani, invites comparison with **Poulenc's** better-known concerto for the same forces, and at moments sounds oddly similar, to the symphony's disadvantage. It again uses a three-note germ-cell and palindromic construction, with metres that gradually lengthen out in the organ and strings but not in the timpani. The *Sinfonia votiva* (*Symphony No. 8*, 1981) is dedicated to the Black Madonna, a major icon in the political turbulence of the period when the symphony was written. The first of two movements is created by clearly audible, overlapping circles, given to various instrumental groups, and is spartan in texture and tone. The second brings together the whole orchestra, but its intention of 'an urgent petition' doesn't quite catch fire. His late works include the *Concertino* (1980), for timpani, percussion and strings, which marks a return to Panufnik's most effective and atmospheric vein; the ninth and tenth symphonies; the *Bassoon Concerto* commemorating the martyred priest Jerzy Popietusko; and the *String Quartet No. 2 'Messages'*, recalling the effect of wind in telegraph lines that Panufnik heard as a small child. All these reportedly made strong impressions.

The relative neglect of Panufnik's immediate and attractive, if uneven, idiom is now coming to an end, as many are beginning to appreciate the finely detailed and immaculately constructed works of this unassuming Polish exile.

Panufnik was director of the Kraków Philharmonic Orchestra (1945–46) and of the Warsaw Philharmonic Orchestra (1946–47), and music director of the Birmingham Symphony Orchestra (1957–59). In her book *Out of the City of Fear* (1956), his first wife Scarlett described their flight from Poland. His daughter (by his second marriage), Roxana, is also a composer.

RECOMMENDED WORKS
Autumn Music (1962) for orchestra
Nocturne (1947) for orchestra
Sinfonia di sfere (Symphony No. 5, 1975)
Sinfonia mistica (Symphony No. 6, 1977)
Sinfonia rustica (Symphony No. 1,

1948 revised 1955)
Sinfonia sacra (Symphony No. 3,
1963)

BIBLIOGRAPHY
A. Panufnik, *Composing Myself*, 1987

Penderecki Krzysztof •••
born 23rd November 1933 at Debica

Krzysztof Penderecki has established himself as one of the leading avant-garde composers of his generation. His music has also appealed to wider audiences than many of his contemporaries, partly because his idiom has been quite wide-ranging and often uses large-scale forms that have met a need in the concert hall. A consistent feature of his output has been the creation of aural soundscapes of seemingly huge dimensions from the forces available. In addition, his music has what might be described as a visual, sculptural quality, as if it were hewn out of great blocks and then shaped, which has appealed to those who have otherwise found the avant-garde elements unfamiliar or disconcerting. His output has been primarily divided between works for orchestra (including concertos) and large-scale choral works of a religious nature.

Owing to the strict cultural control in Poland in the early 1950s, Penderecki only became exposed to the more modern trends in the rest of Europe after 1956, and his first mature work is the *Psalms of David* (1958) for choir, harp, piano and percussion. The vocal techniques include reciting and whispering, and there are fragmentary effects derived from 12-tone techniques. The third psalm has strong echoes of **Orff** in the percussive propulsion and choral writing. There then followed a series of orchestral works in which Penderecki experimented with massed sonorities, creating dense atmospheric soundscapes of great and expressive power. The piece with which he made his name was the *Threnody for the Victims of Hiroshima* (1959–60), which uses 52 strings for a dark work of contemporary effects, reflecting the horror of the subject, and remains as effective and as harrowing today as when it first appeared. *Anaklasis* (1959–60), for 42 strings and percussion, includes a prepared piano used percussively, and the string writing involves the extensive use of quarter-tones and extended instrumental techniques. It is a study in dense-textured cluster sounds, overlayered by pointillistic moments, a transitional piece

between the legacy of serialism and Penderecki's developing command of sonorities. The short and frenetic *String Quartet No. 1* (1960) explored a whole gamut of sound effects, hitherto unheard in the string quartet repertoire, in a simple but effective formal structure. *Polymorphia* (1961) for forty-eight strings developed the idiom, with dense cluster textures, swooping string sounds, massed pluckings, and a series of ebbs and flows culminating in a C major chord. *Fluorescences* (1961) for orchestra is a more extended exploration of expressive and extreme colours. *De Natura Sonoris* (1966) for orchestra breaks up Penderecki's customary dense textures into smaller groupings and transformations, exploring a wider range of sounds, sometimes akin to sounds of electronic music, and at one point infused with jazz rhythms. Meanwhile, in *Dimensions of Time and Silence* (1959–60) for forty-part choir, percussion and strings, Penderecki abandoned the original text in favour of clusters of vowels and consonants. Its tintinabulating opening initiates the sense of ritual in Penderecki's work, and the fantastic sonorities and massed vocal effects point to the later choral works.

His most outstanding success of the 1960s, and one of the seminal works of the period, reached a wide public partly because of its Christian subject and partly because of the intensity and variety of its effects. The *St Luke Passion* (*Passio et mors Domini Nostri Jesu Christi secundum Lucam*, 1963–65) uses a very wide range of avant-garde devices, particularly in the choral and orchestral writing; but they are always in the service of religious effect and drama, and they are combined with obviously tonal effects. The *Passion* showed the viability of linking the emotional, liturgical tradition with judiciously chosen avant-garde techniques. It also proved that such a combination could appeal to a much larger audience than most avant-garde works. In the *Dies Irae* (subtitled *Auschwitz Oratorio*, 1967), for soloists, chorus and orchestra, Penderecki reuses many of the darker effects of the *Passion*, adding the sounds of siren and chain. It is an intensely dramatic and dark work, in which the entire construction, with its massed sounds of horror, aimed at an Expressionist impact. It includes setting of texts from the Bible, contemporary poets and Greek drama, all translated into Latin apart from the Greek fragments.

Perhaps more impressive than either of these two works is the two-part oratorio *Utrenja* (1970–71). Part I, subtitled 'The

Entombment of Christ' for five soloists, two mixed choirs, and orchestra, moves in slow, gradually evolving swathes of dark textures in a contemplative rite. Part I ends in the hope of Resurrection. Part II, subtitled 'The Resurrection', adds a boys' choir to the forces, and provides an emotional contrast to Part I. Here there is a feeling of a tumultuous ritual, of the energy of the crowd, the vocal cries and shouts supported by clappers, bells, rattles and glockenspiels. Against this is set a chorale in the Orthodox tradition. There is a kind of visual abandon to this work: blocks of events happen, stop, and start again, retaining their dense textures. Although the composer agreed to the two parts being performed separately, they are best heard together, with the two emotional worlds balancing each other.

Similar musical effects were used theatrically in the opera *The Devils of Loudun* (1968), drawn from the book by Aldous Huxley, via a German translation by Erich Fried of a play by John Whiting. The complex story, based on a true incident in 17th-century France, centres on the figure of a powerful priest whose liaisons lead to a false accusation of devilry by an Ursuline Sister sexually obsessed with him; he eventually achieves a transcendence when faced with the inevitability of events. The story combines politics, religious hysteria, and sexual excess and repression; it presents a society overcome by obsessive madness, with obvious parallels to the 20th century. The opera, in three short acts divided into succinct, sometimes overlapping scenes, is intensely dramatic and theatrically compelling. The enormous orchestra (including electric bass guitar) is used mainly for a multiplicity of colour combinations, almost all dark, and only rarely for massed effect; the vocal styles range from sections of speech or near-speech to musical lines of heightened tension; there are considerable roles for chorus. The focus is on the drama and the theatrical experience, to which the music adds an extra dimension rather than being at the forefront of the creation. Not the least of its achievements is the strength of characterisation, with one aspect of each character highlighted. It is a harrowing work, but a powerful experience.

In the middle of the 1970s Penderecki suddenly moved away from his considerable development of new sounds and effects, and seemed to step right back into a tonal world. The first piece to suggest such a change was *Przebudzenie Jakuba* (*The Awakening of Jacob*, sometimes titled *Jacob's Dream*, 1974) for orchestra, a tone-painting of huge atmospheric sonorities with neo-Romantic overtones in the massed layers of sound. The trend continued in the large, bold *Violin Concerto No. 1* (1976–77), a work whose soaring solo lines followed the tradition of the virtuoso Romantic concerto with a duality between the quick and happy, and the dark. The experience of his more avant-garde style is sometime apparent, especially in the darker, clustered moments from the orchestra.

The impetus behind this new direction in Penderecki's style was a very large-scale opera, *Paradise Lost* (1975–78), whose theatrical demands are so great it has been rarely performed. From it, Penderecki drew a five-minute suite, the *Adagietto* (1978), made up of instrumental ideas from the opera – an openly Romantic work virtually without a dissonance or massed sonority. However, the work in this new aesthetic that aroused the greatest controversy was the *Symphony No. 2 'Wigilijna'* ('Christmas Symphony', 1979–80), which can only be described as Brucknerian. To those who had supported and admired Penderecki's work, the absence of Penderecki's earlier stylistic concerns seemed a negation of all that he had previously achieved. Given knowledge of Penderecki's earlier music, it is difficult to be objective about this symphony, though taken in isolation it is a powerful work constructed in a large arch, with the theme of 'Silent Night' threading through it at unexpected moments.

Even more obviously neo-Romantic is the *Te Deum* (1980), for soloists, chorus and orchestra, which has strong Polish resonances both in the choice of the text and in some of the musical idiom. It combines very old-fashioned writing with some of the polyphonic choral and vocal effects derived from Penderecki's earlier style. Influenced by traditional liturgical music, it comes as a shock after the brilliant spiritual illumination of his earlier religious works, though the internal shifts from the old-fashioned to the more contemporary are handled with great mastery. This combination ought to appeal to anyone who is just exploring some of the sonorities and effects of the avant-garde, encased as they are here in more familiar surroundings.

This neo-Romantic trend has continued, though considerably tempered, in the *Cello Concerto No. 2* (1982) and the *Viola Concerto* (1983). The Brucknerian element has disappeared in these works, replaced with precise rhythmic punctuation and instrumental detail that seem ultimately to descend from **Stravinsky's** neo-classicism and the vigour of **Hindemith**. The opening of the impressive *Cello Concerto No. 2* recalls Vivaldi, with dropping string lines that overlap with those that remain static to create dissonant effects. The solo writing is expressively restrained but highly virtuoso, the lyricism tempered by a bold, sometimes aggressive ruggedness, sounding against a combination of pithy comments handed around the orchestra. The ending is a whirlwind of different stylistic effects (notably percussion set against the soloist), synthesized into a unified whole, before a relatively tranquil close. The *Viola Concerto* is another large-scale single-movement concerto, Romantic in the opening and in the solo writing, but then injected with orchestral colours derived from his earlier style, as if continuing the attempt at synthesis. The overall image is of a rough-hewn block, while the orchestral chisel is wielded with sharp, angered strokes – unexpected in a concerto for viola, which is usually treated lyrically. One can't help but feel that there is an element of annoyed response to his critics in both these works. Less successful is the *Polish Requiem* (1980–84) for soloists, two choruses and orchestra, whose throwback to the grand 19th-century manner is unconvincing.

Penderecki returned to a tortured, extreme story in the one-act opera *The Black Mask* (1989). Set in 17th-century Silesia, it is a dark work about death, sex, exploitation and corruption. Behind the work lies the shadow of the Black Death; on stage, a dancer symbolises the black death mask of the title, and the plainchant *Dies irae* is a recurring musical theme. Penderecki employs two orchestras, the main pit orchestra and a backstage woodwind orchestra, for a musical idiom that combines generally conventional writing with expressive and dramatic vocal lines. There are few purely solo moments apart from a long aria for the heroine. The orchestral colours are muted and dark, the textures lean and linear in comparison with earlier works, and it gradually builds in variety over the course of its ninety-minute duration.

It is perhaps too early to judge the impact of Penderecki's new outlook, and in particular how general audiences will respond, given his previous reputation as a member of the avant-garde. His earlier works, quite apart from their expressive power, have an important historical place in the development of new sonorities, and his sophisticated handling of these aural effects has had a considerable influence on other contemporary composers.

RECOMMENDED WORKS
> *The Awakening of Jacob* (1974) for orchestra
> Cello Concerto No. 2 (1982)
> opera *The Devils of Loudun* (1968)
> *Dies Irae (Auschwitz Oratorio)* (1967) for soloist, chorus and orchestra
> *Dimensions of Time and Silence* (1959–60) for choir, percussion and string
> *St Luke Passion* (1963–55) for soloists, chorus and orchestra
> String Quartet No. 1 (1960)
> Symphony No. 2 *Christmas Symphony* (1979–80)
> *Te Deum* (1980) for soloists, chorus and orchestra
> *Threnody for the Victims of Hiroshima* (1960) for 52 strings
> Violin Concerto No. 1 (1976–77)

BIBLIOGRAPHY
> R. Robinson, *Penderecki: a Guide to his Works*, 1983

Szymanowski Karol**

born 6th October 1882 at Timashovka (Ukraine)
died 29th March 1937 at Lausanne

The relative obscurity of the music of Karol Szymanowski seems quite inexplicable. No one has ever exceeded him for sheer intensity of sensuous, ecstatic beauty, and of his limited number of works (69 opus numbers) at least three would seem to have all the requirements to maintain a firm hold on the hearts of music-lovers.

His output, after early works influenced by Chopin and German masters, falls into two distinct periods. The first followed his encounter with the music of **Debussy** during a World War I visit to Russia, and his discovery of Islamic culture during a visit to Sicily and North Africa in 1914. In the works that followed, brilliant orchestration of large forces is combined with intricate detail, exotic effects, Oriental rhythms, and large-scale architecture to create music of sensual power and ecstasy. These works are characterised by high expressive violin lines, increasingly chromatic harmonies, and Oriental sonorities. While the overall effect is Impressionistic, the expression of sensuality, the attention to brilliance of detail, and the choice of words, where applicable, are Oriental in origin.

Szymanowski's *Symphony No. 1* (1908–09) was withdrawn, but the richly orchestrated *Symphony No. 2* (1909–10, revisions 1934) stands between the Germanic influence of his earliest works and the full-blown sensuousness that was to follow. Its unusual structure is cast in two parts, the first (opening with a solo violin as if it were a concerto) audibly lies under the wing of **Strauss**, while the second is a series of linked variations culminating in a fugue. The highly charged one-act opera *Hagith* (1913, not performed until 1922), based on the biblical story, still has echoes of **Strauss**, but is closer in idiom to the **Bartók** of *Bluebeard's Castle*, with a mood of ecstasy replacing the brooding of the Hungarian. By the *Symphony No. 3 'Pieśń o nocy' (Song of the Night*, 1914–16) for tenor, chorus and orchestra, one of Szymanowski's finest works, the Straussian voluptuousness had been joined by an Impressionist delicacy. The mystical text (in Polish) is drawn from the Persian 13th-century Sufi poet Djālal-al-Dī Rūmī; the score allows for performance without tenor, but not without chorus. An orchestral introduction sets the sultry, richly perfumed nocturnal atmosphere, quickly joined by the tenor and a chorus line whose textures are folded into the whole orchestral image. The mysterious tone is maintained throughout the work (which is in one continuous flow), sometimes interrupted by fanfare figures or orchestral passages that suggest Bacchanalian dances under a hot night sky. The music is pinpointed with instrumental detail, a tambourine providing a continuous thread; the solo writing follows the inflections of speech. The sense of hushed passion bursting its restraints is maintained to the end in one of the headiest of all symphonies.

At the same time Szymanowski was working on an even finer work, the *Violin Concerto No. 1* (1915–16). With its thinner and more Impressionist textures, this marks the summit of his ability to elicit an orchestral ecstasy, constantly in fervent motion. It was inspired by another night poem, 'May Night' by Tadeusz Miciński, and although there is no overt programmatic content, the concerto follows the exotic imagery and colour contrasts of the poem, with soaring rich solo writing whose sensuous tension is increased by contrasts with the orchestral material. This is one of the most passionate and beautiful of all violin concertos. The *String Quartet No. 1*

(1917) brings some of the yearning beauty of the concerto into the chamber medium, but in a much more restrained fashion. The lovely slow movement (bringing **Ravel** to mind) is followed by a fugal finale in which the voices enter a minor third apart and create polytonal effects until the final resolution. The first two of the three *Mythes* (1915) for violin and piano have an attractive languid Impressionism, especially the first, 'La Fontaine d'Aréthuse', where the singing solo line has almost the role of a story-teller. The third, 'Dryades et Pan', is dramatically more wide-ranging, a miniature tone poem, in which the sound of Pan's pipes are convincingly rendered by high harmonics on the violin.

The summit of this period of Szymanowski's output was the opera *King Roger* (1918–26). The libretto by Jarosław Iwaszkiewicz, is about the 12th-century Norman King of Sicily, Roger II, who surrounded himself with one of the most intellectually advanced and multi-cultural courts of the period. It exactly suited the composer's mixture of mysticism, Arab influence and rich sensuousness. Roger is confronted by a pantheistic figure (the Shepherd) who converts his wife Roxanna, and eventually Roger himself, and is revealed as Dionysus; the distant source for the work is Euripides' *The Bacchae*. On one level this represents the conflict between Christianity and paganism, on another that between Apollo and Dionysus, but this complex, multi-layered libretto, full of allusion, is ultimately best analysed in Jungian terms. The relationship between Roger and the Shepherd has homoerotic undertones; Szymanowski wrote a homosexual novel during this period, but the manuscript was destroyed in the Nazi invasion. The opera is inclined to produce mixed reactions: for some, the continuously charged atmosphere and exotic, sensual musical treatment is too overwhelming in such a long work; for others, it is a continuously fascinating interplay of colour and psychological ideas that raises complex questions of spirituality. Either way, there are glorious moments, such as the huge choral opening in the cathedral (redolent of Byzantine church music, it is one of the most exciting openings to any opera), as well as 'Roxanne's Song', and the vision of Apollonian sunlight at the close.

Following Szymanowski's research into Polish folk music in the late 1920s, the ecstatic sweep of his music was tempered by a more rugged mode of expression. These later works incorporate folk elements either in direct quotation or in spirit, using unusual scales, harmonies and duple rhythms. The exotic colours and cantabile lines remain, but are combined with more immediate, folk-inspired rhythms, and a more direct contrapuntal writing. The orchestration is less dense, and the overall effect is more violent and improvisatory. The hinge work between these two styles is the ballet *Harnasie* (1923–31) for tenor, chorus and orchestra, reflecting the life of the highland Tatra peasants, in which a robber baron rescues a maiden from forced marriage to a much older farmer. It contains marvellous moments, such as the orchestral evocation of the Carpathians and the Tatra folk songs used in the pre-marriage ceremonies, but divorced from its stage setting the music is diffuse overall. The *String Quartet No. 2* (1927), however, is one of Szymanowski's finest works; once heard, the first movement is difficult to forget, with its rocking opening, over which emerges a sad, almost apologetic theme, its autumnal colours, and its moments of fretful mournfulness. The leaner textures, the more formal organisation, and the lingering sensuousness of melodic lines of Szymanowski's later period culminated in two concertante works. The *Symphonie concertante* (*Symphony No. 4*, 1932) for piano and orchestra is more brittle than his earlier works, straying into neo-classical areas, with the piano melded into the general orchestral texture; this lack of highlighted solo display has hampered its wider performance. The *Violin Concerto No. 2* (1933) makes a worthy companion to the first, imbued with the spirit of the folk dance.

Szymanowski was himself a concert pianist, and piano works occupy an important part of his output and a significant place in Polish music. The earlier works are influenced by Chopin or **Scriabin**, but *Métopes* (1915) reflect his sensual period. More likely to be encountered are the *Mazurkas* (two sets, 1924–25). No trace of Chopin lingers in these works; they are subtle and elusive, like delicate perfumes, veering off into unexpected melodic lines and rhythmic effects, often with an improvisatory feel.

Szymanowski's songs also occupy an important place in Polish music; their obscurity outside Poland must be partly due to the language difficulties. The earliest songs are influenced by Chopin, and then there is an increasing chromaticism, as in the considerable demands of 'Ryez

burzo!' ('Howl, storm'), the fourth of *Cztery peiśni* (*Four Songs*, 1904–05). One of the *Fünf Gesänge* (*Five Songs*, 1905–07) sets a poem from the *Das Knaben Wunderhorn* collection; the *Zwölf Lieder* (*Twelve Songs*, 1907) show the influence of **Strauss**. The *Sześć pieśni* (*Six Songs*) herald the interest in the sensual and exotic in both texts and music, and in the two sets of *Des Hafis Liebeslieder* (*Love Songs of Hafiz*, 1914) he reached a mature individual voice in his songs; he orchestrated a number of them. The most representative songs of this period are the cycles *Pieśni ksiezniczki z baśni* (*Songs of the Fairy Princess*, 1915) and *Pieśni muezina szalonego* (*Songs of the Infatuated Muezzin*, 1918). The persona of the former, for coloratura soprano and piano, is a Princess who, in a series of fantastical love poems, sings of sensual longing and physical yearning, with voluptuous vocal lines. The latter, to texts by Iwaszkiewicz, includes the evocation of a Muezzin's call to prayer. *Rymy dzieciece* (*Children's Rhymes*, 1922–23) are a series of twenty miniature songs evoking childhood for soprano and piano, suitable for a child as well as an adult to sing.

The later songs include settings of poems from Joyce's *Chamber Music* (*Four Songs*, 1926), but most show folk influence, notably the *Dwanaście pieśni kurpiowskich* (*Twelve Kurpian Songs*, 1930–32), the most potent expression of Szymanowski's involvement with his folk music heritage. His finest vocal work, considered by many to be his finest work in any genre, is the *Stabat Mater* (1925–26), for contralto, baritone, chorus and orchestra. Aiming at a simplicity and clarity of expression, and mostly slow, it is small in scale but not in effect. It is infused with an ecstatic spiritual intensity, drawing on Eastern church music and on the inflections of folk song in the vocal lines. There is a noble climax to end the penultimate section before the most magical music in the piece, the opening of the finale. It is directly antecedent to **Górecki's** *Symphony No. 3*, but is a more varied and more satisfying work.

Szymanowski stands in a similar relation to Polish music as **Bartók** to Hungarian music, and if he is not as significant an innovator, his emotional range can be as compelling in his best works; he deserves to be far more widely appreciated. He was principal of the Warsaw Conservatory (1927–30), and died in a Swiss sanatorium of tuberculosis.

RECOMMENDED WORKS
opera *King Roger* (1918–25, revisions 1934)
Mythes (1915) for violin and piano
Stabat Mater (1925–26) for contralto, baritone, chorus and orchestra
String Quartet No. 2 (1927)
Symphonie concertante (Symphony No. 4, 1932) for piano and orchestra
Symphony No. 3 (*Song of the Night*) (1914–16)
Violin Concerto No. 1 (1915–16)
Violin Concerto No. 2 (1933)

BIBLIOGRAPHY
J. Samson, *The Music of Szymanowski,* 1980

Portugal

Introduction

Modern music in Portugal has not received as much attention as that in neighbouring Spain, although Portugal too has a long musical history: the Chair of Music at the University of Coimbra was founded in the 14th century. As in Spain, Portuguese music in the 19th century was dominated by Italian opera, and there was a similar move towards the end of the century to initiate a Portuguese opera, notably by Augusto Machado (1845–1924) and Alfredo Keil (1850–1907) – the latter's opera *A Serrana* was the first in Portuguese. In the 20th century, Luis de Freitas Branco (1890–1955) was the leading Portuguese composer to adopt a neo-classical idiom, while Frederico de Freitas (1902–80) introduced polyrhythms and polytonality into his music. The operatic tradition was continued by Ruy (Rui) Coelho (1891–1986), who studied with Schoenberg. Among the younger composers, Emmanuel Nunes (born 1941) has attracted attention with his slow, gentle textures and use of repetition. But the Portuguese composer most likely to be encountered is José **Vianna da Motta** (1868–1948).

Portuguese Music Information Centre:
Fundacao Calouste Gulbenkian
Avenida de Berna
P-1093 Lisboa
45-A codex
Portugal
tel: +351 1 793 5131
fax: +351 1 795 5139

Vianna da Motta José
born 22nd April 1868 at Isle St Thomas
died 31st May 1948 at Lisbon

Best known as a composer of piano music, Vianna da Motta was also celebrated as a pianist (and interpreter of Bach, Beethoven, and his friend **Busoni**). Having studied in Germany, where his teachers included Liszt and von Bülow, he emerged as the leader of a group of Portuguese composers who looked to folk music, and he was also the first modern Portuguese composer to use symphonic form. In spite of this German background (which contrasted with the French orientation of his Spanish contemporaries), he turned to

Portuguese folk traditions for the inspiration of his own works, helping to create a Portuguese musical nationalism chiefly through such piano works as the three *Cenas portuguesas* (*Portuguese Scenes*) and the *Five Portuguese Rhapsodies*. His earliest works (such as the lilting *Barcarolle*, published 1905 for piano) reflected his teaching, and the *Ballada* suggests grand 19th-century models. A change occurs in the first of the three series of *Cenas portuguesas*: although the influence of Chopin and Liszt is still pervasive, a very definite Iberian flavour appears in the opening and close, and a folk dance forms the basis of the middle piece. Echoes of guitar sounds appear in *Vito*, while *Trez improvisos sobre motivos populares* treat popular Portuguese themes in a restrained, unpretentious manner that is sometimes almost Impressionistic.

Vianna da Motta taught at the Geneva Conservatory (1915–17) and was director of the National Conservatory in Lisbon (1918–38). He made transcriptions of the French composer Alkan, and was co-editor of Liszt's complete piano works for the publishers Breitkopf & Härtel.

BIBLIOGRAPHY

J. de Freitas Branco, *Vianna da Motta*, 1972 (in Portuguese)

Romania

Introduction

A single figure, the violinist and composer George **Enescu** (1881–1955), towers over 20th-century Romanian classical music. One of the major composers of the twilight of Romanticism, he evolved in his later works an individual, complex, and leaner style with elements of folk music.

Enescu, out of necessity, spent much of his working life outside Romania, and no other major Romanian composer emerged in the first half of the century. Paul Constantinescu (1909–63) produced mainly late-Romantic concertos, of which the *Violin Concerto* (1957) is pleasant but unremarkable. The second half was dominated by the repressive communist regime, and the paucity of musical quality scarcely deserves comment. Composers such as Doru Popovici (born 1932) and Sigismund Toduță (born 1908) seem to have retreated into a soft regurgitation of early Romanian musics, while the *Symphony No. 4 'From West to East'* by Serban Nichifor (born 1954) has to rank among the worst ever written – a set of musical postcards of all that is most kitsch in American music, both popular and serious. There is also a *Symphony No. 3 'From East to West'*. As Romania develops after the liberation from communism and more of its music becomes disseminated, a clearer picture of the music of such composers as Stefan Niculescu (born 1927) may emerge to revise this otherwise gloomy picture.

Two composers of Romanian origin who left their native country deserve mention. Roman Vlad (born 1919) moved to Italy in 1938, becoming an Italian citizen in 1951. Marius **Constant** (born 1925) settled in Paris following his studies there in the late 1940s.

There is no Romanian music information centre.

Constant Marius*
born 7th February, 1925 at Bucharest

Constant, who moved to Paris in 1945, has pursued an unconventional path using conventional means, drawing on an eclectic range of styles, often with a touch of humour, regularly with jazz elements. He came to prominence with the *Twenty-Four Preludes* (1958) for orchestra, and his subsequent orchestral works include *Turner* (1961), a reaction to three Turner paintings. In *Les chants de Maldoror* (1962) a reciter's words prompt reaction from the conductor, and consequently from the orchestra of twenty-three instrumentalists in aleatoric fashion, while ten cellos have predetermined material.

Constant's concertos are entertaining and sometimes startling: the *Barrel Organ Concerto* (1988) includes reworkings of music for mechanical organ by Mozart and Beethoven, and produces an astonishing range of sonorities from the solo instrument. *Chorus and Interludes* (1988) for horn and orchestra is almost pure jazz, with improvisatory tenor saxophone, double bass, piano and drums, the colours of the first two neatly matching those of the solo instrument. He collaborated with Peter Brook in the famous reworking of Bizet's *Carmen* (1981), and he has written a number of ballets and music theatre works with Roland Petit, while *Candide* (1970, concert version for harpsichord and orchestra, 1971) was written for the famous mime artist Marcel Marceau.

Constant has been a notable conductor of new music, and he founded the celebrated ensemble Ars Nova in 1963.

RECOMMENDED WORK
Barrel Organ Concerto

Enescu George (also spelt Enesco, Georges)**
born 19th August 1881 at Liveni-Virnar
died 4th May 1955 at Paris

George Enescu, acknowledged as the father of modern Romanian music, was also one of the greatest violinists of the century, an infant prodigy who entered the Vienna Conservatory at the age of seven. He was also a pianist, organist and cellist, a distinguished teacher (the violinists Menuhin and Grumiaux, and the pianist Lipatti were among his pupils) and, to a lesser extent, a conductor. He always claimed that composition was for him the most important of his activities, although his output (thirty-three acknowledged works) was necessarily limited.

He studied in Paris (1893–97), and spent much of his life in France, with regular visits to his estate in Romania. A delicate French romantic charm pervades such works as the *Sept chansons de Clément Marot* (1908), and French sensibilities remained a factor in his music, but it was with music of a strong Romanian folk flavour that he first came to fame, notably the two *Romanian Rhapsodies* for orchestra of 1901 and 1902. These, in particular the stunningly exciting *No. 1* – perhaps the most convincing fusion of folk (here Romany) rhythms and orchestral forces yet written – have threatened to eclipse the rest of his compositional achievement outside his native country. His music is one of the last flowerings of the Romantic age, and is tinged throughout with the suggestions of Romanian folk music, but only rarely brings an overt folk idiom to the fore. He is in many respects the Romanian equivalent of such composers as the Pole **Szymanowski** and the Czech **Suk**; and, like the latter, his own personal language only achieved full fruition in his last works.

The thick and opulent late-Romantic textures of his symphonies have deterred many, but would probably attract as many more were they better known. In the *Symphony No. 1* (1905) the strong echoes are those of Brahms, but the work has an effective, rather sensuous slow movement, and a rousing ending. The *Symphony No. 2* (1912–14) is a less obviously earnest, more complex work, with sensual echoes of **Strauss** and **Szymanowski**, some folk influences, and with cyclic construction. It is a mixed work, at times demanding emotional attention, at others long-winded, but the opulence of the polyphony of the closing music, ending in a kind of Edwardian disintegration, is as rich as anything of the period. The rhapsodic *Symphony No. 3* (1916–18, written while the composer was looking after wounded troops on his estate in Romania) uses piano, organ and wordless chorus as well as orchestra, not for the massed effect one might expect from the previous works, but for an intense, rich and lyrical, sometimes almost introverted, expression of colour effects. The work is more a triptych of symphonic poems than a symphony. Two more symphonies were left incomplete on his death.

Of his other orchestral music, the three orchestral *Suites* are in many ways more rewarding than the symphonies, as the narrower scale seems better suited to Enescu's language. The *Suite No. 1* (1903) has a remarkable opening for strings and timpani, while the very attractive *Suite No. 2* (1915) is one of the earliest works to have a strong neo-classical flavour, with extended polyphonic writing in the first movement (prefiguring **Roussel** and **Martinů**, complete with piano in the orchestra), recalling Enescu's encyclopedic knowledge of the music of Bach. This is combined with touches of Enescu's typically sensuous and heady colours and with Romanian folk music, in a work that deserves wider appreciation, standing as it does at the crossroads between two musical epochs. The appealing *Suite No. 3* (1937), subtitled *Suite villageoise* (*Village Suite*), is different in tone and intent, describing his childhood village with contemplative transformations of folk material within a more complex and more dissonant harmonic language.

Enescu's chamber music includes three works for larger chamber forces, the *Deux intermèdes* (*Two Intermezzi*, 1902–03) for strings, the *Dixtuor* (1906) for wind instruments – gentle and sonorous in spite of its symphonic scale, with a touch of the exotic in its middle movement – and the very assured *Octet* (1900) for strings, the whole of which is one sonata form, divided in four movements. His *String Quartet No. 1* (1920) is over-long, and the *String Quartet No. 2* (1950–53) is full of French colour effects. Of his violin sonatas, the third (1926), with its strong Romanian influences, is the best known, and the second (1899) exemplifies the twin influences of the French and of Brahms.

The youthful *Octet* apart, Enescu's masterpieces are to be found among his last works. Here he changed the polyphonic flow into a more complex and more personal harmonic style, and converted the thick orchestral textures into a more luminous use of colour. Chief among these works is his only opera, *Oedipus*, which he started in 1921 (though it had been conceived earlier) and finished in 1936. Its individuality is founded on its echoes of Romanian folk music sublimated into the general style, and the extensive use of chorus. The libretto, by Edmond Fleg, distils the complete Oedipus story, as told in Sophocles' tragedies, into one opera. The two longer central acts of the four-act form provide the drama; the first act is a prologue, the last an epilogue. The ending is one of reconciliation and peace, with Oedipus retiring peacefully, his eyesight restored, to die as an old man. The score,

with its subtly shifting rhythms, its beautiful details of orchestration, and extensive use of chorus, has a strong French influence entwined with the sensual Mediterranean atmosphere. *Oedipus* is Enescu's finest work, and it is surprising that this opera is not central to the modern repertoire. More likely to be encountered is the marvellous *Vox maris*, a symphonic poem describing a storm overtaking a small craft, the lifeboat being launched, and the sea swallowing up the small craft to the sound of the Sirens. The sea then subsides, satiated. It briefly uses soprano, tenor and chorus to create the human dimension. The shifting rhythms of the sea (including the broken effect of turbulent storm-waves) and the drama are beautifully evoked, and Enescu produces vivid colour effects (including a wind-machine) within the largely Impressionist sound. It was begun in 1929 but not finished until 1951.

Enescu taught at the Ecole Normale (Paris), at the American Conservatory in Romania, and later in New York (1946–50). He founded his own string quartet in 1904, and the George Enescu Symphony Orchestra (now the George Enescu State Philharmonic Orchestra) in Bucharest in 1917, and was notable for his partnerships with Thibaud and Cortot.

RECOMMENDED WORKS

Chamber Symphony (1954)
Octet (1900) for strings
opera *Oedipus* (1921–36)
Romanian Rhapsody No. 1 (1901) for orchestra
Romanian Rhapsody No. 2 (1901) for orchestra
Suite No. 2 in C (1915) for orchestra
Suite No. 3 (*Suite villageoise*) (1937) for orchestra
Symphony No. 3 in C (1919)
Vox maris (1950) for tenor, chorus and orchestra

BIBLIOGRAPHY
N. Malcolm, *George Enescu – His Life and Music*, 1990

Russian Republic and the former Soviet Union

Preface

If this guide had appeared in the 1970s, its entry on the USSR would have looked very different. Firstly, compared with the Russian Republic the USSR commanded a wider range of geography and musical cultures. Secondly, the type of composer of whom the Soviets approved, and whose music was disseminated abroad, followed the particular precepts of Soviet music, with some notable exceptions whose range and quality of music was too great to be ignored. Consequently, it would have been necessary to devote considerable space to these composers as representative of Soviet musical thought.

The dissolution of the former USSR thus poses problems for any survey of 20th-century composers. Some lesser composers have become of importance to the heritage of their new countries; these will be found under those countries, as will such younger composers as **Pärt**, whose focus is on his country of Estonia, not the former USSR. Those better-known composers who spent most or all of their working lives in the USSR, and were promoted internationally as Soviet composers, will be found below, as will older and younger composers who were or are Russian by birth. As for some of the less interesting Soviet composers, it seems highly unlikely that anyone will celebrate their music again, for justifiable social and musical reasons. However, they may be of historical interest, and where appropriate they are surveyed in the introduction.

Introduction

By the turn of the century, Russian composition was divided into two major trends, representing differences of stylistic temperament and academic teaching rather than mutually exclusive outlooks. The first built on the achievement of Peter Ilyich Tchaikovsky (1840–93), especially in the more abstract forms of the symphony and the concerto, and was represented by Sergei Taneiev (also spelled Taneyev, 1856–1915), now best known for his four symphonies and the operatic trilogy *Oresteia*. The second followed the lead of the so-called 'Five' ('Kutchka'): Mily Alexeievich Balakirev (1837–1910), Alexander Borodin (1833–87), César Cui (1835–1918), Modest Mussorgsky (1839–81) and Nicolai Rimsky-Korsakov (1844–1908). These composers developed a nationalist school of rich, graphic tone poems and operas celebrating specifically Russian subjects, and their movement culminated in the brilliant, sumptuous and glittering orchestral magic of Rimsky-Korsakov, who was widely influential on the following generation as a teacher. In the same style were the richly orchestrated miniature tone poems of Anatol Liadov (1855–1914).

This division was clear in the earlier works of the generation coming into maturity after the turn of the century. Sergei **Rachmaninov** (1873–1943) and Nikolai **Medtner** (1880–1951) developed the tradition of Taneiev in piano works of Romantic lyricism and clarity within mostly abstract forms; in terms of the development of classical music, their idiom became increasingly anachronistic, but the sheer genius of Rachmaninov overcomes such limitations. In contrast, the early ballets of Igor **Stravinsky** (1882–1971), still his most popular works and long discussed in terms of their rhythmic and dissonant innovations, can now be seen clearly as a development of the idiom of Rimsky-Korsakov.

The academic was represented by Alexander **Glazunov** (1865–1936), who was an important teacher but whose depth of inspiration in his own works never matched his facility. The maverick of this period was the mercurial figure of Alexander **Scriabin** (1872–1915), who built on the pianistic tradition of Liszt, stretching chromatic harmonies to their breaking-point, and plunging into huge visions of spirituality and mysticism in both orchestral and piano works. His harmonic innovations and the intensity of his personal vision suggested the possibility of alternatives to a younger generation of composers, but his influence was more through example than through specific musical styles, a position analogous to that of his French contemporary **Satie**. Of the other composers working in this period, Alexander Grechaninov (also spelled Gretchaninov, 1864–1956) produced in the *Liturgica Domestica* (1917), for two tenors, baritone, bass, chorus and chamber orchestra, one of the finest of all Russian liturgical settings, strongly recommended to those who respond to Eastern European church musics. His secular music is extremely conservative, following in the tradition of Tchaikovsky. He moved to Paris in 1922, and to the USA in 1939.

As the 1917 Bolshevik Revolution completely destroyed the old cultural and social orders, a new generation of extraordinarily talented composers was emerging, who would form the backbone of 20th-century Russian music. There was **Stravinsky** himself, who moved to Switzerland in 1914, and whose series of abrupt stylistic changes, from the innovation of music theatre works in and immediately after World War I, to the development of neo-classicism in the 1920s and 1930s, and the eventual adoption of 12-tone techniques in the 1950s, made him the dominant international composer of the middle of the century, scorned, derided and exiled by the Soviet authorities. The precocious Sergei **Prokofiev** (1891–1953) produced brilliant, savage, tumultuous and dissonant music, only tenuously holding on to traditional harmonies. After returning to the USSR after a period of exile, he developed a melodically distinctive lyrical style, especially in his ballets and symphonies, that was largely acceptable to the Soviet authorities and which includes some of the most joyous and descriptively memorable music of the century. The more dour Nikolai **Miaskovsky** (1881–1950) concentrated on the traditional forms of the symphony and the quartet.

The finest composer of the following generation was Dmitri **Shostakovich** (1906–75). His life was almost a metaphor for the vicissitudes, the horrors and the triumphs of the Soviet Union itself; much of his music reflects the vacuous requirements of the Soviet authorities, and for long Western critics mistook such musical platitudes for the substance of his music. However, his major works (especially the symphonies and the string quartets) cover the widest expression of human emotions and the most complete fusion of the personal and the public since Beethoven. After his early experimental works, his essentially conservative idiom represents an unusual amalgamation of influences: the dark drive and classical formality of **Hindemith**, the eclecticism and large-scale of **Mahler**, and especially the spare, anguished and intense musical world of Mussorgsky, whose music he knew in its original unadulterated form, rather than in the heavily Romanticised orchestrations by others that were invariably played outside Russia. The influence of **Shostakovich** has been considerable, if subtle: his melodic fingermarks and general sound pervade Russian music after 1945, and

regularly appear in the music of other countries.

The period following the Revolution was one of fertile excitement and experimentation in all the arts, reflecting the new interest in industrialisation and the search for ways of expressing the primacy of the people, exemplified in the work of the poet Mayakovsky; the philosophical gulf between **Scriabin's** late theosophist visions of 1905–1910 and **Prokofiev's** *Age of Steel* ballet of 1925–26 is vast. The major musical equivalent to Constructivism was the music of Alexander Mosolov (1900–73). His *Zavod* (*Iron Foundry*), a short orchestral mechanical whirlwind drawn from the ballet *Steel* (1926–28) became a *cause célèbre*; much derided by critics, it remains the powerful epitome of motoric music. His *Piano Concerto No. 1* (1926–27) is equally insistent and anti-Romantic, with its harsh dissonances held in the iron claw of motoric rhythm and an extraordinary polystylism in the near-atonal central movement. This brash, outrageous work deserves revival, as it so encapsulates an aspect of its age.

Under the aegis of two major musical groups, the Russian Association of Proletarian Music and the Association for Contemporary Music, opera turned to an anti-Romantic, direct declamatory style, exemplified by *The North Wind* (1930) by Lev Knipper (1898–1974; see under 'Georgia, Introduction'). Repertoire operas were rewritten with proletarian librettos, and such contemporary works as **Berg's** *Wozzeck* were heard. At the same time the genre of the massed song was being developed by serious composers, leading to a genre of the large-scale patriotic oratorio. An historically interesting and occasionally effective early example of this is Knipper's *Symphony No. 4 'Poem about the Komsomol Fighter'* (1934), in which the essentially simple folk material (including the famous song 'Poliushko') is laid in a huge, epic-scale orchestral bed.

This experimental period in Soviet music came to an abrupt end with the rise of Stalin and the imposition of the official Soviet line of 'socialist realism' in 1932. Applied to music, it meant a return to straightforward 19th-century tonal harmonies in bright orchestral colours; harmonic experimentation was denounced as 'formalism'. The preferred forms were epic-scale symphonies, large oratorios, and operas with communist or patriotic subjects; the required tone was the joy or triumph of the Soviet system and the Soviet people, that had to overcome any tragic elements. This inevitably leaned towards programmatic rather than abstract music. **Shostakovich** was one of the first to fall foul of this Philistine aesthetic: his highly successful opera *Lady Macbeth of the Mtsensk District* (1934) was condemned for its psychological realism by Stalin in 1936, leading to the composer's withdrawal of the *Symphony No. 4* (1936) and to his placatory (but musically sincere) response in the lyrical-epic *Symphony No. 5* (1937).

The leading composers of this period succumbed to this formula. Ivan Dzerzhinsky (1909–78) combined a revolutionary story, Cossack folk songs, and a direct and dramatic melodic idiom in the opera *Quiet Flows the Don* (1935), based on the famous novel written – or apparently plagiarised – by Sholokhov. Yuri Shaporin (1887–1966), whose early works had included such modernist pieces as the suite *The Flea* (the orchestration of which includes wind, sixteen domras, three bayans, flexaton and percussion), now produced such works as the cantata *Battle for the Russian Land* (1944), an effective example of its patriotic genre, and the quintessential Soviet opera, *The Decembrists* (1925–53).

The most convincing composer of a socialist realist style was Georgi **Sviridov** (1915–98), for its limitations suited his own temperament. His work, influenced by Kursk folk songs, reflected another trend promoted by the Soviet authorities, the inclusion in classical music of the widely varying folk musics of the different 'autonomous Republics'. Mikhail Ippolitov-Ivanov (1859–1935) had provided a model in his best-known works, the two colourful, late-Romantic suites of *Caucasian Sketches* (No. 1, 1894, No. 2, 1896). Uzeir Gadzhibekov (1885–1948) established an Azerbaijani nationalistic style, although the first Azerbaijani opera was *Shah-Senem*, by the Ukrainian Reinhold **Glière** (1875–1956). Glière's ballet *The Red Poppy* (1927) was also the first Soviet ballet to present a heroic revolutionary theme, and he retained official approval throughout his career. Zakhary **Paliashvili** (1872–1933; see under 'Georgia') pioneered the application of Georgian music to classical forms. Otar Taktakishvili (1924–89) wrote Georgian operas, and his *Symphony No. 2* (1953) was based on Georgian themes. The most notable of the Soviet composers who based much of their art on folk influences was Aram **Khatchaturian** (1903–78; see under 'Armenia'), whose was at his best when incorporating Armenian colours and scales, and at his worst when attempting the full-blown Soviet epic. This nationalist trend continued throughout the Soviet period.

The new generation of mainstream composers was represented by the lyrical, neo-Romantic idiom of Dmitri **Kabalevsky** (1904–87), and by the unfortunate figure of Tikhon Khrennikov (born 1913), who as Secretary-General (appointed 1948) and Chairman of the USSR Composers' Union (1949–1991), imposed the official line. His own music is unimaginative and undistinguished, although the song 'We should be ploughing' from the opera *The Storm* (1939) is exceptionally beautiful in a simplistic fashion, and is worthy of exploration by male-voice choirs. His shallow *Piano Concerto No. 2* (1974) opens with a 12-tone row, as if trying to emulate the coming freedoms, but quickly establishes the home key of C major. The four early symphonies of Vissarion **Shebalin** (1902–63) show his early influences (Borodin and **Miaskovsky**, his teacher, in the *Symphony No. 1*, 1928), his interest in abstract structure (the passacaglia, fugue and coda in *Symphony No. 3*, 1934–35) and his involvement in Soviet themes: the two-movement *Symphony No. 4* (1935) is dedicated to the heroes of Perekop, the site of an heroic action in the civil war. This aspect of Shebalin's output is exemplified in the *Dramatic Symphony 'Lenin'* (1931–32) for soloists, chorus and orchestra, which is one of the first of the particularly Soviet genre of the 'song-symphony'. Planned originally as a much larger work, it has for its text a poem by Mayakovsky on the death of Lenin, but the first of three rather disconnected movements is purely instrumental, and much the most alluring in a work that is otherwise only of historical interest. However, most of his output avoided political or social themes and, apart from some orchestral works, is dominated by the abstract form of the string quartet.

In 1948 a wave of repression was triggered by the gentle dissonances in the opera *The Great Friendship* (1947) by the otherwise innocuous Georgian composer Vano Muradeli (1908–70). The attacks, led by Andrei Zhdanov, included condemnation of **Shostakovich, Prokofiev, Miaskovsky** and Knipper. Shebalin especially suffered, ironically after winning a State Prize in the same year – one of his denouncers was his pupil Khrennikov. The definition of formalism was widened, and it is an indication of the complete exclusion of Western musical trends since the 1930s that when Rodion **Shchedrin** (born 1932) called for opportunities to hear Western contemporary music in a brave article in 1955, he was referring to **Mahler, Debussy** and **Ravel** rather than **Webern, Messiaen** or **Boulez**. The 1950s were perhaps the bleakest period of Soviet music. While **Shostakovich** managed to produce powerful works that responded to the darkness of the times, he also had to write the most Soviet of his symphonies, the programmatic eleventh and twelfth, and his soviet realist works of this period are his most banal. **Shchedrin**, the bright young light of Soviet music, was composing in an idiom that would have found a home fifty years earlier, relieved only by his perky humour. Mosolov, the epitome of the revolutionary 1920s, was reduced to writing pretty but vacuous suites and popular choruses on folk themes. The symphonist Moisei **Vainberg** (1919–96) was praised for his 'reorientation', and partly turned to the inspiration of folk musics as a safe solution.

The thaw of the Khruschov period was musically led by **Shostakovich**, whose collaborations with the young poet Yevgeny Yevtushenko (*Symphony No. 13 'Babi Yar'*, 1962, and *The Execution of Stepan Razin*, 1964) challenged socialist realism. Viacheslav Ovchinikov (born 1936) produced, in his *Symphony No. 1* (1960), a fine, emotive work which is well worth the discovery (his *Symphony No. 2* for strings is actually earlier, being a 1972–73 revision of a 1956 work). Like other younger composers, however, he could still descend into the banality of the cantata *Song-ballad of BAM Builders* (1974) for bass, chorus and orchestra. **Shchedrin** accumulated some of the tricks and techniques of the Western avant-garde, though without yet integrating them into a personal and individual idiom. The Ukrainian Boris Liatoshinsky (1895–1968; see under 'Ukraine') encouraged his pupils to explore the new Western ideas, but the most prominent promoter of new ideas was Edison Denisov (1929–96), who became president of the revived Association of Contemporary Music. In the 1960s he became interested in serialism and in chamber works for unusual instrumental combinations, but his best-known work is the rather elusive *Symphony* (1987; he has also written a *Chamber Symphony*, 1983). This is swaddled in dense layers of overlapping blocks of sound, somewhat in the manner of the Polish avant-garde, and broken into by high tuned percussion and bells. Its power comes from the clash of themes representing the opposition of light and darkness, and the conflict and resolution following those clashes, leading sometimes

to the darker forces gaining the upper hand, sometimes to a dense but limpid beauty and vivid colouristic effects. Denisov's other works include the opera *L'écume des jours* (1981), concertos, and song-cycles.

Boris Tishchenko (born 1939) came to prominence with the *Cello Concerto No. 1* (1959, apparently orchestrated by **Shostakovich**). Written for cello, seventeen wind instruments, percussion and harmonium or organ, this is an intense, troubled, sometimes slightly mawkish work, in which the tone is set by a long, very spare and impassioned solo cello opening. In his symphonies he has preferred five-movement forms. The *Symphony No. 3* (1966), inspired, like the *Requiem* (1966), by Akhmatova's lament for her assassinated husband, is divided into a long opening four-movement arc, 'Meditation', and a shorter 'Postscript'. Written for a chamber-sized orchestra, it includes haunting, disembodied orchestral effects, with plaintive woodwind and brass solos reminiscent of his teacher Shostakovich, and, briefly, two wordless solo voices. The magnificent *Symphony No. 5* (1974), again in five movements, is a tribute to Shostakovich, quoting and remoulding in a more modern guise major passages from his teacher's most important works, as well as quotations from Tishchenko's own music. The symphony, with its plaintive opening and close, is also a commentary on the Soviet epic symphony: Tishchenko is prepared to show darker, more turbulent emotions and the viability of an alternative epic utterance. The *Violin Concerto No. 2* (1982) follows the Shostakovich tradition of mawkish irony on a symphonic scale. An essentially traditional composer who has effectively absorbed aspects of more recent musical developments, Tishchenko may emerge as one of the major Russian voices of his generation. Of other composers of this generation, the later harmonic touches and colours of Andrei Petrov (born 1930) suggest an awareness of such Western composers as **Berg** and **Messiaen**. His idiom is contrapuntal, and includes a mawkish humour; the '*Poem*' *To the Memory of the Victims of the Siege of Leningrad* (1965–66), for strings, organ, four trumpets and percussion (including piano used percussively), is perhaps his best-known work in the West (under various English translations of the title), although here the chromatic harmonic vocabulary is used to rather heavy-handed effect rather than as substance. His opera *Peter I* (1972–75) is on the grandest scale and the most weighty historical subject.

Other composers who worked in styles that did not meet official expectations still await a proper evaluation. Prominent among these is Galina **Ustvolskaya** (born 1919), whose powerful idiom music is gradually becoming more widely appreciated. A number of younger composers, little known until the break-up of the Soviet Union, have since achieved widespread international prominence. Arvo **Pärt** (born 1935) will be found under his home country of Estonia. Alfred **Schnittke** (1934–98), the most important Russian composer of his generation, has evolved an eclectic mainstream idiom of considerable emotional power, especially in works using large orchestral forces. Sofia **Gubaidulina** (born 1931) has attracted attention with her neo-Romantic, sparse idiom that displays a spiritual intensity and sometimes uses religious symbolism. **Shchedrin** seemed to have finally evolved a personal and individual idiom in the 1980s. Of the other younger Russian composers who have absorbed post-Soviet techniques, Elena Firsova (born 1950) and her husband, Dmitri Smirnov (born 1948), many of whose compositions invoke the English poet William Blake, left Russia in 1991.

Glazunov Alexander Konstantinovich**

born 10th August 1865 at St Petersburg
died 21st March 1936 at Paris

Alexander Glazunov is a prime example of a composer whose artistic imagination failed to match his exceptional gifts and his technical facility. His career spanned the change from the Romantic era to that of experimental modernity, with which he was familiar through his directorship of the St Petersburg (later the Leningrad) Conservatory (1895–1928); among his pupils were **Miaskovsky** and **Prokofiev**. He himself gradually evolved from Russian Romanticism to a sterner classicism, and was one of the last composers in the Russian 19th-century tradition, although unlike most of his precursors he concentrated on tone poems, ballets and symphonies, and he did not compose an opera.

The two main features of his work are a vibrant sense of orchestration, learnt from of one the greatest orchestrators of any age, his teacher Rimsky-Korsakov (1844–1908), and a consistent sense of optimism. There is little that is dark or

troubled in any of his work, and this absence is one of the reasons for its ultimate failure; another is his inability to create really memorable themes within a style that so often requires them.

His eight symphonies were all written between 1880 and 1905, and are consistent in their general approach and in their technical means. Movements are often monothematic, and Glazunov built his material by the extensive manipulation of those themes, sometimes bringing them back in other movements (for example the motto theme of the *Symphony No. 2*, 1886), or disguised in completely different orchestral colours, and by building up ideas from short fragments. Ultimately the lack of interesting development, and sometimes of interesting countermaterial, becomes tedious. His finales are usually more notable for their exuberant noise than for their invention, and generally the most successful movements are the scherzos, when Glazunov could draw on his flair for colour and rhythm. Perhaps the symphonies are better appreciated if approached more in the spirit of colourful orchestral scores than for their symphonic language. The *Symphony No. 1* (1880) is an extraordinarily assured work for someone who had not reached the age of sixteen, and was responsible for the formation of the important and distinguished Russian publishing house, Belyaev: its founder was so moved by the first performance that he determined there and then to publish music. The *Symphony No. 3* (1892, possibly 1890) was dedicated to Tchaikovsky, while the happy influence of his ballet music is evident in the scherzo of the *Symphony No. 4* (1893), subtitled *The Lyrical*. The *Symphony No. 5* (1895) has more epic pretensions, with echoes of Wagner, though again its scherzo is the most successful movement, with celesta and glockenspiel prominent in the atmospheric orchestration. In the *Symphony No. 6* (1896), Glazunov's increasing interest in a more formal classical style is evident in the almost neo-classical intermezzo third movement. Otherwise this is the symphony most overtly indebted to the example of Tchaikovsky. The *Symphony No. 7* (1902) has sometimes been singled out for praise, and its mood reflects its intentional allusion to Beethoven's *Pastoral* symphony in its F major key and in the open fifths of its opening theme. Its scherzo quotes from a Slav folk tune. The *Symphony No. 8* (1905) has attracted the most adherents and detractors alike. A ninth symphony, begun in 1910, was left incomplete at Glazunov's death.

The *Violin Concerto* (1904), perhaps Glazunov's best-known work, follows the tradition of the virtuoso violin concerto. Its lyricism is unashamedly Romantic, and the attention is focused on the flowing solo line, further emphasised by the seamless three-movement form, played without a break. The characteristic lack of a really memorable theme is a handicap, but it is redeemed by the song-like nature of the solo writing. The one-movement *Saxophone Concerto* (1934) is a beguiling work, of chamber proportions, written for alto saxophone. There is no suggestion of jazz influence, but rather a gentle pastoralism, as if we were being slowly transported by the lazy movement of the soloist's boat down a pleasant river, with its varying river-bank scenery. But the best music is undoubtably that for the ballets *Raymonda* (1896–97) and *The Seasons* (1899–1901), once a perennial favourite in concert programmes and still refreshing in its colours and vivacity. Some of his numerous smaller orchestral works, such as the tone poems *Spring* (*Vesna*, 1891) and *Stenka Razin* (1885), telling the story of the Cossack rebel-hero, display Glazunov's virtues at their best, while minimising his weaknesses. They lack the punch and depth of similar works by **Bax**, **Suk** or **Sibelius**, but make pleasant diversions; American readers might respond to the *Triumphal March* (1892) that creates an indeed triumphal version of the American song 'John Brown's Body', while just avoiding bombast.

Glazunov was historically an important figure as a dedicated and skilful, if conservative, teacher. With Rimsky-Korsakov he was also responsible for the sorting and preservation of Borodin's music (he reconstructed the overture and sections of Act III of the opera *Prince Igor* from his prodigious memory). He emigrated to Paris in 1928, when the Soviet regime became more repressive after the death of Lenin, and it was there that **Prokofiev** found him, a rather pathetic and broken alcoholic figure. The *Violin Concerto* and the two major ballets seem destined to survive for their exuberant colour, and certainly make a worthy change for jaded palettes.

RECOMMENDED WORKS
  ballet *Raymonda* (1896–97)
  Saxophone Concerto (1934)
  ballet *The Seasons* (1899–1901)
  Symphony No. 7 (1902)

Symphony No. 8 (1905)
Violin Concerto (1904)

Glière (Glier) Reinhold (Reyngol'd) Moritzovich*
born 11th January 1875 at Kiev
died 23rd June 1956 at Moscow

The prolific Reinhold Glière, of Belgian descent, was the grand old man of Soviet composition. His revolutionary credentials were solid enough (he prudently left Russia for two years in 1905, having signed a protest manifesto), and his music, firmly rooted in the Russian Romantic tradition and generally avoiding the darker or more tragic moods, could be upheld as a model against 'formalism'.

Of his output of more than five hundred compositions, only a few, mainly orchestral works are likely to be encountered. The *Symphony No. 1* (1899–1900) is an assured if derivative work in the tradition of Tchaikovsky, with a perky scherzo that could have come from a ballet score, and a general youthful exuberance. The *Symphony No. 2* (1908) is an altogether finer work, while maintaining the same tradition, with something of the towering monumentality of **Sibelius** in the first movement. The rest of the symphony is less inspired but maintains its interest, especially in the variations of the third movement and the thrust of the finale; the symphony is well worth investigation by those who enjoy the still undervalued genre of the late-Romantic symphony. Glière's masterpiece is generally considered to be the *Symphony No. 3 'Ilya Murometz'* (1910–11). The full scope of this programmatic symphony is epic: it is some ninety minutes in length, and is usually heard in versions that cut it down to a more manageable size; opinions are divided as to whether in its full length it outstays its welcome, or whether it needs to be heard in its monumental whole. Vibrant, teeming and heady, with a first movement heroic in tone and scale, its has a sensuous abandon in its atmosphere and tone-painting, with Impressionistic touches in the second movement. But perhaps his best work is the gorgeous tone poem *The Sirens* (1908), musically invoking not the Mediterranean but the misty Nordic world of **Sibelius**, as if the sirens were calling from the fjords. This atmosphere is combined with a rich, almost Impressionistic orchestral tapestry, a fervour worthy of **Bax**, and a Russian sense of purpose in the rhythms and the main melodies.

The most popular work by Glière has probably been the ballet *The Red Poppy* (1927), the first Soviet ballet to present an heroic revolutionary theme. Although set in China, it is a model of Soviet Socialist Realism, with a traditional harmonic idiom, clean poster-paint colours tinged with Eastern exoticisms, and a suitable touch of sentimentality in the tunes; the 'Scene and Dance with Goldfingers' will particularly appeal to devotees of epic Hollywood film scores. Its success was followed by that of the ballet *The Bronze Horseman* (1949), based on Pushkin; both works are expertly crafted for the ballet stage. The unashamedly Romantic and attractive *Harp Concerto* (1938) has maintained a precarious hold on the repertoire, partly because of the shortage of such works.

In the 1920s Glière made extensive studies of the indigenous music of Azerbaijan, and later Uzbekistan and his home area of Ukraine. The opera *Shah-Senem* (1925, revised 1934), used Azerbaijani folk songs, telling the story of a poor champion of the people who wins the right to the hand of the Princess (of the title) in a musical contest, and eventually gains her after an uprising of the people. Of his later operas, *Hulsara* drew on Ukrainian folk music, *Rachael* was based on Guy de Maupassant, and *Mademoiselle Fifi* was set in the Franco-Prussian war of 1870–71.

Glière was director of the Kiev Conservatory (1914–20) and taught at the Moscow Conservatoire (1921–56). His many pupils included **Khatchaturian**, Knipper, **Miaskovsky**, Mosolov and **Prokofiev**.

RECOMMENDED WORKS
Symphony No. 2 op.25 (1908)
Symphony No. 3 *Ilya Murometz* op.42 (1909–11)
ballet *The Red Poppy* (1927)
The Sirens op.33 (1908) for orchestra

Gubaidulina Sophia*
born 24th October 1931 at Christopol (Tartar Republic)

Sophia Gubaidulina is one of the Soviet composers who emerged after *glasnost*, and immediately attracted some attention outside the (then) USSR. Her avant-garde techniques were presumably responsible for her obscurity before the cultural relaxations, and helped attract the interest of Western commentators curious to encounter a more 'advanced' ex-Soviet composer. Her music, like that of a number of other Eastern European composers who came into prominence in the 1980s, is imbued with an intense spirituality, exemplified in the *Seven Last Words* (1982) for bayan, cello and string orchestra, where the bayan (a type of accordion) represents the human and the cello the spiritual.

The works that established her reputation suggested a composer of considerable talents, whose more advanced qualities had already been covered by the major Western composers of the avant-garde period of the 1960s and 1970s. For example the *Homage to Maria Svetsvaya* (1974) for unaccompanied choir uses many of the choral devices familiar to the 1960s avant-garde, from cluster effects to half-spoken passages and pointillism; it is quite effective (especially with the element of rich Russian bass lines), but less striking than a host of similar choral works from the Europe of the 1960s and 1970s.

It was with the violin concerto *Offertorium* (1979–80, subsequent revisions) that Gubaidulina achieved a distinctive and individual voice. It opens with a theme from Bach's *Musical Offering*, which creates a 12-tone row (though with repeated notes), and is treated pointillistically among the instruments in the manner of **Webern**. Various devices are then used to suggest 'conversion', such as the shortening of the theme by one note at the beginning and one at the end in a series of variations. The last of three sections reconstructs the theme from the centre out, but in reverse; in the coda, the final D of the original theme (omitted from the opening statement) is given to provide resolution. This highly organised formal structure is of interest in itself, but also as a background to the expressive qualities of the work. The first section covers a wide range of textures and colours, with telling details of instrumental emphasis and effects, and moments creating hushed expectations of impending mysteries, all forming a kind of discursive exploration. The middle section concentrates on a beautiful, hymn-like meditation from the soloist with an accompaniment giving the effect of an improvisatory folk orchestra; the third section is a return to the more fragmented moods of the first, and knowledge of the structure is useful in threading through what might otherwise seem rather fragmented ideas.

The mastery evident in *Offertorium* was confirmed in the *Symphony 'Stimmen . . . Verstummen'* (1986), using an organ in the orchestration. Its structure is unusual: twelve movements in which a motto-like section of magical delicacy and dancing movement recurs, transformed by the passages that precede each recurrence, and providing a thread of organic development. This structure is logical and easy to follow, even if it does not carry quite the impact of more conventional symphonic developments. Much of the content draws on techniques developed by the Polish avant-garde: step-like motion up and down, blending the colours and textures of the orchestra as it moves, creating fluctuating strata of sound. But this is handled with great surety and an ear for colour, and is allied with more Russian elements, the tolling of a bell, horns over a plucked bass, sonorous climaxes. The emotional range is considerable, and if it does not have the rigorous logic of a more conventional structure (at times the work can seem like a very sophisticated suite), the symphony is a compelling and memorable work.

Gubaidulina also shows a predilection for the minutiae of instrumental technique and the manipulation of instruments. She sometimes creates the effect of two or more instruments acting almost independently, as in the bare lines and plucking effects of the introverted *String Quartet No. 3* (1987) or in the five movements of *Rejoice!* (1981) for violin and cello, inspired by the Ukrainian philosopher Grigory Skovoroda; indeed these effects are more interesting than the rest of the content. A similar concern for bare lines emerges in *Hommage à TS Eliot* (1987) for octet and soprano, where the octave swoops, given harmonic uncertainty by being set against a contrasting note (for example a major seventh) are reminiscent of late **Shostakovich**. The voice has only a small part to play, and the effects include very tonal fanfares from the horn, eventually creating an atmosphere that recalls **Britten**; the piece was composed in both English and Russian versions of the texts, drawn from *The Four Quartets*. The short *String Quartet No. 2* (1987) opens with tense, overlapping departures from a central, repeated G; even when the lines attempt to open up in a more wide-ranging lyricism, there is still a feeling of constriction and containment, of material straining to be released and never being allowed to. The *String Quartet No. 4* (1994) uses tape.

It is still too early to provide comprehensive assessment of Gubaidulina's achievement; little of her earlier music has appeared in the West, and her finest achievements would appear to have been her more recent music, suggesting a composer still in the full flight of late development, and one well worth encountering.

RECOMMENDED WORKS
> *Hommage à TS Eliot* (1987) for octet and soprano
> violin concerto *Offertorium* (1979–80)
> Symphony *Stimmen ... Verstummen* (1986)

Kabalevsky Dmitri Borisovich
born 30th December 1904 at St Petersburg
died 14th February 1987 at Moscow

The undemanding and melodious idiom of Dmitri Kabalevsky, firmly rooted in the harmonies and structures of the 19th century, commended him to the Soviet authorities. However, if a large number of his works reflect political aims (such as *The Song of the Party Membership Card*, 1956, for chorus and orchestra), there are a number that happily reflect his cheerful and lyrical voice, unencumbered by political messages.

Chief among these are the three concertos written with young people in mind (though not necessarily to be played *by* the less experienced), which are neo-classical in form and in the clarity of orchestration, but have a Romantic lyricism. The glory of the first of these, the *Violin Concerto* (1948), is the bitter-sweet lyrical outpouring of the slow movement, that requires a mellow richness of solo tone for full effect. Its simplicity is perfectly judged (as in the arpeggio solo passages over the theme in the orchestral violins), and it is framed by a dancing opening movement that flashes by at a canter, and a finale that gradually changes the mood to the boisterous and the perky. Within its intended limitations this is a most infectious concerto. The other two youth concertos follow a similar format. The *Cello Concerto No. 1* (1948–49) is again richly lyrical, its slow movement more lamenting as if haunted by past tragedy, and the finale has a pleasant folkish lilt. The *Piano Concerto No. 3 'Youth'* (1952) has its memorable moments, but has too many pale reminders of **Rachmaninov**, **Shostakovich** (of the first piano concerto) and, especially, **Prokofiev** to achieve an independent identity.

Of his symphonies, the first two include chorus and are on patriotic subjects, while the *Symphony No. 4* (1954) has a very beguiling first movement, in which the beautiful, slow, plaintive opening is countered by an epic theme and by lyrical tone-painting. The slow second movement, which has musical connections with the opera *The Family of Taras*, continues the plaintive-epic mood; the scherzo is a waltz, and while the finale is too brazen and obvious for comfort, this is an attractive while undemanding symphony. The suite *The Comedians* (1940) used to be quite well known; based on music for a children's play, it is bright, perky and well orchestrated, belonging to the world of the Pops orchestra.

The best known of his operas is *Colas Breugnon* (1936–38, also known as *The Craftsman of Clamecy*), based on the novel by the French writer (and excellent music critic) Romain Rolland. Rolland was displeased with the libretto, and Kabalevsky revised the opera, first in 1953, and then again in 1969, attempting to return the libretto to the spirit of the book and its central character. The background is 16th-century rural France; the hero is a carver and sculptor, for whom laughter and a bubbling joy of life overcome misfortunes. There is little of the direct social comment common in Soviet operas, although the Duke and the priest are given unsympathetic portraits. The opera, which covers some forty years, is written in a folk-opera style and a completely tonal, lyrical idiom, and is full of pleasant tunes. There is no attempt to use the musical opportunities of the period; idiomatically, the setting could be 19th-century Russia, and even the *Dies irae* is in Orthodox style. The libretto is perhaps more interesting than the music, and the colourful overture is better known than the whole opera, which is perhaps as it should be. The opera *Before Moscow* (1942) concerned the events of the repulsion of the Nazis at Moscow in 1941, while the heroine of *The Family of Taras* (1944–47), based on Gogol, is a young Komsomol woman. Kabalevsky's songs include settings of Shakespeare sonnets.

Kabalevsky's piano pieces for children and beginners are particularly recommended; all written with charm, they range from the extreme simplicity of *A Game* to complex and exacting pieces, and make an interesting alternative to the usual repertoire; a specific skill is developed or tested in each piece.

RECOMMENDED WORKS
Cello Concerto No. 1 (1948–49)
Symphony No. 4 (1956)
Violin Concerto (1948)

Khatchaturian
see under Armenia

Medtner (Metner) Nikolai Karlovich[*]
born 5th January 1880 at Moscow
died 13th November 1951 at London

Although he wrote little, Medtner was a composer of refined sensibilities, with classical tendencies and a Romantic imagination. He left Russia in 1921 and lived in Germany (1921–24) and Paris (1926–36) before finally settling in Britain. Apart from three piano concertos and about a hundred songs, all his output was for piano or small chamber forces, and has enjoyed a minor revival since the 1970s. His music might have fallen into complete obscurity had it not been for the Maharajah of Mysor, the patron of a Medtner Society that arranged, from 1948, for Medtner to make recordings of his compositions.

On hearing the *Piano Concerto No. 1* (1914–18), it is not difficult to see why Medtner's music has its adherents. It has, at the base, an easily assimilable harmonic idiom in the tradition of the 19th century, an unusual construction to keep the intellectual attention, and enough unexpected rhythmic and harmonic effects to add a twist of modernism without undue threat. Constructed in one movement in sonata form, with each section of the form acting as the equivalent of a movement, it opens in the grand virtuoso Romantic manner, but immediately its chromatic twists and rhythmic irregularities and shifts indicate an unusual sensibility. The idiom might be described as **Rachmaninov** with more difficulties and volatility, a fascinating, anachronistic attempt to draw out 19th-century sensibilities into the 20th (one would scarcely credit without knowing its dates that the composer had witnessed World War I and the Bolshevik Revolution during its composition). Within those limitations, it is a work of great accomplishment and interest, and will enrich the repertoire of those who feel incapable of moving beyond the 19th-century in their musical tastes. By the *Piano Concerto No. 3* (c. 1940–43), his style had become even more reminiscent of early Rachmaninov, in phrasing, in the relationship between the soloist and orchestra, and in its emotional mould. Here the rhythmic irregularities and chromaticism are less evident than in the first concerto, and there are occasional echoes of Tchaikovsky. But it is not entirely a clone (as is, for example, the

Harty piano concerto), and there is enough conviction in the consistent lyrical flow to make this concerto well worth hearing for those who enjoy such an idiom.

The twelve piano sonatas follow much the same pattern as the concertos, with formal designs contained in single spans, internally divided into sections corresponding to movements, and often with a single linking idea. The other piano music ranges from the delightful and precocious *Stimmungsbilde* (*Mood Pictures* 1896–97) to ten sets of *Fairy Tales*, a series of miniatures that cover much of his compositional life. Another fine work which occupied much of Medtner's life is the *Piano Quintet* (1903–49), which by the standards of 19th-century conventions is unusual in form: the weight is shifted to the finale (the only sonata movement), which includes themes from the previous movements. It must be said that if one heard this work 'blind' one would be fairly astonished to discover that it was written in the 20th century.

RECOMMENDED WORKS
    Piano Concerto No. 1 (1914–18)
    Piano Concerto No. 3 (c. 1940–43)
    Piano Quintet (1903–49)

Miaskovsky (Myaskovsky) Nikolai Yakovlevich**
born 20th April 1881 at Novogiorgievsk (near Warsaw)
died 8th August 1950 at Moscow

The music of the prolific Nikolai Miaskovsky has been overshadowed by that of his contemporary **Prokofiev** and the younger **Shostakovich**, but after those two composers he is the major Russian symphonist of the first half of the century. He has the reputation of an extreme conservative, but this is a mistaken one, largely based on such later works as the *Violin Concerto* and the *Symphony No. 23*. For while neither a harmonic nor a formal revolutionary, he developed a complex and unsettled idiom within the forms and general harmonic usage of a continuing tradition, much as **Bax** and **Vaughan Williams** did in their symphonies, before turning to a simpler and more direct utterance. The emotional struggles in these works are as much of the 20th century as those of such contemporaries (Miaskovsky himself described the struggle as that between subjective emotional response and objective classical serenity); what they lack are the distinctive personal idiomatic touches

that might have secured him a more lasting place in the repertoire. Nonetheless, the sincerity of that struggle is palpable in the best of his works, and well worth hearing. Through all his output runs a streak of melancholy or nostalgia, often counterpoised by brighter material as if Miaskovsky was determined to overcome it. This emerges as a lament for transience, particularly that of the countryside (overt in the *Symphony No. 5*); there is a strong pastoral streak in his music, which in his late works evolves into echoes of folk idioms.

At the heart of his output are twenty-seven symphonies and thirteen string quartets. His earlier works were influenced by **Scriabin**, most obviously in such works as the *Piano Sonata No. 3* (actually the eighth written), where the heavily chromatic, quasi-improvisatory writing has a similar heady atmosphere of the visionary mystic. The *Symphony No. 3* (1914), in two movements, still shows the influence of Scriabin and **Glière**, but Miaskovsky then developed a symphonic idiom of complex shapes, unusual construction (often built on thematic cells, and sometimes with two- or one-movement structures), and, within the basic dichotomy already outlined, turbulent emotions, all founded on a traditional sense of harmony and structure. The *Symphony No. 5* (1918), in four movements, seems to reflect the contrast between the former peacefulness of the countryside Medtner saw on the retreat from Galacia while serving in the army, and the horrors of the war. It opens with forest murmurings, and a lovely broad counter-theme, while the lullaby second movement has a dark, unsettling, nightmarish aspect. A Galacian Christmas carol is used in the trio of the bucolic scherzo. The fine *Symphony No. 6* (1922–23), for chorus and orchestra, using folk song, French revolutionary songs and the *Dies irae*, reflected his growing social awareness. The *Symphony No. 7* (1922) brings the turbulent emotions to the fore in a musically unsettled mood where there are touches of Mahlerian influence in the treatment, if not the layout. The two movements are played without a break, creating the feel of one span, especially as the theme of the first movement returns in the second. The concise span of the *Symphony No. 10* (1927) makes it one of the most effective of his symphonies, with the kind of murmuring opening at which Miaskovsky was so skilled, and a general contrast between a plaintive and a disturbed, angry mood. The *Symphony No.*

12 (1931–32) symbolized life on the collective farms, and the introverted *Symphony No. 13* (1933) and the *Symphony No. 17* (1936–37) have been highly regarded. By the *Symphony No. 21* (1939–40), a short, one-movement symphony that progresses from the big and brazen towards a warm, noble mood, the emotional content was being held over longer spans, with less sudden change. The *Symphony No. 22* (1941) reflected the events that preceded it (the peace before the war and the Nazi invasion) in one movement divided into three sections. With the very attractive *Symphony No. 23* (1942), subtitled 'Symphonic Suite on Caucasian Themes', Miaskovsky moved to a simpler, very direct idiom incorporating folk-music elements, partly out of a desire to reach the widest possible audience. The heart of the work lies in the first two of three movements: in the first there is a slow and melancholic mood framing a fast and perky dance, unmistakably in a folk idiom; the second is a lyrical slow movement in the mould of 19th-century Russian nationalism. The finale (unlike so many Soviet symphonies, which attempt the huge and triumphant) is a suitably short folk dance with a contrasting melancholic passage. This clean-cut, straightforward symphony, which is probably his best known, is close to the later symphonic idiom of Miaskovsky's close friend **Prokofiev**, and indeed shares themes with the latter's *String Quartet No. 2.* Perhaps the finest of all his symphonies is the last. The *Symphony No. 27* (1949–50) harks back to an Edwardian idiom, and is valedictory in tone. Inexplicably, given the open, easily approachable nature of his later music, Miaskovsky had been denounced in the notorious Zhdanov decree of 1948 for 'formalism', and this symphony was his answer; he was also dying of cancer. The slow opening music lays out one of his country landscapes, but the slow movement is full of a new sad valedictory power, opening with rich brass sonorities in an idiom that recalls Dvořák's ninth symphony. The finale movement has a nobility worthy of **Elgar**, and an attempt at a triumphal march that ends in a minor key. This sincere and moving work should be far better known.

Of his other works, the *Sinfonietta* (1929) uses solo violin passages in the first and second of three movements, but is of little interest. Far more appealing is the *Violin Concerto* (1938), where the lyrical idiom is unashamedly Romantic, with an exceptionally long cadenza in the first movement and a pastoral slow movement.

The *Cello Concerto* (1945) has an Elgarian nobility. A lighter side of Miaskovsky is seen in the sunny *Lyric Concertino* (1929) for string orchestra, which is full of country pictorialism (including the effect of a hurdy-gurdy) and has intense but gentle slow movement, as if describing a landscape at dusk. This shy and introverted composer was also capable of self-assertive musical jokes. The *String Quartet No. 3* (1909; actually the second, but published third), written while Miaskovsky was still a student, opens with a theme using letters from the name Edvard Grieg, whom he admired but whom his teacher Liadov despised. The second movement contains a musical code for the words 'Beware of Liadov'. It is otherwise an innocuous and mournfully beautiful work.

Miaskovsky was himself a celebrated teacher, and among his pupils at the Moscow Conservatory, where he taught from 1921 to 1950, were **Kabalevsky** and **Khatchaturian.**

RECOMMENDED WORKS
Cello Concerto (1945)
Symphony No. 5 (1918)
Symphony No. 6 (1922–23)
Symphony No. 7 (1922)
Symphony No. 10 (1927)
Symphony No. 17 (1936–37)
Symphony No. 21 (1939–40)
Symphony No. 23 (1942)
Symphony No. 27 (1949)
Violin Concerto (1938)

Pärt (sometimes spelt Pårt, Piart, Pyart)
see under Estonia

Prokofiev Sergei Sergeivich***
born 23rd April 1891 at Sontsovka (Ukraine)
died 5th March 1953 at Moscow

The music of Sergei Prokofiev is one of the delights of the 20th century. Never academic, rarely intellectual, only sometimes profound (but then forcibly so), it always shows the distinctive stamp of the musical character and incisive, sometimes compulsive, and yet supremely lyrical temperament of its composer. For Prokofiev is the 20th-century composer who best understood the power and artistic impact of fantasy. Fantasy allows an artist whose natural bent is optimistic and joyfully bright a freedom of expression that retains those qualities without being hackneyed or commonplace. It also has the power to contain more profound statements and emotions than its surface gloss would suggest, often obliquely, especially in an ironic cast or through the archetypal areas of programmatic or stage works. All these qualities Prokofiev had in profusion, together with a wealth of imagination. Only when he became literal (notably to meet the requirements of Soviet realism) does that imagination flag, and fortunately those times are relatively few and far between.

Perhaps the supreme expression of fantasy in music is the ballet, with its expression of archetypes, and it is no coincidence that Prokofiev became one of the greatest ballet composers of all time. Yet the other major expression of his genius comes at the other pole of musical expression, and is still far too little known by many music-lovers. Prokofiev's series of nine piano sonatas (a tenth was left incomplete) represent the greatest contribution to the genre by any composer in the 20th century: Prokofiev was himself a brilliant pianist. If the earliest represent a youthful and still maturing composer, the later sonatas are the closest Prokofiev came to an expression of his private, interior world.

There are two distinct strands in Prokofiev's musical make-up, and they intertwine through his entire output. One is the mercurial, aggressive, brilliant, experimental and sometimes shocking; this was the first strand to emerge in his adult works and gave him the reputation of an *enfant terrible*. Associated with it are clashing dissonances (always used against a tonal backdrop), driving, pulsing and sometimes motoric rhythms, and the impact of repetition. This side of Prokofiev was linked to his piano playing and writing, cascading with notes and textures. The other side is lyrical, often tender, sometimes dreamy, and capable of extending into the grand or the epic. Associated with this aspect are Prokofiev's lovely long-limbed tunes, a clarity of orchestration that loved the lower tones of the woodwind, provided a bass line constantly on the move, and delighted in the punctuation of brass or bright, upper-range instruments. This side is exemplified by his ballets; but in both cases, Prokofiev's music is hardly ever still, and the march, from the grand to the tongue-in-cheek ironical, usually occurs somewhere in a Prokofiev work. The sweep comes in the long tunes, rarely in extended still passages, and even in these moments of long-phrased lyricism the lower voices are usually mobile and plastic or else creating repetitive ideas. This impulse, imparting an enthusiasm for life, is one of the happiest characteristics of the composer. In his best works, both these strands appear to varying degrees, modifying each other. His structures are usually Classical in origin, but he inclined towards episodic ideas rather than closely argued development, again an advantage in such genres as the ballet.

Prokofiev's output is also complex, embracing a wider variety of genres and styles than those familiar only with his best-known works might suspect. Like **Shostakovich**, it is further complicated by the presence of some works of lesser quality that were clearly written for political correctness; Prokofiev, however, with his natural bent towards writing music that would appeal to people, suffered less than his contemporary artistically. Setting aside his prodigious childhood output, his earliest works are mostly brilliant and explosive. He settled in France in 1920, and gradually the lyrical aspects of his musical personality came into prominence. He revisited the USSR in 1933, and returned permanently in 1936. For the main part, his idiom then became simplified, and this period includes his best-known ballets. However, he bore the main brunt of Zhdanov's attacks in 1948, and suffered a heart attack in 1949, and his last works have generally been held to reflect the adverse effects of these events. His major works are to be found among his seven symphonies, his seven concertos, his nine completed piano sonatas, two of his operas and two of his ballets, but there is enough fine work in other genres to confound such an easy classification.

Two of Prokofiev's symphonies are among his most commonly heard works. His first symphony is a work of astonishing vitality, verve, and consummate proportions. The title of *Symphony No. 1 'Classical'* (1917) describes the tone of the work: Prokofiev threw off any shackles of the Romantic tradition in the genre by producing a symphony that looked back to the forms and the proportions of a pre-Romantic age. By using chromatic devices to ease from key to key with fluidity, he welded from this basis an entirely modern work – the first neo-classical symphony. It also allowed him to indulge in a favourite idiom, the dance, and in the kind of melodies that the dance can engender. It is a brilliant, instantly infectious work, dazzlingly executed, and is full of typical Prokofiev touches such as the quirky, jovial delight typified by pitting a solo bassoon against upper strings, or the contrasts of slower grandeur and rushing passages, the lower brass pumping almost motorically. Part of its contemporary feel is created by the fluent shifts between a chamber-orchestra sound (in Classical style) and a much larger, grander orchestral idiom. It has remained one of the most popular, if not the most popular, of all 20th-century symphonies.

The next three symphonies are much less well known. The second and third symphonies reflect Prokofiev in his more daring, aggressive and modernist vein, and have generally been discounted as being too problematic. They burst with ideas, especially the first movement of the *Symphony No. 2* (1924–25), with its huge orchestral textures, its massed lines of counterpoint: an amazing, garish, fascinating and brutal construct of the iron and steel, constructivism on the symphonic stage. To listen to it, one needs to be prepared for the onslaught and to expect nothing of the lyrical Prokofiev. Its two-movement form is based on Beethoven's *Piano Sonata No. 32*, the second movement being a theme and variations with some marvellously imaginative and memorable writing. The *Symphony No. 3* (1928), built on material from Prokofiev's opera *The Fiery Angel* (see below), tones down some of the massive passion of the second, and again is full of stunningly inventive material and foretastes of the better-known ballets, from the pastel tapestry of the andante to the huge, almost literal, orchestral slide into the abyss in the last movement. The problem with both these symphonies is that they teem with ideas that can scarcely be contained by the symphonic argument: one remembers individual passages rather than the overall cast or impact (and indeed some of Prokofiev's most memorable ideas and effects occur in these two symphonies). Within their symphonic limitations they both make for an exhilarating experience; if they do lack symphonic cohesion, that in part reflects the emotive range of a young composer who himself had not yet learned to contain his ideas within a more mature framework. The *Symphony No. 4* (1929–30) was also based on other material, in this case the ballet *The Prodigal Son*, and is less extravagant than its immediate predecessors, although the symphonic argument is still weak in comparison with the later symphonies – or indeed the first. However, the contrasts of a surging drive and more pastoral material give the first movement real impact, while the balletic qualities of the original material delightfully intrude into the last (especially in the original version). It exists in two versions, due to a revision made by Prokofiev in 1947; he lengthened the symphony, adding introductions to all movements, and improved some of the developmentary material. The first version (op. 47) is more biting, more earthy, perhaps more immediate; the second (op. 112) more symphonically cohesive, and orchestrally more assured. Preferences will depend on individual tastes, but in either version the symphony contains too much arresting material to be ignored.

In terms of structure, Prokofiev matured as a symphonic composer in the final three symphonies, and not merely because he simplified his style on his return to the Soviet Union. The proportions, both of emotional material and symphonic structure, are more controlled and better judged, and musical ideas more integrated into a whole, though some may regret the passing of the sheer raw vitality of the preceding works. These last three symphonies are similar in manner, but very different in tone. The *Symphony No. 5* (1944) has remained, with the first, the most popular of Prokofiev's symphonies, and understandably so, for it is instantly attractive. Yet the epic grandeur of the first movement, mixed with a touch of the pastoral, the sleigh-ride delight of the substantial scherzo, a bitter-sweet slow movement that eventually reflects the war during which it was written, and the boisterous delight of the finale, also contain an undercurrent of deeper concern and unease. The *Symphony No. 7* (1951–52) has often been criticised as being too easy, having the charm of the fifth but not the underlying substance. However, it was begun as a work for children, and it seems entirely appropriate that Prokofiev should complete his symphonies with a work that has elements of the child-like, though never childish. For it has a simple flow of appealing music (such as the magisterial theme of the first movement that returns at the end of the work), and, if approached in the spirit of its origins, it is entirely delightful. But Prokofiev's symphonic masterpiece is the *Symphony No. 6* (1945–47). It is full of his characteristic musical fingerprints, but they are metamorphosed into vehicles for emotions of a darker, more introverted intensity rare in his output, closely argued in a three-movement form. The brutal chords of the opening will come as a shock to those used to Prokofiev's more easy vein, just as the opening of **Vaughan Williams's** fourth symphony sounds so devastating to those only familiar with his pastoral mood. The march of the first movement has uncomfortable undertones and a touch of menace, the slow movement unfolds in a terrible darkness, its own march biting and half-satirical, while the melodies of the lighter-hearted finale go harmonically awry, and the symphony ends in genuine tragedy.

Three of Prokofiev's concertos have a firm hold on the repertoire, and of these the best known is the *Piano Concerto No. 3* (1917–21). The opening can be only described as Impressionistic, with a cascade of glittering notes after a clarinet introduction, but then the piano dashes into a short movement of dazzling fluency and drive; there is a marvellous sense of virtuoso fantasy here, as if a box of toy figures has been opened, and they are all rejoicing in their freedom. The central andante, a theme and variations, provides a complete contrast, with beautiful piano writing ranging right across the upper end of the keyboard, and a wide range of mood that includes the lazily mysterious. The finale provides another contrast: bubbling amusement, a hint of playful pomposity, a touch of the grotesque, as well as the lyrical. The concerto is as fluent as the first symphony, and the combination of instant appeal and effortless virtuosity will give pleasure to the newcomer and the specialist alike. The *Violin Concerto No. 1* (1916–17) is far less obviously a display piece: there is no cadenza, and the soloist and orchestra are essentially in consort rather than in dialogue. Its opening is gentle and exceptionally beautiful, leading the listener into an overall form in which two predominantly slower movements frame a faster one. The solo line is constantly singing, and there is a magical, fantastical section of high harmonics to the end of the first movement. The central movement is full of bouncing, swooping delights and a more ponderous march, the soloist descending into gruffer regions. The finale opens with another march but is soon subverted to a more lyrical mood of song, both tender and melancholic, and at the end delicately nostalgic. There is little that is sentimental about this concerto, but much that celebrates joy and beauty. The *Violin Concerto No. 2* (1935) is less well known but equally beautiful; more circumspect and thoughtful, it expresses more of an uncomplicated inward contemplation; it

offers no real fireworks, just a sustained lyricism.

Some of the lesser-known concertos provide an equally remarkable, if less immediately appealing experience. The short but entirely effective *Piano Concerto No. 1* (1911–12) begins with one of the most arresting opening ideas of any concerto: the piano creates a rising and falling phrase which takes flight, and eventually returns at the end of the concerto. The concerto is one of youthful brilliance; in which the occasional backward looks to the Romantic tradition are combined with more dissonant propulsion into modernism. When eventually a Wagnerian horn call rings out, the piano launches away into a spiky, cock-a-snook cadenza, as if to say that this is where one era is ending and another beginning. Indeed it was, and that change is taken further in the *Piano Concerto No. 2* (revised 1923), an expression of the psychological turbulence of youth. The magnificent first movement, one of the finest in all the piano concerto repertoire, is a huge upswelling of emotion, combining motoric rhythms with more subtle and mysterious colours, leading to a gigantic cadenza of awesome power and a return of the orchestra that takes one's breath away in its inevitability and its impact. The whole movement is an expression of the yearning to break free, and many may dislike it precisely because of those bursting passions. While containing some memorable writing, the rest of the concerto is too long; but the concerto is worth discovering for the first movement alone.

The fourth and fifth have fallen into obscurity. The rather ponderous *Piano Concerto No. 4* (1931) was written for the left hand only. It is chiefly of interest for the restrained beauty of its slow movement, apart from the sheer virtuosity of the one-handed piano writing. The five-movement *Piano Concerto No. 5* (1931–32) is more interesting, though neither concerto has the impact of the earlier works. The *Cello Concerto* (1933–38) was extensively revised to form what is essentially a new work, the *Symphony-Concerto for Cello and Orchestra* (1950–52), in which form it is more usually encountered. It is a long and substantial work in which the soloist takes an equal place with the orchestra (as the revised title would imply); its overall tone is gentle and rather ruminative, and it can be an effective work when in the hands of a soloist capable of a rich and expressive tone.

Piano music forms a substantial part of

Prokofiev's output. Three of the first four sonatas have their origins in student works, the third and fourth being rewritings, both carrying the subtitle 'D'après des vieux cahiers' ('From old notebooks'). The *Piano Sonata No. 1* (1909) originally had three movements, but Prokofiev published only the revised allegro, thus making a short, obviously derivative, but energetic and pianistic work. The much longer four-movement *Piano Sonata No. 2* (1912) is incisively clear-cut, but tamer than many of Prokofiev's works of the period, with a lovely lilting Russian feel to the slow movement, as if Mussorgsky's oxencarts were somewhere in the back of Prokofiev's mind. The finale is characteristically lithe, like swift-running rivulets spinning over slower eddies. The short one-movement *Piano Sonata No. 3* (1917, rewriting of 1907 sonata) is the best known of the earlier sonatas. It opens in a torrent of notes before settling down to a typically melodic second subject and a tempestuous development out of which the more tranquil mood emerges triumphant. In the beguiling *Piano Sonata No. 4* (1917, rewriting of 1908 sonata), two quicker movements frame its major attraction, a slower andante that explores an evolving and gently fantastical soundscape, from a sense of the march to a lilting lyricism that heralds the later Prokofiev. Any traces of derivative elements have disappeared by the *Piano Sonata No. 5* (1923), revised as op. 135 in 1953. This is Prokofiev in his delicate vein, full of charm; chromatic colours and running threads add shades to a delightful sonata whose andantino has elements of child-like fantasy, and where perhaps only the very ending of the whole work fails to convince. In the *Piano Sonata No. 6* (1939) Prokofiev expanded the layout into four movements, producing a work of symphonic proportions. There are echoes of the 'barbaric' young Prokofiev, but now combined with simplified clearer textures, less violently driven by juxtapositions of contrasting material.

The next two sonatas, both in B flat major, are among the masterpieces of the piano repertoire. The *Piano Sonata No. 7* (1939–44) has become the best known of the sonatas, and a challenge to pianists for the power and control it requires. Its angular opening idea announces the uneasy edge that pervades the whole sonata. The march into which this develops is equally uncomfortable; the quiet, lyrical moments of the first movement are touched with anxiety; much of the slow movement inhabits the lower, darker reaches of the keyboard, and its central climax reaches up towards the ecstasy of the cadenza of the second piano concerto, but without the same sense of hope and confidence. All this is framed by the rhythmic drive of the faster sections of the opening movement, and the dynamism of the last, marked 'precipito', one of the most mercurial movements Prokofiev wrote. Recurrent themes reiterate with pounding force, especially the hurtling and menacing three-note idea of the finale (which made its brief first appearance in the piano cycle *Visions fugitives*). The *Piano Sonata No. 8* (1939–44) is more introverted, but no less powerful. The first movement is Beethovenesque in its feel and import and almost symphonic in scale, with a development section of tragedy and anguish combined with angry utterance; a sense of fate stalks through this music, framed by the quieter hiatus of the opening and the close. The short second opens with even clearer reminders of Beethoven, albeit to a more jaunty rhythm, the whole movement combining irony with nostalgia. The third movement follows without a break, mercurial, insistent, sometimes motoric, ultimately terrifying and despairing, with references to the opening movement of the second piano concerto and to Chopin's B flat minor piano sonata. It seems simply unbelievable that such heartfelt and searching music as the sixth, seventh and eighth sonatas should have been singled out and condemned by the Soviet authorities in 1948 as too complicated. Perhaps even more than **Shostakovich's** work (which almost always had elements of protest), these three sonatas stand as bulwarks against the madness of cultural philistinism and dictatorship. The four-movement *Piano Sonata No. 9* (1947) explores a different tone from the wartime sonatas. At its base is a classical simplicity and clarity, the harmonies following a more classical pattern, the textures leaner, the feel more ruminating, the rhythms calmer. But by no means is it a simplistic work; here, more than in any of the other sonatas, Prokofiev seems to be conducting a lovers' dialogue with the keyboard for its own sake, albeit it a muted one – as if, in closing his sequence of sonatas, he is asking for contemplation and meditation on the part of the listener.

Besides the sonatas there is a considerable body of other piano music, ranging from the fiery to the music of affection and lyricism for children. The famous *Suggestion diabolique* is the last of the *Four*

Pieces (1908–09); all four short pieces look back to the heavy chromaticism and virtuoso style of Liszt, and this final one is a furious helter-skelter, its diabolic tone based on the use of the tritone (once associated with the devil), even more effective when the first three pieces of the set have already been heard. Equally ferocious, and more motoric in its repeated sixteenth notes, is the *Toccata* (1912). Both these works represent Prokofiev the *enfant terrible*. More organised, and more assured, while still maintaining the element of experimentation, are the five *Sarcasms* (1912–14): the jerky, granular No. 2 is one of the few Prokofiev pieces without a key, while No. 3, propelled by ostinati, has two simultaneous keys. No. 4 is especially effective, with the initial bell sounds, set against a high scanning right-hand, eventually turning into something very delicate – sarcasm is but one aspect of this effective set. The finest of these piano sets, showing Prokofiev at his most seriously experimental, are the *Visions fugitives* (1915–17). Composed of twenty short pieces, they are largely introspective, delicate, sometimes moving into a more emphatic tone (as in No. XIV, *Feroce*); but throughout there is a strange disembodied effect, both intimate and distancing and often with a ghostly beauty, created in part by the consistent use of the high, bright registers of the keyboard.

Prokofiev was the most important composer of classical ballet since Tchaikovsky. He had an unerring gift for conjuring up musical atmosphere for the ballet stage, to such an extent that the suites from his ballets have achieved widespread popularity in their own right. The only one to have lapsed into oblivion is *On the Dnieper* (1930), originally commissioned by the Paris Opéra. His first ballet, *Chout* (*The Buffoon*, 1915, revised 1920) has a story too unfortunate, initially violent, and typically Russian, to receive regular staging, in spite of its strong irony: a buffoon apparently whips his wife to death, brings her back to life again, and encourages seven friends to do the same, but without the same outcome. The rest of the ballet humorously describes his successful attempts to elude their revenge. But the music is atmospheric and lively, with dissonant energy and vitality, and is usually heard in the form of a twelve-section suite. *Pas d'acier* (*The Age of Steel*, 1925) is a mixture of the constructivist and the lyrical Prokofiev, with a touch of jazzy syncopation, and is interesting precisely because of its mechanistic elements. The

music for *The Prodigal Son* (1928–29) is best encountered in its reincarnations in the two versions of the fourth symphony. But it was with *Romeo and Juliet* (1935–36), based on the Shakespeare play, that Prokofiev matured as a ballet composer. His ability to portray anger and conflict as well as lyricism was ideally suited to the subject, and he produced a score of passion, immediacy, and rhythmic drive, in which the characters and the events are vividly drawn. He is at his best in the music surrounding conflict ('Montagues and Capulets', 'Tybalt's death') rather than in the love music between Romeo and Juliet, whose urgently sensuous teenage passion was less well suited to Prokofiev's lyricism than the romantic purity of the subject of his next ballet, *Cinderella*, where the love music is finer. *Romeo and Juliet* is most likely to be heard in the first two of the three suites Prokofiev drew from the ballet (No. 1 and No. 2, 1936, No. 3, 1946), which have become staples of the orchestral repertoire. Both these first two suites actually contain differences from the ballet, which was revised during the first rehearsal (after the two suites had been made) to reduce the orchestral weight. Many conductors also create their own preferred suite, drawing from all three.

Cinderella (1940–44) is his finest ballet, classical in format and full-length in scale. The characters are sharply drawn, the flow of melody is continuous, the invention of effect, colour and atmosphere on a consistently high level. Above all, Prokofiev identified with and understands the spiritual rather than physical love of the main character, and there are three moods associated with Cinderella in the ballet: the abused, the chaste and pure, and the happy woman in love. The complete ballet, although long, is so fine that it is worth encountering it in its entirety, but there are also three orchestral suites drawn from the ballet (all 1946), as well as three sets of piano pieces (1942, 1943 and 1944), and an *Adagio* (1944) for cello and piano. Prokofiev's final ballet was another large-scale work, in four acts with a prologue. *The Stone Flower* (1948–53) reflected his love of the Ural mountains, for its scenario is drawn from Pavel Bazhov's *Ural Tales*. Danilo wishes to craft a malachite vase as simple and as beautiful as a live flower; having released the spirit of the stone he follows it. The ballet recounts his adventures, including being shown a wondrous stone flower and having his love of his Katarina tested. The central theme – the desire to capture simplicity and beauty – is a metaphor for Prokofiev's own compositional motives, and if the ballet does not have the tuneful immediacy of *Cinderella*, he succeeded in creating a score of clarity and simplicity with a background of folk song, without being patronising or shallow. Prokofiev made a short suite of three of the forty-six sections, which is occasionally heard.

Two of Prokofiev's operas have achieved widespread recognition, and they could scarcely be more contrasted. *Love for Three Oranges* (1919) combines the composer's love for the fantastical and the fairy tale with his enjoyment of irony and satire. Based on a farce by Gozzi, it tells the story of a Prince afflicted by the melancholic humours, who, on laughing at a witch, is cursed – he will not be happy until he falls in love with three oranges and they with him. This, by various extraordinary means, he eventually does. The work satirises the traditions of Romantic opera, but is exceptionally entertaining in its own right, and its march has become famous. Prokofiev turned some of the music, including the march, into a suite (1924), and although the opera is regularly performed, it is this suite which is more likely to be encountered. *War and Peace* (1941–43), based on Tolstoy's epic novel, is now recognised as a masterpiece, but is rarely performed because of its huge scale and the forces required, and any production is a major international event. Its genius lies in the conviction with which it reduces the massive spread of the novel to the operatic stage, and in the expression of both individual and large-scale collective emotions. Prokofiev assumed a knowledge of the novel, and for audiences approaching the reduction to eleven scenes, a basic knowledge of its plot is helpful. The scenes are divided between those involving more intimate individual relationships and grand-scale panoramas expressing collective concerns, centred around the Battle of Borodino; the action concentrates on the events of 1812, rather than the events of the first part of Tolstoy's novel, but is divided into two parts, peace and war. The consistently fine score moves easily between grandeur and intimacy, and its highlights include Prokofiev's integration of the waltz into the general texture, and the famous and stirring aria for the Russian Field Marshal Kutuzov, eventually reiterated at the end of the opera by the whole chorus.

Prokofiev's other operas are less well known. *Maddalena* (1911–13) is a very early work (but even so had been preceded by five childhood operas). *The Gambler* (1915–17, revised 1927–28) is based on a story by Dostoyevsky. Much more effective is *The Fiery Angel* (1919–26), set in medieval times, and based on Bryusov's (autobiographical) novel of passionate, obsessive love, combined with religious fanaticism, madness and the Inquisition. Prokofiev latched on to the psychological aspects of the obsession, producing a score in his aggressive, *enfant terrible* style that is worth encountering for its passionate power, but which fails overall in dramatic and musical structure. (Unknown to Prokofiev, while composing the opera in Paris he was actually living next door to the woman who inspired the novel.) *Semyon Kotko* (1939) was an attempt to write an opera about ordinary people *for* ordinary people, and was based on Katayev's novel *I, Son of the Working People*, about a Ukrainian partisan. The oddest of these operas, *The Story of a Real Man* (1947–48) was another attempt to produce an opera for a popular audience, based on a story by Polevoi of an airman who has a leg amputated, but succeeds in returning to action. Both these operas have passages of musical and dramatic interest (notably the love scene in *Semyon Kotko*, and some of the interactions in the hospital in *Story of a Real Man*), but both are doomed by their librettos. Perhaps the opera of most interest after the two famous works is *Betrothal in a Monastery* (1940, first performance 1946), where Sheridan's comedy of errors (the source is the play *The Duenna*, and the opera is sometimes known – incorrectly – by that title) suited Prokofiev's gift for ironic humour and perky comedy. The basis of the story, turned into a libretto by Prokofiev's second wife, Mira Mendelssohn, is the familiar tale of old men desiring to marry young women, and being thwarted by a welter of subterfuges. The style harks back to opera buffa, but with the magic of Prokofiev's orchestral colours and a strong Slavic injection when the setting moves to the monastery of the title. It is a vivid and entertaining work.

Besides these series of works in a specific genre, there are a number of Prokofiev scores that either are already very well known or deserve to be. Chief among these must be *Peter and the Wolf* (1936) for narrator and orchestra, which is as perfect a score as he ever wrote, and one of those very rare works of art that appeal in differing ways to both children and adults. In the simple but resonant story of Peter's capture of a wolf that has been prowling around the farm, a separate instrument is assigned to each of the characters, so that the work is also a guide to the orchestra. The musical characterisation, of both animals and humans, is a delight, but so is that of the action, using the full range of Prokofiev's mastery of bright and direct orchestral colours; the narration has the advantage of being alterable to suit different educational philosophies. Those who enjoy this work might like to explore two other delightful, if less brilliant, scores, *Summer's Day* for orchestra, (1941, from *Music for Children* for piano), and *Winter Bonfire* (1949) for reciter, boys' chorus and orchestra. The *Scythian Suite* (1914–15) is a reworking of the discarded early ballet *Ala and Lolly*. Clearly under the influence of the 'barbaric' elements of **Stravinsky's** *The Rite of Spring*, it takes the orchestral expression of violent primitivism yet further, rolling together touches of exotic Orientalism, aggressive ostinati, and dissonant and brilliant orchestral effects. If it lacks the finesse of Stravinsky's ballet, it has an exuberance that has ensured it a regular place in the repertoire.

Two of Prokofiev's film scores have become regular concert works in their own right. The story of a film about a non-existent lieutenant was exactly one to appeal to Prokofiev's sense of fantasy and irony: owing to a clerical error the Tsar comes to believe in the non-existent lieutenant, and rather than admit the error, the army invents a complete life and death for the fictitious character. Prokofiev's witty and tuneful (if lightweight) response is to be found in the pictorial and brilliantly orchestrated suite that he drew from the film, *Lieutenant Kijé* (1934). The score he created for Eisenstein's 1938 film about Alexander Nevsky, the Russian hero of the 13th-century war with Sweden, is very different, and he turned it into a full-scale cantata, *Alexander Nevsky* (1939) for mezzo-soprano, chorus and orchestra, which has become one of the best known of all Russian choral works. It manages to be epic without being bombastic, as well as extending the Russian choral tradition, and at its centre is the famous depiction of the battle on the ice, almost completely orchestral, in which Prokofiev combined his sense of aggressive orchestral colour and motoric rhythms with his lyricism to unforgettable effect. The passage is even more exciting when heard in its original context of the film. In the same mould, and also based on music for an Eisenstein film, is the oratorio *Ivan the Terrible* (1942) for

narrator, soloists, chorus and orchestra, successfully arranged into oratorio form by Abram Stasevich. This has sections which rival the earlier film score in power and effect, but is less concise.

There are also two particularly effective and little-known choral works. The experimental *Seven, They are Seven* (1917–18, revised 1933 and sometimes known as *They are Seven*) is a brief but explosive work for chorus and orchestra that reflects the contemporary Constructivist movement. The *Cantata on the Twentieth Anniversary of the October Revolution* (1937, not to be confused with the completely vacuous celebrations he wrote ten years later) is not at all the Soviet socialist realist hack work one might expect; based on various texts describing the experience of the revolutionary events, it is scored for huge forces, two choruses, military band, accordions, percussion and orchestra. Those who enjoy *Alexander Nevsky* may care to investigate this work; it has the same direct, urgent impulse.

There are number of smaller-scale works which are also of interest. The attractive *Violin Sonata* No. 2 (1943–44) is actually a reworking of the *Flute Sonata* (1943), although with its very natural and idiomatic violin writing it has entirely overshadowed the original. The overall tone is Classical and restrained, the models being Haydn and Handel, and it has perhaps found more favour with performers than audiences, for it misses some of the sparkle characteristic of the composer. The *Overture on Hebrew Themes* (1919), for clarinet and piano quintet is a compelling and direct score using two Hebrew tunes that are mutated into Prokofiev's own voice; there is an orchestral version, but it is much more effective in chamber form. Of the two string quartets, the *String Quartet* No. 2 (1941) was influenced by Caucasian folk music, and has a beautiful slow movement.

Prokofiev remained all his life a composer and pianist (touring extensively between 1914 and 1936), and did not teach. His diary–autobiography of his early life reveals a writer of considerable charm and talent. He died an hour before Stalin; the news was withheld so as not to conflict, an irony he himself would probably have appreciated.

RECOMMENDED WORKS
cantata *Alexander Nevsky* (1939)
opera *Betrothal in a Monastery* (1940)
ballet *Cinderella* (1940–44)
suite *Lieutenant Kijé* (1934) for

orchestra
opera *The Love for Three Oranges*
(1919)
Overture on Hebrew Themes (1919) for
chamber ensemble
Peter and the Wolf (1936) for narrator
and orchestra
Piano Concerto No. 1 (1911–12)
Piano Concerto No. 2 (1924–25)
Piano Concerto No. 3 (1928)
Piano Sonata No. 3 (1917)
Piano Sonata No. 5 (1923, revised
1952–53)
Piano Sonata No. 6 (1939–40)
Piano Sonata No. 7 (1939–42)
Piano Sonata No. 8 (1939–44)
Piano Sonata No. 9 (1941)
ballet *Romeo and Juliet* (1935–36)
Sarcasms (1912–14) for piano
Scythian Suite (1915) for orchestra
Symphony No. 1 (1916–17)
Symphony No. 4 (1929–30)
Symphony No. 5 (1931–32)
Symphony No. 6 (1945–47)
Symphony No. 7 (1951–52)
cantata *They are Seven* (1917–18) for
soloists and orchestra
song cycle *The Ugly Duckling* (1914)
Violin Concerto No. 1 (1916–17)
Violin Concerto No. 2 (1935)
Visions fugitives (1915–17) for piano
opera *War and Peace* (1941–43)

BIBLIOGRAPHY
S. Prokofiev, *Diary 1927 and other
writings*, 1991
E. & L. Hanson, *Prokofiev*, 1964
H. Robinson, *Sergei Prokofiev*, 1987

Rachmaninov Sergei Vassilievich***

born 1st April 1873 at Oneg estate,
near Novgorod
died 28th March 1943 at Beverly Hills,
California

Almost all who compose largely in the
styles and idioms of the preceding generation are doomed, at best, to a passing fame.
They fail to reflect the potency and concerns of their own age, and almost inevitably lack the depth of understanding of
their predecessors. However, once in a
while an artist appears who is incapable of
working in any other idiom than that of an
earlier generation, and yet has the genius
to infuse something new into that idiom.
Sergei Rachmaninov was just such a genius. He was for much of the century reviled
because his style, especially in his piano

works, for he seemed to belong more to the
age of Tchaikovsky than to the era in
which he worked (and certainly could not
be associated with any of the moods of
European even after 1905).

Rachmaninov's works fall into fairly
distinct periods separated by near silence
brought about by force of circumstance
and his arduous tours as one of the foremost pianists of his day. His earlier music
was especially influenced by Tchaikovsky
and Chopin, culminating in the *Symphony
No. 1* (c.1895–97). The success of the *Piano
Concerto No. 2* (1900–01) heralded his most
productive years, with a spate of works
until 1917 that reflected his mature, nostalgic idiom of haunting beauty. From 1927
until his death he produced six major
works in which the nostalgia is replaced by
a more rugged and positive beauty. His
appeal is founded on a melodiousness
whose main features are nostalgia and
beautiful regret, wrapped in languishing
cadences; all his symphonies and piano
concertos are in minor keys. This basic
appeal to sentiment (much less overt in the
last works) has infuriated some critics, and
his treatment until recently has often been
shabby. For such sentiment is a perfectly
valid aspect of the human experience, and
it was Rachmaninov's singular achievement to express it in musical structures
and idioms that are never trite and usually
exceptionally accomplished. Against a
strong streak of melancholy and a nostalgic regret for things past is set a desire for
more powerful and positive utterance, and
this basic struggle of Rachmaninov's personality provides an undercurrent to much
of his music. It is this substratum that
makes Rachmaninov much more than a
spinner of beautiful, sentimental tunes in
long cantabile lines, often with brilliant
virtuoso pianistic effects.

His earliest works, such as the mis-
named '*Youth*' *Symphony* (1891, probably
intended as the first movement of an
abandoned symphony), show a precocious
technical command and musical imagination. They are heavily influenced by Tchaikovsky, and in the piano music by Chopin,
though the finest of them, *Prince Rotislav*
(1891), is a graphic tone-painting in the
manner of Borodin, based on a ballad by A.
K. Tolstoy. The form is tripartite (slow–
fast–slow), and the misty waterscape of
the opening especially atmospheric. Rachmaninov reached symphonic maturity
with the *Symphony No. 1* (1895–97), but he
was so disillusioned with the reception

given to the first performance, which apparently was appallingly conducted by **Glazunov**, that he destroyed the score. However, the parts survived, and the symphony was reconstructed and heard again in 1945. It emerged as one of Rachmaninov's finest works, heroic in tone, obviously indebted to Tchaikovsky and Borodin, but constructed with a flow of symphonic purpose and devoid of the kind of nostalgic limpid beauty that pervades his later work. The slow movement has real menace to its opening, before evolving into an almost Mahlerian intensity and scope, the finale that Russian blaze of uplifting glory, combined with a darker dramatic urgency, that was the inheritance of Tchaikovsky. With its Russian colours and sound and epic late-Romantic scale, it achieves what Glazunov's own symphonies so often unsuccessfully attempted. However, it does belong to the late 19th century, and it may appeal more to those with a love for pre-Soviet Russian music than to those who enjoy Rachmaninov's later works. The *Symphony No. 2* (1907) is highly attractive and popular, but lacks the symphonic and emotional muscle of the first. The melodies are long and sentimental; the big, broad opening, with yearning strings supported by a more rugged bass, is most effective, as is the lovely slow movement, but the brash close lacks incision. The *Symphony No. 3* (1935–36) seems intended to have a brighter, more positive outlook, but the underground struggle with Rachmaninov's instinctive melancholia keeps threatening, especially in the last of three movements; where the emotional changes are swift and turbulent, with the hint of a mawkish Prokofievian march, and a descent almost into pathos in the penultimate bars. The broad cantabile melody of the slow movement haunts the memory long after the symphony has finished. Finer than any of these symphonies, but not nearly so well known, is the symphonic poem *The Isle of the Dead* (1909). It was inspired by a painting by Böcklin, and in resonant dark colours and rocking and swelling tone-painting brilliantly creates an atmosphere of a slow crossing to the dark, mist-shrouded and mysterious island of the painting. The effect is a perfectly judged combination of seascape and dream picture, impelled from the lower depths of the orchestra, suggesting the silence and desolation. It interweaves the plainchant *Dies irae* that became a recurring theme in Rachmaninov's music.

The *Piano Concerto No. 1* (1891, revised 1917) has, at least in its revised form, so many beautiful ideas in the bitter-sweet melodic style at which Rachmaninov so excelled, that it is surprising that it is not better known. It carries with it a certain portentousness (especially in the very opening), where the student is attempting to emulate Tchaikovsky, but has a misty, rather restrained slow movement, and a youthful boisterousness in the final movement unmatched in Rachmaninov's later works. The *Piano Concerto No. 2* (1900–01) scarcely needs any introduction, as it is one of the best-known works of all classical music, with its opening of expectation breaking out into flowing melody, its haunting slow movement of beauty lost and gained, its glittering and brilliant finale, its virtuoso solo writing, and its general quality of the piano telling a tale. It also represents one of the earliest triumphs for the practice of psychoanalysis. Rachmaninov had found it impossible to compose after the failure of his *Symphony No. 1*, and sought treatment from the early Freudian Dr Nikolai Dahl; the concerto was the result. Much of its appeal is a combination of the sparkle of the solo writing and the allure of its sentiment.

The *Piano Concerto No. 3* (1909) marks a new phase in Rachmaninov's writing. Here the emotion is more deeply imbedded in the music, just as the solo writing is more integrated with the orchestra. The finest of his concertos, it has a linear impulse – announced in the strolling rhythm and gentle insinuation of the opening – that is maintained throughout the piece and made all the more cohesive by thematic interrelations between the three movements. The orchestra and soloist do not compete, but rather support each other in the discourse, even when, in the forceful middle movement, the complex piano writing sets up a dominating tapestry. It is a work of complex and mature emotions, none stated starkly but rather eliding into each other, culminating in a kind of joyous satisfaction; it is also an exceedingly difficult work for the soloist, partly because Rachmaninov had a huge hand-span, and wrote accordingly. The concerto is sometimes heard with cuts sanctioned by the composer, but these are unnecessary.

The rather diffuse *Piano Concerto No. 4* (1926) has never achieved the popularity of the earlier works. It seems to be searching for a style, and rather unexpectedly it is the sparkling finale that contains the most attractive music. No such problems occur with Rachmaninov's last work for piano and orchestra, the *Rhapsody on a Theme of Paganini* (1934). The theme had already been used by Brahms, Liszt and Schumann, but Rachmaninov's is the most brilliant and satisfying treatment, in twenty-five variations with the theme stated in full after the first variation. The piano writing is brilliant and virtuoso, while the range of emotional mood and colour is considerable, from grand power to the percussive Variation IX or the broken, almost pointillistic orchestration of Variation XVI. The *Dies irae* plainchant threads through the work, and there is a glorious moment when a new treatment suddenly appears, as if out of nowhere, in Variation XVIII, and is capped by the scintillating spin of strings that follows.

The most powerful expression of Rachmaninov's pianistic imagination is to be found in the *Twenty-Four Preludes* for piano. These consist of three groups: the famous *C# minor Prelude* (originally the second of the *Morceaux de fantaisie*, 1892); the *Ten Preludes* op. 23 (1903); and the *Thirteen Preludes* op. 32 (1910), which Rachmaninov decided to write in order to make a complete set of works, each in a different key, following Chopin. The *C sharp minor Prelude* allows a slow, almost cumbersome and very Russian tune to take flight. The op. 23 *Preludes* are in the best tradition of such works: direct thoughts that simultaneously make statements about pianism and about inner emotions. Influenced by Chopin, especially in the revolutionary atmosphere of No. 5, they range from the heroic utterance of No. 2, through the rippling flow of semiquavers in No. 8, to the unsettling lilt of No. 9. The op. 32 set are more circumspect, exploratory and elusive, as if taking up an insubstantial element absent from the earlier preludes. The rhythms are more unsettled and shifting, and when characteristic melodies appear, as in No. 9, they are encased in more complex surroundings. Op. 32 No. 10, one of the finest of the 1910 set, was inspired by another Böcklin painting, and the last turns the key of the *C sharp minor Prelude* into an euphoric D flat major. Of his other piano works, the most effective writing is found in the two sets of *Études tableaux* (1911 and 1916–17) and the *Piano Sonata No. 2* (1913). After an inauspicious opening, the *Cello Sonata* (1900) is a fine, large-scale work with a delicate, withdrawn beauty even in the vigorous scherzo. In the lifts to moments of passion, the often florid piano writing impels the cello; the slow movement is more outward-looking and less limpid than

one might expect in a work that followed the *Piano Concerto No. 2*.

Rachmaninov's songs are yearningly melodious, equally effective both in the piano versions and with the added colours of orchestration. Vocal lines are lyrical and flowing, sometimes ecstatically so; the accompaniment looks back to Chopin in the earlier songs, and is more integrated and individual in the later. If not usually profound, they are often exceptionally beautiful, and the major songs, such as *How Fair this Spot*, op. 21 No. 7, *Lilacs* op. 21 No. 5 (1900–06), or *O Cease Thy Singing* op. 4 No. 4 (c.1890), or the glorious *Spring Waters* op. 14 No. 11 (1896) have become standards of the repertoire. The wordless *Vocalise* op. 34 No. 14 (1912), for soprano and piano is usually heard with its orchestral accompaniment, a sinuous nostalgic outpouring touched with melancholy; Rachmaninov also made an orchestral version, assuming the vocal line to the violins.

Rachmaninov wrote three choral masterpieces. *Kolokola* (*The Bells*, 1913) for soprano, tenor, baritone, chorus and orchestra, is a large-scale, symphonically organized work based on an adaptation by Belmont of Edgar Allan Poe. In the first movement the bells are the jingle bells of sleighs, associated with birth and youth; in the second they are bells of marriage, in the third of terror and fire, and in the finale of death, but death as a culmination, with a luminosity reminiscent of **Strauss**. This cycle of birth and death has a strong undercurrent of the Russian countryside and folk music (especially in the rhythms of the last movement), but sophisticated vocal and orchestral writing with an urgent energy and rich colours. As magnificent is the almost unknown *Divine Liturgy of St John Chrysostom* (1910) for unaccompanied choir. As in Tchaikovsky's earlier setting, there is little that is immediately recognizable as the composer's style, but instead a marvellous combination of Orthodox Church choral sound and modes, strong suggestions of Russian folk songs with their vistas of vast Russian landscapes, and complex choral writing with sonorous bass lines. The equally neglected *Vesper Mass* (1915) follows a similar style.

Rachmaninov left Russia after the 1917 revolution, eventually settling in Switzerland, and moved to the USA in 1939.

RECOMMENDED WORKS
   Cello Sonata (1901)
   Divine Liturgy of St John Chrysostom
      (1910) for chorus

tone poem *The Isle of the Dead* (1909)
Piano Concerto No. 1 (1891, rev. 1917)
Piano Concerto No. 2 (1901)
Piano Concerto No. 3 (1909)
Preludes (1892) for piano
Preludes (1904) for piano
Preludes (1910) for piano
tone poem *Prince Rotislav* (1891)
Rhapsody on a Theme of Paganini
    (1934) for piano and orchestra
Symphony No. 1 (1895–97)
Symphony No. 2 (1907)
Symphony No. 3 (1936)

BIBLIOGRAPHY
    G. Norris, *Rakhmaninov*, 1976

Schnittke Alfred Harrievich (also spelled Schnitke, Shnitke)··

born 24th November 1934 at Engels, Autonomous Soviet Republic of Volga Gumans (now Saratov)
died 3rd August 1998 at Hamburg

Schnittke has emerged as one of the major composers of the late 20th century, and perhaps the finest of the Russian composers in the generation after **Shostakovich**. Hardly known in the West until the 1970s, his achievement received rapid recognition after the collapse of hard-line communism in the USSR. He composed within the tradition of symphonies, concertos, and chamber and vocal works, and there is a tonal base to his idiom, overlaid with the experience of 12-tone techniques. He uses chromatic effects, and regularly adds a distant note or notes to give an ethereal, unsettled feel to what otherwise might be a conventional harmony. His eclecticism is legendary, borrowing from a multitude of musical sources, but is an integral part of his musical inspiration and method, firmly locked into his own idiom. Usually such stylistic borrowings create a launch-pad from which his own music can take off, but sometimes they have allusive effects, such as the appearance of an idea from **Britten's** *Billy Budd* in the *Symphony No. 3*, where a potent message can be found encrypted if one knows the words of the original chorus. Almost all his later works open and close with a quiet expressiveness or contemplation within which there is turbulent, often tragic drama.

Schnittke's earlier music followed conventional Soviet principles, and his later output includes over sixty film scores. However, following a visit to Moscow by **Nono** in 1962, he absorbed many of the techniques of the European developments of the 1960s and 1970s, particularly in the handling of dissonances, in the use of orchestral colours and sonorities (with bells and tuned percussion often prominent, and a harpsichord or celesta often woven into the texture), and in the juxtaposition of massed orchestral blocks of colour and timbre. After a period of serialism, which included the *String Quartet No. 1* (1966), and the development of collages that made reference to older musics, in the mid-1970s his idiom moved into the mainstream of European composition. One strand of that idiom has explored a spare, lean, slow-moving, often ritualistic sound, relying on changes of sonorities, not dissimilar to that of **Pärt**. Another presents a larger, more monumental sound, sometimes emphasised by the contrast between urgent, driving counterpoint and more static blocks. A regular device is that of lines moving upward in steps, often cut away without resolution. In many of his later works, these two strands of his idiom are combined (most prominently in the *Concerto for Piano and Strings*), and there is often a sense of distancing or alienation, as if the music was heard from far away through a distorting veil. Suggestions of earlier musics, like a half-triggered recall, continue to seep into his later works, but they are fully integrated into the contemporary idiom. His music, often dramatic in cast, presents an emotional impact and appeal in the Russian tradition, intended to reflect the human condition; the intellectual construct, although often formidable, is secondary to this drive. Again in common with **Pärt**, his music embraces a strong religious feel and outlook, and one of his favourite devices is an ending of ethereal beauty.

The most widely circulated work that includes synthesis of old musics is the *Concerto Grosso No. 1* (1976–77), for two violins, strings, cembalo and prepared piano. Built on an infectious pastiche of lively Baroque music, the underlying material is subjected to contemporary instrumental textures and transformations to give it an anachronistic gloss.

Such refocusing of earlier material is quite widespread in modern music, but this particular example has a verve and sense of aural humour that produce plenty of incident and entertainment. The 'musical game' *Moz-Art à la Haydn* (1977), for two violins, two small chamber orchestras, double bass and conductor is derived from music Mozart wrote for a pantomime, of which only the violin part survives. Various events (including sudden lighting changes) ensue, until the ending emulates that of Haydn's 'Farewell' symphony. A later example is *(K)ein Sommernachtstraum ((Not) a Midsummer Night's Dream*, 1985), which uses pastiche Mozartian and Schubertian tunes.

Schnittke's *Symphony No. 1* (1969–72) pitted tonal against atonal elements, in an exploration of the continuing viability of the medium of the symphony. Something of that questioning of the possibilities still open to the symphonist survives in the *Symphony No. 3* (1981), with part of the answer being an eclecticism of material, aural allusion, and pictorialism, that had been initiated by **Mahler.** A shimmering mass of glittering sonority opens the symphony, three times gaining in intensity to a mighty climax, in a kind of 20th-century equivalent to the opening of Wagner's *Das Rheingold.* Overtones build up, and then break away to form new overtones; the actual material of this study in sonority is derived from the monograms of over thirty German composers. This stunning first movement of considerable orchestral virtuosity acts as an introduction to the succeeding three, laid out in conventional form. The following allegro in sonata form has strong echoes of **Shostakovich** in its perky, waltz-like material, before moving into a typical counter-theme founded on scurrying ostinato strings; its climax includes an organ, and towards the end of the movement a piano is heard playing Mozart, as if from a far nostalgic distance, both in space and time. The short scherzo starts demurely, as a kind of Prokofievian march overlaid with unusual orchestral colours, but then wanders into odder, more disturbed regions and a huge and menacing mechanism. This leads straight into the large, silent wastelands of the opening (for strings alone) of the final movement, following the example of the slow movement of Shostakovich's fifth symphony. This adagio finale is the longest movement of the work, aiming towards an ending that combines triumph with uncertainty before a peaceful close, complete with bells.

The *Symphony No. 4* (1984), for piano, vocal soloists, choir and chamber orchestra, is an odd work, both in symphonic layout and overall effect. Constructed in one movement divided into seven sections, it has a programmatic content: its inspiration is that of the Catholic rosary, and its relationship to the life of Christ (seen through Mary's eyes). Themes composed of tetrachords represent the Catholic, the Orthodox and the Lutheran faiths, and a three-note theme represents ancient chant; all are brought together in the final

chorus. None of this programme is necessary for the enjoyment of the work, which succeeds in purely abstract terms, though its liturgical origins are suggested by the overall tone. The second section is for piano alone, joined by the tenor; apart from a wordless counter-tenor vocalise, the other vocal forces appear only in the delicate and beautiful final section, where an archaic-sounding chant builds in complexity, adding layers to reach a luminous climax with the sounding of bells that slowly die away. In this symphony Schnittke's spare, austere style, as in the bell sonorities of the orchestra against piano and harpsichord in the opening, is juxtaposed with his large-scale assertive utterances. The melodic material is often of gentle, slow-moving simplicity matched by the orchestral colours, but overlaid with harmonies that have the effect of distancing that simplicity. This strange but moving work, one feels, belongs in the cathedral rather than the concert hall. The *Symphony No. 5* (1988) also bears the title *Concerto Grosso No. 4,* the juxtaposition suggesting its general tone, with a metamorphosis of the Baroque style complete with an intermittent harpsichord continuo. The material of the second movement is based on the unfinished second movement of **Mahler's** early piano quartet. With its raucous climaxes and solo violin writing in the style of earlier **Stravinsky,** it has some interest as a concerto grosso, but as a symphony its grander vision seems too calculated.

Concertos form a major strand in Schnittke's output. The short *Concerto for Oboe, Harp and Strings* (1971) has a single arch movement, with a typically quiet opening and close. Funereal in tone, serial in style, it lacks the impact of many of Schnittke's other works. The piano concertos are unnumbered. The first, the *Piano Concerto* (1960), is for piano and large orchestra; the second is titled *Music for Piano and Chamber Orchestra* (1964), and the one-movement third is titled *Concerto for Piano and Strings* (1979). In the last, material based on Russian church music intertwines with that based on a 12-tone row, and the main theme is not stated in its entirety until the end. The solo line has ruminative, almost doodling moments, contrasting with virtuoso and extrovert effects (including massed clusters on the keyboard). Its series of attractive and sometimes violent incidents have echoes of (and one short quote from) **Shostakovich,** and also recall **Prokofiev** in some of the more barbaric piano moments, though the overall effect is Schnittke's alone. The compelling *Concerts for Piano, Four Hands and Orchestra* (1988) is violent and dense, harrowing even in quieter moments.

In the *Violin Concerto No. 3* (1978), for violin, nine winds, four brass and strings, one of Schnittke's finest works, he dispenses with traditional development, although the three movements roughly correspond to a condensed sonata form. Instead there is a sense of linear flow evolving as the events require, propelled by the solo line: the violin acts not as a virtuoso soloist, but as a kind of continuous and expressive emotional thread running through the more broken orchestral contribution. The material almost always suggests a tonal axis, but this is skewed by the accretion of a multiplicity of styles, totally integrated into the flow: 12-tone, serialism, and microtonal variations (especially in the solo line). The concerto opens with a long solo, gradually joined by the winds and brass.

The middle movement is more raucous, using the panoply of atonal and serial techniques, from under which suddenly emerges, in complete contrast, a quiet Dvořák-like tune, developed by the violin. It ends quietly and contemplatively. This is a concerto of many shifting moods, but whose continuity of expressive purpose is continually supported by the solo writing, as if the character underlying the emotional changes remains constant. The *Viola Concerto* (1985) is perhaps even more impressive, with a solo line that veers between soaring lyricism and rushing passages menaced by the orchestral writing. The mawkish, Mahlerian second movement has haunting colours in the orchestration and one terrifying outburst. The ending is reminiscent of that of **Shostakovich's** fourth symphony, almost suggesting a tribute. There is a threatening air to this work, as if lyrical beauty was in danger of being stamped underfoot; this proved prophetic, as Schnittke suffered a severe heart attack on completing it.

The central concept of the *Cello Concerto No. 1* (1985–86), from the explosive orchestral outburst that crashes in on the quiet and lyrical opening, is of the individual (the soloist) faced with his or her surroundings (the orchestra). The emotional conflict between the song-like solo line and an orchestra that looms over it gradually evolves into the soloist seeking answers to the relationship. The second movement is lyrical and contemplative, until it moves into an unsettled climactic

close, as if this path did not provide the answers for the soloist. The short third movement is a mawkish march, reminiscent of **Shostakovich**, with the soloist and orchestra acting in concert, until this compromise reaches a violent, dissonant and inconclusive climax in which material from the second movement intrudes. In the final movement, building on these experiences, the soloist finds a solution as the lyrical, hymn-like cello line is gradually joined by the orchestra for a massive hymn of praise and understanding. Apart from its intrinsic impact, the concerto is also of interest in that its basis – the struggle of the hero leading to an optimistic end – is essentially that of the ideal Soviet socialist symphonic construction, though here the ends are entirely philosophical rather than political, with no trace of musical bombast or ideology.

Besides the symphonies, there are a number of works for large orchestra. *Pianissimo* (1967–68) is for a very large orchestra, including electric guitar and two pianos. Constructed as twelve intermeshed variations, and using a tone-row only stated in its entirety at the end, it reflects Schnittke's exploration of European avant-garde techniques in its study of rising crescendos and the massing of sonorities. *Ritual* (1984–85), dedicated to the victims of World War II, is a short work of commemoration, half joyously expectant, half dirge, concentrating on sonorities, with a long, delicate and memorable close of high bells. The slow-moving, thick-textured undulations of sonorities in the *Passacaglia* (1985) were inspired by a wonderment at nature, and particularly nature expressed by the sea, caught in the great swelling crescendo of a storm.

String quartets form the heart of Schnittke's chamber output. The *String Quartet No. 1* (1966) is a 12-tone work, concentrating on atmospheric string sonorities. It uses the device of a melodic line being slightly modified by the different instruments, each repetition partially offset in time, giving an improvisatory feel. Its opening, sounding like the cries of beached whales, is particularly effective. Atmospheric high harmonics launch the tense, tragic mood of the *String Quartet No. 2* (1980), whose material is derived from ancient Russian church song. It is an intense work full of dramatic action, regularly creating choral sounds, from the rushing chords of the opening movement to the icy alienation of the beginning of the slow third movement. Changes of string colour and tonal base take place with great rapidity, and the offset repetition of lines is again used. The quartet was written following the death of a friend, and the urgency of tragic expression, combined with a philosophical questioning in the distortion of the church material, permeates this emotive work, which ends in a fashion as extraordinary as its opening. The three-movement *String Quartet No. 3* (1983) is more contemplative, though it is not without its dramatic moments. It opens with a quiet, hymn-like effect, quoting from Lasso and Beethoven, and using **Shostakovich's** initials as a motto (D–Eb–C–B, or in German D–S–C–H) to provide the basic material and three different moods. Schnittke uses a technique he developed in the 1980s of material that seems to be leading somewhere, and then collapses, and he again employs rising steps. The quartet has a wistful, distant feel, offset by rigorous passages of driving counterpoint. The *Piano Quintet* (1972–76) was written following the death of the composer's mother, and is one of his most tragically expressive works. The second movement includes a waltz, grotesquely manipulated, based on the motto B–A–C–H, and the last movement is a mirror-image passacaglia. Schnittke orchestrated the *Quintet* in 1978, titling it *In Memoriam*, and this version uses all Schnittke's considerable powers of orchestration (including an organ), in which the waltz, against a cluster of rising strings, has especial menace. The result is virtually a new work, for the impacts of the two versions do differ: spare, elegiac, heartfelt in the chamber guise; powerful, more extrovert and with a greater range of timbre in the orchestral. The *Violin Sonata No. 2* ('quasi una sonata', 1968), which also uses the B–A–C–H motto in its single-movement design, was similarly orchestrated for violin and chamber orchestra in 1987. Full of tense incident punctuated by silences, it again reflects Schnittke's period of avant-garde exploration, as well as the influence of **Stravinsky**. The *Cello Sonata* (1978), in three linked movements, is large-scale in design and intent, more conventional in its material. The cello and piano have equal weight in their own right, rather like two explorers independently pursuing parallel routes across the same terrains towards the same geographic goal. The stark *Prelude to the Memory of Dmitri Shostakovich* (1975) for two violins uses the D–S–C–H motto, with one violin intended to be played behind a screen with amplification, or pre-recorded. Schnittke's vocal music sometimes

shows the influence of **Orff**, both in the ostinato orchestral accompaniments and in the choral writing. The *Requiem* (1974–75), for soloists, chorus, organ and instruments is in his sparser, more ritualistic style, though it includes a jazzy section in the Credo. Noteworthy is the Tuba Mirum, where a monotone chant, influenced by Eastern musics, is set against extraordinary and menacing instrumental sonorities. The *Faust Cantata* (1982–83), for soloists, chorus and orchestra, based on Goethe, arose from ideas for a projected opera. It is more dramatic and more immediate than the *Requiem*, telling the story of the final moments of Faust's life as he is taken by the devil on the stroke of midnight; the influence of **Orff**, obvious in the opening, extends to a monumental contralto tango solo. The opera *Life with an Idiot* (1990–91) is more problematic. Based on the novel by Victor Erofeyev, and with a libretto by the author, it is a grotesque story in the tradition of **Shostakovich's** *The Nose*, with allegories of dictatorship and communism, and a theme of the distortion between reality and madness. It is also extremely violent. A couple, as punishment, have to take an idiot into their home; he despoils their kitchen with his ablutions, and the wife has an affair with him. The husband then takes the sexual place of the wife, as madness overtakes them all, and the idiot eventually decapitates the wife. The context in which the violence against women is placed is disturbing, because it is partly glorified. In addition, the opera suffers from the literary brilliance of its text, where much of the action is reported speech; consequently the results sometimes have elements of the dramatic oratorio, however much dressed up by stage action, and one feels a potentially much better opera lurks behind this one. Schnittke's setting is full of parody and grotesquerie.

Schnittke's music is not immediately recognisable by its melodic material, in the manner of **Prokofiev** or **Shostakovich**, and the use of many earlier styles within a contemporary framework might suggest a lack of that individuality which has always marked the best composers. But Schnittke's style concentrates on sonorities and colours rather than melodic line, and familiarity soon allows recognition of his very particular voice. The interweaving of earlier musics – polystylism – is an integral part of that vision, linking it to the inheritance of the past that any modern composer carries. Schnittke was essentially a Romantic composer, and not merely because he returned to the tonal base of neo-Romanticism. He himself suggested that his music is an attempt to express his inner sonic or visual visions. Throughout there is a suggestion of the struggle between conflicting forces of the human condition, and an exploration of the conflicts inherent in the natural forces working on the human condition, that belong to a Romantic outlook. He combines this with, ultimately, a sense of optimism (and of beauty) that often permeates the final pages of his scores, and which is unusual for contemporary composers; but that optimism is never bland, because of the struggles that have preceded it. His powers of orchestration and of formal design support the expressive intent: he has combined the Romantic musical tradition with many of the expressive devices of the European avant-garde, to ensure that his music both lives within a tradition and extends it.

Schnittke taught at the Moscow Conservatory (1961–72), and from 1972 at the Tchaikovsky Conservatory.

RECOMMENDED WORKS
Cello Concerto No. 1 (1985–86)
Concerto Grosso No. 1 (1976–77)
In Memoriam (1978) for orchestra (from Piano Quintet)
Piano Quintet (1972–76)
Ritual (1984–85) for large orchestra
String Quartet No. 2 (1980)
Symphony No. 3 (1981)
Viola Concerto (1985)
Violin Concerto No. 3 (1978)

Scriabin (also spelled Skryabin) Alexander Nikolaievich**
born 6th January 1872 at Moscow
died 27th April 1915 at Moscow

Scriabin was like a brief comet flaring in the musical sky, scattering remnants of his trail after him but leaving little lasting impression. Steeped in theosophy and mysticism, possessed by the kind of sensuous, grand *fin de siècle* vision that was snuffed out by World War I, he was emblematic of his age. His output reflects an aesthetic that belongs to the late 19th century rather than the 20th. Musically, it is also debatable whether his idiom belongs to the 20th century, as it represents the last flare-up of Lisztian Romanticism, tottering in its massed chromaticism on the edge of a new harmonic world, but

harnessed by the voluptuousness of late 19th-century pianism.

However, certain aspects of Scriabin's harmonic development do herald 20th-century usage, though in very different contexts. Scriabin's developments of Lisztian Romanticism include an interest in the system of harmonic overtones, building chords on the natural sequence. This led to massive chromaticism and the abandonment of key-signatures in his work. Perhaps his most important hallmark was the development of chords based on the interval of the fourth (as opposed to the traditional tonal interval of the third), anticipating a common feature of later 20th-century music. The whole-tone scale appears in his later works.

His output divides into eight works for orchestral forces and a mass of piano works, of which the most important are the fifteen sets of *Preludes* (1888–1914) and the extraordinary series of ten piano sonatas. Of the orchestral works, the *Piano Concerto* (1896) is a highly-charged late-Romantic work teeming with pianistic effect, of interest for its affinities to the music of his fellow-student **Rachmaninov**. The *Symphony No. 1* (1899–1900) uses a chorus in the finale, but it is the last three orchestral works that are of chief interest. By this period, Scriabin was striving for a mystical expression of a vision of the cosmos in which the inner emotions and the outer ecstatic glory are joined; his intent was to so move the audience that they would share in this metaphysical ecstasy. The *Symphony No. 3 'The Divine Poem'* (1902–04) is a surging tone poem in three sections ('Struggles', 'Sensual Pleasures' and 'Divine Joy'), played continuously. The glimpses of the divine are heard through swirling mists, broken into by woodwind cries or blasts from the brass, the whole symphony building from the quiet of the opening to rolling climaxes, and ridden with late-Romantic tension. *Le poème de l'extase* (Poem of Ecstasy, 1905–08) for orchestra has a philosophical programme of heady, orgiastic voluptuousness with music to match, and the summit of his atmospheric mysticism is reached in *Prométhée, le poème de feu* (*Prometheus, the Poem of Fire*, 1908–10), for orchestra, chorus and colour organ, an instrument designed to provide different lights and colours for different notes, and their combinations, to match the music.

Scriabin's most valuable legacy is to be found in the piano sonatas. The *Piano*

Sonata No. 1 (1891) is a large late-Romantic work in four movements, each unusually in the same key, joined by a recurring motto phrase. The *Piano Sonata No. 3* (1897) is essentially a tone poem, as if contemplating the ruined castle that is supposed to have inspired the work. The slow movement suggests overgrown trees on the banks of the moat, and the last has something of the atmosphere of Rachmaninov's *Isle of the Dead.* From the turn of the century Scriabin started to develop his mature piano style: ruminative, sometimes with almost formless wisps of idea expanding into a more emphatic mystical and emotional message. Pianistic Northern Lights pulsate and shimmer, changing shape and colour, spinning off into new subsidiary formations, the whole always launching high into the stratosphere with the suggestion and promise of the mystery beyond. The ruminative, almost disjointed opening of the *Piano Sonata No. 4* (1899–1903), in two movements played without a break, flutters into action and eventual climax. In spite of the use of fourths, this sonata keeps one foot in Scriabin's earlier style; he then pulls it away in the upward chromatic swirl and subsequent disembodied bare rumination of the *Piano Sonata No. 5* (1907), in one movement. Its almost Impressionistic moments, a feature of Scriabin's later piano music, are created by the absence of a sense of recognisable pulse and by wisps of ideas meandering out of the central core. The *Piano Sonata No. 6* (1911) draws the listener into a mysterious inner world; the *Piano Sonata No. 7 'White Mass'* (1911) turns that inner world into a rite of violent fervour, while the *Piano Sonata No. 9 'Black Mass'* (1912–13) creates an almost nebulous world alternating between nervous, disjointed energy and evanescent lyricism, though it is not as dark or furious as its name (coined by Scriabin's friend Alexander Podgaetsky) might suggest. By this sonata the piano writing appears almost totally fluid, reaching its culmination in the luminous *Piano Sonata No. 10* (1913).

Scriabin's last sets of études and preludes are of interest. The *Trois études* (1912) cover diminishing extremes of interval spans: a major ninth in the first, like a bright jewel giving off prismatic reflections and dancing light as it slowly turns; a minor seventh in the slow, Impressionistic second; and perfect fifths in the third. The language of the first of the *Five Preludes* (1914) is reduced to a bare minimum of dissonant sounds; the subsequent preludes range from a ghostly march to the brief flare of the fifth, as if describing thunderclouds building up and altering shape. Throughout the set, the conjunction of overtones, often left hanging, forms a major feature of the music.

At the end of his life, Scriabin was working on a *mysterium* that would embrace all the art forms in a gigantic work (opening with bells suspended above the Himalayas to start the week-long conception). He had made the briefest of sketches for its 'Prefatory Action', which were turned into a full-scale work, titled *Universe*, by Alexander Nemtin (born 1936). While containing little Scriabin, this is a powerful Scriabinesque work in its own right.

RECOMMENDED WORKS
Symphony No. 3 *'The Divine Poem'* (1902–04)
Le poème de l'extase (*Poem of Ecstasy*, 1905–08) for orchestra
Prométhée, le poème de feu (*Prometheus, the Poem of Fire*, 1908–10) for orchestra, chorus and colour organ
Piano Sonatas 3–10 (1897–1913)
Five Preludes (1914)
Trois études (1912)

BIBLIOGRAPHY
H. Macdonald, *Scryabin*, 1978

Shchedrin Rodion*
born 16th December 1932 at Moscow

Rodion Shchedrin emerged in the 1960s and the 1970s as the major Soviet composer of the generation following **Shostakovich** and **Prokofiev** in favour with the authorities. He responded with a populist style, suitably spiced with elements of modernism, sufficiently diluted for him to be promoted by the Soviet authorities as an example of their forward-looking musical ideas. At his best, he has displayed a voice of great expertise, especially in orchestration; at his worst, he can infuriate by his eclectic borrowings (including older musics), his half-assimilated modern Western ideas (including serialism), and a general impression of trite surface glitter. Much of this reaction was based on a misapprehension by both the Soviet authorities and the Western critics, for until the 1980s his art was essentially founded on folk music, especially the wit and play of the form of the 'chastushka', a street-song genre based on a kind of limerick or ditty whose particular humour and rhythms have formed a thread through much of his music. To this he wedded classical forms and borrowings, imitations of Tchaikovsky and **Rachmaninov**, the occasional instrumental playfulness of **Stravinsky**, and, especially, the melodic shapes and instrumental usage of **Shostakovich**. Ballet has also been a major influence on his music, and his own ballets have been created for his wife, the ballerina Maya Plisetskaya. However, in the 1980s his music started to take a new direction, shorn of much of the eclecticism, as if with the new freedoms in Russia he could cast off his role as the bright young light of Soviet music, and find a personal voice.

Shchedrin's works of the 1950s passed virtually unnoticed outside the USSR. The *Piano Concerto No. 1* (1954) rather ineffectually crossed **Rachmaninov** with **Prokofiev**, though it is not Shchedrin's fault that the opening sounds like a variation on the *Star Wars* theme; the lively last movement is based on popular songs. The *Symphony No. 1* (1956–58) is a big, Soviet-epic work, traditional in its language, tinged with melancholy, that, with its direct, uncluttered orchestration, suggested promise rather than substance; in spite of its symphonic argument, it seems to be constantly flirting with the descriptive idiom of the ballet suite. The ballet *The Hunchbacked Horse* (1955) achieved considerable success in the Soviet Union, while the opera *Not Only Love* (1961, sometimes known as *Not Love Alone*), to a libretto by V. Katanyan based on the stories of S. Antonov, has for its central character the woman chairperson of a collective farm. The suite from the opera, for soprano and orchestra, which includes the main aria for the soloist, is heavily under the spell of **Prokofiev** and suffers in the comparison.

Shchedrin came to wider attention through two orchestral works. The *Concerto No. 1 for Orchestra* (1963), subtitled 'Ozorni'ye chashtushki' ('Merry Ditties' or 'Naughty Limericks'), a glittering showpiece for orchestra that comes perilously close to 'light' music, demonstrated Shchedrin's orchestral skill, his perky wit, and the adoption of the 'chastushka'. But he achieved international notoriety with the *Carmen Ballet* (1967), a scintillating orchestration of themes from Bizet's opera that is all glitter, brilliant colours, stunning effect – and little substance when divorced from its stage context – but masterful when seen as a ballet. The scoring is for strings and percussion (or rather percussion, especially tuned percussion, and strings) and the music is such outrageous fun that it should be at least sampled once. The partly atonal *Symphony No. 2* (1965) suggested an awareness of contemporary musical developments in Poland, while the *Piano Concerto No. 2* (1966) was again influenced by **Prokofiev**. *Chimes* (1968) for orchestra drew inspiration from Russian icons, with quasi-serial elements and the influence of Russian bells, and the oratorio *Lenin in the People's Heart* (1969) included a number of quasi-avant-garde vocal effects; it is historically interesting as the most stylistically extreme of any post-war Soviet cantata on such a fundamental Soviet subject, and surprisingly effective in some of its passages, but is now presumably doomed to oblivion. The ballet *Anna Karenina* (1972), in which the adaptation of Tolstoy's novel concentrates on the Anna–Karenin–Vronsky love triangle, was a major event in Soviet ballet. The score is suffused with the rhythms and sometimes onomatopoeic sounds of trains, and Bellini is invoked in a scene at the Italian Opera. However, divorced from its period staging and often tumultuous story, its music, intentionally aping Tchaikovsky, often seems dull. The non-tonal *Piano Concerto No. 3* (1973) was built around a theme and variations. In the opera *Dead Souls* (1977), Shchedrin replaced the violins with choral writing, and the staging used multi-level action; however, the opera was criticised for watering down Gogol's message of the pain and suffering of the Russian people.

In the 1980s Shchedrin developed an orchestral style that is simpler and more personal, but as direct as his earlier works. The works of this period have the stamp of a personal and thoughtful voice, and those new to his idiom, or who are put off by the surface glitter of his earlier music, should turn to these first. The hiccups of modernism are to all intents and purposes abandoned, but while the harmonic language is relatively straightforward, these works are by no means traditional. The orchestral palette is spare; slow swirls of subdued strings usually predominate, broken into by woodwind or brass or the tinkling of the celesta. Movement is unhurried, and contrasts are provided by blocks of colour, where Shchedrin carefully uses the overlapping ranges of families of instruments to create homogeneous blends. Shades of **Shostakovich** and sometimes **Mahler** still stalk through these scores, but they have been melded into a more personal voice.

The emotional range is not as profound as that of **Schnittke**, and the spiritual effect cannot match that of **Pärt**, but they have a compelling and insinuating sense of presence that grows on increased acquaintance. The attractive *The Frescoes of Dionysus* (1982), for wind ensemble, cello and celesta, is a reaction of instrumental colour and timbre to the frescoes and icons in the Feropontov Monastery in northern Russia. The powerful *Self-Portrait* (1984) for orchestra paints a subdued, almost dour picture, of a man quietly and acceptingly wedded to the earth, into whose equanimity break unbidden visions of luminous beauty or angry intensity. *Music for the Town of Köthen* (1984–85) for small orchestra (with a prominent harpsichord) is a three-movement neo-Baroque suite, gently pleasant and spacious, with a whimsical falling idea that adds a compelling dash of modernity and creates thrust in the first movement. *Music for String, Oboes, Horns and Celesta*, drawn from the ballet *The Lady with the Lap-Dog*, grows in stature on repeated hearings; generally solemn and subdued in mood, it is imbued with an atmosphere of winter festivities by the delicate decorations of the celesta and by the block use of oboes and horns, whose colours merge. Of his other works of the period, *Three Shepherds* (1988), for flute, oboe and clarinet, recreates the spirit of traditional competitions between peasant musicians. *The Echo Sonata* (1985) for violin, celebrating the 300th anniversary of J. S. Bach's birth, includes gentle echoes of Bach in an effect akin to electronic transformation, but its theme is not interesting enough to sustain its nine variations and epilogue.

Shchedrin is a concert pianist of stature, and his own piano music provides a microcosm of his development, without being especially arresting. *Poem* (1954) for piano shows indebtedness to **Prokofiev**, the *Humoresque* (1957) to **Shostakovich**, while the *Twenty-Four Preludes and Fugues* (1963–64) are more obviously neo-Bachian than those of Shostakovich, in spite of the moments of extreme chromatic edge. The *Piano Sonata* (1962) shows Shchedrin's eclecticism at its least flattering: with sections of virtuoso showmanship, the opening of the sonata seems to lope along through street scenery of modernist noises for their own sake, while the middle movement is brilliant but empty, as if dispossessed.

Shchedrin was a member of the ill-fated parliament dissolved by President Yeltsin in 1993, and emerged as a staunch anti-communist, who described communism as being 'anti-biological'. His earlier outspokenness, sometimes steering close to the Soviet wind, was marred by his lead in the vicious 1965 attack on a composer of more avant-garde tendencies, Edison Denisov, and his current position as politician-composer has been sullied by his refusal to allow his music to be played on the same programmes as that of Denisov.

RECOMMENDED WORKS
The Carmen Ballet (1967)
Concerto No. 1 for Orchestra (1963)
The Frescoes of Dionysus (1982) for wind, cello and celesta
Music for Strings, Oboes, Horns and Celesta
Self-Portrait (1984) for orchestra

Shostakovich Dmitri Dmitriyevich***

born 25th September 1906 at St Petersburg
died 9th August 1975 at Moscow

Dmitri Shostakovich is one of the most complex musical personalities of the 20th century, whose overall achievement in virtually every musical genre is still widely misunderstood, or not fully appreciated. He has a claim to be, after **Mahler**, the greatest symphonist and, with **Bartók**, the most important composer of string quartets in the 20th century. His symphonies are now universally known and admired, although this is a relatively recent phenomenon. His string quartets, apart from the eighth, are less frequently heard and are undervalued. Perhaps more than any other composer of the 20th century he has reflected the tenor of much of the century, expressing the multitude of emotions, from the very dark to the reflection of beauty, and the desolate cruelty as well as the compassion of 20th-century societies.

That Shostakovich was for many years treated equivocally by critics (and sometimes still is) seems to be due to three factors. The first is that, in technical musical terms, he was not an innovator, aside from youthful experimentation that responded to Western trends until the artistic clampdown of the Stalinist years. He preferred extending traditional forms and harmonic language, moulding them to his own expressive purpose, and innovators have always received more contemporary attention than the technically conservative. The second is that, owing to the circumstances of the Soviet state, he produced a number of works in the style of Soviet Socialist Realism that are often catchy, efficient and workmanlike, but also vacuous, and it was often these works that the Soviet apparatus promoted externally. This presents a problem for listeners, who should not be put off if they encounter such works and are disappointed: they represent a necessary shell, not the kernel of the composer. The third is more complex. Shostakovich was a very direct composer, expressing in an immediate style both his own personal emotions and his reactions to the culture in which he worked. **Mahler** had shown that a more eclectic range of musical ideas and depiction, traditionally excluded from such a serious form as the symphony, could be woven into the symphonic fabric and increase the range of expression within the form. Shostakovich extended this emotional range to include material inspired by immediate topical events, and, at his most successful, mould that particular to the universal. There is inherent in his music a very particular political and social involvement, filtered through his own emotions (though it is far removed from the Soviet posturing his society required), and such a role for music has traditionally been suspect. If his Romantic predecessors can be poorly and loosely defined as expressing the psychological interaction between the individual and Nature in their music, Shostakovich expresses the psychological interaction of the individual and modern society, his very directness allowing a vast emotional range. But this emotional range, which he achieved with such conviction, and which has so appealed to audiences, has not appealed to all critics. In this sense of the purpose, if not the technical means, of his music Shostakovich was an innovator, paralleling modernist developments in other artistic fields.

Although his music is distinctive from the very beginning, his large output falls into three periods. Influenced by **Hindemith** and by **Prokofiev**, his early music was often experimental, responding to Western developments and to the sense of experimentation so excitingly rife in the early Soviet state. Irony and humour are inherent from the start, but also a sense of bubbling joy. With the rise of Stalin, Shostakovich's music became more monumental, more rugged, often with a controlled anger. He was heavily attacked twice, first in 1936 after Stalin violently objected to his opera *Lady Macbeth of the Mtsensk District*, and then in 1948 in the notorious Zhdanov condemnation of 'formalism'. In one sense, all his major music from 1936 onwards reflects some aspect of an artist's relationship with such an experience; at the same time, he churned out a large number of suitable cantatas and film scores along Soviet socialist realist lines, and the period 1954 to 1959 was particularly bleak, with no major personal (as opposed to publicly safe) works except the sixth string quartet. After 1960, his music became increasingly bitter, lean and sad, and later obsessed with death. This later music is his finest, eventually so spare that it seems to work almost instinctively; these are also his most difficult works to assimilate and understand, and the best of them have rightly been compared with late Beethoven. From the late 1940s, he increasingly used self-quotation in his works, clearly with an autobiographical and extra-musical intent whose full import is still not fully understood. Equally significant is the use of the motto theme of his name (D SCHostakovich) D–S–C–H (in German notation D–E♭–C–B: E♭ being 'Es', B natural 'H').

A number of characteristics are observable throughout his output. Apart from a few early works, his idiom is traditionally tonal, admitting chromatic dissonance usually for emotional effect. Only towards the end of his life did he start to use atonal passages and 12-tone rows, and these are essentially utilisations of the harmonic and melodic possibilities they afford within a tonal framework. His structures are generally classical in form (though with increasing freedom and departure from the norm in the late works), and if it were not for the directness and involvement of the emotional utterance, totally unclassical in aesthetic, he might have been regarded as a neo-classical composer. Bach and Beethoven are the major mentors for his mature works, the former for his mastery of counterpoint, the latter for the example of expressing the most intimate of thoughts in the sparest of forms. Indeed, it may be that when the mass of politically correct music by Shostakovich is finally discarded and as forgotten as Beethoven's once wildly popular *Wellington's Victory*, Shostakovich's achievement may be seen as a 20th-century emotional counterpart to Beethoven, but without the latter's technical advances.

A favourite Shostakovich device is to use an adagio opening, with a simple, uncluttered initial idea (whose general casts are reminiscent of **Hindemith**) and a driving energy propelled in linear, rather than vertical lines. His middle movements often include a mawkish, ironic, sometimes demonic humour and energy. He delighted in rich string sonorities, especially in the string quartets. His slow movements aim at simplicity and beauty of texture, sometimes exploding into outbursts – strong contrasts of emotional tone and material are important, and Shostakovich became increasingly adept at handling their transition and juxtaposition in his middle period. In the later works he developed the ability to move from the barest textures to massive, grinding climaxes with complete freedom and conviction. The orchestration, often masterly but seldom used merely for effect, is characterised by clear, often sparse textures, long melodic lines, and colour shades of solo woodwind, solo brass, or small groups of wind or tuned percussion (xylophone, celesta) against massed strings. His output covers all the traditional genres of classical music; but his true genius, and his consummate achievement, are to be found in the series of fifteen string quartets. These are also the most concentrated and difficult of his works to grasp, especially the later quartets, and it is his symphonies that have commanded the most attention, and which, along with the concertos, provide the best introduction to his music.

Shostakovich's symphonies fall into distinct groups, with very differing aims. Four (Nos. 2, 3, 11 and 12) have specifically communist programmatic elements. Nos. 7, 8 and 9 reflect the experience of the war, although they are essentially abstract. Nos. 1, 4, 5, 6 and 10 are the major works in which Shostakovich explores the traditional structure of the symphony. Two of the last three symphonies (Nos. 13, 14) extensively employ vocal forces, and form a group with the last (No. 15) in extending beyond the traditional parameters of the symphony and expressing a very personal and particular emotional world. He burst into international prominence with the *Symphony No. 1* (1924–25), an extraordinary enough work in its own right, but remarkable considering he was only eighteen when he wrote it, and even more remarkable in that instead of being largely derivative it is full of Shostakovich fingerprints. Exuberant, dashing, often full of humour, throwing off the shackles of Romanticism with a happy abandon (and an occasional wry backward glance) as well as a delight in manipulating orchestral colours, it has remained one of Shostakovich's most popular works.

The next two symphonies reflected the optimism and experimental drive of the young Soviet state. The *Symphony No. 2 'To October'* (1927) is in one futurist movement, its opening a gradual emergence of solid ideas from a dark, thick-textured, muted atonal melée, and the whole symphony thrusts towards its long choral finale celebrating the October revolution, via some extremely raucous and insistent music. This little-known symphony is interesting for its experimentation (including combined polyrhythms and polytonality), and for its suggestions of the directions Shostakovich might have taken had he continued in a different cultural climate. The *Symphony No. 3 'The First of May'* (1929), for chorus and orchestra, is the most neglected of Shostakovich's symphonies, and, partly from its lack of thematic development, is the least successful, though there are many interesting episodes in it; with its sunny mood and fervour it is worth the acquaintance. Again in one movement, it includes another choral ending with a joyful socialist message (some Western performances have therefore omitted the chorus).

The hour-long *Symphony No. 4* (1935–36) was withdrawn while in rehearsal, and not heard until 1961. It is the most Mahlerian of the symphonies (especially the funeral march of the largo), episodic rather than traditional in form. In it many of Shostakovich's symphonic hallmarks – ostinati, a directness of pulse over long time spans, rhythmic devices – here reach a maturity of purpose. It is also a powerful work: tragic, brooding, dark, angry and intense. If it is too long, and its ideas overabundant, such failings are compensated by a demonic insistence, a wealth of inspired detail, and an extraordinary final movement ending with a huge ostinato that fades into emptiness, one of the most expressive passages in Shostakovich's whole output; Shostakovich was to return to its technique, colours and mood in the final movement of his last symphony. It was withdrawn primarily for political reasons, although one can't help wondering whether Shostakovich also felt he had also not yet completely achieved the marriage of content and form. His next symphony solved both problems, and has remained perhaps the best known. The *Symphony No. 5* (1937) is subtitled 'A Soviet Artist's Reply to Just Criticism', and in it Shostakovich channelled his impulse for a plethora of ideas into tauter and more controlled forms. The slow tempi and dark opening colours of the sonata-form first movement ideally suited Shostakovich's musical temperament, and most of the subsequent symphonies open in similar fashion. The largo slow movement is extremely beautiful, with beguiling simplicity and open textures dominated by the strings. The finale has long been the subject of debate; ostensibly it attempts the swagger of the official triumphant finale, but, apparently intentionally, fails, the final blare belied by the central slow section. The *Symphony No. 6* (1939), if less overtly appealing, is perhaps more interesting. The range of emotion and expression is much wider (particularly in the long opening largo that dominates the three-movement symphony); the symphonic solutions are more ambiguous, and the finale is more successful, its closing verve alloyed by memories of the opening movement.

The first of the war symphonies, the *Symphony No. 7* (sometimes called '*Leningrad*', 1942), was partly written during the siege of Leningrad, and has become notorious for its first movement. After a slow, bucolic opening, a march theme quietly appears and builds towards a massive climax, through a long succession of inexorable motoric repeats. In the hands of most conductors and orchestras it sounds banal; in the hands of a great conductor and orchestra, it can be hideously menacing, grinding, and monolithic (as Toscanini showed in the first Western performance), which was surely its exact intention. The notoriety of this movement has unfortunately overshadowed the rest of the symphony, which is largely tragic in feel, its slow movement impassioned, its finale grim and uncertain in its optimism until the closing pages. The equally large-scale *Symphony No. 8* (1943) continues the overall idiom of the seventh, but in a tauter fashion, and is one of Shostakovich's finest works. In place of a hollow optimism is an abject pessimism, a depiction of and compassionate response to the horror and suffering of war. It is cast in five movements, the last three linked, and opens with a slow and desolate adagio, a despoiled landscape from which emerges a drained, weeping, anguished extended climax that emphasises the desolation that returns. The short second movement is a mawkish march, suggesting martial splendour and barbed-wire whips. The third movement is another relentlessly urgent rhythmic creation, punctuated by orchestral explosions, that evolves into a trumpet tune over bass drum of phenomenal, determined energy; nothing else Shostakovich ever wrote has such white-hot, angry propulsion. This turns into the fourth-movement passacaglia, wispy, mist over total desolation, and similar in tone to the final movement of **Vaughan Williams's** sixth symphony. The final movement explodes into a huge, quasi-triumphant climax, that is whittled away by a demonic fiddler into a kind of weary, thankful peace. There is no glory in this symphony, only pity and desolation. Its successor is in its own way even finer. Authorities and audiences alike were expecting the *Symphony No. 9* (1945) to be choral, large in scale, and triumphant in tone, not just because of the end of the war with Germany, but also because of the tradition of Beethoven's ninth symphony. What they got instead was a short, five-movement, perfectly integrated and proportioned gem of a symphony, that is one of the few 20th-century works to combine genuine infectious humour with a contemporary idiom and a seriousness of purpose. For this is by no means a work of superficial gloss: underneath the bouncing surface is a wide range of mood, from the ironic to the tragic and the elegiac, the manic elements of the hilarious ending exemplifying the more disturbing elements of the symphony, and it is one of those rare works whose sum seems to contain far more than its parts would allow.

The gradual convergence of content and form in the sixth, eighth and ninth symphonies, and the evolving mastery of the musical expression of complex and often contradictory emotions, culminated in the *Symphony No. 10* (1953), one of the masterpieces of the 20th century. Its symphonic architecture is completely integrated, without the episodic elements of the earlier symphonies. Furthermore its emotional tension is consistent, from the tragic elements of the opening movement, through the propulsive drive of the second, the haunting, shattering, deliberate outburst of the third (a technique he had developed in his quartets), to a completely successful finale that arrives at a suitable emphatic conclusion without sacrificing the overall tone of the symphony. That this was an intensely personal document for the composer is obvious from the music (it followed Stalin's death, and has been seen as reflecting Shostakovich's anger and despair at the society he created), and is reinforced by the use of the motto D–S–C–H. The next two symphonies, as if retreating from such a personal and intense utterance, are programmatic:, *Symphony No. 11 '1905'* (1957) depicts the abortive uprising of 1905, the *Symphony*

No. 12 '1917' (1961) the October Revolution. Both are more appropriately treated as symphonic poems than as symphonies, in spite of their symphonic structures, for the programmatic elements presuppose an outward reflection, a commentary, rather than the internally-generated passions of all Shostakovich's other mature symphonies. Nor should they be dismissed on that score: the *Symphony No. 11* in particular contains some of Shostakovich's finest descriptive music, brilliantly scored, its emotional commentary often hard-hitting, as in the intense build-up to the climax of the shooting in the square, and in the harrowing effect of the music of shattering quietness that follows it.

With the *Symphony No. 13 'Babi Yar'* (1962) Shostakovich changed direction, as if he had said all he had needed to say in the traditional symphonic structure with the tenth symphony, and fulfilled his programmatic needs or commitments in the eleventh and twelfth. Scored for bass, choir and orchestra, it is a setting in five movements of poems by Yevgeny Yevtushenko. It is Shostakovich's most public statement of the collision between private feelings of anger, despair and biting satire against the oppressive Soviet system, and the public artistic utterance. Although Yevtushenko's verses can be construed as politically correct, they are consistently subversive through their ambiguity, and Shostakovich uses echoes of the Russian tradition, particularly of massed male voices, to contrast the aspirations with the realities. It opens with the title poem about the mass graves of Babi Yar, evidence of a massacre officially attributed to the Nazis, but then rumoured to be the work of Stalin (Yevtushenko's poem never mentions the perpetrators or the Communist Party). The second movement ('Humour') summarises Shostakovich's mordant wit, and its psychological necessity. The Finale ('A Career') uses a poem about Galileo to offer a savage indictment of the position of the artist under the Soviet regime. There are few works of music so powerfully expressing the protest of the humanist artist. The *Symphony No. 14* (1969), for soprano, bass and chamber orchestra, transferred the tone and the vocal means of the thirteenth, with the common denominator of the tolling bell, to a more introspective, equally anguished work. Dedicated to Benjamin **Britten**, it is a cycle of eleven settings of poems by Lorca, Apollinaire, Küchelbecker and Rilke. Its subject is death, treated in a variety of tones, all dark, from the barren, spare textures and swooping

double-basses of the opening song, through touches of bitter irony, to an ending preceded by near-silence that offers little hope or resolution. The orchestration is spartan, merely strings against the bright or harsh colours of a percussion section dominated by tuned instruments and excluding timpani; the textures are often reduced to the absolute minimum: music stripped to its barest necessities. This bleak work is hardly touched by moments of lighter beauty; it is a consideration of death unleavened by the transfiguration of the last works of **Mahler** or **Strauss**, but in its own way it is as profound, its musical qualities matching the particularly distinguished poetry. It looks into the abyss of profound depression, as if the only way to avoid that abyss and counter the depression was to express it in music; such a contemplation is not comfortable for the listener, but it is a confrontation with an experience all too central to our century.

Shostakovich's final symphony, the *Symphony No. 15* (1971) is perhaps his most extraordinary. It combines the spare language and the direct, clear textures of its immediate predecessors with the symphonic and purely instrumental effect of the tenth symphony. It uses, for reasons still not yet fully understood, quotations from Rossini's *William Tell* overture and from Wagner's *Ring* cycle. On the one hand the symphony can be approached as a purely abstract work, in which the often disparate ideas flow with a remarkable spontaneity and natural fluidity. On the other hand, it is clearly an intensely personal emotional document, using the D–S–C–H motto and quoting extensively from Shostakovich's own work (including the ninth and eleventh symphonies, *The Execution of Stepan Razin*, the quartets, and the concertos), whose full secrets have yet to be deciphered. It also adds a kind of serene peace and reconciliation to the experience of the fourteenth symphony, still without a strong impulse of hope, but with a spellbinding ending of chattering percussion and tinkling bells against a rumbling timpani theme and held strings, echoing the fourth symphony, that suggests 'I have done what I can'.

Shostakovich wrote six concertos, and each has claim to a regular place in the repertoire. The *Piano Concerto No. 1* (1933), properly titled *Concerto for Piano, Trumpet and String Orchestra*, is an affair of riotous delight, carried on between piano and trumpet as much as the orchestra, especially in the rushing refusal of either instrument to finish the concerto – it is a concerto counterpart to the exuberance of the first symphony. The *Piano Concerto No. 2* (1957) is very different: Romantically hued, with one of the most beautiful slow movements of all piano concertos, it was written for his (then) teenage son, and follows the tradition of **Rachmaninov**. This delightful, unassuming work will appeal to almost every music lover. The two violin concertos are more serious in intent. The *Violin Concerto No. 1* (1947–48, revised 1955) has connections with the tenth symphony and the fifth string quartet, using the D–S–C–H motive, and, in the opening of the third and final movement, incorporates music too close to a section of the film score of *Zoya* (1944) to be a coincidence. It opens with a nocturne and a thoughtful solo line, moves to a scherzo that is a merry-go-round whirl, and ends, after a monumental opening to the finale, with a passacaglia with lovely, less angular solo writing. The *Violin Concerto No. 2* (1967) is more obviously lyrical and subdued, with a plaintive beauty, and omits the usual Shostakovich scherzo. The compelling *Cello Concerto No. 1* (1959), another of Shostakovich's most popular works, is a single-minded concerto (being largely based on one theme heard at the opening), with a slow movement whose idiom is ideal for the richness of the solo instrument, and a bouncy ending. The *Cello Concerto No. 2* (1966) seems to have been inexplicably neglected. Less direct than its predecessor, it is the most haunting, sad and introspective of the concertos, a parallel to the later quartets, lightly scored for the typical late Shostakovich colours of double woodwind, two horns, two harps, percussion including tuned instruments, and strings.

Most of Shostakovich's serious vocal music (as opposed to the poster-paint Soviet socialist realist cantatas) dates from late in his life, when he also orchestrated two earlier song-cycles. The song-cycle *From Jewish Folk Poetry* (1948, orchestrated 1964) for soprano, contralto, tenor and chorus, is both the most Mahlerian of his works and one of the most appealing. The folk poetry is wide ranging in sentiment, and Shostakovich was able to indulge in the grotesque and the satirical, as well as the lyrical (in the lovely duet describing winter). Yet darkness and despair hover in the background throughout, and the chief feature of the song-cycle is a deep feeling of compassion for those in the ballad stories of the poetry, each of

which has a protagonist. It is considerably more powerful in its orchestrated version. *The Execution of Stepan Razin* (1964), for bass, chorus and orchestra, is a dramatic cantata that continued the submerged protest of the *Symphony No. 13*, using verses by the same poet. Ostensibly Yevtushenko's dramatic narrative poem, telling of the execution of a Cossack hero whose severed head laughs at the Tsar, tows the party line. Underneath Yevtushenko's writing is subversive (the Tsar's world is easily equated with the communist regime), and it is this side that Shostakovich emphasised and amplified in the music, which is far from Soviet Socialist Realism. The Soviet authorities did not appear to realise this, but neither have Western musicians, for this most dramatic (aside from the operas) of Shostakovich's works is almost completely unknown. The cantata seems to be following the large-scale declamatory style of 'official' works, but within this framework the writing is bitter, ironic, occasionally mawkish, satirising that official style but at the same time having its own considerable force and brute impact.

Shostakovich's stage works comprise three ballets, of which *The Age of Gold* (1927–30) is the most interesting, two operas, and one operetta. The ballet suites attributed to him are compilations by others of music from his film scores and ballets, and are best avoided: although individual items can be entertaining and witty, generally the material is of a lesser quality, unlike the best of the many film scores (*Hamlet*, 1963, not to be confused with the earlier incidental music, *King Lear*, 1970, and *Zoya*, 1944). The two operas are both major works. *The Nose* (1927–28) is based on Gogol's biting satire of social manners and politics in which a nose takes on an independent life, and is perhaps Shostakovich's most inventive and experimental work. In a rapid series of tableaux employing a huge number of characters (a deterrent to performance) Shostakovich vividly matches the Gogol humour, allowing full rein to his own sense of irony and satire. The often startling and brightly coloured effects tumble over each other with the sharpness of a satirist's pen, there are passages of incisive originality (such as that for a battery of unaccompanied percussion), and the vocal writing closely follows natural speech; the entire opera is a complete break from the 19th century tradition. It is perhaps more correctly described as a piece of music theatre than as an opera, for Shostakovich's intent was to match the Gogol rather than any operatic musical development, and in this he brilliantly succeeded. His second opera, *Lady Macbeth of the Mtsensk District* (1930–32) is a seminal work in his output. On a grand scale, its libretto by Aleksander Preys is based on a story by Nikolai Leskov, with borrowings from Ostrovsky's *The Storm*. It tells of a married woman whose love for a clerk leads her to murder, arrest, deportation and suicide; its powerful plot combines graphic and savage psychological portraits of the central protagonists with hard-hitting social commentary. The complex central character stands for those oppressed by stifling provincial life. It allowed Shostakovich to employ his full range of emotional effects, from incisive mockery to long melodic vocal lines, his instinct for lyricism, his ability to depict anger and violence, and, especially in the last act, his ability to create a vast orchestral landscape. Following Stalin's outrage at the work, it was not heard after its initial run until 1963, when it reappeared in revised form as *Katerina Ismailova* (revision 1956), with, among other changes, the verbal depiction of the psycho-sexual motivation of Katerina toned down. The earlier version is generally preferred, on political grounds as much as anything else, but it should be noted that Shostakovich also took the opportunity for some effective musical alterations in the later version, especially the bleak vision of convict life in the last scene. He started a third opera, *The Gamblers* (1941), but abandoned it (although some of it survives), apparently disillusioned by the official condemnation of both his earlier operas, and the 20th century lost an opera composer of considerable achievement and potential. The operetta, *Moscow, Cheryomushki ...* (1958) is Shostakovich in an unconvincing populist vein, with some good tunes crudely treated and little else.

Following the *Symphony No. 13*, Shostakovich wrote two song-cycles, and revised and orchestrated an earlier one, that express that same dark world, the rejection of the society around him, and the contemplation of death as a release. All three works have a lean strength and power, combined with an other-worldly simplicity, that make them among the most potent of his works. The *Six Songs to Lyrics by English Poets* (1973) for bass voice and orchestra, are orchestrations of a 1942 cycle (op. 62), and set Burns, Raleigh and Shakespeare. *Six Songs to Poems by Marina Tsvetayeva* (1973) explore the place of the artist within a brutal culture, ending with a tribute to the poet Akhmatova. The *Suite on Verses by Michelangelo Buonarroti* (1974) for bass and piano or orchestra set late Michelangelo sonnets that ruminate, sometimes angrily, on the condition of the world, impending death, and immortality achieved through friendship. In all three works Shostakovich favours low dark sounds (lower strings) and high, bright, ethereal sounds (percussion, celesta, high strings), leaving the middle ground to moments of climax and to the funereal or haunting martial sounds of the horn; in the two cycles with bass voice the very colour of the vocal line adds to the frightening bleakness.

The symphony provided Shostakovich with the larger public forum. Through the medium of the string quartet he expressed his more personal, intimate feelings, and it is in them that Shostakovich's most complete utterance is found, unclotted by official demands on the Soviet artist. They are much more consistent in quality than the symphonies, partly because all but two of the fifteen were written after he had reached the age of forty; it is all too easy to forget, when being critical of the earlier symphonies, that he was still only thirty-seven when he wrote the *Symphony No. 8*. The string quartets fall loosely into two types: the works of his middle period, where the intent is almost symphonic in scale and design and which are influenced by the symphonies, and the later quartets in which his expression becomes increasingly rarefied, almost spiritual, and which influenced the last three symphonies. In both cases, these quartets are much more than the abstract exploration of content and form for which the medium has been such a successful vehicle. They are deeply expressive personal documents, through which one can sense the personality and character of the composer, and for this reason they have been compared with Beethoven's quartets. The short *String Quartet No. 1* (1938) is an unassuming, genial and relaxed work, and it is the *String Quartet No. 2* (1944) that starts the series of quartets that are symphonic in weight and proportions. It is built round a long and beautiful tragic adagio, titled 'Recitative and Romance', in which Shostakovich developed his penchant for long solo instrumental recitative. It also uses suggestions of folk music, particularly in the drone-like accompaniments and in the dance ideas, an idiom that permeates the entire cycle of quartets. The five-movement *String Quartet No. 3* (1946) is one of the finest, with its jaunty angular opening tune, an unforgettable march-like staccato passage in the second movement and a powerful scherzo (both anticipating the tenth symphony). Then comes a slow-moving passacaglia, followed by a contemplative finale whose ending, with a high solo violin over a drone, punctuated by pizzicato interjections, is a characteristic Shostakovich effect.

The *String Quartet No. 4* (1949) is a ruminative piece, three of its movements marked allegretto, the fourth andantino. Subtle changes of texture and colour predominate, and a rather sad lyricism pervades this gentle, lucid and beguiling work, which Shostakovich withheld until after Stalin's death. A complete contrast is provided by the *String Quartet No. 5* (1952), one of Shostakovich's most rigorous and unyielding works, which has close affinities with the *Symphony No. 10* and the *Violin Concerto No. 1*. Its three movements are continuous, and the opening adagio is of symphonic ambitions, completely fulfilled in the driving energy and dense linear quartet writing, which creates a more massive sound than the forces would suggest. It moves, through a mysterious passage using harmonics, straight into the central andante, a haunted vista of slow-moving, tenuous simplicity and concerted writing, and thence into the finale. There a slow waltz turns into a massive climax, again stretching the massed sonorities of the medium to its limits and using themes from all the three movements, before subsiding to a quiet but still tenuous close. Another contrast is provided by the *String Quartet No. 6* (1956), which opens with a Haydnesque grace and is more relaxed and genial, each movement ending with the same falling cadence, with a meditative passacaglia for the slow movement – music for a late-night contemplation.

The *String Quartet No. 7* and the *String Quartet No. 8*, both written in 1960, form something of an emotional pair. The former is dedicated to the memory of the composer's first wife, and the latter has a kind of double programme: first a reaction to a visit to Dresden, still desolated after wartime destruction, and then a personal autobiographical document of impassioned intensity. The *String Quartet No. 7* is short (twelve minutes), initiates the more rarefied language and texture that was to be developed in the late quartets, is tightly knit by shared material in the three movements played continuously, and is desolately sad. The *String Quartet No. 8*, the

most immediately affecting and best known of the cycle, quotes extensively from Shostakovich's own work, from the first symphony to the second piano trio, and is in five short movements. Its opens with a disarming largo that starts with Shostakovich's D–S–C–H motto, and then smashes out in a second movement of rigidly controlled frenzy and pounding drive. The lilt of the third movement is broken by stabbing chords that herald the fourth, and the quiet finale ends with a cheerless return to the D–S–C–H motif, wrenchingly sad. The control and tautness of the whole quartet is considerable, the anger, bitterness and sadness palpable. The drones of the second movement have been equated with the sound of bombers over Dresden, but Shostakovich had used the technique before (and was to do so again) without any such programmatic intent. The *String Quartet No. 9* (in five movements that are thematically linked and played without a break) and the *String Quartet No. 10*, both written in 1964, also form a pair in that they are less troubled, more serene, the former with its unassuming pastoral dance opening, the latter with its gently jaunty ending. Both have moments of disturbance, especially the snarling and furious second movement of the tenth, but these two quartets seem to reflect Shostakovich's contemplation of personal and private moments away from turbulence. A number of the middle string quartets have been successfully orchestrated for chamber orchestra by Rudolf Barshai, with the composer's approval.

With the rather perplexing *String Quartet No. 11* (1966) Shostakovich changed direction, and it forms a bridge between the earlier quartets and the final four; each of the quartets nos. 11–14 was dedicated to a different member of the Beethoven Quartet, and in each the instrument of the dedicatee is highlighted. The form of the eleventh is unusual: seven very short movements, internally linked, in what is itself a short work. The language is more rarefied than in the earlier works, its tone enigmatic, as if engaged in some private dialogue to which there are few external clues, but it has a curious simplicity and a quirky logic. The eleventh quartet initiates unusual structures; with the *String Quartet No. 12* (1968) Shostakovich added atonal elements and 12-tone rows, though since the basis of the work is tonal (and the argument partly between atonal ideas and a tonal outcome) these extend the harmonic and melodic possibilities rather than constitute an alternative harmonic system. It is cast in two movements, a short moderato acting as prelude to the long second movement in four sections. This is one of Shostakovich's finest creations, very wide-ranging in mood, captivating in idea – it feels as if Shostakovich succeeded in reconciling his disparate musical and personal traits in this movement. Darkness and depression return in the arch-form, single-movement *String Quartet No. 13* (1970), which continues the use of 12-note rows in a concentrated work that almost abandons any possibility of comfort, ending in despairing sadness from the viola, accompanied by the isolated knocking of the bow on the wood of the instruments. The *String Quartet No. 14* (1973) combines the enigmatic qualities of the eleventh with the two-movement form of the twelfth, and is unified by a repeating idea on the viola; the first movement is almost bewildering in its folding and unfolding of emotional mood, and in the second Shostakovich seems to have retreated into a luminous inner world. The reduction into a completely spare emotional idiom and rarification of musical thought is completed in the *String Quartet No. 15* (1974), in six slow movements, all marked adagio except the penultimate funeral march. The means, but not the emotional intensity, are reduced to the barest essentials, and the effect is of a rare, ethereal world that is disturbing but profound in its sad inwardness.

The rest of Shostakovich's mature chamber output is commensurate with the quality of the string quartets. The intense and satisfying *Piano Trio No. 2* (1944), cast in three movements and dedicated to the memory of a friend who had died in a Nazi concentration camp, is a highlight in Shostakovich's middle period. It is dominated by the intensity of the last two linked movements, a passacaglia largo of heartbreaking sorrow, and a memorable finale that seems like a bitter folk dance. The *Piano Quintet* (1940) is almost as fine, with a solemn opening of rich sonorities, often bare two-part writing for the piano, and an unusual lightness to the last movement. The late *Violin Sonata* (1968) and the *Viola Sonata* (1975) inhabit the same sparse world as the late quartets. The former is the more terse of the two in tone; the latter is the last work Shostakovich completed, a very beautiful swan-song, making references to other works, that redeems the sadness of the fifteenth quartet. He described its opening movement as a 'short story', and it quotes **Berg's** *Violin Concerto*, with both piano and viola heavily involved in the story-telling. The scherzo is less demonic than many of Shostakovich's scherzos, with more of a folk flavour, while the finale adagio is a tribute to Beethoven, brilliantly based on the rhythmic and melodic design of the 'Moonlight Sonata' while remaining quintessential Shostakovich, and, at its end, just emptying away. His piano music is not extensive, although Shostakovich himself was a considerable pianist until Parkinson's disease curtailed his playing. The major piano works are two marvellous sets inspired by Bach, the *Twenty-Four Preludes* (1932–33) and the *Twenty-Four Preludes and Fugues* (1950–51), of which the second set is the more substantial and rewarding.

The impact of Shostakovich's music is based on a powerful duality: on the one hand, the immediate, direct, and physically and psychologically realistic idiom; on the other, an underlying expression, sometimes almost coded, of the emotions of the composer – the conflict between the outward appearance and the inner experience. That Shostakovich was not the committed communist that he has often been painted (it has emerged that many of his public statements and articles were written by others) seems inherent in his musical expression, though it was clearly the repressive state that he was protesting against, rather than for any ideal, and such a protest can be applied to any such state or society regardless of ideology. Much of this contradiction and personal anger and anguish has emerged in an extraordinary book, *Testimony*, supposedly based on conversations between the composer and S. Volkov. The exact provenance of these conversations is suspect; but their substance seems believable.

Shostakovich taught at the Moscow Conservatory from 1942, and his influence is widely evident in the music of the next generation of composers in what was the USSR.

RECOMMENDED WORKS

Symphonies: All the symphonies are recommended. Those new to Shostakovich might try the fifth, then the first, and then the tenth. The second, third and twelfth symphonies are of lesser interest.

Concertos: All the concertos are recommended.

Chamber Music: All Shostakovich's chamber music is recommended, as are the *Twenty-four Preludes and*

Fugues for piano, though the early *Two Pieces* for octet and the *Piano Trio No. 1* are of lesser interest. The *Piano Trio No. 2*, the eighth and third string quartets, the *Piano Quintet*, and then the seventh string quartet might be a sensible order of initial exploration.

Operas: Both Shostakovich's operas are recommended.

Vocal Works: song-cycles *From Jewish Folk Poetry, Six Poems of Marina Tsvetaeva, Six Romances on words by Japanese Poets, Seven Romances on Poems of Alexander Blok, Suite on Verses of Michelangelo Buonarroti, Four Verses of Capitan Lebjadkin*; cantata *The Execution of Stepan Razin*

BIBLIOGRAPHY

D. Shostakovich and S. Volkov, *Testimony*, 1979 (Eng. trans.) (see text)

N. Kay, *Shostakovich*, 1971

I. MacDonald, *The New Shostakovich*, 1990

C. Norris, *Shostakovich, the Man and his Music*, 1982

E. Wilson, *Shostakovich: A Life Remembered*, 1994

Stravinsky Igor Fedorovich•••
born 17th June 1882 at Oranienbaum
died 6th April 1971 at New York

Igor Stravinsky was for many years the most influential and highly acclaimed of 20th-century composers, the yardstick by which others were judged. The residue of this eminence remains, in that the older generation of current musicians, composers, and critics formed their musical outlook when Stravinsky was to all intents and purposes infallible. Yet that infallibility has been tested in the toughest crucible of all, that of regular performances; in spite of his eminence, Stravinsky's later works are little known even by the musically literate, only a handful of the neo-classical works are in the repertoire, and his general reputation rests on three early ballets which are among the best known of all works in classical music. This position is exemplified by his opera *The Rake's Progress*, esteemed by many brought up to admire Stravinsky, but rarely performed, a specialist item in record stores.

The roots of both this esteem and his current position are one and the same.

Stravinsky was an innovator, but an unusual one. Firstly, he was essentially a stylistic innovator, mining and reshaping other musics to forge his particular stylistic idioms, rather than inventing or developing new harmonic structures or sonorities. Little that he innovated was not being independently developed elsewhere in some fashion, but it was his genius to have such command of each new stylistic idiom that it attracted international attention. Secondly, he was not content (as have been most innovators) to develop a new idiom and then expand it into a life's work, extending and deepening it. Instead, he was inclined to explore one new idiom or stylistic innovation, and then move on to another. Thirdly, he was the most prominent of the composers who, in reaction to Romanticism, emphasized craftsmanship and the abstract, structural, architectural components of music, preferring the intellectual content of abstract construction to the emotional content of the expression of the human condition.

All these aspects of his innovations attracted the attention of contemporary composers and critics, and Stravinsky's influence on other composers is enormous. In a number of cases, an idiom he had initiated was developed by another composer into a lifetime's work: **Orff's** particular individuality is directly developed from *Les Noces*, for example, while the impetus for a central idea of much of **Martinů's** later work is to be found in a short phrase in Stravinsky's *Oedipus Rex*. Similarly, Stravinsky's music continues to appeal to musicologists, who have always found it much easier to analyse music for its abstract mechanical qualities than to identify the impact on audiences. Yet, while Stravinsky's central emphasis on craftsmanship and the abstract suited the spirit of the middle decades of the century, it holds less appeal to later generations: the balance between form and content, between the cerebral and the emotional qualities that informs all lasting art, is shifted too much to the former (there is a parallel in the architecture of the period). There is a certain kind of sterility to much of Stravinsky's music, however fantastically well crafted (as it almost always is), as if his concentration on the magic of putting things together was less an aesthetic principle than an attempt to avoid expressing or exploring his own deeper emotions, and his shifting of styles an escape from facing their personal implications. It is no coincidence that two of Stravinsky's most popular works are the most emotionally expressive of his output.

Stravinsky's musical roots were in the tradition of the Russian nationalists and Tchaikovsky, whom he saw conduct as a boy and whose influence is evident in the early and Romantic *Piano Sonata* (1902–04). This heritage was furthered by his studies with Rimsky-Korsakov, the finest orchestrator of his day, and by 1908 the influences had included an awareness of the French Impressionists. This is evident in *Fireworks* (1908), the earliest Stravinsky work to be heard regularly today; this short and brilliant, if vacuous, orchestral showpiece anticipates the more famous ballets that followed, and it also brought Stravinsky to the attention of Diaghilev, and, through the collaboration, international fame.

The first original Stravinsky ballet for Diaghilev was *The Firebird* (*L'oiseau de feu*, 1909–10), a stunningly vivid and direct transliteration of visual ideas into musical impact. Based on the story of the phoenix, it is still derivative: the influence of French Impressionism is strong, especially in the opening passages, there are echoes of Wagnerian horn-calls, and the fingerprints of Rimsky-Korsakov mark the whole score, notably in the slower passages and melodic ideas. The derivative aspects, however, were long masked by the sheer impact of the new elements, most obviously the urgent barbaric earthiness, the sculptural incision, the violence of contrast between tone and mood. Behind these lies Stravinsky's great contribution to 20th-century music: the emancipation of rhythm from a more traditional ordered element into something urgent, motivic, catalystic, in which the tension and release of changing and unusual rhythmic patterns becomes a central structural component of the score. A particular aspect of modern music, formerly contained and often subordinate, started to be unleashed in *The Firebird*, and it shocked many and excited still more.

The ballet *Petrushka* (1910–11) takes up where *The Firebird* left off, in the bright pictorialism of the opening carnival scene, but it is a much more individual and less derivative score. The story contains two aspects of instant appeal: the general setting of a carnival (a Shrove-Tuesday fair in St Petersburg), and a central character who is an ugly but touching puppet. The new element in this widely-loved score is the introduction of an intentional and carefully crafted naïvety, in the sounds of the hurdy-gurdy, the toy-box, the glittering

high percussion, in the passages of simple textures that foreshadow **Copland**, in the semi-humorous writing that is clearly influenced by **Dukas**'s *Sorcerer's Apprentice*. At the same time Stravinsky started to explore a concept (in part suggested by the scenario) that he was to use and develop throughout his career, and which has become a staple of later 20th-century writing: overlapping planes of idea, be it a new key superimposed over the old and emerging on its own, a new melody, or idea of orchestration or rhythm, while motoric ostinati (one of the effects available from the new rhythmic freedom) start to make their presence and excitement felt. Some of these effects are apparent in the short hymn-like cantata *Le roi des étoiles* (*The King of the Stars*, 1911, original Russian title *Zvezdolikiy*), for male voice choir and orchestra, with its polymodal and polytonal effects in the writing for two groups of twelve tenors and twelve basses.

They came to their fore in the most explosive of all Stravinsky scores, the ballet *The Rite of Spring* (*Le sacre du printemps*, 1911–13). Subtitled 'Scenes of Pagan Russia', it is divided into two parts, the first the adoration of the earth and the new spring expressed in rituals and games, the second the propitiation of the earth by the sacrifice of a virgin, with its attendant rituals. The very scenario showed a willingness to express the deep elemental archetypes and urges that the 19th century had preferred to keep repressed, or at least unexpressed. Stravinsky responded with a score that also unleashed those musically repressed aspects, while still using the apparatus of the huge late-Romantic orchestra. Rhythmic power and change dominate: the listener is aware of the changes in basic pulse (multiplied regularly or irregularly) before anything else, and it is this pulse that gives the work its urgency. It is often referred to as 'primitivism', but there is little primitive about the score, with its extraordinary precision of driving rhythms, independent percussive groups, polytonal and polyrhythmic effects, miraculous orchestration, and perfect proportion and sense of pace and pacing. Rather it might be described as 'elemental', since it expresses those elemental emotions that the previous epoch mistakenly equated only with primitive peoples. The influence of *The Rite of Spring* has resonated throughout our century. Rarely has any musical work so completely evoked the scenario it was designed to present.

Stravinsky then allied two aspects of his

emerging idiom, the concentration on rhythm and the expansion of the use of percussion, in a single work. The melodic content of the 'choreographic scenes' *Les Noces* (1914–23) is minimal; the orchestration started off with a full-size orchestra, but ended up in its third revision (1923) with the forces that ideally suit the music: four pianos, a mass of percussion, four vocal soloists and chorus. The subject matter is a wedding, but it is treated not with specific characters and events, but as a conglomerate of ritual, custom, snatches of conversations, and religious material. The entire piece, in which the singing is constant, relies on repetitions and ostinati emphasised by the percussive colours and by the superimposition of planes of rhythmic and melodic idea and chant-like vocal lines. The effect is ritualistic, the lack of orchestral colour giving it a primitive, stripped-down, archetypal power, but it is also powerfully dynamic, the rhythmic patterns constantly changing and impelling the linear motion. In many ways it is as revolutionary as *The Rite of Spring*, as it has no obvious antecedents. In particular, it showed the potential of percussion instruments, using tuned percussion (and percussive piano) to appropriate the functions of the rest of the orchestra while emphasising the rhythmic element. Those who respond to the music of **Orff** will enjoy this work, the direct predecessor of Orff's idiom.

A rather different form of simplicity informs the stage burlesque *Renard* (1915–16), for four mime-artists (dancers), four singers and small instrumental ensemble. This work opens a period in Stravinsky's output where, partly because of the economies of the wartime years, but partly out of a desire to withdraw from the large-scale late-Romantic orchestral forces, he explored the possibility of small-scale stage works. The story is of clowns taking on animal roles, based on Aesop's fable of the fox. The four stage characters (a fox, a cat, a cock and a goat) mime the parts sung by their respective singers. The colours are sharp, like a bright rustic Russian picture, the textures correspondingly clear, the rhythms animated, while the tone is that of burlesque, or of a comical travelling troupe. The direct simplicity of story-line, the bright colours, and the small scale of *Renard* were developed in a work that has become the cornerstone of the development of music theatre, *L'histoire du soldat* (*The Soldier's Tale*, 1918) for speakers, dancers and instrumental ensemble of seven players. Its form harks back to the 18th-century dance suite (its dances include a jazzy 'Ragtime'), but its story – of a soldier who sells his fiddle, symbol of his soul, to the Devil in exchange for riches – has a sardonic bitterness. One of its achievements is that its central character is an ordinary person, a simple soldier; and with its ingenuous music, reminiscent of simpler, folk styles, developing the quasi-naïve idioms heard in *Petrushka*, it punctured the special aura around serious music.

Stravinsky furthered his penchant for jazz in *Ragtime for Eleven Instruments* (1918) and *Piano-Rag Music* (1919). But he developed a major shift in emphasis and direction in the 'ballet with songs', *Pulcinella* (1919–20), which with its return to the structures of Baroque music and of the dance suite, gave an important impetus to the emerging movement of neo-classicism. The ballet was based on a number of themes then erroneously attributed to Pergolesi (1710–36); Stravinsky himself likened this neo-classical idiom to embracing Apollonianism (celebrating the intellectual) after the Dionysianism of his earlier works. *Symphonies for Wind Instruments* (1920, revised 1945–47) has little relation to symphonic construction, the title merely referring to 'sounding together'; instead Stravinsky explored block construction with what he called 'litanies', meaning short blocks of different instrumental groupings, joined together.

The opera *Oedipus Rex* (1926–27) looked beyond the musical Classical period to an earlier classical age, that of Greek tragedy. The concise and taut libretto in two short acts by Jean Cocteau after Sophocles concerns Oedipus's discovery of his patricide, his mother Jocasta's suicide, and his own self-inflicted blinding and exile. The text, apart from the linking narration, is in Latin, itself an innovation for an opera. The chorus act as a Greek chorus; the tone is rigid, ritualistic, formal, with an atmosphere of ceremonial nobility. The solo vocal lines often have an archaic, recitative quality, and a noble lyricism in the writing for Jocasta; blocks of differing tone, like panels of a carved relief, are set against each other in sequence. The whole effect, with the rigidity of ostinati pulse, is to emphasise the inevitability of fate, contrasted with the emotional anguish of the central characters, in what is one of Stravinsky's most powerful works. The invocation to Apollo is overt in the ballet *Apollo* (originally titled *Apollon musagète*, 1927–28), where the two scenes concern

Apollo's birth and his meeting with the Muses (each of whom has a variation), and where the rhythms are inspired by verse metres.

The *Symphony of Psalms* (1930), for chorus and an orchestra that excludes clarinets, violins and viola but includes two pianos (for a distinctive set of colours), has proved to be one of the most enduring of Stravinsky's works. Its three movements, setting two psalms each, become progressively longer. Its tone, with the dark colours of lower strings, its rhythmic vitality, its fugal slow movement, the nobility of its ending, and its whole sense of a pagan delight in the glory of the Lord, has proved more popular in the concert hall than in liturgical surroundings. Ballet continued to occupy an important place in Stravinsky's output. *Jeu de cartes* (*Card Game*, 1936) is a 'ballet in three deals' about a card game in which the dancers are the cards. The music is continuous, the scenes are short, and there are hints of earlier styles of music, but it is neither particularly memorable nor profound when taken out of its theatrical context. The climax of Stravinsky's neo-classical period came with three works written in his late fifties: the concerto for string orchestra *Dumbarton Oaks* (1938), the *Symphony in C* (1938–40), and the exciting *Symphony in Three Movements* (1942–45). *Dumbarton Oaks* (originally *Concerto in E flat*) is a modern equivalent to a Baroque concerto for strings; its nickname comes from the name of the estate of the Americans who commissioned it, and it has retained its place in the repertoire. The *Symphony in C* combines the vigour of Haydn with a Beethovenesque motion around the orchestra in its first movement, creating a classical feel through the regularity of metre and a Stravinskian cast through the perky melodies and the sense of orchestral blocks. The equally vigorous finale has more metric variety and more consorted textures, and these frame a larghetto that has strong hints of **Prokofiev** and a bright allegretto with echoes of the dance; each of the movements has an almost throw-away Mozartian ending. The effect is entirely one of a delight in craftsmanship, like some intricate architectural model. The *Symphony in Three Movements* summarised Stravinsky's development, harking back to the form of the Haydn and pre-Haydn symphony, but constructed with blocks of ideas, and shot through with a rhythmic excitement that recalls *The Rite of Spring*

(but in a much more refined orchestral texture); it also includes reminders of the circus music in *Petrushka*, a theme from the *Concerto for Two Pianos*, and figures from the *Capriccio* for piano and the *Symphony in C*. Stravinsky claimed that the symphony was inspired by cinematographic images of the war, but any such programme is essentially spurious, for this is abstract music at its most vital and communicative, seemingly reconnecting Stravinsky to his Russian roots, and achieving a renewal of emotional impact within a very formal style.

A final embrace with neo-classicism emerged in Stravinsky's only full-length opera, *The Rake's Progress* (1948–51). The libretto, by W. H. Auden and Chester Kallman, apes the atmosphere, characters and story-lines of 18th-century English literature: the rake of the title unexpectedly inherits a fortune, goes to London, leaving his love in the country, visits brothels, gets involved with a bearded circus lady, becomes generally disillusioned with his life, discovers his helping friend is a Mephistopholean figure, and ends up in a madhouse, where he is metaphorically if not physically redeemed by the constancy of his country love. There are magnificent moments in the work (such as when his friend reveals his true nature), and it has always had its supporters among Stravinsky addicts, but the opera essentially misfires and has never secured a permanent place in the repertoire. The milieu of the libretto requires something of the earthy, Rabelaisian tone of its literary antecedents; both the libretto and the music fail to capture that, concentrating on a gloss that can appear affected, occupying the arena of cerebral wit and style, and lacking the undercurrent of emotional power. *The Rake's Progress* was a conscious attempt to recapture the magic of a Mozartian operatic world, but, when compared with the understanding of **Strauss** and Hofmannsthal, it has to be seen as an unsuccessful one.

Stravinsky returned to jazz in his adopted country with his *Ebony Concerto* (1945), for clarinet and jazz ensemble, written for Woody Herman and combining Baroque features with a jazz idiom. It is a quirky but appealing little work, whose central attraction is the constantly unravelling changes of instrumental colour and effect within the context of jazzy rhythms: craftsmanship at its most effective. There then followed a period of transition in

Stravinsky's output, and (*The Rake's Progress* apart) the subsequent works are the least generally known. *Orpheus* (1946), a ballet in three scenes, has an emotional distance (such as the use of a plaintive trumpet over strings), an almost Impressionist limpid quality in its opening, crystalline textures and an exceptionally smooth rhythmic flow, and an affection for the lyrical. The emotional distancing is more potent (because of the religious text) in the very effective and underrated *Mass* (1948) for two child soloists, chorus, wind and brass. The haunting opening to the Gloria, with intertwining brass, has its roots in the age of Gabrielli; the soloists follow; then a rhythmically ritualistic chorus reach out to **Orff**, and these three alternating elements form the idiom of the work, with shades of Monteverdi in the Sanctus. The *Cantata* (1951–52) for mezzo-soprano, tenor, chorus, two flutes, two oboes (one alternating with English horn) and cello, is based on four anonymous 15th- and 16th-century English popular poems, three of them semi-sacred, the fourth a love poem, each ending with a common refrain. In its delicate, archaic tone, and its simple feel, created in part by the warm colours and restrained sounds of the instrumental accompaniment, it is an equivalent to **Britten's** small-scale choral works, especially in some of the cadences.

In this transitional period, Stravinsky, to the astonishment of his admirers and to the consternation of some critics, turned to 12-tone techniques, following the lead of **Webern** as much as **Schoenberg**. In retrospect, Stravinsky's restless penchant for exploration and his consummate grasp of formal construction made such a move less startling than it must have then appeared; also the death of Schoenberg, whom Stravinsky hated, psychologically allowed such a development. Initially he employed 12-tone rows as an harmonic element within a wider harmonic variety. The transition is exemplified by *Agon* (1953–54 and 1956–57), an abstract ballet of twelve dances for twelve dancers, which looks back to the French court dances of the 17th century. The earlier sections of the ballet have a rhythmic vitality drawn from Stravinsky's earlier modes, the later sections 12-tone elements, while the whole is framed by fanfares; the large orchestra is used sparingly in different instrumental combinations. *In Memoriam Dylan Thomas* (1954) for tenor, string quartet and trombone quartet, sets the poet's most famous poem,

on the death of his father. However, it is questionable whether this tense work adds anything to what is an exceptionally musical poem. *Canticum Sacrum* (1955) celebrated Venice in a short five-movement work for tenor, baritone, chorus and an orchestra without upper strings, and further explores the integration of 12-tone rows. With *Threni* (*Threnodies*, 1957–58), subtitled '*id es lamentationes Jeremiae Prophetae*' ('being the lamentations of the Prophet Jeremiah'), for six soloists, chorus and orchestra, Stravinsky based an entire work on 12-tone technique. It transcribes the insistent monumentality and emotional distancing of such earlier works as *Oedipus Rex* into the new harmonic scheme, with a dark and austere formality. The 12-tone rows are used with considerable freedom, but with strict formal integrity (such as combining elements of two rows to make a third), and the rows chosen suggest tonal connections.

These later works, for all their exploration of a new harmonic expression, contain elements of technical play and suggestions that Stravinsky was combining aspects of earlier experience with the new style. *Abraham and Isaac* (1962–63), for baritone and chamber orchestra, based on Genesis (in Hebrew), has a florid, archaic vocal line intertwining with an orchestra often reduced to single instrumental lines. The *Orchestral Variations* (1963–64) are a short (five-minute) set of transmutations on a 12-note series, in which the underlying pulse is constant, the tempo varied. The formality of the neo-classical Stravinsky keeps trying to peek through the Webernesque economy. In *Introitus* (1965), subtitled 'TS Eliot in Memoriam', the tenors and basses intone the Introitus as a chant or whispered imprecation, while the accompaniment employs the 12-note row, announced in full by the timpani. *Requiem Canticles* (1965–66) for soloists, chorus and orchestra, employs two rows, and a frame of differing instrumental forces (string prelude, wind-instrument prelude, percussion postlude). This, his last completed major work, has a rarefied beauty in which Stravinsky's use of 12-tone techniques has become completely integrated into his idiom. It is perhaps ironic that the wider dissemination of these later works, sparse but formally fascinating, and with their own impact in the distillation of the old and the new, should have been so hampered by the popularity of Stravinsky's earlier work, and by his reputation as the major mid-century alternative to the Second Viennese School.

Stravinsky was voluble in print and interview, and collaborated on a series of books with Robert Craft: *Conversations* (1959), *Memories and Commentaries* (1960), *Expositions and Developments* (1962), *Dialogues and a Diary* (1963), *Themes and Episodes* (1966), *Stravinsky in Pictures and Documents* (1968), *Retrospectives and Conclusions* (1969). He left Russia for Switzerland in 1914, moved to France in 1920, and became a French citizen in 1934. He emigrated to the USA in 1939 and became an American citizen in 1945. He returned to the USSR for a visit in 1962.

RECOMMENDED WORKS

Stravinsky was an extremely prolific composer, and all of the works mentioned in the main text above are recommended, with those reservations noted. The core of Stravinsky's works will be found in:
ballet *The Firebird* (1909–10)
opera *Oedipus Rex* (1926–27)
ballet *Les Noces* (1914–23)
ballet *Pulcinella* (1919–20)
Requiem Canticles (1965–66) for soloists, chorus and orchestra
ballet *The Rite of Spring* (1911–13)
music theatre *The Soldier's Tale* (1918)
Symphony in C (1939–40)
Symphony in Three Movements (1942–45)
Symphony of Psalms (1930) for chorus and orchestra
Threni (1957–58) for six soloists, chorus and orchestra
Those following Stravinsky's development might consider exploring his major ballet music, which makes an interesting continuity within a single genre. In chronological order: *The Firebird, Petrushka, The Rite of Spring, Renard, Les Noces, Pulcinella, Apollo, Le baiser de la fée, Perséphone, Jeu de cartes, Orpheus* and *Agon*.

BIBLIOGRAPHY
I. Stravinsky, *An Autobiography*, 1936, reissued 1975
Poetics of Music, 1947
B. Asafyev, *A Book about Stravinsky*, 1982
S. Walsh, The Music of *Stravinsky*, 1993
E. W. White, *Stravinsky*, 1966, second edition 1979

Sviridov Georgi*
born 16th December 1915 at Fatezh (Kursk region)
died 6th January 1998 at Moscow

The Soviet musical genre of socialist realism met with such a scathing response from critics in the West, that it is easy to forget that the bright, optimistic and conservative demands of the Socialist Realism idiom genuinely suited the temperaments, both musical and ideological, of some Soviet composers. The best of these was Georgi Sviridov. Those not prepared to adjust to a usually conservative harmonic idiom, occasionally deceptively simple ideas, and a sometimes ideological content may wish to pass by Sviridov, but they would miss the more personal, musically advanced and intimate smaller pieces of the 1970s. The large-scale 1950s Soviet pieces for which he is best known display his surety of touch within the sonorities of the Russian vocal tradition; his melodic gifts are combined with an inherent conviction that is particularly appealing. He is the master of the long floating solo line over the shimmering sonorities of a distant orchestral or vocal (regularly a cappella) backdrop. He was the leading exponent of the Soviet dramatic vocal cycle, a genre designed to appeal to wide audiences, intellectually naïve but popular, and occupying an important position in Soviet music – a position perhaps analogous to that of the American musical in relation to more 'serious' music theatre.

Sviridov studied with **Shostakovich**, and his earlier works, which mainly concentrate on chamber music, also include three symphones. After a period of apparent uncertainty (1947–50), he found his own *métier* (heralded by settings of the Russian poet Avetik Isaakian and of Robert Burns) in two large-scale vocal-dramatic scores, the *Poem in Memory of Sergei Esenin* (1955) for tenor, choir and orchestra, and the *Oratorio pathétique* (1959), for mezzo-soprano, bass, chorus and orchestra. They are contrasting in mood, though similar in the limitations of their idiom, which, like most of Sviridov's settings, involves a close integration of music and words in song-cycle formats. Indeed, the message of the words is paramount, with the music providing an atmospheric synthesis, and his works are much more impressive when one can follow the texts. The later oratorio reflects the vigour and vivid imagery of the revolutionary poet Mayakovsky, with the bass taking a declamatory narrator role. The *Poem in Memory of Sergei Esenin* is more lyrical and introverted, with the feel of the Russian countryside, especially in the first of two sections; the second reflects the new dynamism following the 1917 Revolution. Sviridov's preferred poets are those with large-scale imagery or political intent (Mayakovsky, Esenin, Blók). But his most appealing music dates from the 1960s and 1970s, and is smaller in scale, coloured with a sense of the melancholic, and reflects the folk poetry (real or imitated) and the countryside of his native Kursk. This inspiration is direct in the *Kursk Songs* (1963), a short cycle of songs based on folk tunes describing peasant life before the Revolution, for mezzo-soprano, tenor, bass, chorus and orchestra. The restrained but colourful orchestration is beguiling, the actual folk tunes imbued with a touch of Eastern exoticism. Alongside the sense of Russian choral spaciousness, there are echoes of Carl **Orff** in the orchestral writing, and these are overt in the ostinato first movement of the marvellous short *Spring Cantata* (1972), for chorus and orchestra, which unexpectedly (and unwittingly) links **Orff** with the minimalism of John **Adams**. Based on poems published a century earlier by Nikolai Nekrasov, the slow second movement is a more conventional dialogue between female and male choruses; the orchestral third is deliberately archaic, setting two oboes against a shimmer of bells, celesta, vibraphone and harp; the last ('Mother Russia') is a grand finale, just avoiding poster-colour extroversion. More obviously unconventional is the powerful and haunting *Concerto in Memory of A. A. Yurlov* (1973), a technically very taxing vocalise (no words) for a cappella chorus with soprano solo; its opening uses cluster harmonies reminiscent of **Ligeti** (though shifting on a more regular rhythmic basis). All these later works have a strong awareness of the Russian choral tradition, metamorphosed in the 1970s by the increasing use of more contemporary choral and harmonic idioms.

While it would be fatuous to suggest that Sviridov's music approaches the range or depth of such composers as **Shostakovich**, **Prokofiev** or **Schnittke**, his vocal-dramatic works nonetheless represent an important historical facet of Soviet thought and culture. They have their own appealing and attractive merits, while the much more advanced smaller choral pieces are particularly satisfying, and the *Concerto in Memory of A. A. Yurlov* is one of the finest choral works to have come out of Soviet Russia. Sviridov succeeded **Shostakovich** as first secretary to the Composers' Congress of the Russian Federation in 1960, a post he held until 1973.

RECOMMENDED WORKS
> *Concerto in Memory of A. A. Yurlov* (1973) for soprano and a cappella choir
> *Kursk Songs* (1963) for soloists, chorus and orchestra
> *Oratorio pathétique* (1958) for soloists, chorus and orchestra
> *Poem in Memory of Sergei Esenin* (1955) for soloists, chorus and orchestra
> *Spring Cantata* (1973) for chorus and orchestra

BIBLIOGRAPHY
> G. Sviridov, *Noto-bibliograficheski spravochnik* (compiled by D. Person), 1974

Ustvolskaya Galina*
born 17th June 1919 at St Petersburg

Ustvolskaya is one of the composers of her generation whose music was virtually unknown outside the USSR until *glasnost*. Although she wrote a number of works in Socialist Realist style (including the cantata *Dawn Over The Homeland*, 1952, and the symphonic poem *Young Pioneers*, 1950), her more personal music concentrated on chamber music with a tough, uncompromising emotional tone.

The dark *Clarinet Trio* (1949) stands as a more introverted companion to the *Piano Trio* of **Shostakovich**, whose music she may have influenced in the 1950s; the trio is quoted in his fifth quartet. In a similar vein is the grim and insistent *Octet* (1949–50) for two oboes, four violins, timpani and piano, which is not only one of her finest works to appear so far, but one of the masterpieces of the Russian chamber repertoire. The piano and the timpani, sometimes like a funeral drum, sometimes like gun-shots, revolve around a central core of strings and wind, moving towards an atonally dissonant thematic idiom with a sharp acerbic edge. If there was ever music that reflected the intellectual desolation under the iron vice of repression, this is it. Of her six piano sonatas, the *Piano Sonata No. 3* (1952, not performed until 1972) takes Bach as a model, while the unconventional *Piano Sonata No. 5* (1986), in ten movements, carries echoes of her earlier sparse style in a deconstructed and very bare idiom of sharp contrasts, dissonant outbursts, movements stripped to the bare bones, and passages of insistent, almost motoric, chordal repetitions. The idiom of this sonata had been heralded in the *Duet* (1964) for violin and piano. Her more recent work has included a number of unconventional symphonies using voice and setting religious texts by the 11th-century German monk Hermannus Contractus. Of these, the *Symphony No. 4 'Prayer'* (1985–87) is written for contralto, trumpet, tamtam and piano, and lasts only eight minutes.

RECOMMENDED WORKS
    Clarinet Trio (1949)
    Octet (1949–50)
    Piano Sonata No. 5 (1986)

Vainberg Moisei Samuilovich (sometimes spelt Weinberg)
    born 8th December 1919 at Warsaw
    died 27th February 1996 at Moscow

Born in Poland, Vainberg fled to the USSR when his home was invaded by the Nazis in 1941. He remained there after the war, his compositions admired in the Soviet Union but little heard in the West. His earlier music was criticised in the strictures of 1948, and he was arrested (because of his Jewish faith) in 1953, but he was soon praised for his 'reorientation'.

Jewish and Moldavian folk elements appear in his traditional idiom, which shows affinities with **Shostakovich**, especially in the use of marches, in the discursive, flowing melodic ideas, and in the phrase construction. His later works also suggest a development, in the orchestral language and general extension of a traditional harmonic idiom, similar to that of the later **Shostakovich**. Some may find these affinities too close for comfort, but the tone of Vainberg's works (as opposed to their means) is different, suggesting an outgoing musical personality under constant restraint, as if standing apart from his material with a disembodied effect, especially in his elusive, angular melodic lines.

Vainberg was primarily a composer of symphonies and string quartets, but his work encompasses all genres, and more needs to be heard for a full assessment. Of his twenty-two symphonies, the *Symphony No. 4* (1961) illustrates a number of the features of his style. The vigour of its opening movement is offset by the unsettled rhythmic shifts and by the strange, introverted close. The second movement has an enigmatic and restrained discussion between orchestral instruments. The slow movement is a gentle but ghostly ride through the Russian countryside, with **Mahler** standing on the horizon. The five-movement *Symphony No. 6* (1963) for boys' chorus, violin and orchestra, includes a Moldavian folk tune, with a literary programme ranging from a small boy making a violin and playing it, to a memorial to the victims of fascism, and the peacefulness of the present. More straightforward than the fourth, there is nonetheless a darker undercurrent to this symphony, subtle and probing, and confirmed by the wild, almost grotesque folk dance of an allegro and the quiet ending. The *Symphony No. 7* (1964) is for harpsichord and strings, and the *Symphony No. 12* (1976) is subtitled 'In Memoriam Dmitri Shostakovich'. Of his concertos, the four-movement *Violin Concerto* (1959) is a fine and neglected work, alternating between an aggressive vigour and an enigmatic lyricism, especially in the lovely slow movement, foregoing direct appeal in favour of a more tangential lyrical utterance. The *Cello Concerto* (1964) is widely admired in Russia. The *Trumpet Concerto* (1968) is a particularly interesting work, very large in scale and scope, unsettling in its sudden emotional and idiomatic shifts. It is full of humour, sometimes mawkish and grotesque, with deliberately uncomfortable rhythms in the opening movement, wide swings from the epic to the lyrical in the middle movement, and a totally enigmatic finale. One cannot help wondering if there is not a hidden agenda in this curious concerto. Of his chamber music, the *Piano Quintet* (1943) is reportedly a fine work. He wrote sixteen string quartets, turning to 12-tone techniques in the *String Quartet No. 12* (1969–70).

Serbia

At the turn of the century, Serbian classical music had an established presence, with Romantic idioms influenced by a nationalism based on Serbian folk music. Three composers, all incorporating folk music, formed the basis of 20th-century Serbian composition. Petar Stojanović (1877–1957) concentrated on string works, including seven violin concertos, in a Romantic style that followed Dvořak; his *Double Concerto* (1952) for piano, violin and orchestra, is influenced by jazz. Petar Konjović (1883–1970) is best remembered for his operas, notably *Koštana*, incorporating folk and Oriental influences, including percussive dances. Miloje Milojević (1884–1946) initially followed the examples of **Strauss** and Grieg, then incorporated Impressionism in his songs and atonal expressionism in his choral works. He was an assiduous collector of folk songs. Of the other composers of this generation, the melodically lyrical works of Stevan Hristić (1885–1958) culminated in the opera *Suton* (*Twilight*, 1925), contrasting the decline of the aristocracy and the rise of the middle classes, and *Snovi* (*Dreams*), originally a one-act opera but expanded in 1954 to three acts with the insertion of a ballet.

The next generation of Serbian composers were influenced by the new music in Prague, and especially by the ideas of **Hába**; indigenous Serbian musical life was enhanced by the establishment of an opera house in Belgrade in 1920 and that of Belgrade Academy of Music in 1937. Dragutin Ćolić (born 1907), Milan Ristić (born 1908) and Vojslav Vučković (1910–42) composed a number of quarter-tone and atonal works in the 1930s before adopting more conservative idioms, the first two in response to changed political circumstances, the last influenced by his communist politics. The best-known Serbian composer outside the country has probably been Rudolf Brući (born 1917); after early works with popular elements, he combined colourful orchestration with a welter of harmonic devices, from polytonality to 12-tone techniques, in an idiom that remains traditional at its base. In the *Simfonia lestá* (1965), what amounts to a nocturne, punctuated by almost triumphant climaxes, is framed by two turbulent and brash movements with a thick and agitated orchestral palette. The opening movement gradually introduces elements of a 12-note row that eventually reaches completion. The ballet *Maskal* (1955) takes its title from an Ethiopian celebration, and combines 12-tone tunes, that manage to be almost pastoral, with primitivism and night-music. The symphonies of Aleksandar Obradovič (born 1927) include the tumultuous *Symphony No. 3* (*Microsymphony*, 1967), with electronic tape, and the *Symphony No. 5 'Intima'* (1974), whose five-movement depiction of struggle ends in quiet repose. His other works include a lyrical *Cello Concerto* (1979), *Epitaph H* (1965) for orchestra, which combines classical polyphony with 12-note technique and electronics (and is a protest against atomic warfare – with human sighs on the tape), and the song-cycle *Plameni vjetar* (*Fiery Wind*, 1956), for baritone and orchestra.

Slovakia

Introduction

The history of Slovak music in the 20th century has been intertwined with that of the former Czechoslovakia, though Slovak composers have not been as prominent as those of the Czech lands. Following the formation of Czechoslovakia in 1918, the foundation of the Slovak National Theatre in 1919 initiated Slovak opera, while the teaching of **Novák** (see the Czech Republic) encouraged Slovak composers; he himself was influenced by the music of the Tatras Mountains. The early works of Alexander Moyes (1906–84) showed the influences of jazz and Constructivism, but he then turned his attention to Slovak folk music, with its vital rhythms. During this period he wrote the symphonic suite *Down the Váh* (1935), a set of five symphonic poems following the course of the river in the manner of Smetana's *Vltava*. His later music was influenced by **Stravinsky**, and again contained jazz elements. His output includes nine symphonies, a flute concerto, a piano concerto, and the *Wind Quintet* (1933). The contribution of Ján Cikker (1911–89) was mainly in the field of opera; his earlier operas incorporate folk and nationalist elements, but the later, highly expressive works adopt an atonal and free 12-tone harmonic idiom. *Juro Jánošík* (completed with final revisions 1955) is based on the story of the 18th-century outlaw of the title, the Slovak Robin Hood, to a libretto by Štefan Hoza that adds a love interest and ends with the gallows. *Beg Bajazid* (1955) pits the Turks against the Slovaks, with a folk-like story of a boy captured by the Turks, growing into manhood as a Turk, then returning to his native land and reverting to its values. *Mr Scrooge* (1957–59, revised as *Evening, Night and Morning*, 1963) was based on Dickens. His later operas moved away from the nationalist themes, and tackled powerful literary sources. *Vzkriesenie* (*Resurrection*, 1962) is drawn from Tolstoy's last novel; *Hra láske a smrti* (*The Play of Love and Death*, 1969) is based on a novel by the French writer Romain Rolland; and Shakespeare was set in *Coriolanus* (1972). *The Sentence: Earthquake in Chile* (first performed 1979) is based on Kleist, while the source for his last opera, *Zo Života hmyzu* (*From the Life of Insects*, first performed 1987), was *The Insect Play* by the Čapek brothers. His concert music includes the first Slovak piano concerto, the *Concertino* (1942) for piano and orchestra, two popular symphonic dances (*Dupák*, 1950, and *Verbuňk*, 1951), and the *Slovak Suite* (1953) for orchestra. The most important Slovak composer of this generation is Eugen **Suchoň** (1908–1993), who is again best known for his operas.

Slovak Music Information Centre:
Slovensky Hudobny Fond
Medena 29
811 02 Bratislava
SK-Slovakia
tel: +42 7 331 380
fax: +42 7 333 569

Suchoň Eugen*

born 25th September 1908 at Pezinok
died 5th August 1993 at Bratislava

Eugen Suchoň is the best-known Slovak composer, whose music commended itself to both the Nazi and the Communist regimes. His earlier music is unashamedly Romantic, sometimes with modal inflections, and includes the cycle *Noc čarodejnic* (*The Night of the Witches*, 1927) for orchestra, the *Serenáda* (1932) for wind quintet, arranged for string orchestra in 1933, and the programmatic *Burleska* (1933) for violin and orchestra; to the latter Suchoň added material in 1948 to create a short violin concerto, *Fantázia a burleska*. In the *Baladická suita* (*Ballad Suite*, 1934) for orchestra (also version for piano) the image of the ballad is not prominent; instead a large Romantic orchestra, with the addition of side-drum, creates what amounts to a tone poem, tuneful and colourful, elegiac in the second of four movements, but not especially memorable.

Suchoň also produced a number of vocal works reflecting the Slovak countryside. These included the cycle *O hrách* (*About the Mountains*, 1934–42) for male voice choir, and the grand *Žalm zeme Podkarpatskej* (*Psalm of the sub-Carpathian Lands*, 1938), for tenor, chorus and orchestra, whose twin themes of the beauty of the countryside and the repression of the people appealed to the later communist regime. This nationalist element culminated in the opera *Krútňava* (*The Whirlpool*, 1941–49, revision 1952), to a libretto by Štefan Hoza from a novel by M. Urban. The title refers to a psychological state rather than a physical phenomenon, and the story of jealousy and murder combines social comment with a folk tradition. It is set in the Slovak mountains in the early 1920s and its central character is Katrena, who develops from a shy wife to a decisive independent personality, illustrating the considerable repression of women in this period. The music (especially the choruses) include folk-like songs and dances, and two actual folk songs. *Metamorfózy* (1953) for orchestra are a set of variations on original themes, lushly Romantic, in an idiom that in all intents and purposes looks back to **Novák**: well-wrought, pleasant, with moments of grander triumph and lyrical atmosphere, but too unidiomatic to be of real interest. These works had used extended harmonies drawn from folk music (including chords of elevenths and thirteenths), and in his next opera Suchoň extended his harmonic idiom, using 12-note rows within a wider harmonic cast, and following modal inflections. The national historic grand opera *Svätopluk* (1959) is set in the 9th century, and in spite of the use of 12-tone techniques has a traditional harmonic feel. The most memorable part is the second act, which has some very atmospheric writing for both protagonists and chorus, and exceptionally powerful dramatic sections, with echoes of **Janáček**. Unfortunately, given Suchoň's evident sense of psychological drama and vocal writing, no other operas have appeared. Since the song-cycle *Ad astra* (1961), for soprano and small orchestra or piano, he has embraced a chord structure system ranging from the diatonic to 12-note, leading to writing in multiple modes. He has also used sets of different pieces as components in a larger structure: *Kaleidoskop* (1968), for example, embraces a piano concerto and a work for organ and percussion.

Suchoň taught at the Bratislava Academy from 1933, at the Bratislava High School from 1950, and at Bratislava University (1959–74). He was president of the Czechoslovak Composer Organisation from 1973.

RECOMMENDED WORKS
opera *Krútňava* (*The Whirlpool*, 1941–49, revision 1952)
opera *Svätopluk* (1959)

South Africa

Introduction

South African classical music has not been heard widely outside its borders. The major South African composer, Priaulx **Rainier** (1903–86) spent most of her compositional life in the UK, but her work was influenced by indigenous South African music. Most notable among her contemporaries are John Joubert (born 1927), who taught at Birmingham University in England, and whose works include two symphonies and seven operas, and Herbert Du Plessis, whose piano music shows the influence of **Bartòk**. The most important South African composer of the next generation, Kevin Volans (born 1949), moved to Germany in 1973. African influences are prominent in *She Who Sleeps with a Blanket* (1985) for percussion, and also impel his string quartets, minimalist in feel, which have been widely heard. The *String Quartet No. 1 'White Man Sleeps'* (1987) has delicate repeated patterns grouped in phrases that are interrupted by rhythmic pauses, suggesting sometimes African drumming, sometimes African string music, alluring, rhythmically invigorating, and often with the beauty of sounds heard from afar over a wide landscape. The *String Quartet No. 2 'Hunting: Gathering'* (1987) 'paraphrases' from Ethiopian, Zimbabwean and Malian music, with twenty-three different sections covered in twenty-six minutes, linked in a pseudo-narrative form. It is influenced by **Reich** in the melodic and harmonic figures, but creates its own atmosphere, with ethereal snatches, sometimes weaving little nets of counterpoint. It was followed by the *String Quartet No. 3 'The Songlines'* (1988), and the *String Quartet No. 4 'Ramanujan Notebooks'* (1990). The opera *The Man with the Soles of Wind* (1992) was based on the life of the poet Arthur Rimbaud. Of other South African composers, Allan Stephenson (born 1949 near Liverpool, England) has written two symphonies and a number of concertos in a very conservative style. The infectious little *Oboe Concerto* (1978), for oboe and chamber, would make a pleasant accompaniment to a genteel afternoon tea, its slow movement apparently under the spell of **Rodrigo's** guitar concerto. The *Concertino for Piccolo, Strings and Harpsichord* (1980), a rare work for such an instrument, is in a similar vein.

There is no South African music information centre.

Rainier Priaulx[*]

born 3rd February 1903 at Howick, Natal
died 10th October 1986 at Besse-en-Chandesse (France)

Brought up among a largely Zulu population in her home area in South Africa, which exposed her to the influence of indigenous rhythms and colours, Priaulx Rainier settled in London on completing her musical studies. She became noticed as a composer with the *Three Greek Epigrams* (1937) and the *String Quartet* (1936–39), where the absorbed and abstracted (rather than pictorial) echoes of her childhood appear in the exotic, if sparse, colours (including the use of harmonics), in the insistent ostinato rhythms, and in the wide variety of mood and effect in what is otherwise a largely post-Romantic work.

Her earlier music follows this idiom, concentrating on chamber works and ignoring counterpoint in favour of straightforward melodic patterns. The exception is the *Viola Sonata* (1945), which introduced a characteristic mood of the sombre and rugged. The African influence appeared more directly in the attractive *Two Songs for Tenor and Guitar* (1948), the first having elements of African rhythms, the second being a setting of a Zulu poem, and in the *Barbaric Dance Suite* (1949) for piano. She then wrote two important vocal works for the tenor Peter Pears: the *Cycle for Declamation* (1952) and the *Requiem* (1956) for tenor and unaccompanied choir. The former is for tenor voice alone, setting passages from John Donne's *Devotions*, and indeed uses a declamatory style, the silences between the sentences forming an integral part of the effect. The latter, to texts by David Gascoyne, is forceful and sparse, the soloist and chorus often echoing or merging with each other, the vocal lines characterised by wide leaps and unsettled rhythms and a declamatory feel, with few points of relief from the overall sense of homophonic tension. Then, to emphasise the abstract and unsettled qualities, Rainier evolved a new style with small motifs replacing thematic material, more chromatic harmonies, more complex rhythms, and greater variety of colours and textures. The dark *String Trio* (1966) is composed of fragments of ideas and moods, from the intense to the more ruminative, with the wide leaps seen in the *Requiem* again evident. It has the sense of eavesdropping on a series of circular musical events, rather than a journey between two points; this is an extension of ideas formulated in the oboe quartet *Quanta* (1962), whose title is based on quantum theory. The fragmentary effect of the rhythmic snatches and ideas in the quartet is in keeping with the avant-garde patterns of the day, although the underlying basis remains tonal, and a sense of flow is maintained through this atmospheric and gritty work by the regular merging of one instrument into another. The *Cello Concerto* (1964) is in two movements, with a rhetorical solo line, while the seven continuous sections of the orchestral suite *Aequora lunae* (1967) describe the affective associations of seven of the seas of the moon, together forming a 'cycle of fertility'. The orchestra is divided into two parts which exchange textures: strings with brass, and hard percussion with woodwind and softer percussion. The colour effects include chord clusters and numerous wind solos. Rainier returned to vocal writing with a setting of an extended metaphysical and mystical poem by Edith Sitwell, *The Bee Oracles* (1969), for tenor, flute, oboe, violin, cello and harpsichord. Again there is a fragmentary quality, but it is combined with a exotic feel partly created by the colours of the instrumentation. Sections of intense forcefulness contrast with the more drifting and ruminative. An unusual sense of progression is achieved through an underlying repetitive rhythmic structure for the vocal line, against which the instruments set up more varied rhythmic conjunctions.

Throughout her output, Rainier's voice is often hard and uncompromising, and completely without any sense of sentimentality. Yet underneath this surface lie fragments of sound patterns, a held chord here, a colour texture there, that clearly derive from her childhood inheritance, like a landscape emerging underneath a hard dawn light. These became more striking and recognisable as her idiom became freer, more abstract and more individual. That idiom will not find a wide appeal, but has an inner sincerity and interest for those prepared to tackle its tough exterior. With her distinctive compositional voice she deserves to be more widely known. Rainier taught at the Royal Academy of Music from 1942 to 1961.

RECOMMENDED WORKS
> *The Bee Oracles* (1969) for tenor, flute, oboe, violin, cello and harpsichord
> *Requiem* (1956) for tenor and unaccompanied chorus
> *Quanta* (1962) for oboe quartet
> *String Trio* (1966)
> *Two Songs for Tenor and Guitar* (1948)

Spain

Introduction

Spain has had a long and honourable musical history, whose fortunes have fluctuated with that of the country. By the 19th century it was dominated by Italian opera, but in the second half of the century Spanish composers (like those in a number of other European countries) started to seek a nationalist expression. Francisco Asenjo Barbieri (1823–94), musicologist, composer, itinerant performer and conductor, brought authentic Spanish folk material into his works, and had considerable influence on the next generation of Spanish composers. His example was emulated by Tomás Bretón y Hernández (1850–1923), Ruperto Chapí (y Lorente) (1851–1909) and Amadeo Vives (1871–1932), all of whom concentrated on the traditional form of the *zarzuela*, the comic operetta that usually incorporated spoken dialogue. But the major turn-of-the-century nationalist composer was a Catalan, Felipe Pedrell (1841–1922, not to be confused with his nephew, the Uruguayan composer Carlos Pedrell). Known as the 'Spanish Wagner' for his epic operatic trilogy *Los Pirineos* (*The Pyrenees*), Pedrell revived the classical elements of the *zarzuela*, drawing on folk music and folk tales and on the *tonadilla escénica*, a popular lyrico-dramatic comic form usually revolving around characters from the lower strata of society.

Pedrell was an outstanding teacher, and his most famous pupils, Isaac Albéniz (1860–1909), Manuel de **Falla** (1876–1946) and Enrique Granados (1867–1916), are the most distinguished Spanish composers of any period. Albéniz's major contribution were the four books of piano pieces titled *Iberia* (1909), evoking the colours and traditions of Spain, especially the music of Andalusia. Granados combined a Spanish passion with classical restraint, notably in his suite of piano pieces after Goya, *Goyescas* (1911), and the related opera of the same title (1916), first heard in New York. Their early deaths (Granados died trying to save his wife after their ship was torpedoed) were a blow to Spanish music, but they had introduced the now familiar idioms of traditional Spanish music worldwide. **Falla** helped establish the nationalist idiom in orchestral music, hitherto largely ignored in favour of stage or piano works. Most Spanish composers of the first half

of the century developed the nationalist idiom, with a noticeable divergence into local identities. In Catalonia, the choral society Orfe Catal had been founded in 1881 to present the Spanish polyphonic tradition and to explore Catalan folk music. Francisco Ali (1862–1908) collected Catalan folk songs, while Federico **Mompou** (1893–1987) and, in his earlier music, Roberto **Gerhard** (1896–1970) utilised Catalan themes. Valencia was represented by Eduardo López-Chavarri (1881–1970), who was a poet and a considerable writer on and editor of music as well as a composer, with such works as *Valencianas* for orchestra and *Danzas Valencianas*, for piano, and by the much better-known composer Joaquín **Rodrigo** (born 1901). Oscar Esplá (1886–1976) made use of Alicante traditions, and **Falla**, Joaquín **Turina** (1882–1949) and the guitar virtuoso and composer Angel Barrios (Fernandez) (1882–1964) used those of Andalusia, which, with their strong gipsy and flamenco elements, have become most associated in the popular mind with the Spanish folk tradition. The lyrical and Romantic elements of this Spanish tradition were continued by Ernesto **Halffter** (1905–89), who was for some time considered to be the inheritor of **Falla's** style, until it was realised that Halffter's essentially vivacious outlook materially differed from the lean Spanish concision of Falla's last works. The music of Esplá, influential and important in Spain but little known outside, aimed for the spirit of folk music rather than its transliteration. In his 1915 *Violin Sonata* he started using a 9-note scale that reflected certain aspects of the music of his native Alicante. His major work is the symphonic episode *Don Quijote verlando las armas* (*Don Quixote Guarding his Arms*, 1924), though he is probably best known outside Spain for his simple and affecting piano music.

A movement away from nationalism and towards a more modern European idiom was initiated by the Grupo de los Ocho (the 'Madrid Group'), founded in 1930, which aimed at a more abstract musical idiom. Its chief members were Ernesto **Halffter** (though traditional Spanish idioms continued to play a role in his subsequent works), his brother Rudolfo **Halffter** (1900–87 – see under 'Mexico'), Salvador Bacarisse (1898–1963) and Julián Bautista (1901–61). Bacarisse moved to Paris in 1936, where he spent the rest of his life. His earlier music was advanced for the Spain of the time, employing strong dissonances and polytonality, and an idiom containing little that was Spanish. Later he mellowed, and turned to works with nationalist subjects, particularly the heritage of older Spanish music. The works written in Paris are more neo-Romantic, although he returned to the Spanish tradition in the *Fantasia andaluza* for harp and orchestra, and in the marvellous *Guitar Concertino* (1957), combining it with neo-Baroque elegance and charm. The concertino is symphonically laid out in four movements, and with its appealing neo-Renaissance opening movement, a slow movement that rivals **Rodrigo** in its beauty and Spanish feel, a light scherzo, and a courtly dance of a finale, it is one of the most attractive of all guitar concertos.

Bautista spent much of his life in South America, moving to Buenos Aires in 1940. Many of his scores were lost in the Spanish Civil War, but his surviving music embraces Impressionism, nationalist subjects, neo-classicism and a more contemporary idiom. Among the better-known works are his tribute to Andalusia, the resonant *Tres cuidades* (*Three Cities*, 1937, to texts by Lorca) for voice and piano or orchestra, which displays his concise idiom, sensuous feel, and a use of a raw folk-like Andalusian vocal style, fusing the traditional with the contemporary. Spain's heroic past is evoked in a number of later works, including *Catro poemas calegos* (*Four Galician Poems*, 1946), for voice and orchestra or piano, which combines archaic and modern elements and contrasts the rustic and the sophisticated, and the *Romance del Rey Rodrigo* (1955–56) for a cappella choir, which describes the defeat of Moors by the last Visigothic king of Spain; here polyphonic ideas vie with dissonant harmonies and polyrhythms. Most of his neo-classical works date from the 1930s.

The influence first of **Schoenberg** and then of **Stravinsky's** neo-classicism surfaced in the music of **Rodolfo Halffter**, who later developed a strongly polytonal idiom. Meanwhile, outside this group, **Mompou** explored his own brand of minimal structures and sounds known as 'neo-Primitivism'. At the same time, during the period of the Republic in the early 1930s, Barcelona, fervent with new political and artistic ideas, blossomed as an international centre for the performance of new music, thus introducing the latest European trends to Spanish composers.

The Spanish Civil War (1936–39) and Franco's victory effectively destroyed modern music in Spain for more than a decade. The majority of the more advanced Spanish composers were of Republican convictions, and left Spain: **Falla** and Bautista went to Argentina, **Rodolfo Halffter** to Mexico, Bacarisse to Paris, **Gerhard** to Cambridge, England. None of them returned, and much of Spain's better modern music was then written outside the country. The finest modern Spanish composer, Gerhard, turned in the 1950s to the development of his own individual ideas about the combination of free 12-tone techniques with tonal elements, especially in his orchestral works.

However, in the 1950s a new generation of composers emerged who had not experienced the Civil War as adults. Throughout the 20th century, a consistent thread of Spanish music had been its associations with developments in French music. Pedrell studied with **d'Indy**, and many of the succeeding generation studied in Paris or were influenced by **Debussy** and the Impressionists, who were themselves influenced by Spanish music. Similarly, two of the more successful of this new generation of composers, Xavier **Benguerel** (born 1931) and Luis **de Pablo** (born 1930), after briefly discovering 12-tone techniques, came under the influence of **Boulez** and his circle. Benguerel, however, then followed the example of the exploration of timbre and sonority of the modern Polish composers. Cristóbal **Halffter** (born 1930), nephew of Rudolpho and Ernesto, was briefly influenced by **Bartók** and **Stravinsky** before also turning to the mainstream avant-garde ideas. All three are European rather than Spanish composers, following a trend observable right across the continent, though **Benguerel** began to incorporate Spanish medieval material into his contemporary idiom, thus continuing the Spanish tradition of fusing the traditional with the modern. However, the finest of this generation with Spanish connections, Maurice **Ohana** (1914–92), preferred to work in France. Although of Andalusian parentage, his father was born in Gibraltar (thus conferring on his son British citizenship), and he was born in Morocco, under which heading he will be found. Of the less well-known composers of this generation, Josep Soler (born 1935) has developed Impressionistic elements and come under the influence of **Messiaen**, while Josep Maria Mestres-Quadreny (born 1929) has been eclectic in his exploration of avant-garde means of expression. None of these composers is well known outside Spain, and throughout the past three decades the music of Spain has been more popularly represented by the works of the conservative Joaquín **Rodrigo**, whose guitar concerto *Concierto de Aranjuez*, for better or worse, is one of the best-known pieces of classical music from any period.

Throughout the century, the guitar has been the predominant Spanish instrument. Partly owing to its general use in 'pop' music world-wide from the middle of the century on, it displaced the piano as the most popular worldwide household instrument. Most of the major 20th-century Spanish composers have written for it in some form or another, or been influenced by its techniques (for example, in piano writing), and the influence of Spanish idioms has filtered through to works written for the instrument by composers of other nationalities. Guitar concertos and other guitar works are still the most likely modern Spanish music to be encountered outside Spain, apart from that of Albéniz, Granados and **Falla**; the absence of any Spanish symphony or opera in the general international repertoire is conspicuous.

Mention should also be made of the effect of Spanish musical nationalism on the serious music of South America, both from indigenous traditions going back to colonial times, and from the influence of those Spanish composers who settled in South America at the end of the Spanish Civil War. The Spanish influence also seeped through from Mexico to some of the American composers.

Spain has also produced some exceptional interpreters, notably the pianist Ricardo Viñes (1875–1943), who was closely associated with many French composers, and who introduced contemporary Spanish piano music to international audiences. The cellist Pau (Pablo) Casals (1876–1973), perhaps the finest of this century, left Spain in 1939 but remained attached to his Catalan heritage. More recently, the singers Victoria de Los Angeles and José Carreras have both included 20th-century Spanish songs in their repertoire, while the pianist Alicia de Larrocha and the guitarist Narciso Yepes have performed a similar service for the modern Spanish piano and guitar repertoires. Those seeking a cross-section of the more conservative 20th-century Spanish repertoire will find it in their recorded recitals.

Spain Music Informatic Centre
Centro de Documentación Musical
Torregalindo 10
E-28016 Madrid
Spain
Tel: +34 1 350 8600
Fax: +34 1 359 1579

Benguerel Xavier*
born 9th February 1931 at Barcelona

Benguerel is one of the more interesting Catalan and Spanish composers of his generation, but has achieved little prominence outside Spain, except in Germany. He left Spain as a child and studied in Argentina, but returned to live in Spain in 1954. His earliest music shows the influence first of **Bartók**, and then of **Schoenberg**. There followed a number of concertante works, including the *Concerto for Two Flutes and Strings* (1961), which has a lucidity of lyrical orchestration and melodic line and lively interplay between the two solo instruments, while following 12-tone and strongly contrapuntal ideas. The overall feel is almost pastoral, though with the injection of a more ominous mood in the centre of the slow movement.

With *Música para tres percusionistas* (1967), he turned to the influence of **Boulez**. *Paraules de cada dia* (*Words for Everyday*, 1967, to poems by his father), for mezzo-soprano and chamber ensemble of three flutes, two clarinets, harp, vibraphone, piano, celesta and percussion, is a song-cycle of detailed textures, the colours determined by the Boulez-like instrumentation. Its wide-ranging vocal line and its close match between words and music create a descriptive effect with contemporary means.

During the late 1960s Benguerel extended the idiom to include aleatoric devices. He also turned his exploration to timbre and sonority, in the manner of such Polish avant-garde composers as **Lutosławski** and **Penderecki**. The interest in symphonic colour had been heralded by the *Simfonia per a un festival* (*Symphony for a Festival*, 1966); by the time of *Quasi una fantasia* (1971) for cello and chamber ensemble his idiom had joined the mainstream avant-garde. It is built on the effects of the orchestration of wind, brass, piano and three percussionists (but no strings), and on the juxtaposition of solos and tuttis. The colours and effects are extreme and inventive, with extended technique, often percussive, for the soloist (it was written for the virtuoso Siegfried Palm), and constantly changing rhythmic effects; however, its overall impact does not match its details.

A second concertante work for cello and orchestra, the much more effective *Cello Concerto* of 1977, opens with an extended solo veering between lyricism and extended technique effects. In common with some of Benguerel's other later work, it draws some of its material from early music (the 1137 Codex Calistinus), thus continuing a tradition observable throughout 20th-century Spanish music. The primary expression is of tension and contrast, sometimes with a blaring intensity, though with an atmospheric central section that directly quotes the Codex material against complex modern orchestral textures. The *Percussion Concerto* (1975), with aleatoric elements, is a study in sonorities from the delicate to the massed. The reworking of medieval material is most obvious in the curiously affecting *Astral* (1979), for guitar, piano (four hands), two percussionists, cello and bass, where the solo guitar is surrounded by contemporary instrumental textures and the deconstruction of phrases. Similarly, *Raices hispanicas* (1978) for orchestra is a collage of various influences, from folk music and the Spanish tradition to a theme from a Renaissance source, with the final emphasis on a formal nobility.

RECOMMENDED WORKS
    Astral (1979) for guitar and 6
        instruments
    Cello Concerto (1977)
    Paraules de cada dia (1967) for
        mezzo-soprano and chamber
        ensemble

Falla (y Matheu) Manuel Maria de•••

born 23rd November 1876 at Cadiz
died 14th November 1946 at Alta
Gracia (Argentina)

In spite of his small output, the Andalusian Manuel de Falla (usually known simply as 'Falla') remains the central figure in the music of 20th-century Spain. He brought orchestral mastery to a national music that had concentrated on opera and pieces for guitar or piano, and developed an aesthetic that was steeped in both a sense of history and a strong expression of spiritual heritage.

In Falla's case the impact of the music has its roots in the qualities of the man. His fastidiousness ensured that all his mature works have a feeling of total surety about them, each element having a consistency of purpose; it was also responsible for his small output. His deep religiousness and self-discipline emerge in a musical rigour through which the richness of the Spanish idiom was filtered; his works gradually became leaner, more concentrated, and more direct. Combined with this is above

all a fervent rhythmic energy, often in repeating patterns that sometimes reflect guitar sounds and tuning, and a tendency towards mixing two or more keys. His contribution to Spanish music was to show that the traditional and colourful Spanish styles could be transmuted into a personal idiom, while retaining their essence, and that this heritage was not incompatible with the move towards compression and the abstract that was taking place elsewhere in Europe. This combination of distinctly Spanish colours and rigorous musicianship has ensured his universal popularity.

Falla's earliest adult works were *zarzuelas* (popular operettas), but his sense of musical heritage was subsequently developed by studies with Felipe Pedrell. His orchestral skills were then honed in Paris (1907–14), where he exchanged ideas with Albéniz, **Debussy** and **Dukas**. Before moving to Paris, he had already written the opera *La vide breve* (*Life is Short*, 1904–05), whose weak drama and characterisation, apart from the central character Salud, has hindered its wider acceptance on the dramatic stage; consequently it is best known through excerpts that have found a popular place in the repertoire. Salud's aria ('All est!') in Act II is the distillation of the Andalusian gipsy in the earthiness and colour of the music, eventually set against a song from a guitar player; the choral dances are vividly exciting. It is primarily an opera of atmosphere and colour, with Spanish folk traditions on the one hand and the influence of the French opera composer Massenet on the other.

Falla's Parisian experience is clear in the *Noches en los jardines de España* (*Nights in the Gardens of Spain*, 1909–15), for piano and orchestra; a triptych of seductive nocturnes, it combines the soft allusiveness of Impressionism with more direct images of Spain. The solo part is an integrated element of the orchestra rather than a concertante role. The four *Pièces espagnoles* (1909) for piano were influenced by Albéniz (to whom they were dedicated), though the last, *Andaluza*, uses the modal harmonies that were to feature in Falla's later work. His attitude to the folk tradition emerged in the 7 *Canciones populares españolas* (*Seven Spanish Popular Songs*, 1914), for voice and piano. While using actual folk tunes, they attempt to recreate the essence of the idiom rather than presenting them in straightforward arrangements. Although the overall effect is lean and intimate, the piano writing is sometimes complex, with reminiscences of the guitar (the songs, like other Falla works, including *Nights in the Gardens of Spain*, have been successfully transcribed for guitar). This attitude to the folk heritage is amplified in the ballet *El amor brujo* (*Love the Magician*, 1914–15, for chamber orchestra, revised for full orchestra), which is steeped in the Andalusian flamenco style without ever directly quoting folk material. It is a fiercely exciting work, vivid with the light and colour of southern Spain, with a vocal part in the gipsy style contrasting with slow Impressionist sections. It has rich orchestration built around string sonorities, biting brass, a touch of Moorish inflection, and a fervour reflecting its rapid composition.

The next major work, *El corregidor y la molinera* (*The Corregidor and the Miller's Wife*, 1917), was revised for Diaghilev and the Ballets Russes as *El sombrero de tres picos* (*The Three-Cornered Hat*) in 1919, in which version it is usually heard, either full-length or in the suite of dances. It makes reference to folk tunes, but it is the taut vigour of the rhythms, their repetitive patterns, and the orchestration that are arresting. Its idiom is steeped in local colour, including castanets and 'olés', but allowing neo-classical moments. The evocations of the cuckoo (by a song for soprano), a cuckoo clock, and a musical box, have a Ravelian magic. The original version, however, is also worth hearing in its own right, for the more austere effect of its chamber-sized orchestration is quite different, with an intimate, charged atmosphere that looks forward to the *Harpsichord Concerto*.

Falla's idiom then became more stylised in the *Fantasia bética* (1919 – Baetica was the Roman name for Andalusia), his best-known piano work, which contains echoes of guitar figurations and characteristic dance rhythms, but also uses modes and polytonality as the basic harmonic material. *El retablo de Maestre Pedro* (*Master Peter's Puppet Show*, 1919–22, based on an episode in *Don Quixote*) is a delight. It is a puppet-show within a puppet-show and an opera all at once. The guests from the inn, who include Don Quixote, are larger marionettes, and the puppet-show they have come to see is played by glove puppets. The singers are placed in the orchestra. The story, which is one of rescue and abduction in Charlemagne's time, is narrated by a boy in a recitative style taken from the story-tellers of Spanish street corners. In the middle, Don Quixote gets confused between artifice and reality, and

attacks the wicked glove puppets. The score includes elements of medieval music and a residue of folk music. The work is now performed all too rarely, and is usually presented with singers replacing the larger marionettes, which destroys some of the theatrical magic.

With the small orchestra of the puppet opera (including harpsichord), the development of Falla's idiom towards a wider variety of effects with leaner forces continued. It reached its culmination in what is perhaps his masterpiece, the short *Harpsichord Concerto* (1923–26), for harpsichord and flute, oboe, clarinet, violin and cello. Traditional Spanish elements are now totally integrated into his individual style, the inheritance of history being expressed in harpsichord writing that is modern while echoing that of Domenico Scarlatti. The gradual concentration of material, evident throughout Falla's work, is complete. He creates a rarefied but expressive effect full of fervour and excitement, with characteristic energy and vigour in the ostinato rhythms, a solemn slow movement, a wide range of colours and instrumental detail, and often a feeling of more than one key. One of the reasons it is not more often heard is that it was written for a modern Pleyel harpsichord, of much larger sonority than the normal harpsichord.

For the final two decades of his life Falla laboured on an enormous 'scenic cantata', *Atlàntida* (1928–46). Written for five sopranos, three mezzo-sopranos, three contraltos, three tenors, baritone, bass, children's chorus, chorus and orchestra, and sung in Catalan, this was to be his expression of the essence of the spirit of Spain. It includes subjects both mythological, such as the story of Hercules in Spain, and historical, such as Columbus's discovery of the New World. Its language continued the spare distillation of the *Harpsichord Concerto* but without its concentration, ranging from grandeur to lyricism, and drawing on medieval modes and forms. It was left in a complex state of partial completion on Falla's death, and his pupil Ernesto **Halffter** eventually created a performing version (1961, revised 1976) – inevitably uneven but a major Spanish work. The failings of this epic originate in the text by the 19th-century Catalan poet Jacint Verdaguer: it is, for a musical work, over-packed with legend and heroic allusion; there is too much emphasis on an allegory of the spiritual connection between classical legend, Spain, and the New World. Both the sentiment and the language belong to the 19th century; so does much of the setting of the first of three parts, in an oratorio style beloved of late 19th-century choral societies. However, the central Part II is more dramatic, musically more individual, and rhythmically more varied and exciting, as in the powerful chorus 'Dixit Dominus', with its half-chanted, half-spoken choral lines. This part deserves to be heard on its own, given that the work as a whole suffers from problems of forces and scale, and from the lack of a clear sense of dramatic or musical shape. The other main work completed in this period is *Homenajes* (1920–39) for orchestra, built on the orchestral version of two instrumental works of tribute, *Le tombeau de Claude Debussy* (1920) for guitar and *Pour le tombeau de Paul Dukas* (1935) for piano, with the addition of a further movement honouring Felipe Pedrell (*Pedrelliana*).

Besides having a number of noted Spanish composers as his pupils, Falla founded the Orquesta Bética de Cámera, and in 1938 Franco named him as president of the Spanish Institute. However, the composer accepted an invitation from Argentina in 1939, and did not return to Spain, although on his death his body was returned for burial in Cadiz Cathedral. The order in his will that none of his works was to be performed on stage after his death has happily been ignored.

RECOMMENDED WORKS (English titles)
Harpsichord Concerto (1926)
ballet *Love the Magician* (1914–15)
Nights in the Gardens of Spain (1911–15) for piano and orchestra
ballet *The Three-Cornered Hat* (1918–19)
puppet opera *Master Peter's Puppet Show* (1919–22)

BIBLIOGRAPHY
S. Demarquez, *Manuel de Falla*, trans. S. Attansio, 1983

Gerhard Roberto **

born 25th September 1896 at Valls (Tarragona)
died 5th January 1970 at Cambridge (UK)

The public reputation of Roberto Gerhard has been confused by his twin allegiances. Although in origins and sometimes aesthetic he is a Spanish composer (albeit with Swiss family origins), he left Spain following Franco's victory in 1939, and settled in the UK, eventually becoming a British citizen in 1960. His striking idiom then followed broad European trends, concentrating on orchestral works, the most notable of which is one of his four symphonies, in which he attempted to extend the formal parameters of the idiom. Although complex formal ideas underlie his later work, notably groups of intervals and an extension of serial ideas into rhythm and duration, Gerhard was at pains to downplay this aspect of his idiom in favour of the purely aural effects of the sonorities and contrasts he developed. His music seems clearly designed to appeal to the emotions more than the intellect, and in this he succeeded. His orchestration is compelling (in the later works always including percussive piano), especially in the clear but busy and almost pointillistic details that are partly the heritage of **Schoenberg**.

He studied in Spain with the Catalan composer Felipe Pedrell, and then with **Schoenberg** in Berlin. The influence of the latter was not to emerge fully until after World War II, but it does show in the few early works written before his mid-thirties, mostly chamber music and songs (notably the *Seven Haiku*, 1922, revised 1958, for high voice, wind instruments and piano). On his return to Spain in 1928 he turned to his Spanish heritage rather than atonal or 12-tone music, producing works with specific Catalan ties, such as the cantata *L'Alta naixença del rei en jaume* (1932), *Albada, interludi i dansa* (1936) for orchestra, and the fourteen *Cançons populars catalanes* (1928), for soprano and piano (six of which he orchestrated). The first works written in England follow this trend, notably the ballet *Don Quixote* (1940–41). This is full of delightful orchestral mosaic detail and wit, exemplified in the use of a tone-row that arises from Quixote's theme to represent the other side of his nature, and which happily merges into the predominantly tonal cast. The ballet *Algérias* (1942), usually heard in the suite of extracts, is a marvellous flamenco evocation, a combination of ironic pastiche and Spanish colour, based on the analogy between bullfight and a wooing, with the bull as the wooer, the torero as the girl; it includes a quote from the funeral march of Chopin's *Piano Sonata No. 2 in Bb minor*. Two works from this period pay tribute to the heritage of Pedrell: the *Cancionero de Pedrell* (1941), for soprano and chamber orchestra and the symphony (not listed in the numbered symphonies) *Homenaje a Pedrell* (1941) on themes from Pedrell's opera *La Celestina*.

Gerhard then returned to Schoenbergian ideas, notably in the *Violin Concerto* (1942–43), which borrows a tone-row from **Schoenberg's** *String Quartet No. 4* for the slow movement, but still has touches of the Spanish heritage (including a reference to Chabrier's *España*). There is a strong emphasis in the concerto on lyricism and sonic effect, hovering on tonality. It oscillates between tonal passages and a more dissonant idiom, and the solo line has a touch of the dance in the outer movements, a whimsical lyricism in the slow movement. With the *Symphony No. 1* (1952–53), he rejected traditional forms: although in three movements, it is non-thematic. Instead each movement grows from within, without repetition or restatements, in a continuously unfolding weave, the final movement building into complex and dramatic climaxes. The result is robust, effective, with a wealth of clear orchestral detail (notably the harp, adding a Spanish touch) combined with a rhythmic flow that is lyrical in impulse. The harmonic idiom that again revolves around tonal associations. In the *String Quartet No. 1* (1950–55) he developed an individual extension of 12-tone ideas to rhythm (a time-series), and subsequently used it to give his later music its particular rhythmic impulse (his series use prime numbers, so that one idea may use five beats, another simultaneous idea seven, and they will not coincide again until 35 beats later). He also started unifying works by having the overall architecture correspond to these internal divisions, and thereafter his music is invariably cast in one continuous structure divided into sections of movements without breaks. Such series are used in the *Symphony No. 2* (1957–59), which was partly revised in 1967, though that revision is incomplete and the published score reverts to the original in the last of the four movements, played without a break. It is a more austere, less individual and rather uncharacteristic work, more obviously related to the contemporary avant-garde, as the orchestration is dominated by percussion, while the interest in unusual sonorities is reflected in the use of an accordion.

In the 1960s Gerhard continued his exploration of sonorities, developing unusual string effects in the *String Quartet No. 2* (1960–62). In the programmatic *Symphony No. 3 'Collages'* (1960) he heightened the drama by opposing the orchestra with an electronic tape using *musique concrète* sounds. Inspired by a plane flight, it is in one movement cast into seven sections, each corresponding to a hymn of praise for a different hour between sunrise and sunset. Alternating between drama and repose, and with a meditative central section without tape, the wide-ranging sonorities from the large orchestra (including piano) match the other-worldliness of the tape, whose sounds are very successfully integrated into the complete pattern. The path of Gerhard's development then reached a logical conclusion in the *Concerto for Orchestra* (1964–65) and in the *Symphony No. 4 'New York'* (1966–67, named after the commissioning orchestra, the New York Philharmonic). The concentration is now entirely on texture and sonorities: structures are built on the contrasts of textures, using all his command of orchestration, and durations predominate over pitch. In the *Concerto* there is a very wide range of sounds, including extensive use of strings as percussion instruments. It is a virtuoso orchestral score, characteristically intense and concentrated, combining three layers: orchestral colour in fast movement, static figurations, and long-breathed slower unfolding. The *Symphony No. 4* feels marvellously organic in its progression of contrasts, in its constantly fluctuating orchestral shapes, and in its huge variety of instrumental effect and colour.

Gerhard's late works continue the exploration of non-thematic evolution and of colourful instrumentation and effect, as in the kaleidoscope of instrumental combinations and figuration in *Libra* (1968), for flute, clarinet, violin, guitar, percussion and piano, or in the more disparate *Leo* (1969), for flute, clarinet, horn, trumpet, trombone, violin, two percussionists, piano and celesta, his last completed work. Both works (from a group known as the *Astrological Series*) end with the moving use of the same folk tune.

Two dramatic scores occupy an important place in Gerhard's other works. The opera *The Duenna* (1945–47, after Sheridan's play) is a neo-classical pastiche, combining tonality for the songs and a more chromatic idiom in a free 12-tone style for the interlinking passages and motifs. *The Plague* (1963–64, after Camus's novel) is unexpectedly a melodrama with narrator, chorus (whose range extends to whispering and shouting) and orchestra. Taking ten episodes from the novel, it is for concert rather than stage use. The *Concerto for Piano and Strings* (1951) moves harmonically from a free idiom to 12-tone, and the tonal associations of 12-tone technique were further explored in the bright *Concerto for Harpsichord, Strings and Percussion* (1956). Among his handful of electronic pieces is a setting of Lorca's *Lament for the Death of a Bullfighter* (1959) for speaker and tape.

Gerhard's music shows a consistent development to the mature and individual works of the 1960s. The earlier Spanish pieces, with their evocative colour, will give pleasure in themselves, but it is the later works which command attention on a number of levels. His personal use of post-Schoenbergian ideas, and the integration of tonal elements with serial elements are of interest in themselves. But the music also appeals through its emotional impact and range of sonorities and colour. This is an idiom that may well appeal to those still hesitant about, or sceptical of, serial developments in music.

Gerhard also edited the quintets of Soler, and was noted for his incidental music, particularly for Shakespeare productions at Stratford. Although he lived in Cambridge from 1939, he did little formal teaching (except at the Dartington and Tanglewood summer schools), but he lectured widely and was visiting professor at the University of Michigan in 1960.

RECOMMENDED WORKS
    ballet suite *Algérias* (1942)
    Concerto for Orchestra (1965)
    Symphony No. 1 (1952–53)
    Symphony No. 3 *Collages* (1960)
    Symphony No. 4 *New York* (1966)
    Violin Concerto (1942–43)

Halffter Cristóbal*
born 24th March 1930 at Madrid

Cristóbal Halffter is the nephew of the Spanish composer Ernesto **Halffter** and the Spanish-Mexican composer Rodolfo **Halffter**. After being influenced by **Bartók** and **Stravinsky** in the 1950s in such works as *Dos movimientos* (*Two Movements*, 1956), which won a UNESCO prize, he then combined tonality with modal influences and elements of serial and 12-tone techniques in the *Misa ducal* (1956), for chorus and orchestra.

In the 1960s he followed this line of development by turning to the ideas of the European avant-garde, particularly in larger-scale works using contrasting sonorities and favouring massed swirling repetitive figures (often in woodwind) set against or within strident interjections.

There is in his mature work an undercurrent of repressed anger and violence which comes to the surface through the avant-garde sonorities, as well as a sense of social comment which, under the Franco dictatorship, had to be covert.

Post-**Webern** ideas surfaced in *Espejos* (*Mirrors*, 1963), for four percussionists and tape, which combines freely improvised elements with strictly controlled rhythms. The mirror of the title is reflected in the form: it ends with both the opening and its retrograde played simultaneously. His individual voice emerged in, for example, *Symposion* (1968), for baritone, choir and orchestra. Here although many of the current avant-garde techniques appear (massed clusters for the chorus, influenced by **Ligeti**, the chattering and talking of the chorus, a section for wood-blocks), there is an epic quality in the sharply contrasting sections, in the declamatory baritone line, and in the insistent opening. This creates a fierce excitement and a personal expressive fervour, which some have seen as a Spanish aspect of his otherwise European idiom.

A similar sense of scale pervades *Secuencias* (1964) for orchestra. A layer of subdued massed string sonorities against declamatory brass creates a long-term sense of swell and subsidence; Halffter regularly divides his orchestra into specified blocks or groups. In *Lineas y puntos* (*Lines and Points*, 1967) for twenty winds and tape, it is the tape which provides the broad sweep, the instruments the foreground detail, now declamatory, now chattering, and eventually lyrical. One of Halffter's most widely known works, commissioned by UNESCO to commemorate the twentieth anniversary of the Universal Declaration of Human Rights, is the dramatic cantata *Yes Speak Out Yes* (1968) for the huge forces of six speakers, soprano, baritone, two choruses, and large orchestra with two conductors. Centred around the progression of key words ('No', 'Why', 'Yes, speak out, yes', 'children', 'peace') and including quotations from the declaration, it utilises avant-garde choral effects (declamatory speech, clusters) with the fervour that is characteristic of the composer. The text is treated atmospherically, and the solo vocal lines use extreme vocal ranges, which merge with declamatory speech from the speakers. In spite of its grand aims, however, it is anger and stridency that leave the final impression. Also on a large scale but much more imposing is the *Elegias a la muerte de tres poetas españoles* (*Elegy on the Death of*

Three Spanish Poets, 1974–75) for large orchestra. With swirls of recurring patterns, resonant layered sonorities and harsh injections, and again with an epic quality, explores the expressive sonorities of the orchestra, both angry and elegiac.

The changes in Spain after the death of Franco (1973), though welcome, did not meet Halffter's artistic hopes and expectations, and he left in 1978. His feelings were graphically expressed in the short harpsichord piece *Adieu* (1978), a combination of gentle nostalgia outbursts of extreme frustration. Of his recent works, he has maintained the main elements of his idiom in the large-scale *Cello Concerto No. 2* (1985), while his *String Quartet No. 3* (1990) suggested a return to more traditional tonal elements.

Cristóbal Halffter was on the staff of Spanish Radio, and conductor of the Orquesta Manuel de Falla (1964–66). He taught at the Madrid Conservatory (1964–66).

RECOMMENDED WORKS
    Elegias a la muerte de tres poetas
      españoles (1974–75) for orchestra
    Symposium (1968) for baritone,
      chorus and orchestra

Halffter Ernesto*

born 16th January 1905 at Madrid
died 5th July 1989 at Madrid

A pupil of **Falla**, Ernesto Halffter was influenced in his early works by the spare and fastidious style of his teacher's *Harpsichord Concerto*, with its echoes of Domenico Scarlatti. The return to classical or earlier models, as in the echoes of Spanish dance styles from all ages in the ballet *Sonatina* (1928), was combined with an awareness of the contemporary vogue for smaller forces and for the abstract neo-classicism initiated by **Stravinsky**. The major work of this period was the *Sinfonietta* (1923–25, revisions until 1927), which had considerable impact in Spain. Following the pattern of a Haydn sinfonia concertante, with instrumental solos, it shows the zest and brilliance that were to remain a feature of his idiom, a tonal idiom leavened by bitonality, and the clear influence of Stravinsky and 'Les Six', in what is for a sinfonietta a long and complex work.

In 1930 he helped to found the Grupo de los Ocho (the 'Madrid Group'), and thereafter the influence of **Ravel** (whom he met in Paris in the late 1920s) shows in works such as the *Rhapsodia portuguesa* (1940,

revised 1951) for piano and orchestra. Between 1954 and 1960, and again through a number of revisions up to 1976, he devoted much of his energies to the reconstruction and completion of **Falla's** huge scenic cantata *Atlàntida*. In the 1960s, under the influence of contemporary post-**Webern** ideas, he refined his own idiom into a more fastidious and economical style (without abandoning a tonal base), most likely to be encountered in the *Guitar Concerto* (1969). This rhythmically vibrant work has a slightly acid touch in its dissonant harmonies, a curiously despondent slow movement with moments suffused with illumination, and a wild dance of a finale, with orchestral outbursts and percussive interjections. He also returned to his earlier neo-classicism (or rather, to the influence of the Spanish Renaissance), in such works as *Gozos de Nuestra Señora* (1970) for chorus and orchestra; these, like other choral works of this late period, also reflects his experience working on Falla's large score.

Ernesto Halffter thus emerges as representative of Spanish neo-classicism, more wide-ranging and sophisticated than **Rodrigo** but in spite of the general appeal of his own stylistic brilliancies without Rodrigo's instant individuality and melodic memorability. In 1924 he was appointed conductor of the Orquesta Bética of Seville, and was director of the National Conservatory in Seville (1934–36). He had close connections with Portugal, his wife being the Portuguese pianist Alicia Càmara Santos.

RECOMMENDED WORK
    Sinfonietta (1923–25) for orchestra

Halffter Rudolfo
see under Mexico

Mompou Federico
born 16th April 1893 at Barcelona
died 30th June 1987 at Barcelona

Mompou's output consists almost entirely of meditative and introvert piano music and songs. He spent much of his life in Paris (1911–14, 1921–41). Influenced by **Satie**, he aimed at a very spare piano style, almost entirely in miniatures or sets of miniatures, with very little modulation or thematic development – a return to a 'primitive' idiom which he called 'recomençament' (or 'recomienzo', beginning anew). The basic material often reflects popular themes, and within its subdued parameters his style used first Impressionistic and then neo-classical elements, often indulging in bell-like sounds. His harmonies regularly have the feel of minor keys, though he dispensed with key signatures and bar divisions. His introspection is reflected in his playing his own music only for friends (in spite of his own pianistic abilities), apart from a complete recording of his piano works late in his life. Even the twelve *Songs and Dances* for piano, spanning the period from 1918 to 1962, are largely slow and melancholic, with a nostalgic quality, and any dissonance confined to stylistic device. The ultimate development of his idiom is found in the four books of *Música callada* (*Silent Music*, 1959, 1962, 1965 and 1967), based on an idea from St John of the Cross suggesting a music that would express the very voice of silence. The miniatures are very austere, with little contrast or change, but with a slow-moving, meditative quality that is rather haunting in its appeal. Of his songs, the song-cycle *Combat del somni* (1942–48) for high voice and piano is typical: delicate and introspective, with three mournful songs comparing dreams, nature and the poet's lover. His only guitar piece of note is the *Suite compostelana* (1962), though his piano music, arranged for guitar, is sometimes heard in recitals. His piano miniatures are best heard in isolation rather than in groups, where the consistency of idiom and emotion is inclined to become wearisome.

RECOMMENDED WORK
Silent Music (1959–67) for piano

BIBLIOGRAPHY
A. Iglesias, *Frederico Mompou*, 1977 (in Spanish)

Ohana Maurice
see under Morocco

de Pablo Luis
born 28th January 1930 at Bilbao

Self-taught as a composer (he studied law at university), de Pablo is a leading Spanish composer who has followed the trends of contemporary European idioms. His early music was influenced by **Stravinsky** and **Bartók**, and in the late 1950s he turned to serialism following his readings of the critic René Leibowitz on the 12-tone composers and his discovery of the ideas of

Messiaen. He later translated writings on **Schoenberg** and **Webern** into Spanish, and published his own book on contemporary music (1968).

In the late 1950s he embraced the major current avant-garde ideas, including free forms, structures based on the concepts of mobiles (e.g *Movil II*, 1958, and *Movil II*, 1968, for two pianos) and collage, and electro-acoustic techniques. Sonorities and the interaction of silences were explored in such works as *Cesuras* (1963) for three woodwind and three strings. He also developed his own technique in what he termed 'modules': the smallest possible expressive units, which are then interchangeable. Thus *Modulos V* (1967) for organ is created from twenty-five fragments, themselves grouped into three episodes, within which the interpreter has choices of register, timbre, and other parameters. The order of the episodes and the order of fragments within the episodes are also open to choice, but at the end comes a fourth episode without such choices. Wispy strands of such fragmentary material form layers in *Modulos III* (1967) for orchestra, and similar techniques are found in the rest of the *Modulos* series (Nos. I–VI, 1965–68, with various instrumental forces). Post-serial developments and similar micro-structures are evident in the often aggressive *Ejercicio* (1965) for string quartet, which displays extremes of dramatic effect and extended technique, with high harmonics, disjointed pointillistic effects, plucking and swoops, and darker held colours. The energetic *Iniciativas* (1966) for orchestra has similarly violent tendencies, contrasting massed string or prominent piano ideas with outbursts from solo or other instrumental groups.

De Pablo then turned to electronic works, with or without other forces, transforming the instrumental group Alea, which he had founded in 1965, into a live electronic ensemble in 1967. He also started to explore theatrical or extra-musical elements, as in his collaborations with J. L. Alexanco (*Soledad interrumpida*, 1971, for tapes and plastic objects, and *Historia natural*, 1972, for instruments, tape, lights and plastic objects). His close alliance with French avant-garde developments is indicated not only by the predominantly French titles in his later works, but also by the French Government creating him an Officier des Arts et des Lettres in 1973.

On the available evidence, de Pablo's music has helped bring Spanish music into the mainstream European avant-garde, but lacks the individual stamp of some of his European contemporaries. Readers may find **Benguerel's** music more idiomatic, and Cristóbal **Halffter's** more individual; all are eclipsed in intellectual rigour and sonic interest by the later music of **Gerhard.** De Pablo has also been active in promoting new music in Spain. He founded the concert series 'Tiempo y Música' (1958–65) and an electronic studio (1965), and has been influential as a teacher at the Madrid Conservatory.

RECOMMENDED WORK
   Ejericio (1965) for string quartet

BIBLIOGRAPHY
   L. de Pablo, *Aproximacin a una esttica de la musica contempornea,* 1968
   T. Marco, *Luis de Pablo,* 1971 (in Spanish)

Rodrigo Joaquín**
born 22nd November 1901 at Sagunto (Valencia)

Blind from the age of three, Joaquín Rodrigo is best known for two works for guitar and orchestra, the *Concierto de Aranjuez* and the *Fantasia para un gentilhombre* – and often dismissed because of it. This is unfortunate, for although his idiom is conservative, he nonetheless showed a steady line of development in a very personal and appealing idiom that concentrated on creating atmosphere and a Spanish ambience. Some of his later works are not only finer than either of these two, the slow movement of the concerto apart, but also progress to a style that may interest many who might otherwise ignore the rest of his considerable output. His works are mainly concertos and vocal music; the former are quite widely disseminated (on the strength of the two popular works), the latter are little known outside Spain.

Where other Spanish composers have turned to recent folk or gipsy traditions for their expression of a national music, Rodrigo has turned as much to an earlier Spanish heritage, being inspired not only by the feel of history so prevalent in Spain, but also by the Spanish composers of the 17th and 18th centuries. In this sense, he is a kind of Spanish neo-classicist, paralleling the Italian neo-madrigale movement. Perhaps he is best described as a pastoral composer, in the sense of the solitary lyricism of the shepherd surveying – with straightforward pleasure, nostalgia and joy – the landscape around him. He is clearly aware of his own historical continuity, suggesting a constant programmatic base to his works. That pastoralism is exemplified in the spare, elemental but lyrical atmosphere of the *4 canciones sefardies (Four Shepherd Songs,* 1963) for low voice and piano, with drones and a pentatonic scale among its colours. There is no sense of *angst* in Rodrigo's music, and that removed him from the general tenor of the music of our time – perhaps some of that solitude stemmed from his blindness. Nonetheless, for all the musical conservatism it entails, it remains a valid part of the human experience. If in some works he continued an essentially unchanged style, in others, such as the magical slow movement of the *Concierto como un divertimento,* he displayed much more idiomatic means in creating a similar ambience. His forms generally follow classical models; his orchestration, which showed a gradually increasing sureness, favours rich colours in spare textures, brass triplets, high wind, and long string lines; his basic material drew on a combination of the classical heritage and folk-music, with a melodic style narrow in range but instantly recognisable and almost always memorable.

His earliest major work is the symphonic poem *Per la flor del lliri blau (For the Flower of the Blue Lily,* 1934) for orchestra. Although it does use traditional songs, the Spanish idioms are not overt in a work that shows the immaturity of his early technique, and is eclectic in its range of material, from a grand march, through contrived dissonances, to a jaunty piccolo tune, with influences from Impressionism to Wagner and Mussorgsky. If at times pompous, it shows Rodrigo's considerable flair for atmosphere, and is worth hearing. It was followed by a work that is among the most popular in the entire classical repertoire, the *Concierto de Aranjuez* (1939) for guitar and orchestra, which has been suborned into countless arrangements, from muzak to jazz (some to Rodrigo's annoyance). Essentially neo-classical in construction, using a small orchestra with prominent solo instruments to balance the guitar, it is an evocation of the haunting atmosphere of the royal palace of Aranjuez, both its colourful joys and its mysterious nocturnal weight of history. The outer movements can be criticised for their lack of orchestral refinement and their over-jaunty tone, but they are infectious. The heart of the work is the central adagio, where Rodrigo brilliantly conjures up the magic of the night air with an almost improvisatory guitar covering a very wide range of colours against a hushed orchestra; for many this is the essence of Spain in music.

Of his other scores for guitar or guitars and orchestra, the *Fantasia para un gentilhombre* (1954), for guitar and orchestra, has achieved almost as much popularity as the *Concerto de Aranjuez* – rather inexplicably, given the greater potential appeal of some of the composer's other works. It is very different in tone, being based on guitar works by the 17th-century composer Gaspar Sanz: early music dressed in the gentle garb of modern Spanish colours, and effective as such. The *Concierto andaluz* (1967), for four guitars and orchestra is, along with the *Concierto heróico* (1942), for piano and orchestra, the least successful of Rodrigo's concertos, overstepping the boundary of banality towards which his music is always in danger of veering. Much finer, and in many ways his most interesting concerto, is the *Concierto madrigal* (1967) for two guitars and orchestra, written for the Romero family of guitarists, who have become closely associated with Rodrigo's music. What distinguishes this concerto is its construction – ten sections using as a central theme the anonymous madrigal *Felices ojos mios* – and the combination of neo-madrigale and folk or dance treatments. The *Concierto para una fiesta* (1982) for guitar and orchestra has the unusual distinction of being commissioned for the social debut of two American sisters (on which occasion it was first performed), and has an extremely difficult solo part. The concerto is more restrained than the title might suggest (except for its opening and the formal nature of the final movement), and while the melodic treatment is typical of the composer, there is greater emphasis on rhythmic variety and less on lyrical ambience.

Of his concertos for other solo instruments, the two for cello are especially effective. The *Concierto en modo galante* (1949) is highly lyrical, while the *Concierto como un divertimento* (1981–82) has an instantly appealing opening movement, with the rhythmic flow (reminiscent of **Sibelius**'s *Karelia Suite*) combined with colourfully Spanish brass and sinuous cello. The andante nostalgico has unusual

orchestral and harmonic effects, with high string, woodwind and tuned percussion figures creating a background tapestry for the lyrical soloist, far distant in technique if not in atmosphere from the earlier works. The solo writing is virtuoso throughout, with an exceptionally difficult cadenza in the slow movement, including quadruple stopping. It is difficult not to warm to this appealing score. The *Concierto de estio* (*Summer Concerto*, 1943) for violin and orchestra was intended to echo the style of Vivaldi, with a rich slow movement in the form of variations. The *Concierto-serenata* (1954) for harp and orchestra is delicate and charming, while the shorter *Sones en la giralda* (1963) for harp and orchestra is an indication of the development of Rodrigo's harmonic language: initially far from traditional tonality while retaining its base, lyrical and flowing, and in one long restrained sweep moving towards more conventional and boundlessly happy material – a rare and valuable addition to the repertoire for harp and orchestra, and beautiful in its own right. The *Concierto pastoral* (1978), for flute and orchestra, is a showcase for the soloist in which the music has a kind of child-like innocence. The tart opening of the first movement develops into a march, with the soloist treated like a very busy fife. The pastoral mood of the little emerges in the slow movement, languid and haunting, much in the style of the *Concierto de Aranjuez*, and there is rustic quality, against chirping flute, to the dances of the final movement.

His vocal works include *Música para un Códice Salmantino sobre letra de Miguel de Unamuno* (1943), for bass, chorus and eleven instruments, where the influence of motets, Gregorian chant and Castilian folk song appeared as well as the ambiguous tonality that was increasingly an element in parts of his later works. *Ausencias de Dulcinea* (1948), for bass, four sopranos and large orchestra, is one of his major works, based on *Don Quixote*, while there are a number of Catalan settings, including *Triptico de Mosén Cinto* (1946) and *Cuarte cançons en llengua catalana* (1946), both for voice and orchestra. This aspect of Rodrigo's output needs to be heard outside Spain.

Música para un jardin (*Music for a Garden*, 1923, 1957) for orchestra reworks four earlier cradle songs for piano, with the titles of the four seasons, and has a short, beguiling and atmospheric score, with delicate orchestration including tuned percussion. A late oddity is the symphonic poem *A la busca del más alla (In Search of the Beyond,* 1978), which has something of the quality of an imaginary neo-Romantic film score, with soaring strings and fluttering flutes combined with some Spanish colour – indeed some passages are strongly reminiscent of **Vaughan Williams's** *Sinfonia Antartica.* In his piano music, Rodrigo also looked back to the Spanish musical heritage, especially that of the keyboard sonatas of the 18th century. The *Cinco sonatas de Castilla con toccata a modo de Prégon* (1950–51) is an attempt to introduce the sonata tradition to a more modern setting. Earlier piano works, such as the *Tres danzas de España* (1941) or *A l'ombre de Torre Bermeja* (1945), follow the lead of Albéniz. His solo guitar music ranges from the early *Zarabande lejana (Distant Zarabande,* written before 1927, that shows his early neo-classical interests (harking back to the lute music of the 16th-century Luis Milán), to the restrained classicism of the *Tres piezas españoles* (1954).

Rodrigo was the first holder of the Manuel de Falla Chair at Madrid University (1947), and among his many honours he was awarded the Grand Cross of the Order of Alfonso X the Wise by the Spanish government in 1953.

RECOMMENDED WORKS
Concierto de Aranjuez (1939) for
    guitar and orchestra
Concierto en modo galante (1949) for
    cello and orchestra
Concierto madrigal (1967) for two
    guitars and orchestra
Música para un jardin (1923–57) for
    orchestra
Sones en la Giralda (1963) for harp
    and orchestra
Four Shepherd Songs (1963) for voice
    and piano

BIBLIOGRAPHY
F. Sopea, *Joaquín Rodrigo,* 1970 (in
    Spanish)

Tórroba Federico Moreno˙
born 3rd March 1891 at Madrid
died 12 September 1982 at Madrid

A conductor as well as a composer, Frederico Tórroba was a leading figure in the revival of the Spanish guitar as a serious concert instrument, writing over a hundred guitar works for such virtuosi as Segovia and Narciso Yepes. However, he first attracted attention with two orchestral works, *La ajorca de oro (The Bracelet of Gold,* 1918) and *Zoraida* (1919), which, together with similar works by such composers as **Turina,** helped revive purely orchestral music in Spain. The descriptive orchestral pieces continued with *Cuadros (Scenes)* and *Cuadros casellanos (Castilian Scenes).* The *Gardens of Grenada* combines rather jaunty dance ideas with evocation, in a neo-classical atmosphere. In general the idiom is tonal, straightforward, but with a mastery of restrained orchestration, guitar textures and techniques, and an integration of the Spanish inheritance with a personal reflective idiom.

However, it is through his guitar works that Tórroba is most likely to be encountered. Of his guitar concertos, the *Concierto de Castilla* is pleasant easy listening, avoiding overt Spanish clichés, while the *Flamenco Concerto* uneasily mixes flamboyant flamenco with orchestral treatment. The most successful is the *Homenaje a la seguidilla* (1962), for guitar and orchestra, attractive and often thoughtful. It is a tribute to flamenco amalgamated with his restrained Romantic style, at times flamboyant without being strident, prepared to wander on occasion into some unusual harmonies, and with a particularly grateful part for the soloist. The Spanish idiom is to the fore, but with lucid and restrained orchestral colours, demonstrating Tórroba's skill in scoring, and combining the tunes of La Mancha with the classic *seguidilla* dance style of Andalusia. His later works included the six-movement *Estampas* for six guitars, the concerto for four guitars and orchestra *Concierto iberico* (1976), making full use of the concertante opportunities of the four soloists, the *Tonada concertante* for four guitars and orchestra and *Diálogos* (1974) for guitar and orchestra.

Besides his writing for guitar, Tórroba scored successes in Spain with his *zarzuelas* (popular operettas), notably *Luisa Fernanda* (1932), which was performed over eight thousand times in the next three decades, and is an entertaining example of the genre. Tórroba was vice-president of the Association of Spanish Composers, director of the Madrid Royal Academy of the Arts, and for ten years a critic for the Madrid daily paper *Informaciones.* He conducted a recording of the *Homenaje a la Seguidilla* at the age of ninety-one.

RECOMMENDED WORK
Homenaje a la seguidilla (1962) for
guitar and orchestra

Turina Joaquín*
born 9th December 1882 at Seville
died 14th January 1949 at Madrid

Turina was an unashamedly descriptive
composer of some importance in Spain for
his evocations of the Spanish heritage. He
is noted, too, with Albéniz, **Falla** and other
lesser composers, for forging a national
style that moved away from the dominance of the musical stage to orchestral
and chamber music. His harmonically conservative idiom developed little, though he
attempted to combine the orchestral
descriptive lessons learnt in a stay in Paris
(studying with **d'Indy** in 1906) to his own
inheritance (encouraged by Albéniz), especially that of his native Andalusia. His
early chamber music follows turn-of-the-
century French models (especially those of
César Franck, as in the *Piano Quintet*,
1907, or the *Violin Sonata No. 1*). The
String Quartet (1911) is cyclical (themes
returning in each movement to provide
unity) in the style propounded by **d'Indy**.
The *Piano Trio No. 2* (1933), though later,
is nonetheless typical, pleasantly lyrical,
well crafted, if completely undemanding.

Turina first came to notice with *La
procesión del rocío* (1913), a vivid tone
poem describing a festive religious festival
in Seville, with lively orchestration and
local pseudo-folk tunes (including a Moorish touch), rhythms and colour. The *Dan-
sas fantásticas* (1920) for orchestra is
probably his best-known work, in three
evocative sections (especially the middle
Ensueño with its lilting main melody) and
with opportunities for solo orchestral virtuosity. The *Rapsodia sinfónica* (1931) for
piano and string orchestra is also occasionally heard. Written in virtuoso style, as if
by a Spanish **Rachmaninov** crossed with a
Spanish **Gershwin**, it has a dramatic opening and a lush lyricism. With figurations
for the piano sometimes echoing guitar
work, it is attractive and often glittering,
without any profundity.

Many of Turina's works reflect his love
of Seville, though after his return from
France he never actually lived there. The
Sinfonia sevillana (1921) has some gorgeously evocative moments, even if the
lush idiom teeters dangerously on the
brink of becoming sentimental. The form is
again cyclical. But his finest work is the
song-cycle *Canto a Sevilla* (1926) for
soprano and piano or orchestra (but much
more effective in its orchestral version) –
moving and evocative, sometimes dramatic, sometimes Impressionistic. His
characteristic idiom here takes on a deeper
intensity, especially in the opening song,
and the solo line combines something of the
rawness of genuine folk music with a
soaring lyrical feel. Orchestral (or piano)
sections intersperse the songs; similarly,
the less impressive but still evocative
Poema en forma de canciones (1918) for
high voice and piano opens with a piano
solo, and mixes Spanish and French idioms.

Turina's extensive piano music (he himself was a renowned pianist) occupies an
important place in his output, although
neglected outside Spain. Again, many are
cycles of shorter descriptive pieces evoking various aspects of Spain or of Seville.
Among his other scores is the unusual *The
Muses of Andalusia* (1942), for soprano,
piano and string quartet, each of whose
nine differently scored movements
describes one of the Muses against an
Andalusian background.

Turina was for many years an influential
critic for Madrid's *El Debate*. He taught at
the Madrid Conservatory (1930–31) and
served in the Ministry of Education under
Franco.

RECOMMENDED WORKS
Canto a Sevilla (1926) for mezzo-
soprano and orchestra
Danzas fantasticas (1920) (piano
version)

Sweden

Introduction

Sweden's 19th-century musical life largely ignored its greatest 19th-century composer, Frank Berwald (1796–1868), best known for his symphonies; he spent much of his life outside the country, mainly in Berlin. At the end of the century there was an expansion in Swedish arts, spurred on by the nationalist '1890s' literary movement and its central figure, August Strindberg. Most of the major musical institutions, such as the Stockholm Concert Society (now the Stockholm Philharmonic) and the Göteborg (Gothenburg) Orchestral Society, were founded in this period. Wagnerian influences were represented by Wilhelm Peterson-Berger (1867–1942), but more central to his idiom was a Nordic Romanticism that followed the example of Grieg. Although he wrote five symphonies, he is best remembered for his songs and smaller piano pieces, and for the opera *Arnljot* (1909), the story of a Viking hero who, having met St Olaf, dies as a Christian. Hugo Alfvén (1872–1960) was the Swedish composer who most successfully integrated national and folk-music elements; Wilhelm Stenhammer (1871–1927) continued a late-Romantic tradition that looked south to Germany for its models. These three composers laid the foundations of 20th-century Swedish music.

Kurt Atterberg (1887–1974) and Oskar Lindberg (1887–1955) continued the Nordic Romanticism, while Ture Rangström (1884–1947) became the major Swedish song composer. Adolf Wiklund (1879–1950) is best remembered for his two piano concertos, attractive if unremarkable late-Romantic works, and for his combination of Nordic Impressionism and Romantic imagery in such works as the appealing, straightforward *Sommernatt och soluppgång* (*Summer Night and Sunrise*, 1918) for orchestra. The reaction against this period of nationalism in Swedish music came with the foundation of the '1920s group', led by Hilding Rosenberg (1892–1985), whose contrapuntal style was influenced by Hindemith. The core of his oeuvre are eight symphonies, powerful and communicative, and it is extraordinary that the work of one of Sweden's most important 20th-century composers is not better known outside Sweden. Also associated with this group was another symphonist, Gösta Nystroem (1890–1966). A

neo-classical reaction was represented by Dag Wirén (1905–86) and Lars-Erik Larsson (1908–86), best known in Sweden for his *Pastoral Suite* (1938) for small orchestra. His *Violin Concerto* (1959) is a fine work, lyrical, slightly melancholic and astringent, that deserves to be better known. His output includes a series of twelve concertinos (1955–57) for different instruments with string orchestra, designed for use by community orchestras; he later adopted 12-tone techniques in such works as the *Three Pieces for Orchestra* (1960) and the *Orchestral Variations* (1962).

Another resurgence of Swedish composition followed the foundation, during World War II, of the 'Monday Group', an influential gathering of composers, instrumentalists and musicologists, many of whom were pupils of Rosenberg. Their studies and discussions ranged across contemporary music; from the departure point of the ideas of Hindemith, they were particularly concerned with tonal relationships. The major figure of the group was Karl-Birger Blomdahl (1916–68), who in 1959 produced the first sci-fi opera, *Aniara*, which received world-wide attention. Other members included Sven-Erik Bäck (1919–94) and Ingvar Lidholm (born 1921). The symphonic tradition was continued by Allan Pettersson (1911–80) in a post-Mahlerian idiom, and by the Estonian Eduard Tubin (1905–82 – see under 'Estonia'). Edvin Kalistenius (1881–1967), who had earlier evolved a personal tonal language, adopted 12-tone techniques, as did Hilding Hallnäs (1903–84). The idiom of Gunnar Bucht (born 1927) follows what might be described as European mainstream, drawing on the experience of the avant-garde for effect, but within a more traditional framework. His opera *Kongsemnerne* (*The Pretenders*, 1961–66) was based on the play by Ibsen. His vocal music includes a number of settings of Swedish poetry written in Finland, notably the rarefied and expressive *Hund skenar glad* (*Dog Runs Happy*, 1961), for soprano, women's chorus and orchestra, setting poems by Gunnar Björling.

The avant-garde in Sweden was led by Bengt Hambraeus, who wrote the first Swedish electronic piece, but who moved to Canada in 1972. Bo Nilsson (born 1937) pioneered total serialism and aleatoric methods in Sweden in the 1950s, usually in short aphoristic works for small ensembles, with detailed, sharp textures. A series of four *Szenes* (1961) included the uncompromisingly aggressive *Szene III*.

His later work started to incorporate more traditional elements: *Revue* (1967) for orchestra turns in mid course from avant-garde techniques to a Romantic elegy for strings, while the woodwind quintet *Déjà connu* (1973) uses tonal harmonies. Vocal music has been an important component of his output, making use of the phonetic qualities of the texts. *Brief an Gösta Oswald* (*Letter to Gösta Oswald*, 1959), for soprano, alto, women's choir, loudspeakers and large orchestra is influenced by **Boulez**, finishing with an extended setting of an Oswald poem. Karl-Erik Welin (1934–92) and Jan Morthenson (born 1940) have been noted for their avant-garde organ music, incorporating new techniques. Perhaps the most eccentric Swedish composer is Ralph Lundsten (born 1936), whose combination of folk legends, popular elements and atmospheric effects, all realised electronically and often for ballets, requires eclectic tastes; but it can be hauntingly beautiful, as in the final 'Amen' (using a boys' choir) from *Fadervår* (*Paternoster*, 1971), or quirkily entrancing in such works as *Nordik Natursymponi No. 1 'Stromkarlen'* (*Nordic Naturesymphony No. 1 'The Neck'*, 1972).

Swedish 20th-century music has not achieved the prominence of that of the other Scandinavian countries, partly because of the conservative nature of Swedish musical circles, that have reacted strongly against the kind of developments initiated by **Rosenberg** in the middle of the century, and **Hambraeus** in the 1960s. Although Sweden has not produced a composer of the stature of **Nordheim** or **Sallinen**, some Swedish composers of the second half of the century have become known outside their own country. The composers of the first half of the century, on the other hand, little known internationally in their own times, deserve a wider audience, especially **Stenhammar** and **Rosenberg**. Sweden also has a fine tradition of choral singing, dating back to the community choirs of the mid 1800s, and now noted especially for a cappella singing. Swedish composers have responded to this stimulus, and although language problems have hampered wider dissemination of Swedish choral music, there is much of great interest to be explored.

Swedish Music Information Centre:
Svensk Musik
Sandhamnsgaten 79
S–102 54 Stockholm
tel: +46 8 783 8800
fax: +46 8 783 9510

Alfvén Hugo (Emil)*
born 1st May 1872 at Stockholm
died 8th May 1960 at Uppsala

Alfvén was the father of Swedish nationalism in the revival of Swedish music at the turn of the century and lived on as the grand figure of Swedish music. His work is often inconsequential and usually programmatic, but redeemed by its sheer delight. He was the first Swedish composer of note to integrate folk material into symphonic composition. He was also instrumental in the development of the modern choral tradition in Sweden, now so highly regarded. Remarkably he conducted the Siljan Choir for over fifty years (1904–57), and was director of the Orphei Drängar (1910–47), as well as being Director Musices at Uppsala University (1910–39).

His symphonies are wonderfully self-indulgent pieces of late nationalist Romanticism, less sure in their over-sized symphonic structure than in their orchestral colour and evocation. The *Symphony No. 1* (1896–97, revised 1903–04) is the least convincing, at its best in the nobility of its first movement, but the *Symphony No. 2* (1897–98) has a Brahmsian sweep to its opening themes, a nobility to its slow movement, and a more troubled but over-long finale. The *Symphony No. 3* (1905) is the sunniest, and was started in Italy. The most unusual is the *Symphony No. 4* (1918–19), titled *Från Havsbandet* (poetically translatable as *From the Seaward Skerries*), which evokes the atmosphere of the outer skerries of the Swedish archipelago on the one hand, and a sensual love affair on the other (it was long referred to as the *Sinfonia erotica*). Scored for soprano and tenor (singing wordlessly), and a huge late-Romantic orchestra, it has been either vilified as a symphony or rather admired for its atmospheric expression. Regarded purely as a tone poem (Alfvén provided a programme), evoking images of the sea and of sensuousness, this one-movement work is a gloriously rich and heady, if over-long, work, laced with falling or sinuous woodwind figures, brass surges, and an erotic solo line (a kind of Swedish equivalent to **Szymanowski**). Its hugely self-indulgent score deserves to be treated indulgently as Sweden's major tone poem of the era of the **Strauss** tone poems. The *Symphony No. 5* (1942–52), not started until twenty-three years after the fourth, is incomplete in its present form, although the first movement is sometimes given separately.

However, it is for his shorter, lighter, and generally more exuberant works that Alfvén is best known and most loved. The first of these, the *Swedish Rhapsody No. 1* *'Midsommarvaka'* (*Midsummer Vigil*, conceived 1892–95, published 1903) is known the world over and, like much of Alfvén's more popular music, has its basis in folk music. From its unforgettable jaunty opening tune, via its ruminative slow section, a large-scale midsummer landscape and a ride punctuated with myriad bells, to the peasant dance of the close, it is the Swedish equivalent of **Enescu's** *Romanian Rhapsody No. 1*, joyously orchestrated for a series of prominent wind solos, massed strings and brass support. The successors, the *Swedish Rhapsody No. 2 'Uppsala Rhapsody'* (1901), which draws on older Swedish musical material, and the more introspective *Swedish Rhapsody No. 3 'Dalecarlia Rhapsody'* (1931, published 1937), are less well known. His next international success was with *Festspel* (*Festival Piece*, 1907), a rather overblown short festive dance piece for large orchestra. The ballet-pantomime *Bergakungen* (*The Mountain King*, 1916–23, usually heard in a four-movement dance-suite version) is a different matter, infused with folk spirit (though with little genuine folk material), scored for large orchestra, utterly Nordic in its evocation, lying mid way between Grieg and **Sibelius**. Its tone is quite sensuous, sometimes delicate, at times almost Impressionistic in orchestration, its three mood-painting sections leading to a well-known rousing dance *Vallflickans dans* (*Handmaiden's Dance*). The final work to achieve international popularity is the spritely and rather more formal ballet *Den förlorade sonen* (*The Prodigal Son*, 1957, usually heard in its orchestral suite version). Anachronistic, but infectiously irresistible in its polkas, it is a remarkably youthful achievement for a composer of 85.

Alfvén's songs are not as highly regarded as those of his contemporaries **Rangström** and **Stenhammar**, but his choral music occupies an important place in Swedish music-making. Best known are *Afton* (*Evening*, probably 1907) for baritone and chorus, and *Gryning vid havet* (*Dawn over the Ocean*, 1933) for tenor and male voice choir. Alfvén himself had strong affection for the oratorio *Herrens bön* (*The Lord's Prayer*, 1899–1900), for

soprano, alto, baritone, chorus and orchestra – with good reason, for it is an unpretentious and attractive work, setting a poem by Stagnelius in which the widow of a knight teaches her son to pray. It is almost two works: the long final fifth movement (itself in four sections) is imposing in style, with fugal writing, while the middle movements have a bright, calculated simplicity that has affinities with **Fauré's** *Requiem*.

RECOMMENDED WORKS
> *Herrens bön* (1899–1900) for soprano,
> alto, baritone, chorus and orchestra
> *Swedish Rhapsody No. 1*
> (*Midsommarvaka*, 1892–95)
> Symphony No. 3 (1905)
> Symphony No. 4 (1918–19)

BIBLIOGRAPHY
> Alfvén published four volumes of
> autobiography, of which excerpts
> appear in a fifth, 1946–76

Atterberg Kurt (Magnus)*
born 12th December 1887 at Göteborg
died 15th February 1974 at Stockholm

Kurt Atterberg is one of a number of Scandinavian composers whose former prominence has been eclipsed by the reaction against Romanticism. He is chiefly known for his sometimes abstract Romantic orchestral works, his use of folk material, and especially his nine symphonies.

The symphonies are bold in colouring and generally bright in tone. The *Symphony No. 1* (1909–11) is, like those of many earlier northern composers, under the influence of Brahms, but the *Symphony No. 2* (1911–13) is more individual and more Nordic, especially in the combined slow and scherzo movement. The programmatic *Symphony No. 3 'Västkustbilder'* (*West Coast Pictures*, 1914–16) is more of a seascape symphonic suite than a symphony, integrating folk material. It is touched with delicate strokes, Impressionist in its opening, with a vivid and lushly scored storm. If treated as an evocation of mood, it has many fine passages. Actual quotations of folk material are used in the smaller-scale *Symphony No. 4 'Sinfonia piccola'* (1918), often considered his best symphony. Of the later symphonies, which include some polytonal passages, the *Symphony No. 6* (1927–28) used to be the best known, as it won the Schubert centennial prize. Scored for a Schubertian-sized orchestra, it is rather an unusual combination of Nordic seascape painting and clear symphonic structure, at its most interesting in the slow movement, when Atterberg can more indulge in the mood-painting that is his forte. Atterburg remained a Romantic until the end of his long compositional life; the *Symphony No. 7* (1942) is actually subtitled '*Sinfonia romantica*' His distaste for 12-tone developments was expressed in the *Symphony No. 9 'Sinfonia visionaria'* (1955–56) for soloists, chorus and orchestra, based on texts from the Old Norse epic the *Voluspa*, in which a 12-tone motif and a diminished seventh represent evil.

Atterberg also wrote nine suites for various orchestral forces, of which the *Suite No. 3* op. 19 No. 1 (1917) for violin, viola and strings is easily the best loved. Drawn from music written in 1916 for Maeterlinck's *Sister Beatrice,* it is a sad and lyrical work, in which the two solo strings intertwine cantabile lines, and the central section has a strongly modal flavour. There is one of his smaller masterpieces that is completely neglected. The slow movement of the *Horn Concerto* (1927) is among the loveliest of its kind ever written; a mellow, nostalgic tune from the horn is answered by a raindrop landscape in the strings, and it builds to a marvellous, misty Impressionistic image. This movement has all the potential to join other famous adagios in the affection of a very wide public. Later suites include the *Suite barocco* (Suite No. 5, 1923), using Baroque dance forms, but rather gentle and meandering – the Baroque through an Edwardian glint. The *Suite pastorale (In modo antico)* (Suite No. 8, 1931) is in much the same vein. The suite from the ballet *De fåvitska jungfrurna (The Wise and Foolish Virgins,* 1920) has retained some popularity as a rhapsodic set of variations on an old folk chorale. Of his string quartets, the *String Quartet No. 2* (1916) shares with the second symphony the effect of containing two contrasting moods within a movement. He also wrote five operas, of which only *Fanal* (1932), the story of a hangman's love (with a happy ending), attracted much attention.

Atterberg was particularly active in Swedish musical life as a conductor, cellist and long-serving music critic (of the *Stockholms-Tidningen,* 1919–57) as well as a composer. He co-founded the Swedish Composers Society and was its president from 1924 to 1947. He was attached to the Swedish Patent and Registration Office as an engineer from 1912 until the 1960s.

RECOMMENDED WORKS:
Horn Concerto (1927)
Suite No. 3 (1917) for violin, viola and strings
Symphony No. 3 *West Coast Pictures* (1914–16)
Symphony No. 4 '*Sinfonia piccola*' (1918)

Bäck Sven-Erik
born 16th September 1919 at Stockholm
died 10th January 1994 at Stockholm

A violinist and string quartet player as well as a composer, and a member of the 'Monday Group' in the 1940s, Bäck had a high profile in Sweden, but little recognition elsewhere. His earliest works, like others of the group, were influenced by his teacher **Rosenberg** and by **Hindemith**, and by his own studies of older styles; these are shades of the 18th century in the *Sinfonia per archi* (*Symphony for Strings,* 1951). Bäck himself was a noted interpreter of Renaissance and Baroque music. He quickly embraced the avant-garde trends in Europe, adopting serialism, pointillism (*Chamber Symphony,* 1955) and electronic music (including two electronic ballet scores). However, two other strains have run through his output: a religious sense and a penchant for dramatic works. The former has included the influence of Gregorian chant (exemplified in the series of unaccompanied motets that followed *Behold, I make all things new,* 1968).

Bäck adopted 12-tone technique in the *Sinfonia da camera* (1955). A *Game around a Game* (1959) for strings and percussion translated into musical terms the energetic sculpture by Björn Evenson that inspired it, with a large battery of percussion instruments. The *Violin Concerto* (1957, revised 1960) combines a decorated solo line, lyrical in the slow movement, with pointillism and percussion. The success of his operas inside Sweden has been partly responsible for his reputation there. The first, *Tranfjädrarna (The Crane Feathers,* 1956), a chamber opera originally written for television, but successful as a stage work both in Sweden and beyond, is probably the best known. Based on a simple Japanese folk tale, it tells of a farmer unknowingly married to a crane in human form – if he sees her in her bird form she will have to leave. Using a children's chorus and a small orchestra, it is concise and effective, with a clarity of instrumental colour (often dominated by isolated percussion) and a simplicity of vocal line that closely follows speech-patterns. It was followed by *Gästabudet* (*The Banquet*, 1958) and *Fågeln* (*The Birds*, 1961), a heavily symbolist work drawn from a radio play by the Serbian writer Aleksander Obrenovic. *Kattresan* (*Cat Journey*, 1952) is a cantata for young children, using a children's choir and common percussion instruments. Of his chamber music, the *String Quartet No. 3* (1962) is a rather severe essay in serialism.

Bäck was appointed director of the Swedish Radio Music School in 1959, having led its school and youth orchestras since 1954.

RECOMMENDED WORKS
   A Game around a Game (1959) for
     strings and percussion
   chamber opera *Tranfjädrarna* (*The
     Crane Feathers*, 1956)

Blomdahl Karl-Birger*
born 19th October 1916 at Växjö
died 14th June 1968 at Kungsngen

Although his output is small, Blomdahl remains one of Sweden's most important composers. He combined a love of the scientific (he originally wanted to become an engineer or a scientist) with an idiom that is at its base more conservative that the more extreme elements would suggest, and which draws on many divergent styles, from the lyrical to the ultra-modern. A sense of disillusion at the human condition is often an undercurrent in this personal synthesis. He came to prominence after World War II as the leader of the group founded in 1944 and known as the 'Monday Group', which included Sven-Erik **Bäck** and Ingvar **Lidhol** and which was particularly influenced by **Hindemith**. A pioneer of Swedish electronic music, he remained at the forefront of the Scandinavian avant-garde until his premature death in 1968., He himself followed many of the trends of the period, being one of the first Swedes to use serial techniques.

His earlier work included the neo-Baroque *Concerto grosso* (1944) and the *Concerto for Violin and Strings* (1946, not to be confused with the 1941 *Violin Concerto*) in a style indebted to Bach. Rhythmic patterns, characteristic of his sense of rhythmic vitality, were prominent in the *Pastoral Suite* (1948), while the three-movement *Symphony No. 2* (1947), the culmination of this period in Blomdahl's output, was still influenced by his teacher **Rosenberg**. In its vigorously contrapuntal opening and closing movements built on fanfare themes, it has echoes of **Hindemith** and **Shostakovich**. With a gentle passacaglia as the middle movement, the dynamic objectivity of the symphony makes it worth hearing.

Blomdahl then started to explore 12-tone technique, and his first major work to attract attention outside Sweden, and one of the first Swedish pieces to use elements of serial techniques, was the *Symphony No. 3 'Facetter'* (*Facets*, 1950), built in an arch structure. However, the 12-note series on the flute, from which all the material of the one-movement symphony is derived (and to which the symphony returns), is mournfully lyrical. Blomdahl sets up a commanding tension between the lyricism (including a sense of mysterious atmosphere in the repetitive figures on high strings) and the gritty rhythms, creating an aggressive insistence of purpose that includes a grotesque parody. Fine and convincing though the symphony is, with a sense of the whole work constantly pushing towards its close, it is not a work of 'total serialism'. The orchestration and the rhythmic development are firmly in the mainstream of the European tradition, and its linearity is an echo of **Honegger**. The harmonic constructs from the 12-note series (the 'facets' of the title) are also tame by comparison with the experimenters of the time.

The cantata *I speglarnas sal* (*In the Hall of Mirrors*, 1951–52), for soloists, chorus, speaker and orchestra, was written to radical verses by his regular collaborator, the writer Erik Lindegren; it combines 12-tone writing with colouristic effects, notably the tinkling glassy opening (harp, celesta, and strings playing behind the bridge, a technique earlier utilised by **Pettersson**). It is highly eclectic in its material, which is chosen to suit the immediate effect rather than follow any overall system or pattern, a trend increasingly apparent in Blomdahl's music. Here contemporary popular elements and the blues vie with spoken choral sections and recitation. The polyphonic style then returned in the *Kammarkonsert* (*Chamber Concerto*, 1953), for piano, woodwinds and percussion, with a single thematic idea linking its movements; it illustrates Blomdahl's recurring interest in dance-like music.

Blomdahl then gained world-wide attention with the opera *Aniara* (1957–58). Set in outer space, and concerning the dying and doomed personnel of a spaceship that had left a destroyed earth, it has a text by Lindegren based on an epic poem by Harry Martinson. The overall tenor of the music is traditional, with set numbers and sometimes a strong jazz influence, though electronic music is used for the machine Mima (with a distorted nonsense-language). The comment in the opera is as much an allegory on political structures and the contemporary sense of hopelessness as any sci-fi flight of fancy. Again there is an eclectic flavour to this opera, which produces moments of great effectiveness (particularly some of the ethereal electronic effects and choruses) but also sections of banality, lessening the overall impression until the middle of the second of two acts, where a beautiful lyrical soprano aria is followed by a climactic scene of singular dramatic power, drive and visionary fervour. A later opera, *Herr von Hancken* (1962–63), has achieved less prominence; at time of his death Blomdahl was working on a third opera that again reflected his scientific interests and the element of disillusion, *Sagan om den stora datan* (*Tale of the Big Computer*).

Of his later works, the sonorous *Forma ferritonans* (1961) for orchestra matches intervals to the Atomic Table, with atomic weight determining progressions, and atomic number the tone relationships. *Spel för åtta* (*Game for Eight*, 1962), a choreographic suite in eight movements (and for eight dancers and full orchestra), manages to be not only fragmentary (in the uses of short snatches of phrases), but also lyrically flowing and rhythmically vital, with motoric elements and serially organised time-values. The sections veer from echoes of **Varèse** and cluster timbres and colours, to jazz influences. The electronic *Altisonans* (1966) is a large-scale sound-picture, taking snatches drawn from satellite communication signals, voices, and the electronic interference from sunspots, and creating an electronic montage; it is unusual in that the sound sources are already electronically generated and existent prior to the musical/electronic process. It is an effective work, which shows that electronic scores can still be vitally compelling, and not necessarily daunting to those unused to them.

Blomdahl worked extensively in radio and television, latterly as director of the Swedish radio music department (1965–68), and was an influential teacher. He was professor at the Stockholm Conservatory from 1960 to 1964. His earlier pupils included **Pettersson**. With his eclectic style, Blomdahl is not an easy composer

to quantify; in the vigorous counterpoint and abstract craftsmanship of his earlier music he can be seen as a Scandinavian counterpart of **Hindemith**, while his later music represents an individual attempt to fuse new elements into a continuity of musical development.

RECOMMENDED WORKS
    opera *Aniara* (1957–58)
    Forma ferritonans (1961) for
      orchestra
    choreographic suite *Game for Eight*
      (1962)
    Symphony No. 2 (1947)
    Symphony No. 3 *Facets* (1950)

Hambraeus Bengt*
born 29th January 1928 at Stockholm

Bengt Hambraeus was the leading avant-garde Swedish composer of the 1950s and 1960s, introducing to Sweden the latest techniques from the Darmstadt school and from non-European musical traditions. As such, his influence and standing in Sweden has been considerable, and during that period his music attracted attention on both sides of the Atlantic. However, in 1972 he moved to Montrèal, Canada, and to a culture that has mostly ignored him (apart from McGill University, where he teaches), although on the evidence of his earlier work he is, with Murray **Schafer**, probably the finest composer in Canada today. His output, especially for the organ (he is an accomplished organist) is both interesting and thoughtful. It is a matter of regret that many Canadians involved in music have never even heard of him.

His earliest music, like that of many of his Swedish contemporaries, was influenced by **Hindemith**, and especially by his own considerable study of medieval and Renaissance music (he was librarian and amanuensis at the Uppsala Musicological Institution, 1948–56). He was largely self-taught, and the works of this period (*Music for Ancient Strings*, 1948, *Cantigas de Santa Maria*, 1948) reflect these studies. With *Music for Organ* (1950), showing the colouristic influence of **Messiaen**, he established a more mature voice, and in the early 1950s, when he studied with Messiaen, he quickly embraced the serialist ideas of avant-garde Europe.

Since *Music for Organ*, Hambraeus has primarily concentrated on sonority, timbre and colour in his music, whatever the stylistic means, while this direction has been tempered by the clarity of line and detail of effect developed from his studies of older music. At times those stylistic means have reflected contemporary developments, such as the soft colours (alto flute, viola, vibraphone and harp) of *Mikrogram* (1961), clearly influenced by **Boulez**. At others the music of the Far East has tempered the colours (as in the three flutes and six percussion players of *Introduzione – sequenze – coda*, 1959). In works with voices, the emphasis on colour is reflected in the use of vocalise (*Spectogram*, 1953, for soprano, flute and percussion, *Antiphones en rondes*, 1953, for orchestra with soprano, and *Crystal Sequence*, 1954, for orchestra with chorus). However, it is the works that utilise organ or electronics, sometimes in combination with each other and other forces, that are of particular interest, especially as modern compositions for the organ using the latest ideas are relatively rare.

Doppelrohr II (*Double-reed II*, 1955), realised in Cologne, was the first Swedish electronic piece. The organ and electronic and other means were then combined in the series *Constellations*, originating in *Constellation I* (1958), a short organ piece. This evolved into *Constellations II* (1959), the electronic elaboration of that piece in which the organ sounds are combined with an electronic realisation of the sounds of a dawn chorus of bird-song that Hambraeus heard in Milan. The effect, intentionally, is of the huge space of the title, in what amounts to a tone poem for organ and tape, contrasting spacious sonorities from the organ with more detailed electronic sounds. In *Constellations III* the tape from *Constellations II* was combined with a new organ piece; in *Constellations IV* percussion joined the same tape. *Constellations V*, for two amplified solo sopranos, chorus and organ (1982–83), was a much later addition, inspired by St Paul's praise of liberty from Corinthians. With *Interferences* (1961–62) for organ, Hambraeus extended the ideas developed in the *Constellations* series, in particular redefining the organ sonorities until they converged with the type of electronic sounds which he had already explored. He utilitised the similarities between overtone sounds and variations available through avant-garde organ-playing techniques (subsequently and similarly used by such composers as **Ligeti** and **Kagel**); also the parallel sounds produced by purely electronic means, including clusters and the slow effect of disintegration when the electric power supply to the organ is turned off. The effect is less obviously of tone-painting, more

abstract and disjointed, but still with the same sense of vast space.

Some of those organ effects are used in the powerful *Motetum Arcangeli Michaelis* (1967), for chorus and organ. Here the vocal writing is primarily concerned with large-scale colour and effect, spacious polyphonic writing merging with more fragmentary declamatory passages. The mosaic-like *Fresque sonore* uses instruments and a wordless soprano voice, recorded individually, and then combined with limited electronic transformation; filigrees of sounds, including a harp, wisping in and out of the landscape. The tendency to group works into 'families' also produced series *Transit*, consisting of both electronic and instrumental music; the last in the series, *Transfiguration* (1963), reflecting Hambraeus's attachment to an ethereal religious mood, is a large-scale work for orchestra. It is an extended study in massed sonorities, again aimed at slow-moving, large-scale effect, and includes characteristic bell sounds influenced by Far Eastern music, clusters, and falling string lines reminiscent of the organ sounds produced by switching the organ off.

In *Rota I* (1956–62), he combined electronic tape with three orchestras, whereas *Rota II* (1963) is a slow-moving, ritualistic tape piece, combining heavily filtered orchestral sounds (including gamelan sounds) with more obviously direct instrumental recordings (including the organ). Ritual reappears in another tape with instrumental recordings, *Tetragon* (1965), which opens with a series of fanfares underpinned by gently knocking percussion, into which slide purely electronic sounds. The textures are much leaner, an unravelling of overlapping events with highly contrasted colours gradually gaining in density, like a dream-like procession heard at a great distance and distorted by the intervening space. It includes allusions to other music, notably in a harpsichord passage. Hambraeus returned to such allusions more directly in *Rencontres* (1968–71) for orchestra, with references to Beethoven, Wagner, **Scriabin**, Reger and **Varèse**, combined with fragments from his own works.

The major work written since Hambraeus's move to Canada is probably the *Livre d'orgue* (*Organ Book*, 1981), four sets of organ pieces intended for teaching purposes as well as performance. The pieces progress from the relatively easy to the complex and virtuoso, and include modern techniques such as clusters and stop-manipulation to alter timbre. For the general listener, the most interesting pieces from this series are perhaps those which most exploit extreme techniques, such as the extraordinary massed sonorities in *Les timbres irisés*, using half-pulled-out stops to site overtones and strange colour relationships on top of each other. *Sheng* (1983), for the unusual combination of oboe and organ, again explores the sonorities of the organ, which sometimes sounds almost like an electronic instrument. However, the Oriental influence is apparent in the woodwind line ('sheng' is a Chinese mouth organ), and apart from climactic central moments the overall feel is almost pastoral. *Carillon* (1974) for two pianos returns to bell motifs. The two pianos are placed at great distance from each other, and the spatial dimension is reinforced by reverberation from undamped strings. It quotes from earlier composers, notably Beethoven and Chopin, in a kind of piano music-drama in which the pianists try to recall earlier repertoire. Of his other Canadian works, *Tides* (1974) is an aurally graphic tape work, its evocation of sea-sounds created electronically rather than by *musique concrète* means; its harsher companion, *Tornado* (1976), is less interesting. The short but effective *Intrada: 'Calls'* (1975) is an electronic transformation of thirsty fragments of brass calls and African kalimba ('thumb-piano') sounds, recalling the cowherd signals of Sweden.

RECOMMENDED WORKS
　　Constellations II (1959) for organ
　　　　sounds
　　Interferences (1961–62) for organ
　　Motetum Arcangeli Michaelis (1967)
　　　　for chorus and organ
　　Rencontres (1968–71) for orchestra
　　electronic *Tetragon* (1965)
　　electronic *Tides* (1974)

Lidholm Ingvar**
born 24th February, 1921 at Jönköping

Ingvar Lidholm was one of the group of radical composers who in the 1940s were known as the 'Monday Group', and who reacted against the prevailing Swedish musical traditions of Romanticism and nationalism. Throughout his career he has continued to be at the forefront of musical ideas in Sweden, and although sometimes he has surprised commentators with a sudden change of direction (as in the neotonal *Piano Sonata* of 1947), generally he has followed mainstream developments in the rest of Europe. Internationally, Lidholm is one of the better-known contemporary Swedish composers.

In his earlier works, he shows some of the rugged drive associated with his teacher **Rosenberg**. Although Lidholm's musical language has changed considerably, this rugged strength remains a feature of his music. **Stravinsky** and early polyphony influenced the three-part *Laudi* (1947) for a cappella chorus, which opens as if it is some choral procession in an ancient church tradition, and continues with great clarity of line and slow-moving contrapuntal textures, evolving from a stark simplicity into contrapuntal and polyphonic brightness. It achieves that rarity, an expression of joy and praise without any accompanying bombast or sentimentality. He turned to 12-note techniques in *Klavierstück* (1949) for piano, and there are echoes of **Bartók** and **Berg** in the *Violin Concerto* of 1951. He later developed serial techniques and improvisatory sections (*Poesis*, 1963, for orchestra). But of the earlier works, the most frequently encountered is the powerful *Music for Strings* (1952), which serves as an excellent introduction to Lidholm's music. Tough and emphatic in its three movements, it exploits the strings' full range of expressive tone qualities, preferring the possibilities of the interaction of the instruments to the use of individual solo lines. Throughout, in spite of attempts to move to a clearer, lighter canvas, there is an underlying sense of tension and trouble, reinforced by the use of suggestive but undeveloped moments and ideas in the final movement.

A similar sense of urgency and tension pervades the ballet *Rites* (1960), and the effective five-movement concert suite drawn from it. Described as a 'ballet with action', it explores the existentialist theme that cruelty is eternal, and that human beings (abstractly portrayed in the ballet) are the victims. By this stage, Lidholm's idiom had broadened to include more angular, less tonal writing; here there are moments of almost Impressionistic effect, and sections (e.g. 'Sacrifice 1 & 2') that are deliberately simple, quasi-improvisatory and almost archaic, with a Pan-like woodwind predominant. Another feature of Lidholm's work is evident in *Rites*: the atmosphere of ritual, of the music serving an almost dramatic purpose beyond the abstract. It recurs in such works as *Kontakion* (1978) for orchestra, where Lidholm's idiom has further evolved, reflecting mainstream developments in European composition. In this one-movement work, the strings are forceful and scurrying, there are cluster effects, different layers of movement, an austere slow section, and moments of trilling woodwind recalling **Debussy**. Predominantly earnest in its weighty, dark orchestral power, it suddenly unfolds into a magical close, with a haunting trumpet solo incanting an Orthodox chant against hushed tremolo strings and the reverberating interjection of tuned percussion. His most widely disseminated work must be the aleatory *Stamp Music* (1970), a score commissioned to appear on a postage stamp to commemorate the 200th anniversary of the Swedish Royal Academy of Music; a soaring melodic solo line revolves around contrasting mutterings.

Ritual also underlies some of the vocal work, of which perhaps the most immediately effective is the haunting and intense *Nausikaa ensam* (*Nausicaa Alone*, 1963) for soprano, chorus and orchestra. Based on verses by Eyvind Johnson describing an episode in the *Odyssey*, it is a kind of semi-dramatic scena, invoking with vivid characterization the internal reactions of Nausicaa to the stranger who has come to the court, while conveying a wider impression of the isolation and interior imagination of the young woman. The vocal writing moves easily between quasi-recitatives and arioso passages. The orchestral writing is primarily concerned with the expressive potential of timbre and colour, and subtle changes. His later choral works increasingly use the sounds of the words as the basis on which to construct the music. In the *Frya körer* (*Four Choruses*, 1953) the emphasis is on colour and block texture, with a declamatory feel, and in the passionate *Efteråt* (*Afterwards*), the use of wordless sounds against a solo soprano. In the series *A cappella-bok* (*A cappella book*, begun 1956) Lidholm created a collection of works, all based on a single 12-note series with tonal implications, that explore a wide range of choral vocal techniques. *Höllandarn* (*The Dutchman*, 1967, based on Strindberg) was the first Swedish opera written for television.

In a European context, Lidholm's music rarely breaks completely new ground, even if he has been a pioneer in Sweden. Nonetheless, his voice is strongly individual, through his rugged sincerity, and especially through his commanding use of mainstream techniques to serve expressive, and not merely musical, ends. That his output is relatively small partly reflects the detail and completeness that his music conveys. Lidholm was a violist with the

Swedish Royal Court Orchestra (1943–46), conductor of the Örebro Symphony Orchestra (1947–56) and professor of composition at the Swedish Royal College of Music (1965–74). He has been particularly active and influential in Swedish radio: he was in charge of chamber music broadcasts (1956–65), and returned in 1974 as head of planning at the music department, in which capacity he has done much to encourage contemporary Swedish music.

RECOMMENDED WORKS
> *Kontakion* (1978) for orchestra
> *Laudi* (1947) for unaccompanied
> chorus
> *Music for Strings* (1952)
> *Nausikaa ensam* (1963) for soprano,
> chorus and orchestra
> *Poesis* (1963) for orchestra
> ballet suite *Rites* (1960)

Nystroem Gösta*
born 13th October 1890 at Silvberg
died 9th August 1966 at Särö

Gösta Nystroem was a well known artist (especially of seascapes) as well as a composer, and took some time to develop a mature compositional voice. After studying Spanish music in Spain in 1912, he moved to Paris, painting in an Impressionistic style combined with expressive colourful effects, and studying composition with **d'Indy**. What little survives of the music of his Parisian period includes symphonic tone poems.

With the *Concerto grosso* (1929) for strings and the *Sinfonia breve* (*Symphony No. 1*, 1929–31) he adopted a purposeful neo-Baroque idiom combined with polyrhythms and harsh dissonances, influenced by **Hindemith** (as were many of his Swedish contemporaries), but also by **Honegger**. He returned to Sweden in 1932, and then produced what is generally considered his finest work, the *Sinfonia espressiva* (*Symphony No. 2*, 1932–35). Taut and expressive, it is conceived in one long sweep, though in four movements, building in density of orchestration and in the organic development of germinal ideas. It exemplifies his combination of a rugged northern expression tempered by Impressionistic orchestral details.

In the works of the 1940s and 1950s, Nystroem developed as a Romantic with a more purposeful hue, the lyricism more evident. In the martial symphonic overture *1945* (1945) there is a morbid edge to the fanfare celebration, the declamatory elements and the driving strings. In the rather long-winded *Sinfonia concertante* (1940–44, revised 1951–52) for cello and orchestra a similar melancholy is set by the solo line in a work that, with the *Viola Concerto 'Hommage à la France'* (1940), expresses the more idyllic side of Nystroem's idiom. His major works of this period explored his favourite visual theme, that of the sea. The *Sinfonia del mare* (Symphony No. 3, 1947–48), perhaps his main popular success, is the most complete expression of that love affair with the sea, built in one large arching movement. It has at its core a song for soprano setting verses by Lindquist, later extracted to stand on its own as *Det en da* (*The Only Thing*, 1951). Similarly, three major song cycles treated the sea as their subject: the Impressionistic *Sånger vid havet* (*Songs beside the Sea*, 1942), alternately lyrical and dramatic; the brief *På reveln* (*On the Reef*, 1949), both for lower voice with either piano or orchestra; and the rather dark and melancholic *Själ och landskap* (*Soul and Soil*, 1952) for lower voice and piano, also to verses by Lindquist. The sea is again central to the radio opera *Herr Arnes penningar* (*Sir Arne's Money*, 1958).

Late in his life, Nystroem returned to the linear contrapuntal style of his earliest works, notably in the last two symphonies, the *Sinfonia seria* (*Symphony No. 5*, 1963) and the *Sinfonia tramontana* (*Symphony No. 6*, 1965), while the harsher harmonies recurred in the *Violin Concerto* (1954) and the two *String Quartets* (1956 and 1961).

Between 1932 and 1947 Nystroem worked as a music critic in Göteborg.

RECOMMENDED WORKS
　Sinfonia espressiva (Symphony No. 2) (1932–35)
　Sinfonia del mare (Symphony No. 3) (1947–48)
　Songs beside the Sea (1942)

Pettersson (Gustaf) Allan**
　born 19th September 1911 at Västra Ryd
　died 20th June 1980 at Stockholm

Allan Pettersson, perhaps more than any other composer, has given expression to that element of introverted dark anguish that characterises the northern spirit, but which in other northern composers is usually an element, rather than predominant. His music is on a gigantic scale, and has aroused passionate advocacy and considerable distaste, as has that of Bruckner and **Mahler** – and Pettersson is the direct successor to the latter. His sixteen symphonies are central to his output, and develop the tortured side of Mahler's idiom. To his detractors, his musical voice is steeped in self-pity; to his admirers, it is the reflection of the horrors of the century. Objectively, there is substance to both views. The tendency to the obsessive in the huge, relentless nature of the music is offset by passages of tremendous power and feeling – for those prepared to accept the former. Undeniably, he gives direct utterance to a childhood of poverty and deprivation, an adulthood racked by crippling arthritis and psychological breakdown, and a strong sense of proletarian suffering.

The Mahlerian inheritance appears in particular in the style of the short-phrased melodic material and its potential extension through repetition. This material is usually treated in sharply delineated blocks, often overlaid in complex webs, with the rhythm being both their doing and their undoing. In a conventional harmonic framework, the juxtaposition of blocks can often create grating dissonances, accentuated by using the extremes of instruments (sometimes with a screaming effect) and awkward intervals. Otherwise the orchestration tends to a homogeny of dark colours. The preferred one-movement form is generally divided into two halves: in the first, usually a huge sort of ostinato structure, the progression is created by crying, yearning phrases and aggressive blocks piled on again and again; in the second, more static half, the ideas are reworked within each other. The endings are usually inconclusive and anticlimactic.

Pettersson's earliest works were chamber music and short songs, and his *Symphony No. 1*, although extant, has never been released. But the *Symphony No. 2* (1952–53) sets the tone; its forty minutes are in Pettersson's favoured single-movement form, here a set of variations. The concept is developed in the very slowly unfolding *Symphony No. 4* (1958–59), which pits the pithy, forward-driving phrases, eventually with the addition of a germinating percussion phrase, against a lyrical choral atmosphere. With this duality, the work moves towards massive climaxes, an increase in contrasts and a Shostakovichian use of haunting woodwind. By now his arthritis was very severe, and the *Symphony No. 5* (1960–62) was the last work he could copy out himself; based on a minimum of material, it provides a link between the contrasting dualities of the earlier symphonies and the more intense later ones. The one-movement *Symphony No. 6* (1963–66), lasting just under an hour, has a sad and serene inevitability among its moments of climactic strength.

The moving *Symphony No. 7* (1967) – and its advocacy by the conductor Anton Dorati – brought him national and international attention. It is a less relentless, more public work, still concerned with the contrast between the interior protest and lyricism, but with the anguish of structural blocks smoothed out, a more convincing sense of structural purpose, and a strong component of resignation in the string writing. The magnificent *Symphony No. 8* (1968–69) is in one continuous forty-five minute arch. A strong linear pulse is set up at the start and never flags throughout the work, regardless of the mood. The central tension is between the lyrical and the martial, who gently spar with each other at the opening of the symphony until an impasse is reached. Turbulence follows; eventually the martial becomes more and more threatening and wild, reinforced by darker bass colours. The lyrical has been transformed by these events, becoming more disjoined, less certain, and the symphony ends in a mood of sad resignation. The enormous *Symphony No. 9* (1970) – seventy uninterrupted minutes – most reflects Pettersson's personal agony. The compelling and turbulent *Symphony No. 10* (1972) marked a change to much shorter symphonies; its twenty-five minutes compress the earlier idiom into a feeling of nervous and frenetic or angry restlessness instead of relentless inevitability; any harmonic security has been removed. Of the later works, the *Symphony No. 12 'The Dead on the Square'* (1972) uses chorus and texts by Pablo Neruda, the *Symphony No. 14* (1978) employs variations on one of the *Barfotasånger* (see below), and the *Symphony No. 16* (1979) is essentially an alto saxophone concerto.

Of his concertos, the *Violin Concerto No. 1* (1949) is for violin and string quartet. The *Violin Concerto No. 2* (1979) was criticised for being more a symphony than a concerto. There are three concertos for string orchestra (1950, 1956 and 1957) which are highly regarded by supporters of his music. His best-known songs are the song-cycle of twenty-four *Barfotasånger* (*Barefoot Songs*, 1943–45), miniatures as spare as the title might suggest, with the

emphasis on the expressive and ruminative vocal lines. *Vox Humana* (1974) for soloists, chorus and orchestra is Pettersson's major vocal work, setting verses of descriptive protest at the human condition, but without any political allegiance, and cast in three parts. The first presents fourteen poems by Latin American worker-poets in emotionally and musically wide-ranging settings using different combinations of the available forces, to create a Mahlerian cycle. The second parts sets three short poems by ancient Indian poets; the third is a small cantata on a longer poem by Pablo Neruda. Both these sections, with their emphasis on choral writing, are different in idiom to the first; Pettersson intended that each could be heard separately. The first section is outstanding, the Mahlerian tendencies counterpoised by the moments of un-Mahlerian choral writing, and deserves to be widely heard on its own.

It may be that (as was once the case with **Mahler**) Pettersson's enormous and heartfelt symphonies have suffered from the lack of performances by sympathetic world-class forces. Apart from scores, virtually the only acquaintance possible with Pettersson's music has been through recordings, often made shortly after premières. Major interpreters may reveal new dimensions to, in particular, the structure of Pettersson's creations; conversely, they may confirm the inability of those structures to hold up such great lengths, troubled emotions, and limitations of thematic material. His music – and in particular the seventh and eighth symphonies – certainly deserves that test.

RECOMMENDED WORKS
  Symphony No. 2 (1954)
  Symphony No. 4 (1958–59)
  Symphony No. 7 (1966–67)
  Symphony No. 8 (1968–69)
  Symphony No. 10 (1972)
  Vox Humana (1974) for soloists,
    chorus and string orchestra

Rangström (Anders Johan) Ture··

born 30th November 1884 at Stockholm
died 11th May 1947 at Stockholm

Rangström is now best known for his songs, of which he is one of the Swedish masters. They range widely in mood (from intimacy to mood painting), in source (but favouring the verses of Bo Bergman), and in subject matter, often using sparse accompaniments. He developed what he called 'speech melody', in which the vocal line reflects an expressive speech rendering of the verse, and the style often changes to suit the particular poetry. Chief among his song-cycles is the dramatic and vivid *Ur Kung Eriks visor (From King Erik's Songs*, 1918), to verses of Gustav Fröding about the tragic and ultimately mad 15th-century Swedish king. Powerful, emotive and rhythmically tense, it exists in versions for both baritone and piano and baritone and orchestra, the colour and drama of the latter adding impact. This Romantic song-cycle deserves to be better known outside Scandinavia. That his songs in general have not travelled is probably due to the unfamiliarity of the language to non-Nordic singers, as they are lyrical miniatures of the highest order; certainly they are well worth hunting out on recordings.

Rangström remained a Romantic composer, echoing the impassioned milieu of his compatriot the writer August Strindberg, and sometimes favouring a harshness in melody and harmony that is associated with the old Swedish tradition. He was also largely self-taught, and his larger-scale works sometimes suffer from structural problems; contrapuntal and polyphonic passages are rare in his work. His four symphonies, which have programmatic titles, all use a large orchestra with considerable flair and colour, and have not always deserved the scorn sometimes heaped upon them by an age out of sympathy with anything Romantic; Rangström himself described them as 'lyrics for orchestra'. The four-movement *Symphony No. 1 'In memoriam August Strindberg'* (1914) is over-ambitious and ineffectual, in spite of some fine moments. The three-movement *Symphony No. 2 'Mitt land' (My Country*, 1919) is more obviously nationalistic (though in common with most of Rangström's work, it does not use actual folk material), darkly Nordic, and the more effective if treated as a tone poem rather than a symphony, since some of the material is banal. However, the *Symphony No. 3 'Sång under stjärnorna' (Song under the stars*, 1929) draws on the experience of both these works for a much tauter one-movement symphony, whose sections of ostinati bass, side-drum snarls, falling or whooping brass and long string lines clearly prefigure the more sparse symphonic world of **Pettersson**. These grimmer passages are set against more Romantic concepts in a powerful and effective work, whose clarity of orchestration, with sharp differentiation between sections of the orchestra, is considerable. Of his other orchestral music, the best known is the *Divertimento elegiaco* (1917) for strings, combining a Nordic expansiveness with the lilt of the dance, but tinged throughout with melancholy – mournfully attractive, but not particularly distinctive.

His piano music includes four *Praeludia (Preludes*, 1910–12), which are full of the fire of youth, and similar in style and tone to the **Rachmaninov** *Preludes*. The later *Improvisata* (1927) for piano, a series of short improvisatory pieces, are more ruminative, with a Nordic opaqueness. Like many of his contemporaries, Rangström was interested in older styles, and this is reflected in two attractive but inconsequential suites for violin and piano. In the *Suite (in modo antico) (In the Old Style*, 1912) the influence of older music (through dance forms and technical details) is filtered through a Romantic hue. Many consider Rangström's finest achievement to be the opera *Kronbruden (The Crown Bride*, 1915), a setting of Strindberg's folk play, in which his lyrical writing and writing for the voice come to the fore. It has remained in Scandinavian opera repertoires. He also wrote the words to one of **Stenhammer's** most important late works, the cantata *Sången (Song*, 1920).

Rangström was a conductor and teacher of singing as well as a composer, and worked as a music critic for *Svenska Dagbladet* (1907–08), *Stokholms Dagblad* (1910–14, 1927–30), and *Nya Dagligt Allehanda* (1938–42). He co-founded the Swedish Society of Composers in 1918.

RECOMMENDED WORKS
 song-cycle *Ur Kung Eriks visor*
  (From King Erik's Songs, 1918)
 opera *Kronbruden* (The Crown Bride,
  1915)
 Symphony No. 3 Sång under
  stjarnorna (1929)

Rosenberg Hilding Constantin**

born 21st June 1892 at Bosjkloster
(Ringsjön, Skåne)
died 19th May 1985 at Stockholm

Hilding Rosenberg occupies an important place in Swedish music, an equivalent to **Vaughan Williams** in the UK. That his music is still so little known outside Scandinavia is something of a mystery, for such works as his *Symphony No. 3* have the power to communicate to a wide audience. Although his oeuvre covers the complete span of traditional genres, he is best known for his eight symphonies and for his fifteen string quartets. His mature style has a noble dignity that is emphasised by a powerful contrapuntal logic and combined with a lyrical sense of delicate beauty, as luminous as the northern light. His orchestral colours are usually dark, with lower strings predominant, and punctuated by brass. In his later works there is a strong feeling of overall momentum spread over long spans.

His earliest music shows the influence of **Sibelius** and **Nielsen,** the leading Scandinavian symphonists the time. He was considered a radical by the 1920s, when his travels introduced him to the latest European developments. However, his mature style emerged with the *Symphony No. 2* (1928–35), for which the contrapuntal art of **Hindemith** was perhaps the major model, tempered by the echo of Sibelius in phrasing and colouring. The vigour, characteristic of the mature works, is founded on the rhythmic drive of bass lines in counterpoint, and on the direct but slowly unfolding logic of his structures; the lyricism emerges in cantilena solo lines and the occasional suggestion of Nordic tonepainting. The harmonic structures are predominantly diatonic, chromaticism being largely used for added effect, or characteristically to give a more angular cast to a melodic line.

The *Symphony No. 2 'Sinfonia grave'* is intense and well wrought, its opening movement alternating energetic passages, insistent percussion to the fore, with more pastoral moments in which woodwind predominate. The slow movement is founded on long soaring string lines, its sense of purpose gradually evolving to a grand climax. The scherzo, where jauntiness is never quite allowed to emerge, has an exotic passage that is almost Oriental in feel. The finale, if the least convincing of the movements, has an impressive moment where snarling trumpets answer diving strings in a series of short antiphonal snatches. The four-movement *Symphony No.3* (1939) is a development of the idiom initiated in the second. It was originally titled *De fyra tidsåldrarna* (*The Four Ages of Man*), and opens with a stark theme that uses all twelve notes of the chromatic scale, while maintaining a sense of tonal base that becomes more overt as the work progresses. With its vigorous counterpoint, sense of purpose, logic and drive, an emotional intensity founded on

the bass lines, and dark hues to the orchestration, this fine symphony, like its predecessor, most recalls **Shostakovich** in affinity, but has the occasional Sibelian touch and a sense of long sweep that firmly shows its northern heritage. The final movement starts off in a happy northern woodland vein, but then unexpectedly evolves into a grimmer march of considerable power. The total neglect outside Sweden of such an emphatic symphony is a cause for considerable regret.

The next two symphonies were choral. The apocalyptic *Symphony No. 4 'Johannes uppenbarelse'* (*Revelations of St John*, 1939–40) is in complete contrast to the third, being a one-hour work for baritone, chorus and orchestra in eight-movement form; with words from Revelations and by the Swedish poet Hjalmar Gullberg in the linking a cappella chorales, it is more in the nature of a Bach Passion than a symphony. Its textures are generally lean, apart from the more climactic choral passages; often one predominant instrumental colour accompanies the soloists to considerable effect – the limpid simplicity of the fifth section is especially affecting. Many commentators consider the *Symphony No. 5 'Örtagårdsmästaren'* (1944, *The Keeper of the Garden*), for chorus and orchestra, to be the finest of all Rosenberg's works. Unfortunately, it has never been recorded.

Rosenberg returned to the purely orchestral symphony with the *Symphony No. 6 'Sinfonia semplice'* (1951, its subtitle a tribute to **Nielsen**, whose sixth symphony is similarly named). Compared with the third symphony, however, its lyricism has a more delicate and reconciled touch, particularly in the cantilena lines that open the first two movements (cellos in the first, French horn in the second). The *Symphony No. 8* (1980, developed from the introduction to the cantata *In candidum*, 1974) was at one point subtitled *Sinfonia serena*. Less immediately direct than the preceding symphonies, it is a complex and dense work in a single movement, its velvet mixed with grit, especially in the patchwork effect of the constantly varying orchestra and the interspersing of more forceful rhythmic snatches. The long stride of the earlier symphonies has become fragmented, interspersed with moments of hazy, almost Debussian Impressionism. This fine work rewards close attention, and completely belies its composer's eighty-odd years, although the abrupt and unexpected ending (it just stops) could perhaps only have been written by someone with the total disregard and confidence of old age.

The first of the two cello concertos (1939) is little known (although the slow movement has been heard in revised form as the *Intermezzo for Solo Cello*), but the *Cello Concerto No. 2* (1953) is one of the better-known concertante works that appeared in the early 1950s; others include the *Piano Concerto* (1950) and the *Violin Concerto No. 2* (1951). Predominantly lyrical, it has some gently beautiful passages, especially the opening of the slow movement, where a horn call is answered by the soloist against muted strings, like a finely shaped branch floating down a lazy river. Overall, the effect is less impressive, that lazy river too often meandering into less interesting backwaters.

Of his other works, the dance suite from the ballet *Orfeus i sta'n (Orpheus in Town*, 1938), describing the awakening of a statue in Stockholm, used to be relatively popular. With its boisterous atmosphere, its tango number and its feel of jazz, suggesting the Berlin of the early 1930s, its subsequent neglect is perhaps undeserved. The initially menacing and then pleasantly bouncy overture to his opera buffa *Marionetter* (1938) is also worth an airing. The *Lento* (1956) for strings is an impassioned dirge responding to the events in Hungary in 1956. The cantata *Den Heliga Natten (The Holy Night*, 1936), with its simplified style, became extremely popular in Sweden, is regularly broadcast each Christmas.

RECOMMENDED WORKS
  Symphony No. 2 (1928–35)
  Symphony No. 3 *The Four Ages of Man* (1939)
  Symphony No. 4 *The Revelation of St John* (1939–40)
  Symphony No. 5 *The Keeper of the Garden* (1944)
  Symphony No. 8 (1974/1980)

BIBLIOGRAPHY
  M. Pergament, *Hilding Rosenberg, a Giant of Modern Swedish Music*, 1956

Stenhammer (Karl) Wilhelm (Eugen)**
  born 7th February 1871 at Stockholm
  died 20th November 1927 at Stockholm

Best known outside Scandinavia for his *Serenade* for orchestra, Stenhammer occupies an important place in the revival of Swedish music. He mostly avoided folk influences, maintaining a more abstract late-Romantic symphonic and string quartet idiom as the 19th century turned into the 20th. He then developed a more formal and personal idiom, thus setting the tone for the following generation of Swedish composers. In terms of aesthetic he occupies much the same place in Swedish music as **Elgar** does in English music, though without the anguish that surfaces in the latter; his is an exuberant, colourful idiom, sometimes shaded with northern melancholia but usually bright and spontaneous.

Those outside Scandinavia are most likely to encounter Stenhammer's orchestral music. The early and extensive *Overture, Excelsior!* (1896), essentially a tone poem, shows strong Germanic influence but has an attractive extroversion and a sure handling of the orchestra. The *Symphony No. 1* (1902–03, never published, as Stenhammer intended to revise it) is a very long work (just over fifty minutes), and derivative, with shades of both Wagner and Bruckner (Stenhammer called it 'idyllic Bruckner'). That being said, it is a gloriously opulent score, memorable in its Brucknerian themes, masterfully orchestrated, especially for brass where the horns are particularly prominent (a feature of Stenhammer's orchestration). The major emphasis is on the outer movements; the slow movement carries less weight than expected from a symphony of this period. A similar structural emphasis applies to the much more frequently heard *Symphony No. 2* (1915). By this time Stenhammer had largely abandoned the Romantic elements for a more personal language partly founded on his extensive study of counterpoint, and this is the finest Swedish symphony of its era. It is Nordic in its opening melancholy (created harmonically by the use of modes), and yet combines this rather dark hue with considerable formal urgency and drive, clarified by the clear-cut orchestration (the brass are again prominent). Some of the rhythms are derived from folk music, the slow movement is a spacious funeral march, and the work ends with a vigorous fourth movement which reflects his counterpoint studies in the expert working of its seven sections, including variations and a double fugue.

The more formal, personal language is repeated in the *Serenade* (1913, revised 1919) for orchestra. This is essentially a nature poem in five movements (but sometimes played with six by including a short *Reverenza* which Stenhammer removed in the revision). It looks forward to neoclassicism in its use of solo strings in 18th-century concertante manner, but remains within the aesthetic of the large late-Romantic orchestra. It is broad and spacious, filled with a Nordic clarity of colour and light, the light humour of the ending having much in common with **Elgar**. The *Piano Concerto No. 1* (1893), although now forgotten, was the first major Swedish work of its kind. The *Piano Concerto No. 2* (1904–07) is a Romantic work, close to **Rachmaninov** in spirit, although the sometimes fiery piano writing is often integrated symphonically into the overall texture, when not in dialogue with the orchestra. The themes are not as memorable as those of the Russian composer, but this often glittering piece is worth seeking out. The two *Sentimentala Romanser* (1910), for violin and orchestra, look to Beethoven as a model, but display a yearning Romanticism in their lyrical outpouring.

However, many consider Stenhammer's string quartets to be the kernel of his work, though they are rarely heard outside Scandinavia. *String Quartet No. 1* (1894) is an early work, but the passionate *String Quartet No. 2* (1896) is modelled on Beethoven, classical in mould. In contrast the *String Quartet No. 3* (1897–1900) is Romantic in inspiration, with a heartfelt lento. The *String Quartet No. 4* in (1904–09) shows the darker side of the Nordic temperament, while the *String Quartet No. 5 'Serenade'* (1910) is a short and lively work (orchestrated by **Nielsen**) using, unusually for Stenhammer, a set of variations on a folk nursery-rhyme instead of a slow movement. The more elusive *String Quartet No. 6* (1916) completes the cycle.

Stenhammer also made important contributions to the Swedish vocal repertoire. The seascape *Ithaka* (1904), for baritone and orchestra, is as much a small cantata as an extended song; its very flowing, rocking solo line is supported by a rich-textured orchestra that graphically matches the words, in a score that inhabits the same area as **Vaughan Williams's** *A Sea Symphony*. Nationalist expression comes to the force in the cantata *Ett folk* (1904–05), whose unaccompanied hymn *Sverige* (Sweden) is one of the best known of all Swedish songs. *Midvinter* (*Midwinter*, 1906–07) is a beautiful 'Swedish Rhapsody' for chorus and orchestra, building slowly on a variant of a traditional hymn, and combining it with echoes of fiddle folk music. The orchestral *Intermezzo* is often extrapolated from the dramatic cantata *Sången* (*The Song*, 1920–21, words by the composer Ture **Rangström**), but the whole cantata, for four soloists, chorus and orchestra, is an important product of Stenhammer's later style. Rangström's poem, divided into two parts, equates sense of place with song in dense imagery; the rich, luxuriant lyricism of Stenhammer's setting places it firmly in the twilight of Romanticism, but tempered by his strong sense of formal choral procedures harking back to the tradition of the oratorio. He himself called it a 'two-movement sinfonia', and this often heady and beautiful work, moving from tense lyricism to exuberant joy and repose, is worthy of the attention of accomplished choral societies. His songs are also particularly effective, notably those written to verses by the poet Bo Bergman. Musical means are closely allied to the nature of the words, with often relatively simple accompaniments. Prominent are the song collection *Visor och stämningar* (1906–09), the cycle *Stockholm Poems* (1918), and the combination of tragedy and lyricism in *Fylgia*. His two early operas both failed, and he did not attempt a third. His piano music includes the *Three Fantasies* (1895) which show the influence of Brahms, but use folk material in the final piece.

Stenhammer was very active in Swedish musical life, as a conductor (notably with the Göteborg Orchestral Society, 1907–22) and pianist (especially in conjunction with the Aulin String Quartet, 1894–1912); consequently his compositional output is limited to forty-four published opuses. He particularly influenced later Swedish music through his pupil **Rosenberg**, the major Swedish composer of the middle of the 20th century. His own Romantic hue has enjoyed something of a revival in recent years; certainly those who enjoy the music of **Elgar** will appreciate the music of his Swedish contemporary.

RECOMMENDED WORKS

*Midvinter (Swedish Rhapsody for
Choir and Orchestra*, 1906–07)
Serenade (1913) for orchestra
String Quartet No. 3 (1897–1900)
String Quartet No. 4 (1904–09)
Symphony No. 2 (1915)

Tubin Eduard
see under Estonia

Wirén Dag Ivar*
born 15th October 1905 at Noraberg
died 19th April 1986 at Stockholm

Dag Wirén's name is widely familiar
through the popularity of a single work,
the pleasant *Serenade for Strings* (1937),
with its well-known march-like theme. His
output was small, reflecting the detail of
craftsmanship evident throughout his
work. His earlier music was Romantic in
idiom, but in the early thirties Wirén lived
in Paris, and, influenced by **Honegger** and
Stravinsky, turned to the new idiom of neo-
classicism, imparting to it his own brand of
gentle humour and melodic skill. To this
period belong the *Symphony No. 1* (1932)
and the *Symphony No. 2* (1939). His idiom
developed further in the 1940s: the language remained tonal, but Wirén started
exploring problems of form, aiming at a
'special form' in each work, especially
creating thematic development and interaction from germinal ideas (recalling **Sibe-**

lius). The main expressions of this
approach were the *Symphony No. 3* (1944)
and the *Symphony No. 4* (1952). The latter,
the best known of his symphonies, is a
marvellously vital work, whose polish and
completeness sparkles. Rhythmically
alive, it still shows a busy injection of neo-
classical verve, and the scoring is search-
ingly lucid. The melodic flair remains predominant, but it is broadened by a darker
streak, especially in the repeated pattern
of two irregular rhythmic figures of the
bass of the first movement, in the sinuous
opening, and in the massed string introduction to the slow movement (recalling
Martinů). This fine symphony is a much
more interesting and rewarding work than
the *Serenade*, and deserves to become
popular in its own right. The development
of Wirén's idiom is also clearly laid out in
the quartets, from the melodic neo-
classicism of the *String Quartet No. 2*
(1935), through the more stringent harmonies of *String Quartet No. 3* (1945), and the
development and reworking of germinal
motifs in *String Quartet No. 4* (1953), to the
economic *String Quartet No. 5* (1970).

Wirén was music critic for the newspa-
per *Svenska Morgonbladet* (1938–46).
Among his lighter compositions was the
Swedish entry for the 1965 Eurovision
Song Contest.

RECOMMENDED WORKS

Serenade for Strings (1937)
Symphony No. 4 (1951–52)

Switzerland

Introduction

Swiss music has inevitably been dominated by the cultural influences of the country's two major language blocks, French and German. Swiss composers concentrated almost exclusively on piano and choral music until the latter half of the 19th century, when Hans Huber (1852–1921) introduced a Swiss awareness into his symphonies and stage and choral works (e.g. his *Symphony No. 1*, titled *Tell*). However, his idiom was still based on German models (Brahms and **Strauss**), and much of the work of Swiss composers in the 20th century has followed developments in Germany or Austria: the heady late-Romantic sensuousness of Otmar **Schoeck** (1886–1957), the formal severity of Willy Burkhard (1900–55), the 12-tone compositions of Rolf Liebermann (1910–99), and now better known as the impresario who revitalised the Paris Opera), or the Germanic avant-garde of such composers as Heinz Holliger (born 1939). The one particularly Swiss emphasis in the output of these composers is the prevalence of vocal and choral works (reflecting a strong choral tradition), and a relatively large number of stage works.

A more obviously nationalist element appeared in the music, especially for voice, of Émile Jaques-Dalcroze (1865–1950) and Gustave Doret (1866–1943), both of whom reflected the folk music of the Suisse Romande (French-speaking Switzerland). The former is also famous for inventing the system of rhythmic education through physical movement with music, known as 'eurhythmics'. A further impetus to French influence was the work of the conductor Ernest Ansermet (1883–1969), who founded the Suisse Romande Orchestra in 1918, and with it became internationally famous for the interpretation of modern French music and of **Mahler**, and for the championing of Swiss composers.

Chief among these were Arthur **Honegger** (1892–1955) and Frank **Martin** (1890–1974), the most distinguished Swiss composers to date, and of international significance. Both show a refinement of sensibility that is a French inheritance, and the former has become permanently associated with French music, especially through his (somewhat spurious) inclusion in the Paris group known as 'Les Six'. The third major Swiss composer of the century, Ernest **Bloch**, also had his musical origins largely in French music; however, he not only emigrated to the USA, becoming deeply involved in musical life there, but also became the leading 20th-century composer to attempt a Jewish aesthetic in his music. Willy Burkhard, now little known outside Switzerland, once had an international reputation for his vocal and choral works, which reflect his deep religious convictions and his love of Bach and the Baroque. His uncompromising severity of technique, based on strict counterpoint and harmonies that include the pentatonic scale and sometimes bitonality, gradually softened, allowing a wider sense of colour and texture. His major works are the oratorio *Das Gesicht Jesajas* (*The Vision of Isaiah*, 1933–35), the dramatic cantata *Das ewige Brausen* (*The Everlasting Roar*, 1936) and the oratorio *Das Jahr* (*The Year*, 1942, describing the four seasons). His final work, *Six Preludes* (1955) for piano, includes 12-note techniques.

More recent Swiss composers have followed international trends, although the work of Klaus Huber (born 1924) continues the predominance of vocal and choral music in the Swiss canon. He is concerned with spiritual matters, and attempts a restatement of the primacy of the spiritual over the excess of the rational, often using medieval, religious, or mystical texts in radical sound-patterns that emphasise spatial sense and effect. His use of avant-garde and serial techniques moves towards a kind of mosaic of effects, in which musical elements are gradually formed 'from the darkness'. The powerful *... inwendig voller figure ...* (1971) has moments of violence, spatial effects, whispered and half-formed texts, and **Ligeti**-like clusters. Other important works include *Tenebrae* (1966–67) for orchestra, with its symbol of a solar eclipse (recalling that event at the hour of Christ's death), and the *Violin Concerto 'Tempora'* (1969–70). In the concerto the solo violin gradually rises out of a structured crescendo of orchestral chaos, and pursues an essentially flowing and lyrical line, interacting with or lying on top of an evolving mobile of orchestral sounds, including guitar and mandolin.

Heinz Holliger is primarily known as the foremost oboe virtuoso of the present day, for whom many contemporary composers have written, but he has been active as a composer of mainly vocal and chamber works. His earliest works follow **Berg** and **Schoenberg**, and were succeeded by a series of small-scale vocal works using serial techniques and cyclical structures. His later vocal work uses texts only for phonometic extraction of sounds and for other unconventional vocal effects. A major theatre piece, *Der magische Tänzer* (*The Magic Dancer*, 1963–65) is of interest more for its imaginative scenario (on a text by Nelly Sachs) than its musical virtues. A number of his later works transfer his experience of extended techniques on the oboe to other instruments; *t(air)e* for solo flute is marvellously written for the instrument, using the whole range of effects from harmonics, breathing and percussive treatment of the keys.

Of Swiss composers once relatively well known but now ignored, two need to be mentioned: Heinrich Sutermeister (1910–95), whose opera *Romeo und Julia* (1940), in an easygoing idiom, was for two decades one of the most successful of all 20th-century operas; and the Russian-born Vladimir Vogal (1896–1984), who developed a form of choral declamation, embraced serial technique, and is best remembered for his gigantic oratorio *Thyl Claes* (1937–45).

At first sight, therefore, most of the classical music of Switzerland would seem to be Swiss adjuncts to German and French traditions, rather than belonging to a recognisably Swiss one. However, many of the diverse works of **Bloch, Honegger** and **Martin** do share an aesthetic of a particular kind of neo-classicism for small forces, infected with bright colours and vigorous rhythms and structures (an echo of the Germanic tradition), nonetheless strong for being relatively unobtrusive. This would seem to be a particularly Swiss combination – the only other important composer who shares a similar aural aesthetic is the Czech **Martinů**, in his later works, and it is perhaps significant that many of those were written while he lived in Switzerland.

A common factor in a large proportion of these works has been the Swiss conductor Paul Sacher (born 1906). All lovers of music are deeply indebted to Sacher for his advocacy of contemporary music, and the extraordinary number of major works he commissioned from composers all over the world for his small orchestra (the Basle Chamber Orchestra, which he founded in 1926), showing an uncanny recognition of which composers have something significant to express. In its own way his achievement is as remarkable as that of the composers he has championed.

Swiss Music Information Centre:
c/o SME
P.O. Box 7851
CH – 6000 Luzern
Switzerland
tel & fax: +41 41 210 6070

Bloch Ernest**

born 24th July 1880 at Geneva
died 15th July 1959 at Portland,
Oregon, USA

Ernest Bloch divided his life between his native Switzerland (1880–1900, 1904–17, 1930–38) and the USA (1917–30, 1938–59), becoming a US citizen in 1924. The Franco-German inheritance was to remain an element of his musical personality (with an occasional touch of the Swiss pastoral); American influences are few; but above all Bloch, especially during the middle of his life, consciously set out to be a Jewish composer. His reputation for local colour in this genre, and the popularity of one work, *Schelom* (*Solomon*, 1916), for cello and orchestra, has obscured the value of the rest of his work, and contributed to his relative neglect.

His earliest work of substance is the *Symphony in C sharp minor* (1903), a large, late-Romantic work indebted to **Strauss**, with a touch of the macabre, skilfully constructed but of interest mainly to the insatiably curious. Impressionism is the main influence in *Hiver–Printemps* (*Winter–Spring*, 1904–05), **Debussy** a major inspiration behind his only opera *Macbeth* (1904–09), which uses cyclical techniques. The opera was a failure at its first production in Paris (1910), but a considerable success in an Italian revival (1938). It has recently been re-evaluated for its dramatic and musical qualities.

With the *Trois poèmes juifs* (*Three Jewish Poems*, 1913–14) for orchestra, Bloch initiated a number of works that have become known as the 'Jewish cycle'. In these works he tried, in an emotional (rather than an intellectual) Romantic fashion, to create a music that, without employing direct quotation of Jewish folk and religious songs, would reflect the essence of the Jewish cultural heritage. Certain stylistic traits give the music its exotic (often Middle Eastern) touches of the 'Oriental': the harmony employs augmented seconds, and bare fourths and fifths, the melodies have long chanting lines originating in synagogue cantor singing, the rhythms echo the Hebrew accent on the penultimate or last syllable, and the orchestration favours brass fanfares and bright exotic colours. Typically he uses the violin or the cello (both instruments well suited to the rhapsodic, Romantic nature of the style), as in *Baal Shem* (1923, orchestrated 1939) for violin and piano, or his best-known work, the 'Hebraic Rhapsody' *Schelom* (1916). The singing cello, using the contrasts of the higher and the lowest registers and Oriental touches, is pitted against the opulent orchestral sound in wide-ranging, large-scale and grandiose emotional moods. The symphony *Israel* (1912–16) for five solo voices and orchestra, is the only work of the 'Jewish cycle' to quote actual Jewish material. *The Voice in the Wilderness* (1936) for cello and orchestra, still sometimes encountered, continues the idea of *Schelom*, but is irritating in its combination of brilliance (the powerful cadenza, the haunted orchestral landscape of the opening) and banality (the suggestions of Hollywood film music). In ethnic terms, the culmination of the Jewish works is the *Avodath Hakodesh* (*Sacred Service*, 1933), which is imposing enough with its combination of a Western choral tradition and elements of Middle Eastern colour, but really too slim in musical interest to hold the attention when divorced from its context.

These works, relying on emotional impact rather than intellectual depth, will find a ready and undemanding response. The drawback is that they have tended to obscure the rest of Bloch's output, which is wider in range than is commonly supposed. The huge 'epic rhapsody' *America* (1926), for orchestra with choral ending (designed for audience participation, and which he hoped might become a national anthem) is a grandiose curiosity of a work, bombastically fascinating in its mixture of neo-Baroque fanfares, American-Indian tunes, shanties, spirituals, hymns and quasi-jazz, but otherwise best forgotten. A motto theme based on an American-Indian idea with an associated rhythmic figure is also found in the much more successful rhapsodic *Violin Concerto* (1938), which, avoiding virtuoso fireworks although employing a very large orchestra, has both Oriental touches and neo-classical elements. Of his large-scale late works, both the *Sinfonia breve* (1952) and the virtually unheard *Symphony in E flat major* (1954–55) use 12-tone themes, but in a strictly tonal milieu.

The works that listeners may find ultimately more rewarding are more intimate in tone, and generally characterised by a gradual abstraction and refinement of idiom, and tauter structures than the rhapsodic abandon of the better-known music. The neo-classical *Concerto Grosso No. 1* (1925) for string orchestra with piano obbligato may have been written as a demonstration piece for students, but it is an arresting work in its own right, with vigorous outer movements and a gently alluring *Pastorale* incorporating Swiss tunes. The *Concerto Grosso No. 2* (1952) for string orchestra (with a central quartet), is even more overtly neo-classical, austere and abstract. The two *Violin Sonatas* (1920 and 1924, No. 2 subtitled *Poème mystique*) have long been popular with violinists. All the five string quartets have an emotional intensity and command of string writing powerful enough to deserve a place in the repertoire; they use the French cyclical structure, with movements sharing a motif, as in many of Bloch's works. The *String Quartet No. 1* (1916) is violent and lengthy, and was once greatly admired; the terse *String Quartet No. 2* (1945) is atonal and the *String Quartet No. 3* (1951–52) is lighter and more joyful in feel while being more concentrated in structure. The final two quartets (1953 and 1954) are introverted, ascetic works: thoughtful and ethereal (notwithstanding the strange off-key dance in No. 4), tautly argued, they are not immediately obvious but repay close study. Perhaps the most successful of these chamber works, consistent, powerful and immediate, is the *Piano Quintet No. 1* (1923). Using quarter-tones as an expressive device to great effect, it moves from a driving, dark, urgent first movement, overlaid with soaring melodic lines, through a tortured, highly-charged central movement, to a finale of a kind of impassioned resolution; the music is never allowed to stay still, and constantly has exotic touches (high harmonics, swoops and sudden bursts). The angrier *Piano Quintet No. 2* (1957) has a haunting slow movement.

In all Bloch's music there is a sense of the rhapsodic, with little suggestion of traditional thematic development, but he is at his best when that feeling of freedom is allied to an internal logic of structure. His overall tone has the strong emotional expression of reaching out of the turbulence of humanity towards resolution. This essentially Romantic notion will appeal to some more than others, and the relatively small number of major works will probably ensure his music is left to the occasional airing. However, his influence, especially on American music, will endure through the results of his extensive teaching; his pupils included **Antheil** and **Sessions**. He was director of the Cleveland Institute of Music (1920–25).

RECOMMENDED WORKS
Concerto Grosso No. 1 (1925)
Concerto Grosso No. 2 (1952)
Piano Quintet No. 1 (1921–23)
Piano Quintet No. 2 (1957)
rhapsody for cello and orchestra
    Schelom (1915)
String Quartet No. 2 (1945)
String Quartet No. 4 (1953)
String Quartet No. 5 (1956)

BIBLIOGRAPHY
E. Bloch, *Biography and Comment*, 1925
S. Bloch and I. Heskes, *Ernest Bloch, Creative Spirit: A program Source Book*, 1976
D. Kushner, *Ernest Bloch and his Music*, 1973
R. Strassburg, *Ernest Bloch, Voice in the Wilderness: a Biographical Study*, 1977

Honegger Arthur···
born 10th March 1892 at Le Havre
died 27th November 1955 at Paris

Caught between his native country, German-speaking Switzerland, and his regular country of residence, France, and between the tug of modernism and the tow of Romanticism, Honegger is now better known by name than by his music. However, it is his general style that is currently out of fashion rather than his abilities or accomplishments, and it seems likely that some of his works will filter back into greater prominence as fashions change.

His earliest works showed the influence of the two major models of the day, Wagner and **Debussy**. However, his studies in Paris, and his return there after Swiss military service in 1916, led to his association with movements reacting against these twin influences. In 1918 he became a member of 'Les Nouveaux Jeunes', with Auric, **Poulenc**, Roland-Manuel and Tailleferre; then (thanks to an article by Henri Collet) he joined the group known universally as 'Les Six' (1920), whose other members were Auric, Durey, **Milhaud**, **Poulenc** and Tailleferre. However, the label was misleading, for Honegger was not in sympathy with their musical mentor, **Satie**, and although he occasionally

worked with the group's intellectual mentor, Jean Cocteau, and collaborated with other members of the group (particularly Milhaud) on numerous films, these were incidental to the main thrust of his music, and his occasional modernism was of a different hue. The aesthetic of Parisian café and jazz music of the 1920s and early 1930s was alien to his background, although it is an indication of his wide-ranging tastes and abilities that he could collaborate with **Ibert** in the Offenbachian trifle of an opera *L'aiglon* (1935), and sometimes echo jazz patterns (e.g. in the last movement of the *Concertino* for piano and orchestra, 1924).

The first work in which his individuality was established was the *String Quartet No. 1* (1916–17), which has a rigorous rhythmic drive and polyphonic and contrapuntal techniques that echo Honegger's love of Bach. From then on his music, for all its considerable diversity of styles and influences, follows an essentially consistent pattern. The chief characteristic is its structural integrity and logic, the result of a meticulous sense of craftsmanship. Sonata structures are regularly used, as well as variation techniques and extensive thematic development (often in sonata form with a return of the second subject before the first). The flow is polyphonic, and tends to be emphasised by incisive rhythms; webs of melodic lines (the melodies themselves long and flowing) or chordal structures interweave in a 20th-century counterpart to Bach, also echoed by chorale elements. The orchestration varies from the wildly savage and mechanistic to a neo-classical simplicity. The emotional tone has three predominant features: a sense of grandeur, a suggestion of mischief or fun (from the grotesque to the macabre), and an underlying feeling of sombreness or tragedy (exemplified in the darker orchestral colours). The restraint that is often a feature of his music is not just a temperamental trait or merely a consequence of the logical craftsmanship, but also a result of the desire to reach out to a wide audience.

Against this general structural pattern appears a temperamental contrast or duality, overt in the earlier works, latent in the later. On the one hand are simplicity and lyricism (and also gentle modal harmonies); on the other, aggressive rhythms, massive instrumentation, and complex polytonal elaborations. The former are exemplified by the Impressionist *Pastorale d'été* (*Summer Pastorale*, 1920), the latter by *Prélude pour 'La Tempête'* (*Prelude to 'The Tempest'*, 1923), both for orchestra, and by the 'mime-symphony' *Horace victorieux* (1921), which has echoes of **Strauss** and is now largely forgotten. In subsequent works these two traits co-exist.

Although Honegger wrote extensively in all fields, his major works (and those most likely to be encountered), fall into three areas: the short orchestral pieces (mostly written in the 1920s), the large-scale quasi-dramatic works (mostly 1920s and 1930s), and the numbered symphonies (1930, 1942–51). Such is the impact of the orchestral pieces, and their conciseness and internal logic, that it seems surprising that they have not held their place in the concert hall. *Pastorale d'été* is a gentle delight, as if trying to move away from Impressionism but still having it caught by the coat-tails. *Pacific 231* (1923) was once a *cause célèbre*, and remarks a stunning *tour de force* of motoric depiction, inspired by a type of express steam railway locomotive (231 stands for the wheel configuration, classed by the British as Pacific). Its unabashed futurism, far removed from Parisian models, was closer to the Russian aesthetic of **Stravinsky** or **Prokofiev**, and the work influenced numerous composers, from the Russian Mosolov to the American **Antheil.** It still stands as a touchstone to the understanding of art in the 20th century. *Rugby* (premièred in the interval of the England vs. France international rugby game of 1928) takes the genre yet further, but musically the most impressive of these shorter pieces is *Prélude pour 'La Tempête'*, with its wild, powerful and violent orchestration and harmonic clashes.

Apart from *Pacific 231*, Honegger's reputation was built on his dramatic cantatas (large-scale 'frescos'), and it is partly the public's loss of interest in the genre that has been responsible for a decline in Honegger's popularity. The dramatic psalm *Le Roi David* (*King David*, 1921, reorchestrated for concert platform 1923), consists of twenty-seven short sections in three parts, linked, like other Honegger works, by a narrator; it succeeds by its underlying simplicity (choruses often in only two parts, a sense of the antique), by its mixture of styles (from quasi-Handel to Primitivism via Impressionism, mixed with the aggression of some of the polytonal choruses), and by the radiant sincerity that successfully binds them together. The dramatic oratorio/opera *Jeanne d'Arc au bûcher* (*Joan of Arc at the Stake*, 1935, prelude added 1944), is equally consistent,

more demanding, and more powerful, offering a major opportunity for an actress rather than a singer in the title role. The last of this type of vocal work is an unusual Christmas cantata, *Une cantata de Noël* (1953), which is of considerably more depth than most works of this type. With carols woven into the general texture, it moves from a mood of despair (with an unusual division between a wordless, chordal chorus, and busier sections of the orchestra) to a general sense of joy. Honegger's operatic masterpiece is the forty-five-minute *Antigone* (1927), a collaboration with Cocteau (after Sophocles). Honegger plays close attention to the text, setting it syllabically (a single note being assigned to each syllable), often with unexpected stresses. The result is a white-hot work of relentless tension in both vocal and orchestral writing, with scarcely a moment of repose. There are virtually no lyrical aspirations at all, but as music drama it is concise and powerful. Single orchestral colours often emerge for the unsettled orchestra to point up the emotional tensions, and the chorus provides passages of climax that serve to provide a breathing space from the flow of solo lines, if not from the psychological anguish.

Of the five numbered symphonies, the underrated *Symphony No. 1* (1929–30) is a good introduction to Honegger's styles and concerns. The bleak *Symphony No. 2* (1942) for strings with a trumpet chorale at the end (deliberately kept silent in the first performance in occupied Paris), is not easily forgotten, its stark neo-classicism unmistakable in intent, its closing chorale tremulously hopeful. The *Symphony No. 3* (1945–46) is subtitled *Liturgique*, referring to the mood and the titles of the movements rather than any musical quotation. It is a protest at the barbarism of the times, with a return to aggressive motoric rhythms and violence, an anguished but moving slow movement, and an extraordinary epilogue of hope. The *Symphony No. 4 'Deliciae basiliensis'* (*Delights of Basle*, 1946) is a more relaxed work incorporating Swiss tunes, rhythmic but pastoral, and not without its darker hues. The *Symphony No. 5* (1951), subtitled *Di tre re* as each movement ends on a D, is enigmatic, tragic and noble. The best of these symphonies (Nos. 2, 3 & 5) are not especially easy to grasp, in spite of their surface accessibility. Their scale seems more intimate than is customary for the form, and their idiom requires close concentration. But, with their attendant extra-musical themes, they are powerful and thoughtful works, worthy of a period that our art still prefers to forget.

Of his chamber music, the two *Violin Sonatas* (1916–18, 1919), the sombre *Cello Sonata* (1920) and the *String Quartet No. 1* (1916–17) are the most interesting. His other works include numerous film scores such as *Mayerling* (1935) and *Pygmalion* (1938). His strong streak of pessimism is evident in the macabre subjects of some of the ballets and works with voice.

Honegger was a noted music critic, and taught at the Ecole Normale de Musique in Paris. If his music can be criticised for eclecticism of style and for over-meticulousness, there is no denying the sincerity of purpose or effectiveness of his best works.

RECOMMENDED WORKS
opera *Antigone* (1927)
dramatic psalm *Le roi David* (1921)
Pacific 231 (1923) for orchestra
Pastorale d'été (1920) for orchestra
Prélude pour 'La Tempête' (1923) for orchestra
Rugby (1928) for orchestra
String Quartet No. 1 (1916–17)
Symphony No. 2 (1942) for strings and trumpet
Symphony No. 3 *Liturgique* (1946)
Symphony No. 4 *Deliciae basiliensis* (1946)
Symphony No. 5 *Di tre re* (1951)

BIBLIOGRAPHY
A. Honegger, *Incantation aux fossiles*, 1948
Je suis compositeur, 1951 (English trans. *I am a Composer*, 1966)
A. Gauthier, *Arthur Honegger*, 1957

Martin Frank**
born 15th September 1890 at Geneva
died 21st November 1974 at Naarden, Holland

The music of Frank Martin is slowly becoming recognised as a major musical achievement of the 20th century, an intensely individual and personal voice that is all the more extraordinary for its late development. Martin did not evolve his own style until the completion of the oratorio *Le vin herbé* (*The Doctored Wine*) in 1941, when he was fifty-one. In marked contrast to his major Swiss contemporaries **Bloch** and **Honegger** (whose successes came early), all his most valuable works were written after this date, and the only 20th-century parallel is that of **Janáček**.

Martin instigated no startling innovations, again like Janáček, but used elements of contemporary ideas to forge an idiom that is so personal that he has had no imitators.

His works divide broadly into vocal works, mainly with orchestra and often on religious subjects, and orchestral music, mostly for smaller forces; there is very little piano music, and only a modest body of chamber music. His hallmark is a wonderful lucidity, a lightness of feel, a transparency of texture (often with very unusual instrumental combinations) that at its best feels almost transcendental. There is little that is overtly dramatic or exotic in colour – Martin's art is one of subtlety, which therefore grows in stature on repeated acquaintance.

His earliest works reflect the duality of his country, for he was influenced first by German Romanticism and Franck, and then after 1915 by the French Impressionists. His search for an idiom that would satisfy him led, in the period from 1925 to 1932, to rhythmic exploration (Oriental, Bulgarian and ancient music), exemplified in *Rhythms* for orchestra (1926), and to an interest in folk music. But at the end of this period he adopted the 12-tone principles of **Schoenberg**, notably in the *String Trio* (1936); he was one of the first composers outside Schoenberg's circle to do so. But the *Piano Concerto No. 1* (1933–34, discussed below) showed how little Martin sympathised with Schoenberg's aesthetic, for it is a dramatic, quasi-Romantic work in which serialism is used only for the construction of some of the thematic ideas. As his subsequent music showed, Martin was not by temperament a serial or 12-tone composer.

Instead, he realised that the kind of harmonies and changing harmonic patterns that he was looking for (tonal pathways in an atonal landscape) could arise from the interaction of 12-tone principles and the traditional major/minor triads. Thus melodic lines, constructed on the 12-tone principle, could have the anchor of an usually static bass. Alternatively the row could be the bass-line beneath traditional harmony. This use of serial thematic material is the antithesis of Schoenberg's objectives, and ensured that Martin remained an essentially tonal composer, emphasising harmonic concerns. The work with which he established this style was the secular dramatic oratorio *Le vin herbé* (*The Doctored Wine*, 1938–41), for twelve solo voices, seven strings and piano, based on a modern treatment of the medieval Tristan legend. Various voices individually take

12-note themes, and the tonality, briefly established by the characteristic triads in the accompaniment or by the bass-line, is constantly in motion. The story follows the legend closely, with its medieval twists and turns and symbolism, and is dramatic enough to make it virtually an opera without staging. Martin's beautiful score, sometimes restrained and formal (expressed in the often homophonic choral writing), sometimes broadening from this base into a more passionate expression of emotions, captures that sense of distancing inherent in such legends. In both literary style and musical treatment, it is an antidote to Wagner's more celebrated treatment of the same tale, and if on first acquaintance it seems restrained, the virtues of its subtle scoring and exact evocation of the spirit of the original soon weave their own spell.

Le vin herbé initiated a series of vocal works that developed its idiom. It was followed by the dark and hauntingly expressive *Die Weise von Liebe und Tod des Cornets Christoph Rilke* (*Lay of the Love and Death of Cornet Christoph Rilke*, 1942–43, also known as *Cornet Rilke*). The stream of the alto vocal line, with its feel of the inflections of emotional speech, is harmonically supported by a sparsely-used chamber orchestra that typically includes a piano. The eventual drama is all the more powerful for the restraint. *Jedermann* (*Everyman*, 1943, orchestrated 1949) for baritone and piano or orchestra continued the style, again with chromatically-shifting triads. The four parts of the short oratorio *In terra pax* (1944) for soloists, two choruses and orchestra, representing the Four Horses of the Apocalypse, express the despair of wartime, the joys of earthly peace, human reconciliation, and the joys of heavenly peace. The two choirs are often used antiphonally, the final Sanctus is particularly beautiful, and there is a haunting moment when the tenor cries 'Watchman, what of the night' over sustained high strings. Martin then turned to the concept of a Passion work. The lengthy oratorio *Golgotha* (1945–48) for soloists, chorus and orchestra is divided into seven 'pictures' of the events of the Passion, divided by settings of the meditations of St Augustine. It is rather a lean work, regularly allowing the intimate story-telling to be carried on the barest of melodic textures, with many moments of affecting beauty. The scenic oratorio *Le mystère de la Nativité* (1957–59), based on part of a 15th-century mystery play, is of almost operatic dimensions, and was intended to

have stage elements. *Pilate* (1964) for soloists, chorus and orchestra is a cantata drawn from the same mystery play cycle. The sense of restraint, of the exploration of the detailed and subtle meaning of a text rather than its immediate outward effect, culminated in the sombre but moving *Requiem* (1971–72), for soloists, chorus, organ and orchestra. Its lines swell from a grave contemplation into passionate expression or luminous soft held major chords, with gripping unearthly orchestral sonorities, and with snarling percussion and half-spoken vocal lines in the opening of the *Dies irae*.

Martin transferred the ideas initiated in *Le vin herbé* to the orchestra in his most popular work, the *Petite symphonie concertante* (1945). The instrumentation (harpsichord, harp, piano and two string orchestras) is unusual, as with many of Martin's later works, setting the kind of technical problem that inspired him, and gaining the clarity needed to express the harmonic feel and to create a matching transparency of timbre. In the same vein is the delightful and beautiful *Concerto for Harpsichord and Small Orchestra* (1952), whose rocking opening was inspired by the waves of the North Sea. In both these works the use of rows in the opening material, the harmonies (minor thirds predominant in the *Harpsichord Concerto*) and the cast of the melodic lines give a darker hue to the tonal base. This contrasts with the other aspects of the style: the lucid orchestration, each instrument finely placed; the rhythmic verve founded on emphatic 'walking' bass lines; and the often jaunty expression. The resulting impression is of a number of layers of emotions occurring simultaneously; but technically this duality of idiom is so perfectly integrated that those emotions appear as different faces of the same coin, and it is this holistic completeness that makes Martin's mature idiom so effective.

The *Concerto for Seven Wind Instruments, Timpani, Percussion and String Orchestra* (1949) is more rumbustious. In the lively first movement, different ideas are allocated to each instrument in dialogue, and full use is made of the contrasting timbres and sonorities of the solo instruments; the middle movement takes on the mantle of a passionate slow march, with eerie colour combinations in the orchestration; and the finale has a Parisian bounce and a lively series of highlights for each soloist, with a return of the march. The proportions of the whole work, which lasts about eighteen minutes, seem perfectly suited both to its material and its orchestral composition, a modern equivalent to the delights of the 18th-century classical concerto. A similar clarity pervades the *Violin Concerto* (1950–51). The *Études* (1956) for string orchestra maintain the general idiom, while concentrating on various techniques that justify the title. A prelude for the whole string orchestra opens the work. The first study passes chromatic lines between string voices; in the second, bows are discarded entirely; the third, for violas and cellos, is slow and expressive; and the last opens with a double fugue with accompaniment, turns to a chorale, and reverts to the fugue. Such is the skill of the writing, there is not a hint of academicism throughout the work, and the technical tricks serve the expressive content. Martin's religious awareness and the refinement of instrumental texture combine in the suite *Polyptyque* (1972–73), for violin and two string orchestras, which is a series of musical images reflecting the Passion of Christ. The writing is more consciously lyrical than in the works of the 1940s, with soaring lines for the soloist, and paradoxically it sounds more old-fashioned and less finely shaped than those earlier works. The operas *Der Sturm* (*The Tempest*, 1952–55, based on Shakespeare's play) and *Monsieur de Pourceaugnac* (1961–62, based on Molière) failed to establish a place in the repertoire, although the orchestral overture to *Der Sturm* is sometimes heard on its own. Well worth hearing it is, too, tone-painting a rocking seascape whose delicate orchestration, lyrical moments and rhythmic effects are strongly reminiscent of **Britten**.

In addition to these orchestral works, there is a series of rhapsodic *Ballades* for solo instrument and orchestra, cast in one-movement forms divided into sections. Brilliant effects characterise the *Ballade for Flute, String Orchestra and Piano* (1939, orchestrated 1941), which was originally written as a competition set work. The *Ballade for Piano and Orchestra* (1939) is in the nature of a discursive conversation piece, the soloist sometimes providing arpeggio commentary, at other times taking the lead. The *Ballade for Trombone and Orchestra* (1940) provides a rare concertante opportunity for the trombone, while the much later *Ballade for Viola, Wind Instruments and Percussion* (1972) uses the harp and the harpsichord percussively, and is a more delicate and

ethereal work, with lyrical writing for the solo instrument. The two piano concertos span a major part of Martin's compositional career. The *Piano Concerto No. 1* (1933–34) disappeared from the repertoire after its initial success, but it deserves better. The intimate feel of the later concertos is evident, but the fusion of 12-tone elements and a tonal base is less complete and less satisfactory. Rhythmically alive, it has a long slow orchestral introduction that foreshadows later works, and includes a 12-tone row taken up by the piano on its entry. The piano writing is often florid, a remnant from more Romantic idioms, except when the influence of 12-tone technique twists the melodic lines into angular shapes. The finale combines the infectiously boisterous with a still, calm lyricism. At the end of his career, Martin produced a work to match the interest and delicacy of the earlier concertos. The *Piano Concerto No. 2* (1968–69) is not so obviously immediate as those earlier works, but at the same time seems to reforge many of his earlier concerns: a bouncy jauntiness, moments of discursive writing for the soloist, an infectious sense of the delight in instrumentation, a jazzy moment for saxophone. The restrained beauty of the second movement is built in the form of a passacaglia on a 12-note row, but again the use of 12-tone elements and the technical facility are totally integrated into the expressive content, which has the assured luminosity of old age.

Martin's achievement was to fuse many of the sound-patterns that had been realised through 12-tone techniques with a predominantly tonal idiom. In this fusion of a new aural experience and an older tradition he was perhaps ahead of his time, without gaining the kind of attention that a pure experimenter would command. But few have married the two so successfully and naturally, or forged such a personal, if often self-effacing idiom. He is primarily a composer of intimate reflection rather than display or power, even at more emphatic moments giving a rather demure sheen to his expression. As such, he is not a composer to grab the listener by the scruff of the neck; rather his best works demand contemplation, a willingness to savour, and the desire to enter a very personal musical world.

Martin moved from Switzerland to the Netherlands in 1946, and taught at the Cologne Hochschule für Musik (1950–57), where **Stockhausen** was among his pupils.

RECOMMENDED WORKS
Concerto for Harpsichord and Small
Orchestra (1951–52)
Concerto for Seven Wind
Instruments, Timpani, Percussion
and String Orchestra (1949)
Études (1955–56) for string orchestra
oratorio *Golgotha* (1945–48)
oratorio *In terra pax* (1944)
song-cycle *Lay of the love and Death
of Cornet Rilke* (1942–43)
Maria Triptychon (1967–68) for
soprano, violin and orchestra
Petite symphonie concertante (1945)
Piano Concerto No. 2 (1968–69)
Requiem (1971–72)
Violin Concerto (1950–51)

BIBLIOGRAPHY
B. Martin, *Frank Martin ou la réalité
du rêve*, 1973 (in French)

Schoeck Othmar**
born 1st September 1886 at Brunnen
died 8th March 1957 at Zurich

Othmar Schoeck is one of the neglected
minor masters of 20th-century music.
Very gradually, however, his outstanding
works are being appreciated outside Germany (he was German-speaking) and his
native Switzerland. There would seem to
be three reasons for this neglect. Firstly,
he belongs to the final flush of Romanticism, that expressive introversion brought
to fruition by **Mahler**, the earlier works of
Schoenberg, and such composers as **Zemlinsky**, but he was composing at a time
when musical attention was directed to
reactions against Romanticism. Secondly,
(unlike the composers just mentioned), his
art is essentially that of the miniaturist,
never a popular area. Lastly, his melodic
invention, while perfectly suited to his
idiom, is not of the type that is instantly
memorable. His music divided, broadly,
into two periods. Before World War I, his
idiom was lyrically Romantic, its emotions
essentially sunny though tinged with a
bitter-sweet melancholy. After the war,
his harmonic idiom became increasingly
chromatic and occasionally almost Expressionist, and his central emotional concerns
turned to the insubstantiality of life and a
wonder at the natural world.

Although Schoeck composed a number
of non-vocal works, his primary achievement is in music for the voice, expressed in
over four hundred songs. His fusion of
music and the underlying sense of words is
uncommonly close, a last flowering of the
German Romantic tradition of the lied
(hence the lack of necessity for memorable
melodies: the music seldom relies merely
on surface colour). The art of lieder writing
requires the skills of the miniaturist – the
completeness of form within a short time-
frame, and the accuracy of detail – and in
these Schoeck excels. But he also wished
to express human concerns on a grander
scale, and larger emotions than could be
contained in individual songs or a small
collection. He therefore evolved lengthy
song-cycles, expanding the accompaniment to include a string quartet, chamber
orchestra, and full orchestra. Vocal lines
do not have obvious melodic beauty, but
rather follow the inflections and rhythms
of the text, lengthened at moments of
passion. Underneath this, the accompaniments regularly have a distinct independence, the meaning of the text usually
supported through harmonic interchange.
Time and time again in his songs a slight
harmonic change subtly points up the text
or shifts the tone. The chromaticism is
generally expressed through the melodic
lines rather than in dissonant clashes, and
is inherent to Schoeck's idiom, rather than
being used for colour effects. The combination of all these elements creates a distinctive lyrical beauty.

The most inspired of these song-cycles
set the Swiss poet Gottfried Keller
(1819–90), whose work remained an abiding influence on the composer. In doing so,
Schoeck developed the one aspect of late-
Romanticism that has continued to fascinate the 20th century: the relationship
between the individual psychology and the
transcendental, and its concomitant, the
fear of death. The first Keller cycle, *Gase-
len* (*Ghazels* – love poems, 1923) is coloured by the accompaniment (flute, bass
clarinet, trumpet, percussion and piano) in
a combination of satire and the ecstasy of
love. His masterpiece is *Lebendig begra-
ben* (*Buried Alive*, 1926) for baritone and
orchestra, an extensive cycle of the poetry
of despair, of being buried alive, of winter,
and of the extended metaphor of the
trapped mind. Setting fourteen of Keller's
poems, the cycle describes the imaginings
and the memories of the buried man, who
hears the clock strike and the sexton
arguing. After the explosive opening, with
an emotional power to match that of Zemlinsky's *Lyric Symphony*, the tone is one of
gradual acceptance. The orchestral writing (which includes organ and piano) is
constantly shifting its colours and forces,
often in chamber-sized combinations. The
poetry itself is unusual and memorable;

with Schoeck's passionate and sensitive setting, it is unforgettable. *Unter Sternen* (*Under Stars*, 1941–49) for lower voice and piano sets twenty-five Keller songs divided into two parts, the first describing the experience of the night, the second contemplating ideas of death, into which the metaphor of light and dark is interwoven. The nineteenth song, *In der Trauer*, has a Schubertian delicacy and simplicity. In *Das Stille Leuchten* (*The Quiet Lights*, 1946) for lower voice and piano, Schoeck turned to the poetry of another Swiss poet of solitude, Ferdinand Meyer. The twenty-eight songs are divided into two groups, the first titled 'Mystery and Parable', the second 'Mountain and Sea', thus moving from abstract to concrete images, a movement that clearly attracted Schoeck in his choice of poetry. Much of the cycle is soft and delicate, with simple accompaniments to the very fluid and solo writing, occasionally swelling up to moments of passion.

Of his other cycles, the marvellous *Notturno* (1931–34) for baritone and string quartet, is divided into five movements on a symphonic scale. All the poems are by Lenau, except the last, by Keller. The first part sets four Lenau songs, and pivots between yearning and thwarted desire in nature and in human life, the pivot being a long interlude for the string quartet, followed by a magical entry of the voice with the words 'The dark clouds hang down.' The second part is a nightmare, the string quartet brilliantly describing the restlessness of the dreamer before he awakes and retells the dream, with Expressionist extremes of vocal writing. Life as illusion forms the theme of the third part, expressed through nature and through fears; the fourth is dank and slow, meditating on faded love and death, with a haunting Mahlerian change of harmony on the last word. The final part considers solitude, with bitter-sweet textures from the string quartet introducing an epilogue of a Keller poem contemplating the Big Dipper in the night sky. The structure of this song-cycle is masterful, both in the overall layout and in the complex internal connections of the poetry chosen. The string quartet writing is rich and plastic, clearly drawn from the sounds of the stream that forms an important image in Part I; the vocal writing encompasses the whole range of Schoeck's expressive idiom.

Schoeck was also an important composer of stage works, and his achievement in this field is starting to receive a wider appreciation. The central theme in his operas and stage works (three operas, a *Singspiel*, a pantomime scene, a stage cantata and a dramatic ballad) is an exploration of the feminine aspect of humanity; that is, not only of the relationship between the sexes, but also of the feminine within the masculine (what Jungians would term the 'anima'); and his various stage works explore different aspects of this theme. His operatic masterpiece is the 'music drama' *Penthesilea* (1924–25), to a libretto by the composer after the play by Kleist; this is a tight psychological drama, where the masculine and feminine principles are combined with the motivations of love and hate when the Amazon warrior queen Penthesilea meets Achilles. The setting is through-composed to create a music drama; the music mines the psychological layers in rich orchestral textures, sometimes Impressionistic, almost always sensuous, with dramatic outbursts and very free flowing vocal lines. *Massimilla Doni* (1935), based on a Balzac story set in Venice in the 1830s, is marred by its libretto by Armin Rüger; *Venus* (1920), based on Mérimée, is reportedly more effective.

Of his orchestral works, the lovely, rich *Concerto quasi una fantasia* (1911–12, usually referred to as the *Violin Concerto*) for violin and orchestra represents Schoeck's pre-war Romanticism; it contains a beguiling violin idea in the passionate first movement, yearning tumult with a touch of the funereal in the central movement, and a weighty finale that turns into a lively headlong tumble with a ruminative interlude. This is such an attractive and energetic concerto, with considerable opportunities for the soloist, that it should be rescued from obscurity. He did not turn again to the concerto form until thirty-five years later. The *Concerto for Cello and String Orchestra* (1947) is too long and varied in quality, but has some beautiful moments, reminiscent of the late works of **Strauss**. More effective is the autumnal *Concerto for Horn and String Orchestra* (1951), where the flowing horn lines sound like a lieder voice, Falstaffian at times. The beautiful and equally mellow 'pastoral intermezzo' *Sommernacht* (1945) for string orchestra is again in a late-Romantic idiom, its programmatic description of harvesting at night inspired by a Keller poem; this would make an interesting companion piece to **Strauss's** *Metamorphosen*. Of Schoeck's four-movement *Cello Sonata* (1957) the three movements that were left complete on his death are not of the same quality.

Schoeck's music will never attract a

wide public. But for those who enjoy the combination of poetry of high quality and the added depth of musical setting of great power and understanding, it may well come as a revelation. His general late-Romantic idiom, like that of **Bax,** is now being appreciated once again, and it is time that Schoeck took his place as one of the specialised masters of the 20th century.

RECOMMENDED WORKS
> song-cycle *Lebendig begraben* (1926)
> > for baritone and orchestra
> opera *Penthesilea* (1924–25)
> song-cycle *Notturno* (1933) for
> > baritone and string quartet
> *Sommernacht* (1945) for string
> > orchestra
> song-cycle *Unter Sternen* (1941–43)
> > for lower voice and piano

Turkey

The development of Turkish classical composition followed the transformation of Turkey after the abolition of the Caliphate in 1924 and the rise of Kemal Atatürk. It was led by a group of composers known as the 'Turkish Five': Necil Kazim Akses (born 1908), Assan Ferid Alnar (1906–78), Ulvi Cemal Erkin (1906–72), Cemal Resid Rey (1904–85) and Ahmet Adnan Saygun (1907–91). Rey's works, which include two symphonies, a number of concertos, and the opera *Celebi* (1943), use indigenous Middle Eastern idioms within Western contexts. The most important of the group was Saygun, who studied with **d'Indy** and collected folk songs with **Bartók.** His idiom combines an Impressionism with Turkish and Oriental inflections, and his output includes three symphonies, a cello concerto, a piano concerto (1958), a viola concerto (1978) and three string quartets. He came to international attention with the oratorio *Yunus Emre* (1946) for soloists, chorus and orchestra, which sets poems by the thirteenth-century poet of that name that move from contemplation of beauty and the inevitability of death to communion with the Divine.

Ukraine

The colourful Ukrainian folk culture is perhaps the best known of all the folk heritages of the former Soviet Union, in part because of the robust Ukrainian communities in other countries. Much of the Soviet classical Ukrainian music was coloured by this heritage. The best-known Ukrainian-born composers were Sergei **Prokofiev** (1891–1953) and Alexander **Mossolov** (1900–73), both of whom spent most of their lives in Russia, and will be found under that heading. Yuri Shaporin (1887–1966), a modernist in his youth, produced quintessential Soviet works, such as the cantata *Battle for the Russian Land* (1944), an effective example of its patriotic genre, and *The Decembrists* (1925–53). The output of Boris Liatoshinsky (1895–1968) included five symphonies, the operas *The Golden Hoop* (completed 1929), with a backdrop of the 13th-century struggles of the Ukrainians against the Mongolians, and *Schors* (1937), telling the story of a Civil War hero, and the cantata *Zapovit*, setting the words of the most famous of Ukrainian poets, Taras Shevchenko. His idiom was traditional, and his orchestral music is too bland to be of real interest; however, he encouraged his pupils to encounter contemporary Western European musical developments. Among those Ukrainian composers who met official approval in the Soviet period was Andrei Shtogarenko (1902–92); his works include three symphonies. Valentin Silvestrov (born 1937) used serial techniques in the 1960s in spite of official condemnation, before turning to a more tonal idiom in the 1970s, while Leonid Hrabovsky (born 1935) has adopted a minimalist style.

Ukrainian Music Information Centre:
Music Information Centre of the Ukraine
Composers Union
Ul. Sofiuska 16/16
252006 Kiev 1
Ukraine
tel: +380 44 228 3304
fax: +380 44 229 6940

United Kingdom

Introduction

The history of British music in the 20th century is a remarkable one. Between the glorious days of Tudor music and the end of the 19th century, British music was essentially defunct, producing not a single work of note except for the satirical operas of Gilbert and Sullivan, its only event of consequence being the work of the German Handel in London. By the 1990s, Britain had not only produced a handful of major international composers, but many of the larger number of accomplished secondary British composers had become familiar internationally.

The genesis of this Renaissance was in large part due to the Irishman Sir Charles Villiers **Stanford** (1852–1924 – see under 'Eire'), who revitalized music teaching at Cambridge University, and included many of the most celebrated of the next generation of British composers among his pupils. Other important contributions were made by Sir Hubert Parry (1848–1918), professor of music at Oxford for eight years, by Sir George Grove (1820–1900), who edited the massive and extraordinary music dictionary that bears his name, and by Sir Henry Wood (1869–1944), who took charge of the Promenade Concerts in 1895, and who included the works of the latest British and foreign composers in his programmes. What convinced the general musical public that Britain had a composer to match the works of such as Mendelssohn, Grieg and Dvořák, was the music, especially such popular music as marches and patriotic songs, of Sir Edward **Elgar** (1857–1934). The power and impact of his most important works took longer to be internationally recognised, but he has now taken his place as one of the major figures of late-Romantic music. Frederick **Delius** (1862–1934) was the main British composer to embrace Impressionism, combining it with the settings and sensibilities of English subjects, with a colourful passion drawn partly from his experience in Florida, and with a Germanic ruggedness and philosophical impulse in his major choral works. His cosmopolitan achievement influenced and encouraged a number of later British composers.

The other celebrated figure of his generation was Dame Ethyl Smyth (1858–1944), writer, composer and suffragette. She found a more ready response to her music in Germany and Austria, and her output awaits a comprehensive reassessment. Her best-known work is the overture to the opera *The Wreckers* (1906), a powerful and well-constructed tone poem that bursts into passion with a memorable march. The opera itself is built around the wrecking and plunder of ships on the Cornish coast, and the attempts by a sailor and a Methodist minister's wife to prevent the practice. The noble music is dominated by the stirring writing for chorus. The *Mass in D* (1891) for soloists, chorus and orchestra with organ, an advanced work in the British context of its time, is the finest of all British 19th-century choral works – big, richly textured, Germanic and late-Romantic. In some ways it looks back to the grandeur of Berlioz, but the magnificent Credo, with its dramatic changes of mood, complex and often luminous interweaving of voices, and undercurrent of gigantic power, looks forward to **Mahler's** *Symphony No. 8*. The *Concerto for Violin, Horn and Orchestra* and *The Prison* (1925), for chorus and orchestra were the most highly regarded of her other works.

Cyril Scott (1879–1970), another composer who deserves reassessment, was seen as the English modernist of the Edwardian period. He is now remembered more as a spiritualist and the author of *Music: Its Secret Influence Throughout the Ages* (1933) and other occult books. Works such as his *Piano Concerto No. 1* (1913–14), with its exotic touches and an extended role for the glockenspiel, the *Piano Concerto No. 2* (c.1956), with its highly chromatic writing, constant rhythmic changes, and touches of mysticism, and the rich, sometimes languid chromaticism of the *Piano Sonata No. 3* (1956) suggest the possibility of interesting music that needs to be unearthed. Even more eccentric was Lord Berners (Gerald Hugh Tyrwhitt-Wilson, 1883–1950), whose works are infused with wit, glittering colours, and a Gallic grace and craftsmanship. Best known is the ballet *The Triumph of Neptune* (1926), written for Diaghilev. The scenario is based on figures from pantomime, and it tells the story of a sailor who sees Fairyland through a telescope, visits, returns to find his wife with a beau, is turned into a prince, and marries Neptune's daughter. The music is full of verve, delightful colour, instrumental wit, and a hazy lyricism in its series of miniatures. His piano music has the influence of Impressionism (*Le poisson d'or*) and something of the satirical wit of **Satie** (*Three Little Funeral Marches*, commemorating a

statesman, a canary and an aunt). The prolific Bernard van Dieren (1887–1936, born in Holland of Dutch and Irish parents) was influenced by **Busoni**, initially experimental in harmony, occasionally Impressionistic (following **Delius**), later more tonal; on available evidence, he is a composer whose experimenting nature was not matched by a personal, idiomatic voice; he was perhaps hampered by his regular illnesses. His earlier piano music, such as the *Six Sketches* (1910–11), is essentially atonal, with a sense of introverted exploration. His fourth and fifth string quartets include a double-bass in the quartet; the Delian *Chinese Symphony* (1914), for soloist, chorus and orchestra uses the same poems as **Mahler's** *Das Lied von der Erde*. His songs, wide-ranging in idiom, are perhaps his most permanent legacy.

With the exception of **Elgar**, all these composers were essentially widening the range of British composition to acknowledge and include the various contemporary developments in European music, and as such remain at a tangent to the British musical renaissance. For that renaissance, propelled by the generation of composers born in the 1870s and 1880s, was founded on two elements that created a specifically British idiom: the resurgence of the English song, in parallel with the new literary vitality of English poetry, and the rediscovery of English folk music that led to the sound of English pastoralism, in parallel with a renewed social awareness of the English landscape and heritage. The revival of English folk music was led by Cecil Sharp (1859–1924), who founded the English Folk Dance Society (1911), and by the towering figure of the late developer Ralph **Vaughan Williams** (1872–1958). His best-loved works are in the pastoral style, but went far beyond its limitations in his large output, especially in his nine symphonies, the finest by any British composer. The melodic content of the English pastoral style is often founded on folk music; the harmonic content is largely traditional, but gains a distinctive sound from the use of Church and Renaissance modes that arose from the reappreciation of English Tudor music. The most distinctive aspect of the idiom is its uncanny evocation of the varied English landscape, with a joy and wonder in its contemplation intertwined with a nostalgia for its history and heritage. Arthur Somervell (1863–1937), John **Ireland** (1879–1962), George Butterworth (1885–1916) and Ernest **Moeran** (1894–1950) are all best remembered for works deeply imbued with the spirit of the English landscape and British folk music. Herbert **Howells** (1892–1983) embraced the idiom in his chamber music, and incorporated its influence in church music. Gerald **Finzi** (1901–56) turned the idiom, and the English literary heritage, to effective use in choral works. Gustav **Holst** (1874–1934), best known for his orchestral suite *The Planets* (which is not typical of his work), combined the pastoral style with Eastern philosophies and musical influences. The roots of Frank **Bridge** (1879–1941) were in the pastoral tradition, but part by in reaction to the horrors of World War I, he developed a more rugged, advanced, and pessimistic idiom, extending beyond conventional tonality.

An offshoot of this tradition was a renewal of interest in the Celtic heritage. The major composer of this movement, and one of the finest British composers of the century, was Sir Arnold **Bax** (1883–1953), who composed in a late-Romantic idiom, stretching tonality, and whose, seething, complex textures and emotions are at their finest in his seven symphonies. Sir Granville **Bantock** (1868–1946) veered between Celtic orchestral works and music reflecting his deep interest in Persian and Arabic culture. The output of Rebecca Clarke (1886–1979) was small but fine, especially the *Viola Sonata* (1919), a late-Romantic work influenced by **Bloch** and tempered in the central short vivace by Impressionism, and the *Piano Trio* (1921), a grittier work that starts where the sonata had left off.

All these composers contributed to the resurgence of the English song, in which the English landscape, its characters and its history play a major part. The most significant poetic impulse of this resurgence was perhaps the poetry of A. E. Housman (1859–1936), whose combination of the evocation of the Shropshire landscape, a consistent sense of loss and regret that came to seem especially pertinent in the emotional aftermath of World War I, and the exceptionally musical verse attracted almost all the main English composers. Anyone wishing to explore a cross-section of English song in the first half of the century could well simply explore settings of his poetry. Perhaps the finest of the song-composers was Ivor **Gurney** (1890–1937). The most arresting work of the psychologically disturbed Peter Warlock (real name Philip Heseltine, 1894–1930), who edited three hundred old English songs, is the song-cycle *The Curlew* (1920–21), for tenor, string quartet,

flute and cor anglais. In its linked settings of four W. B. Yeats poems, the cor anglais reflects the sound of the bird of the title and the overall mood is one of desolation. Many of his other songs, easy-flowing but with subtle shadings and detail, and ranging from nursery songs to works of jauntiness and profound sadness, are very fine. Roger Quilter (1887–1953) is now remembered entirely for his songs.

Some younger composers, such as William **Alwyn** (1905–85), continued to have their roots in English pastoralism, but the reaction against the general style came in the 1930s, in part reflecting the political and social concerns of the period. Sir William **Walton** (1902–83) echoed **Satie** in his *Façade* (1923), but then injected a new sense of power and turmoil (heralded by **Bax**) into his *Symphony No. 1* (1935); **Vaughan Williams** found a similar explosive quality in his *Symphony No. 1* (1931–34). Walton's oratorio *Belshazzar's Feast* (1931) introduced an element of barbarism into a rather moribund English oratorio tradition. Its self-confident brashness influenced the marvellous short cantata *The Blacksmiths* (1934), for mixed chorus and orchestra or strings, two pianos, timpani and percussion, by Sir George Dyson (1883–1964). An adaptation of an alliterative Middle English text, it is dramatic, percussive in feel, taut in its word setting, unexpected in its direct power of portraiture. His other choral works have been largely forgotten, but the thick-textured cantata *Sweet Thames Run Softly* (1955) for baritone, chorus and orchestra, with its echoes of **Delius** and the English pastoral tradition, well matches its title. Of other composers less influenced by pastoralism, Edmund **Rubbra** (1901–86) concentrated on symphonies of contrapuntal energy, the later works reflecting religious themes. Sir Lennox **Berkeley** (1903–89) emerged as the most abstract of English composers, delighting in craftsmanship, instrumental precision, and a restrained pleasure in music-making. Alan Rawsthorne (1905–71) also brought an accomplished craftsmanship and a northern English ruggedness to largely abstract works, influenced by **Hindemith**.

Throughout the 19th and 20th centuries, London's Covent Garden continued to be a major international opera house, but English opera remained parochial, and its one masterpiece, **Vaughan Williams's** *Riders to the Sea* (1936), largely unnoticed, until the advent of two major composers, Benjamin **Britten** (1913–76) and Michael **Tippett** (1905–98), and the first performance of the former's *Peter Grimes* in 1945. Britten's musical idiom broke no new ground, but his instinctive response to words, his sure musico-dramatic sense, his pervasive theme of innocence lost and its consequences, and his strongly personal idiomatic musical language created a most distinctive and individual voice. Tippett has been more exploratory within a mainstream heritage, and his operas have been built around Jungian principles. For both composers opera was merely the central aspect of their genius; Britten's song-cycles and choral works are as powerful as his operas, and Tippett has extended his idiom into such forms as the symphony.

By the end of World War II, English music, although now well established, was essentially conservative and insular in spirit. Elizabeth Lutyens (1906–83) had been one of the first composers to embrace 12-tone techniques after hearing **Webern** in 1938, but her music was generally overlooked in the 1950s and 1960s, and her large output deserves reappraisal. Much of her finest work involves the voice, ranging from the delicacy of the setting of Rimbaud's *O saisons, o châteaux* (1946) for soprano, guitar, harp, violin and strings, through the use of baritone and soprano in the largely orchestra *Quincunx* (1959–60), to the Quasimodo setting *And Suddenly it's Evening* (1966) for tenor and eleven instruments. Her output includes a large body of chamber music, and stage works such as the music-theatre *The Linnet from the Leaf* (1972) and the 'scena' *One and the Same* which uses mime. The music of Nicholas Maw (born 1935) absorbed a wide range of contemporary European influences, and went through a serial phase, before arriving at a sumptuous sound in *Scenes and Arias* (1962), for soprano, mezzo-soprano, contralto and orchestra (setting a *c.*14th-century love-letter and the reply). His stylistic journeys have culminated in the gigantic *Odyssey* (1974–89) for orchestra, over ninety minutes in length.

Alexander Goehr (born in Berlin, 1932) infused a younger generation of composers with new Continental ideas and the examples of **Stravinsky** and **Schoenberg**, although his own compositions did not have the same impact. A group of these younger composers became known in the 1950s as the 'Manchester school'; the major figures were Harrison **Birtwistle** (born 1934), whose especial achievement has been ritualistic operas and music-theatre works of a singular individuality, and Peter Maxwell **Davies** (born 1934), whose

idiom has ranged from hard-hitting avant-garde instrumental, orchestral and music-theatre works to attractive music aimed at a wider audience and inspired by his adopted home of the Orkney Islands. The Marxist Cornelius Cardew (1936–81) was the most extreme of the British avant-garde composers, a brief flare of a phenomenon now best remembered for his 'scratch orchestra' consisting of musicians of widely varying talents. David Bedford (born 1937) produced some of the most promising music of the English avant-garde, especially the *Two Patchen Poems* (1966) for choir, influenced by **Ligeti**, and *Star's End* (1974) for orchestra. Using amplified guitars in the orchestra to memorable and haunting effect, this is one of the finest British orchestral works of its period, creating emotive vistas of the night sky and the explosion of the star of the title in a forthright structure. He then moved through an unfortunate phase of ineffectual quasi-pop music, and his more recent works have not had the impact of the earlier. In a more mainstream tradition, John McCabe (born 1939) was influenced by **Hartmann**, to whom he paid tribute in the *Variations on a Theme of Karl Amadeus Hartmann* (1964) for orchestra, mixing the rugged with the delicate in clear-cut colours. His output includes three symphonies, an opera based on CS Lewis, *The Lion, the Witch and the Wardrobe* (1969), and the most effective song-cycle *Notturni ed alba* (1970), for soprano and orchestra, where the often sensual orchestral textures (including a large percussion section) graphically support the four poems of night and sleep based on Latin medieval texts. His best-known work is the orchestral suite *Chagall Windows* (1974), an abstract evocation of Chagall's twelve stained-glass windows at the Hadassah-Hebrew University in Jerusalem, organised symphonically, where McCabe's clear-cut sense of bright orchestral colour admirably matches the inspiration. This generation also includes the more conservative Malcolm Lipkin (born 1932) and David Morgan (born 1933), whose neo-Romantic music, following a European mainstream tradition, includes a beautiful and sensuously passionate *Violin Concerto* (1967), four symphonies and six string quartets.

The generation of British composers born in the later 1940s and 1950s has been especially interesting, deserving more coverage that this *Guide* can accommodate. Many of these composers have come to the fore in the late 1980s and 1990s, and seem destined to produce their most significant work in the 21st century; certainly all the composers discussed in the following are worth encountering. The depth of quality and quantity of these composers partly reflects the emancipation of British music from more insular and conservative outlooks, and particularly the gradual disappearance of music critics brought up in an age that viewed Continental musical developments with deep mistrust. Brian **Ferneyhough** (born 1943) continued to develop total serialism into what has become known as the 'New Complexity'. The music of Michael Finnissy (born 1946), also springing from the avant-garde, can appear similarly complex, but includes such works as *Cabaret vert* (1985), for voice and two instrumentalists that uses the simplest of effects and means drawn from Eastern folk-musics. Other musics have sometimes been the starting-point of his own inspiration, such as the intervals of a Romanian folk song in *Câtana* (1984) for ensemble. His *String Trio* (1986) uses **Mahler's** *Symphony No. 9* as its general source, its melodic material drawn from the symphony, its twenty-eight sections following the symphony's tempo markings. Himself a formidable pianist, Finnissy is probably best known for his piano music, notably the long *English Country Tunes* (1979), characteristically wide-ranging in effect and emotion.

The minimalist movement is represented by Michael **Nyman** (born 1944), the more mainstream integration of avant-garde techniques by Michael **Berkeley** (born 1948) and Oliver **Knussen** (born 1952). Robin Holloway (born 1943) has a kind of sumptuous Viennese *fin-de-siècle* imagination transported into the late 20th century. The *Scenes from Schumann* (1971) for orchestra use Schumann tunes as their base in a welter of allusion; the vibrant, sometimes raucous and perhaps over-lush *Concerto No. 2* (1979) uses block procedures and dabs of orchestral colour, constantly tugging towards the neo-Romantic, to which it eventually succumbs in an orgy of orchestral sound. The *Viola Concerto* (1983–84) is a lyrical work in four movements. A major achievement was his opera *Clarissa* (begun 1971, performed 1990), based on Richardson's novel and recreating the mood but not the musical styles of the 18th century. After earlier explorations of serialism, a similar richness of orchestral colour and complexity of effect is found in the music of Colin Matthews (born 1946) in such works as the series of orchestral 'sonatas', the *Cello*

Concerto (1983–84) or, in more fragmented fashion, in *Sun Dance* (1985) for orchestra.

The earlier music of Gavin Bryers (born 1943) followed the model of **Cage**, culminating in an evocation of the disaster of *The Sinking of the Titanic* (1969). After the opera *Medea* (1982–84) his idiom has become eclectic, drawing on inspirational sources as far apart as jazz and the chromaticism of Viennese music at the turn of the century, often with repetitive rhythmic elements. It is infused throughout with a gentle sense of irony and wit, exemplified in his choices of texts for the vocal works, with something of the lateral view of the world of one of his major influences, Marcel Duchamp. Brian Elias (born 1948) has written emotional and passionate works in a post-**Berg** milieu influenced by his teacher Lutyens, lean and with a touch of the archaic in the vocal lines of *Somnia* (1979), for tenor and orchestra, emotionally and sometimes lyrically expressive in *L'Eylah* (1984) for orchestra. Nigel Osborne (born 1948) adopted the less startling effects and procedures of the legacy of the avant-garde for an expressive idiom with heightened emotions, sometimes inspired by Soviet poets. (Voznesenky in *I am Goya*, 1977, for baritone and chamber ensemble, Mayakovsky and Esenin in *The Sickle*, 1975, for soprano with chamber ensemble, the flute and guitar prominent). *Poem Without a Hero* (1980) for voices and instruments, is based on Anna Akhmatova in what amounts to a dramatic cantata, using speech effects and extended vocal techniques. This Russian interest culminated in the opera *The Electrification of the Soviet Union* (1987), using a chamber orchestra with tape and based on a Pasternak story. His music also has a more subdued lyrical side, as in the slow movement of the virtuoso *Concerto for Flute and Chamber Orchestra* (1980), while the *Sinfonia* (1982) has a more direct appeal, coloured with an almost neo-Romantic hue in the slow first movement (using a Gaelic folk song and reflecting events in Northern Ireland) and Caribbean-inspired drums in the second.

John Casken (born 1949) was initially influenced by **Lutosławski** and the Polish avant-garde, in such works as *Amarantos* (1978) for nine instruments, with its slow block-like movement, but progressed to an uneasy lyricism (with touches of Near East inflections) in the *Cello Concerto*. *Golem* (completed 1989) tells the story of the clay man who comes to life, his effect on a Jewish family and community, and eventual demise, in an interesting opera of the interaction of subconscious and conscious forces, using electronic and instrumental forces. It is a combination of more disjointed post avant-garde effects and a lyricism drawn with more traditional harmonic brush-strokes that does not quite match the potential of the libretto. Dominic Muldowney (born 1952), who studied with **Birtwistle** and succeeded him as musical director at the National Theatre, has been noted for his concertos, including the *Saxophone Concerto* (1984), incorporating jazz elements, the *Percussion Concerto* (1991) and *Violin Concerto* (1992), and his vocal settings of Brecht. His style can include an astute compendium of different traits, ranging from the neo-Romantically lyrical to the hard-hewn serial in the *String Quartet No. 2* (1980).

Robert Saxton (born 1953) has developed a sound of intense orchestral or instrumental density, often furious movement, and colourful tapestry effects, founded on the movement of harmonies that hover between the tonal and the more acerbic, looking for resolutions. Many of his works have literary inspirations; there is a vitality, a young almost explosive energy to the *Concerto for Orchestra* (1984), inspired by the Kabbala, whose panache is continued in such works as the *Violin Concerto*. The theme of his opera *Caritas* (1991), to a libretto by Arnold Wesker, is the immurement of a young woman in a medieval church. George Benjamin (born 1960) has written aural landscapes using post-avant-garde techniques, ranging from the bold colour and timbral effects of *At First Light* (1982), inspired by a Turner painting of a castle against the sun, to the rarefied, distilled effects of the fragile *Antara* (1987), with electronics.

Classical composition in Wales is largely a 20th-century achievement, in spite of the reputation of the Welsh as singers. The founders of modern Welsh music were Grace **Williams** (1906–77), whose haunting atmospheric idiom owed much to **Vaughan Williams**, and Daniel **Jones** (1912–93), whose principal achievement was in the field of the symphony and string quartet. Alun **Hoddinott** (born 1929) has combined modern mainstream elements with a strong sense of the Welsh Celtic heritage, while William **Mathias** (1934–92) was chiefly noted for his choral music. Of other Welsh composers, David Wynne (1900–83) was influenced by **Bartók**, and his strong chamber music is well worth encountering. Mervyn Burtch (born 1929) has concentrated on vocal works, particularly works and operas for children. John Metcalf

(born 1946) has become a major figure in Welsh opera composition.

Scottish composition has been dominated by the figure of Peter Maxwell **Davies**, who although born in Manchester, has recently adopted an idiom drawing on tradition Scottish music. Iain Hamilton (born 1922), a serialist in the 1950s, is now best known for his operas, notably *The Royal Hunt of the Sun* (1967–69), based on the Peter Shaffer play, and *Anna Karenina* (1981), based on Tolstoy. Edward Harper (born 1941) has followed a mainstream path: the *Symphony* (1978) draws on **Elgar** for its basic material, though the result is contemporary, and his *Clarinet Concerto* (1982) is an attractive work, neo-Romantic in spirit. Judith Weir (born 1954) has developed a striking instinct for dramatic works, often economical and precise, as in the ten-minute 'grand opera' *King Harald's Saga* (1979) and *The Vanishing Bridegroom* (1990), using Scottish folk-themes. Her sources of inspiration have been eclectic. The appealing *Airs from Another Planet* (1986) for chamber ensemble, conjures up a picture of Scottish settlers in Mars. The opera *A Night at the Chinese Opera* (1987) is one of a number of works drawing on Chinese culture; and the Bayeaux Tapestry inspired *Thread!* (1981) for narrator and ensemble.

An incomparable element in the development of British music from obscurity to international eminence has been the work of the British Broadcasting Corporation (the BBC) founded in 1922. Its Radio Three (formerly the Third Programme) has the highest standards of any classical music radio station in the world, thanks to the enlightened and so far prevailing view that the hidden benefits in promoting British musical culture far outweigh the immediate economics of its relatively small audience. It also supports its own orchestras, and the finest and most comprehensive series of concerts anywhere in the world, the Promenade Concerts at the Albert Hall, London. In the 1990s these standards and achievements have been under threat from that curse of late 20th-century societies, the philistine American corporate mentality; it is to be hoped that erosion of the BBC's standards will continue to be resisted.

Music Information Centres: Britain has three music centres, reflecting the three constituent countries of the mainland:

British Music Information Centre
10 Stratford Place
London W1N 9AE

tel: +44 0171 499 8567 (to dial from outside the UK, omit the 0 from 0171)
fax: +44 0171 499 479 (to dial from outside the UK, omit the 0 from 0171)

Scottish Music Information Centre
1, Bowmont Gardens
Glasgow G12 9LR
tel: +441 41 334 6393
fax: +441 41 334 8132

Guild for the Promotion of Welsh Music
Angel Chambers
94, Walter Road
Swansea SA1 5QA
tel: +441 1792 464623
fax: +441 1792 648501

Alwyn William*
born 7th November 1905 at Northampton
died 11th September 1985 at Southwold

William Alwyn is probably better known for his film music (over sixty scores) than for his rather conservative concert music, which nonetheless has continued to have strong adherents, and may well appeal to those who enjoy a traditional but ruggedly individual and cosmopolitan idiom. A painter and writer as well as a composer, he acknowledged only the works written after 1939, when he reappraised his position and in particular his technique, which he considered inadequate.

The major earlier works were the *Piano Concerto* (1930) and the oratorio *The Marriage of Heaven and Hell* (1936). There followed a period of neo-classical music (including three *Concerti Grossi* for orchestra, 1942, 1951, 1964), until he turned to a number of unashamedly Romantic works (now termed 'neo-Romantic') in the middle of the 1950s, in a self-professed search for musical beauty. By the 1960s he had adapted the uses of rows from 12-tone techniques, marrying them to his tonal base, as in the short and pithy *String Trio* (1961), which is also under the influence of Indian classical music and scales. His style, however, is lyrical and usually rhapsodic throughout, moulding and exploring soft orchestral colours. It is free in feel, usually using ostinati and ground basses in preference to any strong sense of counterpoint. What prevents his lyrical idiom from appearing merely anachronistic is the unobtrusive but highly refined craftsmanship. This

gives a feeling of strength and sometimes of ruggedness that blends with and supports the lyricism. Drama is sometimes inherent (especially in the symphonies), but is muted by his long melodic lines.

The core of his output are five symphonies, which attracted attention both inside and outside Britain as they became more widely known in the 1970s, and three string quartets. The conventional *Symphony No. 1* (1949) is in the grand style, rather rambling and unmemorable, but with characteristically clear and prominent brass writing. In the next three symphonies he developed his use of rows, building material from the initial row: in both the third and the fourth symphonies the row is divided to provide two interacting and contrasting keys. The *Symphony No. 3* (1956) includes a romantic and beautiful ending (with soaring violins in octaves). The *Symphony No. 4* (1959) is more muted, ending with a passacaglia, whereas the *Symphony No. 5* (1973), inspired by the 17th-century prose writer Sir Thomas Browne, is perhaps the most immediately compelling, with a strong sense of drama and changing mood. Also inspired by extra-musical associations (here the mystical poetry of the 17th-century English poet Fletcher) is the very attractive and rhapsodic *Concerto for Harp and String Orchestra 'Lyra Angelica'* (1954), where the harp is closely integrated into the orchestral colours, and where there is an English sense of nobility.

Of his chamber music, the lyrical, sometimes yearning *String Quartet No. 1* (1955) concentrates on tone colour rather than formal matters, and is eclectic in its synthesis of romantic influences. The *String Quartet No. 2 (Spring Waters*, 1975), which, like the first, has something of the atmosphere of **Janáček's** two string quartets, is a haunting, valedictory, but affirmative work, loosely following hopes and disillusions from youth to old age. The *String Quartet No. 3* followed in 1984. The three *Concerti Grossi*, of which the second is a rather indistinctive work for strings, and the third explores different colours in each movement (brass, woodwind and strings), was followed by the first *Sinfonietta* (1970) for strings. His piano music includes a set of eleven *Fantasy-Waltzes*, neo-classical remouldings of the salon music tradition. His vocal output is small; the song-cycle *Mirages* is a setting of his own verse. In the 1970s he concentrated on two major large-scale operas. *Don Juan or the Libertine* (1972–76) is a symbolic and sometimes ironic modern retelling of the

406 **United Kingdom,** Alwyn

Don Juan story. The highly-charged *Miss Julie* (1977) is based on Strindberg's play, the vocal lines having the flow of speech, the orchestral textures in constant flux. It is ultimately overwhelmed by the strength of the play on which it is based, in spite of the powerful portrait of the title role.

Alwyn was also a flautist and a conductor, and taught at the Royal Academy of Music from 1926 to 1955.

RECOMMENDED WORKS
Concerto for Harp and String
Orchestra (*Lyra Angelica*) (1954)
String Quartet No. 1 in D minor (1955)
Symphony No. 5 (*Hydriotaphia*)
(1973)

Arnold Malcolm Henry*
born 21st October 1921 at
Northampton

Malcolm Arnold is something of an anomaly in modern English music: a prolific, sometimes brilliant but often depressingly banal composer totally out of touch with the developments of the second half of the 20th century. His orchestral command is sometimes powerful enough to have an infectious sparkle, but he writes in an idiom whose basis is so anachronistic that – apart from the music written for pure entertainment, which carries its own built-in purpose – it seems to have little relevance.

Arnold's mastery of the orchestra came from his years as an orchestral trumpeter, with the London Philharmonic Orchestra (1941–42 and 1946–48) and with the BBC Symphony Orchestra (1942–46). His diatonic harmonic idiom is usually conservative but his orchestration is always strikingly clear, and sometimes he delights both in using unexpected but effective combinations of instruments, and in including some element of surprise in a work – a sudden change of dynamic, an unexpected change of emotional direction. His structures are usually conventional, but within them he will often propound a theme, examine it, and then reject it.

The best of his brilliant orchestral showpieces are so full of deft touches, infectious tunes and humour that they deserve to survive. The comedy overture *Beckus the Dandipratt* (1943) abounds in odd and impish instrumental juxtapositions and the lively urgency of the urchin of the title. The orchestral folk-song suites *English Dances* and the *Four Scottish Dances* (1957) are vividly entertaining, especially

the latter, with their grandiose opening and a Hebridean slow dance. With the exception of a Robert Burns tune in the Scottish set, they do not use actual folk songs but original tunes in the appropriate style. But the best of these occasional pieces is the marvellous overture *Tam O'Shanter* (1955), a miniature tone poem with a strong Scottish flavour built around a graphic storm that owes much to the example of Berlioz.

With his flair for melody rather than for formal construction, Arnold's symphonies are too amorphous to be of real interest, and the *Symphony No. 4* (1960), with its Afro-Cuban percussion section, and a Hollywood-style finale with touches of the macabre of **Shostakovich**, must be one of the most banal ever written. The impressive moments, such as the gentle and restrained slow movement in the *Symphony No. 6* (1967) or the impressive slow movement of the *Symphony No. 2* (influenced by **Sibelius**), only makes their many facile passages the more disappointing. All too often the darker emotions seem assumed, rather than inherent. The exception is perhaps the *Symphony No. 5* (1961), where the popular elements are much more rigorously examined and then transformed, and what emerges is an eclectic and unsettling work.

The large number of concertos are essentially works of pleasant music-making, exemplified by the easygoing *Organ Concerto* (1955). The one most likely to be encountered is the *Guitar Concerto* (1959), complete with the usual memorable tune in the first movement. A different side of Arnold's output is shown in his chamber pieces, written with strong sensitivity for the instruments concerned, and mixing humour and melodiousness with an effortless, armchair charm. They sometimes have structural tricks, such as the passacaglia of the *Piano Trio* (1956), where each entry moves up a semitone until all twelve notes are covered. They include the deftly characterised series of short *Sonatinas* for solo wind instruments and piano (1948, 1951, 1951, 1953), and the much more virtuoso series of short *Fantasies* (1966), for solo wind. (1966). His best-known chamber work is probably the *Three Sea Shanties* (1943), for wind quintet, full of felicitous discordancies. But these works, too, lack an individual voice or a sensibility beyond the superficial; for all that, they will give relaxing pleasure to many who like their music mainly as a divertissement.

As his style would suggest, Arnold has

been a conspicuously successful and prolific composer of film scores, notably *The Bridge on the River Kwai* (1959), for which he won an Oscar.

RECOMMENDED WORKS
> overture *Tam O'Shanter* (1955)
> Sinfonietta No. 1 (1954)
> Symphony No. 5 (1960)

Bantock (Sir) Granville*
born 7th August 1868 at London
died 16th September 1946 at London

Sir Granville Bantock's fame, certainly in the earlier part of his life, was out of all proportion to his current reputation, which has suffered from the reaction in the 1930s against his style of music. In addition, the very large-scale nature, often in both duration and size of forces, of the best of his huge output has militated against revival.

His rich idiom was derived from late-Romanticism and the example of Wagner, but his interest in exotic (especially Eastern), Greek, and Celtic subjects is very British, as is his Romantic treatment of such material. Indeed, it is Bantock, rather than **Elgar**, who represents in music that exploring, enquiring, slightly gullible wandering spirit of the best of the late-Victorian English Romantics. He is also the one English composer whose idiom belongs to the late-Romantic rich outpouring that includes **Zemlinsky** and **Pfitzner**. His two masterpieces both include choral forces: the huge three-part setting of Fitzgerald's *Omar Khayyám* (1906), and the 'choral symphony' *Atalanta in Calydon* (1912). The former is essentially a song-cycle for soloists, chorus and orchestra, though very long, at around two hours. It comes partly from the tradition of the English oratorio (in the part-writing for chorus), partly from the Wagnerian Germanic tradition. But at the same time there is some wonderfully delicate tone-painting in the orchestration, occasionally almost Impressionistic, to contrast with larger moments, and above all a linear flow. This drive, with sinuous lines of counterpoint, gives a rarefied undulating thrust that epitomises the work. Although it suffers from its considerable length, just when the inspiration seems to flag a new moment of swell and flow almost invariably emerges to recapture the attention. This is an English masterpiece full of the warmest fervour, and it deserves to be unearthed. *Atalanta in Calydon* is for unaccompanied choir, divided into three to correspond to the tone colours of sections of an orchestra. The first, a six-part mixed choir, parallels the string section; the second, a three-part mixed choir, the woodwind; the third, a four-part male voice choir, the brass.

Of his orchestral music, the best known is *Fifine at the Fair* (1901), the third in a set of *Six Tone Poems*. Based on Browning, it is a lively, richly scored and descriptive work, well worth hearing. The *Hebridean Symphony* (1915), descriptive of the sea, was quite widely admired at the time of its composition. It is a splendid work, more a tone poem than a symphony, with a very wide range of mood and drama. Bantock's skill at orchestral colour blazes out, and there are polyrhythmic moments, as well as a distinct nod in the direction of Mendelssohn's *Hebrides Overture* in the very opening. Those who enjoy the best of **Bax**'s tone poems will find this equally rewarding. The *Pagan Symphony* (1923) is a wonderfully sumptuous one-movement tone poem divided into four symphonic sections, its orchestration decadently rich, its tone a pictorial representation of the sensuousness of a pre-Christian, Nature-orientated world. The *Celtic Symphony* (1940) for strings and six harps, in which Hebridean folk songs are used, is a rich and beautiful work in one movement, divided into sections matching those of a symphony. It follows the English tradition of large-scale string works, here with the addition of the sonorous textures of the harps and with broad and memorable melodies.

There is much music by Bantock waiting to be explored, and it may be, judging by the quality of some of the work that does have the occasional outing, that interesting and important works will surface in an age more indulgent to his idiom. Bantock was also an important and influential teacher, with more advanced views than his own music might suggest. He was principal of the Birmingham School of Music (1900–08), and professor at Birmingham University (1908–34). He was knighted in 1930.

RECOMMENDED WORKS
> choral symphony *Atalanta in Calydon* (1912)
> *Celtic Symphony* (1940) for strings and six harps
> tone poem *Fifine at the Fair* (1901)
> *Omar Khayyám* (1906) for soloists, chorus and orchestra
> *Hebridean Symphony* (1915)
> *Pagan Symphony* (1928)

BIBLIOGRAPHY
> M. Bantock, *Granville Bantock*, 1972

Bax (Sir) Arnold Edward Trevor°°

born 8th November 1883 at London
died 3rd October 1953 at Cork

The music of Arnold Bax, for so long a neglected British master, has undergone an astonishing revival in the last few years, mainly owing to the advocacy of a handful of British conductors and the enterprise of one British recording company. His name, deservedly, is now known throughout the arena of Western classical music, a position unthinkable in the 1970s.

The leading composer of the Celtic revival in Britain, Bax was deeply influenced by Irish thought and culture, and indeed successfully wrote Irish stories under the name Dermont O'Bryne. Throughout his work, his idiom is Romantic, usually within the framework of traditional structures, and his evocation of mood is often prompted by non-musical events or places. His style displays a fecundity of idea and effect, whose virtue is the multiplicity of invention, and whose vice is a tendency to over-complex detail and ornamentation, leading occasionally to apparent disjointedness. However, that complexity is necessary to his harmonic palette, which is sensual and richly chromatic, extending traditional harmony to its boundaries, although in later works the chromatic colours are used against a diatonic base. His compelling orchestration, usually of large or very large forces, is thick in texture, sometimes brilliant in detail, and often explores the extreme ranges of more unusual instruments; the use of the lowest register of a darker coloured instrument can give a sense of great aural space or depth, especially in the symphonies. His idiom requires rapid changes of mood, emphasis and rhythm, and it was partly the difficulties that orchestral players had with these, and the consequent unsatisfactory performances, that caused his neglect until orchestras became used to playing much more complex modern music. In addition, his later works sometimes avoided the denser, emotional Celticism, with mixed results, leading to an impression of creative decline.

His most effective works are for the medium of the tone poem, the symphony or chamber music. His early works (mainly chamber music and songs) are excessively complex in technique and melodic invention, but a relative simplification coincided with his desire to express Celtic mythology in music. This led to a series of orchestral tone poems on Celtic subjects, epic in intent, rich in texture and melodic expression, and portraying a wide range of moods and emotions. In *Spring Fire* (1913), inspired by Swinburne and the paganism of Diaghilev's ballet company, the luxuriance of invention is out of control, though its marvellous passionate moments of orchestral power make it worth hearing. This was followed by Bax's three finest tone poems, in which he concentrated his musical imagination while retaining all his descriptive powers. In *The Garden of Fand* (1913–16) a miraculous mid-Atlantic island is described in music conveying the rise and fall of the sea, with harp and celesta creating sparkling effects, a restless storm, and a gradual change of mood towards the calm end. *November Woods* (1917) is turbulent, while *Tintagel* (1917–19), the finest of these Celtic-inspired works, describes the Cornish seat of King Mark in the Tristan story. It has a rugged, sometimes explosive vigour, with a Sibelian mystery in the opening and an allusion to Wagner's *Tristan und Isolde*. The fourth tone poem of this period, *The Happy Forest* (1914–21), is more Russian in feel, with exuberant fifes and drums and a lovely broad theme. Of his later and shorter orchestral works, *Mediterranean* (1920, orchestrated 1922) is a kind of Spanish waltz, and of the three *Northern Ballads* (c. 1927–34) inspired by the 'fiery romantic life' of the historical Scottish Highlands, the second is a powerful work, the third the most interesting – expansive, constantly changing mood, and emotionally complex. The once popular *Overture to a Picaresque Comedy* (1930) is great fun, if not characteristic of Bax's general idiom. Describing various characters from theatrical comedy, it combines an intentionally Straussian cast (with many near references) with an English rumbustiousness.

Bax wrote a number of concertante works. The *Phantasy for Viola and Orchestra* (1920) includes one of Bax's rare quotes of an actual Irish folk song. The Edwardian flavour of the *Cello Concerto* (1932) rambles too much to be of real interest, in spite of an atmospheric slow movement. Much finer is the *Violin Concerto* (1938), with a slow and thoughtful central movement framed by two dance movements, in the first of which the sweetly lyrical second subject at one point almost turns into a spiritual. This attractive concerto, with lighter textures than Bax commonly employed, deserves to be better known. More likely to be encountered are the two works for piano and orchestra. In the relatively few major works for piano and orchestra from the highly chromatic twilight of late-Romanticism, Bax's *Symphonic Variations* (1914–17) occupies an important place. A big work (forty-five minutes, though Bax produced shortened and simplified versions), its six variations with an intermezzo seem to follow an autobiographical journey, each variation having a descriptive title. The piano writing is densely textured, the idiom ranging from the Celtic mystery of 'Nocturne', through Impressionist and exotic effects in 'Temple' to a triumphant close. It will not appeal to everyone; its grandeur comes from the density of texture and shifting restlessness rather than from the bold flourish, and there is no obviously memorable theme. *Winter Legends* (1930), for piano and orchestra, is equally long, ranging in widely mood from the percussively barbaric to the lyrical, and less sure of its structure.

The complex emotions and dense shifting textures of Bax's idiom found their finest expression in the form of the symphony. On first encounter their three-movement forms, largely based on sonata principles, can appear amorphous. But while the progress from emotion to emotion is the dominant feature, the construction of these symphonies is much more subtle than first appears, often built on small cells of notes whose interaction becomes clearer on familiarity. A striking feature is the unity of the whole series of seven symphonies, creating (like those of **Sibelius**) a clear emotional progression, from the turbulence and anger of the first two, through a more lyrical reassessment in the third and fourth, a combination of emotional turbulence and sea-painting in the fifth, and a more mature summation of all these emotions in the sixth, to an understanding and acceptance in the seventh. The *Symphony No. 1* (1921) is a tremendous work, exploding with power and anger, and seeming to reflect the emotional legacy of World War I and the Irish Easter Rising. In three taut movements, unified by the return of the opening material as a triumphant march at the end, the scurrying rhythms of the first move

ment, the brooding basses and huge climax of the middle movement, and the heightened emotions were unlike anything written in Britain before. Some of its mood returns in the turbulent and martial third movement of the *Symphony No. 2* (1924–25), which includes organ and piano in the orchestration. The previous two movements are more relaxed, with solo lines and colours more prominent in the opening movement, emerging from the detailed textures, and with a sonorous and expressive lyricism in the slow movement, verging on the feel of the blues.

These two symphonies are the antithesis of both Edwardian musical self-satisfaction and the English pastoral movement; the *Symphony No. 3* (1929) is more accessible but less arresting. The textures are much thinner, with linear woodwind prominent, and it has moments of Mahlerian beauty in the first movement, a nocturnal atmosphere in the slow movement. An initially rather brash finale progresses through an Elgarian slow march to the innovative close, a beautiful and wistful epilogue that causes one to re-evaluate the early emotional progression of the work. The *Symphony No. 4* (1931), the most brazen and outgoing of the symphonies, is lighter in tone; inspired by the sea, it was written for a very large orchestra, including organ. The *Symphony No. 5* (1932) is dedicated to **Sibelius**, and with its quiet troubled opening and general construction it has affinities with the Finnish composer, although it is by no means an imitation. The first movement covers a wide sweep of mood, from brooding melancholy to a brutal quality emphasised by ostinato figures. The broad, homogeneous textures of the slow movement create the main weight of the work, still with an undercurrent of melancholy, but lightened by sparkling figures. The final movement, grappling with conflicting emotions towards a broad nobility and a final blaze, tries to reconcile the earlier conflict; throughout the symphony the sound vistas are huge and deep, including great subterranean hammer-blows, as if Bax was equating mood-painting of the northern seas with a complex internal struggle.

The symphonic experience of all these symphonies culminates in the magnificent *Symphony No. 6* (1934). The pulse and tension of the opening movement has a fabulous energy and momentum, with ostinato figures interrupted by huge chords, moments of more studied contemplation always hauled back into the tempestuous restlessness. The tone-painting of the central movement, with slowly swirling textures and lazily drifting melodies that gradually evolve into a shadowy march-like image, creates a disturbing ambiguity. Both these movements are preparation for the extraordinary final movement, cast in three sections: introduction, scherzo with trio, and epilogue. Its opening, with a long clarinet solo, is gentle, nostalgic, slightly melancholy, opposed by the dance of the scherzo, which is interrupted by the gently swaying strings and harps of the trio before returning in the guise of a demonic storm, as the emotional culmination of Bax's turbulence. This final outpouring dies down into the lovely epilogue. Hence the horns, harps and hushed strings are prominent in the delicate textures, disturbed by ostinato figures and distant mutterings from timpani. The final mood is one of peace and acceptance, a reconciliation of all the moods not only of this symphony, but of the earlier ones as well. The *Symphony No. 7* (1939) is freer and more fluid in construction, bolder and brighter, with distinctly Elgarian elements (as well as the Tristan quote used in *Tintagel*). Heard on its own it might seem too nebulous, too easily positive, but the most effective way to hear this symphony is to listen to it immediately after the sixth, when the true character of this last symphony becomes apparent: a triumphant affirmation of the sixth's epilogue, an emotional movement from reconciliation to a positive understanding.

Bax was perfectly capable of writing dull music, and the *Sinfonietta* (1932) is no match for the symphonies. Likewise, the considerable body of chamber music varies from some of the most effective of all British chamber music to such relatively uninteresting works as the *Piano Trio* (1945). The finest of the chamber works is the *Viola Sonata* (1921), powerful and yet lyrical, single-minded in its emotional mood. Works such as *Piano Quintet* (1914–15), the *Harp Quintet* (1919), the short and tempestuous *Piano Quartet* (1922, later orchestrated as *Saga Fragment*), and the *Cello Sonata No. 1* (1923) represent Bax in his Celtic turbulence mood, with rapid changes of colour and emotion; the *Cello Sonata* uses the device of a quiet epilogue to close a three-movement work that is almost symphonic in scale. In contrast, there are a number of unpretentious and melodious chamber works, the scale more intimate, the emphasis on a more charming lyricism, including the rather rambling *Violin Sonata No. 1*

(1910–15), the light and flowing *String Quartet No. 1* (1918), the pastoral *Oboe Quintet* (1922) and the fine *Nonet* (1931) for flute, oboe, clarinet, harp and strings. The *String Quartet No. 2* (1924) is exceptionally austere, while the *String Quartet No. 3* (1936) successfully combines some of the darker, brooding Baxian emotions, including a ghostly marching dance at the core of the troubled second movement, with moments of pastoral contemplation in the opening movement, a classical serenity in the third, and an almost Bartókian dance in the last. The *Sonata for Harp and Viola* (1928) brings together two of Bax's favourite instruments, with writing of considerable technical virtuosity.

At the heart of Bax's piano music are four sonatas, the first three epic in scale. The Romantically passionate one-movement *Piano Sonata No. 1* (1910, finale 1920) was largely written in the Ukraine. Its descriptive qualities, full of rippling pianism, are clearly inspired by the Russian landscape (it ends with the pealing of bells), while its form is modelled on Liszt. The more rugged *Piano Sonata No. 2* (1919), also in one movement, represents a hero's conflict with the powers of evil, and the *Piano Sonata No. 3* (1926) continues the epic mood in the first of three movements. The *Piano Sonata No. 4* (1932), however, inhabits a different emotional and musical world: it has clear-cut textures, a more formal classical three-movement structure, a compelling second movement with echoes of Impressionism built on a mesmerising pedal point, and an harmonically gritty finale that sometimes glitters, sometimes follows a rhythmic harshness, but ends in a rather abrupt tone of triumph. Many of Bax's smaller piano pieces are reflections of nature; of the more important works *Mountain Mood* (1915, in variation form) and the tone poem *Winter Waters* (1915) stand out.

His finest vocal work is the magnificent motet *Mater ora Filium* (1921) for unaccompanied double choir, recreating Renaissance polyphony in an entirely modern idiom; its counterpoint is so brilliant and complex that it was considered virtually unsingable until the general Bax revival. The cantata *Enchanted Summer* (1910), for two sopranos, chorus and orchestra, setting Act II of Shelley's *Prometheus Unbound*, is also very fine: a combination of a rich and luxurious English pastoralism and pre-Raphaelite vision, with a sumptuous mosaic of orchestral textures and ethereal floating choral writing, especially for the sections with women's voices, which look forward to the choral writing of **Holst**. Of his songs, *A Lyke-Wake* (1908) for tenor and orchestra makes an interesting and worthy comparison with **Britten's** more celebrated setting in his *Serenade*, while songs such as *Far in a Western Brookland* (1918), to words by Housman, display a more lyrical side of his idiom, and his sensitivity to words.

Bax's idiom, with its Romantic emotional complexity, turbulence and luxuriance, will not appeal to everyone; his lesser works are best forgotten; but the considerable body of very fine music reflects a very particular sensibility of the Celtic Romantic struggling to express both his internal conflicts and a vision that retained an imaginative wonder at the world in which that struggle took place. His music regularly walks a knife-edge between high impact and disappointing failure, and a work that appears uninteresting in a poor performance can be arresting in a fine one. Bax was knighted in 1937, and was appointed Master of the King's Musick in 1941.

RECOMMENDED WORKS
Mater ora Filium (1921) for unaccompanied double choir
Nonet (1931) for flute, oboe, clarinet, harp and strings
Northern Ballad No. 3 (1933)
Overture to a Picaresque Comedy (1930)
Piano Quartet (1922)
Piano Sonata No. 4 in G minor (1934)
Symphonic Variations for Piano and Orchestra (1918)
Symphonies 1–7 (1921–39)
tone poem *The Garden of Fand* (1916)
tone poem *Tintagel* (1917)
Viola Sonata (1921)
Violin Concerto (1937)
Winter Legends (1930) for piano and orchestra

BIBLIOGRAPHY
A. Bax, *Farewell My Youth*, 1943
C. Scott-Sutherland, *Arnold Bax*, 1973

Berkeley (Sir) Lennox*

born 12th May 1903 at Boar's Hill (nr Oxford)
died 26th December 1989 at London

Sir Lennox Berkeley occupies a strange place in English music. His output of around one hundred works was (and remains) critically admired, but failed to maintain any permanent place in the repertoire. Recordings of his music can be difficult to find, performances are relatively rare, and his achievement awaits the kind of general reassessment that has to be given to so many other English composers. One of the reasons for this may be that his clear and precise idiom looked to the charm and elegance of French music, following his studies with Nadia Boulanger. A composer with more musical affinities to **Poulenc** and **Stravinsky** than to **Vaughan Williams** or **Britten**, he essentially stood outside the main thrust of English music (though he collaborated with Britten in the *Mont Juic Suite* of four Catalan dances in 1937).

Berkeley's idiom is essentially abstract and founded on classical forms, reflected in so many of his titles. He delights in polished craftsmanship, crystal-clear instrumental and orchestral colours, transparent textures, and in making the absolute precision with which events unfold appear effortless. His harmonies invariably have a tonal base, though he occasionally experimented with such devices as eight-note rows, and his melodies are usually self-effacing. The emphasis is on an intellectual enjoyment, the emotions are generally restrained, and charm is the prominent feature. On first hearing, a Berkeley work can sometimes sound bland, but he is a composer whose works deserve a second hearing, for on familiarity they usually reveal a quiet underlying strength, subtle emotional statements, and a sense of restrained joy in brighter passages.

These characteristics are exemplified in the two works most likely to be encountered, the *Trio for Violin, Horn and Piano* (1952) and the *Guitar Concerto* (1975). The former, written for the same forces as Brahms's trio, has a Gallic lightness and airiness to the instrumental dialogue, with a rather solemn lento where the horn and violin try to lift the mood and the piano eventually succeeds, leading to a lovely, calm close. The final movement is a theme and ten variations, where the pleasure comes from the variety of the variations on an uninteresting theme, alternating between the jaunty mood of the first movement and the slower and more lyrical mood of the second. The *Guitar Concerto* avoids all Spanish connotations, and concentrates on fastidious but effortless detail. The rather pastoral opening movement has beautifully woven textures following the opening horn calls, the slow movement is a gentle contemplation with delicate, overlapping textures, and in the bright and bouncy finale the guitar bounds off and against the orchestral textures. The concerto is not as immediately arresting as some, but so full of subtle delights that it is well worth knowing.

Berkeley wrote four symphonies (No. 1, 1940, No. 2, 1957, revised 1976, No. 3, 1969, No. 4 1976–78) that concentrate on a sophisticated orchestral idiom rather than emotional impact; they are elegant in their construction, precise and effective in their orchestral colours. The third is in a single movement, divided into three sections, and uses the principle of continuous development from germinal material. The *Serenade for Strings* (1939) and the *Divertimento* (1943) for small orchestra, both in four movements, exemplify Berkeley's wit and sensibilities, and are primarily designed to entertain. Of his other concertos, the attractive *Violin Concerto* (1961) uses a Classical-sized orchestra, with a central passacaglia, and deserves to be better known. His chamber music repertoire is limited, but includes the attractive *Viola Sonata* (1945), the *String Trio* (1944), which is full of grace and an easy flow, and the *Quintet for Wind and Piano* (1975), which expertly explores the available colours, with a theme-and-variations finale. He wrote three chamber operas for the Aldeburgh Festival, of which *Ruth* (1956), based on the biblical story, is reportedly the best. His three-act opera *Nelson* (1953–54), concentrating on the relationship between Nelson and Emma Hamilton, caused a certain amount of interest, but has not been revived. His piano music is often short in duration, but usually precise and concentrated in content.

There is though, another side of Berkeley's idiom, expressed in religious music of spiritual intensity, including the fine *Stabat Mater* (1947), for six solo voices and twelve instruments. The impressive *Four Poems of St Teresa of Avila* (1947) for contralto and strings, has affinities with **Britten**, and is laid out as a small symphonic song-cycle, each poem corresponding to a different movement. The underlying passion of the cycle emerges in the restless harmonies of the opening song, in the sombre third song, resonating low in string and vocal range, and especially in the interaction and opposition of vocal line and strings, with transparent textures. A similar intense ecstasy informs the purely secular song-cycle *Four Ronsard Sonnets (Set 2)* (1963) for tenor and orchestra, the four poems being addressed to Helen. The restrained precision of the orchestra in the first two songs gives the impression of a lover-protagonist who does not normally declare his emotions, but is here overwhelmed by love. The third song explodes, all restraint cast aside, with a passion and power that will astonish those who only know Berkeley's more playful music; and the final song opens with anguished harmonies and complex textures before thinning into a quiet conclusion – most, if not all, passion spent.

Berkeley taught at the Royal Academy from 1946 to 1968; among his pupils was John **Tavener**. He was knighted in 1974.

RECOMMENDED WORKS

> song-cycle *Four Poems of St Teresa of Avila* (1947) for contralto and strings
> song-cycle *Four Ronsard Sonnets (Set 2)* (1963) for tenor and orchestra
> Guitar Concerto (1975)
> *Serenade for Strings* (1939)
> Trio for Violin, Horn and Piano (1952)

Berkeley Michael
born 29th May 1948 at London

Michael Berkeley has emerged as a powerful mainstream voice in English music, who has gradually assimilated techniques and sounds developed by the avant-garde into a style originally rooted in tradition. This combination has found a ready audience; but as he has developed, he has gradually moved away from those traditional roots towards a more radical voice, and he seems to have carried that audience with him.

Like his father, Sir Lennox **Berkeley**, he was blessed with considerable technical facility, and his earlier, more conventional works suffer from a similar flaw: an emotional reticence that blanched the impact of the music, in his case not mitigated by the delight in style and grace that characterise Sir Lennox's music. These earlier works included the *Piano Trio* (1981) and the clear-textured *Clarinet Quintet* (1983), which is full of neat little tricks and ends in a characteristic and lovely lullaby lament. The *Chamber Symphony* (1980), the most radical of these earlier works, simultaneously portends his later music and reveals his earlier influences. The idiom of **Shostakovich** briefly appears, especially in some of the melodic figures, as well as some of the rhythmic bounce of **Stravinsky**. Both are memorably combined in the second section, in a work that is a symphony only in the Stravinskian sense of 'sounding together', with passages drawn from jazz and from **Messiaen**. Berkeley's technical skills are considerable, and he manages to forge this eclectic work into an effective whole.

The work that brought Berkeley wider attention was the oratorio *Or Shall We Die?* (1982) for soprano, baritone, chorus and orchestra, written with the poet Ian McEwan (including quotations from Blake). A big, expressive and often melodious work, it is a protest against the futility of a future nuclear holocaust and a call for a change in human thinking. It contains some very beautiful writing, including distant echoes of the English visionary pastoral set in a more contemporary and uneasy harmonic context, with touches of the chorale as well as a dramatic stridency, whose power is spoiled by the quasi-pop music that ends the piece. In hindsight it seems a work particular to its times (or rather, to the late 1960s and early 1970s), but also one seminal to Berkeley's development, in which the immediacy of the subject let loose something in his musical psychology. The results may have too much emotional multiplicity for comfort, but he was able to draw on them individually in subsequent works.

Many of these earlier works included an element that was essentially at odds with the prevailing mainstream style (such as the extraordinary piano effects, playing the strings, in the *Piano Trio*, or the pop music at the end of *Or Shall We Die?*), which suggested that Berkeley was uneasy with his idiom and was searching for a more expressive and personal voice. The *String Quartet No. 2* (1983), in a single-movement arch form, favoured the expressive over the intellectual but remained self-effacing. In *Fierce Tears I* (1984) for oboe and piano, one can hear the anger trying to break out in the falling cries of the oboe at the opening and close, which is otherwise safely encased in musical precision. *For the Savage Messiah* (1985) for piano, violin, viola, cello and contra-bassoon bursts out of this mould like **Honegger**'s Pacific steam engine running out of control, with motoric ostinati, an attempt at lyricism from the cello, near-silence after the crash before starting again, ending with a tortured upward gazing series of cries before the final apotheosis. It was the first of Berkeley's works to lay bare a powerful individual character behind the music, and its main feature – a furious anger, almost palpably aimed at injustice, and a kind of personal frustration at not being able to do more –

has remained a key element in his music to date.

In *Songs of Awakening Love* (1986), for soprano and small orchestra, setting poems by Elizabeth Barrett Browning and Christina Rossetti, Berkeley developed the lyrical side of his idiom. But gone is the easy, sweet melodiousness of some of the earlier music; in its place is a darker lyricism of much greater impact, supported by a more plastic rhythmic freedom (one of his major technical advances in his more recent works), ranging from the spare simplicity of the string opening to a teeming fertility. The harmonic idiom, too, is almost completely divorced from traditional procedures, but always founded on a recognisable centre-point, and, like the modern Polish composers, using the combination of colour and what once might have been considered dissonant intervals to create effects of considerable beauty. But the work that signalled a new maturity was the magnificent *Organ Concerto* (1987, since revised), in which the recently-found harmonic and rhythm fluidity combines with the anger to create work of ferocious emotion and intensity. The organ and the careful instrumentation (favouring colours to match the organ) explode together in a massive assault, breaking the last chains of stylistic politeness that still clung to his idiom. The anger descends into the dark string lyricism developed in *Songs of Awakening Love*, and emerges into a hushed beauty with a dense texture of woodwind and harp. It is as if, having gone through the catharsis, the wondering protagonist has emerged in a completely new and unimagined landscape. The concerto, in one continuous span, ends in a new awareness, a chorale-like expression of nobility and beauty, wrapped in an ethereal dissonance, and ending with the tolling of a bell.

Coronach (1988) for string orchestra reverts to a more formal attire, in which neo-classicism hovers on the margins. But *Entertaining Master Punch* (1990–91) for chamber ensemble broke new ground, especially in the interaction of colours, textures, and repetitive ideas, influenced by gamelan music. Written in part as a preparation for the opera *Baa Baa Black Sheep*, especially in the exploration of texture, it has a sense of ritual, with a constant harmonic language and a strong linear thrust, in which passages of near silence (but not stasis) mark division points, and from which individual colours or densities emerge vertically as if momentarily diverting from a central line. The linear flow and the dynamic use of silence were further extended in another piece connected with the opera, the one-movement *Clarinet Concerto* (1991). In this haunting, uneasy work the solo attempts to forge lyricism out of cold, steel-coloured pain, while the orchestra first puts out long streamers to prevent it but eventually aids in the attempt with cries of anguish leading to a calm apotheosis. This marvellous work is technically complex (if not to the ear), and its procedures, owing much to Berkeley's experience in the earlier works but here put to quite different ends, are entirely original.

The opera *Baa Baa Black Sheep* (1993), chamber in scale but large in scope, is so far the culmination of this new phase. The inspired libretto by the Australian David Malouf is drawn from an autobiographical story by Kipling, which describes how he and his sister were sent to England from India, into a household where he was repeatedly beaten and abused. This experience led to the concept of the child among the animals in *The Jungle Book*, and the opera juxtaposes this actual scenario with elements of the *Jungle Book*, each character having an animal counterpart. The result addresses not only the darkness of abuse, but the release of fantasy. Berkeley's score draws heavily on the experience of the preparatory works, with gamelan (rather than any trace of Indian music) representing the East. It has aspects of the fairy tale – the appalling woman who looks after the children is more of a caricature than a character – and the music, drawing on parody and chorus writing reminiscent of **Britten**, creates a powerful, sometimes savage linear thrust and fantastical atmospheres. Musically, it lacks the vocal idiomatic touches that might raise it above a powerful stage work, but as a first opera it suggests that a very distinctive operatic voice is emerging. Certainly those who formed their opinion of Michael Berkeley's music from the widely publicised earlier works are strongly advised to encounter the later ones.

RECOMMENDED WORKS
opera *Baa Baa Black Sheep* (1993)
Chamber Symphony (1980)
For the Savage Messiah (1985) for piano, violin, viola, cello and contra-bassoon
Organ Concerto (1987)
Songs of Awakening Love (1986) for soprano and small orchestra

Birtwistle (Sir) Harrison•••
born 15th July 1934 at Accrington

Harrison Birtwistle is one of the true outsiders of modern music, a composer whose aesthetic is unique, and arose virtually fully formed, before he flowered in the middle 1960s into one of the most recondite but original musical thinkers. His mind is like that of some scholastic alchemist, delighting in the arcane and ritualistic, searching out hidden symmetries, exploring the possibilities of cyclical events or structures, and finding mathematical balances – not for the mathematics but for the symbolisms. Theatre underlies all his musical thinking, whether for the concert hall or the stage. The delight in the potency, the potentialities of a word – the word as signifying a plethora of subconscious and conscious meanings – is another medieval conceit, most overt in the titles of the seventeen arches over which Orpheus must pass in *The Mask of Orpheus*. His music, with its strong sculptural qualities, especially in the use of blocks of sound, invests each event with an added dimension, as if it requires to be examined from every angle. Yet at the same time amid all this complexity there is a kind of ingenuousness that appears in the simplest of songs or chants. It is as if some Lancashire ploughman of the Middle Ages, steeped in oral stories passed down from the Greeks and interwoven with the folk myths of his own time and place, had found himself transported with a massive intellect into the musical world of the late 20th century, and yet has never forgotten the pleasure – or symbolism – of setting the ploughshare to the soil, while delighting in the sounds of clockwork and the mechanical. There is, too, a touch of the childish. He has never outgrown the small child's delight in charging around a house banging a tin drum at full volume, and this effect is heard throughout his entire output, although it becomes more sophisticated. He seems to inhabit some nether world that is an amalgam of the intellectual adult and the child at the intuitive, amoral stage – and that is precisely the amalgam of the orally transmitted folk tale, with its irrationality, time-distortion, and sometimes violence, but underlying cohesion. It is this quality, combined with influence of the archetypal structures and juxtapositions of classical Greek theatre, that has found a ready response in audiences, once they have overcome the shock of the contemporary musical idiom.

Much of Birtwistle's output has been for

unusual forces or instrumental combinations, designed to suit the particular work, but also to enhance that sense of the essence of the Greek or the medieval being transferred into a contemporary context; the bamboo flute and pipes, oboes, penny whistles and percussion of the music-theatre *Bow Down* provide an extreme example. Brass, percussion and woodwind predominate in his sound-world, partly because they are all capable of sudden, raucous attack. Consequently his works have not been as widely heard as they should; it is difficult for many ensembles to gather the appropriate forces, and his orchestral works are few.

His output before 1960 was very small, and most influenced by **Varèse**, as shown by the juxtaposed blocks of idea in *Refrains and Choruses* (1957), for wind quintet. His maturity came with *Tragoedia* (*'Goat-Dance'*, 1965) for ensemble divided into three groups. Its structure draws on classical Greek verse forms and rhythms; it launches an aural assault at its opening, and then creates a series of blocks, all with an underlying sense of pulse, some of clockwork insistence, others almost mellifluous, and including a redolent and mocking dance. The extrovert and compelling *Verses for Ensembles* (1969) uses only Birtwistle's favourite instrumental sounds, wind (including brass) and percussion, grouped into ensembles on the stage. The structure, using large-scale and detailed repetitions, suggests a static, ritualistic cast, within which blocks of events or incidents are laid over one another, meandering or eruptive, their differentiation sharpened by what Birtwistle has called 'strata' of instrumental registers. Much of the block incident has the quality of dramatic conversation or vocal statement, heightened by the strong characterisation achieved by the use of individual instruments: the effect is like walking in a gallery where a number of loud, separate but interlocking discourses are going on, sometimes repeating; but it is a gallery, and when one has left, those voices remain inside, bound by the walls, and, for all one knows, still continuing.

The culmination of Birtwistle's music of the 1960s was the opera *Punch and Judy* (1966–67, discussed below); the music of *Tragoedia* is used in the opera. Much of his work of the 1970s was a prelude to, or a study for, the opera *The Mask of Orpheus* (1973–83). The often harsh juxtaposition of blocks with striking, hard-edged colours was joined by more mellow, watercolour timbral effects, a less hard pulse and a

more fluid, mobile construction where a central idea is gradually turned to show different facets. The more contemplative and mellow elements are immediately apparent in *Nenia – The Death of Orpheus* (1970) for soprano and instrumental ensemble; the title refers to a Roman funeral dirge. The instruments are grouped in uniform timbres, and often used to create homogeneous and delicate textures; the vocal range is very wide, from arioso to speech, as is the dramatic effect, creating what amounts to a monodrama. In *The Fields of Sorrow* (1971), for two sopranos, chorus and ensemble, to a text by Ausonius from the *Aeneid* describing the souls of lost lovers wandering around the underworld, the sense of pulse is reduced to a minimum, with generally static swathes of choral, ritualistic nearchant, and a simple melodic sense to the fore. *The Triumph of Time* (1970–72) for orchestra is based on a painting of that name by Peter Breughel the Elder. It is a more direct expression of a running thread in Birtwistle's work: the contrast between the mechanical action of time and the perceived or imaginable variance of its workings. Its layers match those of the painting: Time followed by Death and Fate in the foreground, in slow-moving funeral music, the everyday of ordinary life behind, with the two musically interconnected. *Silbury Air* (1976–77) for large ensemble was the work that alerted a wider audience to Birtwistle, and remains an effective introduction to his music. Birtwistle has disclaimed any literal representation of the prehistoric mound in Wiltshire of the title, but the melodic patterns have a definite sense of the circular within the juxtaposition of sounds, some sculptural, some softer, which parallels the juxtaposition of the static, constructed object against the undulating landscape. Throughout this evocative work, a sense of pulse and repetition dominates on a monolithic base, eventually dying away to drum interjections like some winding-down clockwork toy and reinforcing the circular motion by recalling the opening repeated note. *Carmen Arcadiae Mechnaicae Perpetuum* (*The Perpetual Song of Mechanical Arcady*, 1978) concentrates on the mechanics of the title, with six different types of musical machinery creating a conglomerate of clockworks, divided by still moments of held notes. But there is a sense of melodic motion here, albeit built from brief snatches, that softens the purely mechanical edge.

However, Birtwistle had by no means

416 United Kingdom, Birtwistle

abandoned the power of sharp percussive interjection. *For O, for O, the Hobby-Horse is Forgot* (1976) is a 'ceremony' for six percussionists, its title taken from Shakespeare's *Hamlet*. Two players (King and Queen) take the lead; the other four are the Chorus, and the score indicates stage movement. Musically, the long ceremony surges forward, with continuous movement created by rolls or the equivalent of heartbeats, sliced into by whips and thuds. Sometimes the harshness endemic to Birtwistle's idiom can appear unremitting. In *... agm ...* (1979) for sixteen voices and three instrumental groups, the singers sing fragments of poems attributed to Sappho against a group of eleven upper register instruments, nine lower register and six other punctuation instruments (piano, three harps, three percussion). The title refers to a fragment of Sappho found on a papyrus (*agma* = fragment), but could also could mean net, and the work (in three parts) is indeed a thick net of choral swathes or planes against raucous instruments, especially brass and percussion, and all the material is related to a central pitch (E) and pulse. The result, especially in the first part, is akin to putting one's head inside a metal case that is being systematically hit by a sledgehammer, and even in the more delicate second part, dominated by intertwining choral lines, the continuous short, sharp vocal shocks have the effect of chalk being scraped across a blackboard. But individual moments are highly effective, such as the gradual movement from a slow reiterated pulse and haunted, disembodied sounds to clattering percussion, instrumental interjections, and a break-up of that pulse. *Secret Theatre* (1984), for large ensemble, its title drawn from Robert Graves, enacts an undisclosed ritual, played between two layers, a changing body of 'Cantus' instrumentalists at the front of the stage, and a 'Continuum' to the rear; the rite takes place in the musical and physical interaction of the two. *Earth Dances* (1986) for orchestra, grouped according to register rather than colour, uses up to six separate layers of material organised vertically or horizontally, and these strata sway into importance and then recede again in a flow that allows for evolution of textures and effect. This, one of the most effective and approachable of all Birtwistle's works, is underpinned throughout by three basic motions: the long slow sway like some vast undulation of the earth, the sharp incision of mechanical clockwork, and a forward momentum between the two; these are

matched by the strong differentiation of timbre associated with each momentum. The various strata and momentums are aurally immediately clear, there are long melodic threads (although the work is based on intervals rather than thematic melodies), and an enormous and yet detailed landscape is created to singular effect.

Birtwistle's first opera *Punch and Judy* (1967) set the general nature of his dramatic works. The libretto by Stephen Pruslin is freely based on the Punch and Judy story, with considerable violence; its tone is a combination of pantomime, Greek drama (with a chorus) and, above all, fairy tale or myth, in the unadulterated form where surface morality or consequential action or logic is replaced by an underground message through symbolism and an overall effect best analysed in structuralist terms. The influence of the Bach passions is evident in the three chorales that punctuate the action; like many unadulterated fairy tales, the tragic and comic elements are merged, though the work claims at its end to be a comedy. Birtwistle's setting is in the line of Weill's *Threepenny Opera* and more distantly Gay's *Beggar's Opera*, for in part it apes operatic conceptions from an earthy, popular angle, thus commenting on the nature of opera, and uses a similar progression of 'numbers' (often in themselves melodically memorable). The idiom is thoroughly contemporary, but alloyed with effects that give a hint of the street-band rather than the opera orchestra, and the violence of the story is matched by the stridency of the music in a complex, multi-layered but scintillating work. The smaller-scale music theatre of *Down by the Greenwood Side* (1969), for five singers and nine instrumentalists, and *Bow Down* (1977), for five actors and four instrumentalists applied a similar formula, inspired by medieval strolling players and folk-myth themes, though with a strong component of Greek theatrical ritual. The very violent central action of *Bow Down* has been as much misunderstood as the violence in *Punch and Judy*, mainly by those who respond only to the literal and overlook the psychosymbolic.

The opera *The Mask of Orpheus* (1973–83), to a libretto by Peter Zinovieff, provided the central core of Birtwistle's thinking for a decade. It successfully takes opera's ability to present multi-layered ideas and events to their extreme, while still being founded on the combination of folk-story, myth, and Greek elements; the added element is the breakdown of linear time or an ordered sequence of events, leading to simultaneous presentation of distantly connected views or events. It examines the Orpheus myth from many different angles and points of view, using three dramatic layers: singers, puppets (with off-stage singing), and mime, the last including six points of dramatic stasis where the music is electronic. Many of its components are again 'numbers', but here often overlapping; the orchestra provides another complete layer, an independent protagonist that structurally comes into consort with the vocal music only at the climax of the last act. Perhaps inevitably its complex stage events, relying heavily on allegory and symbolism, recall the ritualism of the operas, stage celebrations and masques of the age of Monteverdi; again, there is an implicit commentary on opera itself, with the final event being the decay of the myth of Orpheus. The theatrical complexities of this opera have proved too difficult for regular production.

Yan Tan Tethera (1984), with a libretto by Tony Harrison, reverted to the countryside elements and folk tales, centred around a tale of two rival shepherds and including a number of (human) sheep; it again is strongly ritualistic, mesmerisingly interesting but less powerful than the two earlier large-scale works. Birtwistle called it a 'mechanical pastoral', and as in so much of Birtwistle's musical thinking, 'mechanical' could surely refer both to the physical sense and to Shakespeare's 'mechanics'. *Sir Gawain and the Green Knight* (1989–91, revised 1994), to a libretto by David Harsent, is based on the famous Middle English poem of the same title, telling of a knight at King Arthur's court who takes up the challenge of the Green Man to strike him with an axe, and receive the same blow from the Green Man at the Green Chapel a year later. The expressive treatment includes a masque and ritual passages, ornate and declamatory vocal writing, and courtly dances. *The Second Mrs Kong* (1994) continues the theme of time in the disparity between memory and the present; Kong (based on the celebrated film gorilla) and Pearl exist in two different worlds, which can meet but not merge. The libretto, by Russell Hoban, is full of allusions and symbolism; specific references link the opera not only to specific myths but also to Birtwistle's previous works: Orpheus appears, but (recalling *Gawain*) as a severed head, while personifications of the abstract such as Despair and Doubt echo morality plays. The setting makes considerable use of modern technology (television screens, computers, film), which itself can call up other references (such as snatches of celebrated films, including *King Kong*). With its wide range of vocal styles, from the lyrical to *Sprechstimme*, *The Second Mrs Kong* would seem to consolidate Birtwistle's position as the leading composer of post-modernist opera, combining an amalgam of past references, placed in a contemporary framework, with his deep understanding of the potency of myth.

Birtwistle taught at Cranbourne Chase School (1962–65) and was appointed musical director of the National Theatre, London, in 1975. He was knighted in 1988.

RECOMMENDED WORKS
    music theatre *Bow Down* (1977)
    Earth Dances (1986) for orchestra
    For O, for O, the Hobby-Horse is
       Forgot (1976) for 6 percussionists
    opera *The Mask of Orpheus* (1973–83)
    Nenia – the Death of Orpheus (1970)
       for soprano and 5 instruments
    opera *Punch and Judy* (1966–67)
    opera *Sir Gawain and the Green*
       Knight (1989–91, revised 1994)
    The Triumph of Time (1972) for
       orchestra
    Verses for Ensembles (1969) for
       instrumental ensemble

BIBLIOGRAPHY
    M. Hall, *Harrison Birtwistle*, 1984

Bliss (Sir) Arthur Edward Drummond*

born 2nd August 1891 at London
died 27th March 1975 at London

Sir Arthur Bliss's music never quite seems to fulfil the reputation he held during his lifetime, although he continues to have strong advocates. At his best in passages of a martial anguish (doubtless the legacy of his experiences in World War I), his well-constructed works, becoming more neo-Romantic through his career, often have striking individual moments but always seem to be reaching for a level of import and depth that is never achieved.

His earlier music was bold and experimental for the British context of its time, leaning towards a Stravinskian neo-classicism, but his best-known work, *A Colour Symphony* (1921–22, revised 1932), signalled a change to a more conservative Romantic approach. The four movements (Purple, Red, Blue, Green) were inspired by the colour associations used in heraldry, each with an associated mood. It shows both Bliss's strengths and his weaknesses: it has a clarity of construction and orchestration, a rhythmic vigour, moments of forthright beauty in the slow movement and strength in the last, together with light-hearted elements; but overall it lacks a conviction of individuality or deep commitment, and is ultimately disappointing. The 'Symphony for Orator, Chorus and Orchestra', *Morning Heroes* (1930), similarly ceremonial in feel, is a more arresting work, perhaps because its inspiration – the slaughter of the First World War – reflected Bliss's own experiences, including being wounded in 1916 and gassed in 1918, and the death of his brother at the Somme. It sets texts from the *Iliad*, Walt Whitman, Wilfred Owen, Robert Nichols and the Chinese poet Li T'ai-po. The oration is most effectively woven into the form, its import amplified by the music; the slow movement contrasts Li T'ai-po's poem of a wife whose husband is away at war with Whitman's of a soldier thinking of home.

The *Piano Concerto* (1939) is a virtuoso piece appropriate to the festive occasion for which it was commissioned (the New York World Fair), while the late *Cello Concerto* (1970) is perhaps the most immediate of Bliss's works, well contained within the limitations of his idiom and using a classical-sized orchestra with the addition of harp and celesta. Rhapsodic in tone, its genial vigour regularly contemplates a sad melancholy, almost gets caught up in it, but always withdraws.

Two of Bliss's ballets have had life beyond the stage. The staged chess-game of *Checkmate* (1937) is a metaphor for medieval power-games, including the seduction of the Red Knight by the Black Queen, and a concluding battle and checkmate, signalling the fall of a kingdom. The music uses elements of pre-classical dance forms and shows influences of plainchant, but is suffused with Bliss's bright vigour. *Adam Zero* (1946) follows the seven ages of man, at whose end a new Adam is born. Bliss's chamber music is elegantly wrought, rather emotionally disengaged, occasionally rich and enjoyable, but not especially memorable. The finest is the *Clarinet Quintet* (1929), with sonorous string writing, confident contrapuntal writing, and rich, vigorous solo lines. Of his other vocal music, *Pastoral 'Lie Strewn the White Flocks'* (1928) for mezzo-soprano, chorus, flute, timpani and string orchestra, evokes the Mediterranean; Pan and the flute are prominent, and it ends with dusk and the night. *A Knot of Riddles* (1963) for baritone and eleven instruments sets Anglo-Saxon riddles with nature imagery; the baritone sings the solution after each one.

Bliss lived in the United States from 1923 to 1925, was knighted in 1950, and was appointed Master of the Queen's Musick in 1953, in which capacity his idiom suited the ceremonial requirements. He was director of music at the BBC from 1942 to 1944.

RECOMMENDED WORKS
Cello Concerto (1970)
Clarinet Quintet (1929)
Morning Heroes (1930) for orator, chorus and orchestra

Brian Havergal**
born 29th January 1876 at Dresden (Staffordshire.)
died 28th November 1972 at Shoreham

In this guide will be found a number of reclusive and eccentric composers for whom devotees have made extravagant claims that on closer inspection turn out to be chimeric. At first glance, Havergal Brian would seem to be such a composer. But between the ages of forty-three and fifty-one he produced one of the world's artistic masterpieces: in vision, grandeur, and in the combination of complexity and luminosity the *Symphony No. 1 'Gothic'* (1919–27) is worthy to stand alongside the great cathedrals of the age that inspired it. (It is sometimes called the second symphony; an earlier symphony was discarded, and this led to confusion in the numbering.) Arguably it is, more than any other late-Romantic work, the climax of the Romantic age, because it incorporates the power and optimistic vision of the late 19th century as well as its turmoil. Not for nothing was it called the Gothic, for its forces are truly gigantic, but more pertinently it is charged with the sheer energy that is palpable in Gothic architecture. Probably the largest symphony ever written, it uses four soloists, four large mixed choirs, a greatly extended orchestra, four separate brass bands, and organ. But these huge forces are neither inflated nor gratuitous; instead they are used for moments of almost unimaginable power to launch the symphony to the heavens, at other times reduced to near chamber textures, with the exception of the deep lower instruments (including a bass tuba) that provide massive foundations for the structure of the sound. Much of the orchestration is built around brass, against which woodwind often act as busy border colours. The harmonies are late-Romantic and heavily chromatic, but to these are added polyrhythms and a natural use of semitonal clashes (with almost cluster effects in the choral writing of the last movement). These, together with some of the passages that use percussion, suggest an element of Brian's musical vision that was moving beyond the confines of the late-Romantic.

Above all, this gigantic symphony is truly symphonic. There is a movement from D minor to E minor in the first of two parts, and from D major to E major in the second; material is developed, transformed or reused in different contexts that give audible organic unity to such a large work, and the more one lives with it the more one realises the complexity and surety of those ties. Part I is divided into three movements, and is purely orchestral; the idiom is distantly related to that of **Mahler**. The first movement launches a journey of gripping excitement, thunderous turmoil and energy, and sudden withdrawals into a mystical atmosphere that explodes out again. The second movement, again of a vast soundscape, is more troubled, arriving at a Sibelian climax, sinking into motion in the shadows like the passing of great, warm-blooded dinosaurs, and producing triumphant fanfares that dissolve into ruin and return to the opening material. The third scherzo movement contains one of the most phenomenal and unprecedented passages in all late-Romantic music. A huge percussive storm erupts, with an extraordinary movement of rhythmic pulse. Great swells punctuate it, rising from the depths of the enormous orchestra. Out of this emerge high tinkling sounds, the xylophone prominent, into a polyrhythmic mêlée of precise structure and effect, whose components come together into a huge ominous climax, eventually greeted by silence and the soft spiritual close that is immediately echoed in the opening of the second part.

Part II, again in three movements and twice as long as the first, uses the large choral forces in a setting of the Te Deum. It is difficult to convey the sheer exaltation – and exultation – of this music, complex brass fanfares often re-energising the momentum, the choral writing of polyphonic complexity and visionary feel, the energy never flagging. Not Handel at his most joyful, Berlioz at his most grand,

Mahler at his most visionary, or **Messiaen** at his most ecstatic, has approached this effect of overwhelming praise, for which the huge forces are entirely justified. The fifth movement, which traverses the tremendous horror of the Judgement and an ending of monumental power, and uses only four words in the choral writing, includes a central section that is the unearthly passage of the scherzo transformed almost (but not quite) out of recognition, as if reforged in the choral ecstasy that had preceded it. The choral sound often has a medieval cast, and some of the spacious movement of Eastern Orthodox music, but also complex polytonal effects. It is entirely characteristic of this massive work that it should end quietly, shorn of almost all its forces, on an unaccompanied chorale-like choral line.

This symphony is an experience quite unlike anything else in music. However, it has only received three public performances: a semi-amateur one in 1961, a performance under Boult in 1966, and another under Ole Schmidt in 1980. Unfortunately, the only commercially available recording (made outside Britain) is a travesty, and readers are warned not to judge this work on its evidence, as sadly must have happened: beside the Schmidt performance it seems like a body stripped of all its flesh and muscle (and most of the lower instruments that are so crucial to the overall sound). It is a disgrace to British music that, at the time of writing, this masterpiece has not received a major British recording.

The course of British music, and certainly of Havergal Brian's career, might have been very different had this symphony been performed in the 1920s, though its advanced elements might have been misunderstood. The rest of Brian's composing life is equally remarkable: although he never again (on the still too scant evidence) produced a work of such unadulterated genius, he went on to write another thirty-one symphonies of a very high quality, of which twenty-one were composed after he had reached the age of eighty, and they are by no means works of dotage. Symphonic argument forms the core of Brian's thinking, and he gradually developed more and more concise encapsulations of symphonic development, while retaining the large orchestral forces for a flexibility of effect. Thus, by the time of the very short later symphonies, Brian was in the unusual situation of a composer using a traditional medium rooted in tonality who had arrived at the compression and emphasis on the detail of the individual moment that had taken place in more experimental forms. In the more compressed works, the harmonic organisation can become complex and the emotional changes swift, creating tough but never academic works that gain in stature on increased acquaintance. Overall, he explores the darker side of the human experience, sometimes using march elements, but regularly juxtaposed with moment of tranquillity, sometimes with solo violin lines; the vital energy apparent in the *Gothic Symphony* is maintained even to the works written in his nineties. Brass, often with fanfare effects, continue to play prominent roles in the orchestration, and the percussion section is elevated far beyond the role of added colour or effect.

Symphony No. 2 (1930–31), *Symphony No. 3* (1931–32) and *Symphony No. 4 'Das Siegeslied' (Psalm of Victory*, 1932–33) form a group of large-scale symphonies. The scherzo of the third, with its sixteen horns grouped in fours joined by two pianos and three timpani, has been highly praised. The fourth is choral, a setting of Psalm 68, and has been described as a masterpiece by those fortunate enough to encounter it. The *Symphony No. 5 'Wine of Summer'* (1937) is for middle-voice and orchestra, setting a poem by Lord Alfred Douglas. The single-movement *Symphony No. 6 'Sinfonia tragica'* (1947–48) is so arresting that its neglect is unfortunate. It was inspired by J. M. Synge's *Deirdre of the Sorrows* (the harp giving a brief Celtic touch at the opening) and uses traditional harmonies, but its open textures, its use of silence, its sudden turns from delicate chamber writing to large effects, and its eclectic imagery all help to create an entirely modern effect, and its symphonic argument is clear.

The eighth, ninth and tenth symphonies form another group. The four-movement *Symphony No. 7* (1948) is quite different in character, the flow more linear, with strong martial overtones; but just when one expects the work to settle down on fairly conventional lines, a switch of orchestral effect or an abrupt change of tone shatters any complacency. It illustrates another aspect of Brian's idiom that takes getting used to: the individual movements are not easy to characterise in mood (as are those by, say, **Vaughan Williams** or **Prokofiev**). Rather there is a conglomeration of moods within a movement, and a gradual shift of overall emotion through the symphony (here from self-confidence

to an angry uncertainty and the diffidence of wisdom), to which the individual movements contribute. Bells of various kinds sound through the symphony, and each movement ends with the ringing of an individual percussion instrument left naked to decay. The magical overlapping ostinati of the beginning of the third movement create another striking and original effect, like swallows darting around Gothic columns, airy and full of lightness.

The next three symphonies form another group. The *Symphony No. 8* (1949) is in a single movement for a large orchestra including piano, and with the euphonium and bass tuba prominent; here the overall mood is one of mourning, the conflict of the symphony unresolved at the end. Unlike the eighth, the tragic *Symphony No. 9* (1951) for large orchestra with organ uses sonata form in the outer of three movements. The *Symphony No. 10* (1953–54) combines the moods of the predecessors in a single movement, from desolation to a funeral march in a heroic-tragic cast.

From this period the symphonies become increasingly preoccupied with concision, though they retain his idiomatic and emotional hallmarks; in effect they are almost variations on a symphonic problem, with common emotional content (nos. 12 to 32 were all written in his eighties and nineties) but differing symphonic contexts and solutions. In the sixteen-minute *Symphony No. 16* (1960), for example, the initially daunting kaleidoscope of events becomes much clearer when one is familiar with the six sections into which the single movement is divided, and the symphony emerges as a tough, rugged work with a touch of pastoralism and a marvellous sense of assertion at the end: a gathering of the symphonic skirts. The less intense *Symphony No. 21* (1963) reverts to four movements, but the two-movement *Symphony No. 22 'Symphonia brevis'* (1964–65) lasts just nine minutes, and still manages to include the characteristic swell to climax in the second movement, ending in melancholy before a final luminosity, and a turbulent first movement culminating in an Elgarian nobilmente, so that the short length by no means precludes large statements. He maintained his symphonic incisiveness to the last works, written in his nineties. The thirteen-minute one-movement *Symphony No. 31* (1967–68), in four distinct sections, has a feeling of playfulness, lucid orchestral textures, and yet rapid injections of gritty power.

It is still difficult to arrive at an accurate

assessment of Brian's works other than the symphonies. The 'comedy overture' *Tinker's Wedding* (1948) for orchestra is Brian in a lighter mood, inspired by J. M. Synge. The piano music includes the *Double Fugue in E major*, where the contrapuntal framework provides opportunities for excursions into contrasting emotions that deviate from the linear logic, while some of the earlier small pieces have Satiesque qualities. One would like to know how his structural instincts and surety of choral writing translate to the opera stage, in *The Tigers* (1917–20, revised 1925–32), a satire on the military (the title refers to a military unit), *Agamemnon* (1957), or especially two operas that invite comparisons with well-known treatments, *Turandot* (1950–51) and *Faust* (1955–56).

Havergal Brian was one of those rarities, an experimenter within established traditional forms, from the gigantic to the concentrated; deservedly his music is now being rescued from obscurity. He was assistant editor of *Musical Opinion* from 1918 to 1939.

RECOMMENDED WORKS

Symphony No. 1 *Gothic* (1919–27)
Symphony No. 4 *Das Siegeslied* (1932–33) (see text)
Symphony No. 6 *Sinfonia tragica* (1947–48)
Symphony No. 7 (1948)
Symphony No. 16 (1960)
Symphony No. 22 *Symphonia brevis* (1964–65)

BIBLIOGRAPHY

M. MacDonald, *The Symphonies of Havergal Brian* (3 vols.), 1975–84

Bridge Frank**

born 26th February 1879 at Brighton
died 10th January 1941 at Eastbourne

Frank Bridge is best remembered as the teacher of, and mentor to, Benjamin **Britten**, which has unfortunately overshadowed his own striking achievement as an innovative and introverted composer essentially standing apart from the interwar development of English music. His concentration on rarefied chamber works has contributed to that limited appreciation: he himself was a viola player of note, with the Joachim String Quartet and then the English String Quartet. His development from a late-Romantic idiom, flowing but delicate, controlled by precision of

intellect, to an harmonic idiom similar to that of **Berg** was an entirely natural one, an object-lesson to those who think the 20th-century harmonic revolution necessitated abrupt changes of style. This later harmonic palette was far too advanced for the conservative English audiences of his time, and this circumstance has contributed to his relative neglect. Emotionally, his music is dark, sometimes troubled, an attempt to reconcile the traumatic horror of World War I to his pacifist temperament, though his few orchestral works are palpably more outgoing, showing the public rather than the private side of the composer.

Bridge's early works are influenced by Brahms and **Fauré**, with a warm Romantic richness. They include the *String Quartet No. 1* (1906) and the *Phantasie* piano trio (1907), built in an arch shape, and touched with an English melancholy devoid of anguish. This period also includes two superb orchestral works. The *Dance Rhapsody* (1908) deceives with its quasi-ceremonial opening, for it immediately launches into a buoyant surging brilliance with the infectious delight of **Enescu's** *Romanian Rhapsodies*, which surely must have influenced this work. It moves into broader planes, but there is a whiff of the ocean in the major theme of the opening and in atmospheric moments, and it was that which was invoked in his finest orchestral work, the suite *The Sea* (1910–11), cast in four movements. Although there is the occasional nod in the direction of Impressionism, this picture of the sea is born of the undercurrents and the interplay of the energy of water and air, rather than the experience of the boat on the surface that is found in **Debussy's** *La mer*.

The events of World War I, palpable in a setting of Francis Thompson's poem 'What shall I your true love tell' (1919), with its bare vocal lines, permeated Bridge's music not so much in a rapid change of style as in a change of emotional content. *Lament* (1915) for two violas (also orchestrated for strings) was clearly an immediate response, anguished and dark, commemorating a little girl drowned in the sinking of the *Lusitania*. Less graphic, the rhapsodic and flowing *Cello Sonata* (1917) has an Edwardian richness in its two movements, the second combining slow movement and finale, but there is a sense of loss and lamentation in the cello writing, made more poignant by the attempts of the piano to provide a more optimistic, ecstatic context. The short opera *The Christmas*

Rose (1919, orchestrated 1929) seems to have been an attempt to find rebirth from the horror. It uses a deceptively simple story of the shepherd girl and boy who are left behind when the shepherds, on hearing the angels, go to the stable to offer gifts to the Christ-child. The children follow but, having no gifts, are about to leave without seeing the child, when roses sprout and bloom in the snow, and the children recognise that they have their gifts. As an opera, the dramatic structure is too diffuse for impact; as a psychological document it is more noteworthy. Its introduction is almost entirely within the pastoral tradition, but this breaks down into a tougher idiom, echoing the collapse of pre-war English ideals, with metaphors such as the ravaging of the sheep by the wolves serving as a reminder of the slaughter. This new mood is expressed in **Holst**-like choral and vocal writing, and that final image of hope through the innocence of children. If treated as such (rather than as a stage work), this opera repays those interested in the period; and its central concept was, of course, to emerge as the basic theme of much of **Britten's** work. At the same time, the suite of three pieces titled *The Hour Glass* (1920) for piano show no traces of the trauma of the war: the idiom is more Impressionist, with something of the delicacy of **Ravel** in the opening piece, 'Dusk', and with **Debussy** palpable in the powerful 'The Midnight Tide'.

Bridge's final foray into nature painting was the fine *Enter Spring* (1927) for orchestra, which combined the English tradition with an awareness of the new ideas emerging on the Continent. With the *Piano Sonata* (1921–24), written in memory of a friend killed in the war, Bridge had started to infiltrate his rhapsodic flow with more dissonant harmonies that, in the powerful, dark *String Quartet No. 3* (1926), led to the abandonment of a specified key in a combination of passionate emotion and technical refinement that has affinities with **Berg**. The unearthly *Rhapsody* (1928) for string trio would be entirely atonal were it not for the regular return to a tonal lodestone, yet this is an entirely natural progression from his earlier work, the piano writing having been removed, so to speak, from the *Cello Sonata*, and the harmonies of the cello line extended and rarefied beyond the tonal tradition. Indeed, in the *Rhapsody* the idiom regularly and convincingly slips into rhapsodic moments (the rest is much more taut than the title would suggest), so that we are all

the more aware of both the emotional development forged by the events between 1914 and 1918, and the continuity of the underlying character.

By the time he wrote the *Rhapsody* Bridge had developed from the technically very adept and emotionally passionate but not overtly individual pre-war composer, to one at the forefront of contemporary European writing, though at the time this was hardly realised. The large-scale and widely admired *Piano Trio No. 2* (1929) seems a retreat from the implications of the *Rhapsody*, in spite of its use of bitonality. The piano writing of the opening has Impressionist echoes, if not setting, eventually emerging as a sparse stillness, but in spite of the elusive darting effects and trenchant harmonies, the legacy of the richer Edwardian flow is here more obvious.

There then followed two major works with orchestra. *Oration 'concerto elegiaco'* (1930), for cello and orchestra, is a funeral oration for those who fell in the war, juxtaposing a personal, introverted idiom, notably in the opening and in the beautiful, restful ending in the epilogue, with a more extrovert public pronouncement. This extroversion occurs in the march that emerges from the opening, in the central march that manages to interpolate a funeral march into a pastoral idiom, and in the grotesque nightmarish march, ending in bugle calls, that descends into fragmentation and thus to the epilogue. The striking large-scale *Phantasm* (1931) for piano and orchestra, like the *Oration* a long single movement with closely integrated episodes, explored the realm of dream and nightmare. Its opening episode and much of the later material seem like a cross between early Expressionist **Schoenberg** and the texturally detailed richness of **Szymanowski**; a central turbulent episode, more direct, elicits a nightmare with feverish echoes of the waltz dreams of confusion, and this strange work ends unfulfilled yet fortified. The direction of the *Rhapsody* was realised in the marvellous *String Quartet No. 4* (1937), a work of Classical lucidity and clarity of construction, with complex polyphony in the opening movement, combined with an assured immersion in the atonal harmonic idiom. The spare delicacy has more affinities with **Webern** than with **Berg**, and the rhapsodic elements have evolved into touches of the dance; indeed the central movement is marked 'quasi minuetto'. It is difficult not to conclude that in the *Oration* he was publicly fulfilling his need for commemoration and in the *Phantasm* was working out the turbulence of his subconscious; these necessities complete, he could arrive at a personal resolution through the development of an advanced personal language in the *String Quartet No. 4*, a conclusion reinforced by the (for Bridge) optimistic ending of the quartet. Indeed, the overture *Rebus* (1940) for orchestra, with a more traditional harmonic cast, is brighter, expansive, sometimes almost playful, using a theme that gradually expands and then gets distorted (the working title was 'rumour'; the current title refers to a pictorial device signifying a name). Bridge's songs (there are over fifty) often show the lighter side of his idiom; most date from earlier in his career, and two of the more popular, the Tennyson setting *Go not, happy day* (1916) and the Mary Coleridge setting *Love went a-riding* (1914), have florid, cascading piano writing supporting a long flowing vocal line, suitable for encore pieces.

Bridge was active as a conductor as well as violist; he took no teaching post, but **Britten** was a private pupil.

RECOMMENDED WORKS
Cello Sonata (1917)
Enter Spring (1927) for orchestra
Dance Rhapsody (1908) for orchestra
Oration 'concerto elegiaco' (1930) for cello and orchestra
Phantasm (1931) for piano and orchestra
Piano Sonata (1921–24)
Piano Trio No. 2 (1929)
Rhapsody (1928) for string trio
String Quartet No. 3 (1926)
String Quartet No. 4 (1937)

BIBLIOGRAPHY
A. Payne, *Frank Bridge*, 1984

Britten (Edward) Benjamin (Baron Britten of Aldeburgh)•••
born 22nd November 1913 at Lowestoft
died 4th December 1976 at Aldeburgh

Of all the major 20th-century composers, Benjamin Britten was among those least motivated solely by purely musical considerations, and the most concerned to illuminate and amplify those aspects of the human condition that have usually been expressed in literature. His inspiration is above all the written word and its associations, particularly the landscape, the populace and the traditional heritage of his native Suffolk. His major works therefore revolve around the human voice (though not exclusively), and with **Berg, Janáček** and **Strauss** he is the most convincing opera composer of our century. A second and important strand was the close association both with writers (notably W. H. Auden, William Plomer and Myfanwy Piper) and with the performers of his works (especially his companion, the singer Peter Pears, and the cellist Mstislav Rostropovich). Consequently, much of his music was written with specific performers in mind, creating the sense of personal intimacy and rapport between music and performer that is another feature of his music.

Musically, Britten was a conservative composer. Since his objective was the expression of emotional conflicts, technical innovation was secondary, and his idiom is largely diatonic and lyrical, his favoured structures the suite or the theme and variations; his operas are built on essentially traditional forms. Melodic line is an important factor in his idiom, emerging in a variety of styles, though often characterised by an upward leap. His idiom is also eclectic, in that he synthesized influences from and aspects of various composers, notably **Mahler, Shostakovich** (especially in the use of parody, in bass phrases, and in some orchestral colours), **Grainger** (in the return to nature) and, in the later works, **Schoenberg**. Within that framework, his ability to extend tradition with personal hallmarks (such as the use of bitonality and the juxtaposition of semitones), and the adaptation of one tradition to another (such as the use of theme and variation structure in opera or the reworking of Japanese Noh techniques in the Church parables) created a voice that is entirely individual, and usually immediately recognisable as Britten's.

One single human theme is an undercurrent to almost all Britten's work: the corruption of innocence, be it an expression of that innocence (for example, the cantata *A Boy was Born*); its betrayal (the opera *The Turn of the Screw*); the resulting torments of middle age (the opera *Peter Grimes*); the sense of loss and mourning (the orchestral *Sinfonia da Requiem*); the desire for its return (the opera *Death in Venice*); a combination of all of these, either literally (the song-cycle *Winter Words*) or symbolically (the vocal *Spring*

Symphony); or its reduction to the complicated interaction of good and evil (the opera *Billy Budd*). It is perhaps pertinent that Britten was a homosexual, and for most of his life lived in an age where such an orientation was still illegal and taboo. Although his treatment of the theme of innocence far transcends any considerations of gender, his particular understanding makes him perhaps the only composer whose homosexuality, in the face of such stigma, led him to expressive insight, and not just the expression of internal conflict that is found in the music of such other homosexual composers as Tchaikovsky.

It was Britten's technique to pare away superficial emotional and musical complications to present the primary emotion or theme of the textual moment. Musically this is achieved by often bare textures that have a chamber-like intimacy, or by the virtual personification of individual instruments to support the moment (for example, the horn in the *Serenade*, the fanfares in the *War Requiem*, or the flute in *Billy Budd*). His orchestration highlights individual instruments, contrasted by massed surges in which strings predominate, and similar techniques are found in his choral writing. Harmonic devices support the tendency to characterisation, such as the semitone expressing darkness and turmoil, often expressed in two keys a semitone apart, the triad representing the ethereal and the innocence of beauty, or the use of the key of A major expressing Apollonian beauty. Combined with a love for such intellectual devices as the canon, and with the distancing effects of the high vocal lines he preferred, this can seem a rather dry, cognitive outlook – hence the criticism levelled at Britten that he has pity for his characters, but not compassion.

This superficial distancing was necessary, so that Britten could concentrate on the particular human theme (his stage works, for example, are largely devoid of secondary stories or sub-texts). Consequently, most of his works are serious in intent; even the more light-hearted children's pieces, such as *Let's Make an Opera* or the *Young Person's Guide to the Orchestra*, have a didactic purpose. His genius lies in the other layers of emotional content that Britten almost invariably adds. His choice of poetry or text – always of a very high literary standard – concentrates on those that contain complex metaphysical or symbolic allusions, often with a relatively black-and-white surface message or story. Britten powerfully expresses both layers in his music: the intellectual tackles

the surface, the emotional the hidden intent, so that it revolves around two apparently opposed poles, brought together by the medium of music. Those who have little sympathy for the allusionary or the symbolic generally admire his music, but are not moved by it. Those who do respond find that Britten's idiom has extraordinary impact, and when these deeper layers have a very wide relevance – such as the musical symbol of the sea as the unconscious in *Peter Grimes*, or the combination of innocence and Christian symbolism in *A Ceremony of Carols* – the relevant works have achieved very wide popularity.

An important device gradually developed through Britten's output is the layering of different sound worlds within a single unit, adding spatial as well as emotional perspectives. It can be seen in such simple examples as the use of the solo harp, set apart from the voices, in *A Ceremony of Carols*, as well as in larger designs, such as the evocation of the sea in the four *Sea Interludes* of the opera *Peter Grimes*, the change of focus from the interior of Captain Vere's monologues to the ship-board world in *Billy Budd*, or the contrast between Aschenbach's piano-accompanied recitatives and the orchestral responses to Venice and the other characters in *Death in Venice*. The culmination is in the *War Requiem*, where three layers are carefully delineated, coming together in the final moments: the foreground of the war poems of Wilfed Owen assigned to the soloists and chamber orchestra; the middle layer of the Latin Requiem text for chorus and orchestra; and the ethereal distance of a boys' choir accompanied by a chamber organ. The musical intent appears to be for clarity of expression; the emotional intent to define and present different emotions simultaneously in the composer's constant search to untangle and delineate the complex web of different and often opposing emotional states that is the human personality.

Britten's musical maturity dates from the works of the 1940s, notably the lovely little canticle *Hymn to St Cecilia* (1942) and the opera *Peter Grimes* (1944–45), which rocketed English opera into a serious art form after an interval of two hundred years. Two major motivations were his return from his stay in the USA (1939–42) and the start of his collaboration with Peter Pears. His music before this period includes over thirty film scores for the General Post Office (of which his collaboration with W. H. Auden in *Night*

Mail is a masterpiece), the diverting *Sinfonietta* (1932) for orchestra, the popular *Variations on a Theme of Frank Bridge* (1937) for string orchestra, the virtuoso *Piano Concerto* (1938, revised 1945) and works of political intent, notably the song-cycle *Ballad of Heroes* (1939), written in response to the Spanish Civil War. While there are musical elements that herald later developments, the theme of innocence betrayed (although present from his youthful works onwards) is largely suppressed, the separation of the intellectual and the emotional less overt; but there is a surety and a range of fervour and expression in these earlier works that have often appealed to those who do not respond to his later idiom, and which has caused speculation on the other avenues of development Britten might have taken.

Outstanding among these earlier works, and deserving of wider recognition, are the chamber works, (the *String Quartet in D*, 1931, revised 1974, the *String Quartet No. 1*, 1941, the *String Quartet No. 2*, 1945, and the *Phantasy Quartet* for oboe and strings, 1932), the song-cycle *Our Hunting Fathers* (1936), and the *Violin Concerto* (1939, revised 1958). The W. H. Auden text of *Our Hunting Fathers* revolves around the relationship between hunting and animals, and inspired strikingly original music of assertively wide range and expressive effect, though with momentary echoes of some of the eclecticism of **Mahler**, the gritty orchestral exhortation of **Vaughan Williams's** *Job* or the angularity of **Walton**. The much undervalued *Violin Concerto* (1939) is one of the finest and most beautiful of 20th-century concertos. The very difficult solo writing regularly lies very high; in the first movement the roles of lyrical solo and nervous, repetitive ideas in the orchestra are swapped in the middle, to magical effect, and then reversed again. The central movement is a furious and passionate scherzo, which comes close to **Shostakovich** in feel, the cadenza picking up the nervous motto from the first movement. The finale, a passacaglia, leads to a beautifully visionary, peaceful close. In this concerto Britten takes the ecstatic element of the English pastoral tradition, sets it in the context of a much tougher, more agitated, structurally dissonant idiom, and forges a concerto in which bliss and sadness are melted together. The internal theme of innocence lost is absent; this is an outward struggle. It promised the possibility of a new aesthetic and harmonic direction that Britten was never to explore, although the music of the

preparations for the battle in *Billy Budd* is directly heralded in the first movement, and a chordal progression in the opera in the last.

From the same period comes one of the least known of Britten's stage works, but one of his most instantly appealing. *Paul Bunyan* (1940–41, revised 1974) is part operetta, part American musical, and closest to the Brechtian operas of **Weill**, while reflecting the contemporary American genre of the socially aware 'high-school opera'. Its text by W. H. Auden, drawing on the combination of surrealism, humour and seriousness of the poet's earlier plays, celebrates the American frontier as an allegory of the pioneer in all fields; the music ranges from operatic arias to cowboy songs.

In the operas the theme of innocence and betrayal, as already outlined, is paramount, and text and libretto take on a primacy rare in opera. Britten's concentration is on individual character, to the extent that all his operas were written with specific performers in mind (the television opera *Owen Wingrave* was actually cast before it was written), creating detailed characterisation even in minor roles, and allowing a sense of intimacy however broad the subject. Location is an important factor, selected for more than mere atmosphere by reinforcing the human concerns through symbolism. *Peter Grimes* (1944–45), still his most popular opera, is centred on the tragic story of the fisherman Grimes, a loner who cannot overcome his frustrations and anger, which is indirectly responsible for the deaths of the boys who one by one assist him. Of the two other protagonists who dominate the story, one is collective and one is abstract. The Borough – the community who oppose Grimes – is represented by traditional populist elements (folk-like choruses including echoes of shanties and church music) that are a feature of Britten's work. Second, the sea is always present, in broad and often huge seascape music, notably in the orchestral interludes, four of which are often encountered in the concert hall as the *Four Sea Interludes*. Dramatically, the work draws on conventional dramatic elements, and includes scenes at a courthouse and a pub, and a storm.

Peter Grimes is a grand opera, a form which Britten turned to again in *Billy Budd* (discussed below) and in *Gloriana* (1953). This Coronation work is a character study of Queen Elizabeth I, exploring the contrast between the pomp and pageantry of her court and the personal conflict of her relationship with Essex, with its denial of sexuality. It was a failure in the Coronation year, but subsequent revivals have shown its musical strength, especially in its ensembles and the dances combining on-stage and pit orchestras, and again drawing on Britten's sense of archaic tradition. These are sometimes heard on their own. Meanwhile, Britten had turned to chamber opera, partly from practical necessity, partly from a musical preference, and from this grew the English Opera Group, for whom most of the subsequent operas were written. The first two chamber operas present dramatic problems. *The Rape of Lucretia* (1946) is based on a Latin story of trust and love betrayed, spare in style and texture and with elements of Greek drama. The overlay of Christian message (expressed by two singers as chorus) sits ill with the early Roman setting. *Albert Herring* (1947) is a humorous counterpart to *Peter Grimes*, a comedy of rural English manners in which the youth of the title has the choice between following the repressive mores of his elders or a personal fulfilment expressed by his friends. His innocence is lost, but he has not been corrupted. The opera continues to appeal to audiences who do not wish to delve deeper than the attractive and entertaining surface, and this is probably Britten's most popular opera; the satire on the English class system has found a ready response in widely different cultures. But it is also full of many disturbing dramatic anomalies and hidden emotional tensions, inherent in both libretto and music. These are largely unresolved, and for those responsive to them the comic framework of *Albert Herring* can appear an uncomfortable vehicle for such deeper resonances, and the opera emerges as a flawed and unsatisfying experience.

With *The Turn of the Screw* (1954) Britten found a subject better suited to both his concerns and his chamber-opera conceptions. The libretto by Myfanwy Piper on the celebrated ghost story by Henry James combines innocence betrayed (in the destruction of the two children) and ambiguity, in that it is possible to interpret the ghosts and the events – in other words, the entire opera – as some projection of the neuroses of the character who plays the children's governess. Britten's music brings out the layer of the supernatural and the breakdown of mental states; as such this is a drama of the psyche. The tension is heightened by the use of high tessitura and by the prominent

piano, and the taut structure is cast in a theme (a 12-tone row representing the governess's neurosis) and a series of variations in which the different expressions of the theme seem to explore psychological states. The technique, if inspired by **Schoenberg**, is not strictly dodecaphonic: as in subsequent works employing rows there remains a sense of a tonal base, and the contrasts of keys continue to play an important symbolic role.

A Midsummer's Night Dream (1960) is based on Shakespeare's words, with a counter-tenor in the part of Oberon. It introduced into his operas a theme already present in the song-cycles, that of dreams and the night, the area of the subconscious and therefore in touch with the innocence otherwise lost. There are three layers: the Athenians with their urban sophistication; the rustics, humorous but earthy; and the fairy-world of innocence. There are parallel musical layers: children singing against tuned percussion and harp, chordal ideas based on all twelve tones, Puck speaking rather than singing, and represented musically by a trumpet and drum, Oberon associated with the celesta. Britten looks back to the operas of his English operatic predecessor, Purcell (1659–95), while the rustics parody styles ranging from Italian opera to the music hall. Act II is constructed around four chords allocated to different orchestral groups. This is Britten's most delightful and successful comedy.

Owen Wingrave (1970), again based on a Henry James story adapted by Myfanwy Piper, was especially written for television. With its cross-cutting and cinematic techniques it was perhaps the first opera to embrace the technical possibilities of the medium, and as such has failed to transfer successfully to the opera stage. Its subject is pacifism, one of Britten's most deeply held principles, and the opposition in the strange story is between the pacifist Owen and the military traditions of his family, with a supernatural element representing psychological forces. Again, 12-tone elements (with eight different rows) are used, and structurally the aria and ensemble predominate. With its uncompromising message, it seems destined to remain one of Britten's less performed works, in spite of the impact of the music.

Meanwhile in the 1960s Britten developed an aspect that had been latent in earlier works: the element of ritualistic and liturgical theatre for church settings developed from the traditions of Christian mystery plays. In transferring this tradition to a modern aesthetic, Britten was influenced both by the formal theatre of Japanese Noh plays, and by the textures and patterns of Balinese gamelan music, which Britten had discovered in the 1940s and first employed in the extrovert ballet *The Prince of the Pagodas* (1956). The result was the three 'Parables for Church Performance', *Curlew River* (1964), *The Burning Fiery Furnace* (1966) and *The Prodigal Son* (1968), representing respectively hope, faith, and charity. These music-theatre works share features: a simple story amplified by elements of ritual, slow-moving symbolic action and music, and the use of plainchant and procession to introduce and conclude. Bells are prominent, as is the use of heterophony (two independent lines of music presented simultaneously). The atmosphere of these works draws us into an age when man was closer to nature and the impact of ritual, and they need to be experienced in the particular setting, lighting and acoustics of a church to achieve their full impact.

His final opera, *Death in Venice* (1973), based on Thomas Mann's famous novella, is an extraordinary work, a kind of rarefied distillation of Britten's emotional and musical preoccupations (including untouched innocence, the corruption represented by disease, the sea of the Venetian setting, parody, and the musical layers). Here they are seen through an elderly man's eyes, combined with a tragic attempt at rejuvenation and the eventual redemption of death within the sight of innocence. The thematic development parallels Aschenbach's gradual psychological change, and the Venetian characters have aspects of archetypes (as have the ballets through which the boy and his family express themselves and which are associated with gamelan-like percussion). The work has something of the visionary quality of a composer approaching old age, and surely a strong autobiographical element – here the intimacy of deep personal knowledge and experience translated through the allegory of the story. With its implied opposition of Apollo and Dionysus, *Death in Venice* invokes (like the city of its setting) the metaphysical; as such it has a fascinating, if rarefied, appeal.

Britten's operatic masterpiece, however, is *Billy Budd* (1951, revised 1961) – even if it has from the point of view of opera companies one major flaw: an all-male cast. Based on Herman Melville's short novella, to a libretto by E. M. Forster and Eric Crozier, and set on a British naval

ship in 1797, the deceptively simple story of the opposition of good and evil has immediate impact. But closer acquaintance reveals layer after layer of allusion, symbol and spiritual dimension, inherent in Melville's original story, but perfectly integrated into the libretto. It emerges as an exceptionally complex work, from the presentation of the Iago-like Claggart and the innocent Billy Budd as but two aspects of the same force, through the problems of moral choices imposed by human society on a natural order, to the ultimate parable of the theme of action and redemption, with the ship as the symbol of the world. Much of this is perceived subliminally, a perfect medium for a musical setting, and to this Britten responded with music of disarming simplicity. However, the music itself gradually reveals layers of emotional intent, from the detail of instrumental colour and the use of recurrent themes, the duality of a semitone (B flat major/B minor), the expression of humanity through adapted sea-shanties, to broad seascape chords that take on the aspect of the spiritual. It is one of the few operas where the addition of music actually improves and illuminates the impact of a literary masterpiece.

Of his works for soloists, chorus and orchestra, *Spring Symphony* (1949) for soloists, chorus, boys' chorus and orchestra is more an extended song-cycle than a symphony; its subject is the chill of winter leavened by the promise of spring. Its trumpet fanfares set against solo voice look forward to the *War Requiem*, while much of the choral writing anticipates that of *Billy Budd*, though the use of boys whistling is typical of Britten's sense of unusual colour effects, as are the rattling percussion and distant, conch-like call of the opening of the finale. It is perhaps a work to turn to after acquaintance with the better-known scores, fascinating for its moments of ethereal chill and vivacious expectancy, and for its pre-echo of later works. The *War Requiem* (1962), for soprano, tenor, baritone, chorus, boys' chorus, chamber ensemble and orchestra, is very large in scale and liturgical in form, following the Requiem Mass but interspersed with Wilfred Owen's poems. Its subject is 'the pity of war', and it has an undeniable and harrowing impact. Indeed it has sometimes been called Britten's masterpiece; but it is also a cold and almost calculated work. Perhaps because of the subject matter, it misses the element of personal intimacy that informs so much of Britten's best music. Compassion does here almost turn to pity, but it is the haunting individual moments (particularly the apotheosis of the setting of Owen's 'Strange Meeting') that remain in the memory, rather than the overall effect.

Britten's song-cycles stand in the same relationship to his operas as **Shostakovitch's** string quartets do to his symphonies: interior expressions of those same human concerns that are given more extrovert treatment in the larger works. Again, there is a concentration on the importance of the written word, with melodic lines supporting the clarity of expression. The mature song-cycles with orchestra have a common thread in the theme of night and dreams. *Les Illuminations* (1939) for high voice and string orchestra sets the complex imagery of the French poet Rimbaud. The vocal line and the strings act with a spontaneous independence, and the lithe dancing feel of the string colours, from their fanfare opening, remains highly memorable. In the *Serenade* (1943) for tenor, horn and strings it is the shimmering expectancy, sometimes striding forward, sometimes still, but always with a sense of nostalgia reinforced by the high vocal writing and the haunting use of the horn, that has made it the best known of the song-cycles.

Of the song-cycles for high voice and piano, *The Holy Sonnets of John Donne* (1945) is perhaps Britten's most spiritual work. Intense and deeply interior, it was written in reaction to giving a concert with Yehudi Menuhin in one of the newly liberated Nazi death-camps. Sparse accompaniments alternate with pianistic fervour, against long vocal lines with often unexpected phrasing; the central 'Since she whom I loved' transmutes love to a metaphysical plane, and is one of the most beautiful of all English songs. The example of Schubert stands behind *Winter Words* (1953) to poems by Thomas Hardy, the most characteristic of all Britten's song-cycles. Here imbued with a kind of ruggedness, the central Britten themes abound: the innocence of young boys, the ballad, the tradition of liturgical music, oppositions of character, death. The marvellous final song 'A time there was', with its tragic cry ('how long, how long') can stand as a summation of the concept of innocence lost. The five *Canticles* (No. I *My Beloved is Mine*, 1947, No. II *Abraham and Isaac*, 1952, No. III *Still Falls the Rain*, 1954, No. IV *Journey of the Magi*, 1971, No. V *The Death of St Narcissus*, 1974) are settings of single extended poems chosen from sources as varied as a mystery play and T. S.

Eliot. Written with specific performers in mind, they are personal, austere and effective; No. II is almost a miniature dramatic cantata.

An important area of Britten's output are the cello works written for Rostropovich. The *Cello Symphony* (1962–63) integrates the soloist into the orchestra, although the cello part was written for the particular sound of the Russian soloist, and is commensurately virtuoso. The orchestral textures tone down middle ranges (the area of the cello) but emphasise such extremes as the bassoon and the tuba. Unmotivated by any extra-musical associations, the idiom is chromatic and dense, with the largest sonata first movement Britten wrote, again using 12-note elements, and a restraint of pure lyricism until the bright light of the coda. Of the three *Suites* for solo cello (No. 1 op. 72, No. 2 op. 80, No. 3 op. 87), the third includes the use of Russian folk songs, and all show an assimilation of the idiom of **Shostakovich**. The three mature string quartets (No. 1 op. 25, 1941, No. 2 op. 36, 1945, No. 3 op. 94, 1975) demonstrate Britten's concern with the intricacies of form, including sonata form, the chaconne and the passacaglia, and the *String Quartet No. 3 'La Serenissima'* is closely related to *Death In Venice*, using ideas from the opera. Britten himself played the viola, and his sole work for the instrument, *Lachrymae* (for viola and piano, 1950; version for viola and strings, 1976), is unjustly neglected. With a wide range of austere expression, it is based on a song by John Dowland (1563–1626), and reflects on various aspects of the song in variation form before presenting it whole at the end.

Britten's output is striking for the consistency of seriousness and quality. He is one of those rare composers whose lesser-known works almost always reward those seeking them out. With his contemporary and friend **Shostakovich**, he is the composer of the 20th century most motivated by the expression of the psychology of the human condition, and its tragic and traumatic manifestations. As with the Russian composer, this seems to have been fuelled by his own tensions and position as an artist, and in these terms his operas and song-cycles provide a counterpart to the symphonies and string quartets of Shostakovich. He was a staunch supporter of the recording studio, and one of the best interpreters of his own music, recording a large number of his works with the performers for which they were written – a unique legacy. He was also active as a pianist (in chamber music and as accompanist) and as conductor of a wide range of repertoire, with recordings ranging from Schubert songs (with Peter Pears) to **Elgar's** *The Dream of Gerontius*. He also made many arrangements of folk songs, and realisations of the music of Purcell. With Pears and others he founded the famous annual Aldeburgh Festival (1948), set in his home village in Suffolk, and the Britten–Pears School for Advanced Musical Studies. He was created a Companion of Honour in 1953, and raised to the peerage as Baron Britten of Aldeburgh in 1976.

RECOMMENDED WORKS

opera *Billy Budd* (1950–51)
A Ceremony of Carols (1942) for treble voices and harp
Cello Symphony (1962–63)
church parable *Curlew River* (1964)
opera *Death in Venice* (1971–73)
song-cycle *Holy Sonnets of John Donne* (1945)
song-cycle *Les Illuminations* (1939) for high voice and strings
Hymn to St Cecilia (1942) for chorus
Lachrymae for viola and piano (1950)
opera *A Midsummer Night's Dream* (1959–60)
song-cycle *Our Hunting Fathers* (1936) for high voice and orchestra
operetta *Paul Bunyan*
opera *Peter Grimes* (1945)
song-cycle *Serenade* (1943) for tenor, horn and strings
Sinfonia da Requiem (1940) for orchestra
song-cycle *Songs and Proverbs of William Blake* (1965)
String Quartet No. 2 in C (1945)
String Quartet No. 3 (1975)
opera *The Turn of the Screw* (1954)
Variations on a Theme of Frank Bridge (1937) for string orchestra
Violin Concerto (1939)
War Requiem (1961)
song-cycle *Winter Words* (1953)

BIBLIOGRAPHY

H. Carpenter, *Benjamin Britten: A Biography*, 1992
C. Headington, *Britten*, 1981
I. Holst, *Britten*, 1966, revised 1980
M. Kennedy, *Britten*, 1981
C. Palmer (ed.), *The Britten Companion*, 1984
E. W. White, *Benjamin Britten: His Life and Operas*, 1970, revised 1983

Davies (Sir) Peter Maxwell**
born 8th September 1934 at Manchester

Internationally regarded as the leading (if the least emulated) British composer of his generation, Peter Maxwell Davies has shown a totally individual consistency of intent, concern and style, while his music has gradually evolved from infuriating the establishment to dismaying the admirers of the new. Encompassing all forms, it ranges from the arcane and highly complex to the most happily straightforward, but almost always with an unmistakable voice and underlying seriousness of purpose.

His works show a number of consistent features within this wide range of styles. Firstly, he is steeped in the symbolism and psychology (rather than the religious dogma) of Christianity, which for him seems to serve as the expression of, or the metaphor for, a collective unconscious that underlies all human action, including the creation of music. A feature of this symbolism has been his use of archetypes (the King, the Fiddler, the Jester) in vocal or dramatic works. Secondly, he is fascinated by the interaction and indivisibility of thesis and antithesis, be it in human character or in musical structure, and this is linked to the Christian heritage in particular by an exploration of good and evil, and especially of the betrayal that links the two. Thirdly, he has used pre-Classical music of various periods and types, as a regular starting-point for his own music (often with an element of parody). The music is linked to Christianity by allusions to religious works, and to thesis and antithesis both by the contrast of the old and the new and by the choice of subject matter in works with words. Finally, since his discovery of the Orkney Islands in Scotland (in particular the island of Hoy) in 1970 and his subsequent move there, his output has been steeped in Orcadian tradition and a sense of community and local purpose, and he has succeeded in combining these with the themes of betrayal and opposites, the Christian themes, and the utilisation of old forms and musical ideas.

Stylistically, Maxwell Davies has always shown great individuality. His structures, while latterly including recognised forms (such as the symphony), have regularly been built on arcane, and particularly medieval, ideas. These have included proportion (time signatures changing according to ancient proportional rules), number symbolism (such as the use of nine, as in nine movements, or fourteen, representing the Stations of the Cross), but most pertinently the use of the 'magic square'. In this construction the elements of the square are typically pitch and/or duration, and the square can be read across, up-and-down or diagonally, and includes symmetry. Maxwell Davies uses these lines to create a sequence of rows, and although most of these effects are sensed by the listener rather than recognised, they do create a strong sense of structure. Harmonically, the atonal (and often dissonant) palette is tempered by a sense of direction towards a tonal point (often aided by the repetition of a tonal centre created by the symmetry or palindromic effect of the 'magic squares'). This rarely acts as a resolution, but more often as a launching point for new directions, reinforced by the inconclusive endings of many of his works, particularly in the 1960s and 1970s. In his extensive music for children and amateurs his harmonic concepts are much more conventional, and his more sophisticated works have recently followed suit. The extensive recall of old music is usually filtered through this harmonic language, creating distortions that often amount to parody or pastiche. This sense of imbalance is reinforced by the gestural exaggerations, and by contrasts of expression, though again these have mellowed in recent works and have been absent in much of the simpler music. The instrumentation favours bright, incisive colours, with extremes of register, though bells have been an important colour element, reaching their culmination in the sonorous *Turris campanarum sonantium* (1971) for one percussionist and tape, and then evolving to the softer colours of tuned percussion.

After the initial discovery of the European post-Webern movement, in conjunction with Harrison **Birtwistle**, Alexander Goehr, the pianist John Ogden and the trumpeter Elgar Howarth (collectively and briefly known as the 'Manchester School'), and in study with **Petrassi** and **Sessions**, he eventually found his personal idiom with a group of works based on the reforging of material from Monteverdi's *Vespers 1610* (the *String Quartet*, 1961, the *Leopardi Fragments*, for soprano, contralto and instrumental ensemble, 1962, and the rather boring *Sinfonia*, 1962). They were followed by a series of works centred around the opera *Taverner* (1962–70), and including elements of the Tudor master's music. The opera itself, based on a (probably erroneous) version of Taverner's life with a theme of betrayal

(Taverner moves from musician of the Catholic church to its persecutor, while a parallel desiccation takes place in his own art), uses a declamatory vocal style and a contrast between the orchestra (Taverner's thoughts and reactions) and ancient instruments (other characters and events). In parallel with this opera appeared *Three Fantasies on an In Nomine of John Taverner* (1962, 1964, and 1963–64): the first for orchestra, the second a single-movement symphony, with a sense of irony and distortion in the otherwise grand statement, and the third containing rather strident writing for wind quintet, harp, and string quartet.

With the founding (with **Birtwistle**) of the chamber ensemble the Pierrot Players in 1967, and its evolution in 1970 into the Fires of London (without Birtwistle), Maxwell Davies's writing entered a new phase. To this day the scale and instrumentation of many of his works have been determined by the forces of the Fires of London. The themes of Christianity, betrayal and distortion of medieval music continued in *Antechrist* (1967) for piccolo, bass clarinet, violin, cello, and three percussionists, but new elements of parody, particularly the foxtrot of Thirties dance bands, were added to the scheme. The large-scale orchestral work *St Thomas Wake* (1969) exemplifies many of Davies's concerns and traits of this period, and because of its populist elements is one of the most effective ways to approach his idiom. It is built in three layers: a pavane by John Bull (1562–1628), the purity of ancient music here associated with the harp; a Thirties band that plays, with an element of nostalgia, a series of foxtrots based on that pavane; and a modern orchestra, distant and alien in feel but often (with a number of unusual instruments) powerful in its range of colours and blocks of uncompromising effect. With such a structure, it becomes a moving montage of three time periods.

However, of the music written for the Pierrot Players and then the Fires of London, it is the music-theatre pieces that have attracted most attention. The unstaged *Revelation and Fall* (1966), for soprano and sixteen players, had already used savage contrasts between a more subdued vocal writing and primal outbursts (through a loudhailer). *Missa super l'homme armé* (1968, revised 1971) contained antithesis, in the form of a figure in robes of the opposite sex, and the theme of spiritual betrayal, while the pastiche includes Victorian songs, foxtrots, barn-yard noises, pop music and machinery. It employs harsh extremes and has a ninefold structure. The extraordinary *Eight Songs for a Mad King* (1969) showed that the format of **Schoenberg**'s *Pierrot Lunaire*, whose scale, approach and broad aims it shares, was not an isolated event. The highly expressive instrumental ensemble (in cages, representing the bullfinches to whom the mad King is trying to teach music) react to a soloist who must use the very extremes of vocal expression to por-tray the mad King, on texts by Robert Stow after George III. Quotations from Handel and other music of the period are woven into the fabric, and the sense not only of the protagonist's madness, but also of the narrow division between the audien-ce's state of mind and that of the King make this one of the most compelling pieces ever written for music theatre. The idiom was further refined (with the instru-mental group more obviously supporting the soloist) in the sympathetic study of a deranged woman, *Miss Donnithorne's Maggot* (1974) for mezzo-soprano and instrumental group. The *Vesalii icones* (1969) for ensemble, cello and dancer brought together the foxtrot and the betrayal of Christ. This avenue has been further explored in the music-theatre pieces *Blind Man's Bluff* (1972) and *Le Jongleur de Notre-Dame* (1978), using instrumentalists as actors. The larger-scale opera *The Lighthouse* (1979) has maintained a peripheral place in the mod-ern repertoire. In the same period appeared one of his most beautiful works, and one of the easiest to approach, *A Mirror of Whitening Light* (1976–77), for fourteen instruments.

With his move to the Orkneys, a further element has been added to his music. On an obvious level there have been a series of lighter and approachable works (including many for children) that have had a strong Scottish flavour (notably the highly colour-ful *An Orkney Wedding with Sunrise*, 1985, for orchestra, which is the equivalent of a **Sibelius** or **Nielsen** tone poem). But a number of haunting and sometimes tragic song-cycles, especially to the words of the Hebridean poet George Mackay Brown, have specifically reflected the influence of Orkney life and the colour and light of the sea and the islands, with a more direct lyrical flow, while still employing Maxwell Davies's idioms and harmonic designs. Thus *From Stone to Thorne* (1971) for soprano, bass clarinet, harpsichord, guitar and percussion creates a relationship between the Stations of the Cross and the agricultural seasons. The vocal line, unlike many of his other vocal works, allows the soloist a number of notes on one syllable, with softer instrumental colours. The *Hymn to St Magnus* (1972) for mezzo-soprano and orchestra combines the vio-lence of martyrdom and the violence of the sea, founded on the famous 12th-century Orcadian hymn, while the dour, brooding *Dark Angels* (1973) effectively combines the guitar with the soprano. The parable opera *The Martyrdom of St Magnus* (1976), with instrumentation of sextet, guitar and brass trio, shows a return to the themes of betrayal and savagery and again uses the foxtrot as the music of evil. *Into the Labyrinth* (1983) for tenor and cham-ber orchestra sets poetry of Mackay Brown, and exactly mirrors the clear, monochromatic light of the north, with distant echoes of **Sibelius** in the ending. The overall effect is of a natural simplicity, with a flowing, lyrical vocal line and spar-tan, well-defined orchestral textures. The *Sinfonietta accademica* (1983) for cham-ber orchestra, in spite of its title, again reflects the sights and sounds of the Ork-ney landscape, interwoven with plainsong chant. It opens with a drunken reel, and has moments of humour throughout, though its general tone is a rather bleak seriousness, like an early winter northern landscape.

At the same time, Maxwell Davies has continued to expand his larger scale forms, attempting, as in the specifically Orcadian works, to evolve a simpler and 'stronger' language that can still cope with complex forms. The *Symphony No. 1* (1978 from material begun in 1973) is a complex, difficult and sometimes ghostly work, dominated by the colours of the large tuned percussion section, and including the use of the plainsong 'Ave Maris Stella'. The influence of **Sibelius**, only implicit in this work, is more obvious in both the *Symphony No. 2* (1980) – the extent of harmonic evolution is indicated by its des-ignation with a key, B – and the *Symphony No. 3* (1985), with their more direct orches-tral sound and the influence of the sea. Two more symphonies have followed; the *Sym-phony No. 5* (1994) is, at twenty-five minutes, the shortest to date. Another more direct work is the full-scale, two-hour ballet *Salome* (1978), full of stunning and often very graphic orchestral effects, from the delicate to the use of raucous noise makers. It is especially rewarding in its *Dance Suite* form (1979). The some-times droll but rather nebulous *Sinfonia* *concertante* (1982) is a distant reflection of the classical period, with a wind quintet and timpani as the concertante instruments. The *Violin Concerto* (1985) is in a big Romantic style, only lightly tempered by Maxwell Davies's usual harmonic language. The influence of the Scottish dance weaves in and out, and the end of the cadenza is especially beautiful, although the large scale sits rather uneasily with his idiom. A major chamber work of the period is the powerful and tense *Image, Reflection, Shadow* (1982) for chamber ensemble, whose instrumentation includes a cimbalom.

Among his more recent works has been the ninety-minute opera *The Resurrection* (1988), for seven singers, five dancers, and an orchestra that includes a pop group, a Salvation Army band, and pre-recorded tape. Maxwell Davies had been planning this work, an attack on the commercialism of American popular culture and the concept of instant material gratification, for twenty-five years. Its range is eclectic, including twenty-four television commercials, eight pop songs, and various transmutations of plainsong, while drawing on Dürer's Apocalypse woodcuts and Jung's alchemic illustrations. The central plot is of a 'Hero' who is abused by family and school, is transformed by Four Surgeons, and is resurrected as a huge monster figure.

His works for children and for schools were originally inspired by a period of teaching at Cirencester Grammar School (1959–62), and his continuing achievements in this field have been widely admired. They include *The Shepherd's Calendar* (1965) for voices and a large instrumental ensemble, piano music, songs for young children, and two operas for children: *The Two Fiddlers* (1978) who travel the path of wisdom to combat philistinism, and *Cinderella* (1978–79) for younger children.

In 1977 Maxwell Davies founded the highly successful St Magnus Festival in Kirkwall, the Orkneys, and since 1985 he has been associate composer/conductor of the Scottish Chamber Orchestra. He was knighted in 1987.

RECOMMENDED WORKS
  Dark Angels (1974) for soprano and
    guitar
  music theatre *Eight Songs for a Mad
    King* (1969)
  A Mirror of Whitening Light
    (1976–1977) for 14 instruments
  music theatre *Miss Donnithorne's
    Maggot* (1974)

  sextet *Image, Reflection, Shadow*
    (1982)
  Into the Labyrinth (1983) for tenor
    and orchestra
  An Orkney Wedding with Sunrise
    (1985) for orchestra
  St Thomas Wake (1969) for orchestra
  Turris campanarum sonantium
    (1971) for percussionist

BIBLIOGRAPHY
  P. Griffiths, *Peter Maxwell Davies*,
    1982

Delius Frederick Theodore Albert**

born 29th January 1862 at Bradford
died 10th June 1934 at Grez-sur-Loing
(France)

The music of Frederick Delius occupies a unique position in the English tradition. Often incorrectly called Impressionistic, it consists rather of a rich tapestry of sensuous textures that have touches of Impressionism (although Delius developed his style independently of such potential French models as **Debussy**), but equally stretch back to a heady Germanic lushness. The Impressionist sense of time suspended, where the end of a work folds back on its beginning, is largely absent in Delius's work; the complex fluidity of Delius's rhythmic flow can create this Impressionistic effect, but it is more purposeful, the linear progression aiming at distinct goals. In addition, Delius adds an English sensibility to his idiom, and this element, often half-submerged in the surrounding textures, has affinities with English pastoralism. His musical temperament is a poetic response to nature, sometimes wistfully sad, sometimes ecstatic.

His music is far less popular now than it used to be, or perhaps deserves to be. Part of the reason is that unusual position; part is his relatively narrow range of idiom and type of work; another part may be ascribed to the fact that, from the age of twenty-one he lived abroad, first in Florida and elsewhere in the United States (1882–86), and from 1888 to the end of his life in France. His American stay recurs as an influence in his music. The most enduring output is to be found in his orchestral tone poems and a number of visionary choral works; to them may be added a number of characteristic but never wholly successful operas, and four concertos. These genres intermingle throughout his career: there is no period of particular concentration on one. His idiom was never suited to large-scale orchestral works, or the more traditional forms such as the symphony or the string quartet. His relatively small output was hampered from the age of sixty by the effects of syphilis, and his major works written after 1928 (and which include often extensive reworking of earlier material) were constructed with the help of a young amanuensis, Eric Fenby, a remarkable story in itself.

The first of his major orchestral works was the 'nocturne for orchestra' *Paris – The Song of a Great City* (1899). It evokes Whistler rather than the Impressionists, a sultry Paris night, redolent of the lazy flow of the Seine, but also of the glitter and dazzle of a city still awake and enjoying itself. There are touches of **Strauss**, but the pattern of textures and the fluid rhythmic interplay are Delian. *Appalachia* (1898–1903) added a chorus to the orchestra, and is based on a theme that Delius heard on a Virginia tobacco plantation ('Oh honey, I am coming down the river in the morning'). *In a Summer Garden* (1908), *Summer Night on the River* (1911) and *On Hearing the First Cuckoo in Spring* (1912) represented the application of Delius's idiom to a more obvious nature-painting, on a smaller scale and decidedly French in quality (though the last uses a Norwegian folk song Delius probably learnt from Grieg), and have remained his most popular works. The earlier *Brigg Fair* (1907), using a large orchestra, is equally Delian, in spite of its English title. *Eventyr* (1917) seeks to evoke the spirit of Norwegian folk myths, peopled by goblins, sprites and elves, and although these characters do charge across the rich textured landscape that has touches of northern tone-painting, here Delius's lack of focus and strong emotional contrasts works to his disadvantage.

Delius's concertos have sometimes been described as more rhapsodies than concertos, partly because of the single-movement forms. The early and rather uncharacteristic *Piano Concerto* (1897, often revised) includes rather grand Romantic gestures in its arsenal, but indeed has a rhapsodic and continuous flow. The short *Double Concerto* (1915–16) for violin, cello and orchestra, and the *Violin Concerto* (1916), however, have a complex and assured evolution of thematic ideas across the general sections into which the one-movement forms are divided, creating genuine, if unconventional, concerto-symphonic development. The *Violin Concerto* is one of Delius's finer works, whereas the rhapsodic *Cello Concerto* (1921), which was his own favourite among the concertos (because of the melodic invention), is too meandering to match the earlier string works.

Arguably the finest and most characteristic music of Delius uses voice and chorus. The reasons for its neglect are understandable: the mixture of sensuous and visionary ecstasy (to texts by Nietzsche, Whitman, and the most mystic and ecstatic passages of the Bible), a pantheistic and essentially Eastern philosophy, and Impressionistic tone colours (with the chorus often submerged in that tone-painting) has not appealed to the English choral tradition, and has been disparaged by critics, although the philosophy and the idiom have proved far more enduring than his detractors suggested, and lie well within the scope of current experience. The *Requiem* (1914–16) for tenor, chorus and orchestra is a much finer work than its general reputation would suggest, sensuous and ecstatic, rich in texture in its huge orchestra, with moments of more acerbic harmony than is usual in Delius. Its text (by Delius, drawing on the Bible), is pantheistic in feel, expressing the duality of life in death and death in life. It is the English equivalent of the sensuous sound of **Szymanowski**, and musically and spiritually is very far removed from the usual Requiem text, which probably explains its almost total neglect. It is also more tautly concise than the work usually acknowledged as Delius's masterpiece, the *Mass of Life* (1904–05) for soloists, chorus and orchestra, which, although uneven, encapsulates Delius's musical vision and philosophy. Based on Nietzsche's *Also Sprach Zarathustra*, this long work in two parts displays Delius's soaring passion, his sense of the elemental mysteries of the hours of the day and the feeling of noble joy in the equation of night and death, as well as moments of intense drama, as in the opening invocation. *Sea Drift* (1903–04) for baritone, chorus and orchestra is a setting of the central part of Walt Whitman's famous poem. Whitman's poetic style of densely packed imagery suited Delius's equally richly textured musical style, with its dense choral writing, and this idiom was further developed in one of his finest works, the neglected *Songs of Sunset* (1906–08) for mezzo, baritone, chorus and orchestra. The eight poems by the 19th-century poet Ernest Dowson, set in a continuous flow, are again rich in sensuous imagery, framed by the theme of the dream, and there is marked convergence of forces into a single general texture, suffused in joyous sunset colours, even when touched by pale amber autumnal shades. The third song is almost entirely Impressionist, time suspended, woodwind figures adding detail, until the final bars of solo violin that break the spell. Whitman was again the inspiration for the fine *Songs of Farewell* (1930–32) for chorus and orchestra. Delius wrote some sixty songs, influenced by Brahms and Grieg and mostly dating from before 1902.

Of Delius's operas the best known is *A Village Romeo and Juliet* (1900–01, revised 1910), to a libretto by Jelka Delius based on a story by the Swiss poet Gottfried Keller set in 19th-century Switzerland. It bears no relationship to Shakespeare's tale whatsoever, apart from the common theme of two fathers who quarrel and whose children fall in love and die. It is one of those operas that ought to work, but misfires; the simple plot, that on first sight would seem entirely suitable for Delius's idiom, in fact works against it. Where another composer might have seized on the archetypal symbolism (the blind fiddler, the boatman of death), Delius treats their emotions literally in a heady sensual richness (in part derived from Wagner) that becomes wearisome in its regularity. But it represented a development in Delius's handling of fine orchestral detail (with a huge orchestra used sparingly), and one purely orchestral passage has become celebrated in the concert hall as *A Walk to the Paradise Gardens*, a poetical evocation of a slow summer stroll enveloped in love. *Koanga* (1895–97) has a much more interesting, if bizarre, plot, set in the kind of Louisiana plantation known to Delius in his youth, and involving a captured African chieftain, sexual predation, incest and destruction, all contained within the framework of a tale told on the verandah of the plantation house. Delius salvaged the best music of *Margot-la-rouge* (1902) for a vocal-orchestral work, *Idyll* (1930–32) for soprano, baritone and orchestra. A text was drawn from Whitman to create a rich love duet, but apart from the very beautiful orchestral introduction the result is turgid until it takes life in the duets of the close. The opera itself, long thought lost, was resurrected by Fenby from a piano score made by **Ravel**.

Delius was undoubtedly a composer who limited himself to a narrow range of idiom, and reactions to his music are usually marked: it is reasonable to suggest that if

one does not respond to a particular piece, one is unlikely to appreciate the rest, and vice-versa. His importance to British music is generally underestimated. He was one of the first composers of the English revival to raise English music to high standards, and his idiom opened up possibilities for other English composers.

RECOMMENDED WORKS
> *Double Concerto* (1915–16) for violin cello and orchestra
> *A Mass of Life* (1904–05) for soloists, chorus and orchestra
> *Paris – The Song of a Great City* (1899) for orchestra
> *Requiem* (1914–16) for soprano, baritone, chorus and orchestra
> *Sea Drift* (1903–04) for baritone, chorus and orch.
> *Songs of Sunset* (1906–08) for mezzo-soprano, baritone, chorus and orchestra
> opera *A Village Romeo and Juliet* (1900–01)
> Violin Concerto (1916)

BIBLIOGRAPHY
> E. Fenby, *Delius as I Knew Him*, 1936, 1981
> C. Redwood (ed.), *A Delius Companion*, 1976

Elgar (Sir) Edward William***
born 2nd June 1857 at Broadheath (Worcestershire)
died 23rd February 1934 at Worcester

Elgar remains the figurehead of the revival of British music, the first English composer since Purcell with an internationally appreciated, distinctively individual voice. His reputation (justly) rests on a handful of works, and his output, which is mainly orchestral and choral, divides into three broad groups which all reflect aspects of his complex personality. The first are the masterpieces that have, slowly but surely, established his status as an international master: the *Enigma Variations*, the *Introduction and Allegro* for strings, the two symphonies, the two concertos, and the oratorio *The Dream of Gerontius*. What distinguishes the power and pertinence of these works (with the exception of the *Introduction and Allegro*, and less obviously in the *Enigma Variations*) is that, amid the undoubted grandeur and expressions of joy, sometimes ecstasy, is an anguished psychological drama. It is not the personal angst of the

Romanticism from which Elgar evolved; rather it is a deep sense of uncertainty, of insecurity, of loss or hopelessness, inextricably woven into the fabric. Such an aesthetic is particularly a 20th-century experience, and is why his music (like that of his contemporary **Mahler**) is finding an increasing international response, however much it may use the remnants of 19th-century orchestral means. This unusual combination was responsible for much of the misunderstanding of Elgar's work. His reputation was coloured by distaste for his salon or ceremonial music, a failure of differentiation still unthinkingly found in some musical circles today. That such an aesthetic was capable of musical evolution into more modern techniques was subsequently shown by **Walton**, who in many respects continues the Elgarian tradition.

The second group are works that, while often of great beauty, nobility or interest, do not carry such a personal message. Some, like the oratorios *The Apostles* and *The Kingdom*, are bound up in the complex but dying choral tradition of the previous epoch; others, like the tone poem *Falstaff*, have particularly English cultural associations; while in works such as the five *Pomp and Circumstance Marches*, or the shorter pieces for strings, the scale of form is more miniature.

The third group belongs to a different aesthetic, the residue of Victorian English music values, and is a response to the Edwardian fervour (but rarely, in spite of his reputation, jingoism) and the fey cloying sentimentality of the day. This aesthetic is alien to modern tastes; readers exploring his lesser-known music should not expect the same quality as in the more celebrated scores. Nor is this division necessarily chronological: the salon ordinariness of the suite from *The Starlight Express* (1915), for example, postdates both the symphonies and the violin concerto.

His idiom is Romantic, drawing on the broad sweep of Brahms and the shifting harmonic example of Wagner, alloyed by a Gallic clarity which has elements in common with the music of the French composer Jules Massenet (1842–1912). Although Elgar is often referred to as quintessentially English, such a description is very misleading (and confusing, for abroad it is his ceremonial works that are associated with the 'English'). For his music belongs to the general European context of the time and the Austro-Germanic tradition in particular. He has little in common with the succeeding generation of English nationalists (and was not affected by the folk music renaissance). His legacy to them was the inspiration of his pioneering career as a professional composer rather than his musical idiom.

His ability to express the nobility of the human condition (with his favourite marking 'nobilmente') is unmatched. His orchestration is among the most assured of any in any age, often mixing tone colours in rapid succession but always with clarity, and building climaxes by the development of colour (especially brass comment) as well as thematic ideas. Smaller changes of mood are usually initiated by the momentary comment of a new colour, such as the harp, and timpani are prominent. Strong bass lines, often emphasised in the orchestral colours, impart a sense of solid foundation and purposeful momentum. The sense of insecurity, of loss, is regularly achieved by yearning strings in broad falling ideas, backed by muted, punctuating orchestral colours, and by rapidly shifting keys. Thematic ideas, often profuse, build from shorter phrases, adding to a feel of a rich orchestral palette, and structural unity is regularly reinforced by returning themes, either with a cyclical intent or in the form of motto themes. There is a prevalent rhythmic feel of being somewhat restlessly on the move, often varied by a characteristic use of triplets, but creating a very natural, almost evolutionary sense of progression from one episode of emotional mood to another.

Almost entirely self-taught (and thus partly divorced from the stifling Victorian English music education), he was already in his forties when a trio of works brought him recognition. The song-cycle *Sea Pictures* (1897–99) for contralto and large orchestra with organ obbligato is in the English vocal tradition revitalised by **Stanford**, but its melodiousness (if not its indifferent verse) has assured it a permanent place in the repertoire. The *Variations on an Original Theme* (*Enigma*), invariably known as the *Enigma Variations* (1898) for orchestra, is Elgar's first masterpiece and remains perhaps his best-known large-scale work. In spite of a hidden counter-theme that has never been successfully identified and the portraits of friends (and himself) in the thirteen variations and finale, the music's impact is abstract, with a wide range of mood developed from the grandeur of the theme in masterful orchestral colours (including hushed timpani played with coins). Three sides of Elgar's idiom are present: the broad, impressive sweep, the distant sense of interior tragedy, and a delight in bustling vigour.

The visionary power of *The Dream of Gerontius* (1898–1900) for soloists, chorus and orchestra, has triumphed in spite of Cardinal Newman's unusual text, describing the passage of the soul of a dying man into the eventual presence of God, which many have found difficult to accept. Its dramatic intensity and structure are almost operatic in fervour, heightened by the use of a semi-chorus as well as a chorus, and marked a new departure for the English choral tradition. Repeated motifs bind the work together, and the massive orchestra, with its stunning climax in the introduction (eventually answered in the vision of God at the end), is almost a protagonist in itself. The mood varies from grandeur to haunted resignation and serene acceptance, and the part of Gerontius requires as much expression of character as any operatic role.

The *Introduction and Allegro* (1901–05), for string quartet and string orchestra, is a vigorous and sometimes lyrical abstract evocation recalling the composer's love of his native landscape, with a tune for viola inspired by a song Elgar heard in Wales. It is also a study in rich and bold string textures, the string quartet at times taking an almost concertante role, with the powerful contrapuntal writing that is such a feature of Elgar's idiom. But perhaps the best of Elgar is found in the two symphonies, both extensive and very wide-ranging in mood, with something of the breadth of Bruckner, especially in the slow movements. In the *Symphony No. 1* (1907–08), the more sunlit of the two, the pulse is constantly varied, with a sense of small-scale ebb and flow (sometimes within a phrase) merging into larger emotional changes. This is achieved by a profusion of smaller themes in addition to the main ideas (including a motto theme), and by the constant flow of orchestral colours, often assigning different elements of an idea to different instruments or instrumental blocks and creating an effect of rapidly changing light and shade. The scherzo, full of powerful energy, is more direct, and the emotional weight is reserved for an adagio that is orchestrally broadened by divided strings. The marvellously assertive ending exemplifies another Elgarian touch: surging snatches of orchestral phrases set against the broad main idea, creating a feeling of excitement and nobility. The *Symphony No. 2* (1903–11, but whose ideas were brought

together in only seven weeks, 1911) is both a more difficult work and an achievement of greater spiritual weight, suffused with a sense of disillusionment. All the complexities of Elgar's personality emerge, from the combination of nobility and restless uncertainty in the opening, the mixture of yearning and fear in the rondo, to the quiet resignation of the ending, all passion spent. The heart of the work is the larghetto, sometimes referred to as a funeral march; this is misleading, for it is much more a lament in which warm affection and still unresigned disillusionment are merged, to be seen as but two sides of the same emotion. That characteristic surging effect here reaches its culmination, with unforgettable impact.

The relative obscurity of the *Violin Concerto* (1909–10) is largely due to the difficult nature, both technically and emotionally, of the solo part, and the limited number of soloists prepared to tackle it. Although full of virtuoso requirements, the almost continuous solo line, predominantly lyrical though in constant fluctuation, is discursive and sometimes almost philosophical, and requires unremitting emotional as well as musical interplay between the soloist and orchestra. The *Cello Concerto* (1919, arranged as a *Viola Concerto* by Lionel Tertis with the composer's approval, 1933) is Elgar's swan-song – the handful of subsequent works are minor in design and intent. Its emergence in the last three decades as a standard work of the concerto repertoire has been responsible as much as anything else for the renewed recognition of Elgar's genius. With a four-movement form (linked in pairs), the orchestra is much more restrained than in Elgar's previous works, and the cello dominates. The mood is that of a rich sunset shot through with sadness but with passages of bright gold, and the solo line is song-like almost throughout; in the slow movement it is continuous except for one bar, overwhelmingly sad but never sentimental.

Much of Elgar's music was inspired by people he knew, and in the symphonic poem *Falstaff* (1913, from earlier sketches), he brought his versatile powers of portraiture – from the boisterous to the tender, from the subtle to the extrovert – to bear on the Shakespearean character. As fine, and perhaps more immediate, is the vivid orchestral portrait of London in the concert overture *Cockaigne* (*In London Town*) (1901), a tone poem in its own right. The five *Pomp and Circumstance*

Marches (1901–30) need little introduction, as the first has become an alternative British national anthem. It has rather overshadowed the infectious merits of the other four, which are as much full of joy as pomp; No. 5 is especially satisfying. The concerto overture *In the South (Alassio)* (1903–04) is another tone poem, inspired by the Italian light and landscape, and by the tumult of ancient conflicts. To set alongside the *Introduction and Allegro* are two lovely, deeply emotional and introverted pieces, the *Elegy for Strings* (1909) and *Sospiri* (1914), for strings, harp and organ. The *Serenade for Strings* (1892) is equally attractive, the first of its three movements slightly ruminative, the second predominately still, broad and lyrical. The two *Wand of Youth Suites* (1907 and 1908), which are sometimes heard, are diverting reworkings of childhood compositions.

The huge oratorios, *The Apostles* (1903) and *The Kingdom* (1901–06), two parts of a projected trilogy, present considerable problems. Both are Wagnerian in inspiration (*The Apostles* has eighty leitmotifs, *The Kingdom* seventy-eight), and there are some inspirational moments, notably in some of the choral writing. However, with the exception of Judas, the strong characterisation of Gerontius is absent, the overall impression is too dense, too swollen, and these works are rarely performed. Apart from some early salon pieces, his three chamber works (the *Violin Sonata in E minor*, 1918, the *String Quartet*, 1918, and the *Piano Quintet*, 1918–19) were all written in the same period as the *Cello Concerto*. Those already convinced by Elgar's idiom will respond to the leaner textures; others may feel that the strengths of the works, particularly the seriousness of the quintet and the element of the pastoral in the quartet, do not mitigate the uneven inspiration or the absence of the depth of expression Elgar found in the colours of his orchestration. Of his transcriptions of the works of other composers, his orchestration of JS Bach's *Fantasia and Fugue in C minor* and of Parry's famous song *Jerusalem* are outstanding, while his version of the British national anthem (*God Save the King*) is the most impressive yet penned.

So long dismissed by so many as a relic of the Edwardian period, a repository of the sentiments of a dying imperial culture, Elgar has emerged as composer who, while at times reflecting his era in an immediately recognisable and individual language that belongs to the culmination of the Romantic tradition, also expressed conflicts of emotions and personality that seem timeless.

He taught for a short and stormy period at Birmingham University (1906–08), and held various conducting posts. He became a member of the Order of Merit (a distinguished royal honour) in 1911, Master of the King's Musick in 1924, was knighted in 1928, made a baronet in 1931, and received further royal honours in 1933. He was one of the first composers to take a keen professional interest in the new medium of gramophone recordings, so that his distinguished interpretations of many of his major works survive.

RECOMMENDED WORKS
  Cello Concerto (1919)
  oratorio *Dream of Gerontius* (1899–1900)
  Elegy for Strings (1909)
  Enigma Variations (1899) for orchestra
  tone-poem *Falstaff* (1913)
  Introduction and Allegro (1904–05) for strings
  Pomp and Circumstance Marches 1–5 (1901–30) for orchestra
  song-cycle *Sea Pictures* (1899)
  Sospiri (1914) for strings, harp and organ
  Symphony No. 1 in A (1908)
  Symphony No. 2 in E (1910)
  Violin Concerto (1910)

BIBLIOGRAPHY
  M. Kennedy, *Portrait of Elgar*, 1968
  J. N. Moore, *Edward Elgar: A Creative Life*, 1984
  P. M. Young, *Elgar O.M.*, 1955

Ferneyhough Brian*
born 16th January 1943 at Coventry

Brian Ferneyhough has the reputation of being one of the most intractable of post-**Webern** composers, taking serialism to its limits. He has become the leader of the British 'New Complexity' movement, although he has lived outside Britain since the early 1970s. His formidable reputation was established by the length (over forty minutes) and dense details of the *Sonatas for String Quartet* (1967–75), while his writings on his own works have added to the daunting image.

In reality, this bogey-dragon turns out to have a benign breath, rather than an sulphurous one. Ferneyhough's almost Rococo imagination creates larger-scale works which teem with decoration and detail and hence have a complex fecundity, but which are following carefully organised patterns. The basic conception is serial, with each element of the music independently organised, but it is a serialisation that is extended to include those decorations as well as instrumental or vocal effects and details. The longer spans are created from the mass of this detail, changing their interactions and contours, with internal connections between the short sections that many Ferneyhough works employ. These constructions can be extremely complex (and difficult to perform), requiring close attention to understand; but, such is the sense of logic underlying the idiom, the sympathetic listener can identify these shapes without necessarily grasping all their workings. The resultant idiom is very expressive and often forthright, creating an unusual sound world that has considerable impact.

The *Sonatas for String Quartet* are in twenty-four short movements; their intense idiom, bound by internal repetitions and recognizable figures within the sections, is relieved by cadenza-like passages for the individual instruments. But as good a place as any to dispel any preconceptions about Ferneyhough's music is the *String Quartet No. 2* (1980). It is an ascetically sensuous work, direct and expressive, with nimble detail of movement over denser textures in a combination of independent and convergent lines. There is an unusual atmosphere in this quartet that appears in many Ferneyhough works: the short, darting phrases and the chattering effects seem like live creatures – perhaps birds, flitting purposefully here and there, their paths crossing, reaching some undefined boundary, and swinging back again.

A tendency in Ferneyhough's output has been to maintain a concept through a series or group of works. The central series of the 1970s were the *Time and Motion Studies*: No. 1 for bass clarinet (1971–77), No. 2 for cello, delay tape, modulation and amplification (1973–76), and No. 3 for sixteen voices, percussion and tape (1974). Central to the 1980s was the cycle *Carceri d'invenzione* (1981–86), which continues the concept of the boundary so audibly palpable in the *String Quartet No. 2*. The title, inspired by Piranesi etchings, means both 'dungeons of invention' and 'imaginary dungeons'. The pieces are wide-ranging in format, but have a common element in the sound of the flute family, moving

from the piccolo to the bass flute as the series progresses. Three works form the core of the series: *Carceri d'invenzione I* (1982) for chamber orchestra, one of Ferneyhough's densest works in which the patterns turn in on themselves with a feeling of claustrophobia; what amounts to a flute concerto in *Carceri d'invenzione IIa* (1984) for flute and chamber orchestra; and *Carceri d'invenzione III* (1986) for eighteen winds and three percussion. Around these are ranged works for smaller forces. The series opens with *Superscriptio* (1981), a high, fast, darting piccolo solo, and ends with *Mnemosyne* (1986) for bass flute and tape, a wistful, tranquil and very beautiful work with the fluttering and humming of the bass flute set against held notes on the tape, producing non-dissonant resonances that will present listening problems to no one. *Intermedio alla ciaccona* (1986) for violin deliberately adds a hard, ugly edge to the sound, but the most substantial of these works is *Etudes transcendentales* (1982–85) for soprano and ensemble including harpsichord. This song-cycle sets nine short and pithy poems by Ernst Meister and Alrun Moll contemplating transience, each with a different instrumental combination. The conjunction of logic and dynamic expression is formidable, cast with great clarity; the strict control of material leads to an almost improvisatory freedom (the oboe writing of the opening song having almost a pastoral cast). The constant leaps of the phrases form regular aural patterns, and the vocal writing is dramatic and expressive, with hum and trill effects. The whole of the song-cycle moves from a pure clarity to the more dense.

Ferneyhough's other works have a consistency of idiom but a wide range of means. These include a two-minute caprice in *Adagissima* (1983) for string quartet; vocal effects and lyrical and rhapsodic elements in *Transit* (1972–74, revised 1975) for six amplified voices and chamber orchestra drawing on metaphysical-philosophical sources (Heraclitus, Paracelsus, Trismegistus); and eighth-tones in *La chute d'Icare* (1988) for clarinet and seven instruments, in which the gradual disintegration matches the title. The *String Quartet No. 3* (1987) organises twenty-three types of texture, and the *String Quartet No. 4* (1990), with soprano solo, takes its inspiration from **Schoenberg's** second, for the same forces.

Ferneyhough has taught in Germany for

over twenty years, at Freiburg (1973–86) and at Darmstadt since 1976.

RECOMMENDED WORKS
song-cycle *Etudes transcendentales* (1982–85) for soprano and small ensemble
Mnemosyne (1986) for bass flute and tape
String Quartet No. 2 (1980)

Finzi Gerald*
born 14th June 1901 at London
died 27th September 1956 at Oxford

Gerald Finzi was the most thoughtful of the composers who formed the core of the English musical renaissance, and his fastidious craftsmanship is reflected in his small number of works. His music idiom emerged from the examples and pastoral writing of **Vaughan Williams** and Finzi's older contemporaries, but the influence of Bach is also apparent, directly in such works as the *Grand Fantasia and Toccata* (1954) for piano and orchestra, more subtly in some of the construction and figuration of other works. The chief temperamental trait is an introverted awareness of the transience of life (as well as of the disappearing English countryside), and this is reflected in his choice of poetry to set and also in the fragile beauty and underlying sadness of some of his other works.

Finzi's most celebrated work also encapsulates his music and emotional idiom. The *Dies natalis* (begun mid-1920s, completed 1938–39) for high voice and strings sets texts of the little-known 17th-century mystical cleric Thomas Traherne, in which the world is seen with innocent wonder through the eyes of a new-born child. The awareness of transience is immediate in the darker hues of the otherwise pastoral string 'Intrada'. At the centre of the work, the second part of 'Rapture' is expressed as a dance, flanked by two mystically contemplative sections where the high vocal writing adds to the tone of metaphysical ecstasy. The final 'Salutation' is in the form of a chorale prelude, concluding a work of compelling but restrained beauty. Wordsworth's 'Ode on Intimations of Immortality' has a very similar basis to the metaphysics of Traherne, and Finzi's other major vocal work with orchestra, *Intimations of Immortality* (1936–50), sets it for tenor, chorus and orchestra. *Farewell to Arms* for tenor and strings is in the form of an introduction (1940), setting Ralph Knevet and using recitative elements, and aria

(1926–28), setting the late 16th-century poet George Peerle and with a vocal line that has the long flow and shape of 17th-century models.

Finzi responded strongly to the poetry of Thomas Hardy, with whom he shared many concerns: the fleeting nature of life, the futility of war, the sense of the beauty of nature in which humankind was an element, not the dominant force, and the power of memory to re-energise the past. Five of his song-cycles are Hardy settings (*A Young Man's Exhortation*, 1926–29, *Earth and Air and Rain*, 1928–49, *Before and After Summer*, 1938–39, *Till Earth Outwears*, 1927–56, and *I Said to Love*, 1928–56). Hardy's language is often complex and knotty, and Finzi's settings unravel its more thorny aspects in a most natural way. Finzi's settings are highly crafted, often delicate, sometimes in the form of dramatic ballads with forthright characterisation or story-lines. His Shakespeare settings in the song-cycle *Let Us Garlands Ring* (1942) are sensitive and individual, with lively characterisation in the piano, from the rocking effects in 'Come away, come away, death' to the interplay and bird calls and final joyful chords of 'It was a lover and his lass'.

Although Finzi is best known for his choral works and his songs, his concertos have become increasingly admired since his death. The very opening of the *Clarinet Concerto* (1948–49) for clarinet and strings suggests **Stravinsky**, but with the entry of the soloist it settles into a mellifluous flow, whose contours have been aptly compared to those of the rolling English downs. The solo writing consistently aims at warmer tones, especially in the almost shyly sensuous meditation of the slow movement which swells into mystical passion. The shallower finale has an easy going bounce. The *Cello Concerto* (1955) takes Finzi into unexpectedly grand and bold orchestral regions and thicker textures, while retaining the inflections of vocal lines in the cello writing. Less distinctive than the clarinet concerto, it is nonetheless worth the occasional hearing. The *Eclogue* (1956), for piano and strings, originally intended as the movement of a piano concerto, is a lovely meditation with Bachian touches underneath the pastoral atmosphere; music for a warm summer's evening. Finzi's limited output of chamber music is less interesting than his vocal music or the concertos.

Finzi taught at the Royal Academy from 1930 to 1933. He rescued several varieties of English apple from extinction in his private orchard.

RECOMMENDED WORKS
Clarinet Concerto (1948–1949) for clarinet and strings
cantata *Dies natalis* (1939) for high voice and strings
Eclogue (1956) for piano and orchestra
song-cycle *Let Us Garlands Bring* (1942)
song-cycles of Hardy poems (see text)

Gerhard, Roberto
see under Spain

Gurney Ivor Bertie*
born 28th August 1890 at Gloucester
died 26th December 1937 at Dartford

Although his life was marred by the effects of mustard-gas in the treaches in 1917, which partly led to many years in a mental institution before his premature death, Gurney remains one of the finest song-writers in the revival of the English song; his other works are few in number, but include *A Gloucestershire Rhapsody* for orchestra and five string quartets. The majority of his eighty-seven published songs were written between 1919 and 1922, though he composed some two hundred more, in various states of completion. Most of his settings are of contemporary English poets, and are spontaneous in feel, with a sense of privacy and personal utterance. The music is closely moulded to the words, the flowing linear piano writing an integral part of the word setting rather than an accompaniment (listening with the printed words is almost essential for full appreciation of his idiom). His melodic gift has a natural sense of improvisation, little affected by the contemporary interest in English folk song, and is often tinged with the echoes of an anguished yearning, or (as in *All Night under the Moon*, 1918) with a delicate lyricism. The harmonies are late-Romantic in idiom. He is particularly responsive to poetry with an element of story-telling, as in his settings of W. B. Yeats (such as *The Folly of being Comforted*, 1917, or *The Cloths of Heaven*, 1919 or 1920). But his finest achievements are the two cycles to poems by A. E. Housman, *Ludlow and Teme* (1919) and especially *The Western Playland* (1908–20), both for voice and piano quintet. *The Western Playland* is at times lyrical, at times dramatic, with an element of anger and

anguish, and the interpretation of the poetry is sometimes so unusual in comparison with the many other settings of the same poems as to cast a new light on them. The accompanying textures are complex, with a sense of the motivation of nervous, yearning energy. Such consort between words and music partly reflects Gurney's other artistic field: he was himself a fine poet (though he rarely set his own words), his publications including *Severn and Somme* (1917) and *War's Embers* (1918).

RECOMMENDED WORKS
song-cycle *The Western Playland* (1908–20) for voice and piano quintet
song-cycle *Ludlow and Teme* (1919) for voice and piano quintet

BIBLIOGRAPHY
M. Hurd, *The Ordeal of Ivor Gurney*, 1978
P. J. Kavanagh (ed.), *collected Poems of Ivor Gurney*, 1982

Harty (Sir) Hamilton
see under Eire

Harvey Jonathan Dean
born 3rd May 1939 at Sutton Coldfield

Jonathan Harvey's music has had surprisingly little general exposure, but his name is well-known among those who follow contemporary music. His chief inspirations are Christian mysticism and Eastern philosophies, and much of his output is for religious purposes. Even his non-religious music is almost invariably coloured by a spiritual impulse and the desire to express the visionary in terms of modern music. Influenced by **Stockhausen** (on whom he has written a book) and by Eastern musics, he has evolved a personal style which has increasingly used electronics (sometimes manipulated in real time), usually in combination with other instruments, on a foundation of carefully detailed structures derived from serial principles.

His most widely disseminated work has been *Mortuos plango, vivos voco* (1980), composed at the IRCAM studios in Paris. One of the most atmospheric of all electronic pieces, it uses the sounds of the tolling of a Winchester Cathedral bell and the treble singing of the composer's son to the text of the inscription on the bell (meaning 'I toll the dead, I summon the living'), from which the title is taken.

These form the basis of computer-manipulated sounds; both also sound out unadulterated in the resultant tape. The slow-moving layers and strands of sound, unimaginable by any other means, are of a spiritual purity that is exceptionally beautiful, often hauntingly so. It will usually be encountered in recording, but in concert-hall performance the effect is even more formidable, with the electronic sounds all around the audience, and the great tolling of the huge bell sounding as if it were suspended above the audience's heads. *Ritual Tape* (1980), in contrast, was created entirely from computer-generated sounds, though these were made to emulate chant and various Eastern instruments. Unfortunately the results sound too similar for comfort to the much earlier and more arresting work of the Swede Ralph Lunsden (using analogue and concrete sounds).

The series *Inner Light* pays homage to the Christian philosopher Rudolph Steiner, an abiding influence on Harvey, who has attempted musical equivalents to Steiner's conception of expansion of the human consciousness within itself to the final goal of fusion with the Deity. *Inner Light I* (1973) is for six instruments and tape; *Inner Light II* (1977) expands the forces into five solo voices and a chamber ensemble with synthesizer and tape; *Inner Light III* (1975) arrives at full orchestra with a quadraphonic tape, the electronic sounds sometimes mimicking the orchestra, sometimes extending the sound beyond instrumental capabilities, and surrounding the audience. The tape maintains the continuity, against big effects or short flurries of ideas from the orchestra. Cast in three main sections, this substantial piece ends with the orchestra frequency in the Alpha brainwave range, associated with meditative states; the orchestra dies away, leaving the tape. The success of the meditative effect is questionable, especially as the inner light is often turbulent, but this does not detract from a complex but striking work. *Bhakti* (1982), for instrumental ensemble and quadraphonic tape, combines serial organisation, the thematic material based on a 12-note row, with freer ideas influenced by Eastern musics. The device of the expansion or mirroring of vertical material above and below a central point is also found in other works, such as the *String Quartet No. 2* (1988).

Song Offerings (1985) for soprano and chamber ensemble (setting Tagore) and *From Silence* (1988) for soprano, violin, viola, three synthesizers and three electronic technicians show two sides of Harvey's idiom. Both have flowing, Expressionist vocal lines, and in both the instrumental accompaniment is dramatic and with descriptive elements. The distant ancestor of the former is **Schoenberg's** *Pierrot lunaire*, and with the purely acoustic accompaniment the idiom is flowing and linear, often with delicate effects. The electronics in the latter create different planes and depths of sound, and in spite of the mystical texts, the instrumental writing (like that of *Inner Light III*) is often violent and fragmented against the electronics. The silence refers to a state of repose rather than physical fact, apart from the opening (a cymbal appearing slowly out of silence) and the ending. The largest of his works for church use was an opera in twelve scenes, *Passion and Resurrection* (1981), designed for performance in a church, using the organ and a small orchestra. His more recent works include a *Cello Concerto* (1990) and an opera of a journey into the afterlife, *Inquest of Love* (1991–92), combining Christian and Buddhist spirituality, and using electronic sounds.

Harvey has taught at Southampton University (1964–77) and at Sussex University since 1977.

RECOMMENDED WORKS
    Cello Concerto (1990)
    Inner Light III (1975) for orchestra
    electronic *Mortuos plango, vivos voco* (1980)
    Song Offerings (1985) for soprano and chamber ensemble

Hoddinott Alun[**]
born 11th August 1929 at Bargoed

The Welsh composer Alun Hoddinott has been the most accomplished of the Principality's composers to date. He first came to prominence with the slightly neo-classical *Clarinet Concerto No. 1* (1950), a lithe and lively work with characteristically sinuous solo lines, and was later incorrectly branded as a serial composer by the more conservative critics. Although he has used serial techniques, the bulk of his work combines serial elements (such as use and transformation of rows as basic material) with an harmonic idiom that is often chromatic, and which usually centres around a tonal base. In this he was out of step with the main developments of the 1960s, but with the rejection of serialism by so many composers in the late 1970s and early 1980s, his idiom can now be seen as a mainstream development. He has continued to extend traditional forms, particularly the symphony and the sonata, but often employs novel structural means, such as the continuous development of source material through short sections. His very large and very uneven output has hampered wider appreciation, but the best of his music, so often influenced by extra-musical influences, is strongly atmospheric and forceful, and shows two main strands. The first is a very individual dark, solemn vein (the title 'Nocturne' appears regularly) that has a strong sense of mysticism reflecting his Celtic heritage, and which is reinforced by rich orchestration, often with points of brightness (especially percussion) dotting the large dark-hued landscape. The second is a sense of dance, with lively and varied time signatures, which can threaten to note-spin in the lesser works.

The *Clarinet Concerto No. 2* (1987) reflects Hoddinott's later style. It has an ominous mystery in the orchestral opening of the slow movement, using the tolling of a bell and delicate tuned percussion, out of which arises a legato solo line. The overall imagery is atmospheric, even in the faster passages of the ending. Given the paucity of clarinet concertos, both his concertos are useful additions to the repertoire. The *Triple Concerto* (1986), for piano trio and orchestra, in one continuous movement in three parts, derives all its material from the opening ideas, and is a work of rather nervous intensity and thick textures.

Of his symphonic works, the *Symphony No. 5* (1973) is in two movements, the first having passacaglia elements, the second being a series of variations, or six 'panels' on an arch structure using some of the material from the first movement. The *Symphony No. 6* (originally subtitled *Odyssey*, 1984) is in a single unfolding movement with seven sections, typically lively in its orchestral colours and in its sinuous, dance-like rhythms, tonally centred but with serial elements. Its symphonic argument is based on the gradual evolution of the initial set-idea to its final transformation and ecstatic ending. Some of his most effective scores have been for orchestra, where he has been able to indulge in his delight in Celtic mysticism and rich orchestral colours in a freer framework, with a broadening of textures in the 1970s. The vivid *The Sun, the Great Luminary of the Universe* (1970), the title of which comes from a passage by James

Joyce describing the end of the world, draws on a Lutheran chorale and the plainchant of the *Dies irae*, heard at the climax. Densely textured, it combines moments of hushed luminosity with a tense and growing sense of expectation, the climax of which is deliberately held back to launch a scurrying apocalypse and a hushed sense of the end of time. It was followed by the equally atmospheric *Lanterne des Morts* No. 2 (1981). The first of two sets of *Welsh Dances* (1958 and 1979), based on original rather than traditional tunes, and the *Investiture Dances* (1969), all entertaining diversions in a light idiom, have achieved some popularity.

Hoddinott's major output between 1974 and 1981 was opera; of the five written in this period (three with the librettist Myfanwy Piper), the most successful was the entertaining and evocative children's opera *What the Old Man Does is Always Right* (1977). The most ambitious was *The Trumpet Major* (1981), based on Thomas Hardy's novel, but its grand opera pretensions seem dated. His wistful, sometimes mournful ecstasy is also captured in such works as the song-cycle *A Contemplation upon Flowers* (1976) for soprano and orchestra, part of a large vocal output. His chamber music, usually well wrought and often amiable in its sinuous solo lines, is less individual, missing the element of orchestral colour; here the serial elements are sometimes more to the fore.

Hoddinott taught at Cardiff University (1967–87) and was founder and artistic director of the Cardiff Festival (1967–89), which introduced many contemporary and new works to Wales.

RECOMMENDED WORKS
  Lanterne des Morts No. 2 (1981) for
    orchestra
  Symphony No. 6 (1984)
  *The Sun, the Great Luminary of the
    Universe* (1970) for orchestra

BIBLIOGRAPHY
  B. Deane, *Alun Hoddinott*, 1977

Holst Gustav(us) Theodore (von)**

born 21st September 1874 at Cheltenham
died 25th May 1934 at London

Gustav Holst's achievement is entirely overshadowed by the justified success of one exceptionally popular work, the orchestral suite *The Planets* (1914–16).

Scored for a huge orchestra, late-Romantic in idiom though with a touch of a more modern dissonance, it is inspired less by astrology than by the Classical or spiritual associations with the heavenly bodies. Brilliantly orchestrated, full of emotional passion, part of its appeal is the clear musical delineation of each of its movements, from the violence and anger of Mars to the Elgarian nobility of Jupiter. At the same time it is a synthesis of many contemporary influences, moulded into an individual whole and in which nothing seems out of place, with an ethereal use of a wordless women's chorus in the closing Neptune. Its precursor had been the orchestral *Beni Mora*, op. 21 No. 1 (1910), with its heady Oriental atmosphere and evocative Russian echoes. Yet as an example of Holst's music *The Planets* is totally uncharacteristic. Most of his output is introvert in tone and scale, sometimes visionary or spiritual in intent, (especially influenced by Sanskrit literature) and finely calibrated in effect, with the addition of the influence of English folk music. His emphasis on the precision of rhythm is contrasted with a counter sense of restrained introversion. Unusually, he wrote no chamber music apart from some early works and one later minor piece.

Of his other orchestral music, *Egdon Heath* (1927) is a picture of a bleak landscape inspired by Thomas Hardy, while the fine, rhapsodic *Lyric Movement* (1933) for viola and small orchestra marries the English pastoral tradition with introspection; given the scarcity of works for viola and orchestra, it deserves to be more widely known. The *St Paul's Suite* (1913) is a joyous set of dances for string orchestra (including a version of the folk song 'Greensleeves'), while the *Brook Green Suite* (1933) for strings is neo-classical in inspiration, and rather unexpectedly gives the shape of classical phrasing to melodies which sound like folk songs. Two late orchestral works, the contrapuntal *Fugal Concerto* (1923) for flute, oboe and strings, and the *Double Concerto* (1929) for two violins and orchestra are rarely heard. The work that comes nearest to *The Planets* in scale and intent is the uneven *Choral Symphony*, (1924) based on poems by Keats. Often close to the idiom of Holst's friend **Vaughan Williams** (especially in the folk-song inspiration of the second section) it has moments of exceptional beauty, as well as some of the playfulness observable in *The Planets*. The harmonies are spiced by bitonality, the reticent orchestra by

clarity of colour; if the problems of combining symphonic structure with a series of poems are not fully solved, the beauties of this work are reward enough.

It is in his choral music that Holst's vision is best appreciated. The four groups of *Choral Hymns from the Rig Veda* (1908–12) are based on different combinations (Group 1 for voices and orchestra, Group 2 for female voices and orchestra, Group 3 for female voices and harp, Group 4 for male voices and orchestra). The *Ode to Death* (1919), for chorus and orchestra, based on verses by Walt Whitman, has a resigned beauty, and provides an interesting comparison with settings of the same words by **Hindemith** and **Piston**. The *Hymn of Jesus* (1917) and the *Choral Fantasia* (1930) are perhaps his finest choral works. The former, for chorus, organ and orchestra, is an ecstatic paean of praise, with constantly overlapping dancing waves of vocal writing for a chorus divided into two with the addition of a semi-chorus; with its moments of acerbic harmonies and bitonal writing, it was a new departure for English choral music. The latter, for soloists, chorus, organ and chamber orchestra, is a difficult work. Its wide range of idiom, from complex harmonies to the simplicity of plainchant, clearly comes from a very private source.

Although the extravagant early opera *Sita* (1900–06) was Wagnerian in intent and scope, his published operas are small in scale. *At the Boar's Head* (1924), drawn from Shakespeare's portraits of Falstaff, is inspired by country dance tunes, and with its unsatisfactory libretto is better heard than seen, while the humour of *The Wandering Scholar* (1929–30) is musically rather heavy-handed. The ballet suite drawn from the otherwise forgotten *The Perfect Fool* (1918–22) has retained its popularity, but it is the opera *Savitri* (1908, chorus revised 1917), based on a Sanskrit tale of a woodcutter's wife who prevents death from taking her husband, that is his finest achievement in the genre. This short (thirty-minute) work is breathtaking in its balance and simplicity. The two string quartets, bass, two flutes and English horn of the orchestra are reinforced by a wordless women's chorus. Its delicacy and power give it something of the feel of Yeats's contemporary drama, but its ethereal feel (apart from one echo of Wagner) and its chamber scale were unique at the time, anticipating the much later developments of music theatre.

Ultimately, Holst's music has something in common with the art of the miniaturist, being narrow in emotional scope, strong in appeal to those who find themselves in sympathy but somewhat chill to those who do not. The smaller orchestral works are always engaging and beautifully balanced, but lack the impact of *The Planets*. The best of the choral works require a spiritual affinity. For these reasons *The Planets* seems destined to remain the one work known to a wide public.

Holst spent 1918 and 1919 organising musical groups in the Balkans and Turkey at the behest of the YMCA. Among his teaching posts he taught at St Paul's Girls' School in Hammersmith, London, from 1905 until his death; among his students at Yale in 1932 was Elliott **Carter.**

RECOMMENDED WORKS
  A Choral Fantasia (1931) for soloists,
    chorus, organ and orchestra
  Choral Symphony (1924)
  Hymn of Jesus (1917) for chorus,
    organ and orchestra
  The Planets (1914–16) for orchestra
  opera *Savitri* (1908)

BIBLIOGRAPHY
  I. Holst, *Gustav Holst: a Biography*,
    1969 (2nd edition)
    The Music of Gustav Holst, 1975
    (3rd edition)
  E. Rubbra, *Gustav Holst*, 1973
    (revised)

Howells Herbert Norman*
born 17th October 1892 at Lydney
died 23rd February 1983 at London

Herbert Howells is best known for his liturgical music for the Anglican church, still in widespread use. Its combination of the direct, the lyrical and the atmospheric, with a strong feel for church acoustics, often makes few concessions to choral technical abilities. Like many English composers of his generation, Howells was profoundly affected by his discovery of the English musical heritage of the 16th and 17th centuries. This influence becomes filtered through his own idiom, especially in the modal feel to his extensive harmonic palette, which ranges from unison choral writing to diatonic passages of counterpoint, often at the service of long melodies. The culmination of his vocal writing is the radiant and powerful *Hymnus paradisi* (1938, but not heard until 1950), for soloists, chorus and orchestra, based on biblical and liturgical texts. Among his solo

songs, *King David* (1918) has retained its popularity.

Less well known are his chamber works, mostly written during or immediately after World War I. They include some of the most attractive of all English chamber music, written in response to the qualities of the English landscape. Eschewing drama or intellectual rigour, the feel is predominantly lyrical and rhapsodic, influenced by English folk music (although usually using his own tunes in folk style) and a strong sense of repose. Those who enjoy the English pastoral style will find an immediate response to his poetic sensibilities. In such works as the *String Quartet No. 3 'In Gloucestershire'* (rewritten 1930 from earlier material) the influence of the landscape is inherent, the textures of the quartet typically blended rather than contrasted. Two of the most effective works combine strings with other colours: the lovely *Piano Quartet* (1916) and the joyous *Rhapsodic Quintet* (1917), for clarinet and string quartet. The *Phantasy Quartet* (1918) for string quartet continues the idiom. Equally lovely and intimate is the much later *Oboe Sonata* (1943). Howells' orchestral music, including two piano concertos (again mostly dating from his earlier years), is all but forgotten, but includes the *Fantasia* (1937) for cello and orchestra, which he later intended to turn into a cello concerto but never completed. It is affecting enough but lacks the intimacy of the chamber music or the spirituality of the vocal works.

Howells taught at the Royal College of Music, where he had an extraordinary long tenure (1920–72).

RECOMMENDED WORKS
  Phantasy Quartet (1918) for string
    quartet
  cantata *Hymnus Paradisi* (1938)
  Piano Quartet in A minor (1916)
  Rhapsodic Quintet (1917) for piano
    and string quartet

Ireland John Nicholson*
born 13th August 1879 at Bowdon
(Cheshire)
died 12th June 1962 at Washington
(Sussex)

Ireland was a composer of meticulous craftsmanship who combined the heritage of **Elgar** with elements of the emerging English pastoral idiom, adding discreet touches of the less radical continental developments; his style remained generally consistent throughout his career. His music is given added colour by his interest in the pagan and pan-Nature atmosphere of the writings of Arthur Machen, with its suggestion of the shades of the past that inhabit the British landscape, and by his sensibility for the beauties of the Channel Islands (as in the orchestral *Forgotten Rite*, 1913, or *Sarnia: an Island Sequence*, 1941, for piano).

His most enduring works are probably his songs, but his output includes a number of orchestral scores. Best of these is the symphonic rhapsody *Mai Dun* (1921), inspired by Maiden Castle, the large prehistoric earthwork in Dorset, beloved of Thomas Hardy. The scene painting is big and vital, Elgarian in hue rather than pastoral. His other major large-scale work is the derivative *Piano Concerto* (1930), which has been the subject of exaggerated advocacy and excessive vilification, and deserves neither. It is a likeable but not particularly profound work, with some bravura writing for the soloist. Its bright first movement evolves into an almost improvisatory lyrical rhapsodising; the slow movement, wandering from an Elgarian opening to a Rachmaninovian lyricism, aims at big passions and just misses. The finale includes a quote from a string quartet by the pianist Helen Perkin, who inspired the concerto; its perkiness (sounding like **Rodrigo**) is a little wearisome, but is leavened by Impressionistic moments and the influence of **Prokofiev**, especially in the fine march.

Ireland's songs number over 100, and cover a wide range of mood, from the dark resonant harmonies of the Hardy setting *Her Song* (1925) to the English jolliness of *I Have Twelve Oxen* (1918). The general idiom remains consistent: an easy flow, a close correspondence between vocal line and piano writing, except when the piano is decoratively descriptive (as in *A Thanksgiving*), and melodic ideas that are derived from the English folk idiom. *Sea Fever* (1913), to the celebrated poem by Masefield, is the best known of his songs, and its popularity brought Ireland to the attention of a wider public. Ireland's major choral work is *These Things Shall Be* (1937), for baritone, chorus and orchestra, setting an optimistic vision of a just world without war by John Addington Symonds, in four sections with orchestral interludes.

The streak of sentimentality that occurs in the songs is less apparent in the piano music. The *Piano Sonata* (1920), the *Piano Sonatina* (1927), *Sarnia: an Island*

Sequence (1941) and the three descriptive pieces of *Decorations* (1913) are but a few fine examples of one of the most accomplished and least-known sides of Ireland's music. The gentle *Holy Boy* (1912) for piano is sometimes heard in its versions for string orchestra (1914) and string quartet (1941), or as a sung carol for soprano and organ. The *Piano Trio No. 2* (1917) and the *Fantasy Sonata* (1943) for clarinet and piano are the most interesting of his chamber works.

Ireland was organist at St Luke's Chelsea from 1904 to 1926, and an important teacher at the Royal College of Music (1923–39); his pupils included **Britten** and **Moeran**.

RECOMMENDED WORKS
Ireland's songs are recommended.
Mai Dun (1921)
Piano Concerto (1930)
Sarnia: an Island Sequence (1941) for piano

BIBLIOGRAPHY
M. V. Searle, *John Ireland* (1979)

Jones Daniel Jenkyn*
born 7th December 1912 at Pembroke
died 23rd April 1993 at Newton (near Swansea)

The music of Daniel Jones, with Grace **Williams** the first Welsh composer of real note, belongs to a mainstream cosmopolitan tradition, essentially tonal (though with recognisable tonal centres rather than key structures) and emotionally expressive, but with certain unusual stylistic features that mark it out as individual. Chief among these is his concept of 'complex metres', formulated in 1935, in which complex rhythmic patterns are created by irregular metres (e.g. 3+2+2) repeated in regular patterns. This creates a sense of unusual and subtle movement within recognisable patterns (subsequently mathematically developed from Jones's ideas by the German composer Boris **Blacher**, and now assimilated into the works of many composers). The rhythmic concentration infects all of Jones's music after that date, as can be most obviously seen in the *Sonata for Three Unaccompanied Kettledrums* (1947), one of the first and most successful works for solo timpani. A second feature is the exploration of unusual forms within generally traditional structural frameworks, inherent in his twelve symphonies (the first dating from

1948), which are the core of his achievement.

The symphonies are remarkable in that each one has a different tonal centre, one for each of the twelve notes – an idea intentionally embraced when about half the symphonies had been written. The basic structures are usually classical in form, but thematic development is generally organic, the basic material stated at the outset (often including a significant interval) and then extended or metamorphosed in all the subsequent movements. The *Symphony No. 4 'In Memory of Dylan Thomas'* (1954, A flat), the first of his symphonies to attract wider attention, includes a typical stylistic trick in the final three bars of the symphony inverting the opening theme. Characteristic of his interest in unusual structures within traditional frameworks is the scherzo, whose central section is a theme and variations. It is a fluent and deeply felt work in three movements, dark in colour and texture, elegiac in tone. The best of these earlier symphonies, the *Symphony No. 6* (1964, D) consists of six sections paired into three movements, with an expansive feel, again dark in its colours, and an energetic flow. These symphonies appear approachable, but with their shifting changes of mood require close attention, and perhaps evoke respect rather than affection. In the five-movement structures of the *Symphony No. 7* (1971, F sharp) and the *Symphony No. 8* (1972, F) Jones seemed to be attempting to extend the range of his idiom, particularly in the handling of the orchestra, which was always inclined towards the monochromatic. The eighth is the more playful, its five movements having elements of the suite, and both can be seen as transitional works. For the later symphonies become tauter, more astringent, and are of considerable interest, the emotional development closely matched to the thematic and harmonic argument. The material for the cogent four-movement *Symphony No. 9* (1974, C) is contained in the opening, where the triumph implied by the tonal centre emerges from darkness but is tempered by a semitonal clash, and the movement broadens into an uneasy turbulence. The second, slow movement attempts to resolve this unease and fails; it takes the dancing bounce of the third to inject optimism, though it is still a struggle, and the finale, including the spirit of the march, provides resolution only at the very close. The *Symphony No. 10* (1981, B flat) is the most formidable of these symphonies, emotionally less reticent than its predecessor, surging with repressed anger and tension even in the dance movement with its characteristic irregular rhythms, the colours dark as if summoned up from the subterranean depths by the bell that tolls the opening and the close. Each movement has a brief moment of lighter lyricism, as if being pierced by a ray of sunlight. The work is concluded by a moment of extraordinary illumination as the very opening material returns and throws the whole of the symphony into a different cast. The less immediately arresting *Symphony No. 11* (1982, E flat), like the sixth, has a sound cast that might have come from a Scandinavian composer, with an underlying sadness as if the shadows were slowly lengthening over its fjords. The *Symphony No. 12* (1985, G) is valediction with a smile: in place of the customary dark introduction, the opening is airy, almost pastoral; the bounce of the scherzo nearly puts a thumb to the nose; and the final movement of this compact and self-assured work starts with a bugle call of farewell but ends happily. Jones in fact wrote one further symphony, *In Memory of John Fussell* (1992), but it is titled, rather than numbered.

Jones was also a prolific composer of string quartets, preferring to date them in the title rather than assign them numbers; there are at least nine (the exact number is currently unclear: his own 1988 catalogue listed seven, plus his last posthumous quartet, but nine are known, and there were earlier, unacknowledged quartets). These are perhaps finer works than the symphonies, though they will appeal to a narrower audience. While the general idiom is similar, Jones allowed himself a more experimental and more assertive development of traditional forms (such as a palindromic scherzo). The quartets also concentrate on a tone generally absent in the symphonies, of a dark but passionate tragedy or yearning, often expressed in high solo writing against held chords or more subdued ideas from the other three instruments, best expressed in the *String Quartet 1978*, or in the attractive and well-argued *String Quartet 1957*. The *String Quartet 1975* has a delightful 'whispering' scherzo on muted strings. The *String Trio No. 1* (1970) is in a similar dreamy vein.

The sense of dance that figures prominently in the scherzos of the symphonies culminates in the marvellous *Dance Fantasy* (1976) for orchestra, which uses 'complex metres' but (according to the composer) can be danced to. Two other works deserve mention, and provide perhaps the most immediately appealing introduction to Jones's work, for they give reign to a melodic lyricism generally restrained in the symphonies and string quartets. The *Oboe Concerto* (1982) is intentionally limited in its aims, but nonetheless delightful, while *The Country Beyond the Stars* (1958), for chorus and orchestra, has a visionary beauty, and is much more effective than the rather stern oratorio *St Peter* (1962).

Daniel Jones belongs to that generation of symphonic composers, like **Rubbra** or Vagn **Holmboe**, whose combination of cogent symphonic argument, developed from traditional patterns, and a restrained emotional exploration was overshadowed by other musical events. As the tradition of classical music in Wales develops, it seems almost certain that his significance will grow in stature; certainly his tenth symphony deserves a wide audience. He edited the collected edition of his friend Dylan Thomas's poems (1971), and wrote the music for the famous radio play *Under Milk Wood* (1954); his personal memoir of the friendship was published as *My Friend Dylan Thomas* (1977). He worked at the famous Bletchley Park in World War II, decoding Japanese cyphers.

RECOMMENDED WORKS
> *The Country Beyond the Stars* (1958)
>   for chorus and orchestra
> *Dance Fantasy* (1976) for orchestra
> Oboe Concerto (1982)
> *Sonata for Three Unaccompanied*
>   *Kettledrums* (1947)
> *String Quartet 1957* (1957)
> *String Quartet 1978* (1978)
> Symphony No. 4 *In Memory of Dylan*
>   *Thomas* (1954)
> Symphony No. 6 (1964)
> Symphony No. 10 (1980)
> Symphony No. 12 (1985)

Knussen Oliver*
born 12th June, 1952 at Glasgow

Oliver Knussen burst in on British composition at a very young age, with a remarkably self-assured idiom that until then had exercised little hold on British music: Expressionism. After a fluent *Symphony No. 1* (1967), touched with influences of **Britten**, and a *Concerto for Orchestra* (1967–70) that included jazz elements, his *Symphony No. 2* (1970–71, various revisions to 1983) for soprano and orchestra was quite unlike any earlier British composition. The pattern of the four-movement

symphony is combined with that of the Mahlerian song-cycle, with settings of poems by Georg Trakl and Sylvia Plath. The immediate antecedent of the latter was **Berg's** *Altenberg Songs*; however the surrealistic mood built around the moon and death, an atmosphere that dominates this period of Knussen's output, ultimately looks back to the **Schoenberg** of *Erwartung* and *Pierrot Lunaire*. Yet the lithe sinuousness of some of the orchestral writing (its textures and colours skilfully chosen) is from a different tradition, as is the movement from a 12-tone base to a more consonant harmonic idiom in the last movement, while the cinematographic cross-cutting techniques and superimposed layers owed something to Knussen's discovery of **Carter**.

Trumpets (1975), for soprano and three clarinets continued this tone in a setting of another Trakl poem, with a sonata form compressed into four minutes, and sinuous Expressionist polyphony from the clarinets. *Ophelia Dances, Book 1* (1975) for nine instruments, developed from an abandoned movement of the third symphony, creates an atmosphere of almost obsessive order that is simultaneously given a slightly deranged cast. The dances are those of an introverted, wispy Ophelia living entirely in her own mental world, with only scattered connections to outside reality; the close moves to a portrait of still waters, with delicate effects from the celesta, ending with a final ripple.

From this point Knussen developed his skills of pointed detail within larger effects. The *Cantata* (1977) for oboe and string trio tones down the Expressionism in favour of an exploration of colours and timbres as a setting for a solo instrument, and the experience of these works culminated in the *Symphony No. 3* (1973–79). This fifteen-minute work, originally conceived as an 'Introduction and Masque' followed by a 'Cortège', is a diptych consisting of a tense, jagged section of bold contrasts and a slow passacaglia with a powerful central double climax, the whole preceded by a more fantastical introduction whose opening material is repeated at the end of the work to create a circular unity. Underneath this work lies the heritage of the more conventional symphony, in the shape, in the moments of melodic progression that break to the surface, and in the large climaxes of the third section, succeeded by surrealistic fanfares. But this heritage is fractured into overlaps and fissures, like one of those frozen rivers where the ice has compressed into fantastical and irregular shapes. The introduction uses interjectory percussion, half disruptive, half commentating, surely drawn from the influence of **Birtwistle**; the powerful passacaglia has an eerie atmospheric flow, in which the surface writing is busy but vainly immobile, and the strength is in the undercurrent, until a kind of dissolution or acceptance after the climaxes.

Knussen had considerable difficulty finding the final forms of these works, and since that spate in the 1970s his output has been very small, dominated by two short 'fantasy' operas, using large operatic forces and resources, including a huge panoply of percussion instruments, that turned his surrealistic instinct from Expressionism to the fantastical, designed to appeal to children and adults alike. Both operas are drawn from the well-known, largely visual children's books by Maurice Sendak, with librettos by the writer and composer. *Where the Wild Things Are* (1979–83) has as its central character a boy who seems a first cousin to the wilful and angry child of **Ravel's** *L'enfant et les sortilèges*. After altercations with his mother, he goes to a fantasy island where the wild monsters are; the work is an allegory of a child trying to tame the anarchic elements of his nature. Knussen's setting tones down some of the more fractured elements of his idiom, and uses ideas from Mussorgsky and **Debussy** as basic musical material (including the Coronation music from *Boris Godunov* at a climatic point), evolving a form of nine scenes. His ability for a musical hurly-burly is especially effective, but there is also lyrical writing. It does not displace Ravel's masterpiece as the finest of all such children-adult operas, but enhanced by the stage recreation of Stendak's drawings, it makes compelling theatre. Some commentators have pointed to the 'difficulty' of the contemporary musical idiom, but this applies mainly to those parents unused to modern music; children, less brainwashed into the dogma of traditional harmony, generally have no such problems. However, divorced from the stage delights, the careful musical construction of the piece gains strength and the recording is more for adults. *Higglety Pigglety Pop!* (1984–90), along much the same lines, creates a double bill for the two fantasy operas. His more recent works have included the short *Variations* for piano (1989), the octet *Songs without Voices* (1991–92), and settings of Rilke and Whitman.

Knussen is a very fine conductor of contemporary music. He was appointed artistic director of the Aldeburgh Festival in 1983, and has headed contemporary music activities at Tanglewood since 1986.

RECOMMENDED WORKS

opera *Higglety Pigglety Pop!* (1984–90
Ophelia Dances, Book 1 (1975) for
nine players
Symphony No. 2 (1970–71)
Symphony No. 3 (1973–79)
opera *Where the Wild Things Are*
(1979–83)

Lloyd George Walter Selwyn
born 28th June 1913 at St Ives
(Cornwall)
died 3rd July 1998 at London

George Lloyd's music is perfect for those who wish to ignore the fact that they are living at the end of the 20th century. Harmonically his ultra-conservative idiom to all intents and purposes predates Wagner, and it concentrates on the form of the symphony. There do seem to be personal reasons for this style: Lloyd suffered a breakdown after being shell-shocked on the terrible Arctic convoy duty in 1942, and retired to become a carnation and mushroom farmer. His return to composition clearly had a therapeutic element. However, it does not express the traumas of that experience – to discover such personal anguish and tragedy readers should turn to the symphonies of **Petterson**. Lloyd's idiom is usually good-humoured and characterised by lyrical slow movements and colourful if conventional orchestration, and only very occasionally does a dissonant climax, or a more modern rhythm, appear.

Unfortunately, conservative critics, following their now-forgotten counterparts down the ages, have in recent years seized on his works (like those of **Tubin**) to mollify 'an intelligent musical public, looking for contemporary works with which they can identify'. Lloyd's works, however, are contemporary only in date, and the response is less a question of identification than an avoidance of any kind of challenge. For those wishing to explore approachable symphonies with far more compelling content there are many alternatives to be found in this guide.

Lloyd's music, with the possible exception of the *Symphony No. 7* and occasional moments in other works, essentially belongs either to the realm of the tone poem or to the world of light music. With that in mind, the *Symphony No. 2* (1933 revised 1982) has an energetic opening movement, typically buoyant and joyous (a cross between a storm and a picture of a hunt), a sentimental slow movement, a straightforward march for the scherzo, and a touch of polytonality (by juxtaposing two tunes) in the finale. Those expecting the long *Symphony No. 4 'Arctic'* (1945–46) to reflect Lloyd's wartime experiences on the convoys are likely to be disappointed, as it is pictorial rather than experiential. The slow movement is a beautiful and restrained picture of a peaceful northern landscape that could stand on its own, but its effect is nullified by the trite scherzo that follows. The opening of the finale could come straight out of **Sibelius**, but the development of the movement has none of that master's genius. The *Symphony No. 5* (1947) is another large-scale work, with an effective march in the opening movement, and a touch of Tchaikovsky in the dance-like patterns. The *Symphony No. 6* is much shorter than its immediate predecessors, and in light-music vein after an opening idea that could have been written by Walton. The *Symphony No. 7* reverts to a greater length (three movements, lasting some fifty minutes), and was inspired by the Greek legend of Persephone. Its opening, with Straussian string figures against glockenspiel, has a magical atmosphere (the idea returns later in the work), and throughout there is a greater sense of passion, evidenced in the big climaxes, although these are offset by the areas of more trite idiom, such as the second of the opening ideas. However, for those exploring this composer's work, this may be the place to start. The *Symphony No. 9* (1969) is light-hearted, its three movements representing the dancing of a young girl, a reminiscing and grieving old woman, and the merry-go-round. The slow movement is the finest, again having moments of powerful emotion. The *Symphony No. 10 'November Journeys'*, inspired by visits to English cathedrals, is for brass ensemble. The five-movement *Symphony No. 11* (1985) is perhaps the least interesting of the series.

Of his other works, his opera *Iernin* (1914) was produced when the composer was only twenty-one. The *Piano Concerto No. 4* (1970, orchestrated 1983) is in an entirely Romantic virtuoso vein, indulging in a combination of sentimentality and syncopation.

RECOMMENDED WORK
Symphony No. 7

Mathias William*
born 1st November 1934 at Whitland (Dyfed)
died 29th July 1992 at Bangor (Gwynedd)

Of the four main composers Wales has produced to date (the other three being Alan **Hoddinott**, Daniel **Jones** and Grace **Williams**), William Mathias is probably the best known but ultimately, with the exception of his church music, the least interesting. This is partly because his prolific idiom was inclined to be derivative and sometimes dated, and partly because of his inclination towards superficiality rather than substance. In particular, his rather inflexible rhythmic invention failed to illuminate his other areas of technical command. His large output includes many concertos, three symphonies, and chamber and organ works; many of his works were for ceremonial or church use, and in these he excelled, producing attractive music with enough modern touches to sound contemporary, but within an idiom that would be widely appreciated.

His best music is choral, as he had a natural affinity for writing for the voice. This includes the deft *This Worlde's Joie* (1974) for chorus and orchestra, with its happy mixture of archaic hints and modern effects, of bawdy and serious elements, and *Lux aeterna* (1982) for soprano, mezzo-soprano, contralto, children's chorus, chorus, organ and orchestra. *Lux aeterna* is a multi-layered, direct and appealing piece, with echoes of **Britten** and **Tippett** well assimilated. The choral writing, in particular, is full of ethereal effects and shimmering textures, with a division between straightforward tonal directness (though with archaic touches) and heavily chromatic passages. The impassioned solo writing is less inspired, but the orchestral texture is very atmospheric, and it is perhaps Mathias's best work. His large output of church music sometimes required choirs of high, if not exceptional, abilities; typical of these is the fine *Rex gloriæ* (1981), four motets for unaccompanied chorus, where a lively sense of pleasure in singing is combined with some beautiful effects, the harmonies regularly sliding through a functional dissonance to provide momentum between moments of resolution. Surprisingly, his mastery of vocal writing was not reflected in his opera

The Servants (1980), to a unconvincing libretto by the novelist Iris Murdoch; it attempted the manner of a grand 19th-century opera and an historical setting in an age which had little need of either. The music reflects those aspirations, with an uneasy balance between voice and orchestra.

Mathias came to attention with the assured *Divertimento* (1958) for string orchestra, in which the outer movements shows traces of French neo-classicism, and the rocking slow movement develops into a forceful, sonorous passion. By the *Prelude, Aria and Finale* (1964) for strings, the sonorous dominates over the neo-classical, the elegant restraint tempered by a stronger sense of atmosphere. His chamber music inclines towards Gallic charm and, while gratifying to play, can be rather an academic listening experience, exemplified by the perky *Wind Quintet* (1963). His music is more effective when propelled by a nervous and sonorous energy, as in the *String Quartet No. 1* (1968), in one continuous movement divided in four sections. The *String Quartet No. 2* (1981), inspired in part by medieval music, is more varied, with a folk-like second movement making effective use of pizzicato, but never goes beyond the restraints that good taste might dictate, and thus take flight. The *Symphony No. 3* (1991) is the most tautly constructed and interesting of the symphonies. Of his concertos, the fine *Piano Concerto No. 3* (1968) juxtaposes the turbulent against the poetic and mysterious in all its three movements. A notable example of his many organ works is the *Partita* (1962), in which two dancing movements frame a heartfelt lento.

Mathias taught at the University of Wales, Bangor (1970–88).

RECOMMENDED WORKS
> *Lux aeterna* (1983) for soloists, chorus, organ and orchestra
> String Quartet No. 2 (1981)
> Symphony No. 3 (1991)
> *This World's Joie* (1974) for chorus and orchestra

Maconchy Elizabeth*
born 19th March 1907 at Broxbourne (Hertfordshire)
died 11th November 1994 at Norwich (Norfolk)

Although the music of Elizabeth Maconchy covers most genres, at the heart of her output are her thirteen string quartets: expressive, involving, often beautiful works that deserve to be better known. She called the medium of the quartet 'impassioned argument', and in hers there is a strong sense of debate, which can be rhythmically forceful, and is regularly lyrical in the earlier works, stark in the later. The counterpoint is often rhythmic as well as harmonic; clear and usual concise motifs form the basis of the material, but the intellectual rigour is always used for expressive and emotional ends. Until the eighth quartet the harmonic idiom is traditional but heavily chromatic; from the eighth onwards the language veers towards the atonal.

The early quartets are taut and economical. The *String Quartet No. 1* (1932–33) is in four contrasted movements, but lasts only some fourteen minutes. In the more introspective *String Quartet No. 2* (1936) the movements are connected by related material, a practice retained in the later works. The four-movement *String Quartet No. 3* (1938) is cast in a single compressed movement. The *String Quartet No. 5* (1948) uses rhythmic counterpoint, with the opening material returning transformed in the finale, and the overall mood is dark and impassioned. The opening passacaglia theme of the *String Quartet No. 6* (1950) provides the central idea in another sonorous, sombre work with an expressive slow movement. The *String Quartet No. 7* (1955–56) is built in an arch, with a central slow movement flanked by two scherzi (the second entirely pizzicato) and two outer movements, all internally linked with germinal motifs and with the main material brought together at the end. All these quartets have something of **Bartók** in their direct emotional impact and general technical proceedures, culminating in the searching emotional range of the very fine seventh quartet, which has more resolutions to the emotions than its predecessors. The *String Quartet No. 8* (1966) retains the driving Bartókian rhythms, and is built on a chord of two perfect fifths superimposed at an interval of a minor fifth. The sound world changed considerably in the interval of ten years, with a loss of a sense of tonality, the lyricism more acerbic, and with a slow movement in questioning, searching mood, written without bar-lines. The *String Quartet No. 9* (1968–69) inhabits a spare, stark world, the slow movement inspired by the Soviet invasion of Prague. The very condensed and equally severe *String Quartet No. 10* (1971–72) and the *String Quartet No. 11* (1977) both employ one-movement forms, the latter with more clearly defined sections, the starkness emerging into a kind of resolve. The four-movement *String Quartet No. 12* (1979) is equally short, but lifts out of the darker moods of its predecessors with some magical string effects and a dynamic, yearning lyricism. Written as a test piece, the *String Quartet No. 13* '*Quartetto Corto*' (1984) lasts seven and a half minutes, condensing a fast-slow-fast structure into a single movement.

Of her other works, the vigorous *Symphony* (1953) for double string orchestra drives towards the final passacaglia with interplay between the divided groups, while the *Serenata concertante* (1962) for violin and orchestra is in a lighter vein, the solo part integrated into the whole, rather than in virtuoso opposition to the orchestra. In the long gap between the seventh and eight string quartets she mostly concentrated on vocal music and opera, including the trilogy of one-act operas: *The Sofa* (1956–57), to a libretto by Ursula Vaughan Williams, *The Three Strangers* (1958–67), based on Hardy, and *The Departure* (1960–61). *The King of the Golden River* (1974–75), based on Ruskin, is one of a number of works written for children.

Elizabeth Maconchy's second daughter, Nicola LeFanu (born 1947), is also a composer.

RECOMMENDED WORKS
String Quartet No. 7 (1955)
String Quartet No. 8 (1967)
String Quartet No. 12 (1979)
Symphony (1953) for double string orchestra

Moeran Ernest John*
born 31st December 1894 at Heston (Middlesex)
died 1st December 1950 at Kenmare (Ireland)

Moeran's name is probably better known than his music, apart from the *Symphony in G minor* (1934–37), which has maintained a peripheral place in the English repertoire. Until the success of the symphony he wrote primarily chamber music and songs, in a folk-song style influenced by **Ireland** and **Delius**, and with a poetic sense of nature. He collected Norfolk folk songs in 1915 and 1921. His harmonic language is traditional, though with increasingly chromatic decoration until the symphony, when he started to simplify that decorative content; he later adapted his rhapsodic idiom to larger-scale forms. The chamber music is fluid and evocative, to be appreciated on the level of texture and warm colours rather than intellectual musical argument. For those who respond to the English pastoral, this is attractive music, especially the *String Quartet* (1921) and the *String Trio* (1931). *Whythorne's Shadow* (1931) for orchestra reflects an interest common to so many English composers of the time in the Elizabethan madrigal. His later works were mainly orchestral, including a *Violin Concerto* (1942) that contrasts exuberance with lyricism, and a lyrical *Cello Concerto* (1945). A series of orchestral pieces represents a late flowering of the English folk idiom in richly coloured rhapsodic orchestral garb, although usually the folk-like melodies are Moeran's own rather than traditional. The tone-painting of *In the Mountain Country* (1921) is the simplest and perhaps the most immediate of these. The *First Rhapsody* (1922) is a similar but more varied landscape evocation, ranging from a Delian warmth to anticipations of **Vaughan Williams's** *Sinfonia Antartica*. The *Second Rhapsody* (1923, revised for smaller orchestra 1941) is more obviously and directly indebted to folk music, with a sense of Irish boisterousness. The pleasing if unmemorable *Third Rhapsody* (*Rhapsody in F sharp*, 1943) is more a miniature grand concerto for piano and orchestra than a mood-evoking work, and has extraordinary modulations in the cadenza which are almost worth hearing in their own right. The *Symphony in G* itself combines a grandeur with the lyricism of his landscape painting, and structurally is built on developmental growth of germ themes, in the style of **Sibelius**. The other work most likely to be encountered besides the symphony is the *Sinfonietta* (1944), a virtuoso work which culminates his gradual movement towards contrapuntal writing. His best-known song-cycle, *Ludlow Town* (1920), to poems of A. E. Housman, is rather florid in accompaniment, earnest in the vocal line.

Moeran's sense of melody and skill at orchestral colour will appeal to those already exploring the English pastoral tradition; otherwise, while pleasant listening, his relatively unremarkable invention and individuality make him a peripheral rather than a central figure.

RECOMMENDED WORKS
  In the Mountain Country (1921) for
    orchestra
  String Trio (1931)
  String Quartet in A minor (1921)
  Symphony in G minor (1937)

BIBLIOGRAPHY:
  S. Wild, *E. J. Moeran*, 1973

Nyman Michael•
born 23rd March, 1944 at London

Michael Nyman has become the doyen of English minimalists and, like the American minimalists **Glass** and **Reich**, formed an instrumental group to perform his music. His own brand of repetitive patterns undergoing slow metamorphosis has been more forceful than that of either the American composers, creating in its colours and in its movement towards unresolvable situations an obsessive, slightly neurotic quality; some of his earlier works had no concrete ending, but simply stopped in mid-stream.

This ideally suited the equally obsessive and surrealistic idiom of the film-maker Peter Greenaway, and Nyman's music became very well known through his film scores, the suites from which stand successfully on their own. The music for *The Draughtsman's Contract* (1982) overtly recreated Baroque models, with something of the driving basses of Vivaldi, but with a major difference in the replacement of Baroque harmonic progressions with a largely static harmonic base. The music drawn from *Prospero's Books* (1991) is essentially an extended song-cycle setting words from Shakespeare's *The Tempest*. Its high vocal writing, ranging from delicate repetitive tapestries to aggressive patterns, is interspersed by instrumental sections with a pop-music flavour.

His concert works are musically more substantive. *Back Fools, Double Relishes and Springers* (1981) for two violins initially pits a yearning phrase against dancing patterns, and gradually metamorphises the general shape in a mesmerisingly effective weave. *Think Slow, Act Fast* (1981–82, the title coming from Buster Keaton) for ensemble is derived from a bass-line (and its chordal equivalent) originally conceived for an aborted new version of the 'Ride of the Valkyries'. In this marvellously pungent work the infectious rollicking basic figure is given bite by the scoring for saxophones, and offset by the quite different effect of the piano, before ending in warmth and vibrancy. *Time's Up* (1985) was written for a gamelan orchestra, and although it does not use traditional gamelan procedures, his idiom is well suited to such a body, designed for music with repetitive elements and slow, long-term changes. There is a spirit of warmth and delight in this short and effective work. Nyman's first opera, *The Man who Mistook his Wife for a Hat* (1986), was based on the case history by Oliver Sachs of an Alzheimer patient, and uses three characters (the man, his wife and the psychiatrist) and an ensemble for strings, harp and piano. The libretto is effective, but Nyman's idiom proved too one-dimensional to delve underneath its implications. The vocal writing, often very high, is an unfortunate combination of awkward notes and syllables awkward to sing, but the unusual dramatic content of this opera makes it worth the encounter.

The Piano Concerto (1993; the title includes the definite article) was reworked from the score to the film *The Piano* (1991–92). Splendid in the context of the film but over-sentimental as a concerto, this is a musical equivalent to purple prose, though passages such as the jazzy feel of the opening of the third movement are superficially attractive. Far more effective is *MGV* (1993) for instrumental ensemble and orchestra; the title stands for 'musique à grande vitesse', referring to the French high-speed train for whose inauguration the work was commissioned. Its opening has a marvellously infectious bounce in its interplay of rhythms and colours, managing to convey the excitement of a fast-moving train without being too obviously pictorial, apart from the train whistles. This opening manages to impel the rest of the piece, which is in five continuous sections, and though the inspiration falters in the subsequent material – there is simply not enough contrast or interesting variety – the excitement returns at the end, and *MGV* is recommended for its sheer vitality.

Some of Nyman's most attractive and energetic music is found in his string quartets. The *String Quartet No. 1* (1985) draws material from the 17th-century John Bull's *Walsingham Variations* and from **Schoenberg's** *String Quartet No. 2*. The *String Quartet No. 2* (1988) was written as both an independent string quartet and as the score for a solo South Indian dance. It has a beautiful contemplative slow section, juxtaposed with compelling fast sections, and is one of Nyman's most attractive works. The *String Quartet No. 3* (1990) emerged from a choral work, *Out of the Ruins*.

RECOMMENDED WORKS
    film score *The Draughtsman's Contract* (1982)
    opera *The Man who Mistook his Wife for a Hat* (1986)
    MGV (1993) for instrumental ensemble and orchestra
    String Quartet No. 2 (1988)
    Think Slow, Act Fast (1981–82) for ensemble
    Time's Up (1985) for gamelan orchestra

Panufnik, Andrzej
see under Poland

Rubbra Edmund**
born 23rd May 1901 at Northampton
died 13th February 1986 at Gerrard's Cross

The considerable neglect of the music of Edmund Rubbra, as in the case of his contemporary the Dane Vagn **Holmboe** (with whom he has much in common), remains a mystery, especially in a culture that has so successfully reassessed its heritage of 20th-century music. His idiom may not include an instantly memorable melodic style, or arresting idiomatic fingerprints, but it combines a musical imagination of eloquent craftsmanship with an ardent intensity, sometimes powerful and rugged, sometimes (especially in works with religious inspiration) austerely luminous.

His musical roots are an unusual combination. The heritage of the English pastoral tradition informs some of his melodic patterns and general textures, together with the influence of **Holst's** choral writing and some of the intricacy of **Bax**. An admiration of **Ravel** leads to some Impressionistic moments in his earlier works. Above all, Tudor polyphonic music is an abiding influence, and he applied many of the techniques of the music of this period to his own idiom, leading to a style of assured and powerful counterpoint. Temperamentally, there is a vigorous strength, usually dressed in darker orchestral colours, that has affinities with the Scandinavian composers, especially in the eleven symphonies that form the core of his output. The harmonies are tonal, though with modal inflections, but they are complicated and extended by the interplay of counterpoint and polytonality, and by such devices as delaying an expected harmonic change and then producing it with a sudden shift. The rhythmic energy is considerable, often motivic, and regularly built around the repetition of small figures; a favourite device is to hold these repetitions, with only small changes, while the surrounding material undergoes changes generated by the counterpoint, producing shifting points over a stiller, insistent base.

Rubbra's immersion in the polyphonic heritage is exemplified by the early and lovely *Dormi Jesu* (1921) for a cappella choir. It sounds exactly as if it had been written in the 16th century, until in its middle the soprano line rises in the English pastoral melodic idiom, and one suddenly realises this is a 20th-century work. This direct assimilation was later echoed in such works as the *Improvisations on Virginal Pieces by Farnaby* (1939) for orchestra, where Rubbra keeps to the spirit and much of the music of the originals in homogeneous colours. The most effective *Violin Sonata No. 2* (1932) displays all his roots: a slightly yearning English melodiousness in the violin writing, Ravelian Impressionistic ripples in the piano writing, and a touch of Bartókian folk inflection in the central lament, reinforced by the fast dance of the final movement. This general idiom was developed in the more assured *String Quartet No. 1* (1933, withdrawn, revised with a new finale 1946); this attractive and uncomplicated work makes an interesting introduction to Rubbra's music.

Rubbra's first two symphonies were both criticised for their lack of variety in their orchestral colour, but this homogeneous quality is endemic to Rubbra's idiom, allowing close polyphonic interplay and the unified development of counterpoint. Throughout the symphonies the emphasis is on the organic growth of material, often built from motivic cells or ideas, and on the organic growth of the counterpoint with considerable symphonic imagination; consequently there are not the strong thematic contrasts one might expect from more traditional development. This growth propels structure, rather than the evolution and contrast of keys. The emotions can appear restrained (through the lack of surface drama), but are no means dry: rather they operate over long spans, with the feel of philosophical or metaphysical contemplation (no doubt arising from Rubbra's abiding interest in a mystical Christianity and in Buddhism) often propelled by powerful undercurrents. Movements to build up slowly to great climaxes, then fall away again, and this process has led to comparison with Bruckner, although the context is very different. The rugged strength is most obvious in the first two symphonies; the middle symphonies are less monochromatic, and the later symphonies are suffused with a spiritual quality. The development of material in the first movement of the *Symphony No. 1* (1935–37) is built on the opening horn and trumpet theme, rather than by sonata principles, and elements of that basic theme emerge in the play of counterpoint. In spite of its uniform shades of dark colours, the *Symphony No. 2* (1937, revised 1950) has an elemental power and a fluent inevitability of the unfolding of events, the restraint of the opening idea (a chant-like theme on violins in unison) characteristic of the composer. The granite-hewn power of the movement gradually swells to tough climaxes, with an undercurrent of brusque, emphatic force; the second movement has a northern turbulence, the sombre third movement is almost a funeral march with a great central swell, and the finale is suitably lithe. The *Symphony No. 3* (1939) and the *Symphony No. 4* (1941) are more varied orchestrally (the third uses a classical-sized orchestra with trombones), and have been very highly regarded by those fortunate enough to have heard them. The *Symphony No. 5* (1947–48) is probably the best known. It is lighter in feel and more deft in orchestration than the second, and if more approachable, is not as arresting or as interesting until the impressive slow movement: noble, sometimes languorous, it emerges into an Elgarian march, leads fluently into the finale, which uses the main material of the previous movements, and ends with the orchestral evocation of bells before its characteristically quiet close. The tune on which the scherzo is based moves through all twelve keys in the course of the movement, although this was not a predetermined effect. The *Symphony No. 6* (1954) has another beautiful slow movement, and is developed from an initial four-note idea. The last, slow, movement of the three-movement *Symphony No. 7* (1957) is in the form of a passacaglia

and fugue. The element of spiritual intensity emerges in the more lyrical *Symphony No. 8 'Hommage à Teilhard de Chardin'* (1968), and culminates in the visionary *Symphony No. 9 'Sinfonia sacra'* (1971–72) for soloists, choir and orchestra on the theme of the Resurrection; its sections are played continuously, and it uses 17th-century tunes and Bachian chorales. The serene *Symphony No. 10 'Sinfonia da camera'* (1974), in contrast, is the most condensed of the symphonies, lasting just over a quarter of an hour and using chamber forces. It is the symphony closest to **Sibelius** in its sound and development of germinal material, in one continuous movement in sonata form that contains within it three sections corresponding to the three movements of a classical symphony. Of his other orchestral works, the lovely *Tribute to Vaughan Williams* (1942) deserves mention, especially the slow unfolding polyphony of its first half; although it does not actually quote from **Vaughan Williams's** music, its English pastoralism is a clear tribute.

Rubbra's long musical spans and closely argued counterpoint have been more of a disadvantage in the concertos, for the lack of display has discouraged performance. The *Piano Concerto in G* (1955) was Rubbra's second (the first dating from 1931–32), and has claims to be his finest work. Each of the movements, although internally varied, has the feel of overall purposeful sweep and linear flow, the piano exploring a metaphysical mystery with the orchestra. Its opening is magical, a visionary contemplation that gradually expands into a musical dawn in the orchestra, with the piano providing decoration. Its mood gradually gets more assertive, the piano in concert with the orchestra, and arrives at a noble, almost ecstatic Brucknerian climax that dissolves into bright joyfulness, before a quiet, restful ending. The slow movement finds the piano quietly musing over a subdued orchestra with a slow but intense passion, eventually singing a liquid solo song tinged with sadness and emerging into almost exotic ideas and a huge swell of a climax. The finale crashes in with an urgently lyrical piano against thundering timpani, and then has a spiky instrumental flow, with comments interjected by various instruments, before arriving at an orchestral noblimente; the timpani proudly underline the mood, and the piano adds a descant that emerges into an extended cadenza broken up by the timpani for a final joyous race to the abrupt end.

The darker and more turbulent *Violin Concerto* (1959) is less effective. The soloist sounds rather like a lost soul in the first movement; the slow movement has a somewhat desolate beauty, but the attempt to lighten the mood in the last movement does not fully succeed and peters out. The *Viola Concerto* (1952) surrounds a lively central movement with two slow movements, while the serene *Improvisation* (1956), for violin and orchestra uses material from the *Fantasia* for violin and orchestra of 1934. Of his other chamber works, the ruminative *Oboe Sonata* (1958) is very effective, while the *String Quartet No. 2* (1950–51) is one of his finest works. The construction is built on an initial four-note idea in the first movement, echoed in the close, and is full of subtle devices, in the mirroring of motifs, in the shades of string colour, and especially in the rhythmic fluidity. The quartet has a flowing spontaneity about it, sombre and undemonstratively intense in the first movement, dancing to elliptical rhythms in the *moto perpetuo* second. The third movement has the spirit of a slow madrigal, and the finale is ruminative until a transcendental touch at the close.

His choral works have an austere spirituality; the best known are probably the *Missa cantuariensis* (1946), using a double choir unaccompanied except in the Credo, where it is joined by an organ for extra emphasis, and the more concise *Missa in honorem Sancti Dominici* (1948). A number of his vocal works were inspired by St Teresa of Avila. His little-known songs cover an extraordinary range of texts, from Ancient Greek through Irish medieval Christian texts and Icelandic ballads, to modern American and English poetry.

Rubbra pursued a career as a pianist (notably in the Rubbra–Gruenberg––Pleeth Trio), and taught at Oxford University (1947–68) and at the Guildhall School of Music from 1961.

BIBLIOGRAPHY

L. Foreman (ed.), *Edmund Rubbra: Composer*, 1977

Simpson Robert Wilfred Levick

born 2nd March 1921 at Leamington
died 21st November 1997 at Tralee, Eire

Sometimes a composer emerges who would seem to have all the prerequisites for impact and success: considerable technical facility, a probing mind capable of creating imaginative and interesting structures, a concentration on and development of a particular form. Yet the spark that would give life to the music, and not mere existence, is, for whatever reason, missing.

Robert Simpson was just such a composer. Heavily influenced by Scandinavian composers as well as by late Beethoven, he concentrated on symphonies and string quartets that extend traditional harmonies and forms (especially building up material from germ themes or cells). His musical logic is impeccable, his grasp of the possibilities of unusual departures from traditional structures and forms enviable, and his music usually evinces a dark and rugged northern cast. Time and time again an interesting procedure captures the intellect, a passage fires the imagination, but then peters out into a still birth. One major cause is the lack of memorable material, of the details of content within a span or concept that is inherently interesting; another, rhythms that always have the aura of predictability. In the symphonies this is compounded by dull metallic orchestral colours that, however succinct the orchestration, invariably have a sense of the blanched. It is not enough for a string quartet merely to have an impressive logic of construction, especially in the tradition that Simpson has followed; it must also have emotional impact and a significant content, and in these the music of Simpson, for all its earnest build-ups into climaxes, is simply lacking.

That being said, Simpson's music may be of interest to those whose main concern is the unfolding of largely traditional patterns in new guises, and who do not wish to be challenged by the emotional content; and for those who have already explored the symphonies and string quartets of such composers as **Rubbra** or **Holmboe** there are indeed moments that do fleetingly capture the attention. Of his symphonies, the *Symphony No. 1* (1951) and the *Symphony No. 2* (1955–56), scored for a Classical orchestra, are both in three movements, played continuously in the former. The rugged contrapuntal writing and the use of progressive tonality and conflicting keys in the *Symphony No. 2* are characteristic of Simpson's writing; the still slow movement, cast in a palindrome except for the last few bars, has the feel of a star-scape. The *Symphony No. 3* (1962) is in two movements, the first in B flat, with a pull towards C, the second beginning in B flat, but ending in C. Although there seems little connection between the music and the implied programme (of a sleeper awaking and being infused with energy), this is one of Simpson's more effective symphonies, the first movement having an insistent power, the second more restrained, if losing its way at times. The long (forty-minute) *Symphony No. 4* (1970–72, later revised) has a lovely mystical moment at the end of the first movement, and the extended climactic drive of the end of the symphony is wonderfully clear and sustained. The development of germinal cells in the one-movement *Symphony No. 6* (1976) was inspired by parallels with biology, its big and powerful build-ups full of northern gravity. The *Symphony No. 7* (1977), also in one movement, was designed for recording rather than the concert hall (though there does not seem to be any especial concession or technique). The adagio is the most effective of the three sections. The *Symphony No. 9* (1987) uses palindromic variations in the second half of a one-movement form, and pays tribute to Bruckner. The fifty-five minutes of the *Symphony No. 10* (1988) in four movements are almost completely unmemorable.

The string quartets, largely inspired by the example of Beethoven, are in some ways more sympathetic listening, in part because they lack the regular monotony of those dark grey orchestral colours. The *String Quartet No. 1* (1951) is an attractive and assured two-movement work. The *String Quartet No. 2* (1953) compresses three sections into a single movement, while the *String Quartet No. 3* (1953–54) employs an unbalanced two-movement form, with an adagio introducing a large-scale sonata-allegro. The *String Quartet No. 4* (1973), *No. 5* (1974) and *No. 6* (1975) are all inspired by Beethoven's *Rasumovsky* quartets, being a kind of commentary on and development of them. The *String Quartet No. 9* (1982) is in the form of thirty-two palindromic variations on a theme by Haydn that is itself palindromic. The *String Quartet No. 10* (1983) is in three movements, and is subtitled 'For Peace'. The first of the two movements of the *String Quartet No. 12* (1987) has a stark, icy intensity; the second is a very extended scherzo.

Simpson was on the staff of the BBC from 1951 to 1980, and wrote widely and most effectively on music, especially on the symphony.

RECOMMENDED WORKS
Symphony No. 3 (1962)

BIBLIOGRAPHY
R. Matthew-Walker, *The Symphonies of Robert Simpson*, 1991

Stanford (Sir) Charles Villiers
see under Eire

Tavener John Kenneth**
born 28th January, 1944 at London

In the late 1960s the young John Tavener burst into prominence like a flash flood with the topical cantata *The Whale*. The waters then receded until he re-emerged in the 1990s as one of the leading and most popular of British composers. In the interim, however, unheard by a wider public, he was developing an individual and powerful idiom, given impetus by his conversion to the Russian Orthodox faith in 1977.

Almost all his music has a religious impetus, and most of it uses the voice. His earlier works emerged from the tail-end of the avant-garde, and had a powerful sense of drama, often explosive orchestral effects (favouring brass and percussion) and usually a constant ritualistic pulse. With vocal writing influenced by Eastern chants and the layered effects developed by the avant-garde, the result was a distinctive ritualistic idiom. By the late 1970s, the more disruptive elements of his style were becoming smoothed out, and by *Prayer for the World* (1980) for sixteen solo voices and *Ikon of Light* (1983) for chorus and string trio he had developed a spare, almost minimal, ethereal polyphony drawn from his earlier experience with the layering of choral writing, and with the intent of creating a mystical contemplative religious atmosphere. This style is not dissimilar to that independently developed by **Pärt**, and by the 1990s had proved equally popular. Throughout, he has ignored traditional forms and structures; instead these have been founded on the ritualistic needs of the individual piece, or the demands of a given text, usually with a strong and effective sense of logic that often includes palindromic shapes (the second section of *Ultimos ritos*, for example, is a double arch, ABCBAABCBA). Besides the more obvious influences of religious ritual and Russian orthodoxy, a Greek thread has also wound through his work, in settings of Sappho and Seferis and elsewhere, as if it provides a metaphorical meeting-place between the Western European and the Byzantine elements of the Russian Orthodox.

One psychological theme runs through this development of Tavener's idiom: the abnegation of the self. It haunts his earlier work, as if he is trying to find a context for self-effacement: in Jonah's burial in the belly of *The Whale*, in the children's chanted mockery of an adult sound-world in *Celtic Requiem*, in the contemplation of the Cross in *Ultimos ritos*, in the crisis of faith of Ste Thérèse of Lisieux in the short opera *Thérèse* (1973–76), and in the extinction of Antigone in *The Immurement of Antigone*. *Akhmatova: Requiem* pays tribute to a poetess who had been blotted out by a political system, but fought back. In these terms, his conversion to the Russian Orthodox faith, and his subsequent musical style, become a logical solution to the problem: the atmosphere of highly ritualised distancing of the rites of the church, and the musical sounds of pure, rarefied contemplation dissolves the self into the mystical soul. His more recent works suggest a new phase in this quest, and if it continues to be a major motivator in his music, it could be overall an examination of one particular aspect of human spirituality analogous to **Britten's** concern with the theme of lost innocence.

The Whale (1966) for speaker, mezzo-soprano, baritone, chorus and orchestra, used spoken words from the *Encyclopaedia Britannica*, sung Biblical texts, shades of **Ligeti**-like choral writing, interjectory, declamatory and chant-like elements, and occasional echoes from the British choral tradition to create a raw, flawed, but compelling piece, touched with bells and echoes from pop music (it was recorded by the Beatles' recording label). But it was the little-known and more concise *Celtic Requiem* (1969) for soloists, chorus, children's voices and orchestra that indicated the presence of a major composer with dramatic powers and strong religious leanings. It mixes deliberately naïve elements not normally associated with a requiem (children's nursery rhyme chants, recorders) with complex and sophisticated writing. Its ethereal, gossamer moments herald the better-known, later works, but it has its own entirely distinctive mould: the E flat major chord that rises up at the opening, joined by the sound of shaken percussion and children's chants, and which explodes into layers of singular clarity, combining solo soprano voice,

chants, and the children; the terrible groaning and crashing of whips after the 'Kyrie'; the sudden cataclysmic interjection of the organ that turns into a hymn; and the return of the opening crescendo at the end. Each layer carries its own momentum and pace, and the overall effect is of some great rite where the pagan spirit, contained in the children's nursery rhymes, is handing over to Christianity, but at the same time refusing to relinquish its influence. The *Celtic Requiem* was followed by one of Tavener's finest works, for the sheer magnetism of its logic, its emotional power, and its brilliance at bringing together unexpected elements in a very specific setting – that of a cathedral. *Ultimos ritos* (*Last Rites*, 1972), for soloists, chorus, organ and orchestra is even less well known than the *Celtic Requiem*, and it drew on the experience of combining Bachian elements with the layered choral writing in *Coplas* (1970) for voices and tape, in one of the finest of British church pieces in the second half of the 20th century. It is a kind of abstract church drama, centred on the contemplation of the Cross, with the central movement (of five) using just the word 'Jesu'. The atmosphere is strongly ritualist and generally slow-moving, making full use of the size and acoustic space afforded by a cathedral. The basic elements include complex and beautiful fanfares, cataclysmic and insistent orchestral effects, layered choral writing, chanting influenced by Eastern models, and a counter-movement, like some ancient processional, suggesting medieval tabor and pipes. All this material is derived from J. S. Bach's 'Crucifixus' from the *Mass in B minor*; completely disguised at first, it is barely discernible in the fanfares of the second section, but gets stronger until eventually it dominates the more modern elements at the end of the work, to stunning effect. *Requiem for Father Malachy* (1972) for chorus and ensemble follows this general cast, but on a chamber scale, using plainsong and chant, and musical glasses in the instrumental ensemble.

At the cusp between Tavener's earlier work and the later minimal style appeared one of his few non-religious, orchestral works, significantly titled *Palintropos* (*Turning Back*, 1977) for piano with an orchestra of brass, percussion, harp, celesta and strings. Each of its four sections, divided by 'musical columns', attempts to repeat its opening, but never succeeds, and a pivotal note of C is sounded at the beginning and the end by double basses.

The piano writing is in consort with the orchestra, at times emulating the sound of the cimbalom, at others woven into the general textures (brilliantly decorative in the opening). The tone alternates between mystical tapestries, sometimes still and contemplative and shadowed by the figure of **Messiaen**, and more assertive effects. *The Immurement of Antigone* (1978), a powerfully dramatic rendition of the death of Antigone which was written for soprano and orchestra but can also be staged, retains the ritualistic pulse effects (eventually becoming a funereal drum), but the block-like interjections and orchestral writing are toned down in favour of more linear effects, with long vocal lines that combine the angular with the flowing. As she is being immured, the orchestral textures become increasingly dense, the vocal lines more edgy, and the orchestra reiterates repeated harrowing phrases until the immurement is complete, and all one hears is the sound of tinkling bells, dying away. The climax of this second phase of Tavener's output was *Akhmatova: Requiem* (1970–80), for soprano, bass, brass, percussion and strings. The soprano sings settings of Akhmatova (in Russian, and built around her experiences of trying to find news of her imprisoned son, eventually leading to thoughts of death and madness); the bass sings largely Russian Orthodox liturgical interpolations between the poems; and then the two soloists join for the penultimate contemplation of the Crucifixion. There is a strong Russian flavour throughout the work, in the opening soprano unaccompanied solo, in the liturgical sections, in the use of bells, and in the palpable influence of **Shostakovich's** later, darker vocal works. The result is something of an anomaly on Tavener's work, as if he had moved to combine his own experience with the modern Russian vocal-symphonic tradition, but it has a dour impact.

Tavener's more ethereal vocal style of the 1980s, heralded by the austere *Divine Liturgy of St John Chrysostom* (1977) for unaccompanied chorus, was turned almost into early Renaissance music in *Funeral Ikon* (1981) for unaccompanied chorus, a setting in English of the Greek funeral service for priests, and reached fruition in the large-scale, mystical *Ikon of Light* (1983) for chorus and string trio, setting a text by the 11th-century St Simeon the New Theologian. Tavener's minimal setting matches the luminescence of the words, the choral writing largely derived from plainchant (with one major melodic idea, together with its inversion), but also including quasi-Renaissance polyphony and, near the opening and end, **Ligeti**-like cluster effects. The trio (representing the 'soul yearning for God') often accompanies this with held basic notes, and intersperses its own harmonically simple contribution. This long work, in which time stands still, has little sense of rhythmic movement, and is designed to be approached in a state of contemplation or meditation. So strong have plainchant and the Renaissance sound become in Tavener's work that one expects the modal-based harmonies of the lovely little carol *The Lamb* (1982), a setting of William Blake for unaccompanied chorus, to resolve into a final major chord – but they never do.

This spare contemplative style reached a huge public with *The Protecting Veil* (1987), for cello and strings, a work without voices, but still religiously inspired. The title refers to a vision of the Virgin Mary in Constantinople in which she held out her veil to protect the Christians against the Saracens. It is cast in eight sections, played continuously and each referring to a different aspect of Mary's life. The cello sings an almost non-stop dolorous lament of great beauty; the harmony is based on the traditional triad (but not classical harmonic progression, as it remains essentially static); the colours are rich, the textures sonorous. It is ironic that when the accompanying strings do break the contemplation of this moving work late in the first section and again repeatedly in subsequent sections, the result is unmistakably the sound of **Respighi**, another composer influenced by plainchant, and whose music has so long been disparaged by critics. There is indeed a turning back.

A different kind of turning back occurs in the opera *Mary of Egypt* (1992). Designed to parallel the visual image of an icon triptych, in five short acts, it tells of Mary the prostitute, who eventually becomes Christian through the example of the priest-monk Zossima. It has one almost fatal flaw. However sincere their religious inspiration, the words of the libretto by Mother Thekla of the Orthodox Normanby Monastery are quite possibly the most banal ever set into music in an opera. There is no characterisation whatsoever, only icons of the good and the fallen, and virtually no psychological tension. In other words, it seems as if the abnegation of the self that threads through Tavener's work has been completed in an opera with non-persons; and, in the absence of any sense of archetype or psychological progression, it becomes a tale without a moral, merely one of pure faith. The Middle Eastern and Indian ritualistic headiness, the sensuousness of the flute music associated with Mary, and the allure of her vocal lines are combined with the massive interjections that are a return to the tortured anger of *Ultimos ritos*. This tone, together with the unintentional sense of repressed masochistic sexuality that haunts the libretto, creates a profound ambiguity between intent and realisation. The mesmerising and often profoundly beautiful score has an underlying emotional passion that can only obliquely be related to the context; perhaps Tavener is moving to a position analogous to that of **Messiaen**, where the contemplation of the divine can be made musically from the stand-point of the emotional self, and not merely projected on to disassociated blocks or pure ethereal tones. However, *The Apocalypse* (1994) for soloists, choir, chorus, and large ensemble, including brass, recorders, percussion, string quartet and string orchestra, returned to a huge scale, in nine 'ikons' with a prologue and epilogue, dealing with the most graphic of visions of self-abnegation.

Tavener's output is considerable and uneven, dominated by works for voices or chorus on religious themes or for religious use, but also including such works as the chamber opera *A Gentle Spirit* (1976), based on Dostoevsky, and the delightful, simple little piano snippet *In Memory of Two Cats* (1986). His focus is necessarily narrow, but he has developed an entirely personal idiom to reflect that focus, and it is fitting that the music of one of the finest contemporary British composers is at last reaching a wider public.

RECOMMENDED WORKS

> *Celtic Requiem* (1969) for soloists, chorus, children's voices and orchestra
> *Ikon of Light* (1983) for chorus and string trio
> *The Immurement of Antigone* (1978) for soprano and orchestra opera
> *Mary of Egypt* (1992)
> *The Protecting Veil* (1987) for cello and strings
> *Ultimos ritos* (1972) for soloists, chorus, organ and orchestra

Tippett (Sir) Michael Kemp***
born 2nd January 1905 at London
died 8th January 1998 at London

It took many years for the singular achievement of Michael Tippett to receive widespread recognition, following derogatory comments by leading conductors, an inability to read across bar-lines by leaders of orchestras, and bewilderment at his first acknowledged opera by critics in the early 1950s. Many have found his idiom extremely difficult to absorb, in part because, misleadingly, it sets up an expectation of a traditional basis. The harmonies, for example, are never especially extreme in modern terms, and most of his works have the starting-point of the traditional genres of symphony, concerto, oratorio or opera. After the earlier works, however, that expectation is completely confounded, and the listener must adapt to an idiom that pursues its own course within the mainstream of our concert experience. However, perseverance brings its rewards, in the shape of a highly individual and incisive mind, whose especial achievement has been to create a genre of Jungian psychological opera.

The development of his style has been consistent, but has undergone evolutionary leaps with each new opera, the musical solutions in those operas spilling over into the non-operatic works that follow them. He has been considered an eclectic composer, but this tag too can be misleading: his procedures have been to absorb the work of other composers (from Gibbons and gamelan music to **Messiaen**, with Beethoven perhaps the predominant mentor) and heighten his own idiom with aspects of those musics that answer particular needs in his own personal style. Counterpoint, stretching back to Renaissance procedures, has been a foundation of his music, but he has developed two aspects of his music into an individual voice. The first has been the use of rhythm, particularly 'additive' rhythms, where the uneven rhythmic accents do not follow the regularity of traditional bar lines (hence the problems of orchestral players in the 1950s, unused to such flexibility) and cross-rhythms, which give his music a lithe, fluid life. The second has been the development of unusual forms within the general framework or flow of a traditional genres; gradually a procedure using blocks of thematic ideas, which are often associated with particular instrumental combinations and which undergo overlapping development (often through changes of tone or colour) has dominated, within more traditional formal divisions. The operas have used cinematic techniques of 'cross-cutting', with overlaps of time. Form, and the overall structures, are crucial to Tippett's music; individual incident is always related to that overall form. Whereas in the work of many composers the accumulative effect of individual sections or incidents gradually reveals the form from within, so that the listener gains the overall impression as the work progresses, this is not the way a Tippett piece generally works, except for the earlier music. Consequently the first hearing of a Tippett work can be confusing or bewildering; after a second or third hearing the overall pattern becomes clear, and then the content and details within that pattern are revealed; it is *always* worth hearing a Tippett work a number of times before making a judgement.

A number of emotional and philosophical themes combine to make Tippett's music especially individual. The first is the strong sense of humanity and compassion, concerned with allowing people to achieve their full potential as individuals. The second is a visionary quality, looking beyond the merely corporal and material towards the spiritual and the psychological, but taking care to relate those to the more mundane world. The third, and perhaps the most important, binding these two themes, is the exploration of Jungian psychology, and the use of music to express those aspects of Jungian psychology that are difficult to express in words, especially the movement towards the 'individuation' of each person. Some understanding of Jungian psychology is really essential for the operas to have their full impact, and also enlightens even his purely abstract works. Associated with this (especially the concept of the 'collective unconscious') is an understanding of time in which larger, non-linear concepts of time predominate over our more ordinary notions of time's progress; this influences Tippett's musical structures.

Tippett later withdrew all the music he wrote before 1935, and his first acknowledged work is the *String Quartet No. 1* (1935, revised 1943), in which two energetic and rhythmically vital outer movements frame a Beethovenesque slow movement of austere and unsentimental lyricism. The *Concerto for Double String Orchestra* (1938–39), still one of his most popular works, was the nearest he came to an English pastoral evocation through its colours, harmonies and sonorities, but it bursts with lithe rhythms (unequal beats, cross accents) that give it a distinctive

sound, and its sonorous slow movement is modelled on Beethoven's *String Quartet in F minor*, op. 95.

The first major indication of Tippett's humanitarian concerns came with the passionate plea against tyrannical oppression that is still probably his best-known work. *A Child of Our Time* (1939–40, first performed 1944) for soloists, chorus and orchestra, is recognisably in the English oratorio tradition, but both subverts and extends it. Firstly, its subject was a contemporary one: the shooting of a German diplomat by a Jewish refugee in Paris in 1938. Secondly the use of the vernacular in combination with forms based on Handel and J. S. Bach's *St Matthew Passion* removed the constraints from such a lofty tradition. Its most striking feature is the use of five Negro spirituals as the equivalent of Bach's chorales; Tippett saw a correspondence between Renaissance music (influencing his own music) and the jazz-blues tradition, and the spirituals arise entirely naturally from the general writing, to striking effect. It also (though entirely covertly) introduced the Jungian into Tippett's work, showing humankind in dire circumstances psychologically battling with its Shadow, and exploring the themes of compassion, tolerance and forgiveness; it remains as potent today as when it was written.

The *Symphony No. 1* (1944–45), although it shows some of the preoccupations that were to be developed in subsequent works, is now the least encountered of the symphonies; the divergence between wealth of musical idea and the creation of a large-scale form to contain it is too obvious. In the *String Quartet No. 3* (1945–46) marvellously lithe fugal writing dominates two of the five movements, and the influence of Beethoven is absorbed into a personal idiom.

However, these works of the late 1930s and 1940s were preludes to the maturity of his musical philosophies, that came to fruition with the opera *The Midsummer Marriage* (1946–52), discussed below. In this period the wonderfully rich sonorities of strings and the vitality of rhythm predominate. The beautiful *Fantasia concertante on a theme of Corelli* (1953) for strings brilliantly combines the ethos of Corelli's music (including a touch of the mood of Corelli's *Christmas Concerto* at the end) with Tippett's rapturous idiom of the period. The *Divertimento on Sellinger's Round* (1953–54) for strings ingeniously blends the dance tune with echoes of earlier English music from the Tudor period to Sullivan. The *Piano Concerto* (1953–55), inspired by Beethoven's *Piano Concerto No. 4*, inhabits the dense lyrical textures of *The Midsummer Marriage*, with which it has musical connections, the sonorities of piano extended by the sound of the celesta. The initial impetus for the *Symphony No. 2* (1956–57) was the pounding basses of Vivaldi's music, and with its atmospheric slow movement, continuing the tone of *The Midsummer Marriage* and the piano concerto, it avoids traditional development in favour of transformations using colour and texture, set against the colours of harp and piano.

With the opera *King Priam* (1958–61, discussed below), Tippett developed a more direct idiom, which had started to emerge in the finale of the *Symphony No. 2*. In this idiom the rich sonorities and lithe dances were evolved into a more rigorous and pungent use of the orchestra, in part derived from the example of **Stravinsky**. Structures are developed by the contrasts and overlaps of blocks of thematic material associated with particular instrumental groups, exemplified in the *Concerto for Orchestra* (1962–63). This method of construction confounds traditional expectations of the progress of the music, giving a spontaneous flow but also a lack of expected resolution; and it is combined with the visionary in *The Vision of St Augustine* (1963–65), for baritone, soprano, chorus and orchestra, where Tippett uses his recently evolved sound in a thicker palette. In three parts, drawn from Augustine's visions in the *Confessions* in Latin and English translation, combined with other religious material, it uses fourteen thematic blocks each of which has its own tempo and pursues its own development, while the chorus writing has layers of effect, from hymns to soaring choral declamation. The work has a ritualistic quality, and touches of the dance emerge, but the flow and the high choral writing imbues this with passion and visionary fervour in what has aptly been described as a 'stream of consciousness'. It is a work of ferment and ecstasy best absorbed by immersion in the sound and text, allowing the construction to be felt intuitively.

The *Symphony No. 3* (1970–72), for soprano and orchestra, followed the experience of the opera *The Knot Garden* (1966–70, discussed below). Underlying it is the combination of the abstract symphonic form and concrete expression through words in the exemplified by Beethoven's *Symphony No. 9* (which is quoted), but here it is a blues which serves

as a modern counterpart to Beethoven's choral ending. It is a symphony of dualities: a two-movement structure combining aspects of sonata form with Tippett's construction by blocks, the opposition of dynamic music, with flamboyant orchestral effects, and quieter music concerned with the release of that energy, in a mood that Tippett has called the 'windless night sky and the tidal wave below'. The *Symphony No. 4* (1976–77), following the opera *The Ice Break* (1973–76, discussed below) is entirely orchestral, in one continuous movement divided into three sections, and overall using three general tempi. The third section absorbs a fantasia by Gibbons, and the symphony is an unusual amalgam of fantasy and symphony, its theme of 'birth-to-death' emphasised by the haunting wind sounds that open and close the work. There are assimilations of **Shostakovich** (the fifteenth symphony is all but quoted) and **Messiaen,** and the work is like some dream in which events seem quite logical at the time, but in retrospect have an elusive, illogical quotient. The *Triple Concerto* (1978–79) for string trio and orchestra also uses a one-movement form, and has a beautiful central section influenced by gamelan music. *The Mask of Time* (1977–82), for voices and instruments is a kaleidoscope of musical, intellectual and literary ideas for large forces (rarely used all together) that traces man's place in the cosmos and his relationship to time. In spite of the moments of vivid imagination and typical power of orchestral expression, it is an uneasy work, partly because the structure is so disparate, and partly because the vocal writing (as opposed to the much more imaginative orchestral writing) is inclined to echo the large-scale oratorio tradition, sounding over-emphatic and feeling curiously dated. The *String Quartet No. 4* (1977–78) again followed a one-movement pattern built around a passionate slow movement; a fifth string quartet appeared in 1992. Mention should also be made of Tippett's four piano sonatas, dating from 1938 to 1984, the third of which contains his most abstract and direct music with little sense of outside influences or absorptions.

However, it is the operas that form the most complete of Tippett's achievements. Their central core is their conscious use of Jungian psychology, which led to bewilderment among audiences and critics until the general facets of Jung's thinking were more widely understood. Just as material from the collective or personal unconscious is expressed in dreams or myth, so it could be expressed in opera, where the combination of stage-symbol, word-symbol and music-symbol, as well as movement (dancing and ritual are major components of Tippett's operas), could be employed to express both idea and communication on a subconscious level. Tippett first developed this concept in the lyrical opera *The Midsummer Marriage* (1946–53), in which he drew on many sources, including Greek myth, the Grail legends, and the illusionary poetics of Eliot's *The Waste Land*. Its antecedents are perhaps Mozart's *The Magic Flute* and **Strauss's** *Die Frau ohne Schatten*; but whereas in those works the psychological symbolism was largely instinctive, here it is used consciously. Two levels are represented and combine: the human and the archetypal, represented by two couples, Bella and Jack, largely living in the conscious (though they have parallel roles in the mythical), and Mark and Jennifer, with elements of the mythical. Both must take the journey into the unconscious to find their own dualities of masculine and feminine, and achieve Jung's process of 'individuation', the central theme of this quest opera. The entire libretto is suffused with symbolism to support these two pairs: archetypal figures, archetypal places, and even archetypal musical forms. The four ritual dances (well known through their concert version for orchestra) represent the state of grace, and the wholeness of the mandala (with four sides). Those unwilling to be immersed in this strange world that crosses back and forth from the conscious to the unconscious will have great difficulty with this work. Nevertheless it is a masterpiece which teems with life, like a fecund representation of nature; its gloriously rich textures are dominated by string colours, with essentially traditional harmonies (extended by the use of superimposed fourths), touches of the Baroque and of Purcell, hints of the masque, marvellous choral writing, and above all a vital, rhythmic and ceaseless energy.

The opera *King Priam* (1958–61) marked a change in Tippett's idiom, a dramatisation of Homer that is closer to the poetics of Brecht than to Eliot. It concentrates on the role of King Priam in the Trojan war, its scenes set against the off-stage war, and is divided into four short acts with the chorus used as 'interludes'. Its theme is that of personal choices, or rather the consequences of personal choices, which are seen to have two aspects: the immediate personal consequences, determined by one's own choices

and actions, and the longer-term pattern where those choices are part of a wider determination whose interactions cannot be predetermined. This is more than just the Greek sense of Fate or Destiny: it is Jungian (specifically in such figures as the old man, and the equation of the three Goddesses with the three human women of the story), although the symbolism is not nearly so overt as that of *The Midsummer Marriage*. Fate unfolds in more a synchronistic than a predestined fashion. The lucid orchestration, often using a single instrument (with no strings in the second act) and with an assimilation of **Stravinsky's** neo-classical orchestral techniques, is striking and powerful, as if each instrument represented some Greek deity standing behind and influencing the human-vocal, whose lines are declamatory rather than lyrical. This is above all an exciting opera – direct, sometimes abrasive, often fast-paced, and with compelling characters.

With *The Knot Garden* (1966–69) Tippett returned to the Jungian allusionary vision. Here the structure is less conventional and draws on a multiplicity of sources, from *The Tempest* and Goethe to Eliot and Virginia Woolf. The 'knot garden' itself provides the primary image of the inner life that the personality may or may not be cultivating, the knots being the twists of that inner life. The theme is that of displaced relationships; each of the seven characters starts the opera without the internal psychological balance (self-knowledge) to make an external relationship successful. The figure of the analyst appears, himself not fully aware of his psychological inner life, and there is little plot, rather a gradual awareness of each individual's personal psyche to the point where successful relationships and interactions are possible. Dysfunctional generational effects from distorted relationships are shown in the figure of Flora, and the whole opera has a sense of therapeutic role-play. The score continues the more direct, spartan orchestral usage of *King Priam*, but to quite different ends; here it is intimately connected with each character, expressing the subconscious and its changes, and the overall moods are both more nervous and more lyrical. One character remains without resolution, but that was provided in the associated *Songs for Dov* (1969–70) for tenor and chamber orchestra.

Tippett's discovery of American culture, which some have seen in *The Knot Garden*, first emerged consciously in *The Ice Break*

(1973–76). Here Tippett explored another archetypal theme: that the domination of the crowd by one archetype leads to personal and social disintegration. When this happens, only the assimilation of the multiplicity of archetypes within the individual allows personal emancipation. Symbolism abounds (the chorus are masked), the words are matched by 'archetypal sounds' in the score, Jung is quoted directly, and the very last words return to the archetypal theme of the maimed fisherman. Tippett has been heavily criticised for his librettos, mostly owing to the non-comprehension of the Jungian content, for (apart from one or two infelicitous phrases), his actual word-usage is generally workmanlike if not poetic. But *The Ice-Break*, which contains some of Tippett's finest music, with its rich and dramatic use of the orchestra, is indeed spoiled by its words, in particular the use of slang, which sounds not only instantly dated, but also affected and somewhat ridiculous in the slower time-frame of sung, rather than spoken, word.

There is an element of George Bernard Shaw in Tippett's musical drama, often masked by the Jungian layers, and the opera *The New Year* (1985–88) has something of the symbolic futuristic fantasy of Shaw's late plays, similarly employing a variety of genres (here including masque, ballet, pantomime and suggestions of the musical theatre). Tippett has identified elements of his own childhood experience in the central male character, the Afro-American Donny; the central female character, Jo Ann, a child psychologist, has suggestions of Joan of Arc. Its two general settings are 'Somewhere and Today' of the turbulent urban present, and 'Nowhere and Tomorrow', an equally uncomfortable futuristic world of time-travel ruled by a domineering woman. The two worlds interact (with the landing of a spaceship), and with the experience of this interaction Jo Ann is transformed from an inability to cope with a violent world to a position of self-confidence, her choice between reality and escapist amnesia being made in a paradise garden. It is a heavily symbolic opera: the characters from the future can clearly be identified with Jungian psychological archetypes, representing her unconscious, and indeed the whole opera can be construed as a psychological projection of Jo Ann. Tippett's music is wildly eclectic, including elements of pop music and 'break dancing', and uses electronics.

Tippett organised music at workcamps for unemployed ironstone miners in 1932, and was a conscientious objector in World War II (and was briefly imprisoned in 1943). He taught at Morley College (1940–51), became President of the Peace Pledge Union in 1959, and was artistic director of the Bath Festival (1970–75). He was knighted in 1966. Marmalade has been his chief solace in times of stress or crisis.

RECOMMENDED WORKS
oratorio *A Child of Our Time* (1939–40) for soloists, chorus and orchestra
Concerto for Double String Orchestra (1938–39)
Concerto for Orchestra (1962–63)
Fantasia concertante on a theme of Corelli (1953) for strings
opera *The Ice Break* (1973–76) see text
opera *King Priam* (1958–61)
opera *The Knot Garden* (1966–69)
The Mask of Time (1977–82) for voices and instruments
opera *The Midsummer Marriage* (1946–53)
opera *The New Year* (1985–88)
Piano Sonata No. 3 (1972–73)
String Quartet No. 4 (1977–78)
Symphony No. 2 (1956–57)
Symphony No. 3 (1970–72) for soprano and orchestra
Symphony No. 4 (1976–77)
The Vision of St Augustine (1963–65) for soloists, chorus and orchestra

BIBLIOGRAPHY
M. Tippett, *Moving into Aquarius*, 1959
D. Matthews, *Michael Tippett: An Introductory Study*, 1980
M. Bowen, *Michael Tippett*, 1982

Vaughan Williams Ralph•••
born 12th October 1872 at Down Ampney (Gloucestershire)
died 26th August 1958 at London

The music of Vaughan Williams, long thought too quintessentially English for successful export, has found an increasing and admiring international response as the durability and the universality of his major works have become more apparent. His output is large and diverse, covering all the major musical genres, and much of it is indeed parochial. Like a number of other similarly nationalist composers of the same period (for example, **Bartók**), he was concerned that serious music should be available to all, and his works extend from music for amateurs with purely local significance to an emotionally complex, large-scale, and sometimes abstract idiom. However much affection the English have for some of the former, it is the latter that are emerging as significant 20th-century works. The relative delay in their general acceptance is partly due to the lack of obvious musical experimentation in Vaughan Williams's language – he was content to develop recognised forms using a traditional harmonic base. Another reason is the over-popularity of some of the less substantial pieces, of which the beautifully crafted, effortlessly lyrical *Fantasia on Greensleeves* (1934) for orchestra is the most obvious example – the best-known arrangement of one of the Western world's best-known tunes.

Behind all of Vaughan Williams's music lie two decisive influences, both rediscoveries for English music when he began to employ them: the English folk song, and the madrigals and polyphonic mastery of Tudor and Elizabethan English composers. He collected English folk songs (he joined the Folk Song Society in 1904), together with fellow composer **Holst** (which again has parallels with the similar activity of such composers as **Bartók** and **Kodály** in the same period), and his interest in hymn and church music was reflected in the editing of the music of *The English Hymnal* (1904–06). His earlier work which is dominated by songs, is direct, usually simple and often lyrical, and shows a keen appreciation of the quality of the literature set and the nuances of the language. A notable example is the song-cycle *Songs of Travel* (completed by 1907) to words by Robert Louis Stevenson.

Then, following a period of study (1908) with **Ravel**, three years his junior, and whose influence recurs indirectly in orchestral colour and effect, Vaughan Williams produced a number of works that mark his late maturity. The *Sea Symphony* (1903–09), for soprano, baritone, chorus and orchestra, is his (and English music's) farewell to the English Romantic tradition of the large-scale oratorio, but its visionary fervour – to the sensuously joyous words of Walt Whitman – looks forward to a later emotional expression. The symphonic form is indicative of his sense of technical craftsmanship, and the nocturnal mystery of the slow movement and the passion of the final movements contain many of his musical hallmarks. The 'Aristophanic Suite' *The Wasps* (1909) contains an English jauntiness that infects much of his output, while at one point rather uncannily foreshadowing the ballet idiom of **Prokofiev**. The song-cycle *On Wenlock Edge* (1909) for tenor, piano and string quartet (setting A. E. Housman) has the long-breathed lyricism associated with his English pastoral style combined with a more fervent Impressionism. But his first masterpiece is the *Fantasia on a theme by Thomas Tallis* (1910) for two string orchestras and string quartet. Using one of the old church modes (the Phrygian) that give so much of Vaughan Williams's music such a distinctive flavour, and the use of which is his main if subtle contribution to 20th-century harmony, the *Fantasia* spins webs of soaring and serene polyphonic sound. The alternation of major and minor creates a nostalgic and yearning flavour in an idiom that is an English neo-Renaissance equivalent to the neo-classical movement.

These works established the essential flavour of Vaughan Williams's idiom, though it was to undergo constant evolution until his death. His range and contrasts of mood are nowhere better expressed than in the nine symphonies which are the backbone of his output (though since Vaughan Williams was such a late developer, he was already seventy-one when he wrote the fifth symphony). All except the seventh use a traditional four-movement pattern, but they contain an exploration of many emotional facets, and although (after the choral first) only one of the symphonies has any kind of detailed programme, it is difficult not to see each symphony as reflecting the *mood* of particular extra-musical events or inspirations, if not a programmatic text. The *Symphony No. 2 'A London Symphony'* (1912–13) – or more accurately, a symphony 'by a Londoner' – emerges from the 19th-century inheritance of the Romantic symphony, its opening redolent of the great city awakening in the gloom, a musical equivalent of a painting by Monet or Whistler. Westminster chimes appear (and they do keep time with the actual progress of the symphony), as well as a lavender-seller's cry and the sounds of street musicians, but this is primarily a symphony of the evocation of mood (sometimes in darker hues than mere celebration). These is one major innovation: the haunting epilogue, coming after the powerful finale, that seems to conjure up the Thames, with wisps of earlier material half-remembered.

The *Symphony No. 3 'A Pastoral Symphony'* (1916–1921), is a combination of a haunting sense of loss (it was started in northern France when Vaughan Williams was serving with an ambulance brigade) and wonder at the beauty of pastoral landscapes, encapsulating the emotions of a generation. Its atmosphere is contemplative throughout, visionary in the feel of its chordal progressions, developing through the metamorphosis of melodic idea rather than through traditional procedures, and using a wordless soprano in the finale. This is one of Vaughan Williams's most beautiful works; it is also of great interest from a purely symphonic point of view, with modal scales and procedures that swing into diatonic scales, a combination which is responsible for many of the haunting effects.

The *Symphony No. 4* (1931–34) burst like a thunderbolt on to Vaughan Williams's mainly pastoral image. Its opening bars unleash anger, a predominant mood in this darker-coloured work, but undermined or opposed by a jaunty buoyancy typical of Vaughan Williams. It is also a concise and taut work, exactly containing what it wants to express, unified by the constant presence of two motifs heard at the opening, and achieving a kind of emotional equilibrium in its finale, almost as if it is smiling at its own outburst. The *Symphony No. 5* (1938–43) again confounded expectations by returning to a serene beauty and to the overlap of the modal and the diatonic. The darker undercurrents are kept at bay by the overall impression of visionary stillness found especially in the opening of the 'romanza' slow movement and in the finale; they are there, notably in the scherzo, but they have the quality of something from the past, something remembered, and the achievement of this symphony is to create an atmosphere in which the spiritually lyrical predominates over the more sinister or tragic without any sense of triumph or domination.

He returned to something of the dark anger of the fourth symphony in the *Symphony No. 6* (1944–47). This, however, is an altogether finer work, where the passions have been held, weighed, and then unleashed. In terms of exploring the more difficult of human emotions (and presumably his own) it is his most searching symphony, and, together with the more lyrical fifth, his finest. Like the fourth, it erupts at its opening, but when the bouncing basses emerge they have a macabre, sardonic edge. An almost Elgarian noble lyricism attempts to oppose this, but ends up in a disconcerting uneasy climax. Now

comes the true dark grit of the work, with menacing reiterated phrases against pallid, haunted strings; a more resolute nobility attempts to overwhelm this, but is itself gets caught up. The sardonic dominates the restless third movement, especially in the sound of saxophones, the whole suggesting some kind of malicious retributive fury, but all this suddenly emerges into the extraordinary epilogue finale. 'We are such stuff as dreams are made on, and our little life is rounded with a sleep,' Vaughan Williams commentated, quoting *The Tempest*, and this movement never rises above *pp*, occupying some remote region of the mind, and inevitably suggests parallels with nuclear oblivion. It is bleak, but also icily beautiful, and completely recasts the effect of the music that has gone before it.

The *Symphony No. 7 'Sinfonia antartica'* (1949–52), with soprano and female chorus, has been treated as the ugly duckling of Vaughan Williams's symphonies, for it was the development of music he had written for a film about Scott of the Antarctic. Each of the five movements is headed by a quotation applicable to Scott's enterprise, and also descriptively to the music of the movement. In idiom it echoes and extends some of the effects of the sixth symphony, turning them to a more descriptive purpose, as if in emotional terms he was trying to reconcile the interior emotions of that work with a place in nature. It is also an instantly attractive work, especially the magisterial third movement, and even if its symphonic argument is weaker than in his other symphonies it deserves a more sympathetic reputation. The last two symphonies are products of the wisdom of old age, caring little about meeting the expectations of younger minds. The sound of the *Symphony No. 8* (1953–55) is enlivened by a battery of percussion instruments, many tuned; its variation form first movement covers many of the composer's different musical hues. The *Symphony No. 9* (1956–57), whose genesis was inspired by the Thomas Hardy landscape around Salisbury, is a tougher and more interesting work. There are touches of his earlier music throughout, but they are distilled into a softer, enigmatic glow, enhanced by saxophones (used lyrically) and the flugelhorn.

Many of Vaughan Williams's other major works group themselves around the symphonies in terms of mood and tone. The beautiful *A Lark Ascending* (1920) for violin and orchestra, with its soaring evocation of the bird over the English landscape, has the pastoral lucidity of the third symphony. *Flos campi* (1925) for viola, wordless chorus and orchestra, with its rich writing for the viola, like the lark descending, has the visionary stillness felt in the fifth symphony, countered by a central dance-march (representing Solomon). *Five Variants of 'Dives and Lazarus'* (1939) for strings and harps combines folk song with the mood of the fifth symphony, as does the last movement of the *String Quartet in A minor (String Quartet No. 2* 1942–44), and especially the attractive small-scale *Concerto for Oboe and Strings* (1944). In the latter, the solo, always lyrical, is sometimes dancing, sometimes with the longer-phrased stillness inherent in the symphony. The dramatic and angry fourth symphony was preceded by a finer but less well-known work, the ballet (or 'masque for dancing') *Job* (1927–30). The scenario by Geoffrey Keynes is based on eight Blake illustrations to the biblical story, in nine scenes in the score. Equally effective as a concert work, the ballet uses a large orchestra augmented by percussion, bass flute, organ and especially saxophones, used to telling effect in the sixth scene, as Satan brings in three Comforters, with its apocalyptic vision of the Devil. The emotional range of the score is striking, from the pastoral to sardonic wild dances and broad visionary vistas. Much of it has a crushing power, leavened by moments of bouncy jauntiness (to which some have objected, but which was an essential part of Vaughan Williams's musical make-up), preventing any sense of distancing. The instrumental experimentation of the eighth symphony was reflected in the *Romance* (1951) for harmonica, strings and piano, and in the *Bass Tuba Concerto* (1954), both lightweight but entertaining works – an old man pottering about and simply enjoying himself without any pretensions.

The summation of all these different emotional aspects of Vaughan Williams's work is the opera *The Pilgrim's Progress* (completed 1949), whose composition covered much of his life. Perceptive listeners will recognise not merely the Romanza movement from the fifth symphony (which he adapted from the opera when he thought he would never complete it) but also echoes of most of his other symphonies. For this work is Vaughan Williams's testament, from which the symphonies are the expansion and pendants. Based on

Bunyan, but considerably condensed by the composer, the story is an allegorical quest rather than a drama, a ritualistic progression that Vaughan Williams called a 'morality'; this has caused problems in staging, but should not in future, following the wider understanding and acceptance of spiritual ritualistic works by **Britten, Glass, Messiaen** and **Tavener.** In any case, *The Pilgrim's Progress* is not without colourful stage settings and characters, in the arming of the pilgrim, for example, or the bustle of Vanity Fair. When familiar with the pastoral folk-lyricism, the bouncy jocularity, or the powerful angry thunder of Vaughan Williams's best-known works, it is easy to forget that underneath those layers he was at heart a visionary, an agnostic with a deep understanding of the humanist and the spiritual, and their importance; hence the deep sincerity of his liturgical music. *The Pilgrim's Progress* is the finest expression of that vision, for the pilgrim himself remains true to it (and the composer made his intentions clear by changing his name from 'Christian' to 'Pilgrim', indicating it is an opera about universal spirituality, untied to any specific religion). The pilgrim passes through those other emotional and musical layers that make up the composer's personality and form the various scenes, and Vaughan Williams's evocation of the visionary could not be more beautiful or more ardent. The work will not appeal to those for whom such spirituality counts for little in their lives; but it can be an extraordinary experience for those prepared to respond.

That Vaughan Williams could write a purely dramatic, psychologically intense opera was demonstrated in *Riders to the Sea* (1925–32). Not only is this arguably his finest single work; it is one of the tautest and most moving of all one-act operas. It sets J. M. Synge's play almost word for word, and Vaughan Williams supplies exactly the musical expansion the play needs, with a huge orchestral backdrop of the sea (including a wind machine) deeply involved in the action as a protagonist, a wrenching portrait of the old woman who loses her sons, sharp secondary characterisation always pointed up by the music, and the sense of the other-worldly visionary common to the idiom of both Synge and Vaughan Williams. It is astonishing that the opera is not more often performed, for it always proves deeply affecting; the problem is finding a companion work that is not emotionally overshadowed by it. His other operas contain some very fine music, but their librettos subscribe to a rose-tinted view of the English past that now seems dated. *Hugh the Drover* (1910–14) is a folk opera, drawing on traditional tunes and including a boxing match in its action. The much more mature *Sir John in Love* (1924–28), based on *The Merry Wives of Windsor*, captures the atmosphere of Shakespeare's underlings aspiring to greater pretensions and to other wives' beds, but lacks a deeper undercurrent; it is, though, very entertaining, and would perhaps be performed more often were it not for its large demands in cast and staging.

Vaughan Williams wrote a large number of choral works, from hymns to full-scale cantatas. The oratorio *Sancta civitas* (1923–25), for tenor, bass, chorus and orchestra, sets texts (in English) drawn from Revelations, Plato and the Roman Missal, and was the first indication of his more angry, powerful voice, as opposed to the ruminative folk-song pastoral with which he was then associated. The cantata *Dona nobis pacem* (1936) includes passages from the Bible, Whitman, John Bright, and Latin prayer; its theme of peace not only looks back to World War I but reflects the turbulence of contemporary European politics. If largely within the English choral tradition, its combination of rhythmic flow, passionate intensity and the quietly lyrical reveals his depth of feeling. The *Mass in G minor* (1920–21) is for unaccompanied double choir with a quartet of solo voices from within the chorus. It is in essence a neo-Renaissance work, merging older polyphonic procedures with the composer's modern directness and is within its particular liturgical purposes, most effective. The *Five Tudor Portraits* (1935) for baritone, contralto and chorus are rather rollicking settings of the early 16th-century poet John Skelton.

Two of his more effective vocal works are unusual hybrids. The *Fantasia on the Old 104th Psalm Tune* (1949) for piano, chorus and orchestra sets the psalm with the old Ravenscroft tune in a series of variations, with the piano playing a fantasia role, in a work that is half choral, half piano concerto. The marvellous *Serenade to Music* (1938) sets words from *The Merchant of Venice*, for sixteen solo voices with orchestra. It has a long, pastorally lyrical orchestral introduction, into which the voices quietly steal (with affinities to both **Holst** and **Delius**) and then weave a gorgeous web, the music entirely matching the magical seduction of the words in one of the finest of all Shakespeare settings. It is, however, rarely performed,

since it does require operatic or oratorio solo voices, and not merely a divided chorus. His many songs are always effective and sympathetic to the words, if (with the exception of the cycles *On Wenlock Edge* and the late *Ten Blake Songs*, 1957, for voice and oboe) not as penetrating as those of some of his English contemporaries. 'Linden Lea' (1900) and 'Silent Noon' (from the cycle of six Rossetti sonnets *The House of Life*, before 1903), with its limpid piano writing and cadences, are two of the best-loved of all English songs.

Vaughan Williams's output was extremely large, and those exploring his lesser-known works should bear in mind that many were written for specific occasions, purposes or performers – he believed that music should be available to all walks of life – and thus not expect the universality of his major works. The neo-Baroque *Concerto grosso* (1950) for string orchestra, for example, uses three bodies of strings: a concertante group (advanced players) against a group of players of intermediate skills and another of beginners. Other works can vary in quality; the ballet *Old King Cole* (1923) will perhaps only appeal to the English, while the Christmas cantata *Hodie* (*This Day*, 1954) contains music of visionary wonderment alongside pedestrian passages.

RECOMMENDED WORKS

> All the symphonies are recommended; those new to Vaughan Williams might care to start with the central symphonies from *A London Symphony* (No. 2) to the *Symphony No. 6.* cantata *Dona nobis pacem* (1936)
> *Fantasia on Greensleeves* (1934) for orchestra
> *Fantasia on a theme by Thomas Tallis* (1910) for two string orchestras and string quartet
> *Flos Campi* (1925) for viola, wordless chorus and orchestra masque for dancing *Job* (1927–30)
> *A Lark Ascending* (1920) for violin and orchestra
> song-cycle *On Wenlock Edge* (1909) for tenor, piano and string quartet

BIBLIOGRAPHY

> R. Vaughan Williams, *National Music*, 1973
> M. Kennedy, *The Works of Ralph Vaughan Williams*, 1964
> H. Ottaway, *Vaughan Williams*, 1966
> U. Vaughan Williams, *R.V.W.*, 1964

Walton (Sir) William Turner[**]
born 29th March 1902 at Oldham
died 8th March 1983 at Ischia (Italy)

William Walton's place in 20th-century music is currently an equivocal one, rather like that of his friend **Hindemith**, with whom he has much in common. Like Hindemith, his works remain on the margins of the repertoire (with the possible exception of the oratorio *Belshazzar's Feast*), while his name remains universally known. An individual voice in English music, he totally ignored the English interest in old English music and in folk song, and developed an idiom usually deriving internally from the technique of composition rather than being inspired, like so many English composers, by extra-musical sources – the orchestral overtures are an exception. His harmonic style, essentially tonal (though later using tonal bases founded on elements of note-rows), and his structures are largely traditional, and in aesthetic he continues an English line initiated by **Elgar**. At the same time his brilliant rhythmic incision and complexity, initially inspired in part by jazz and by **Stravinsky**, were new to English orchestral music. His relatively small output is loosely divided by the war years, after which his insistent rhythmic energy became more mellow, and between a number of shorter occasional works and larger scores of more serious intent.

The work that brought him to fame was a tongue-in-cheek divertissement, the brilliant and witty *Façade* (1921–22, for reciter and string instruments, revised 1926 for larger instrumental group, revised again with additional material in 1979 as *Façade 2*, and turned into two suites without reciter, 1928 and 1939). He never repeated its chamber-scale dramatics (except for echoes in the comic opera *The Bear*), although the ironic intellectual wit remained an element of his style. The poems are 'abstract' but socially ironic experiments by Dame Edith Sitwell; the music is a parody of contemporary Parisian musical manners, with strong jazz overtones.

Walton's preferred medium was that of the large orchestra. Prominent and popular are a number of occasional overtures and marches following the Elgarian tradition, notably *Crown Imperial* (1937) with its noble tune, full of pomp and circumstance, and the 1953 coronation march *Orb and Sceptre*. The overture *Portsmouth Point* (1925), in sonata form, is a busy score, combining a sense of the English pictorial in brilliant orchestral colours with rhythmic diversity. The overture *Scapino* (1940), inspired by a drawing of the *commedia dell'arte* character, is jaunty enough but unconvincing, and, for readers looking for such works, Malcolm **Arnold's** similar overtures are more entertaining and vivid. However, the later *Johannesburg Festival Overture* (1956) and the *Capriccio burlesco* (1968) are abstract works, more clear-cut, the former enlivened by a sense of Afro-Cuban sounds in the percussion, the latter with an almost neo-classical verve. The *Partita for Orchestra* (1957) is a three-movement showpiece for orchestra, brilliantly executed but not very memorable.

The three string concertos have been much admired by critics, but have not achieved a similar popularity with soloists or audiences, and readers are advised to take glowing statements about their richness and warmth with a degree of scepticism. Such lyricism is indeed present in the *Viola Concerto* (1928–29, orchestration revised 1961), premièred by **Hindemith**, but it is compromised by the nervous impetuous energy, an unusual combination which partly explains its marginal place in the repertoire. The *Violin Concerto* (1938–39) starts dreamily, but quickly turns into a virtuoso work for the soloist, again with an unsettled quality to the music. The *Cello Concerto* (1956) is more obviously warm, with a Mediterranean tinge (Walton's home was the island of Ischia, off Naples).

As with so much of Walton's music there is a feeling in these works of the emotional distance between the composer and his material, of an intellectual refinement. It is in the two symphonies (the first being his masterpiece) that the personal involvement is palpable. The dramatic *Symphony No. 1* (1932–35) is savage and shattering, with the influence of **Sibelius** in the build-up of profuse thematic ideas. Its opening phrase, capable of both power and nostalgia, insinuates itself into the memory. The unsettled atmosphere of the work is partly based on the use of the interval of a seventh, partly on the contrast between changing chromatic harmonies and the foundation of long bass pedal points, and partly on the orchestration, that includes saxophone colours. The scherzo has a combination of amiability and menace, and the weakest section is the final fugal movement, more celebratory and restrained, and written some time after the previous three. The three-movement *Symphony*

No. 2 (1959–60) uses a 12-note sequence (with six of the notes in the first movement's second subject, the other six stated in the slow movement, and the full twelve as the theme of the passacaglia theme and variations in the finale). Structurally more assured, the finale is in three large sections, and while much of the bite of the earlier symphony remains, the nervous energy and short terse phrases have broadened. The mood is more light-hearted, with a song-like slow movement in which thick string textures predominate. The later orchestral works include the *Variations on a Theme by Hindemith* (1962–63), each of whose nine variations has a tonality based on a different note of the Hindemith theme (from his *Viola Concerto*). Although sometimes dry, the elegant writing has considerable variety and typically purposeful orchestration.

The oratorio *Belshazzar's Feast* (1931) was a landmark in the English choral tradition. Its rhythmic insistence, pulsing energy, fierce orchestration and total absence of sentimentality represented a new departure at the time, but it now seems much tamer, especially in comparison to the contemporary choral works of composers such as **Prokofiev** or **Orff**. Essentially a vividly descriptive piece rather than a philosophical or spiritual oratorio, it derives much of its bite from the large orchestra, used in clear-cut colours with fierce brass and percussion dominating. The choral writing, marvellously textured, is less overtly incisive, and has its antecedents in **Elgar**. But the work continues to thrill audiences, partly because the vocal writing so often comes close to the limits of acceptance of modernity for amateur choral societies. His two operas have failed to keep a hold in the repertoire. The grand Romantic opera *Troilus and Cressida* (1950–54) is predominantly lyrical, concentrating on vocal line rather than the symphonic development that might have been expected. The one-act comedy of manners, *The Bear* (1965–67), based on Chekhov's 'jest in one act', is totally different, being essentially a work of parody of various operatic styles (including his own earlier opera). The ballet *The Wise Virgins* (1940) is based on orchestrations of music by J. S. Bach.

An important part of Walton's output was his uncompromising music for films, especially for three Shakespeare films, *Henry V*, *Hamlet* and *Richard III*. He was knighted in 1951.

RECOMMENDED WORKS
  oratorio *Belshazzar's Feast* (1931)
  melodrama *Façade* (1921–22, revised 1926)
  Symphony No. 1 (1932–35)
  Symphony No. 2 (1959–60)
  Violin Concerto (1938–39)

BIBLIOGRAPHY
  F. Howes, *The Music of William Walton*, 1965 (2nd edition 1974)

Williams Grace*
born 19th February 1906 at Barry
died 10th February 1977 at Barry

Grace Williams was of especial importance to the music of Wales. She established, with Daniel **Jones**, a place for Welsh classical composition and greatly encouraged the improvements in standards of orchestral performance and composition by her example and her music. Although fairly narrow in range and relatively conservative in its idiom, and without any great profundity, her music does have individuality. It is also exceptionally beautiful, filled with an ecstatic fervour and joy, and would win many friends outside Wales were it better known. She destroyed most of her early works, and her mature idiom has affinities with the choral music of **Holst** and the more visionary side of **Vaughan Williams**, though without the pastoral element and sometimes tinged with unexpected influences from **Strauss** and **Mahler**. What makes her music so attractive is its exceptional fluidity; in many of her works, all the components seem to have been spun out of gossamer. Technically this is achieved by a number of elements. There is an absence of classical procedures, leading to a more spontaneous flow of ideas; her preferred forms were the suite, or were dictated by word-settings. When she attempted a more traditional structure, such as the *Symphony No. 2* (1956, revised 1975), with more turbulent emotional material than was her custom, the traditional harmonic arguments are muted; the *Trumpet Concerto* (1963), highlighting one of her favourite instruments, is structurally more successful. The chromatic harmonies, especially in the 1940s and early 1950s, are often ambiguous (while founded on a diatonic base), sometimes without key signatures, oscillating on modal ideas, and frequently use a scale of alternating semitones and tones, probably derived from **Bartók** (the scale is also **Messiaen's** second mode of transposition). Her rhythms are rarely emphatic, but tend to be full of lithe and subtle changes. The fervour arises from this constant fluidity, the ecstasy often from the high writing for instrumental or vocal lines; the solo vocal writing sometimes encompasses wide leaps, drawn from Viennese influences, but these are so integrated into the general tone that they can go unremarked.

Of her earlier music, *Hen Welia* (1930) for orchestra is a suite of Welsh folk songs and folk-like tunes, while the *Fantasia on Welsh Nursery Tunes* (1940) for orchestra, the best-known of her works which have a nationalist hue, uses eight traditional Welsh lullabies. The short, heartfelt *Elegy for Strings* (1936, revised 1940) exemplifies her aesthetic – rapturous, emotionally undemonstrative, and much of the time harmonically ambiguous. An abiding influence was that of the sea, beside which she lived, and whose constant change and motion is reflected in her music. The suite *Sea Sketches* (1944) for strings is perhaps her most famous work. In five sections, it covers a wide range of mood: the turbulent, the mysterious (with fog-horns subtly sounding), the evocation of breakers rolling over each other, and the final calm in summer, reminiscent of late **Strauss**. The *Sea Sketches* are perhaps the most accurately evocative musical view of the sea ever penned, avoiding any attempt to anthropomorphise or to add spurious colour. The suite *The Dancers* (1951) for soprano, female chorus, strings and harp is the finest of these earlier works, setting five poems from sources as varied as Chesterton and Kathleen Raine. It has a rapturous opening, in which the falling violin line is answered by the soprano. The magical movement of the second song (a setting of Belloc's 'Tarantella') is matched by the lament of the third, in which the soloist repeats a refrain of her lover's death eight times, each at a different pitch, over a floating, chanting chorus.

After 1954 Grace Williams never again utilised an authentic Welsh folk tune; instead, within a framework of less ambiguous key structures, she started to incorporate some of the inflections and accents of the Welsh language into her music. *Penillion* (1955) for orchestra most obviously started this process, for it emulates (in three movements) the traditional Welsh art of vocal improvisation with irregular metrical structures against a repeated melody on the accompanying harp (here replaced by various members of the orchestra). The Welsh style is declamatory, and this infiltrated her vocal writing, notably in the powerful song-cycle *Six Poems by Gerard Manley Hopkins* (1958) for contralto and string sextet. Hopkins's highly musical and alliterative verse is difficult to set, but his metrical systems were themselves influenced by Welsh verse, and Williams's setting succeeds in releasing both the metrical effects and the spiritual beauty, with a distinct echo of **Mahler** in the middle. Perhaps her finest vocal setting is one of her last. *Ave maris stella (Hail, Star of the Sea*, 1973) for unaccompanied choir ossilates between the complex vertical writing of the verses and the soft swell of the refrain. The title refers to the Virgin Mary; the work is suffused with a sense of loving prayer, as well as the movement of the sea. Her one-act comic opera, *The Parlour* (1961), based on a Maupassant story of a cantankerous grandmother whose supposed death leads to family wrangles, confounded when she awakes from a coma, was highly regarded by some of those fortunate enough to encounter it.

RECOMMENDED WORKS
> *Ave maris stella* (1973) for unaccompanied choir
> *Sea Sketches* (1944) for orchestra
> *Six Poems of Gerard Manley Hopkins* (1958) for contralto and strings choral suite *The Dancers* (1951) for soprano, women's chorus, strings and harp

BIBLIOGRAPHY
M. Boyd, *Grace Williams*, 1980

Williamson Malcolm
see under Australia

United States of America

The history of 20th-century classical music in the USA revolves around a continuous series of attempts to formulate novel and especially American forms of musical expression. This can be seen partly as a struggle against the domination of European classical music and ideas, new or old. Some of these attempts have been more successful than others; ironically, most of them have been absorbed and transformed by European traditions. It is difficult not to come to the conclusion that in terms of musical impact, and in the reflection of the wider human condition and the narrower expression of the ethos and ideas of the day, none of the American composers has yet matched their major European counterparts. Elliott Carter (born 1908) and John Cage (1912–93) are the prime contenders, but the demanding idiom of the former seems unlikely to capture the attention of more than a small and highly knowledgable audience; the latter's main achievement, perhaps the primary contribution of a serious American composer to a wider culture, has been through his approach, ideas and liberation from traditional constraints, rather than through his actual music. A large measure of this creative failure may be due to environmental factors rather than to any absence of an innate pool of talent: modern music is woefully under-funded and under-encouraged in the general American culture. The educational system and the dominance of commercial media values simply fail to instil appreciation of cultural knowledge and excitement in a wider public. The academic system, on which American composers' livelihoods now depend, has had an 'ivory tower' effect on composition, shifting the balance to purely intellectual concerns, away from the expression of a wider human condition, and from the reflection of popular American emotions and non-academic concerns. The States has produced, and continues to produce, a remarkably large number of composers. A book such as this cannot possibly do justice to that scale, and this one therefore concentrates on those composers most likely to be encountered, in the States or outside. In addition, the first generation of truly American composers, now coming to the end of their lifetimes, are of such general if not exceptional interest, and their music is so undeservedly neglected even if their names are widely known, that there is an element of bias towards that generation.

A major feature of American music is the long tradition of maverick experimental composers, from Henry Billings (1746–1800), who wrote an atonal hymn, and in whom interest has been revived this century, to John Cage in the present day. But as the 20th century started, American music was anything but original or inventive, being dominated by European example, European training (particularly Germanic), and by European visitors, such as Dvořák (1841–1904) or Mahler. The principal figure of the end of the 19th century was Edward MacDowell (1860–1908), whose idiom was in the German Romantic tradition. Similarly, the group known as the 'New England Classicists' – George Chadwick (1854–1931), Arthur Foote (1853–1937) and Horatio Parker (1863–1919) – followed the example of Brahms. These, the leading composers of the period, concentrated on symphonic and instrumental works; opera meant Italian opera. There were two principal exceptions to this general cast of American composition at the turn of the century. The first was Charles Martin Loeffler (1861–1935), who reflected the *fin-de-siècle* developments of the end of Romanticism in Europe. Drawn to unusual, bizarre or exotic subjects, his outlook was Symbolist, and his main achievements are the orchestral colours and effects of his tone-painting. The evocative *La mort de Tinagles* (1897, revised 1901), a tone poem for viola d'amore and orchestra based on a dark marionette play by Maeterlinck, is similar in style to the music of his British contemporary Bantock and well worth hunting out. Loeffler's output is now little heard; it may be that, in an age more indulgent to his type of idiom, he will emerge as a composer of greater stature than such obscurity would suggest. The second is Charles Ives (1874–1954), whose extraordinary output, anticipating many of the techniques evolved by others later in the century, had no influence at the time of their composition. His place in the history of American music is discussed below. Two other composers might be far better known had their output been larger. After early works influenced by German models, Charles Tomlinson Griffes (1884–1920) developed an Impressionist idiom tinged with Oriental colours and effects, in such evocative tone poems as *The Pleasure Dome of Kubla Khan* (1912–17) for orchestra and *The White*

Peacock (1915, orchestrated 1919, originally the first of four *Roman Sketches* for piano). These, and the fine *Poem* (1918) for flute and orchestra, are well worth the encounter; this talented composer died prematurely just as his music had been discovered, but he helped American music turn away from German influences and look to French music. The output of Carl Ruggles (1876–1971, a painter as well as composer), bold in scale but meticulously crafted, was extremely small (some ten acknowledged works) but of a visionary quality, exploring an atonal harmonic palette. *Sun-Treader* (1926–31, much revised), the third of a triptych of orchestral works, is one of the finest American compositions of the first half of the 20th century, a large, rich sixteen minute score, its roots in late Romanticism, but with an extremely chromatic harmonic palette that (through Ruggles' general unwillingness to repeat a note until some eight others have been heard) sometimes has an atonal cast. The emotional range is considerable, the orchestra regularly swelling up and out in unresolved climaxes that must start again, the whole effect one of Expressionist emotional tension compressed almost to bursting-point, each detail meticulously weighted. An apt comparison is perhaps with the earlier orchestral writing of **Berg**. The two other works of the triptych, *Men and Mountains* (1924, revised 1936) for orchestra and *Angels* (1921, revised 1939) for four muted trumpets and five muted trombones, are equally compressed. The former, for a very large orchestra and in three parts, is in a idiom similar to, but less intensely effective than, that of *Sun-Treader*, while *Angles* is a forty-seven-bar work, muted but anguished. Ruggles spent many years working on an opera, *The Sunken Bell*, based on a play by Gerhardt Hauptmann, but eventually burned the score.

The first, and the most lasting and influential of all specifically American musical developments, was not in the field of 'serious' music, but in the development of jazz. Ironically, the first classical composers to absorb some of the techniques and ideas of jazz into their work were not American at all, but those such as **Martinů**, **Milhaud** and **Stravinsky**, working in Paris in the early 1920s. Nonetheless, it was the element of jazz that provided the impetus for the styles of the first American composers who came to the fore in the late 1920s and early 1930s with music that was instantly recognisable as American, rather than a European clone. The catalyst for this sudden explosion of an American music was also found in Paris, in the teacher Nadia Boulanger. So many Americans studied with her, from **Copland** to **Glass**, that a list of her pupils reads rather like a catalogue of major American composers. She encouraged American composers to seek their own American voices. She also insisted on a detailed and thorough study of basic techniques, which had two effects: on the positive side, she instilled the sense of craftsmanship that is so apparent in the subsequent generation of American composers; on the negative side, she contributed to the obsession with intellectual analysis that has so castrated academic American music. A second thread running through the history of American music has been that of dance. Many of the best-known works of Aaron **Copland** (1900–90) originated as ballets; much of the initial experimental work with percussion by **Cage** and Lou **Harrison** (born 1917) was influenced by dance, and minimalism had its origins in small-scale works for dancers.

However, one of the most lasting legacies of the heritage of American serious music, the symphony, is now also one of the most neglected. The generation of American composers who came to prominence in the 1930s excelled at the traditional form of the symphony (and, to a lesser extent, its interior obserse, the string quartet). What is more, these symphonies, far from being mere copies of European models, proved to be a major vehicle for the expression of ideas, emotions and concerns that reflected the American outlook of their age, especially a sense of broad landscape and a rugged, rough purpose. If the States did not produce a symphonist of the calibre or consistency of **Shostakovich** or **Vaughan Williams**, the best of these symphonies are very fine indeed, and moreover are of especial interest and appeal because they reflect that particularly American spirit. It seems extraordinary that American orchestras have not trumpeted these works at home and abroad, to help build a sense of pride in a musical cultural heritage that is currently so nebulous in the USA, especially when the form of the symphony is one readily accessible to general audiences. The principal American symphonists include (besides **Ives** and **Copland**), Howard **Hanson** (1896–1981), a conservative but a major force in promoting indigenous American music, Roy **Harris** (1898–1979), Walter **Piston** (1894–1976), Wallingford **Riegger** (1885–1961), William **Schuman**

(1910–92) Roger **Sessions** (1896–1985), and the now virtually forgotten Ernst Toch (born Vienna 1887, died 1964), who moved from a Romantic idiom through neo-classicism to 12-tone techniques, and whose music deserves a revival.

This group of symphonists formed the core of American classical music in the 1930s, 1940s and 1950s. Together they established and promoted a specifically American idiom ranging from the American subjects and tone of **Copland** and **Schuman** to the 12-tone techniques of the influential **Sessions**, and developed an American symphonic and operatic style, though much of the latter awaits re-exploration and appraisal. Meanwhile Henry **Cowell** (1897–1965), a major American innovator, had started exploring works dominated by percussion, music for pianos prepared in various ways to change or extend the range of colours, and Eastern musics and rhythms. John **Cage** (1912–1992) and Lou **Harrison** (born 1917) developed this legacy, the former then emerging into an important avant-garde force whose ideas were taken up by a number of experimental American composers. The eccentric Harry Partch (1901–1974) was on a parallel experimental path, but using specially designed instruments with microtonal intervals (dividing the scale into forty-three or more tones). His extraordinary sound world, quite unlike anything until the 1980s (when Eastern sounds became more assimilated into Western music), owes much to traditional Eastern musics, is usually built around his specially designed, tuned percussive instruments, and has a strong ritual and theatrical quality. Unfortunately, his compelling sound world is almost impossible to encounter except on recordings, owing to the uniqueness of the instruments. Of his earlier works, often using voice, *Barstow* (1941–43) is a remarkable setting of eight hobo inscriptions on a railing outside the town of the same name, using two voices, half singing, half speaking, and four players on original instruments; it captures the essence of the period of displaced hitchhikers, a 1940s equivalent to **Reich's** 1980s *Different Trains*. Of his later works, mostly large-scale rituals, *Delusions of Fury* (1963–69) is a music-theatre piece for mime, dancers (also chanting or singing) in two halves, the first based on a Japanese ñoh play, the second a folk-like tale centred around a hobo, and covers the whole gamut of Partch's unusual instruments, infectious rhythms, Oriental colours and microtonal

effects. The RCA Company had been experimenting with electronic instruments since the late 1940s, but Vladimir Ussachevsy (born in Manchuria, 1911, died 1990) and Otto Luening (1900–96) pioneered American electronic music in the late 1950s, establishing a studio in Columbia University that became the Columbia-Princeton Electronic Music Center in 1959. Their example was followed by Mario Davidovsky (born in Buenos Aires, 1934); all three composers are now rarely encountered, but made important contributions to the development of American music.

The 1960s saw a wide variety of American compositional trends. Some composers followed the experiments and examples of **Cage**; others, like Lukas **Foss** (born 1922), had similarities with the European avant-garde. Many more followed the path of 'total serialism' into ever more arcane detail, led by Milton **Babbitt** (born 1916); this also dominated academic composition teaching in the 1960s and 1970s, and still dominates academic musical analysis. **Carter** remained the most interesting and consistent of the American composers, but his idiom was unique. The reaction in the 1970s and 1980s also produced a fragmentation of styles. These included a return to a late-Romantic influence – **Mahler** in the works of David **Del Tredici** (born 1937) and especially in those of George Rochberg (born 1918), whose change from a serial to a tonal neo-Romantic idiom is best heard in his string quartets. Many composers adopted a less specific neo-Romanticism, exemplified in the very attractive if superficial *Violin Concerto* (1979) of Earl Kim (1920–98). Others were influenced by popular music and the Broadway musical, notably Leonard **Bernstein** (1918–90), a major personality and force in American music, although more through his conducting and broadcasting than through his own compositions. John **Corigliano** (born 1938) has incoporated elements of all of these in a stylistic mismash.

However, the movement that has had the most national and international attention and influence, and the only 'school' that has arisen in this period, is that known as 'minimalism'. With its origins in the music of Carl **Orff**, more immediately in the 1960s drone works of the jazz composer LaMonte Young, and particularly in the seminal *In C* (1964) by Terry Riley (born 1935), it was immediately loathed by conservative critics and serialist academics alike, partly because it was a strong reaction to 'highbrow' and, particularly, academic American values. Its earliest manifestation in the 1960s was closely linked to experimental modern dance and small chamber groups, usually using electronic amplification. It then broadened its range and appeal in the 1970s, when the works of Philip **Glass** (born 1937) and Steve **Reich** (born 1936) achieved an enormous following beyond the range of lovers of classical music, and has since spread into all serious musical genres, including opera. While it has had adherents outside America, its use of repetitive evolving patterns has increasingly influenced elements of works by composers who could not by any stretch of the imagination be included in the minimalist school. Adherents of minimalism have been at pains to point out the considerable stylistic differences between the major composers of the school. Such differences are undeniable; but the cast of similarities, particularly the influence of gamelan ideas, the return to a diatonic base, and the altered conception of the time and spatial elements of the construction of music, so markedly set these composers aside from other developments in modern music that the broad grouping is apposite. Whether the movement will be a lasting one, or whether it will prove to be more significant through the influence of its ideas on non-minimalist music remains to be seen; but its main flaw – that it is suited more to broad spiritual undertows than focused, immediate, experiential emotions – suggests the latter.

These, then, are the main outlines and figures of the development of American music, but a number of other composers, for whom there is not enough space for full inclusion in this *Guide*, also deserve mention. John Alden Carpenter (1876–1951) experimented with jazz influences in the very visual ballet *Krazy Kat*, based on a comic strip. The finest work of Ruth Crawford Seeger (1901–53) is her *String Quartet* (1931). Paul Creston (born Guttoveggio, 1906–85) was a cosmopolitan traditionalist, best heard in two of his symphonies. The *Symphony No. 2* (1944), a two-movement work, pits a **Sibelius**-touched 'Introduction and Song' against an 'Interlude and Dance', full of forceful infectious bounce tinged with jazz. The fine, if conventional, *Symphony No. 3* (1950) has a programme representing the mysteries of the Nativity, Crucifixion and Resurrection, but with the American gaiety of the second movement and the contemplative dark third movement, it works better as an abstract work. The unashamedly neoclassical *Partita* (1937) for flute, violin and strings is also most attractive. Gian-Carlo Menotti (born in Italy, 1911) is generally thought of as an American composer, though he retained his Italian citizenship and settled in Scotland in 1974. He is best known for his earlier operas, unchallenging in their morals and in a naïve idiom that came straight from the Italy of 1900, including *The Medium* (1946), *The Telephone* (1947) and *The Consul* (1950). His most successful work was the short, sentimental but attractive *Amahl and the Night Visitors* (1951), woven around a crippled boy who meets the three Magi; it was the first television opera, and on the stage remains a perennial Christmas favourite in North America. David Diamond (born 1915), best known for his *Rounds for Strings* (1944), was primarily a symphonist, his nine symphonies being mostly traditional, attractive, but unmemorable. Vincent Persichetti (1915–87) produced a large body of works in a variety of communicative styles, from the tonal to the atonal, including nine symphonies. The symphonies of Peter Mennin (born Mennini, 1923–83) are large and bold, tinged with an American brashness and syncopation, and, if not as striking as similar works by **Harris** or **Schuman**, worth hearing, especially the *Symphony No. 3* (1946). Ned Rorem (born 1923) is probably better known for his provocative books of musical autobiography and criticism than for his music. His primary achievement is his large body of songs; his style has been gracefully traditional, drawn from French models, and his output has been large. Of his three numbered symphonies, the *Symphony No. 3* (1957) is full of delightful ideas but, with its range from the atmospheric and serious to the light, fails to gel. Of his operas, *Miss Julie* (1960–65, revised into one act, 1975) belongs to the American traditional of lyrical opera, but its vocal fluency does not plumb the psychological depth of the Strindberg play. He is at his worst in such grand-scale works as *An American Oratorio* (1983–85), mixing a 19th-century choral tradition with populist elements and jazz, and at his best in smaller-scale works that give rein to his sense of style and grace. Lejaren Hiller (born 1924) has concentrated on music composed with computers; his *Illiac Suite* (1957) for string quartet (developed with Leonard Issacson) was the first computer-programmed acoustic composition. His *String Quartet No. 5* (1962) is in quarter-tones with a 24-note row, using variation technique in which variation twelve is itself a miniature quartet inside a quartet, all four movements played simultaneously. Earle Brown (born 1926) was a leading advocate of 'indeterminacy', with mobile forms and scores that allowed the players considerable freedom regarding interpretation and the order of events. Ben Johnston (born 1926) is best known for his string quartets using microtonal intervals, notably the *String Quartet No. 2* (1964). Morton Feldman (1926–87), initially influenced by Cage and the avant-garde New York painters, developed an idiom of quiet, sometimes hypnotic strands of sound undergoing slow-moving variation of detail, and used graphic scores in the 1950s before reverting to conventional notation. Jacob Druckman (1928–96) turned from electronic music with instruments (notably the *Animus* series, 1966–69) to a neo-Romantic style that has included references to earlier musics. John Eaton (born 1935), after exploring electronic music in the 1960s, has more recently turned to opera (including *The Tempest*, 1985), where he has used quarter-tones, especially in the orchestral writing, set against more traditional harmonies to considerable effect. Morton Subotnick (born 1933) has produced a series of atmospheric, electronic 'theme' works, aimed at a more popular market; *Silver Apples of the Moon* (1967), designed for an LP, brought him wide attention, but the most effective is *After the Butterfly* (1979) for trumpet ensemble and electronics.

Finally, it should be pointed out that the States has a particularly honourable tradition in the form of the musical, which, with the help of Hollywood versions of Broadway productions, usurped the position of European operetta from the 1930s to the 1960s. Like the symphony, the neglect of the heritage and academic dismissal has led to its decline, and modern American musicals have been eclipsed by their English counterparts. Such works lie outside the scope of this book, but they have influenced American classical music. Many American composers, both US-born (such as **Bernstein**) and immigrants (**Weill**), have made major contributions to the genre, while Broadway's most talented exponent, George **Gershwin** (1898–1937), included works of a more classical idiom in his output.

United States of America Musical Information Centre:

American Music Centre
30 West 26th Street
Suite 1001
New York, NY 10010–2011
tel: +01 212 366 5260
fax: +01 212 366 5265

Adams John**

born 15th February 1947 at Worcester (Massachusetts)

John Adams, who came to prominence with the grand-scale opera *Nixon in China* (1987), is proving to be one of the most fascinating and infuriating of the new wave of minimalist composers who have followed the examples of **Reich** and, in Adams's case, **Glass**. He is also the American minimalist composer most aware of the inheritance of musical tradition, incorporating many influences into the minimal structures of his works, from material that he shares with **Ives** (hymns, marches – such Adams titles as *Common Tones in Simple Time* are clearly an echo of Ives), to a use of ostinati colours that looks back beyond **Orff** and the metallic percussive colours of early **Cage**. Most strikingly, he almost immediately applied minimalist techniques to large-scale orchestras with an almost Impressionist, Ravelian command of orchestral colour. (Adams had the advantage of being composer-in-residence with the San Francisco Symphony Orchestra, in contrast to Reich and Glass, who arrived at writing for larger forces via their own small groups.) His earlier works show his fondness for lyrical ideas as well as the influence of Cage and, in the triptych *American Standard* (1973), Cardew and the Scratch Orchestra, with marches, jazz, and performers adding 'found objects'. The section 'Christian Zeal and Activity', with an almost Wagnerian overtone to the slow unfolding of melodic strand, continues the American tradition of using hymn tunes, and placed Adams firmly in the neo-Romantic movement.

Adams's first major minimalist work is also one of his most effective. *Shaker Loops* (1978), for string septet (version for string orchestra, 1982–83), is inspired by another American phenomenon, the religious sect known as 'Shakers'. Adams's minimalism does not come from the use of very slow changes, the movement in stasis heard in Eastern musics, that is inherent in the music of Reich and Glass, and whose trance-like effect has been so often noted. Instead, Adams's driving, impulsive, and very effective repetitive rhythms are strictly ostinati, emphasising changes of colour and timbre, and closer to neo-classical ostinati usage (a rhythmic parallel to the third movement is **Honegger's** *Pacific 231*). Similarly, there are no sudden key shifts, but a conventional tonal (and neo-Romantic) sense of harmonic progression and eventual resolution: *Phrygian Gates* (1978) for piano is a cycle of fifths. A simple harmonic pattern is the basis of *Common Tones in Simple Time* (1979–80, revised 1986), where the structure is built on common chords (triads) or similarly simple harmonic constructions, and modulation is achieved only through chords with common tones. With an equally simple basic metre (always 4/4 or 2/2), the emphasis is thrown on the changing colours, achieved by such details as the sixteenth notes played by violins and violas, the two pianos being one-sixteenth out of phase with each other, or the two oboes or two trumpets hovering between neighbouring B and C.

The element of banality that has subsequently plagued some of Adams's music then became apparent in *Grand Pianola Music* (1982); it has elements of pastiche, including revivalist hymns and, in the finale, echoes of the modern Hollywood pop epic style in major keys exemplified by the pop composer Vangelis, together with gospel music and marches. In contrast, two works have shown the enormous potential of this composer, both extremely powerful in their own right. In *Harmonium* (1981), for chorus and orchestra, and *Harmonielehre* (1985) for orchestra, rich and sometimes delicate orchestral textures vie with orchestral detail, the long flowing melodies with complex repetitive rhythmic touches. Events unfold especially through changing colours, and through the gradations of dynamics over a very long time-span, leading to great sweeping climaxes in major keys whose power, emotional effect and sheer excitement, thanks to the scale of the orchestral imagination, is unmatched by any other minimalist composer.

The influence of **Glass**, observable particularly in the shifts of the interval of seconds in *Harmonielehre*, unfortunately becomes more overt in Adams's major success to date, the opera *Nixon in China* (1987). The opera deals in a rather uncomfortably surrealistic way with Nixon's trip to China and his meetings with Chairman Mao. Much of the orchestra texture is pared down, the fascination of detail lost, and in spite of some marvellous climactic moments (especially when ecstatic choral texture joins rich orchestral colour), the banality resurfaces, partly caused by the

ugly and whitewashing libretto, which makes some sections seem a minimalist parody of Gilbert and Sullivan. In contrast to Glass's individual vocal writing, Adams's solo vocal lines here belong to another American tradition: that of the American musical, exemplified by Bernstein's *West Side Story*. This type of melody sits very uneasily on the minimalist orchestral writing, sometimes the impetus seems to lose focus, and the long lines become merely note-spinning. Nowhere is this better exemplified than in some sections of *The Chairman Dances* (1985, on material from *Nixon in China*) for orchestra, which feel like muzak, in spite of the thrilling impetus of much of the writing, with influences from Chinese music to **Weill**. However, in *Fearful Symmetries* (1988), for winds, saxophones, synthesiser, strings and brass (the same orchestral complement as *Nixon in China*), Adams combines his sense of forward momentum, climactic moments and delicate touches with a more eclectic synthesis of moods, not the least of which is humour, to create one of his most satisfying and entertaining works.

Adams's second opera, *The Death of Klinghoffer* (1989–91), also to a libretto by Alice Goodman, again treats a contemporary subject: the highjacking of the cruise ship *Achille Lauro* by Palestinian terrorists, with the subsequent death of one of the passengers, Leon Klinghoffer. The aim is a tragedy, rather than the quasi-comedy and parody of *Nixon in China*, and its form is influenced by the Bach Passions, being laid out in clear sections with a conspicuous choral involvement. Although individual moments echo the idiom of the earlier opera, the musical style is more varied, and in many respects more conservative than Adams's earlier work, and the libretto more poetic. Both these operas leave a sense of discomfort, albeit easy to overlook because of the sheer power of some of the music. In spite of the claims of the composer, librettist and director, the treatment of other cultures and ways of looking at the world has exactly the kind of shallow, single-culture viewpoint that bedevils American news. It is instructive that in *Nixon in China*, and even more in *The Death of Klinghoffer*, Adams should turn to what amounts to an equivalent of the 19th-century Grand Opera, a form that inclines to primary colours and shallow simplistic treatment when dealing with political subjects. This has been reinforced by the spectacular, almost melodramatic, stage elements of the operas, such as the appearance of the fuselage of the Boeing when Nixon arrives in China with Kissinger – visually very exciting, but contributing little else.

Whether Adams will continue to develop his individual brand of minimalism, or whether he will continue a populist opera style, remains to be seen. However, those coming new to the genre will find him perhaps the most accessible composer of this new American movement. They should not confuse him with the composer John Luther Adams (born 1953).

RECOMMENDED WORKS
Fearful Symmetries (1988) for
orchestral ensemble
Harmonium (1981) for chorus and
orchestra
Harmonielehre (1985) for orchestra
Shaker Loops (1977–78) for 7 strings

Antheil George Johann Carl*
born 8th July 1900 at Trenton (New Jersey)
died 12th February 1959 at New York

George Antheil was the first modern American composer to attract attention (and controversy) in Europe. He had originally gone to Berlin in 1922, as a pianist, but settled in Paris in 1923, where he was championed by the writers James Joyce and Ezra Pound and where, during the next four years, his anti-Romantic, excessively mechanistic music (influenced by Stravinsky, whom he knew) caused a sensation.

Initially, this was expressed in piano music, especially in a series of sonatas, *Sonata sauvage* (*Sonata No. 2*, 1922 or 1923), *Death of Machines* (*Sonata No. 3*, 1923), the three-minute *Jazz Sonata* (*Sonata No. 4*, 1922), and, most notoriously, the *Airplane Sonata* (*Sonata No. 1*, 1921), with repetitive machine-like rhythms, organised in blocks of different ostinati, and including cluster-like chords. His *Symphony No. 1 'Zingaresca'* (1922, revised 1923) had included jazz elements, developed in the lively, impulsive, witty and short *Jazz Symphony* (1925) for twenty-two instruments (revised for small orchestra, 1955). But the most notorious piece of this period was the *Ballet mécanique* (1923–25), for eight pianos, player piano, four xylophones, percussion and two airplane propellers (version for sixteen pianos and other noise makers, 1927). The version now usually performed is a considerably shortened revision (1953),

and uses four pianos. Again, modular repetitive units are used, under the influence of similar procedures in Cubist painting. The fragments of melodic material (rhythm and percussive colour being much more important) are influenced by Stravinsky. With the pianos used percussively, it is a *tour de force* of mechanistic but sometimes delicate sounds, whose repetitions are masked by other constant changes. In its use of unpitched percussions sounds, and emphasis on organisation by contrasts of rythmic rather than harmonic material, it parallels the work of Varèse and anticipates later percussion developments.

Antheil then turned to a neo-classical style, again following the lead of Stravinsky, but also produced *Transatlantic* (1927–28), an admired satirical opera on American life that uses cinematographic stage techniques, parodies of popular tunes, and his modular and ostinati techniques. The strory revolves around big business trying to influence the outcome of a presidential election. It was the first opera by an American composer to be produced by a foreign opera company. His last major piece written in Europe before his return to the USA in 1933 was the uneven but sometimes fascinating *La femme: 100 têtes* (1933), a set of forty-four preludes and a final dance for piano. These include a return to the steely, percussive (and sometimes noisy) style, as well as parodies of other pianistic styles, from the virtuoso, through Impressionism, to a suggestion of Shostakovich (later a strong influence on Antheil's music); but there is also a visionary feel to the overall set, and an internal programme recalling Antheil's childhood.

From 1935 Antheil became well-known as a film composer working in Hollywood, and in the late 1940s and early 1950s turned to writing operas, of which the most successful was the comic *Volpone* (1949–52). At the same time his style changed considerably, becoming neo-Romantic in orientation, though keeping something of the rhythmic impulse and jazzy rhythms of his experimental period. The most prominent works of this period are the *Symphony No. 4* (1944), showing the influence of Shostakovich, and using intentionally populist melodies, and the infectious *Symphony No. 5 'Joyous'* (1947–48), not to be confused with the *Tragic Symphony*, 1945–46, sometimes called No. 5, with a lively first movement whose language recalls Shostakovich's scherzos, and a slow movement in the American landscape mode. The ballet *The*

Capital of the World (1953) is based on a Hemingway short story about a young bullfighter from a poor village who goes to Madrid, the city of the title, and eventually dies in the ring. First presented on television, it is a colourful and vivacious score, full of Spanish touches, conventional in substance, but with enough American verve to suggest that it would work well on stage.

Among Antheil's many achievements were the writing of a syndicated column of advice to the lovelorn, the co-invention of a new kind of torpedo, and the publication of two books on glandular criminology. His music deserves more prominence, particularly the opera *Transatlantic*, not least for its historic interest.

RECOMMENDED WORKS

Airplane Sonata (Piano Sonata No. 2, 1921)
Ballet mécanique (1926, rev. 1955)
Jazz Symphony (1926, rev. 1955)
La femme: 100 têtes (1933) for piano
Symphony No. 5 *Joyous* (1947)

BIBLIOGRAPHY

G. Antheil, *Bad Boy of Music*, 1945, reissued 1981
E. Pound, *Antheil and the Treatise on Harmony*, 1928, reissued 1968
L. Whitesitt, *The Life and Music of George Antheil*, 1983

Babbitt Milton Byron[*]
born 10th May 1916 at Philadelphia

For better or worse, Milton Babbitt has been – through his writings, his theories and his teaching as well as his music – one of the most influential of American composers since World War II, one whose music is treated outside the circles of his followers more with respect than with affection. Indeed, his works are totally unknown to the vast majority of those who listen to music: the composer himself has stressed the validity of appealing to a small élite. Broadly speaking, his achievement has been to remain in the forefront of the establishment and development of 12-tone music in the USA. More specifically, it has been to reappraise the 12-tone legacy of **Schoenberg; to** ally it with **Webern's** derived sets (a term invented by Babbitt, referring to a 12-note set that is derived from the manipulation of a smaller set of notes); to apply the techniques to all the parameters of music (e.g. duration, dynamics) as well as pitch; and to utilise

the concepts of new mathematics in the resultant systems, and invent (or borrow from mathematics) terms to describe the processes. These terms have become current usage in complex analysis of such works.

The result was the concept of 'total serialism', which European composers such as **Boulez** and **Stockhausen** were arriving at independently following the lead of **Messiaen,** but a year or so later than Babbitt. A major difference has been that, by the mid 1950s, the European composers by and large had dropped the strict application of total serialism as being too restricting; Babbitt, on the other hand, has developed it. His first work of total serialism was *Three Compositions for Piano* (1947–48), a busy, yet austere and sometimes delicate set of abstract miniatures, much more easily appreciated (like most of Babbitt's music) when heard while following a score. It uses a rhythmic set (and its transformations) that corresponds to the pitch set (and its transformations according to 12-tone principles). In the uncompromising, often single-voiced *Composition for Four Instruments* (1948) for flute, violin, clarinet and cello, and *Composition for Twelve Instruments* (1948), the complex serial interrelationships between the various aspects of the music are extended. He then continued to refine the internal mathematical honeycombs of his music, notably in the *String Quartet No. 2* (1954). Here the structure is based on the introduction of the first half of a 12-note series with their own row permutations, with increasingly larger intervals until all six notes are stated consecutively, followed by a similar process with the second six notes; eventually all twelve notes can be sounded. The process of refinement continued with the intervallic relationships of *Partitions* (1957) for piano, the polyphonic network of *Relata I* (1965) for orchestra, the faints jazz touches of *All Set* (1957) for jazz ensemble, and in the *String Quartet No. 3* (1969–70) which the composer has aptly described as 'sonic asceticism'. In all these works the fascination is largely intellectual, the appeal to the mathematical mind, the conceptualisation abstract. To the curious general listener, the most appealing work of this period is probably *Philomel* (1964) for soprano and 4-track tape.

In 1959 Babbitt set up the Columbia-Princeton Electronic Music Center, and himself became one of the earlier American exponents of electronic music. His own use of medium was largely in order to have complete control over the detailed graduations of his strictly total serial concepts, particularly organised changes in timbre and colour, and to exploit the ability to create much faster changes than instrumentalists could, in contrast to the new aural conceptualisations that the Europeans were pursuing. His earliest essay for tape was *Composition for Synthesiser* (1961), the best known probably *Ensembles for Synthesiser* (1962–64).

Babbitt's own achievement has been considerable, even if appreciated by a very few. But there are many who consider that his influence on American music has been unfortunate: that it has produced a whole generation of composers without his talent, erudition or wit who, in the academic circles where much of the funding for new music is available, have slavishly followed intellectual complexities of such convoluted intent that their music has often been excruciating, and totally devoid of any audience other than their fellow practitioners. One might also point to another effect of his influence, which many would consider equally unfortunate: that the main reaction to such intellectual complexity has been a swing of the pendulum to the opposite extreme, the often oversimplified, harmonically naïve trend of minimalism.

Babbitt has taught at Princeton since 1938 (as director of the Columbia-Princeton Electronic Music Center since 1959), and at the Juilliard. He received a Pulitzer Special Citation for Music in 1982.

RECOMMENDED WORKS
Ensembles for Synthesizer (1964)
String Quartet No 2 (1952)

Barber Samuel˙˙
born 9th March 1910 at West Chester
died 23rd January 1981 at New York

Samuel Barber was a more varied and more interesting composer than his current reputation as a conservative in an age of modernism would suggest. His output was small, but beautifully crafted, usually in larger forms. He is often misleadingly called a Romantic composer, but there is rarely any Romantic sensibility or conflict in his music except in the two major operas; instead there is a distillation of potential complexities into their base constituents. He is, though, undoubtably a lyrical composer, the lyricism perhaps stemming from his training as a singer (unusual for a composer) and providing a constant thread throughout his work. This seeming effortless lyrical inspiration is married to a base drawn from neo-classicism, usually using conventional Classical forms, the harmony traditional, though extended in works after 1939. He was a composer of considerable and undemonstrative craftsmanship: his rhythmical sense is often quietly active, adding angles on to the flowing lines, and his orchestration, often for chamber-like forces, is a model of clarity. In this general cast he has in his earlier works much in common with **Kabalevsky** and **Rodrigo**, and indeed can at times coincidentally sound like either (for example, in the first and second movements respectively of the *Violin Concerto*). His later works are more wide-ranging in their idiom, as he discreetly absorbed elements of contemporary developments but also was prepared to vary the means considerably to suit the demands of a particular work.

Two of Barber's best-known works come from early in his career, and make a lyrical introduction to his music. *Dover Beach* (1931) for baritone and string quartet sets Matthew Arnold's descriptive-philosophical poem, and is illustrative of a predominant mood in Barber's music, a kind of wistfulness tinged with lyrical sadness. The quartet creates an almost continuous weave, rocking like the waves, undulating, rhythmically fluid, crossing paths with the melancholic but rhapsodic vocal line. The lovely, sonorous *Adagio for Strings* is actually the slow movement of the *String Quartet* (1936) with expanded forces. A third introduction to Barber's music is the *Piano Sonata* (1949), which goes beyond the purely lyrical image of the composer. Tonal in the sense of using a basic key, it also freely uses ideas drawn from 12-tone techniques. The virtuoso first movement is essentially Romantic, but constantly confounds expectations rhythmically and harmonically; the second is a brief scherzo, twinkling and lissom, like a music-box waltz; the third builds up to passion; and the finale, starting as a fugue, is the most interesting, with boogie-woogie jazz rhythms whose feel has confounded many an accomplished player – this sonata needs a pianist who can get underneath its eclectic idioms if it is to come off, and is fascinating when it does.

Besides the *Adagio* and *Dover Beach*, it is the concertos that are most frequently encountered. The popularity of the *Violin Concerto* (1939) has been hampered by its hybrid nature. The first two movements are gloriously lyrical, with a lovely insinuating opening idea worthy of Dvořák, lucid chamber textures (including piano) and a singing slow movement. But the businessman who commissioned the concerto for his protégé complained that these were too easy to play, whereupon Barber wrote a furious, virtuoso and rather brash finale (which the violinist then claimed he could not play). This sits rather uneasily against the preceding lyricism, though it does illustrate Barber's gradual change to a less obviously Romantic idiom. The *Capricorn Concerto* (1944) for flute, oboe, trumpet and strings has the verve of a **Stravinsky** neo-classical work in a quasi-concerto grosso. The less well-known *Cello Concerto* (1945) is a lovely undemanding work with a first movement pitting energy against lyricism, a Mediterranean glow in the slow movement touched by a hint of wistfulness, and a finale of complex, shifting emotions. The *Piano Concerto* (1962) is a virtuoso work in three movements, each in a sharply contrasting minor key. It is the most obviously Romantic of his concertos, though in the sometimes helter-skelter final movement the writing is eclectically wild, with a touch of humour.

The *Symphony No. 1* (1935–36, revised) is in a single movement with contrasting sections. The second symphony has a somewhat complex history. Titled *Symphony Dedicated to the Army Air Force* (1943–44), and using aeroplane effects and dissonant harmonies, it was revised and then mostly destroyed in 1964 (although it survives in a recording). The exception is the second movement, which was retitled *Night Flight* for orchestra; it is an atmospheric evocation of its title, an American equivalent to a **Respighi** mood-painting. The fine *Essay for Orchestra No. 1* (1937), its title referring to 'a work of a moderate length on a particular subject', is an abstract, largely neo-classical work in one movement but with distinct sections along symphonic lines, tinged with a hint of Dvořák towards the end; it is most effectively constructed on the simplest of themes, that appears in its inversion to round off the work. The music of *Medea's Meditation and Dance of Vengeance* (1946, usually heard in its orchestral tone-poem form, 1955) was originally written for a Martha Graham ballet charting Medea's growing jealousy of Jason and her desire for vengeance, with the characters of the Greek tragedy sometimes assuming the form of a modern woman and man. It is rich

and exotic, its dissonances used for dramatic rather than harmonic ends; the actual dance is American in feel, with its piano ostinato, its jazzy rhythms and colours passed among the orchestra and providing a kind of foretaste of **Bernstein's** *West Side Story*.

The libretto for Barber's opera *Vanessa* (1958), written by Gian-Carlo Menotti, is a romantic tale set around 1905 in northern Europe: Vanessa has waited twenty years for her lover, but it is his son who returns, takes up with her, and leaves with her for Paris. In the process, the son rejects his own lover, who shrouds the house to await his return. All the tricks of Grand Opera (four acts, a ball scene) are employed in this overtly Mills and Boon/Harlequin story, designed to appeal to conservative American audiences not willing to be challenged, and Barber wrote music to suit. His next full-length opera, *Antony and Cleopatra* (1965–66), was also on a grand scale and had a notoriously disastrous première. The libretto by Zeffirelli and Barber, based on Shakespeare, was revised in 1974 by Menotti, who removed much of the spectacle, condensed some sections and added a duet taken from a play by Beaumont and Fletcher (which Barber set with a lyricism worthy of **Puccini**). It deserved reworking, for Barber's music is communicative and attractive, and, if lacking the depth of the Shakespeare, it combines passion, lyricism and a touch of exoticism. In its revised form the opera is worth exploring by those who might have been put off by its original reputation. Less flawed than either of these is the tiny chamber opera *A Hand of Bridge* (1948) for four soloists and chamber orchestra, a comedy with a serious undertone. The frame for the opera is the game; within this the four players are alienated, estranged individuals, thinking respectively of such things as clothes, a mistress, a dying mother, and a boring job, and yet continuing the pretence of their lives through the formalities of bridge. The lithe score has touches of jazz and follows the moods of the players. The smaller scale of this work might seem more suited to Barber's idiom, but he proved that he could write on a large, powerful, and dramatic scale in the scena *Andromache's Farewell* (1962). This is a setting of Euripides: Andromache, widow of Hector, has been told that she cannot take her son with her into exile following the defeat of Troy – he is to be killed, and this extended aria is her farewell to her son and to Troy. It has the richness of **Strauss**, immediately obvious in the opening orchestral outburst, making one wish Barber had created a complete opera from the story. *Knoxville: Summer of 1915* (1947) for soprano and orchestra is an effective setting of a James Agee prose poem about evening in a small American town.

Barber was a composer whose self-effacing and essentially uncomplicated musical view of life becomes increasingly attractive the more one explores it; a minor master whose work now deserves a more sympathetic general treatment.

RECOMMENDED WORKS
Adagio for Strings (1936)
scena *Andromache's Farewell* (1962) for soprano and orchestra
opera *Antony and Cleopatra* (1966, revised 1974)
Essay for Orchestra No. 1 (1937)
chamber opera *A Hand of Bridge* (1959)
Cello Concerto (1945)
Dover Beach (1931) for lower voice and string quartet
Medea's Meditation and Dance of Vengeance (1947) for orchestra
Piano Sonata (1949)
Violin Concerto (1939)

BIBLIOGRAPHY
N. Broder, *Samuel Barber*, 1954

Bernstein Leonard*
born 25th August 1918 at Lawrence (Massachusetts)
died 14th October 1990 at New York

At present, it is difficult to separate Bernstein the composer from Bernstein the media-master, the most brilliant example of American mass high-culture, a marvellous speaker and communicator, and sometimes brilliant, usually wayward conductor. His music is often treated like his personality and his conducting: uncritically, as if such a forceful personality has to be brilliant just because he was such a personality. This very American confusion between style and substance masks the underlying impression that he composed a number of interesting works but only one masterpiece (the musical *West Side Story*) – which, through its genre, lies on the margins of this guide.

Much of Bernstein's more weighty music is touched by his Jewish faith, and the earliest work likely to be encountered,

the programmatic *Symphony No. 1 'Jeremiah'* (1942) uses the Biblical 'Lamentations of Jeremiah' (in Hebrew) in its third and final movement, for mezzo-soprano and orchestra, with an aura of Hebrew melody in the (original) vocal line. The symphony is grand in scale, Mahlerian in the first and third (slow) movement, but with a very American tone to the most attractive middle movement, full of Coplandesque dance syncopations broadening out into a larger American vision (and portraying its intended programme of the dire results of pagan corruption rather unsuccessfully, since it is so vital). The *Symphony No. 2 'Age of Anxiety'* (1947–49, revised 1965) is essentially a piano concerto inspired by the poem by W.H. Auden (in essence a cry for faith), in two parts each divided into three sections, closely following the structure and the content of the poem. It veers eclectically in style, from a late-Romantic florid delicacy, through echoes of **Stravinsky** and grand gestures, to pure jazz, but manages a tenuous internal logic. These two symphonies deserve a place in the canon of the American symphony, if not a prominent one. The *Symphony No. 3 'Kaddish'* (1961–63, revised 1977) for soprano, speaker, chorus, boys' chorus and orchestra, is the least successful of the three. Continuing the theme of faith, it sets the Jewish prayer chanted for the dead, along with English words by Bernstein that do not match the Hebrew or the music in quality: indeed at times the work has similarities to Soviet socialist realist declamatory choral works. The *Mass* (1971), for singers, players and dancers, bears about the same relationship to a liturgical work of depth as does an Andrew Lloyd-Webber musical to a serious modern opera. Using pop elements, including an electric guitar, quasi-Broadway tunes, mixed uneasily with classical touches, and combining embarrassingly corny words with the Mass, it seemed designed for the instant gratification of those for whom there is no other kind.

Bernstein's flair for a more populist idiom had surfaced much more successfully in the ballet *Fancy Free* (1944). The ballet follows a group of sailors on shore leave, trying to find young women; it is Bernstein at his best, bringing together elements of Broadway, jazz, a trace of Kurt **Weill**, in a score of gaiety, verve and rhythmic flow. It was then expanded into the Broadway musical *On the Town* (1944). The witty and entertaining *Prelude, Fugue and Riffs* (1949) for clarinet and ensemble is a cross between Stravinskian neo-classicism and out-and-out jazz. After an adaptation of Voltaire in the musical *Candide* (1956), a work of varying quality that doesn't match its source, the culmination of this trend was Bernstein's masterpiece, the musical *West Side Story* (1957). With a book by Stephen Sondheim, himself a renowned Broadway composer, it reworks *Romeo and Juliet* in modern New York with a brilliant combination of Bernstein's classical and more popular experience, its songs too familiar to be enumerated here. Bernstein turned some of the music into a successful concert suite (*West Side Story – Symphonic Dances*, 1960). His one-act opera *Trouble in Tahiti* (1952) was less successful; he later reworked it into the opera *A Quiet Place* (1983).

Of his other works for the concert platform, two stand out. *Chichester Psalms* (1965) for treble, chorus and orchestra (also version with harp and organ) uses Hebrew texts of the psalms, the idiom ranging from touches of jazz to a cappella writing. In the orchestral song-cycle *Songfest* (1976–77) for six soloists and orchestra Bernstein finally succeeded in integrating the disparate influences on his music into a convincing whole. Although it was written for a festive occasion (the American Bicentenary) and draws on American poets from the 17th-century Anne Bradstreet to Lawrence Ferlinghetti, many of the poems chosen have an undercurrent of protest. The musical idiom draws on a similar range, from Broadway-like tunes through art song to a big-band sound. But whereas so often in Bernstein's work these eclectic sources had been inserted wholesale into a particular passage, here they are melded into a concert-classical base. The Ferlinghetti setting, for example, initially appears to be a jazz piece, but it is also a 12-tone setting, and eventually reaches regions beyond the jazz song, while two poems about the Afro-American experience are brilliantly combined into a single song. The orchestra is huge, but used in different combinations for each song.

Bernstein was music director of the New York City Center Orchestra (1945–48), taught at the Berkshire Music Center (1951–55) and at Brandeis University (1951–56) and was associated with the New York Philharmonic Orchestra as assistant conductor, musical director, and Laureate Conductor from 1943. It was perhaps a measure of his confusion over different idioms that near the end of his life he recorded *West Side Story* with purely operatic voices, with disastrously stilted results.

RECOMMENDED WORKS
Chichester Psalms (1965) for treble, chorus and orchestra (or harp and organ)
ballet *Fancy Free* (1944)
Songfest (1976–77) for six singers and orchestra
Symphonic Dances (from West Side Story) (1960)
Symphony No. 1 *Jeremiah* (1942)
Symphony No. 2 *Age of Anxiety* (1949, rev. 1965)
musical *West Side Story* (1957)

BIBLIOGRAPHY
L. Bernstein, *The Unanswered Question*, 1976
J. Peyser, *Bernstein: A Biography*, 1987

Bolcom William[*]
born 26th May 1938 at Seattle

William Bolcom is as well known as a performer (especially with his third wife, the mezzo-soprano Joan Morris) as a composer. He is also an expert on ragtime music, and his own compositions draw on a wide variety of sources, especially early American music, ragtime, and the occasional touch of cabaret or Broadway. These he has combined into a postmodernist idiom drawing also on the experience of the avant-garde period. Sometimes this mix sits uneasily; at others it can be most effective, and he is always willing to be exploratory. His harmonic idiom is eclectic, ranging from the serial to works with heavy chromatic dissonance with a tonal centre, and to more traditional harmonies. His concert works are often dramatic, and in the 1960s he worked with improvisational theatre groups.

His more important works include songcycles. The huge setting of William Blake's *Songs of Innocence and Experience* (1956–81), for nine solo voices, three choruses, children's chorus and orchestra, includes forty-six songs and took him over two decades to write. The song-cycle *Open House* (1975) for tenor and chamber orchestra, sets seven poems by Theodore Roethke in a sensitive treatment that matches the gently passionate poetry, ranging from the Expressionist, through shades of **Britten** and a sinuous humour reminiscent of **Walton's** *Façade*, to a Broadway influence. The second part of the two-movement *Symphony No. 4* (1986) for mezzo-soprano and orchestra is an extended setting of a Roethke poem, 'The Rose'; the first movement, 'Soundscape', is of Mahlerian proportions and emotional range, longer on effect than substance. The *Symphony No. 5* (1990) drew on Wagner (*Lohengrin* and *Tristan und Isolde*) and the hymn 'Abide with Me'.

His other works are wide-ranging in styles and genres. In the 1960s he attempted collage-like effects, with a Blakeian vision of an American culture moving towards disintegration, and was then increasingly influenced by ragtime and classical music. *Black Host* (1967) for organ, percussion and tape includes a jazz passage and crowd noises on the tape. *Frescoes* (1971) for two pianos doubling harmonium and harpsichord is a rather strange two-part work, inspired by paintings, the first half titled 'War in Heaven', the second 'The Cave of Orcus' (the underworld). It is a declamatory collage of effects, from the monumental to the deliberately naïve, its first part heavily influenced by early American secular music (such as Benjamin Carr's *The Siege of Tripoli* for narrator and piano). The culmination of this collage tendency was the wild *Piano Concerto* (1975–76), which draws on almost every musical style conceivable, ending with a montage of snatches of famous American tunes (such as 'The Battle Hymn of the Republic' – it was written for the Bicentennial). *Commedia* (1971), 'for (almost) 18th-century orchestra', has a contemporary opening which evokes the *commedia dell'arte* and is almost immediately countered by reminders of Papageno's flute. The work then traverses an entertaining amalgam of the old and the new that is aptly titled and well worth encountering; it uses a kaleidoscope structure in which different combinations come into view and are replaced by others. The *Fantasia Concertante* (1986) is entirely Mozartian. Much of his piano music emulates piano rags, which also emerged in *Ragomania* (1982) for orchestra. Works such as the *Duo Fantasy* (1973) for violin and piano move from an almost atonal idiom to a waltz and ragtime, traversing both agitation and sentimentality; one of the more successful combinations of blues and suggestions of old hymns is the laid-back and attractive *Violin Sonata No. 2* (1978). Two of his operas are in cabaret style (there are also two sets of cabaret songs); the rather uninteresting television opera *Matigue* (1993) has an American

Western theme, somewhat hysterical vocal lines, and echoes of Broadway.

Bolcom was composer-in-residence with the Detroit Symphony (in 1987 and 1988), and he was taught at the University of Washington (1965–66), the City University of New York (1966–68), New York University (1969–71), and at the University of Michigan since 1973.

RECOMMENDED WORKS
> *Commedia* (1971) 'for (almost) 18th-century orchestra'
> song-cycle *Open House* (1975) for tenor and chamber orchestra
> *Songs of Innocence and Experience* (1956–81) for nine solo voices, three choruses, children's chorus and orchestra
> Violin Sonata No. 2 (1978)

Cage John (Milton)•••
born 5th September 1912 at Los Angeles
died 12th August 1992 at New York

John Cage was the outstanding American experimenter of the 20th century, and the one who has most deeply influenced other composers the world over. His name has also been vilified by the more orthodox music listener – partly through ignorance and often unfairly, as many who have encountered his music have discovered. His inventive and meticulous mind was matched by a surety of ear that transcends the merely theoretical, and if his more extreme ideas, especially in the 1950s and early 1960s, may have a largely intellectual appeal to a limited number of music lovers prepared to address the extremes of the avant-garde, his earlier music in particular paved the way for the most recent of trends, minimalism. Those music lovers who enjoy minimalism will appreciate and enjoy the music of this remarkable precursor (and find it considerably more rewarding than many of the later minimalist composers).

Cage's earliest scores followed 12-tone principles (he studied briefly with **Schoenberg** in 1934), but it was by following the example of Henry **Cowell**, to whom Cage acknowledged a considerable debt (creating a continuity of eccentric American innovators), that he developed an individual voice. Cowell and **Varèse** had opened up new possibilities with percussion; Cage formed his own percussion group in 1938, and faced an inherent problem in the indeterminate pitch of so many of the percussion instruments he used (including found objects, such as brake drums, and many exotic eastern instruments). The solution was the reliance not on the musical organisation of pitch in the Western tradition, but on the development of the organisation of rhythm (as **Varèse** had done in *Ionization*). Cage's preferred method was to repeat groups of rhythmic patterns, well known to the Eastern musics (e.g. Indian talas), that **Cowell** had introduced Cage to some years before. Such additive groups give a sense of stasis within movement. At the time this was a rhythmic concept alien to the Western tradition, but it now enjoys widespread acceptance thanks to later developments in both popular and classical music. Cage's own version preferred squared proportions in numerical relationships. Typical works of this period are the vividly and metallically coloured, urban-orientated *First Construction (in Metal)* (1939), for a variety of metal-based percussion instruments, and the rather spare-textured *Third Construction* (1941) for percussion, using traditional instruments from all parts of the Americas. This piece, being divided into twenty-four sections, themselves divided in twenty-four bars, illustrates his preoccupation with proportion.

Equally trail-blazing was the addition of variable speed turntables in *Imaginary Landscape No. 1* (1939), and frequency oscillators (producing purely electronic sounds) in *Imaginary Landscape No. 3* (1942), as Cage continued the search for sound sources divorced from traditional concert instruments. **Cowell** had achieved considerable notoriety with his unconventional use of the piano, creating sounds by plucking or sweeping the strings with the hands, and using tone clusters. These were essentially atmospheric accompaniments; Cage extended the range of sounds by meticulously preparing the piano, modifying individual strings by the application of objects (ranging from nuts and bolts to forks and cardboard strips) to the strings themselves, creating what he named (on the score of *Bacchanale* for piano, 1940) the 'prepared piano'. The expression has since received general acceptance. The result was an instrument that was essentially percussive, and a development of the percussive approach already discussed; since Cage initially used prepared piano pieces as music for dance (thus obviating the need for a number of percussion instruments), the modifications became the sounds of the music itself, rather than the essentially accompanying role of Cowell's

innovations. The percussive nature was emphasised by the fact that some of the modifications meant that specific strings could lose their absolute pitch (harmony, in any chordal sense, has a minor place in all of Cage's work). The innovations were allied with the experience of his percussion music, and there appeared series of works which look forward to the minimalists of the 1980s, with slow-moving patterns of sound whose rhythmic progression is drawn from Eastern models, and, in the colours Cage elicited, a strong echo of the timbre and style of the gamelan orchestra, often very delicate in timbre. The characteristic piano sound is almost completely eradicated by Cage's preparations. Typical examples are *The Perilous Night* (1943–45) for prepared piano, with ethereal, beguiling sounds and a mesmerising progression, the monodic *A Valentine out of Season* (1944), and the very minimalist *Music for Marcel Duchamp* (1947). *Amores* (1943) juxtaposes sections for percussion (with the hissing sounds of a pod rattle against tom-toms, a colour contrast found throughout Cage's music) against the softer sounds of a prepared piano. Exceptionally complex preparation and (within the unfolding of longer patterns) intricate polyrhythms, sounding like the multiple rhythms of more recent improvisatory jazz, dominate *Three Dances* (1944–45), for two amplified prepared pianos, again with gamelan overtones, and all strictly notated (and therefore composer-instigated). The *Sonatas and Interludes* (1946–48) were an extended set of works (sixteen sonatas and four interludes) for prepared piano (with mesmerising ostinati in such works as *Sonata V*). The last piece that Cage wrote for prepared piano is generally the most highly regarded, the *Concerto for Prepared Piano and Chamber Orchestra* (1950–51), although most readers may prefer the earlier works already mentioned. This piece, with its nebulous strands and a narrow range of timbres, also used rhythmic structures drawn on charts, and silent sections, and reflects Cage's growing conviction that the composer's role was as a conduit for divine (or natural) influence rather than as a means of self-expression.

The summation of this period is probably the *String Quartet in Four Parts* (1950), in which many of Cage's concerns over the previous years are brought together. The structure, based on square roots, is mathematically precise, with a basic structural unit of twenty-two bars and with small divisions keeping a similar pattern, the overall distribution between the four movements also being based on twenty-two. The string players are expected to play in a very flat style (e.g. with no vibrato) to produce sounds reminiscent of some of the sound effects of the prepared piano. In addition, the movements not only represent seasons: in the first two, places are also represented, and in all four, elements of Indian philosophy. If this sounds impossibly academic, the results, like so much of Cage's music up to this point, are exactly the opposite, with a haunting unadorned unfolding of slow events like the distant distortion of some familiar music, but with an underlying inevitability (the tempo indication is constant) that does indeed reflect the philosophy.

These works had been meticulously notated, with a mathematical exactitude. With *Music of Changes* (for piano, in four volumes, 1951), Cage's ideas took a radical new turn, and one that was to become exceedingly influential. Following his reading of the Chinese *I Ching* (*Book of Changes*), he abandoned his careful delineation of all the parameters of his music, and allowed some of them to be determined by chance (specifically by charts and by the throwing of dice). The music that Cage then notated was therefore partly determined by these procedures; with *Music for Piano I* (1952) Cage took a further step, with the performer rather than the composer choosing the duration of the notes, and the pitch of the notes being determined by imperfections in the music paper. In *Imaginary Landscape No. 4* (1951) for twelve radios the element of chance lies in what is on the air and received by the radios. The intention in all these pieces is to turn the audience's attention away from the self-expression of the composer towards an understanding of the elements of incidental chance and of the sounds around the performance. The latter was brought, in its most famous manifestation, to an extreme expression in *4'33"* (1952) for any number of players (usually a pianist) who remain(s) silent. If anyone thinks this a joke, they should attend a performance; they may not consider the event music, but the result is that one's awareness of the sounds around in (in the hall, outside) is considerably heightened, and one's awareness of the nature of sound enhanced.

Cage then developed chance into indeterminacy, where instead of chance being a factor in notation, it would take place in performance, so that no two performances

of a piece would be the same; the role of the composer was thus further transformed from self-expression into an initiatior of ceremonies. *Music for Piano 1–84* (1953–56), in four parts, may be played all together or in sections, perhaps separately, perhaps simultaneously, by any number of pianists, while the *Concert for Piano and Orchestra* (1957–1958) is totally random, any number of players on any instruments choosing any parts of a score founded on chance, the duration determined by a conductor showing the time. The graphic notation of works of the late 1950s and early 1960s (such as *Variations I* for any number of players, 1958) are almost totally divorced from the musical results, and exist in their own right (Cage was eventually to produce art works). Works such as *Atlas Eclipticalis* (1961–62), consisting of constellation maps translated into musical notes, can be played simultaneously with others like *Winter Music* (1957), for any number of pianists, the score distributed randomly. The *reductio ad absurdum* was probably a necessary measure at the time; its opposite was the exploration of sounds *per se* by electronic means (often in collaboration with David Tudor), from *Williams Mix* (1952), through *Cartridge Music* (1960) to realisations of such works as *Variations II* (1961). Whether anyone would now want to recreate such things other than in the spirit of historical interest is a moot point: the music requires the listener simply to receive the sounds resulting from so much indeterminacy, rather than listen in the conventional sense. If one is in the right frame of mind this can be interesting (though surely more rewarding to create than receive), but mostly the music of this period of Cage's output is significant only from the point of view of musical philosophy or aesthetics. Overall, it is totally boring to the attentive ear, though interesting as background noise.

However, Cage's development of 'happenings', combining this aural hodgepodge with visual elements, belongs to the exploration of new musico-dramatic possibilities that was one of the main legacies of the avant-garde period. His happenings ranged from the stage events of *Water Music* (1952) for piano, which includes pouring water, through *0'0"* (1962), in which Cage made juice from vegetables in an electric blender, to the gigantic multimedia *HPSCHD* (with Lejaren Hiller, 1967–69), including fifty-one tapes, and snatches of the music of past masters, with film, slides, and lights. In *HPSCHD*, the sounds become incidental to the overall creation; when divorced from the other events, they start, wittingly or unwittingly, to create an urban soundscape. This process was furthered in the much more interesting *49 Waltzes for the Five Boroughs* (1977) 'for performer(s) or listener(s) or record maker(s)' – a graphic map of five boroughs of New York, then 149 street addresses divided into groups of three. Like the harpsichord fragments of the earlier work, sounds and fragments of waltzes are distributed by *I Ching* consultation and by dice throwing, and are combined with tapes pre-recorded on location, as specified, and other live sound-makers. The montage of chance sounds of the street, brought into the concert hall and punctuated by distant fragments of music, is atmospheric and evocative.

Cage's later work continued to use chance operations, as well as many of his earlier techniques, with varied results. Some works remain more interesting in the conceptualisation, as in *Score* (1974) for any number of instruments and/or voices, where small drawings from Thoreau's *Journals* are used to determine the music. In others, such as the delicate and ethereal *Hymns and Variations* (1979) for twelve solo singers with echoes of tunes by Henry Billings (1746–1800), there is a return to more conventional soundscape and delineation of forces (and, in this case, to the inheritance of the American tradition).

Cage's place in American and avant-garde music is unquestioned, for his conceptualisations remain of interest to anyone considering the problems of the development of modern music. Whether his actual music will continue to command the respect of performance is a different matter. The earlier works deserve to, and it is greatly to be regretted that so often the place of Cage's earlier music has been overwhelmed by his later innovations. Certainly 20th-century music has been greatly enhanced by the presence of this extraordinary personality, writer, artist (and expert on mushrooms) as well as composer.

RECOMMENDED WORKS
  Amores (1943) for prepared piano and
    percussion
  Concert for Piano and Orchestra
    (1957–58)
  Concerto for Prepared Piano and
    Chamber Orchestra (1951)
  First Construction (in Metal) (1939)
    for percussion
  Sonatas and Interludes (1946–48) for

  prepared piano
  Three Dances (1944–45) for two
    amplified prepared pianos
  Third Construction (1941) for
    percussion quartet
  Thirty Pieces for Five Orchestras
    (1986)
  String Quartet in Four Parts (1950)

BIBLIOGRAPHY
  Cage's own writings include *Empty*
    Words, 1979, *For the Birds*, 1981,
    Mud Book, 1982, *Silence*, 1961,
    Themes and Variations, 1982, and
    A Year from Monday, 1967.
  P. Griffiths, *Cage*, 1981
  R. Kostelanetz (ed.), *John Cage*, 1970

Carter Elliott Cook***
born 11th December 1908 at New York

Elliott Carter was born the day after **Messiaen**, and the two composers are perhaps the most highly regarded of their generation. For Carter, widespread recognition came comparatively late in life, partly because he did not develop a truly individual idiom until his early forties. Since then, however, his musical language has been entirely personal, following none of the systems or trends evident since the 1950s, but displaying an awareness of those developments. His idiom is especially rewarding because it combines conceptual brilliance and complexity of thought with an entirely expressive intent: Carter is inclined to develop the means, the structure of a piece, especially for the intent of that piece, whatever the common threads of his ideas. Thus he has not adhered to any particular system, apart from his use of 'metrical modulations'.

However, both the concepts and the expressive content are usually of considerable complexity, especially in rhythm and metre. In place of development by conventional means (thematic or harmonic), Carter has used in his mature work what he has called 'metric modulation'. Analogous to harmonic modulation (which transforms the sense of key), metric modulation is a gradual transformation of the underlying rhythmic pulse of a passage, sometimes emphasised by the introduction of cross-rhythms to change the metre (as opposed to a sudden shift, such as halving the speed). These changes can mark formal blocks in the structure. His atonal harmonic language is equally plastic, and typical of the way Carter will find novel structural solutions in a particular work is the extraction of a foreground three-note chord from a 12-note background in the *Piano Concerto* (1964–65), which he then developed into more complex five-and seven-note chords in the *Concerto for Orchestra* (1969).

Equally prominent in Carter's work is a sense of duality, both in means and in content. His sense of music-making as a drama or conversation creates tensions with the purely abstract, intellectual intricacies of construction. Part of the solution is to create intentional dualities in the formal layout, whether between instrumental groups that oppose, interact, and overlay each other, or in strong differentiation between the colours, rhythms, harmonic kernels and character of the basic materials – a form of collage. This can lead not only to the considerable aural complexity of much of his work, but an impression of a split between the formal and expressive qualities of his music; much of his evolution has been an increasing mastery of the combination of the two. That complexity requires considerable rehearsal time, and consequently his orchestral music is less often encountered in the concert hall than his chamber music.

Carter's earlier – and now less frequently heard – music had included (after the early influence of **Stravinsky** and neoclassicism) echoes of **Ives** and **Copland**. In such works as the *Holiday Overture* (1944) he had demonstrated a rugged personality, while the *Symphony No. 1* (1942), although its last two movements are in the mainstream American tradition, has an unconventional first movement that progresses by variations on two groups of musical material – a foretaste of Carter's later concerns with unusual structures. The rugged and the vital are paramount in what is perhaps the most effective of the earlier works, the *Piano Sonata* (1945–46). The sense of the overtones of the piano, emphasised by material based on chords of fifths, anticipates later preoccupations with sonority, while the undercurrent of stillness that keeps (magically) emerging as if always latent is another example of Carter's basic duality between the still point and the surrounding activity. The rather dour ballet *Minotaur* (1947, suite 1950) is primarily of interest to those wishing to explore the range of Carter's earlier music.

The work with which Carter (at the age of forty-two) found a totally individual voice, and which initiated a steady evolution of style ever since, was the *String Quartet No. 1* (1951). Here he allowed himself to explore a much more esoteric language, only to be surprised by the enthusiastic reception of the work. Although in three movements, these do not correspond to the sections of the work: rather the breaks are pauses in the flow. The quartet opens with a cello cadenza, giving the basic harmonic material, including a four-note chord in which every interval may be obtained through permutation; this is picked up by the violin at the close, the common link representing real time. Within this frame (suggesting dream time) is a complex layering of independent melodies fastened to each other through polymetric relationships. It is an intensely expressive work, 'a continuous unfolding and changing of characters', as Carter has described it, emotionally charged, sometimes with a dryness reminiscent of the desert area in which it was written. A passage in the adagio exemplifies Carter's metrical manipulation for those new to it, with shifting flows and tempi above a strict 'walking' jazz bass, whose influence is felt even when it has finished.

A similar rugged sense pervades the *Sonata for Flute, Oboe, Cello, and Harpsichord* (1952), in which Carter's sensitivity to texture is paramount, the other instruments picking up the resonances of the harpsichord. Perhaps the most effective work with which to approach his music is the *Variations for Orchestra* (1954–55), one of Carter's more transparent pieces with a synthesis of many different styles (from **Schoenberg** to the American symphonic tradition). The structure, based on continuous variation of material rather than the traditional clearly differentiated sectioning, is particularly approachable, and the working of Carter's complex imagination is clearly exemplified by the two 'ritornelli', in which the tempi characteristically undergo controlled change, and by variations seven, eight and nine – the ninth presents the three successive ideas of the seventh simultaneously over a rhythmic pulse transformed from variation eight. Throughout, the detailed clarity of the orchestration reflects Carter's mastery of sonority; there is an impression, found throughout Carter's music but especially strong here, that he is not following any system, but building his own edifices.

In the *String Quartet No. 2* (1959) the sense of the individuality of the instruments, inherent in the first quartet, becomes overt. This is a kind of modern conversation piece (echoing **Ives**'s *String Quartet No. 2*), with each instrument being associated with different musical gestures, rhythms and expressive content. It is a more condensed work than its predecessor, in both nine sections and four 'movements' played continuously (with each of the first three dominated by one of the instruments). The 'characters' go their own way, imitate each other, sometimes co-operate. In the *Double Concerto* (1959–61) for harpsichord, piano and two chamber orchestras, Carter's characteristic sense of duality is expressed by the different materials for the two soloists, and by their function as intermediaries between the percussion and the two orchestras. The work is not easy to listen to, with its very busy textures. However, it has a convincing arch structure, issuing from chaos to a kind of ordered expression and dissolving back again; its vibrant layers of imagination and event become compelling on renewed acquaintance. The *Piano Concerto* (1964–65) is emotionally more uncompromising; the piano is associated with a concertino septet, in often violent (and unresolved) conflict with the main orchestra; and many will find the concerto, and its widely leaping intervals, excruciatingly difficult music.

The culmination of this period of constructional intensity, complexity and dramatic interplay was the *String Quartet No. 3* (1971). The quartet of instruments is divided into two duos (violin and cello, violin and viola), each of which has different material and a number of different tempi in a formal plan of ten cross-cutting sections. Each of the tempi of one group is at one time or another played against the tempi of the other, as well as on its own (with the other duo silent), and such is the complexity of these ever-shifting strata that the quartet is usually performed with a metronome 'click-track' relayed by headsets to the players. It is a mistake to approach with conventional expectations; instead one has to allow the ear to drop in and pick up the changing patterns and textures in this gritty and forceful work.

The *Duet for Violin and Piano* (1973–74) formed a bridge between these complex works and a more open style that continued to explore new methods of expression while retaining the metrical idiom. At first hearing the song-cycle *A Mirror on which to Dwell* (1975) for soprano and chamber orchestra, setting six poems by Elizabeth Bishop, can appear dour. But underneath this surface is a welter of detail and effect, enhanced by the changing combinations of instruments for each song. In 'Sandpiper', for example, the soprano lines (echoed by the oboe) exactly mimic the stop-go-stop movement of the bird on the shore; in 'Insomnia' there is a haunting play of light in the overlapping textures; while 'A View of the Capitol from the Library of Congress' (the work was commissioned for the Bicentennial) has Ives-like juxtapositions. *A Symphony of Three Orchestras* (1976) was inspired by Hart Crane's poem *The Bridge*. The orchestra is divided into three groups with distinct characters, each of which has four movements, all differing in tempo and harmony, that are cross-cut in the manner of the *String Quartet No. 3*; the whole piece travels, in three parts but one overall motion, from the heights of the opening strings, woodwind and trumpet to the lowest depths. But these complex interactions travel too fast for immediate appreciation; the dominating effect of this powerful work, its textures less dense than earlier orchestral works, its sudden eruptions and outbursts new to Carter's idiom, is of a great, teeming, sometimes pugnacious, momentarily lyrical, urban landscape, in which individual sections or buildings initially present a sense of confusion until they are seen within the broader landscape, matching Crane's epic imagery.

The symphony marked a climax in Carter's output, in which there was an element of reconciliation between the demands of form and of expressive intent. The twenty-minute *Night Fantasies* (1980) for piano retained the considerable complexity, together with virtuoso writing and sharp contrast of episode, but subsequent works have shown a mellowing of the intricacy. *Syringa* (1978) for mezzo-soprano, baritone and orchestra, sets an allusive and ironic view of Orpheus by John Ashbery in a collage with fragments of Greek texts, with a clarity derived from *A Mirror on which to Dwell*. It was joined by another vocal work, *In Sleep, in Thunder* (1981), for tenor and chamber orchestra, setting Robert Lowell, to complete a trilogy. *Triple Duo* (1983) returns to the interplay of character through its juxtapositions and interactions of the duos – sharply contrasting in timbre and colour – of flute (doubling piccolo) and clarinet, violin and cello, and piano and percussion.

Carter's singular achievement has been to create a viable, expressive musical language that eventually owes very little to traditional formal procedures, and yet maintains a link, however tenuous, with that tradition. His other achievement is more subtle: as the century has progressed there has been an increasing understanding that behind all apparent chaos, in whatever field, physical, psychological or social, lie patterns and organisations that have their own rigorous logic, momentum, order and beauty. Carter's music has exactly reflected that understanding.

Carter worked in the Office of War Information during World War II. He taught at the Peabody Conservatory (1946–48), at Columbia University (1948–50), at Yale (1960–62), at the Juilliard (starting in 1963) and briefly at other universities.

RECOMMENDED WORKS

Double Concerto (1959–1961) for harpsichord, piano and two chamber orchestras song-cycle
A Mirror on which to Dwell (1975) for soprano and chamber orchestra song-cycle *In Sleep, in Thunder* (1981) for tenor and chamber orchestra
Piano Sonata (1945–46)
String Quartet No. 1 (1951)
String Quartet No. 2 (1959)
String Quartet No. 3 (1971)
A Symphony of Three Orchestras (1976)
Variations for Orchestra (1954–55)

BIBLIOGRAPHY
E. Carter, *The Writings of Elliott Carter* (ed. E. and K. Stone), 1977
D. Schiff, *The Music of Elliott Carter*, 1983

Copland Aaron***

born 14th November 1900 at New York
died 2nd December 1990 at New York

Aaron Copland was the first composer of classical music whose style and spirit were recognised by a wide public to be specifically American. Although **Ives** and others had consciously forged an 'American' style, they did so in isolation, virtually unnoticed; historically Copland instigated a new outlook, in which younger American composers looked to their fellow composers rather than European contemporaries for their models. Many followed his example of studying with Nadia Boulanger in Paris.

He remains the quintessential American composer, whose basic duality reflects the American landscape: the lyrical and the broad, evoking the wide expanses of the prairies, and the monumental, suggesting the high mountains when lyrical, urban

skyscrapers when dissonant. For Copland, these were not mutually exclusive, but rather the opposite ends of the same pole, mediated by dance rhythms and especially the influence of Latin-American and Mexican music. His primary vehicle was the orchestra, and he saw the timbres of individual instruments as having specific emotional connotations; consequently his orchestration concentrates on eliciting the maximum expression from each instrument and maintaining space between them, giving a purposeful airiness in the sound. The apparent ease and mastery of his rhythmic drive is often achieved by complex rhythmic patterns that have their origin in the syncopations and polyrhythms of jazz, though it should be noted that the jazz influence is rarely that of the intimate club (as it is in **Stravinsky** or **Milhaud**), but that of larger popular dance bands. Traditional and folk material (or invented folk-like tunes) are invariably modified by odd accents and phrasing. Two moods predominate in these dance patterns (corresponding to the basic duality in Copland's work): the undulating and trance-like, and the lively and nervous. Except when using 12-tone techniques, his traditional harmonies are enlivened by clashes and polyharmonies, and development is more often by evolution of rhythm and theme than by any conventional harmonic progression (except when used as an intellectual device in such works as *In the Beginning* for choir, 1947). In general, his music seeks to express the multiplicity and variety of the surface impressions and emotions of the American life around him, as opposed to exploring the profound or the tragic.

Commentators have tried to define periods in Copland's output, but the elements of Copland's distinctive language were formed early on, and his early music brings many of them together, sometimes tumbling over each other. His development was to extract these various strands and to bring them to fruition at various times in different groups of works. The *Symphony for Organ* (1924), revised as *Symphony No. 1* without organ in 1928, introduces a number of Copland characteristics: the broad lyricism, the clear textures, the use of ostinato figures, the syncopated rhythms and the fanfare figures. The organ is generally undemonstrative, and there are acerbic harmonies, especially in the second movement. *Music for the Theater* (1925) for small orchestra is imbued with the dance, the influence of popular band music in evidence. The opening of the

Piano Concerto (1926) establishes a kind of American pastoral, especially with the blues inflections of the piano entry; there are echoes of **Prokofiev** in the piano writing, but the second of two parts (played continuously) is jazzily dissonant and happily raucous. The *Dance Symphony* (1929), reworked from an earlier ballet *Grog* (1922–25), opens with a delightful Stravinskian neo-classicism, moves to the monumental and the rugged, and ends with jazzy touches similar in idiom to **Gershwin's** *An American in Paris*. Even at this early stage the influence of Latin-American percussion is evident. The more inflated *Symphonic Ode* (1928–29, revisions to 1932) traverses broad vistas, and uses a characteristic Copland figure: a short note leaping upwards or downwards (sometimes on the octave) to a longer held note. The *Short Symphony* (1930–33, numbered as *Symphony No. 2*), with a fifteen-minute slow-fast-slow structure all of whose material is derived from the opening idea, is more spiky.

All these earlier works are distinctive, individual, and well worth hearing, but in the 1930s Copland's idiom split into two main strands. The first was a consciously more popular sound, with generally traditional harmonies, colourful rhythms and evocations, and a particular concentration on the broad, lyrical vistas. The second picked up on the more exploratory and dissonant elements inherent in almost all the earlier works, and developed them, eventually with 12-tone elements. These works, less often encountered, reflect the turbulence and the urban energy that Copland saw around him.

A major impulse in the more populist works was Copland's systematical absorption of the idiom of Mexican music, following visits there and through his friendship with **Chávez**. It was a development of great import for indigenous American music, for the Spanish-Mexican influence had infiltrated over the border through the movement of cattle ranching and its popular music, and Copland was thus forging a link with the music of the American West. *El salón Mexico* (1933–36) for orchestra, brilliantly coloured, rhythmically impulsive, and full of 'bounce' (Copland's word), adapted themes from two collections of Mexican folk music. The ballet *Billy the Kid* (1938), whose orchestral suite uses a large portion of the ballet, brought the idiom to the American Western heritage, opening with the wide open prairie, portraying a frontier town, complete with Mexican women and their characteristic music,

using onomatopoeic ideas for the gunfight, and weaving in an authentic cowboy song. The equally entertaining ballet *Rodeo* (1942, symphonic suite in four sections, 1945) is virtually a companion piece, following the adventures of a lonely tomboy who tries to match the riding skills of the men, and eventually dresses as a beautiful woman for the ranch dance and wins her man. *Billy the Kid* is more characterised by its vivid colour, *Rodeo* by its strong vein of humour. The best-known example of this aspect of Copland's output is undoubtably *Appalachian Spring* (1943–44), which exists as the original ballet for thirteen instruments, as a full orchestration of the ballet, and as a suite (omitting some eight minutes) for full orchestra, but sometimes played with the original instrumentation. This glowing, warm-hearted work transports us to Shaker country, that now defunct sect famous for its perfect combination of form and function in its furniture, and for its hymn tunes, of which 'Tis the gift to be simple' forms the heart of the ballet music. Set in the early 1800s, it follows a young couple, about to be married, celebrating their newly-built farmhouse and warned by revivalists about human fate. The *Symphony No. 3* (1944–46) contains a similar idiom in symphonic form, the basic duality being between the lyrical and the monumental and declamatory. Although widely admired, it seems a little stilted alongside the ballets, though it has some magical effects in the fourth movement, which opens (without a break from the third) with the well-known and imposing *Fanfare for the Common Man*, originally written as a separate piece for brass and timpani in 1942. The *Concerto for Clarinet and String Orchestra* (1948) belongs to this group of works, in spite of its intimate jazz touches (with a plucked bass), for the clarinet writing largely reflects the spacious, lyrical tone of the work. Other, shorter pieces in a similar vein are well worth hearing, among them *John Henry* (1940), which celebrates a railroad man. In the same period Copland produced a number of scores for films that celebrated a shared view of the American heritage; *The Red Pony* (1948) in particular contains attractive music. The score for *The Heiress* (1948) won him an Oscar. The attractive song-cycle *Old American Songs* (two sets, 1950–52) most effectively arranges well-known American songs, including the Shaker hymn of *Appalachian Spring*, but the finest of Copland's limited output of vocal works is the song-cycle *Twelve*

Poems of Emily Dickinson (1949–50), which, in general tone, rhythmic variety, and its use of high independent piano writing, is an American first cousin to **Britten**'s song-cycle *Winter Words*.

The culmination of this aspect of Copland's art should have been the opera *The Tender Land* (1952–54), designed for smaller stages (or television) and telling the story of a prairie family whose daughter is seeking escape. Its major failing is that its libretto by Erik Johns is too pat and insubstantial, suggesting an outsider's concept of prairie life, not inside observation or knowledge. Copland's score was designed to appeal to wide audiences, but it does not have enough psychological bite for sophisticated opera audiences, and is unlikely to be seen by the kind of audience who might respond to it. It is best encountered in recording. The last work to explore this side of Copland's idiom was the ballet *Dance Panels* (1959, revised 1962), a set of seven contrasting sections without a storyline.

Copland had written what was virtually an atonal work in his setting of e.e. cummings's *Poet's Song* in 1927, but he initially avoided the example of **Schoenberg** and his followers in order to divorce himself from the Germanic tradition. The *Piano Variations* (1930), a seminal work in American piano literature and one of Copland's finest creations, comes close to the techniques and aesthetic of the Schoenberg circle. However, in its twenty variations in two sets of ten, all based on a seven-note theme, it does not completely break with a tonal base. Copland orchestrated it in 1957 as the *Orchestral Variations*, but it is more effective, aggressively turbulent and remorseless, in its original version. The opening of the influential *Piano Sonata* (1939–41) takes up from the *Piano Variations*, with steel-edged abrasive chords and an unsettled rhythmic percussive lilt. This is followed by a darting wispish scherzo, and the pace only slows in the last movement, whose opening has parallels with the opening of **Ives**'s *Concord Sonata*. The *Piano Quartet* (1950) does use 12-tone techniques, but is totally devoid of any Germanic cast; indeed, Copland deserves more credit for showing, at an early date, that such techniques could serve the mellifluous, here spiced with dissonant moments and a spiky, jovial second movement. *Connotations* (1961–62) for orchestra opens with the 12-tone row piled vertically in chords, which then spread out in a series of variations, the percussive colours

of the orchestra suddenly countered by the colours of a piano. The feel is of the urban landscape, sometimes forceful, almost brutish, often lonely, occasionally fantastical with little flute runs or strings using harmonics. The piece, whose title refers to implications 'in addition to the primary meaning' is one of Copland's finest and least-known works. *Inscape* (1967), Copland's penultimate orchestral work, fittingly brought together the two strands in his aesthetic. It opens with a 12-tone chord, but tonal implications are quickly established, and the gritty urban forcefulness is offset by a broad lyricism.

Besides Copland's compositional contribution to American music, he was a major advocate of new American music in his activities as writer, conductor and broadcaster. Among his many achievements, he co-founded the Copland-Sessions Concerts, which ran from 1928 to 1931, helped organise the American Composers' Alliance (1937), was on the faculty of the summer courses at Tanglewood, and numbered **Bernstein** and **Foss** among his pupils. **Ives** may have been the herald of a truly American classical music; Copland was its father-figure.

RECOMMENDED WORKS

Copland's output was not large, but its quality was consistent, and all his music is recommended. Those new to his work may care to start with the more popular pieces, as outlined above; those familiar with the well-known scores might care to explore the other side of his output – the more abrasive and experimental scores – or the early works.

BIBLIOGRAPHY

A. Copland, *Copland on Music*, 1960
A. Copland and V. Perlis, *Copland*, (2 vols), 1982 & 1989

Corigliano John*

born 16th February 1938 at New York

John Corigliano is emerging as the 'safe' populist American composer, sufficiently in touch with tradition to aim at a mass audience, sufficiently touched with modernism to promote as a contemporary composer, and sufficiently untouched by deep philosophical delving that might challenge audiences.

His earlier works such as *Elegy* (1965)

for orchestra, follow a tonal, popular tradition that stems from such earlier composers as Nelson and Moore, through **Copland**; *Tournaments Overture* (1965) has palpably American tunes, a 'holiday' atmosphere, and just enough dissonant effects to ensure it is not confused with a composition of an earlier epoch. The *Piano Concerto* (1968) has big bold gestures, contrasts of mood, and a fleeting effect in its four movements (including an overtly neo-Romantic slow movement), but is totally unmemorable apart from the rhythmic flow and ostinati impulse of the second movement. The *Oboe Concerto* (1975) emulated the effect of orchestral tuning in its opening, and of Moroccan music in its finale. The fine *Clarinet Concerto* (1977) still relies on the big effect, in its outbursts and in its demanding solo writing reaching into the highest registers, but is much less traditional in its procedures. A series of contrasting emotional states unfold, the possibilities of juxtaposed colours are explored, and there is a broad, lyrical and homogeneously textured slow movement. The *Pied Piper Fantasy* (1978–79) is a programmatic flute concerto, but is less effective, with its corny opening of power and might, its neo-Romantic writing, and such banalities as a tin whistle. Two independent children's orchestras represent the children of the story: they leave, lured by the flute in a work of gesture and effect rather than substance. The *Fantasia on an Ostinato* (1986) for piano (also orchestrated) is based on a passage from Beethoven's seventh symphony, its almost Ravelian repetitive insistence (with an imitation of the decay of repeated notes) evolving into an Impressionistic minimalism. The *Symphony No. 1* (1990) was inspired by the exhibition 'The Quilt', commemorating AIDS victims; three of the four movements commemorate particular friends who died from AIDS, and it ends with an epilogue, intertwining ideas from the earlier movements. It has moments of considerable power – dark marches with climactic interjections, hushed sad passages (and a fine slow movement), piano playing and dances distantly heard as if through nostalgic memory – that succeed in creating a work of emotional substance rather than of the mere effects that sometimes threaten. The extravaganza of an opera *The Ghosts of Versailles* (completed 1991) was commissioned for the 1983 centenary celebration of the Metropolitan Opera, and is overall an opera buffa, based on the third book of the Beaumarchais's Figaro trilogy to a

libretto by William M. Hoffman. It takes place in Marie Antoinette's private theatre at Versaille, where the ghost of Beaumarchais has fallen in love with that of the queen. His love is unrequited, and he offers to put on his new opera, in which the characters from *The Marriage of Figaro* will rewrite history and save the queen, even though it will mean his damnation. She realises the depth of his love, and rejects the alteration of events; the two are united. Its considerable spectacle, rivalling those of contemporary musicals, was more interesting than its music, which draws on a divergent set of styles, new and old. The opera answered an American vogue for entertainment on a lavish scale, but it was a pity that the Met could not have chosen a composer of greater musical depth for their first new opera in a quarter of a century.

Of his other vocal music, the most important is the choral symphony *A Dylan Thomas Trilogy* (1960–76), composed over a sixteen-year period. The first part, 'Fern Hill' (1960–61), is for chorus and orchestra, and the second, 'Poem in October' (1970) for tenor and orchestra. The last, 'Poem on His Birthday' (1976) for baritone, chorus and orchestra, includes material from the earlier movements, and the whole work moves from a simpler idiom to a darker, more anguished tone.

Corigliano teaches at the City University of New York, and, since 1991, at the Julliard School.

RECOMMENDED WORKS
　　Clarinet Concerto (1977)
　　Opera *The Ghosts of Versailles*
　　　　(completed 1991)
　　Symphony No. 1 (1990)

Cowell Henry Dixon**
　　born 11th March 1897 at Menlo Park
　　(California)
　　died 10th December 1965 at Shady
　　(New York)

Henry Cowell is one of the major figures in the American traditions of eccentric music experimentation, and of enthusiastic support for and promotion of the modern music of others. Like a number of those other experimenters, his ideas are now more often heard in the music of the generation of composers who followed him, and who adopted many of his innovations, than through his own music. His output is vast (over 950 works) and eclectic, much of it is now totally ignored (especially in Europe), and currently it is difficult to gain an overall impression of its value, especially as much is unpublished.

As a child he used to hear Oriental music in the Chinatown of San Francisco, which became an abiding influence. Not only did he further this interest, studying non-European musics at the end of the 1920s and the beginning of the 1930s; he also assimilated influences from his Celtic heritage (especially Irish music), and American Midwestern folk tunes. But it was his new ideas on the sounds available on the piano that first brought him and his music into prominence. Chief among these was the concept of the tone cluster (a term he himself invented), which **Ives** had also developed, independently and unnoticed. These clusters Cowell played using the forearm, the palm and the fists, although they are closely delineated and mostly used as support for more conventional melodic ideas (as in *Adventures in Harmony*, 1913, for piano). To this technique he added new ways of actually playing the strings, such as the very atmospheric and haunting swirls and characteristic glissandi played internally on the piano strings in *The Banshee* (1925), which also incorporates the whole-tone scale in a strikingly successful demonstration of new piano colours. Similarly, in the *Aeolian Harp* (c.1923) the strings are plucked and strummed (Cowell termed the instrument thus used the 'string piano'). All these ideas, as well as his innovation of placing objects inside the piano to change the timbre, have been developed by subsequent composers (especially through the influence of **Cage**) to become common parlance in avant-garde piano music; most of them, and their use as background to more conventional writing, are heard in Cowell's *Piano Piece (Paris 1924)*. His widespread tours as a pianist, sensationally received (he was also the first American composer to be invited to tour the USSR in 1929) furthered the influence of his new ideas.

Cowell also used clusters in his orchestral music of the 1920s, notably in the *Piano Concerto* (1928), but meanwhile he had experimented in totally different areas: those of microtones, harmonics and very unconventional and complex rhythmic patterns moving completely independently of each other. These ideas were expressed in two atonal quartets, *Quartet Romantic* (1915–17) for two flutes, violin and viola, and *Quartet Euphometric* (1916–19) for string quartet, which were thought by the composer and others to be unplayable, until new techniques in the

1960s proved otherwise. They have the sense of two worlds colliding: for while the individual melodic lines belong loosely to their period, the uses to which they are put, and the multiplication of simultaneous ideas, are some fifty years ahead of their time. As such, there is an element of the academic about the quartets, and their influence derived from the expounding of these and Cowell's other experimental ideas in the classic theoretical book *New Musical Resources* (1916–19, but not published until 1930). He also developed new sound sources, for example in the concerto *Rhythmicana* (1931) for the early electronic rythmicon and orchestra, and through the widespread use of percussion, notably in the *Ostinato pianissimo* (1934). Scored for two string pianos, eight rice bowls (an early use of 'found objects'), two wood blocks, guiro, tambourine, two bongos, three drums, three gongs and xylophone, this beguiling work has an Eastern sense of progression and colour, which again influenced such composers as **Cage**.

Yet another innovation that Cowell bequeathed (again following the lead of **Ives**) was that of indeterminacy, which he termed 'elastic form', and which he first applied theoretically to dance. In his own work it concerns especially the free order in which events are to be played (*Mosaic Quartet* for string quartet, 1935). The middle of the 1930s marked the end of his particularly experimental period (coinciding with his false imprisonment on a morals charge for four years in 1937); now he increasingly turned to tonality and to more homely idioms, particularly Irish music and the rich tradition of American hymns (exemplified in *Eighteen Hymns and Fuguing Tunes* for diverse instrumental combinations including orchestra, 1944–64).

In the 1950s and 1960s he integrated many of his earlier concerns, especially dissonance and clusters, with a less esoteric approach, particularly the influences of the Near and Far East (*Percussion Concerto*, 1958, and *Koto Concertos No. 1 and No. 2*, 1961–62, 1965). Among the major works of this period, most of which are in a more accessible idiom, are the *Symphony No. 11 'The Seven Rituals of Music'* (1953), in which each of the seven movements is in a different style, matching the seven ages of man. The first sections herald material in the last sections, and the stylistic approach varies from insistent motoric percussion to shades of the big-band and jazz sounds in what is essentially a dance score as much as a symphony. A similar mixture of tradition and exoticism is found in such works as the *Symphony No. 15 'Thesis'* (1961), which opens in the American hymn style, has five tiny movements followed by a sonata-form closing movement, and includes percussive effects and wailing string harmonics, with some very quirky results in its combination of the traditional and the modernistic. The element of Americana is typified by the light and fluffy *Saturday Night at the Firehouse* (1948) for small orchestra, using folk melodies and rhythms.

Both as a composer and as a major historical figure in serious American music, Cowell has still not received his due. His earlier works are both enjoyable and essential to an understanding of the history of modern American music. Among his many pupils at Columbia University and the New School for Social Research were **Cage** and **Gershwin**, and he championed the cause of new American composers through his magazine *New Music* (1927–48), which published gramophone records as well as scores. Among his books, *New Musical Resources* is a classic of the genre, while *Charles Ives and His Music* (written with his wife Sidney Cowell, 1955) is the definitive work on the composer.

RECOMMENDED WORKS
  Ostinato pianissimo (1934) for
    percussion orchestra
  Pulse (1939) for percussion
  Symphony No. 11 *The Seven Rituals
    of Music* (1953)

BIBLIOGRAPHY
  H. Cowell, *New Musical Resources*,
    1930, reprinted 1969
  R. Mead, *Henry Cowell's New Music*,
    1925–1936, 1981

Crumb George··
born 24th October 1929 at Charleston
(West Virginia)

George Crumb became established in the 1960s as one of the more individual of contemporary American composers, and one who commanded a much wider audience than most of the avant-garde. After a number of atonal and then serial scores, his individual voice emerged in a cycle of works (1964–70) for voice and chamber ensemble inspired by, and incorporating sections of, the poetry of Lorca. Crumb responded to the dark, earthy but haunting imagery of the poetry with musical equivalents, especially in the basic atmospheric tension between deep held sonorities and sharp bursts of usually percussion colour.

In the first of these, *Night Music I* (1964) for mezzo-soprano and chamber ensemble, Crumb established a delicate, wispy texture, detailed with dots of subtle percussive colour and deep sonorities, that relied on colour and atmosphere for its effect and to point up the sometimes almost spoken vocal line. In *Madrigals* (1965–69, in four books) for soprano and various chamber forces, Crumb explores a similar world but with a refinement of subtle graduations of instrumental sound (including very precise and controlled modifications such as striking the harp with metal rods). Some of the melodic effects (set against a wide range of vocal styles) suggest a strong Moorish hue (and, in the final madrigal, a folk line against a drone). This Moorish influence is even more overt in the clarinet writing of the *Eleven Echoes of Autumn* (1965) for violin, flute, clarinet and piano (with the instrumentalists at three points intoning a Lorca fragment). In this more austere work Crumb starts to use the high extremes of instruments that he developed in later works as an evocative and effective colouristic device. All these works have a sense of improvisatory freedom (belying the actual precision of detail) that exactly reflects the poetry, but the most successful of this series is also the best known, the song-cycle *Ancient Voices of Children* (1970) for mezzo-soprano, boy soprano, oboe, mandolin, harp, electric piano and percussion. Working from a similar base of delicate detail, the range is extended: there are shimmering vocal and instrumental effects, contrasted with the intensity of the percussion writing in the 'Dance of the Sacred Life-Cycle'. There are many allusions to the style of Spanish music, and the work captures both the earthiness and the ethereal inherent in Lorca's poetry. It deserves to stand alongside the other masterpiece that sets Lorca, **Ohana's** *Llantano por Ignaio Sanchez Mejias*.

The sense of ritual that lies behind these works was more evident in such scores as the Pulitzer Prize-winning *Echoes of Time and the River* (1967) for orchestra. It became fully integrated in his most evocative work, and one which continues to capture the public's imagination when performed, the *Vox Balaenae* (*Voice of the Whale*, 1971) for flute, cello and piano with antique cymbals, all sometimes amplified. In it the high harmonic effects become an instrumental echo of the whales' cries; the highly atmospheric writing is enhanced in stage performance by the use of masks, turning the piece into a 'mystery' in the ritualistic sense. Meanwhile, the underlying humanity of the Lorca settings was sharply contrasted by the harshness of *Black Angels (Images I)* (1970) for electric string quartet. Ethereal, distant wisps of sound, very high, sit behind a foreground of tortured and sometimes brutal electric string expression. Using the plainchant *Dies irae*, snippets of Schubert's *Death and the Maiden* and an Elizabethan madrigal, a spoken voice, and numerical symbolism, its extreme Expressionism centres around black and sinister superstitions – the performance instructions suggest the volume should be 'on the threshold of pain'. Nonetheless, some passages are very evocative. Crumb's preoccupation with tone colours and with atmosphere has been developed in *A Haunted Landscape* (1984) for orchestra with a very large percussion section (forty-five different instruments). Designed to conjure up the sensibilities of landscape, it is indeed a haunting work, pitting foreground colour, sometimes spare (the use of the rattle recalling early Cage), sometimes climactic, against a background that regularly uses a series of tonal chords, reminiscent of the colourless but moving world of the end of **Vaughan Williams's** *Symphony No. 6*.

Crumb's achievement has been to take the pointillistic sound of much serial music, and adapt it to his own (non-serial) exploration of tone colour and atmosphere. Devoid of any system, his music is designed to appeal to the emotions as much as the intellect; and with his very sure sense of colour, restraint and overall structure (usually a number of shorter sections within a larger span), he has succeeded in still sounding modern while appealing to a wider audience, who respond to the emotional aspects. His works are genuinely evocative; and while they have currently been somewhat eclipsed by the vogue of the minimalists, they seem likely to continue to appeal.

Crumb has taught at the University of Colorado (1959–64), and at the University of Pennsylvania from 1965.

RECOMMENDED WORKS
Ancient Voices of Children (1970) for mezzo-soprano, boy soprano and five instruments
Black Angels (1970) for electric string quartet
A Haunted Landscape (1984) for

orchestra
Madrigals (1965–69) for soprano and various forces
Makrokosmos III 'Music for a Summer Evening' (1974) for 2 amplified pianos and percussion
Vox Balaenae (1971) for flute, cello and piano

Del Tredici David Walter*
born 16th March 1937 at Cloverdale (California)

David Del Tredici is one of the most approachable eccentrics of modern American music. His idiom is dominated by three fundamental clashes: the tug between the modern avant-garde of his training and a sumptuous Romanticism that eventually looks to **Strauss** and **Mahler**; the pull between the demands of music for the concert platform and a preference for the operatically dramatic; and the desire to reach both sophisticated and populist audiences. Such a raft of conflicts is perhaps irreconcilable without obsession or humour, and Del Tredici has both in full measure; Oliver **Knussen** has aptly pointed out than even when his music is being serious, it is humorous, and when being humorous it is serious; these conflicts also create a palpable tension in his music. It is perhaps typical of his humour that he often uses the number thirteen (in intervals and time signatures, for example) in his works, punning on the Italian meaning of his name.

After earlier, mainly piano, works, Del Tredici's output has been dominated by two obsessions: between 1958 and 1968 the writing of James Joyce, and since 1968, forming the bulk of his work, Lewis Carroll's *Alice in Wonderland* and *Alice through the Looking Glass*. Both writers, of course, share a delight in odd language connected to tradition, quirky humour (often half-hidden), surrealist imagery, and a lateral, disconcerting logic – all of which are found in Del Tredici's music. The Joyce works are essentially a prelude to the Alice works. Characteristically, in *Syzygy* (1966), for soprano, horn, tubular bells and chamber orchestra, the lithe vocal lines are electronically amplified, to counter the massed sounds from the orchestra. The first of the Alice works was *Pop-pourri* (1968, revised 1972), for amplified soprano, a rock group of saxophones and electric guitars, chorus and orchestra; this provides a good introduction to his quirky humour, rhythmic inventiveness and to the characteristic solo vocal writing, lyrical at its base but with huge leaps, sudden runs, trills, speech and a wide range of colours and inflections. The irreconcilable oppositions in this piece are the 'turtle soup' passage from *Alice* and the Catholic liturgy, represented in part by the (Protestant) Bach chorale 'Es is genug' (used by **Berg** in his *Violin Concerto*), separating each of the five sections and whose first four notes provide the basic material. In the second section the chorus have repetitive chants derived from Del Tredici's memories of interminable hours in church. The turtle soup material is eventually heard played backwards while a trumpet plays forward, and in the final section the Bach chorale is heard in full against interjections of turtle soup material. The result is a piece that can suddenly turn from pathos or a wonderful, childlike humour (especially in some of the tongue-in-cheek instrumental effects) to moments of serious impact. *An Alice Symphony* (1969) followed a similar formula, with a folk group replacing the rock group, but it was with *Final Alice* (1975–76) for amplified soprano, folk group and orchestra that Del Tredici found a less startlingly eclectic idiom to suit the material; its success catapulted him into international prominence. Set in five scenes, it retains the vocal style (including distortions available through the amplification), opening with the soprano narrating; but as soon as the soprano starts singing (against prominent banjo and mandolin) the large orchestra moves into a sumptuous large-scale palette directly derived from **Strauss** and **Mahler**. The harmonies, phrase-shapes and orchestral colours and patterns are instantly recognisable, yet glossed with more modern harmonic effects and the vastly extended range of vocal style. It is as if we were in a parallel world (which is where, of course, the texts place us) in which the known developments of 20th-century music had not happened, and instead classical music had continued directly from the late-Romantic; the effect is remarkable, fiercely dramatic (with Alice eventually denouncing the cards and returning to reality) and strangely moving. Perhaps the dominating emotions in *Final Alice* are a Mahlerian bitter-sweet ecstasy and a Straussian turmoil and triumphant joy.

Final Alice was not, however, final, and even more stunning is *In Memory of a Summer Day* (1980), for amplified soprano and orchestra. This is the first and best-known part of *Child Alice* (1977–81), in which the other parts form the second half of a concert evening when it is given in its entirety. In the earlier Alice works Del Tredici had told various parts of the Alice story; in *In Memory of a Summer Day* he dropped the linear story-telling in favour of an Alice atmosphere, and at the same time omitted the rock or folk groups. While the idiom remains similar, there is a greater emphasis on lyrical calm, as if this were the grown-up Alice looking back and reminiscing. A large number of Del Tredici's other Alice works are reworkings of parts of the major Alice works in different formats, or forming new works: *Virtuoso Alice* (1984), for example, is a fantasy for piano on a theme from *Final Alice*.

Del Tredici's extraordinary idiom is a one-off, inimitable except by parody, a mixture of two eras fused through equally remarkable non-musical inspirations; it certainly provides a unique experience, to which many have responded.

RECOMMENDED WORKS
> *Final Alice* (1975–76) for amplified
> soprano, folk group and orchestra
> *In Memory of a Summer Day* (1979)
> for amplified soprano and orchestra
> *Pop-pourri* (1968) for amplified
> soprano and orchestra

Foss Lukas (né Fuchs)**
born 15th August 1922 at Berlin

Lukas Foss has been one of the most conspicuous of the experimental American composers, tempering his modernity with what often seems a residue of traditional ideas or techniques, and usually incorporating new directions in his own idiom rather than himself being an innovator. He is also well known as an unusual conductor, and an enthusiast for new music. Although born in Germany, he moved with his family to Paris in 1933 and to the USA in 1937, becoming an American citizen in 1942.

His early music was influenced by **Copland**, and until the 1950s he wrote music cast in neo-classical mould, with traditional harmonic structures (including a *Symphony in G*, 1944) and a sense of American colour and nationalism (as in *The Prairie*, 1944, for soloists, chorus and orchestra, or the comic opera *The Jumping Frog of Calaveras County*, 1949). The influence of the Passions of JS Bach lay behind the narrative style of *A Parable of Death* (1952), for narrator, tenor, chorus and orchestra. Using the poetry of Rilke, it has a spare, serene beauty, the narrator taking the major role while the musical forces comment or support. The diversity of styles that he has continued to show was evident in the virtuoso *Piano Concerto No. 2* (1951) and the romantic and sensuous *Song of Songs* (1946), for soprano and orchestra. He continued to write in this broadly mainstream style until the *Symphony of Chorales* (1956–58, based on Bach chorales) and the ten-minute opera *Introductions and Goodbyes* (1959, to a libretto by Gian-Carlo Menotti, by which time he had already started experimenting with improvisation groups at the University of California, Los Angeles (UCLA), where he had taught since 1953. This led to a complete change of style, and it is for the works written since 1959 that he is now best known.

In 1957, following his experiments with his students, Foss founded the Improvisation Chamber Ensemble to explore the possibilities of chance, and the relationship between composer and performer in the control of the performed music. In his own works, notably the Webernesque song-cycle *Time Cycle* (1959–60, versions for soprano and orchestra or chamber ensemble), with a spare vocal line and some tonal, some atonal sections, he started to use serial techniques, strictly composer controlled, in spite of interpolated improvisations (later notated) in the first performance of *Time Cycle*. With *Echoi* (1961–63), for clarinet, cello, piano and percussion, his first more experimental piece, Foss retained the serial basis for the construction of the music, but, building on the experience of the Ensemble, he included limited chance (the players switching to sections of the score on the stroke of an anvil), and achieved a characteristically large-scale sound (including internal piano sonorities) from limited resources. In the extrovert feel of the work there is a sense that the lyrical is never too far away.

Foss then developed the concept of what he called 'multi-diversity': the score is dense with material, but only a small amount is used at any one time and in any given performance. This allows a random element while ensuring control of the actual material. *Elytres* (1964) for solo flute, two solo violins and instrumental ensemble varies the density of forces as well as material. The *Fragments of Archilochos* (1965) for four small choirs, large chorus, percussion, mandolin, guitar, male and female speakers and solo counter-tenor, with considerable use of speech,

allows some choice in rhythm and pitches in its rather dense and declamatory gestures. The elements of the linguistically dramatic and the declamatory (and the rather brutal) were developed in *Paradigm 'for my friends'* (1969), for percussion (doubling conductor), electric guitar and three instruments, with many chance elements.

The influence of the Baroque, evident in the *Symphony of Chorales*, then resurfaced in Foss's new style. From the grand white-noise sonorities and the echoes of the Baroque in the insistently effective *Non-Improvisation* (1967) for four instruments (the very title indicating a change of direction), Foss arrived at the marvellous synthesis of the Baroque and modernist distortion that are the *Baroque Variations* (1967) for orchestra, his most notorious, most popular and most accessible experimental music. Based on Handel, Scarlatti and Bach, it is not in a recognised variation form, but fragments of the originals are seen distorted in a kind of dream (and, in the last movement, nightmare) world, haunting and effective, a reflection both of the 20th century's interest in earlier music, and of the way it becomes a residue in our memories. In the same year, the *Concert for Cello and Orchestra* mixed a live orchestra and the cello recorded on tape, both eventually dividing and distorting a Bach sarabande.

The more recent works have explored a number of these facets of his idiom. Timbre and sonorities are the subject of *Ni Bruit Ni Vitesse* (1973), in which two pianists treat the inside of two pianos percussively, with effects akin to electronic music. The *Salomon Rossi Suite* (1975) for orchestra treats music by the early 17th-century Mantuan composer with great reverence, modifying the original only by orchestration. The almost neo-Romantic idiom of *Night Music for John Lennon* (1980) is cast in neo-classical forms (prelude, fugue and chorale), while *Solo* (1983) for piano is influenced by the repetitions of minimalism.

Foss taught at UCLA (University of California in Los Angeles) from 1953. He was the artistic director of the Buffalo Philharmonic Orchestra (1963–70), conductor of the Brooklyn Philharmonia (now Philharmonic) Orchestra from 1971, and director of the Milwaukee Symphony Orchestra (1981–86). He founded, and became director of, the Buffalo Center for Creative and Performing Arts (1963).

RECOMMENDED WORKS
Baroque Variations (1967) for
orchestra
Ni Bruit Ni Vitesse (1973) for two
pianos
Non-Improvisation (1967) for four
instruments
song-cycle *Time Cycle* (1959–60) for
soprano and orchestra

Gershwin George*
(as classical composer)
born 26th September 1898 at Brooklyn
(New York)
died 11th July 1937 at Hollywood

George Gershwin was one of the finest
popular song-writers of the century, often
with his brother Ira as lyricist; songs such
as 'That Certain Feeling' (1925), ' 'S Wonderful' (1927), 'I've Got a Crush on You'
(1928) and 'I Got Rhythm' (1930) have
become standards, and he brought to the
American musical stage a new sophistication drawn in part from his classical training. These and the shows from which they
came, including *Lady, Be Good!* (1924),
Funny Face (1927), *Show Girl* (1929) and
Strike Up the Band (1927, revised 1930), lie
outside the parameters of this *Guide*. But
Gershwin also wrote a number of works for
the concert stage, colourful, vivacious, and
imbued with the spirit of jazz, blues and
ragtime. *Rhapsody in Blue* has become
one of the best-known of all 20th-century
compositions, and his idiom paved the way
for other American composers to incorporate jazz and popular elements into their
music.

Aside from the *Lullaby* (c.1919) for
string quartet, his first major attempt at a
combination of the popular and the classical was the twenty-minute one-act opera
Blue Monday (1922, original orchestration
by Will Vodery), which used a theme from
the *Lullaby*. Set in a night-club, it was
originally (and disastrously) used within a
musical comedy, and then taken up by the
band leader Paul Whiteman and reorchestrated (1929) by Ferde Grofé under
the title *135th Street*. It was Whiteman
who commissioned the *Rhapsody in Blue*
(1923–24), whose opening upward clarinet
run is pure jazz, before it turns into a
scintillating combination of short piano
concerto and jazz suite. The orchestration
in the version usually heard was again by
Ferde Grofé (best remembered for his
overtly Romantic *Grand Canyon Suite*,

1931, for orchestra); it is more effective,
however, in its original guise for piano and
jazz band. Its instant popularity led to a
commission for the *Piano Concerto* (1925).
This much more ambitious work attempted to extend the idiom of the *Rhapsody*; it
veers into sentimental lushness and into
brashness, but has a memorable lilt and a
bright optimism. More successful is *An
American in Paris* (1928) for orchestra, an
evocation of Gershwin's reactions to the
sights and sounds of Paris (the street
noises including the sounds of taxis),
whose verve and bright colours far outweigh its rather rambling form. The
Cuban Overture (1932) for orchestra incorporated Cuban rhythms, and helped draw
the attention of American composers to
the fertile inspiration of Latin-American
music.

Gershwin's masterpiece, however, is the
opera *Porgy and Bess* (1934–35), to a
libretto by Ira Gershwin and DuBose
Heyward, based on the novel by Heyward.
The story is set among the American black
dockyard community (drawn from Heyward's knowledge of Charleston), and follows the love of a cripple (Porgy) for the
loose woman Bess. Bess is the 'woman' of a
stevedore, Crown, who commits murder in
a crap-game; Porgy gives Bess sanctuary,
until Crown returns and Porgy kills him.
Porgy is taken away by the police (to
identify Crown, not as a suspect as Bess
believes), as Bess is persuaded by another
villain to leave with him for the high life in
New York. When Porgy returns, she is
gone, and the opera ends with him setting
out to follow her. Gershwin correctly
described it as a 'folk-opera', for it is an
equivalent of a ballad opera, drawing on
Negro spirituals as well as jazz, blues and
ragtime; the lovely song 'Summertime' has
become one of the most famous ever written. The opera teems with vitality and
energy, vivid in its evocations and emotions, and it remains, whatever its affinities with the form of the musical, the
classic American opera.

Gershwin died at the age of thirty-eight;
one can only wonder how he might have
continued the synthesis of popular and
classical American styles.

RECOMMENDED WORKS
An American in Paris (1928) for
orchestra
Rhapsody in Blue (1924) for piano and
orchestra or jazz band
opera *Porgy and Bess* (1934–35)

BIBLIOGRAPHY
E. Jablonski, *Gershwin*, 1988
C. Schwartz, *Gershwin*, 1973

Glass Philip**

born 31st January 1937 at Baltimore (Maryland)

Philip Glass is unquestionably the most successful serious American composer of the present day, at least in terms of contemporary public reaction, commanding an international audience that includes lovers of pop and jazz as well as classical music. He is also the popular leader of the reaction to post-serialism and the 1960s avant-garde, known as minimalism, and developed in Glass's case in small-scale works, mainly for dance, before he turned to opera. The essence of his minimalist style is a series of repeating patterns, usually based on the traditional diatonic harmonic triad, that undergo changes by the addition or subtraction of different instrumental colours, sometimes with sharply contrasting dynamics, changes in speed, and sudden gear-shifts in the harmonic patterns. A favourite device is the change from a minor triad to the major triad a major third below, prominent in the haunting *Glassworks* (1981), written like many of his smaller-scale works for his own ensemble. A kind of atmospheric minimalist tone poem, its success launched his world-wide fame and it remains the best introduction to his music.

At his best, these procedures can create mesmerisingly effective atmospheres that are whipped up into ecstatic excitement, often with a fabulous sense of timing, especially in the placing of brass. At his worst (which is often), his music can be horrendously banal and infuriatingly trite; unfortunately, many of his works include passages of both. He has tried to broaden his techniques and range throughout his career, but eventually has seemed trapped in his own success, each repetition of the formula becoming less original and inventive.

His large output is so divergent in quality that this entry concentrates on the more interesting works, especially his major achievements in opera. The early works are best avoided, except by Glass aficionados. The mind-numbing simplicity of *Dance 1–5* (1978–79) for small ensemble serves as an example. A set of mechanistic pieces designed for dance, it shows all Glass's hallmarks – repetitive patterns with additive rhythms, bright colours, rapid rising arpeggios, tonal harmonies rocking on major seconds, and simplistic syncopations, intentionally hypnotic, with characteristic gear-shifts. The music will apparently repeat endlessly, and then (with a change of colour, key, or ostinati length) shift into another extended repeat (sometimes emphasised by a change in instrumentation), usually shifting back again eventually. With *Glassworks* he started to integrate rhythmic and harmonic changes in a more unified fashion, especially in the operas.

Glass's first three operas developed into a trilogy based on historical figures. The first, *Einstein on the Beach*, explored the philosophical and poetical concept of the scientist, the second, *Satyagraha*, that of the humanist, and the third, *Akhnaten*, that of the religious thinker. Theatrically, especially in terms of stylistic ritual, they show a clear thread of development, but musically, *Einstein on the Beach* represents a culmination of Glass's idiom to that point, while the next two operas show the development of a new musical maturity.

Einstein on the Beach (1975), written in collaboration with Robert Wilson, revolves around images connected with Einstein (trains, a bed, a spaceship, Einstein playing the violin) and delves into a post-modernist enquiry into the scientist. It is the most disjointed of Glass's operas, and is best heard (as opposed to seen) section by section. The second work in the trilogy, *Satyagraha* (1979–80) is stylistically much more unified and developed, while acting as a prelude to the full maturity of Glass's idiom in *Akhnaten*. The basis of the opera, to a libretto by Constance de Jong, is the development of Gandhi's concept of 'satyagraha' (resistance by non-violence) while he was in South Africa, and includes a number of incidents during his protest over the treatment of Indians there. The actual text to this plot is in Sanskrit, drawn from the *Bhagavad-Gita*, and each of the three acts has a non-singing character as symbolic mentor: Leo Tolstoy and Rabindranath Tagore (both major influences on Gandhi), and, in the third act, Martin Luther King Jr, representing 'satyagraha' after Gandhi's death. The use of the archaic language, its marriage to the plot, and the symbolic figures create a kind of philosophic mystery-play of an opera, with a strong ritualistic element. Musically there are obvious similarities to *Glassworks*, and a distinctive orchestral colour, using only strings, woodwind and organ. Glass builds terrific energy, especially in Act II, using longer vocal lines with echoes of chant, often in combination or with chorus, over the characteristic repetitive pulses of the orchestral writing. The seams between musical changes, and the long-term movements of the music are not as assured as in *Akhnaten* (*Satyagraha* was the first minimalist work on so large a scale and time-span), but the opera remains a compelling experience.

The final work of the trilogy is Glass's masterpiece, where he found a ritualistic stage format that merged completely with both the subject matter and the mesmeric qualities of his musical style. *Akhnaten* (1982–83), to a libretto by the composer, Shalom Goldman, Robert Israel and Richard Riddell, based on ancient Egyptian texts, opens with the funeral procession of the Pharaoh Amenhotep IV in 1375 BC. It then presents in three acts the ascending to the throne of his son Akhnaten, the revolutionary changes during his reign (including the first concept of a monotheistic, abstract god), and his downfall. It culminates in dual time, with modern tourists visiting the ruins of his city. Its central theme is that of a revolution in philosophical thought, eventually overcome by inherent forces of conservatism. The main protagonist is essentially the orchestra; merged into its everunravelling web are large choruses and ritualistic solo vocal lines, with the title role given to a counter-tenor. The languages are Ancient Egyptian, Akkadian and Hebrew, except for the linking narration and Akhnaten's central hymn of praise, which are in the language of the audience. The progress of the piece evolves over long time-spans, changes to the overall tone created by changes of long-term colours (such as adding drums, the use of solo bells, diminution of forces into a chamber ensemble). The Ancient Egyptian setting, with its strong visual symbolism, its direct, yet allusive, verbal imagery, its sense of huge time-spans, and its ritualistic emphasis, finds its mirror-image in Glass's music, and the work is less an opera than a ritualistic event in which music, words and visual effect merge. Consequently, readers are advised at least to seek out the video of the opera if they are unable to attend a performance, where the full impact of the conjunction of these elements is better experienced. However, a recording is still a compelling experience,

with moments such as the Act II love-duet between Akhnaten and Nefertiti, where a sense of the purity of a Renaissance madrigal is combined with the insistent repetition of Glass's orchestral writing, or Akhnaten's haunting hymn, or the poignancy of the Pharaoh's deserted official, appealing for military help, followed by the massed choral and orchestral power of the mob attacking the Pharaoh's palace.

Glass's other stage works have had less impact. *The Making of the Representative for Planet 8* (1987) was based on a sci-fi novel by Doris Lessing, in which an ice-age on a temperate planet destroys its people, ennobling them in the process. It missed the earlier operas' symbolism and the distancing achieved by the settings of archaic languages. *The Photographer* (1982) is a combination of play, concert music and dance; the final pages of the suite arranged from it for orchestra have a terrific excitement. *The Voyage* (1991–92) was commissioned by the New York Metropolitan Opera to celebrate the 500th anniversary of Columbus's transatlantic voyage. Conventionally laid out in three acts with a prologue and an epilogue, it equates a space journey in 2092 to Columbus's voyage. The two outer acts are the space voyage; the central act is set in the 16th Century. At the opera's close, the heads of the earth states are assassinated, and there are trendy allusions to such figures as Mrs Thatcher and Stephen Hawking. The chief interest is in the scenario and the libretto: the music, with its repetitive schemes, forms a large-scale underframe for the scenarios rather than itself creating subtleties of depth of character or personal interactions. The choral writing, characteristically ecstatic, is effective, but one can't help feeling that this is yet another example of American easy fare for the masses, whose ultimate lack of musical content is conveniently overlooked because of its immediacy and potential for visual appeal.

Of his other works, perhaps the most successful is the *String Quartet No. 2 'Company'* (1983), where the lack of contrasting instrumental colours forces a concentration on the subtleties of other aspects of Glass's repetitions, with most appealing results. The song-cycle *Hydrogen Jukebox* (1989–90) for narrator, vocal and instrumental ensemble promised more than it delivered, being a collaboration with the poet Allen Ginsberg to create a 'portrait' of America from the 1950s to the

1980s through Ginsberg's inimitable poetry. The best parts are the actual narration of poems (by Ginsberg in the Nonesuch recording), at one point against quasi-improvisatory piano, and the insidious pulse of a setting of part of *The Green Automobile*. A trio of symphonically conceived 'portraits of nature' appeared in the late 1980s. The most ambitious is *Itaipú* (1989) for chorus and orchestra, concerned with a hydro-electric dam on the Paraná river. Glass is at his swirling best in the opening, as he builds up power and momentum, and in the ecstatic, triumphant ending. Its weaknesses are trite middle movement that treads a path already covered by David Bedford's equally trite *The Odyssey*, and an opening to the third movement that is an unfortunate cross between Handel's *Zadok the Priest* and **Bernstein's** *Mass*. *The Canyon* (1988) is a huge orchestral ritual dance, effective as such, but not quite achieving the grandeur of its aims. Some of Glass' most successful music is to be found in film scores, notably *Koyaanisqatsi* (1981) and *Powaqqatsi* (1987).

Philip Glass occupies a special place in modern American music. He has filled a void left by the virtual demise of the American musical and of 'popular' opera and operetta, after the former was taken over by the huge-scale, usually British, spectacular, and the latter simply disappeared. His formula has been wildly popular, and deservedly so: it appeals to a much wider audience than the general repertoire of operas. Unfortunately, this has been promoted as something which, with the possible exception of *Akhnaten*, it is not: great 20th-century opera. This is hardly the fault of Philip Glass, who does what he does with panache and effect; but it is a sad commentary on current critical and intellectual standards that something that should simply be celebrated for its particular appeal should instead be awarded an inflated reputation as a thought-provoking creation, let alone an intellectually challenging or emotionally enriching experience, the prerequisite of any great opera. It does, however, make for good box-office.

RECOMMENDED WORKS
opera *Akhnaten* (1982–83)
Glassworks (1981) for ensemble
Itaipú (1989) for chorus and orchestra
opera *Satyagraha* (1979–80)
String Quartet No. 2 *Company* (1983)

BIBLIOGRAPHY
P. Glass, *Opera on the Beach*, 1988

Hanson Howard*
born 28th October 1896 at Wahoo (Nebraska)
died 19th February 1981 at Rochester (New York)

Howard Hanson was one of the major figures of American music, especially through his activities as teacher, conductor, and enthusiast for American music and younger American composers. His own compositions stand on the cusp of the development of American classical music, their late-Romantic idiom drawing on the Scandinavian symphonic tradition (his parents were immigrant Swedes): he was the last of the American Romantics whose models were primarily European, and he is the only one of real stature.

His earlier symphonies are the works most likely to be encountered. The *Symphony No. 1 'Nordic'* (1921–22) sets the tone: a large-scale, three-movement work of vitality and colour, soaring tunes, a luxuriant slow movement and a big, brassy finale that turns into an American equivalent of an Elgarian march to emphasise the sombre undercurrent of the work. The *Symphony No. 2 'Romantic'* (1930) is warmer and more mellow, with a swaying lyricism that suggests (as often in Hanson's music) the motion of the sea, and with a motto theme linking the three movements. The *Symphony No. 3* (1936–38) recalls **Sibelius** in its use of development from germinal cells and a build-up and flow over pedal points. More linear than its predecessors, it includes a touch of the light-hearted, a second movement of smooth textures, an almost primitive effect in the repetitions of the third, and an uplifting finale. The *Symphony No. 4 'The Requiem'* (1943), using a cyclical structure in its four movements, was written in response to the death of the composer's father. The *Symphony No. 5 'Sinfonia sacra'* (1954) is short – a single fifteen-minute movement – dark in hue, rugged in effect, and was inspired by St John's account of the Resurrection. The *Symphony No. 7 'The Sea'* (1977), for chorus and orchestra, draws on the same group of Whitman texts as the sea symphonies of **Vaughan Williams** and **Harris**; its main tone is of joyous affirmation. Of his other orchestral works, *Mosaics* (1956) for orchestra is a set of variations that covers most of Hanson's colours and idioms, including a distinct touch of the English pastoral and a moment of the exotic, besides the Nordic sense of space and ruggedness. The *Piano Concerto* (1948), which comes in and goes out gently, and often has an improvisatory feel to the solo writing, is entertaining but not especially distinctive.

Hanson's major choral work is *The Lament for Beowulf* (1925) for chorus and orchestra. A long orchestral introduction with a repetitive throbbing rhythmic idea and fanfares creates the Nordic mood, and the movement of the sea again infects the linear vocal and orchestral writing, both often bare and exposed. Many of Hanson's other choral works are well worth the encounter, especially his only a cappella work, *A Prayer of the Middle Ages* (1976), a setting with rich dense textures of a 9th-century prayer. Works such as his settings of psalms would make an effective alternative in Anglican services. His opera *Merry Mount* (1933), based on Hawthorne, was well received at its original Metropolitan première, but has disappeared from the repertoire apart from an orchestral suite drawn from the opera.

Hanson's influence on younger American composers was considerable; he encouraged them to experiment and develop, but never attempted to impose his own conservative idiom. He started teaching at the College of the Pacific in San José in 1916, becoming the dean of its school of music in 1919, at the age of twenty-three. He was the director of the Eastman School of Music at the University of Rochester from 1924 to 1964, and his American Music Festivals included works by all the important younger American composers.

RECOMMENDED WORKS
The Lament for Beowulf (1925) for
    chorus and orchestra
Symphony No. 1 *Nordic* (1921–22)
Symphony No. 2 *Romantic* (1930)
Symphony No. 3 (1936–38)
Symphony No. 5 *Sinfonia sacra* (1954)

BIBLIOGRAPHY
H. Hanson, *Music in Contemporary
    American Civilisation*, 1951

Harris Roy**
born 12th February 1898 at Chandler,
Oklahoma
died 1st October 1979 at Santa Monica,
California

Harris is the composer of the wide open American landscapes: his music is expansive, with a quiet strength. He drew material from cowboy songs, the music of the American Civil War, and American hymn tunes, to forge it into an idiom that reflects American rural, rather than urban, life. His contrapuntal idiom is predominantly tonal, with long flowing melodies, but always has an edge sharpened by dissonances and polytonality, and by irregular rhythms, and occasionally by modal harmonies. He is one of the finest American composers, and if he is still too little known both inside and outside his own country, this is partly due to the reaction against the mainstream American evocative composers during the avant-garde period of the 1960s and 1970s. Although his output covers a wide range of genres, including much band music, it is as a symphonist that he is chiefly to be valued.

Like a number of composers of his generation, he studied (none too successfully) with Nadia Boulanger in Paris, and the most important of his early works is the *Concerto for Piano, Clarinet and String Quartet* (1927). His first symphony, titled *Symphony 1933* (1933), is a landmark in the history of American music, the first American symphony unmistakable in its cultural origins. From the vigorous opening onwards, it has a sense of the expansiveness of the American landscape, and a rough pioneer spirit in spite of the sophisticated and characteristic sense of counterpoint. It was also the first American symphony to be recorded, and it stands out in the history of the American symphony much as **Walton's** first does in that of the British. With its vitality and touches of the American folk tradition, it still has impact, in spite of moments where the counterpoint seems to be in danger of stalling the momentum. The second symphony is not a conventional symphony at all, but a fifteen-minute, three-movement work for a cappella choir based on texts by Walt Whitman, and one of Harris's most successful works. Titled *Symphony for Voices* (1935), it is vocally challenging, with eight-part writing, ostinati lines regularly rising in step-like motion with dissonant consequences, and speech-like moments in the middle movement that provide a close match with the essence of the texts. The first movement provides a fascinating contrast with **Vaughan Williams's** setting of the same lines in the *Sea Symphony*.

However, it was the *Symphony No. 3* (1938) that instantly became Harris's best-known work, and which became established as one of the central symphonies in the American repertoire. Its one movement is divided into five contrasting sections, themselves characteristic of Harris's general concerns ('Tragic, Lyric, Pastoral, Fugue-Dramatic, Dramatic-Tragic'). It opens with a long, expansive and almost hymn-like tune, its dark orchestral colours anticipating the more tragic elements of the work. The ease of its flowing construction has gained the admiration of critics. To a wider public, its various moods, from dark expansive sonorities expressive both of the American landscape and the hardships of the pioneer world, through a gentle lyricism, a jaunty boisterousness reminiscent of the traditional cowboy music idiom, to a rugged and dramatic assertion, have seemed a quintessential reflection of the American spirit, its idiom identifiable with the American soil and pioneer values. On both levels, it remains as powerful today.

The *Symphony No. 4* (1939) extends that sense of connection with the soil. Properly titled *Folk-Song Symphony*, it is a fantasia for chorus and orchestra rather than a symphony, its material based on popular American traditional tunes. The *Symphony No. 5* (1942, later revised and shortened) is intentionally heroic, to express the 'will to struggle' inherent in the American dream. In idiom, it is similar to the third; however, the material is not developed along traditional thematic lines, but by metamorphosis of initial motives. The orchestral colours are dominated by horns, and a march-like quality adds spice and piquancy to the otherwise characteristic style. It is well worth hearing in its own right, and some may prefer its more monumental directness, although the final movement almost tips into bombast. The *Symphony No. 6* (1943–44, subtitled *Gettysburg*) was a wartime symphony, dedicated to the armed forces, and was inspired by Lincoln's address. The opening movement, a long crescendo, is atmospherically inspired, the vibraphone adding a brightness to colours centred on string-tones, its motion in search of a key belying its purposefulness. The second picks up the same mood, opening with a long brass tune over a sonorous pulse of a drone in the strings before dissolving into gesture (with fanfare whoops). With a curious lack of contrast, the rich sonorities are extended in the slow movement. The impression is of a deeply flawed work,

especially in the moments of almost populist rhythms in the finale, but one that is nonetheless strangely compelling.

Considerably more successful is the *Symphony No. 7* (1951), where there is a much stronger sense of an internal tension and turmoil. Harris reverted to the one-movement form; the rhythmic drive remains, together with moments of atmospheric sonority. But there are 12-tone elements in the melodic cast, with considerable more acerbity than his earlier symphonies, the orchestration more wide-ranging in short phrases and motifs. In spite of a lighter dance lilt in the centre of the symphony, and the move towards a brighter, more monumental horizon at the close, the overall impression is of the threat of the fragmentation of the American dream. This symphony may not be so immediate, or so obviously American, as the third, but it is perhaps a finer creation. None of his later symphonies have been as successful. The *Symphony No. 10* is for chorus, brass, amplified pianos and percussion; for superstitious reasons the numbered sequence omits thirteen.

Of his concertante works, the most appealing is the *Violin Concerto* (1949, first performed in 1984 – the orchestration of an earlier violin concerto was never completed); this shares some material with the *Symphony No. 7*, though to quite different ends. With a typically exciting, driving opening followed by a rhapsodic violin, it contains strong modal influences, the bouncing feel of the popular, rural dance, and an essentially lyrical view, not unlike the concertos of **Vaughan Williams**. The *Concerto for Piano and Strings* (1960) is a reworking of the 1936 *Piano Quintet*.

The traditional American tune *When Johnny Comes Marching Home* provided the basis for two attractive works of the same title: the first (1934) is a deservedly popular set of symphonic variations subtitled an 'American overture', its boisterousness mixed with more contemplative and expansive moments; the second (1937), a short and effective choral work for a cappella choir, a much more dissonant treatment that is virtually a very sophisticated round.

Harris taught at the Juilliard School (1932–40), at Colorado College (1940–46), at various other institutions, and then at UCLA (University of California in Los Angeles) from 1961 to 1973. He directed the music section of the Overseas Division of the Office of War Information in 1945.

RECOMMENDED WORKS
'American overture' *When Johnny
Comes Marching Home* (1934)
Symphony No. 3 (1939)
Symphony No. 5 (1942)
Symphony No. 7 (1952)
Symphony for Voices (1935) for a
cappella choir

BIBLIOGRAPHY
D. Stehman, *Roy Harris: An
American Musical Pioneer,* 1984

Harrison Lou Silver*
born May 14th 1917 at Portland
(Oregon)

Lou Harrison has made a virtue out of
extreme eclecticism, casting around
widely for the sources of his own distinctive sounds. His music might be better
known if he had been identified with a
particular area of contemporary music, for
his works are almost always inventive and
interesting, and almost invariably breathe
a sense of grace and fun. As a child,
growing up amid the cultural diversity of
the San Francisco area, he heard everything from Cantonese opera to Mexican
music; his own sources as a composer
range from the Baroque through 12-tone
techniques (he was a pupil of **Schoenberg**),
to Eastern musics, especially gamelan
music, which is perhaps the most obvious
feature of his own style. Tuning is an
important concern to the quality of his
sound: often he will require 'just' intonation, where the intervals within the octave
vary slightly (as opposed to the regular
division of 'equal temperament'). Some of
his works (such as the anti-nuclear *Novo
Odo*, 1961–63, for chorus and orchestra)
have a strong political and pacifist content.

Harrison was one of the earlier explorers of the potential of percussion, influenced by **Cowell** and working with **Cage**. In
the *First Concerto* (1939) for flute and
percussion (two players), rhythm is the
main motivator, the flute melodies woven
from the rhythmical patterns, each of
three short movements using different
percussion, with the Eastern flavour
emphasised by the use of gongs. *Suite for
Percussion* (1941) used a number of found
and home-made percussion instruments,
and metrical modulation (altering the
pulse by the overlapping introduction of a
new rhythmic idea); the winsome second
movement opens and closes with rustling
sounds and is otherwise pared to a minimum, with an 'aria' for temple-blocks.

Canticle (1941, revised 1989) for ocarina (a
terracotta flute), guitar and five percussionists is a gently attractive, musing work
when the ocarina is playing, otherwise
with a clockwork-like percussive insistency.

Although Harrison's music on a chamber scale is the most likely to be encountered, he has also written a number of
larger-scale works. The ritualistic and gently paced ballet *Solstice* (1949), usually
heard in its concert suite, has a newly
invented myth as its basis, pitting darkness against light. Its feeling of simplicity,
delicacy and strong colours is most attractive, with prepared ('tack') piano in its
octet forces, and Chinese and gamelan
inflections in its idiom. The *Suite for Symphonic Strings* (1930–42), like many of his
larger works written over a long period,
includes a wide range of styles in its nine
movements, from medieval dances to a
Romantic nocturne. The *Symphony on G*
(1948–54) uses 12-tone techniques while
maintaining a tonal base. The *Symphony
No. 3* (1937–82) is in six movements, the
second, third and fourth short and grouped
into a dance section (a reel, a waltz and an
estampe). It opens in the grand, almost
Romantic manner, with just a hint of the
Oriental, but its moods and idioms are
wide-ranging, more of a suite than a symphony. The attractive *Concerto in slendro*
(1961) for violin and ensemble of specially
tuned celesta, two prepared pianos and
two percussionists has a strong Eastern
flavour, especially in the second movement, where a simple, contemplative violin
melody is answered by gentle comments
from individual members of the ensemble;
the violin writing has the flavour of Eastern folk-singing.

His later music has included many
works written for gamelan orchestras, for
which some of the first American gamelan
instruments were made. *La Koro Sutro*
(1972) is a rather simplistic extended work
for a chorus of a hundred singers, harp,
organ and gamelan orchestra, in its own
fashion anticipating the slightly later New
Age movement. The vocal lines are based
on chanting; the text is the 'Heart Sutra'
translated into Esperanto. A similarly
home-made quality innocently pervades
Varied Trio (1986), for violin, piano and
percussion (including chopsticks and
bakers' pans). A set of three pieces for
gamelan written in 1978 and 1979 highlight
soloists: in *Main bersama-sama* (1978) a
French horn, retuned to match gamelan

tuning and creating unexpectedly effective contrasts of timbres; a violin in *Threnody for Carlos Chávez* (1979). He has also used the gamelan for concertos: the *Double Concerto* (1981–82) is for violin, cello and Javanese gamelan. In the *Piano Concerto* (1985) the black keys are tuned to mathematically precise intervals, the white keys to 'just' intonation, and sections of the orchestra are tuned to one or the other; gamelan is again a strong influence. A *Summerfield Set* (1987, revised 1988) for piano, on the other hand, shows no Eastern influence at all, but is entirely neo-Baroque. *String Quartet Set* (1978–80) looks back to earlier musics: a 12th-century tune, a stamping peasant's dance, the French Baroque and the music of the Turkish court; where appropriate, the body of the string instruments are used as percussion.

Harrison was critic for the *New York Herald Tribune* (1945–48), and a notable champion for the revival of the music of Charles Ives. He has taught widely, notably at San José State College, California (1967–80).

RECOMMENDED WORKS
Harrison's works with gamelan ensembles are recommended, in addition to the following:
Canticle #3 (1941, revised 1989) for ocarina, guitar and five percussionists
Concerto in slendro (1961) for violin and ensemble
First Concerto (1939) for flute and percussion
Symphony No. 3 (1937–82)

BIBLIOGRAPHY
L. Harrison, *Music Primer: Various Items About Music to 1970*, 1971

Hovhaness Alan (Chakmakjian)
born 8th March 1911 at Somerville (Massachusets)

Hovhaness is quite easily the most disappointing of the American composers listed here. He would not appear in this book at all, were it not that a large number of recordings have been devoted to his works, and he has a following in the USA. Therefore readers may be curious about this composer and his works.

His music can only be described as musak with a sophisticated veneer. It is a mishmash of strong Armenian influences

(Hovhaness is of Armenian origin), spiced by the occasional exoticism, served with a sauce of pseudo-philosophising, spread over a tonal base. This conglomeration is ill-digested. The same Armenian tinge appears again and again in the majority of his works, as do the rather plodding square rhythms, and almost invariably there is a long brass line floating somewhere over strings, and usually bells. Occasionally (as in *Khaldis*, 1951, for piano, four trumpets and percussion) there is an attempt at a more contemporary rhythmic moment or harmonic combination, but with integration into the general idiom. Trite dances, often with a folk or exotic flavour, regularly appear, usually with ostinato effects in the strings. Hovhaness is an extremely prolific composer, and it shows. His works sprawl, without any sense of purposeful construction, and sections of works seem to have been plonked alongside each other, like random patches.

This is all the more regrettable, because, just occasionally, Hovhaness will produce an effect or a sonority that can grippingly capture the imagination, in the manner of a good film score. The opening of *Fra Angelico* (1968) for orchestra, for example, has a hushed sense of atmospheric magic. Similarly, the main theme of the *Concerto for Horn and String Orchestra 'Artik'* is gloriously expansive and affecting. This quality is most notable in climactic moments, when Hovhaness has the ability to create a noble statement of brilliant orchestral colours, especially in the timing of harmonic resolutions. Examples of this include the ending of *Fra Angelico* and the bright, visionary feel of the ending of the *Symphony No. 11 'All Men Are Brothers'* (1960, revised 1969). Unfortunately, the rest of these works show such a complete lack of self-discipline or structural judgement as to nullify these moments. Worse, many of his works are intended to reflect philosophical or religious concerns, from Eastern mysticism to 15th-century European artists and Christian themes. One could therefore expect some kind of insight, elucidation or exploration of those themes. However, no such illumination emerges at all.

The one work that rises out of this general mediocrity is the short continuous *Symphony No. 2 'Mysterious Mountain'* (1955), which is as much an extended tone-painting as a symphony. Here Hovhaness's traits are contained within a convincing, linear structure, with a modal edge to the harmonies. The contrapuntal writing with scurrying strings, a Hovhaness hallmark, has a sense of drive and purpose, and the nobility of the climaxes is satisfying. The slow section, with string voices gradually entering and rising over quiet sonorities from horn and harp, has an atmospheric magic. Many will derive considerable pleasure from this symphony. The other work that has attracted wider attention is *And God Created Great Whales* (1970) for orchestra, with taped whale songs; **Crumb's** *Vox Balaenae*, however, is an infinitely more thoughtful contemplation of the same subject.

RECOMMENDED WORK
Symphony No. 2 *Mysterious Mountain* (1955)

Ives Charles Edward***
born 20th October 1874 at Danbury (Connecticut)
died 19th May 1954 at New York

Charles Ives is the supreme individualist of American music, a pioneer whose worth was not fully recognised until some thirty years after his works had been written. He is also among the most American of composers in that the inspiration of his music is deeply rooted in the landscape and history of the United States, and his musical sources in its vernacular musical traditions, especially band and hymn music.

Ives's experimentation came almost entirely from his childhood. His father, a bandmaster, so encouraged his son's musical activities that by the age of thirteen Ives was a church organist. Moreover, his father was ceaselessly curious about sounds of every type – acoustics, clusters, quarter-tones and unusual tunings – and included his children in his experiments. This curiosity was inherited by Ives, and increasingly in his own music he experimented, on a traditional base, with effects originally instilled by these experiences: atonality, polytonality, unusual rhythms, spacial effects, collage effects of widely differing materials, often in different keys and rhythms – all techniques widely incorporated into music later in the 20th century, but at its beginning virtually unheard-of. In addition, he was little exposed to orchestral music of the European tradition then dominant in American music, and thus could develop these ideas relatively unhindered.

Much has therefore been made of Ives the innovator; some even ascribe to him a place in the development of 20th-century music analogous to that of **Schoenberg** or **Stravinsky**. This, however, is misleading. Firstly, his isolation extended to performance (he was much more famous in his lifetime as the author of *the* manual on insurance salesmanship). Little of his music was heard until the late 1930s (he stopped composing after 1926), and the full value of his achievement was not recognised until the 1950s and 1960s, by which time these innovatory procedures had been independently developed elsewhere and were in general use. Secondly, and perhaps more important, Schoenberg was consciously and intellectually attempting to create a system that would extend the development of music, as was, in a very different fashion, Stravinsky in his stylistic changes. There is little sense of such an intellectual conceit in Ives, but rather an instinctive attempt to translate the sounds he heard inside his head in the most accurate form possible, with a largely emotive rather than intellectual intent. Consequently the cast of his music broadly follows the general practices of the late-19th century – almost all his works have a programmatic content, and are vividly descriptive – while its techniques belong firmly to the 20th century. None of this diminishes Ives's place: rather it makes him unique, and the effect of the combination of late-Romanticism and modern effects is extraordinary, producing strong reactions both for and against. His works are also depictions of the memories of childhood, and their effects on the adult life, that are rare in concert music; on the evidence of the music, there is a strong suggestion that the need for such recollections may have been a primary motivation for his composition.

The symphonies and descriptive orchestral evocations form the core of Ives's output. The *Symphony No. 2* (1900–01, first performed 1951) best shows his musical origins, an over-diffuse Romantic work in five movements, with a touch of Beethoven here, and more of Dvořák there, though unexpected modernisms slice in, such as a polyrhythmic side-drum, the injection of fife and drum music, or the hideous final musical joke. But much of it has an attractive clarity and a transcendental gentleness. The much more effective *Symphony No. 3* (1902–04, revised 1909, first performed 1947) uses a small orchestra, and might be subtitled the 'hymn' symphony, for it is based on hymn tunes (from the 1830s and 1860s) and church organ pieces. Sometimes subtitled 'The Camp Meeting', its three movements represent old folks gathering, children's day and communion, and, devoid of Ives's experiments in harmonies and rhythms, this genial work looks forward to **Copland** and **Schuman**, its dominant string sonorities emulating its inspirations. The *Symphony No. 4* (1909–16, first performed in full 1965) for chorus and orchestra is the most startling and the most original, scored for a very large orchestra with two conductors and piano, a modernist work that parallels the aesthetic of such writers as James Joyce. Predominant is collage: the second movement is a huge conglomeration of juxtaposed ideas, images and colours, resolved in the fourth. The opening movement uses the chorus, setting a poem by Lowell Mason that poses the philosophical basis of the symphony (questioning the meaning of life); the third movement is a more restrained adagio for strings. More conservative critics have hated it, and indeed there is a sense that Ives's fertile imagination is out of control, but ironically it should present no problems to those used to the superimposed collage effects of the avant-garde period. Some of its effects are striking, such as sudden movements from loud passages to ghostly ideas as if heard at a distance or in memory, a technique that came into widespread use in the 1970s. It is throughout a fascinating work, Ives's most ambitious and a summation of his musical development.

Perhaps his most frequently heard work is *Three Places in New England* (1903–14) for orchestra (formally titled *Orchestral Set No. 1*). The first movement is an evocation of a procession of dead souls from the Civil War on Boston Common, ghostly, rhythmically and harmonically in flux, the web of misty orchestral swirl highlighted by the emergence of individual instruments, including the piano. The second depicts Putnam's Camp, commemorating a winter military camp in 1778–79, full of marches, quotations from 'The British Grenadiers', and bouncing band music that is combined with completely contrasting material in clashing keys to give a bright, dream-like effect. This collage-juxtaposition effect was extraordinary for its time, a technique that was not fully employed until the avant-garde 1960s. The third depicts the misty morning river at Stockbridge, with distant singing in the church; the orchestral palette remains thick, swirling, again pinpointed with isolated instrumental touches like a fusion between Impressionism and pointillism, and the harmonies of the climax go beyond chromaticism into clusters. The *Orchestral*

Set No. 2 (1909–15, partly based on earlier material) for orchestra and chorus has a similar pattern, but is more extreme in its experimentation. The second movement is remarkable for its disjointed rhythmic effects within a general flow that suggests popular music. The third is an extraordinary concept, inspired by hearing people singing after receiving the news of the sinking of the *Lusitania*; it starts with a distant chorus, continues with a threnody of different simultaneous orchestral layers, ends with an almost Mahlerian climax before the long fade. The *Holidays Symphony* (1904–13) is in the same vein of experimentation and description, and is more of a suite than a symphony, each of the four movements celebrating a national holiday: Washington's Birthday, Decoration Day, The Fourth of July and Thanksgiving. It includes a jews' harp in its orchestration, and the wild and swirling 'Decoration Day' is often heard on its own. Of his other orchestral works, *The Unanswered Question* (1906, performed as theatre interlude 1907, concert première 1946), with its quiet strings, questioning trumpets and answering flutes, and *Central Park in the Dark* (1906, same performance history) are the most gratifying.

Of the two string quartets, the *String Quartet No. 1* (1896) is a conventional early work with echoes of Dvořák in its four movements. However, the key structures are not traditional, and there are moments of polytonality and echoes of American hymns; the fugue was reused in the *Symphony No. 4*. The *String Quartet No. 2* (1907–13) is quite different: Ives described it as a discussion among four men who converse, debate, argue, fight and make up (movements one and two), and eventually walk up the mountain to view the firmament (the third movement). There are quotations from Beethoven, hymns, and Civil War songs, and the harmonic idiom is largely atonal in a complex work, difficult to assimilate, but leading to a transcendental close. Of his piano music, the *Three-Page Sonata* (1905), in three clearly defined sections, is remarkable for its compression, for the way it raises emotional and musical expectations, only to follow other directions, and for its feeling of unreality, created by layers of different harmonies and rhythms. The huge *Piano Sonata No. 2 'Concord'* (1911–15, full subtitle *Concord, Massachusetts, 1840–1860*), with flute and viola (sometimes omitted), is Ives' summation of his philosophy and his admiration for the American Transcendentalists. Partly based on earlier music, it was revised many times and first performed in 1939. Its many revisions have left various alternatives open to performers, and it remains his finest work and a major contribution to 20th-century piano music. Its four movements pay tribute to the Transcendentalists from the town of Concord (Emerson, Hawthorne, The Alcotts and Thoreau); a motto from the four-note opening of Beethoven's fifth symphony pervades the work, and well-known American tunes occasionally make their appearance. 'Emerson' surveys powerful contemplation and complex thought, occasionally leavened by more musing moments; the viola makes a tiny but telling appearance. 'Hawthorne' veers wildly in mood, regularly returning to a mysterious melancholic atmosphere. 'The Alcotts' is delicate, fragrant, counterpoised by passion stirred by the Beethoven motto. 'Thoreau' is the most transcendental of the movements, with the flute representing the mist over Walden Pond. Throughout the sonata the piano writing is usually dense and of considerable virtuosity; those listening to the work for the first time might consider taking one movement at a time. Ives's output also includes fine songs; he wrote some two hundred, ranging from the sweetly sentimental to the acerbically complex.

Ives is a composer best taken in small doses. He is uneven in his inspiration; some of the effects sound just that; and his emotional range is essentially limited to those half-dreamt integrations of childhood memories. Occasionally one wishes for tauter formal structures to bind works together. But at his best his musical visions are compelling, and when rediscovered he made an indelible mark on American music and on American composers of the second half of the 20th century.

The insurance agency he co-founded, Ives and Myrick, eventually became the largest in the United States.

RECOMMENDED WORKS
Piano Sonata No. 2 *Concord* (1911–15, often revised)
String Quartet No. 2 (1907–13)
Symphony No. 3 (1902–04, revised 1909)
Symphony No. 4 (1909–16)
Three-Page Sonata (1905) for piano
Three Places in New England (1903–14) for orchestra
The Unanswered Question (1906) for orchestra
Central Park in the Dark (1906) for orchestra

BIBLIOGRAPHY
C. Ives, *Essays before a Sonata*, 1961
H. and S. Cowell, *Charles Ives and his Music*, 1952, 1969
V. Perlis, *Charles Ives Remembered*, 1974

Piston Walter··
born 20th January 1894 at Rockland (Maine)
died 12th November 1976 at Belmont (Massachusetts)

Piston, who trained as a painter before studying composition with Nadia Boulanger in Paris, is best known for his suite from the ballet *The Incredible Flautist*. However, his reputation rests more securely on the eight symphonies which are at the heart of his output. He has been called a 'neo-classicist' for the elegance at the heart of his output, and the self-contained unity in his musical architecture. Although such a tag contains an element of truth, there is a rugged individuality in his music, combined with concentration on formal devices, that is reminiscent of **Hindemith**. All his works are for orchestral or instrumental forces; there is no vocal music.

Most of the American composers of his generation attempted to infuse their work with a specifically American cast. Piston was one of the first American symphonists for whom the evocation of the American spirit was less important than the more abstract exploration of the form. When elements of American popular influences do appear, particularly in echoes of jazz (notably syncopated rhythms), they are integrated into his abstract goals, and became less obvious as he explored more complex harmonic ideas in the 1960s.

Although Piston was interested in the pattern of thinking of 12-tone composers and in some of their formal devices, his harmonic language remained essentially traditional, based on tonality, and linear counterpoint predominates. The use of particular intervals as a basis of form is a common feature (for example, the rising sixth in the first movement of the *Symphony No. 7*, or the relationship in the slow movement of the *Symphony No. 3* between the intervals of the 12-note row and those of the principal theme of the first movement). Piston is also the most widely known of American theorists, and his textbooks on harmony, counterpoint and orchestration are still standard university works. Some of that academicism perhaps raises its head in his music. The regular presence of passages which are impeccable in their academic credentials, yet fail to have impact beyond that (notably meandering strings), have probably hindered a wider dissemination of his music. On the other hand, his textural clarity, sense of rugged assertion, and moments of a very objective contemplation are far removed from any sense of the academic. His melodic lines have an inevitability about them, sometimes forcefully so, without the tuneful flow of such American contemporaries as **Harris** or **Copland**.

The rather dour *Symphony No. 1* (1937) is, with the seventh, the most obviously neo-classical of the symphonies. The rigid rhythms, offset by syncopations, are characteristic and give a rugged directness to the expression. Forceful strings predominate, and there is an affinity with the hardened steel and concrete purposefulness of the architecture of the period; this symphony is worthy of revival. The next three symphonies probably remain the best known. The three-movement *Symphony No. 2* (1943) extends this rather direct and limited vision, adding a sense of lyrical warmth and much more varied material, including suggestions of the 'cowboy' musical inheritance in the first movement. This adds a touch of optimism that is generally apparent in Piston's output, although a largely sombre mood is maintained until the end: the gentle slow movement becomes more impassioned and persuasively pastoral, but the last movement is short and somewhat facile, an example of Piston at his less inspired. The *Symphony No. 3* (1947) uses a large orchestra, with a notable part for two harps, and a favourite fugato texture in the finale. The key is the optimistic one of C major (with a conventional progression of C–F–G–C in the four movements, and an overall structure of slow-fast-slow-fast), though it opens in a solemn and subdued mood with dark orchestral colours; solo lines (especially woodwind) or blocks emerge from a dense, atmospheric texture. The slow movement has a hymnal quality to its expansiveness, a monumental quality to its climax. In total contrast is the energetic, highly contrapuntal scherzo, jerky and piquant in intent (apart from a meditative central section with solo flute), with touches of the Mexican bounce that **Copland** had developed. A similar tone is adopted in the finale, complete with a march tune, the orchestration reminiscent of the harmonium; and this is the most

obviously 'American' of Piston's symphonies. The similarly orchestrated *Symphony No. 4* (1950) has at its close a different, though related, tonal centre from that of its opening. It starts, unusually, in a light and lyrical mood, and the whole feel is more relaxed, almost to the point of what the English would call 'light' music, dance dominating the scherzo (titled 'Ballando'), the meandering of the strings never more obvious. The slow movement reverts to contemplation, with a massed crescendo, but to less effect than in the earlier symphonies. Overall, in spite of its superficial attractions, this is the least successful of Piston's symphonies.

With the three-movement *Symphony No. 5* (1954), Piston extended the range of his idiom, maintaining the strict classical structures, but adding the use of a tone-row in the opening of the slow movement, and binding the structure with melodic elements that appear throughout (he had used all twelve notes in the slow movement of *Symphony No. 3*, but this was obscured by the purely tonal goals). The effect is both more obviously abstract, and at the same time grittier, with a consistent argument between diatonic and chromatic material, and more spare and pointed textures. The *Symphony No. 6* (1955) is a return to the rather vacuous idiom of the fourth. The three-movement *Symphony No. 7* (1960), on the other hand, is much more lithe and angular in its material, more obviously neo-classical, and with particularly clean textures. The orchestra is used sparingly in clearly differentiated lines, often reduced almost to chamber size. The harmonic exploration, still rooted in tonality, is tense and chromatic, and the finale, for all its brashness, has an acerbic edge. The final *Symphony No. 8* (1964–65), again in three movements, maintains that harmonic edge, but combines it with the sense of the monumental observable in earlier works.

Surveying the symphonies as a whole, it is difficult not to come to the conclusion that their details and individual moments are more impressive than their overall impact. The development of the idiom from first to last is consistent, but limited. They are almost all rewarding in one way or another (with the exception, perhaps, of the fourth and sixth), and are interesting in the honesty of their construction and their clarity of idea. Those interested in the techniques of music will find the fifth perhaps the most appealing; those more receptive to emotional impact, the third. The final two symphonies, in the tension of their harmonic material and its application to so many of Piston's characteristics, are perhaps the most fascinating.

However, the work most likely to be encountered is the completely uncharacteristic suite (1938) from the ballet *The Incredible Flutist* (1938). The scenario is a sleepy village that wakes up to the arrival of a circus band, including the Incredible Flutist. Through his playing, and his dalliance with the Merchant's daughter, the Widow is united with the object of her passion, the Merchant himself. The suite uses about half the full ballet, and largely follows the same action. It is Piston at his most unexpectedly populist, boisterous and colourful. After a characteristically neo-classical start, the idiom ranges the gamut from pseudo-Spanish, through Broadway waltz, quasi-Mexican, a touch of the 19th-century virtuoso piano, hoe-down ideas, to circus music, complete with all the appropriate orchestral colours, unashamedly American in its melting-pot approach. With its distant echoes of *The Sorcerer's Apprentice*, it is a happy reminder that Piston was at one time a pupil of **Dukas**, and a marvellous compendium of the popular influences on American serious music in mid-century.

The five string quartets share many stylistic features with the symphonies, and show great craftsmanship, but possess a more luminous, interior quality. The *String Quartet No. 1* (1933) is essentially lyrical (in spite of the chromatic elements of the first movement) and ruminative, the two outer movements using material that oscillates on a C – D flat axis. The *String Quartet No. 2* (1935) is in much the same vein, but with a haunting and beautiful slow opening to a long first movement that has a wide variety of moods and material. Both works are effective on a purely emotional, as well as intellectual level. The *String Quartet No. 3* (1947) and *String Quartet No. 4* (1953) are more discursive. Both have extremely slow, long-lined slow movements, and the latter a scherzo with something of **Shostakovich's** mawkish humour. The *String Quartet No. 5* (1962) shows the more astringent, almost atonal harmonies that Piston had by then developed, but otherwise follows similar lines. If none of these works is particularly gripping in its entirety, they are nevertheless pleasing, particularly in the clarity of their intellectual construction. However, perhaps Piston's finest chamber work is the *Flute Quintet* (1942). Written for the unusual combination of flute and string quartet, it has a delightfully wispy and flowing opening, the sunlight of **Ravel's** Provence looking over Piston's shoulder, with the flute integrated into the general string texture while providing a parallel colour (the relationship had been foreshadowed in the solo flute passages of *The Incredible Flutist*). The scherzo is spiky, typical of Piston's rhythmical insistence, but with colourful flute writing, and a scurrying finale.

Piston was a celebrated teacher (at Harvard, 1929–60), and among his pupils were two of the most distinguished (and most contrasted) of American composers, **Bernstein** and **Carter**. His writings on theory are *Counterpoint* (1947), *Harmony* (1941), *Orchestration* (1955) and *Principles of Harmonic Analysis* (1933).

RECOMMENDED WORKS
  Flute Quintet (1942)
  ballet *The Incredible Flutist* (1938)
  String Quartet No. 2 (1935)
  Symphony No. 1 (1937)
  Symphony No. 2 (1943)
  Symphony No. 3 (1947)
  Symphony No. 5 (1954)
  Symphony No. 7 (1960)

BIBLIOGRAPHY
  H. Pollack, *Walter Piston*, 1981

Reich Steve**
born 3rd October 1936 at New York

Steve Reich has emerged as the most serious composer of the minimalist movement, and perhaps the one most deserving of attention. His idiom, more uncompromising than that of **Glass**, less populist than that of **Adams**, uses slowly unfolding repetitive patterns not only for effect, but also as solutions to abstract problems, often at the service of descriptive intent. The result can be both intellectually and emotionally mesmerising.

Reich's version of minimalism was initially influenced by La Monte Young (born 1935), who experimented with minimalist repetitive ideas and 'happenings', and by Terry Riley's *In C* (Reich took part in the first performance). Its essence is movement within the repetition by shifts of rhythmic patterns of one or more of the instruments or voices at different times, creating gradual overlapping patterns of changes. This is in contrast to the abrupt gear-changes of **Glass**; for although abrupt changes do regularly occur in Reich's music, they usually appear first in one voice alone to create a new strand in the weave. These changes are often subtle (the replacement of a rest by a beat, for example), and the overlap of the same rhythmic patterns out of phase with each other, with one of them then changing position for a new overlap, has become known as 'phase shifting'; it is analogous to the traditional technique of canons, or indeed double canons when one voice of the pattern moves slowly, another fast (first employed by Reich in the *Octet*). Gradually through his output he has extended these techniques to more complex harmonic as well as rhythmic patterns.

Of his early works, *It's Gonna Rain* (1965), using only the recorded voice of a black preacher, Brother Walter, is fascinating less for its musical effects than as an example of Reich's first experiments with phase shifting. While a single spoken phrase is endlessly repeated, a second recording gradually moves out of synchronicity with the first, creating deepening echo and rhythmic effects. *Violin Phase* (1967), in which a violin is played against one, and then two and three, tracks prerecorded by the violinist, is typical of the early works evolving the phase shifting; the prominence and changes of the resulting patterns are emphasised by the simple device of adjusting the volumes of the tape tracks. With its rigid note patterns and singularity of timbre, however, it seems crude compared with later works.

With *Drumming* (1970–71) for various drums, instruments and voices, Reich took a major step to remedy some of the monotony evident in the earlier works, a step made possible partly by his studies in Africa of Ghanaian drumming. This long work takes in its entirety one and a half hours, but is divided into parts, often heard on their own. By substituting beats for rests as the piece progresses, he creates a series of shifting patterns, and with the resonant and timbral effects of a battery of drums, the result is mesmerising. It progresses from small forces (two bongos) to the full ensemble. The technique was further developed, with a much wider range of colour, in *Music for Mallet Instruments, Voices and Organ* (1973). It is based on two rhythmic cells, whose note values are subject to lengthening and shortening, creating changing patterns of colour, with three abrupt changes of direction. The effect is unexpected: rather than the feeling of rhythmic shifts and overfolding of ideas in Reich's later work, the various individual colours of his forces emerge and recede against the ostinato patterns, like parts of a tapestry coming in

and out of focus. **Stockhausen** had achieved similar effects in *Stimmung* four years earlier. However, with its small but abrupt harmonic shifts, and the feeling of always being on the edge of tonal resolution, *Music for Mallet Instruments* (as it is usually known) is the work that brought Reich attention world-wide, and comes closest to the idiom of Philip **Glass**.

With *Music for Eighteen Instruments* (1976), with its suggestions of jazz, and *Music for a Large Ensemble* (1978, revised 1979), which again uses wordless voices as part of the instrumental texture and changes signalled by the vibraphone, Reich reached a public that included followers of popular music as well as those following the latest classical music. *Variations* (1979) for orchestra of winds, strings and keyboards was Reich's first piece for such large forces. While using subtle shifts of phase, it has considerably more melodic movement, with the emphasis on overlapping and slowly shifting layers of melodic ideas, propelled by the bass-lines of long held notes, essentially static against the higher ostinato layer as a kind of *cantus firmus*. This technique and pattern of sound proved to be a point of departure for another minimalist, John **Adams**.

Variations was quickly followed by the *Octet* (1979), for string quartet, two pianos, two clarinets (doubling bass clarinet, flute and piccolo; ten musicians may be used if necessary, but only eight play at any one time). This is one of Reich's most impressive and closely argued works, built around complex writing for two pianos (four hands). The sense of stasis inherent in repeated phrases slowly undergoing transformation is relieved by the wide leaps of the melodic fragments, giving a feeling of expansion and contraction, and by the dense and tight focus and yet wide range of instrumental colour afforded by the instrumentation. The movement between each of the five sections is also more securely handled, creating an almost unnoticed change and overlap rather than a more abrupt gear-change, and this better suits the complex interlocking of rhythmic ideas that is basic to his idiom.

Reich moved to the actual setting of words (as opposed to voiceless chorus, or speech on tape) in *Tehillim* (1981) for voices and instruments, a Psalm setting that draws on his Jewish heritage, including a melodic influence. There is no fixed metre or metrical pattern, but merely the metre of the text, which is constantly changing. Reich is here starting to move away from a 'pure' minimalism, the repetitions turning to variations and canons in a beautiful flowing tapestry of voices, the instruments providing a slower grounding. The next major work was *Desert Music* (1982–84) for chorus and orchestra, a long work based on excepts from poetry by William Carlos Williams. The structure is an arch form, with the five movements played continuously, the first matching the last, the second the fourth; the central movement is in A–B–A form. The longer melodic lines, initiated in *Tehillim*, are further developed. The effect is less busy than in his earlier works, with a spaciousness that matches the title, and new textures are introduced: a wailing siren imitated on the violas, and signalling a shift to a different movement (rather than the overlaps of the *Octet*) that is smoother and more convincing than those in the works of the 1970s. Much of the sense of being on the edge of harmonic resolution has gone; instead the colours are darker and more chromatic. Some of the rhythmic devices (in particular a beat of 3 against 2) have jazz origins, and, in spite of the respect with which this work was received, they sound pedestrian in comparison with some of Reich's other works; and the realisation of the essence of the poetry is less effective than in *Tehillim*.

In the *Sextet* (1984–85), for percussion instruments, two pianos and two synthesisers, Reich returned to a purer, abstract palette, but with greater harmonic complexity, the changes of tempo made abruptly at the beginning of each of the five movements by metric modulation. *Different Trains* (1988), for string quartet and tape is Reich's masterpiece to date, and marks a change in direction. It is a music docudrama evoking trains of three eras, each filling a movement: the great intercontinental American trains before the war, the trains transporting Holocaust victims during the war, and trains after the war. It is based on repeated snippets of spoken words on tape (looking right back to *It's Gonna Rain*), by Reich's childhood governess, Holocaust survivors, and a retired Pullman porter, together with recordings of trains from the periods; the string quartet, over-recorded four times to create dense patterns, matches the rhythms and speech-melody patterns of these taped snippets and adds its own commentary. From the opening bars, one knows Reich has moved into a denser, far more expressive world while retaining the main features of his idiom; the effect is both exciting and moving, the three atmospheres are clearly delineated, the effects of the train whistles (used as an integral part of the patterns) and the voices are haunting and hard-hitting, the multi-tracked string quartet layers propulsive, descriptive, evocative and gripping. In 1993 his first full-length 'documentary music theatre', the opera-length *The Cave*, was premièred, partly building on his experience in *Different Trains*. The three acts focus on the common ancestor of Abraham in three religions, Jewish, Muslim and Christian, using taped interviews as well as extensive quotations from religious texts. The static, oratorio-like nature of the libretto was countered by extensive and integral use of video techniques.

RECOMMENDED WORKS
  Different Trains (1988) for string
    quartet and tape
  Drumming (1970–71) for various
    drums, instruments and voices
  *Music for Mallet Instruments, Voices
    and Organ* (1973)
  Octet (1979)
  Tehillim (1981) for voices and
    instruments

Riegger Wallingford*
born 29th April 1885 at Albany
(Georgia)
died 2nd April 1961 at New York

Wallingford Riegger belongs to that generation of American composers who forged an American music by casting new ideas in traditional forms. He developed a free and unschematised use of 12-tone techniques, in which often ideas generated in the initial row are used in conventional structures; sometimes this is combined with a sense of tonality, and some works are almost entirely tonal. The chief features of his music are a sense of directness, clarity and logic (sometimes expressed in such forms as the fugue or the passacaglia), and a drive based on forceful rhythms. These were partly the result of his considerable experience of writing for dance; between 1933 and 1941 he wrote nothing else, producing scores (mostly with piano and drums) for most of the notable American modern dancers, including Martha Graham. After this period he concentrated on abstract orchestral and chamber works.

His earliest music was entirely traditional, in the line of Brahms (he admitted to hissing at the first Berlin performance of **Scriabin's** *Poème de l'Extase*), but between 1923 and 1926 he withdrew from composing to rethink his musical stance. He then joined a group of forward-thinking American composers, and became involved in the advanced Pan-American Association of Composers. The first major compositional results of this self-examination were the *Study in Sonority* (1926–27) for ten violins or any multiple thereof, and *Dichotomy* (1931–32) for chamber orchestra. The former, a very advanced and austere American work for its time, shows the influence of **Schoenberg** in its dissonant textures and its wide leaps, and of **Bartók** in its percussive use of string instruments and the incorporation of folk-like thematic fragments; the impulse is of an atonal lyrical flow, the textures getting progressively thicker. The vibrant *Dichotomy* was one of the first American works to employ tone-rows, using two of eleven and ten notes each, and including their standard manipulations – inversion, retrograde inversion (backwards), inverted plus retrograde – although Riegger was unaware at the time of Schoenberg's formal 12-tone theories (whatever some American commentators may have later claimed). However, its percussive energy, leading to a furious ending, is much more apparent than any dissonance, and Riegger does not adhere strictly to his rows, anticipating his later use of the formal 12-tone system.

The *Fantasy and Fugue* (1930–31) for orchestra and organ is ostensibly atonal, though in its carefully matched sonorities (the organ colours being integrated with the orchestra, rather than concertante), its dance-like rhythms and melodic flow, it rarely feels dissonant. In contrast, the *Canon and Fugue* (1941), for either string or full orchestra is representative both of his interest in counterpoint and of his occasional writing in an entirely tonal manner. Riegger withdrew his first two numbered symphonies, and it was with the *Symphony No. 3* (1946–47) that he became known to a wider audience. It has that rugged intensity characteristic of mid-century American symphonies and is perhaps his finest work. The *Symphony No. 4* (1957) is a more diffident work, in a tonal idiom centred on keys without a strong sense of resolution (it ends on a major seventh); the rhythmic sense is here rather nervous, the scoring spare and often assigned to solo woodwinds. The *Variations for Violin and Orchestra* (1959) is the best known of the works based on variations (others include the *Variations for Piano and Orchestra*, 1953, and the *Variations for Violin and Viola*, 1956). With twelve variations and a cadenza, it is based on 12-tone principles (although with some deviations), with a predominantly lyrical singing line for the violin, and more aggressive interpolations from the chamber-sized orchestra. Of his other works, he produced two important scores for brass ensembles, *Music for Brass Choir* (1948–49) and the *Nonet* (1951) for brass, both of which include cluster effects.

Where Riegger differs from the Viennese practitioners of 12-tone technique (apart from his free use of the system) is in his avoidance of the heightened extremes of Expressionism. Instead his idiom appears direct and thoughtfully rugged, individual in its personal use of 12-tone idioms and in their combination with more traditional harmonic and formal patterns. Among his few pupils was Morton Feldman; among his output were a large number of commercial arrangements (under a variety of pseudonyms), done out of financial necessity in the years of the Depression. He died from injuries received falling over a dog's leash in a snowstorm.

RECOMMENDED WORKS
Dichotomy (1931–32) for chamber orchestra
Study in Sonority (1926–27) for 10 violins or multiples thereof
Symphony No. 3 (1946–47)

Schuman William Howard[**]
born 4th August 1910 at New York
died 15th February 1993 at New York

William Schuman was one of the major figures in the mainstream of American music, continuing the tradition of the American symphony as the vehicle for the abstract expression of American life. He had an unusual apprenticeship, writing popular songs (usually arranged by others), before starting a serious study of music at the age of twenty-three. Although most highly regarded for his ten symphonies, he is also noted in America for his choral works. His development was one of consistent extension of his idiom, rather than any radical changes of style.

There is a strong and vital urgency about his music, and he was a public composer in the sense that the bulk of his works seem to express outward events and situations rather than inward emotions. He explored no new boundaries, but extended traditional forms with a strong consensus between form and content –

rarely does anything sound out of place in Schuman's work. His essentially tonal framework, though usually without key signatures, sometimes had dissonant counterpoint or polytonal moments, and characteristically used leaping sevenths and triads. The most immediate aspect of his music is its rhythmic intensity; he favoured a steady pulse overlaid with crossrhythms, sometimes with spectacular rhythmic shifts (as at the end of the *Symphony No. 3*). Dance rhythms also appear in some of his later works, and underlying everything lies the rhythmic example of jazz. On this rhythmic base he places long, often cantabile melodies, allowing broad conceptions. His orchestration often divides the orchestra into groups, and he delights in the sonorities of solo strings. A favourite technique, particularly in the middle and later works, is the overlay of two or more concepts moving at different paces and sometimes in different keys. As a framework for this melodic and rhythmic motivation, he preferred neoclassical forms.

It was with the powerful *Symphony No. 3* (1941) that Schuman came to prominence (he withdrew the previous two symphonies, the second of which was admired by **Copland** but was a disaster at its première). Divided into two movements, each in two parts, it shows Schuman's fondness for ordered neo-classical forms, here the toccata, chorale, passacaglia, and especially the fugue; unusually among 20th-century composers Schuman regularly used the fugue with a strong sense of freedom and lightness as an integral structural catalyst. It is a pulsing, vital work, using its formal framework for vivid shifts of colourful expression and its nocturnal slow section. The *Symphony No. 4* (1941) is more thinly textured, less substantial and less inventive than its predecessor in its combination of three-movement form and outgoing content, in spite of the impressive fugal work of the finale and the driving pulse of the opening movement. The most neo-classical of the symphonies is perhaps the rather intense *Symphony No. 5 (Symphony for Strings*, 1943) for strings alone, with very broad melodic lines and throughout an energetic pulse. The *Symphony No. 6* (1948) is considered by some to be his finest. It is a powerful and densely argued work, in which one plane is dominated by strings and timpani, in long lines or powerful statements, another by the brighter colours of woodwind and solo brass, rhythmically more fragmentary. Its construction is unusual: in its single movement, two

outer slow sections frame four central ones, which themselves have echoes of classical construction (fast opening, scherzo, adagio and finale). The violent, punctuating nature of the presto is particularly effective. This fine achievement is let down, perhaps, only by the rather aimless wandering of the strings at its centre.

After a gap of twelve years, the *Symphony No. 7* (1960) re-established Schuman's position as a symphonic composer. Building on a mood suggested by the sixth symphony, it is darker, more anguished and personally intense than the earlier symphonies. The harmonies are often uncomfortable (pitting upward sevenths against thirds), the orchestral colours brightly embittered by brass fanfares. There is a yearning slow movement – cantabile intensamente – for strings alone. It is one of the finer American symphonies, an uncomfortable and compelling work. The three-movement *Symphony No. 8* (1960–62) has a massive, sometimes harsh feel, the string lines long and thicktextured, offset by woodwind and brass layers, as in the sixth symphony. It creates a sense of slabs grinding against each other, like a geological fault. Its slow movement is equally firm and insistent rather than lyrical, with characteristic short chattering notes in the brass at its climax. The dark *Symphony No. 9 'La fosse ardéatine'* (1968), written in reaction to a visit to the site of Nazi atrocities in Rome, again used a slow-fast-slow construction.

Of his concertante works, the discursive and extended fantasy for cello and orchestra *A Song of Orpheus* (1961), written just after the seventh symphony, is deeply lyrical. Schuman's characteristically long melodic line is fully extended for the solo instrument, pitted against solo woodwind over a neo-classical orchestra before moving to more positive assertion and some deeply expressive writing. His most unusual concertante work is the *Concerto on Old English Rounds* (1973) for viola, women's chorus and orchestra. Here the basic lyricism is tempered by harsher sections, unexpected sonorities are set up by the combination of women's chorus and the solo instrument, and the nature of the material demands constant transformation – in idiom it is perhaps an oldfashioned work, but nonetheless effective and individual. The *Violin Concerto*, originally (1950) in two movements, was revised in 1956, and was then cast again as a two-movement work in 1959; it opposes energetic moments with more contemplative ideas, characteristically using fourths and sevenths. Sometimes forceful, sometimes lyrical, it has considerable impact, making few concessions to any virtuoso Romantic tradition in form or in content.

Two of Schuman's most successful works were written for the choreographer and dancer Martha Graham. The scenario of *Night Journey* (1947, concert version subtitled 'choreographic poem' for fifteen instruments, 1980–81) is based on the Oedipus legend, but seen from the point of view of Jocasta. It combines motoric moments with drawn-out ideas of a neoclassical character, and something of the spare, semi-static nature of Greek drama. *Judith* ('choreographic poem' for orchestra, 1949), was based on the biblical story of Judith, with overtones of earlier fertility rituals. Two clearly different strands of musical line work independently but set up polytonal effects. Within the atmosphere of a rather ritualistic drama, Schuman uses the full orchestra for a wide range of effect, from an intimate chamber quality to large sonorous climaxes. Two other ballets for Martha Graham (*Voyage for a Theater*, 1953, and *The Witch of Endor*, 1965), were later withdrawn. Of his other orchestral music, the *Credendum (Article of Faith*, 1955) for orchestra was the first piece of music to be commissioned directly by a department of the US Government, while his *American Festival Overture* (1939) has retained its popularity. *New England Triptych* (1956) for orchestra is also in Schuman's more popular vein, using hymn tunes by Billings, with a lovely second movement ('When Jesus Wept') and a blockbuster of a finale ('Chester').

A Free Song (1943), the second of two *Secular Cantatas* for chorus, won the first Pulitzer Prize in music. Schuman's major choral work is perhaps the *Carols of Death* (1958), to three poems by Walt Whitman. He wrote it for a cappella choir, using the actual rhythms of the words to govern the structure. With contrasts between broader swathes of choral sound combined with rhythmic detail, and darker harmonies always suggesting an eventual resolution, this short, intimate work is unassumingly effective. His two single-act operas are both lightweight but entertaining. *The Mighty Casey* (1951–53), to a libretto by Jeremy Gury, is based on the most famous of all baseball stories (*Casey at the Bat* by Ernest Lawrence Thayer), which will need no introduction to baseball fans but will probably mystify others. Full of vocal lines that verge on the idiom of the Broadway

musical, it is colourful, boisterous, gently humorous, and in a style designed to appeal to a wide audience: in a word, fun, with a little homespun philosophising and a touch of the bitter-sweet at the end. It was revised as a cantata, *Casey at the Bat* for soprano, baritone, chorus and orchestra in 1976. *A Question of Taste* (1987–88), based on a story by Roald Dahl, with a libretto by J.D. McClatchy, is a little comedy of manners centred around a dinner-party wager concerning wine recognition in which the hand of the host's daughter is bet against half a million dollars. The idiom is again easy going, but darker-hued. Schuman wrote relatively little chamber music, and virtually no piano music. Four of his five string quartets are earlier works, and the *String Quartet No. 1* (1936) was withdrawn. The *String Quartet No. 3* (1939) has cyclical elements, material from the first movement being developed and restated in the next two.

Schuman was a particularly prominent figure in American musical life. At the age of thirty-five he became the director of the Juilliard School (1945–62), where he was an innovative administrator. From 1962 to 1969 he was president of the Lincoln Center for the Performing Arts, and he was appointed chairperson of the MacDowell Colony in 1973. Columbia University named the William Schuman Award for lifetime achievement as a composer in his honour.

RECOMMENDED WORKS
　Carols of Death (1958) for
　　unaccompanied chorus
　opera *Casey at the Bat* (1951–53)
　Concerto on Old English Rounds
　　(1973) for viola, women's chorus
　　and orchestra
　choreographic poem *Judith* (1949)
　Symphony No. 3 (1941)
　Symphony No. 5 (for strings) (1943)
　Symphony No. 6 (1948)
　Symphony No. 7 (1960)
　Symphony No. 8 (1960–62)
　Violin Concerto (1950–59)

BIBLIOGRAPHY
　C. Rouse, *William Schuman: Documentary*, 1980
　F. R. Schreiber and V. Persichetti, *William Schuman*, 1954

Sessions Roger Huntington**

born 28th December 1896 at Brooklyn
(New York)
died 16th March 1985 at Princeton

Roger Sessions was perhaps the most highly regarded American teacher of composition of his generation, but his own music, so prized by a few, has never received the wider attention and exposure that might have been expected. His sympathies were on the one hand with a classical sense of order, and of music being primarily an abstract and technical art (consequently he worked in traditional forms, notably the symphony), and on the other with a Expressionist appreciation of the power of music to reveal the subconscious emotions, the 'energies which animate our psychic life'. His best music keeps the two in balance, with an emphasis on rhythmic energy and variety; during the late 1950s, his technique threatened to suppress the expression, notably in the middle symphonies, but he redressed the balance in the middle 1960s.

His early works were influenced by **Bloch** and then by neo-classicism, and one of these early works, the imposing ballet *The Black Maskers* (1923, suite 1928) remains one his most often heard works. It was reworked from the incidental music to the symbolic play by Andreyev dealing with the dark forces of the unknown, and the music matches the demonic undercurrents, generally late-Romantic in idiom, with dark, clear-cut orchestral colours that are characteristic of his orchestration. From the 1930s he developed an harmonic idiom that was increasingly atonal, and in the early 1950s embraced 12-tone technique, though his usage is not strict. Elastic rhythms, often varying rapidly and used organically in carefully organised structures, were a major feature of his music, with a continuous flow in which events (as **Copland** pointed out) come to the surface and then submerge. This can create a long-breathed overall continuity; at times it only emphasises an academic angularity. His orchestral colours are hard-edged, sometimes suggesting a monumental cast; his music is rarely 'easy', but it is an idiom that increases in effectiveness as one becomes more used to the details and their imagery.

Sessions's development is best seen through his symphonies. The *Symphony No. 1* (1926–27, revised 1929) is the work of a composer trying out his voice, drawing on **Stravinsky, Copland** and neo-classical elements. Rhythmically energetic, especially in the outer of the three movements,

it has a key structure but much harmonic wandering, a slow movement of rather ponderous but attractive lyricism, and a wildly exotic and quixotic finale with jazzy features. The *Symphony No. 2* (1944–46) occupies quite a different sound-world: anguished, dense, swirling, harmonically unstable, regularly losing any sense of basic key; the textures are maintained in the slow movement and the finale, where the undercurrent of Expressionist monumentality against a nebulous surface is confirmed. By the *Symphony No. 3* (1957) he had fully adopted his own brand of 12-tone technique. The *Symphony No. 4* (1958) uses much leaner textures and more pointed orchestration; its three movements were originally conceived as character pieces. It has a nervous, angular cast, with fragments of high colour in the central elegy. The *Symphony No. 5* (1964) retains the angularity and the leaner textures, but is more compressed; the movements are played without a break, changes of mood are more swiftly juxtaposed, and the opening figure recurs throughout the work. It has a hard-edged monumentality, and is more successful than its predecessor in integrating procedure and expression. The next three symphonies were written under the impetus of the Vietnam war, and by the *Symphony No. 7* (1967) he had restored a feeling of expressive dynamic purpose. The symphony is unsettled, with thick textures, urgent, varied rhythms and an elusive, long-breathed angular slow movement. His penultimate symphony is also one of his finest. The *Symphony No. 8* (1968) is in one continuous movement, scored for a large orchestra, and it appears to reconcile Sessions's symphonic make-up, in the easier flow, the less extreme angular leaps, the almost Romantic moment of violin solo, and in the arch of quietly atmospheric opening and close (strings against hushed percussion). It retains the dark hues, the rhythmic interest, and a tone of melancholy that may be tense, but is no longer anguished.

Of his other works, the *Violin Concerto* (1930–35), the work with which he gained a mature style, is perhaps the finest. The long phrasing of the solo line is usually set very high in an elliptical, energetic and expressive work with clean orchestral colours (omitting violins) and edges, an angular lyricism and a sometimes sharply chromatic harmonic language. The *Piano Sonata No. 1* (1927–30) includes dissonant and chromatic passages handled with clarity as Sessions was developing his harmonic language. The *Piano Sonata No.*

2 (1946) is aggressive, restless, elusive, sometimes quasi-humorous, harmonically unsettling with near-cluster effects in the opening. The *Sonata for Violin* (1953) for solo violin was his first work to use a 12-tone structure, with an elusive melancholic lyricism. His two operas have not maintained a place in the repertoire: *The Trial of Lucullus* (1947) has been eclipsed by the treatment of the Brecht play by **Dessau**; *Montezuma* (1941–63, later revisions), relating the overthrow of the Inca Montezuma by the Spanish conquistadors, was more theatrically imposing. The large cantata *When Lilacs Last in the Doorway Bloom'd* (1964–70, but conceived in 1927), for soloists, chorus and orchestra, to words by Walt Whitman, is one of his finest later works, the music often vividly reflecting the descriptive images of the poetry.

Sessions taught at Smith College (1917–21), at the University of California, Berkeley (1945–52), at Princeton (1935–45 and 1953–65), at Berkeley (1966–67), at Harvard (1968–69), and at the Juilliard. He co-founded the Copland–Sessions concerts that introduced new American composers.

RECOMMENDED WORKS
    suite *The Black Maskers* (1923, suite
        1928) for orchestra
    Symphony No. 2 (1944–46)
    Symphony No. 7 (1967)
    Symphony No. 8 (1968)
    Violin Concerto (1930–35)
    cantata *When Lilacs Last in the
        Doorway Bloom'd* (1964–70) for
        soloists, chorus and orchestra

BIBLIOGRAPHY
    R. Sessions, *The Musical Experience
        of Composer, Performer, Listener*,
        1950
    *Roger Sessions on Music: Collected
        Essays*, 1979
    A. Olmstead, *Roger Sessions and his
        Music*, 1985

Thomson Virgil*

born 25th November 1896 at Kansas City
died 30th September 1989 at New York

Virgil Thomson's contribution to American music was made as much through his work as a critic (notably with the *New York Herald Tribune*, 1940–54) and writer as though his own composition. His very large output (much of it short works) embraced a wide range of styles, but his music is characterised throughout by a wit (sometimes ironic), a piquant view of life and a delight in a quasi-naïve simplicity and directness derived in part from the influence of **Satie**, and in part from the writer Gertrude Stein, whom he met in Paris in 1926. His earliest works used jazz (*Two sentimental Tangos*, 1923, for piano or band), a dissonant neo-classicism (the *Sonata da chiesa*, 1926, for clarinet, horn, trumpet, trombone and piano), and modal and Gregorian chant hues in choral works; but he also turned to the American heritage of hymn music that was an abiding thread through his output (*Symphony on a Hymn Tune*, 1928). In the 1930s he concentrated on chamber and string works, including the *Violin Sonata* (1930), the *String Quartet No. 1* (1931) and *String Quartet No. 2* (1932). The last has all the ethos of Schubert's Vienna, with a classical structure and tonality, charm, grace and clarity, and a waltz for a second movement (one wonders how he could have thought it modern, as he did, but that may have been part of his impish humour). He orchestrated it into his *Symphony No. 3* in 1972, in which guise it takes on a completely different character, partly owing to the use of percussion and brass, the charm turning into a kind of forcefulness; the two works make a fascinating comparison. In the late 1930s he returned to American themes, especially in his film scores.

His critical activities took up much of the 1940s and 1950s, but he returned to full-time composing in 1955, consolidating his style and reworking a number of earlier works into new compositions. In *Five Songs of William Blake* (1951), for baritone and orchestra or piano, he applied the simplicity and directness of the American 19th-century parlour song to Blake (including settings of 'Tiger, Tiger' and 'Jerusalem' – a delightful, ironic, contrary setting with a sparkling ripple of an accompaniment); this is an unexpected but effective combination that only briefly flirts with a more complex art-song idiom. Recordings of this work have omitted the fourth song as being racially insensitive, though the censors have missed the irony of the words and the setting, which has the strong flavour of a Stephen Foster song. The fine *Feast of Love* (1964) for baritone and small orchestra, setting translations of Latin texts, ranges from a Stravinskian cast, with a lively pulse in the accompaniment set against the counter-rhythms of the long vocal lines at the opening, to a Romantic hue. The lovely concertino *Autumn* (1964), for harp, strings and percussion opens with the broad chordal movement of a **Copland** work, and the last three of its four movements are reworkings of the *Piano Sonata No. 2* (1929) – the last movement, with bumptious tuned percussion, is a little gem.

However, Thomson's music is now most likely to be encountered in three areas: his operas, his series of 'portraits', and his suites from film scores. His most important work is undoubtably the opera *Four Saints in Three Acts* (1927–28, orchestrated 1933). The libretto by Gertrude Stein, with Cubist juxtapositions of word and image that follow little linear pattern, is less obtuse than it at first appears: in a Prologue and four acts (there is a discussion between the third and fourth as to whether the fourth will take place), it is fanciful, with a huge conglomeration of different images, periods, and symbols, but with an undercurrent that is both serious (touching on spirituality and religious ecstasy) and ironic. Two of the four saints are genuine (St Teresa of Avila and St Ignatius Loyola) and two are invented, and there are host of minor saints. There is no plot as such, but a series of choreographed scenarios, ranging from a monastery and a garden party to the opera house and heaven. Thomson's score is equally eclectic in its inspiration, including suggestions of American folk and hymn tunes, and an actual quote from 'America'; throughout it bubbles with brightness, gentle humour, rhythmic bounce and choral writing of simplicity and vitality. The orchestral writing is deliberately kept undecorated to support the vocal lines and to provide aural simplicity and clarity. Not the least of its achievements is a close association between vocal writing and the inflections of American speech; this, together with its original structure partly dictated by the libretto, makes it the first American opera to depart entirely from the European operatic tradition, a feat not again matched until the operas of **Glass**. The first production also unprecedentedly used an all-American Black cast (a year before **Gershwin's** *Porgy and Bess*). It was followed by *The Mother of Us All* (1946–47), which followed a similar vein, except that the libretto by Stein is more concerned with actual events, centred around the suffragette Susan B. Anthony. Its fantastical elements introduce figures from American history and legend, including John Adams, Indiana Elliott and Ulysses S. Grant, and it uses quotations from literature, speeches and letters. The score has more dissonant elements than its predecessor. Thomson's final opera, *Lord Byron* (1961–68), to a libretto by Jack Larson, was more direct, but failed to achieve the impact of the earlier works.

Throughout his life, and especially in the 1940s, Thomson wrote 'portraits' (the idea was inspired by Stein) for a wide variety of forces and in a diversity of styles. These miniatures range from the angular dissonance of *Bugles and Birds (Portrait of Pablo Picasso)* (1940, orchestrated 1944) for piano, and the contrapuntal severity of *Persistently Pastorale (Portrait of Aaron Copland)* (1941, orchestrated 1945) for piano, through the *Family Portraits* (1972–75) for brass quintet to the *Eight Portraits for Violin Alone* (including a portrait of Gertrude Stein as a young girl). The best have a Satiesque quirkiness; among those he portrayed are **Harrison** and **Sauguet**.

Thomson's film music is distinguished; the best known is probably the score wrote with Marc Blitzstein for the unforgettable documentary *Spanish Earth*, 1937, drawing on Spanish folk music. Three of his film scores stand on their own as orchestral suites. *The Plough that Broke the Plains* (1936, suite 1942) and *The River* (1937, suite 1957) were both written to accompany Department of Agriculture films, and allowed Thomson to express a feel for the American landscape in a broad pictorial style that has affinities with **Copland**. The former includes genuine cowboy songs and a jazz movement, the latter the swagger of the 'Old South', the exuberance of 'Industrial Expansion in the Mississippi Valley', a slow movement ('Soil erosion and Floods') with funereal undertones, and references to well-known American tunes. *Louisiana Story* (1948) was written for another documentary, about the oil industry in the bayou, and includes touches of Impressionism, a folk-tune set against a chorale, and a passacaglia and a fugue for the last two of the four movements. It is the only film score yet to have won a Pulitzer Prize.

RECOMMENDED WORKS
  concertino *Autumn* (1964) for harp, strings and percussion
  opera *Four Saints in Three Acts* (1927–28)
  opera *The Mother of Us All* (1947)
  suite from film *The Plough that Broke the Plains* (1936, suite 1942)
  'portraits' (see text)

suite from film *The River* (1937, suite 1957)

String Quartet No. 2 (1932) / Symphony No. 3 (1972) (see text)

BIBLIOGRAPHY

V. Thomson, *Virgil Thomson*, 1966

K. Hoover and J. Cage, *Virgil Thomson*, 1959

Wuorinen Charles*

born 9th June 1938 at New York

In spite of his nationalist views on American music, the prolific Charles Wuorinen was the major American composer (aside from **Babbitt**) to develop the European heritage of the aftermath of 12-tone techniques and serialism. His music has been widely heard in the States, and his influence as a teacher and (on other academic composers) as a composer has been considerable. However, for all its technical facility and fertility, his music lacks the distinctive individuality or idiomatic personality that distinguishes such contemporaries as **Ferneyhough**, or indeed Babbitt himself. Some have even claimed that Wuorinen has had a baleful influence on American music, and one can't help but feel they have a point, for the ultimate impression of his music is one of sterility.

In his earlier music (represented by such works as the spiky *Flute Variations*, 1963) he developed an idiom that systematised not only the intervals of the row and the rhythm (as Babbitt had done), but also the larger structures of a piece, and this has remained a cornerstone of his technique. These works have abrupt changes of pace and dynamics, block-like effects, darting figures, and a rather severe cast. The *Chamber Concerto* (1963) for cello and ten players exemplifies this idiom, in five movements, each with a different tone for the soloist. The *String Trio* (1967–68) is the best of these earlier works, still exceptionally severe, but with the changes less abrupt.

Wuorinen came to wider notice with the electronic *Time's Encomium* (1968–69), commissioned by Nonesuch records, in which he applied similar techniques (especially the control of duration from the smallest event to overall form) in the electronic medium. It now sounds terribly dated, and excruciatingly dull in comparison with the European electronic works of the 1960s, as if he was doodling with his idiom on the Moog – partly because of the very synthesised sound of the RCA synthesiser on which it was realised, which

was prejudiced towards the use of 12-tone equal temperament. The *Piano Sonata No. 1* (1969) effectively applied the spiky leaps and sudden shifts to the piano, in fast, darting writing with spare textures. *Ringing Changes* (1969–70), for percussion ensemble, is too anonymous in character to be of real interest. In the *String Quartet No. 1* (1970–71) the sudden changes are turned to a more theatrically dramatic cast, with different characterisation for each instrument. When these characters become more homogeneous, the sense of a dramatic conversation is maintained, leading to almost minimalist repetitions of great energy, and this work is a rewarding place to start for those wishing to sample Wuorinen's music.

This shift to the less severe in Wuorinen's idiom was continued in the timbral musings of the *Bassoon Variations* (1971–72) for bassoon, harp and timpani. *Grand Bamboula* (1971) for strings further eroded the severity by combining an energetic Stravinskian neo-classicism with the gestural effects and a more avant-garde harmonic palette, and is worth the encounter. The *Concerto for Amplified Violin and Orchestra* (1971–72) is big and aggressive, again concerned with timbre, the potential lyricism of the solo instrument expunged by the amplification. The *Percussion Symphony* (1976) for twenty-six players, including (like *Ringing Changes*) pianos used as tuned percussion, returns to severity in its first movement, and in spite of some delicate sounds in the slow movement and a momentary echo of jazz in the last, is too cerebral, too academic, to lift off a plane of aggressive self-consciousness. Its three movements are divided by transcriptions of a Dufay setting of Petrarch, providing a restful contrast of mood, like eating a sherbet between courses.

However, in more recent works Wuorinen has developed a more direct sound world, building on his technical experience; he has retained the complex rhythmic shifts and drive, but smoothed out the disjointed effects of his style, so that the vertical components have started to serve a more linear flow. The *Piano Concerto No. 3* (1982–83) has a furious first movement initiated by the piano, to be joined by percussion and, gradually, by other members of the orchestra; a slow movement of angular ideas that builds in complexity after the establishment of the distinctive colours of cow-bells, tom-toms, timpani and drums; and an ebullient, crowded finale. The title of *The Golden Dance* (1986) for orchestra (including piano) refers not only to Californian history, but also to the 'Golden section' (the ratio of 2:1), which matches the relative durations and, inversely, the tempi of the two movements. Its 12-note row is derived from a hymn melody by St Thomas Aquinas; the first movement shifts from tone-painting of colours and textures to a more detailed focus of dense, complex elements, its idiomatic anonymity eventually becoming wearisome; the second movement is more furious but equally vacant.

Wuorinen has taught at Columbia University (1964–71), at the Manhattan School of Music (1971–1979), at Rutgers University since 1954, and was a composer-in-residence to the San Francisco Symphony Orchestra (1985–1989).

RECOMMENDED WORKS
Piano Concerto No. 3 (1982–3)
Grand Bamboula (1971) for strings
String Quartet No. 1 (1970–71)
String Trio (1967–68)

Yugoslavia

During the writing of this *Guide*, the former Yugoslavia partially broke up into constituent states. General information about the composers of Croatia and Serbia will be found under those countries. There is, however, still a Yugoslavian music information centre covering the general region.

Yugoslav Musci Information Centre
(SOKOJ):
Union of Yugoslav Composers'
Organisations
Misarska St 12–14
JU–11000 Beograd
Yugoslavia
tel/fax: +381-11-345 192
fax: +381-11-336 168

Malec, Ivo
see under Croatia

List of Recommended Composers

Composers with ••• recommendations

These are the major composers of 20th-century classical music. Page references are to their main entries.

Bartók *Hungary* p.232
Berg *Austria* p.15
Birtwistle *UK* p.415
Boulez *France* p.126
Britten *UK* p.423
Cage *USA* p.483
Carter *USA* p.486
Copland *USA* p.489
Debussy *France* p.130
Elgar *UK* p.434
Falla *Spain* p.361
Fauré *France* p.137
Henze *Germany* p.181
Hindemith *Germany* p.186
Honegger *Switzerland* p.391
Ives *USA* p.506
Janáček *Czech Republic* p.75
Ligeti *Hungary* p.243
Lutosławski *Poland* p.294
Mahler *Austria* p.25
Martinů *Czech Republic* p.83
Messiaen *France* p.146

Nielsen *Denmark* p.96
Orff *Germany* p.191
Penderecki *Poland* p.299
Prokofiev *Russian Republic* p.319
Puccini *Italy* p.263
Rachmaninov *Russian Republic* p.326
Ravel *France* p.156
Schoenberg *Austria* p.32
Shostakovich *Russian Republic* p.336
Sibelius *Finland* p.114
Stockhausen *Germany* p.200
Strauss *Germany* p.206
Stravinsky *Russian Republic* p.345
Tippett *UK* p.459
Varèse *France* p.166
Vaughan Williams *UK* p.463
Webern *Austria* p.39
Weill *Germany* p.214
Xenakis *Greece* p.221

Composers with •• recommendations

These composers are less well known than those with ••• recommendations, but are still of considerable stature, often of importance in their own country but less heard abroad. Page references are to their main entries.

Adams *USA* p.475
Andriessen *Holland* p.225
Babbitt *USA* p.478
Bacewicz *Poland* p.290
Baird *Poland* p.291
Barber *USA* p.479
Bax *UK* p.408
Berio *Italy* p.249
Bergman *Finland* p.110
Bloch *Switzerland* p.389
Blomdahl *Sweden* p.376
Brian *UK* p.418
Bridge *UK* p.421
Busoni *Italy* p.251
Casella *Italy* p.254
Chávez *Mexico* p.275
Cowell *USA* p.492
Crumb *USA* p.494
d'Indy *France* p.129
Dallapiccola *Italy* p.257
Davies *UK* p.429
Delius *UK* p.432

Dukas *France* p.135
Dutilleux *France* p.136
Egk *Germany* p.176
Eisler *Germany* p.177
Enescu *Romania* p.306
Foerster *Czech Republic* p.72
Foss *USA* p.496
Gerhard *Spain* p.363
Ginastera *Argentina* p.1
Glass *USA* p.498
Glazunov *Russian Republic* p.312
Hába *Czech Republic* p.73
Harris *USA* p.502
Hartmann *Germany* p.179
Hoddinott *UK* p.441
Holmboe *Denmark* p.93
Holst *UK* p.442
Jolivet *France* p.141
Kagel *Argentina* p.3
Kodály *Hungary* p.239
Krenek *Austria* p.22
Kurtág *Hungary* p.241

522 **List of Recommended Composers**

Landowski *France* p.144
Lidholm *Sweden* p.379
Malipiero *Italy* p.258
Martin *Switzerland* p.393
Miaskovsky *Russian Republic* p.317
Milhaud *France* p.151
Nono *Italy* p.260
Nordheim *Norway* p.285
Novak *Czech Republic* p.88
Ohana *Morocco* p.281
Pärt *Estonia* p.106
Petrassi *Italy* p.262
Pettersson *Sweden* p.381
Pfitzner *Germany* p.195
Pijper *Holland* p.227
Piston *USA* p.508
Poulenc *France* p.153
Rangström *Sweden* p.382
Reich *USA* p.510
Respighi *Italy* p.266
Revueltas *Mexico* p.279
Rodrigo *Spain* p.369

Rosenberg *Sweden* p.383
Roussel *France* p.161
Rubbra *UK* p.453
Sallinen *Finland* p.112
Satie *France* p.163
Schafer *Canada* p.59
Schmidt *Austria* p.31
Schnittke *Russian Republic* p.329
Schoeck *Switzerland* p.396
Schuman *USA* p.513
Scriabin *Russian Republic* p.333
Sculthorpe *Australia* p.12
Sessions *USA* p.515
Stenhammer *Sweden* p.385
Suk *Czech Republic* p.89
Szymanowski *Poland* p.301
Takemitsu *Italy* p.270
Tavener *UK* p.456
Villa-Lobos *Brazil* p.51
Walton *UK* p.467
Zemlinsky *Austria* p.43
Zimmermann *Germany* p.218

Index

Composers with main entries are in capitals, with the page reference to their entry in **bold**, thus: **ATTERBERG**